Australia

The Complete Encyclopedia

AMERICAN
WALTHAM WATCH
COMPANY

Australia

The Complete Encyclopedia

Foreword by **PAT O'SHANE**

Introduction by **PETER COSGROVE**

FIREFLY BOOKS

PUBLISHER	Gordon Cheers
ASSOCIATE PUBLISHER	Margaret Olds
MANAGING EDITOR	Mary Halbmeyer
EDITORS	Fiona Doig
	Scott Forbes
	Sue Grose-Hodge
	Ariana Klepac
	Frank Povah
	Sarah Shrubb
ADDITIONAL TEXT	Scott Forbes
	Sue Grose-Hodge
	Rowena Lennox
	Margaret McPhee
	Barbara Scanlon
ART DIRECTOR	Stan Lamond
SENIOR DESIGNER	Mark Thacker
COVER DESIGN	Bob Mitchell
DESIGNERS	Cathy Campbell
	Moyna Smeaton
	Veronica Varetsa
	James Young
CARTOGRAPHER	John Frith
CONTOUR SHADING	John Gittoes
MAP EDITOR	Valerie Marlborough
ARTWORK	Spike Wademan
ILLUSTRATIONS	Mike Gorman
	Frank Povah
	Robert Taylor
GRAPHS	Mike Gorman
TYPESETTING	Dee Rogers
INDEX	Glenda Browne
	Dee Rogers
PUBLISHING ASSISTANT	Erin King
PRODUCTION	Rosemary Barry

Note regarding Indigenous art and images in this book:
The publisher has made every effort to obtain permission from the
owners of all artworks and images to reproduce their works in these
pages, and to correctly credit artists. We apologise for any unintended
omissions and would be pleased to hear from copyright owners in
any such instance.

A FIREFLY BOOK
Published by Firefly Books Ltd., 2001

Illustrations from the Global Illustration Archives
© Global Book Publishing Pty Ltd 2001
Photographs from the Global Photo Library
© Global Book Publishing Pty Ltd 2001
Text © Global Book Publishing Pty Ltd 2001
Maps © Global Book Publishing Pty Ltd 2001

First Printing

National Library of Canada Cataloguing in Publication Data

Australia : the complete encyclopedia

ISBN 1-55297-543-6

1. Australia. I. Cosgrove, Peter
DU96.A79 2001   994   C2001-900550-4

U.S. Cataloging-in-Publication Data
(Library of Congress Standards)

Australia : the complete encyclopedia / foreword by Peter
Cosgrove. – 1st ed.
[912] p. : col. ill. : photos. : maps ;   cm.   +1 CD-ROM
Includes index.
Summary : A comprehensive text including: geography,
geology and ecology, history and culture, arts and science,
government and economy.
ISBN: 1-55297-543-6
1. Australia. I. Cosgrove, Peter. II. Title.
994   21   2001

Published in Canada in 2001 by
Firefly Books Ltd.
3680 Victoria Park Avenue
Willowdale, Ontario
M2H 3K1

Published in the United States in 2001 by
Firefly Books (U.S.) Inc.
P.O. Box 1338, Ellicott Station
Buffalo, New York 14205

Produced by Global Book Publishing Pty Ltd
1/181 High Street, Willoughby, NSW, 2068, Australia
Printed by Sing Cheong Printing Co. Ltd, Hong Kong
Film separation Pica Digital, Singapore

Cover images
Back cover from left to right: Paddle steamer, Echuca, SA; Wine
country, SA; Parliament House, ACT; Dandenong Ranges National
Park, Vic; Mungo National Park, NSW; Pittwater, NSW; Road sign,
NT; Father and daughter, SA.
Front cover from left to right: Rock art, Carnarvon National Park,
Qld; Silverton Hotel, NSW; Diving, Great Barrier Reef, Qld;
Porcupine grass, WA; Surf lifesavers; Caloundra, Qld; Uluru, NT;
Brisbane, Qld; Mt Feathertop, Vic.

Captions for images in the preliminary pages
Page 1: Frilled lizard (*Chlamydosaurus kingii*), NT
Pages 2–3: Opening of the Melbourne Exhibition, Victoria,
15 September, 1888
Page 4: Mt Field National Park, Tas
Page 7: New growth after drought, Qld
Pages 8–9: Salt-water crocodile (*Crocodylus porosous*), NT
Pages 10–11: Cape Bareen Island, Tas
Page 15: Aerial view of Uluru (Ayers Rock), NT
Page 18: Lake Bonney, Barmera, SA

Captions for images on the chapter opening pages can be
located on page 912.

Photographers are acknowledged on page 912.

Contributors

Dr Dick Bryan is Associate Professor in the School of Economics and Political Science at Sydney University where he teaches a course, with Gabrielle Meagher, on the changing structure of the Australian economy. He holds a PhD from Sussex University and has worked in the public sector and at a number of Australian universities. He is author of a number of articles and books about the international economy and Australia including *The Global Economy in Australia* (with M. Rafferty; Allen & Unwin 1999).

Richard Cashman is Associate Professor of History and the Director of the Centre for Olympic Studies, at the University of New South Wales. Since 1989 he has been Managing Director of the Australian Sports Consultancy Pty Ltd and its sports-history publishing division, Walla Walla Press. Richard has published more than 20 books on sports history including *Paradise of Sport: The Rise of Organised Sport in Australia*; he has co-authored a two-volume history of Marrickville; and has written two books on the history of South Asia; and was an editor of the *Oxford Companion to Australian Sport* and editor of *Sporting Traditions*, the journal of the Australian Society for Sports.

Steve Charters lectures in Wine Studies at Edith Cowan University, in Perth, Western Australia. His courses cover the understanding and appreciation of wine, its varying worldwide styles, and marketing and selling wine. Initially qualified as a lawyer in the United Kingdom, Steve was seduced by the allure of wine, and worked in retail and wine education in both London and Sydney. He is one of only 240 members in the world of the Institute of Masters of Wine, and one of only 12 in Australia, having passed its rigorous theory and tasting examination in 1997.

Bruce Elder is a senior journalist with *The Sydney Morning Herald* newspaper, writing regularly about television and popular music. Bruce has been writing about media and popular culture since 1972. In 1996 he was the first popular culture critic to win the Geraldine Pascall Award for Critical Writing.

Claude Forell has been a staff writer for and contributor to *The Age* in Melbourne since 1952, as a State and federal political reporter, and European correspondent, a public affairs columnist and chief editorial writer. He is the author of *How We Are Governed*, used in schools since 1964 and still in print. He was also the founding editor of *The Age Good Food Guide*.

Peter Forrestal was the founding editor of *The Wine Magazine* and is currently its associate editor. As a freelance wine and food writer he wrote *A Taste of the Margaret River*, co-authored *The Western Table* and edited *Discover Australia: Wineries*. He is a former president of the Wine Press Club of Western Australia, a member of the Circle of Wine Writers and of the Australian Society of Wine Educators. He has been wine correspondent for the *West Australian*, the *Western Review* and the *Perth Weekly*.

Ken Gargett is a practicing lawyer as well as a senior writer for *Vine, Wine & Cellar* and a contributor to *The Wine Magazine, Discover Australia: Wineries* and other publications. Based in Queensland's Gold Coast, he is a wine educator for the Wine Society in Queensland and conducts training, and consults within the industry as well as judging. He was the 1993 winner of the Vin de Champagne Award and has conducted Australian wine promotions, seminars and master-of-wine classes internationally.

Ian Glover is one of Australia's most experienced outback travellers, having seen even rarely accessible regions from behind the wheel of a 4WD. He has led many 4WD expeditions in Australia over the past 20

years, including: retracing John Oxley's expedition along the Macquarie River from the Blue Mountains to the Macquarie Marshes (1978); following in the tracks of Kimberley explorers O'Donnell and Carr-Boyd (1984); a transcontinental crossing of each of Australia's major deserts (1990); a search for the Discovery Well in the Great Sandy Desert (1992); and the Calvert Centenary Expedition in the Gibson, Little Sandy and Great Sandy deserts (1995).

Dr Ken Green is a wildlife ecologist specialising in cold-climate biology. His doctoral thesis examined the life of insectivorous marsupials beneath the snows of the Snowy Mountains. He has undertaken seven trips with the Australian Antarctic Division, including a year on the Antarctic continent and another on subantarctic Heard Island. He has published research on feeding and foraging ecology, vocalisations and population numbers of seals; and breeding biology, foraging ecology, diet and numbers of penguins and other seabirds. He has published two books: *Wildlife of the Australian Snow Country* with Will Osborne, and *Snow: a Natural History*; and edited *Uncertain Future*.

Lincoln Hall is editor of the adventure sports magazine *Outdoor Australia* and of *Out There* magazine, and is a former columnist for *The Good Weekend*. Lincoln has been intensively involved with the Australian outdoors for three decades. After discovering rock climbing near his home in Canberra as a teenager, he devoted 15 years to climbing in Australia and around the world. This culminated in his key role in the first Australian ascent of Mt Everest in 1984, the subject of his first book, *White Limbo*. His next book, *The Loneliest Mountain*, is the story of the first ascent of Antarctica's Mt Minto. He has also written a novel, a guide to the Blue Mountains and two biographies, including *Douglas Mawson, The Life Of An Explorer*, published in 2000.

Dr David Horton is retired and lives on his farm at Gundaroo near Canberra. He has been palaeoecologist at the Australian Institute of Aboriginal and Torres Strait Islander Studies, head of Aboriginal Studies Press and General Editor of the *Encyclopaedia of Aboriginal Australia*. Involved in many archaeological excavations, he became interested in the relationship between Aborigines and the environment, publishing dozens of academic papers, monographs, the book and award-winning interactive CD-ROM *Recovering the Tracks*, the map 'Aboriginal Australia' and his latest book, *The Pure State of Nature*. Awarded the rare Doctor of Letters degree, he is currently working on two new books and several articles on environmental issues.

Peter Macinnis is a science writer and broadcaster living in Sydney. He writes the science content for *Webster's World Encyclopedia* CD-ROM and does radio work for ABC Radio National's 'Ockham's Razor' and 'The Science Show'. He has published several children's books including the Whitley award-winning *The Rainforest*, with Jane Bowring and Kim Gamble; the same team is completing a companion volume on the Great Barrier Reef. Peter is currently writing a social and natural history of cane sugar, aimed at an adult audience.

Kate McIntyre is a regular contributor to *The Wine Magazine*. Learning first-hand about vineyards and wineries growing up from the age of nine on her family's estate on Victoria's Mornington Peninsula, Kate began her career in the wine industry at Philip Murphy Wine and Spirits in 1996. In 1998 she was the inaugural winner of the Negociants Working with Wine Fellowship. During 1999 she was wine writer for *The Australian Women's Weekly* and is an occasional contributor to *Divine* magazine.

Kate was also a contributor to *Discover Australia: Wineries*.

Dr George McKay was born in England's Lake District and was educated both there and in Canada, where he developed a fascination with mammals. After university education in Vancouver and Washington, DC, which involved as much field work as possible, he had a short career in zoos before settling into an academic post at Sydney's Macquarie University. During that time he has studied mammals in Europe, North and Central America, Asia and Australia. In 1996 he retired to become an independent biologist dedicated to spending time filling in the gaps in his geographic coverage.

Dr Gabrielle Meagher is Lecturer in the School of Economics and Political Science at the University of Sydney where, together with Dick Bryan, she teaches a course on the changing structure of the Australian economy. She is author of a number of articles about the Australian domestic services industry, women in economics, and social sustainability in Australia.

Alex Mitchell credits her involvement in the 1998 Negociants Working With Wine program as being the turning point in her career in wine. It exposed her to an unprecedented range of imported wines and winning its prestigious Wine Writing Prize led to her writing regularly for *The Wine Magazine*. After many years of nursing and four years in wine retail, she now has her own business. She has taught wine studies at Swinburne University and has contributed to three books, including the *Global Encyclopedia of Wine*. She plans to complete a Bachelor of Oenology with the intention of becoming a winemaker.

David Moon is Vice President of the National Four Wheel Drive Council, having spent two years as President. As Queensland editorial correspondent for Australia's leading 4WD magazine, *4x4 Australia* adventure magazine, he covered the International Rainforest Challenge in Malaysia. David is also a regular official at the ARB/Warn/4x4 Australian Outback Challenge. He is involved in the release of new 4WD models and is also involved in the 4WD aftermarket industry. David presents 4WD segments for the popular Channel 7 'Creek to Coast' program, is a Director of the Australian Off Road Driver Training Centre Pty Ltd, which runs nationally accredited 4WD courses, and is also a qualified Workplace Trainer and Assessor.

Ron and Viv Moon founded the magazine *Action Outdoor Australia* in the early 1980s and also travelled extensively as freelance adventure travel writers. This included canoe trips on the Zambezi River, high-altitude walking jaunts on Mt Kilamanjaro and Mt Kenya in Africa, diving in the Red Sea, Coral Sea and Mediterranean and trekking in New Zealand. Together they have written, produced or contributed to nine guidebooks on remote areas in Australia. Ron is Editor of *4X4 Australia* magazine, and gained an enviable reputation as one of Australia's most widely travelled and 'hands on' 4WD experts. He has been 4WD presenter on Rex Hunt's television fishing show, and consultant and co-presenter for several adventure 4WD television documentaries, 4WD instructional videos for Ford and Mitsubishi and a range of videos on 4WD skills and techniques. He also produced several Australian travel destination videos.

Jeremy Oliver is an independent Australian wine writer, broadcaster, author and speaker. Since 1984, when he became the world's youngest published wine author, he has written nine books and has contributed wine columns to dozens of magazines and newspapers. In addition to his self-published annual guide to Australian wine, *The*

OnWine Australian Wine Annual, and his bi-monthly newsletter, *Jeremy Oliver's OnWine Report*, his current contributions include *The Wine Magazine*, *Personal Investment* and *The Australian Way*. Jeremy is also a regular speaker and master of ceremonies at wine presentations and has a comprehensive, and independent wine website.

Stephen Samuelson is Executive Producer for Fairfax *CitySearch* in Australia. He has followed his first love, sports writing, ever since graduating university with a degree in politics. He has written or contributed to more than ten books in the last four years, including an official publication for the 1999 Cricket World Cup in England. Stephen's articles have appeared in *Inside Sport* and *The Sydney Morning Herald*. During the Sydney 2000 Olympics he worked as a consultant for the American network NBC.

Professor Leon van Schaik is Deputy Vice Chancellor and Professor of Architecture at Royal Melbourne Institute of Technology (RMIT) and Chair of the University Campus Planning Committee. He writes regularly for architectural and other journals and, as an architect, he has worked on projects from housing to complex educational buildings, art galleries and factories.

His many other roles include visiting critic at the Harvard Graduate School of Design, curator in the Adelaide Festival, visiting critic to the Kumamoto Artpolis, Commissioner for the Australia Pavilion at the Venice Biennale 2000, and he is currently on the Advisory Board of the Dutch Architecture Biennale 2002–2004.

Dr Claire Smith is a Senior Lecturer in Archaeology at Flinders University in Adelaide, South Australia. During 2000 to 2001 she was a Fulbright Fellow with the Smithsonian Institution in Washington, DC, where she conducted research on globalisation and indigenous peoples. An active fieldworker, she has extensive experience with indigenous communities in Australia, Asia and North America. She is the author of *Cultures in Contact: Colonisation and an Australian Aboriginal Community* and coeditor, with Graeme K. Ward, of the book *Indigenous Cultures in an Interconnected World*.

Professor Bruce G. Thom, holds the title Emeritus Professor from University of Sydney. He is currently Chair of the Coastal Council of New South Wales and Chair of the State of the Environment Council for the Commonwealth Government. Formerly

Vice-Chancellor at the University of New England (1994–96) he has held many other positions, such as Foundation Professor of Geography at the Royal Military College, Duntroon (University of New South Wales, 1977–84); Professor of Geography, University of Sydney (1985–93); and Pro-Vice-Chancellor of Research, University of Sydney (1990–93).

John Wrigley operates a plantation growing native tropical rainforest foliage for the florist trade. He has published eight books on the cultivation of native plants. John's botanical career began when he became Curator of the then new Canberra Botanic Gardens (now the Australian National Botanic Gardens) in 1967. He was made the first Honorary Life Member of the Society for Growing Australian Plants (New South Wales) after serving his first year as Federal President and Newsletter Editor. In 1981, after 15 years as Curator, he left to establish a horticultural consultancy near Coffs Harbour, New South Wales, where he and his wife also developed a 7 ha (17.3 acre) property as a private botanic garden. He was made a Member of the Order of Australia in 1983. As a consultant, he has designed regional botanic gardens at Coffs Harbour, Mildura and Tamworth, Australia.

C O N T

Contributors 8

Foreword by Pat O'Shane 14

PART 1
THE STORY OF AUSTRALIA 16

Introduction by Peter Cosgrove 19

**THE NATURAL HISTORY
OF AUSTRALIA** 20

Physical map: Australia 22

Political map: Australia and
 External Territories 24

Physical geography 25

Fauna 42

Flora 60

Antarctica and the Subantarctic
 islands 74

**THE HUMAN HISTORY
OF AUSTRALIA** 84

Indigenous history 86

History since European
 contact 104

Science and technology 130

**GOVERNMENT AND
THE ECONOMY** 142

Government 144

The economy 158

CULTURE AND THE ARTS 172

Indigenous art and culture 174

Culture and society 190

Media and the arts 204

Architecture 222

Sport 232

PART 2
PLACES IN AUSTRALIA 246

VICTORIA 248

Melbourne 254

Adventure activities in Victoria 258

South-West Victoria 260

North-West Victoria 284

South-East Victoria 294

North-East Victoria 316

Maps of Victoria 334

NEW SOUTH WALES 346

Sydney 352

Adventure activities in
 New South Wales 356

South-East New South Wales 358

Central-East New South Wales 378

North-East New South Wales 404

North-West New South Wales 426

South-West New South Wales 440

Maps of New South Wales 452

**AUSTRALIAN CAPITAL
TERRITORY** 466

Canberra 470

Maps of the Australian Capital
 Territory 476

QUEENSLAND 478

Brisbane 484

Adventure activities in
 Queensland 486

E N T S

South-East Queensland **488**

Central-East Queensland **508**

North Queensland **518**

Outback Queensland **530**

South-West Queensland **538**

Cape York and Cairns **544**

Maps of Queensland **554**

NORTHERN TERRITORY **570**

Darwin **576**

Adventure activities in the
 Northern Territory **578**

The Top End **580**

Central Northern Territory **594**

Southern Northern Territory **600**

Maps of the Northern
 Territory **611**

WESTERN AUSTRALIA **620**

Perth **626**

Adventure activities in
 Western Australia **628**

South-West Western Australia **630**

Central-West Western
 Australia **658**

Central-East and South-East
 Western Australia **670**

The Kimberley **678**

The Pilbara **690**

Maps of Western Australia **703**

SOUTH AUSTRALIA **716**

Adelaide **722**

Adventure activities in South
 Australia **724**

South-East South Australia **726**

Western South Australia **738**

Central-East South Australia **746**

North-East South Australia **776**

Maps of South Australia **785**

TASMANIA **794**

Hobart **800**

Adventure activities in
 Tasmania **802**

Northern Tasmania **804**

Southern Tasmania **824**

Maps of Tasmania **837**

**ROAD MAPS KEY AND
DISTANCE BARS** **846**

INDEX **848**

Index to Part 1 **849**

Index to Part 2 **859**

Acknowledgements **912**

Foreword

Her mountains worn smooth; her plains swept bare; apparently benign: Australia. 'The Timeless Land' (as one pre-eminent Australian author, Eleanor Dark, named it) is the oldest continent on Earth. And the Indigenous people of this Timeless Land have the oldest surviving cultures on Earth. In a word, we are unique— that gives us a great deal to celebrate.

Even prior to the advent of modern Australian society in 1788, this land has, at once, both fascinated and repelled those from other lands. Many have seen it as dry, inhospitable, impenetrable desert or rainforest. Others have seen it as having an endless sameness about it, at the same time as acknowledging that it stretches through every climatic zone from hot tropical to cold antarctic; from mountains and rainforest-covered escarpment to desert plateaus and long gentle beaches. It is a land of many parts.

Since 1788, when the first shiploads of English convicts were dumped on our shores at Port Jackson (named by Captain James Cook in 1770) our social mix has grown to include people from every nation on Earth, from every religious background, and from every cultural persuasion. We Australians are people of many parts.

Yet, despite all of this diversity of land and people, many Australians still experience alienation from the land that is Australia. Their alienation is manifested in the large-scale denudation of the native forests, and the replacement of those forests with a variety of exotic trees, shrubs and other plants. It is expressed in excessive use and waste of water, our most scarce resource; and the constant misuse and abuse of the thin arable soils. It is acted out in the rejection of Aboriginal and Torres Strait Islander cultures, the denigration of the people, together with the cynical commercial exploitation of those aspects which so loudly proclaim to the rest of the world our uniqueness.

Happily these negative behaviour patterns informed by ignorant, outmoded habits of thinking and feeling are passing. In place thereof, our schools, our community groups, our political and business leaders—our people all, are beginning to acknowledge that we cannot continue the futile battle against Nature, the land as it is with its scarce basic resources. We now acknowledge, as our Indigenous people learnt experientially over millennia, that we must nurture Nature if we are to survive happily in peaceful coexistence, not only with each other, but with all other species as well. We now acknowledge that we all have something to celebrate in being able to draw spiritual and emotional strength, guidance and wisdom from the oldest surviving cultures in the world.

We acknowledge that the history of each of our component parts is the history of all of us, for all of us.

PAT O'SHANE

Dr P.J. O'Shane MA undertook Law studies at the University of New South Wales, graduating in 1976, the first Indigenous person to do so in Australia. She practised at the NSW Bar and in the Northern Territory, where she worked with the Central Australian Aboriginal Legal Aid Service. In 1981, Dr O'Shane went to Canberra and worked for a brief time as a Senior Policy Advisor in the Office of Women's Affairs, while commencing postgraduate studies in Law at the University of Sydney. She was soon appointed as 'permanent head' of the newly established Ministry of Aboriginal Affairs, a position she held for five years. In 1984 Dr O'Shane was awarded a Member of the Order of Australia. She graduated with a Master of Laws in 1986 and was appointed a Magistrate of the Local Courts of New South Wales. She is married and has two adult daughters. In 1998 Pat O'Shane was voted one of Australia's Living National Treasures.

PART I

THE STORY OF AUSTRALIA

Introduction

Like most other young Australians of my generation, at school I learnt the words of Dorothea Mackellar's wonderful poem, 'My Country', written in 1908. How evocative those words are still, when describing this great land in which we live, Australia. The richness of its starkly contrasting landscape, the vagaries of its climate, its beauty, its cruelty, the fortitude of its people; they are all magically captured in Mackellar's words.

Australia's story continues to unfold as we come to grips with who we were, who we are, and what we hope to be. Our nation and its society are a rich mixture of many things: our land, our people, our past and our heritage. But as Dorothea Mackellar recognised, it is our land that is the common bond that holds us together as Australians.

In my dual roles as Australia's chief soldier and, in the Year of the Centenary of our Federation, the Australian of the Year, I enjoy the privilege of travelling all over this vast land and meeting a tremendous number of my fellow Australians. I am struck by the common themes I constantly encounter: pride in what we are and what we have achieved, confidence in our future, but above all that, the enduring Australian characteristic of mateship.

In my military life it is a characteristic we value above all others along with courage and a fair go. As a nation we see it constantly on the sporting field, and all too often in adversity when the vagaries of either human-made or natural disaster strike. It is a characteristic which sets us apart from many other nations. And for me it strikes a chord of national pride when I see our young women and men serving overseas demonstrating those same characteristics in often difficult, dangerous and trying circumstances. As Dorothea Mackellar recognised, it is to our native land that our thoughts turn when circumstance or opportunity takes us from its shores.

As you journey through *Australia: The Complete Story* remember that it is a story yet to be fully told. Question what you read and what you see; and learn from the experience. I have great optimism from the confidence I encounter in Australians wherever I go, that in the next 100 years we will continue to grow as a nation, as that rich mixture I mentioned earlier grows, changes and develops. And at the heart of that growth will be that sunburnt country, a land of sweeping plains, a land whose story you are about to discover, Australia.

LIEUTENANT GENERAL PETER COSGROVE

Lieutenant General P.J. Cosgrove, AC, MC entered the Royal Military College in 1965. In his early career in the Royal Australian Infantry Corps he served in Australia, Malaysia and South Vietnam and was awarded the Military Cross for service in Vietnam. His many career postings in Australia included Commanding Officer of the 1st Battalion, RAR and he was subsequently appointed a member of the military division of the Order of Australia for his service there. He became Commander 1st Division and Deployable Joint Force Headquarters in March 1998, and commanded INTERFET (International Forces for East Timor). In March 2000 he was appointed a Companion in the Military Division of the Order of Australia and a Companion of the New Zealand Order of Merit in recognition of his services in East Timor. Lieutenant General Cosgrove assumed his current appointment as Chief of Army on 16 July 2000. He is married to Lynne and has three sons: Stephen, Philip and David. Peter Cosgrove is Australian of the Year in 2001.

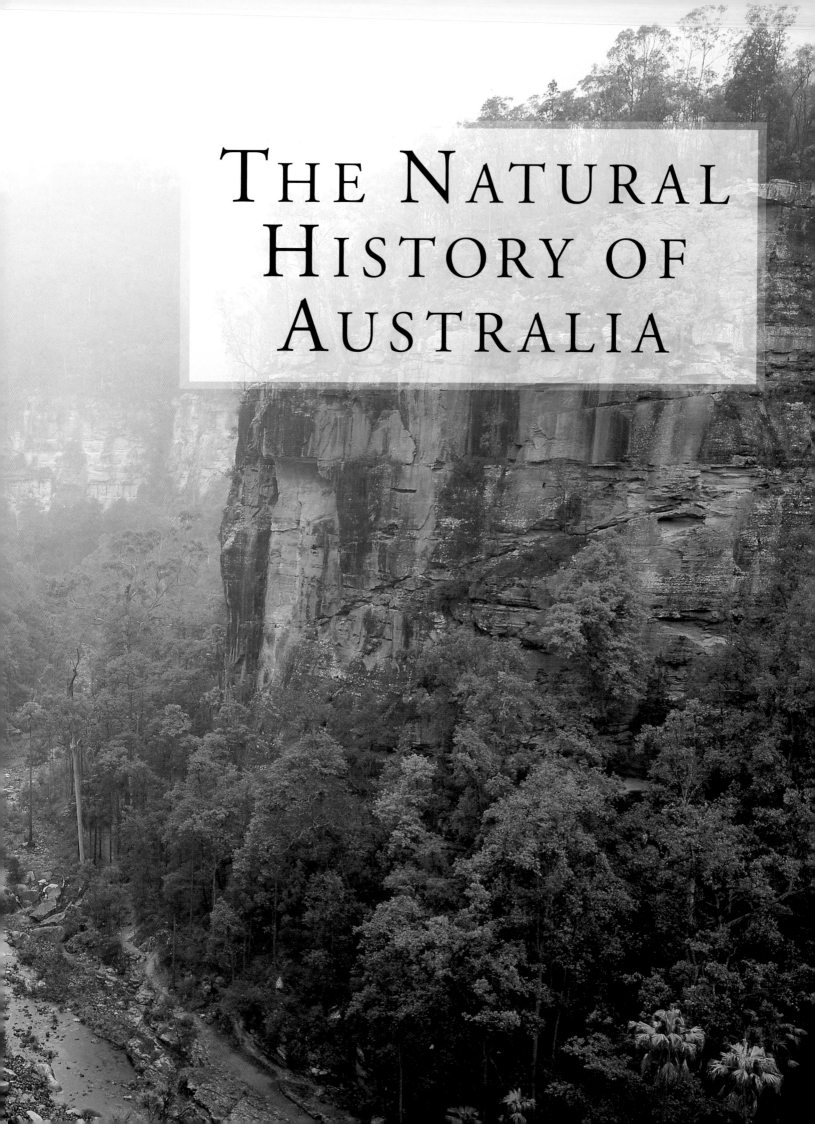

The Natural History of Australia

Australia Fact File

Official name Commonwealth of Australia

Capital Canberra

Land area 7,692,030 sq. km (2,970,125 square miles)

Highest point Mount Kosciuszko, NSW, 2228 m (7310 feet)

Lowest point Lake Eyre South, SA, 11.9 m (39 feet) below sea level

Longest river Darling River 2740 km (1703 miles)

Largest lake Lake Eyre 9300 sq. km (3590 square miles)

Highest average annual rainfall Happy Valley, Qld, 4436 mm (175 inches)

Lowest average annual rainfall Lake Eyre region, SA, 100 mm (3.9 inches)

Highest recorded temperature 53.1°C (127.5°F) at Cloncurry, Qld, January 1889

Lowest recorded temperature −23°C (−9.4°F) at Charlotte Pass, NSW, 29 June 1994

Population 19,400,000 (2001 est.)
Indigenous population 427,094 (June 2001 est.)

Population density 2.5 per sq. km (6.5 per square mile), but 84% of the population occupy 1% of the land

Urban v. rural population 84.6% urban, 15.4% rural (1997)

Population growth rate 1.2% (1999–2000)

Projected population 2051 24–28 million

Birth rate 13.3 per 1000 population (1998)

Death rate 6 per 1000 population (1998)

Life expectancy 76 for males, 82 for females (1997–99)
Indigenous life expectancy 56 for males, 63 for females (1997–99)

Infant mortality 5.3 per 1000 births (1999)
Indigenous infant mortality 14 per 1000 births (1999)

Country of birth of population Australia 76.4%, UK & Ireland 6.5%, New Zealand 1.9%, Italy 1.3%, Former Yugoslavia 1.1%, Vietnam 0.9%, China 0.8%, Greece 0.7%, Germany 0.7%, Netherlands 0.5%, Philippines 0.5%, Hong Kong 0.3%, other 8.4% (1999 est.)

Country of birth of migrants New Zealand 17.1%, UK & Ireland 12.3%, China 8%, Former Yugoslavia 6.7 %, South Africa 4.6%, Hong Kong 3.7%, other 47.6% (1995–99)

First language English 84.5%, Italian 2.3%, Greek 1.6%, Cantonese 1.2%, Arabic 1%, Vietnamese 0.8%, German 0.6%, Mandarin 0.5%, Spanish 0.5%, Macedonian 0.4%, Tagalog (Filipino) 0.4%, other 6.2% (1996)

Religious affiliation Catholic 27%, Anglican 22%, other Christian 21.9%, non-Christian 3.5%, no religion 16.6%, not stated 9% (1996)

Employment by sector Services 82%, industry 12%, agriculture and mining 6% (1999)

GDP $591,546 million (total 1999), $30,487 (per capita 1999)

Major exports Coal 9%, gold 5%, crude petroleum products 5%, iron ore 4%, wheat 4%, alumina 4% (1999–2000)

Major imports Motor vehicles 6%, telecommunications equipment 6%, crude petroleum oils 5%, computer equipment 4%, aircraft 4% (1999–2000)

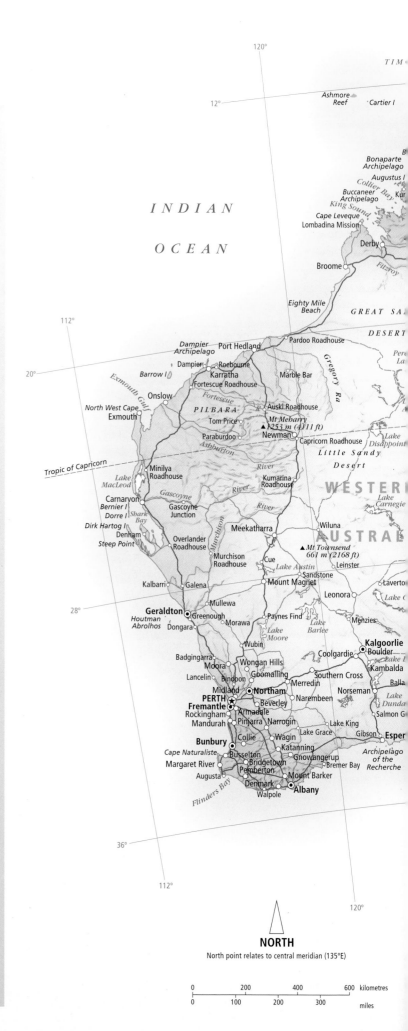

NORTH

North point relates to central meridian (135°E)

Australia and External Territories

Scale approx 1:40,000,000 at latitude 25°S
Projection: Orthogonal

0   500   1000   kilometres
0   300   600   miles

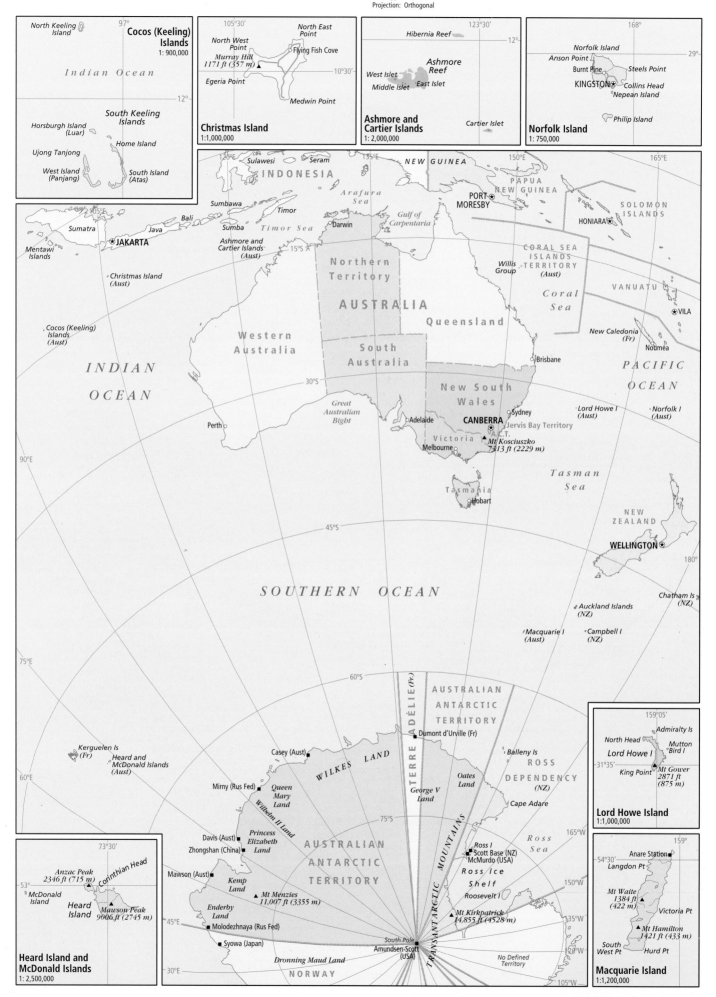

Cocos (Keeling) Islands
1: 900,000

North Keeling Island
Indian Ocean
97°
12°
South Keeling Islands
Horsburgh Island (Luar)
Ujong Tanjong
West Island (Panjang)
Home Island
South Island (Atas)

Christmas Island
1:1,000,000

105°30'
North West Point
North East Point
Murray Hill 1171 ft (357 m)
Flying Fish Cove
10°30'
Egeria Point
Medwin Point

Ashmore and Cartier Islands
1: 2,000,000

Hibernia Reef
123°30'
12°
Ashmore Reef
West Islet
Middle Islet
East Islet
Cartier Islet

Norfolk Island
1: 750,000

168°
Norfolk Island
Anson Point
29°
Burnt Pine
Steels Point
KINGSTON
Collins Head
Nepean Island
Philip Island

Heard Island and McDonald Islands
1: 2,500,000

73°30'
Anzac Peak 2346 ft (715 m)
Corinthian Head
53°
McDonald Island
Heard Island
Mawson Peak 9006 ft (2745 m)
45°E
30°E

Macquarie Island
1:1,200,000

159°
Anare Station
54°30'
Langdon Pt
Mt Waite 1384 ft (422 m)
Victoria Pt
Mt Hamilton 1421 ft (433 m)
South West Pt
Hurd Pt

Lord Howe Island
1:1,000,000

159°05'
Admiralty Is
North Head
Lord Howe I
Mutton Bird I
31°35'
King Point
Mt Gower 2871 ft (875 m)

INDONESIA
Sulawesi
Seram
NEW GUINEA
150°E
135°E
120°E
PAPUA NEW GUINEA
SOLOMON ISLANDS
Sumbawa
Timor
Arafura Sea
Gulf of Carpentaria
PORT MORESBY
Bali
Java
Sumba
Timor Sea
Darwin
HONIARA
Sumatra
JAKARTA
Ashmore and Cartier Islands (Aust)
15°S
CORAL SEA ISLANDS TERRITORY (Aust)
165°E
Mentawi Islands
Christmas Island (Aust)
Northern Territory
Willis Group
Coral Sea
VANUATU
VILA
AUSTRALIA
New Caledonia (Fr)
Noumea
Cocos (Keeling) Islands (Aust)
Western Australia
Queensland
South Australia
Brisbane
INDIAN OCEAN
30°S
New South Wales
PACIFIC OCEAN
Great Australian Bight
Perth
Adelaide
CANBERRA
Sydney
Lord Howe I (Aust)
Norfolk I (Aust)
A.C.T.
Jervis Bay Territory
Victoria
Mt Kosciuszko 7313 ft (2229 m)
Melbourne
90°E
Tasman Sea
Tasmania
Hobart
NEW ZEALAND
45°S
WELLINGTON
180°
75°E
SOUTHERN OCEAN
Chatham Is (NZ)
Auckland Islands (NZ)
Macquarie I (Aust)
Campbell I (NZ)
60°S
TERRE ADÉLIE (Fr)
AUSTRALIAN ANTARCTIC TERRITORY
Kerguelen Is (Fr)
Heard and McDonald Islands (Aust)
Dumont d'Urville (Fr)
60°E
Casey (Aust)
WILKES LAND
Balleny Is
ROSS DEPENDENCY (NZ)
Mirny (Rus Fed)
Queen Mary Land
Oates Land
George V Land
Cape Adare
75°S
165°W
Davis (Aust)
Princess Elizabeth Land
Wilhelm II Land
AUSTRALIAN ANTARCTIC TERRITORY
Ross Sea
Zhongshan (China)
Ross I
Scott Base (NZ)
McMurdo (USA)
150°W
Mawson (Aust)
Kemp Land
Mt Menzies 11,007 ft (3355 m)
TRANSANTARCTIC MOUNTAINS
Ross Ice Shelf
Roosevelt I
Enderby Land
Mt Kirkpatrick 14,855 ft (4528 m)
135°W
Molodezhnaya (Rus Fed)
45°E
Syowa (Japan)
South Pole
Amundsen-Scott (USA)
No Defined Territory
Dronning Maud Land
120°W
NORWAY
30°E
105°W

PHYSICAL GEOGRAPHY

Our Geologic Inheritance

A geologist views history in millions of years. For some countries and regions of the Earth, the geologic perspective is confined to as little as a few hundred million or even less than fifty million years. Australia, by contrast, is extraordinarily privileged. Our nation is rich in geologic history, one of the few countries that embraces almost the full spectrum of geologic time since the Earth's crust was established more than 4 billion years ago.

Australia's geologic inheritance in so many ways drives the identity of the nation. This is evident in its remoteness, its vastness, its latitudinal position, its dominating aridity, its ancient landscapes carved in rocks far from the sea, and in its enormous wealth of minerals. Our continental land mass extends seawards to embrace the surrounding continental shelf, narrow on the eastern margin—where to the north-east it is covered by the magnificent Great Barrier Reef—and wider on the north-west shelf, a large area rich in petroleum and natural gas.

The core of ancient Australia is in the west. Here occur those so-called 'blocks' of metamorphic and igneous rocks formed by the intrusion of molten magmas into the Earth's primeval crust and subjected to heat and pressure in that earliest period of Earth's history, the Archaean. As our atmosphere slowly evolved to include oxygen, sediments derived from the blocks began to accumulate with banded layers of precipitated iron oxide, the backbone of a mineral resource which has become vital to today's export-driven economy (for example the rich iron deposits of the Hamersley Range).

By 1500 million years ago (mya), the ancient rock masses of the western half of the continent could be identified as a vast plateau. Within the shallow seas bordering this region, early life forms appeared as far back as 3.5 billion years. It is through the fossil record trapped in sediments that we can trace the evolution over geologic time of plants and animals—including events causing mass extinctions.

To the older western core of Australia were added more sedimentary rocks. Gradually the forces of mountain building produced the folded and intruded rock sequences of what are now termed the Eastern Highlands. Between 600 and 300 mya, these rocks were intruded by molten rocks from below the Earth's crust, in places enriched in gold and other precious metals. As in the west, shallow basins between the

Spectacular Chambers Pillar in the Simpson Desert south of Alice Springs in the Northern Territory. An eroded sandstone remnant, it is at the southern margin of the Palaeozoic rocks that form the ranges of central Australia and was named by J. McDouall Stuart after an Adelaide horse dealer known as 'Greenhide' Chambers.

As awe-inspiring as they are ancient: the sandstone bluffs of the Rainbow Valley Conservation Reserve in the Northern Territory. Fronting a vast claypan, they are seen at their best in the late afternoon, when the lowering sun highlights bands of iron in the white sandstone.

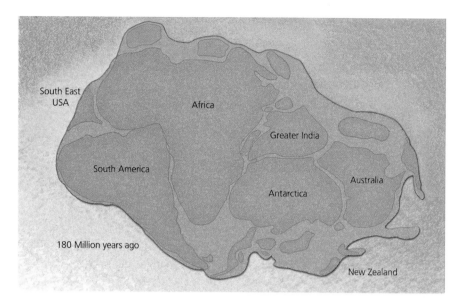

The great supercontinent of Gondwana at approximately 180 million years ago, highlighting opportunities for migration of plants and animals from one continental mass to another.

folded mountain ranges trapped sediments washed into the seas, so becoming the site of extensive peat swamps which over time were transformed into coal deposits of Permian age (280–245 mya), as occur in the Hunter Valley of New South Wales. The dominating sandstone foundations so characteristic of the Sydney region were also formed around this time, during the Triassic (245–205 mya).

The ancestral continents

Until relatively recently in geologic time (over the past 100 million years), Australia did not become an identified continental landmass. Then, just over 200 mya, the great supercontinent of Pangaea, the 'One Earth', broke into two major land regions, Laurasia in the Northern Hemisphere and Gondwana in the Southern Hemisphere. The splitting and subsequent collision of the 'drifting' continental masses is a result of what is known as plate tectonics. Australia is now

part of the Indo–Australia Plate which extends from southern India, through parts of Indonesia then to the south-east, where it takes in a section of New Zealand. Until approximately 100 mya this plate was attached to Africa and Antarctica and even joined onto South America. Flora and fauna of these now separate continents had much in common as is seen, for instance, in fossils of the Permian coal deposits.

This separation and movement of the continental plates has left its mark on many elements of the Australian landscape. On the eastern margin, the steep continental slope and narrow shelf and the elevation of the Eastern Highlands reflect the opening of the Tasman Sea between 60 and 80 mya. Rivers flowing east at this time started to entrench themselves not only into the Eastern Highlands, but also onto the shelf that later would be invaded and overwhelmed by rising sea levels. In marked contrast are the traces of the old rivers which once flowed northwards across the flatter landscapes of south-western Australia; these watercourses had their highland origins in Antarctica!

Over the past 50 to 100 million years Australia drifted northward at the rate of about 8 to 12 cm (3 to 5 inches) per year, thereby distancing itself from Antarctica, and it was during this time that the distinctive nature of the continent's recent geology, biota and climates began to unfold. Only at the margins of the plate—across Indonesia and in the newly emerging mountains of Papua New Guinea, as well as along the south-west Pacific's island chain, including New Zealand—did volcanism and earthquake activity dominate the landscape. Although smaller volcanoes and lava flows did occur in eastern Australia as the older rocks of the crust passed over hot spots from within the Earth's mantle, Australia became a relatively quiescent landscape, with whole land surfaces slowly transformed by the weathering of rocks and by river and marine erosion and deposition. Vast areas of

Avalon, one of Sydney's northern beaches. Erosion by wave and water over millions of years has shaped the spectacular sandstone bluffs and headlands so characteristic of the Sydney region today.

inland Australia forming the Central Lowlands were flooded by shallow seas which progressively retreated to the present shoreline positions, leaving behind subterranean reservoirs of salty waters, which would later become a source of much concern to farmers and graziers. During this period, the early Cretaceous, Australia was divided into a number of large islands.

Birth of a continent

Connections to other continental land masses once allowed for migrations of plants and animals adapted to different climatic and soil conditions. But as the continents separated, Australia became more isolated. So it is that over the past 50 to 100 million years, biota began to evolve in relative isolation in response to selection pressures from changing environments. While some remnants of Gondwanan biota have survived, members of the Proteaceae family of plants for instance, the distinctive character of present-day vegetation slowly emerged as the Australian continent moved closer to Asia.

Dinosaurs, the egg-laying mammals known as monotremes, crocodiles and birds were among the animals present in the early Cretaceous landscapes of around 100 mya. The changing environments of the late Cretaceous, from 95 to 65 mya, saw the retreat of the seas, and with the continent moving northward into warmer, more humid climates, flowering plants became more dominant. The catastrophic event which resulted in the termination of the Cretaceous at 65 mya, presumably caused by an asteroid impact, led to mass extinctions including those of Australian dinosaurs. A new era of geologic time commenced,

the Cainozoic, which continues today and includes two geologic periods, the Tertiary (65 mya–2 mya) and the Quaternary (1.65 million to present).

The warmer and wetter conditions of the early Tertiary permitted rainforest growth across much of the continent which by 40 million years ago was separated by a deep sea strait from Antarctica. This separation was a critical event in Australia's history, as it led to a drying of its climates. Oceanic currents surrounded Antarctica, facilitating the establishment of ice on its land surface with a cooling elsewhere in

The glistening saltpans and lakes of the arid inland, like this one at Kambalda, Western Australia, are reminders of a wetter past.

The characteristically dry bed of the Todd River near Alice Springs, Northern Territory. Flowing only after heavy rains, the Todd's water disappears in the sands of the Simpson Desert.

The southern African *Protea* belongs to the same plant family that includes Australian natives such as the waratahs and the banksias.

RIGHT: *Temperate rainforest was common in Australia 20 million years ago. Eucalypts, were found only on poorer, drier soils.*

the world and a drop in sea levels. Precisely what happened to Australian biota at this time is unclear. However, by 20 to 25 mya a relatively rich fauna living in temperate rainforest conditions with an abundance of freshwater rivers and lakes has been documented. Eucalypts were relatively scarce in these moist climates although they may have been more abundant on nutrient-deficient soils.

By about 20 mya the northern edge of Australia was at roughly 20°S latitude and temperatures were warmer and rainfall more variable. Plants and animals had to adapt to changing and stressful conditions with much of the abundant fauna found in fossil-rich sites such as Riversleigh in Queensland becoming extinct. Riversleigh is now a World Heritage Site, and more than 280 fossil assemblages have produced over 300 vertebrate and invertebrate species characteristic of cool, wet, lowland forests.

Although global temperatures continued to fall from 10 mya, there is evidence that patterns of aridity so characteristic of today's Australia were already beginning to emerge. A shift occurs towards dry sclerophyllous forests with *Casuarina, Eucalyptus,* and *Angophora* trees as the more dominant types of vegetation. However, details of the rate and character of change occurring among biota over this period for Australia as a whole is quite scanty and the extent of true grasslands before 2 mya is debatable.

Australia today

Today the island continent of Australia extends from about 10°S to 45°S and covers an area of 7,686,850 sq. km (2,967,896 sq. miles). It embraces a range of climates greatly influenced by the surrounding oceans, but it is from its geology that this continental nation has received the inheritance which created environmental and cultural conditions of significance—first of all to its indigenous inhabitants, and more recently to the arrivals from the Northern Hemisphere. The exploitation of iron and bauxite from ancient and weathered rocks; the finding of precious metals deep underground such as at Kalgoorlie, Broken Hill and Mount Isa; an abundance of black and brown coal in Queensland, New South Wales and Victoria for both export and energy generation; and the availability of oil and natural gas in continental-shelf as well as onshore reservoirs; all provide the economy with a strength which should underpin wealth creation for many years to come. Moreover it is the geology and the moulding of the land surface, an inexorable process occurring over millions of years, which have formed the distinctive soil types upon which Australian agriculture is so dependent. These soils have in so many ways demonstrated themselves to be fragile, demanding of agriculturists an understanding of their history and character far beyond that which is necessary for the management of the younger and more fertile agricultural lands of Europe, Asia and North America.

GEOLOGY AND MAJOR MINERAL DEPOSITS

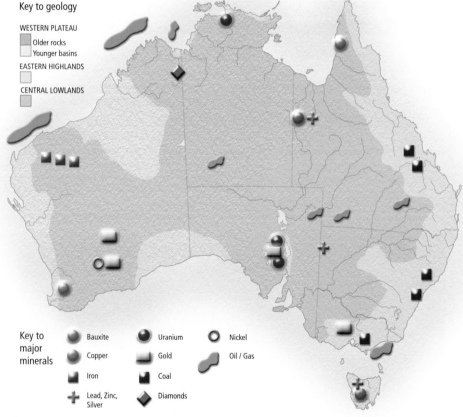

Key to geology

WESTERN PLATEAU
  Older rocks
  Younger basins
EASTERN HIGHLANDS
CENTRAL LOWLANDS

Key to major minerals
  Bauxite   Uranium   Nickel
  Copper   Gold   Oil / Gas
  Iron   Coal
  Lead, Zinc, Silver   Diamonds

| PHYSICAL GEOGRAPHY TIMELINE | 2500 MILLION YBP Formation of the Hamersley Range, now in north-west Australia, which absorbs large quantities of iron from ocean. | 750 MILLION YBP Severe ice age covers much of continent in ice sheets. | 540 MILLION YBP Plate movements give rise to volcanic islands, beginning buildup of eastern part of continent. Sediments accumulate around islands. | 325 MILLION YBP Onset of another ice age as continent drifts toward South Pole. Sediments continue to accumulate in east. | 260 MILLION YBP Climate becomes gradually warmer and wetter; large areas of cool-temperate swamps give rise to continent's vast coal deposits. | 155 MILLION YBP Gondwana begins to break up. Rift appears between Australasia and Antarctica, widening gradually over the next 100 million years. | 80–60 MILLION YBP Tasmantis—New Zealand, New Caledonia, Norfolk, Lord Howe, Kermadec and the Chatham islands—splits from Australia. |

670 MILLION YBP Glaciers cloak continent during another ice age.

| 3500 MILLION YBP Formation of the continent's oldest geological formations, the Yilgarn and Pilbara blocks. Sediments then begin to accumulate around them. | 1500 MILLION YBP Further accumulation of sediments around existing blocks begins to form Western Australian Plateau. | 600 MILLION YBP Australasia joins with South America, Africa, India and Antarctica to form Gondwana. Collision creates huge (now eroded) Petermann Mountains. | 360 MILLION YBP Gondwana merges with Northern-Hemisphere landmasses to form Pangaea. | 285 MILLION YBP Sediments unite Western Plateau and eastern mountains, bringing continent to today's dimensions. | 245 MILLION YBP Pangaea begins to break up, leaving Gondwana isolated once more. | 140 MILLION YBP Rising sea levels flood interior, dividing continent into four blocks. | 55 MILLION YBP Australia, now separated from Antarctica, begins to drift northward. |

40 MILLION YBP
Temperatures drop and weather becomes increasingly seasonal with periods of heavy rain followed by periods of aridity.

14–10 MILLION YBP
Australia collides with Pacific Ocean Plate. Temperatures drop and sea levels fall, forming land bridge between Australia and New Guinea.

2 MILLION YBP
Following long, alternating periods of dry and wet spells, climate approaches current levels of aridity in interior.

20,000 YBP Last major ice age at its peak; ends 15,000 ybp.
10,000 YBP Melting ice raises sea level, cutting land bridges to Asia and Tasmania.

1788 Governor Arthur Phillip records a minor earthquake on 22 June.
1859 Regular official weather reports first compiled in Sydney.

1939 Black Friday bushfires in Vic. leave 71 people dead and destroy 1.2 million ha (3 million acres) of forest.
1955–56 Floods in NSW kill 22 people.

1982–83 Major drought affects much of eastern Australia.
1983 Ash Wednesday fires destroy homes in SA and Vic, accounting for 70 lives.

1990 Floods engulf Nyngan, NSW, leading to evacuation of entire town.
1994 Worst bushfires in 30 years strike NSW, threatening to engulf parts of Sydney.

25 MILLION YBP
Large area of ocean floor at southern edge of continent lifted above sea level forming Nullarbor Plain.

4 MILLION YBP Sea levels rise and more frequent dry spells occur.

1.65 MILLION YBP
Start of series of 20 glacial and interglacials, results in greater diversification and specialisation of biota.

8000 YBP Great Barrier Reef begins to reform.
6000 YBP Mount Gambier, Australia's last active volcano, erupts. Sea levels reach those of today.

1877 First weather map published in Australia.
1895–1903 Severe drought afflicts much of country. Other droughts follow in 1911–16 and 1918–20.

1974 Cyclone Tracy strikes Darwin on Christmas Day, destroying 90 per cent of the city's buildings and claiming 65 lives. Severe wave erosion along east coast in May.

1989 An earthquake measuring 5.6 on the Richter Scale hits Newcastle, NSW, on 28 December, toppling buildings and killing 13.

1999 Damaging hailstorm strikes parts of Sydney.
2000 Floods in NSW devastate crops, causing more than $0.5 billion of damage.

Ice Ages and Australia

Wetlands such as these at Bool Lagoon, South Australia, are a precious resource in Australia, the world's driest inhabited continent.

RIGHT: Fraser Island, the world's largest sand island, is quite young in geological terms. Parts of its interior support rainforest. The age of the dunes can be traced by the plant communities which occupy them.

FAR RIGHT: The Walls of Jerusalem, Tasmania. Flora and fauna which have adapted to environments such as this may be threatened by the onset of global warming.

BELOW: Trends in temperature and precipitation over the past 50 million years in Australia and surrounding regions. Present conditions are characterised by oscillations in temperature with colder, more arid periods.

The global onset of colder 'icehouse' conditions in the Late Cainozoic Era involved first the accumulation of ice sheets in Antarctica and Greenland. During the past 2 million years (the Quaternary Period) there has been a distinctive cyclic pattern to the periodic extension of ice sheets, especially in the Northern Hemisphere. A pattern of cool to cold (glacial) conditions separated by shorter, warmer intervals known as interglacials is a feature of this latest period of Earth's history. Currently, we are in an interglacial referred to as the Holocene. Though the trigger for this cyclic behaviour of the Earth's climatic system is unclear, its impact on all the planet's biota, including the evolution of humans, was most profound.

While Australia was touched only lightly by the periodic growth of the ice caps, evidence of which can be seen in the uplands of Tasmania and on the Snowy Mountains, vast areas of northern and western Europe and North America were overwhelmed by spreading ice sheets.

The long descents into full glacial conditions, when average air temperatures fell some 5 to 10°C (9 to 18°F) below those characteristic of the interglacial periods, were accompanied by cooling oceanic temperatures, the displacement of weather systems and ocean currents, falling sea levels, and the migration of ecosystems. Only the core areas of tropical rainforests were relatively unaffected by these shifts, with glaciers growing dramatically, even on the peaks of equatorial mountains in places such as Papua New Guinea. During the rapid return to the interglacials, which occupied only 10 per cent of Quaternary time, plants and animals had to adjust to the warmer and regionally much wetter conditions than had dominated the preceding glacial event. Each glacial event lasted 100,000 years or more.

Thus the Quaternary can be characterised as a period of oscillation, with biota seeking stable niches which all too soon were disturbed by natural forces and, somewhat later, by a combination of those forces and the activities of humans.

The drying of Australia

Within this global context, Australia reached its current latitudinal position and tended to become progressively drier. While wet sclerophyll forests and rainforests persisted in wetter pockets even during the coldest, windiest and driest of the full glacial events, there has emerged on this continent a biota which has successfully adapted itself to aridity or episodes of it. Now-familiar landforms such as saline lakes and dune fields became a more characteristic part of vast areas of Australia and, as far as can be determined, aridity of the kind seen in modern Australia was evident about 500,000 to 700,000 years ago.

The story of Australia during the Quaternary is in some ways just about as dramatic as that of Europe. It was not the advance and retreat of glaciers which our landscape endured, but the spread and reduction of surface waters. During the height of each glacial episode, aridity intensified and wind-blown sand and dust extended across most of the continent including coastal areas. The last of these episodes occurred only 15,000 to 25,000 years ago. A picture of this time reflects a harshness to which the indigenous occupants somehow adapted, having benefited from much moister conditions 30,000 to 40,000 years ago when freshwater lakes and flowing rivers rich in fish and other wildlife were a feature of the landscape, at least across southern Australia. Such places became sites of intensive human occupancy as at Lake Mungo in south-west New South Wales and many other places in what are now Australia's arid lands.

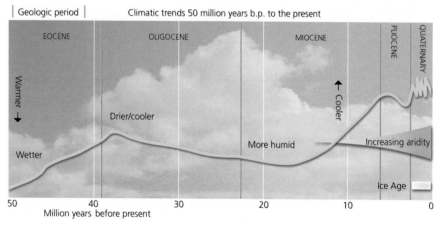

Geologic period				Climatic trends 50 million years b.p. to the present	
EOCENE	OLIGOCENE	MIOCENE	PLIOCENE	QUATERNARY	

Warmer ↓ / Wetter

Drier/cooler

More humid

Increasing aridity

↑ Cooler

Ice Age

50   40   30   20   10   0
Million years before present

Glacial growth and decay leads to worldwide falls and rises in sea level. Although barely perceptible on a yearly basis, changes in sea level measuring as little as 10 to 15 mm (⅜–⅝ inch) per year can have a significant impact on shoreline position. Unlike those areas where mountain-building is active, or where coastal margins are subject to earthquakes caused by plate motion, or even in those places where glaciers are loading or unloading Earth's crust, Australia's continental shelves are comparatively stable. Therefore, world-wide (eustatic) oscillations of sea level, involving a total rise and fall of 100 to 120 m (330 to 390 feet), can drown or expose all river valleys or flat plains built by river deltas and wave deposits. Sand blown off retreating shorelines by onshore winds progressively accumulated to form the massive coastal dunes on the east coast in southern Queensland (as at Fraser Island), or along the west coast (at Shark Bay, for example). Another response to changing sea levels has been the repeated cycles of upward growth, followed by exposure and erosion, then the upward growth again of corals and associated organisms, thereby forming tropical coral reefs. The Great Barrier Reef stands as one of Earth's natural wonders, rising from its continental-shelf bed as a multi-layered sequence of limestone reefs which has kept pace with, or been killed off by, sea-level changes.

Environmental change

Rapid environmental changes of the sort undergone by Australia during the Quaternary had a profound impact on flora and fauna. Investigation of the fossil-rich limestones at Riversleigh, in north Queensland, points to mammal diversity in today's wet tropics being about half that of the early Miocene (some 20 mya). Extinctions probably were at their greatest during full glacial periods when conditions were at their harshest. Aridity was, however, a condition that called for adaptation if species were to survive. Unreliable water supplies permitted those biota equipped to withstand long droughts to begin to dominate. Another factor, fire, became more prominent in the landscape leading to an increase in plant species that could easily reproduce after burning. Eucalypts, grasses and heathy shrubs now found themselves as the characteristic plants. They were

When Europeans arrived in Australia, the impact of their introduced animals was nowhere more dramatic than in the fragile arid zone. Here, rabbits have stripped the vegetation, and wind erosion has then exposed the roots of this tree by removing vast amounts of topsoil.

Much of Australia's flora, such as this eucalypt, have evolved to be at least partly dependent on fire as a trigger for reproduction.

utilised, in part, by an array of grazing and browsing mammals, among them the so-called megafauna such as the giant kangaroo (*Procoptodon*), wombat (*Phascolonus*) and the rhinoceros-sized *Diprotodon*, the largest marsupial that has ever lived. These herbivores were preyed upon by such creatures as *Thylocoleo*, the marsupial 'lion'. The demise of these giants is quite contentious although most would appear to have become extinct somewhere around 35,000 years ago, at some time after humans arrived on the continent.

The arrival of humans

Exact times of arrival of humans in Australia prior to European settlement are unknown. However, it was at least 40,000 to 50,000 years ago, and some archaeologists suggest the time frame is considerably longer. This was during an early phase of the last glacial period when sea levels were lower. Their spread was undoubtedly aided by the milder, wetter conditions preceding the glacial maximum, and by the great abundance of food-rich lagoons and estuaries on now-drowned continental shelves. Contact with more northern peoples continued throughout the period of changing sea levels with the more recent arrival, about 5000 years ago, of the native 'dog' (the dingo, in reality a wolf) as evidence of interaction prior to the coming of the Europeans.

Of great interest is the impact of the early humans on Australia's biota. The question of the demise of the megafauna is only one issue. What is evident is the use by Aborigines of fire for a variety of purposes. Increased incidence of fire in the landscape after 50,000 years ago is seen in charcoal records of peat and lake deposits. In some areas casuarinas may have become a less dominant tree as the fire-hardy species responded to conditions more favourable to their spread. Rainforests, already contracted, probably were more restricted, and grasslands which had more timber cover prior to Aboriginal burning, now were prone to a pattern of frequent fires which suppressed tree growth. The Aborigines made their way across the landbridge to Tasmania, where they sheltered from the onslaught of full glacial icecap growth in caves, continuing to burn large areas. The human occupation of windier, more arid parts of the continent declined as people took advantage of richer plant and animal resources in the more humid areas. Conditions were milder during the Holocene and it is possible that humans again spread to inhabit most ecosystems, developing new tool techniques for hunting and new methods of handling food plants. As the sea level around Australia reached approximately its present position 6000 years ago, there was sufficient time for marine and estuarine habitats to flourish and yield abundant resources for groups of Aborigines who lived on or visited the coast.

Natural Forces and Australian Landscapes

The ancient history of Australia, which embraces its geology and includes the arrival and impact of the indigenous peoples, has made a strong imprint on contemporary Australia. Natural forces and human activities had many times modified ecosystems, long before British settlement. The pace of change may have been relatively slow, but we now know enough to understand that climate, vegetation and soils are dynamic phenomena, and what was first documented by the early European explorers was just a snapshot in time of an ever-changing natural history.

Indigenous Australians had long since recognised and adjusted to the vagaries of Australia's climatic systems. However, the early European settlers, more attuned to the reliable seasonal rains and milder temperatures of western Europe, were soon beset by problems, even to the point of starvation. Learning to cope became a major challenge; and still the learning process continues, as Australians come to not only appreciate the peculiarities of their environments, but also begin to come to grips with the consequences of the many mistakes made in trying to subdue and make productive what to them was a new world ripe for exploitation. In a mere two hundred years these new settlers have modified Australian landscapes at rates far in excess of those of nature and the country's original inhabitants combined.

Mineral resources aside, the natural factors which influence Australian land use and society are climate, vegetation and wildlife, soils, and various marine factors. Of critical importance is the variable nature of climatic systems that influence, either directly or indirectly, these other factors as well as human lifestyles. Few places on Earth possess such 'liveable' climatic conditions, even though for the first hundred years or so of white settlement there was an aversion to living and working in the hot and humid tropics by those of British origin.

Climate types

Australia's latitudinal position and continental size make for a mix of climatic types. The dominating atmospheric system is the subtropical high-pressure belt; this embraces pressure cells which migrate from west to east across the continent, as well as seasonally northwards in winter and southwards in summer. Dry, descending warm air ensures that the lands beneath these 'highs' remain rainless for long periods. Fortunately for northern Australia, the summer monsoon brings lower pressures and rainfall, especially to coastal sections, but in some years these rains reach well into the interior, where they trigger the rapid reproduction of plants and their dependent fauna as

Europeans have greatly modified Australian landscapes, and are still doing so. As the population becomes more aware of the challenges posed by climatic change, practices such as clear-felling of native forests are being increasingly questioned.

Much of Australia is subject to 'all or nothing' cycles of drought and flood and agriculturists have been forced to adapt to these erratic climatic patterns.

RAINFALL AND OCEAN CURRENTS

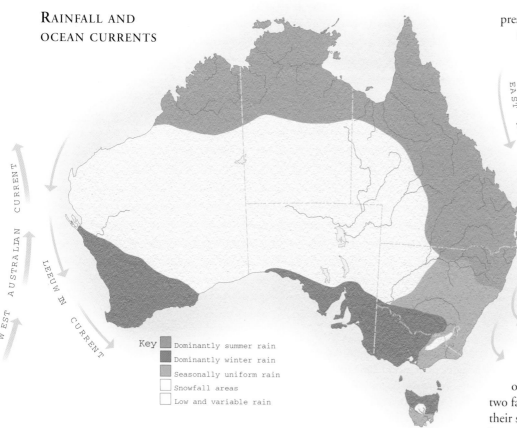

WEST AUSTRALIAN CURRENT

LEEUWIN CURRENT

EAST AUSTRALIAN CURRENT

Key
- Dominantly summer rain
- Dominantly winter rain
- Seasonally uniform rain
- Snowfall areas
- Low and variable rain

RIGHT: In 1994 a series of bushfires threatened parts of suburban Sydney. Here windsurfers in Pittwater near Palm Beach ride their boards against a fiery backdrop. Changes in the fire regime since European settlement have seen a rise in frequency of 'wild' fires.

Many of Australia's ancient soils are nutrient-poor and extremely fragile. Poor management in the past led to degradation in many areas, particularly the arid lands.

they exploit these infrequent flooding events. In contrast, southern Australia is predominantly an area of winter rainfall traversed by low-pressure cells which bring strong westerly winds, rain, sleet and even large quantities of snow to mountains in Tasmania and the south-east corner of the 'mainland'. The east coast receives its rainfall from various sources including travelling winter depressions; intense east-coast lows that generate enormous wind energy and rainfall in the Tasman Sea; tropical trade-wind moisture on the north-east highlands; and, of course, devastating winds, deluges of rain and sea-level surges generated by tropical cyclones.

Droughts and flooding rains

Natural hazards in Australia are largely climatically induced events. The continent does experience the odd sensational earthquake, such as the one which hit Newcastle with deadly force on 28 December 1989. But tropical cyclones are expected each year on north-western and eastern coasts, their tracks and intensity largely unpredictable. Since European settlement many lives and much property have been lost to furious storms such as Cyclone Tracy which struck Darwin on Christmas Day 1974, almost completely destroying the city. Flooding rains, especially in the eastern half of the continent, are associated with wet years which see waters slowly spread westward across the vast interior networks of rivers into the Lake Eyre and Murray–Darling basins. Wet years like this are usually associated with meteorological events known as La Niña, a period of generally lower atmospheric

pressure over the western Pacific and Indonesia. Contrasting conditions, called El Niño, occur as higher pressures build up to the north of the continent. The dominance of these conditions can lead to severe, prolonged drought, especially in northern and eastern regions as in 1982–83 and 1994–95. Coping with limited rainfall for several years on end is one of the great challenges that has always and will continue to beset Australian society. Drought periods such as these frequently permit drying of forests, sometimes leading to severe bushfires on the margins of towns and cities or even within cities, as in Hobart in 1967 and Sydney in 1994.

Plant and soil associations

Vegetation and soil types are closely inter-related in Australia. Landscapes receive much of their character from the ways in which these two factors are associated with landforms through their shared inheritance from the continent's geologic history. Persistent aridity provides opportunities for drought (and fire) resistant plants to cover much of the interior extending towards the west coast. Mulga, mallee eucalypts and spinifex, and their associated animals, cover vast areas of sand dunes and rocky surfaces. Plants' adaptive mechanisms include hardened leaves and long roots to capture moisture from deep in the soil or rock crevices. Native grasslands, perhaps the result of Aboriginal burning, are characteristic of the semi-arid areas of the northern and eastern plains and are the resource on which the sheep and cattle pastoral industry is based.

The highly species-diverse shrub and timbered landscapes formed on weathered rocks in south-west Australia, the Eastern Highlands and adjoining ranges (the Grampians in Victoria, for example), and in Tasmania, represent adaptations by Australia's flora to soils of varying nutrient status. *Eucalyptus, Casuarina* and *Acacia* species proliferate in these areas with their shrub understoreys or separate heathlands all supporting vast riches in mammals, birds and insects. Locally, on wetter slopes and in valleys, both tropical and temperate rainforests of different genera occur, remnants of a far more expansive ecosystem extending back into the Tertiary period. Here resides much of the continent's bat and insect fauna, perhaps waiting for another climatic shift to spread once again over now drier areas. Our knowledge of much of the animal life is limited—it is estimated that somewhat less than half of the existing invertebrates unique to this continent are known to science.

The oceans

As an island continent, Australia is not just 'girt by sea', but is also significantly influenced by the oceans, whose currents swirl around two-thirds of the Earth's surface. From the South and North Pacific and the Indian and Southern Oceans emanate marine waters of varying temperature and nutrient status. Along the West Australian coast there is an interplay between colder current, upwelling flows from the south and west, and the warm, inshore Leeuwin Current which pulses southward from the Indonesian Archipelago, even reaching across the southern continental shelf.

The East Australia Current emerges from equatorial flows of the south-west Pacific through the Coral Sea. It warms the coastal waters of the Great Barrier Reef and dissipates in the Tasman Sea as a series of giant eddies reaching to New Zealand.

The continent's weather systems are influenced, in ways still poorly understood, by oceanic flows and variations in water temperatures. Waves generated at sea move sand onshore to form the majestic beaches of southern Australia, although during great east-coast storm periods—such as those which occurred along the New South Wales and southern Queensland coasts in 1974—deep water-waves that exceed 10 m (33 feet) in height can scour these sands and erode dunes and cliffs, causing considerable property damage. The oceans bring biotic diversity to the continental shelves and coasts, permitting the setting up of a fishing economy well established by indigenous Australians and continued to the present. Unfortunately, the relative lack of nutrients in Australian waters, due to the warmth of much of our surrounding sea, means that to sustain the industry into the future, delicate management decisions must be made to ensure continuing and sustainable harvests of edible species. But the warmth of these waters, along with the growth of corals and the formation of magnificent beaches, makes for localities as attractive to international tourists as they are to the local inhabitants. As Australia enters the twenty-first century, coastal tourism has become a phenomenon of great importance to Australia's economy, long reliant on exports, and dependent for its existence on the many environmental factors of past and present origin.

In contrast to most others in the world, Australia's deserts are well vegetated and home to a wide variety of species. Though much of the flora is ephemeral and most of the fauna is small and unobtrusive, the diversity is great.

Australian beaches are by any standards spectacular. Relatively unspoiled and uncrowded, they act as a magnet for tourists and make a valuable contribution to the national economy.

The Great Barrier Reef

ABOVE AND BELOW: Storybook coral islands, warm translucent waters, coral reefs and shoals and an abundance of colourful marine life make the Great Barrier Reef one of Australia's top attractions.

Australia is custodian of the world's largest system of interconnected coral reefs, the Great Barrier Reef (GBR). Located off the northern coast of the State of Queensland, the system stretches for 2500 km (1550 miles), from approximately latitude 10°S to 24°S. It contains innumerable coral growths rising from many metres below sea level towards the low-water mark, forming between 2500 and 3000 identifiable reef shoals locally surmounted by sand or coral rubble constituting at least 350 islands. Mapping and defining these separate reef areas and islands is an on-going activity given the vastness of the GBR and the ever-changing character of its surface, constantly subjected to the forces of current, wind, wave and tide.

When looked at in detail, the GBR is a mixture of different reef types reflecting oceanic conditions, tidal heights, width of continental shelf and distance from land. There exist to the north true ribbon or barrier reefs, elongated structures sitting atop the edge of the continental shelf and breached by narrow 'passes' through which tidal waters flow. More common are the platform and smaller patch reefs located along the length of the GBR. Some of these possess sandy 'cays' or islands at their northern ends. These are the 'low islands', partly fringed by mangroves in northern regions, and home to millions of nesting seabirds and seasonally visited by several species of marine turtles when the females come ashore to deposit their eggs in

the sand. The windward or south-east corners of some of these reefs contain very large accumulations of cemented coral rubble cast up by cyclonic storms.

In addition there are the 'high islands', about two-thirds of all GBR islands, formed of continental rock around which grow fringing reefs. Where rivers are absent, these reefs may also grow out from the mainland coast into the shallow waters of the GBR.

The GBR is not the product of a single geologic event. Slow subsidence of the continental margin combined with many oscillations of sea level during the 'ice ages' (or Quaternary Period), allowed colonies of marine plants and animals to grow on exposed limestone outcrops as the rising sea inundated the continental shelf during each episode of glacial-ice disintegration. These colonies have hard skeletons which add to the limestone of previous periods of growth, resulting in sequences of reef development

and exposure repeated over the past two million or so years. The latest episode of marine transgression reached present sea level, or perhaps a metre (3 feet) higher, around 6000 years ago. Consequently the most recent geologic unit constituting the GBR is only rarely more than 10 metres (33 feet) thick and less than 10,000 years old.

A cauldron of life

The GBR is vast, both in area and in the number of living organisms which make their home in it. Its waters are bathed in warmth from solar radiation and the south-flowing East Australian current which sweeps out of the Coral Sea. Many discrete habitats occur within the reef system, which is home to 1500–2000 species of fish, some 4000 mollusc types, abundant marine mammals, sea grasses, mangroves and other organisms including 350 hard or reef-building corals. Individual coral fragments comprise numerous species of algae, both soft and hard, along with burrowing worms and shells.

The waters of the reef, while comparatively low in nutrients, are capable of supporting an incredible wonderland of life, a great joy to those who observe from the air, peer through glass-bottomed boats, or more intimately, find themselves beneath the surface immersed in a world

of contrasting colour and movement. However, turbid river waters bring soil eroded from canefields and the grazed hinterland, now increasingly seen as disturbing the harmony of the dynamic reef system and perhaps encouraging outbreaks of the dreaded, coral-browsing crown-of-thorns starfish.

Management problems

Although in the past pressures to mine reef limestone and drill for oil threatened the integrity of the GBR, the declaration in 1975 of the Great Barrier Reef Marine Park, along with agreements of cooperation between Commonwealth and State governments, have led to more considered management and planning that should benefit future generations. However, in 2001, new proposals for oil exploration adjacent to the reef look set to once more become an issue. Tourism is a major industry in coastal Queensland, fuelled in no small way by the GBR. Strict zonings control the activities of tourism operations, fishing and shipping, but there is always the threat posed by a large ship running aground within reef channels, a threat that became real in late 2000 with the grounding of a Malaysian freighter. Named a World Heritage area in 1981, the park is 344,000 sq. km (133,000 sq. miles) of stunning beauty and diversity visited by millions each year. Its attractions support local and regional economies on a scale that is not represented elsewhere in Australia.

The loggerhead turtle (Caretta caretta) thrives in the warm waters of the Reef. It lays about 100 eggs each year in all seasons but winter.

Snorkelling on the Great Barrier Reef. Its custodians must remain vigilant against over-exploitation and inappropriate use if it is to keep its place among the great natural attractions of the world.

Land Exploitation and Conservation

Grain silos similar to these near Toowoomba, Queensland, are a common sight in rural Australia. However, over-clearing in many areas has had dramatic and far-reaching consequences.

Much has been written about how Australians since European settlement have abused the country's lands, waters and soils. Even the Governor-General in his Centenary of Federation address made on 1 January 2001, noted the need to acknowledge and rectify the damage we have done to the continent.

As a continental nation, modern Australia is the custodian of a huge area of land and territorial sea; these are formed into regions of great biological diversity influenced not only seasonally and annually, but over decades and far longer periods by variable atmospheric, hydrological and oceanographic conditions. Human activities since 1788 have greatly reduced that diversity and affected in countless ways the waters of our creeks, rivers and lakes and those of our groundwater systems; catastrophically denuded or damaged much of our soils; and introduced animal and plant pests which we must manage if they are not to ruin more native biota and reduce the nation's agricultural productivity.

Recognition of impacts of changes to ecosystems is part of an ongoing imperative to sustainably manage our natural resources. Unfortunately, it will be too late for a large number of species. At least 17 species of vertebrate have become extinct including seven marsupials, the Tasmanian thylacine. among them. Regionally, there is a noticeable decline in biodiversity, for instance on intensely farmed plains and around urban areas. Causes of these declines are many, ranging from the deliberate extermination of whole populations, introduction of predatory pests (cats, dogs, foxes, etc.), habitat modification, which includes such things as new fire regimes and the impact of rabbits, and the application to landscapes of agricultural practices on a vast scale through the clearing of tree and shrub cover, introduction of monocultures, use of fertilisers and pesticides, removal of soils thereby disturbing the supporting microflora and -fauna, and the impact on land and water conditions of overgrazing and overcropping in times of drought.

Although the first European settlers in the Sydney Basin found it extremely difficult to establish a productive farming community, those that later utilised the cleared coastal valleys and inland plains found land systems which could generate wealth. Invasion of these lands by hard-hoofed animals, especially by sheep and cattle for whose products markets could be found in Europe, offered opportunities for large-scale grazing and for selection of smaller farming blocks encouraging intensification of settlement. The concept that 'rain would follow the plough' was quickly dispelled. It was soon recognised that semi-arid, marginal agricultural land was unfit for wheat growing, for instance, in South Australia north of the so-called Goyder's Line, and in western New South Wales. But while the devastating impact of drought on these areas became widely known, the push to farm and graze, involving massive tree and shrub clearance, continued. The wheat belt of south-western Western Australia and the grazing lands of central Queensland are two areas of more recent extensive modification encouraged by both Federal and State governments supportive of short-term rural economic growth. Longer-term viability on the scale first envisaged in these regions has now become highly questionable given the vagaries of the Australian climate and soils.

This tea plantation in north Queensland is an example of the diversification that has allowed many small farmers to weather the vagaries of the economic climate. However, modern trends in 'agribusiness' have seen a rise in land clearing in many regions.

Salt in the wounds

One environmental factor which has come to haunt Australian agriculture is salinity. Salt, inherited at least in part from the ancient soils and seas of Cretaceous and Tertiary age, has long been part of this continent. During Quaternary dry periods, salt rose to the surface in many depressions and in dried up

lake basins. When wetter conditions returned, the deep-rooted plants gradually stabilised the nearly bare surfaces and assisted in driving water tables to lower depths. But as settlers cleared vegetation in the nineteenth and twentieth centuries, replacing the native plants with shallow-rooted pasture grasses, food crops or orchards, they facilitated the rise of saline water tables. Irrigation assisted this process. The impact has been cruel to many farmers as soils across vast tracts of southern Australia have lost what limited fertility they once had. At least 2.5 million ha (6.2 million acres or 5 per cent of cultivated land) are currently affected by dryland salinity and the trend continues. The impact is not just on-farm; rivers and creeks are also becoming more saline, reducing the quality of drinking water for both livestock and humans. It is possible that Adelaide will within 20 years fail World Health Organisation drinking-water quality standards on two days out of five.

Soil conditions suitable for crops and pastures are highly dependent on nutrient status. With very few exceptions (volcanic soils are one), most agricultural lands in Australia are low in the two critical elements nitrogen and phosphorus. Even trace elements like boron were shown to be lacking in some farmed areas. Again, the cause of such deficiencies can be linked to the ancient history of weathered rocks not reworked by the grinding and eroding forces of glaciation and degradation as was experienced in the rich, productive farmlands of the Northern Hemisphere. The addition of fertiliser became a factor not only in the survival of crop economies, but also in enhancing levels of output to ensure continued export growth for cereal crops and the maintenance of 'improved' pastures. While it is true that higher productivity has been achieved, there have been some serious environmental consequences. Overuse of phosphates, in particular, has resulted in blue-green algal outbreaks in rivers and lakes. It could also be argued that farming practices have been encouraged on marginal soils. During periods of intense runoff these have become prone to the formation of gullies and to sheet erosion, thereby losing much soil cover and causing siltation of water channels and loss of habitat in wetlands. In semi-arid areas, the exposure of tilled and fertilised lands to winds during droughts has led to dust storms sweeping valuable topsoil across coastal cities (as in Melbourne in 1983) and on into the ocean.

In Tasmania, south-western Western Australia and all along the Eastern Highlands from Victoria into Queensland, extensive forests survived the clearing of the last two centuries. The importance of various tree

Australia's agricultural industries rely heavily on irrigation, but there is an increasingly high price to pay. Creeping salinity, the effects of which can be seen in this photo taken near Lyrup Lyrup in South Australia, renders large areas unproductive. Even in places where irrigation is not an issue, overclearing of native tree and shrub cover has seen water tables rise, threatening even the buildings in some rural centres. Forward-thinking landowners and organisations such as Landcare are now fighting to stem the rising saline tide.

Though there are many marine species in Australian waters, only a few are in populations large enough to be exploited on a commercial scale. Australia is surrounded by vast oceans but a combination of factors make the waters of the continental shelf relatively low in the nutrients fish need.

types for timber initially led to expansion of coastal settlements. In New South Wales and Queensland, red cedar *(Toona australis)* was highly prized, but was quickly over-exploited. Forestry interests have somehow managed to continue their operations in the face of continuing and growing opposition to clear-felling, the introduction of non-native species (such as *Pinus radiata*), and the use of valuable timber for low-grade products through the production of wood chips. Forests cover about 41 million ha (101 million acres) of which 16 per cent is protected in national parks. Much has been done in recent years to expand areas of forest protection as well as to encourage the return

of degraded farmlands to forest. Although there are now about 1 million ha (2.5 million acres) of tree plantations, only 5 per cent consist of natives.

Difficult decisions

In the year 2000, the author Eric Rolls asked: 'What can be done to cure Australia?' Many politicians, scientists, natural historians, farmers and others have asked the same question in slightly different ways over the years. Inquiries by various colonial, State and Commonwealth governments since the late nineteenth century, have pointed to mistakes, abuses of legislation and other causes of land degradation. The concept of 'conservation of natural resources' is not new in Australia or elsewhere. Failure to develop conservation strategies, what we now refer to as sustainable practices, can be seen as a factor in the demise of several past civilisations. Many attempts to promote the 'conservation ethic' at both community and individual levels have been to a large degree unsuccessful in Australia, despite the intentions, plans and policies of various governments and landowners. There is an underlying

Tree plantations are becoming increasingly common in rural Australia. Though large-scale plantings of exotics—chiefly conifers—have been undertaken for many years, it is only recently that native hardwoods have been considered for plantations.

tension between exploitation/use of natural resources (soil, water, vegetation, minerals, etc.) and long-term conservation of environmental values. Pressure from short-term market interests, supported by a deeply entrenched 'property-rights' philosophy as well as a political system which is sometimes overly protective of rural interests, frequently give rise to decisions that over time can be shown to lead to land degradation. Tensions are most apparent during 'hard' times as defined by droughts or depressed commodity prices, or, as in the 1890s, 1930s and again in the early 1980s, by a combination of both. The inappropriate exploitation for irrigation of low river flows, over-stocking to ensure some monetary return, or even more vegetation clearance to create 'fresh' pastures, all can have damaging longer-term impacts, even after moisture returns to the land.

Water and soil together require a degree of care and management on a scale beyond the scope of the individual farm. Excessive use of water for cropping, pasture or stock (let alone for urban purposes), creates demands on river and groundwater systems that far exceed supply. Natural ecosystems are losing out to these demands as witnessed in the diversion of Snowy River waters to the west. But increasingly there is a recognition that nature is taking revenge. Land and water management on a catchment scale, way beyond the farm gate, is fundamental if some of the conse-quences of past mismanagement are to be addressed and overcome. The twin goals of sustaining both economic productivity and environmental values are requiring hard decisions with intervention by govern-ments being part of the process despite the innate conservatism of land owners and their demands to be able to manage their own property as they see fit. Some decisions include, for instance, the re-diversion of river flows. Allowing the Snowy River to attain discharges many times that permitted at present is one example of this. A reduction in the number of irrigation licences and/or changing irrigation tech-niques may also be necessary as could be the removal of some dams, and making available for environ-mental purposes (wetland and river flushing) large amounts of water during wet periods. There is also the need for many leased areas and some freehold land to be permanently protected, with appropriate compensation, from the impact of tillage and hoofed animals. If rabbits and similar pests can be controlled, kangaroo 'farming' in such areas may be a far more efficient use of the land. As well, large tracts of land should revert to the national estate, possibly to be managed by the indigenous peoples.

The Commonwealth Government has introduced Landcare and other programs in an effort to promote broader awareness of better management practices. There continues to be a need to promote awareness of these practices, but defining what is 'best' for variable regional landscapes subject to changing climatic conditions and degraded soils is not easy to proscribe. Uncertainties faced by landowners and land users may very likely increase as global warming,

due to the enhanced 'greenhouse effect', gathers pace. This further increases the urgent need for a stronger community-based approach to natural-resource management at scales appropriate to water and soil use. Such an approach should be based on an increased awareness and understanding of those ecosystems which need protecting and conserving if sustainable environments, economies and societies are to be achieved in Australia.

Australia inherited vast mineral deposits from its geologic past. Its exports in large part consist of the output of mines and their associated works such as this copper-flotation plant operated by CMT, Tasmania.

History of the Australian Fauna

Muttaburrasaurus langdoni, *a plant-eating dinosaur, lived during the early Cretaceous Period, about 120 million years ago, when flowering plants began to appear. Its bird-like beak would have helped it to rip leaves and flowers from the vegetation.*

Australia has about 270 species of mammal, 770 bird species and more than 960 species of reptiles and amphibians and unknown numbers of insects, with more being discovered every year. Many of these species are endemic with their ancestry going back to Gondwana, the ancient southern super-continent which once included New Guinea, New Zealand, Antarctica, South America, Africa and India and was itself part of a larger landmass called Pangaea. One type of ant, for example, is the most primitive living ant in the world. In 1931, two unusual ants were found in a collection of insects from coastal heathland in south-west Australia. They were identical, it was discovered, to 60-million-year-old fossil ants called *Nothomyrmecia macrops*. It was not until 46 years later that a living colony was finally found, on the Eyre Peninsula in South Australia, more than 2000 km (1240 miles) away to the east.

The Gondwanan fauna

By the time Gondwana and Laurasia, the northern supercontinent (comprising North America, Europe and Asia) split from Pangaea, around 254 million

Lush rainforest, which supported an extraordinary number of different species of fauna, covered much of what is now Australia in Gondwanan times when the climate was wetter than it is now.

A model of the fearsome predator Kronosaurus queenslandicus bares its impressive-looking teeth. It was an enormous (13-m/43-ft) marine dinosaur which lived about 120 million years ago.

LEFT: Tree frogs are found in many parts of the world from sea level to altitudes as high as 4575 m (15,000 feet). They are members of an ancient family which originated in Gondwana. Most frog species live in Australasia and South America, which were once joined. At about 13 cm (5 in) the white-lipped tree frog (Litoria infrafrenata) is one of the largest frogs in the world.

no endemic Australian groups. Even among presumably Gondwanan groups such as land snails, giant earthworms and some spiders Australia only has a tiny fraction of endemic families.

Perhaps the most distinctive of the Gondwanan animals are the marsupials. Although marsupial fossils appeared first in Laurasian landmasses and only later invaded Gondwana, they did not persist there and placental animals such as antelopes, bears, cats and primates are now dominant. South America still has a rich marsupial diversity despite a massive North American invasion of animals at the time when the Panama Isthmus closed, when North and South America collided, about three million years ago. In Australia, it was thought for a long time that marsupials had always dominated the continent but we now know that placental mammals—relatives of hedgehogs—travelled to Australia in Gondwanan times because their fossils have been found alongside those of dinosaurs in southern Australia. So at the time of the break with Antarctica, around 55 million years ago, there were both marsupials and placentals in Australia. Although it is not certain what happened, it is likely that the early placentals were overwhelmed by the rapid marsupial radiation for they later died out. The bats and rodents which live here now arrived after Australia became an island continent.

Interestingly, the marsupial radiation produced a remarkably similar range of forms to the placental animals evolving elsewhere, so in Australia there are wombats filling the ecological niche of marmots, thylacines in place of the dog family and marsupial lions as equivalents for the cat family. There are strong resemblances between many Australian possums, such as the gum-feeding sugar glider (*Petaurus breviceps*) and the Madagascan fork-crowned lemur (*Phaner furcifer*) and between the insect-eating striped possum (*Dactylopsila trivirgata*) and the Madagascan aye-aye (*Daubentonia madagascariensis*). Even more remarkable is the astounding similarity between Australian marsupial moles and the golden moles of southern Africa, both of which lack both eyes and ears, and appear to 'swim' through the loose desert sand without making a permanent burrow. Such resemblance is a product of an evolutionary process called convergence, where unrelated plants and animals in different places develop in similar ways as a response to similar climates, ways of living and habitats.

years ago, all the major groups of animals had already evolved. Laurasia and Gondwana each inherited Pangaean animals which is why the fauna and particularly the flora of the world, though distinctive, comprise the same basic groups. There are still interesting echoes from this time. For instance, the ancient velvet worm (*Peripatus*) only occurs as a fossil in North America, but persists as a living animal in Australia and other southern continents. Today's marsupials still exist in two of the continents which were once joined as Gondwana, so there are opossums in South America and possums in New Guinea and Australia.

After the separation from Laurasia, Gondwana began evolving its own suite of animals and birds. The climate in Gondwanan times was much warmer and wetter than it is now, and rainforest covered most of the land, resulting in an amazing diversity of fauna. From the discovery of fossil feathers, birds are known to have been present in Australia at least as early as 120 million years ago, even before the first flowering plants migrated around the margins of Gondwana and at the same time as major rifting commenced between Africa and South America. The budgerigar, malleefowl, cockatiel, little button-quail, black-eared cuckoo and white-backed swallow are just a few of the many Australian bird species which have an ancient ancestry in Gondwana. Australia's many species of tree frogs, southern frogs and burrowing frogs are also Gondwanan in origin.

Most invertebrate classes and many families of fauna had already differentiated before the breakup of Pangaea, so at the higher taxonomic levels there are

Marsupials now dominate the Australian continent, though they once shared it with early placental animals. The marsupial quokka (Setonix brachyurus) is a wallaby, the last survivor of an evolutionary line which branched off from the early browsing macropods. It is distinguished from other wallabies by its short tail and small ears.

Ancestors of today's male bower-birds have been making their intricate courting spaces for at least 20 million years. The spotted bowerbird (Chlamydera maculata) above has decorated his bower, woven of twigs and grass stems, with an arrangement of snailshells, bones and glass.

Australia is dominated by elapids, poisonous front-fanged snakes originally from Asia. The brown tree snake (Boiga irregularis) is one of the few species here to represent the generally non-venomous colubrids, the largest snake group in the world.

Echoes of ancient times

Twenty million years ago at least six different species of koala and a variety of possums ranging from minus-cule to cuscus-sized inhabited the rainforest canopies sheltering a greatly expanded Lake Eyre (now the driest part of the continent). Songbirds—ancestors of today's robins, scrub wrens, sitellas, pardalotes, wood-swallows, butcherbirds, bowerbirds, warblers and honeyeaters—were prevalent. Several types of dipro-todont marsupials, resembling cow-sized wombats, browsed the rainforest shrubs. On the ground lived smaller marsupials such as rat-kangaroos, bandicoots and insectivorous dasyurids. Crawling through the understorey were types of goanna, dragons and skinks as well as large snakes which also hung in thick 6-m (20-foot) loops from rainforest trees, making today's 2-m (6.5-foot) long desert-dwelling pythons look like worms in comparison. The permanent inland bodies of water supported an incredible variety of animals and birds: there were flamingoes, cormorants, ducks, geese, rails, grebes, large crocodiles, turtles, catfish, lungfish and large platypuses. There were even fresh-water dolphins in the ancestral Lake Frome area which was not far north of present-day Adelaide. It is likely that bats, perhaps Australia's first Asian immigrants, had also arrived here at that time.

Other Asian immigrants came from the sea. Somewhere between 20 and 15 million years ago, snakes similar to today's Asian coral snakes arrived on Australia's shores. Genetic studies suggest that from this single influx of egg-laying snakes arose the largest group of Australian snakes, the elapids, or front-fanged snakes, the same family (Elapidae) as the cobras of Africa and Asia and very similar to them

in form and behaviour. The elapids can be divided into two main groups: the small, nocturnal snakes such as the red-naped, brown-headed and golden-crowned snakes which are mostly lizard-eaters; and the larger snakes, such as brown-snakes, black-snakes and taipans, which are mostly active by day and have more general diets. This group includes some of the deadliest snakes on Earth.

Retreat of the rainforests

As Australia drifted north towards Asia the rainforests continued to contract and by eight million years ago the characteristic rainforest fauna had disappeared from most of the continent. One of the best windows into this time is a fossil site two hours north of Alice Springs. In the small area of pebbly terrain at the foot of a series of flat-topped desert mesas can be found the remains of dromornithids—several species of behemoth birds which weigh more than 350 kg (770 pounds) and stand 3 m (10 feet) tall. These ground-dwelling birds were able to exploit the ex-panding savanna habitat. Diprotodontid marsupials were also abundant at nearby Alcoota, ranging in dimension from sheep-sized *Kolopsis* to water-buffalo-sized *Pyramios*. In between were hippopotamus-like *Plaisiodon* and tapir-like *Palorchestes*.

The predators in this community were primitive thylacines and the marsupial 'leopard', *Wakaleo alcootaensis*. Aquatic predators included large fero-cious crocodiles equipped with teeth like serrated knifes. Flamingoes and turtles were also common. *Hadronomus*, the relative of the first true kangaroos, also made an appearance at this time, possibly in response to the increasing grasslands.

This was the era of the megafauna in Australia, which included the large diprotodontids *Diprotodon* and *Zygomaturus*, the giant wombat *Phascolonus* and the colossal kangaroos *Protemnodon*, *Sthenurus* and *Procoptodon*. The wildlife at the beginning of the Pleistocene also included small macropodids like the modern bettong, the Tasmanian devil and various species of possum. Rodents, which first appeared in eastern Queensland about four and half million years ago, were now also found in southern and central Australia. In moving inland they diversified considerably, evolving into forms like the stick-nest rat and a spinifex hopping-mouse.

By five to three million years ago, the fragmentation of rainforest and expansion of open savanna environments continued paralleling the abundance of grazing and browsing macropodids. These included the grazing kangaroo (*Prionotemnus palankarinnicus*) which lived close to Lake Palankarinna (near Lake Eyre) which probably had a similar diet to the modern agile wallaby.

Rapid change

Climatically, the past million years has oscillated between ice ages (glacials) and interglacials (our current climate). In Australia, this climatic yoyo has translated into the breaking-up and re-forming of habitats which in turn has been a potent mechanism for the generation of new species. The appearance of the bandicoot (*Ischnodon australis*) at this time represents the first clear adaptation to arid and semi-arid grasslands. It was very similar to the modern-day bilby which has a diet in which grass seed is important. The continual breaking-up and re-forming of forest patches catalysed the evolution of another 30 genera of birds which, today, have close relatives around the coast. Inland, the blue bonnet, crested bellbird, whitefaces, striped honeyeater, pied honeyeater group, spiny-cheeked honeyeater, chats and several birds of prey now evolved.

Only a few bones of the extinct marsupial Palorchestes survive, but from these and the evidence of Aboriginal rock paintings, we can deduce that it looked rather like a tapir with a short trunk and sturdy limbs with long claws.

By the late Pleistocene, 50,000 years ago, most of Australia's wildlife, apart from the megafauna, was similar and in some cases identical to today's animals. Since then the cycles of glaciation and interglacials, increasing aridity and the actions of human hunters have led to a number of changes. As a result of all these changes the megafauna are gone and only a few species such as emus, the grey kangaroos and wombats remain as midget descendants of their giant ancestors. In addition, many smaller species declined to the stage that they were already rare by the time of European 'discovery'. Thylacines (a wolf-like marsupial) and devils (carnivorous marsupials) which once roamed the mainland were now restricted to Tasmania. The stage of Australia was set for a human-dominated fauna.

Enormous kangaroos such as Sthenurus, the short-faced kangaroo, roamed Australia during the Pleistocene Period. They were over 2.5 m (8 ft) tall and weighed nearly 300 kg (660 pounds). They became extinct about 35,000 years ago.

The blue-tongued lizards (Tiliqua species) are common and wide-spread in Australia; equally at home in the deserts of the west, the tropical north, and the suburban gardens of the eastern seaboard. Their slow metabolism means that they can go for long periods without food or water when necessary.

Adaptations to a unique environment

Much of inland Australia is arid, a place driven by extremes rather than averages. Seventy per cent of the continent is desert with a low and unpredictable rainfall. In this mostly infertile land with a capricious climate most animals are unable to survive. Despite this, over time a surprising number of plants and animals have evolved to carve out a successful niche for themselves.

Most seed-eating birds can only survive in the desert by regularly visiting waterholes, but truly desert-adapted animals do not need to search for water. Insectivorous birds, mammals and some lizards, for instance, derive enough moisture from the juices of their prey. Energy-expensive desert mammals such as the spinifex hopping mouse (*Notomys fuscus*) have adapted to obtain water by metabolism of carbohydrates, so that they do not need to drink, but even these animals supplement their diet with moisture-containing insects. Like all desert mammals these mice produce highly concentrated urine as a means of conserving scarce water.

While it is easy to be fascinated by these sorts of adaptations, it is important to remember that they are extreme, only one end of a spectrum of incredible life-history strategies. Indeed, most of Australia's desert-living animals have behavioural rather than physiological adaptations. For instance, many animals will build burrows to create their own micro-climate. Creatures from the size of tiny mice and frogs to the large and robust wombat have adopted the strategy of making tunnels and burrows in which to escape the desert heat. Another behavioural ploy is to feed when it is cooler. Kangaroos and wallabies, for example, are all nocturnal or crepuscular—that is, they look for nourishment mainly at dawn or dusk. At the other end of the spectrum are the environmental adaptations. Animals in the rainforests have adapted to climb into the canopy for their living—even the kangaroos. The tree kangaroos (*Dendrolagus* spp.) have shorter hindlimbs and more powerful forelimbs than their ground-dwelling cousins.

Amphibians in Australia have had plenty of time over the millennia to come up with ingenious adaptations to the increasing aridity of their environment. Australian frogs, like frogs everywhere, need moisture to survive, and 35 per cent of the Australian frog fauna

Human intervention in the landscape (land-clearing and dam-building) has benefitted galahs (Cacatua roseicapilla) which prefer to live in open country near water. When resources are scarce inland, they are often seen in towns.

fill themselves up with water when it is available and then burrow to conserve it. These species have structures called metatarsal tubercles, like little spades, on the undersurface of their feet which aid in digging. Some of these frogs dig to considerable depths and entomb themselves for a period, waiting for enough percolating water to free them so that they can begin their breeding cycle. They only respond to rain in the summer; in winter, the temperatures are not high enough to accelerate the developmental rate from egg to tadpole to frog.

So successful are they at adapting to their surroundings that even in the apparently inhospitable red sand and spinifex plains that cover around 30 per cent of Australia there are up to 50 frogs per ha (25 per acre). These are the 'water-holding' frogs and they have evolved a unique method of surviving in the absence of water. Instead of eating their old, dead outer skin when it is sloughed off in the process normal to most frogs, the water-holding frog keeps it and uses it as an external cocoon. In this way, well protected by a plastic film-like wrap, the mucous-coated frog is able to conserve its natural moisture and resist being dried out.

Coping with the vagaries of the weather has become a way of life with the kangaroo family and the reproductive system of the red kangaroo is a finely balanced adaptation to an arid and uncertain climate. After the female gives birth she immediately comes into oestrus and mates again. The second embryo stops developing after a few days and remains in a dormant state in the mother's uterus. In times of abundant food the first baby continues to suckle and grow in the pouch, then continues suckling from outside the pouch until almost a year old. During this suckling period the second embryo remains dormant. But if drought or the death of the first young should cause suckling to cease, the dormant embryo will recommence development. In this way the female red kangaroo is able to maximise her chances of breeding in the unpredictable desert climate.

Mammals

Only in Australia and in New Guinea can one see the full range of the three different branches of mammalian life: the monotremes, marsupials and placentals. Monotremes are an ancient lineage with many primitive anatomical and reproductive characteristics. They lay soft-shelled eggs, which are incubated by the mother for a very short time—about 10 days to two weeks. The hatchlings are nursed from mammary glands which have no teats or nipples but simply open as pores on the mother's belly.

Marsupials have a brief internal development where the embryo develops inside an egg membrane within the mother's uterus. After a very short gestation the young (called 'joeys') are born looking like 'external embryos'; they make their way independently to the mother's pouch and attach themselves to a teat where they will continue developing.

Primitive placentals have a short gestation and the newborn young are blind, naked and helpless. In more advanced forms, gestation is longer and the newborn are alert, fully furred and can run around actively within hours of birth. The range of specialisation and adaptation of these modern mammals demonstrates how the evolution of the placenta and increased length of gestation has increased the newborns' chances of survival.

Monotremes

Monotremes first occurred in the fossil record in 120-million-year-old opal deposits found in Australia and were long thought to be unique to the continent.

Then, in 1991, a single monotreme tooth was described from 60-million-year-old deposits in Patagonia, South America. These fossils are remarkably similar to each other and to later fossil platypus from Australia indicating that the monotremes are an ancient Gondwanan group just like the marsupials.

THE PLATYPUS

The aquatic platypus (*Ornithorhynchus anatinus*) is common in the freshwater rivers and lakes of eastern Australia from north Queensland to Tasmania. Its strong jaws, covered with a leathery beak, are armed not with teeth but with horny pads, which it uses to crush its prey. It is an energetic animal and has a voracious appetite. Its diet includes worms, molluscs, insect larvae and crustaceans. The platypus often hunts in the dark or forages for food in muddy water. In effect, it is blind and deaf because when submerged, its eyes and ears are enclosed by a flap of skin for protection. However, it is able to locate its prey underwater by touch and by remarkable sensors on its duck-like beak which detect electrical impulses from the prey's muscles. Although both front and hind feet are webbed, only the front feet are used in swimming. The webs on these front feet have an extra flap which can be conveniently extended during swimming and folded back when digging. Male platypuses have a prominent spur connected to a venom gland on each hind leg. Naturalists have puzzled over the function of this spur for over 200 years but the truth is still unknown. Females lay one to three eggs, which they incubate in a nest within their burrow.

The short-beaked echidna (Tachyglossus aculeatus) *is a monotreme, a subclass of the ancient mammal group which has lived in Australasia for over 100 million years. Only this member of the genus is now present in Australia, though several genera of long-beaked echidnas were widespread here up to 10,000 years ago.*

From fossil evidence we now know that toothed ancestors of the platypus lived in Australia at least 120 million years ago. The discovery of fossil 'platypus' teeth in South America, dated to 60 million years ago, is evidence of a Gondwanan distribution of the monotremes.

The thylacine was a carnivorous marsupial, also known as the Tasmanian wolf or tiger. Probably driven from the mainland by competition from the dingo thousands of years ago, it was hunted to extinction in the 1930s by European settlers in Tasmania who regarded it as a pest.

ECHIDNAS

Although they belong to the same group of mammals, echidnas, with their spiny coats and pointed beaks, bear little outward resemblance to platypuses. Two types once roamed Australia and both still occur in New Guinea but only the short-beaked form has survived in Australia. This form (*Tachyglossus aculeatus*) has become specialised to feed on ants and termites with a sticky tongue which can be extended to 18 cm (7 in). They crush food between their tongues and spines on the roof of their mouth, for they have no teeth. Female echidnas develop a pouch on the belly, which they use to incubate their single egg and the offspring when it is very young. As soon as the baby's spines begin to develop, it is parked in a nest in a hollow log or burrow where the mother will continue to look after it. To conserve energy, echidnas can drop their body temperature to become torpid.

Although most of the desert-adapted species of bandicoot have been pushed to the brink of extinction, three of the coastal species remain common and a fourth is widespread in Tasmania, where campers are likely to see them if they leave food out.

Marsupials

Marsupials are not unique to Australia, but the majority of marsupials live here—about 140 species. They range in size from the tiny planigale, at a weight of only a few grams, to the red kangaroo, which can grow to over 90 kg (200 pounds) and they can be found in many environments, from snowfields to deserts. Some marsupials have incredibly specialised diets, while others are omnivorous. The life cycles of some species have evolved to overcome drought.

CARNIVORES

The carnivorous marsupials are a group of three families, two of which have only a single species each (the thylacine—now extinct—and the numbat). The numbat (*Myrmecobius fasciatus*), one of Australia's only two diurnal marsupials, specialises in eating termites which it collects from their foraging galleries or pathways under the leaf litter of the forest floor. Once widespread over southern Australia, it is now restricted to south-western Western Australia. The third family, the Dasyuridae, is Australia's largest marsupial family with 53 species. Dasyurids range in size from the planigale and ningaui, which live in the cracks of the parched earth, to the predatory cat-sized quolls and the Tasmanian devil (*Sarcophilus harrisii*), Tasmania's largest predator and an efficient scavenger.

HERBIVORES

Bandicoots and their allies (*Isoodon* spp.) share some characteristics with the most primitive of marsupials but others, such as the reduction of toes on the hind foot, with the most specialised herbivorous marsupials. Current opinion favours dividing them into three families: one for the bilbies and pig-footed bandicoot (Thylacomyidae), a second (Peroryctidae) for the spiny bandicoots of New Guinea and Indonesia (one of which occurs on Cape York), and the third (Peramelidae) for the remainder. Bandicoots have the trait of having the highest potential reproductive rates for marsupials: females mature at three months, multiple litters per year are normal and gestation, at 12.5 days, is the shortest of any mammal. It is ironic that such prolific breeders should be among Australia's most endangered species.

Wombats (Vombatidae) are Australia's most highly specialised grazing marsupials. Their teeth are open-rooted and continuously growing to compensate for wear, a trait shared with horses and cows and many grass-eating rodents. This allows them to grind the stems and leaves of grasses which contain crystals of calcium silicate which deter grazing animals. Like horses and elephants, they gain their nutrition from fermenting the finely chewed grass in an enormously distended hind gut with the aid of symbiotic bacteria. All wombats live in burrows which are interconnected and also lead to grazing areas by well-trodden paths. The three living species occupy only a fraction of their former habitat and one, the northern hairy-nosed wombat (*Lasiorhinus krefftii*), is extremely rare.

TREE AND FOREST DWELLERS

Australia's rainforest legacy is still evident in the diversity of arboreal, or tree-dwelling, marsupials. In all, six different lineages of possums, as well as the koala (which is not a possum but an arboreal wombat), have survived from the ten or more groups that came to evolve into arboreal specialists. One of the most fascinating possums is the tiny honey possum (*Tarsipes rostratus*), which lives entirely on a diet of nectar and pollen, which is fermented in its specialised stomach. This possum is restricted to south-western Western Australia where banksias and other nectar-producing flowers bloom year-round.

Apart from the gum-feeding petaurids, the remainder of the possums are specialised herbivores or leaf-eaters. The cuscuses and brushtails (Phalangeridae) and the ringtails (Pseudocheiridae) are widespread throughout Australia and New Guinea but the koala (*Phascolarctos cinereus*), is native only to the eucalypt forests of eastern Australia. The koala, the common brushtail and several of the ringtails actually thrive on the toxic leaves of certain eucalypts. Their guts—in effect huge fermentation chambers—are geared to neutralising the leaves' poisonous phenols and gaining extra nutrients by bacterial fermentation of normally indigestible fibre. Another aspect of this peculiar diet is that koalas have the lowest energy requirements of all marsupials. The koala's population has undergone several fluctuations due to a bacterial infection called *Chlamidia psittaci* and as a result of the continued fragmentation of its forest habitat.

Reinventing the wing has been tried at least three times in the possum group. Patagia, or gliding membranes, have evolved in three completely different groups: the gliding possums (*Petaurus* spp.), one of the ringtails (the greater glider, *Petauridoides volans*) and the feathertail glider (*Acrobates pygmaeus*).

Two families of the possum lineage developed in a different direction from their arboreal ancestors. The potoroos, or rat-kangaroos, and kangaroos proliferated during the retreat of the rainforests. The most primitive of the potoroo family, the musky rat-kangaroo (*Hypsiprymnodon moschatus*), remains a rainforest dweller and forages on all fours for fallen fruits. The other members of this family, the potoroos and bettongs, are

Possums are members of the most widespread group of Australian marsupials, the Phalangerida. The ringtail possum (Pseudocheirus peregrinus) is an expert climber. Its feet are well adapted for gripping (two toes are opposable to the other three) and it uses its tail as an extra limb to hang onto branches. It has adapted to living closely with humans on the eastern mainland.

LEFT: There has been some confusion in classifying the koala. Initially described variously as a native bear, monkey or a New Holland sloth, it is actually most closely related to the wombat, sharing the suborder, Vombatiformes. Both animals have backward opening pouches and nearly invisible, short tails.

A mountain brushtail possum (Trichosurus caninus) baby clings tightly to its mother's back. It will stay with her for up to three years, much longer than the ringtail (above) which is weaned at about seven months. It is abundant where its habitat of tall forests still occurs in the south-east of Australia.

Baby kangaroos (joeys) continue to suckle for about seven months after they have left the pouch.

RIGHT: Little red flying foxes (Pteropus scapulatus) are nomadic bats, often travelling considerable distances to find eucalypts in flower.

Kangaroos are social animals and stay together in groups, known as mobs, for safety. Until they are fully independent, joeys are at risk from predators such as dingoes, eagles and introduced animals such as foxes.

widespread but declining in numbers. Most seem to have a varied diet but, in cases where they have been studied, all appear to have a particular fondness for species of fungi, a habit which may well have an important part in dispersing and propagating fungi.

KANGAROOS

Members of the kangaroo family (Macropodidae) have evolved from browsers to specialised grazing animals. Unlike the possums and wombats, which have developed a horse-like hindgut fermentation system, the kangaroos have evolved a complex stomach, similar to that of sheep or cows. The solid fraction of the finely chewed leaves is selectively retained in the sack-like stomach and fermented by symbiotic bacteria.

Chewing grass into the fine shreds needed for this process causes wear to the grinding teeth. Kangaroos have responded to this challenge by evolving a system of gradual tooth eruption where the teeth grow slowly and move forward in the jaw during the life of the animal. Most kangaroos only have four or five grinding teeth in each quadrant of the jaw so in time they eventually run out of teeth, but the tiny nabarlek, or little rock-wallaby (*Petrogale concinna*) seems to have an unlimited supply and keeps on producing more and more teeth through its lifetime. A similar system of tooth replacement is found among placental mammals in elephants and manatees.

Placentals

The ancient Gondwanan placentals left no descendants in Australia but other groups of placental mammals have repeatedly invaded the continent in the last 40 million years. The earliest known invasions were microbats—small insectivorous bats which have been found in enormous numbers as fossils in the Riversleigh deposits of north Queensland. Other bats must soon have followed for Australia now has a rich and varied bat fauna.

BATS

Flying foxes, or fruit bats, are a group of Old World tropical bats that play an important role in the pollination and seed dispersal of many forest plants. The smaller species have long snouts and protrusible brush-tipped tongues which they use to gather nectar and pollen. They are generally shy rainforest dwellers and are seldom seen. The larger fruit bats are much more visible and frequently come into conflict with orchardists and urban-dwelling humans. These bats are especially fond of the flowers of *Melaleuca* and *Angophora* and can be seen in great numbers during the flowering seasons of these trees.

| **FAUNA TIMELINE** | **570 MILLION YBP** First appearance of multicelled animals in Australian fossil record, including sea anemone (*Inaria*) and jellyfish (*Tribrachidium*). | **420 MILLION YBP** Arthropods emerge from water, as indicated by tracks in Murchison Gorge near Kalbarri, WA, formed by sea scorpions called *Eurypterids*. | **400 MILLION YBP** First vertebrates emerge from water, as evidenced by tracks found at Glenisla Homestead, Vic, thought to belong to newt-like tetrapod. | **230 MILLION YBP** Emergence of reptiles, which have a distinct advantage over amphibians in that they are capable of laying eggs on land. | **70–55 MILLION YBP** Marsupials spread to Antarctica and Australia from South America. **65 MILLION YBP** Mass extinction of dinosaurs. | **23–20 MILLION YBP** Ancestors of today's fauna widespread, including koalas, carnivorous kangaroos and VIP silvabestius (sheep-sized marsupial). | **35,000 YBP** Extinction of megafauna, possibly as a result of overhunting by humans or drastic and sudden climate change. |

| **3500 MILLION YBP** Emergence of micro-organisms known as stromatolites in north-west Australia. Still found in WA, these may be oldest living things on Earth. | **470 MILLION YBP** Emergence of bony-skinned jawless fishes, *Arandaspis*, first Australian vertebrates. | **410 MILLION YBP** Appearance of trilobites in fossil record, which subsequently become abundant. Soon afterward, first jawed fishes appear. | **240 MILLION YBP** Late Permian extinction, perhaps caused by falling sea levels, wipes out half of all animal families and 80 per cent of planet's sea creatures. | **210 MILLION YBP** Dinosaurs appear and dominate for 145 million years. **120 MILLION YBP** Appearance of monotremes and birds in fossil record. | **55 MILLION YBP** Australia separates from Gondwana and begins long period of isolation. Marsupials start to outcompete placental mammals. | **15 MILLION YBP** Giant animals, or megafauna, become common. **4.5 MILLION YBP** First wave of rodents colonises Australia. | **6000–3500 YBP** of dingo from South-Asia; soon after, thylacin Tasmanian devil beco extinct on mainlan |

Most of Australia's microbats are either widespread species such as the common bentwing bat (*Miniopterus* spp.) or close relatives of similar forms in Asia. Two highly specialised species are the ghost bat (*Macroderma gigas*) and the large-footed myotis (*Myotis adversus*). The ghost bat, which has relatives in Asia and Africa, is Australia's only carnivorous bat and hunts small rodents and roosting birds. The large-footed myotis rakes the surface of lakes and streams with the sharp claws of its enormous feet to collect its diet of water beetles and other aquatic insects.

The fluke of a humpback whale breaks the water just before diving. Once hunted almost to extinction, their numbers are now increasing along the east coast. Their continued wellbeing is now important to the tourist industry which runs popular whale-watching expeditions.

THE MOST SUCCESSFUL MAMMALS

Invasion by rodents—now almost universal mammals—must have occurred on several separate occasions, as evidenced by the four distinctly different groups of rodent now native to Australia. Two of these groups, the water rats and the conilurines, have closer affinities to rodents from the Philippines than those from mainland Asia and are the oldest colonists. The mosaic-tailed rats are more recent invaders from Indonesia via New Guinea and most recent of all are 'true rats' of the genus *Rattus*, some brought by European settlers, which are now widespread.

The 'boom and bust' conditions which occur sporadically in the Australian climate are not a barrier to rats and mice. Reproductive speed is the key which gave them their evolutionary edge and allowed the Muridae to become the dominant mammalian family worldwide (29 per cent of living mammals are murids). As well, strategies such as extracting water from seeds and digging burrows to conserve water have enabled mice to conquer the desert. Hopping is another way these mice have adapted to desert life, using the same principles of energy conservation as kangaroos. Each time the hopper lands, energy is stored in elastic tendons of the heel as the foot bends. This stored energy means that each succeeding bound uses less metabolic energy than the first jump.

MARINE MAMMALS

Many other mammals occur in the seas around Australia, including dolphins, whales and dugongs. Dugongs (Family Dugongidae) and the seagrasses on which they depend are now an endangered ecosystem, threatened not so much by hunting as by over-development of their fragile habitat. On the brighter side, stocks of humpback whales (*Megaptera novaeangliae*) appear to be increasing. Their well-known patterns of migration from their feeding grounds in Antarctica to the east and west coasts of Australia were once used by hunters to plan their slaughter, but are now proving an advantage to the flourishing ecotourism industry. The southern right whale (*Eubalaena australis*) is also recovering from earlier exploitation and returning to Australia's coastal bays to calve. Likewise, sea lions and fur seals are recovering from former decimation and are expanding to recolonise many of their former rookeries.

INTRODUCTIONS

Perhaps the most sinister mammalian invasion of Australia is that of the 21 species of mammal which were introduced by humans, mainly the Europeans, for a variety of reasons and which have established feral populations across Australia. Some have had only a localised impact but ten of these, plus the introduction of domestic sheep and cattle, have had an enormous impact on the landscape, flora and fauna of Australia.

The earliest introduction was the dingo (*Canis lupus dingo*). Descended from Indian wolves, dingoes were spread by traders through southeast Asia and eastward through the archipelagos to Australia from 6000 to 3500 years ago. Once they reached Australia they spread widely across the mainland and probably contributed to the extinction of several species including the thylacine and Tasmanian devil on the mainland. Dingoes themselves are now threatened by poisoning campaigns and by interbreeding with domestic dogs.

In the nineteenth century, hunters killed so many fur-seals that they had to turn to slaughtering elephant seals and penguins to fill their quota of oil. The Southern fur-seal (Artocephalus pusillus) is now protected in Australian waters.

97 John Macarthur introduces merino sheep.
40 Recording of assumed nction of lesser stick-nest ong-eared hopping mouse Darling hopping mouse.

1933 Last-known thylacine dies at Hobart Zoo, though sightings continue to be reported today.
1935 Introduction of cane toad to Qld.

1996 IUCN Red List records that Australia has 58 mammal, 45 bird, 25 amphibian, 37 reptile, 27 fish and 281 invertebrate species in danger of extinction.

1859 Release of 24 rabbits near Geelong, Vic., allows species to multiply. By 1900, it has spread throughout NSW, SA, much of Qld and reached WA.

1961 Rediscovery of Leadbetter's possum, which had been presumed extinct for over 50 years, at Marysville, Vic.

1999 Australian Museum announces plan to clone thylacine using DNA obtained from preserved specimen.

The rufous-banded honeyeater (Conopophila albogularis) is a member of the largest bird family in Australia, the Meliphagidae. It inhabits the northern edge of the continent, nesting in diverse environments from monsoon forest and coastal scrub to suburban gardens.

Birds

RIGHT: The bony casque, or helmet, of the flightless southern cassowary helps to protect its head as it negotiates dense undergrowth. It lives in the rainforests of Queensland.

The emu is Australia's largest bird, and the second largest in the world after the ostrich. Now found only on the mainland, there were once two distinct forms in Tasmania and on King and Kangaroo Islands.

Australia is rich in bird life, with over 770 species spread over the continent. Several groups have evolved into a large number of families and now occupy many ecological niches. Honeyeaters (Family Meliphagidae), for example, with about 72 species, are the largest Australian bird family and have colonised all areas of the continent.

An ancient lineage

Australia's endemic families include the plains wanderer, lyrebirds, scrub-birds and Australian mud-nest builders. A further nine Australian-centred families of birds extend no further than New Guinea. These include the fairy-wrens, pardalotes and the Australian treecreepers and babblers, as well as the cassowaries and the emu family (Dromaiidae). This family is a member of a Gondwanan group of flightless birds, the ratites (Order Struthioniforms), which includes ostriches and rheas. The emu (*Dromaius novae-hollandiae*) browses on herbs, shrubs and some fruits and is still fairly abundant across much of Australia. Cassowaries (*Casuarius casuarius*) feed on fallen fruit in tropical rainforests and the Australian species is endangered by fragmentation of its habitat.

Another group of primitive birds is the mound-builders (Family Megapodiidae). These birds exhibit a most un-birdlike method of incubation. Males build a large mound of earth and decaying vegetation in which they dig holes for the females to lay eggs. The heat generated by the rotting plant material, rather than the body temperature of the parents, incubates the eggs. Getting the temperature right is crucial, and the male malleefowl (*Leipoa ocellata*) spends much time and effort trying to ensure optimum conditions. He does this either by adding sand or scraping it away from the mound according to the heat of the sun and the time of day. On hatching, the young not only

make their own way to the surface but begin foraging independently as soon as they emerge. The orange-footed scrubfowl (*Megapodius reinwardt*) is the most widespread species, ranging from the Nicobar Islands to tropical Australia, the Philippines and New Hebrides. It favours the lowland rainforest and monsoonal scrubs. Another mound-builder is the Australian brush-turkey (*Alectura lathami*) which lives in a wide variety of habitats from Cape York to south-east New South Wales. The now rare malleefowl is patchily distributed in drier habitats across southern Australia.

Diversity of parrots

Australian parrots display a greater variety of form than anywhere else in the world and make up about 15 per cent of the world's parrot fauna. Two families of parrot occur in Australia, the typical parrots (Psittacidae) which are pantropical and the cockatoos (Cacatuidae), which occur primarily in Australia although a few species extend to the Philippines and Solomon Islands. Some species of cockatoo are adept at collecting small seeds from the ground, others extract tubers from the ground or wood-boring insect larvae from tree stems, and the glossy black cockatoo (*Calyptorhynchus lathami*) uses its massive bill for cracking open the tough fruiting cones of *Casuarina*. All species of cockatoo nest in hollows in large trees and are extremely vulnerable to habitat destruction and fragmentation. Because individuals live so long, declines in breeding numbers may not be noticed for many years and even apparently prolific species may be slowly disappearing from the landscape.

The 40 Australian species in the Psittacidae belong to five subfamilies and show a wide array of adaptations. Five species of lorikeet have brush-tipped tongues for feeding on pollen and nectar. The tiny double-eyed fig parrot (*Cyclopsitta diophthalma*) is a highly variable species which occurs also in Papua New Guinea and is represented by three distinct subspecies. Its appearance is so different it was long considered to be a separate species. In the broad-tailed parrot subfamily the three species of rosella also show much geographic variation. Rosellas eat grass seeds and other fallen seeds which they gather on the ground. Perhaps the best-known Australian parrot is the budgerigar (*Melopsittacus undulatus*), kept worldwide as a cage bird, which can be seen in large flocks through-

out arid inland areas. Least known are the secretive green night parrot (*Pezoporus occidentalis*) and ground parrot (*P. wallicus*), two species which have adapted to skulking in dense low vegetation and seldom fly.

Environmental specialists

The gradual changes of terrain over the ages have had an effect on how some species have adapted and diversified. The chestnut quail-thrush (*Cinclosoma castanotus*) inhabits a system of dunes which connects the populations living in the western central and eastern areas of the Great Victorian Desert. The same system severed two main populations of the cinnamon quail-thrush: one group of cinnamon quail-thrush (*C. cinnamomeum*) now lives in the low shrublands of the Lake Eyre Basin and the other lives in a similar habitat on the Nullarbor. This bird, which is now distinguished as the Nullarbor quail-thrush, is evolving away from the parental form. The same process has caused speciation within babblers so that today three closely related species—the white-browed babbler, chestnut-crowned babbler and Hall's babbler—now overlap without interbreeding.

Australia's ranges, even though low, are themselves a primary source of divergence and radiation within the desert avifauna. The Hamersley Ranges in Western Australia and the central ranges, including the

Red-winged parrots (Aprosmictus erythropterus) are seed and berry eaters.

LEFT: Early European settlers in the north mistook the enormous mounds of the malleefowl for Aboriginal burial monuments.

The blue-winged kookaburra (Dacelo leachii) hunts insects, skinks and snakes.

The male variegated wren (Malurus lamberti) is very similar in appearance to the male blue-breasted wren (Malurus pulcherrimus) and their voices are also similar. The females of both species also look alike—an echo of their relatively recent common ancestry, and membership of the great songbird order Passeriformes.

RIGHT: The peaceful dove (Geopelia striata) belongs to the only surviving family in the order Columbiformes. It competes for food with the spotted turtle-dove.

The nocturnal tawny frogmouth (Podargus strigoides) is an expert in disguise. It only nests in trees, the bark of which exactly resembles the markings on its feathers, rendering it virtually invisible during the day.

world's crow family also includes nutcrackers, birds of paradise, Australian magpies and currawongs, butcherbirds and woodswallows, the Borneo bristlehead and the Old World orioles, cuckoo-shrikes and trillers. These birds represent an ancient, endemic, basically Australasian group which not only radiated far beyond the continent but, more recently (geologically speaking), recontributed members back into Australia, such as the genus *Corvus*, which contains Australia's better-known crows, and the orioles.

Fossil evidence in the northern hemisphere, which shows no remains of songbirds in otherwise rich fossil beds of birds, supports the findings that Australia's birds evolved in Australia and did not migrate here from the northern hemisphere. Also absent in the Old World fossil evidence are groups such as pigeons and parrots, which are both found in abundance in Australia. It is possible that all of these originated in the southern hemisphere and migrated to the northern hemisphere after 55 million years ago. New research suggests that all the world's songbirds did indeed originate in Gondwana and later migrated into Europe, rather than the other way around.

MacDonnells, have been particularly important refuges during dry glacial times. Subspecies of spinifex pigeon, ringneck, streaked and dusky grass-wrens and western bowerbirds, for instance, probably diverged in the last glacial, around 15,000 years ago. When the climate ameliorated these birds spread out to overlap with their relatives, now too different to interbreed. This explains why similar-looking birds such as pairs of red-capped and scarlet robins, variegated and blue-breasted fairy-wrens, and grey-fronted and yellow-plumed honeyeaters occur together today.

A Gondwanan origin for songbirds

The evolutionary story of Australian birds is fascinating. Up until very recently it was thought impossible that this antipodean outpost could have its own unique bird fauna. The prevailing view, despite strong evidence against it, was that most of Australia's birds must have migrated here from Asia.

Then, in 1986, a revolutionary phylogenetic, or family tree, of the world's birds was created, drawing on new information from the field of molecular biology. Using this information in conjunction with knowledge of plate tectonics, or continental drift, a more convincing story of the origin of the world's avifauna has emerged. It showed that the

Life in Estuaries and Rivers

Crocodiles

Of the two crocodile species which exist in Australia, only the freshwater crocodile (*Crocodylus johnstoni*) is endemic; the estuarine, or saltwater crocodile (*Crocodylus porosus*) ranges from India to the western Pacific. The freshwater crocodile only occurs in the creeks and rivers of the north. Growing to a maximum of 3 m (10 feet), it is smaller than the saltwater crocodile, the largest of its species in the world, which can grow up to 9 m (30 feet). The freshwater crocodile is not a threat to people, but the saltwater species is the cause of a number of sometimes fatal attacks on unwary bathers. Crocodile share several traits with birds, perhaps because of their common dinosaur affinity, including a strong maternal bond with the young. Female crocodiles lay their eggs in a nest of vegetation near a river or billabong (waterhole). She guards the nest assiduously against predators. The eggs are incubated by the heat from the decaying nest material. At the time of hatching the babies begin to grunt, signalling the mother to uncover the nest. She then assists the hatchlings to get to water by carrying them gently in her mouth. They stay under her protection for a few days and then disperse.

Turtles

Two families of freshwater turtle are found in Australia. The family Chelidae, commonly called 'tortoises' in Australia, occur here and in South America. Several species occur widely throughout Australia and New Guinea, living in streams, lakes and swamps. More unusual is the pig-nosed turtle (*Carettochelys insculpta*), a monotypic family with affinities to a related family in North America, Africa and Asia. This peculiar looking animal, which has a leathery, pitted skin and paddle-like flippers like a sea turtle, was thought to occur only in New Guinea but it has recently been found to be widely distributed in Australia's Northern Territory.

Fishes

Australia's fish fauna is poor compared to the rest of the world's continents and contains few truly freshwater species. Many species, like barramundi (*Lates calcarifer*) and Australian bass (*Macquaria novemaculeata*) either migrate regularly between fresh and saltwaters or are marine species which only occasionally venture upstream. Other non-migratory forms such as the perches and cods of the major river systems (*Macquaria* and *Maccullochella* spp.) are recent descendants of these species. Many of the large inland river systems have or had endemic fish species and it is now recognised that the Cooper Creek/Lake Eyre population of golden perch is a separate species from that of the Murray/Darling.

Two groups of freshwater fishes are of interest. The galaxiids (Galaxiidae) are found only in the southern hemisphere and 18 of the 20 species found in Australia are endemic. The Australian lungfish (*Neoceratodus forsteri*) is an ancient species, one of a group of Gondwanan families. Lungfishes have a unique place in the evolutionary family tree of vertebrates, close to the ancestors of the amphibians. Unlike their African and South American relatives, Australian lungfishes cannot hibernate in a mud cocoon but need standing water all year round. They survive only in Queensland's Mary and Burnett Rivers.

Short-necked river turtles (Emydura spp.) live in fresh water and are commonly seen in the rivers and creeks of eastern and northern Australia.

TOP: The freshwater crocodile has a long slender snout—one way of distinguishing it from its dangerous saltwater relative.

A saltwater crocodile drifts in classic crocodile pose, with its head and eyes just above the water, lying in wait for prey. Like the freshwater, it lives in the estuaries and rivers of the north.

Hunters and Prey of the Spinifex

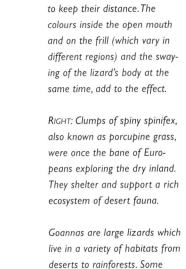

A spectacular warning display by the harmless frilled lizard (Chlamydosaurus kingii) convinces most predators to keep their distance. The colours inside the open mouth and on the frill (which vary in different regions) and the swaying of the lizard's body at the same time, add to the effect.

RIGHT: Clumps of spiny spinifex, also known as porcupine grass, were once the bane of Europeans exploring the dry inland. They shelter and support a rich ecosystem of desert fauna.

Goannas are large lizards which live in a variety of habitats from deserts to rainforests. Some species, like the lace monitor (Varanus varius) are good at climbing and scale trees to find one of their favourite foods.

Lizards

Lizards are a spectacular example of evolutionary success, colonising specific habitats, particularly the expanding spinifex-covered sandy deserts and acacia-dominated shrublands. In the spinifex grasslands just south-west of Alice Springs, up to 440 lizards per ha (176 per acre) have been recorded and up to 42 different species can be found living together. Their coexistence has no ecological parallel anywhere else in the world. A remarkable 90 per cent of the more than 750 reptile species found in Australia occur nowhere else, and new species are being described every year. The clue to their survival and diversity in such apparently inhospitable conditions lies in their cold-bloodedness (in terms of energy, this means that they do not have to maintain a constant temperature in areas of extreme heat and cold) and in their ability to become inactive, virtually switching off during periods of stress.

Of the lizards, the varanids are the top predators in spinifex grasslands. Although the varanids are relatively late immigrants, they have had an explosive radiation—25 of the world's 30 varanid species occur in Australia. The largest Australian varanid, the perentie (Varanus giganteus), grows up to 2 m (6.5 feet) long and is the second largest lizard in the world (after Indonesia's komodo dragon). The smallest species, V. caudolineatus, is only 30 cm (1 foot) long.

Of the shrub-preferring lizards at least eight species of dragon, gecko and skink have crossed from the deserts of the west to the deserts of the east through the shrubby band of acacia known as the Giles Corridor. This corridor is the only continuous ribbon of shrublands through the Great Victoria Desert in Western Australia—an undulating sandy region which is dominated by sandridges, sandplains and salt lakes. Dragons in the family Agamidae, including the thorny devil (Moloch horridus), are the only group of lizards known to be partial to feeding on ants.

Geckos form the bulk of Australia's abundant nocturnal lizards. In order to cope with their hot and sometimes crowded and competitive environment, some geckos burrow; one species, Gehyra pilbara, even lives inside termite mounds; some, like G. variegata, climb trees; some live in caves and cliffs; some, like Diplodactylus ciliaris, prefer the wide open spaces. (In the north of Australia some inhabit human homes.) In the Great Victoria Desert as many as nine different geckos can be found living closely together. They manage to coexist by partitioning space and food. For example, geckos with larger heads, like the knob-tailed gecko (Nephrurus spp.), hunt larger prey than those with smaller heads, who prey on animals further down the size scale.

Closely related to the geckos are the Pygopodids, legless worm-like or snake-like lizards. These are the only lizard family endemic to the region, occurring only in mainland Australia and New Guinea.

One of the physiological adaptations animals can undergo when adapting to life in the desert is a reduction in the size of limbs—or even their complete loss. In this way they can more easily move—or, more accurately, swim—through the sand. The best example of limb reduction occurs in the Australian skinks of the genus *Lerista*. This is the second largest group of lizards in Australia, with over 50 species, and is one of the most graphic demonstrations of a possible course of evolution. While some species have retained their limbs and toes, others are limbless. Following the evidence of the fossil record, these species of *Lerista* show all the stages of limb reduction, starting with the loss of bones from the toes. Incredibly, *Lerista* gains vertebrae at the same rate as it loses its toes, giving it more length and agility for moving through sand.

Ants and termites

If lizards are the hunters of the infertile grasslands, termites are the miniature 'game'. As well as being food for lizards, termites are also prey to numerous animals—other insects, echidnas, the numbat, birds, frogs and snakes, including blind snakes which live underground. So well adapted are they to their environment that they exist in enormous numbers.

Termites need cellulose to survive and to get it they eat foodstuffs such as wood and animal dung which is inedible to just about any other animal. Their cumulative weight reflects the cellulose glut

in the environment: termites under the ground easily weigh as much as all the kangaroos and cattle on top of it! One species alone harvests 100 kg per ha (88 pounds per acre) of dry weight annually. In the Tanami Desert north of Alice Springs, there are at least 800 termite mounds per ha (320 per acre).

Just as abundant but startlingly diverse are the ants, particularly in the arid zone. There are thousands of species in Australia, with more being discovered all the time, and most occur in the desert regions. This is unusual because in global terms the diversity of ants is related to latitude (and hence temperature) so that, generally, the richest ant fauna is found in the equatorial tropics. Australia has double its latitudinal quota. Here, there are an astonishing 100 species in a plot only 20 × 40 m (66 × 130 feet) and, in one region at the southern edge of the arid zone, an extraordinary 250 species have been recorded.

The reasons for such diversity are complex. One explanation is the horizontal diversity in the Australian environment—in other words, the variability occurs across the landscape rather than vertically, as it does in a forest. Ants respond well to this horizontal change. In the arid zone ants can be found virtually everywhere—nesting in trees, in litter, under logs or stones and in mind-boggling numbers in soil; some species are even soil-specific. They can work throughout the day and night foraging singly, loosely or in columns and are able to cope with temperatures as high as 65°C (149°F). Another important factor influencing the prevalence of ants is the incredible mass of one of their favourite foods—termites—everywhere. They also eat a wide variety of plant material including seeds (which some ants harvest) and other insects,

Dominant ant species affect the behaviour patterns of other species. The tyranny of the native *Iridomyrmex purpureus*, colloquially known as the 'meatant'—caused by inquisitiveness, aggression and sheer force of numbers—enforces a pattern in space and time with which other ants must conform. For instance, the lone forager ant *Melophorus* is forced to hunt when *Iridomyrmex* does not—in the middle of the day. *Melophorus* species have adapted to these rules by further partitioning the time available to them according to their colour: dark species (which cope less well with the heat) forage when the temperature is around a relatively cool 45°C (113°F) while the red-headed or yellow species are active during the hotter 50°C (122°C) timeslot.

Their rudimentary eyes allow them to distinguish between light and dark, but blind snakes (Family Typhlopidae) have little use for sight as they spend much of their time underground, feeding on termites, worms and ants. Parts of their skeletal anatomy (a lizard-like skull, and the vestiges of a pelvis) suggest that they may once have had legs.

The shape and size of termite mounds varies according to the type of environment and the species of termite. The spinifex termite (Nasutitermes triodiae) builds mounds of up to 6 m (18 feet) high. The thick, fortress-like walls and construction of air vents provide temperature control which enables termites to survive the scorching heat of the desert.

Land of Extinctions

*In an age when hawks were killed as pests, this bird was also known as the brown hawk or chicken hawk. Luckily, the brown falcon (*Falco berigora*) escaped the attention of European settlers. It is one of Australia's most widespread and common birds of prey.*

TOP: *Logging is sometimes a controversial issue when it comes to environment conservation.*

RIGHT: *European agricultural methods (such as irrigation of 'thirsty' crops like cotton) deplete the water table and result in the salination of many bodies of water, with the loss of native vegetation and wildlife.*

There are around 4000 species of mammal currently living in the world, and the extinction rate is about one species every 400 years, and for birds, one species every 200 years. In Australia, since the beginning of the Tertiary period which started about 65 million years ago, many species have evolved or disappeared for many reasons. Major climatic change and geological upheavals, along with the natural evolution of a species and their survival as distinct species, causes these changes. However, Australia alone has a record of loss over the past 200 years of 40 times the worldwide extinction rate, based on the current list of 20 species of mammals known to have become extinct since 1788. For birds, Australia has 20 times the worldwide extinction rate.

Unfortunately, human intervention is now the main cause of these extinctions. There are two main reasons—the way the land is managed (land-clearing and inappropriate management) and the introduction of new species of animals and plants. In the last 200 years, Australia has lost 75 per cent of its rainforests and 43 per cent of its forests. Some regions have been particularly affected, such as areas in the east and south-west which have been extensively cleared for agricultural use. Tragically, the greatest loss of vegetation has occurred only in the last 50 years with the result that a further 85 species of mammals, birds and reptiles are on the verge of extinction.

Nowhere is this most evident than in the outback where the enforced movement of Aboriginal people into settlements in the 1930s and 1940s ushered in the return of uncontrolled wildfires. A number of desert mammals such as the burrowing bettong (*Bettongia lesueur*), the golden bandicoot (*Isoodon auratus*)

and desert bandicoot (*Perameles eremiana*) which were known to be widespread before this have since vanished. Other animals are critically endangered. The rufous hare-wallaby (*Lagorchestes hirsutus*), for example, a shaggy, sandy-coloured animal about the size of a European hare, was once one of the most abundant and widespread macropods in inland Australia. Now the species is known only from the Bernier and Dorre Islands off Western Australia and from a small region of the Tanami Desert.

To many European settlers, the Australian terrain, and particularly its unfamiliar wildlife, were unlovely. Animals which were seen as troublesome, such as wombats, rat-kangaroos, the thylacine, wedge-tailed eagles, any species of hawk, ravens, dingoes, native cats, tiger-cats and goannas were poisoned or shot for such sins as poultry-raiding or egg-eating. Throughout the nineteenth century, and well into the twentieth, homesick Europeans living in Australia tried to bend

the country to suit their ideal of how it should be—in fact, to create a second England in the antipodes. The greatest enthusiasts of this folly were those belonging to the Acclimatisation Societies. Their objective was to homogenise Australia by the introduction from Britain and her colonies of 'innocuous' animals which were familiar or thought to be useful.

The definition of what was harmless, however, proved problematic. Some members, for instance, thought that monkeys would be a terrific acquisition 'for the amusement of the wayfarer whom their gambols would delight as he lay under some gum-tree in the forest on a sultry day'. This desire to populate the country with interesting and useful species was so great that the Melbourne Royal Park and Botanic Gardens (now the Melbourne Zoo) complained that there were hardly any animals left as they were being liberated with abandon by Acclimatisation Societies.

These century-old attitudes would make us laugh if they hadn't led to such serious consequences for Australian biodiversity. For instance, three species of bird released by the Victorian Acclimatisation Society—the Indian mynah, the English starling and the house sparrow—now dominate some Australian habitats to the detriment of native birds. Some of these proved to be pests immediately and were regretted at the time. The sparrows, for example, introduced to eat the caterpillars that were ruining the livelihood of many orchardists, preferred to eat the fruit instead. And starlings, too, devoured fruit crops. In all, 96 species of bird have at one time or another been introduced to Australia since European settlement.

English pond fishes—tench (*Tinca tinca*), roach (*Rutilus rutilus*) and goldfish (*Carassius auratus*)—and redfin perch (Family Percidae) and European carp (*Cyprinus carpio*) were introduced to Australian waterways in various localities. Now any pool of water in south-east Australia is likely to have carp or goldfish in it. Redfin have increased to such levels that they eat themselves out of food and European carp destroy their habitat by sucking up mud in their search for food and spitting out the remains, as well as killing native fishes and amphibians.

There are now at least 80 species of introduced animals from all over the world that have established wild populations in Australia. Among those causing

public concern are rabbits, foxes (introduced for hunting), cats, pigs, goats, donkeys, deer, camels from the Middle East, swamp buffaloes from Asia, mosquito-fish, Nile perch, house mice and other rodents, and cane toads from Hawaii.

Of all the animals introduced to Australia, rabbits have probably caused the most damage to the environment and to agriculture. They compete with native wildlife for food and shelter, and contribute to the decline in the numbers of many native plants and animals. In particular, they have been closely implicated with the disappearance, late last century and earlier this century, of many medium-sized ground-dwelling native mammals. At this time, the combined effect of sheep grazing, plagues of rabbits and drought seriously reduced the carrying capacity of the land, and brought about a wave of extinctions. Animals such as burrowing bettongs (*Bettongia lesueur*), brush-tailed bettongs (*Bettongia penicillata*) and bridled nail-tail wallabies (*Onychogalea fraenata*) disappeared from most of their former ranges before the end of the nineteenth century. Many other species such as the pig-footed bandicoot (*Chaeropus ecaudatus*), eastern hare-wallaby (*Lagorchestes leporides*) and crescent nailtail wallaby (*Onychogalea lunata*) disappeared completely.

At this rate of extinctions, the picture for the future apparently looks grim, but Australia still remains a land of surprises. In the last decade, at least one new species each of carnivorous marsupial and desert rodent has been discovered every year and others previously known only from a few old, misidentified museum specimens have been rediscovered as living populations. As well, the night parrot (*Pezoporus occidentalis*), long thought to be extinct here, has been confirmed to be still extant.

Perhaps most surprising change is the increasing concern for conservation. Successes like the rehabilitation of Port Jackson (Sydney Harbour) and Port Phillip Bay (in Melbourne) do not yet outnumber losses such as the massive clearing of brigalow or diversion of water from rivers and wetlands to irrigate cotton. But on a smaller scale, changes to legislation on the control of dogs and cats and schemes such as Landcare, Coastcare and Land for Wildlife indicate that the attitudes of most Australians are gradually changing the emphasis from development to sustainability.

This cruel-looking instrument was used to trap the thylacine, also known as the Tasmanian tiger. Regarded as a nuisance to livestock, efforts to eradicate it proved all too successful: the last thylacine died in a zoo in 1933.

LEFT: The swamp buffalo (Bubalus bubalis), the mainstay of Asia's agriculture, was introduced last century to serve as food for settlers. Since then it has gone wild and its numbers have increased drastically. Buffaloes have caused much damage to the environment by compacting mud with their hooves and by overgrazing delicate ecosystems.

The warrung, or crescent nailtail wallaby, may have survived in some regions up to the late 1950s. The species is now extinct, victim to competition, loss of environment and attack from introduced animals.

FLORA

An Ancient and Diverse Flora

Wollemia nobilis. *This rare conifer, discovered near Sydney in 1994, is being propagated at the Royal Botanic Gardens, Sydney. It will be released to the trade in 2005, and funds raised will be used to ensure its long-term conservation.*

The flora of Australia varies greatly with the climate. The map shows six major regions, and within the South-west region five further ecological zones. The boundaries of the regions are arbitrary, and many species will overlap. Specific floral systems within these regions are labelled and marked in green.

FLORAL SYSTEMS OF AUSTRALIA

Angiosperms—plants which have their seeds enclosed in an ovary—evolved some 110 million years ago. Before that, flora was dominated by ferns and gymnosperms (conifers and cycads). Ferns reproduced by spores and gymnosperms produced their seeds on organs known as sporophylls or cones. One genus of pre-angiosperm flora (*Araucaria*) and several angiosperm genera (*Nothofagus, Lomatia* and *Eucryphia*) are common to both the east coast of Australia and the west coast of South America, reflecting the relationship between these two continents—they were both part of ancient Gondwana. Proteaceae is believed to be one of the oldest Australian angiosperm families. Leaf fossils probably representing *Persoonia*, a member of the Proteaceae family, have been found in Upper Cretaceous deposits over 100 million years old, and fruiting cones of *Banksia* have been found in late Eocene deposits, dated at about 50 million years old.

As well as age, the isolation and size of the land are factors which have contributed to the remarkable diversity of the continent's flora. This diversity so impressed Banks and Solander, the botanists travelling with Captain Cook, that the site of the first settlement was named Botany Bay. However, despite their enthusiasm, many of the early settlers, homesick for Britain, were not enthralled by the flora in their new country. Robert Brown, a botanist financed by Banks to collect plant specimens, wrote in 1803: 'There is an endless variety of genera and species of shrub, but the general impression is dismal.'

Over 21,000 species have been recognised, 85 per cent of which are found nowhere else. *Acacia*, with over 950 species, and *Eucalyptus* (including *Corymbia*), with nearly 800, are the two dominant genera. Eucalypts are particularly well adapted to a harsh climate: their leaves tend to hang vertically and turn as the sun moves across the sky, so that their edge is always facing the sun, reducing transpiration. Some families reach their peak of diversity here: Myrtaceae, for instance, has almost 1900 species in 89 genera and Proteaceae has more than 1100 species in 46 genera. In addition to flowering plants, Australian flora is comparatively rich in ferns, fern allies and gymnosperms (conifers and cycads). These tend to be concentrated in the wetter coastal areas and ranges, but occasionally they are also found in more arid places. Some 390 species of fern, 44 species of conifer and 69 cycads have been recorded as native. Of particular significance was the discovery in 1994 of a new genus of conifer, the Wollemi pine (*Wollemia nobilis*). This rare plant, which is considered a relic, with characteristics related to fossil species in the family Araucariaceae, was found in a deep gorge surrounded by sandstone cliffs, only 200 km

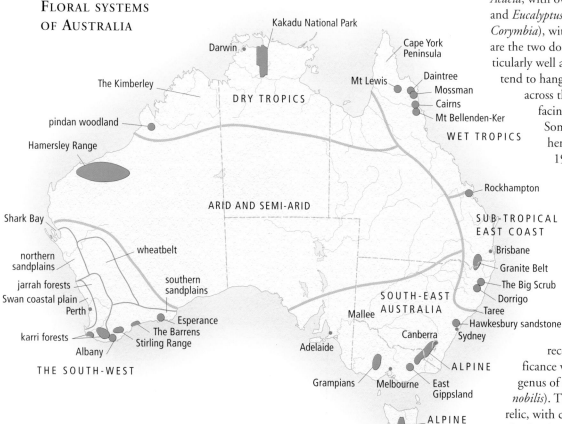

Kakadu National Park
Darwin
Cape York Peninsula
The Kimberley
Daintree
Mt Lewis
Mossman
DRY TROPICS
Cairns
pindan woodland
Mt Bellenden-Ker
Hamersley Range
WET TROPICS
Shark Bay
ARID AND SEMI-ARID
Rockhampton
northern sandplains
wheatbelt
SUB-TROPICAL EAST COAST
jarrah forests
southern sandplains
Brisbane
Swan coastal plain
Granite Belt
Perth
The Big Scrub
SOUTH-EAST AUSTRALIA
Dorrigo
karri forests
Esperance
Mallee
Taree
The Barrens
Hawkesbury sandstone
Albany
Stirling Range
Canberra
Sydney
Adelaide
ALPINE
THE SOUTH-WEST
Grampians
Melbourne
East Gippsland
ALPINE
Hobart

(125 miles) from Sydney. One of the reasons for such diversity is Australia's range of environments and climates—from the subtropical north, with its distinctly seasonal rainfall, to the generally arid interior, to the alpine areas of Tasmania and Victoria.

Fire—seasonal bushfires and the human strategy of burning off areas of vegetation—has also been an important factor in the evolution of our flora, and different species have adopted varying strategies to cope with it. The eucalypts possess epicormic (dormant) buds, which sprout new shoots from the trunk after fire. Many members of the Proteaceae family develop a lignotuber (a swollen base), which shoots after fire. Other families have seeds with hard coats, which germinate after fires and the following rains crack the seed coat.

Nearly 5 per cent of Australian flora—about 76 taxa—have become extinct since European settlement, and an additional 1009 are considered threatened. Reasons for this include the expansion of suburbia around capital cities, the development of major towns and the clearing of land for agriculture and mining. The setting up of national parks and reserves in all states and territories has alleviated the situation, and recovery plans have been put into place to assist certain vulnerable species. The first national park in Australia—the Royal National Park, on the southern outskirts of Sydney—was established in 1879, only seven years after the world's first national park, Yellowstone, in the USA. Even before this, in 1872, King's Park in Perth was gazetted as a public park and place of recreation—it remains a significant conservation area today.

Palm Valley is a refuge for the Central Australian Cabbage Tree Palm (Livistona mariae). Here on the Finke River lives this remnant from millions of years ago, when the land was much wetter. It occurs over about 60 sq. km (23 sq. miles), in an area where the unique geological formations allow water to seep down from the tops of gorges to the rocky shales beneath.

The lemon-flowered gum (Eucalyptus woodwardii) grows in deep sandy loam east of Kalgoorlie, Western Australia, where the annual rainfall is about 220 mm (8.5 inches). It has thick grey leaves, which help it to conserve moisture.

The South-East

The heath banksia (Banksia ericifolia) is a common shrub of the Hawkesbury sandstone heaths around Sydney. Its flower spikes can reach up to 30 cm (12 inches) long in autumn.

Grass trees belong to the endemic genus Xanthorrhoea. There are 28 species. While some are trunkless, others, like this one, X. quadrangulata, near Adelaide, develop huge, sometimes branched trunks. They often occur in fire-prone areas, and although their trunks blacken, the growing shoots remain undamaged.

Dry sclerophyll forest

This type of forest is made up of a low to medium-height tree canopy under which flourishes a diverse ground layer of shrubs and herbs which tend to be drought-resistant. Dry sclerophyll forest occupies much of south-eastern Australia, and it is in this environment that floral diversity reaches its peak. The soils, usually derived from siliceous rocks, are well drained but poor in nutrients, particularly phosphorous and nitrogen. Many shrubs have adapted to these poor soils by modifying their root structure. Members of the Proteaceae family, for example, produce a mass of tiny roots called proteoid roots near the surface of the leaf litter in order to absorb the maximum amount of nutrition from the precious elements present. These roots are short-lived, developing with a growth flush prompted by rain. This environment is also subject to frequent fires, and many species have developed strategies to allow them to survive in this hazardous habitat.

The canopy is usually dominated by a variety of small to medium-sized eucalypts, frequently with twisted or contorted trunks. The scribbly gum (*Eucalyptus haemastoma*), with its white trunk and scribble-like bark markings, is very common in the forests around Sydney. Stringybark eucalypts, such as the red stringybark (*E. macrorhyncha*), the broad-leaved peppermint (*E. dives*) and the Sydney red gum (*Angophora costata*), are also dominant here.

The Hawkesbury sandstone area surrounding Sydney and extending into the Blue Mountains has a rich flora, with shrubs such as the floral emblem of New South Wales, the Sydney waratah (*Telopea speciosissima*), the heath banksia (*Banksia ericifolia*), the woody pear (*Xylomelum pyriforme*) and several *Grevillea* species representing the Proteaceae family. Both the banksia and the woody pear retain their seed in their fruits until fire causes the follicles to open and release them. Wattles, pea flowers and some members of the Rutaceae family have a hard seed coat, which also responds to fire by cracking and permitting moisture to reach the embryo.

Further south, in western Victoria, the Grampian Mountains offer another opportunity to view this dry sclerophyll vegetation at its best. Almost one-third of the Victorian flora occurs in this relatively small mountain range. Steep sandstone cliffs conceal a vast variety of colourful flowers, including the Grampians thryptomene (*Thryptomene calycina*) and showy bauera (*Bauera sessiliflora*), two of the 20 or more species endemic to the Grampians.

Wet sclerophyll forest

The wet sclerophyll forests of the south-east are typified by the blackbutt (*Eucalyptus pilularis*) forests of New South Wales and the huge mountain ash (*E. regnans*) forests of east Gippsland in Victoria. While these forests are impressive in their size and grandeur, there is less diversity in their understorey, as the dense canopy restricts the amount of sunlight reaching the ground.

Temperate rainforest

The mainland temperate rainforests lack the species diversity of the tropical and subtropical forests further north. Tree ferns and palms, however, flourish in the deep gullies. The cabbage tree palm (*Livistona australis*) forms huge populations in these shady refuges, and is often

accompanied by the soft tree fern (*Dicksonia antarctica*), with trunks up to 5 m (16 feet) tall and fronds to 3 m (10 feet). The dominant trees are the sweetly scented southern sassafras (*Atherosperma moschatum*), coachwood (*Ceratopetalum apetalum*) and the lilly pilly (*Acmena australis*).

While the myrtle beech (*Nothofagus cunninghamii*) does grow in the Otway Ranges of Victoria, it reaches its best development in Tasmania, where it is seen in company with several conifers. These wet, mossy forests are unique in Australia, where conifers are not usually among the dominant species. Here, in the south-west of Tasmania, the giant Huon pine (*Lagarostrobus franklinii*) can be found, along with the celery-top pine (*Phyllocladus aspleniifolius*) and the King Billy pine (*Athrotaxis selaginoides*).

Mallee

The word 'mallee' is derived from an Aboriginal word used to describe eucalypts with surface roots from which water could be obtained. It is now used to designate huge areas of dry, inland south-western New South Wales, north-western Victoria and parts of South Australia and Western Australia dominated by multi-trunked eucalypts that develop massive swollen bases known as lignotubers. This habit is believed to be a response to several factors—fire, frost, drought and possibly the grazing of native animals. Several species of eucalypt are conspicuous in these areas: the red mallees (*Eucalyptus socialis* and *E. oleosa*) occur over most of the mallee area.

The mallee appears at first glance to be colourless, but the range of small shrubs and ephemeral plants is extensive. Brilliant yellow wattles (*Acacia* spp.) and cassias (*Senna* spp.) and emu bushes (*Eremophila* spp.) are prominent in the shrub layer. Broombush (*Melaleuca uncinata*) often forms dense stands—its stems are harvested to make brush fences. Small perennials, such as the blue *Dampiera* and yellow *Goodenia* species, light the ground layer in spring. After rain, the annuals soon appear, with poached egg daisies (*Myriocephalus stuartii*) and orange immortelles (*Waitzia acuminata*) flowering among the prickly spinifex (*Triodia* spp.) clumps.

Temperate rainforest in Mt Baw Baw National Park in eastern Victoria. Moss-covered logs serve as nurseries, providing the perfect place for ferns to germinate in the humid forest environment.

LEFT: The Sydney waratah (Telopea speciosissima) was formally gazetted as the floral emblem of New South Wales on 4 October 1962. Its image can be seen in old Sydney buildings such as the GPO, the Mitchell Library and the Lands Department building.

Snow Country

The snow gum (Eucalyptus niphophila) bends with the wind in the severe environment of the Australian alps.

Snow daisies (Celmisia asteliifolia) are probably the most common flowers above the snow line. They flower in summer, with a variety of other colourful daisies, buttercups and herbs.

Strictly speaking, the truly alpine areas of Australia are those above the tree line, which on mainland Australia are those above 1800 m (5900 feet). In Tasmania, much further south, they are usually above 1000 m (3300 feet). However, what is usually referred to as 'snow country' may be 300–400 m (985–1310 feet) below these altitudes. The snow country occupies about 6500 sq. km (2510 sq. miles) in Tasmania and about 5200 sq. km (2010 sq. miles) on the mainland. In total, this is only about 0.15 per cent of the Australian landmass. Despite often extreme conditions in these areas, certain species of plant survive and thrive. In New South Wales' Kosciuzko National Park alone, there are about 200 species of native plants, of which some 21 are endemic to the park. Within Kosciuzko there are several different habitats, including the tall and short alpine herbfields, which occupy well over 90 per cent of the park. These are often very rocky areas, where plants receive some shelter and benefit from the heat absorbed by the rocks during the day.

Heath, in the snow country, consists of generally taller woody plants which tend to colonise more protected areas. Here, the snow gum (*Eucalyptus niphophila*) adopts an almost mallee-like habit, with low, twisted branches and colourful blotched bark. It offers shelter to a variety of colourful shrubs.

Bogs here are permanently wet areas, often with sphagnum moss, where small herbaceous plants thrive. These plants are nurtured in the icy waters of melting snows and act as retention areas to prevent erosion in the gullies. One of the more common species here is *Astelia alpina*, which resembles small pineapple plants and in Tasmania is known as pineapple grass. There are also small shrubs, including the candle heath (*Richea continentis*); the tiny insectivorous sundew (*Drosera arcturi*) grows here too.

The feldmark, a high-altitude community characterised by scattered dwarf prostrate plants, often with a mat or cushion-like habit, is the harshest environment in the snow country. Occasionally some parts of it are covered with snow for the whole year. In other parts, the plants receive constant blasts from freezing winds and the snow cover is blown away, leaving the vegetation exposed. Only the hardiest of species can survive in these conditions, but some of the most beautiful alpine plants are amongst them— the alpine buttercup (*Ranunculus anemoneus*) and the Australian eidelweiss (*Ewartia nubigena*), which forms silvery mats among the exposed rocks. Perhaps unexpected in the feldmark is the small-leaved heath (*Epacris microphylla*), which grows here as a small twisted shrub, very different from the sparse, often single-stemmed shrub of the coastal heaths.

Subtropical East Coast

This area has a unique variety of ecological zones, due to a large extent to its rainfall pattern and warmer climate. It has a distinct wet and dry season pattern, with a dry late winter and spring and high rainfall in summer and early autumn, with high humidity.

Rainforest

Much of the region's subtropical rainforest has been cleared for agricultural purposes. The largest area, east of Lismore in New South Wales, was originally known as the Big Scrub, and contained around 75,000 ha (185,325 acres) of rainforest. It has now been reduced to less than 300 ha (740 acres), part of which has been logged. Several national parks and nature reserves have been established to conserve the remaining areas. Parts of Dorrigo National Park and the Border Ranges National Park are still intact, and contain important remnants of rainforest.

One of the targets of loggers early in the last century was the red cedar (*Toona ciliata*). This deciduous tree is no longer common, but surviving trees are readily identified in spring, when their prominent new red growth is seen. Strangler figs (*Ficus watkinsiana*), which begin life as epiphytes and wrap their enormous root system around their doomed host, are common, as are vines and other epiphytes. Ferns, mosses and orchids adorn huge forest trees which are frequently buttressed by enormous roots. The understorey is usually sparse, as a result of low light levels.

Eucalypt forest

Both wet and dry sclerophyll forests are found in this region. The wet forests are frequently dominated by the smooth-barked flooded gum (*Eucalyptus grandis*) and the rough fibrous-barked tallowwood (*E. microcorys*), both of which are fine timber trees. The poorer soils of the granite belt, which extends over the border of Queensland and into New South Wales near Wallangarra, support an area of much drier forest and a number of endemic shrubs, such as the yellow-flowered *Phebalium whitei* and the white-blossomed *Leionema ambiens*, which are conserved in the Girraween National Park.

Coastal sand dunes

The harsh environment where the land meets the sea has its own very specialised flora. Here, the dunes are stabilised by plants resistant to the salt-laden winds, such as beach spinifex (*Spinifex hirsutus*) and creeping plants (*Ipomoea pes-caprae* ssp. *brasiliensis* and the guinea flower, *Hibbertia scandens*). Behind them are shrubs of coastal wattle (*Acacia sophorae*), the grey-foliaged *Sophora tomentosa* and small trees of coastal banksia (*Banksia integrifolia*), horse-tailed she-oak (*Casuarina equisitifolia* ssp. *incana*) and tuckeroo (*Cupaniopsis anacardioides*). Much of this coastal dune area was mined for titanium in the mid-twentieth century and revegetated with species that were not local to the region, including the native coastal tea tree (*Leptospermum laevigatum*) and the South African bitou bush (*Chrysanthemoides monilifera*). These plants have naturalised, and have now become serious weeds.

Heath

Rainfall on the grey sandy soil of this region drains quickly from the surface, but the water table is usually not far below the surface, allowing moisture to be available by capillary action. The heath here is particularly rich, and many coastal national parks have been established to conserve it. Three national parks stretch almost continuously from Red Rock, just north of Coffs Harbour, to near Ballina. Here, boronias, baueras, several *Epacris* species, flannel flowers (*Actinotus helianthi*) and many pea flowers appear in spring; summer sees fields of Christmas bells (*Blandfordia grandiflora*) blossoming, and in autumn there are several species of banksia (*Banksia ericifolia*, *B. aemula* and *B. oblongifolia*) and geebungs (*Persoonia* spp.). In south-east Queensland, the low-lying and poorly drained coastal heath is known as 'wallum', an Aboriginal word for *Banksia aemula*, a common shrub of this area. These low-nutrient soils support a colourful array of low-growing shrubs.

The young crozier of a tree fern begins to unfold to produce the huge fronds of the soft tree fern (Dicksonia antarctica). These young growths are edible, but they have a slimy, somewhat bitter taste.

The coastal banksia (Banksia integrifolia) is at home on exposed headlands and behind sand dunes—in places where it is battered by strong, salt-laden winds. The nectar of its flowers is a favourite of honeyeaters and colourful lorikeets.

The South-West

Kangaroo paws (Anigozanthos spp.) are widespread throughout the south-west. Eleven species have been described. Due to their horticultural potential, plant breeders have created many hybrids, to improve hardiness and variety of colour. The plant illustrated is such a hybrid.

The karri tree (Eucalyptus diversicolor)—along with the mountain ash (E. regnans) of East Gippsland, Victoria—is the tallest tree in the Australian flora. It yields a valuable timber of great strength.

This is the richest and most diverse region of Australia in terms of plants, with almost 6000 species of native plants, 68 per cent of them endemic. It experiences a Mediterranean-type climate, with dry summers and wet winters, and is a total contrast to the humid east coast (it has no rainforests). Several characteristically Australian families reach their maximum diversity here. These include Proteaceae, Goodeniaceae, Myrtaceae and Stylidiaceae. The heath, mallee, forests and woodlands of the region are all made up of sclerophyllous plants.

Woodlands and shrublands

The coastal fringe, from some 100 km (60 miles) north of Perth to the south coast east of Albany, includes such floristically important areas as the Swan coastal plain, the Darling Scarp, the Stirling Ranges and the Barrens.

The major trees of the coastal plain are the tuart (*Eucalyptus gomphocephala*), which can grow up to 40 m (130 feet) in favourable sites, the marri (*E. calophylla*), common in eastern parts of the plain, and the she-oak (*Allocasuarina fraseriana*). The bull banksia (*Banksia grandis*) can occur as a tree growing to 10 m (33 feet) in woodland or as a spreading shrub on exposed headlands. Red and green kangaroo paws (*Anigozanthos manglesii*) occur here in great numbers, as does the firewood banksia (*B. menziesii*).

Near the south coast and inland from Albany lie the Stirling Ranges, where many endemic plants, such as mountain bells (*Darwinia* spp.), grow. Further east, the Barrens form a range of isolated peaks reaching 530 m (1740 feet). Some 600 species of plants have been recorded here, 10 per cent of them endemic. Among the most spectacular is the royal hakea (*Hakea victoria*), with large, prickly-edged foliage presenting colours of yellow and red and becoming brighter as the plant ages.

Karri forest

The karri tree (*Eucalyptus diversicolor*) is among the tallest of Australia's native trees, with a specimen of 90 m (295 feet) high being recorded. Karri forests occupy only a small area of the south-west— where the rainfall is higher, over 1000 mm (40 inches), and more evenly distributed throughout the year. The understorey of these forests is dense but not particularly diverse, as the canopy is closed and allows only limited light into the understorey. Also, regular fires have caused certain species that germinate well after burning to dominate the area at the expense of other plants. Acacias, especially the karri wattle (*Acacia pentadenia*), and other legumes, are common.

Jarrah forest

The jarrah (*Eucalyptus marginata*) is one of the world's finest hardwoods, and it occurs in forests which extend from near Perth to north of Albany, inland from the coastal plain. In contrast to the dense karri forests, trees in jarrah forests tend to be widely spaced, allowing more light into the understorey and thus a much more diverse flora there. Orchids and the native iris (*Patersonia* spp.) are common, as is the blue lechenaultia (*Lechenaultia biloba*), one of the few true blue flowers of the Australian flora, plus blue boy (*Stirlingia latifolia*), drumsticks (*Isopogon* spp.) and cone-sticks (*Petrophile* spp.). The family Proteaceae is also well represented, as it is in much of the south-west.

Sandplains

There are two distinct areas of sandplain in the south-west. The southern sandplains extend from near Lake Grace to Israelite Bay in the east. The northern sandplains stretch from Shark Bay in the north to the Moore River, 100 km (62 miles) north of Perth.

The southern sandplains are relatively flat, with low rainfall and few rivers. There are several salt lakes towards the north of the region. Soils are generally sandy, with exposed granite peaks offering some relief in the topography. The vegetation is mostly heath, with areas of taller mallees; again, the Myrtaceae and Proteaceae families dominate. Some small eucalypts— the four-winged mallee (*E. tetraptera*), red-flowered

The southern sandplains of the south-west with spring wildflowers: white and yellow feather flowers (Verticordia spp.) and the wispy grey of a smoke bush (Conospermum spp.) flower amongst the spent light brown heads of spinifex (Triodia spp.).

moort (*E. nutans*), tallerack (*E. tetragona*) and bell-fruited mallee (*E. preissima*)—are common.

The northern sandplains are also floristically diverse, with many endemic species. There are a number of *Banksia*, *Hakea* and *Grevillea* species, and several smoke bush species (*Conospermum* spp.).

The wheatbelt

The wheatbelt extends to the east of the jarrah forests and north of the southern sandplains. The area has been mainly cleared for agriculture, but remnants of the original woodland vegetation still exist. The tree flora is dominated by the York gum (*Eucalyptus loxophleba*), the salmon gum (*E. salmonophloia*), the wandoo (*E. wandoo*) and the spirally twisted trunks of the gimlet (*E. salubris*). Grevilleas, hakeas and verticordias are common in the shrub layer.

LEFT: Wilson's grevillea (Grevillea wilsonii) grows in the lateritic soils of the Darling Scarp, just east of Perth. Its brilliant flowers rise above prickly green foliage.

Arid and Semi-Arid Regions

The fruits of the mulga (Acacia aneura). This species is widespread in arid areas of all mainland states. Its beautifully figured timber is used to make ornaments, and it is considered one of the best fodder trees.

By far the largest part of mainland Australia is arid or semi-arid, with an average annual rainfall of less than 250 mm (10 inches). Some areas may endure years with virtually no rain while in other years, flooding may occur. Various plant communities are found in these environments—tussock grasslands, acacia woodlands, cypress pine, belah and wilga woodlands and saltbush plains are but a few. When the rains come, many ephemeral plants flower almost immediately, bringing the desert into bloom.

Tussock grasslands

Tussock grasslands consist of perennial grasses, with the Mitchell grasses (*Astrebla* spp.) and spinifex (*Triodia* spp.) being the most common genera. After rain, many annual daisies appear, often with papery yellow, pink or white bracts—*Bracteantha, Rhodanthe, Myriocephalus* or *Schoenia* species. Black box (*Eucalyptus largiflorens*) and coolibah (*E. microtheca*) are seen along drainage lines in these communities.

Acacia woodlands

Wattles such as mulga (*Acacia aneura*), the gidgee (*A. cambagei*), the brigalow (*A. harpophylla*) and the myall (*A. pendula*) are a common sight in arid Australia. Other plants in acacia woodlands include beefwood (*Grevillea striata*) and scattered eucalypts, with an understorey of emu bushes (*Eremophila* spp.), hop bushes (*Dodonaea* spp.) and lantern bushes (*Abutilon* spp.). The grey appearance of many of these desert plants is caused by minute hairs on the leaves, which help reduce transpiration and thus conserve moisture in the harsh environment. In western regions mullamullas (*Ptilotus* spp.) and Sturt's desert pea (*Willdampia formosa*) add colour after rain.

Other woodland communities

White cypress pines (*Callitris glaucophylla*) often form dense populations, sometimes associated with bimble box (*Eucalyptus populnea*). An understorey of wattles,

A flock of emus is seen here in an area of bluebush (Maireana spp.). These birds are common in many parts of Australia, and cause considerable damage to wheat crops. Bluebush is grazed by sheep and cattle.

FLORA TIMELINE							
1000 MILLION YBP Emergence of first nucleate plant cells in the form of algae. One group, the green algae, are the forebears of all higher plants.	**415 MILLION YBP** Emergence of first higher plants, evidenced by fossil remains of *Cooksonia*, a moss-like plant that occurs worldwide at this time.	**325 MILLION YBP** Ice age leads to extinction of giant clubmoss forests; flora now dominated by low-diversity seed ferns.	**260 MILLION YBP** Conifers, cycads and ginkgos develop modifications, including the ability to reproduce by seeds, that allow them to colonise higher, drier areas.	**100 MILLION YBP** Appearance of first flowering plants, including an ancestral form of holly, Proteaceae, and the Antarctic beech (*Nothofagus*).	**30 MILLION YBP** Rainforest dominates but as continent dries slightly, some plants develop adaptations to drought. First eucalypts and mangroves emerge.	**2 MILLION YBP** Continent reaches today's aridity levels. Flora of interior increasingly dominated by opportunist species adapted to heat and drought.

| **2500 MILLION YBP** Certain bacteria develop the chemical process of photosynthesis, adding oxygen to air and developing green colour that characterises plants. | **420 MILLION YBP** First plants (similar to liverworts and mosses) appear on land, but need for moisture confines them to shorelines and wetlands. | **385 MILLION YBP** Structural developments allow plants to produce wood and grow into trees. This leads to formation of giant clubmoss forests of the Devonian period. | **275 MILLION YBP** Ice dwindles, giving rise to large cool-temperate swamps inhabited by horsetails, mosses, ferns and seed ferns. | **208 MILLION YBP** Jurassic flora dominated by large conifers, cycads and ferns, an environment similar to modern-day warm temperate rainforest. | **60 MILLION YBP** Appearance of Myrtaceae. **55 MILLION YBP** Australia separates from Gondwana. Antarctic beech rainforest widespread. | **14–10 MILLION YBP** Lowering of temperatures and rainfall sees rainforests shrink and sclerophyllous forests and grasslands expand. Myrtaceae begins to dominate flora. | **1.65 MILLION Y** Beginning of series of g and interglacials that w for next 1.64 million greatly increasing specie habitat diversificatio |

hakeas, budda (*Eremophila mitchellii*) or warrior bush (*Apophyllum anomalum*) can also be seen in these arid and semi-arid areas. The warrior bush is host to the caper white butterfly in summer. In southern and western districts, the mallee pine (*C. verrucosa*) replaces the white cypress pine. Belah (*Casuarina cristata*) and wilga (*Geijera parviflora*), a handsome weeping tree, may also form dense communities; the wilga is sometimes seen with the leopardwood (*Flindersia maculosa*), so named because of its wonderfully spotted trunk of cream, orange and grey.

,000 YBP Spread of e-tolerant vegetation.	**1770** Joseph Banks and Daniel Solander compile first studies of Australian flora.	**1982** Federal Government announces National Tree Program, which aims to plant one billion new trees to make up for deforestation.
00 YBP Growing use e by humans transforms e areas of woodlands to open grasslands.	**1795** European settlers begin to harvest red cedar; by 1890 most is cleared.	
10,000 YBP Warmer, wetter climate gives rise to plant distribution found today.	**1880s** Introduction of *Mimosa pigra*, which gradually devastates wetlands.	**1999** Government scientists estimate that almost half Australia's native forests and 75 per cent of rainforests have been cleared since European settlement.
1688 First records of Australian plants made by William Dampier.	**1940** Prickly pear, a widespread pest in Qld and NSW, is finally eradicated.	

Saltbush plains

Saltbush plains are found on soils that are rich in sodium and usually have a high clay content, and occupy about 7 per cent of inland Australia. They are virtually treeless, dominated by plants of the family Chenopodiaceae. The vegetation rarely exceeds 2 m (6.5 feet) in height, and the plants are frequently grey-leaved (*Atriplex* spp., *Maireana* spp.) or succulent (*Sarcocornia* spp., *Halosarcia* spp.), as they need to be both drought and salt-tolerant in order to withstand extended dry periods. The latter two genera are often found on the edges of salt lakes.

Atriplex nummularia is known as old man saltbush, and is often used as a wind protection hedge around inland homesteads because of its dense habit and resistance to dry conditions. *Maireana* species are collectively known as bluebushes, and are sometimes seen as monospecific stands covering many hectares. Their occurrence usually indicates the presence of lime in the soil. These plants are frequently heavily grazed by sheep and cattle.

Much of the Hamersley Ranges in the north-west of Western Australia has been made into the Karijini National Park, in order to conserve its unique flora. Here clumps of porcupine grass or spinifex (Triodia spp.) are seen with the white barked snappy gum (Eucalyptus leucophloia).

Giant boab trees (Adansonia gregorii) are a feature of the western Kimberley. The large fluffy white flowers are fragrant and seen in the wet season. Aboriginals blended the sap of the tree with water to make a tasty drink; the pith surrounding the seeds is also edible.

One of several paperbark trees that are common in the dry tropics, this species, Melaleuca viridiflora, can have red or green flowers. It is found on swampy ground or on hillsides where the water table is not far below the surface. The flowers produce copious nectar, which attracts birds and small mammals.

Dry Tropics

The areas of north Western Australia and the northern parts of the Northern Territory are generally referred to as the dry tropics. They experience very distinct wet and dry seasons, with the summer rains often being associated with cyclones and heavy storms. The dry season is extended and accompanied by temperatures of over 30°C (86°F), and plants have had to develop particular—and unusual—survival strategies to deal with these harsh conditions. For example, eucalypts are often semi-deciduous during the dry season, and some plants develop huge underground tubers which retain moisture. When the cyclonic rains come, the run-off causes erosion, and over millions of years huge gorges have been formed in the ranges. These gorges function as refuges for both plants and animals, as permanent water is usually found at their base.

Gorges

The gorges of the Hamersley Range, the Kimberley, Kakadu National Park and Katherine are typical of the important plant sanctuaries found in these parts of Australia. They are usually lined by river red gums (*Eucalyptus camaldulensis*) and a variety of paperbarks (*Melaleuca* spp.), with *M. leucadendra* and *M. argentea* being the most common. Ferns can often be seen in the crevices of the steep walls of the gorges, and occasionally dense populations of the screw pine (*Pandanus aquaticus*) border the rivers.

Grasslands

The western Kimberley district is predominantly grassland, with *Sorghum* and *Plectrachne* species the most common grasses. Some tree cover occurs in areas where the rainfall is slightly higher.

Woodland

The woodland of the western Kimberley is dominated by *Acacia* species and a variety of emergent eucalypts. It is known as 'pindan', from an Aboriginal word—meaning 'wild, arid or waterless country'—which is used here to describe the vegetation. Shrubs include several species of grevillea and the deciduous helicopter tree (*Gyrocarpus americanus*), with its unique winged seeds that spin to the ground when they are mature. Groups of immense boab trees (*Adansonia gregorii*), with their swollen trunks, are scattered here too. Their trunks serve as reservoirs for moisture; the boab loses its leaves in the dry season to further assist its conservation of water.

In Kakadu, the woodland is much denser, with the Darwin stringybark (*Eucalyptus tetrodonta*) and the red-flowered Darwin woollybutt (*E. miniata*) predominating. The understorey here is different from the western Kimberley, with palms and cycads indicating a higher rainfall—dwarf fan palms (*Livistona humilis*) and cycads (*Cycas armstrongii*) are very common in these lowland forests.

The sacred lotus (Nelumbo nucifera) raises its umbrella-like leaves above the surface of the northern billabongs and creeks. Its large flowers are various shades of pink. These waterholes are also home to the saltwater crocodile, so visitors must be cautious in these areas.

Wetlands

The floodplains of Kakadu are a haven for water birds, and also contain a fascinating range of flora. During the wet season the flooded area is extensive, but in the dry, the wet area is reduced to scattered waterholes. Here the beautiful pink lotus flower (*Nelumbo nucifera*) makes a beautiful display, ably assisted by waterlilies (*Nymphaea* spp.) and several diminutive *Nymphoides* species.

The swamp mahogany (*Eucalyptus ptychocarpa*), paperbarks and an occasional Leichhardt tree (*Nauclea orientalis*) are the trees most often seen surrounding these permanent waterholes.

Vine forests

These occur in the northern parts of the Kimberley and in patches over the Northern Territory, where almost 300 species of plant live, including several which are endemic, such as the commonly cultivated palm *Carpentaria acuminata*. Vine forests comprise a unique collection of rainforest trees, shrubs and vines but very few epiphytes, as the long dry season would not permit their survival. The majority of the species that occur here are seasonally deciduous, as most trees are leafless to conserve precious moisture. Once the wet season arrives, everything changes, and the forest soon becomes lush and green.

The Victoria River in Gregory National Park, Northern Territory is bordered by paperbark trees, which spend much of their time partly immersed in water. The sandstone escarpment in the background is typical of the gorges in the dry tropics.

Wet Tropics

Colourful rainforest fruits are often seen on the forest floor. These are usually consumed by small native mammals or wild pigs, which do untold damage to the ground flora.

The wet tropics lie in the eastern parts of Queensland, north of the Tropic of Capricorn. They include pockets of tropical rainforest and extensive areas of woodland with isolated paperbark swamps and rich coastal mangrove populations. The rainfall is seasonal, with very wet summers and drier winters, and varies considerably, from as little as 1000 mm (40 inches) in the southern areas to over 3700 mm (144 inches) near the Daintree River. Isolated high peaks, such as Mt Bellenden-Ker, (1615 m/5300 feet) and Mt Lewis (1224 m/4015 feet), and the lowland rainforest of the Daintree River, are home to many endemic species.

Tropical rainforest

Tropical rainforests are restricted to areas between Proserpine and Mackay and then north of Townsville in Queensland. Of the lowland rainforests, the Daintree World Heritage Area is one of the most diverse areas of plant species, with a very high proportion of primitive flowering plants and gymnosperms. The tall cycad *Lepidozamia hopei* reaches more than 20 m (65 feet) high in this area. Epiphytes and palms are common, including almost pure stands of the fan palm (*Licuala ramsayi*). Australia's only *Phalaenopsis* orchid (*P. rosenstromii*) also occurs here. The Mossman Gorge National Park is home to the Mt Spurgeon pine (*Prumnopitys ladei*), and to many rare and threatened epiphytic orchids.

Highland tropical rainforests occur on the Atherton Tablelands and on the high peaks. While some species are found in both lowland and highland forests, most occur in one or the other. In the highland forests, there are generally fewer lianes, and at the highest altitudes the tree canopy is much lower, and lichens and mosses festoon the trees. Clouds and mist are present most of the time, and the high humidity allows epiphytes and lithophytes (plants growing on rocks) to thrive. Australia's only *Rhododendron* species (*R. lochiae* and *R. notiale*) are found here. Both have red flowers and occur as lithophytes. The beautiful heath *Dracophyllum sayeri*, with its long tapering leaves and inflorescences of candlestick-like pale pink flowers, can also be seen here.

Woodlands

While rainforests occupy isolated pockets in the wet tropics, woodlands are widespread. These are generally open and dominated by eucalypts, Moreton Bay ash (*Eucalyptus tessellaris*), ghost gum (*E. papuana*), long-fruited bloodwood (*E. [Corymbia] polycarpa*) and the semi-deciduous white gum (*E. alba*) being some of the most common. The conifer *Callitris intratropica*, which can reach 30 m (100 feet), is also widespread on sandy soils. The shrubs in these areas are varied, with several *Grevillea* species common.

A typical creek in the rainforests of north Queensland, lined with native gingers (Alpinia spp.) and tree ferns (Cyathea spp.). Several species of native freshwater fish inhabit these creeks, including the amazing archer fish, which spits at its prey in order to capture it.

Wetlands

The extent of the wetlands varies greatly with the season, but the permanent waterholes, also called billabongs, are home to many interesting aquatic plants. Several species of paperbark inhabit these wetlands, as do waterlilies (*Nymphaea* spp.), marshwort (*Nymphoides* spp.), the pink lotus flower (*Nelumbo nucifera*), the unique carnivorous pitcher plant (*Nepenthes mirabilis*) and unusual insectivorous liverworts.

As well as these permanent residents of the wetlands, there are also many ephemeral plants that thrive in the wet season and shortly afterwards and then die as the water subsides, their seed awaiting the following seasonal rains. These also include a few insectivorous species, such as sundews (*Drosera* spp.) and *Byblis linifolia*, which possesses sticky hairs on its stems and leaves with which to trap insects.

Mangroves

The mangroves of the Australian wet tropics are a diverse group, with some 48 species representing many different families. They form a very important role in the ecology of the sea and river estuary shores, preventing erosion and providing many fish species with their breeding grounds. They are also home to the saltwater crocodile. Because mangroves grow in mud that is virtually airless, most produce roots which are exposed to the air at least at low tide. The exposed roots, known as pneumatophores, are filled with a spongy tissue and have numerous small holes in their bark through which oxygen is transferred to the below-water root system. These prop roots sometimes form almost impenetrable forests.

The degree to which mangroves can stand saline conditions varies with the species. Some, known as freshwater mangroves, require regular flooding with fresh water from river flows to survive. One such species is the mangrove palm, *Nypa fruticans*, which produces huge, prostrate, subterranean stems with giant fronds up to 9 m (30 feet) long arising from the growing tip. Another species that prefers some fresh water is the cannon ball mangrove, *Xylocarpus granatum*, which can grow to 8 m (26 feet), and which has red-grained timber and globular fruits that can be up to 20 cm (8 inches) in diameter.

Mangroves play an important role in the ecology of rivers and estuaries. Here we see the grey mangrove (Avicennia marina) near a sandy beach. It is the most widespread of the Australian mangroves, found from Victoria up the east coast to northern Australia and extending down the west coast to near Bunbury, just south of Perth.

The female fruit of the Mt Spurgeon black pine (Prumnopitys ladei). This rare conifer occurs in well-developed mountain rainforest, in soils derived from granite, in the Mt Spurgeon–Mt Lewis area of north Queensland. It grows slowly, and is popular as an indoor potted plant.

ANTARCTICA AND THE SUBANTARCTIC ISLANDS

Early Discoveries

Antarctic exploration was often perilous before the days of ice-breaking ships. Here, the ship Endurance *is slowly crushed to pieces in pack-ice in 1915.*

Twelve countries maintain the 65 bases in Antarctica. Of these, seven claim a slice of Antarctic territory, some of which overlap and are neither recognised or refuted. The South Pole is shown as the southernmost point of the Earth, as opposed to the South Magnetic Pole which moves with Earth's magnetic field, a few kilometres a year.

Although the presence of a great landmass in the south (to 'balance' the land of the northern hemisphere) was intuited by the ancient Greeks, including Pythagoras and Plato, it was not until the eighteenth century that more concrete evidence of its existence was discovered. Initially, Captain Cook had reached 71°S (the furthest south anyone had sailed at that stage) without seeing any land. On a later voyage of exploration in 1775, however, he sighted South Georgia and reasoned that all the ice spread over the Southern Ocean must come from land still closer to the Pole. However, it was not until January 1820 that Antarctica was discovered when the Russian explorer Fabian Gottleib von Bellingshausen and the British Royal Navy's Edward Bransfield found the continent within three days of each other. John Davis, an American sealer, probably made the first landing at Hughes Bay on the Antarctic Peninsula next year, but this was largely unknown until his log was found in 1952. It wasn't until 1895 that a whaling party that included Carsten Borchgrevink, a Norwegian who migrated to Australia at the age of 24, made the first undisputed

landing on the Antarctic continent. What was to become the Australian sector was not sighted until John Biscoe's discovery of the area he named Enderby Land in 1831; the territory was joined soon after by Kemp Land, discovered by Peter Kemp in the *Magnet* in 1833, and Wilkes Land, which is named after Charles Wilkes, who discovered it in 1840.

The next stage of Antarctic history is known as the heroic age because of the number of hazardous expeditions undertaken by various countries, including Australia, in their efforts to discover more about this previously uncharted territory. The first group to stay throughout winter south of the Antarctic Circle was the Belgian Antarctic Expedition under Adrien de Gerlache from 1898 to 1899. His ship, the *Belgica*, was trapped in the ice off the Antarctic Peninsula and it remained there, slowly drifting westwards with the pack-ice for a further 13 months. Among the crew were two men whose names would become associated with the South and North Poles respectively, first mate Roald Amundsen and ship's surgeon Frederick Cook. Borchgrevink led the British Antarctic Expedition (on which all but three of its members were Norwegian) during the first winter spent ashore in Antarctica at Cape Adare.

This period also saw several attempts in the race to be the first to reach the South Pole. Ernest Shackleton, a member of Englishman Robert Falcon Scott's first expedition, returned later with the British Antarctic Expedition in 1908. This team came to within 180 km (112 miles) of their goal before they eventually turned back. Some of the party—T.W. Edgeworth David, Douglas Mawson and Alistair Mackay—did, however, become the first people to reach the South Magnetic Pole in early 1909. Scott and his companions reached the true South Pole on their second expedition, begun in 1910, but on 17 January 1912 they discovered to their dismay that they had been beaten in the race by Amundsen who had got there a month before. Scott and his entire group subsequently died on the return trek.

In the same year another feat of heroism was made necessary when the 1911–14 Australasian Antarctic Expedition, led by Douglas Mawson, ran into trouble. After the loss of Belgrave Ninnis down a crevasse with the party's tent, spare clothes and most of the food, as well as the best dogs, Mawson and Xavier Mertz turned back to trek the 500 km (310 miles) to Cape Denison. They had to travel slowly, killing the weakest dog to feed the others and themselves. Mertz died within a week from vitamin A poisoning, a consequence of eating husky livers. Very weak, frostbitten and also suffering from the poison that killed his companion, Mawson sawed the sled in half to lighten his load and faced the last 160 km (99 miles) alone. He arrived at Cape Denison just in time to see the departure of his supply ship, the *Aurora*. Despite contacting the ship by radio, it was unable to return and Mawson and the six men who had waited for him then had to settle in for a second full year in Antarctica.

Shackleton's later attempt, in 1915, to cross the Antarctic continent came to nothing when the ship *Endurance* was crushed in the ice of the Weddell Sea after being trapped for nine months. After a further

five months camped on the ice the crew took the ship's boats to Elephant Island. Leaving the bulk of the party there, Shackleton and some of the crew continued to South Georgia in an open boat to get help, a journey of 1290 km (800 miles). Two weeks later they arrived, but landed on the wrong side of the island, making a crossing of the interior necessary, and becoming the first people to do so. Eventually they found help at the whaling station at Stromness Bay and were able to return to Elephant Island to find all 22 crew still alive after 105 days of camping under the ship's boats

The south polar continent of Antarctica covers 14 million sq. km (5,405,400 million sq. miles).

The hut of Australian explorer Douglas Mawson still stands as a monument to his memory in Commonwealth Bay.

Research and Exploitation

Commercial exploitation

Many of the early journeys of exploration of the Antarctic were followed by those whose interests were commercial. Only 15 years after Cook discovered South Georgia, sealers, mainly American, set up on the island and wreaked havoc on the seal population. At one stage nearly 120,000 seal skins were taken in a year. The same thing happened after George Vancouver discovered Snares Island south of New Zealand in 1791: the seals were wiped out within 20 years. And a similar pattern occurred on Macquarie Island, discovered in 1810 by Frederick Hasselborough, and the South Shetland Islands, discovered in 1819. Within ten years all the seals were gone. In 1881 the British government was forced to introduce regulations in order to control sealing.

Whaling was another industry to take advantage of the apparently inexhaustible bounty of the Antarctic seas in the early days. In 1904 Carl Larsen set up a whaling base at Grytviken on South Georgia and in 1923 established a factory ship based industry in the Ross Sea. The use of these factory ships made whalers independent of fixed bases and soon Antarctic waters were thick with their vessels. An attempt was made to regulate the slaughter in 1937 when nine nations signed the International Convention on

Whaling, but to little avail: during the summer of that year whaling peaked, with a record number of 46,000 animals being taken. In another effort to stem the depredations on whale populations, an International Whaling Commission was established after the war in 1946 but apart from protecting right whales and humpbacks in the Antarctic, it did little to conserve other species such as the blue whale. In the season of 1950–51 there were over 32,500 whales taken. From 1962 onwards catches declined dramatically as stocks plummeted and the whaling station on South Georgia was forced to close due to the shortage. From this point whalers had to travel further with factory ship-based hunting. By 1982 the situation was such that the International Whaling Commission voted to end all commercial whaling from 1986 but due to a legal loophole so-called 'scientific whaling' has been able to continue.

The exploitation of resources is now carefully monitored. It was intended to ban mining for 40 years when the Minerals Convention was adopted in 1988 but this document was never ratified. However, although minerals such as gold and silver have been found in Antarctica, along with coal and iron ore, they do not occur in commercial quantities and so there is currently no mining activity. The possibility of danger from accidents resulting from oil extraction

Krill (Euphausia superba) *is a small, shrimp-like crustacean that is a vital part of the Antarctic food chain. It is the staple food of the crabeater seal, Adelie and gentoo penguins and the sole diet of baleen whales. People harvest it too, as a base for human food.*

Tourists trek the last few kilometres of Ernest Shackleton's route into Stromness whaling station at South Georgia.

Zealand and France. Australia claims two gigantic tracts of land totalling 6 million sq. km (2315 sq. miles) or almost 42 per cent of the continent. This claim is based on the activities of Douglas Mawson and the later occupancy of the western sector with the establishment of Mawson Station in 1954. There has been no attempt by Australia to strengthen its claim to the eastern sector by occupation. Two outcomes of the Treaty when it came into effect in 1961, however, were that territorial claims are neither recognised nor refuted, but are held in abeyance and that the Antarctic continent south of 60°S is open to all for scientific research. Signatories currently number 44. Research is now, at least ostensibly, the major reason for occupation of Antarctica although activities such as the birth of a child at an Argentinean base in 1978 may be aimed at bolstering territorial claims.

There are now over 40 permanent Antarctic bases and a number of abandoned or seasonal bases. ANARE (Australian National Antarctic Research Expeditions) has four permanent Antarctic bases, three on the continent (Mawson, Davis and Casey) and one on Macquarie Island. The oldest, at Mawson, was set up in 1954; Davis, established in 1957, is the furthest south; and Casey, opened in 1969 as a replacement for Wilkes, was acquired from the Americans. The original ANARE base, at Atlas Cove on Heard Island, was abandoned in 1954 to set up Mawson and is now used only occasionally for summer visits although a party of five spent 14 months on the island in 1992, wintering at Spit Bay. These, then, make up the Australian Antarctic and Subantarctic outposts and together they add a quite fascinating dimension to the study of the natural history of Australia.

Some of the science conducted in Antarctica cannot be conducted elsewhere. As well as the biological studies of native animals and plants and investigations into the earth's magnetic field and glaciology, the study of past climates through the evidence of ice cores and the gases trapped in air bubbles, has contributed significantly towards an understanding of the causes of global warming. Possibly the most spectacular success of Antarctic science was the discovery of the hole in the ozone layer in 1984. It was found that this gap had been there since as far back as 1970, but until that time had gone unnoticed by temperate zone physicists.

Four species of seals live in the Antarctic—crabeater, leopard, Ross and Weddell. Unafraid of people, they were an easy target for hunters in the early years of Antarctic exploitation.

A whaling ship with its bounty alongside. The largest concentration of whales in the world live in Antarctic waters.

Penguins, like many animals in the Antarctic, don't see people as a threat, enabling people to watch them at close range. A tourist here observes a chinstrap penguin (Pygoscelis antarctica).

will have to be dealt with should future finds lead to exploitation. At present the main extractive industry is of Antarctic krill, which is used in food products for humans and domestic animals. In order to protect the natural consumers of krill—whales, penguins, seals and other predators—the Commission for the Conservation of Antarctic Marine Living Resources (CCAMLR), established in 1981, manages and monitors the numbers of krill-dependent predators as a safeguard against over-exploitation.

Today, however, the fastest growing industry in Antarctica is tourism. Apart from a few commercial flights in 1956, Antarctic tourism really began in 1965 with the advent of cruises to the area. The most popular route is from Punta Arenas or Ushuaia in South America to the Antarctic Peninsula. Air tourism restarted in 1977 with day trips by Qantas but only two years later tragedy struck when an Air New Zealand DC 10 with 257 people on board crashed into Mt Erebus. Air travel is still the major tourist route between Australia and the Australian sectors because travelling by ship takes weeks. This guarantees that they will remain comparatively undeveloped as tourism destinations for some years to come.

Scientific research

The International Geophysical Year was held in 1957, heralding a big increase in the activities of scientists in the Antarctic. The number of bases established on the continent increased from 28 to 40 and includes one at the South Pole itself. Out of the IGY came the Antarctic Treaty, signed in 1959 by 12 nations, including Australia, one of seven countries to claim territory in the region. The other six countries are Argentina, Great Britain, Norway, Chile, New

Physical Geography

One of the few flowering plants in the Antarctic regions is the ballflower, which grows on the Subantarctic islands.

Huge glaciers continue to shape the landscape of Antarctica.

Landforms

Around 140 million years ago—the land mass of Antarctica was joined to Australia, India, Africa and South America, making up the supercontinent of Gondwana, in which offshore New Zealand was a part of the continental shelf. It contains two distinct sections—the ancient continental shield of East Antarctica and the more recent rock of West Antarctica, divided by the Transantarctic Mountains. Much of this land is buried beneath about 30 million cubic km (18,630,000 cubic miles) of ice—in some places greater than 4500 m (14,765 feet) thick—and lacks any life larger than bacteria or algae. In East Antarctica the ice is so heavy that it has depressed the land by about 1000 m (3280 feet) so that in places where the ice has melted uplift occurs. This can be seen in the Australian sector most spectacularly at the Vestfold Hills at Davis Station where arms of the sea had become trapped by uplift to form lakes that, depending on the amount of inflow, extend from freshwater to salinity up to nine times that of seawater. One of these, Deep Lake, is so salty it remains liquid even in midwinter. Most of the Antarctic coastline consists of icecliffs or glaciers and includes the 200 km (125 mile) wide Amery Ice Shelf, the seaward extension of the Lambert Glacier. This glacier, at 400 km (250 miles) long and more than 40 km (25 miles) wide and draining one million sq. km (385,000 sq. miles), is the largest in the world. Generally, the ice slopes back from the sea to the height of the Antarctic plateau at 4100 m (13,450 feet).

Antarctica is the highest continent on Earth, and averages 2300 m (7550 feet), way over Australia's average of 340 m (1115 feet) to get the idea. The highest exposed land in Antarctica is outside the Australian sector at Vinson Massif (5140 m/16,865 feet).

Subantarctic Heard Island lies on the world's largest marine plateau. An active volcano, its glaciers extend from its highest point, Mawson Peak, to sea level so that an amazing 80 per cent of the land is ice-covered.

Further to the east lies Macquarie Island, which rises to 425 m (1400 feet). It is oceanic in origin, part of a system of trenches and ridges called the Macquarie Ridge Complex. This island arose with the uplifting of a block of ocean-floor material that was subsequently reshaped by erosion, sea level changes and periglacial action. The degree of glaciation on the island in the past, if any, is still being debated but there are no present-day glaciers on the island.

Weather and climate

As well as being the highest continent, Antarctica is also the driest (although it contains 90 per cent of the world's fresh water, the snow accumulation on the plateau is only about 50 mm (2 inches) water equivalent per year), coldest (the lowest temperature

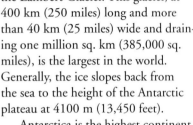

recorded in the Australian Antarctic Territory at Vostok is also a world record at –89.6°C (–129°F) and windiest (at Commonwealth Bay in 1912–13 Mawson recorded winds averaging greater than 65 km (40 miles) per hour for over 60 per cent of the time). Antarctica is not just subject to the weather, it dominates it, helping to generate the circling low pressure systems that bring westerly winds and precipitation to both the Subantarctic islands and the southern Australian mainland and finally dissipate at about 60°S. On the coast the temperatures average –15°C to –30°C (5°F to –22°F) in winter and about freezing point in summer. Temperatures inland in the winter months may average as low as –70°C (–94°F).

Where the cold Antarctic waters meet the warmer subtropical waters at an area known as the Antarctic Convergence, the water temperature drops from 4°C to 2°C (39°F to 36°F) in just 250 km (155 miles). The Convergence passes to the north of Heard Island but to the south of Macquarie Island so that Heard Island has snow to sea level for three months of the year whereas the snow falling in Macquarie Island is ephemeral. Average temperatures on Heard Island at sea level in the coolest and warmest month are –1.5°C and 3.5°C (29°F and 38°F), whereas on Macquarie Island they are 3.5°C (38°F) in the coolest month to 7°C (45°F) in the summer.

Flora

Although the combination of cold and dryness in Antarctica is generally inimical to life, lichens, which are able to function at low temperatures with low light and water levels, can be found on rocks within 400 km (250 miles) of the South Pole and in the Vestfold Hills, where high salinity is added to cold

and dryness, algae may even grow under pieces of quartz where sufficient sunlight for photosynthesis is transmitted through the rock. The most common plants that occur in Antarctica are mosses and lichens but there is a species of grass (*Deschampsia antarctica*) and a pearlwort (*Colobanthus quitensis*) that are found in the Antarctic Peninsula region.

By contrast, both Heard and Macquarie Islands are comparatively blooming. Although both islands are approximately the same size, Heard Island has less area available for plant growth as only 20 per cent of the land surface is free from glaciers and it is subject to a harsher environment. There are about 42 species of moss, 40–50 lichens, about 20 liverworts and 11 species of vascular plants (mostly grasses). As well, there is *Acaena* with its well-known barbed seeds, a species of buttercup (*Ranunculus crassipes*), Kerguelen cabbage (*Pringlea anticorbutica*, which is a member of the same family as domestic cabbage), used in the past as a remedy against scurvy by sealers, while a major colonising species found inland is *Azorella*, a species of cushion plant. Plants thrive more readily on Macquarie Island, which has 45 native vascular plants and another three species that have been introduced by humans.

Two researchers using weather balloons to collect meteorological data. From 1960, daily weather reports have been sent from the Antarctic stations to Australia.

Most of Heard Island is ice-covered and actively volcanic. Its summit, Mawson Peak, is the highest point in Australian territory at 2745 m (9000 feet).

ANTARCTICA TIMELINE	150 MILLION YBP Gondwana begins to break up. 100 MILLION YBP Continent reaches current position.	1820 Russian explorer Fabian von Bellingshausen sights Antarctica on 20 Jan; two days later British mariner Edward Bransfield also records sighting.	1895 Norwegian whaling ship *Antarctic* makes first confirmed landing on continent, at Cape Adare.	1911 Norwegian expedition led by Amundsen reaches South Pole on 11 Dec. British expedition led by Scott arrives one month later, but party perishes during return.	1957 Beginning of International Geophysical Year (IGY), an international program of scientific research which led to establishment of numerous scientific bases.	1983 Russian base Vostok records lowest air temperature ever measured: –129°F (–89.6°C). 1984 Discovery of hole in ozone layer over Antarctica.	2000 US begins construction of new South Pole research station. Iceberg B-15 measuring 11,000 sq. km (4250 square miles) breaks off Ross Ice Shelf.
	600 MILLION YBP Antarctica becomes part of large southern landmass called Gondwana, along with Australasia, India, Africa and South America.	1775 Captain James Cook becomes first to cross Antarctic Circle; he correctly assumes that pack ice must come from a large landmass to the south.	1821 American sealer John Davis lands on continent at Hughes Bay, but his feat goes unrecognised as he dies and his journal is not discovered until 1952.	1898 Belgian Antarctic Expedition led by Adrien de Gerlache is trapped in ice for 13 months, thus becoming first party to winter in Antarctica.	1936 A large area of East Antarctica is declared Australian Antarctic Territory. 1937 Whaling in Southern Ocean reaches a peak, with 46,000 animals killed.	1959 Signing of Antarctic Treaty, which establishes suspension of territorial claims, peaceful use of continent and freedom of scientific enquiry throughout region.	1994 International Whaling Commission establishes whale sanctuary to protect major feeding grounds. 1998 Annual tourist numbers reach 10,000.

Fauna

Adelie penguins (Pygoscelis adeliae) are the smallest of the Antarctic penguins.

Emperor penguin chicks (Aptenodytes forsteri) will huddle close for warmth).

For most Antarctic animals the main determining factor in their distribution is their access to the sea or, for parasites, their access to the animals of the sea. The animals of the inland include threadworms, tartigrades and rotifers at the smallest end of the scale, and at the largest, springtails, mites and even three species of fly—*Belgica antarctica*, *Parochlus steinenii* and *Telmatogeton magellanicus*. More closely allied to the harvest from the sea are the parasites found on birds and seals—lice, mites and ticks and the Antarctic flea, *Glaciopsyllus antarcticus*. On the islands, the larger of the invertebrates include earthworms, snails, spiders, springtails, beetles and crustaceans, as well as a species of wasp, *Antarctopria latigaster*, on Macquarie Island. Smaller invertebrates include mites, thrips, aphids, tartigrades, threadworms and booklice which, as well as books, also feed on fungi and plant tissue.

Life on the fast ice

The coastline and the stable ice offshore (known as fast ice) teems with life wherever there is bare ground exposed for nesting for the two main species that breed there—the emperor penguin, *Aptenodytes forsteri*, and the Weddell seal, *Leptonychotes weddelli*. The female 30 kg (66 pound) emperor penguin lays her single egg on the ice in April or May and the male then incubates it on his feet for 60 days. At about the time of hatching the females return with food. The chicks are then brooded on the feet for a further 40 days. Weddell seals' pupping season begins in spring when the young are born at a weight of 25 kg (55 pounds) and grow rapidly to over 100 kg (220 pounds) at weaning. During this time the males stake out underwater territories and feed on crustaceans and fish from the shallow water. By the end of December the males are out on the ice, resting and recovering from wounds; the mothers try to coax their pups into the water. Once the ice starts to break up the seals move out to sea and their diet changes to more pelagic fish.

For another species of penguin, the Adelie (*Pygoscelis adeliae*) the extent of the ice is critical to the survival of their young. Too much ice means that the adults have to use up more energy, and consequently make fewer trips to the sea to bring krill and fish back for their growing chicks. One animal associated with the Adelie is the leopard seal, *Hydrurga leptonyx*, which feeds inshore on Adelies during their breeding season and is the key reason for the penguins' hesitancy when entering water. Other birds which need access to the sea but are less constrained by the extent of fast ice are the petrels. Antarctic petrels (*Thalassoica antarctica*), Cape petrels (*Daption capense*) and southern fulmars (*Fulmarus glacialoides*) all nest on exposed rock ledges from December, while snow petrels (*Pagodroma nivea*) and the tiny Wilson's storm petrel (*Oceanites oceanicus*) nest under the cover of rocks to hide from predatory skuas. Southern

giant petrels (*Macronectes giganteus*) breed near the Australian stations at Casey and Davis, which is the furthest south they will breed but, possibly for the same unresolved reason as the decline of elephant seals, numbers have been falling for years.

Pack-ice inhabitants

The pack-ice—the great barrier of detached floating ice surrounding the continent—provides not only resting sites for penguins but breeding grounds for three species of seal—the Ross (*Ommatophoca rossi*), crabeater (*Lobodon carcinophagus*) and leopard (*Hydrurga leptonyx*). The crabeater is the most common seal in the world and feeds mainly on krill. Far less is known about Ross and leopard seals, mainly because they breed deep in the pack-ice. Although the leopard seal feeds on penguins, fish and krill, it also attacks seal pups. The rare Ross seal has backwardly curved canines and incisors which help it to grip its rather slippery food of squid.

Adelie penguins nest in their thousands in rookeries on rocky headlands. Each bird chooses a site at the same distance from its neighbours to avoid territorial disputes. The nests are made of pebbles, collected by the male.

The sharp teeth and wide jaws of the leopard seal (Hydrurga leptonyx) enables it to tear chunks out of its prey. It feeds mainly on penguins but also eats fish, squid and krill.

The islands

Heard Island differs from Macquarie Island in that it does not have any introduced animals (or plants, for that matter). On Macquarie Island feral cats and rats play havoc with nesting petrels, and rabbits destroy the vegetation—these pests are subject to ongoing control programs by the Tasmanian Parks and Wildlife Service. (The environment on Heard Island may have been too severe to support these species.) Apart from that, both islands share a rather similar fauna that includes elephant seals, fur seals, four species of penguin, albatrosses, petrels and cormorants and an abundant invertebrate population.

Wind plays quite a significant part in the islands' ecology. Macquarie Island, for example, receives visits from landbirds blown off course from Australia (once including a racing pigeon released in Mount Gambier en route to Tasmania). While strong winds bring some ocean wanderers such as the light mantled sooty albatross (*Phoebetria palpebrata*) and wandering albatross (*Diomedea exulans*) to both islands, and in addition the grey-headed (*D. chrysostoma*) and black-browed albatrosses (*D. melanophris*) to Macquarie, they can also be restrictive to birds with a smaller wingspan. Both islands have endemic cormorants that only forage 20 km (12 miles) or so away from land and on Heard Island one bird, the lesser sheathbill (*Chionis minor*), doesn't go to sea at all. It is still a puzzle as to how this landbird arrived there. Wind also affects the insect population, resulting in the evolution of wingless moths, flies that walk and, on Macquarie Island, a wasp without wings, *Antarctopria latigaster*.

Elephant seal populations at both Macquarie and Islands Heard have declined from the first census figures taken in the 1940s and '50s to less than half that number, with the cause still under investigation. Weighing up to 4000 kg (8820 pounds) and often reaching a length of over 6 m (20 feet), the southern elephant seal (*Mirounga leonina*) is the largest of the world's seals and dives the deepest, to about 2000 m (6560 feet), where it can remain submerged for up to two hours. Elephant seals feed on squid and fish as far away as the mainland waters of Australia and Antarctica. The males come ashore in September/October to establish territories where they collect a harem of up to 20–30 females. The defence of their breeding rights can lead to very bloody fights, with the result that many adult bulls are covered with battle scars. More often, however, a veteran bull will use intimidation—a roared challenge, upright posture with open mouth and inflated proboscis and, occasionally, a sudden charge—to deter a less experienced rival.

Fur seals may also defend a harem but numbers in these groups are much smaller, consisting of about five females. On Heard Island the population consists of Antarctic fur seals (*Arctocephalus gazella*); while at Macquarie Island there is an interbreeding Antarctic/Subantarctic fur seal population (*A. tropicalis*) as

TOP: The northern giant petrel (Macronectes halli) breeds on Macquarie Island.

LEFT: The Antarctic skua (Cath-aracta skua) is also known as the robber gull for its habit of chasing other birds and forcing them to disgorge their food.

well as a population of non-breeding New Zealand fur seals (*A. forsteri*). Unlike southern elephant seals, fur seal numbers are booming worldwide, possibly due to the fall-off in competition for krill from reduced numbers of whales.

Both Macquarie and Heard islands support four species of breeding penguin—king, rockhopper, gentoo and macaroni (Heard) or royal, *Eudyptes schlegeli* (Macquarie). The macaroni penguin (*E. chrysolophus*) is unusual in that the first egg is always discarded as soon as the second is laid so that the penguin only raises one chick, a phenomenon still not understood. Both the gentoo (*Pygoscelis papua*) and rockhopper (*Eudyptes chrysocome*) penguins forage in shallower waters, while the macaroni and royal penguins tend to go further afield and may dive regularly to around 60 m (200 feet). King penguins (*Aptenodytes patagonica*) also range out to sea but they can dive to as deep as 240 m (790 feet).

Of the other birds, the land-based sheathbill (*Chionis minor*) makes its living by scavenging and even vampirism. This habit may have been started by opportunism (picking at the wounds of elephant seals) but it now extends to the deliberate picking of the hind flipper of these and leopard seals in order to drink their blood. The main scavengers of seals are the Subantarctic skuas, *Catharacta lonnbergi* (larger than their Antarctic cousins), and both the northern and southern giant petrels (*Macronectes halli* and *M. giganteus*). Cape petrels also breed at Heard Island and they scavenge in the sea around carcasses of seals and penguins killed by leopard seals. As well, gulls and terns make a living from the shallow nearshore area. The most numerous birds found at Heard Island are the smaller petrels—South Georgia diving petrel (*Pelecanoides georgicus*) and common diving petrel

(*P. urinatrix*), dove (or Antarctic) prion (*Pachyptila desolata*) and fulmar prion (*P. crassirostris*) and the ubiquitous Wilson's storm petrel. All of these birds feed on plankton and generally come ashore to their nests each night. The birds that breed on Macquarie Island include the blue petrel (*Halobaena caerulea*), the white-chinned petrel (*Procellaria aequinoctalis*), the Antarctic and fairy prions (*Pachyptila turtur*), the sooty shearwater (*Puffinus griseus*), the grey-backed storm petrel (*Garrodia nereis*) and also the common diving petrel (*Pelecanoides urinatrix*).

Gentoo penguins (Pygoscelis papua) live on both Heard and Macquarie Islands.

THE HUMAN HISTORY OF AUSTRALIA

Ancient Australia

In the year 2000 many thousands of people marched across the Sydney Harbour Bridge to express their support for the process of reconciliation between Aboriginal and non-Aboriginal Australians. Among the crowd were many Aboriginal people, young and old. They had come from all over Australia, and although there would later be marches in other cities, on this day all had converged on Sydney. It was here, in 1788, that the first act of the long drama that would eventually lead to the need for the marches was played out. It is possible that among the marchers was a small group of people whose forebears were the very first to cross the harbour many thousands of years before.

The march for reconciliation was an act of contemporary political significance with a historical depth of 212 years of often troubled relationships between black and white.

Early Sydneysiders

People had been crossing the harbour in canoes for thousands of years, and before that there had been a long period when the inhabitants could virtually walk across the area, with just a short river crossing.

The first residents of what is now Sydney may have set up camp on a piece of ground now submerged by the deep waters of the harbour. They might have reached the spot by following the river down from the hills, or by following it in from the beach many kilometres away; perhaps they travelled

overland from the Hawkesbury River. They almost certainly had relatives in those areas and had moved on as a family group to explore new hunting grounds, much as the English were to begin doing in 1788.

These people were at home in their environment. By the time they reached Sydney their ancestors had several thousand years of experience in making a living in Australia. It is easy to forget that a century is four or five generations; 1000 years, then, is perhaps 50, and 3000 years 150 generations, time spans that are so long they are difficult to grasp. Few people of British descent can trace their ancestry back 1000 years (in AD 1000, Britain was just emerging from the Dark Ages). Just 2000 years ago the Romans were in Britain, and 3000 years ago is well before any written history is known from Britain, although written records were beginning to emerge in Egypt and the Middle East. Advances in technology mean that our

TOP: Flaked stone tools found in Queensland. Over thousands of years new tools, including those made from bone, teeth and wood, were invented in response to changes in Australia's environment. Artefacts made of stone make up most of the archaeological record because they survive the longest.

RIGHT: Body painting (colours and design) and forms of headdress (style and materials) for ceremonial purposes varied from region to region and between different clans. These men are from New South Wales.

In the year 2000 some tens of thousands of Aboriginal and non-Aboriginal Australians crossed the Sydney Harbour Bridge in a march for reconciliation. The bridge crosses an area where Aboriginal people had lived for millennia, long before the coming of the First Fleet in 1788.

understanding of Aboriginal prehistory is under constant review. Of this we can be sure: if ever we discover just when people first landed in Australia or created the first painting on this country's ancient rock, the time scale will still defy the imagination.

The world's first mariners

When we say that ancestral Aboriginals arrived in Australia at least 50,000 years ago, and 'quickly' spread over the whole continent, it is worth remembering that these are relative terms—the process actually took 2000–3000 years.

By 50,000–40,000 years ago, humans had evolved to the point where they can be called 'modern' and were just beginning to spread throughout Europe and Asia from their African homeland. By now they were using fire and relatively simple stone and wooden tools, but the first great technological innovation we know about is the watercraft used by the ancestors of Australia's Aboriginals to make the sea crossing to Australia.

The voyage may have occurred at a time when low sea levels made the strait to be crossed relatively narrow, but even at the times of lowest sea level, the distance of the sea crossing between Asia and Australia (including the eastern Indonesian islands and New Guinea) was so great that land on the other side would have been invisible to an observer.

In all probability the journey to Australia was a deliberate act, and if so was almost certainly inspired by the sighting of distant smoke from bushfires. It has been suggested that the early arrivals may have been accidental—fishing craft blown away from home by storms or strong winds—but if this were the case then there would have been no follow-up voyages by other people. While it has been pointed out that, theoretically, one pregnant woman accidentally landing on the coast could populate the country, this is extremely unlikely. To successfully populate a new continent you would need sufficient people not only to ensure adequate genetic variety but, perhaps more importantly, also to provide social, cultural and technological support.

Those first humans arrived in Australia well prepared for success. Some have thought that there would have needed to be a big readjustment, and much trial and error before people could learn to live here in an environment apparently very different from that of South-East Asia. However, some plants are common to both regions, and there is in fact a gradual change in fauna and flora between the two rather than an abrupt one so the difficulties may not have been so great.

People who live by hunting and gathering learn to live with the total ecology of their environment. In Australia, as elsewhere, the first settlers would have looked for shellfish, seabirds and waterfowl and their eggs, tree-dwelling herbivores, grass-eating mammals,

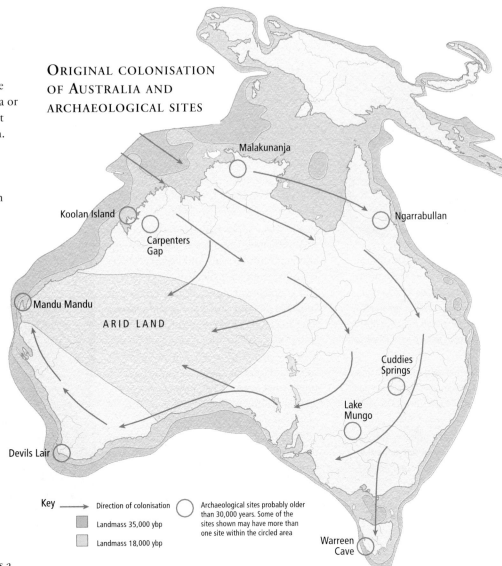

ORIGINAL COLONISATION OF AUSTRALIA AND ARCHAEOLOGICAL SITES

Malakunanja

Koolan Island

Carpenters Gap

Ngarrabullan

Mandu Mandu

ARID LAND

Cuddies Springs

Lake Mungo

Devils Lair

Warreen Cave

Key — Direction of colonisation

Landmass 35,000 ybp

Landmass 18,000 ybp

Archaeological sites probably older than 30,000 years. Some of the sites shown may have more than one site within the circled area

reptiles, rodents, beehives and fish. Initially, they would not have needed specialised local knowledge to identify which species could be hunted and eaten. Similarly, among plants they would have been looking for grasses with harvestable seed, legumes, root crops, and fruits and nuts which were eaten by birds. Although lack of familiarity may have led to a few accidental poisonings, in theory the newcomers could have been putting together their first meal within hours of landing. Later, trial and error would lead to the invention of processes to remove toxins from fruits and berries.

As the first people spread over the continent they encountered a variety of different environmental conditions. Their building styles reflected this variety and included houses on poles and dwellings made of stone and timber. This shelter, in northern Queensland, is made from palm leaves.

Sandstone from Queensland showing grooves where spears and other tools have been sharpened over long periods. Similar grinding grooves are found in most parts of Australia.

RIGHT: A man from north Queensland with body decoration and ceremonial clothing. His headdress is similar to that of the Deri people of Torres Strait. Similarities in culture are the result of contact over many thousands of years.

Of the more than 100 islands in Torres Strait, only 20 have sufficient fresh water supplies for permanent settlement. The indigenous population was probably around 4000 at the time of European annexation; today there are about 9000 people living on the Islands. Torres Strait Islander culture is distinctive from mainland culture in language, music, ceremony, economy and material culture.

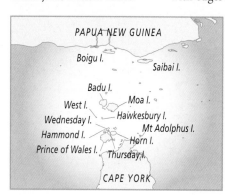

The peopling of Australia

As the population began to grow, small family groups would spread out to find new hunting grounds. The best areas—woodlands and sea shores—were filled first. There was plenty of food, plenty of water and, over much of northern Australia, comfortable temperatures. The desert areas were probably investigated last, at least with a view to permanent settlement. People needed to develop containers for carrying and keeping water, learn the complex ecology of the desert and gradually memorise its landscapes. In later years the young ones would learn long stories in which the sequences of waterholes and their locations were memorised—vital information for travel and survival. However, deserts occupied a much smaller area when humans first arrived on the continent, and there was plenty of more-productive land.

As people spread out across the country, they gradually began to encounter ecology that was different from that to which their now distant ancestors had adapted. Conditions become colder as you travel south, and were colder than they are today. Clothing and housing became more important and new kinds of traps and weapons would have been needed to obtain the different kinds of animals found in the new environments.

There was scope now for people in different areas to behave differently as they specialised for each environment. They also began to come to terms with the universe in different ways, as various styles of artistic expression developed and the philosophy of the Dreaming provided explanations of how things had come to be the way they were in different places.

It is difficult to say much about the tools that were used in different regions of Australia. Almost all that has survived is the stone that was used for making them. The wood and string and fur and fabric and other perishable materials are long gone. The stone tools themselves were mainly relatively simple sharp-edged flakes of stone used for cutting and scraping. But there were also large stone axes with edges sharpened by grinding, a technology not used elsewhere until tens of thousands of years later. And somewhere along the way the boomerang was invented, rare fragments being found preserved in a South Australian swamp.

Artistic expression in the early part of Australian history seems to have mainly involved engraving. The oldest known examples are those in a southern cave where simple lines are scratched into the soft walls. Then comes the representation of symbols,

including animal tracks, on rocky outcrops, and then the depiction of the animals themselves. There are also engravings on the walls of rock shelters. However, the idea that people only engraved in early times may be misleading. It is quite possible that the engravings were filled with pigments. If they had used paint, it would not have survived for paint would not last on the exposed rocks where many engravings are found. The earliest evidence of painting that has survived dates from perhaps 20,000 years ago.

It has been suggested that at various times groups of people from different places and with differing genetic backgrounds came to Australia. If this is so it is surprising that the evidence for it is so thin, and it currently seems unlikely to have been the case.

Those people of long ago achieved a great deal. They gradually learned to live in every part of Australia, evolving different cultures in order to do so, and establishing the framework from which their descendants would develop a complex and civilised society. They developed art, religion, philosophy, language and social structures in ways that would come to be seen as uniquely Aboriginal.

Although there are arguments to the contrary, they appear to have caused no great environmental damage over a long period of time. Although they used fire, the Australian continent was accustomed to natural fires, and the few additional fires lit by humans would have had little impact on the vegetation or animals. Although they hunted animals they did so in a way that enabled populations of species to be maintained.

They also dealt with massive climatic change and its consequences. Towards the middle of the period we are discussing, the climate became considerably drier, with the central desert expanding and most parts of Australia low in available water. A significant consequence of this was the extinction of many large animals which could not adapt to what may have been the driest period in a few million years. The loss of these large species, such as diprotodon (a huge marsupial the size of a rhinoceros) which would have been hunted only occasionally by people living in small groups with no means to preserve food, was probably of little significance. But they did have to adjust to the harsh new conditions and live through them, perhaps temporarily occupying a smaller area of the continent—although there were people living in present-day southern Tasmania about 20,000 years ago. When conditions eased, around 10,000 years before the present, people could again spread out and make full use of the whole continent.

Australia now was somewhat smaller and the movement of people more restricted than it had been. Former coastal areas were under water. One population of the ancient people had been cut off in Tasmania, which had become an island, and from that time on would have their own separate history. In the north, what had once been hills along the track from Cape York to New Guinea were now islands. Although there would continue to be contact between Australia and New Guinea, from now on it would have to be made by canoe, and some epic voyages would be undertaken in the years to come.

Eighteenth-century etchng of a Tasmanian man. Separated from the mainland 10,000 years ago, Tasmanians developed different languages, music, clothing, art, tools and weapons to that of the rest of Australia, and had distinctive physical attributes, such as a tendency for tightly curled hair.

Although Aboriginals had lived through times of change and adapted to great environmental shifts, they seem to have done so while maintaining a great deal of consistency in their culture and the way they exploited the environment. Then, a few thousand years ago, for reasons no one yet understands, there was a major change in Aboriginal Australia.

Rock engravings from N'dhala Gorge in the Northern Territory showing mythological figures. Engravings are found virtually wherever there is a suitable rock face in all parts of Australia.

Before Colonisation

Examples of a finely shaped and decorated wooden shield and throwing sticks. This kind of refined woodwork may have begun to develop 5000 to 3000 years ago when new types of stone tool were invented.

TOP RIGHT: Rock engravings from Mt Augustus in Western Australia. The meanings of symbolic designs like this one, are often unknown.

BOTTOM RIGHT: A man hunting, with several tools, including a finely worked spear, through a recently burnt landscape.

If we could go back in time to see Australia 10,000 or 20,000 years ago, its Aboriginal societies and cultures would probably bear little resemblance to those we are familiar with today. There would have been some similarities, but every detail of daily life from the tools people used to the way they hunted, from the way their camps were organised to their clothing and their art would all have been different. When did modern Aboriginal society begin to develop?

Around 5000–3000 years ago there was a substantial change in Aboriginal culture and society reflected in the development of a range of smaller stone tools made with more refined techniques. These small blades and points in turn suggest equally refined techniques for woodworking, and probably also the use of complex methods of combining stone and wood to make composite tools and weapons.

The arrival of the dingo in Australia at around the same time not only confirms the level of contact with the outside world, but would in itself have had an impact on hunting behaviour and performance.

An Australian renaissance

New art styles also seem to have arisen during this period, suggesting not only different ways of seeing the world, but in some cases showing the changing technologies of such weapons as spears and boomerangs and changes in clothing.

It is unfortunately impossible to be accurate about the exact timing of any of these changes. Rock art itself is extremely difficult to date due to difficulties in dating technology and the many differences and schools of interpretation. As well, the archaeological record is sparse and uncertain. However, we know that changes in art and technology didn't occur overnight, but developed gradually over thousands of years.

If the evidence had survived, we could probably trace a direct line back from the rich diversity of recent Aboriginal culture and ways of thinking to their origins thousands of years ago. However, the richness is composed of things largely invisible to archaeology—kinship arrangements, religion, ceremony, song, body painting and costumes, dance, bark paintings and wooden artefacts.

Trading of goods may have begun in a small way with the swapping of commodities such as particularly good examples of stone or ochre to neighbouring groups, perhaps for the production of artefacts like spears or boomerangs. Eventually there was to be a huge network of trade routes covering the whole continent from north to south and east to west. In this way it was possible for goods made or found in Queensland to end up in southern South Australia or the north-west of Western Australia. Trade with the people of Torres Strait may also have increased at this time as in theory it was possible for canoes to under-take long voyages down both the east and west coasts of Cape York.

MAJOR ABORIGINAL TRADE ROUTES AND OUTSIDE CONTACTS

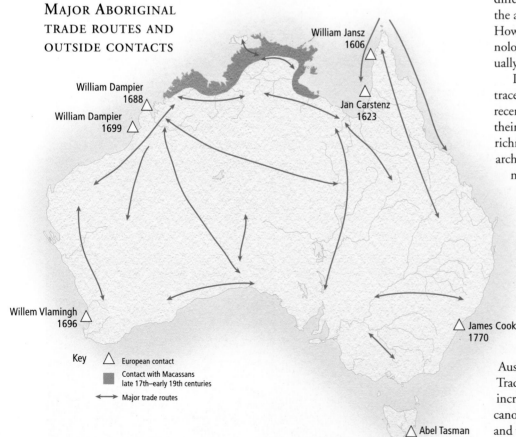

William Jansz 1606

William Dampier 1688

William Dampier 1699

Jan Carstenz 1623

Willem Vlamingh 1696

James Cook 1770

Key
△ European contact
▨ Contact with Macassans late 17th–early 19th centuries
⟷ Major trade routes

Abel Tasman 1642

Beautifully carved and painted Pukumani poles in the Northern Territory, used as part of the long sequence of ceremonies after a burial. An example of the extraordinarily rich artistic and ceremonial life of Aboriginals.

Trading involved not only the movement of goods, but the coming together of large numbers of people. There were big gatherings for ceremonies, so that news and ideas could be exchanged and marriages arranged, new songs and dances learned, and new ways of making things copied. It may be that this trade network not only developed as part of the renaissance, but helped to cause it and helped to accelerate the development and dissemination of ideas around the country.

Ceremonial life

The people who assembled for these great gatherings were entertained by ceremonies and music. Bodies were painted in complex patterns, with clothing, ornaments and headdresses added to the decoration. A unique musical and dance tradition developed.

Alongside this came the development of ceremonial and religious structure in the form of earth mounds and banks, stone structures, carved trees and poles. To take one example, there was often a sequence of ceremonies extending over many months when someone died. Burials involved coffins of various kinds, cremation, or burial with grave goods in the ground.

Around the country in rock shelters, on the earth and on rocky outcrops, and probably on bark, many styles of art were developed. Some were naturalistic and depicted people in costumes, dancing figures and hunting scenes with animals. Animals were painted in great detail, one style depicting body cavities and internal organs, as if in an X-ray. This style gradually became complex and decorative. Other paintings were highly symbolic, with marks whose purpose and meaning are now lost. Supporting this artistic ferment were changes in economic life.

The technology changes

Aboriginals would remain hunters and gatherers, but in the last few thousand years of this era they would refine food-collecting techniques to levels never before seen. In Victoria, for example, long canals were dug to link swamps harbouring eels, not only making the eels easier to catch, but leading to an increase in their numbers. In Queensland and elsewhere in northern Australia, large areas of reef flats were crisscrossed by stone walls to make fish traps by utilising the rise and fall of the tides. In inland Australia, native seeding grasses were harvested and laid out in abundance to dry in the sun. People probably also planted seeds of favoured plants. In the north, yams and other root crops were replanted after harvesting. Complex fish traps were built in inland rivers, and nets capable of catching large numbers of birds were made. Fishhooks were fashioned from shell and twine woven to make fishing lines.

Food was processed in new ways to allow the use of some valuable foods which were also poisonous, toxins being removed by long and difficult processes. Grindstones began to be used to process seeds into flour. Fruits were dried and stored.

Change was facilitated by the use of the new stone tools to make better spears and knives, as well as chisels, planes and files for the working of wood, shell and bone, and the stone itself was shaped in new

A fish trap laid out over many hectares of reef flat. At low tide the traps were visited to harvest the fish. Enormous cooperative effort was needed to build and repair such big structures, which generated enough food to maintain large populations.

Rock art in Kakadu National Park, Northern Territory. Paintings and engravings survive in numerous rock shelters in this region, possibly spanning more than 10,000 years and providing evidence of an unbroken tradition which embraces both continuity and change in Aboriginal art.

and subtle ways. Among other major technological developments came new and improved canoe designs, permitting longer voyages and the exploration and exploitation of offshore islands. The fashioning of skin bags for carrying large volumes of water made the movement into arid areas to obtain food a practical and safer proposition.

These innovations in production led to greater efficiency in the art of survival—larger numbers of people could now be supported, and more permanent settlements were possible. In some areas substantial houses were constructed and settlements grew in size. With access to more food, larger ceremonial gatherings could now take place.

Cultural diversity increases

A larger population and a more complex economic and cultural life led to wider cultural diversity across Australia. Aboriginals had responded to the different climatic and environmental zones by developing some 18 major regional variants of the basic culture. People from the desert areas in Australia—Arnhem Land, Cape York, the Kimberley, the south-east and so on—would lead very distinctive lives. And beyond that, groups of people within each region developed distinctive cultural practices based on the differences inherited from their own particular social group—

carrying slightly different weapons, holding different ceremonies, decorating their bodies in different ways and singing different songs. A number of distinctive languages developed, probably some 500 in total, each with different dialects spoken by smaller groups.

Individual groups were clear about which piece of land they owned and were responsible for, the knowledge of sites and boundaries having been handed down over generations. Each group also developed and enforced complex rules about which individuals owned and were responsible for particular parts of the land and the songs and ceremonies and art associated with it. The rules also governed almost every aspect of communal life from marriage and hunting to the arrangement of a campsite.

While all this was going on, the Aboriginal people of Tasmania, isolated from the rest of Australia, developed their own unique culture. While in some ways the island can be seen as just another region, thanks to its isolation, it was perhaps the most distinctive of all. It would later become perhaps even more distinctive as a result of European colonisation.

Australia itself had experienced little contact from the rest of the world, leaving it to develop its own culture and society, as had been the case with many other regions—China, north America, Central America, west Africa, Hawaii and New Zealand, for example. Life was to change in all of these countries as the Europeans, and other races, began to break free from their own isolation and explore the world.

In fact, Australia had never been totally isolated as there was a constant interchange with other people through the Torres Strait Islands, with big canoes bringing songs and dances and musical instruments and stories— and the canoes themselves—and probably much else into Cape York Peninsula. But the culture of the people of Torres Strait was not enormously different to that of northern Australia and ideas and goods could be slowly assimilated into the living cultures of the peninsula. Now visitors were about to begin calling from the unimaginably different world beyond Torres Strait, and nothing in Australia would ever be the same again.

MAJOR REGIONS OF INDIGENOUS AUSTRALIA

Merriam, Muralag

Gagadju, Gooniyandi, Gunibidji, Gunwingu, Larrakiya, Ngarinyin, Tiwi, Yolngu

Djabuganjdji, Gayardilt, Kuku-Yalanji, Lardil, Waanyi, Wik, Yanuwa, Yidinjdji

Alyawarra, Arrernte, Kukatja, Pintupi, Pitjantjatjarra, Wangkatha, Warlpiri, Warrumungu, Yindjibarndi

Adnyamathanha, Awabakal, Barkindji, Bundjalung, Daingatti, Dharug, Dieri, Eora, Gunditjmara, Kalkadoon, Kamilaroi, Kaurna, Kurnai, Ngarrindjeri, Ngunawal, WakaWaka, Wiradjri, Wurendjeri, Yorta Yorta, Yuggera

Nyungar, Wajuk

some named groups listed for each region

Key
- Northern
- Desert
- Cape
- Torres Strait
- Eastern
- Tasmanian
- South-western

Lairmairrener, Nuenonne, Paredarerme

Colonial History

The first visitors we know about for certain came in 1606, aboard a little Dutch ship named *Duyfken*, meaning 'dove'. The Dutch were colonising Indonesia, and their route to the 'Spice Islands' led to not-infrequent contact with the western and northern coasts of Australia. But there was nothing for the Dutch here, and they were met with resistance from the Aboriginals. *Duyfken*, making contact on the western shores of Cape York, was met with hostility, and one of its sailors killed. Another Dutch boat, the *Pera*, also sailed into the gulf a few years later (1623) and, met by fierce resistance, the crew killed one of the 200 Aboriginals opposing their landing. Every European boat, up to and including the *Endeavour*, would find itself opposed by Aboriginals.

Along with the Dutch, the English, too, were on the move in the seventeenth century, and in 1688 William Dampier made his first visit to Australian shores, landing in the north-west of Western Australia. He would make a second visit in 1699.

None of these visits had much impact on either the Aboriginals or the European visitors to Australia, apart from an occasional death on both sides. The foreigners' visits were brief, involving neither settlement nor trading. Aboriginal artists might occasionally represent a sailing ship in a painting, but that seems to have been about it. As far as the indigenous peoples were concerned, the appearance and pattern of behaviour of the foreigners was so threatening that resistance to their landings was the only possible course of action to take.

Relations with the Macassans

Not long after Dampier's second visit, however, a different group of people began to call in the north, and they were treated far more warmly.

The Macassans were fisherfolk from Indonesia. The boats probably came from a number of different Indonesian islands but 'Macassan' has come to be used as a general term for all of them. They came not to conquer but to fish, not in large boats but in small ones, and they weren't aggressive. Fishing was an occupation understood and carried out by both groups and their interactions seem to have been entirely amicable. There may well have been payment or trade involved for the right to visit fishing grounds. The Macassans built temporary structures for drying their catch of trepang (bêche-de-mer) and didn't try to settle permanently, but the relationship endured for long enough for stories and songs to be written, and for paintings and stoneworks to record their visits. Even more revealingly, Macassan words appeared in Aboriginal languages (a sure sign that communication was good) and there seem to have been relationships formed between Macassan men and Aboriginal women.

Much in the way that cooperative links were forged with the people of Torres Strait, resulting in an exchange of culture, so too were bonds formed with the people of the southern part of Indonesia.

The British come calling

When Captain James Cook came sailing into the waters of what would later be named Botany Bay in 1770 he was by no means the first European to make contact with Aboriginals. The reaction of the Botany Bay people was exactly the same as that of every other group that had seen sailing ships call on the Australian coast. They regarded the strangers as a threat and tried to protect themselves. After watching some of the crew disembark from a boat, two Tharawal men, after sending away their women and children, bravely resisted Cook's landing as far as they were able to. The events which followed must have seemed the stuff of which nightmares are made.

An Englishman, William Dampier, visited Western Australia in 1688 and 1699, one of a number of European explorers who had contact with Aboriginal people and wrote about his experience. On his second visit he was resisted by men with spears who forced him to retreat. He shot and killed one of them.

An artist's impression of Cook's first landing in Australia, opposed by two brave Tharawal men. Everywhere that Europeans came ashore in Australia over a period of some 150 years, they were met with resistance by men throwing spears, or setting fire to the bush; brave acts against guns and cannon.

In 1824 a penal settlement was established at Redcliffe on Moreton Bay in Queensland (and later moved to the present site of Brisbane). To the Aboriginal people living in the area, some of whom are shown here watching, the expanding frontier meant loss of their land and hunting grounds and the arrival of such diseases as smallpox, measles, pneumonia, tuberculosis and venereal disease, to which they had no immunity.

Truganini was the last survivor of a group of Tasmanians captured and shipped to Flinders Island in an effort by Europeans to 'sweep' Tasmania of its original inhabitants. Later, as disease took its toll, the group were brought back to Hobart, where they died. Truganini died in 1876 aged 64. Descendants of Tasmanian Aboriginals survived on other Bass Strait Islands and later returned to Tasmania.

'We then threw them some nails, beads etc. ashore which they took up and seem'd not ill pleased in so much that I thought that they beckoned to us to come ashore; but in this we were much mistaken, for as soon as we put the boat in they again came to oppose us upon which I fired a musket between the two which had no other effect than to make them retire back where bundles of their darts lay, and one of them took up a stone and threw it at us which caused my firing a second musket load with small shot, and although some of the shot struck the man yet it had no other effect than to make him lay hold of a shield or target to defend himself. Immediately after this we landed which we had no sooner done than they threw two darts at us, this obliged me to fire a third shot soon after which they both made off ...'

It was no wonder that Cook would later say: '... all they seemed to want was for us to be gone.'

This was just the first of the battles that would be fought on Australian soil over some 150 years. Arthur Phillip landed unopposed, but around the perimeter of his little colony the Aboriginals of Sydney, being displaced after some 45,000 years of occupation, fought a guerrilla war.

The perimeter or frontier of the colony quickly began to expand out from Sydney, and later from new colonies in Hobart, Melbourne and Brisbane. For many white Australians, maps that show the expanding frontier are a source of some pride. In art and literature the frontier is the scene of hard work, sacrifice and achievements against great odds, of 'conquering a wilderness', of carving a nation out of a new land. To Aboriginals, the expanding frontier meant the loss of their land and hunting grounds, their ceremonial and sacred sites. It meant death and destruction. Even before the frontier arrived in a district it was preceded by diseases like smallpox, which brought death on a large scale even before the colonisers began using guns.

The wars for a continent

To Aboriginals, then, the frontier was the battleground, where (as in many parts of the world, even today) they would fight with such weapons as spears and boomerangs against rifles, cannon, and troopers mounted on horses.

It was guerrilla warfare, just like that which the French Resistance fought against the German army. Lightly armed civilians can't stand and fight battles against heavily armed regular troops, so they strike and run and live to fight another day.

In areas where guerrilla tactics became too successful, the colonial governments brought in Native Troopers, Aboriginals from other parts of Australia who knew all the tactics, and how to track, and didn't mind fighting against strangers. Themselves dispossessed and, in many cases, brutalised by their white commanders, they were successful—and feared and hated by those they hunted.

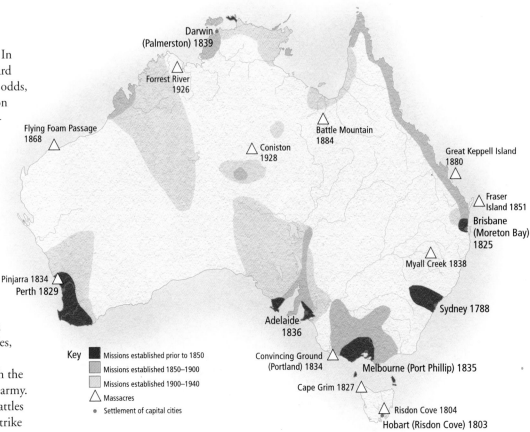

Key
■ Missions established prior to 1850
▨ Missions established 1850–1900
□ Missions established 1900–1940
△ Massacres
● Settlement of capital cities

On many parts of the frontier, local people simply took the law into their own hands. If there was resistance, if a sheep was stolen, or if people were simply in the way, a mob would form and go hunting. It wasn't publicised. Nor usually was it publicised when the police did the same thing. How many incidents there were, and how many people were killed will never be known, but it was certainly in the tens of thousands. Attempted reconstructions now are impossible because records were not kept, and nothing was said (except perhaps in drunken boasting in outback pubs to an audience who would say nothing outside). On rare occasions there were prosecutions, but they were rarely successful.

The last known massacre was in central Australia, the last frontier, in 1928 at a place called Coniston. Over a period of nearly a year, large numbers of Aboriginals were killed by police in savage reprisal for the death of a prospector (or possibly a dog scalper) from unknown causes.

The Christian missionaries

The next major influence on Aboriginals was Christianity. Close to the frontier, wherever it might be, were the missionaries. Missions were established all over Australia by all denominations. Some performed a vital role as a safe haven where people could retreat and find protection from fighting. They also provided the only educational and health facilities available to Aboriginal people. Many people survived who would otherwise have died from diseases. Many children received an education that would give them some way of functioning in the new society that was being created behind the frontier.

MISSIONS AND SOME MASSACRES

LEFT: These pictures, posted on trees in Tasmania, implied equal justice for all. While it was true that Aboriginals who killed whites would be hung, the reverse wasn't.

The grave of the stationmaster at remote Barrow Creek in central Australia. He was killed by Kaytej men during an attack on the telegraph station in 1874, one of hundreds of incidents in the guerrilla warfare Aboriginal people conducted against the expanding frontier. Many Kaytej men were later killed in revenge.

People at Lake Tyers Mission in Gippsland, Victoria. An Anglican mission established in 1861, it was one of many institutions which, as a result of missionary attitudes, economic, social and health problems, and attitudes of whites in surrounding areas, caused enormous distress to its inhabitants. It was later government-controlled, with the same end results.

A pub in outback Australia. In many outback areas, the dynamic between Aboriginals, pubs, alcohol, whites and government regulations, has led to friction and terrible health and social consequences.

On the other hand, the missionaries frequently became the agencies that would disrupt Aboriginal society to an even greater extent. In many cases mission children were not allowed to see their parents or other relatives, were not permitted to speak their own language and were forbidden to take part in the religious and ceremonial activities of their people. The aim was to totally sever them from their culture in order to 'assimilate' them. It generally left them feeling at home in neither society, and with an enormous sense of loss.

The impact of government

The third major influence on Aboriginal lives was government—the various colonial and, later, state governments and the Commonwealth. There were three main ways in which the effects were felt. First, there were government settlements, which worked in a similar manner to the religious missions. They also provided safe havens and services, but because people could be coerced into moving into the settlements, and because the settlements (and the missions) crowded together people from many different (and sometimes hostile) groups, often in poor conditions and with no possible economic activity, they became places with enormous social and health problems.

Then there were government agencies in the form of various kinds of 'protection' boards (later often called Welfare Boards). These agencies had enormous power over the lives of Aboriginal people and could determine where they could live, who they could marry, what would happen to their children, how their money (if any) would be spent and what work they were allowed to do. Perceived infringements of their draconian and wide-ranging framework of rules could lead to the removal of the offender to an even worse settlement or imprisonment. Welfare Boards may at times have been run by well-meaning people, but good intentions notwithstanding, their effects were often devastating in terms of the psychological trauma of broken families and the loss of their connection to the land.

Finally there were government policies and the laws to enforce those policies. In general terms the policies initially were based on the idea that Aboriginals would gradually die out and that governments should try to make this as painless a process as possible. When it became clear that this was not going to happen, the government's aim was then to assimilate Aboriginals, another form of rendering them invisible—to make them disappear by absorbing them into the white community.

Throughout this whole period, the moving frontier marked the point at which Aboriginal people were removed from their land and dispossessed of it. Even where they had survived, they had been moved on to missions or government settlements, often far from their own country, or were living on cattle and sheep stations on what had been their land, working for their keep, which was often meagre.

While the land was important materially in providing a living, in terms of Aboriginal culture, society and religion, it was essential. Now the fundamental link between Aboriginal people and land, vital for the wellbeing of both society and the individual had been broken, and the effects were devastating. In 1937 a man was born who would, by his efforts, try to reverse this process where it could be reversed. His name was Eddie Mabo.

Modern History

The year after Eddie Mabo was born marked the symbolic beginning of modern Aboriginal political activity. The year 1938 marked the 150th anniversary of the landing at Sydney Cove and the decade of the 1930s saw a stirring of political activity in Australia, bringing with it a new awareness of the history of Aboriginal people throughout those years.

Two organisations were founded in this decade—the Australian Aboriginals League (1932) and Aboriginals Progressive Association (1937)—although there had been one preceding organisation, the Australian Aboriginals Progressive Association, which functioned in New South Wales in the mid-1920s. This latter organisation, under the presidency of Fred Maynard, held conferences, but it was effectively destroyed by the actions of the Aboriginal Welfare Board (which was not prepared to allow criticism of its behaviour by Aboriginal people). Also in the 1930s came the formation of Aboriginals Advancement Leagues in some States, and while these were a welcome sign that white Australians were recognising that there were matters that needed to be addressed in relation to Aboriginal affairs, there was little if any involvement in these organisations by Aboriginals themselves. The other two organisations would be different.

The Day of Mourning

The Australian Aboriginals League began in Victoria, founded by William Cooper and Ebenezer Lovett. Later members of the League would include Doug Nicholls (for a time, remarkably, appointed Governor of South Australia), Bill Onus, Eric Onus, Reg Saunders and Margaret Tucker. The League approached those in power, petitioning the King to have special Aboriginal electorates, and asking the government of the day to establish a national department of Aboriginal affairs.

The Aboriginals Progressive Association was formed by a group including William Ferguson, John Patten, Bert Groves and Pearl Gibbs. It petitioned the Federal Government to take over Aboriginal affairs, and to grant citizenship to Aboriginal people. Another important aim of the Association was to improve living conditions on Aboriginal reserves, and to have Aboriginal people involved in the control of the Aboriginal Welfare Board (asking that half the board members be Aboriginal). If the Federal Government had listened to and acted upon these requests at the time, it would have made an enormous difference to the future

welfare of Aboriginal people, and radically changed the future course of the politics of Aboriginal affairs to the present day.

The two organisations combined forces to hold a 'Day of Mourning' protest on Australia Day 1938, including a conference to discuss the situation and needs of Aboriginal people in New South Wales and Victoria and ideas for future political action. Unfortunately, international events in the form of World War II put the brakes on this political momentum, and although both organisations resumed for a short time after the war, and some of the same people remained active, it would take a new generation and new organisations to achieve some of their goals in the 1960s and 1970s.

At war again

World War II put a stop to political activity, and not simply because the political agenda was solely concerned with the war. It also came to a stop because Aboriginal people were themselves heavily involved in the conflict.

Designed by Harold Thomas in 1971, the Aboriginal flag has been an effective symbol of protest, resistance and pride over the years. It was carried by Aboriginal runner Cathy Freeman in 1994 (along with the Australian flag) when she won a gold medal in the Commonwealth Games in Canada, an event which inspired some controversy. In 1995 Federal Cabinet proclaimed it an official flag of Australia.

Aboriginal soldiers from a special platoon of volunteers, Wangaratta, Victoria, in the 1940s. Officials tried to discourage Aboriginals joining the armed forces in both World Wars, but thousands succeeded in enlisting and fought in all the services. This was the only Aboriginal squad in the Australian Military Forces.

The house of Albert Namatjira in the Northern Territory. Namatjira, one of Australia's best-known artists—white or black—fought for years to be granted citizenship after being refused the right to buy land and then a house. He eventually achieved citizenship but later received a jail term in 1959 for supplying alcohol to a relative. Although the sentence was commuted, the experience broke his spirit and he died one year later at the age of 57.

In World War I several hundred Aboriginal men had enlisted as soldiers. There were probably considerably more, but many hid their identity because Aboriginal people were discouraged and in many cases actively prevented from joining the army.

The same prejudice occurred in recruiting centres in World War II, but when it became public the ensuing fuss caused the restrictions to be relaxed, and eventually thousands of Aboriginal men enlisted in all three services, and many Aboriginal women joined the women's services. Many other Aboriginals in Torres Strait and the north of Australia were involved in the Coast Watch, which provided intelligence on the movements of enemy ships and planes. Among the many who distinguished themselves in the services were Reg Saunders (who held officer rank in the army), Len Waters (who became a pilot) and Oodgeroo Noonuccal (who served in the Women's Army Service).

The contrast between army life (during which servicemen and women were treated relatively equally) and life after the war (when Aboriginal ex-service personnel returned to restrictions and prejudice based on their race) radicalised many Aboriginal people and was the basis for them becoming politically active in the 1950s and 1960s.

Recognition as Australians

The best known of the new organisations for change was the Federal Council for the Advancement of Aboriginals and Torres Strait Islanders, or FCAATSI. This umbrella group for a range of Aboriginal advancement organisations began in 1958 with a conference, the first of many annual conferences it held on Aboriginal affairs. It lobbied and fought on many different issues including education and wages, the aftermath of nuclear tests at Maralinga, justice for the artist Albert Namatjira, and voting rights. Its greatest achievement was the 1967 referendum. It lobbied for years to have the referendum held, having realised that efforts over the previous few decades to have the Federal Government act in Aboriginal affairs had failed because of obstacles posed by the Constitution. The referendum aimed to rectify matters by having removed from Section 51 (xxvi) the words: 'other than the aboriginal race'. This section enabled the Commonwealth to make laws 'for the people of any race [other than the aboriginal race in any State] for whom it is deemed necessary to make special laws.' This was the critical part of the referendum, the other part—to remove the provision (Section 127) preventing Aboriginals from being included in population figures—was seen as being largely of symbolic importance, although data on Aboriginal people would be crucial in introducing new programs.

The referenda were both passed by 'Yes' votes of around 90 per cent, the most successful results ever obtained in any Australian referendum. However, in some areas there were large numbers of 'No' votes, reflecting unchanging views.

Aboriginal children celebrate their culture through their paintings at Wannabirri pre-school, Redfern, Sydney. The fight for improved educational opportunities has been one of the main thrusts of Aboriginal political activity over the last three decades.

The Land Rights movement

The result was seen as a watershed moment in Aboriginal affairs, both as an indication that the mood of the public was in mostly in favour of starting to deal with the problems that Aboriginal people faced, and as the start of federal involvement in the area. However it was not until 1972 that a Federal Government made use of its new powers in this area and began to develop programs. FCAATSI had achieved its major aims and in the 1970s was eventually to disappear.

At the same time as the referendum campaign was under way, a group of Sydney University students in 1965 set out on a bus journey called the Freedom Ride (a name derived from similar events in the US). The aim was both to investigate and publicise the plight of Aboriginals throughout New South Wales. The group, which included the late Charles Perkins, Jim Spigelman and Reverend Tedd Noffs (now also deceased), found poor living conditions and discrimination everywhere they went. Two incidents in particular attracted national attention. At Moree, in the State's north, they desegregated a swimming pool which barred Aboriginal children; at Walgett, in the west, they demonstrated outside the Returned Servicemen's Club which barred Aboriginal ex-servicemen from entry. At both places they were met by angry crowds and riots. These events brought to the attention of the media features of Aboriginal–white relations, that had been kept out of sight.

In 1966 a quite different event in a quite different part of Australia also focused media attention on other significant aspects of Aboriginal affairs. In August of that year, Aboriginal stockmen and staff went on strike at Wave Hill cattle station, demanding better pay and conditions (there was a long history in the cattle industry of not paying wages to Aboriginal people but having them work for their 'keep'). There was also a demand for the right to own their own

A land rights demonstration at Sydney Town Hall, one of many in the last 35 years to keep up the pressure on successive State and Federal Governments.

Bull riding in the outback. Aboriginal stockmen have been the mainstay of the cattle industry for over a century.

An Aboriginal 'tent embassy' in Glebe, Sydney, during the 2000 Olympic Games. Such demonstrations are modelled on the original tent embassy protest outside Parliament House in Canberra in 1972 and have proved a practical—and symbolic—rallying point for protest about Aboriginal issues.

The fight for equal pay and conditions in the cattle industry has been long and hard for Aboriginal stockmen. A protracted strike by 200 workers at Wave Hill Station, south of Darwin, in 1966 eventually achieved their goals and provided an impetus for the land rights movement.

land and run their own station. In this they were eventually to be successful. The strike and subsequent events were important in raising issues of Aboriginal ownership of land, and the mechanisms for achieving this (both through legislation and the purchase of properties by governments) which would also be important for many other Aboriginal groups.

The 'tent embassy' was another major event aimed at drawing the attention of the media to Aboriginal issues. It was also the beginning of the modern focus on 'Land Rights' as a significant issue in Aboriginal affairs, although there had never been a time since 1788 when the issue was unimportant to Aboriginal people. In 1972 the prime minister, William 'Billy' McMahon, had announced the creation of a new kind of land lease specifically for Aboriginals which would depend upon their 'intention and ability to make reasonable economic and social use of the land' and specifically excluded mineral and forestry rights.

Aboriginal people were outraged at the conditions, and many felt that they were 'foreigners in their own country' while they were not permitted to have freehold title to any part of it.

To symbolise this feeling a group of Aboriginal people established an 'Embassy to the People of Australia' in a tent on the lawns of the national parliament on 26 January 1972. From July onwards there

---

INDIGENOUS HISTORY TIMELINE

25,500 YBP Date of evidence for cremation of human remains found at Lake Mungo—the earliest evidence of human cremation ever discovered.

5000–3000 YBP Appearance of more sophisticated stone tools in archaeological record. Dingo brought to Australia.

1770 Tharawal people attempt to drive off landing party from Cook's *Endeavour*. Total indigenous population at this time between 300,000 and 750,000.

1825 First missions set up in NSW, beginning a wave of mission building that wanes around 1850.

1835 Last Tasmanian Aboriginals exiled.
1838 Following massacre of 28 Aboriginals at Myall Creek, NSW, seven white men are tried and hanged.

1914 World War I breaks out; 500 Aboriginals enlist.
1918 Aborigines Ordinance allows Commonwealth to remove children from Aboriginal mother if father is white.

1932 Founding of Australian Aboriginals League and, in 1937, Aboriginals Progressive Association reflects new political awareness emerging among indigenous peoples.

25,000 YBP First stone axes appear.
10,000 YBP Melting ice raises sea level, isolating Tasmanian Aboriginals and cutting off land bridge to Asia.

50,000–40,000 YBP Aboriginal peoples arrive in Australia and begin to spread out across the continent.

1606 Dutch ship *Duyfken* lands on Cape York; local people respond to perceived threat and a sailor is killed.
c.1650 Macassan fisherfolk begin to visit north.

1778 Following establishment of colony at Sydney, local Aboriginal peoples resist its expansion with guerilla tactics, many under command of famous warrior Pemulwuy.

1830 In Tasmania, government organises Black Line, a line of 3000 settlers and soldiers that sweeps across the island, forcing Aboriginals into Tasman Peninsula.

1860 Beginning of second wave of mission building which lasts until 1890.
1876 Death of Truganini, last full-blooded Tasmanian Aboriginal, at Hobart.

1928 Following murder of European settler, police posse massacres 60–70 Warlpiri people at Coniston Station, near Yuendumu, NT.

1939 Following outbreak of World War II, 2000 Aboriginal people enlist.
1951 Federal Government reasserts policy of assimilation of Aboriginals.

were attempts to tear down the tents and there was a series of violent clashes with police. The embassy managed to survive the attacks (which in themselves resulted in great media interest) and would continue to stand until 1975, although it has been re-formed at various times since then.

In 1973 the Federal Government established a Land Rights Commission to look at issues concerning land and Aboriginals in the Northern Territory. It would eventually result in the Aboriginal Land Rights Act (NT) of 1976, under which various Aboriginal groups in the Northern Territory have been able to claim their traditional lands.

In 1975 the government established the Aboriginal Land Fund Commission in order to purchase freehold land on behalf of traditional owners. One of the first purchases (influenced by the Wave Hill strike) was that of Daguragu for the Gurindji people, the handover being accompanied by the now-famous image of Prime Minister Gough Whitlam pouring soil into the hand of Vincent Lingiari to symbolise the transfer of ownership.

Both legislation and land purchases as mechanisms for providing land ownership to Aboriginal people suffered from the fact that they were based on the premise that Aboriginals had no rights to land and that if they were to get any it would be by the goodwill of the Australian people and their government. When Captain James Cook had claimed the country on behalf of the British Crown he did so on the grounds that the land was *terra nullius*—that is, it was owned by no one. Whatever Aboriginal people lived here (and *terra nullius* didn't mean the Crown didn't recognise prior occupation), and whatever system of ownership of land, if any, had existed, all such title had been lost at the time the country was claimed by the Crown.

The Mabo Case

In 1982, Eddie Mabo and a group of friends decided to challenge this assumption in the courts, in a case that was not only to change the whole understanding of the meaning of land rights in Australia, but also the nature of non-Aboriginal title to land. It was a move that was inevitably going to be both controversial and of enormous significance.

The Mabo Case, as it came to be called, was based on establishing Eddie's traditional ownership to a piece of land in the Torres Strait Islands. The case

NTARIA LAND TRUST
LIQUOR ACT
WARNING
RESTRICTED AREA

THE POSSESSION OR CONSUMPTION OF LIQUOR IN THIS COMMUNITY WITHOUT A PERMIT IS A SERIOUS OFFENCE. VEHICLES CARRYING LIQUOR MAY BE SEIZED AND FORFEITED AND THE FOLLOWING PENALTIES MAY ALSO APPLY.

| FIRST OFFENCE: | UP TO $1000 FINE OR 6 MONTHS GOAL. |
| SECOND OR SUBSEQUENT OFFENCE: | UP TO $2000 FINE OR 12 MONTHS GOAL. |

The problems associated with alcohol abuse among Aboriginal people has been addressed by both Aboriginal elders and local authorities. Some communities have decided to restrict and monitor the consumption of alcohol on their own lands.

The Central Land Council office in Tennant Creek. The Council was originally established under the Northern Territory Land Rights Act of 1976 to coordinate and argue claims for land by Aboriginal traditional owners in the south of the Territory. There is also a Northern Land Council.

58 Creation of Federal il for the Advancement boriginals and Torres it Islanders (FCAATSI) h begins lobbying on of indigenous peoples.

1965 Group of Aboriginals led by Charles Perkins, Jim Spigelman and Reverend Ted Noffs embarks on Freedom Rides aimed at ending segregation, especially in rural areas.

1966 Aboriginal workers at Wave Hill Cattle Station, NT, begin strike for better conditions and right to own traditional land.

1967 Referendum proposing that Commonwealth be allowed to legislate for Aboriginals and that indigenous people be included in census is passed overwhelmingly.

1971 Aboriginal flag, designed by Luritja man Harold Thomas, raised for first time, in Adelaide. Liberal politician Neville Bonner becomes first Aboriginal MP.

1972 Conditions imposed on land rights prompt founding of Tent Embassy outside Federal Parliament. Department of Aboriginal Affairs set up.

1975 Government creates Aboriginal Land Fund Commission to buy freehold land on behalf of traditional owners. First beneficiaries include Gurindji at Wave Hill.

1976 Following investigation by a federal commission, Aboriginal Land Rights Act (NT) establishes first procedures for land rights claims anywhere in Australia.

1985 Uluru, NT, and surrounding land returned to traditional owners, the Anangu people.
1986 Pat O'Shane becomes first Aboriginal magistrate.

1990 Creation of Aboriginal and Torres Strait Islander Commission (ATSIC). Council for Aboriginal Reconciliation established.

1991 Royal Commission into deaths in custody condemns actions of police forces in managing prisoners and recommends wide-ranging reforms.

1992 In response to land rights claim led by Eddie Mabo, High Court rejects *terra nullius* and declares that indigenous peoples hold title to ancestral lands.

1993 Federal Government passes Native Title Act to recognise and protect land rights of indigenous peoples and establish procedures for native title claims.

1996 With the so-called Wik Decision, the High Court rules that pastoral leases do not necessarily extinguish native title.

1997 Report of enquiry into 'stolen generations' highlights trauma caused by assimilation and recommends that Aboriginal peoples receive compensation and apology.

2000 In Sydney, 300,000 people march across Harbour Bridge to express support for National Reconciliation Week.

The Stuart Town Jail in Alice Springs, central Australia, built in 1908 and now a museum. Aboriginal people continue to be over-represented in Australian jails and the introduction of mandatory sentencing has exacerbated the problem. The result can be fatal—Aboriginal deaths in custody are an ongoing social and personal tragedy.

went through the Queensland court system (which has jurisdiction in the Strait) then to the High Court of Australia. The decision was handed down in 1992 (a few months after Eddie Mabo's death), the Court ruling that people on the island of Mer had owned their land before white occupation and overturning *terra nullius* as a basis for the original settlement.

The Federal Government would introduce a Native Title Act in order to establish Land Rights, given the new understandings of the legal situation.

There remained some doubt as to whether the Mabo decision, applying as it did in Torres Strait, to a different people with a somewhat different system of land use and tenure and a history different from the rest of Australia, could provide a firm legal basis for 'Native Title' elsewhere in the country.

While it was clear, for example, that freehold title, which applied to much of Australia, extinguished any previous Native Title, other forms of title might not. On the other hand, land that had always been Crown Land retained Native Title. In between came, in particular, the vexed question of pastoral leases in some parts of Australia. These leases, for land to be used for a particular purpose (i.e. grazing stock), were in an uncertain position. This was clarified by the 'Wik Case' in Cape York, where it was established that pastoral leases and Native Title could both apply to a particular piece of land (since the leases did not carry with them all rights to the use of land to the exclusion of all others).

The Mabo and Wik Cases and the Native Title legislation resulted in enormous public debate and political controversy and acrimony. Following the election of a conservative Federal Government in

March 1996, changes to the legislation were introduced that would once again greatly restrict Aboriginal rights to land.

This issue in itself was to cause a considerable rupture between the government and the Aboriginal people. Other matters would exacerbate the problem.

Black Deaths and Stolen Generations

In 1987, following the death of yet another Aboriginal man in police custody (the sixteenth in that year alone), the Federal Government established a Royal Commission to inquire into the causes of what would eventually be 99 deaths. The commission produced its final report in 1991, finding that few of the deaths were the result of actions by custodians (which had been widely seen as the major cause). But in any case, the large number of deaths (one-third self-inflicted, one-half due either to natural causes or substance abuse) among a people representing a small fraction of the Australian population—but a large percentage of the prisoners in jails—required explanation and remedy. An enormous number of recommendations (339) were made, covering a whole raft of reforms over many different areas including housing and education, police relations, reform of the justice system, tackling substance abuse, better economic basis for communities, land rights and many others. A significant aim was to try to reduce the disproportionate number of Aboriginal prisoners.

Some of the recommendations were acted upon by the States. Late in the 1990s it came to public attention (again through deaths in custody) that both the Northern Territory and Western Australia had enacted laws covered by the general term 'mandatory sentencing'. Whatever the merits of the process, the end result was undoubtedly again to increase the number of Aboriginal prisoners, frequently (again) in jail for minor offences. The death of a young boy sparked demands that the Federal Government overturn the Northern Territory legislation. It would not do so.

Officer of the Aboriginal Legal Service at work in Sydney. Such services now exist nationwide to help Aboriginal people become aware of their rights and to provide services in a friendly and culturally appropriate way.

Reconciliation and Self-determination

Many of the threads of Aboriginal dispossession and disadvantage, the frequently brutal interaction between black and white, and the attempts in recent years to try to improve this relationship, were meant to be addressed by the Reconciliation Council, established in 1990.

This Council, with a ten-year life span, brought together Aboriginal and non-Aboriginal people to improve relationships between the two communities and conducted many educational activities during its term. However, reconciliation as a process was compromised by the increasing friction between the Aboriginal community and the government. The long-time Chair of the Council, Pat Dodson, resigned and was replaced by Evelyn Scott.

The friction has come to be symbolised by the lack of an official apology. The Council's ten-year term ended, and the government has announced its replacement—a body with fewer political teeth. The end of the Council's term was marked by the march over the Sydney Harbour Bridge, by which tens of thousands of people suggested that it was time to recognise the mistakes of the past and move on together and continuing calls for both an apology and a formal treaty. It is impossible to know if, at some time in the future, another historian will see it as a major turning point in our troubled history.

Isolated outback communities often have a hard time in their battle for self-determination. One company in Alice Springs— the Centre for Alternative Technology—aims to provide Aboriginal communities with technology that is useful in their conditions and for their needs. Here a student is welding a barbecue.

Another enquiry that was to look in effect at the whole history of black–white relations in an attempt to find some solutions to continued disadvantage, was the so called 'stolen generations' enquiry. This was set up in 1995 by the Human Rights and Equal Opportunities Commission in response to a request from the Federal Government. It reported back with its findings in 1997.

The enquiry was established to look into the extent and effects of the official practice of removing Aboriginal children from their families. This was a practice begun very early (in 1815) in the history of Australia, which reached its peak from the 1930s to through to the 1950s, and continued into the 1970s. (However, it seems that old attitudes die hard: as recently as 1998 police in Western Australia again proposed separating Aboriginal children from their parents.) The removals were carried out by police acting for the Welfare Boards, or by Board officers, or by missions. Many Aboriginal people believe that the trauma it caused, both to individuals and to communities, has played a major role in Aboriginal disadvantage right up to the present day.

The enquiry interviewed many Aboriginal people. It made a series of recommendations, the two most controversial of which involved compensation and the issuing by the prime minister of a formal apology on behalf of the people of Australia. While the government has responded to many of the commission's recommendations, it has refused to act on these two.

The refusal of the prime minister to 'say sorry' as his stance has come to be characterised, has been another major cause of friction with the Aboriginal community. This has been exacerbated by the response of the government and a number of conservative commentators, all suggesting that the problem has been greatly exaggerated, and, essentially, that whatever removal of children did occur was done legally and for the best of motives.

Carpentry training for young Aboriginal boys at the Centre for Alternative Technology. Education in such skills is vital for many communities trying to survive.

Maritime Exploration and Colonisation

The main settlement on Norfolk Island. Reoccupied as a penal settlement in 1825, Governor Darling wished the island to become a place of 'the extremest punishment short of Death'.

Aboriginal people arrived in Australia at least as long as 40,000 years ago, possibly earlier, island-hopping along the broken chain of land that once connected the continent to the islands of what is now Indonesia. It was inevitable that other groups in the region would have explored the area between that time and European settlement in 1788. It is likely that Chinese and Arab mariners visited Australia in the fifteenth century, possibly bringing pottery, cloth and metal tools with them. From about the seventeenth century the Macassans of Sulawesi came to the northern coasts to fish for trepang (sea cucumber) for sale in the markets of Canton. They remained for several months each monsoon during which they harvested and processed their catch, a procedure which involved gutting, boiling and smoking.

First sightings

On the other side of the world, the Europeans had for centuries been attracted by often fanciful stories of a mysterious southern continent. Referred to as *Terra Australis Incognita* ('Unknown Southern Land'), the fabled continent was believed to be a place of great wealth inhabited by wondrous beasts.

Spanish, Portuguese and Dutch explorers looked for new trade routes and commercial opportunities in South-East Asia and the Pacific during the sixteenth and seventeenth centuries. In 1606 both the Dutch and the Spanish were in the same area. At the end of 1605 two Spanish ships under the command of Pedro Fernandez de Quiros sailed from Peru in the hope of discovering another America and with a mission to convert its inhabitants to Christianity. De Quiros thought he had achieved this goal when he reached an island of the New Hebrides (Vanuatu) in 1606, which he named Australia del Espiritu Santo. Luis Vaez de Torres, on the other ship, proved de Quiros wrong when he circumnavigated the island and then sailed west to discover the strait between Australia and New Guinea that now bears his name. At the beginning of the same year, the East India Company ship *Duyfken*, under Dutchman Willem Jansz, made landfall on the western side of Cape York Peninsula. Jansz was the first European known to have set foot on Australia, but he was unimpressed with the new-found land and its inhabitants.

The Dutch continued to chart the west coast but none judged the new land worthy of settlement: ten years after Jansz, skipper Dirck Hartog sighted the western coast of Australia, landing at Shark Bay and leaving behind a pewter plate with his name on it. Other ships reached Cape Leeuwin in 1622, sighting Rottnest Island (named for the many quokkas, a small wallaby, which live on the island and which were thought by the sailors to be rats) along the way, and in 1627 Francois Thijssen sailed for about 1000 nautical miles (1.85 km or 1.15 miles = 1 nm) along the southern coast east from Cape Leeuwin.

In 1642, another Dutchman, Abel Janszoon Tasman, set off to find a route from the East Indies to South America. Sighting land on 24 November 1642 he named it Van Diemen's Land, after the governor-general of Batavia. Tasman then turned eastward, sailing on to the South Island of New Zealand. During a second voyage in 1644, the Dutchman mapped the southern and western shores of the Gulf of Carpentaria.

A map from the world's first ever printed atlas. The postulated southern land mass is obscurely defined and bears names first dreamed up by Marco Polo.

TYPVS ORBIS TERRARVM

TERRA AVSTRALIS NONDVM COGNITA

QVID EI POTEST VIDERI MAGNVM IN REBVS HVMANIS, CVI AETERNITAS OMNIS, TOTIVSQVE MVNDI NOTA SIT MAGNITVDO. CICERO:

Dutch explorers were joined by the British and French by the late seventeenth century. Englishman William Dampier was a member of the ship *Cygnet* which visited the west coast, around King Sound, in 1688. Dampier endorsed the Dutch assessment of the country in a book on his voyage. According to him, the land was unsuitable for settlement and inhabited by the 'miserablest people in the world'.

Another Englishman, Captain James Cook, was appointed by the British Admiralty to command the *Endeavour* on a voyage of exploration to the south seas. He was also under instructions from the Royal Society (Britain's premier scientific institution) to observe the transit of Venus in 1769 at Tahiti. Also aboard the ship was a group of scientists, including the naturalist Joseph Banks. After circumnavigating New Zealand, Cook sighted the east coast of Australia at what is now called Cape Everard on 19 April 1770. He travelled north, charting the coast as he went, and anchoring at Possession Island in Torres Strait on 21 August 1770. Claiming possession of the east coast of New Holland for Britain, and naming it New South Wales, Cook sailed through Torres Strait.

Colonial beginnings

During the 1770s and 1780s the French closely shadowed the British in the Pacific region. Coincidentally, two ships under the command of Jean-François de La Pérouse called in at Botany Bay to make repairs only days after the First Fleet anchored there in January 1788. They left shortly afterwards, never to be seen again. (Years later, in 1986, the wrecks were investigated by an Australian-led expedition to Vanikoro, in the Santa Cruz group of islands .)

European colonisation of Australia commenced on 26 January 1788 when a group of ships under the command of Captain Arthur Phillip landed at Sydney Cove. (Six days earlier the fleet had arrived at Botany Bay but Phillip decided that it was unsuitable for settlement.) Those 11 ships of the First Fleet, which had sailed from Portsmouth, England, on 13 May 1787, arrived in Australia with 736 convicts (548 of them men and 188 women) as well as four companies of marines and some officials. The ships also carried horses, cattle, sheep, goats, poultry and food enough to last the colonisers for two years.

When Governor Phillip took possession of the land and hoisted his country's flag, he assumed that because its inhabitants were nomadic, they could not be considered as owners of the land. Thus the idea of *terra nullius*—an empty land—was born, vindicating the colonisers' right to take the land for themselves.

Historians continue to debate the motives for establishing a permanent settlement in such a remote continent. At the time there was a perceived need for somewhere to send Britain's burgeoning convict population. Since 1718, 30,000 convicts had been transported to America, but after the loss of those colonies in 1776, the prison hulks (old ships used to house convicts) had become dangerously overcrowded. There may also have been wider strategic and trade objectives. A colony in New South Wales would be perfectly located for further expansion in the Pacific and could be a way of countering French ambitions in the region. There was also a belief that the new continent might provide supplies of flax for sailcloth and timber for ships, and even its own industries such as whaling. Perhaps, too, the colony would provide another link for trade with Asia and the Pacific.

Tasmania's spectacular, though forbidding Tasman Peninsula. Named for Abel Tasman, who sighted this coast in 1642, this later became the site of the notorious Port Arthur prison.

The Early Years

Hobart's St George's church was built by convicts. Its architect, James Blackburn, was himself a convict, transported for forgery.

The character of convict society has been a matter of much historical debate and our attitudes towards the convicts have changed. Were they hardened criminals or victims of a harsh penal system, transported for no more than stealing a mere loaf of bread or a petty act of poaching? Although research has shown that most convicts were part of a growing urban criminal sub-culture, economic and social circumstances of the time were harsh for those at the bottom of the class system. For earlier generations of Australians, convict ancestry was regarded as an embarrassment but in recent decades it has become a matter of some pride to find one of Australia's first (invol-untary) European settlers in the branches of a family tree.

Survival proved difficult in the first two years of settle-ment. Plantings of vegetables and grain failed, cattle wandered off into the bush and most of the sheep soon died. When some supply ships failed to reach the colony, rations were drastically cut and the inhabitants were close to star-vation when the Second Fleet arrived with fresh supplies in mid-1790. Conditions on board the ships of this fleet were appalling and 267 convicts out of a total of over 1000 died on the voyage from England.

Self-sufficiency became a reality in the next few years when small farms at Parramatta and along the Hawkesbury River produced good yields of maize. Some of these farms were cultivated by emancipists, convicts who had been set free and given modest land grants. Whalers and sealers also began operating from Sydney. To make the settlement more self-sufficient free immigrants were attracted to the colony from 1792 by the promise of a free passage, a land grant and convict labour. When Governor Phillip departed Sydney in December 1792 he predicted that the new colony would become 'the most valuable acquisition that Great Britain ever made'.

The ball and chain formed part of the punishment for convicts on the brutal 'iron gangs'.

Establishment of new settlements

From 1803 several new settlements were established. There were a number of reasons for this. One was the need to house the increasing flow of convicts coming to Australia—between 1788 and 1820, 28,410 people were transported, compared with a mere trickle of about 4500 free settlers. There was also a belief that the worst convicts should be removed from the 'advantages and comforts' of Sydney and sent to remote places. To this end new jails were established at Port Macquarie, north of New-castle (1821), at Macquarie on Tasmania's west coast (1822) and at Port Arthur, on the south-east coast of that island (1832). Jails such as the one at Port Arthur became infamous for their cruelties in the form of floggings, 'dumb cells' and long periods of solitary confinement. Another reason for establishing new territory was the pressing need for agricultural land. By the 1820s and 1830s free settlers moved beyond the bounds of settlement to find suitable land for pasture south of the Murray River, over 600 km (370 miles) from Sydney.

Because of the continuing presence of French ships until the 1820s, there was also a fear that France would attempt to carve out its own territory in some unprotected parts of the country, particularly along the unsettled southern and western coasts. The arrival at Van Diemen's Land of a fleet of French ships in 1802 only served to revive the settlers' insecurities. To strengthen the British presence, a group of 49 convicts in the charge of Lieutenant Bowen estab-lished a settlement at Risdon Cove on the Derwent River, Tasmania, in 1803.

Fear of the French was the prime reason for another brief, and abortive, settle-ment in the south, this time at Port Phillip in October 1803, by a party of marines, free settlers and convicts

A copper engraving by Philip Slaeger of early Parramatta, as seen from the north side of the river. The name is taken from the Darug Aboriginal word for eel, once common here.

Concern that the French might also settle in Western Australia led initially to the establishment of a military outpost at Albany in 1826, and then the founding of the Swan River Colony in 1829, under the command of Captain James Stirling, with Fremantle as its port and Perth the township. Large land grants, in total some 400,000 ha (988,400 acres) were offered to entice settlers to migrate to the new colony. However, because of the impoverished, sandy soil and the scarcity of labour, only 40 ha (100 acres) had been brought into cultivation by 1832. Ironically, the long-term solution to the shortage of labour in the western colony was the importation of convicts in the 1850s, at a time when the eastern colonies had begun abandoning convictism.

Francois Peron was the naturalist on Nicolas Baudin's expedition of 1800. It was suspicion of French intentions that fuelled expansion of settlement in Australia. Prisons such as that at Port Arthur (above left) were built to house convicts who had been removed from the 'comforts' of Sydney.

under Lieutenant-Governor David Collins. However, the failure of the experiment had by December forced Collins to move to a second site, Hobart Town, on the western shore of Sullivans Cove in Van Diemen's Land. Meanwhile, another group of 181 convicts under the command of Lieutenant Colonel Paterson settled on the Tamar River to the north, later to become the site of Launceston. The early years in Van Diemen's Land proved as tough as Sydney's had been, with crop failures and desertions. However, Hobart Town, later shortened to Hobart, with its excellent deepwater port, became a thriving whaling and ship-building hub and by the 1820s was rivalling Sydney as a commercial centre. By 1825 Van Diemen's Land had become independent of New South Wales.

Up the east coast, to the north, Moreton Bay was established as a convict settlement in 1824, although within a year the settlement had been moved further up the river to the site of what would later become Brisbane. A relatively small number of freed convicts made their way to Moreton Bay when the district was opened to settlement in 1842.

The upper Swan, in Western Australia, drawn by J.W. Huggins during Stirling's 1827 exploration of the river.

The Frontier Expands

Stiff-necked and prudish though he may have been, Lachlan Macquarie's governorship saw great advances in the colony. He was taken by Flinders' suggestion of Australia as a name for England's southern acquisition.

The Blue Mountains for many years presented a seemingly impassable barrier to the colonists on the coastal plains.

Exploration

The initial exploration of the continent was by sea, and Matthew Flinders was one of the outstanding navigators of his time, eventually circumnavigating the entire land mass. George Bass and Matthew Flinders explored the south coast of New South Wales from 1795, and by 1799 they had proved that Van Diemen's Land was an island with the discovery of a strait of water between it and the mainland. In the following year Flinders sailed north, looking for suitable harbours and navigable rivers by which to venture inland, eventually reaching Bundaberg.

Flinders, who published *A Voyage to Terra Australis* in 1814, contributed to the adoption of 'Australia' as the name for the whole continent in preference to New Holland, which applied specifically to only half of it. The idea appealed greatly to Governor Lachlan Macquarie when he read of Flinders' suggestion.

By the second decade of the nineteenth century the growth of pastoral industries made landward exploration a priority. A succession of expeditions from 1797 had failed to penetrate inland because of the ruggedness of the barrier to the west, the Blue Mountains. There was considerable speculation about what lay beyond, ranging from settlers' dreams of good grazing land to the fancies of convicts, some of whom were convinced that if they could only escape over the mountains, they could reach China and from there make their way back to England.

It was not until 1813 that three graziers—William Lawson, Gregory Blaxland and William Charles Wentworth—successfully effected a crossing by carefully following the ridges rather than walking through the valleys. Later that year a party led by George William Evans extended the trio's discoveries, reporting the prospect of good land on the western plains. Evans went on to name the Lachlan River. A road across the Blue Mountains was constructed soon afterwards, heralding the advent of farming on the western plains, where in 1815 Bathurst was founded.

The crossing of the mountains stimulated many expeditions to inland New South Wales, Victoria and Queensland. One of the questions that intrigued explorers was what happened to the inland rivers that flowed west. Did they perhaps flow into an inland sea? Surveyor-General John Oxley was one of the first official explorers of inland New South Wales and on

expeditions in 1817 and 1818 followed the Lachlan, Macquarie and Castlereagh Rivers in his search for an inland sea. The search was unsuccessful, but he did discover fertile land for settlement before finding himself at an estuary with a good harbour which he named Port Macquarie after the governor.

Graziers Hamilton Hume and William Hovell in 1824 left Hume's property at Gunning for Western Port, but instead reached Corio Bay. They discovered good land on the way, but their insistence that they had reached Western Port, not Corio Bay, delayed the settlement of Victoria for another decade.

Botanist and explorer Allan Cunningham and his party travelled north from the Liverpool Plains in 1827 in search of land suitable for settlement. They found an inland route through the mountains beyond Moreton Bay to a large area of good grazing country which they named Darling Downs.

Captain Charles Sturt, surely one of the most determined explorers of his day, was keen to survey the river system which continued to mystify the settlers. In 1829 he and Hamilton Hume followed and mapped the Macquarie and Bogan Rivers, and then a river they named the Darling. In the following year Sturt felt he had succeeded when on 9 February his party, which had rowed down the Murrumbidgee in a whaleboat, reached the mouth of the Murray at a freshwater lake which they named Lake Alexandrina. It took a superhuman effort to row back against the current and by the time they returned the crew were exhausted and in poor shape.

The challenge of exploring the outback, in particular the remote and seemingly inhospitable north, also inspired many explorers in the mid-nineteenth century. One of the most famous of these was a young Prussian naturalist, Friedrich Wilhelm Ludwig Leichhardt (1813–1848?), who arrived in Australia in 1842 and led an expedition from Brisbane to Port Essington—a distance of 4800 km (2980 miles)— from 1844 to 1845. Given up for dead, the party's return to Sydney created a sensation. The aim of his second expedition, to cross the northern part of the continent and travel down the west coast to Perth, ended in failure after only 800 km (500 miles), due to bad weather and quarrelling between the expeditioners. Leichhardt and his party disappeared on their third transcontinental expedition which left from Roma, 480 km (300 miles) west of Brisbane, heading again for the north. Nine major search parties over the next 90 years failed to find any clues to the party's disappearance and the mystery of the fate of Ludwig Leichhardt's expedition remains.

Another expedition that ended in tragedy was the epic attempt of Robert O'Hara Burke and W.J. Wills to reach the Gulf of Carpentaria via the Darling River and Cooper Creek. Great crowds gathered in the city of Melbourne to farewell the explorers on 20 August 1860. The party had the backing of the Victorian government and was well equipped; it even boasted 25 camels, specially imported for the journey. When on 11 February the expedition reached the Gulf of Carpentaria, it was hampered by the wet season and suffering from a shortage of provisions, scurvy, attacks by Aborigines and quarrelling among the members. Some poor decisions by Burke cut off the two explorers from their relief party, with the tragic result that they starved to death at Cooper Creek.

However, the expedition of Burke and Wills was not a total failure. Reports of abundant grazing land encouraged settlers to drive their livestock there and by the end of the 1860s a number of cattle and sheep runs had been established in the remote north. Partly

In this watercolour by Augustus Earle, a party of convicts breaks stones on the summit of Mt York during the building of the first road over the Blue Mountains. The view is towards the west and the Bathurst Plains.

telegraph line and the undersea cable to Java enabled Darwin to survive as a permanent settlement. As well, a gold-rush at Pine Creek, 250 km (155 miles) south of the town and the discovery of pearlshell in the nearby seas and in the Torres Strait attracted Asian migrants and helped establish a polyglot community.

Expansion

Although the British authorities continued to send large numbers of convicts to Australia in the 1820s, it became clear that the country's financial and social prospects were good. It also had potential as a source of raw materials, as a focus for fresh avenues of investment and as a growing market for British goods. The temperate climate and the abundance of land were ideal for large-scale farming, enabling Australian-grown wool in particular to reduce British dependence on foreign supplies. From this time on there were increasing numbers of free settlers who chose to emigrate to Australia.

Other colonies were founded on the mainland. Farmers from Van Diemen's Land, frustrated by the shortage of land, now looked across Bass Strait to Port Phillip Bay in Victoria, as yet unsettled. Thomas Henty and his sons applied for permission to acquire land there, but their request was refused by the Colonial Office. While their second request was under consideration, one of the sons, Edward Henty, in 1834 sailed to Portland Bay, the chosen site for their farm. This action triggered a response by a group of Launceston pastoralists who formed the Port Phillip Association. John Batman, acting on their behalf, explored the country around Port Phillip Bay in May

Camels made ideal beasts of burden in outback Australia. Government camel studs were established in various places.

because of the scarcity of suitable grazing, station boundaries stretched enormous distances, with properties measured in square miles rather than acres.

The South Australia-backed expedition in the 'race for the north' was more successful. At his third attempt John McDouall Stuart's horseback expedition crossed the continent from Adelaide to the Arafura Sea, arriving 65 km (40 miles) east of the Northern Territory's Adelaide River on 17 July 1862. Stuart's expedition solved the question of whether or not there was an inland sea—Sturt proved that there was no significant body of water there—and pioneered a suitable corridor through the centre of the continent for the construction of an overland telegraph.

Frustrating French ambitions and developing trade with Asia were the motivating factors behind many of the attempts to create a settlement in the Northern Territory. Military garrisons established at Fort Dundas on Melville Island (1824–28), at Fort Wellington (1824–29) and Victoria (1838–49) on the remote Cobourg Peninsula were short-lived and another settlement in 1864 at Escape Cliffs, 58 km (36 miles) north-east of Darwin, was abandoned after only a few years. Darwin, known as Palmerston until 1911, was established in 1869. Although hopes of agricultural development and trade with Asia failed to materialise, the link with the overland

John Batman persuaded Victorian Aborigines to place their totem marks on a 'title deed' in return for trinkets. It is doubtful if the gifts included the pistol shown in the foreground.

HISTORY SINCE EUROPEAN CONTACT TIMELINE

1642 Another Dutch mariner, Abel Tasman, explores southern coast of Australia, landing on Tasmania and naming it Van Diemen's Land; sails on to New Zealand.

1788 First Fleet lands at Sydney Cove on 26 January and establishes penal colony. **1792** First free settlers attracted to colony by free passage and land grants.

1813 Gregory Blaxland, William Wentworth and William Lawson find a way across the Blue Mountains, previously a major barrier to westward expansion.

1835 John Batman explores Port Phillip area. Later that year, John Pascoe Fawkner occupies land on the Yarra and effectively founds Melbourne.

1858 Overland Telegraph links Adelaide, Melbourne, and Sydney, then Darwin in 1872. **1859** Moreton Bay area becomes separate colony, to be known as Queensland.

1880 Ned Kelly hanged at Melbourne Gaol on 11 November. **1890s** Stock market crashes and droughts lead to decade of economic depression.

1914 Outbreak of World War I. Thousands of Australians fight heroically at Gallipoli in April of the following year, 8700 dying.

1606 Dutch East India ship *Duyfken*, under the command of Willem Jansz, lands on west coast of Cape York **1616** Dutch explorer Dirck Hartog lands at Shark Bay.

1770 Captain James Cook reaches east coast, names it New South Wales and claims it for Britain. His favourable reports inspire British plan to establish penal colonies.

1803 Lieutenant-Governor David Collins leads unsuccessful attempt to create settlement at Port Phillip; he and his party establish township at Hobart the following year.

1824 Penal colony established at Moreton Bay. **1826** Establishment of military garrison leads to founding of Swan River Colony and WA three years later.

1836 A colony for free settlers set up in SA, but struggles to prosper initially. **1851** Discovery of gold at Ophir, NSW, triggers gold-rushes locally and in Victoria.

1868 Following abolition of transportation in Qld (1842), NSW (1852), Tas. (1853), the system finally comes to an end when convict shipments to Western Australia cease.

1901 Following a series of referenda held in all colonies, federation takes place, and the Commonwealth of Australia is subsequently proclaimed on 1 January.

1917 Temperance ment succeeds in fo introduction of 6 p. in pubs. Transcontinen route between Sydne Perth completed

This landscape near Cowra, New South Wales, shows clearly the rich country made available to the settlers once the daunting crossing of the Blue Mountains had been achieved.

1835 and claimed to have had a conveyancing document to some 600,000 acres (243,000 ha) signed by the local Aborigines in return for an assortment of blankets, looking-glasses, beads and other trifles.

The real founder of the city of Melbourne, however, was John Pascoe Fawkner who led another party from Launceston later that same year. He took over land on the Yarra River on 30 August 1835 and on it erected Melbourne's first building. By the end of the year this de facto settlement had gained official recognition. Pastoralists now moved into Victoria from New South Wales and Van Diemen's Land, rapidly swelling the population. By 1842 Melbourne had a population of 4000 and served as a shipping, supply and banking centre for its hinterland.

Adelaide was settled in 1836. Colonel William Light, the first Surveyor-General of South Australia, developed a grid plan on which the city was based. South Australia was founded as a model and planned colony for free settlers on the basis of principles laid down by Edmund Gibbon Wakefield, who argued for systematic colonisation, a balance of classes, sexes and occupations and the sale of land at reasonable prices to independent farmers. South Australia's promoters also aimed to encourage settlers who valued civil and religious liberty. From its inception Adelaide had a high proportion of religious dissenters, and was later to become known as the 'city of churches'. The free colony of South Australia struggled in its first decade. The discovery of copper in 1845 helped save the colony from a threatened collapse.

Criticism of the transportation system increased during the 1830s, some arguing that convictism led to degraded communities. Others contended that transportation discouraged free settlers, who were becoming vital to the economy. In the event, transportation of convicts did not come to an end until 1842 in Queensland, was abolished in New South Wales in 1852 and the last transported felons landed in Tasmania in 1853. To overcome the acute shortage of labour in Western Australia, the transportation of convicts to that colony, which had begun in 1850, continued between 1852 and 1868. In all, about 185,000 people were transported to Australia. Some were broken by the brutality of the system but others prospered in the new land.

Portland, Victoria's first permanent colonial settlement, was a sealing port from 1828. It thrived on whaling until the 1840s when whale numbers declined. A decade later, the town's prosperity revived on the wave of the goldrushes. It has survived as an international shipping port.

8 War ends. Of the ore than 400,000 alians who enlisted, 60,000 have died and have been wounded.

1920 Australia's first airline, Qantas, founded at Winton, Qld.
1927 Federal Parliament moves to new Parliament House in Canberra.

1929 Stock market crash on Wall Street leads to worldwide economic slump. By 1932, one-third of all Australian workers are unemployed.

1939 Britain joins France in declaring war on Germany; Australia follows suit.
1942 Japanese bomb Darwin, killing 243 people and raising fears of invasion.

1945 Japanese surrender on 6 August and war ends. Of the one million Australians who enlisted, 34,000 have lost their lives.

1950 Australia agrees to support United States by sending troops to fight in Korean War.
1953 British nuclear tests begin at Emu, SA.

1966 Prime Minister Harold Holt agrees to send troops to Vietnam. Around 50,000 serve and 500 are killed. Decimal currency introduced; pound replaced by dollar.

1967 In a referendum, voters choose to end discrimination against Aboriginal peoples, granting them citizenship and including them in subsequent censuses.

1970 Anti-Vietnam War protestors stage largest demonstrations ever held in Australia.
1972 Labor government comes to power and introduces wide-ranging reforms.

1975 Labor government dismissed by Governor-General Sir John Kerr.
1984 Introduction of Medicare, a tax-funded public health system.

1988 Australians celebrate bicentenary of arrival of First Fleet at Sydney Cove. Indigenous peoples mark the day with protests against the invasion of Australia.

1992 Land rights claim led by Eddie Mabo results in High Court rejecting idea of *terra nullius* and declaring that indigenous peoples hold native title to ancestral lands.

1996 Gunman Martin Bryant massacres 36 people at Port Arthur historic site in Tas. The incident prompts the introduction of tighter gun controls nationwide.

1996 With Wik Decision, High Court rules that pastoral leases do not necessarily extinguish native title.
1997 Landslide at Thredbo kills 18 people.

1999 Voters reject republican model presented at referendum, thereby retaining constitutional monarchy. Australian troops lead peacekeeping efforts in East Timor.

2000 Sydney hosts highly successful Olympic Games.
2001 Centenary of Federation celebrated throughout the country on 1 January.

The goldrushes

Although gold had been found by 1840, the matter was kept quiet by the colonial authorities because they feared a goldrush would lead to civil chaos and dislocation. However, by 1851 the authorities could see the advantages of goldmining and were even offering incentives to potential prospectors. Using techniques he had learned on the goldfields of California, Edmund Hargraves proclaimed that he had discovered gold near Bathurst and, although he had panned only a few specks of the precious metal, claimed the huge government reward of £10,000.

So began the chaos that is a goldrush. Fulfilling the direst predictions of the authorities, many young men abandoned their jobs in the towns, deserted ships and left sheep runs in the rush to get rich.

Prospecting for gold offered not only the prospect of sudden wealth but an escape from the drab routine of everyday life. It acted as a magnet not only to Australian hopefuls, but to adventurers from all over the world. Within the space of a few months the rush in New South Wales was overshadowed by incredibly rich finds at Ballarat, Bendigo, Buninyong and Mount Alexander in Victoria. By the end of 1851 there were 20,000 people on the Victorian diggings.

Resentment over the high cost of a miner's right, a licence costing £1 10s a month, led to a celebrated clash between government troops and goldminers at Eureka near Ballarat on 3 December 1854. The aggrieved miners erected a stockade over which they flew a blue-and-white flag featuring the Southern Cross. During the brief clash, 300 soldiers charged 150 poorly armed diggers, killing 30 of them; six soldiers were killed. Although the miners had been defeated, there was public outrage at the government's brutality and the leaders of the uprising who were charged were later acquitted and their demands—the abolition of the licence fee and the right to vote—met.

The discovery of gold had a dramatic effect on both Australian society and the local economy. The population of Australia, less than half a million in 1851, doubled in a decade. Victoria's population jumped from a mere 77,345 on the eve of the rush to 540,322 in 1861. The goldrush attracted a larger body of more affluent immigrants than before, people who were able to pay their own fare and who were free with their money. Most of the new arrivals were British and Irish but large numbers of Americans, French, Italians, Germans, Poles and Hungarians also came. Some 40,000 Chinese made up the largest foreign contingent. There were some ugly outbreaks of racial violence against the Chinese when the gold discoveries began to peter out.

Gold launched a period of economic expansion, optimism and further immigration. Gold bullion worth millions of pounds was shipped to London and in return Australians were able to afford more British goods. In the early 1850s the Australian colonies took 15 per cent of British exports.

There was a series of later goldrushes in north Queensland in the 1870s and 1880s and in the arid countryside around Coolgardie and Kalgoorlie in Western Australia in the 1890s. There were also fresh finds in New South Wales, but none was as large or as spectacular as the Victorian goldrush of the 1850s.

A New Society

The bush

Although most Australians live by or near the coastal fringe, the bush—the country's untamed heart—has always exerted a powerful influence on the national imagination. In the second half of the nineteenth century, Australian artists discovered the bush as a source of unique subject matter and spectacular light. The stockman became an icon for the new country—independent, egalitarian and staunchly loyal to his mates. In recent years, however, feminist historians of this outback hero view his fondness for the life of the bush as a repudiation of domestic responsibility.

During the colonial era, bushrangers (a sort of rural highwayman) were a real threat to travellers and settlers. Their daring deeds were romanticised and celebrated in song, reflecting the Australian fondness for disrespect of authority. One of them operated in the Hawkesbury–Nepean area in the late 1820s and although he made life difficult for many settlers, his exploits were celebrated in 'Bold Jack Donahoe', a bush ballad that was, and still is, widely sung in many pubs. Later, some of the bushrangers of the 1860s and 1870s encouraged the public's tendency to mythologising their exploits by adopting colourful and romantic aliases such as 'Thunderbolt' (Frederick Ward) and 'Captain Moonlite' (Andrew Scott).

Frank Gardiner, Ben Hall and John Gilbert, all the sons of poor settlers in rural New South Wales, intercepted gold deliveries and stole horses from wealthy squatters in the 1850s. In the 1860s 'Bold' Ben Hall led a notorious gang which intercepted coaches, robbed banks and held up hotels. But of them all, Ned Kelly and his gang are Australia's most famous bush-rangers and the saga of their deeds continues to fascinate artists and writers. The son of a poor Irish ex-convict, Ned grew up resenting those who had land and privilege and exercised authority. The Kelly gang held up coaches, robbed banks and even held Jerilderie, a New South Wales town, to ransom for two days. They relied on the sympathy and support of many poor farmers and labourers, people in a

The death of the bushranger Thunderbolt near Uralla, New South Wales. Many in Australia still see these outlaws of the past as romantic enemies of tyranny.

A stockman sits on his swag and contemplates the waterhole at Combo, in Queensland. It is here that the poem Waltzing Matilda is supposedly set.

The sea is a strong presence in Tasmania, Australia's island State. These fishing boats are moored at Hobart's Victoria Dock.

Bourke Street, Melbourne. The commercial centre was financed by the gold-wealth of the mid-nineteenth century, which transformed colonial society beyond recognition.

The cities

From the 1820s to 1900 Australia transformed itself from a largely rural society to a highly urban one: the percentage of Australians living in towns of 2500 or more increased from 30 per cent in 1828 to 55 per cent by 1911, making the country considerably more urbanised than Argentina (50 per cent), the United States (46 per cent) or Canada (37 per cent).

The most spectacular population growth took place in Melbourne which until 1851 had been a small outpost and part of New South Wales. Thanks to the gold-rush—Victoria was producing one-third of the world's gold by the 1850s—the city's population increased dramatically. For the next 40 years, Melbourne, and Victoria, grew faster than anywhere else in Australia. Not until the 1890s did Sydney's population match that of Melbourne.

During the nineteenth century there was intense rivalry between Sydney and Melbourne—a rivalry that continues today. The latter's main claim to superiority was that it had been established by free settlers, not convicts. Much of its appeal lies in the fact that it was a well-planned city with well-located suburban development supported by a good transport system. Sydney's development, by contrast, was more haphazard. However, while Sydney had to endure criticism of its convict origins and a more raffish population, it could boast of the superior attractions of its harbour and extensive waterways.

situation similar to their own, who were frustrated with the corruption and indifference of the police force and those who saw themselves as landed gentry (known as the 'squattocracy') to their plight. In a final shoot-out with the police, Ned Kelly donned home-made heavy 'armour' and a helmet with a narrow slit. The surreal outfit inspired a series of famous paintings by Sidney Nolan and even featured in the Opening Ceremony of the Sydney Olympic Games in the year 2000. Edward Kelly was hanged on 11 November 1880, aged 25, at the Melbourne jail while thousands of his supporters held a quiet vigil outside.

Other cities enjoyed spurts of growth later in the century: Adelaide grew fastest in the 1870s and Brisbane in the 1880s and Perth, benefiting from the Kalgoorlie and Coolgardie goldrushes, in the 1890s.

Communications and transport

The 'tyranny of distance', a very apt phrase coined by the twentieth-century historian Geoffrey Blainey, has always been a central theme of Australian history. Communications between the colonies and the outside world before the 1850s were primitive. Transportation, primarily by sailing ships, was equally slow in this period, leaving the new settlers isolated from the wider world and, to a lesser extent, from each other. Before 1852 the only communication between Australia and Europe involved a journey of as long as six months by sailing ship. In May of that year the P&O (Peninsula and Oriental Steam Navigation Co.) steamer *Chusan* left Southampton, arriving with the Royal Mail in Sydney on 6 August, the forerunner of quicker, more reliable transport and communications. Because of its importance the service was heavily subsidised by colonial governments.

Following the end of the Crimean War in the mid-nineteenth century, the geographical remoteness of Australia gave rise to much irrational fear that the Russians might invade. The completion in 1857 of Fort Denison on Pinchgut Island in Sydney Harbour was one measure designed to augment the defences of colonial New South Wales. Later in the century it was believed that the primary threat to the colonies might come from the peoples of Asia.

From the 1850s land transport was dominated by the now legendary firm of Cobb & Co. Recognising that transport between Melbourne and the Victorian goldfields was poor, American Freeman Cobb with three of his country-men imported several coaches from the United States. These 'Concord' coaches (they were built in Concord, New Hampshire, for use in conditions like those to be found on the Australian goldfields) with their leather 'suspension' and sturdy frames, proved ideally suited to Australian bush roads and began a service which became highly popular and profitable, soon spreading to the outback and eventually throughout the eastern States. Vehicles bearing

the legend Cobb & Co. plied many routes in eastern Australia until 1924, though the company had by then changed hands many times.

However, by the 1880s, horse-drawn coaches were superseded by a network of railways, which linked many country towns with metropolitan areas. From this time Cobb & Co. coaches survived by providing services to more remote communities. Because each colony had developed independently of the others, each had different railway gauges and customs posts at the borders. This amazing lack of uniformity was yet another incentive in the push for the Federation of Australia. However, although Federation went ahead in 1901, a common rail gauge was not to be achieved until many decades later.

The coming of the overland telegraph linked Adelaide, Melbourne and Sydney by 1858. Tasmania was added to the network in 1859, when a submarine cable was laid in Bass Strait. Brisbane followed soon after in 1861. The completion in 1872 of the line from Port Augusta in South Australia to Darwin in the Northern Territory (a distance of 2900 km or 1800 miles) was achieved in the face of extreme hardship. It was scheduled to be built in 18 months, but took over two years at a cost of £480,000 and six lives. The telegraph service was provided by operators who lived in small huts, most of them in extreme isolation. Public banquets were held in Adelaide, Sydney and London to celebrate the great achievement, and thereafter, telegraph messages travelled by submarine cable to Java (Indonesia) and overland, via Asia, to Europe. The line to Perth, completing the national network, was not completed until 1877.

From 1878, a mere two years after Bell first demonstrated his invention, trunk calls made with the telephone also helped reduce the tyranny of

Work on a standard-gauge railway line across Australia did not end until 1995. A passenger travelling from Brisbane to Perth once suffered nine changes of train, and was carried on lines of five different gauges.

From its inauspicious beginnings as Queensland and Northern Territory Air Services, Qantas rose to a place of prominence in international air travel.

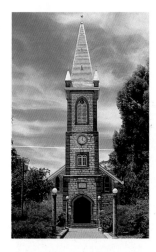

Many Germans emigrated to Australia during the goldrushes. In South Australia they built churches and schools in all the towns they established.

distance. Telephone exchanges originally operated privately but government-run services had become the norm by the 1880s.

The first decades of the twentieth century were witness to a number of remarkable feats of aviation. The Smith brothers won £10,000 for flying to Australia from Britain in under 30 days, and Ray Parer and J.C. McIntosh made the first single-engined aircraft flight from Britain in 1920. Eight years later, Bert Hinkler made the first solo flight from Britain to Australia. These events were avidly followed by the Australian public and the world's media and inspired many commercial and government initiatives. Also in 1920, Hudson Fysh and Paul McGinness, who had been flyers during the war, founded Queensland and Northern Territory Aerial Services, later to achieve fame as Qantas. The first airmail service in Australia was launched in 1921 and in 1928 the Flying Doctor Service—a medical initiative that sought to overcome the isolation of outback communities—was started in Melbourne by the Reverend John Flynn.

Immigration to 1900

Continuing goldrushes saw impressive increases in the Australian population over five decades from the 1850s. Numbers grew from less than half a million in 1851 to 3,773,801 by 1901. Unlike the period prior to the 1850s, when immigrants came as convicts or were assisted to emigrate under government schemes, many of the new settlers paid their own way, attracted by reports of a growing and dynamic economy.

At the time of Federation (1901), 98 per cent of new Australians were predominantly British or Irish. The Irish, roughly one-third of the population, were the most significant minority and as their religion was different from the Protestants who held the reins of power, sectarianism was a lively issue in Australia well into the twentieth century.

Significant minorities from many other European cultures also migrated to Australia in the second half of the nineteenth century. Forming one of the largest groups were the Germans who arrived at the time of the goldrushes, settling mainly in South Australia and Queensland. People also migrated in large numbers from the United States. For the most part such communities fitted into Australian society, though the Germans did experience some harassment, official and otherwise, at the time of World War I.

It was a different story with the Chinese, the largest non-European group in Australia and easily identifiable by their different appearance, customs, language and religion. At the time of the goldrushes there were some 2000 Chinese resident here, but gold brought another 40,000 (mostly male) Chinese to Australia. During the frenetic Victorian goldrushes of the 1850s, the Chinese formed 8 per cent of the population. One of the causes of resentment towards them was their habit of working separately from the other miners. When gold discoveries began to peter out, the frustration of the other miners vented itself in racism towards this easily identifiable group. The Chinese digger now became a target for ridicule and violence, stereotyped as a dirty, disease-ridden opium smoker. One of the worst instances of violence occurred on 30 June 1861 at Lambing Flat, later renamed Young, in New South Wales, when a large mob attacked Chinese prospectors, burnt their tents and drove them off the diggings. New acts were passed which made it more difficult for Chinese to come to New South Wales and even excluded them specifically from some of the goldfields.

From 1863 to 1904 approximately 61,000 Pacific Islanders, known as 'Kanakas', were recruited

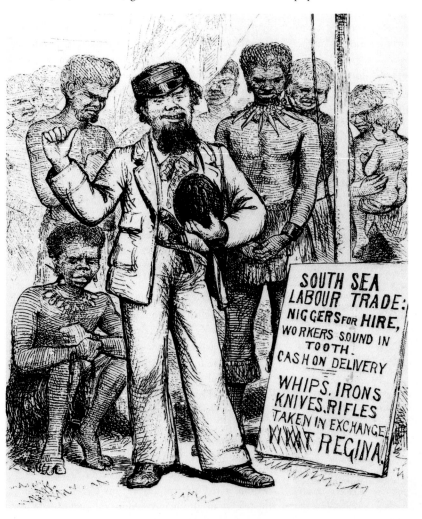

Kanakas—from the Hawaiian word for 'man'—came mainly from Vanuatu. Often removed at gunpoint from their homes, they were brought to Australia to work at tasks 'unsuited to white men'.

to provide cheap labour for the sugar and cotton industries in Queensland and northern New South Wales. While some immigrants from Vanuatu, the Solomon Islands and the New Britain archipelago came voluntarily, others were the victims of 'black-birding', kidnapped at the point of a gun. Kanakas worked initially as indentured labourers but the harsh conditions of work, sub-standard housing and food produced a high mortality rate and this, along with poor wages, led many critics to view the process as a form of slavery. Eventually Queensland's government recognised in 1885 that blackbirding involved at best employment under false pretences and at worst kidnapping. In the years after federation some 462 ex-labourers were repatriated by the Commonwealth Government, although some were permitted to stay. Some opposed their continuing presence because it went against the concept of a 'White Australia'.

This idea, which gathered momentum around the centenary of European settlement, was prompted by a great and at times almost hysterical fear of what was often popularly referred to as the 'Yellow Peril'—the notion that unchecked multitudes of people from Asia, China in particular, would flood Australia and threaten white dominance. It sprang in part from a belief that a mixture of races was socially dangerous and a source of pollution, both moral and physical.

The Chinese, who had migrated to Australia in significant numbers in the 1850s, had long been the object of suspicion. Because of their willingness to work for low wages, it was believed they threatened the jobs of Australian workers. This was far from the truth: in fact, many of the Chinese in Australia were self-employed as market gardeners and as owners of restaurants and laundries. By this time, however, Anti-Chinese Leagues had been formed in a number of cities. Feelings against 'John Chinaman' reached a peak in 1888 when a ship carrying immigrants from Hong Kong was met by howling mobs and could not land its passengers in either Sydney or Melbourne.

At the height of this anti-Chinese feeling an inter-colonial Conference of Premiers debated the 'Chinese question'. The participants favoured a severe curtailment of Chinese immigration to Australia and even restrictions on the movement of Chinese from one colony to another. This stance led to debate between the British Secretary of State, Lord Knutsford, and the various colonial governments. Knutsford pointed out that the Hong Kong Chinese were citizens of the British Empire and that he opposed the development of an immigration policy which was based on race. Moreover, he contended that such an action would also be detrimental to trading relations with China. However, his points were ignored, and by the 1890s the colonial governments' racist policies had been broadened to include all so-called 'coloured' peoples. (One exception was the government of Queensland which tried to exclude Kanakas from this definition because of their usefulness to the economy.)

One of the first pieces of legislation passed by the new Federal Parliament in 1901 was the *Immigration Restriction Act* which installed the White Australia

At the height of the goldrush the Chinese in Australia numbered about 40,000. This group is probably on its way to the Palmer rush, on Cape York Peninsula.

The Australian Labor Party had its beginnings in the great strike of 1890, in which the shearers played a prominent role. Scab labour was recruited for work on the wharves (right), the shearing sheds and other vital industries, and received police protection.

Policy as the national priority. While many of the colonies had moved to restricted immigration policies before 1901, this Act endorsed and provided more prominence and publicity to this odious concept of immigration based on race.

The unions and the Labor Party 1850–1915

The discovery of gold in the 1850s made Australia a prosperous nation and workers were able to achieve better rates of pay and conditions than their counterparts in many other countries. Their better conditions were won, in part, by the active agency of the trade unions who were instrumental in maintaining a fair wage and reasonable hours, together with a safe work environment for members. By the 1890s workers in the largest industries—wharf labourers and railway workers in the cities, and miners and shearers in rural areas—were unionised. However, with falling wool prices during the depression of the 1890s, employers feared reduced profits and sought to cut wages and introduce non-union labour. As a result there ensued a classic confrontation between the employers, who favoured freedom of contract, on the one hand, and on the other the unions, who wanted a closed shop.

The clash precipitated the great maritime strike of 1890. Beginning on the ships, the dispute spread to the wharves, sheep stations and mines. Employers hit back with the employment of non-union labour. Many people were desperate for employment and as a consequence some—vilified as 'scabs' and 'blacklegs'

It is 1 January 1901. Under a plaster-of-Paris dome built for the occasion, the Commonwealth of Australia comes into being.

by the strikers—were prepared to work under less-favourable conditions. Inevitably this led to pitched battles when unionists clashed with the scabs, who were supported by soldiers and mounted police.

At Barcaldine in central Queensland, shearers and shed-hands raised the Southern Cross—the flag of the Eureka stockade—and took up arms, declaring that they would fight for their rights. However, the unions were crushed and humiliated wherever they fought, their leaders arrested and jailed, and their funds confiscated. The employers, the army and the police, with the backing of the courts, won a number of similar battles over the employment conditions of shearers and miners during the next decade.

The trade unions had learnt a bitter lesson—they could not fight alone for the rights of workers, they required parliamentary allies to support their cause. In 1891 workers gathered beneath a spreading gum tree at Barcaldine, Queensland, to choose a labour candidate for Parliament. It was the beginning of the trade-union based labour parties which soon emerged in the various colonies and began to make their presence felt. In New South Wales, for example, 36 Labor candidates were elected to the Legislative Assembly in 1891 and held the balance of power. Labor also held the balance of power in Queensland in 1893.

South Australia in 1894 became the first colony to enfranchise women. A few years later, following the passage of a bill through the Federal Parliament in 1902, most women (women of non-European backgound, including Aboriginal women, were for the most part excluded) could vote in federal elections.

Labor won 14 of the 75 seats in the first election for the Federal House of Representatives in 1901 and its support of the Protectionists, led by Deakin, (who favoured tariffs on imports as a means of protecting Australian produce) enabled it to form government. A Labor minority government, led by J.C. Watson, held office for four months in 1904 and yet another minority Labor government, under Andrew Fisher, was in power for seven months in 1909. Labor held power in its own right for the first time in 1910 following Fisher's resounding victory at the polls, which saw it win 43 of the 75 seats. However, it was not until 1915 that a national labour organisation, the Australian Labor Party, was established.

World War I

The Anzac tradition

When Britain declared war on Germany on 4 August 1914 there was great initial enthusiasm in Australia, and by the end of the year 50,000 men had enlisted for service. Leader of the Labor Opposition Andrew Fisher, who was elected Prime Minister the following month, declared that Australia would fight for the mother country to 'our last man and our last shilling'.

Australian soldiers were initially sent to Egypt where they fought alongside New Zealand troops in the Australian and New Zealand Army Corps, at first abbreviated to A & NZAC then later entering the language as Anzac. The Australian troops were also known as 'diggers', a name probably originating in the goldrushes and perhaps referring to the fact that they seemed always to be digging trenches.

In the early dawn of 25 April 1915 Australian troops landed at Gallipoli, Turkey, and stormed the precipitous slopes. Unable to dislodge the Turks, the Anzacs dug in and refused to be budged. Another major attack was mounted at Lone Pine, above Anzac Cove, on 6 August 1915 when the Anzacs again charged the enemy, who was barely 100 m (330 feet) away. In only a few days some 4000 Anzacs lost their lives. Despite the fact that 8000 men had been killed during the campaign, the evacuation of Gallipoli, which took place five days before Christmas 1915, was a skilful operation and Anzacs were seen as heroes who had fought with great bravery despite the poor planning and execution of their largely British commanders. English journalist Ellis Ashmead Bartlett, for example, declared that there had been 'no finer feat in this war' than the glorious defeat at Gallipoli and English poet John Masefield further encouraged the myth-making by describing the Anzacs as 'those smiling and glorious young giants' and praising their 'physical beauty and nobility of bearing'. However, it was Australian historian C.E.W. Bean who elevated the Anzacs to their now-legendary status, making a connection between the land and its progeny, writing that 'the wild independent pastoral life of Australia, if it makes rather wild men, makes superb soldiers'.

Since Australia had never fought a war in its own right, the Anzacs' performance at Gallipoli was seen as a proving ground for the nation's courage. The landing was celebrated in Australia on 25 April 1916 as Anzac Day and thereafter became a public holiday with a dawn service to mark the time of the landing. Despite today's different attitudes to war, the annual dawn ceremonies held at Gallipoli and throughout Australia continue to attract large numbers, many younger people among them, and continues to inspire both writers, composers and film-makers.

As the war dragged on for years rather than the mere months that had been anticipated, enlistment figures fell dramatically. To rectify this situation Prime Minister Billy Hughes (who became known as the 'Little Digger' because of his efforts during and after the war) in 1917 proposed two controversial referenda to introduce conscription. After much bitter and divisive debate, along with vigorous opposition from a loose coalition of trade unionists, farmers and Irish–Australians, both referenda were defeated.

War memorials are a feature of almost every Australian town and city. Hardly surprising when one considers that in some small communities virtually every male who could do so enlisted.

William Morris Hughes being applauded by troops in 1917. Feted as the 'Little Digger' for his militaristic stance, Hughes favoured conscription during the Great War.

The unlicensed playing of two-up, or swy, a game in which a kip is used to toss two coins in the air (above and at right) and bets placed on the face they will show on landing, is still illegal in most of Australia. However, the call to battle against the odds, 'Come in spinner', may still be heard in many places throughout the land.

The war had a profound and long-lasting impact on Australia, with virtually every community and family contributing members. From a population of approximately five million some 417,000 enlisted, with 330,000 of these sent to Europe and Africa, 59,000 were killed and another 174,000 wounded. For their services, returning troops were promised land grants and as a result nearly 40,000 former soldiers were settled on small holdings, many of them in areas newly opened to settlement.

Drinkers, gamblers and wowsers

The absence of so many men on war service enabled the temperance movement, bolstered by a conservative alliance of Protestants, some trade unions and a home-based women's vote, to secure an important victory in 1917: a majority of those Australians who remained at home voted in the affirmative in a referendum to decide whether or not hotels should close at 6 p.m. It led to the infamous custom known as the 'six o'clock swill' in which, during the last minutes before closing patrons lined up a succession of full beer glasses which they raced to finish in the time remaining. To accommodate the inevitable spillage of beer, pubs had tiled walls and floors which could be cleaned simply by hosing them down.

This state of affairs lasted until the 1960s when conservative forces became less influential, resulting in a liberalisation of the liquor laws. The maintenance of Sunday as the Sabbath, another key item in the Protestant agenda, also declined, leading to larger audiences at public entertainments such as cinemas and sporting events.

Before and after the goldrush of the 1850s there had been few restrictions on drinking and gambling, which had been popular recreations for convicts. By that time 'two-up', a game in which coins are spun and the outcome bet on, had become the archetypal Australian pastime. Much gambling was also focused on the popular sport of horseracing.

From the late nineteenth century on, however, middle-class Protestants joined with conservative political parties to stop what they saw as profligate behaviour. Irish–Australians and the Labor Party, on the other hand, frequently opposed this agenda which they saw as an attempt to restrict the leisure activities of the working classes. Their efforts notwithstanding, 'local option' legislation was passed in New South Wales in 1905, enabling individual local electorates to determine the closing times of hotels sited within their boundaries. Legislation was also introduced in a number of State parliaments to restrict and control gambling. The term 'wowser', meaning 'killjoy', was used to describe these activities. It has been attributed to John Norton of the Sydney newspaper *Truth*, who invented the word as an acronym of We Only Want Social Evils Remedied. However, by the end of World War I, organised Protestantism was in decline and State governments began to welcome the additional revenue generated by official gaming and betting.

The Australian government continued its laissez-faire attitude towards gambling, giving its citizens more opportunities to gamble than those in most other countries. Many new forms of gambling have been introduced, including the on-course totalisator, the legalisation of poker machines (in 1956), the establishment of the TAB (Totalizator Agency Board), first established in Victoria in 1960, and the opening of casinos in all the major cities following on from the opening of the Wrest Point Casino in Hobart in 1973. There is also a host of lotteries along with games offering instant prize-money.

Although politicians regularly debate the social problems arising from gambling, the revenue it brings to government coffers continues to grow, providing no incentive for State governments to intervene. And whatever the merits or problems of gambling, most people in the country pause to enjoy a flutter on the running of the annual Melbourne Cup horse race, which, with good reason, has been described as 'the race that stops a nation'.

More like public toilets than hotels. The ceramic tiles that lined many eastern States hotels allowed the bars to be hosed out after the orgy of drinking that was the 'six o'clock swill'.

The Depression and the 1930s

The stockmarket crash on Wall Street in October 1929 marked the formal beginning of a world-wide economic slump, the Great Depression. Australia suffered earlier and more severely than many other countries because its economy was based heavily on the export of primary products, notably wool and wheat, and on overseas borrowings.

The Depression created a dramatic rise in unemployment: about one in three workers in Australia were out of work by 1932. The country also suffered from ballooning foreign debt and soon consumed about half the amount of revenue earned previously by exports. Government at all levels appeared powerless to solve the social and economic problems of the day. Local councils and the Salvation Army organised soup kitchens and other community projects to help. Those without jobs received a small 'dole' and State governments established a system known as sustenance, or 'susso', whereby the out-of-work received some assistance in the form of food and clothing in return for involvement in public works, such as clearing land or building roads.

There were mass demonstrations by those out of work in 1930 and 1931. City-dwellers who could not afford to pay rents were evicted and thousands of the unemployed took to bush roads with a swag (a rolled bundle of belongings) and a billy (a container for boiling water). Others gravitated to the shanty towns which sprang up on wasteland and riverbanks. The Communist Party started the Unemployed Workers' Movement in 1930 which organised marches on government offices and took up the cause of tenants evicted by landlords. 'Rabbitohs' (the catchers and sellers of wild-rabbit meat) now became familiar figures on suburban streets. The unremitting gloom engendered by the Depression saw the achievements of cricketer Don Bradman and the racehorse Phar Lap eagerly seized upon by a public yearning for some good news. Escapist movies were also popular.

The economic and social emergency brought on by the Depression strained the country's democratic traditions, widening the social gap between the out-of-work and the employed and leading to the growth of extremist political groups. The Labor government of James Scullin, elected at the time of the Wall Street crash, was defeated in a landslide by the conservative United Australia Party, led by Joe Lyons, in December 1931. In New South Wales, however, Labor leader Jack Lang was in 1930 elected for a second time on a radical platform to restore employment by increased public works and and his proposal to withhold the interest payments on overseas loans. Lang's stance helped spawn the quasi-military New Guard, inspired by the European Fascists and Nazis, which achieved notoriety when one of its members, F.E. de Groot, slashed the ribbon ahead of the premier to open the Sydney Harbour Bridge in 1932. De Groot declared that he did so 'in the name of His Majesty the King and all decent people'. The Lang government came to a spectacular end, dismissed by the Governor of New South Wales, Sir Philip Game, in the same year, for what Game called Lang's 'defiance of the law' in managing the State's fiscal policy.

Although the worst years of the Depression were from 1930 to 1934, it took most of the 1930s for the Australian economy to recover from its effects. There was considerable growth in the manufacturing sector by the late 1930s but rural recovery was much slower. By 1939 there had been no real return to the more prosperous conditions seen in the 1920s.

It is 1932 and the arch of the Sydney Harbour Bridge is about to be joined. Until the bridge's completion, Sydney relied greatly on the harbour ferries.

Victims of the Great Crash. These men living in a rock shelter in Sydney's Domain in the 1930s may have left behind wives and children to 'tramp for work'.

World War II and the 1940s

Following the Japanese bombing of Darwin in 1942, there was a scramble to strengthen defences. This bunker is at Buffalo Creek in the Northern Territory.

Perhaps because World War I had been so protracted and traumatic, there was far less public enthusiasm to support the 'mother country' when Britain declared war on Germany on 3 September 1939. The Prime Minister Robert Menzies, however, declared that as Britain was at war, therefore Australia was also at war. However, Australia's deferential attitude to her overseas allies was to change with a change of leadership later in the war. In 1942 Prime Minister John Curtin, despite pressure from Winston Churchill and the US President Franklin Roosevelt who wanted them sent to Rangoon, brought the Australian troops home.

In August 1944 about 1100 Japanese prisoners broke out of the prison camp at Cowra, New South Wales. A memorial garden to the 234 Japanese and four guards who died now attracts many visitors to the town.

At the outset of hostilities the Communist Party was outlawed because of its opposition to war. Later, the Curtin government also restructured the economy so that wages, prices and rents were fixed and there were extensive controls on industry and employment. Women played a significant role in this war. In July 1942, a national Women's Land Army was formed, with a permanent force of over 2000, to assist with rural production. Women also relieved a labour shortage in many jobs in war industries, factories and transport. In 1944, 52,000 were serving in the three services and in various nursing and auxiliary services.

The first Australian troops to participate in the war fought in the Middle East and Greece, helping to achieve notable successes at Tobruk in North Africa, where they played a crucial role in preventing a major German victory, and El Alamein in Egypt's Western Desert. Their enemies dubbed them the 'Rats of Tobruk', paying a back-handed compliment to their tenacity and heroism in this arena.

Japan's entry into the hostilities in December 1941, when they bombed the US naval base at Pearl Harbor, dramatically changed the war in the Pacific. Soon after the attack a number of divisions, notably the 6th and 7th, were shipped from Europe to this new theatre. The Japanese quickly took control of the Philippines, Hong Kong, Malaya and Burma and swept through South-East Asia. In the process the two leading British ships, *Prince of Wales* and *Repulse*, were sunk off Malaya on 10 December. The surrender of Singapore on 15 February 1942 was considered a disaster for the Allied forces because it had formerly been regarded as impregnable. The Japanese took 130,000 prisoners, 15,384 Australians among them. In Burma they forced Allied prisoners of war and Asian labourers to work in appalling conditions on a railway link between Burma and Thailand. Of Japan's 275,000 prisoners, 94,000 died. Australian army surgeon Edward 'Weary' Dunlop, whose diaries were published in 1986, showed great courage and ingenuity in helping Australian soldiers cope with a range of tropical diseases and became a hero, almost a saint, to many whom he helped to survive.

With the British defeats by land and sea in South-East Asia, Australia appeared vulnerable to invasion and its worst fears were realised when the Japanese bombed Darwin on 19 February 1942. Eight ships in the harbour were sunk, many buildings destroyed and 243 people killed. The small coastal town of Broome, in Western Australia, was also bombed on 3 March, leaving 70 people dead. In May that same year, five Japanese submarines surfaced 16 km (10 miles) off Sydney and three midget submarines made their way into Sydney Harbour. One was destroyed, another was caught in a net and the third escaped, there was near panic among the population: plans for evacuations were developed, air-raid shelters built, trenches dug, and many women and children fled from the cities to the country. By July 1942 the Japanese forces had reached New Guinea and it seemed an invasion of Australia was imminent.

It was now that Curtin appealed to America for help. The new Australia–US alliance was quickly put in place when Curtin surrendered military control of the country to General MacArthur, Supreme Commander of the Allied forces in the south-west Pacific, in March 1942. For the Americans, Australia was a convenient base for their war against Japan in the Pacific and from that time US servicemen were a highly visible presence in Australia. Almost a million visited in total, though there were never more than 100,000 in the country at any one time.

Although the Australian cruiser HMAS *Perth* and the USS *Houston* had been sunk in the Java Sea in March 1942, a joint Australian–US fleet inflicted the first defeat over the Japanese in the Battle of the Coral Sea in May of that year, followed by another naval victory at Midway in June. On land in New Guinea, Australian and American soldiers struggled hard to thwart the Japanese, fighting in the dense jungle of

Indigenous Papuans carried supplies and acted as stretcher bearers, often at great personal risk. Their efforts earned them the name 'Fuzzy-wuzzy angels'.

the highlands, more often than not in heavy mud and rain. The battle for control of the Kokoda Trail, a crude track over the forbidding Owen Stanley Range, cost the lives of 12,000 Japanese, 2000 Australians and approximately 500 indigenous Papuans, whose heroic support of the Australian troops earned them the title 'Fuzzy-wuzzy angels'. Two months later Australian troops halted the Japanese advance in New Guinea at Milne Bay on the south-eastern tip of Papua, the first victory gained by land forces over the Japanese.

Three more years of hard, bitter fighting were to be endured before the Japanese surrendered on 6 August 1945. Approximately 37,000 Australians died in World War II, about half as many as died in World War I. It is disturbing, too, to note that of the 30,000 Australians taken prisoner during the war (about 22,000 of them held by the Japanese), only some 14,000 lived to return to their homes in Australia.

Veterans of the bitter fighting in New Guinea. Troops of Australia's 39th Battalion.

After the War

Asian immigration has had many positive influences. This Buddhist temple near Wollongong, New South Wales, provides many services to the local community.

Barbara Ann Porritt, aged 21, was Australia's one millionth post-war immigrant. She landed with her husband Dennis in Melbourne on 8 November 1955.

Populate or perish

In the late 1940s Labor immigration minister Arthur Calwell's racist quip that 'two Wongs don't make a white' echoed widespread fears of the Yellow Peril which were as strong as ever after the war and were now fuelled by hatred of the Japanese. However, because of the public anxiety that Australia's small population would have been unable to withstand invasion during the conflict, a succession of governments now pushed the line that Australia needed to 'populate or perish'. Immigration also provided a means to further develop the economy and to secure labour for ambitious projects such as the Snowy River Hydro-Electric Scheme, begun in 1945. After World War II Australia became an attractive destination for a variety of displaced people and refugees, mainly from a number of European countries. Although Britons in particular were encouraged to migrate to Australia, paying only a nominal £10 passage fee, thereby entering Australian folklore as '£10 Poms', an insufficient number were prepared to do so, and the government looked elsewhere to fill its immigrant quotas. From 1945 to 1965 1.5 million Europeans

migrated to Australia: among them were Italians, Greeks, Yugoslavs, Dutch, Germans and Poles. Life for many of these new arrivals was initially difficult and discouraging. They were crammed into 'migrant hostels' with primitive accommodation and facilities and many were treated as second-class citizens and had to endure xenophobic labels such as 'dago', 'wog', 'reffo', 'Balt' and 'spag'.

During the 1970s there was even more diversity in the immigrant flow, with a growing number of the newcomers of non-European, non-English-speaking and, in some instances, non-Christian background. The Middle East provided a significant source with numbers of immigrants arriving from countries such as Egypt, Lebanon and Turkey.

By the 1980s migration from Asia, particularly Vietnam and China, became possible following the relaxation of the White Australia Policy in the 1960s, and migrants from these countries became the fastest-growing group. Again, prejudice reared its head and Asian immigration once more became a matter of controversy, as it had been during the goldrushes. In 1984, historian Geoffrey Blainey initiated a campaign to reduce the total immigrant intake, arguing that the

increasing number of non-Europeans was testing the community's tolerance and could only lead in the end to long-term social problems.

In the 1990s One Nation leader Pauline Hanson played on the perceptions of the disenfranchised, in particular those living in economically depressed rural areas, that migrants were to blame for unemployment and a host of other ills, and campaigned against Asian immigration. During the decade, significant numbers of immigrants came from New Zealand and the small island countries of Oceania.

Assimilation was the guiding government philosophy in the 1950s. It was believed that in a matter of time migrants would forgo their native culture and language and blend invisibly into the Australian way of life. However, by the 1970s, multiculturalism, the policy which celebrated the diversity and richness of Australia's different ethnic populations, was preferred by governments. Multiculturalism was based on the belief that immigrants need not forgo their cultural legacy and that the resulting diversity could only enhance the cultural life of the nation. There are in Australia those who are still wary of multiculturalism—and who have their uncertainties exploited by those on the far right of politics—but the idea is well accepted in the areas of sport (encouraged by the success of talented athletes and players from overseas now representing Australia) and cuisine. Immigration has very subtly changed the country, almost without people realising it. An increasing proportion of people from non-British backgrounds was seen as one reason why the movement for Australia to become a republic gained fresh impetus in the 1990s.

The 1950s and the Menzies years

The decade of the 1950s was a period of prosperity, stability and almost full employment, and Australians were able to afford many of the new labour-saving devices developed in the United States: washing machines, refrigerators and vacuum cleaners, along with a 'Hills hoist' rotary clothesline, a home-grown invention of the period. A family car, usually an Australia-made Holden, was also a 'must-have'. Subsidised by the government, the first Holdens had rolled off the assembly line in 1948. The success of

The Holden car became an Australian icon almost from the moment the first model rolled off the line in November 1948.

the Melbourne Olympic Games in November 1956, the 'Friendly Games', also contributed to a feeling of wellbeing and, later, nostalgia, for the decade.

The figure of Sir Robert Gordon Menzies, leader of the Liberal Party and Australia's longest-serving prime minister (1949–66), loomed large over the 1950s. Menzies led a conservative and confident Australia which seemed untroubled by self-doubt. He fostered a 'middle-of-the-road' liberal image and was a witty debater and a polished public speaker.

Menzies was proud of the country's British and imperial heritage and was never shy of stating that he was 'British to the boot-heels'. During the visit in 1954 of the newly crowned Queen Elizabeth II, the first English monarch to visit Australia, the prime minister was moved to quote the sixteenth-century words of Barnabe Googe to convey his deep respect for the royal personage: 'I did but see her passing by, And yet I love her till I die.'

Although the 1950s was a time of comfort and contentment for most Australians, there were, however, significant perceived threats from outside the country. Menzies exploited the popular fear of Communism to win a succession of elections: there was great concern about a 'fifth column' operating within Australia and a fear of the 'Red Menace' in Asia, especially after China became a Communist country in 1949. In 1950 Australia came to the aid of the United States in the Korean War, aimed at curbing the spread of Communism. However, the High Court rejected a Communist Party Dissolution Bill and a referendum to outlaw the party failed in September 1951. Menzies also profited from the 1956 split in the Labor Party, over the issue of Communism, which saw the formation of the Democratic Labor Party or DLP.

There was also a shift away from Britain towards the United States, and later Japan, in terms of trade and investment. Britain contributed to this movement in 1961 when it began negotiations to join the European Economic Community, a shift that Australia saw as excluding it from its once-secure market.

The 'Great Australian Dream'. The post-war prosperity of the 1950s allowed many couples to purchase their own modest home on a suburban block.

The Old Order Changes

The repercussions of Prime Minister Menzies' decision to commit young Australians to the war in Vietnam are still being felt.

Huge protest marches, like this one in Melbourne, were a feature of demonstrations against the Vietnam war during the 1970s.

Vietnam

When after 16 years Menzies finally stepped down as prime minister on 20 January 1966 Australia was a more complex and less complacent country with a range of new problems and controversies. Menzies had in 1965 committed a battalion of Australian troops to help the US war effort in Vietnam, arguing that if North Vietnam was not contained and the Viet Cong defeated in South Vietnam, governments in South-East Asia would collapse like a row of dominoes, leaving Australia vulnerable. Although there was some initial support for the war, it soon became unpopular in many circles because it involved a form of conscription, introduced by the Menzies Liberal government in 1964. Under this system every 20-year-old male had to register for National Service and those born on certain dates (drawn from a barrel as in a lottery) had to serve in Vietnam. Menzies' deputy and successor, Harold Holt, pledged support for the war when he visited US President Lyndon Baines Johnson in the White House in July 1966 and declared that the country would 'go all the way with LBJ'. President Johnson visited Australia just a few months later and was greeted by protestors, though a majority of spectators gave him a positive welcome. Benefiting from the good feeling thus generated, Holt was successful in the election held shortly afterwards. However, his term as prime minister was cut short just over a year later, on 17 December 1967, when he disappeared while swimming in surf in wild weather, near Portsea in Victoria.

He was succeeded by the Liberal politician John Gray Gorton, the first prime minister chosen from the Senate. In contrast to Menzies, Gorton projected a more down-to-earth, homespun image, saying 'I am Australian to my boot-heels'. Perhaps as a sign of its shifting loyalties, Australia adopted decimal currency on 14 February 1966, with the pound being replaced by a dollar valued at 10 shillings. Fortunately perhaps for future generations, the name favoured by Menzies for the new monetary unit, the royal, received only limited public support.

As the conflict in Vietnam dragged on and the US forces suffered defeat in the Tet offensive in 1968, the war became increasingly unpopular in Australia, as it was in the United States. An anti-war moratorium in May 1970 resulted in the largest street marches ever seen in Australia. When a Labor government was elected in 1972 it promised to end Australia's involvement in Vietnam. By the time the war ended, in 1975, 50,000 Australians had served there, with some 500 killed and another 2000 wounded.

Anti-Vietnam protests were just one part of the lively counter-culture sweeping Europe, Australia and the United States at this time. It questioned many aspects of society, from consumerism to conventional morality, and manifested itself in long hair, beards, marijuana-smoking and protest music. Other young people were inspired by left internationalism, first popularised by Leon Trotsky, and the New Left was prominent on many Australian campuses in the late 1960s, as it did in many other parts of the world.

The National Trust became more active in the 1960s, joining with unions to oppose the unwanted destruction by developers of traditional fabric of the cityscape. The Australian Conservation Foundation, formed in 1965, was one of the first of what would soon become many environmental lobby groups.

The Whitlam era

The election of the Labor party to government in December 1972 ended 23 years of Coalition rule and was a significant watershed in Australia. Although the Labor government, under the leadership of Gough Whitlam, held office for only two shortened terms, its reforming zeal and vision for Australia altered the political and social agendas for decades after.

The Whitlam government presided over a period when there was a new sense of purpose and identity in Australia. It adopted a more independent stance internationally, withdrawing troops from Vietnam, abolishing conscription and recognising Communist China. At home, it abolished fees for tertiary students and introduced a publicly funded health system, Medicare, along with many social and welfare reforms including support for single parent families. And, demonstrating how far it had come from the days of the Menzies government, it initiated a quest for a new national anthem, announcing in 1974 that *Advance Australia Fair* would replace *God Save the Queen*. The Whitlam government also promoted Australia as a more pluralistic society, championing the interests of indigenous people, equal pay for women, the arts, multiculturalism and the environment.

For many, the unravelling of Menzies' vision of Australia was too reckless and too radical. Inflation and unemployment, rising with an oncoming recession, further troubled the Whitlam government until, beset by a succession of crises, it was dismissed on 11 November 1975 by the Governor-General, Sir John Kerr, thereby creating the most serious constitutional crisis in Australia's history. Kerr had acted to resolve a political crisis after the Liberal–Country Party coalition had blocked supply in the Senate, thereby cutting off the government's source of money. Many of Labor's supporters were outraged by the dismissal carried out by the Queen's representative, but in the ensuing election in December 1975 Labor was easily defeated by Malcolm Fraser's Liberals. Despite the dismissal, the Whitlam legacy survived the Fraser years and beyond— many of its reforms such as Medicare, free tertiary education and support for the arts remained intact or were only gradually whittled away.

The protest movements begun in the previous decade gathered further momentum during the 1970s. In 1969 a small group of women met at Adelaide University to launch the women's liberation movement in South Australia, and one year later expatriate author Germaine Greer had published *The Female Eunuch*, a critique of traditional femininity which, in the opinion of one journalist, was 'guaranteed to offend nearly everybody'. At about the same time, Gay Liberation developed a political voice with the formation in 1970 of CAMP, (Campaign Against Moral Persecution). Sydney's Gay Mardi Gras, first staged in 1978 as a protest march against intolerance, encountered opposition from police and morals crusaders, but soon became a well-publicised and commercial annual street festival.

Other movements to enhance both the built and natural environments emerged in the 1970s. The conservation movement attracted a wide variety of people from both middle- and working-class interest groups, including Jack Mundey, the high-profile secretary of the New South Wales branch of one of the country's most powerful unions, the Builders' Labourers Federation. The BLF placed a number of very successful 'green' bans on city and suburban developments considered to be detrimental to the urban heritage and environment.

The politics of the bomb came to Australia on 14 February 1978 when an explosion claimed two lives outside Sydney's Hilton Hotel, the venue for a Commonwealth Heads of Government meeting. It was held at the time that the bombing was the work of Ananda Marga, a religious sect who claimed it was being persecuted by the Indian government, and three of its members were imprisoned. However, further investigation led to their pardoning in 1987.

Today's growing acceptance of different lifestyles owes much to the counter-culture that swept Australia in the 1970s.

A Labor Party rally in the Sydney Domain, 1975. The bitterness engendered by the dismissal by the Queen's representative of the Whitlam Labor Government in that year persists today.

Towards a New Millennium

All Australia's coinage is made at the Royal Australian Mint in Canberra. It has the capacity to produce 2 million coins each day.

Boom and bust: the 1980s

Malcolm Fraser, tall, patrician, aloof and, at times, awkward, was elected prime minister for the third time in 1980, thereby becoming the longest-serving incumbent since Menzies. Fraser had attempted to reduce inflation and unemployment by savagely cutting federal expenditure and the public service and by the encouragement of private enterprise. Despite his rhetoric the Canberra bureaucracy did not shrink and the power of the centre remained intact.

Fraser was defeated in 1983 by the former trade union leader Robert 'Bob' Hawke, a man of very different character who prided himself on the level of communication he was able to achieve with ordinary people. As a leader he was pragmatic, valuing greatly consensus between employers and workers. Hawke introduced a succession of price and income accords by which workers would agree to forego wage rises in return for job creation. A second strand to Labor's strategy was financial deregulation, which included the floating of the dollar and the lifting of restrictions on foreign banks and other financial institutions. It was believed that this would give rise to a more competitive Australian economy.

Australia enjoyed considerable prosperity for much of the 1980s and the unemployment rate fell from over 10 per cent to around 6 per cent by the end of the decade. The Hawke government was re-elected for a third time in 1987, creating a record for the Australian Labor Party.

Prominent during the economic boom of the mid-1980s were many corporate high-flyers such as Alan Bond, Christopher Skase, both since discredited, and Robert Holmes á Court. Bond's syndicate under-wrote the successful campaign of the yacht *Australia II* which won the America's Cup in dramatic circum-stances on 27 September 1983. The event epitomised a period of intense nationalism and attendant pride in

In Sydney, a fleet of tall ships was a highlight of the celebrations which in 1988 marked the bicentenary of the European settlement of Australia.

Australian achievement. Bond's companies also con-tributed A$200 million to the country's first private university, Bond University, which admitted its first students on 16 May 1989.

However, deregulation also exposed Australia to the judgment of international markets and by 1986 the Australia dollar had slid to a new low, leading to the then Treasurer Paul Keating's quip that without cuts in public spending and wage restraint Australia was likely to become a 'banana republic'. After the stockmarket crash of 21 October 1987 there were some spectacular corporate falls. By 1989 the Bond Corporation was recording huge financial losses and Christopher Skase's Quintex Australia group was rushing headlong into receivership.

The issue of the environment rose to greater prominence during the 1980s. There was a clash in 1983 between the Federal Labor Government led by Bob Hawke and the Tasmanian Liberal Government, under Robin Gray, over the construction of a hydro-electric dam on the Gordon River below its junction with the Franklin, with the Federal Government using its power to quash the development.

The disappearance of a baby, Azaria Chamberlain, reported missing from a campsite near Uluru (Ayers Rock) on 19 August 1980, sparked a media frenzy and much bizarre speculation about her fate. While some blamed the disappearance on a dingo, there were also bizarre rumours of devil worship and ritual sacrifice, perhaps sparked by public ignorance about Seventh Day Adventism, the faith to which the parents adhered. In 1982, Mrs Lindy Chamberlain was found guilty in a Darwin court of the murder of her daughter and sentenced to life imprisonment. She was released after serving more than three years in jail, when new evidence casting serious doubt on the original judgment was presented. Lindy and her hus-band Michael were pardoned by the government of the Northern Territory and the 1982 convictions were finally quashed in 1988.

In 1988 many Australians celebrated the occasion of the arrival of the First Fleet 200 years previously. On 26 January of that year some two million people thronged the shores and crowded the waters of Sydney Harbour to watch the arrival of a fleet of tall ships from all over the world, a centrepiece of the Bicenten-ary celebrations. However, indigenous people and their supporters, some some 20,000 of them, marched through Sydney streets mourning the European invasion and the problems it had caused for Australia's indigenous communities. In Queensland Brisbane put on an enormous exhibition, Expo, which attracted visitors by the hundreds of thousands.

The 1990s and the Future

Although Bob Hawke had led the Australian Labor Party to four successive election victories and was Australia's second longest-serving prime minister, he was dumped as federal leader on 20 December 1991, the result of a political ambush by his deputy, Paul Keating, in federal Caucus. Hawke lost the vote by 56 votes to 51 and Keating became prime minister.

The Keating years were similar in some respects to the Whitlam era. Like Whitlam, Keating's period in power was relatively brief—1991 to 1996—and his interest, too, was in 'big picture' issues: the republic, reconciliation and Australia's special relationship with Asia. However, at the same time Keating was deeply committed to the mantra shared by all parties in the 1990s, that of economic rationalism, leading to greater privatisation and the reduction of government services, particularly to the bush.

When he was opposed in the 1993 election by the doctrinaire and inexperienced Liberal leader Dr John Hewson, Keating cleverly exploited popular fears of a GST (goods and services tax), the centrepiece of the Hewson platform. Although Keating proclaimed his election success as a victory for 'true believers', he was soon to lose touch with many of Labor's traditional blue-collar supporters.

Having learnt its lesson, the Liberal Party turned to the cautious political veteran John Howard, who made of himself as small a target as was possible by repeatedly espousing the middle ground. Howard benefited by a strong anti-Keating mood to win the 1996 federal election by a landslide.

After this 1996 election, a political unknown, Pauline Hanson, the owner of a fish-and-chips shop in Ipswich, Queensland, ignited a new populist bushfire with racially inflammatory statements. The party she formed, One Nation, promoted a grab bag of policies which included a dislike of Aborigines,

Asian immigration, multiculturalism and economic rationalism, and opposition to restrictions on gun laws. For a year or two One Nation achieved massive media coverage and considerable support at the ballot box before internal dissension and the lack of any coherent policy wrecked its chances, though the party did win seats in two State elections.

Despite the fact that the GST probably cost Hewson the 1993 election, Howard was so deeply committed to tax reform that he ran in favour of the GST at the 1998 polls. Although he won a second term in office, his majority was halved, with the Liberals and its National Party partner securing fewer votes than the Labor Party and the balance of power in the hands of the Democrats. The support of the Democrats was needed to steer the GST legislation through the Senate in 1999 and in return, the Democrats were able to secure minor changes to the legislation, such as the removal of the GST on some items of food.

Although it was believed in the 1990s that a majority of Australians favoured a republic, a referendum in late 1999 failed because republicans were split between those who favoured a model where the president was elected by the people and those who preferred a president selected by Parliament. Many believe that John Howard, an ardent royalist, had framed the referendum question in just this way so as to split the republican vote, thereby maintaining Australia's status quo as a constitutional monarchy.

By 2000 there were an increasing number of public marches and demonstrations in favour of formal reconciliation between indigenous and other Australians. However, at the time of the centenary of Federation, 1 January 2001, this matter seemed no closer to being resolved.

Pre-1788 and the Early Days

New growth after a fire, in the Litchfield National Park, Northern Territory. Fire was used as a land management technique by the Aboriginal peoples; it burnt off undergrowth, thus protecting against bushfire, and ensured new growth—food itself—which would attract animals.

Painting of the First Fleet entering Port Jackson, on 26 January 1788. The fleet had first landed at Botany Bay, but soon realised that there was not a satisfactory fresh water supply there.

Strictly speaking, Australian science and technology began when the first Australians arrived, 40,000 or more years ago, and began managing the land with fire. This brought new plant growth, which supported animal populations for hunting and did no damage to the precious topsoil. They brought stone-working skills with them, and went on to create string for fishing lines and nets, boats, wooden implements and tools, using local materials. At some point, they invented the world's first aerofoil, the returning boomerang. In the absence of animals that could be herded or used as transport, and with no crops that favoured agriculture, the first Australians lived a life that matched the climate and available resources. Their methods were suited to the environment and worked successfully to sustain both them and the land, until the Europeans arrived in force.

Oddly, the shock to the Australian environment that we call 'European settlement' was driven origi-

nally by a thirst for science. Captain James Cook had been sent to Tahiti to observe the 1769 transit of Venus—the time when that planet would come between the earth and the sun—so that European astronomers could combine these observations with others made around the world and thus estimate the size of our solar system. Cook was also instructed to seek out the Great South Land—some believed it must exist, in order to counterbalance the land mass of Europe, or the world would wobble!

Various navigators had been bumping into bits of Australia for 150 years or more so, ignoring the wobble theory, so it probably seemed sensible to take a closer look at the area Dutchman Abel Tasman had sailed around in the 1640s, to see just what was there. Cook had two botanists on the voyage, Daniel Solander and Joseph Banks. Elected President of the Royal Society, Britain's leading scientific body, in 1778, Banks was an important person, and it was partly

Before long, the small penal colony was the centre of a much larger pattern of settlement, and soon free settlers began to arrive, attracted by the cheap land here, but before about 1850, the efforts of most scientists were devoted to identifying land that would make good farms, and to mapping the new continent. The early European explorers were able to find their way largely by following the paths that had been created by generations of Aboriginal feet; their main role was to survey and map the route, which is why the most famous 'explorers', such as John Oxley and Thomas Mitchell, were actually surveyors. Collectors and botanists accompanied the explorers, gathering specimens and samples as they went and sending them back to Britain for scientists to examine, providing much food for European thought. Robert Brown, famous among physicists for discovering Brownian motion, and to biologists for discovering that the cell has a nucleus, was just one of the botanists who collected plants in Australia; he was with Matthew Flinders on his circumnavigation of the continent in 1802.

Just as evidence from the Americas had made European scientists rethink their assumptions, now they had the added challenge of an entirely unknown flora and fauna to fit into their scheme of how the world worked. The new biology and novel geology of the Antipodes helped drive the advance of world science, and the cross-fertilisation of ideas between Australian and European scientists, plus the interest in science in this part of the world, stimulated Australian science. By 1827, the elite of the now thriving colony in Sydney felt the time was ripe to found an Australian museum to store a truly local collection of natural wonders.

Matthew Flinders (1774–1814) was the first to circumnavigate both Tasmania and, later, Australia. Some of his charts are still in use today.

TOP LEFT: Cannon at Dawes Point in Sydney, New South Wales, site of Australia's first observatory.

LEFT: The medallion made by Josiah Wedgwood (1730–95), from the first Australian clay exported to Britain.

The Museum of South Australia, which opened in 1862. There was interest in learning and sharing knowledge of the new land from the very start.

through his influence that the destination of the First Fleet would be Botany Bay, where he had discovered many new plant specimens. The application of a little more science in selecting the place might have been useful, however, for while the shores of Botany Bay supported a wealth of plant species, the soil was extremely poor. Mostly composed of sand, it was worthless as farmland, so within a few days the First Fleet shifted north up the coast, to Sydney Harbour: a place where good anchorages, good water and good soil were available. There, on 26 January 1788, the British flag was raised on the shore at Sydney Cove. European science and technology had now reached Australia and established a toehold from which to reshape the landscape.

A science of survival and opportunity

The people in the infant colony had simple priorities: to find materials with which they could feed, house and clothe themselves, to defend themselves against attack from the French or Spanish, and to establish as accurately as possible the longitude of Sydney, so vessels could set their chronometers accurately. The naval officers quickly set up batteries of cannon—to fire on any enemy shipping—and a small observatory under Lieutenant William Dawes, but they were poorly equipped for their other tasks.

The First Fleet brought many felons who gave their trade as 'pedlar', but few artisans who could make anything for pedlars to sell. There were not many people with farming experience in the First Fleet—the convicts at this time were drawn mainly from the urban poor—so the colony had no geologists or soil scientists, no mineralogists and no engineers. It did bring surgeon John White, and he was responsible for the first two exports for technological application from Australia: a sample of clay, from which Josiah Wedgwood made a medallion, and a sample of eucalyptus oil.

Australian Science Takes Off

The Main Quadrangle of the University of Sydney. The university was legislated in 1850, and began teaching in 1852, with a mere three professors and 30 students. Now there are more than 2200 academic staff and 36,000 students at the university's ten campuses.

The platypus, Ornithorhynchus paradoxus, *was described as 'an amphibious animal of the mole kind, which inhabits the banks of the fresh water lagoons of New South Wales'. This early drawing by David Collins was published in* An Account of the English Colony of New South Wales, Vol 2.

Through the 1830s and 1840s, geologists and collectors crisscrossed the continent, mapping, collecting and keeping an eye out for geological riches. In a sense, Britain saw the drive of scientific enquiry in Australia as existing solely to serve the needs and reputation of British scientists.

So, while Richard Owen, doyen of English zoologists, cultivated his Australian contacts for specimens, it seems that one of his aims was to stop French scientists with evolutionary ideas from getting their hands on a platypus skin to prove their theory of a 'missing link'. Collectors were largely funded by individual patrons and, later, institutions interested in discovering more about the continent, a pattern which has been retained to this day.

Gold was discovered in small amounts, but it wasn't until Australian prospectors started returning from the goldfields of California that Australia's own gold rush started. That, in turn, would fund a great deal of science and technology.

With the finding of gold, Melbourne found itself supporting a large class of wealthy people. Some were rich from prospecting, some from selling supplies to the miners, and some were already rich from their

landholdings, but all had new money to spare. They set out to take up 'genteel pursuits', science among them, and the 1860s saw Melbourne rivalling Sydney in its aspirations. Melbourne had more money, but Sydney had more tradition, and intercolonial rivalry became intense, with universities having opened in both cities—everywhere there was that supreme confidence of the Victorian era that applied science was the way to even greater riches.

Patronage and the scientific visitors

Even before gold was found, the colony at Sydney supported a large middle class, keen to pay attention to developments in science and to pay court to visiting scientists. Governor Brisbane established an observatory at Government House in Parramatta, just as Sydney reached a critical mass of collectors and observers, and the governor of Van Diemen's Land, Sir John Franklin, and his wife encouraged the sciences in the growing colony. Scientific visitors such as naval captain James Clark Ross and botanist Joseph Dalton Hooker called upon Sir John and Lady Franklin, and during the Franklins' time in Hobart the brotherhood of polar explorers beat a regular path to their door. Other names of note from overseas included Charles Darwin, Captain Charles Wilkes and his geologist, James Dana, and even T.H. Huxley, later famous as 'Darwin's bulldog'. Some, such as the collector and botanist Allan Cunningham and explorer Ludwig Leichhardt, came here as visitors and stayed, mapping the continent and making collections. A number of

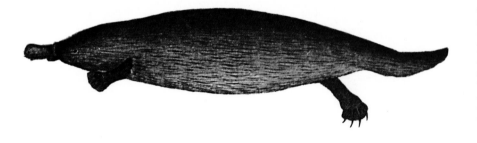

Polish hero Kosciuszko (when it was discovered that a nearby peak was actually higher, the name 'Kosciusko' was quietly transferred to the higher peak—it has only recently had its Polish spelling reinstated).

Australia's own scientists

In the middle of the nineteenth century both Sydney and Melbourne created universities to educate their young men (the women would have to wait a few years more). Now Australia could train its own scientists, and soon its graduates were beginning to make their mark. The Reverend W.B. Clarke and Samuel Stutchbury did original geological survey work in the 1850s, and from then until 1889, so did the Reverend Julian Tenison Woods. This priest (who may one day become the world's first geologist saint, if some Australian Catholics have their way) located and described fossils in South Australia, Queensland, New South Wales and Tasmania. Later, Edgeworth David and Griffith Taylor would explain the continent's geological history, though many of their conclusions have since been superseded. Australian science was still directed at practical ends, so people such as Ferdinand von Mueller crossed the country describing the geology and collecting biological specimens and, towards the end of the century, writing descriptions and taxonomic keys to Australia's plants, while in Sydney, Joseph Henry Maiden and his colleagues carried out detailed research on the production of eucalyptus oil from different species of gum tree, collecting seed from the most productive strains, and exploring medical and commercial uses for it.

A tradition of astronomy

The Parramatta observatory had closed in 1848, but by 1858 a new Sydney observatory had been estab-

other nations, especially France, sent exploring expeditions to Australia; they probably still had hopes of founding a colony on some unclaimed part of the enormous island continent.

Philip Parker King, another famous name in the scientific world, mapped the area around Tierra del Fuego and parts of the Australian coast. Everybody who was anybody called upon King, including Darwin when he came to Sydney in 1836, before sailing on to Hobart. Count Paul Edmond de Strzelecki, adventurer, explorer, geologist and Polish patriot, visited Australia in 1840, and many scientific toasts were drained in Sydney to Polish freedom. While Strzelecki was detailing the geology of the Snowy Mountains, he named Australia's highest mountain after the

An 1844 drawing of explorer Ludwig Leichhardt (1813–?48). Leichhardt came to Australia in 1842, and became well known after his expedition from Brisbane to Port Essington (near Darwin) in 1844–45. His next expedition, in 1846, was to cross Australia from east to west— from the Darling Downs (Qld) to the coast of WA. He did not succeed. He tried again in 1848, but the entire expedition disappeared, and no trace of it has been found to this day.

The Inauguration of the University of Sydney, as seen in The Illustrated London News of 29 January 1853. The university's Faculty of Science was established in 1879, with Englishman Archibald Liversidge, Professor of Geology, as its founding dean.

Lord Howard Florey (1898–1968). Florey, with E.B. Chain, and with some crucial help from Alexander Fleming, discovered the antimicrobial properties of penicillin, for which he and Chain were awarded the Nobel Prize for Medicine in 1945.

RIGHT: The Parkes, New South Wales, radiotelescope, which was built in 1961. Australian radio astronomy has helped monitor NASA's Apollo and Voyager space missions, and identified the existence of radio galaxies, plus many pulsars and quasars.

The Mount Stromlo Observatory, near Canberra, opened in 1924 and is now part of the Australian National University's Research School of Astronomy and Astrophysics. The observatory was home to the Starlab project (a wide-field free-flying ultraviolet telescope) in the 1980s.

lished on Observatory Hill, where it stands to this day. The first government astronomer was a Cambridge-trained clergyman, but after that, Australia bred its own astronomers. In 1861, John Tebbutt opened his own observatory at Windsor, outside Sydney, and from this centre, and a second larger observatory built in 1879, he wrote more than 300 papers on astronomy, as well as discovering, in 1861 and 1881, comets which now bear his name.

In 1862, the Victorian colonial parliament voted the money to build the largest equatorially mounted reflector telescope in the world, a 48 inch (122 cm) Cassegrain reflector; while the device was greatly admired, and helped put Australia on the astronomical map, it never achieved much, and the best astronomy continued to come from Sydney.

In 1874, there was another transit of Venus, the first since the event in 1769 that brought Cook and Banks to the Pacific, but now Australia had its own astronomers, and the Sydney-born government astronomer sent expeditions out to observe the transit from different vantage points. These transits come in pairs, more than a century apart, and by the next transit, in 1882, Australia was a recognised part of the world astronomical community.

In 1995, the year of the most recent transit, Australia was a major world centre for visual and radio astronomy, offering a platform which is seismically and politically stable from which to search the southern skies. Looking ahead, Australian astronomers hope the transit of 2004 will see north-western Australia selected as the site for the 'Square Kilometre

Array', the first of the next generation of radio telescopes. Other developments in astronomy include the Parkes radio telescope, best known to Australians as the dish used to receive television shots of the first moon landing in July 1969; in November 1998, the hard-working telescope located its 1000th pulsar. Australia also has the Culgoora Solar Observatory's radiospectrograph, which carries on the earlier work of the radioheliograph, a major source of information and early warnings on ionospheric and geomagnetic disturbance in the region.

Australian science established

The end of the nineteenth century saw science established as a field in its own right, separate from its applications. There would continue to be visits by overseas scientists to Australia, but now they were likely to find scientific skills here that matched their own. Australia now produces an estimated 2 per cent of the world's scientific publications, and has produced a number of Nobel Prize winners: Howard Florey (1945), Sir Frank Macfarlane Burnet (1960), Sir John Eccles (1963), John Cornforth (1975) and Peter Doherty (1996). With the exception of Cornforth, whose prize was for chemistry, all were in the category 'physiology or medicine'.

Australia has repaid the British investment in Australia many times over, and has even provided two scientists— Sir Howard Florey and Sir Robert May— to fill the presidential shoes of Sir Joseph Banks at the Royal Society, something which surely would never have happened if Banks had not been President of the Royal Society and had not then used his influence to dispatch the First Fleet to Botany Bay.

The Ingenious Tinkerers

That ability which Americans celebrate as 'Yankee ingenuity' seems to have been just as common in Australia. Far from centres of manufacture, rural Australians had to make their own solutions, using the materials that were available: bags and other packing that came around stores, fencing wire, sheets of stringybark from trees, rawhide and the available timber. Using these unlikely materials, ordinary people could make everything from a comfortable chair to a self-closing gate, a toasting fork to a better mousetrap, while those with more technical skills were busy inventing new agricultural machinery.

Henry Sutton was one of the most imaginative and prolific of these self-taught amateurs. Born in a tent on the Ballarat goldfields, he is said to have invented many things, though he only patented two. At the age of 14, he thought up what later became known as the 'Gramme motor', named after the Belgian professor who independently invented the same motor in the following year, and he also made a clockwork-powered flying machine at the same time. At the age of 20, within a year of Bell's first telephone, Sutton invented some 20 different variations on the device and put some of them to practical use, linking his family's music store with their warehouse, for example. A number of these developments were later patented by others overseas. Sutton also developed the first portable radio (which had a range of about 500 m/1640 feet), an electric storage battery with copper and lead/mercury electrodes and copper sulphate as the electrolyte. He also invented a mercury vacuum pump, which was widely used to make lamp bulbs after further development by others.

In the late 1870s, Sutton developed an incandescent light bulb, and around 1885, he came up with the idea for a device called the telephane, the first theoretically feasible television, which he planned to use to transmit the Melbourne Cup horse race over telegraph lines to Ballarat, 150 km (93 miles) away. (The device was never actually built, and would have failed in any case, as the existing lines would not have been able to carry the necessary information.)

Lawrence Hargrave, who arrived in Sydney at the age of 15, became an early and unselfish pioneer of aviation, inventing the box kite design that lay behind early biplanes, the aerofoil section (which the Wright brothers may have invented independently, though they did have access to Hargrave's work, and which featured in the boomerang, even earlier) and the radial engine which drove most aircraft until about 1920. Hargrave shared his ideas widely and patented nothing.

Inventions inspired by the land

Australia's tinkering tradition saw its grandest moment with the stump-jump plough. Clearing land in Australia to plant crops involved ringbarking trees

The Hills Hoist clothesline, a result of Australia's 'tinkering', an endeavour that has always been very responsive to both the environment and our isolation. The design certainly uses more space than could be afforded in more crowded parts of the world, but it also makes good use of the sun and the wind—and it has the added benefit of being a great plaything for thousands of Australian children.

A rare photograph of Lawrence Hargrave (1850–1915) with some of his box kites at Stanwell Park, south of Sydney, a spot that is still popular with hang gliders. During experiments with box kites here, he succeeded in having four kites lift him 16 feet (about 5 metres) off the ground.

An example of old, probably improvised, farm equipment, at Pioneer Park in Parkes, New South Wales. While such equipment is now well out of date, the ability to put things together in unusual ways is still with us.

A wheat harvester, in Streaky Bay, South Australia. Australian agricultural technology now uses GPS (Global Positioning System) to accurately direct ploughing and planting. Airborne high-resolution imagery is used to analyse soil and vegetation.

which were then gradually felled to make open fields, with the trees being burned to return minerals to the soil. The stumps were left to rot, resulting in impediments to ploughs, which would either bend or snap. In 1876, Robert Bowyer Smith, an engineer-turned-farmer, invented a system of levers and adjustable weights (to cope with different types of soil) which allowed the plough to flip back and ride over the stump before dropping down again. Sadly for Smith, every colony had its own patents system, and others claimed to have invented better ploughs. However, his work was eventually recognised by the South Australian parliament, which voted him £500 and 260 acres (105 ha) of land.

The shortage of capital which made farmers keen to start working their land was matched by a shortage of labourers at harvest time, for new arrivals were hungry for land of their own. This led to the development of the first stripper harvesters, machines which would gather wheat quickly and efficiently. For many years, Australian inventors developed machinery in parallel with, and sometimes ahead of, the American firms of Deering and McCormick.

William Farrer, a Cambridge graduate in mathematics who came to Australia in 1870 aged 25, built into the Australian consciousness a clear understanding of the economic value of applied genetics. Farrer had planned to farm sheep, but became a surveyor instead, before settling into the work that made him famous—as a breeder of new wheat strains. At a time when Gregor Mendel's work was still lying unnoticed on most library shelves, Farrer was instinctively applying the same principles in his attempts to develop strains of wheat which provided both a high yield and resistance to disease, and he was highly successful in both these aims. Australia remains a major world centre of genetic improvement and manipulation of stock and crops—'gene shears' (ribozymes which can snip a gene at a predetermined position) were an Australian invention. It will be for a future generation to determine whether or not these successes explain why Australians are generally less alarmed about genetic manipulation than Europeans or Americans are.

Another invention which solved a specifically Australian problem was refrigeration. While primary products such as grain, wood, hides and tallow could be successfully exported overseas, meat had to be salted or smoked to last the long distances. This changed when Eugene Nicolle, a French migrant, began experimenting with refrigeration. In partnership with Thomas Mort, a migrant from England, he developed cold storage systems and worked on practical refrigeration to operate on ships. After a number of setbacks, the first frozen beef reached Britain on board the *Strathleven* in 1879.

All of a sudden, new export markets were opened to Australia (and to Argentina, which also benefited from refrigerated ships). The development of ice-making machinery also allowed the more affluent to have an 'ice-chest' at home; poorer homes used another Australian invention, the cheaper 'Coolgardie safe', which relied on the principle of evaporative cooling. New South Wales Surveyor-General and explorer Sir Thomas Mitchell used the same cooling principle when he copied the kangaroo skin water bags used by Aborigines to make the canvas water bag—this is still seen today, hanging from the front of many vehicles in the outback.

SCIENCE AND TECHNOLOGY TIMELINE							
1770 Botanists Daniel Solander and Joseph Banks, later president of the Royal Society, Britain's principal scientific body, visit eastern Australia with Captain Cook.	**1827** Government grants funds for founding of Australian Museum in Sydney. **1836** Charles Darwin visits Australia; his observations influence theory of evolution.	**1858** Overland Telegraph links Adelaide, Melbourne and Sydney; reaches Darwin 1872. **1861** John Tebbutt builds observatory at Windsor, NSW, and begins pioneering studies.	**1879** First consignment of frozen meat shipped to UK by Thomas Mort and Eugene Nicolle. **1880** First telephone exchange opens in Melbourne.	**1886** William Farrer begins developing new strains of Australian wheat. **1888** Founding of Australian Association for the Advancement of Science (AAAS).	**1907** First trunk telephone line established between Sydney and Melbourne. **1914** H.S. Taylor's header harvester, on which modern harvesters are based, trialled.	**1918** First radio message sent between London and Sydney. **1919** Ross and Keith Smith become first to fly from Britain to Australia.
c.40,000–20,000 BP Aboriginal peoples invent boomerang, world's first aerofoil. In south-east, some groups construct elaborate systems of dams to trap fish.	**1788** Lieutenant William Dawes arrives with First Fleet and sets up first observatory. **1809–17** Elizabeth Macarthur breeds merino sheep for wool production.	**1841** Introduction of gas street lighting in Sydney. **1850** Founding of first Australian university in Sydney. Melbourne University founded three years later.	**1871** First international telegram received via cable between Port Darwin and Java. **1876** Stump-jump plough invented by Richard B. Smith at Kalkaburry, SA.	**1883** Train service between Sydney and Melbourne begins. **1885** Hugh McKay patents Sunshine Harvester. Henry Sutton constructs the 'telephane', a kind of television.	**1894** Lawrence Hargrave lifts himself off the ground using four box kites **1897** Henry Austin builds Australia's first car with internal combustion engine.	**1916** First forerunner of CSIRO, Advisory Council of Science and Industry, set up. **1917** Transcontinental rail link opens between Sydney and Perth.	**1920** Qantas foun Winton, Qld. Found second forerunner of Commonwealth Insti Science and Industr Howard invents rota

Wheat and silos, at Goondiwindi, Queensland. Around one-third of Australia's wheat exports go to noodle production; scientists are helping the industry stay competitive. Researchers have found that noodle colour, which is important, can be influenced by the level of a particular plant enzyme. Screening for this in breeding programs may improve noodle colour. Gene technology is also helping discover which wheat lines have the starch characteristics the Japanese noodle market requires. This is paying big dividends, as the premium noodle wheats command high prices.

Refrigeration meant new foods could be marketed in both the domestic and export markets, but these needed to be developed locally. Up until this time, crops and animals were European imports. Although some of these were unsuited to Australia, there was a belief that just as natural selection weeded out the less fit, so, too, human beings could selectively replace what they regarded as 'worthless' local plants and animals with their own 'superior' imported breeds. One example of this was the success of John Macarthur's merino sheep-breeding program, due mostly to the work of his wife (who had no choice in the matter as her husband slipped inexorably into an insanity which had no cure before the age of antibiotics).

The inspiration for the 'ute', or utility, came from a modified vehicle noticed by Lewis Brandt, a Ford engineer, in 1930. A truck with an open back, giving it a 'sawn-off' look, was obviously ideal for the amount of loading and unloading necessary in a busy farmer's life. The first ute was made at Ford in 1933 and—it is known to Americans as a 'pickup'.

Other practical inventions for everyday use included the Victa mower, a rotary two-stroke lawnmower seen as so symbolic of Australian life that it featured in the opening ceremony of the 2000 Olympics in Sydney. The prototype used an old tin can to hold the fuel, but the machines took off in a slightly more sophisticated form, and have since spread across the world.

Four men (J.A.B. Little, R.B. Paterson, C. Todd and A.J. Mitchell) who worked on the Overland Telegraph line between Adelaide and Darwin. Charles Todd supervised the project. The price of one word went from 10 shillings in 1872 to one shilling in 1901.

The old Telegraph Station at Alice Springs, Northern Territory, part of the Overland Telegraph line. The line was completed in 1872, allowing direct communication between Australia and Europe.

First radio stations broadcasting in Sydney, Melbourne and Perth.
First international flight, from Darwin to Singapore.

1926 Founding of the Council for Scientific and Industrial Research (CSIR), third forerunner of CSIRO.
1930 First international telephone call made.

1932 Sydney Harbour Bridge opens, on 19 March.
1941 Norman Gregg demonstrates link between rubella and birth defects.

1945 Howard Florey named joint winner of Nobel Prize for Medicine for his work on development of penicillin. Founding of Australian National University (ANU).

1946 Hills Hoist invented by Lance Hill.
1949 CSIRO founded. Beginning of Snowy Mountains Hydroelectric Scheme, completed in 1972.

1952 Victa rotary lawnmower invented by Mervyn Richardson.
1954 Australian Academy of Science established.

1956 Television broadcasting begins in Australia.
1958 Australia's first nuclear reactor opens at Lucas Heights, near Sydney.

1960 Sir Macfarlane Burnet declared joint winner of Nobel Prize for Medicine for his work on acquired immunological tolerance.

1961 William McBride establishes link between thalidomide and birth defects. Parkes radio telescope begins operating.

1963 Sir John Eccles awarded Nobel Prize for Physiology or Medicine for his work on transmission of nerve impulses.

1966 First television programs from UK transmitted to Australia via satellite.
1968 First Australian heart transplant at St Vincent's Hospital, Sydney.

1975 Sir John Warcup Cornforth shares Nobel Prize for Chemistry for his work on the three-dimensional structure of molecules.

1983 Cochlear set up as company to advance 'bionic ear' created by Graeme Clarke.
1984 World's first frozen embryo baby born in Melbourne.

1992 Fred Hollows Foundation set up to continue work of surgeon who pioneered treatment of cataract blindness among indigenous peoples here and overseas.

1996 Peter Doherty receives Nobel Prize for Physiology or Medicine for research into cell-mediated immune defence.

1999 Australian-made Relenza becomes world's first approved influenza therapy.

Science in the Twentieth Century

The Sydney Harbour Bridge, partway through its construction. Designs were drafted as early as 1912, but building did not start until 1923. The completion of the construction was celebrated at the opening ceremony, held on 20 March 1932.

The twentieth century was the age of great engineering feats. The Trans-Australia railway, for example, eventually overcame that lasting legacy of colonial rivalry, the gauge mismatch, which saw three rail gauges in use in a single nation, forcing rail travellers until 1962 to change trains at the border when they travelled between Sydney and Melbourne. The nation's first great bridge, over Sydney Harbour, became an icon for all of Australia; opened in 1932, it was the widest and heaviest single-arch bridge in the

A section of the Trans-Australia railway, near the Nullarbor Plain, in Western Australia. Railways appeared in Australia in the 1850s, the first being lines between cities and their ports. Railways outside main cities were all taken over by governments by the 1860s; they were seen as agents of expansion, of development. They were the nation's major development project in the late nineteenth century, and the source of much political bickering, as not being on a new line could turn a prosperous centre into a ghost town.

world. The Snowy Mountains Hydroelectric Scheme, begun in the 1940s, was seen as a victory over the old enemy, drought. It came into effect in stages, and was officially completed in 1972. Today, however, damage to the environment is part of its legacy—the once-proud Snowy River is now deprived of most of its water and there are salination problems caused by irrigation using waters from the scheme. In late 2000, agreement was reached to return some of the diverted water to the river.

The glorious tradition of amateur gadgetry continued when ANZAC forces had to retreat from their landings at Gallipoli in 1915 and did so without loss, due to the success of a variety of jury-rigged timing systems based on candles, dripping cans of water and weights and strings, which fired random shots, giving their Turkish enemies the impression that they were still in their trenches.

After World War I, a stream of talented scientists began to flow away from Australia, with Britain the main source of attraction for people such as Howard Florey, who shared the Nobel Prize for his work on penicillin. The reason was simple—there was no tradition of basic research in Australia. Many, however, such as Sir Mark Oliphant, later returned to Australia, where the Australian National University, the Commonwealth Scientific and Industrial Research Organisation (CSIRO) and the larger universities were all attracting talent, as well as more funding from such bodies as the Australian Research Grants Commission (ARGC). Australia's scientific progress since, while often astonishing, has also been erratic, and has occurred in some perhaps surprising fields.

Medicine and biology

Some of the unsung heroes of Australian science are those who made medical discoveries. Ashburton Thompson and Frank Tidswell, for example, identified the way in which fleas spread bubonic plague from rats when Sydney was one of many Pacific seaports affected by the plague in 1900. Joseph Bancroft, who migrated to Brisbane, demonsrated that a worm causes the parasitic disease filariasis, and his son, Thomas Lane Bancroft, proved in 1904 that dengue fever is transmitted by a mosquito.

Others have received more official recognition: in 1935, Sir Frank Macfarlane Burnet and Dame Jean Macnamara showed that there are at least two polio viruses, and Burnet later identified the causative agent of Q fever. In 1941, Sir Norman Gregg showed that rubella (German measles) in early pregnancy can cause foetal congenital deafness or blindness, and in 1961 William McBride, in Sydney, was the first to link the drug thalidomide to birth defects.

The unthinking English importer of rabbits into Victoria, Thomas Austin, believed that he was benefiting the population by introducing a food animal, but within a few years rabbits had spread across the continent, doing great damage to crops and native vegetation and competing with native fauna for resources.

The scientific solution—the introduction of a disease, myxomatosis, in the 1950s—sent rabbit numbers crashing, but most farmers failed to follow this up with baiting, shooting and warren destruction, and before long normal evolutionary forces had produced a strain of resistant rabbits and strains of less ferocious myxoma virus.

Over the years we have learned more about biological control. The *Opuntia* cactus, known as prickly pear, had come to Australia from South America in the 1850s and run wild. It blocked access to millions of hectares of grazing land until the *Cactoblastis* moth (also from South America) was brought in to control it. The introduction of African dung beetles is also a success story—they have reduced the numbers of 'bush flies', which previously bred to plague proportions in the dung of another non-native species—cattle. The cane toad, however, which was introduced to control the cane beetle, which was ravaging sugar plantations, was a total disaster, because the toad not only did not eat the cane beetle (it couldn't jump high enough to reach it), it also out-competed some endemic amphibians and poisoned many native mammals and birds.

As a result of past experience, when a new virus, calicivirus, was introduced into Australia to control rabbits, it was carefully planned, the intention being to maximise its impact by using other forms of control at the same time, but despite good intentions, the virus escaped and began to spread through the nation's rabbit population. It remains to be seen how long the effects will last.

Rabbits are not the only problem—Australia has many introduced birds that are now feral, as well as wild populations of mice, rats, hares, pigs, goats, donkeys, horses, several species of cattle, and even camels which are exported to the Middle East. Australia also has many endemic species now under threat, so wildlife management is a major challenge for the future.

A racecourse 'tote'. Mechanised totes were in use from as early as 1879; the first totalisator machine was used in Western Australia in 1916.

TOP LEFT: *Carp are an introduced freshwater species whose population exploded in the 1970s. They may be associated with increased turbidity and bank instability, and with a decline in native species.*

Ultrasound scans, which use inaudible pressure waves, are a safe, non-invasive way to image foetuses and internal organs.

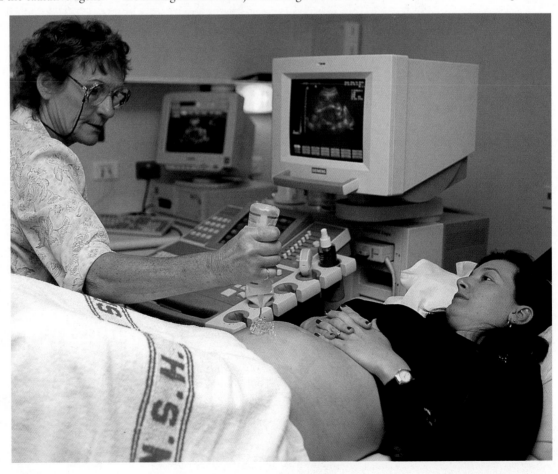

Notable firsts in technology

The surf rescue reel was invented in 1906 (and, the following year, used to rescue a boy called Charlie Smith, who later became famous as the aviator Charles Kingsford-Smith) and the first racecourse totalisator (a mechanical computer to manage betting) was invented by an Australian, George Julius (though the first 'tote' office opened in Auckland in 1913), who later—from 1926 until 1945—headed the Council for Scientific and Industrial Research, the early version of the CSIRO.

Australians invented the world's first heart pacemaker (1926), ultrasound scanners, the 'black box'

The new National Museum of Australia, in Canberra, opened in March 2001. The museum includes the Children's Museum (right). The museum's three themes are Australian society and its history since 1788, the interaction of people with the Australian environment, and Aboriginal and Torres Strait Islander cultures and histories. The museum plans to develop this framework—Land, People and Nation—using both traditional (economic, political) history and non-traditional history (migration, urban, environmental and personal).

aeroplane flight recorder, the pedal wireless, the first mine-detector, the pop-top can, the wine cask, the race-cam and stump-cam, and techniques such as the flotation process in mining (for separating out ore after crushing), and discovered the value of lithium as a treatment for manic depressives. Australia has also given the world latex gloves, polymer bank notes which defeat the most determined counterfeiter, cloud-seeding to generate rain, bionic ears, spun concrete pipes and improved photovoltaic cells.

Institutions

One of the outstanding successes in the development of Australian science in the mid-twentieth century was the establishment of the Commonwealth Scientific and Industrial Research Organisation (CSIRO), which began slowly as the Commonwealth Institute of Science and Industry in 1920 and expanded greatly after about 1950. Its main thrust of research has been in areas related to minerals and agriculture.

At the end of the century a new model for applied science and technology emerged, the Cooperative Research Centre (CRC). Under this scheme, universities, government and the private sector all contribute funds and even researchers. There are now 63 CRCs across Australia, covering six industry sectors: manufacturing technology, information and communication technology, mining and energy, agriculture and rural-based manufacturing, environment and

NOW SHOWI[NG]

IMAX THEATR[E]

ALASKA
SPIRIT OF THE WIL[D]

21 October 2000 – 4 February 2001

Body Art, produced by Australian Museum, Sydney.
Rated M

A campus of museum

Melbourne museum

Life. No[w]

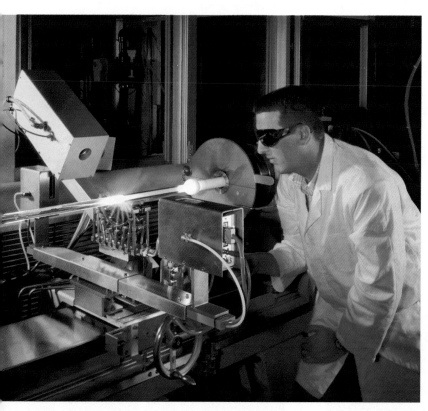

example, a contact lens designed specifically for the 1.3 billion people in the Asia Pacific region who need some form of vision correction has been developed. As well, there has been the successful commercial release of the new generation System-24 bionic ear, used by more than 16,000 people worldwide.

The future

Australian science has had major successes when applied to agriculture and mining, and Australian scientists are among the world leaders in areas such as new and applied technology, sustainable environments, radio astronomy and proteomics (an Australian term for the study of proteins), which is likely to become one of the major sciences of the next 20 years. All that is lacking is some form of national leadership, national resolve and national investment—a lesson that Australians are slowly beginning to learn. Australia's brain drain has now slowed to a trickle, and is probably balanced by the inflow of talent from overseas. There are still young Australians who, driven by a vital curiosity, are attracted to careers in science, and enough older and experienced scientists in the system to provide the infrastructure for them to flourish.

Preform lathe: this is the first stage in the production of application-specific optical fibre at the Australian Technology Park (ATP) in Redfern, New South Wales. The ATP is a focal point for innovative science and technology, housing a mixture of high-tech businesses, including start-ups, cooperative research centres and sections of several universities. Its aim is to promote links between theory and practice, between R&D and commerce.

AUSSAT 1 and 2, Australia's first communications satellites were launched aboard the US space shuttle Discovery in 1985. Since then, Australia has joined both the COSPAS-SARSAT network, the international satellite system that provides distress alert and location data to search and rescue operations worldwide, and the ERS-1 (Earth-observing) satellite program, whose purpose is to study oceans, atmospheric conditions, ice caps and coastal regions in order to help monitor environmental damage.

tourism, and medical science and technology. Initially, each CRC is given a seven-year life span, plus a serious amount of funding, and all are reviewed regularly to ensure that they are meeting their key objectives.

One of the most successful is the Australian Photonics CRC, which has already set up three spin-off companies aimed at commercialising its research. Photonics (the art of transmitting information by optic fibre) is ideally suited to a country where the centres of population are far from each other, and even further from the rest of the world, so furthering the development of this industry is essential to Australia's future as an IT-intensive nation.

Other products which have come from CRCs include new methods of extracting gold from ore, new welding techniques, the development of ATM super-systems for banks, new alloys, food packaging systems, sustainable forestry methods, new legume strains with deep root systems, anti-fungal genes for use in crop plants, and software systems for wine-makers. Yet other CRCs have made advances in more traditional areas of concern, such as premium quality wool, wheat, sugar and beef, and newer forms of Australian agriculture, including aquaculture and cotton.

The CRC for Cellular Growth Factors has funded a high-speed computer, Caduceus, which can screen millions of chemical compounds, and will help in the design of new pharmaceuticals, and the CRC for Molecular Engineering and Technology has created the world's first functioning nanomachine—the biosensor, which can detect minuscule amounts of substances, such as microbial infections.

Belatedly, Australia has recognised the mistakes of the past, and a number of CRCs specialise in aspects of environmental management and repair, as well as medical research which is region-specific. For

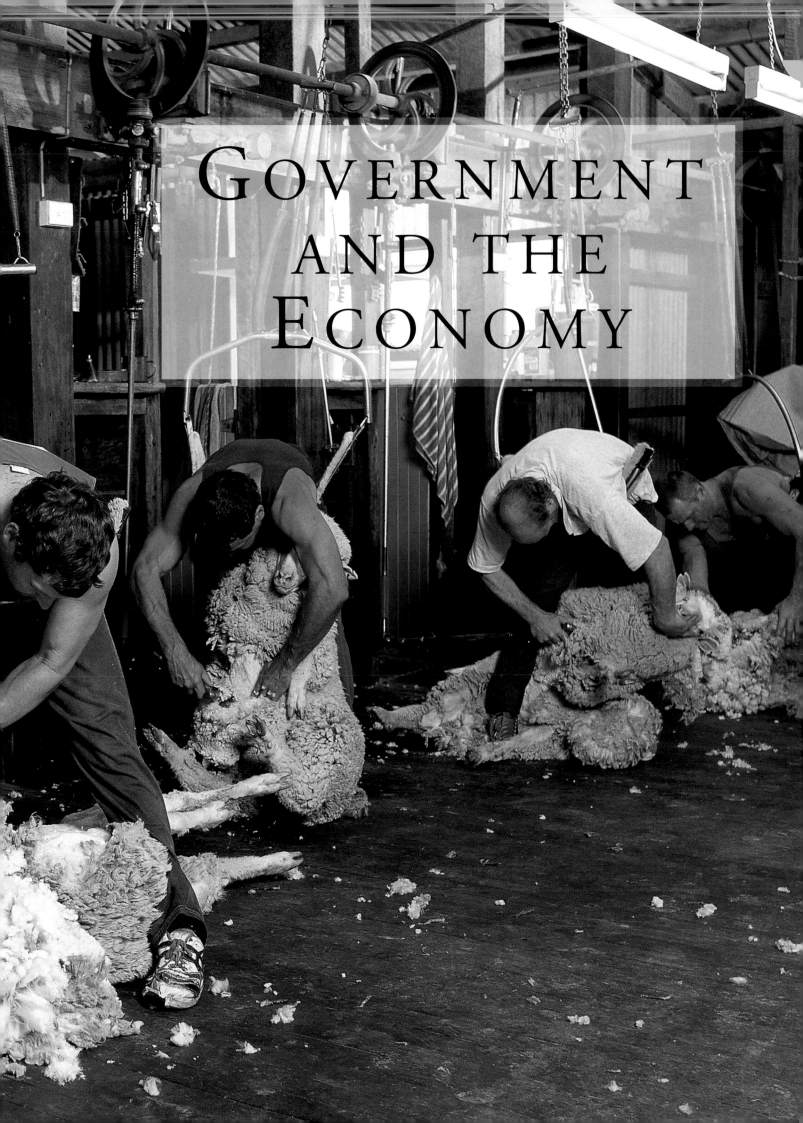

GOVERNMENT AND THE ECONOMY

GOVERNMENT

Political History

Australia's national day, 26 January, celebrates the founding of the first permanent European settlement in 1788. Many Australians commemorate this anniversary with a mixture of national pride and shame for the infant colony of New South Wales was born as a penal establishment under military rule and signalled the dispersal, dispossession and numberless deaths of its Aboriginal inhabitants. Yet in little more than 200 years, from these inauspicious beginnings has grown a free, democratic and civilised nation.

This development was a gradual progress, marked more by small, largely forgotten milestones rather than by such notable occurrences as the federation of six separate colonies into the Commonwealth of Australia on 1 January 1901. Even that event took decades to evolve. Australia's political history has had no popular revolution, military victory or declaration of independence on which to anchor a truly national day of celebration. That may yet come, if and when Australia becomes a republic.

Meanwhile, Australia remains a constitutional monarchy, as well as a parliamentary democracy and a federation of States. Each of these terms describes a different aspect of its system of government and can be properly understood only in the broad context of the country's British heritage, rather than within the narrow bounds of its written constitution. Yet in spite of the lingering formal nexus with a shared, absentee and hereditary monarch, Australia is, in international law and for all practical purposes, a fully independent nation, fully responsible for its own governance and for its own constitutional future.

Towards democracy

The struggle for self-government and parliamentary democracy under the English crown was largely won in the nineteenth century. Subject only to a distant imperial parliament and the common and statute law of England, the first governor of New South Wales, Captain Arthur Phillip, ruled from Sydney over the whole eastern section of the continent. Tasmania (originally called Van Diemen's Land) became a separate colony in 1825. Establishment of Western Australia as a colony in 1829 completed British possession of the continent. Boundaries were redrawn to make way for the new colonies of South Australia in 1836, Victoria (settled by adventurers from Tasmania in the 1830s) in 1851, and Queensland in 1859.

Pressure from the growing numbers of free settlers and emancipated convicts saw the progressive development of representative, responsible government in each of the colonies. In New South Wales, a legislative council of nominated officials was appointed in 1823 to advise the governor. In 1842 the council was expanded to comprise a two-thirds majority of elected representatives. In 1856, the concept of responsible government was introduced with the addition of a legislative assembly from which, as in the House of Commons in London, an executive (the cabinet) was chosen from the majority of members to form a government.

Introduction of this, the so-called Westminster system of government—with two Houses of Parliament and the government responsible to the lower house—followed a similar pattern in the other colonies. Not that it was, at first, fully democratic. The colonial governors (and the British government) reserved certain powers of veto. Each of the legislative councils for a long time kept restrictive

membership and voting qualifications aimed at curbing any democratic 'excesses' by the more popularly elected assemblies. But the right of most men and, later, women to elect their parliamentary representatives by secret ballot was won in the colonies long before these reforms were introduced in England.

Federation

The tyranny of distance was both an impediment and an impetus to federal government. A sparse population spread over a vast continent, widely separated administrative capitals and poor communications—not to mention parochial jealousies, political rivalries and conflicting interests—all militated against the development of an overriding central government. Yet the problems of defending the continent and the examples of the United States and Canada were clear signposts to the logic of a federal union and Britain was more than eager for the colonies to share the costs and responsibilities of defence.

Many colonists were alarmed by potential threats from other European powers seen to have imperial ambitions, and harboured a fear, sparked by the arrival during the goldrushes of fairly large numbers of Chinese gold prospectors, of Asian immigration. As well, the citizens of some border towns were irritated by the customs and trade barriers between the colonies. However, there was mutual, deep suspicion between the free trade merchants of New South Wales, on the one hand, and Victoria's protectionist manufacturers and their workers on the other.

'A Nation for a Continent and a Continent for a Nation'. The long-held dream of the federationists at last came true on 1 January 1901 and crowds throughout Australia celebrated the birth of the new nation.

The commemorative coin, designed by Wojciech Pietranik, struck to mark the centenary of Australian nationhood.

Although the idea of federation had been raised much earlier, it took more than 20 years of patient advocacy, sporadic agitation and periodic debate to overcome the doubts and opposition. And that just to convince the majority of colonial politicians. A Federal Constitution was drafted, refined and approved by a series of intercolonial conventions in the 1880s and late 1890s before being endorsed by two sets of referenda in 1898 and 1899. New Zealand took part in one meeting but decided to stay apart.

Queen Victoria assented to the draft Constitution on 9 July 1900 and the fledgling Commonwealth of Australia came into being by an Act of the Imperial Parliament on 1 January 1901.

Australia's Parliament inherited by default many of the traditions of its English parent. Although Labor governments usually do away with the trappings of ceremonial office, such as the regalia of the Serjeant-at-Arms, they are reinstated when the conservative parties are in office.

The Commonwealth Constitution

The Constitution of the Commonwealth contains two essential elements. It sets out the formal structure of the federal government and limits the scope of its responsibilities. 'Formal' is the operative word here, because nothing is as simple as a literal reading of its text might suggest. The founding fathers imbued the written Constitution with certain assumptions based on their British heritage. These embraced their loyalty to the Crown, their understanding of the Westminster system of government and their faith in the rule of law and the traditional liberties of the monarch's subject. They did not see the need to spell out the conventions of responsible government or include a comprehensive bill of civil rights.

But even while adopting the principle of federalism, they were also eager to restrict the powers of the new federal government. They ceded a list of specific national responsibilities to the Commonwealth and left the rest with the individual States, as the former colonies were now to be styled. A few powers were to be shared (said to be concurrent), and others could be referred to the Commonwealth by the States if they wished. The main exclusive powers include defence, foreign affairs, international trade, communications, immigration, citizenship, pensions and the currency. Examples of concurrent responsibilities are health, education and welfare. An important change for the colonists was that trade between the States was to be free and that the Commonwealth would have the exclusive right to levy customs and excise duties (later held to include sales taxes).

In spite of these limitations, the Commonwealth has been able to expand its authority, in large part through its superior taxing powers but also partly by the rather liberal interpretation of some its specific powers. The authors of the Constitution also made it very difficult to change their document by legislation and, with only a few exceptions, notable as they are, successive federal governments have been unable to increase the Commonwealth's powers through constitutional amendments, which must have popular as well as parliamentary approval.

Australia's first ministry. Among the first legislation enacted by the infant government was an Act to restrict the entry of non-British peoples. This 'White Australia Policy', aimed chiefly at Asians, had wide public support.

Rt. Hon. Sir George Turner P.C. K.C.M.G.   Hon. Alfred Deakin.   Rt. Hon. Edmund Barton. P.C.   Hon. Sir John Forrest G.C.M.G.   Hon. C.C. Kingston

Hon. Sir Wm Lyne K.C.M.G.   Hon. J.G. Drake   Hon. Sir Philip Fysh K.C.M.G.   Hon. R.E. O'Connor

COMMONWEALTH MINISTRY.

Federal Parliament

The first three chapters of the Constitution lay down the traditional separation of powers between the legislature, the executive and the judicature. However, unlike the case in the United States, where these three are indeed strictly separate, in Australia, as in Britain, the executive is drawn from and accountable to the legislature. Formally, Parliament comprises the Queen (represented by the governor-general), the Senate and the House of Representatives. All legislation must be approved by both Houses and then given Royal (that is, vice-regal) assent.

The Constitution provides that the House of Representatives should have about twice as many members as the Senate. At present, the House has 148 members, popularly elected for three-year terms from single-member constituencies with a roughly equal number of voters. As in the British House of Commons, it is in the 'House of Reps' that governments are basically made and unmade.

The Senate was intended to serve a dual purpose—the traditional upper-house role as a chamber of review, and its federal function of safeguarding the interests of the States. Owing to the dominance of party politics, it does not fulfil the latter to any significant extent. In deference to the federal principle, each of the States is represented by 12 Senators, and there are two each from the Northern Territory and the Australian Capital Territory, a total of 76. Senators are elected with each State and Territory serving as a single (but widely unequal) electorate. Normally, Senators serve six-year terms, half their number retiring every three years. The Australian Senate is both more democratic (being directly elected by the people) and powerful than Britain's partly hereditary, partly appointed House of Lords. From 1967 to 1975 and again since 1981, no federal government has had a reliable majority in the Senate, which has at times obstructed, delayed or forced significant amendments to legislation. It can even force a government prematurely to the polls by denying 'supply' (that is, approval of vital expenditure).

Executive government

The Constitution would appear to give the governor-general, as the Queen's representative, almost totalitarian powers, including the right to summon and dissolve Parliament, to withhold assent to legislation, dismiss ministers of State and command the armed forces. One hint that these powers are not as sweeping as they may seem is the proviso that most of them must be exercised on the advice of an Executive Council whose members sit in Parliament. Another more effective limitation is the constitutional requirement for parliamentary approval of the raising and spending of revenue. (This was the historic means by which the British Parliament curbed the absolute power of the monarchy.)

In the United States, the president is both head of State and head of government. In Australia, following the British model, the governor-general's role as surrogate head of State is largely formal and ceremonial. The effective head of government is the prime minister, the leader of the parliamentary political party or coalition with a majority of members in the House of Representatives. He (up until the present day, no woman has been elected prime minister) or his party choose a cabinet or ministry, whose members are sworn in as members of the Executive Council and most of whom are given specific portfolios (responsibility for particular government departments). Nowadays, the term cabinet usually applies to an inner group of the more senior ministers, who meet on a more regular basis, while the term ministry covers all the ministers of State. Sitting opposite the prime minister and his 'front bench' of ministers in the House of Representatives are the leader of the opposition and the 'shadow ministers'— in effect, the alternative government.

Although the Constitution implies that the prime minister is chosen by the governor-general, the reality is the reverse. The governor-general is appointed, usually for an agreed term, by the Queen on the advice of the prime minister. By convention, he (again, so far no woman has been appointed) generally acts on the advice of the prime minister or other ministers,

Usher of the Black Rod is a central figure in the ceremonial opening of Parliament. A detail of the staff of office is shown at the centre of the page.

Old Parliament House, Canberra. Despite the cramped conditions of its later years, many MPs of long standing say that they miss the accessibility it offered both constituents and colleagues. Intended as a temporary seat of government, it was not replaced until 1988, more than sixty years after it opened.

Australia's federal Parliament consists of two 'houses', known popularly as the Lower House and the Upper House, or Senate. Pictured above, the Senate acts as house of review for legislation introduced into the Lower House.

whether it be the calling or dissolving of Parliament, assenting to legislation passed by Parliament, making regulations or appointing officials. In earlier years, governors-general tended to be British aristocrats or retired military officers. Now it is accepted that the holder of the office should be Australian, and they are more likely to be elder statesmen, respected professors or distinguished judges.

The governor-general is more than an ornamental cipher. As the British constitutional historian Walter Bagehot put it, he has a right to be consulted, to encourage and to warn. He also has discretionary powers in a crisis, although their exercise may embroil him in controversy. This happened in 1975, when the then governor-general, Sir John Kerr, dismissed the Whitlam Labor government, which had been denied supply by a hostile Senate. 'The Dismissal', as it is still called, sharply divided the nation, and fostered a rise in republican sentiments. Ironically, Kerr acted solely on his own initiative, without reference to the Queen. Whatever doubts remain about his timing and judgment, the underlying problem lay in the Constitution, which allowed the Senate to precipitate the crisis in a way no longer possible in Britain, and the governor-general to intervene in a manner which would be unthinkable by a modern British monarch.

The rare risk of dismissal aside, an Australian prime minister is in some respects in a stronger position than is a United States president, and so is his government. Though his tenure might depend on the confidence of his colleagues and his government's survival rest on its success at periodical elections, and though his policy proposals are subject to cabinet and/or parliamentary party approval, passage of his government's legislation through the House of Representatives is usually guaranteed through party discipline. A prime minister has another advantage over his counterpart in the United States: he can call an earlier than necessary election if political circumstances are opportune. Unsuccessful opposition leaders, on the other hand, face the greater hazard of being replaced by their party colleagues.

Sir John Kerr, at right, at his swearing-in as Governor-General in 1974. The following year, Kerr dismissed the government of the day led by Gough Whitlam, here seen standing on Kerr's right.

The Judicature and Legal System

The rule of law as a bulwark against arbitrary government and guarantee of civil rights is a fundamental principle of the Australian system of justice. Most civil and criminal law in Australia derives either from State legislation and regulations, or from the British heritage of common law as interpreted by the courts. Federal law is limited by the scope of the powers laid down in the Constitution, but a valid Federal law may override an inconsistent State law.

The High Court of seven justices is adjudicator of the Commonwealth Constitution and Australia's final court of appeal from both Federal and State jurisdictions. It has original jurisdiction over serious matters involving interpretation of the Constitution, those matters involving Commonwealth–State or interstate disputes, matters arising from international treaties and agreements and disputes to which the Federal government is a party. In the notable Mabo case in 1992, the High Court ruled that indigenous peoples' customary rights to their land survived white settlement, thus dispelling the legal theory that Australia had been a continent vacant for the taking. However, native title has largely been extinguished by legislation (for example, over all freehold land), and land still open to claims may be subject to negotiation or arbitration under the most stringent of conditions.

Two subordinate federal courts are the Federal Court (covering bankruptcy, corporation law, industrial relations, taxation and trade practices matters) and the Family Court (matrimonial disputes and divorce). Supreme Courts in each State and Territory conduct the most serious civil and criminal cases, and hear appeals from lower courts. The County Court in Victoria and the District Courts in the other mainland States have civil and criminal jurisdiction of intermediate importance. Magistrates preside over courts of summary jurisdiction, which have different names in different States. These courts deal with minor offences, disputes and claims, and also hold preliminary hearings of more serious criminal charges to decide whether or not they should be tried in a higher court.

Both the Commonwealth and State governments have a range of quasi-judicial tribunals to deal with such matters as administrative and planning appeals, industrial relations, Aboriginal land claims, human rights and discrimination issues, small claims, tenancy disputes and criminal compensation. The former (federal) Arbitration and Conciliation Commission was once a powerful body which adjudicated in national labour disputes and served as a central wage-fixing authority. However, its role has been largely replaced by a decentralised system of enterprise agreements and private contracts.

Changing the Constitution

The onerous provisions laid down by the founding fathers of federation and the sceptical conservatism of the Australian electorate have made it extremely difficult to change the Constitution. Formal amendments require legislation by the Federal Parliament that must be approved in a referendum by a majority of voters overall and in at least four of the six States. Since 1901, only eight of 44 referendum proposals have passed this formidable barrier. The most significant changes approved have been to give the Commonwealth control over social services including medical and hospital benefits (1946) and power to legislate on Aboriginal affairs (1967). Some notable defeats included federal attempts to ban the Australian Communist Party (1951), to nationalise monopolies (1913 and 1919), acquire wide-ranging powers over industry and commerce (1926) and to control prices and incomes (1973). More recently, in 2000, the proposal for an Australian republic was defeated at a referendum. More often than not, federal political rivalry, the suspicions of the smaller States and a reluctance on the part of the public to invest any government with more power have proven to be insuperable barriers.

The Northern Territory's Supreme Court building in Darwin. The Territory Government has recently come under attack for its 'mandatory sentencing' laws, seen as draconian by many in the legal profession.

LEFT: Australia's legal system draws heavily on English jurisprudence, represented by the reigning monarch.

Many early courthouses reflect the optimism of their day. This one in Maryborough, Queensland, was completed in 1877 and occupies the site of the former Immigration Barracks.

State and Territory Governments

The Constitution allows for the creation of new States within the Commonwealth, but sporadic movements in parts of Queensland and New South Wales for subdivision (and in Western Australia for secession) have come to nothing. The sparsely settled and largely self-governing Northern Territory is likely to be the first new State since federation.

The structure of government and parliamentary systems within the original six States is similar to that of the Federal system. Each State has a governor (who directly represents the Queen and is not subordinate to the governor-general), and two Houses of Parliament (with the exception of Queensland, which in 1922 abolished its Legislative Council). State governments are headed by a premier, who is the parliamentary leader of the majority party or parties in the lower houses, known as Legislative Assemblies or Houses of Assembly.

The Northern Territory was separated from South Australia in 1911 to be administered as a federal territory. Self-government approaching full Statehood has developed over the years, but the Commonwealth retains control over Aboriginal affairs, national parks and uranium mining, as well as the right to amend or override Territory laws. The Territory has an administrator, responsible to the Federal Government, and a chief minister, who is responsible to the Legislative Assembly, fulfils the functions of a State premier.

The Australian Capital Territory (ACT) was also established in 1911. As a compromise between the claims of Melbourne and Sydney, the Constitution provided for a national capital—Canberra—to be built in New South Wales at least 100 miles (160 kms) south of Sydney in the direction of Victoria. Until the first Parliament

Parliament House. Darwin. There is a strong push for Statehood for the Northern Territory which is largely self-governing, though it still relies heavily on subsidies from the Commonwealth.

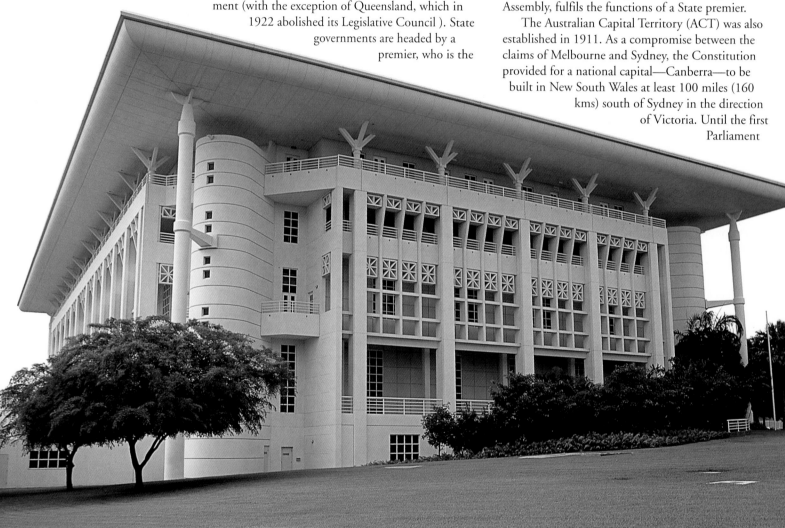

GOVERNMENT TIMELINE

1788 Captain Arthur Phillip hoists the British flag at Sydney Cove, claiming the colony of NSW for the Crown.

1808 The so-called Rum Rebellion sees soldiers depose Governor Bligh and run colony until Lachlan Macquarie becomes governor in 1810.

1823 With NSW Judicature Act, Britain grants colony a degree of self-government by setting up Legislative Council, a panel of citizens presided over by governor.

1825 Van Diemen's Land becomes separate colony under Lieutenant-Governor George Arthur.

1829 Western Australia becomes a separate colony with founding of Swan River Colony.

1836 Boundaries of NSW redrawn to create colony of SA.

1842 NSW's Legislative Council expanded to 24 elected members and 12 appointed members.

1851 Colony of Victoria created as a result of Australian Colonies Government Act of 1850, which also recognised desire for self-government in colonies.

1856 Legislative Assembly created in NSW. Universal male suffrage introduced in SA and later in Vic. (1857), NSW (1858), Qld. (1872), WA (1893), Tas. (1900).

1859 Moreton Bay area becomes separate colony, to be known as Queensland.

1890 Founding of Labor Party in NSW. It becomes a national party in 1901.

1894 Women given the right to vote in SA. WA follows suit in 1899, the Commonwealth in 1902.

1898 First referendum on federation of colonies is inconclusive. A second referendum in the following year sees all states except WA vote in favour of federation.

1901 Federation proceeds and the Commonwealth of Australia is proclaimed on 1 January. The colonies become states and federal parliament opens in Melbourne on 9 May.

1908 Canberra is chosen as site for proposed new federal capital.

1909 Liberal Party formed following merger of Free-Traders and Protectionists.

1915 Introduction of compulsory voting in Qld. Later introduced by Commonwealth (1924), Vic. (1926), NSW and Tas. (1928) and WA (1939).

1918 Introduction erential voting sy

1927 Federal Par moves to new Parl House in Canbe

Like the Commonwealth, each State and Territory has its coat of arms. Pictured above is that of the Northern Territory.

TOP LEFT: Tasmania's Parliament House was purposely built in close proximity to the waterfront. In its early years it did joint duty as the Customs House.

House was opened in Canberra in 1927 the national Parliament sat in Melbourne. The first building was considered temporary, but it was not until 1988, the bicentenary of European settlement, that a majestic new Parliament House on Capital Hill was opened. The ACT has a more limited form of self-government than that of the Northern Territory.

Australia's sovereignty over offshore territories has diminished over the years. The former Australian territories of Papua and New Guinea became a single independent nation in 1975, and the small Pacific island of Nauru achieved its independence in 1968. Australia is still responsible for Norfolk Island, the Cocos Islands and Christmas Island. All three have limited local government under the administration of the federal government. Australian Antarctic Territory has several research stations under federal control.

Federal–State relations

Over the past century, the powers and responsibilities of the Commonwealth over those of the States have expanded to an extent that few of the federation's architects would have wished and only the most prescient of them could have foreseen. This dominance is only marginally due to those constitutional amendments approved by the Australian electorate. Other significant factors have been the formal referral by all or some of the States of their jurisdiction (such as civil aviation and industrial relations), extension of existing Commonwealth powers into new areas (posts and telegraphs, for example, now includes radio and television broadcasting), reliance on its external affairs powers to legislate on matters impinging on United Nations treaties (such as those on anti-discrimination and human rights), and liberal interpretation by the High Court of Commonwealth powers in such areas as environmental protection.

The most potent instrument of federal intrusion on State sovereignty, however, has been, and remains, the power of the purse. The Constitution gave to the

Commonwealth the exclusive right to levy excise and customs duties, which the High Court later ruled to include sales tax. In 1942, as a wartime emergency measure, the States agreed to give the responsibility for collecting income tax (including company tax and capital gains taxes) wholly to the Commonwealth in return for a share of the revenue. For many years the Commonwealth also exercised strict controls over borrowing by the States.

This is now the nub of a continual conflict, for not only has the Commonwealth gained the preponderance of lucrative taxing powers, it but also retains the right to decide how much of the collected revenue it will return to the States, and on what terms. The States have for long complained that their financial resources are inadequate to pay for expensive works and services, and that the Federal Government has increasingly used its power to make specific-purpose grants to interfere in such State responsibilities as education and health.

In 2000, the Federal Government replaced the existing sales tax regime with a very controversial and more comprehensive new goods and services tax—the GST—the proceeds of which are to be directed to the States and Territories. This arrangement should help strengthen State revenues, but the more populous among them resent having to subsidise the financially weaker States by revenue sharing.

Dissension over money matters aside, a form of 'cooperative federalism' has gradually evolved through regular meetings of State ministers and officials to discuss those problems of common concern. However, the centralists and constitutional reformers are of the opinion that the Commonwealth still does not have sufficient power to manage a modern economy at a time of increasing globalisation, while the federalists wish for a clearer distinction and a fairer balance between Federal and State revenues and responsibilities.

As the site of the Commonwealth Government, Canberra is also home to the embassies of foreign governments. Many, like that of Papua New Gunea, are housed in buildings of striking design.

| 2 Australia adopts of Westminster of which awarded all colonies equal status with the UK. | 1945 Modern Liberal Party created by Robert Menzies. 1946 Commonwealth Government granted control of social services following amendment to Constitution. | 1957 Formation of anticommunist Democratic Labor Party splits Labor vote, effectively keeping party out of government for next 15 years. | 1972 Labor returns to power when Gough Whitlam's party is elected to Federal Government. Whitlam immediately begins sweeping social reforms. | 1977 'Advance Australia Fair' is adopted as national anthem. Founding of Australian Democrats under Don Chipp, with slogan 'Keep the Bastards Honest'. | 1986 Proclamation of Australia Act is signed by the Queen, ending executive powers of Crown in Australia and right of British Parliament to legislate for Australia. | 1993 Liberal Party's intention to introduce GST if successful in federal election contributes to their defeat at polls. Labor, now led by Paul Keating, increases its majority. | 1998 Coalition government returned and honours pledge to set up Constitutional Convention to examine move to a republic. NT voters reject statehood in referendum. |
| 1943 Enid Lyons and Dorothy Tangney become first female members elected to federal parliament. | 1949 Liberal and Country party coalition gains power and governs for 23 years. 1951 Referendum proposingbanning of Communist Party is defeated. | 1967 Prime Minister Harold Holt disappears while swimming at Portsea, Vic. Constitution amended to give Federal Government control of Aboriginal affairs. | 1975 Whitlam government dismissed by Governor-General Sir John Kerr. At subsequent election, Liberal and National parties takes power under Malcolm Fraser. | 1978 NT becomes self-governing. ACT follows suit in 1989. 1983 Labor wins federal election, making Bob Hawke prime minister. | 1987 Labor re-elected. 1990 Hawke government re-elected. Carmen Lawrence elected premier of WA, becoming Australia's first woman premier. | 1996 John Howard leads Liberal Party to landslide victory at federal election. 1997 Independent MP Pauline Hanson founds One Nation Party in Ipswich, Qld. | 1999 Voters reject republican model presented at national referendum by 55% to 45%, thus opting to retain constitutional monarchy. |

The Political System

Part of the chamber housing the Legislative Assembly, Parliament House, Canberra. This, the Lower House, is where legislation is first introduced and debated.

The Westminster system of parliamentary democracy depends on the competition of different political parties to run for office in periodical elections to ensure that one party (or a coalition) has a cohesive parliamentary majority and can form a government. Under this system these parties formulate public policies, select candidates for election and campaign for electoral victory. In Australia over the past one hundred years, the main division in Federal and State parliaments has been between the Australian Labor Party and Liberal–other conservative alliances, each side fighting to capture the middle ground occupied by most voters. Smaller parties rise and fall over the years, and independents may from time to time win a few seats in Parliament.

Australian Labor Party

William 'Billy' Hughes had a stormy political career. Of Welsh parents, Hughes migrated to Australia in 1884 and worked at jobs as diverse as boundary rider and ship's cook. In 1916, many of his first cabinet resigned over Hughes' support for conscription to military service.

The Australian Labor Party (ALP) is the country's oldest political party with continuous representation in its parliaments. In 2000 it was the ruling party in New South Wales, Victoria, Queensland and Tasmania. It grew from, and is still linked, with the trade union movement. After long maritime and shearers' strikes failed in 1890–91, union leaders turned to political action as an alternative means of improving conditions for workers. By 1901, Labor

candidates had been elected to most colonial/State parliaments and to the first federal Parliament. The party adopted its present name in 1918.

For much of the twentieth century the ALP proclaimed socialist objectives, among them the nationalisation of key industries. But the party has always been more pragmatic than ideological, more nationalist than internationalist, and more intent on sharing the benefits of the capitalist system than on overthrowing it. Now the ALP also favours Australia becoming a republic.

These days, the Labor Party is essentially a social democratic party and, with trade union membership declining, has to win significant middle-class support to govern. It has long abandoned its original insistence on a 'White Australia' policy in favour of a more egalitarian, humanitarian and anti-racist stance. The Commonwealth governments led by Gough Whitlam (1972–75), Bob Hawke (1983–91) and especially Paul Keating (1991–96) radically modified many of Labor's traditional collectivist principles to make the Australian economy more productive, competitive and resilient in the international marketplace, to win business confidence and to convince voters of their party's economic competence. Labor administrations have gone further along the paths of free trade, fiscal rectitude, financial deregulation, and even that of privatisation of government enterprises than would have seemed imaginable 30 years ago. At the same time, the party believes in a fairer distribution of incomes and wealth through tax policies, social security and community services, stronger environmental protection and better opportunities for the vulnerable and disadvantaged. The present leader, Kim Beazley, is unlikely to turn back the clock.

Both in national structure and its parliamentary memberships, the ALP has demanded greater loyalty and enforced stronger discipline than its more loosely organised opponents. But it is also more sharply divided into factions and sub-factions, which struggle for policy dominance, parliamentary preselection and executive positions. The factions range from the often militant Socialist Left to the more pragmatic Irish-Catholic Right, spanning both the party's trade union affiliates and its local branch members. In 1954 a deep, bitter and long-lasting schism developed over allegations by the federal Labor

FIRST HUGHES MINISTRY
27 -10 -1915
TO
14 - 11 -1916

leader, Dr H.V. Evatt, that a secretive, Catholic-inspired movement, formed to fight the Communist dominance of some trade unions, was trying to take control of the ALP. Many Labor members quit to form the new right-wing Democratic Labor Party which split the Labor vote and effectively kept the mainstream ALP out of office in Canberra and some States for nearly two decades.

Liberal Party

The present-day Liberal Party was formed in 1945 by Robert Gordon Menzies from the main non-Labor parties that evolved from informal political groupings in the earlier colonial parliaments. Menzies, who led the Liberals to power in Canberra in 1949, was one of Australia's most influential political leaders. An Anglophile and ardent monarchist, Menzies envisaged the Liberal Party as a bastion of free enterprise, personal opportunity and balanced federalism against what he portrayed as the restrictive, coercive forces of socialism and bureaucratic centralism.

In practice, he and his successors proved to be more flexible and opportunistic than their official platform and the pre-1972 Labor Party. In the structure of its organisation, the Liberal Party is federal rather than national, exerts less control over its parliamentary members, and accords its leaders (while

successful) more authority. Unlike Labor, it has no formal factions, but there have long been divisions between the party's 'small-l liberal', socially permissive, consensus-seeking and welfare-oriented elements (sometimes called the 'wets') and the now more dominant social conservatives and hardline economic rationalists (known as the 'drys').

The present Federal Coalition Government led by the Liberal prime minister, John Howard, since 1996 faces another election in 2001. His administration has pursued a radical program of tax reform and economic restructuring, has introduced rigorous industrial relations and social security regimes. Mr Howard is a strong advocate of 'family values', an opponent of the republican movement (which many of his colleagues support) and has provoked much controversy over his seemingly uncompromising attitudes to more liberal immigration, Aboriginal reconciliation and some United Nations committees.

National Party

Its former name, the Australian Country Party, is a truer indication of the National Party's regional base and rural focus. It grew rapidly in membership and influence in the early 1920s, drawing support from farmers' associations who were dissatisfied with wartime marketing schemes for primary products.

Feeding the chooks. 'Impromptu' press conferences are part and parcel of political life. Here, Palestinian protestors and the press confront Anthony Albanese, Parliamentary Secretary to the Shadow Minister for Family and Community Services.

The National Party is strongest in Queensland, where it is the leading non-Labor party in the State Parliament, and parts of New South Wales. Federally, it has been a junior coalition partner in every non-Labor government since 1940. Socially conservative and staunchly pro-monarchist, the party is primarily concerned with the interests of farmers and those in rural towns in issues ranging from trade access, commodity prices and marketing arrangements to better delivery of government services. Telecommunications has recently become a major issue.

At times the National Party has formed strategic alliances with city-based manufacturers (offering support for tariff protection in return for farm subsidies) and multinational mining corporations. Its need to influence public policy on behalf of its rural constituents and yet to collaborate with the more broadly based, urban-oriented Liberals has often led to internal and mutual tensions—such as the issue of gun control—and to occasional schisms in some States.

Minor political parties

While many special-interest groups, independents and splinter parties contest elections, in recent years only three minor parties have managed to achieve parliamentary representation in Canberra and/or more than one State.

AUSTRALIAN DEMOCRATS

The Democrats, formed in 1975 as a middle-of-the-road 'third force' under the leadership of a former Liberal minister, has been the most influential of the minor groups. Drawing on popular disenchantment with the major parties by promising to 'keep the bastards honest', it has at times (as at present) held the balance of power in the Senate. It has used this

position to frustrate or force modifications of aspects of many aspects of the Howard Liberal government's tax, industrial relations, social security, privatisation and environmental policies.

GREENS

The Greens have significant support in Tasmania, and have several state MPs and one senator. They have also won some support in Western Australia by their opposition to logging and seeking greater protection of heritage wilderness areas.

ONE NATION

Founded by a small-town businesswoman, Pauline Hanson, this party achieved international notoriety in the past few years with its racicst anti-immigration rhetoric, naïve economic prescriptions and strident opposition to Aboriginal land rights. Internal squabbling, culminating in a split, electoral deregistration and litigation eclipsed its limited initial electoral success, but in 2001 it experienced a resurgence of support in two State elections.

The electoral system

Compulsory electoral enrolment and voting, first introduced in 1915, is one distinctive feature of Australian elections. All adult citizens (aged 18 and over) in Australia are not only entitled to vote in elections for Federal and State parliaments but are required by law to do so. All elections, including those for local government, are by secret ballot and are conducted with scrupulous honesty by an independent electoral commission.

Preferential voting, dating from 1918, is another distinguishing feature of the Australian elections, and is used for the House of Representatives and most

State assemblies. Under this system, voters must mark ballot papers with consecutive numbers in order of their preference (or as advised by their preferred party). If one candidate does not win an outright majority, the one polling the least votes is eliminated and the voters' second preferences are distributed, and so on, until one candidate wins a majority. Minor parties, by advising supporters how to allocate their preferences, can often determine which of the major parties will win particular seats or even gain office.

Forms of proportional representation, with each State as a single, multi-member electorate, are used in elections for the Senate and the Legislative Councils (upper houses) of New South Wales and South Australia. Tasmania uses proportional representation, based on five seven-member electorates, for its House of Assembly. To simplify voting for the Senate, electors may now mark a single block vote for their preferred party or grouping, rather than having to fill in numbers for 50 to 70 or more individual candidates.

All elections make provision for the casting of both absentee and postal votes by those unable to attend their local polling booth. Since 1984, the Commonwealth Electoral Commission has allocated public funding to political parties for their election campaigns, and has required certain disclosures of other campaign contributions.

Voting for local councils, once restricted to property owners, is open to all adult residents and in some States is compulsory. The lord mayors of Sydney and Brisbane are directly elected by voters, while most other mayors and shire presidents are elected by their councils. The Labor Party endorses candidates in some urban areas, but most aspiring councillors are either independents or supported by local business or residential interest groups.

Public administration and local government

Australia has followed, federally and in each State, the British model of a non-political, permanent public service that continues the task of impartial policy advice and administration regardless of changes of government. However, this system is no longer as clear-cut as it was. Incoming governments now often appoint new heads of departments and other senior executives, mostly from outside the service and on fixed contracts, whom they regard as more in tune with their programs. Ministers now also have their own expert and political advisers, who may be more influential than their departmental officers.

Much of the work of government, which in other countries is left to government departments or private enterprise, has traditionally been undertaken in Australia by semi-autonomous statutory corporations, commissions and authorities. Some of those established to provide essential services such as savings banks, public transport, and gas and electricity, have been privatised in recent years, in the ostensible interests of efficiency, competition and debt-reduction. There are still some powerful regulatory authorities, however, like the Australian Competition and Consumer Commission.

A uniquely structured and independent federal statutory authority is ATSIC, the Aboriginal and Torres Strait Islander Commission. Its 18 members are delegates from 35 directly elected regional councils. It advises governments on indigenous affairs, advocates indigenous interests in national and international forums, and administers programs relating to land rights, community support and welfare. However, its position is now under review.

Local government in Australia dates from the colonial era, when settled areas were divided into rural shires and urban centres classed as cities, towns or boroughs. Although often called the third tier of government, local government is subject to State or Territory law and supervision. Its scope of mandatory and optional responsibilities is more limited than in many other countries, such services as police, schools, hospitals, main roads and public transport being state-run operations. Local councils are generally responsible for the maintenance of local roads, street lighting and cleaning, garbage disposal, traffic control and parking, planning and building permits, local parks and gardens, recreational and cultural activities and local community and health services. Local councils derive most of their revenue from rates based on property values and from government grants.

Today, many shire and municipal councils are fighting to stay afloat, a far cry from the age of certainty that saw the building of this town hall in Collingwood, a suburb of Melbourne, Victoria.

LEFT: Voting in Australia is by secret ballot and, in State and Federal elections, is compulsory.

The politics of local government engenders election campaigns as bitter as any fought in the federal sphere. Here, Hobart's Mayor, Rob Valentine, adjusts a sign canvassing votes.

Evolution to Nationhood

The new federal government announced a competition on 29 April 1901 to design the Australian flag. The prize money of £200 was divided between five winners whose designs all included the Australian Blue Ensign. For many years this flag was restricted to official use only, until the 1953 Flags Act was passed, establishing theAustralian Blue Ensign as the Australian National Flag.

The seat of Australia's Federal Government, Parliament House, Canberra. Unlike the national flag, its design seems to have gained widespread approval..

Australia's growth from colonial status to that of sovereign independence has been gradual, as Britain progressively relinquished its imperial controls and Australians began increasingly to assert their separate interests. Just before Federation, Australia achieved 'dominion' status within the British Empire, with the recognition of internal self-government, considerable independence in foreign relations and at least implied equality with the 'mother country'. This was more clearly defined in the 1926 Balfour Declaration and the 1931 Statute of Westminster, which Australia did not bother formally to adopt until 1942.

Further milestones have included the following.

Australian citizenship was introduced in 1949; up until this time, Australians were regarded as British subjects and carried British passports.

In 1997 *Advance Australia Fair* was adopted as the national song in place of *God Save the Queen*; attempts to change the national flag have not as yet succeeded.

The High Court was recognised as the final court of appeal with the ending of the right of appeal to the Judicial Committee of the Privy Council in London from the year 1985–86.

The passing of the *Australia Act of 1986* formally relieved the Queen of any remaining (though long-disused) executive powers over the Commonwealth of Australia and the States, severed the dormant right of the British Parliament to legislate for Australia and the application of some old imperial statutes.

During World War II Australia realised that it could no longer rely on the Royal Navy to defend its shores and the wartime prime minister, Labor's John Curtin, made a dramatic appeal to the United States of America for support against the prospect of a Japanese invasion. Since then, Australia has continued to look to the United States as a strategic guardian (as evidenced by its active participation in the controversial and divisive Vietnam War, and ongoing joint defence, surveillance and communications facilities), while forging strong trade links with Japan and other nations of the Asian-Pacific region.

Australia was a founding member of the United Nations and has always played a prominent role in many of its agencies and peace-keeping missions (most recently in East Timor). It is also active in a number of world trade and regional economic organisations. As a relatively isolated, sparsely populated, trade-dependent, medium-sized power, Australia is now responding to pressures to pursue a more self-reliant defence policy, foster more cooperative relationships with its Asian–Pacific neighbours, and push for lower trade barriers and to negotiate better prices for its exports.

Towards a republic

In a national referendum in November 1999, voters rejected by about 55 per cent to 45 a proposal that Australia become a republic. This will not be the end of the debate. Like the federation movement more than a century earlier, the momentum is expected to resume and eventually succeed. The former Labor prime minister, Paul Keating, strongly advocated the constitutional change, proposing a 'minimalist' model that would formally replace the governor-general with an appointed president, fulfilling much the same limited functions. His Liberal successor, John Howard, although personally opposed to change, honoured an election commitment to convene a Constitutional Convention and, if it favoured a republic, put the question to a popular referendum.

The Convention, consisting of 152 appointed and elected delegates, met in 1998. A majority soon agreed in principle that Australia should become a republic; the challenge was to recommend what form it should take. There was no impetus for a radical change to an American-style executive presidency that would be incompatible with the country's Westminster parliamentary system. The main division was between those who wanted a directly elected head of State—the popular choice, according to opinion polls—and those who thought a president should be appointed by Parliament.

The Convention finally recommended more or less the model suggested by Mr Keating: that the president be an eminent citizen acceptable to the prime minister and opposition leader and appointed for an agreed term by a two-thirds majority of Federal Parliament. When put to a referendum, however, the proposal failed. Opponents played not so much on royalist sentiments, which are undoubtedly diminishing in Australia, as on a popular mistrust of politicians and a prevailing preference for an elected president.

A change of government in Canberra is likely to revive the question, probably by first holding a plebiscite to determine whether most Australians favour a republic in principle, before seeking approval for a particular form of change. The main problem with a directly elected head of state is that it could politicise an office at present held by an in the main respected, impartial and unifying figure above the fray of partisan politics, and possibly lead to a constitutional crisis if some future president, claiming a personal mandate, contravened the advice of the prime minister. Some critics of the Keating model believe, however, that this would weaken some of the subtle checks and balances of the present system.

Many, if not most, Australians feel that a republic is the logical next step on the long road to national maturity, even though such a largely symbolic assertion would make little practical difference. But meanwhile there are more pressing problems to engage the nation and its leaders—how best to reap the benefits of an increasingly global economy, a volatile financial marketplace and the bewilderingly fast technological revolution, for instance, while at the same time mitigating their socially damaging and polarising impacts. And how best to achieve reconciliation with the indigenous peoples of Australia and enhance relations with the nation's regional neighbours, strategic allies and trading partners and in a spirit of cooperative self-reliance. Such challenges of national security, prosperity and welfare have a deeper resonance than a renewed clash of constitutional symbols.

Economic Structure and Evolution

Coal loader at Newcastle, New South Wales. In the 1960s, a coal-mining boom turned Australia into a mineral-driven export-oriented economy almost overnight.

The Akubra hat factory, Kempsey, northern New South Wales. The lifting of tariffs on clothing imports had adversely affected many rural centres.

In the century following white settlement, agriculture and some mining, mostly gold, fuelled Australia's economy. Manufacturing industries began to emerge as cities grew in the second half of the nineteenth century, but the adage 'Australia rides on the sheep's back' remained true. Colonial ties reinforced the economic importance of agriculture: Australia exported cheap agricultural goods to Britain and provided a market for its manufactures. Australia exported about half of its total production and spent about half of national income on imported goods and services, a level of trade not again achieved until the late 1990s.

With Federation and independence, the push to develop manufacturing industries grew. In the battle between 'free-traders' and the 'protectionists' seeking taxes (tariffs) and/or prohibitions on imports, the protectionists won. The alliance between emerging manufacturers looking to capture the Australian market and trade unions seeking secure jobs became a powerful political force.

As protection grew, so did manufacturing, related employment and the influence of trade unions, and Australia developed a highly regulated economy.

When farmers protested that tariffs were raising their costs, policy shifted to what soon became known as 'protection all round'—various marketing boards and subsidies were introduced to match the assistance given to manufacturers.

Primary industries

In the mid-1960s mining developed with a rush, iron ore and coal turned Australia almost overnight into an export-oriented, low-cost mining economy. After a shaky period in the late 1960s, when trading frenzy made gambling chips of mining shares, the mining sector expanded and diversified, making Australia a major producer of minerals, ranging from alumina to diamonds to iron ore.

The battle between free traders and protectionists was rejoined in the 1970s, and this time it was the free traders who won. Successive governments cut tariffs and manufacturing went into relative decline, its share of national production falling from 20 per cent in 1974 to 12 per cent in 2000. The steel, motor vehicle, textiles and clothing and footwear industries were the hardest hit.

Although primary industries have been important to Australia's economic history, their contribution to national production is relatively small. In the year ended June 2000, agriculture, forestry and fishing together contributed about 3 per cent and mining 4 per cent, little different from the position they held 25 years before. Nonetheless, primary industries continue to have a significance beyond mere figures. This is partly cultural, Australia's national identity remains at least partly rooted in the idea of 'the bush', and agriculture and mining remain as Australia's major export industries. Indeed, the current expansion of our agricultural exports looks set to rival the golden age of wool. A good example can be found in the

wine industry, discussed in the following pages, which is still experiencing phenomenal growth in both production and exports.

However, the boom in the agricultural sector and the continuing growth in mining and other primary industries pose questions which must be addressed. Concerns about indigenous peoples' rights to their land and environmental sustainability are widespread. Meaningful land rights for the indigenous peoples, erosion and salination of farmland, the loss of bio-diversity due to logging in old-growth forests and the long-term implications of mining uranium are but a few of the challenges facing Australians in the effort to balance present and future prosperity.

The services sector

Services has always been the largest sector in the Australian economy and at June 2000 accounted for almost 73 per cent of gross domestic product (GDP). It is perhaps a surprising figure, but if you think about where most people work, then banks, schools, hospitals, shops, restaurants and offices come to mind. Figure 1 shows the contribution to GDP of some major service industries. The most pronounced change during the past 25 years has been the growth of the finance, insurance, property and business services. Their combined contribution to national production has grown more than 5 per cent since 1974, corresponding to the decline in the manufacturing sector. Economic data on the

significance of tourism in the Australian economy have only just become available in the Australian Bureau of Statistics' (ABS) innovative Tourism Satellite Account. The ABS estimates that for the year 1997–98 tourism contributed 4.5 per cent of GDP— almost $1 in every $20 of national production.

The decline in manufacturing and the growth in the service industries have wrought much change on the Australian economy. Union membership, once almost universal, has halved since 1976 and economic

Wool classing. The wool industry was the source of much of Australia's wealth until the early 1950s.

Figure 1
Selected service industries, contribution to national production, 1974–2000

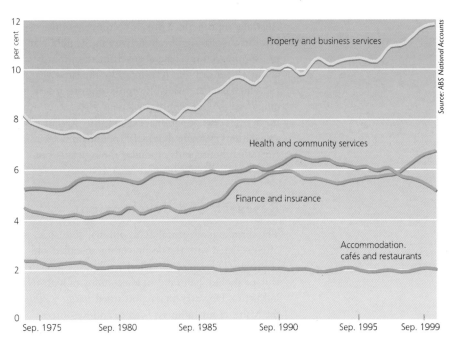

Source: ABS National Accounts

A coal train passing through the suburbs of Newcastle, New South Wales. Despite the demise of the steelworks in the city, Newcastle remains an important port for the export of primary produce.

activity has become increasingly concentrated in the metropolitan areas. As small textile and clothing manufacturers in country towns and steel makers in provincial cities closed, the financial centres of the capital cities, especially Sydney, have boomed and an increasing number of people are employed in small consulting firms, in many cases working from home.

Another way of understanding the structure of the economy is to look at the distribution of economic activity between the institutions that organise it. Australia is primarily a private-sector economy, but there is also significant activity in the public and non-profit sectors. General government output is about 18 per cent of GDP. In 1996, the latest year for which data are available, non-profit organisations employed 6.5 per cent of the labour force, accounting for 5.5 per cent of national expenditure. Recent ABS calculations estimate that in 1997, unpaid work in Australian households produced the equivalent of 50 per cent of GDP in goods and services.

Research and development

The shrinking of Australia's 'traditional' industries is often equated with the decline of the so-called 'old' economy. There is much talk that all future growth will, or should, be in the 'new' economy of high-tech industries. However, in a report titled *Industry 2000*, the Minister for Industry, Science and Resources remarked that while new-economy factors had been important in boosting growth in the US economy, this does not appear to be so in Australia. A 'brain drain' of scientists seizing more lucrative opportunities in the United States of America and Europe, along with the tendency for Australian inventions to be sold for development elsewhere are two of the contributing factors. Many commentators express concern because high-tech industries are the likely source of future export growth, and a recent survey by the ABS on the use of information technology shows that although almost two-thirds of all employing businesses in Australia used computers in 1998, the nation produces little of this equipment.

Research and development (R&D) is at the centre of the new-economy industries. However, the 1997 *Review of Business Programs* reported that although Australian government support for R&D is at about the average level for advanced industrial countries, private-sector investment is lagging well behind. Not unpredictably, the ABS survey of innovation in manufacturing records that though many companies blame this unwillingness to invest in R&D on a lack of government assistance, they also contend that there is little need for research and development because others' innovations can be copied. However, as the impact of global competition is increasingly felt, such industries will need to expand. Whether or not this happens will depend partly on government policies and partly on where individual companies fit into the global competitive system.

Australia has a reputation as a supplier of agricultural produce of uniformly high standards. The work undertaken at Institutions such as this cheese facility at Charles Sturt University, Wagga Wagga, have played a large part in establishing this reputation.

Many regional universities focus their research efforts on the advancement of agriculture. This is the winery operated by Charles Sturt University in the Riverina district of New South Wales.

The Wine Industry

White steel wine vats in the Barossa Valley, South Australia. The majority of wine produced in Australia is sold as 'bulk-wine' based on multiregional blends.

While the small players in Australia's agricultural sector are placing increasing reliance on diversifying their production to fill niche markets and exploit the country's image—justified or not—as a 'clean, green' source of agricultural produce, the large companies are beginning to dominate the growing of crops such as cotton, edible oil-seeds and wine grapes. In the wine industry, for example, there has been a proliferation of small, family-owned 'boutique' wineries, but both the domestic and export markets are dominated by the large corporations.

At the same time, a growing interest in wine has provoked the new phenomenon of wine tourism. People have been visiting wine regions for years, but deliberately encouraging tourists with tours, accommodation, good food and other attractions has today become a major industry in Australia.

Modern developments

Wine has been made in Australia for almost two centuries, but the current growth in production has its beginnings in an increase in the consumption of wine with meals as Australian society changed its dining habits over the past 35 years, a trend which has in recent years been influenced in no small way by the emergence of an 'Australian cuisine', which draws its inspiration from the national commitment to the concept of multiculturalism.

These recent developments are characterised by an industry structure in which most wine is made by just a few large companies, a willingness to ignore European tradition to produce interregional blends and an emphasis on technological development.

Often forgotten in the pursuit of world-renowned wines like Penfold's Grange and Henschke's Hill of Grace is the fact that half of all the wine consumed in

The tasting room at McWilliam's Mount Pleasant Winery in the Hunter Valley, New South Wales. A growing national interest in wine has seen the rapid growth of winery-based tourism in Australia.

Australia is bulk wine, which is usually purchased in 4 litre (1 gallon) casks. The basis of this wine—and of many of the cheaper bottles of Australian wine sold in supermarkets around the world—is the multiregional blend. The statement, 'Wine of south-eastern Australia' on a label means that the bottle's contents could have originated from almost anywhere except Western Australia—that is to say, from anywhere in 98 per cent of the nation's vineyard area. Such wine may well be sold as varietal blends and will be distinctively Australian, but will fly in the face of traditional European concepts of 'terroir', regional wines influenced by the soils in which the grapes grow. However, this does not mean the wines are of poorer quality. Australia's fruity wines have revolutionised the international market over the past two decades and even the nation's greatest wine, Grange, is traditionally a blend from several regions.

Two factors can be singled out to explain Australia's rapid rise to prominence on the world wine scene. The first is the emphasis placed on technology. Australian wines are often criticised for being too clean, made as they are with a focus on hygiene. However, the crisp, fresh, value-for-money chardonnay that seems run-of-the-mill today barely existed 20 years ago. Australia came to large-scale wine production free of the long-entrenched winemaking traditions of the older countries, and with the capital to invest in state-of-the-art equipment and a determination to pursue technological perfection that is also emphasised in excellent university courses in viticulture and winemaking.

The second factor is the willingness, even keenness, of Australian winemakers to share ideas and to learn from their colleagues. An extension of this, the 'show system' of wine competitions spawned by winemakers exhibiting at regional agricultural shows, has been of inestimable value in raising the quality of Australian wine. Notwithstanding the obvious marketing benefits gained by winning medals, many winemakers use these events to learn from the judges the strengths and weaknesses of their wines.

The growing domestic popularity of Australian wine has been mirrored by the growth in exports—from 39 million l (10.3 million gallons) in 1987 to 216 million l (57 million gallons) in 1998–99. Most exports are to the United Kingdom (45 per cent), but the United States of America, Canada, Japan and Scandinavia are also important.

The big players

In common with recent trends in many industries, a number of large companies have emerged, among which just one, Southcorp, is responsible for almost 30 per cent of wine production and owns many of the country's historic brand names. Australia's largest wine company, Southcorp Wines also claims to be the seventh largest in the world. With 1999 sales reaching A\$660 million (US\$400 million), of which A\$313 million (US\$190 million) were exports, the company produces around 30 per cent by value of all Australian wine. This spectacular international expansion has been responsible for annual earnings growth of about 20 per cent in recent years.

Southcorp's 6,000 ha (15,000 acres) of vines make it Australia's dominant vineyard owner, and quite possibly the world's largest. Of the 25 vineyards the company owns, three-quarters are in South Australia and the remainder in New South Wales, Victoria and Western Australia. In 1999, these wineries crushed 224,000 tonnes (247,000 tons) of grapes. Even before its current program to double its red-wine processing ability, Southcorp claimed to be the world's largest maker of premium red wine. Announced in late 1997, the \$A405 million (US\$245 million) investment over five years involves spending \$A145 million

(US\$88 million) directly on vineyard and winery expansion, the most significant investment ever in the history of Australian winemaking.

Outside Australia, Southcorp produces La Perouse wines in the Languedoc-Roussillon region of France and in 1999 acquired the James Herrick brand in the same region. In the USA, the company makes Seven Peaks wines in partnership with Paragon Vineyards in the Edna Valley, and in 1997 bought land for a new vineyard development near Paso Robles, California.

Also important are BRL Hardy, Orlando Wyndham (itself owned by the French company Pernod Ricard), Mildara Blass and Simeon Wines (most of whose production is sold in bulk). Between them, they control more than 70 per cent of all production. A number of renowned middle-ranking producers, such as McWilliams and Rosemount, are still family owned, but of the more than 1100 wine companies operating in Australia, 98 per cent produce less than 5 per cent of all wine.

This concentration of production is also mirrored geographically. The State of South Australia makes more than half of all Australian wine and is home to the largest producers, while Tasmania, the island State, has 8 per cent of the wine-making companies, and yet accounts for less than 0.5 percent of the nation's wine production.

Wynn's Coonawarra winery and vineyard. South Australia's Coonawarra region is renowned throughout the world for its elegant cabernet sauvignon.

Medals won at wine-judging competitions are held in high regard by both the winemakers and the consumer.

Economic Policy

The electronic share-price display board at the stock exchange (ASX) in Sydney. Australians are now among the world's leading owners of shares.

For most of the twentieth century State and Federal governments increased their share of national income. Income taxes rose, new sales taxes were introduced, and the public sector employed a substantial proportion of Australia's workers. Governments also tightly regulated international trade and the labour market. But the government role in the Australian economy has been changing markedly since the 1980s. Political ideas have been important, notably that economic activity is best carried out by the private sector and that government 'interference' impedes efficiency and compromises individual liberty. Globalisation has also exerted strong pressure on governments to conform to what Thomas Friedman calls 'the golden strait-jacket' of deregulation, free trade, a shrinking public sector and balanced budgets. In Australia, governments, both Labor and Liberal–National Party, have embraced the broad thrust of these changes in pursuit of low inflation and economic growth. Since the mid 1990s, a National Competition Policy has provided the framework for further sweeping changes in the organisation of economic activity within and between the public, private and non-profit sectors.

Deregulation

One of the signal themes of policy development since the 1980s has been 'deregulation'. The term is something of a misnomer, because no economy is able to function without a system of rules and social infrastructure provided by government. But deregulation is widely used to describe the withdrawal of many of the government controls on economic activity that

have been accumulated during the twentieth century. In Australia the most notable deregulations have been the reductions in tariff protection, the decentralisation since the 1980s of wage fixing, the floating of the exchange rate in 1983, and the lifting of controls on movements of funds in and out of Australia. Tariffs of several hundred per cent on some goods—notably clothing—have been cut to less than 10 per cent today. Workers now negotiate their wages and working conditions at enterprise rather than industry level, often without union representation. Foreign banks now trade in Australia, and money market transactions move many billions of Australian dollars around the world, literally at the speed of light. These changes are certainly consistent with the belief in market forces, but government regulation remains essential. There are today more people employed in financial-sector regulation than was the case at the beginning of the 1980s, and legislation on individual worker's rights proliferates.

An element of the philosophical shift towards small government is the view that individual citizens, not governments, should choose how their income is spent. Accordingly, governments have been steadily reducing their spending relative to GDP, and along with reducing controls on market activities, successive Australian governments have been contracting out, corporatising, and privatising their own activities, at the same time introducing or increasing charges for a range of publicly provided services.

Corporatisation increasingly has organisations across the public sector run like businesses. New systems of public administration emphasise efficiency, financial accountability and customer focus. Many public utilities—once the hallmark of community—have been sold in a wave of privatisations over the past decade. Former national icons such as the Commonwealth Bank, Qantas and the majority share of the telecommunications company Telstra are now in private hands. Many government-owned properties have been sold and the premises rented back at market rates by the postal service and other remaining public-sector organisations. Some State governments have sold water, power, and parts of their public transportation services. Construction of main roads is now typically contracted out to corporations which often gain the right to charge tolls. Even the justice system has been caught up in the push to privatisation as State governments put out to tender the provision of prison services and buildings.

Hamilton State School, Victoria. When the GST was introduced, the Federal Government pledged to pass on the benefits directly to the States to be used for services such as education and health.

Port Kembla steelworks, New South Wales. The lifting of tariffs on many imports had a profound effect on the steel industry, which shed thousands of employees.

In addition to passing many of its own activities partly or wholly to the private sector in these ways, the current Government is increasing incentives for Australians to look to private provision of health care and education. All these developments have reduced the relative contribution of the public sector to GDP, and increased the role of both the private and non-profit sectors. A further consequence of privatisation has been a massive increase in the rate of share ownership in Australia. More than 41 per cent of the adult population now directly owns shares, more than double the number in May 1997 and one of the world's highest rates of share ownership. However, most investors hold small portfolios with shares in just one or two companies; only those households which enjoy very high incomes tend to hold large, diversified share portfolios.

For some, change in the role and size of the public sector has been too rapid. The privatisation of utilities and the privatising of prisons means that essential services are now run as profit-making concerns but without some of the caution and guarantees (and probably expense) that make essential community services failsafe. This debate is likely to be a central issue in the economic platforms of Australia's political parties well into the future.

Taxation policy

Tax policy has also recently changed significantly. Despite popular perceptions, Australia is a relatively low-tax country (see Figure 2). However, it is not always seen that way because the Australian tax system has been weighted by the Commonwealth unusually heavily towards income taxes levied on wages, earned interest and profits. On 1 July 2000, the introduction of a new tax system lowered income tax rates and introduced a sweeping consumption tax, the GST, on most goods and services. The Federal Government pledged that revenue from the GST will pass directly to State and Territory governments, which have the primary responsibility for delivering social and community services including health and education. At the time of writing, it is projected that the new tax will yield more revenue than originally expected, perhaps going some way towards reversing the trend to shrinking expenditure in these areas.

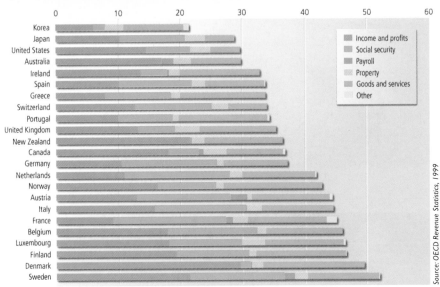

Source: OECD Revenue Statistics, 1999

Figure 2
Main sources of tax revenue as a percentage of GDP, 1997

ECONOMY TIMELINE

1820s Whaling and sealing are main economic activities.
1834 Wool exports overtake fisheries exports.
1840–42 Colony experiences economic depression.

1807 John Macarthur sends first export of merino wool to Britain.
1817 Colony's first bank, the Bank of NSW, founded. In 1982, it is renamed Westpac.

1864 First sugar produced from Qld cane fields.
1875 Wool industry booming; sheep population 50 million. Public works fuel growth of manufacturing.

1850 Australia supplying 50% of British wool imports; sheep population 15 million.
1851 Gold rushes result in increase in scale of economy. Gold exports overtake wool.

1890s Stock crashes and droughts contribute to major economic depression. Results in greater diversification, with meat, dairy and wheat becoming more important.

1883 Discovery of silver at Broken Hill, NSW, leads to founding of BHP.
1886–90 Manufacturing grows. Farming spreads into marginal land.

1920s Government steadily increases import tariffs.
1929 Worldwide economic depression. Within three years, one-third of Australian work force unemployed.

1910–11 Employment by industry: agriculture and related industries (forestry, fishing) 26%, mining 6%, manufacturing 21%, other (mainly services) 47%.

1954 Unemployment falls to less than 3%.
1960 Reserve Bank founded.
1961 'Credit squeeze' recession follows mini-boom of 1960. Mining boom begins.

1939–44 Factory employment rises to 50% of workforce. Unemployment: 1.1%.
1945 Government white paper announces aim for full employment.

1983 Unemployment rises above 10%. Government floats Australian dollar on money markets and continues to reduce import tariffs.
1987 Stock market crash.

1966 Decimal currency introduced; dollar replaces pound.
1973 UK joins EEC (now EU), depriving Australia of preferential access to British markets.

1999 Employment by industry: agriculture and related industries 5%, mining 1%, manufacturing 12%, other (mainly services) 82%.

1991 Most remaining tariffs and quotas removed. Downturn leads to unemployment of 10.9% by 1993.
1994 Gross foreign debt balloons to $210 million.

Working Life

ABOVE: A worker at Copper Mines of Tasmania's processing plant. Jobs such as this, once held by a full-time unionised workforce, are increasingly changing to part-time positions with conditions negotiated by individual contract or workplace agreement.

TOP: Servicing a cattle-mustering helicopter at Katherine, in the Northern Territory. Skilled trades in Australia are almost exclusively a male domain and there is still a tendency at some levels for women to work in the people-focused industries, and for men to work with machines.

Changes in the structure of industry and business behaviour, along with policy shifts, have since the 1970s profoundly reshaped the way Australians work. More Australian adults work now than was the case 20 years ago; the labour-force participation rate stood at 63.3 per cent at the end of 2000, up from 61.4 per cent in 1980. However, behind this broad pattern are profound changes in the composition of the labour force, and in the dynamics of the labour market. Men's participation rate has fallen from 78.6 per cent to 72.4 per cent, while women's participation rate has increased from 44.8 per cent to 54.5 per cent during the same period.

For the first time since the Great Depression, unemployment emerged as a serious problem in the 1970s, and still persists at disturbingly high levels. Just over 6 per cent of workers were unemployed in late 1980 and at the end of 2000. But during two recessions, one in the early 1980s the other in the early 1990s, the unemployment rate reached double figures, peaking at over 12 per cent in late 1992. The proportion of long-term unemployed, people who for more than a year have been unable to find work, has climbed over the past 20 years, now sitting at around 32 per cent of the total number of unemployed at the end of 2000, despite the introduction of a range of labour-market programs to assist job seekers.

Changing work patterns

Perhaps the most significant labour market change of recent decades has been the rise of what might be termed 'non-standard work', propelled by employers' pursuit of workplace flexibility and by the shift of industrial-relations bargaining to the enterprise level. The 'male breadwinner' in secure, full-time employment, the traditional picture of the Australian worker, is no longer the norm: full-time male workers now comprise fewer than half the total workforce and more than a quarter of all workers—the majority of them women—are employed part-time.

Not only are more men working part-time, but a growing proportion in full-time work are employed casually, that is, without security of employment and without access to many benefits including sick leave and holiday pay. Many of these people work in those industries that we expect to offer standard, full-time employment such as mining, building construction, manufacturing, and transport and storage. The ABS Labour Force Survey reveals that during the ten-year period 1988 to 1998, the number of male casual employees increased by 115 per cent, while over the same period the number of non-casual male employees decreased by 2 per cent, indicating a major shift in the structure of the male workforce.

More than 26 per cent of Australian workers are employed as casuals—the second highest rate among the OECD countries. Researchers at the Australian Centre for Industrial Relations Research and Training argue that this 'casualisation' means that managers now have tighter control over how labour is deployed on the job and so can ensure that all hours worked are productive. However, they also point out that there may be some limits to the increases in labour productivity achievable in this way. Removing idle time from workplaces by the use of casual workers hired only at times of peak load has increased productivity during the 1990s, but these same casual workers can hardly be expected to be loyal and committed employees. Nor are they likely to contribute to the same productivity increases engendered by high trust/high commitment settings.

Despite the alarming increase in the number of men in casual full-time work, most of those in casual work are women and young people, particularly students. These groups often prefer part-time work because it allows time for their other commitments, but this preference pushes them into the service sector, as waiters and so on, where casual, part-time jobs are disproportionately clustered.

Gender and the workforce

In fact, Australia has one of the most sex-segregated labour markets in the world. More than 45 per cent of all working women are employed in retail trade, health and community services, and education, whereas less than 21 per cent of working men find jobs in these industries. On the other hand, men predominate in agriculture, manufacturing, mining, construction, wholesale trade and transport and storage. Women in Australia, it seems, work with people and men work with machines. The large and female worker-dominated retail industry does employ more than one in eight male workers, but many of these are young students working in low-skilled,

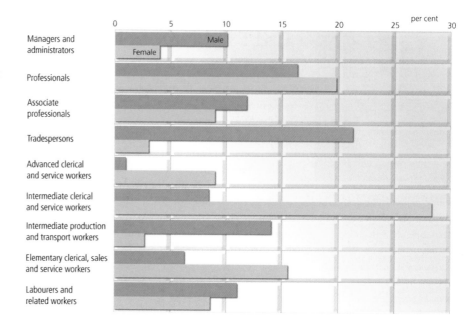

Figure 3
Employed persons by occupation and proportion employed, 1998–99

poorly paid jobs, to supplement their income. These young men will move on to other industries after they have completed their education.

Figure 3 shows the distribution of Australian working men and women between occupations. The idea underpinning the classification of occupations is a rough hierarchy of skill, with managers and administrators at the top and labourers at the bottom. Men are more than twice as likely as women to be managers and more than seven times as likely to work in a skilled trade. Women with a trade are crowded into hairdressing, the only trade dominated by women. Figure 3 also shows that women predominate among professionals. But this broad category obscures much starker divergence in the jobs professional men and women do. For example, about nine out of 10 nurses are women, but most engineers are men.

Under- and over-employment are also problems in the labour market—the working hours of many of those in full-time employment are increasing while at least one-fifth of part-time workers are reported as wanting to work more hours.

Not all work done in the Australian economy is paid. Under pressure to maintain productivity, many workers now do unpaid overtime. Other work is undertaken outside the market, by voluntary workers and by householders in their own homes. The most recent ABS survey revealed that volunteers worked 8.3 million hours in 1995, in educational, welfare and community organisations, in sport and hobby clubs and for religious and arts organisations. Economist Duncan Ironmonger has valued this work as being equivalent to about 8 per cent of GDP. Men and women contribute differently to unpaid work in the home. Time-use surveys by the ABS show that men remain largely responsible for outdoor work and home maintenance, while women continue to do much of the cooking, cleaning and laundry. These last are more time-consuming—women in couples spend nearly twice as much time on unpaid domestic work than do men.

LEFT: Blundstone boot factory, Tasmania. Australia has one of the most gender-divided labour markets in the world and women predominate in the textile. clothing and footwear sectors.

BELOW: A weary firefighter takes a well-earned break. Volunteers in many fields contribute more than 8 million hours of labour to the economy each year.

Earning and Spending

A modern farm office near Armidale, New South Wales. Australians are enthusiastic adopters of new technology, particularly in communications, but little of the hardware is manufactured here.

Developments in both the labour market and in government policy also have significant implications for the Australian standard of living. A simple gauge of national living standards is GDP per capita. By this measure, World Bank data show that Australians live in the twentieth richest country in the world, with annual income of 22,448 'international dollars' per capita in 1999. However, we can get a better understanding of how Australians live by looking at how income is distributed between individuals and households, at patterns of redistribution by governments, and at how people spend their income and time.

Income distribution

Australians have traditionally prided themselves on living in a classless society, a myth, albeit a pleasing one. During the 1990s, the gap between households at the top of the income-distribution ladder and those at the bottom increased. Those households enjoying high incomes have increased their share of total disposable income, while those with low and middle incomes have had their share reduced. Changes in the composition of both the labour force and the wages structure largely explain these developments.

Two-income families tend to be clustered higher in income distribution than other types of families. When a woman whose husband works takes a job, even part-time, she increases the household's income. On the other hand, if a married man is unemployed, his wife is also very likely to be unemployed, leaving them to rely on the relatively low level of income support provided by government. Lone parents, who in 1997 represented 20 per cent of all families with dependants, are also less likely than married parents to be in paid employment.

The government policy of decentralising wage bargaining has also increased earnings inequality between individuals. In the past, relatively centralised

As the gap between high and low income earners widens and work patterns change, owning one's own home may become an increasingly remote possibility for many Australians.

wage fixing meant that most workers benefited when powerful groups won wage increases. Now workers with bargaining power, members of trade unions for example, fare much better than those without. Moreover, many of the new service-sector jobs are poorly paid compared to the manufacturing jobs that were lost during structural change.

The gender gap

Another dimension of income inequality is seen in the 'gender wages gap'. In 1998, the average weekly earnings of Australian women were just under two-thirds of those of men. Women are more likely to work part time, accounting for some of the gap, but even those working full time receive on average only 80 per cent of male earnings. Even when we take account of the 'glass ceiling' and compare the earnings of non-managerial employees only, those women working full time still receive on average only 88 per cent of male earnings—in 1998, in every broad occupational group, women earned less on average than men. Segregation by occupation is a crucial factor here. A recent inquiry by the New South Wales Industrial Relations Commission found that women's work has been traditionally undervalued: the skills involved in the jobs women typically hold are neither recognised nor justly remunerated.

The labour market is not the only institution through which income is distributed. Government taxes, transfers and social expenditures also redistribute resources to alter the living standards of many households. The latest available ABS research into the impact of government benefits and taxes on household income demonstrates that increased inequality of income from paid work and investments between 1984 and 1994 was, at least in part, compensated for by progressive income taxes to fund income support, particularly for older people and sole parents. Governments also redistribute income from households without dependant children to those with children by way of cash benefits and by providing health, education, and other community services. Although significant redistribution still takes place in this way, the extent of redistribution via taxes and benefits may possibly have fallen since the mid-1990s. Recent changes to the tax system have reduced income tax rates and increased the rate of indirect taxes. This means that people with higher incomes will pay proportionately less tax than was previously the case. At the same time, the Commonwealth Government has made access to income-support payments more difficult and greatly reduced expenditure on health and education.

Home ownership

A look at home ownership and spending patterns helps flesh out the picture. Of all the world's peoples, Australians are among those most likely to own their own homes. The Australian Housing Survey shows that in 1999, 70 per cent (7.2 million households) owned or were buying the home in which they were currently living. Other households rented homes, primarily from private landlords. Fewer than one Australian household in 20 lives in a home rented from a public housing authority.

Household spending

Australian households spent an average 34.6 per cent of total weekly expenditure on housing, domestic fuel and food in 1998–99. The ABS Household Expenditure Survey shows that the richest 20 per cent of households spend on average less than 31 per cent of their weekly income on these essential items, whereas the poorest 20 per cent spend nearly 40 per cent. Figure 4 shows some interesting divergences in discretionary spending among income groups . Richer households spend a greater proportion of their income on recreation and dining out and a far smaller proportion on tobacco products. Total spending on dining out (including takeaway meals) in Australia increased by 10 per cent between 1984 and 1994, fuelling the proliferation of restaurants and cafes in Australian cities and regional centres.

Australians are famous for their rapid uptake of new technologies. The ABS survey of information technology use found that in May 1999 about 47 per cent of Australian households had a computer, and nearly half of these had internet access, a massive 57 per cent increase over May 1998. But access to the internet is strongly skewed towards high-income households, leading some commentators to talk about an emerging 'digital divide'. Those households with incomes of $50,000 or more were twice as likely to

have access to a computer at home than those with incomes under $50,000 (75 per cent compared to 37 per cent) and nearly three times as likely to have access to the Internet at home (51 per cent compared to 19 per cent).

Australia is a wealthy society in which most people enjoy a good standard of living. However, significant and increasing inequalities in income, expenditure on discretionary goods and services and access to emerging technologies raises many concerns. Indigenous Australians remain greatly disadvantaged. The rise of employment in the service industries has seen the encroachment by the working week into weekends for many workers, and this increase in full-time working hours may lead to 'time poverty' even as it raises income. Thus may our increasing wealth in other ways impoverish us.

The service industries have experienced some of the highest growth rates of recent years. Childcare is no exception, aided in part by increasingly long hours worked by those in full-time work and a rise in casual employment among women.

Figure 4
Proportion of total household expenditure on selected items, 1998–99

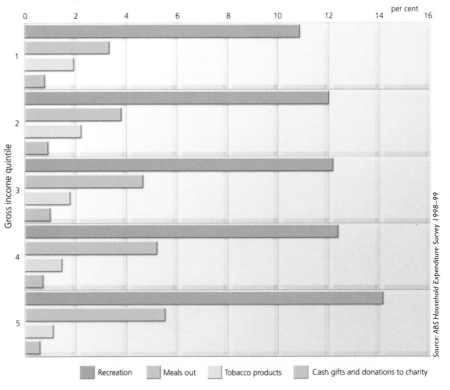

Recreation   Meals out   Tobacco products   Cash gifts and donations to charity

Source: ABS Household Expenditure Survey 1998–99

Australia in the Global Economy

Australia floated its dollar in December 1983 as part of the push towards deregulation of the financial market.

'Globalisation' is the process by which economic activity transcends national boundaries and refers to changes that have been occurring worldwide at an increasing rate over the past 20 years. There are three dimensions to the global integration of economic activity: international trade, international investment and international finance.

International trade

Colonial Australia produced wheat, wool, timber and minerals for Britain, receiving in return manufactured goods. Australia now trades with many countries—over 60 per cent of our exports go to Asia—but the nineteenth-century pattern of specialisation in trade continues. Although agricultural goods and minerals account for just 6 per cent of Australia's production, they contribute 48 per cent of its exports of goods and services and 62 per cent of goods alone.

Conversely, all but a tiny portion of Australia's imports are manufactures and, not surprisingly many would argue, the nation imports considerably more than it exports—as Australians become richer they want more manufactured goods. At the other end of the spectrum, as inequalities in income increase throughout the world, the rich are demanding more sophisticated high-tech manufactures and services rather than food and simple, metal-intensive manufactured goods, while the poor, whose numbers are increasing, can afford neither. As a result, the demand for Australia's agricultural and mineral commodities is limited but Australians keep importing. Herein lies the basis of arguments for developing a skills-based economy, to make the country a producer of high-tech manufactures for the world market.

The other aspect of trade seen in the context of globalisation is that a growing amount of the nation's consumption is imported and an increasing portion of its production is exported. Currently, exports plus imports are equal to about 45 per cent of GDP—that is to say, about 22 per cent of production is exported and about 23 per cent of the goods and services the nation consumes is imported. A significant increase from a steady total of about 33 per cent from the 1950s to the 1980s, though still less than the 50 per cent total when ties with Britain dictated trade.

Foreign investment

Levels of foreign investment in Australia have always been high, and both credit and direct investment by transnational corporations looking to operate here have been significant. Britain dominated until after World War II, when companies from the United States were the leading investors. By the 1970s Australia was one of the world's largest recipients of investment by transnational corporations. In the early years of that decade three-fifths of mining and half of all mineral exploration were under foreign control, as was a third of all manufacturing and insurance.

Economic nationalism saw Australian governments restrict foreign ownership, especially in mining, the media and real estate, from the early 1970s. Foreign investment did continue—especially Japanese investment in the resource industries—but now increasingly in partnership with Australian-owned companies. However, with the growth from

RIGHT: Livestock for export being loaded at the port of Fremantle, Western Australia. In many respects, Australia's overseas trade still follows the pattern established in the nineteenth century, and agricultural and mineral exports predominate.

Despite mining operations carried out on a vast scale and extracting minerals mainly for the overseas market, like the Super Pit goldmine at Kalgoorlie Western Australia, Australia still imports more than it exports.

the early 1980s of a much more globally integrated economy, these controls have been steadily whittled away. Moreover, this global integration has made for an increasing diversity in the origins of companies investing in Australia.

Increased global integration since the 1980s has also involved international investment by companies of Australian origin. A few Australian companies had long invested internationally, some since the 1890s, but the 1980s saw Australian companies rushing to do the same. Much of this activity was short-lived and associated with the activities of companies such as Bond Corp. and Quintex, all insolvent by the end of the decade. Since the 1990s, Australian international investment, lead by financial institutions, has grown far more cautiously. Interestingly, although Australian companies export chiefly to Asia, they invest mainly in Europe and North America.

Figure 5 demonstrates that the level of Australian investment abroad remains about half the value of foreign investment in Australia, though as ownership structures become more complex it is increasingly difficult to say which are 'Australian' companies and which are 'foreign'. Whether, for example, News Corporation, with a head office in Adelaide, its boss now a US citizen and most of its assets, production and shareholders outside Australia, can still be called Australian is a moot point.

Financial markets

The global integration of financial markets has been the most profound change of the past two decades. Australia, along with most industrial countries, from the 1970s began lifting some controls on international financial flows. The floating of the dollar in December 1983 and the subsequent entry of foreign banks formed a major turning point. Since that time, Australian-based financial institutions have themselves spread across the globe.

However, there is more to the globalisation of finance than the question of who owns the financial institutions. First, with funds free to chase profits around the world, companies in Australia have found it cheaper to borrow overseas—indeed, some foreign companies have chosen to borrow within Australia. Many economists contend that overseas borrowing creates a foreign-debt problem, but others argue that because these loans are predominantly privately contracted, they are not a debt of the nation.

Second, the Australian dollar is now traded freely on international financial markets, its value fluctuating with supply and demand. Australia's foreign exchange market turns over around $US75 billion each day, though less than half of that involves trade in the Australian dollar, most of which occurs outside Australia. This latter fact signals that the country's central bank, the Reserve Bank of Australia, has only a limited capacity to affect the value of the nation's currency and can only do so by acting as a big trader in international currency markets.

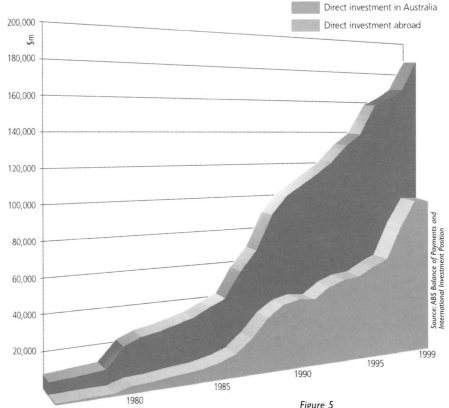

Source: ABS Balance of Payments and International Investment Position

Figure 5
Levels of foreign investment in Australia and of Australian investment abroad.

Some observers of this top-level currency trading call it speculation, akin to gambling. The speculators do 'play the markets', but many companies are also 'hedging', trading to cover themselves against price or exchange-rate movements. The volatility of prices for agricultural goods and minerals makes hedging especially important for Australian companies and partly explains why the Australian dollar is now the world's fifth most traded currency.

Government responses

Globalisation has integrated world economic activity, resulting in increased flows of goods and services, investment and finance between Australia and the rest of the world. This has triggered debate about whether economic volatility is increasing and whether or not Australia's economic sovereignty is being undermined. Some argue that to compete for globally mobile investment, the Australian Government is effectively compelled to adopt policies it believes are pleasing to transnational companies—lower company taxes, selective subsidies and a relatively non-unionised, flexible, trained workforce. In this view, the financial markets are even more powerful and government policies seen as intrusive and not approved of by these markets will see the Australian dollar sold off and assets moved offshore, perhaps explaining the shift towards privatisation, deregulation and small government—the free-market ideology of financial markets being transmitted to governments. It is not clear if these are the only feasible policy responses to globalisation and the rules of Australia's engagement with the global economy are still being written.

The worlwide interest in the Indigenous art and culture of Australia sees large numbers of tourists visit the country each year. Tourism contributes greatly to GDP, but recognition of the indigenous peoples' contribution is slow in coming.

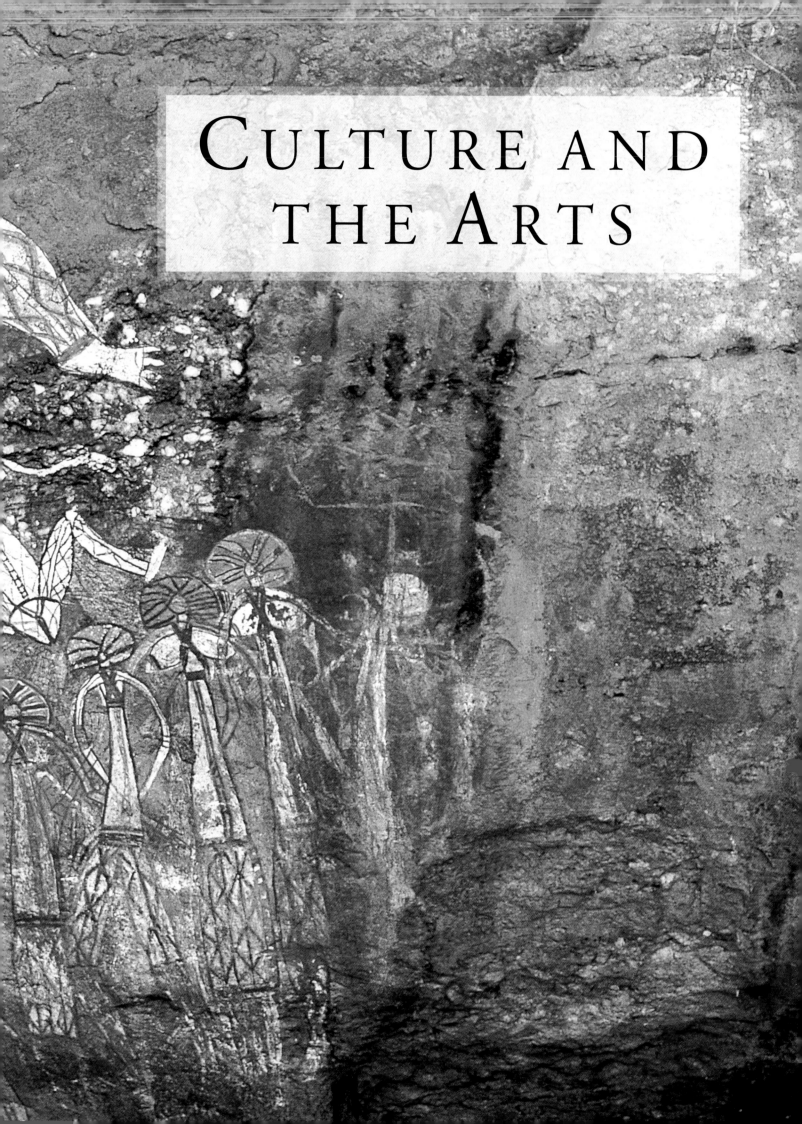

CULTURE AND THE ARTS

Art and Society

In pre-European Australia the didgeridoo was confined to the northern and north-westernparts of the continent. However, a revival of pride in indigenous culture has seen its enthusiastic adoption by Aboriginal people everywhere. These children are pupils of the Kuranda State School in Queensland.

The English invasion of Australia in January 1788 has often been portrayed as the beginning of the end for the Australian Aboriginal and Torres Strait Islander cultures. Today, it is clear that these cultures have survived. While they have faced radical changes, indigenous Australians have drawn upon the flexibility and strengths inherent in their cultures to ensure their on-going survival. The result has taken different forms in different parts of the country, in the same way that indigenous cultures took different forms in pre-European times. The result is a wide diversity of indigenous cultures in the present that matches the diversity of those cultures in the past.

Australia has two distinct indigenous populations with distinct cultures and different histories. There are approximately 360,000 Aboriginal people and about 35,000 Torres Strait Islanders, together comprising about 2 per cent of the total population. The Aboriginal people inhabit the mainland and many of the offshore islands, while the Torres Strait Islanders come from the many islands of the Torres Strait, the narrow waterway between Cape York in Queensland and Papua New Guinea.

The sovereignty of these indigenous Australians is represented in their flags, both now officially recognised by the Federal Government. Designed by Harold Thomas and flown for the first time in 1972, the Aboriginal flag uses a pallet of traditional colours. The people are symbolised by the black upper band, the land by the lower red band, and the life-giving sun shines on both. Attributed to the late Bernard Namok of Thursday Island, the central motif of the Torres Strait flag is a white headdress. The five main island groups and the navigational importance of stars to a seafaring people are depicted by a white, five-pointed star, green and blue bands represent land and sea, while the narrow, black stripes separating them symbolise the people. These flags, both now widely accepted, are outstanding symbols of the diversity and unity of indigenous Australian cultures.

Whether produced in the past or the present, indigenous Australian art forms are concerned with connecting people to the world around them. They express ancestral relationships to land, explore individual identity, make a protest against the injustices of colonialism, and are always a statement of cultural survival. Whether a bark painting or ceremonial rite that is actually a title deed to land, a dance that confronts the challenges of urban life or a song lamenting the loss of a child stolen because of a government's assimilation policies, indigenous art is political

It is important not to think of indigenous peoples primarily in terms of the differences between 'us' and 'them', as this can reinforce stereotypes that lock them into an idealised past and serve to reinforce racist assumptions. It is important, however, to recognise the significant differences in the ways in which indigenous and non-indigenous Australians construct knowledge. In indigenous systems, knowledge is rarely definitive. Grounded in oral tradition, it has many levels and is open to alternative interpretations according to the particular situation. Knowledge is not 'open' in the sense that all people have an equal right to acquire it; rather it is cared for by people with appropriate qualifications and personalities. The right to knowledge has to be earned.

Different notions of time

Similarly, there are differences in the ways time is perceived. Principally, Western notions of time are linear, in that the past is thought of as being separated from the present, whereas indigenous Australians see the past as actively influencing the present (Figure 1).

This can be seen in the current debate over reconciliation. Some Australians argue that they are not responsible for the actions of their forebears—a linear view—while many indigenous people hold that the actions of the past must be confronted and reconciled in the present, because the past continues to affect the present. Schooled in a tradition of collective ownership, they maintain that non-indigenous Australians are, in one sense at least, collectively responsible for the actions of their forebears, for not only have they inherited the benefits of past actions but with these benefits a responsibility to redress past wrongs.

Visual and performing arts

The visual and performing arts of Aboriginal and Torres Strait Islander Australians encompass drawings on the human body, rocks and 'Western' media, and dance, music and song. Though each of these forms is full of meaning, none is produced solely for its aesthetic value or for its religious significance. Part of the sophisticated and complex ways of defining one's self, one's relatives and one's place in the world, these art forms arise from complex social systems that communicate information about societies as a whole and about the individual's place within them. Each art form is interdependent on the others and a fusion of forms may be necessary to properly express an idea.

Until recently poorly known and little valued, Australia's indigenous arts were for the most part confined to museums. The paintings were categorised as artefacts, traditional music and dance were recorded for academic audiences only, and contemporary arts were virtually ignored. Today, they take their place in the mainstream and are recognised as extending the world's oldest, continuous, living cultural traditions.

The fact that paintings were produced using natural pigments on natural surfaces served to have them categorised as 'primitive' and inhibited their adoption by a world that valued material permanency. In fact, Aboriginal and Torres Straits Islander arts only really entered the cultural mainstream once the artists began using media such as acrylic paints and canvas, providing works that could be made the subject of serious investment. In comparison, international interest in music and dance tends to focus on the authenticity of indigenous voice and a concern with understanding the contemporary experiences of the indigenous peoples.

The cultures of Torres Strait are stylistically very distinctive and in many ways different, both from the Aboriginal cultures to the south and those of New Guinea in the north, though links to the latter can be seen in the elaborate masks and deri (headdresses) worn for ceremonies. In 'Broken', the language that arose after European contact, the Islanders' culture is called *Ailan Kastom* (Island Custom), a dynamic force, continually open to innovation. There are regional variations within Torres Strait in the same way as there are regional variations in mainland cultures.

Aboriginal entertainers dancing at Currumbin, Queensland. Tourism has provided many indigenous communities with an opportunity to generate income at the same time as celebrating and reinforcing their culture.

BELOW LEFT: Alicia Entata works on a painting at Ntaria Arts Centre, Hermannsburg, once a Lutheran mission in Central Australia. Though the colours and media she is using are non-traditional, the work is based on inherited, individually owned designs.

BELOW: Figure 1 Aboriginal Australians see the past and present as being interactive and indivisible.

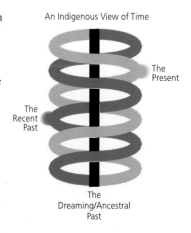

An Indigenous View of Time

The Present

The Recent Past

The Dreaming/Ancestral Past

The Concept of the Dreaming

Fruits of the rainforest tree, Elaeocarpus grandis. Indigenous knowledge of the nutritional and medicinal properties of plants was and is profound, though much priceless information has been lost in many areas. A large supermarket chain is now stocking 'bush tucker' lines.

The Devils Marbles, near Tennant Creek, in the Northern Territory. To all but the most sceptical viewer, the reverence in which Aboriginal people hold such landforms, and the power with which they are imbued, is immediately understandable.

For many Aboriginal people, art is embedded in the rules established in an ancestral past that still, somehow, exists in the present. Aboriginal people inhabit landscapes that are full of meaning; landscapes that are inherently powerful and potentially dangerous. These landscapes were created in the Dreaming, the creation time during which ancestral beings travelled in the land, creating by their actions its topography and finally 'sitting down' in one place, becoming forever a living part of that place. The Dreaming is both 'then' and 'now', encompassing events of the ancestral past and existing in the present.

Within the Aboriginal cosmos, power flows from ancestral beings, themselves inherently powerful, to the land, which is imbued with a potency given to it by the actions of people and the ancestors in the past. In this way, every facet and feature of the landscape became steeped in ancestral associations and social identity. Finally, the power flows through to living people, some of whom have the ability to call upon the forces and authority inherent in both the land and the ancestral beings. People do not see themselves as having power in their own right, but rather as having the ability to call upon the power which is held by the ancestors and permeates the land.

The land is an important facet of Aboriginal and Torres Islander identity, closely tied to the sophisticated social systems that have structured relationships to it. An integral part of growing up is learning about one's relationships to one's country. As people move through their lands they learn about the relationships between place and ancestors and by this learn about themselves and their particular rights and responsibilities to land. Rock art sites play an important role in this process of identification. Kinship relationships link ancestors, contemporary peoples, specific places and 'country'. In this sense, there is no separation of land, kinship, inheritance and religion.

Throughout Australia, the indigenous peoples interpret and use the land in ways that are distinctly Aboriginal or Torres Strait Islander. Aboriginal ways of relating to place exist in a variety of forms, varying according to the historical situation of individuals and groups. These exist in spite of, and in some cases in response to, the pressures arising from European colonisation. Common threads are an enduring sense of identity, which is inextricably linked to place, and an understanding of place as being of itself inherently powerful and potentially dangerous.

Food and medicine

In many regions, indigenous relationships to place are established through the transference of oral histories and regular visits to places important to the country of a particular group or individual. An important aspect of this practice is in teaching to children their history and passing on knowledge of traditional foods and medicines. Throughout Australia, the main body of knowledge about food and medicines in any region was in the custody of senior people, in the case of medicine, often older women.

The people of the Torres Strait were renowned seafarers and their trading canoes are known to have travelled for long distances down the mainland coast. Despite their close proximity to and contact with the indigenous cultures of mainland Australia and New Guinea, the Torres Strait Islanders developed and maintain a culture and way of life that is theirs alone.

Where feasible, such activities are carried out on the hereditary lands of the people involved. This sometimes occurs without indigenous people themselves being fully aware of the links between their own behaviour and that of their ancestors. Connell Perry, from Mount Isa, has said that he always returns to particular tracts of land but that other Kalkadoon people go back to different tracts. Each person goes to the place that they were taken to as a child and in taking their own children to this place they replicate and reinforce traditional Aboriginal land-use patterns. The information is transferred down the generations.

For most of Australia's human history, indigenous peoples obtained food through hunting, gathering and fishing. Largely ignorant of the techniques being used, European colonists assumed that Aboriginal Australians did not practice husbandry or manipulate their food resources when, in fact, they did so in numerous ways, from the replanting of yam tops in the north to the damming of watercourses to preserve fish populations during dry periods in the south. One of the major ways by which indigenous Australians manipulated their environment, however, was by so-called 'firestick farming'. This involved the regular burning of land in order to regenerate plant species and improve the habitat for game animals, which also became more visible in the cleared environment. The mosaic patterning of areas that were at intervals regularly burnt at low-levels of intensity or 'cool burning', allowed animals to escape; a sharp contrast to the devastating, high-intensity 'hot' bushfires of more recent times. Practical measures for manipulating the environment were augmented by ceremonies devoted to the increase of species and social customs that permitted people to seasonally visit neighbouring lands and to draw upon a neighbour's resources in times of extreme environmental stress.

Nor did the Europeans pay much attention to the wide range of plant foods eaten by the indigenous peoples, but in fact hundreds of species were used, from the mineral-rich seeds of pigweed on the inland plains to the marine resources of the coasts and Torres Strait. Some foods formed the centrepiece of great ceremonial gatherings, the bunya nuts of Queensland and the summer hordes of bogong moths in the Australian Alps providing just two examples. Indigenous medicines and healing techniques, both physical and psychological, can be very effective—in many cases at least as effective as Western medicine. Drugs are available to treat a wide range of conditions, from allergies to menopause and may be applied in many ways including rubbing, ingesting, chewing or even blowing smoke from a burning plant over the patient. Passing this information down from generation to generation is a vitally important way of keeping alive these aspects of indigenous Australian cultures.

There are many still puzzled by the fact that the indigenous Australians did not take up the cultivation of plants or animal husbandry. Even in the northernmost islands of the Torres Strait, where the people had regular contact with the garden culture of New Guinea, such practices were fairly limited. This was put forward by early observers as proof of their 'primitiveness' and lowly position on the ladder of human evolution. However, the refusal of indigenous Australians to invest in time-consuming agriculture was not a failure on their part. Rather, it was the result of a conscious choice to pursue a different lifestyle.

A family photographed near Alice Springs in Central Australia. To Aboriginal people living more urbanised lives, people such as these, living in their own country, can be a source of inspiration and knowledge.

The Importance of 'Country'

Travel in some Aboriginal lands is restricted and requires a permit. However, permit holders are forbidden access to important sites, which can be visited only by those with special knowledge. These restrictions, resented by some non-Aboriginals, serve to give Aboriginal people a measure of control over their own lives and helps protect their culture.

The existence of distinctly indigenous relationships to land in all parts of Australia has been recognised in both State and Federal legislation. Initially, this was brought about by the passage of a series of Aboriginal land rights acts during the 1970s and 1980s, each of which is specific to a particular State or Territory. The underlying premise of this legislation is that indigenous relationships to land—and, in cases where it is part of their country, to the sea—are fundamentally different from those of non-indigenous people. More recently, recognition of Aboriginal sovereignty at the time of contact was made in the 1992 High Court decision for Torres Strait Islander Eddie Mabo. By rejecting the doctrine of 'terra nullius', this decision recognised that Aboriginal and Torres Strait Islander people held a form of native title over the lands of Australia at the time of contact. Terra nullius was the legal basis for the British acquisition of Australian land so that, in effect, settlement became sovereignty.

The Federal *Native Title Act of 1993* formally recognised native rights and interests in Australian land and waters. This Act established the National Native Title Tribunal and gave to the Federal Court jurisdiction in matters pertaining to native title. The first mainland native title agreement to be resolved by this tribunal awarded compensation to the Dunghutti people of Crescent Head on the New South Wales north coast. From an indigenous perspective, the recent legislation has merely caused land to be recognised in law as indigenous or non-indigenous land. Nowhere in Australia did the indigenous peoples ever appear to have considered the land to be legitimately owned by anyone other than themselves.

Recently, indigenous groups have argued for sea and other water rights as a logical extension of land rights. The traditional country of indigenous groups along the coast often extends into the sea, and its Dreaming tracks may include sites which became

The imposing bulk of Crescent Head, at Port Macquarie on the New South Wales mid-north coast. Its traditional occupants, the Dunghutti people, were beneficiaries of Australia's first native title agreement.

submerged with the rising of the seas a few thousand years ago. A test case has been put forward by the traditional owners of Croker Island, which is off the coast of Arnhem Land, in the Northern Territory. In 1998 the Federal Court recognised the existence of native title to the sea but found that these rights were non-exclusive and non-commercial. The court's finding allowed for common-law public rights to fish and navigate these waters and thereby prevented exclusive indigenous possession, occupation, exploitation and enjoyment of the areas.

Sacred sites

In a world in which the Dreaming exists, Australian contemporary landscapes are imbued with Aboriginal spiritual values, knowledge of which is passed down through the generations, affecting the way in which the land is used. Sites such as Tooloom Falls in northeast New South Wales have been formally gazetted as Aboriginal Places on the basis of their cultural significance to Aboriginal people. Tooloom Falls has been protected from vandalism and destruction so that it can continue to fulfil its very important function of educating Aboriginal children in their legends and heritage, along with the beliefs of their people.

Throughout Australia sacred sites are identified as being both potent and dangerous. For instance, Dome Mountain in northern New South Wales is avoided by adult men, as the area is believed to be dangerous to them, even though the exact knowledge of why this is so has been lost. In other regions of Australia, the significance of a site may be fully understood by elders and custodians, but younger people may only know to avoid that place, without fully understanding the reason why it is dangerous. For Aboriginal people, travel through their lands is something that needs to be negotiated. It is essential

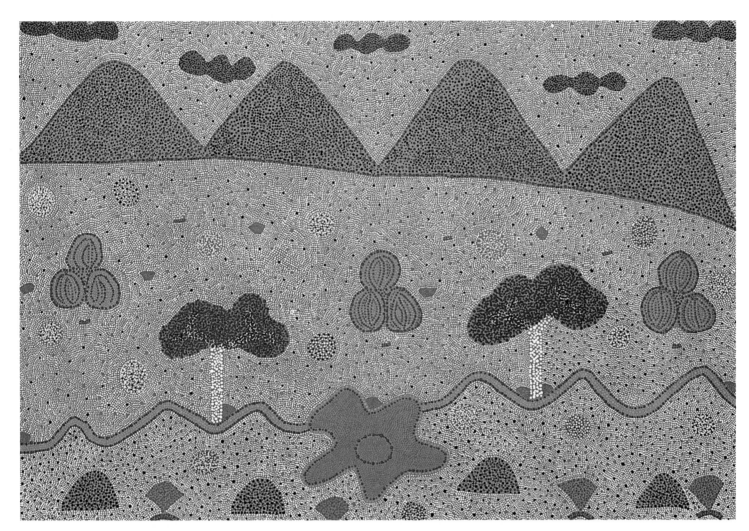

that people be aware of how they are interacting with, and how their actions may impinge upon, what are essentially living landscapes. Not only have the landscapes been shaped by human action over numberless generations, they also shape human action.

Rock art

Rock art sites in Aboriginal Australia, are not silent and inert depictions of mythological or long-vanished pasts. Rather, they have direct and potent relevance to the present. Rock art is part of a vibrant, living tradition, that taps into unbroken and vital sources of ancestral power.

There is enormous diversity in the kinds of rock art found throughout Australia. In the Sydney region there are engravings of fish and sea animals. In Tasmania the engravings mostly comprise geometric circles and lines. The same also holds true for central Australia but the designs are different, while on Cape York, recent rock art is mostly figurative painting. In the Kimberley, in Western Australia, there are the Wandjina figures, paintings of the ancestors who once lived at that place and whose spirits still reside there. Hand stencils, which signify a person's relationship to a particular place, are found throughout Australia.

Relationships between moieties, colours and dimensions

Short | Long
Red (DHUWA) | Yellow (YIRRITJA)
Black | White

In parts of northern and western Australia, caring for rock art is one way in which Aboriginal elders can demonstrate that they are looking after their country and their culture. This strengthens both the past and the present. Rock, as part of land, comes already laden with facets of social identity, such as language group, clan affiliation and moiety. This information does not need to be communicated in the rock art itself, because it is already encoded in place.

Moiety is a very important means by which the Aboriginal people of the Barunga region in north of the Northern Territory, conceive of the world around them. During the Dreaming, ancestral beings assigned everything in the world—people, animals, plants, places—to either the Dhuwa or Yirritja moiety, and each moiety is associated with particular colours and proportions. Dhuwa is associated with dark colours, such as black and red, while Yirritja is associated with light colours, such as white and yellow. Similarly, Dhuwa is associated with shortness and Yirritja with tallness. Thus, the black cockatoo is Dhuwa and the white cockatoo is Yirritja. Likewise, the short-necked turtle is Dhuwa and the long-necked turtle Yirritja.

An important principle followed by Barunga artists is that of joining Dhuwa and Yirritja moieties

'Other Side of Ammaroo', a contemporary painting by Alana Holmes Kngwarrey. The artist has used a mix of traditional and non-traditional colours to vividly portray the range country in the central east of the Northern Territory. (Artists of Ampilawatja.)

LEFT: FIGURE 2
Artists of the Northern Territory's Barunga region are careful to have the moieties, representing different aspects of being, 'in company': dark and light, short and tall, and so on.

Engravings at the Punda Art Site near Newman in the Pilbara region of Western Australia. The meanings behind many such ancient engravings are unclear, but they represent a rich legacy and oral tradition inherited by the artists of today.

so that they are 'in company'. Nearly all art forms combine light and dark colours, irrespective of the identity of the artist or the audience for which the art is produced. In rock art, however, moiety is already encoded in place, partly through the colour of the rock and partly through the moiety of the land, so there is no need to join moieties through colour. Thus, a rock painting can still properly conform to the principle of bringing together Dhuwa and Yirritja even if the painting is in a single colour. For this reason rock art cannot always be looked on as being typical of other contemporaneous art forms.

Rock art styles

Aboriginal people living in the north of the Northern Territory recognise three kinds of rock art site. The first of these is very old and includes both paintings and engravings. It is identified as having been made, either by the *mimi* (spirits) or ancestral beings, or as the actual bodies of these beings who placed them-

selves on the rock wall. Sometimes such artworks are in extremely inaccessible places and their location is cited as proof that they could not have been put there by people. Paintings such as these are much valued by Aboriginal people, not only for their great antiquity but because they are an embodiment of the ancestral beings from the Dreaming.

The second category of rock art was produced by ancestors in the Dreaming but can be renewed by its Aboriginal custodians in the present. The renewal of such images not only strengthens the Dreaming but also acts as a focus of the power that emanates from the ancestral past. The brightness of the renewed painting gives people today a visual message that the custodians are caring for their culture.

The third category of rock art is new paintings, usually secular scenes of families hunting or fishing and often explained as narratives of imagined or past events. Access to these sites is not restricted and they can be viewed by all members of the society.

It is important to Aboriginal people that rock paintings be 'right' for a particular place, both at the general and specific levels. At the general level is a painting by traditional custodian Jack Chadum of a man catching a barramundi. This rock art site is located at a local fishing spot called Dodluk. When he made this painting Jack Chadum described the man as being from that country. However, the basic theme of man and barramundi might be appropriate to many sites throughout the region. At the more specific level is Jack's painting of the rock kangaroo Dorria, which is at a place called Yalkmurlering. The rock kangaroo is an important part of the ancestral history of that place.

Throughout Australia, artists painting on rock, and occasionally in other media, have signed their work with a hand stencil. Not only does this serve as a reminder of the individual artist, it also refers to the artist's rights of residence. Senior artist Paddy Ford-ham Wainburranga explains that the hand stencils will endure long after other reminders have perished.

Petroglyphs at Rocky Bar, in the Northern Territory. Among the oldest of Australian art forms, petroglyphs, along with many engravings, are but poorly understood, though sufficiently so to be recognised as sites of great significance. The Australian Government in 1981 ratified the 'Burra Charter', a document embodying principles for the conservation and preservation of monuments and significant sites.

Future generations will not only be reminded of those who have gone before, evoking their continuing link with country and the interaction of past and future, but will gain a sense of self, of belonging.

Tradition and innovation

While the production of rock art is now rare, the creation of paintings on bark and other media are important facets of cultural expression—and provide essential income to people in communities with little or no industry. Bark paintings became popular with collectors during the 1940s and 1950s and are now widely produced for sale. Made on sheets of eucalypt bark (often a type of stringybark) that have been flattened, dried and smoothed prior to being painted with natural pigments of red, yellow, black and white, they are produced primarily in the northern parts of the Northern Territory, where suitable trees occur. Bark paintings are a powerful form of art because in taking the bark from the tree, the tree is often killed, thereby imbuing the painting with the tree's spirit.

Certain dances, songs and designs are held in the custodianship of individuals and have been inherited from their forebears in the same way that they have inherited the rights to their land or to the enactment of particular roles in ceremonies. Though these art forms are still in the process of evolution, as indeed all art forms are, the philosophy is conservative, and looks to the past for direction and validation. Billy Lukanawi, a senior male artist, told of how his father and uncle explained the importance of adhering to this inherited tradition. It is important to do so for the precise reason that it is inherited. His country, his style of painting, and his subject matter.

When in remote communities art forms are made in ceremonial contexts, there is little, if any, room for innovation. The principal concern here becomes the way in which these art forms articulate with ancestral dictates and their aesthetic value is judged by how correctly the artist is able to represent the decrees and stories of the ancestors.

Dances, songs and designs are all believed to have their genesis in the actions of the ancestral beings and it is this that endows them with their power. It is no coincidence that most senior artists also inherit and perform major roles in ceremonies and that those whose work is most respected by their peers are important ritual leaders. This is because they are the recognised custodians of ancestral knowledge.

A treasure trove of stencil art in Carnarvon National Park, south-east Queensland. Boomerangs, hands and arms, nets and carrying dishes are among the stencils at this rich site.

Aboriginal art, in common with art everywhere, is constantly evolving. This gallery at Jay Creek in the Northern Territory includes scenes from the cattle industry.

Commercial Art

A growing interest in the Papunya Tula style of painting has seen a proliferation of works painted on everyday objects. (Artworks by C. Young and R. Ryder, Keringke Arts Centre, Alice Springs.)

Didgeridoos like these, produced for sale to non-Aboriginals, are more lavishly decorated than those made for ceremonial use. (Sacred Sounds, Cairns.)

Room for innovation arises when art is produced for non-Aboriginals, demonstrating that the identity of the audience has an important influence on style. In northern Australia, art produced for Aboriginal ceremonies is stylistically much simpler than that produced for sale to tourists. Didgeridoos, ancient instruments made from termite-hollowed tree limbs, provide a striking example. Producing a complex humming sound, they are used in ceremonies but are also made for sale elsewhere. Didgeridoos produced for traditional audiences are made 'plain way', the wood simply polished or painted in plain, geometric bands. This rule is strictly adhered to, even if modern materials are used in the manufacture. Those sold to tourists, however, are made 'flash', cross-hatched and incorporating a wide range of figurative motifs. In some respects, then, there are two artistic systems, one aimed at selling to non-Aboriginal people and making use of a variety of mostly figurative motifs, the other for viewing by Aboriginal people only and using a limited range of primarily geometric motifs.

It seems, therefore, that Aboriginal artists in the northern communities are acting cooperatively to protect the more secret or private features of their culture, while at the same time taking advantage of the growing economic opportunities presented by the non-Aboriginal art market.

Women's art

In some parts of Australia there is clear differentiation in art according to gender. In the Barunga region of northern Australia, women work mainly with animal and vegetable fibres, producing baskets, containers and mats, while the men use wood and paint to make carvings, didgeridoos and paintings. These gender-based differences in art arise from, and reinforce, the gender differences in these societies.

A growing market for indigenous art, and a willingness to explore new forms of expression, has seen items such as these fired clay pots being produced for sale. The fibre arts, of which this basket is an example, were until recently mainly purchased for the collections of museums. (Desart Gallery, Alice Springs.)

For male artists in this region, the depiction of totemic species and ancestral figures links their art to the spiritual realm, offering material proof that the artist is meeting his responsibilities to the ancestral world, maintaining and empowering it. Aboriginal people say that men's art has 'meaning'. This art actively communicates information concerning the Dreaming, and its production is tied to the land and the rights of inheritance.

Women's fibre arts, on the other hand, do not have this explicit spiritual dimension or any clearly defined ties to land but their production also follows social rules. In the Barunga region, though open-weave string bags, which are long, are attributed to the Yirritja moiety and woven bags, which are short, are attributed to the Dhuwa moiety, they do not hold the layers of meaning that are incorporated in men's paintings. Women in this region describe their art as having 'patterning' rather than meaning. However, this should not be taken to imply that women do not have religious power or knowledge. It is simply that this knowledge and authority has different material outcomes to that of men.

Rarely do women's arts command a commercial return commensurate with the labour and skill used to produce them. The basic supposition has always been that men produce 'art' while women produce 'craft', with the latter assumed to involve less skill and hence command a lower price on the open market. However, there is tremendous skill involved in the production of fibre arts. The making of string bags, for example, involves collecting the raw materials from the surrounding countryside, producing the string by rolling vegetable fibres along the thigh to twist them together, dyeing the finished string and, finally, making the bag. The artist then has to find a market for her work. In many remote areas, these markets are limited and people may have to accept very little for work that has taken several days.

Art movements

There are important traditions in all contemporary Aboriginal arts, including distinct art 'schools'. Albert Namatjira, an Aranda man of central Australia, was one of the first indigenous artists to gain international recognition. On the basis of his artistic achievements he was granted citizenship in the 1960s, at a time when this right was denied to all but a few Aboriginal and Torres Strait Islander people. He was presented to the English Queen and feted by mainstream society. Consistent with his Aboriginal outlook and heritage, Albert Namatjira's paintings were mainly landscapes

A view from the former home of Albert Namatjira, Hermannsburg, Northern Territory. When this artist's watercolours, painted in the European style, were first seen by critics, many of whom had never left the cities, they were dismissed by some as mere 'chocolate-box' art. Nevertheless, his first exhibition of 41 paintings held in Melbourne in 1938, sold out in three days. As more Australians visited the almost fantastic landscapes of what was once called the 'Dead Heart', Namatjira's landscapes were recognised as being accurate renditions of the artist's country.

Western Desert art has at its centre traditional themes. Some of the motifs in this painting by Judy Napangaradi Watson, of Yuendumu, can also be found on woodcarvings made in the region. (Desart Gallery, Alice Springs.)

RIGHT: Desert designs adorning a VW Kombi.

A pot by Clara Inkamala of Hermannsburg. (Desart Gallery.)

depicting his country. Many other artists from this region, some of them relatives of Namatjira, began painting in the same style, creating a recognisable art school and giving the outside world its first glimpse of Aboriginal art using Western media.

Other styles also broke new ground. The Western Desert style has its genesis in the remote community of Papunya, and is sometimes called the Papunya Tula school. These paintings, mainly done with acrylics on canvas, are visually distinctive. Deriving from body decoration and ceremonial ground-paintings, they depict a relatively limited number of geometric motifs, each rich in symbolic meaning. Circles, for example, may represent a campsite or water-hole, while arcs may depict the marks a person's legs leave after they have been sitting in the sand, or the shape of a vessel used to carry grass seeds, fruit and the like. Invariably, these motifs can have several meanings, the multi-layering allowing Aboriginal people freedom to exploit the possibilities of a commercial market while at the same time protecting sacred knowledge.

The production of such paintings is flourishing in many remote communities in the Western Desert, from Balgo in the east of Western Australia to Yuendumu and Lajamanu, north-west of Alice Springs. It is very interesting to note that each of these communities has developed its individual sub-style. Papunya artists, for example, tend to use a traditional, four-coloured pallet, while those from Yuendumu lean towards works incorporating a wide range of non-traditional colours including blues and greens. The production and obvious commercial success of these paintings stand as a potent example of the inherent adaptability of indigenous Australians, and of a flexibility that is manifested in the use of non-traditional media. Some very fine examples have been made on very innovative materials, such as doors, cars, transistor radios and even a pair of sandshoes.

Through these new media, Western Desert artists have discovered a way of exploring their indigenous heritage, re-established their connections to the land and created a commanding and respected presence in the international art world.

The Urban People

The visual and performing arts of rural and urban indigenous peoples have different challenges. In order to understand these art forms it is necessary to know something of the history and social and economic circumstances of indigenous Australians. Aboriginal and Torres Strait Islanders live shorter lives and have poorer health than other Australians. Aboriginals can expect to live almost 20 fewer years than the national average—life expectancy for Aboriginal men is just 57 years as compared to 75 years for non-Aboriginals, and for women 62 years and 81 years respectively. Aboriginal people are admitted to hospital three times more often than other Australians and their infant mortality rate is three times higher than that for the non-Aboriginal population. They have significantly less disposable income than other Australians and their rate of unemployment, 23 per cent, is nearly four times the national average. Aboriginal people are more likely to have their children taken from them and placed in government custody; the National Aboriginal and Torres Strait Islander Survey of 1995 showed that 10 per cent of indigenous people aged 25 and over had been taken from their families, suffering the trauma of separation and attempts at assimilation. The Aboriginal survivors of colonialism have endured official policies that at various times have attempted to displace, convert, segregate and assimilate them. Today's indigenous peoples still live with the consequences of these failed policies and, as we have seen, social indicators for health, employment and education display enormous disparity in comparison to those of non-Aboriginal people.

So, what do these issues have to do with Torres Strait Islander and Aboriginal arts and cultures today? A little and a lot. A little, in that these issues are rarely referred to in the work of artists living in remote, outback communities. This may be because there is

little room for innovation in traditions so closely tied to ancestral dictates, but on the other hand it may also be due to a conscious tendency to 'make things small', to minimise that which people feel cannot be changed. And yet these same issues are critical to the work of artists in rural and urban areas, for they are the muses that inspire and motivate them.

Aboriginal buskers are now a familiar site at tourist venues throughout Australia. This trio is performing at the Mindal Beach Night Markets in Darwin.

Assertion of identity

The theme that dominates the visual and performing arts of rural and urban areas is the construction and assertion of an Aboriginal and Torres Strait Islander identity. This is particularly acute for artists who were taken from their Aboriginal homes under successive Australian government's assimilation policies.

The contemporary artworks of rural and urban indigenous communities give some visibility to these 'invisible' Aboriginal people. The art is vibrant, expressive, and often disturbing. As visual and performing artists interpret their histories and lived experiences from discrete Aboriginal perspectives, they redefine the contact history of Australia, placing Aboriginal people at the centre.

What makes the art forms of urban and rural Aboriginal people distinctly different from similar forms by non-Aboriginal people? In what manner does the Aboriginal identity of these artists, dancers and song writers make their work

Northern Territory artist Dorothy Napangardi at work in Gallery Gondwana in Sydney. In conjunction with an exhibition of her works in the gallery, the artist was available to talk about her work and show her works in progress to urban people.

Members of the Tjapukai Dance Theatre, Kuranda, Queensland. Providing training and career opportunities for local indigenous youth, the group has its own 300-seat theatre where up to fourteen performances are staged each week. In 1990 they completed a world tour as ambassadors for the Australian Tourism Commission and Qantas.

Individual life histories inform much of the art. The paintings of Ian Abdulla, for example, fuse a nostalgic concern with his own family history with an interest in Aboriginal spiritual relationships to land. His paintings depict his family living and working in rural South Australia. They evoke the strength of Aboriginal family relationships forged in times of hardship and later remembered in tranquillity.

Other paintings might be regarded as shocking—but they are certainly no more shocking than the histories that prompted them. These are angry and very disturbing works, focusing as they do on past and present conflicts between indigenous and non-indigenous people.

Gordon Bennett's 'ABC' series is particularly brutal since it exposes the coarseness and physical cruelty associated with early European contact. ABC alludes to the racist epithets 'Abo', 'Boong' and 'Coon' and so links the atrocities of the past to racism in the present. Paintings such as these undermine European readings of Australian history by replacing the Eurocentric view with an Aboriginal perspective—the colonial vision is challenged and, finally, usurped by an indigenous interpretation of history. Gordon Bennett moves the focus of colonial vision from the European occupiers to Aboriginals and in doing so redefines the history of European occupation, so that it becomes primarily Aboriginal history.

unique? Stylistically, it is by the use of patterning, techniques and motifs that derive from much older art forms. Thematically, this identity is expressed in terms of a special connection between people and the land, an emphasis on family relationships, an enduring spirituality, a concern with ritual and with regeneration, a preoccupation with dispossession and concealed histories, and an ongoing perception of disenfranchisement and oppression.

Indigenous artists from Australia's rural and urban communities make contact with and express their origins in three principal ways. Some Aboriginal artists learn directly from their counterparts in remote outback communities. Some use symbolism, imagery or techniques emanating from such communities but are careful to avoid the use of images that have sacred significance. Others derive inspiration from ancient traditional rock art, peopling contemporary landscape with totemic ancestors and spirit figures, making ancestral images resonate in contemporary contexts. Not surprisingly, there is an emphasis on earth tones, though the use of vibrant colours is certainly part of the contemporary tradition. Similarly, the symbolism of art by various Aboriginal and Torres Strait Islander clans can be combined stylistically with some related influences from European art movements.

Artists such as Judy Watson and Robert Campbell Jnr concern themselves with what are contemporary issues: the tragedy of Aboriginal deaths in custody, institutionalisation, segregation and land rights. The artists' approaches vary, from the confrontationalism of Bennett to the subtle allusions of Watson's work to the barbed humour of Campbell's narratives. His 'Roped off at the Pictures' investigates power relationships between Aboriginal and non-Aboriginal people by depicting segregation in cinemas. This is not a work drawing on a scene from some distant past—such segregation was still practised in many parts of Australia in the 1970s.

INDIGENOUS ART AND CULTURE TIMELINE							
39,000 YBP Date of ochre fragments found at Carpenter's Gap in the Kimberley, which may be the remains of earlier rock paintings.	**20,000–15,000 YBP** Rock art consisting of patterns and lines painted at Koonalda Cave on the Nullarbor Plain.	**8000 YBP** Regionalisation of art styles indicates higher levels of territorialism. **7000 YBP** Earliest examples of necklaces made from animal teeth, found in NSW.	**3000–2000 YBP** Development of 'x-ray' style of painting in Western Arnhem Land, now most readily seen in works at Ubirr, Kakadu National Park.	**1000 YBP** Dramatic increase in rock painting at Laura, Cape York, possibly indicating population increase or changes in artistic behaviours or belief systems.	**c.1800** Depictions of European sailors and settlers start to appear in rock art. **1860s** William Barak and Tommy McRae depict impact of Europeans on local culture.	**1929** National Museum of Victoria hosts first major exhibition of indigenous art. *Native Legends* by David Unaipon, first book by an Aboriginal writer to be published.
50,000 YBP Date of high-quality ochre pigments found at Malakunanya II, indicating some type of artistic activity, most likely rock art or body painting.	**30,000 YBP** Burial of Willandra Lakes Hominid 3 (Mungo III), male corpse decorated with red ochre transported from 200 km (124 miles) away.	**14,400 YBP** Geometric rock engravings at Sandy Creek 1, Cape York, Qld. **13,000 YBP** Rock engravings at Early Man Shelter, Cape York.	**6000 YBP** First appearances of rainbow serpent in rock art. Appearance of 'yam figures' in Western Arnhem Land and red-ochre Bradshaw paintings in Kimberley.	**1500 YBP** Beginning of Wandjina tradition in the Kimberley, characterised by depiction of Wandjina spirits, stylised figures with halo-like shape around head.	**c.1700** Macassan mariners and cultural artefacts depicted in rock art and stone arrangements of north coast and islands.	**1879** Bark paintings from NT displayed in Sydney. **1912** First official collection of indigenous art assembled by Baldwin Spencer for National Museum of Victoria.	**1936** Albert Nam[ ] begins to paint water[ ] at Hermannsburg. **1938** In Melbou[ ] Namatjira holds firs[ ] exhibition by Aborigina[ ]

Music, Dance and a Global Audience

Bangarra Dance Theatre at the Opera House, Sydney. Bangarra has achieved worldwide acclaim for its innovative performances incorporating modern Western and traditional Aboriginal and Torres Strait Island dance forms.

Like art, music, song and dance are vehicles used to explore indigenous peoples' identities, at both the individual and group level, and to further political aspirations. Survival is a dominant theme running through indigenous performing arts, referring not only to surviving the abuses of colonialism but also to conquering the challenges of the present.

Companies such as the Bangarra and Tjapukai dance theatres draw for inspiration upon indigenous and non-indigenous traditions, in the process creating works that are thoughtful, confronting and challenging. Established in 1989, the Bangarra Dance Theatre melds traditional instruments with modern musical technology and blends the cultural traditions of the Aboriginal and Islander people with contemporary Western dance movements, juxtaposing indigenous and Western traditions. For the theatre's director Stephen Page, the inspiration comes from traditional family kinship and the need to maintain its strength by passing on stories at the same time as imparting direction and advice.

Music today

Contemporary Aboriginal music encompasses many forms, rock and roll and country music among them. The titles of songs such as *Kimberley Roadtrain* and *Cattle Camp Reverie*, both sung by Kevin Gunn, evoke images of the Australian outback and appeal to Australians of differing backgrounds on many levels. Other songs, Kerri-Anne Cox's *Stolen Children* for example, are more clearly concerned with issues identified as particularly Aboriginal, in this case the alienation and grief felt by Aboriginal people when their children were taken from them under successive governments' assimilation policies. Others, such as

Members of the Tjapukai theatre group light a fire in the ancient manner. Performances like this help demonstrate to Aboriginal youth the value and uniqueness of their cultural legacy.

5 **Harold Blair** begins music at conservato- Melbourne—the first nal person to work in rn musical tradition.

1948 US–Australian scientific expedition to Arnhem Land collects 275 bark paintings and numerous carvings, many of which are placed in state galleries.

1964 *We Are Going* by Kath Walker (Oodgeroo Noonuccal), first book of verse by an Aboriginal writer to be published.

1966 Bark painting by Central Arnhem Land artist David Malangi used by Commonwealth as design for first Australian dollar note— without his permission.

1972 *The Two Worlds of Jimmie Barker*, one of first of many Aboriginal autobiographies. First performance of play by Aboriginal author, *The Dreamers* by Jack Davis.

1981 First major exhibition of indigenous art, *Aboriginal Australia*, shown in Vic., WA, Qld and NSW. *Day of the Dog*, novel by Archie Weller, later filmed as *Blackfellas*.

1988 *Barunga Statement*, painting calling for treaty with Commonwealth, presented to PM Bob Hawke.
1989 Bangarra Dance Company founded in Sydney.

1997 Emily Kame Kngwarreye, Judy Watson and Yvonne Koolmatrie represent Australia at Venice Biennale. *Festival of the Dreaming* held in Sydney.

1947 T.G.H. Strehlow publishes *Aranda Traditions*, a collection of Aboriginal legends and stories which highlights the richness of indigenous traditions.

1963 Yolngu people of Yirrkala in Arnhem Land send protest about mining on their land, in the form of a petition on a bark painting, to Canberra.

1965 *Wild Cat Falling* by Colin Johnson (Mudrooroo), first novel by an Aboriginal author to be published.

1971 Geoffrey Bardon takes up position as art teacher at Papunya, NT, and encourages local people to paint traditional designs, thus initiating Papunya Tula movement.

1976 *Warlugulong*, first large-scale canvas by Western Desert artists Clifford Possum Tjapaltjarra and Tim Leura Tjapaltjarra.

1983 *Dreamings: The Art of Aboriginal Australia* tours USA and Australia.
1987 Magabala Books, first indigenous publishing house, founded in Broome.

1990 Rover Thomas and Trevor Nickolls become first indigenous artists to represent Australia at Venice Biennale. *Paperbark*, an influential collection of Aboriginal writings.

2000 *Papunya Tula: Genesis and Genius* retrospective of Western Desert art held in Sydney. *Snake Circle* completes Roberta Sykes' autobiographical *Snake* trilogy.

the popular hit *My Island Home,* sung by Torres Strait Islander Christine Anu, pay homage to the artist's country and the seafaring heritage of her people.

The Aboriginal music group enjoying the greatest international recognition is no doubt Yothu Yindi, a rock band from Yirrkala, a small, Northern Territory coastal community of around 800 Yolngu people. Yothu Yindi translates from Yolngu to English as 'child and mother', and the band describes itself as the contemporary cultural voice of the Yolngu people of Yirrkala. The band has an explicit philosophy, one of balance and mutual respect between Aboriginal and non-Aboriginal Australians. In 1991 the band's second album, 'Tribal Voice', gained extensive media attention. A single from the album, *Treaty* calls for a

Participants in a traditional dance near Darwin, the capital of the Northern Territory. The red loin cloth, or naga, may have been introduced by Macassan fishermen who regularly visited northern Australia from the mid-eighteenth century.

formal treaty between the Australian government and Aboriginal people and spent 22 weeks in the national charts—the first song in an Aboriginal language to gain international recognition. The 'Tribal Voice' album generated international recording and touring contracts for Yothu Yindi, securing their place in the international music arena.

Yothu Yindi's commercial success provided the groundwork for the establishment of the Yothu Yindi Foundation Aboriginal Corporation. Its goal is to support and further the maintenance, development, teaching and commercial potential of Yolngu cultural life and activity. The foundation aims to provide such cultural services for the major community centres in the region and in the surrounding homeland centres.

Different Aboriginal communities in remote areas have other concerns. Historically, their performing arts have been enacted in both ceremonial and non-ceremonial contexts. In today's northern Australia, people make a distinction between 'corroboree' and 'business'. Corroborees—from a Darug (Sydney region) word—are ceremonies that can be viewed by all members of the community. Included under this rubric are the open sections of mortuary ceremonies in which the spirits of dead people are laid to rest. 'Business', on the other hand, refers to ceremonies which are conducted by senior people and which can only be viewed by people of the same gender. Both 'women's business' and 'men's business' exist. They include special songs, dances and body paintings, each specific to a particular ceremony. Access to certain sites at which ceremonies are being conducted is restricted to those of the appropriate gender during the duration. Today, these ceremonies are located closer to the community centres rather than in the more remote areas of the country in which they were enacted in the past.

Looking to the future

Globalisation presents indigenous Australians with new challenges and fresh opportunities. Increasingly, Aboriginal people are using the internet to reach out to a global audience. Aboriginal websites have a wide diversity of functions. Cultural groups such as the Bangarra Dance Theatre and Yothu Yindi establish them not only to promote their work but also to express in their own words their aims and ideals. Aboriginal communities in remote areas can increase their national and international profile without infringing upon their autonomy, avoiding extended contact with non-Aboriginal people and providing greater security for indigenous values. The website for Australia's former principal indigenous agency, the Aboriginal and Torres Strait Islander Commission, promoted the political agendas of Aboriginal Australians and challenged the place of all indigenous Australians in colonial histories. The site provided a directory of corporate and information publications, the commission's view on government policy and information on programmes along with a strong

A young Aboriginal girl of Mt Isa, Queensland. A growing awareness of the inherited rights, cultural and otherwise, of the world's indigenous peoples may secure for her a brighter future.

LEFT: Australians were quick to embrace the communications revolution, and the indigenous people were no exception. Aboriginal people in remote areas use video conferencing and the worldwide web to conduct 'law business' and to disseminate knowledge. This photograph was taken during classes at the Alice Springs Centre for Appropriate Technology, Northern Territory.

section which confronted the many myths that still exist about indigenous Australians. Pwerte Marnte Marnte Aboriginal Corporation in Central Australia hosts a website which coordinates cultural, tourism and economic enterprises. The site includes a 'didgeridoo university' which gives a step-by-step guide to playing the instrument, and also provides an on-line venue for purchasing didgeridoos and other artworks.

The Internet age

New technologies furnish a much-needed venue for indigenous voice, providing people with an opportunity to present themselves and their communities from their own viewpoint, without the intervention of non-Aboriginal interpreters. Publication on the worldwide web has the potential to overcome the frustration many indigenous arts and cultural groups have felt at being marginalised by mainstream media. Indigenous websites have the ability to project a sense of community that is immediate and authoritative. Given without interpretation by non-indigenous people, this can be a powerful message.

Communication technologies not only have the potential to sustain and fortify indigenous cultures, but also provide a means by which international alliances between indigenous peoples can be realised. There are both community-specific and globally shared issues of importance that need to be addressed. While all indigenous groups do not share the same history or circumstances, they often share a history of marginalisation within their respective countries and it is around political issues such as this that these international alliances are likely to form. Given their histories of interconnectedness, the predisposition of their cultures towards visual forms of communication and the level of control that they can have over how they are represented, it is hardly surprising that indigenous Australians are proving eager to embrace the new communications technologies.

There are challenges as well. For cultures locked into the fluidity and mediation of oral tradition there is the real fear that multi-media technology will 'fix' information in a way that is antithetical to indigenous systems of knowledge. Increasingly, Aboriginal people

are focusing on the ownership, control and protection of their cultural and intellectual property. The renowned example here is the misuse of one of David Malangi's paintings by the Reserve Bank of Australia. Without consulting the artist, the bank used a painting depicting a funeral scene in the design for the $1 note when it was introduced in 1966. Malangi sought compensation for this misappropriation of his design and subsequently was awarded a medal, a dinghy, an army tent and $500. Malangi is now among the most well respected of Australian Aboriginal artists and his work is exhibited in private collections and galleries throughout the world. This case was important because it established that Aboriginal designs are owned, and has set a precedent by which Aboriginal people receive commercial benefit from their cultural and intellectual property.

The indigenous peoples' need to have control over their cultural and intellectual property is not being met by existing legislation. However, some countries that are home to indigenous people are considering a range of legislative changes in order to accommodate indigenous ways of learning and curating knowledge. Among the issues being addressed are the revision of legislation relating to patents so that it recognises the contribution made by indigenous knowledge to the development of new medicines; changing copyright legislation to recognise the communal and multi-levelled ownership of designs and cultural knowledge; and changing legislation relating to performers' rights to recognise the secret and restricted nature of certain indigenous performances. These developments are critical if Australia's indigenous arts and cultures are to continue to flourish.

Indigenous art and culture is now a major component of Australia's tourist industry and makes a large contribution to the nation's export earnings. Pictured are the Alice Springs premises of a company built around the work of artists from Papunya, in the desert country west of Alice Springs. Artists from here were the first to commercially produce work in the now-familiar 'dot' style, giving rise to what is sometimes called 'the Papunya Tula School'.

The Myth of the Australian Character

The Australian character is a complex mixture of many traits, a brew based on its convict past and seasoned by an influx of cultures from many lands.

When John Douglas Pringle, a highly esteemed Scots-born journalist who later became editor of the *Sydney Morning Herald,* analysed the culture of his adopted country in his book *Australian Accent* in 1958 he declared: 'Only one profound book has been written about Australia. It is D.H. Lawrence's novel *Kangaroo* ... most of it is as true today as when it was written thirty-five years ago.' In this he was mimicking the infamous academic who, asked to deliver a lecture on Australian literature, replied that, as there was no real Australian literature, he would instead deliver a lecture on Lawrence's *Kangaroo.*

How could this have happened less than 50 years ago? Is it really true that there was no distinctive Australian culture then? And what is the situation now? Certainly on a superficial level, the way in which Australians view their culture has changed. No academic would now be foolhardy or ill-informed enough to maintain that there is no real Australian literature. The problem, for all commentators, is to determine exactly what Australian culture is and to detect those defining differences which separate Australian society from others in the world.

Part of the issue lies in that Australia is a land of great contradictions. It is, for example, one of the oldest countries on earth, and at the same time one of the newest. While Aboriginal Australia can trace its uninterrupted ancestry back at least 40,000 years (and there are those who argue that Aborigines may have been here for three times as long as that), European Australia can, at best, only claim a little more than 200 years of occupation. For every year of Aboriginal settlement, Europeans have lived on the continent for less than 24 hours .

Yet another paradox is the fact that Australia is among the most urbanised societies on Earth—more than 80 per cent of the population lives in cities and along the eastern seaboard—yet it largely depends for its imagery and iconography on the desert and the outback. And though there are more women than men in the population, the notion of male mateship, which some argue was forged on the battlefields of the Great War, plays an important part in national identity. And this admiration for old-fashioned self-sacrifice sits oddly with the hedonism of Sydney's Gay and Lesbian Mardi Gras, the world's largest celebration of gay pride. Is this a contradiction or is it, as some would have it, proof that Australian mateship is just an expression of repressed homosexuality?

These anomalies are part of the complex fabric of a society so new it scarcely knows itself. What are the truths about modern Australian society and culture? Australia certainly promotes itself aggressively as an egalitarian society, a great and abiding meritocracy in which human beings are measured by their individual behaviour rather than their background or wealth. In keeping with this principle of a 'fair go' for everyone, Australia is about as close as the world has ever got to a working-class utopia. The average Australian still prefers a beer to a wine, a meat pie or a hamburger to *haute cuisine*, an action movie to an art film, commercial television to the ABC or SBS, popular music to classical, a night out at the local club to a night at the opera. According to this view, Australia is essentially a working-class society made good (in European terms *petit bourgeois*), motivated by simple pleasures and uncomplicated desires, the dream of the philosophers of eighteenth- and nineteenth-century Europe. But

The paradox that is Australia. This rodeo competitor at Bungendore, in the ACT, may to many people personify Australia's rural-based heritage. In fact, the style of his clothing, the horse's gear and the event, calf-roping, are imports from the United States. The ringers on Australia's vast cattle stations use entirely different methods to handle stock.

would Rousseau, Voltaire, Marx, John Stuart Mill and Engels really admire the reality? When they dreamed of an ideal working-class society did they really have modern day Australian in mind?

Forging a national identity

It is a characteristic of 'new' societies that they worry about the nature of their national identity and it is equally true that older societies find such a preoccupation rather strange. The English, for example, with their long history as a nation, know exactly who they are and instead of navel-gazing spend a lot of time gently sending up their own idiosyncrasies. Since the nineteenth century the United States of America has seen literally thousands of books attempting to define just what it is. Some, like Frederick Turner's famous *Frontier Thesis* (which argued that the character of its people had been forged in the cauldron of an unceasing desire to move ever further westward to find new territory to develop), have themselves become part of that nation's identity.

Australia is no exception to this rule. Its obsession with the 'national character' has given rise to a large number of books, many of which have enjoyed wide commercial success and some, most notably Donald Horne's *The Lucky Country* and historian Geoffrey Blainey's *The Tyranny of Distance*, have actually

entered the language as cliched, and often misunderstood and misinterpreted, explanations for why the Australians are the way they are.

Australia's current notion of character is today still influenced by two major forces of the past still active today: Federation (that day in 1901 when six separate colonies came together as a nation) and World War I which followed soon after. Prior to Federation there had been a lively interest in national identity at the same time as it was acknowledged that antagonisms and competitiveness existed between the colonies.

ABOVE: *Despite grumblings on the far right of politics, Australia is a largely harmonious multi-cultural society. Its remaining so is in the hands of children like these.*

TOP: *Australians may profess to have their roots in the bush, but they have always been a nation of coast-hugging city dwellers.*

Home-grown films were popular with Australians in the years between the First and Second World Wars. Above is a still from a film based on Steele Rudd's On Our Selection, which played to big audiences in 1920. Dad and Dave, a radio serial based on Rudd's work, was still drawing listeners in the 1950s.

Influence of the *Bulletin*

In the *Bulletin* magazine of the 1880s and 1890s, under the editorship of the remarkable Jules F. Archibald, this nascent interest in a national character finally found a voice. During this time Archibald actively nurtured a generation of talented local writers and cartoonists, notable among them Andrew 'Banjo' Paterson, Henry Lawson, Steele Rudd (Arthur Hoey Davis) and Price Warung (William Astey). Though not always conscious of what they were doing, these writers created a series of enduring Australian cultural archetypes—the Little Aussie Battler (Paterson's Man from Snowy River is braver than his master and will ultimately triumph in the end; coincidentally, the Battler also happened to be an exceptional horseman and bushman), the All-Suffering Woman (Henry Lawson's Drover's Wife dedicates her life to the follies of her hard-working man), the City Spiv (beautifully captured in Banjo Paterson's poem 'The Man from Ironbark') and the Naïve Larrikin (symbolised by Paterson's character of Mulga Bill who to experience 'modernity' buys a bicycle and nearly kills himself on it). As well, they drew on an endless sense of humour about the travails of ordinary life (perfectly captured by Lawson in his short story *The Loaded Dog* and by Paterson in 'A Bush Christening') and the constant conflict between the country and the city (distilled into a single event in Paterson's 'The Geebung Polo Club' where the bush and city take each other on in a symbolic battle to the death). Steele Rudd's stories of Dad and Dave (first published as *On Our Selection*) epitomised the rewards of honest toil through the efforts of a large rural family who slowly better themselves, one of them eventually entering Parliament, and come to enjoy modest prosperity. Price Warung looked at the Australian character through the prism of history and left-wing politics. Born in Liverpool, England, in 1855, Warung came to prominence in the pages of the *Bulletin* in the early 1890s. Warung's stories of European settlement were collected into volumes like *Tales of the Convict System* and *Tales of the Early Days,* giving a perspective on colonial life as harsh and a view of convicts as essentially decent working people oppressed and maltreated.

Whether or not these images are still true is a moot point, but they persist. Even today there is still a very open antagonism between 'the bush' and the city with the bush having its own political party (the National Party, once called the Country Party, rarely contests city-based elections) and its own sense of values. Equally, the images of the Naïve Larrikin, the Little Aussie Battler and the All-Suffering Woman, even if they no longer really exist, are still very much part of the nation's iconography.

Masculinity dominates

These images were soon to become part of Australia's identity as a separate and independent nation. But they were soon modified and overwhelmed by the events of World War I. Only 13 years after coming to nationhood Australia, deeply committed to Britain and the notion of a British Empire, went off to fight in that grand folly known as The War to End All Wars. One of the earliest campaigns was that around Gallipoli on the shores of the Dardanelles in Turkey. Here, Australian and New Zealand forces, fighting a battle which could never be won because of the

Sometimes half-disparagingly referred to as 'big, bronzed Aussie surfers', surf life-savers are an Australian icon nevertheless. These men are competitors in a surfboat race, a gruelling event which in heavy surf can be as dangerous as it is exhilarating.

terrain and the incompetence of their military leaders, were to demonstrate such levels of bravery that the infant nation viewed these young soldiers as being symbolic of the kind of national character it wanted to develop.

C.E.W. Bean, Australia's official war historian, gave a voice to this feeling when he wrote of the ANZAC forces: 'It lay in the mettle of the men themselves. To be the sort of man who would give way when his mates were trusting to his firmness; to be the sort of man who would fail when the line, the whole force, and the allied cause required his endurance; to have made it necessary for another unit to do his own unit's work; to live the rest of his life haunted by the knowledge that he had set his hand to a soldier's task and had lacked the grit to carry it through—that was the prospect which these men could not face. Life was very dear, but life was not worth living unless they could be true to their idea of Australian manhood. Standing upon that alone, when help failed and hope faded, when the end loomed clear in front of them, when the whole world seemed to crumble and the heaven to fall in, they faced its ruin undismayed.'

This became the enduring myth of the Australian character. It was entirely masculine (women weren't considered in the equation), deeply committed to a notion of mateship and unbelievably courageous (determined to fight on regardless of the risks that involved). Tell that to your average young city slicker in the twenty-first century and, while he or she might agree with Bean's ideals, in reality the circumstances in which they live would give them little chance to bear out this strange notion of Australian identity. It is one of the great contemporary ironies that an increasing number of young men and women, mostly twenty-something backpackers wandering around Europe, now go to Anzac Cove each year on Anzac Day to commemorate the tragic loss of life and to somehow celebrate and participate in this grand Australian myth. They are, in every imaginable sense, far removed from those brave innocents who gave their lives fighting for Britain.

If World War I gave rise to the myth of the brave ANZAC soldier, then the following decade saw the emergence of a new national icon, the Bronzed Aussie, epitomising the 'manly' pursuits—excellence in sport, a love of the outdoors and a preoccupation with physical fitness. Like so many modern images the Bronzed Aussie was part reality (there was a huge growth in the popularity of surfing and beach culture in the 1920s) and partly movie myth-making. And the quintessential Bronzed Aussie was a real person. Snowy Baker, who was born in Surry Hills in Sydney, was a hugely talented sportsman excelling at swimming, water polo, Rugby Union (he represented New South Wales), rowing, fencing, wrestling and boxing (famously winning three matches in one day). After the war he starred in a number of movies—essentially as himself—the first in a long line to represent what was now seen as the ideal Australian man. Over the years Snowy Baker has been followed by the likes of Chips Rafferty, Jack Thompson, Bryan Brown, Mel Gibson and Heath Ledger.

Who is the modern Australian? Well, statistically she is female (more than 50 per cent of the country's population are now women), she lives in one of the country's main cities and is likely to live close to the coast. She is very much influenced by global fashions, whether that involves wearing what is currently fashionable in New York and London, going to movies which have enjoyed international success or watching the latest soaps and sitcoms from Britain and the United States. Australians do like to see themselves on television and in the movies but it is equally true that such a sense of nationalism can be easily over-ruled by the desire to be part of the wider world, of the new 'global village'. She is also less likely to be of British or Irish descent than was the case just a generation ago, though people from this group still predominate.

An Australian gun crew at the hell that was Ypres, Belgium, in 1917. The Anzacs' disrespect for authority that so appalled the English officers contributed greatly to Australians' perceptions of themselves.

A nation of sports lovers, though increasingly as spectators rather than participants, Australians flocked in their thousands to the 2000 Olympic and Paralympic games in Sydney. Many foreign visitors were bewildered when Australian barrackers cheered competitors who had just beaten the local hero.

The Modern Australian Character

Defiant to the end, Edward Kelly faces the troopers at Glenrowan in 1880. Born to impoverished Irish settlers, Ned is still seen as the epitome of the ongoing struggle against all the odds between the Little Aussie Battler and an uncaring Establishment in the form of everything from banks and bosses to telephone companies and the government of the day.

There is no doubt, as the country enters the twenty-first century, that Australia has established a definable national character and identity. However, this identity is a complex mixture of traits which, like any series of generalisations, is open to dispute and question.

Egalitarianism and the Irish

The first generalisation is that Australia is a truly egalitarian society. Modern Australia is full of stories of poor people, particularly immigrants from Eastern Europe after World War II, who stepped off refugee boats penniless and ended up as multi-millionaires. Theoretically, it is possible for anyone in Australia to move through the imaginary levels of society, though most of the country's Aboriginal population would hotly dispute that. It is true that compared to older and more hierarchical societies there is no obvious aristocracy in Australia.

The so-called upper echelons of society comprise anyone who has made a mark, or who has enough money. Thus the country's self-styled aristocrats are really more power brokers than blue bloods and can include millionaire builders, TV and radio personalities, restaurateurs and media owners as well as those whose families may have had money for a few generations.

Part of the reason for this apparent egalitarianism is that Australia is essentially a post-industrial society. The British settlers had no time to develop either a rural aristocracy (and those who now exist are asset rich and cash poor) or a rural peasantry. To this egalitarianism has to be added the vital ingredient of the Irish in Australia.

RIGHT: In 1954 Queen Elizabeth visited Australia; this was the first visit by a reigning monarch. At this time, most Australians still saw themselves as being a part of the British Empire, and Empire Day was celebrated each year.

Their national traits of scepticism (particularly in regard to the English and the English Establishment), independence, and a healthy disregard for formality and status were similar to certain traits of the English working class. When these two strands came together in a society which was founded on the conflict between the Establishment and those who flouted authority it was inevitable that they would have an impact on the Australian character. It is equally no accident that one of Australia's most potent icons was a man of Irish descent, the bushranger Edward 'Ned' Kelly.

Ned epitomises Irish independence and scepticism in his famous 'Jerilderie Letter' in which he wrote: 'And is my brothers and sisters and my mother not to be pitied also who has no alternative only to put up with the brutal and cowardly conduct of a parcel of big ugly fat-necked wombat-headed big-bellied magpie-legged narrow-hipped splay-footed sons of Irish bailiffs or English landlords which is better known as officers of justice or Victorian Police who some calls honest gentlemen?' Kelly truly epitomises the Australian dislike for formality, pretentiousness and pomp. He is also a potent symbol of the deep Australian suspicion of the forces which rule society.

Naturally, the forces which rule society insist that this defiance is really the 'tall poppy syndrome' at work. By this they refer to the tendency of some to mock and dismiss those who have achieved greatness or power. But while there is great admiration for anyone who, with enterprise and a little bit of luck, has managed to create a fortune by doing anything from running a chain of liquor outlets to becoming a movie star, Australians have a passionate dislike for those who reach positions of power but seem to lose contact with the 'ordinary people'. The cutting down of tall poppies is usually reserved for those who are seen to be 'getting above themselves'.

ABOVE: *A third-generation descendant of Scots settlers, Ham Bickett of Parkes, New South Wales, would for many personify the 'face of Australia'. In reality, Australia has always had many faces.*

From Anglophile to Republican

Until the 1960s Australia saw itself as nothing more than an adjunct of the British Empire. We loved 'Mother England' and some even talked about it as 'home'. In 1954, Australians poured onto the streets to welcome Elizabeth II, the new Queen of England and Australia and the first reigning monarch to visit Britain's former colony in the south. The greatest sporting competition in the country was the Ashes, a cricket match contested by England and Australia. The ABC was peopled by announcers who spoke a strange antipodean variant of standard BBC English. For many, an Australian diet closely resembled that of the 'mother country'—roast beef and Yorkshire pudding was a staple along with white bread, tea, lots of gravy and two vegetables. The Australian legal and political system were imitations of the British model. The consequence of this was, predictably, a huge sense of cultural cringe. Nothing we did was as good as the English—our television wasn't as good, our literature wasn't as good, our plays weren't as good. Real culture was seen to reside in London and anyone with cultural aspirations—Clive James, Barry Humphries and Germaine Greer were just three of our more famous cultural refugees—headed off to England to experience it.

The great migrations from Greece and Italy in the 1950s began, slowly and inexorably, to change this. The new migrants felt no particular allegiance to Britain, and brought with them their customs, culture and food. Also that old Irish spirit continued to assert itself, recognising that, even though they weren't sure who a real Australian was, they knew real Australians weren't culturally cringing Anglophiles. By the early 1970s—and the Whitlam era from 1972–75 is now seen as being emblematic— Australian movies were telling Australian stories, Australian food was reflecting Italian and Asian

influences, and Australian culture, epitomised by novelist Patrick White winning the Nobel Prize for Literature in 1973 for *The Eye of the Storm*, was starting to be taken seriously. Out of this impetus towards independence was born the debate on Republicanism with its national referendum in 1999. Polls indicated that the majority of Australians wanted to cut ties with Britain to become a republic, but the referendum was lost primarily because the debate was hijacked by conservatives eager to maintain old ties with England. Instead of holding off until a genuinely acceptable model for a republic could be reached (and therefore achieving a broad measure of public agreement) a timetable was established which meant a rushed, and possibly flawed, model for a republic was offered. That Australia will become an independent republic is inevitable. All that is needed is the political will and a determination to reach a broadly based agreement on the shape of the new order.

ABOVE LEFT: *Another face of Australia. Several generations of Ah Toys stand outside their family-run store, established in 1935, at Katherine, in the Northern Territory. The Chinese have a long history in Australia.*

As Australia gropes its way towards the future, Aboriginal Australians, whose histories encompass more than 1300 generations, are demanding that they, too, be allowed to take their rightful place in society.

What Australia Looks Like

There is hardly a community project in rural Australia that was not partly funded by a 'lamington drive', the sale of small cakes made of (originally) reject sponge-cake, cocoa and dried coconut. 'Lammoes' are still a popular entry in the baking section of Australia's country agricultural shows.

As a nation, Australia came into existence after the invention of the motor car and electricity. It was, from its very beginning, a truly modern society which depended on technology rather than tradition and where regional food, styles of housing, languages and dialects simply did not have the time to develop.

Food

Consider the importance of food, upon which part of a nation's cultural identity depends. If Europeans had arrived in Australia before the advent of the Industrial Revolution, there is no doubt that kangaroo meat, the vegetables and berries of the bush, emu, crocodile and probably goanna and snake would all have become an integral part of a unique Australian cuisine. Instead, the early settlers produced a cuisine of necessity based on the animals they had brought with them (sheep and cattle), along with a few easy-to-grow vegetables and grains raised in Britain (mainly wheat and potatoes), all cooked in a very British kind of way. Stew, comprising mutton, potatoes, wheat-based dumplings and maybe carrots, and cooked over an

open fire for most of the day, became the rural staple. It was ideal food for out in the bush because the cook never knew when the men would come in from clearing the land. It was often supplemented by damper (the most basic bread imaginable) and tea brewed over an open fire.

Interestingly, this is now changing in the national cuisine. Many country restaurants focus on locally grown produce and a plethora of growers' markets in the cities sell everything from truffles (now grown in Tasmania) to Sydney rock lobster. At the end of the twentieth century and into the second millennium Australia has finally embraced multiculturalism and food has played a very large part. It is hard to believe, when strolling around the cosmopolitan cafes in any large city, that the nearest thing to pâté used to be meat loaf, and that citizens of Darwin once believed that lychees (now exported worldwide from Australia) were part of a Chinese plot to drug them. Eating habits have been slow to change, as the Europeans who migrated after the war were to discover to their disappointment. At the end of the nineteenth century when meat was abundant and relatively cheap, the

Most Australians today enjoy a choice of foods that were largely unknown only a couple of generations ago. Australian chefs are gaining world attention for their willingness to experiment with the ingredients and cooking styles of many cultures as they create an Australian cuisine.

CULTURE AND SOCIETY TIMELINE							
1788 First Fleet establishes penal colony at Port Jackson. Aboriginal population estimated at between 300,000 and 750,000, speaking around 250 languages.	**1851** Gold Rush attracts large numbers of Chinese prospectors, with 24,000 living on Victorian goldfields by 1861. States respond by limiting Chinese immigration.	**1901** Population: 3.8 million (98% British/Irish origin, only 93,000 Aboriginal). Life expectancy: 55.2 for males, 58.8 for females. Immigration Restriction Act introduced.	**1942** General Douglas Macarthur made commander of Allied Forces in the SW Pacific. Thousands of US soldiers arrive, helping to disseminate American culture.	**1952** Following agreement in 1947 with International Refugee Organisation, 170,000 European displaced persons settle in Australia.	**1981–91** Number of Asian immigrants rises 156 per cent between 1981 and 1991, with Vietnamese, Malaysians and Filipinos forming the largest groups.	**1999** Population reaches 19 million. Life expectancy: 76 for males, 82 for females; but for indigenous Australians, only 56 for males and 63 for females.

40,000–50,000 YBP Aboriginal peoples spread across continent from north. Most develop a nomadic lifestyle, meeting other groups to trade and hold ceremonies.

1831 Government establishes assisted migration program to attract large numbers of settlers. Most are British, though a large proportion is Irish.

1891 Industrialisation results in increasing urbanisation, with Sydney's population reaching 400,000 and Melbourne's coming close to 500,000.

1919–29 More than 300,000 British migrants arrive. Growth in popularity of outdoor sports such as swimming and surfing creates image of 'Bronzed Aussie'.

1947 Government offers assisted passage to British ex-servicemen and women. By 1955, one million migrants, or '£10 Poms', have taken advantage of the scheme.

1965–69 Half of migrants arriving are still British, but 18 per cent now come from Italy and Greece. These two groups soon make a major impression on local culture.

1996 More than 200 languages in use, led by English, Italian, Greek and Cantonese. About 48,000 indigenous people speak one of 48 indigenous languages.

national consumption was 135 kg (300 lb) per person per year—more than twice as much as their British counterparts. Australians stuck to 'traditional' cooking ('meat and two veg.'), regarding anything more exotic than spaghetti bolognaise with deep suspicion. While Chinese restaurants have been part of the Australian scene since the 1850s, the dishes had to be altered to suit local tastes, so everything seemed to come with pineapple chunks and sweet and sour sauce. Many migrant biographies tell of miserable childhood experiences when xenophobic attitudes translated into criticism of their eating habits and they were made to feel ashamed if their parents packed anything as exotic as a salami sandwich in their school lunch.

Away from Australia in the 1950s, the homesick expatriate might crave a lamington (stale sponge cake dipped in chocolate and covered with shredded, dried coconut), a pavlova (meringue filled with fresh fruit and cream, created in 1935 by an Australian chef to celebrate the visit of the ballerina, a claim ardently disputed by New Zealanders, who claim the pavlova as their own), a chiko roll (chicken and vegetables rolled in a pastry cylinder and deep-fried), a battered sav (a saveloy or frankfurt fried in batter and served with tomato sauce), or the ubiquitous Vegemite sandwich (Vegemite is a yeast-based spread), still loved by 'happy little Vegemites', as it has been for generations according to the company's advertising jingle.

All this was to change, although very gradually, as immigrants, unable to find the ingredients for their own styles of cooking, or to enjoy a meal out, opened shops and restaurants. New eating patterns, more appropriate to Australia's climate and lifestyle, began to emerge. In the 1990s, Italian and Thai cuisine, and

'fusion' food (blending influences from a number of different culinary styles) were popular. Indigenous ingredients such as native fruits, emu, kangaroo, barramundi fish and even witjuti grubs began appearing on menus and fuelled a bush foods industry. These days for their Christmas lunch, Australians are just as likely to sit down to fresh seafood as they are to roast turkey with all the trimmings, and to finish the meal with tropical fruit rather than plum pudding.

Housing

Although in the beginning housing was responsive to local circumstances, it later followed the British model, with little regard for topography or climate. In long-established societies there is a unique and practical use of products native to a particular area, with an emphasis on their suitability to the environment. Local honey-coloured stone characterises many areas in southern England, for example, and in the south of Greece every house has an area upstairs where the inhabitants can sleep when the warm winds blow north off the Sahara. In inland Australia, the early settlers built simple residences of wattle and daub and in western Queensland, where the local Aborigines actively opposed the European invasion, thick stone

It took more than half a century for the Europeans in Australia to realise that the houses they were used to were for the most part totally unsuited to the local climate. One result was the 'Queenslander', an airy, timber building that provided respite from the heat, humidity and frequent floods of the tropical and subtropical coasts.

houses with small windows were constructed almost as fortresses. In the nineteenth century different areas of settlement in Australia began to show similar signs of regional differences. The coastal areas of Queensland, characterised by lush forests rich in cedar and oppressively hot tropical and subtropical summers, developed the distinctive 'Queenslander', a wooden house built on stilts to allow breezes to cool the house in summer. Along the New South Wales coast certain towns became 'timber' towns because of the local abundance of suitable timber.

Unfortunately, the growth of modern Australia coincided with a time when regional variations, particularly in housing, were in decline and conformity in domestic architecture was the order of the day. The result has been an extraordinary homogeneity from one end of the continent to the other. For example, a house in the outer suburbs of Perth is likely to be identical to a suburban house in the outer suburbs of Melbourne, the simple full-brick 'Federation home' can be seen as easily in certain suburbs of Sydney and Melbourne as in certain areas of Goulburn, Ballarat or Wagga Wagga, and the 1950s fibro house (now

largely out of favour because of the negative 'poor-peoples' housing' connotations it has acquired) is as much a part of suburban Wollongong as it is of Dubbo, Geelong or Gin Gin. Since the 1960s the project home—a style of house designed to fit any new suburb anywhere in Australia—has become popular, and project-home companies have established their own particular styles from Darwin to Hobart and from Carnarvon to Sydney.

Language

Then, finally, there is the issue of language. In preindustrialised Europe, centuries of geographical isolation resulted in unique variations in dialect and accent. In places such as Britain these differences have persisted, and linguistic geographers can even identify speakers from neighbouring villages. And despite the speed of modern communications, cities which are now only a couple of hours drive from each other—Liverpool and Birmingham, for example—still have quite distinctive ways of speaking. In Australia, on the other hand, it is virtually impossible to detect from a person's speech whether they come from Western Australia or Queensland, Hobart or Hunters Hill, and even though vast distances are involved there are no distinct accents and very few regionally unique words. Although there are minor variations in pronunciation and phraseology in some areas these are not significant. The result of all this has been that, in habits and appearance at least, Australia is a remarkably homogeneous society. Whether this is a good or a bad thing is difficult to say, but Australia's is certainly a uniquely modern post-industrial society.

Entire suburbs of 'project homes', usually built by one developer and almost indistinguishable one from the other, can be found on the outer fringes of towns and cities all over Australia.

A Multicultural Society

On mainland Australia and Tasmania, the indigenous people belonged to the same racial group and had lived as successful hunters and gatherers for at least 40,000 years before the coming of the Europeans. This situation changed dramatically with the arrival of the First Fleet in 1788 which brought approximately 1000 Europeans to Australia. Only one person among its cargo of convicts, a third of whom were from London, was black. Originally from the island of Madagascar, this man, nicknamed 'Black Caesar', became Australia's first bushranger.

Anglo-Saxon origins

During the penal colony era some 900 convicts, of whom 120 were born in Britain, were non-white. By 1853, when transportation to eastern Australia ended, 29,466 Irish men and 9104 Irish women—nearly one-quarter of all convicts and many of them of the Catholic faith—had arrived in Australia. However, the first recorded Roman Catholic mass on Australian soil did not occur until 1803, and the first officially appointed priests did not arrive in the colony until 1820. In spite of the presence of blacks and Irish Catholics the overwhelming majority of emigrants were white Anglo-Saxon Protestants from England and, because they held the positions of power, they determined the attitudes and values of Australia for the next century and a half.

Ethnic waves

From the earliest times the country was in need of labour, leading to waves of immigration of different ethnic groups from different places. A contingent of nearly 500 labourers from the Indian subcontinent came to Australia between 1837 and 1844 . In 1838–39 a group of 500 Lutherans from Prussian Silesia arrived in South Australia. Jewish migration began slowly but accelerated during World War II. They were a minor group on the First Fleet; no one knows the precise number but it is thought that between eight and fourteen Jewish convicts were transported. By 1830 only 400 Jewish convicts had arrived and by 1845 that number had only reached 800. In 1851 there were still only 2000 Jews in the country. A decade later, largely due to the goldrushes which had brought people to Australia from all over the world, the Jewish population had grown to 5000. In the 1880s a wave of anti-Semitism swept Eastern

Indians have had a presence in Australia since colonial times. The South Australian mining town of Burra Burra received its name from Burra Creek, which was named by Indian shepherds working in the area. Burra in Hindustani means 'great'.

Indochinese refugees arriving at Canberra in 1979. By June 1987, Australia had received about 107,000 people from this region. Contrary to popular belief, the vast majority of Vietnamese now living in Australia were selected from refugee camps in South-East Asia. In the decade from 1977, only 2097 'boat people' came directly to Australia.

method Australia resisted settlement by Asians and actively discouraged Asian immigration for 100 years. Changes occurred only very slowly. In the 1950s the Colombo Plan brought to study in Australia students from the countries of South-East Asia. Their numbers were expanded as fee-paying students from Asia were permitted to study at the country's secondary and tertiary educational institutions. Asians are now for the most part welcome in Australia and are coming to settle in increasing numbers. In 1991 there were 404,600 Australians of South-East Asian origin, an increase of 64 per cent on the 246,900 who were resident in 1981. In 1991, Australia's largest Asian groups were the Vietnamese (133,400), Malaysians (84,100), Filipinos (74,300), people from Hong Kong (73,200), China (68,500) and India (65,400).

In 1863 the first Pacific Islanders arrived from the New Hebrides and Loyalty Islands to work on the Queensland canefields. Between that year and 1904, 61,160 of these immigrants, known as 'kanakas', worked as indentured labourers in a state of virtual slavery. The practice eventually stopped in 1904.

Post-war migrants

At the beginning of World War II and for many years afterwards, and in spite of these waves of migration, Australia was still an aggressively Anglo-Saxon society, determined to maintain its links with the British monarchy and believing that the British legacy, in terms of the country's legal and political systems, were part of a heritage which should never be altered. After the war, however, frightened by a perception that the country was in imminent danger of being overrun by Asians, Australia began an active campaign to attract migrants of European descent. Preference was given to the British, who were offered assisted passage. The plan worked, and by 1955 the postwar immigration boom had brought one million migrants to Australia. The first wave brought refugees from war-torn Europe, mainly from Eastern Europe. The second wave in the 1950s came from the Mediterranean countries, with Italians making up about a third of the intake. By the mid-1970s Australia had assisted-immigration plans in place with Italy, Greece, West Germany, Yugoslavia, Holland, Poland and Austria.

More than those from any other minority groups, migrants from Italy and Greece have had a profound effect on the Australian way of life. It is hard to imagine an Australian city without pizza, cappuccino, pasta and wine, and games such as soccer have become an integral part of Australian culture. Italian immigration to Australia is essentially a post-war phenomenon. It began in a very small way with just one convict of Italian descent on the First Fleet. By the time of the first census in 1871, 960 Italians were recorded as living in Australia. A substantial number of Italians

Australia's acceptance of multiculturalism, by which people can become Australians while still acknowledging and celebrating their ethnic origins has, by and large, been a great success. While events in the former homelands are still of great concern, the country is remarkably free of incidents like those that plague immigrants in other societies.

CENTRE: A stained-glass window in the Synagogue, Margaret Street, Brisbane. The first eight Jews arrived in Australia as convicts on the First Fleet. The first Jewish parliamentarian, Lionel Samson, was elected to the Western Australian legislature in 1849.

Europe, with tens of thousands of Jews fleeing from Russia and Poland, many coming to Australia. The rise of Nazism in 1938 saw 2000 Jews from Europe seeking refugee status in Australia every week.

The Asian and Islander impact

The most significant non-white emigration to Australia was from 1848 to 1852 when 3000 Chinese came to work as indentured labourers on farms. Their arrival saw the first signs of racial disharmony. The 'coolies' were paid as little as £1 a month and this was widely seen as a threat to the stability of the white workforce. The situation was exacerbated by the massive immigration which occurred as a result of the discovery of gold. In Victoria in 1854 there were only 2000 Chinese. Over the next 18 months 15,000 Chinese arrived on the Victorian goldfields and by 1861 there were over 24,000. By then, 60 per cent of all the people on the New South Wales gold-fields and 25 per cent of the people on the Victorian goldfields were Chinese. This influx of people who looked different, spoke a different language, had different religious beliefs, ate different food and lived in tightly knit and separate communities challenged the predominantly European nature of Australian society. There were race riots on the goldfields and by 1855 Victoria had enacted anti-Chinese legislation which was followed by restrictive legislation in South Australia (1857) and New South Wales (1861). These pieces of legislation were the precursors to Australia's discriminatory 'White Australia' policy by which came to work on the Queensland sugarcane fields in the 1890s and by the time of the 1921 census there were over 8000 Italians. By 1933 this figure had grown to 26,500. Following World War II, the Australian government agreed to provide assisted passage for selected Italian families, and between 1945 and 1973, 379,000 Italians who saw Australia as a land of opportunity emigrated here. By the 1980s more than 20 per cent of all first-generation Italians were self-employed in enterprises as diverse as corner stores, wholesale and retail greengroceries, cafes, restaurants and construction companies.

The fourth largest ethnic group in Australia is the Greeks. They form a significant minority with over half a million Australians claiming Greek ancestry, although as late as 1891 there were fewer than 500 Greeks living in Australia; by 1939 this number had only risen to 15,000. The main period of Greek immigration began in the early 1950s when over 30,000 arrived in Australia. This pattern of migration continued into the 1960s with an average of nearly 16,000 Greeks a year arriving to settle.

Today, Australia is a genuinely multicultural society. The forces which evolved over the past two centuries have slowly coalesced to produce a society which, while English-speaking and firmly committed to many British legal and political structures, is a diverse mixture of races, cultures, religions and customs. Whether Australia is a successful multicultural society is an open question. Inevitably, some believe that the country is being overrun by Asians, that the glories and virtues of the 'British way of life' are disappearing and that there are too many non-Christian, non-English speaking people in positions of power and authority. This viewpoint, articulated by a small and very conservative right-wing political party, Pauline Hanson's One Nation, in the 1990s became the catchcry for the disenfranchised; particularly some older Australians and rural people affected by falling world prices for wool, wheat and beef. However, despite these minority views, Australia is in the main a remarkably tolerant, egalitarian and essentially easygoing society which, despite the difficulties posed by isolation and size, remains, in the eyes of many inhabitants, a well-kept secret of which they are proud.

The Australian Customs Service is responsible for a coastline more than 37,000 km (23,000 miles) long, much of it only sparsely populated, if at all.

The largest numbers of Greeks came to Australia in the years 1954–66. Many have made their mark in fields ranging from biophysics to cultured pearls.

How we Celebrate our Identity

It is not so long ago that people of non-British origins were expected to keep a low profile, to the point of becoming invisible. Nowadays, a community festival without a contribution from all minorities living in the locality would be almost unthinkable.

RIGHT: The word 'Koori' was adopted by the Aboriginal people of south-eastern Australia partly as a means of promoting political unity. Other States adopted other terms, such as Nyungar in south-western Australia. People living in less-urbanised environments still prefer to use their traditional group names.

OPPOSITE: The beach is an important part of Australian life. Surf carnivals are likely to always be part of our lifestyle.

Other societies have national days which are deeply embedded in the consciousness of their history and evolution. America's Thanksgiving Day, for example, is a celebration of the success of the Pilgrim Fathers who founded modern America and Bastille Day in France is a reminder of how modern France threw off the yoke of aristocratic rule.

In Australia there are few events of great moment in the nation's history. Yet, as most Australians love a party and are always looking for an excuse to celebrate, the country's national day, Australia Day, commemorates what any other society in the same situation might prefer to forget, that modern Australia was basically a dumping ground for England's unwanted criminals, a result of the fact that the United States, having fought its War of Independence, refused to accept any more convict ships from Britain. Seeing its jails getting out of control, England decided to send the overflow elsewhere—to the far side of the world, where in 1770 Captain James Cook had claimed half of the continent of Australia for the British Empire. Eighteen years later, the British decided to turn this isolated land into a prison.

So what does Australia Day mean? To indigenous Australia, it symbolises the day on which Europeans disrupted the way of life of an ancient people who had successfully survived for at least 40,000 years, by bringing with them disease, maltreatment and war, albeit undeclared. The Aboriginal population, which may have numbered upwards of half a million in 1788, had dropped to about 100,000 by the end of

the nineteenth century. Regardless of this, on Australia Day, 26 January, 'ambassadors' (usually celebrities) travel to towns and suburbs around the country where, with typical Australian casualness, there are a few speeches, a few local dignitaries receive awards, and a few immigrants become citizens. This might then be followed by a barbecue.

In their heart of hearts, most Australians know that this date doesn't really rate with Bastille Day or even Thanksgiving. Consequently, as a nation, they search for other days of significance. In recent years the dawn ceremony on 25 April, Anzac Day, which commemorates the landing of Australian and New Zealand troops at Gallipoli in 1915, has grown in popularity with notable increases in crowd attendance around the country. Although it might be considered odd to rejoice in the fact that Australia's decision in 1914 to send troops to Europe to fight for the British Empire decimated an entire generation of young men, and had a cruel impact on almost every town and city in the country, the crowds who now gather at memorial services in Australia and at Anzac Cove in Turkey are probably acknowledging the continuing feeling of community loss rather than analysing the politics of that past era.

Then there is Sydney's Gay and Lesbian Mardi Gras, now over 20 years old, which attracts audiences of over 500,000 people each year and injects tens of millions of dollars into the city's economy. Similar to Rio's Carnivale in its exuberance, the opportunity to celebrate sexual diversity and to poke fun at wowserism and intolerance in its many forms has resulted in the largest single entertainment event in Australia, with people travelling to Sydney from all over the world as the city goes on one huge party.

The Big Picture

Non-indigenous Australia is only a little over 200 years old. Compared to most of the rest of the world, it is a young culture and because it is so recent, it raises a myriad of complex, and perhaps unanswerable, questions both about the nature of art and about the place and importance of modern art in a technological, postmodern world. Australia in the twenty-first century is a small, sports-loving, mass media-orientated, egalitarian society dominated by plebeian, rather than patrician, tastes and sensibilities. It is a society created by three great impulses—incarceration (from 1788 until the 1840s), the lust for gold (from the 1840s to the 1880s) and multicultural expectations of a better life (from the 1940s to the present). It is a predominantly European culture characterised by the country's geographic isolation from other European societies and by a certain level of alienation from the Asian and Pacific Island cultures which surround it. To understand Australian culture it is necessary to be aware that it is not simply a transposed European culture. Nor can be it measured or understood by some ill-considered set of international benchmarks.

Firstly, there is the question of population. Australia, with only 19 million inhabitants, is still a very small country and while it is probably true that both Sydney and Melbourne enjoy a cultural richness and diversity equal to many similar-sized cities around the world, the arts are necessarily dependent largely on government grants. One result of this is that many of Australia's most talented artists, writers and performers have chosen to pursue their careers overseas. Opera divas Dame Nellie Melba and Dame Joan Sutherland, for example, could never have survived artistically if they had chosen their home country as their primary residence and performance destination. Equally, many of Australia's cultural commentators and critics—people such as Robert Hughes, Clive James, Phillip Knightley, John Baxter and Germaine Greer—have established international reputations only by living outside the country.

Secondly, there is the issue of time. Some commentators argue that Australia hasn't had time to develop a distinct cultural identity. And the institutions which traditionally nurture the arts over time—museums, grants, foundations and benevolent funds—have not flourished in an egalitarian climate in which wealthy people have no desire to immortalise themselves as patrons.

Thirdly, it is an undeniable fact that many Australians are obsessed with sport and outdoor living—entirely reasonable impulses in a country which enjoys such extended periods of excellent weather. Consequently, art is often regarded as an essentially snobbish and elitist activity reserved for professional and tertiary-educated people. Numerous surveys try to demonstrate that audiences at the opera are actually full of truck drivers and labourers, but nobody really believes this fiction. Equally, the popularity of outdoor operatic events (Opera in the Vines, Opera in the Park, Opera in the Desert), and of folk and jazz and other music festivals, is often cited as evidence of the broad appeal of such activities. Yet the size of these outdoor audiences never converts into substantial record sales or concert hall attendances. The fact that these activities are well patronised seems to have more to do with the enjoyment of being outdoors than a genuine appreciation of opera, jazz, folk or other styles of music.

The nation's artistic and cultural interests are more to be found in the domain of the popular arts. Australians are good at making small, wry, human interest movies. They are good at making television soap operas, and have had reasonable success with popular music. Australia has produced some exceptional cartoonists, and many of its popular novelists (particularly Morris West and Colleen McCullough) enjoy international reputations. Nowhere was this sense of mass culture populism more potently demonstrated than at the closing of the Sydney 2000 Olympic Games, where the organisers, searching for the icons and symbols of contemporary Australia

which would be recognisable to an international audience, chose popular movies (*Priscilla, Queen of the Desert, Crocodile Dundee, Strictly Ballroom*), television and pop personalities (Kylie Minogue, Vanessa Amorosi), sporting stars (Greg Norman) and supermodels (Elle Macpherson). With the exception of soprano Yvonne Kenny, who sang the Olympic anthem, there wasn't a 'high art' image in sight.

In this sense, the majority of today's Australian art is a modern, post-industrial cultural experience. Its

references are not to an ancient shared past; therefore, when assessing the nation's artistic endeavours, they should be measured in terms of the country's relatively short history of European settlement, and its aspirations. Australian art has been a powerful force in defining the national character, and is still important in any discussion of modern Australia. This is ironic, given that the enduring themes and symbols in the way Australians represented themselves—the swagman underdog in 'Waltzing Matilda'; in painting, the brave stockman in Tom Roberts' *The Breakaway* and the tireless shearers in *Shearing the Rams*, and the stoicism and loneliness of the bush settler in Frederick McCubbin's *The Pioneer* and *The Lost Child*; in literature, the laconic humour of Tom Collins' *Such is Life* and the great truths about emigration contained in Henry Handel Richardson's *The Fortunes of Richard Mahony*—which are all rural and nineteenth century, still define us more than a century later, when nearly 90 per cent of the country's population lives in cities which cling to the continent's coastline. Modern writers and artists continue to recycle the same preoccupations. *The Tree of Man* by Patrick White, for example, is about rural Australia battling against fire, flood and drought, and *Voss*, a retelling of the story of the Prussian-born explorer Ludwig Leichhardt, also has a largely rural setting. Equally, the subject of Sidney Nolan's most famous cycle of paintings was not contemporary Australia but the nineteenth-century bushranger, Ned Kelly. It is illuminating that Kelly still plays an important part in the nation's intellectual landscape, by being the subject of a recent book (*True History of the Kelly Gang*) by well-known expatriate Australian novelist Peter Carey.

David Hockney's Grand Canyon, *in the National Gallery of Australia in Canberra. The Gallery was opened in 1982. It has a collection of over 100,000 works. The Gallery has four major focuses—Australian, Aboriginal and Torres Strait Islander, Asian, and International art—and its collection includes paintings, prints, barks, sculpture, photography, posters, textiles, illustrated books and decorative arts.*

Magnolia and Palm sculpture, by Bronwyn Oliver. The sculpture is part of Sydney's Sculpture Walk, which is made up of up to 20 site-specific commissioned works. This sculpture is nestled among trees near Sydney's Farm Cove. The oversized seed pods are made of copper rods, branching upwards from a granite base, and the surface is covered with curling tendrils of copper.

J.F. Archibald (1856–1919), journalist, co-founder and, for many years, editor of the Bulletin. *His legacy includes the Archibald Prize, Australia's most prestigious portraiture prize.*

Henry Lawson (1867–1922), Australia's most loved balladist and short story writer. Writing for the Bulletin, *he produced laconic but realistic tales of bush life. His work and his place in Australian literature still provoke debate.*

Literature

Australia's small population (and even smaller book-buying population) imposes restrictions on locally produced literature. The economics of publishing mean that publishers have to rely on overseas interest before committing themselves to large print runs. Inevitably this has had some effect on content, and some would argue that it favours popular, rather than literary fiction, leading literary authors to rely on grants, awards and part-time jobs to supplement their income. Australian authors at home and overseas continue to explore local themes. As well as recently drawing on the story of Ned Kelly, the Australian convict Magwitch in Charles Dickens' *Great Expectations* was Peter Carey's inspiration for *Jack Maggs*. Other Australian writers popular with an overseas readership include Colleen McCullough, whose romantic saga *The Thorn Birds* (1977) set a record by selling over 100,000 hardback copies in Australia alone (the paperback rights were sold in the United States for US$1.9 million), Bryce Courtenay, author of *The Potato Factory* (1995) and *The Power of One* (1996), and Thomas Keneally, whose novel *Schindler's Ark* (1982) was later filmed as *Schindler's List*. Many

if not most writers, however, do not enjoy wide popularity beyond Australia. This group includes Tim Winton, David Foster, Rodney Hall, Kate Grenville, Christopher Koch, Jessica Anderson, Helen Garner, Thea Astley and David Ireland. Aside from the politics of publishing, one of the reasons may be a lingering belief left over from colonial days that anything Australian must be second-rate.

This belief was long reflected in the curricula of Australian universities, where courses in literature concentrated on British classics and largely ignored the achievements of Australian writers. Over the past 40 years, however, there has been a concerted effort to integrate Australian literature into both secondary and tertiary curricula. Critical to this process was the emergence of Sydney-based Currency Press, which started publishing contemporary Australian plays. Works by young playwrights such as Peter Kenna, David Williamson, Alex Buzo and Jack Hibberd became commonplace on high school curricula. However, it has only been in the past 15 years or so that universities have taken steps to create Chairs of Australian Literature and subsequently a whole new interest in the history of Australian writing has occurred.

It is a history which goes back before European settlement occurred in 1788. The hugely successful *Voyage to New Holland*, a description of his journey to the antipodes, was published in 1702 by William Dampier, for example. However, in the very early years of settlement there was virtually no published writing by either soldiers or convicts, the emphasis being rather on formal government documents and on recording, in words and pictures, the flora and fauna of the new continent. A little later memoirs and histories began to make an appearance. The first novel to be written in Australia was Henry Savery's *Quintus Servington*, a picaresque allegory about a convict of the same name, published in 1830.

However, if great novels, plays and poetry were not yet being produced, some impressive works on natural history were, and were coming to public attention. Matthew Flinders' botanist, Robert Brown, published *Prodromus Florae Novae Hollandiae* in

1810—it was hailed as 'the greatest botanical work that has ever appeared'. In 1840 John Gould started publishing his groundbreaking 36-part work, *The Birds of Australia.*

It wasn't until the 1850s that Australian literature began to assert itself as an important cultural force. While traditional literary styles were still employed, local themes were increasingly evident. In 1859, Henry Kingsley enjoyed considerable success with the historical romance *The Recollections of Geoffry Hamlyn,* a generational saga of three families which included the familiar devices of Victorian melodrama (elopement, forgery, thwarted love and murder) with local detail (bushranging, attacks by Aborigines and bushfires). The lyric poetry of Henry Kendall in *Poems and Songs* (1862), *Leaves from Australian Forests* (1869) and *Songs from the Mountains* (1880) described the beauty and melancholy of the bush and established him as a favourite for generations of schoolchildren. The 1870s saw a number of literary landmarks, including Marcus Clarke's *For the Term of His Natural Life*, a portrait of the harshness of convict life in Van Diemen's Land, and a collection of poems by Adam Lindsay Gordon titled *Bush Ballads and Galloping Rhymes,* which many critics see as the beginning of the great 'bush ballad' tradition, and would reach its high point a decade later.

The next 30 years (from 1880 to 1910) were a golden age for Australian literature. In 1886, David Mackenzie Angus and George Robertson, both from Scotland, established a bookselling and publishing company which, for over a century, was responsible for publishing virtually every famous Australian author, including Marcus Clarke, Henry Lawson, Banjo Paterson, Miles Franklin and hundreds of others. (Today, after a chequered history of takeovers and mergers, Angus & Robertson survives as the Australian imprint of the multinational company HarperCollins.) This was also the time when the *Bulletin*, Australia's popular weekly 'bushman's bible', was at its height. Radical, funny and anti-British, it flourished under the editorship of J.F. Archibald in the 1880s and promoted the work of talented local writers such as Banjo Paterson, Henry Lawson, Steele Rudd and Norman Lindsay. (Between 1940 and 1960 the *Bulletin* supported the talent of poets Judith Wright and Rosemary Dobson, and novelist and poet Hal Porter, and published anthologies.) Its tone, which had always been xenophobic on the matter of immigration (in the 1890s it was against the Chinese), became increasingly shrill in its later years ('Australia for the White Man' was the magazine's slogan until 1960).

Australian themes continued in Rolf Boldrewood's (Thomas Alexander Browne) popular *Robbery Under Arms* (first published as a serial in 1882–83 and then in book form in 1889), a bushranging adventure, and such enduring classics as Banjo Paterson's poems 'Clancy of the Overflow' (1889), 'The Man from Snowy River' (1890) and Australia's unofficial national anthem, 'Waltzing Matilda', all set in the bush. His collection of poems, *The Man from Snowy River and Other Verses,* sold a staggering 10,000 copies in less than 12 months.

Ethel Turner's enduring classic novel for children, *Seven Little Australians*, about the escapades of an engaging, high-spirited family, was first published in 1894 and frequently reprinted. The following year Steele Rudd (Arthur Hoey Davis) created the world of the Rudd family, rural 'battlers' who included Dad and Dave, two characters who began life in the *Bulletin* and won national fame through their subsequent appearances in novels, stage adaptations, films and comic strips.

In the new century many authors continued to write of their own lives, in autobiographies and in fiction. Australians could learn about the diverse realities of life on their island continent by reading of the stifling dependence of a woman's lot in Miles Franklin's *My Brilliant Career* (1901), the picaresque adventures of anti-hero Tom Collins and his bush companions in Joseph Furphy's *Such is Life* (1903), the point of view of a European settler living on a huge property in the Northern Territory in Mrs

Flying Squirrel (sugar glider possum), Petaurus australis, *painted in 1813 by T. Richard Browne, part of the album by Lieutenant Thomas Skottowe,* Select Specimens from Nature of the Birds, Animals, etc. of New South Wales. *Not much is known of T.R. Browne, other than that he was probably a convict and he lived in Newcastle.*

CENTRE: *An illustration from Norman Lindsay's* The Magic Pudding. *Lindsay (1878–1969) both wrote and illustrated the story. Here we see Albert, the grumpy—but self-replenishing— pudding himself, with his vagabond owners, Bunyip Bluegum, Bill Barnacle and Sam Sawnoff, whose task it is to save Albert from the ever-present pudding thieves who want to steal him. These characters have been loved by generations of Australians.*

A memorial statue to Dorothea Mackellar (1883–1968), best-known for her poem 'My Country', first published in 1908. The statue is in Gunnedah, New South Wales.

RIGHT: Author Christina Stead (1902–83). Stead lived much of her life abroad, and her work was little recognised in Australia, because of her Marxist politics, until the 1970s.

Steele Rudd's mythical Snake Gully family—Dad, Dave, Mum and Mabel—immortalised a few kilometres outside Gundagai, New South Wales, home of the real Snake Gully.

Aeneas Gunn's *We of the Never-Never* (1908), and life on a desert island in E.J. Banfield's *Confessions of a Beachcomber* (1908).

Surprisingly, the four years of the Great War also yielded a number of highly regarded works, including the children's favourites *The Magic Pudding* (1918) by Norman Lindsay, a tale about a pudding which magically grows complete again every time it is eaten, *Snugglepot and Cuddlepie* (1918) by May Gibbs, a story in which the characters were the flora of the Australian bush, and the classic *The Sentimental Bloke* (1915) by C.J. Dennis, a series of poems about a wide-eyed Australian innocent. These years also saw the publication of Henry Handel Richardson's (Ethel Florence Lindesay Robertson) *Australia Felix*, the first part of her trilogy, which became known as *The Fortunes of Richard Mahony*. Its theme, the sense of dislocation caused by emigration, was an eternal dilemma, here given a particularly Australian interpretation.

The late 1930s and the 1940s saw the emergence of a generation of Australian writers who would come to dominate the nation's literary landscape for nearly half a century. These writers were unapologetically nationalistic in their choice of themes, and were popular overseas as well as in Australia. They included Christina Stead, Morris West, the poet Judith Wright and Patrick White, whose international career was launched by the publication, in both New York and London, of *The Aunt's Story* in 1948.

A small number of Australians also made international reputations for themselves in the field of non-fiction. Germaine Greer's feminist tract *The*

Female Eunuch (1970), Derek Llewellyn-Jones' advice for women *Everywoman* (1971) and Robert Hughes' polemic analysis of the origins of modern Australia, *The Fatal Shore* (1987), are three fine examples.

Within Australia, biographies, autobiographies and novels revealed much about the nature of identity, both on a personal and a national level. The experience of immigrants has been part of the fabric of Australian literature since settlement, reflected early on in convict novels such as Marcus Clarke's *For the Term of His Natural Life* (1874). After World War II there was more writing by 'New Australians', which revealed much of the migrant perspective, not all of it positive. Much of this writing would have stemmed from the pressure to assimilate, which has slowly, and not without some resistance, changed over the years to an acceptance, and even celebration, of cultural difference. Judah Waten's *Alien Son* (1952) explores the hardship experienced by a Russian Jewish family who emigrated to Australia at the beginning of the century. The main character in Rosa Cappiello's ironically titled novel *Oh Lucky Country* (1984), a feisty, working class Italian, challenges the assumptions of superiority many Australians felt obliged to defend in the face of change. The voice in Angelo Loukakis' *Messenger* (1992) speaks eloquently of the responsibilities second generation migrant Australian children have faced in mediating between the new world and the old for migrant parents who found it difficult to negotiate cultural change.

Today, the policy of encouraging multiculturalism has resulted in a burgeoning diversity in literature, reflecting the pluralistic nature of Australian society. However, the issue of multicultural literature as a separate genre can be problematic. For example, should Melina Marchetta's *Looking for Alibrandi* (2000) be seen as a rites of passage novel about a young girl growing up in Australia, or an exploration of the Italian-Australian experience? In the past some migrants Anglicised their names in order to be less conspicuous, but in an odd, and highly publicised, reversal of history one author, Helen Demidenko, actually appropriated a Ukrainian background in order to lend credibility to her novel, *The Hand that Signed the Paper* (1994), a credibility which was damaged when her surname was revealed to be Darville.

Other books which reflected different aspects of Australian life included Frank Hardy's novel *Power Without Glory* (1950), a vivid account of Melbourne life between 1895 and 1945 with thinly disguised portraits of various

well-known local identities (as a result of which he was unsuccessfully sued for libel), Donald Horne's *The Lucky Country* (1964), one of the first serious attempts to analyse the character of modern Australia and its people, George Johnston's novel *My Brother Jack* (1964), a semi-autobiographical account of growing up after the Great War, and A.B. Facey's *A Fortunate Life* (1981), an unselfpitying look back at a childhood of extreme poverty in the Australian bush at the turn of the century. Other such novels written by women include Gabrielle Carey and Kathy Lette's *Puberty Blues* (1979), a girls' take on the macho world of suburban surfing culture, Robyn Davidson's *Tracks* (1980), an account of the author's brave solo trek by camel across the deserts of central Australia, and Jill Ker Conway's *The Road from Coorain* (1989), about the author's progress from rural origins to her current international business success.

Until his death in 1990, Patrick White dominated the landscape of literary fiction in Australia. His consistently brilliant career included novels, essays, memoirs (*Flaws in the Glass*, published in 1981) and plays, and earned him the Nobel Prize for Literature in 1973 for *The Eye of the Storm*, a remarkable novel about an old Sydney woman's search for the meaning of life. White had few competitors until Peter Carey's work became popular. Carey was awarded the Booker Prize for *Oscar and Lucinda* (1988). Equally impressive are both the poet Les Murray, famed for his ability to write about the ordinariness of Australian rural life, and poet-turned-novelist David Malouf, whose novel *Remembering Babylon* (1996) won the IMPAC Dublin Literary Award, at A\$212,000, the world's richest literary prize. And there is, of course, a new generation rising: Andrew McGahan, Julia Leigh, Christos Tsolkas … the tradition continues.

Germaine Greer (b. 1939), a woman whose strong views, plus her ability to argue them, have made her a highly respected—and sometimes slightly feared—force in Australian feminism. Her best-known works are The Female Eunuch (1970), Sex and Destiny (1984), The Change: Women, Ageing and the Menopause (1991), and The Whole Woman (1999). She is eloquent, outrageous, irrepressible, rude and fearless, changes her mind and her targets repeatedly, and remains a successful author and academic.

Patrick White (1912–90), a dominating figure in Australian literature for more than 40 years. White had an ambivalent relationship with Australia. His best-known works—The Tree of Man (1955), Voss (1957) and Riders in the Chariot (1961)—are all set in Australia, though they focus on 'the land of the mind'.

Theatre

David Williamson (b. 1942), in younger days. Williamson is perhaps Australia's best known and most successful playwright; his plays deal with the foibles and greed and weaknesses of the educated middle classes—the people who are his audience.

This G. Lacey watercolour shows a perhaps slightly romanticised view of the diggings. The gold rush towns, for all their hardship, roughness and danger, were also arts centres—the still-young colonies enthusiastically built theatres and brought theatre companies and other performing artists to the bush.

The crisis in theatre throughout the world for at least the past 40 years, the result of competition with other forms of entertainment (particularly film and television), has impacted on Australia, particularly more adventurous and experimental theatre. Big budget, big production plays and musicals (many of them from overseas) and new works from reliably middle-brow Australian playwrights (most notably David Williamson) as well as the marketing of 'season tickets', are the strategies now followed by theatre companies in their battle for financial survival.

Australian theatre started in 1789, only a year after the arrival of the First Fleet, when a group of convicts performed George Farquhar's *The Recruiting Officer*. By 1796 a company of convict actors had been formed for the entertainment of the colony but their activities were short-lived and very strictly monitored. The country's first playwright of note was David Burn, a free settler from Scotland who migrated to Van Diemen's Land in 1826. Burn was responsible for a number of plays including *The Bushrangers* (a play loosely based on the life of bushranger Matthew Brady) and *Sydney Delivered*. These plays, while not being particularly memorable, were important because they explored local themes—and they gave notice that the bushranger would be a continuing image in Australian iconography.

The start of a truly national theatre came in 1833 with the opening of the Theatre Royal. It continued to operate for the next five years, and some 400 plays were performed there. It was followed by the establishment of theatres throughout the colonies. The Royal Victoria took over from the Theatre Royal in Sydney and remained a dominant cultural force until the late 1840s. The Queen's Theatre Royal was established in Melbourne, the Theatre Royal in Hobart Town, and the Queen's Theatre in Adelaide. With these theatres came professional actors, influential impresarios and the development of a local culture of playwriting. Locally written plays produced around this time included Henry Melville's *The Bushrangers*, Evan Henry Thomas' *The Bandit of the Rhine*, Charles Harpur's blank verse drama *The Tragedy of Donohoe* (later changed to *The Bushrangers,* clearly a hugely popular topic at the time) and *The Currency Lass,* a musical comedy with a local background, by convict playwright Edward Geoghegan, which is still widely known and studied.

A dramatic change in the life of Australian theatre occurred with the goldrushes of the 1850s. Suddenly the country seemed to be awash with people eager to spend their spare cash in pursuit of pleasure—and that included theatre. Theatres were built in most of the major goldrush towns, including Ballarat, Bendigo, Bathurst and Gulgong, and the size and number of playhouses in the major cities increased, with both Sydney and Melbourne boasting two of the largest—the Prince of Wales in Sydney and the Theatre Royal in Melbourne—capable of seating audiences of 3000 people. Public entertainment progressed in a rather haphazard way from the 1880s through to the 1940s. There was always a commercial theatre but, as at present, it relied heavily on overseas playwrights, productions and even actors to maintain its viability. So while the famous actress Sarah Bernhardt, for example, drew crowds when she toured Australia in 1891, few Australian playwrights or local plays of that time survived for long or are now remembered.

The watershed occurred after World War II, when a group of young playwrights started writing about contemporary Australia and, with the help of a number of dynamic theatre groups, forged a new theatrical climate for the country. Symbolic of this change was an enduring masterpiece, Ray Lawler's *Summer of the Seventeenth Doll* (1955), a study of Australian mateship closely tied to the complex conflicts which existed in suburban society between a sense of freedom and a sense of responsibility.

At the same time, Australian radio (particularly the ABC) was offering new opportunities to play-

Hullo! Tom, here's a speck— Cricket

wrights, resulting in a number of radio plays, the most successful and enduring of which were Douglas Stewart's *Fire on the Snow* and *Ned Kelly*. The latter subsequently became a successful stage play. The success of these plays and playwrights was partly due to the creation of a fringe theatre, which was spearheaded by the Independent Theatre at North Sydney and the left-wing New Theatre, which established itself in the country's major cities. Out of these changes came more theatre groups, most notably the Ensemble Theatre in Sydney, the Pram Factory and Cafe la Mama in Melbourne and later the Jane Street Theatre and Nimrod Street Theatre in Sydney. It was in this reinvigorated environment that a generation of talented and innovative playwrights was nurtured. Jack Hibberd's *Dimboola* (1969), a hilarious send-up of a rural wedding set in a country town (Dimboola), has been produced more often than any other Australian play, and John Romeril's *The Floating World* (1974) dissected the philistinism and hypocrisy of a typically unreflective Australian man on his way to Japan on a cruise ship. Although he has been criticised for the narrow focus of his plays (the rather self-conscious concerns of the self-indulgent middle classes), David Williamson, Australia's most successful playwright, continues to attract audiences with his entertaining satires. His first, *The Coming of Stork,* was staged in 1970, and his success has continued with, among others, *Don's Party* (1973), *The Club* (1977), *Emerald City* (1987), *Brilliant Lies* (1993), *Dead White Males* (1995) and *Up for Grabs* (2000).

Objectively, it is hard to argue that live theatre, in all its manifestations, is particularly healthy in Australia at the beginning of the twenty-first century. Experimental theatre has become an increasingly fringe activity, and large-scale overseas musicals (*Cats, Phantom of the Opera* et al), satirical and high camp revues (Bob Downe, Barry Humphries) and reliable old theatrical stalwarts (Shakespeare, Oscar Wilde,

Arthur Miller, Neil Simon), often with overseas stars in the leading roles, still seem to be the staple diet of the majority of Australian theatre-goers.

In response, theatre has moved away from independent companies to substantial, government-financed organisations in both Western Australia and New South Wales. (John Bell, who was part of the experimental fabric of the Nimrod Street Theatre, is an exception, and now runs his own Bell Shakespeare Company in the style of a nineteenth-century theatrical impresario.) During a period of economic rationalism, the graduates of the National Institute of Dramatic Art in Sydney now focus more on the lucrative film industry than on theatre. And exciting young talents such as Barry Kosky, Baz Luhrmann and Michael Gow, rather than establishing themselves exclusively in live theatre, now move from film to theatre to opera, and to all points in between.

Street theatre is popular entertainment in Australian cities, for children and adults. This kind of informal, humorous, sometimes politically savvy, performance suits the Australian climate, love of outdoor life and irreverent sense of humour.

J.C. Williamson (1845–1913), and his first wife, US actress Maggie Moore (1851–1926). Williamson, also an American actor, in 1882 set up the theatre company now known as J.C. Williamson's Ltd, which long remained Australia's dominant theatre company.

J.C. WILLIAMSON.   MAGGIE MOORE.

The Fine Arts

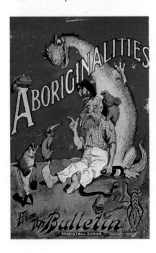

The first published European depiction of Australian fauna occurred as early as 1593, when *Speculum Orbis Terrae*, a Latin geography of the known world, depicted a kangaroo on the title page. Throughout the seventeenth and eighteenth centuries the Dutch, recording the topography of the coast of Western Australia, illustrated books with images of 'New Holland'. When William Dampier's famous books on his voyages were published in England in 1697 they included drawings of birds and fish. This tradition continued with the arrival, exploration and settlement of the east coast. Both French and English publishers were eager to show their readers images of the new continent, its inhabitants and its fauna and flora. Artists accompanied journeys of exploration, and both military officers and convicts were eager to draw and paint the new land. Prominent among these artists were John Glover, who lived and worked in Tasmania, and Conrad Martens, who painted superb watercolours of Sydney Harbour.

The discovery of gold in the middle of the nineteenth century was vital for the development of art in Australia. The wealth of the goldfields attracted vast numbers of people to Australia, including a number of distinguished artists. The most famous of these was Samuel Thomas Gill, whose sketches of life on the diggings are still admired, George Rowe, who became famous for his panoramas, Eugene von Guèrard, Nicholas Chevalier and Louis Buvelot.

The chain of wealth which generated art on the goldfields led to the establishment of the National Gallery of Victoria in 1861. In the next two decades, other states, eager to keep up with Victoria, built their own galleries: the Tasmanian Museum and Art Gallery (1863), the Art Gallery of New South Wales (1874), the Art Gallery of South Australia (1879), the Art Gallery of Western Australia and the Queensland Art Gallery (both in 1895).

Towards the end of the century a small group of artists who became known as the Heidelberg School changed the face of Australian painting forever by establishing a new 'way of seeing' the Australian landscape in all its different light, colour and forms. Tom Roberts and Frederick McCubbin set up an artists' camp at Box Hill, near Melbourne, and painted 'from life', emphasising the local palette, which included both the dazzling blues and golds which are so often seen in Roberts' landscapes and the more subdued greys and greens of McCubbin's bush themes. They emulated the French Impressionists' methods of capturing the moment, but chose national themes. They were later joined by others, among them Charles Condor, Arthur Streeton and Louis Abrahams. While some artists portrayed idyllic landscapes and heroic workers (*Shearing the Rams*, by Tom Roberts, is one example of this), others showed a continuing anxiety about their place in a country still strange and sometimes hostile; this is evident in their titles (such as McCubbin's *The Lost Child*, *Down on his Luck* and *Bush Burial*).

Around this time Australia also developed a fascination with sketching, etching and black and white newspaper and magazine illustration. The rise of the *Bulletin* and *Smith's Weekly*, and the publication of the *Picturesque Atlas of Australasia* (all of which used etchings and sketches) saw artists such as David Low, Norman and Lionel Lindsay, Julian Ashton, Will Dyson and Phil May all establishing another great Australian art tradition.

With the arrival of the twentieth century it was clear that while artists' subject matter would be uniquely Australian, fashionable techniques—be they Modernism, Impressionism, or Abstract Expressionism—would be borrowed from overseas. By World War II Australia was awash with a new generation of immensely talented artists: the remarkable and controversial modernist portrait painter William Dobell; Donald Friend, who was much influenced by Asian art through time he spent living in Bali; Sidney Nolan, whose most famous series of images was of Australian icon Ned Kelly; Albert Tucker, who built his reputation redefining the way we look at the continent, particularly the desert; John Passmore, who loved and recorded the intense beauty of Sydney Harbour in his Cezanne-influenced works; Russell Drysdale, perhaps the quintessential painter of the outback; John Perceval, with his strange, dark visions of the land; Arthur Boyd, whose love affair with the Australian landscape found its finest flowering at his home, 'Bundanon', near Nowra on the NSW south coast; Lloyd Rees, with his evocative and dreamy land and seascapes; Clifton Pugh, whose painting of Gough Whitlam is still the finest portrait ever painted of an Australian prime minister; John Brack, whose haunting painting of workers in Collins Street, Melbourne, is one of the nation's iconic suburban images; Charles Blackman, who achieved fame with his naïve Alice in Wonderland-like images; and Fred Williams who, with his lyrical love of the bush, bridged the gap between older artists such as Tom Roberts and more contemporary visions of landscape. In many ways the influences some of these artists brought back to Australia from overseas revolutionised the way Australians saw their own country, their own landscape.

Today, art is very much alive and well in Australia. At the popular end of the scale are artists such as Ken Done, whose bright and breezy images of Sydney and Australia cleverly hover between Modernism and advertising, Tim Storrier, who has achieved great success with a hyper-realistic style, and Martin Sharp, once a cartoonist for *Oz* magazine, who progressed to designing covers for 1960s' rock bands and then started to pursue his lifetime fascination with Tiny Tim and Sydney's Luna Park. The late Brett Whiteley, whose works cover a broad range of functions and styles, from the Dire Straits' *Brothers in Arms* album cover to huge canvasses—now to be found in most of the country's major galleries—has been so successful that there is now a permanent gallery to his memory in Sydney. Cartoonist/portraitist Bill Leak regularly wins the People's Choice award at the Archibald Prize for portraiture and is a powerful political cartoonist with *The Australian* newspaper.

'Fossicking', a lithograph from *Victoria Gold Diggings and Diggers as They Are* (1852), by S.T. Gill (1818–80). Gill came to Australia as a young man, and always worked as an artist. He is best known for his goldfields work, but he also accompanied an expedition to Spencers Gulf, and did a deal of work depicting city life in Melbourne.

FAR LEFT: Artist William Dobell (1899–1970). Dobell studied and worked overseas for many years, returning to Australia in 1938. He is perhaps best remembered for his portrait of Joshua Smith, which won the Archibald Prize in 1944 and was then challenged in court on the grounds that it was caricature rather than portraiture.

LEFT: Artist Arthur Boyd (1920–99), perhaps the best-known member of the Boyd art dynasty, in his studio at 'Bundanon' in 1981. Boyd's early work was Impressionist in style, but he later moved to a more Expressionist mode. His interests in Aboriginal themes and in landscape were evident in his art from as early as the 1950s.

Popular Music

The Big Guitar, at Tamworth, New South Wales. Tamworth is the home of the biggest country music festival in the land, held each January. The festival has been running for 29 years now, and is still growing. There is a multitude of activities, including the well-known Golden Guitar awards, the Bush Laureate poetry competition, songwriting awards, talent quests, and even a harmonica competition.

Johnny O'Keefe (1935–78), was Australia's first rock'n'roll sensation. He began his singing career in the 1950s, and ended up with twenty-nine Top 40 hits here. He helped establish Australia's recording industry, battling to get air play and TV experience for local artists. He wrote and produced hits for Australian artists, managed artists, compered TV shows, toured, and helped set up the 'Mo' entertainment awards. He died young, in the sad tradition of many a true rock star.

Regardless of style or fashion, there has always been an Australian act offering a unique local spin. By the 1950s Australia was already under the cultural influence of the United States as a result of the war, so it's not surprising that Australia's first pop star, Johnny O'Keefe, emulated American role models. He sang American songs, dressed like Elvis Presley and Jerry Lee Lewis, adopted the Presley onstage moves and travelled to the United States, where he became known as 'The Boomerang Kid'. At the time, other acts, notably Col Joye and the Joy Boys (a kind of Australian equivalent of Cliff Richard in the United Kingdom) also enjoyed success, and by 1958 the country's first Top 40 chart, devised by radio station 2UE in Sydney, appeared. This same year, 1958, was also the year Channel 9 introduced the hugely popular television pop show *Bandstand*.

From the beginning there have been three strands to the Australian popular music scene: locally produced music which has not enjoyed success overseas, music which has enjoyed international success and individuals and groups who have succeeded both at home and overseas. Over the years many artists have tried their luck overseas with groups such as the Easybeats, the Saints, the Birthday Party, Icehouse and Kylie Minogue having some success in Britain and INXS, the Little River Band, Air Supply, Midnight Oil, Cold Chisel and Savage Garden making it in the United States. The first Australian to have a significant international pop career was Frank Ifield, a country-style yodelling singer from Sydney, who had a string of hits in England between 1962 and 1964. Ifield's 'I Remember You' also became a Top 5 hit in the United States, the first Australian record to achieve that level of international success.

Australia, like every other Western country around the world, experienced the British boom of the 1960s and was influenced by the Beatles (who toured Australia in 1964), the Rolling Stones and the dozens of pop groups who were part of that overall movement. Surprisingly, the musical influence wasn't all one way, and Australian talent fed back into the British music scene. Between 1965 and 1967 (at the height of Beatlemania) the Australian group the Seekers, led by Judith Durham, had no fewer than eight Top 10 hits (including two No. 1s and two No. 2s) in Britain. Equally rewarding for solo artists was Britain's penchant for novelty songs. Over the years, successes have included such songs as 'The Pub With No Beer' (1959) from Slim Dusty, Gary Shearston's 'I Get A Kick Out of You' (1974), Sherbet's 'Howzat' (1976) and Joe Dolce's 'Shaddap You Face' (1980).

The Australian pop music stars of the early 1960s were groups such as the Easybeats (their 'Friday on my Mind' was a hit in both Australia and Britain in 1966), Billy Thorpe and the Aztecs, Ray Columbus and the Invaders (one of the first groups to arrive from New Zealand), Ray Brown and the Whispers, and individuals such as Normie Rowe, whose rocking versions of the old standards 'Que Sera Sera' and 'It Ain't Necessarily So' were hits in 1965. By the end of the decade Australia was also producing groups such as Tully and Taman Shud, who were more album-orientated, and whose music reflected what was going on in San Francisco and London after the Beatles' success with *Sergeant Pepper's Lonely Hearts Club Band*. This more complex, and obviously drug-influenced, music arrived on the local charts in 1969, when Russell Morris reached No. 1 with 'The Real Thing (Parts 1 & 2)'.

In the 1970s, again reflecting the musical changes occurring in Britain and the United States, the Australian music industry saw the creation of independent record companies. The most successful of these, Mushroom in Melbourne and Regular Records in Sydney, signed up and promoted groups such as Mental as Anything, Skyhooks and Split Enz. 1974 and 1975 were watershed years. In 1974 Skyhooks released 'Living in the 70s', which went on to sell 230,000 records and become the most successful Australian record ever. In that same year, *Countdown*, an ABC TV program compered by Ian (Molly) Meldrum, started broadcasting. It had an enormous impact on the pop purchasing patterns of Australians. Not only did it do much to promote local talent, but it was also largely responsible for the huge success in Australia of bands such as ABBA, Queen, Pussycat and Fox. In the following year, 1975, 2JJ (Double Jay), the ABC's national youth radio network, began, with the release of a debut album by AC/DC, who would go on to become one of the world's premiere hard rock acts. The arrival of punk in Britain in 1976–77 was complemented in Australia by bands such as the Saints and Radio Birdman, but, interestingly, it was the success of New Zealand export Split Enz at this time that most impressed overseas markets.

The 1980s were characterised by great diversity. At the pop end were bands and individuals such as Moving Pictures (their hit 'What About Me?' reached No. 1 in 1982), the Swingers, Billy Field, Australian Crawl, Icehouse, the Church, Goanna, the Divinyls, Men at Work, Jimmy Barnes and INXS, a great dance/funk band. At the album end of the market, often promoting themselves as non-commercial, were bands such as Midnight Oil, who were driven by political commitment, the Birthday Party, dark, arty and very post-punk, the Triffids, the Laughing Clowns, Severed Heads and dozens of smaller bands who enjoyed considerable popularity in the burgeoning club and pub scene. The more successful bands of this era commonly found their support in the huge pubs in the outer suburbs of major cities, rising to prominence by honing their performing skills and developing a powerful stage presence. This was the decade when popular music split into a myriad different forms and styles.

Australian international success since then has reflected this diversity: in the United Kingdom Kylie Minogue creates clever disposable pop; Savage Garden exploits the teen pop charts; silverchair is Australia's answer to the Seattle grunge scene; Tina Arena is the Australian equivalent of Celine Dion and Maria Carey; Human Nature is the country's mandatory boy close harmony group; and John Farnham does sophisticated pop for ageing babyboomers.

Kylie Minogue (b. 1968), whose career took off with a role in Neighbours, one of Australia's most successful—at home and abroad—TV soaps. Her first hit was a remake of 'Do the Locomotion'; it was followed by a number of hit singles and her first (self-titled) album (1988). Since then she has worked with other singers and groups, released several more albums, in a range of musical styles, and done some film acting.

Film

Some of the earliest films ever created were produced in Australia, though there is some debate concerning whether the Salvation Army's famous *Soldiers of the Cross*, made as early as 1900, is the first feature film. Certainly it comes only six years after Thomas Edison's Kinetoscope parlours opened in New York and it was made on a scale unknown overseas. Equally important is *The Story of the Kelly Gang*, an hour-long film which was made in 1906 and was some years ahead of similar length films that were being produced in either North America or Europe.

From this promising begin-ning the Australian film indus-try prospered. Throughout the 1910s and 1920s a large num-ber of silent films were made, many of which enjoyed great commercial success, as did their stars—actors such as Charles Chauvel (later a director), Raymond Longford and Lottie Lyell (who became producer-partners) and Bert Bailey. Some films were early versions of Australian literary works like *Robbery Under Arms, The Sentimental Bloke, On Our Selection* and *For the Term of His Natural Life*. By the late 1920s sound had developed and Hollywood was starting to develop as a major supplier of popular movies to the world. During the 1930s, until the

outbreak of war in 1939, the industry continued to flourish, with Ken G. Hall making such admired works in this decade as *The Silence of Dean Maitland, Tall Timbers*, and *Dad and Dave Come to Town*.

After World War II, as a result of the increased output from Hollywood, there was a corresponding boom in the number of large picture theatres in Aus-tralia. American films were now all the rage, and local filmmakers struggled to find an audience. Then Holly-wood saw the potential in Australia and turned its attention to producing films with local content on location. *On the Beach* (1959), starring Ava Gardner, was filmed in and around Melbourne, and in South Australia, *The Sundowners* (1960), with Robert Mitchum. This had a pro-found effect on Australian filmmaking that would persist for two decades. In 1971 two of the greatest films ever made in Australia—Ted Kotcheff's *Wake in Fright* (retitled *Outback* in the United States) and Nicolas Roeg's *Walkabout*—were produced with a fine combination of Australian and overseas talent.

In 1969 the federal government, under Prime Minister John Gorton, set up a Film Committee. This led, in 1971, to the establishment of the Aus-

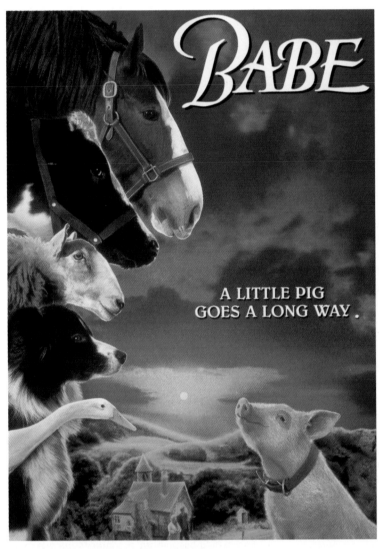

BABE

A LITTLE PIG
GOES A LONG WAY.

Schepisi made *The Devil's Playground* (1976) and *The Chant of Jimmie Blacksmith* (1978); Phillip Noyce's career in Australia included *Backroads* (1977), *Newsfront* (1978) and *Dead Calm* (1989); George Miller's initial success was with the Mad Max trilogy (local accents in *The Road Warrior* were dubbed in the United States) and he went on to produce *The Year My Voice Broke* (1987), *Flirting* (1990), *Babe* (1995) and *Babe: Pig in the City* (1998); Gilllian Armstrong's first major box office hit was *My Brilliant Career* (1979); Bruce Beresford's commercial filmmaking career started in 1972 with *The Adventures of Barry McKenzie* and was followed two years later by the equally successful *Barry McKenzie Holds His Own*. He continued to work in Australia, producing such 1970s' classics as *Don's Party, The Getting of Wisdom, Blue Fin* and *Breaker Morant*; this success extended into the 1980s, with the screen version of David Williamson's play *The Club* (1980) and *Puberty Blues* (1981). Other directors followed, and also made their mark, including Dutch-born Australian Paul Cox, whose early successes included *Lonely Hearts* (1981), *Man of Flowers* (1983) and *My First Wife* (1984). He went on to make *Vincent: The Life and Death of Vincent Van Gogh* (1987), *Island* (1989), *Exile* (1994) and, in 1999, *Father Damien*. And Peter Faiman achieved instant success with *Crocodile Dundee* in 1986.

Today, the Australian film industry is remarkably healthy. It continues to prouce popular local movies and, intermittently, films which achieve recognition and financial success outside the country. Recent international hits have included movies such as *Strictly Ballroom, Muriel's Wedding, Priscilla, Queen of the Desert* and *The Castle*.

However, in a fickle industry, success is measured only in box office returns. Recently, 1999 was a bad year, yet it was followed by an exceptionally good one—a year in which film industry profits nearly doubled those of the previous 12 months. And the successes were in very varied films: by September 2000 *The Wog Boy* had grossed A$11.4 million, *Looking for Alibrandi* had taken A$8.2 million, *Chopper* had taken A$5 million and *Me Myself I* had earned A$3 million.

LEFT: Babe (1995) was directed by Chris Noonan. It is a sweet, humorous film about an orphan pig taken in by a soft-hearted farmer and raised by a range of farm animals, including a duck and a sheepdog. The film follows Babe, who wants to be the greatest sheep pig (as opposed to sheepdog) of all time. It was a huge success both in Australia and overseas, taking a total US$240.7 million worldwide.

A poster from the 1932 film version of Steele Rudd's famous book. (Bert Bailey has a writing credit as well as being the star here.) The book has been filmed three times. The first time was in 1920—a black and white and silent film, directed by Raymond Longford. The most recent version, Dad and Dave: On Our Selection (1995), was directed by George Whaley.

tralian Film Development Corporation (later the Australian Film Commission) and, a few years later, the setting up of the Australian Film and Television School. Federal support was matched, to different degrees, by the states. The government-run South Australian Film Corporation, for example, had a major involvement in commercially successful and critically acclaimed films such as *Sunday Too Far Away* (1975*)*, *Storm Boy* (1976) and *Breaker Morant* (1977*)*.

Apart from a brief period in the 1970s and 1980s when the country became obsessed with costume dramas, possibly looking to the past for a sense of identity (*My Brilliant Career, The Getting of Wisdom, Eliza Fraser, Picnic at Hanging Rock*), the strength of the Australian film industry, both commercial and artistic, has been in comedy (*They're a Weird Mob, Crocodile Dundee, The Adventures of Barry McKenzie, Strictly Ballroom, Muriel's Wedding, Priscilla, Queen of the Desert, The Castle* and *The Wog Boy*) and dramas (*Caddie, The Devil's Playground, Storm Boy, The Chant of Jimmie Blacksmith, Newsfront* and even the first of the *Mad Max* movies).

At this time a generation of directors began to make films in Australia and establish reputations which would later take them overseas to work: Peter Weir started his feature film career with the much admired *The Cars that Ate Paris* in 1974; Fred

Broadcasting

Joseph Benedict (Ben) Chifley (1885–1951), was prime minister from 1945 until 1949, the year in which his government proposed establishing a national TV network. Chifley is a much revered Labor figure—he began his working life on the railways, helped set up a union and rebuild the Labor Party.

DJ Clarry 'spinning discs' on CAAMA Radio in Alice Springs, NorthernTerritory.The CAAMA Group is an Aboriginal-owned media organisation which works in radio, music, film, retailing and satellite television. It was set up in 1988 to promote and encourage Aboriginal culture, music and language.

Radio

Australian radio in the twenty-first century is in a parlous state. Once a glittering jewel in the crowns of the major media empires, it was characterised by a rich diversity of programming and a strong sense of broad-based entertainment. Now it is mainly reduced to predictable formatting which focuses on comedy, talkback and popular music. The reason for this demise is simple. In the 1980s companies paid too much money for radio licences and thus had to focus all their efforts on trying to generate sufficient advertising revenue to service their loans. This meant they were forced to play safe. The consequence has been frightening. Only the ABC, itself now almost totally emasculated by government cuts which have occurred continuously for over a decade, is the only radio network providing diversity.

In the days before television, radio stations were the centre of home entertainment, and offered all sorts of things: popular music, educational programs, programs for women during the day, news and reports on finance and country matters at lunchtime, sentimental and romantic serials in the early afternoon, programs for children in the early evening, and comedy shows, variety shows, quiz shows and serious dramas later in the evening.

The Wireless Telegraphy Act of 1905 was one of the first Acts passed by the new federal government, but it wasn't until 13 years later that radio in Australia really got underway. Between 1918 and 1924 the infant medium grew quickly. On 22 September 1918 the first direct overseas radio transmissions from Britain to Australia were heard; a year later (13 August 1919) the first public demonstration of radio was given to the Royal Society of New South Wales. On

23 November 1923, at 8.00 pm, the first concert was broadcast by the Sydney radio station 2SB, and in the same year two radio stations began broadcasting, in both Melbourne (3AR) and Perth (6WF).

In 1928 the government established the Australian Broadcasting Commission. This was changed to a national broadcasting service in 1932. From its inception, ABC radio was modelled on the BBC in Britain. This changed rather dramatically in 1975, when the ABC, responding to changing attitudes towards radio, established 2JJ (known as 'Double Jay'), a radical, youth-orientated station. Perhaps the most significant recent changes in radio have been the introduction of the FM radio band, which has greatly improved the quality of sound and led to the proliferation of music-based radio stations, and the continuing growth of community radio stations.

Television

As early as 1934 (two years before the BBC began transmission in England) there were experimental television transmissions in Brisbane. The arrival of television in Australia was slowed down by the war and then by successive governments, who tried to develop the system carefully and systematically. In 1948 the Australian Broadcasting Control Board was founded, and the following year the Chifley Labor government announced that a national television network would be established. Chifley's aim was to create a single channel owned by the Australian people, but he lost the next election to Robert Menzies, whose preferred model was a mixture of public and commercial broadcasters, similar to radio.

The Menzies government handed out television station licences in what was described at the time as 'an example of looking after old friends'. The Fairfax-Associated Newspapers and Macquarie Broadcasting Group in Sydney (an organisation which at the time owned the *Sydney Morning Herald*, the *Sun*, radio 2GB and a number of country radio stations) was given a licence to set up Channel 7 (in Sydney), and Frank Packer, a longtime active supporter of Menzies and publisher of the *Daily Telegraph* and the *Australian Women's Weekly*, won the licence for Channel 9 (also in Sydney).

Once the licences had been granted, the race to be the first television station to begin transmitting was on. Packer won, and on the evening of Sunday 16 September 1956 his new station, TCN9, managed to put four hours of programming together and transmit it from their half-built studio in the Sydney suburb of Willoughby. The first face seen on Australian television was that of Bruce Gyngell, who would go on to have a long and distinguished career in television, which included heading Channel 7 and the Australian Broadcasting Tribunal.

Australian television is now divided between four, often competing, interests. The Australian Broadcasting Commission (ABC) is the public broadcaster. Funded by the federal government and ever more tightly squeezed for funds, it is under increasing pressure to broaden its appeal and become more commercial. In recent years its budget has been shaved to a point where it has become increasingly dependent on overseas productions, mainly from the BBC. Its traditional sports base is now virtually nonexistent, reduced to a half hour comedy show in which sport, covered on the commercial channels, is discussed.

A second government network, the Special Broadcasting Service (SBS), was established in 1980. It broadcasts multilingual programs (its policy is that half its programming will be in languages other than English) and overseas news coverage as well as locally produced arts, sport and current affairs programs. Its ability to advertise (restricted to time slots between programs) has ensured its ongoing economic viability.

The commercial free-to-air channels—7, 9 and 10—cover the cities, and a number of smaller operations service rural Australia by combining the city material with locally made products (most usually the local news). Roughly speaking, Channel 9 dominates sports, news and current affairs and focuses on the over 35 demographic, Channel 10 is an overtly downmarket teen and twentysomething channel which imports popular American programs, and Channel 7 fits

somewhere between the two, though it is probably closer to Channel 9 in terms of advertising and mass appeal. All three are virtually identical when it comes to movies, reality TV and DIY shows.

The fourth sector is pay TV (known elsewhere as cable or satellite TV). Offering in excess of 40 channels, this market is controlled by Optus (a telephony provider), Foxtel (combined media and telephony interests) and Austar (specialising in servicing areas outside capital cities). More than 1.3 million Australian homes now have pay TV. It has huge potential, but is currently hamstrung by legislation that prohibits the live transmission of major sporting events involving Australian teams.

The cast of Blue Hills, *a hugely popular radio serial, in 1949, when the program began. It ran for 27 years. Locally produced radio, and later TV, serials are an enduring feature of Australian broadcasting.*

An Indy car is taken through its paces at the Gold Coast, Queensland. Live Australian sport, still on free-to-air TV—pay TV is fighting this—now includes several world class motor sport events.

Print Media

Here printers are checking material as it comes off the press at Media Press, a publisher of ethnic newspapers in Marrickville, New South Wales. An enormous number of languages are spoken in Australian homes, and there are locally produced newspapers for all these ethnic groups.

A printing press came to Australia with the First Fleet and the colony's first newspaper, the *Sydney Gazette*, was published 15 years later, on 5 March 1803. Its existence was dependent on the permission of the governor, and it was carefully censored to remove any possible anti-administration material. It lasted until 1842 and, while abused by some of the more intelligent members of the colony as a paper full of 'flattery of Government officials and inane twaddle on other matter', it did serve its purpose as a general information bulletin for the colony.

By 1824 censorship had been lifted, and on 14 October of that year the *Australian* (not the ancestor of the current national daily) joined the *Gazette*. Two years later the *Monitor* appeared. This gave Sydney three papers, all of which had to find enough local material to fill their pages. None of them was a daily. The trend was for a paper to first appear weekly then, after a trial period, to be produced twice weekly. In fact it wasn't until 1840 that the *Sydney Morning Herald*, which had started nine years earlier, actually felt confident enough to go daily.

By early in the 1840s South Australia had five weekly papers, all being printed on different days of the week, and by 1854 Tasmania had 11 papers. With so much choice available, both the circulation and the size of these publications tended to be very small. In 1873 the *Adelaide Register* was selling 300 copies; ten years later it had only doubled its circulation.

Between 1840 and 1860, and helped by high immigration and the goldrushes, the country newspaper became an important part of the Australian mass media. By 1886 New South Wales could boast 143 country newspapers. Not surprisingly, competition was fierce, and when proprietors found a recipe for success, they stuck to it. By the mid-nineteenth century a thriving business in 'sex and scandal' had led to high circulations and low reporting standards. A typical success story of the time is that of Samuel Bennett and the Sydney *Evening News*. When the paper was launched in 1867 it had a modest circulation of 2000. By 1884 the circulation had risen to 40,000, due to what was criticised at the time as 'graphic accounts of the brutal prizefight, the "sickening details" of the horrible murder, the lascivious disclosures of the divorce or breach-of-promise case'.

Concurrent with the rise of newspapers was the appearance of broadsides—single sheets of paper with sensational accounts of 'battles, atrocious piracies, calamitous shipwrecks, proclamations, deaths of the

MEDIA AND THE ARTS TIMELINE

1803 First newspaper, the *Sydney Gazette*, published.
1824 Publication of the *Australian*, the colony's first independent newspaper (not related to today's *Australian*).

1789 First play performed in the colony: *The Recruiting Officer* by George Farquhar.
1794 *A Direct North General View of Sydney Cove*, painting by Thomas Watling.

1833 Opening of the Theatre Royal. Sydney.
1854 First issue of the *Age* appears in Melbourne. *The First Subscription Ball, Ballarat*, painting by S.T. Gill.

1830 *Quintus Servinton* by Henry Savery, the colony's first novel is published.
1831 Publication of *Sydney Herald* newspaper (*Sydney Morning Herald* from 1842).

1870 *Bush Ballads and Galloping Rhymes*, Adam Lindsay Gordon.
1874 *For the Term of His Natural Life*, novel by Marcus Clarke.

1859 *The Recollections of Geoffry Hamlyn*, novel by Henry Kingsley.
1862 *Poems and Songs*, Henry Kendall.

1895 *The Man from Snowy River and Other Verses*, by Andrew 'Banjo' Paterson.
1896 *While the Billy Boils*, book of short stories by Henry Lawson.

1880 Founding of the *Bulletin* magazine by J.F. Archibald and John Haynes.
1890 *Shearing the Rams*, painting by Tom Roberts.

1903 *Such Is Life*, novel by Joseph Furphy.
1908 *We of the Never Never*, autobiographical account of bush life by Mrs Aeneas Gunn.

1900 Salvation Army film *Soldiers of the Cross*, one of the world's first feature films.
1901 *My Brilliant Career*, novel by Miles Franklin.

1918 *The Magic Pudding*, children's book by Norman Lindsay; *Snugglepot and Cuddlepie*, children's book by May Gibbs.

1915 *The Sock Knitter*, painting by Grace Cossington Smith, an early example of Australian modernism.

1931 Australian Ballet established in Sydney.
1932 *On Our Selection*, film by Ken G. Hall.
1933 First publication of *Australian Women's Weekly*.

1928 Founding of Australian Broadcasting Corporation (ABC).
1930 *The Fortunes of Richard Mahony*, novel by Henry Handel Richardson.

1940 *The Man Loved Children*, no Christina Stea
1941 Max Harris *Angry Penguins* maga a focus for avant-ga

great, remarkable events and phenomena, intriguing mysteries, horrid enormities and tragedies, villainies of all kinds'. Significantly, broadsides often had larger circulations than newspapers. They flourished from the foundation of the colony until 1855, when they disappeared, presumably overwhelmed by the rise in 'sex and scandal' newspapers. Alongside the broadsides and the sensationalist newspapers were publications dull in both layout and subject matter. Such a paper was the early *Sydney Morning Herald,* which included extensive reporting of parliamentary proceedings and columns of closely packed type without illustrations or sub-headings.

In 1872 a major news and communication breakthrough occurred when the Overland Telegraph Line, which ran 3200 km (2000 miles) from Port Augusta in South Australia to Port Darwin in the Northern Territory, was completed. At the time it was a technological miracle with far-reaching consequences. Instead of news taking four to six weeks to arrive by sea from Europe, it was now received within hours via a submarine cable which linked Darwin to Banyuwangi in Java and thus to the telegraphic networks of Asia and Europe. This led to the establishment of the Australian Associated Press service from London and, for Australian newspapers, to access to the services of the international news agency Reuters.

The era of the press barons emerged during the period 1890–1930. In August 1890 the first issue of John Norton's *Truth* appeared. It heralded a new period of journalism where competition was intense and ruthless. A Sydney-based newspaper company owned by Hugh Denison tried to invade Melbourne. It was repulsed by Keith Murdoch's Herald and Weekly Times organisation which, in typical style, bought them out. During the 1920s and 1930s Murdoch continued to buy up papers and magazines. By the mid-1930s Murdoch and his Herald and Weekly Times group were Australia's largest media proprietors. While Murdoch's empire was expanding, so too were those of Warwick Fairfax, Frank Packer and his father, and John and Ezra Norton. As a result, between 1923 and 1933 the number of newspaper owners dropped from 21 to 10.

By this time the newspaper business was dominated by just a few families—the Fairfaxes, Packers, Nortons and Murdochs. With increased wealth came influence and power. In the l950s the balance was altered when Sir Keith Murdoch died. Control of the Herald and Weekly Times group passed to a board of

directors, though Murdoch's son, Rupert, was given the *Adelaide News.* Since the 1950s, Rupert Murdoch has built a new press empire—News Limited—and in the process has absorbed most of what was once owned by the Norton family.

Today, Australia's newspapers are controlled by too few people. At the end of the nineteenth century there were 17 independent proprietors who owned 21 daily papers in the capital cities. As late as 1923 it was estimated that 21 independent proprietors controlled 26 metropolitan dailies. But by the 1930s the Australian press was controlled by four men. And that has not changed since then.

It is a pattern which has also been a characteristic of both the magazine industry (now dominated by Kerry Packer's ACP (Australian Consolidated Press) and the radio and television industries. Over the years there have been numerous attempts to broaden the base by placing controls on the major proprietors, but this has been difficult, as the owners, being few but therefore extremely powerful, are capable of wielding enormous political influence; if they turn against a government, they can affect the outcomes of elections by waging political campaigns.

Kerry and Ros Packer at a film premiere in Sydney. The Packer family has been one of the dominant Australian media owners since the 1930s. Kerry Packer and his family currently have controlling interests in both print (newspapers and magazines) and broadcast (free-to-air and pay TV) media in Australia. Packer is both admired and disliked, often for the same things: his determination, his outspokenness, his love of sport, his impatience with politicians.

SYDNEY MAIL
MELBOURNE
OCTOBER 17TH., 1934.
CENTENARY NUMBER

The Sydney Mail was the weekly stablemate of the Sydney Morning Herald, and was published between 1860 and 1938. As a weekly, it aimed to work for the rural community, who had no access to daily newspapers, and the urban poor, who couldn't afford daily papers. The weekly would have it all—news, advice to farmers, and light, even literary reading, including Rolf Boldrewood's Robbery Under Arms, in 1882–83.

William Dobell wins
~~ Prize for his por-
~~ua *Smith,* prompting
~~ of artists to issue a
~~nst the judges; they
ensuing court case.

1948 *The Harp in the South,* novel by Ruth Park.
1950 *Power Without Glory,* novel by Frank Hardy, prompts businessman John Wren to sue for libel.

1958 Foundation of National Institute for Dramatic Art (NIDA) in Sydney. First Top 40 popular music chart issued by Radio 2UE. Channel 9 launches TV show *Bandstand.*

1964 *The Lucky Country,* a survey of Australia by Donald Horne. *We Are Going* by Kath Walker (Oodgeroo Noonuccal), first published book of verse by an Aboriginal writer.

1969 *Dimboola,* play by Jack Hibberd. Roger Woodward cofounds, with Sir Bernard Heinze, the International Sydney Piano Competition.

1974 Pop music program *Countdown* begins on ABC TV.
1975 Introduction of colour television. Founding of ABC radio 2JJ. *Picnic at Hanging Rock,* film by Peter Weir.

1983 Thomas Kenneally wins the Booker Prize for *Schindler's Ark* (1982).
1986 *Crocodile Dundee* becomes the most successful Australian film ever.

1993 *The Piano* wins the Palme d'Or at the Cannes Film Festival.
1995 Australia's first pay TV service, Galaxy, begins broadcasting.

1944 Russell Drysdale begins paintings of drought-stricken areas.
1946 *Ned Kelly,* painting by Sidney Nolan. *The Moving Image,* poems by Judith Wright.

1955 *Summer of the Seventeenth Doll,* play by Ray Lawler. *The Wandering Islands,* poems by A.D. Hope.
1956 Channel TCN9 transmits first TV programs.

1958–60 Arthur Boyd produces *Love, Marriage and Death of a Half-Caste* suite of paintings.
1963 *You-Yang Landscape I,* painting by Fred Williams.

1965 *Wild Cat Falling* by Colin Johnson (Murdrooroo), first published novel by an Aboriginal author. *Sun Music I,* composition by Peter Sculthorpe.

1970 *The Female Eunuch,* a feminist analysis of sexuality and society by Germaine Greer.
1972 *The Removalists,* play by David Williamson.

1976 1976 Patrick White awarded Nobel Prize for Literature, the first Australian to receive the award.
1980 Multicultural TV channel SBS begins broadcasting.

1987 *The Fatal Shore,* a history of the early days of Australia by Robert Hughes.
1988 Peter Carey wins the Booker Prize for *Oscar and Lucinda.*

1997 Geoffrey Rush wins Best Actor Oscar for his performance in *Shine.*
2000 Les Murray is awarded Queen's Gold Medal for Poetry.

ARCHITECTURE

Taming the Landscape

The clean lines and simple form of a lighthouse in Port Adelaide, South Australia. Utilitarian structures such as these show a functional engineering beauty evident in much of the earliest Australian architecture.

To arrive in Australia by air is to experience the awesome single-mindedness of two centuries of the old settler ambition to control and own the surface of this continent. From Port Hedland to Sydney fence lines cut across the patterns of ancient flash floods, evidence of indifference to nature and a determination to control and exploit the land which has ultimately led to deforestation and salinity problems across areas the size of Western Europe. The vastness of the land highlights the painful learning incursions of the colonists, attempting to override the tension between the comfortable coastal fringe and the haunting abstractions of the centre.

The European settlers moved into the hinterland from their fledgling cities with faltering but persistent steps, clear-felling the land bit by bit, slowly turning Australia into a place like the one they had left behind. While the first settlers made do with the available resources such as local timber, bark and mud, later generations were able to indulge their whims with imported materials and a new knowledge of how to adapt their buildings to the climate.

Phases of settlement

A flour mill at Portarlington in Victoria, built by architect Andrew McWilliams in 1857 in classical Georgian style. In the colony's early days it was hoped that the style's harmonious proportions and associations with 'civilising' influences would inspire order in the often unruly new settlement.

The first step in the building of a city was to establish a grid, the form of colony since the establishment of the ancient Greek colonies around the Mediterranean. Colonel William Light, Adelaide's Surveyor-General, agonised over the location of the grid for the city, dreaming at night that he was excavating it from the bones of the land as if by clearing in the right place he would find the place where the city was

always meant to be. Melbourne's grid is draped from one hill to another with a stream down its centre, as the surveyors sought to rationalise the settlement that had sprung up at this watery junction. Across the river another larger grid was set out true north to accommodate the imperial institutions of government. In Adelaide too, the settler grid is separated and angled away from the administrative grid.

To begin with, architecture was utilitarian: bridges, lighthouses, piers, gun-emplacements, ports and shearing sheds, often austerely handsome in appearance. Some of the earliest buildings were prisons, as the continent equipped itself for its mission of accommodating the criminality exported from Britain. Prisons took on the control model invented by Jeremy Bentham, and panopticon plans were built across the country allowing one warder at the hub to see all of the cells down every spoke. Often the severe utility of the conception was offset by charming Georgian houses for the governor and staff, as if the civilising influence of the architecture would anchor their behaviour in the better half of human values.

Mechanics Institutes, societies dedicated to the furtherance of literacy and skills, were among the first institutions to be established in most settlements. As befitted their mission, the institutes were usually portico-fronted classical structures, simple and rational in form. Churches, too, were established early on, those of Anglican denomination often sited on low ground near the seat of administration, the Catholic on the highest adjacent site, with other denominations spread in between. They signalled their relationship to the mysteries above with a variety of styles—high church neo-Gothic, austere neo-classical and the innovative, neo-Romanesque of Unitarianism. Schools, too, proclaimed their aims in their building styles: neo-Gothic for the traditionalists, neo-classical for the rationalists and, in due course, modernism for the pragmatists.

As the population grew, pressure for living space increased. The Chartist belief in the need for separation from the State through the independent ownership of land resulted in houses being built away from the administrative centre. The first suburbs, like Fitzroy in Melbourne, were laid out on grids with large three or four-storey houses at the junctions

between major and minor streets, two to three-storey houses along the major streets and single-storey cottages in terraces along the minor streets. It was a fabric which encompassed all classes and echoed styles recognisable in other colonial cities around the British Empire.

The economic forces and architectural ambitions that ordered these places flowed like tides, running for a generation, then receding and returning but altered and flowing somewhere else, carrying the intentions of the next generation. An example is Lancefield in the granite boulder country north of Melbourne. Here, at a crossroads, buoyed up on the expectations of apparently endlessly expanding wealth from the goldfields, a three-storey city building was erected, complete with party walls. It sits there to this day, isolated and still awaiting the rest of the boulevard its builders envisaged.

Which style for the environment?

In the nineteenth century a booming economy was reflected in a profusion of Victorian styles—among them Georgian, Regency, Egyptian, Classical, Italianate, Tudor, Queen Anne and Arts and Crafts. While many of these appealed to prevailing fashions, there was often little regard to the practicalities of climate and topography. Then came the Federation bungalow. This single-storeyed house with its shady verandas was designed in the days of the British Raj in India, and was thought to be particularly well suited to the Australian climate. Later styles continued to mimic international trends, some of them with more relevance to the local topography than others. Mediterranean and Spanish mission styles established

themselves in the temperate belt of the continent, their open courtyards, shuttered windows and arcaded loggias providing welcome relief from the Australian summer heat.

In the post-war period, although Australia continued to be influenced by overseas trends (particularly the International style), regional styles began to have an impact in Melbourne and Brisbane, particularly in domestic architecture. This impetus was taken up from the 1960s onward in Sydney, Perth and Adelaide. Organic architecture made use of natural materials like stone, mud brick and timber, and sites which took advantage of topography and available sun and wind. In the far north of the Northern Territory and Western Australia, architectural ideas evolved to accommodate the mostly humid climate in that region. Instead of bricks, houses were now constructed in timber or steel, roofs were extended to protect verandas from rain and sun, windows were shaded or louvred to provide a cross-breeze and provided with flyscreens.

In the cities there was a reaction against Brutalism which asserted itself in strong, aggressive and boldly conceived public buildings: Structuralist design made its mark in Melbourne with the contour-embracing Myer Music Bowl (1959) and later (1985) the airy Exhibition Centre in Sydney's Darling Harbour.

It is hard to predict where architectural style is going next if cities are accurate indicators of where the next architectural tide rises first. What should we make of mock-Georgian houses with shrunken porticoes and paned windows in the suburbs; and what of mini-Manhattans of gleaming glass and granite where people live in towers, once the sole preserve of corporations?

The nineteenth-century gold boom in Victoria coincided with the high Italianate style in architecture as shown in these Melbourne terraces.

TOP LEFT: Richmond Bridge, Tasmania, built by convicts in 1823, overlooked by the Church. The utilitarian and the religious needs of the settlers were the first to be satisfied by early architects.

Grosvenor House, Sydney, designed by Harry Seidler, a proponent of the International style. Simple lines, shaded windows and landscaping are in harmony with the environment.

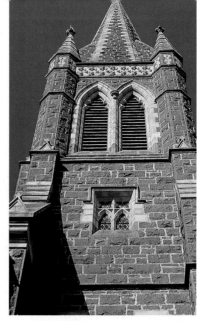

Hamilton: a Microcosm

Almost any small Australian settlement can reveal the whole of this history of European inhabitation. Hamilton, for example, 250 km (155 miles) from Melbourne, is a thriving rural centre of 11,000 people. It was founded by Scottish pastoralists and German settlers from South Australia. The town was at first laid out on one simple grid, which centred on a crossroad intersection.

The hill to the west was set aside for a botanical garden while the flatter land to the east was reserved for the city hall, library and art gallery. Between these the commercial strip was built. Once it must have been almost fully protected with pavement canopies, as once was metropolitan Bourke Street in Melbourne several hours drive to the east. Here, the ambitions of the commercial class can still be seen in the imposing classical edifices proclaiming a family name as well as the simple clapboard structures with painted signs

obscuring changing fortunes. Corners are taken up with banks in a variety of styles—classical, gothic and modern—some of which have inevitably been turned to other uses.

The houses between the administrative and commercial streets have largely been swallowed up in the expansion of those activities. Walk from the commercial street to the Botanical Gardens, however, and the history of taste and the ambitions it portrays are still evident. The houses drip with symbols of where they are and what they stand for. There is both nationalism rampant, and nationalism strident but unsure of itself. High on the hill, with a belvedere snatching views to the west is an Italianate villa, grey behind its cypress hedges, insisting on a closer linkage to the Italy of the romantic novels of the day than any part of Kensington in London ever achieved. Below, on a corner facing the city entrance to the Botanical

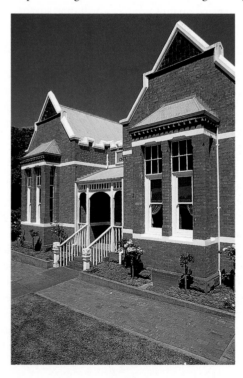

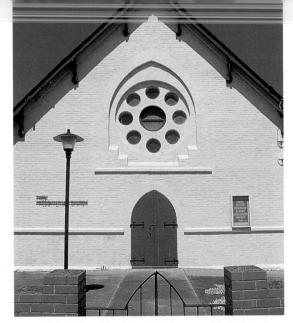

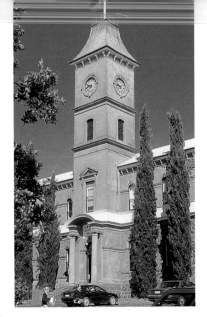

TOP, LEFT TO RIGHT: Mechanics Institute, c.1860: its Classical style emphasises gravitas and tradition.

The Gothic windows and rough-hewn stone of Hamilton's Anglican church, Christ Church.

Filigree ironwork adorns 'Ivanhoe' (1860), a Victorian bungalow.

The Greek-inspired facade of the Free Presbyterian Church, 1870.

The elegant cypresses flanking Hamilton College (1871) emphasise its Italianate style.

BOTTOM, LEFT TO RIGHT: Post offices, like this one, built in 1878, were often housed in grand buildings, reflecting their civic status.

Dundas Shire Office and Hall, 1892, show an Arts and Crafts influence in the roof design.

Tudor-style decorative beams and mullioned windows decorate 'The Gables', built in 1907.

Uniting Church manse, 1913, from front and side: simply decorated timber verandas give the manse a homely quality.

A simple, single-storey bungalow of the type built around 1950.

Gardens is a Queen Anne-style mansion, a breathtaking composition of turrets and cupolas in creamy plaster and rosy red brick. It rises three storeys to an attic with dormers, and twists around the corner so effectively that the house has been split into two without an obvious division between where one part begins and the other ends. This is the High Edwardian moment of Empire, when it was at its most confident. Further up the hill there are the smaller, more uncertain manifestations of Federation. This is a style of over-determination, insisting on a place for everything: a corner turret room for afternoon tea, a veranda for quoits, a terrace for drinks. As this is Australia, the finials are terracotta kangaroos.

Around the corner lies the immediate antidote to historical frippery, the Californian bungalow. Here was a style that was embraced enthusiastically by Australians, a style that was optimistic, New World, untainted by the foolishness of Europe. And yet, paradoxically, it is also dark and fortress-like, predicated on the home-as-castle mentality with its sloping columns and heavily closed eaves. Wood panelled inside, the bungalow owes much to the Arts and Craft movement and a popularisation of English architect Charles Voysey's neo-vernacular cottages. Slowly this is edged out by a more austere architecture, one that is more sober, more affordable and more economical in its use of materials: skillion roofs open up towards the light, large sheets of glass reveal an inside as bare as the cropped lawn outside, thin structural poles support flying cantilevers of improbable elegance. Reason returns with these houses. They proclaim that with careful consideration there is enough for everyone, that we can live in the present and make use of available materials, without the legends of other people's pasts, and that it is possible to live in easily maintained spaces.

These houses are part of the post-war optimism. But by the mid 1970s a mood of pessimism returns with the dismissal of the Whitlam government and with it a reversion to settler legend and narrative in house styles. Neo-Federation takes the elements of the style and shrinks them into symbols for the symbols that they were: in this interpretation narrow, unusable verandas clad the sides of houses, windows shrink and brick is present as a veneer.

The Cities

The military Garrison Church in the Rocks area in Sydney was designed by Henry Ginn and enlarged by Edmund Blacket in 1878. Here, as in Britain, military values are endorsed in Gothic style, an architectural tradition which drew on a romantic past to legitimise its imperial ambitions.

RIGHT: The old General Post Office in Sydney was built in grand Classical style in 1866 and covers an entire city block. Its magnificence is a reminder of the days when the postal service enjoyed a prominent place in government, employing thousands of people to maintain communication both within and outside Australia. The building has since been converted to commercial use—though it still houses a small post office.

Customs House at Circular Quay in Sydney displays another grand facade. It was designed by James Barnet in 1885. In the entrance hall is a swastika, symbol of good luck and prosperity long before the Nazis appropriated it.

Different cities have different stories to tell, different agendas to pursue and different moods to promote. The atmosphere in each Australian city is affected by its climate zone and quality of light and the surrounding landscape. Architecture in these places is manifested as a varying relationship between the tectonics—the innate logic of building, which is inspired and affected by its surroundings—and the scenographic—the unfolding history of the human events which have shaped it. Boom times, economic depressions and world wars have left their mark on the settlement of Australia. The story of architecture in this country has moved through a comprehensive catalogue of international building styles. An example of just one style from each period gives an idea of the scope of choice: Colonial Regency, Victorian Italianate, Federation Gothic, Inter-War California Bungalow, Post-War International, Late Twentieth-Century Organic. Rural and urban Australia display examples of these and many more overseas and regional styles in both its public and private buildings.

Post-war architects who have emerged as practitioners of a distinctively Australian way of seeing include Ken Woolley, Harry Seidler, Philip Cox, Robin Boyd, Daryl Jackson and Glenn Murcutt. While inevitably their work owes a debt to overseas influence, references to a national vernacular can be seen in Woolley's 'Lowline' solution to the problem of building on steep sites; in Seidler's modernist Customs Building in Brisbane with its sun-facing windows calibrated for shade and its veranda; in Cox's elegant and ephemeral-looking tent-like structures at Yulara tourist resort in the ancient landscape near Uluru; in Boyd's idea of integrating the garden with the house; in Jackson's use of timber; and Murcutt's love of corrugated iron.

Sydney

The architecture of Sydney (and Hobart) was influenced by organically pragmatic, harbour-seeking decisions. Then followed landing places, ramps and roads, all dictated by the particular topography of the site. Not until the mid-nineteenth century did the organising mind of administration begin to impose order, capturing the writhing streets and closing them in with a surveyor's grid. In the early days, the buildings of government were simplified versions of the Georgian classical style popular in Britain, in accord with prevailing notions of how a well-proportioned city should look, and staking a claim for the civilising influence of the new settlers. One of the first people to shape the architecture of the new colony was a convict, Francis Greenway, an architect who had been transported for forgery in 1814. His abilities were recognised by Governor Macquarie, who appointed him Civil Architect in 1816, and earned him his freedom in 1818. Harmonious proportions and simplification of detail are hallmarks of his style. He designed 40 buildings, of which 11 still stand, including

Hyde Park Barracks in Macquarie Street, the Government House stables (now the Conservatorium of Music) and St James' Church in King Street. In contrast, commercial development bowled along in an unchecked boom from the harbour to George Street. There, buildings were assembled in a riot of styles and symbols, later culminating in the froth of the Romanesque-style Queen Victoria Building, designed by George McRae and built between 1893 and 1898. The tussle between the forces of order and the heady risk-taking gambol of the commercial is embedded in Sydney's architecture to this day.

Despite its affection for racy origins, Sydney architecture has in the main opted for the philosophy in which the structure of buildings is made simple and apparent, clad with elements designed only to mediate between the interior and the climate. This school focuses on climate and materials, moving from the thousands of self-cleaning tiles on the sail-like shells of the Sydney Opera House (begun in 1959 and completed in 1973) and evolving into an explicit green agenda in the design of the Olympic village and stadium at Homebush Bay in 2000. The Opera House, designed by the winner of an international design competition, Danish architect Joern Utzon, underwent a metamorphosis in construction after Utzon quit the project in 1966. His original concept for the interior was changed and although the building is Australia's most recognisable icon and has been nominated for World Heritage listing, its function as a venue for opera has been criticised.

Hobart

Many of Hobart's early buildings are still intact, so that much of the original plan laid out by Governor Macquarie can be seen, and nearly 100 are classified by the National Trust. The English influence is evident in Arthur Circus where cottages crowd around a traditional village green and in a variety of styles from the Victorian Tudor of Government House to the Romanesque Revival of the Congregational Church in New Town. James Blackburn and John Lee Archer, two of the early colony's most accomplished architects, designed a number of public buildings including St George's, said to be Australia's finest Grecian church.

More of Hobart's history would be visible if the city had not been overlaid by imported bureaucratic architecture in the 1970s and 1980s when an array of ugly boxes was erected across some of the most prominent ridges. However, led by the persistent and sensitive intelligence of architects like Leigh Woolley, the bones of the original topography are surfacing again with a series of infill developments. In Salamanca Place, a row of old sandstone warehouses has been converted for contemporary use into offices, galleries,

restaurants and shops. On this ideal site, tucked into a slope, there are places where sun can be captured and people can relax, as well as a renewed respect for the natural wonders of the site, the mountain and the long sea vistas. The inner suburbs also take advantage of the sea views and the sight of snow on Mount Wellington. The modern efficiency of the hospital is designed on the principles of flow rather than that of containment. Up a winding road which follows every good gradient away from the harbour is the brewery, situated on the last flat space before the base of the mountain, high enough to ensure a good supply of uncontaminated water. The section between this factory and the artificial plane of the harbour quays is a good example of how architecture ensures a successsful engagement with place. In this way, Hobart's architects are rediscovering the qualities that make it a unique place to live.

Melbourne

Melbourne's flat topography and its need to differentiate itself from Sydney's commercial culture created a distinctive architecture. Surveyor Robert Hoddle designed the heart of the city on a grid 1 mile (1.6 km) wide and half a mile (805 m) wide with plenty of space for parks and gardens. Swanston Street, Melbourne's civic spine, encompasses both local city government and retail buildings and links the imperial government zone across the Yarra River to the university and the cemetery in one direction, and to the original bayside resort of St Kilda in the other.

A house designed by Leigh Woolley in Freycinet National Park, Tasmania. It was assembled on site to avoid damage to trees, and nestles in the environment, rather than dominating it. Its wooden surfaces have been feathered away at their edges, adding to the ephemeral effect.

The functional design of Australia's oldest brewery has endured the test of time, unlike many another historic building—beer is still brewed here.

The Royal Exhibition Building in Melbourne would not look out of place in Italy. Built in 1880, its dome is said to be supported by the largest timber roof trusses in the southern hemisphere.

RIGHT: Gas flares draw the eye to the gold facade of the Crown Casino in Melbourne. Built in 1997 by architects Bates Smart, Daryl Jackson and Perrot Lyon Mathieson, the building marks the last transition of the Yarra River embankment from working dock to commercial enclave.

The acclaimed facade of RMIT's building on Swanston Street, Melbourne. The design reflects and reinterprets aspects of the city's traditions, from local architectural references to the colours worn by the players of Australian Rules football.

Australian's colonial past, its British heritage and its links with Europe form one of the many architectural layers in Melbourne's built environment. The buildings of government are all neo-classical with a strongly Italianate influence, exemplified in the Florentine dome of the Royal Exhibition Building, designed by David Mitchell in 1880. Opened in 1856, the reading room of the State Library is similar in proportion and shape to that of the British Museum in London. Also emphasising a shared heritage is St Paul's Cathedral, an example of Gothic Revival style which stands on the site of a church from the 1850s, with a floor mosaic copied from Glastonbury Abbey. St James' Old Cathedral, Melbourne's oldest structure, is Georgian in style and possesses a twelfth-century marble font, given to Governor La Trobe by Queen Victoria.

Present-day architects continue to reinterpret and add to past achievements. Set amidst a flurry of skyscrapers coeval with Chicago's, Capitol House is one of the only buildings in Melbourne designed by Walter Burley Griffin, the American architect who won the competition to design Canberra. Inside is an extraordinary crystalline ceiling, designed by his wife, Marion Mahoney, creating an Aladdin's Cave of effects. The award-winning facade of the buildings of RMIT (the Royal Melbourne Institute of Technology, the original self-help education centre, once the city's Mechanics Institute) was redesigned in 1993 by Peter Corrigan and Maggie Edmond. RMIT Storey Hall is an architectural breakthrough, utilising Penrose's mathematical formula to reduce the number of tile shapes needed to cover any surface from over 200 to two. Designed by Ashton Raggatt McDougal, the interior of this building was the first to benefit from the new mathematics in its design. Tiling, in the form of a facetted curtain in Federation Square, is also trans-

forming and questioning the way the city is perceived: its effect is to capture and reflect the evening light in a shimmering kaleidoscope that dissolves and reforms the static faces of the cathedral, its neighbours and Flinders Street station, a metaphor for the continuous but ever-changing relationship between the old and the new.

Adelaide

Like Melbourne, Adelaide was laid out on a grid and has many magnificent public buildings. Colonel Light, designed a grid 1 mile (1.6 km) square. Within the grid are four squares, with Victoria Square in the middle. Parks surround the city, some planted with rows of olive trees, and the more prosperous areas are generously provided with gardens, or 'paradise garden' apartment blocks in which views are all focussed on a symmetrically organised patch of greenery.

The handsome buildings of North Terrace, one of the city's main thoroughfares, encompass a cornucopia of architectural fashions. Regency-style Ayers House, owned by and named after Sir Henry Ayers, premier of South Australia, was originally built as a cottage in 1846, but grew into a bluestone mansion with 40 rooms. Its farsighted underground living accommodation is still perfectly suited to the fierce heat of an Adelaide summer. Parliament House, with its Corinthian columns, Government House (1838–40) and Holy Trinity Church, the state's first Anglican church, are also situated on North Terrace.

Later buildings include the nineteenth-century Botanic Chambers Hotel with its towering series of balconies, an exaggerated archetype of the Australian country hotel, neo-Gothic Tobin House, designed by F.K. Milne in 1927–28, Adelaide University's library, built of reinforced concrete with a classical façade in 1932 by W.H. Bagot and Bonython Hall, part of the University of Adelaide, a recreation of the Tudor style favoured by many academic institutions, built in 1933 by the architectural company of Woods, Bagot, Laybourne-Smith & Irwin.

Nowadays there is a ruthless pragmatism evident in home-grown commercial and institutional work, almost as if people were afraid of the seductive qual-

ities of the beauty the first settlers celebrated in their buildings, places which, within too short a span of generations, have ended up empty and embarrassingly divorced from their founding intentions. One example is the railway station, once the proud entry point to this city, and now housing the city casino.

Large areas of Adelaide—places like McLaren Vale and Clare Valley—lie well beyond the city grid. The founders of these suburbs discovered the Arcadian qualities of these locations and built their dream houses there.

Perth

Perth was founded in 1829. Isolated and west-facing, the central grid of the city, designed by Surveyor-General John Septimus Roe, snuggles under the ridge of Kings Park, as if relieved to be done with the ocean. On these gentle slopes beside the Swan River the founders seem to have dreamed of Hampton Court and the 'sweetly flowing' Thames, adopting the Tudor as its badge of respectability. The buildings of the administration seem to join this masquerade, for example, the arch of the Old Pensioners' Barracks, designed by Richard Roach Jewell in 1863. Some of the buildings in the commercial district follow suit: Elizabethan-looking London Court, a shopping mall with elaborate towers, diamond-paned windows and old-fashioned hanging signs, was built in 1937. However, Perth has in its Tudor precinct perhaps the finest modern administration building on the continent, Council House. Geoffrey Powlett's classic modernist slab, while incorporating the linear components of the structure as both supports and sunscreens, remains in sympathy with its Tudor-style neighbours. St George's Terrace, too, is a mixture of the old and the new, with some of the city's oldest institutions rubbing shoulders with newcomers like Allendale Tower, an elegant aluminium-clad skyscraper designed by Cameron, Chisholm & Nicol which sprang up in the building boom of the mid-1970s.

The Commonwealth Games in the 1960s opened up suburban tracts like Coolbinia that filled with some of the finest modern houses in the country, awesome in their intelligent use of the fall of each site, the simplicity of their materials, the maximising

of space and the minimising of distinctions between inside and out. Some of this tradition remains in the crematorium designed by Bernard Seeber, in the houses of Paul Odden and in the houses and schools of Donaldson and Warn. This is Perth at its brave best, proudly of its time and making the most of its remarkably privileged geographical situation.

Darwin

Darwin faces north into the Indonesian archipelago, looking across the sea to neighbours who are closer than Australia's eastern cities. It was the only city to be bombed by Japan in World War II and continues to be subject to severe tropical storms. A generation ago the city was devastated by Cyclone Tracey which destroyed 95 per cent of its domestic architecture. Few public buildings survived intact: the stone walls

Adelaide's old railway station is now a casino with a hotel and convention centre.

TOP LEFT: Wackily House, Adelaide (1956), designed by Robin Boyd a strong proponent of modernist regional domestic architecture.

BOTTOM LEFT: Government House, Perth, built between 1859 and 1864, one of many Tudor-inspired government buildings in the city.

This council building in Perth narrowly escaped demolition in 1997, its style now recognised as a classic of its time.

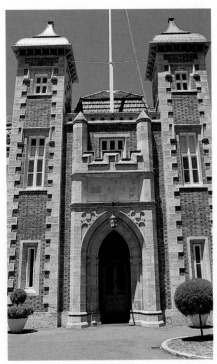

RIGHT: This house in the Myilly Point Historic Precinct in Darwin survived the many tropical storms which have battered the city. Designed to cope with the vagaries of the weather in the tropical far north, it stands on stilts, a precaution against floods, and an aid to the circulation of air through the house.

RIGHT: This house in the Myilly Point Historic Precinct in Darwin survived the many tropical storms which have battered the city. Designed to cope with the vagaries of the weather in the tropical far north, it stands on stilts, a precaution against floods, and an aid to the circulation of air through the house.

BOTTOM: Virtually all the living space is outside in this cool and practical modern house in the Northern Territory.

Cullen Bay Marina development, Darwin: light, tropical colours, shady balconies, landscaping and proximity to the water add up to an architecture that is in tune with its place.

of Christ Church Cathedral, built in 1902, the old naval headquarters and Brown's Mart, the oldest building in the city (1885) have all had to be either extensively repaired or rebuilt. New buildings must now comply with cyclone-resistant regulations.

Unfortunately, much new building lacks the charm that comes from attunement to local conditions, relying instead on air conditioning and thus lacking a sense of connection to place. Troppo Architects, on the other hand, aim to work with the climate instead of against it. Their philosophy is to allow their buildings to 'hear' the thundering rain of the Wet and the drip of water off broad leaves and to acknowledge the brightness of the sun in the Dry. Their prefabricated houses are made of easily transported and assembled material (essential for a widely spread and often remote population). Adjustable 'skins' enable the buildings to adjust to the often dramatically changing climate; gable or pyramid roofs cope with heavy rain and allow natural ventilation; and bathrooms are open-sided to avoid mould and condensation. In the city, the Territory Insurance Office, designed by Stapledon Architects in 1982, has fixed louvres on a frame around the building's shell which protect it from the sun yet do not impede the view. Myilly Point Historic Precinct, which was built in the 1930s and is still standing, demonstrates the viability of architecture which features elevated buildings, casement windows and louvres.

Brisbane

The river port of Brisbane in the subtropical north sits in the loop of its mangrove-lined river surrounded by low hills, its climate and topography providing a challenge for generations of architects. Much of the city's domestic architecture has been influenced by these factors, the 'Queenslander' being its most characteristic invention. This house, an evolution of the ubiquitous bungalow, is usually built of timber and corrugated iron and generally has four rooms divided by a corridor on a square plan. Raised on timber stumps to take advantage of passing breezes, all four sides of the house have verandas screened with lattice and a central exterior staircase. The walls are made of single skins of clapboard. The result creates areas of darkness and breezy shade.

In the city a central road divides the governmental side from the commercial, and the cultural institutions have migrated across the river to another loop, where the modern art gallery, museum and theatre complex is linked through the gardens of the 1988 Expo site. A love of opulence is reflected in several grand buildings of the Victorian era as well as in the mirrored high-rise structures of the twentieth century. Compare the extravagance of the Treasury building, for example, with the 135 m (443 feet) AMP building. Some of these buildings have lost their original function (the Treasury is now a casino), or prominence (the grand Italianate tower of City Hall is now hemmed in by skyscrapers), others have adapted to different times and different expectations. The university's European-inspired quad of enormous proportions, for example, has been redeemed

by a series of humanely scaled modern colleges by James Birrell. Parliament House, designed by Charles Tiffin in 1865, the winner of an architectural contest, and finished in 1889, was built in elaborate French Second Empire style but its annexe is modern.

Canberra

Canberra is a planned city, bringing together on one site the works of some of the best architects in Australia and overseas. The city has wide tree-lined avenues, long vistas and a lake and was designed to harmonise with its bushland setting. As well, representatives of over 250 countries are based in Canberra, their embassy buildings often reflecting their own material and cultural heritage.

American architect Walter Burley Griffin won the international contest to design the nation's seat of government. Although his vision was never fully achieved due to bureaucratic and political wrangling, much of his original plan was carried out. The impressive concrete and glass structures housing the National Gallery and the High Court, designed by Edwards, Madigan, Torzillo & Briggs in 1974, are among the best works of their kind in the world. The new parliament building, built into the hill behind Old Parliament House, was completed in 1988, the crowning achievement of US-based Italian architect Romaldo Giurgola. The new National Museum, designed by Ashton Raggatt & McDougall, borrows a footprint from the most poignant work of the twentieth century—the Jewish Museum in Berlin. This building can be seen as a symbol of the work that lies ahead for Australia—the reconciliation between tens of thousands of years of dreaming this continent into being and the raw 200-year-old story that we have begun to discover and tell through our architecture, writing and song.

The future

The cities and settlements of Australia are stories of ambition and its fortunes, an amalgam of many philosophies and styles which ebb and flow according to different expectations over the years. Often these tides begin as influences from elsewhere, but their significance lies not in how appropriate they were in the past, but in how they survive and change in the face of local events and traditions today.

In this way, and in millions of separate acts each year, some positive, some negative, Australians endeavour to align themselves architecturally with their continent. Their houses and gardens are all attempts at establishing 'abiding events'—in other words, permanent stories to testify to their existence.

Living above the ground is cooler in the steamy subtropics. The 'Queenslander' is an adaptation of one of Australia's favourite designs, the bungalow, with the verandas closed in.

TOP: In Brisbane, the classical facade of the Customs building no longer dominates the street-scape as it had since 1889, with the modernist Seidler tower now calling for attention.

The classical proportions of the National Library of Australia in Canberra reflect Greco-Roman architecture. Designed by Walter Bunning and situated on the foreshores of Lake Burley Griffin, the National Library was opened in August 1968.

SPORT

The Culture of Sport

As one of only a very few Western countries to gain its independence in the twentieth century, Australia has struggled to gain international recognition in political, economic and military affairs. Emerging from the shadows of the economic power-houses, and the traditional European sense of history, the nation has managed to excel in the cultural and sporting arenas of the world.

When Edmund Barton was sworn in as Australia's first Prime Minister on 1 January 1901, the country had already fielded 10 captains in 56 cricket Tests against England, two rugby captains in internationals against Great Britain, and had won six gold medals in Olympic competition. As sport played a part in gaining for Australia international recognition, so it was an integral ingredient in the federation of the six disparate British colonies on the Australian continent.

The 1882 Ashes Test match at The Oval, London, when 'Demon' Fred Spofforth tore apart the English batting line-up and gave his team a famous victory, did more than just provide the beginnings of one of the world's great sporting series. It brought a sense of national identity to the colonies, with Victoria, New South Wales and South Australia all represented in the victorious squad.

The sporting public

Australia reveres its sporting heroes more than it does its film stars, rock musicians, painters and political leaders. In the 40 years between 1960 and the close of the twentieth century, no less than 11 sportsmen and women claimed the Australian of the Year award.

In the first 21 year-history of the Young Australian of the Year awards, nine of the winners were in the sporting sphere. Sporting icons are prominent features in the country's cultural institutions, be it a stuffed horse hide in the Museum of Victoria or famous racing yachts in the Australian Maritime Museum.

This need to succeed on the world stage, seemingly driven by a deep and enduring insecurity, has produced as many martyrs as heroes. When in 1932 the mighty Phar Lap was found dead in a San Francisco stable, the presumption was that the Americans had poisoned the Australasian champion, despite a lack of any conclusive evidence to prove so. And it appears to matter little that few outside of Australia and New Zealand have heard of the champion horse, the legend of Phar Lap is passed on through the generations, as is the myth that the dastardly Yanks nobbled our great champion.

But it's perhaps Australians' appreciation of the sporting contest that sets us apart from the rest of the world. When the Sydney Olympics ended, the International Olympic Committee (IOC) and representatives of the international media, almost without exception praised Australian audiences and the warm reception they gave to the world's athletes. That's not to say Australians are not at times overly parochial, but what motivates the cheering is not necessarily the winning or losing, but the spirit of competition. President of the IOC Juan Antonio Samaranch intimated as much when he awarded Sydneysiders the Olympic order—the first time a host city had been given such an honour. He cited the case of the long jump competition when Cuban Ivan Pedroso was cheered loudly down the runway for his last jump as he managed, by just six centimetres (2.3 inches), to pip Australian Jai Taurima for the gold medal.

Likewise Australians do not appreciate boorish, arrogant (as opposed to confident) or unsporting behaviour from their own or others' athletes—a trait

Australia is a nation of sports lovers and the top events attract spectators of all ages and from all backgrounds. This couple are on the way to the 2000 Sydney Paralympic Games.

Accolades that in other countries are showered on rulers and film stars are in Australia reserved for its sporting heroes. Here a street parade of Olympic athletes is cheered on by an adoring crowd.

often wrongly referred to as Australia's 'tall poppy syndrome', a label properly attached to other sorts of behaviour. In Adelaide in 1998, cricketer Mark Waugh was booed as he made his way to the batting crease, after it had been revealed he had accepted money from bookmakers to provide information about the pitch and weather conditions. After Greg Chappell had shamefully instructed his brother Trevor to bowl underarm during a Test match against New Zealand, barrackers at the Sydney Cricket Ground (SCG) hoisted a sign reading: 'It's not lawn bowls Greggy'.

The breadth of participation

Australians have made their marks in many sports. In some, surfing for example, one would expect them to perform well, yet the country has also produced world champions in alpine and freestyle skiing events. From archery to yachting, Australia has produced a multitude of world champions, and sport sits on a pedestal above all other endeavours. This is perhaps best illustrated by the remarks made by then Prime Minister Bob Hawke in 1983, the year that *Australia II* became the first boat to wrest the America's Cup

ABOVE: When Bondi, arguably Australia's most famous beach, was named as the site for beach volleyball at the 2000 Olympic Games in Sydney, controversy raged for months. However, anger was eclipsed by euphoria when the gold-medal was won by the Australian women's team.

Though in Australia there is a growing concern among sporting bodies that participation rates are falling, events such as Masters games attract increasing numbers of contestants. This photo was taken at the 2000 games in Alice Springs.

When Sydney was named host city for the 2000 Olympics, the public's enthusiasm knew no bounds. This celebratory graffiti is on rocks at Nambucca Heads, New South Wales.

RIGHT: *A benign climate and good facilities have no doubt played a part in Australia's prominence at swimming, but organisations aimed at youngsters, such as Surf Life Saving's Nippers, have an important role.*

Hardly a town of any size does not have its lawn bowls club. Though the sport is presently going through a difficult period, its administrators are working to attract young people.

from the Americans since they first won it in 1851. Hawke declared that any boss who sacked a worker for not showing up that day would be 'a bum'.

For what is a relatively small country, Australia has produced a number of world-class golfers, but three stand out from the pack: Greg Norman, Peter Thompson and arguably the greatest woman player ever, Karrie Webb. The Australian golf circuit has also been popular, with Jack Nicklaus once describing the Australian Open as the 'fifth major', although many top players are reluctant to take the long trek down under after an arduous northern hemisphere season.

In an era when a reconciliation with Australia's indigenous population is high on the public—if not the government—agenda, it's perhaps fitting that it was a sporting moment that most epitomised this desire. While hundreds of thousands marched for the

cause in Australian cities during the year 2000, perhaps the most enduring image will be that of an Aboriginal runner, representative of an ancient and proud—though much abused—culture, holding aloft a torch to light the Olympic flame in the focus of the world's cameras.

Cathy Freeman reprised this feat 10 days later by winning the 400 m sprint in front of an estimated Australian television audience of 10 million, a record. Cathy Freeman has not been the country's only Aboriginal champion, but has been by far the most feted. The country's indigenous population has produced many champions: in AFL, both rugby union and rugby league, hockey, netball and basketball. It has thrown up world-champion boxers and even a Wimbledon champion in tennis. However it was 1996 before a person with indigenous forebears, Jason Gillespie, played cricket for Australia.

Although millions of dollars are poured into elite sport in Australia, its strength lies in its grass-roots participation, backed by a warm climate and what is a seemingly endless array of facilities. When asked why Australia was so successful at swimming, after the country won three-quarters of the available gold medals at the 1994 Commonwealth Games, the head coach of England pointed out that there were only three Olympic-size swimming pools in Great Britain. There are 10 times that number in Sydney alone.

Drive through most metropolitan suburbs or country towns in Australia, and you will see acres of grassed sports fields, asphalt netball and basketball courts, lawn-bowls greens and golf courses, and every surf beach near a population centre has volunteer life savers. For all these sporting facilities there are clubs that play on them, clubs that are part of the country's social fabric. Every weekend parents take the children off to junior cricket and football matches or little athletics or junior life saving (the Nippers) events.

Although not every Australian is enamoured of sport, and of horseracing in particular, the Melbourne Cup is truly 'the race that stops a nation'. Its appeal lies in its equality, in its epitomising of the 'fair go'. The race has never been about proving which horse is the best in the land; it's a handicap event and some absolute no names have run off with the trophy as the better horses in the field are forced to carry punishing weights around the track.

On the first Tuesday in November each year, almost the entire country downs tools and indulges in a betting frenzy on a sport that few know little of. On Cup Day in the year 2000, more than $100 million were plunged on the race, and when 3.30 p.m. rolled

likely the triumph of human endeavour that captivates the national imagination. Most Australians wouldn't dream of tackling the treacherous seas of Bass Strait, and for that reason admire the salty souls who do so year after year.

Australian sporting successes are many and encompass a wide range of sports. The squash player Heather McKay won the British Open 16 times in succession

Eulogised since colonial times by poets such as 'Banjo' Paterson, horseracing still holds much romantic appeal for Australians. Picnic race meetings at bush courses, like this one at Coober Pedy, South Australia, are still important social events in the remote outback.

around, Australians sat glued for more than three minutes to television and radio sets, barracking loudly for a horse whose name they'd only come to know that morning. All over the nation, from the smallest outback town to the biggest city, organisations of all types hold fund-raising Cup Day luncheons and fashion shows, and employees in workplaces organise a Melbourne Cup 'sweep'.

The 'well-to-do' sport of sailing also has its iconic event, the Sydney–Hobart yacht race, but just why this race is so popular is harder to pinpoint. As with the Melbourne Cup, it's a handicap race, but it's most

and lost only twice during her career. Authorities in the 1930s had to change the laws of billiards to curb the dominance of Walter Lindrum, whose world record for the largest break still stands. The boxer Jeff Fenech won four world professional titles, while the Aboriginal pugilist Lionel Rose overcame great odds to claim his world bantamweight title in 1968. Many surfers have also won world titles. And the rest of the world sometimes finds it difficult to believe Australia's successes. When in 1999 Zali Steggall became world slalom champion in alpine skiing, the US organisers played the Armenian national anthem.

Though some clubs are taking innovative steps to broaden their youth membership, yachting is still seen in Australia as a sport for the well-off. However, this does not lessen the appeal of the Sydney–Hobart race. The Boxing Day start attracts large crowds to Sydney Harbour and the tragic events of the 1999–2000 race probably served only to deepen its mystique in the public eye.

Cricket

The Australian sporting landscape owes a large debt to its former colonial master. The country's premier summer sport and still the only truly national game, cricket came to Australia with the English and was the first modern team sport played in this country. Since that first match on Australian soil, played in 1803 on a Sydney lawn by crewmen of HMS *Calcutta*, cricket has grown to become arguably the country's number-one sport, and at the dawn of the new millennium, Australia can justifiably lay claim to being the world's greatest exponent of the game, boasting a better wins-to-losses record than any other Test-playing nation. In the shortened version of the game, only the West Indies has won as many World Cups (two), while Australia remains the only country to appear in four finals.

The first team of Australian cricketers to tour England was made up of Aborigines from Victoria's Lake Wallace district. Though there have been some notable Aboriginal cricketers, social disadvantage and past elitism have largely excluded them from the game.

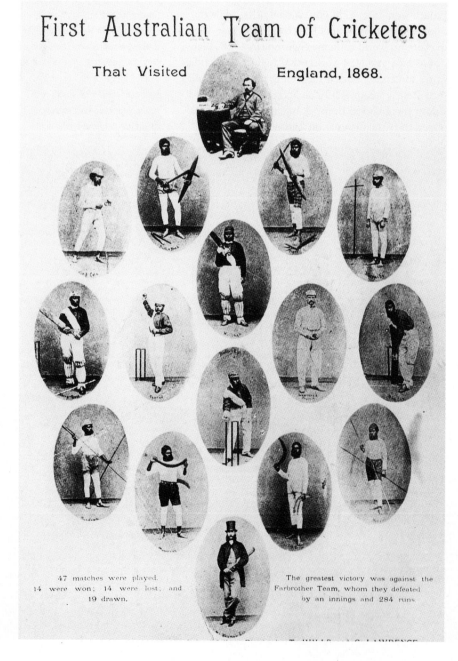

First Australian Team of Cricketers
That Visited England, 1868.

47 matches were played.
14 were won; 14 were lost; and
19 drawn.

The greatest victory was against the
Farbrother Team, whom they defeated
by an innings and 284 runs.

Like every other Test-playing country, Australia brings its own unique characteristics to the international scene: hard wickets, a tradition of fast bowling and mysterious leg spin, tough men never short of a word and blazing batsmen whose play off the back foot is second to none.

First-class cricket was played on these shores for the first time in 1851, and in 1868 an all-Aboriginal team from western Victoria toured England, notching up 14 wins and 19 draws in 47 matches. Sadly, there was much of the circus about the demonstrations of spear and boomerang throwing at the matches and though the sporting press generally praised the team's efforts, particularly 'Johnny Mullagh's' 73 in an hour and 20 minutes against Surrey, the establishment did not take them seriously.

The game did not come of age in the Australian colonies until 1877, when James Lillywhite's touring team played a combined New South Wales–Victoria XI at the MCG. And thanks to Charles Bannerman's unbeaten 165, Australia won by 45 runs in what was later recognised as the first-ever Test match.

Both countries regularly played each other over the next 20 years, with what is arguably the most famous encounter taking place at The Oval, London, in 1882. Courtesy of a devastating spell of bowling by Demon Spofforth—who took 14/90 (14 dismissals at a cost of 90 runs)—Australia beat, by seven runs, the best-ever England team fielded to that point, and the Ashes was born. The result gave the colonies a sense of nationhood and England realised they now had a foe to be reckoned with.

World War I brought the first interruption since 1858 to first-class cricket in Australia, but after the war, Armstrong's Australians swept all before them. Such greats as Bill Ponsford, Clarrie Grimmett and Jack Gregory helped Australia dominate not only England, but South Africa also. Although the great Wally Hammond, Jock Hobbs, Herbert Sutcliffe and Maurice Tate gained the 'Mother Country' some respite in the late 1920s, the arrival on the scene of Don Bradman made Australia virtually untouchable until the grand man's retirement in 1948.

Simply put, 'The Don' was the greatest cricketer who has ever lived. English batsman Denis Compton described him as 'not a once-in-a-lifetime player', but as one who arises 'once in a life of a game'. When in March 2001 he died, aged 92, he was as famous as ever he was, despite not having graced the Test arena for more than 52 years. In his final years, Bradman still received more than 200 letters a day from an adoring public. During his Test career, Australia lost just two series: his first in 1928–29 and the infamous 'Bodyline' series of 1932–33. The latter involved dubious tactics by arch villain Douglas Jardine. He instructed his bowlers to intimidate the Australians with a mixture of a legside field placing and bouncers.

For the opposing batsmen the equation was simple—get out or get hit. With Australia in the midst of the Great Depression, and Bradman's status as national hero, outrage was felt across the nation. So much so that the series led to diplomatic exchanges between the Australian and British governments.

At the end of his career, Bradman captained what many consider to be Australia's greatest-ever side, the Invincibles, who swept undefeated through England in 1948. Upon his retirement Australian cricket went into a state of relative decline not to be invigorated until 10 years later under the captaincy of Richie Benaud. The New South Wales leg spinner led with flair, and under his leadership Australia did not lose a series, with the most memorable encounter being the legendary 'Tied Test' played against the West Indies in 1960.

The aggressive and ultra-competitive Ian Chappell continued the tradition. With a side featuring what was possibly Australia's greatest-ever fast-bowling combination—Dennis Lillee and Jeff Thomson—he waged all-out war against England and the West Indies, Australia not going down in a series between 1972 and 1977. But it was perhaps Chappell's involvement in the establishment of World Series Cricket which had a greater impact on the game.

Media magnate Kerry Packer, denied television rights to the game by the Australian Cricket Board, in 1977 bought some of the world's best cricketers and established a competition of his own. With the official Australian XI (in effect it was a second or third XI) losing badly, the establishment couldn't compete and within two years a peace deal, heavily

favouring Packer, brought the two camps together. And the legacy was great. Australian players became better paid and could afford to compete as full-time professionals, one-day cricket proliferated, and the exciting day–night matches were introduced.

After a brief resurgence during the early 1980s, Australian cricket entered its darkest period. Many put this down to the simultaneous retirements of Lillee, Greg Chappell and Rod Marsh following the Fifth Test against Pakistan in 1983–84. However, a more important factor was the 'rebel tour', under Kim Hughes, to the recalcitrant Republic of South Africa. This tour deprived new captain Allan Border of 17 of the country's top 30 players, leaving a lack of depth that was sorely evident between 1985 and 1988. Riding out the bad times, Border moulded a competitive outfit, and by the time of his retirement in 1994, he not only had broken many of the game's aggregate records, but had discovered the deadly leg spinner, Shane Warne.

His successor Mark Taylor took the team to the top of world cricket. Under him, Australia wrested the Sir Frank Worrell Trophy from the West Indies in 1994–95—the 'Windies' first loss in over 15 years. 'Tubby' Taylor was so well regarded that he was made Australian of the Year in 1999.

His successor, Steve Waugh has led the team to another World Cup, a record 16-straight Test wins, and international one-day victories. With the unofficial motto 'never satisfied', Australia is set to enter another golden era at the dawn of a new century.

The Australian women's team also has a proud record. They've won four of the seven World Cups staged—and twice finished runners-up—and when in 1998 Wisden, long regarded as the bible of cricket, launched its inaugural Australian edition, it named as the first Australian cricketer of the year a woman; the Australian captain Belinda Clark.

The man known to generations of Australians as 'The Don'. Sir Donald Bradman, born in New South Wales in 1908, was revered throughout the cricketing world as the greatest batsman who has ever lived. His death in 2001 was mourned by cricket lovers everywhere, from retirees in Darwin to schoolchildren in Bombay; from cabbies in London to street vendors in Barbados.

Australia plays England at Lords, London, in 1886. When in 1882 'Demon' Fred Spofforth bowled Australia back from the brink of defeat by an England team seen as unbeatable, London's Sporting Times published an obituary to English cricket, announcing that its ashes would be interred at the Melbourne Cricket Ground, and from that time on, test matches between England and Australia have been played for the Ashes.

Football Codes

If cricket can lay claim to be a great uniting force in Australia, then footy—both inter- and intra-codes—is surely the great divider.

It's difficult to measure which is the more bitter: intra-code rivalries such as New South Wales versus Queensland in State of Origin rugby league, Western and South Australia against Victoria in Australian Football League (AFL), or both rugby codes versus AFL. Northerners dismiss the southern code as aerial ping-pong, while the south will not have a bar of 'thugby'. Even the rugby codes have their rivalries; Union is seen as the game of the well-to-do, whereas League, with its professional origins, is the domain of the working class. Soccer, despite a large participation rate, particularly among schoolchildren, still remains a poor cousin to the lot.

Australian Rules

Known simply and fondly as 'footy', Australian Rules Football was developed in 1858 by Thomas Wills, a renowned sportsman of his day, and his cousin H.C. Harrison, in part as a way of keeping cricketers fit during the off-season. Similar to, and borrowing much from Gaelic football, the game also has some of its roots in rugby. In terms of spectator numbers alone, footy is the most popular of all the codes. The game crosses class lines—clubs such as Melbourne and Hawthorn have their origins in educational institutions, and working-class suburbs were championed by St Kilda and Footscray.

Despite recent matches played against Ireland under so-called 'International Rules', Aussie Rules is the only football code that lacks truly international competition. Formal domestic competition began in 1877 with the establishment of the Victorian Football Association, but the contests were flawed in two main respects: the rules tended to encourage defensive play and some clubs lacked supporters, with the popular teams propping up the competition. It was an untenable situation which came to a head in 1897 when eight clubs—Melbourne, South Melbourne, St Kilda, Collingwood, Carlton, Fitzroy, Geelong and Essendon—broke away to form the Victorian Football League. Although South Australia, Western Australia and Tasmania had their own competitions, the VFL became the hegemonic body of the game. The rules were changed to promote a more attacking style of play, perhaps the most significant being the introduction of behind posts, (a ball kicked between them scores one point, through the goalposts six). This makes drawn matches rare, and encourages teams to seek scoring chances rather than defend a score.

The new league remained relatively unchanged for nearly 90 years, with Hawthorn, Footscray and North Melbourne—all joining in 1925—the only additions. South Melbourne, which was suffering financial problems, became the league's first guinea-pig for expansion when the club relocated to Sydney in 1982, where it was renamed the Sydney Swans. After struggling for many years, the Swans are now a permanent and popular fixture in this bastion of

rugby. The year 1987 saw another foray into rugby territory, this time in Queensland, with the establishment of the Brisbane Bears. The same year also saw the addition of Perth's West Coast Eagles from another footy stronghold, Western Australia. The Adelaide Crows, from South Australia, another footy-dominated State, joined in 1991, and the Fremantle Dockers (WA) signed up in 1995. Port Adelaide Power (SA) joined in 1998, replacing Fitzroy (Vic.) which, unable to survive in its own right, had earlier merged with Brisbane to form the Brisbane Lions.

The Australian Football League is the country's premier competition. It attracts crowds greater than those attending any other sport and with interest in the game not restricted only to the footy oval. Indeed, songs about the game such as *Up there, Cazaly* and *There's only one Tony Lockett* have appeared in the Top 40, and there is a seemingly never-ending stream of AFL talk shows on both radio and television. Unlike rugby league, AFL has never had to retreat from the areas to which it has expanded. The most successful and popular clubs field three of the foundation teams: Carlton, Essendon and Collingwood.

Along with rugby league and boxing, Australian Rules football has been the prime avenue of sporting success for Australia's indigenous population and, following some ugly incidents in the 1990s, the code has been to the fore in the fight against racism. While this stance can primarily be attributed to the strong advocacy of players such as Michael Long, there is a strong heritage of Aboriginal champions in the sport, and to have allowed such an ugly issue to fester would have besmirched their fine contributions. Players of the calibre of Graham 'Polly' Farmer, Doug Nicholls (who later defied all the odds and became Governor

of South Australia), the Krakouer brothers, Jim and Phil, and Gavin Wanganeen, rate as among the finest the code has produced.

It's perhaps not surprising that AFL, boxing and rugby league have produced so many indigenous champions for, in terms of equipment, they are minimalist sports. Disadvantaged communities do not have swimming pools, squash courts and golf courses. AFL and league require only a ball and some open space, while all boxing calls for are fast hands and nerves. To Australia's indigenous peoples, sport is not the expression of a cultural cringe, it's a celebration of what comes naturally. More often than not, their champions are the antithesis of the clinical professional who drops flair for the percentage game.

Rugby Codes

RUGBY UNION

Rugby football first appeared in Australia in 1865, some 30 years after the development of the game in Great Britain. Unlike today's clubs which represent geographical areas, the early teams, such as Wallaroo, in Sydney were made up of 'like-minded' men. The phenomenon spread to country New South Wales and then to Queensland, where the growth of the game allowed inter-colony contests to take place from the 1880s. A suburban competition was established in Sydney in 1896 and within three years Australia made its first appearance on the international stage, beating Great Britain at the Sydney Cricket Ground. Despite this initial success, the Wallabies, as the team and its members are known, spent the first 80 years of the twentieth century on the periphery of the elite, never really keeping up with the world powers, New Zealand, South Africa and Wales.

The inability of the code to spread beyond New South Wales and Queensland limited the pool of talent available for national selection and the founding in 1908 of rugby league continued to deprive it of the best and brightest.

However, all that changed in the 1980s, when the Wallabies, with the famous Mark Ella, David Campese, Michael Lynagh, Nick Farr-Jones and Simon Poidevin began amassing wins at an unprecedented rate. Then in 1984, they became the first Australian team to take the Grand Slam of wins from a tour of England, Wales, Scotland and Ireland and, two years later, became the first Australian team in 38 years to win a Bledisloe Cup series in New Zealand. Failure to qualify for the inaugural world cup final in 1987 was a case of one step backwards before two leaps

Carlton plays Melbourne in 1881. Australian Rules Football had its beginnings in the working-class Melbourne of the mid-1850s and its barrackers soon became renowned for their parochial fanaticism.

forward. With talented youngsters such as John Eales, Tim Horan, Phil Kearns and Jason Little joining the likes of Lynagh, Farr-Jones, Poidevin and Campese, the Wallabies were an irrepressible force in the second world cup series, beating England in the final at the latter's famous home, Twickenham in London.

The win was a boon for the sport in Australia and it made the first of its great surges. For the next three years, the Wallabies remained virtually unbeatable, losing just three of their matches. Australia's public broadcasting network, the ABC, which had for so long covered the game, lost the rights as commercial networks started to offer big money to broadcast Australia's international matches. There was, too, the steely determination of administrators to halt the flood of defections to the professional game, rugby league, of talented union players. In fact, when the Super League war began in 1995, rugby officials in Australia, and to a lesser extent in New Zealand and South Africa, were so concerned the new competition would lead to a player drain, that they forced union to turn professional, ending 125 years of amateur competition. The rest of the world followed suit.

However, at the next world cup in 1995, the world caught up with the Wallabies, and they again stumbled when they were expected to succeed. Bumbled out in the quarterfinals by a last-minute field goal from England, Australia for three years

wandered in rugby's wilderness, before former New South Wales flanker Rod Macqueen took the helm. His reign as coach ushered Australia into its most successful period. Under his command, the Wallabies lost barely a game.

With the star halves George Gregan and Stephen Larkham joining the 'youngsters'-turned-seasoned-professionals of the 1991 world cup side, the team won the 1999 world cup, a success followed by three successive Bledisloe Cup series victories. By the time the Wallabies won the Tri-Nations title in 2000, every available trophy was in their cabinet.

RUGBY LEAGUE

It is something of a coincidence that the sport that began as a breakaway from rugby union and with strong working-class appeal, has been bitterly divided by big business less than 100 years later.

For most of the twentieth century, rugby league overshadowed its close relative in Australia. Although the game was first played in the north of England in 1895, it did not appear in the antipodes until 1907 when a New Zealand team—in Australia en route to England—poached Australia's best rugby player, Herbert 'Dally' Messenger. The following April, when Messenger returned from England, nine clubs had formed the inaugural New South Wales rugby league competition, with South Sydney winning the first of its record 20 premierships.

In the early years, league relied on converts from rugby union and it received a big fillip when most of the 1908 Wallabies squad, gold medal winners at the London Olympics, switched codes. By the time league had formed its own junior base, the number of defections had decreased, although there were many notable transfers over the years, Russell Fairfax, Rex Mossop, Ray Price and Michael O'Connor among them. The most successful team of the postwar era is St George. The team hailing from Sydney's south won a staggering 11 successive premierships between 1956 and 1966. The club rugby league competition has always been more popular than its union counterpart, but bitter

Youngsters playing Aussie Rules at Mataranka in the Northern Territory. Requiring only minimal equipment, both rugby codes and Australian Rules have always been popular with the country's indigenous peoples, who have given many champions to all three football games.

SPORT TIMELINE

1810 First official horse race takes place at Hyde Park, Sydney.
1814 Convicts John Parton and Charles Sefton compete in colony's first boxing match.

1826 First club cricket match, in Hyde Park, Sydney.
1827 First sailing competition held in Tas.
1829 Soldiers in Sydney play first football match.

1851 Victoria and Tasmania meet in the first intercolonial cricket match.
1858 Group led by Tom Wills sets some rules for Australian Rules football.

1865 First club football match played in Sydney; following rules of rugby union.
1868 Aboriginal cricket team tours Britain.

1877 Australia wins first cricket test match against England at Melbourne Cricket Ground. Victorian Football Association (VFA) founded.

1896 Edwin Flack wins 800 m and 1500 m at Athens Olympics.
1897 Eight clubs break away from VFA to form Victorian Football League (VFL).

1928 First Australian Formula I Grand Prix, Melbourne.
1930 Phar Lap wins Melbourne Cup. First rugby league Grand Final played.

1795 First recorded game of billiards played in Australia.
1803 First cricket match played in Sydney by group of sailors.

1818 John Piper wins first recorded rowing competition, at Bradleys Head, Sydney.
1825 Sydney Turf Club founded.

1838 Melbourne Cricket Club (MCC) founded.
1842 Australian Jockey Club (AJC) founded.

1861 Victorian Turf Club runs first Melbourne Cup, won by a horse called Archer.
1862 English national cricket team tours Australia for the first time.

1873 Melbourne wins the first intercolonial regatta against teams from Sydney, Hobart, Geelong and Ballarat.

1882 Australia defeats England at the Oval, London. Stumps and bails used are burnt to commemorate 'death of English cricket'—the origin of the Ashes.

1907 Rugby league breaks away from rugby union.
1924 First Brownlow Medal awarded to Geelong player Edward Greeves.

1932 Phar Lap di Beginning of inf 'Bodyline' series o test matche
1945 First Syd Hobart Yacht Rac

power plays within the sport have undermined its appeal, with many pundits predicting the game will once again merge with rugby union.

After World War II, the wealthier Sydney clubs slowly but surely drained the playing talent from the Queensland and country competitions, leading to a disparity in representative matches between City and Country and New South Wales and Queensland.

The solution proved a watershed: State of Origin, introduced in 1980 became the pinnacle of the sport, surpassing even international football. Soon after, the league launched an ambitious expansion campaign that saw teams formed in Canberra, Perth, Wollongong, Brisbane, the Gold Coast, Newcastle, Auckland (New Zealand), Townsville, Adelaide and Melbourne. Many did not survive as the sport was ripped apart by a bitter row, inspired by Pay TV. Foundation club South Sydney was booted out of the competition in 1999, while others were forced to merge, leaving Eastern Suburbs, now the Sydney Roosters, as the only intact 1908 club.

Internationally, Australia struggled to keep up with Great Britain and France, until 1950 winning just one series against these teams. For the next 28 years, England and Australia engaged in some classic struggles, but by 1978 Australia had emerged as the dominant nation, not losing a series during the remainder of the twentieth century. Only New Zealand regularly threatened Australia's dominance, with wins in one-off test matches, and a couple of close calls in the 1985 three-test series and again in the 1999 Tri-Nation series.

Soccer

It's an anomaly, but Australia's highest-paid football players are not in its most popular code. Soccer has one of the largest junior participation rates, but can't convert this strong foundation to mass spectator interest. The problem is twofold. Clubs originally formed along national lines dominate the domestic competition, with those of Italian, Serb, Greek and Croat descent predominating, thus narrowing the following of each team. On top of this, all the top players go overseas to chase their fortunes, and with Australian audiences used to the best in cricket, AFL and the rugby codes, watching second-tier soccer players compete at club level holds little appeal. Indeed, the English Premier League is more popular with Australians than is the National Soccer League (NSL).

What began as a trickle has become a flood. It started with Joe Marston in the 1950s; he played for Preston North End in the English FA Cup final in 1954, and the turn of the century saw more than 50 Australians playing in the European professional leagues. Most notable of these are Harry Kewell and Mark Viduka at Leeds and Mark Bosnich who went to Manchester United and now plays at Chelsea.

The NSL didn't kick off in Australia until 1977, and although leagues were formed from 1880, the game didn't really get a start until the huge boom in immigration following World War II. Clubs such as Sydney Prague, St George Budapest, Perth's Azzuri and South Melbourne Hellas sprang into being. With their unscrupulous recruiting of overseas talent, these clubs angered FIFA, the world governing body, and earned Australia a brief international ban in the late 1950s and early 1960s.

Internationally, Australia has made soccer's world cup finals only once—in Germany in 1974—but at junior level they have performed much better, with a second place in the 1999 Under-17 World Championship and a fourth place at the Barcelona Olympics. Perhaps Australia's effort in qualifying for the 1998 world cup sums up the state of the sport in Australia. After leading Iran 2–0, with 20 minutes to play in front of a packed crowd at the MCG, two defensive lapses allowed the Iranians to equalise, with the Persian Gulf country booking the last place for the finals. For Australia it was another case of so much promise, too few results.

The great Mal Meninga in full flight. Playing Rugby League for Australia in no less than 18 test matches, Meninga always gave 100 per cent of his talents for his team and is among the great indigenous players who have graced the game.

an Bradman retires average of 99.94. Walter Lindrum naving remained as world billiards on since 1932.

1960 Playing against the West Indies in a test match, Alan Davidson takes 10 wickets and scores 120 runs. At Rome Olympics, Herb Elliott wins 1500 m on track.

1965 Peter Thompson wins British Open for fifth time.
1966 St George wins its eleventh successive rugby league premiership.

1970 Margaret Court becomes second woman to win tennis Grand Slam. AFL Grand Final between Carlton and Collingwood draws a record crowd of 121,696.
1977 Kerry Packer establishes World Series cricket competition.

1976 Heather McKay wins first Women's World Squash Championship.

1982 Brisbane hosts XII Commonwealth Games. Mark Richards wins fourth successive world surfing championship.
1983 *Australia II* wins America's Cup.

1990 Greg Norman wins US PGA Championship.
1991 Jeff Fenech wins his fourth world boxing title.
1995 Australian cricket team wins Sir Frank Worrell Trophy.

1998 Pat Rafter wins second successive US Open. Mick Doohan wins fifth 500cc motorcycle championship.
1999 Wallabies win rugby union World Cup.

1956 Olympic Games held in Melbourne. Australia wins 35 medals. Peter Thompson wins British Open golf championship for third successive year.

1964 Midget Farrelly wins first amateur world surfing championship. Dawn Fraser becomes first woman to win the same title (100 m freestyle) at three successive Olympics.

1968 Aboriginal boxer Lionel Rose wins world bantamweight title.
1969 Rod Laver wins fourth Wimbledon title and second Grand Slam.

1972 At Munich Olympics, Shane Gould wins record five medals and sprinter Raelene Boyle wins two silvers.
1974 Australia reaches the soccer World Cup finals.

1980 Evonne Goolagong wins Wimbledon.
1981 Australian Institute of Sport (AIS) opens. In golf, David Graham becomes first Australian to win US Open.

1984 Wallabies win first Grand Slam during tour of UK. Robert de Castella wins Boston Marathon.
1987 Pat Cash wins Wimbledon Championship.

1996 At Atlanta Olympics, Australia wins 41 medals, including 9 golds. At the Paralympics, Louise Sauvage wins four gold medals on the track.

2000 Sydney stages Olympic Games. Australia wins 58 medals, including 16 golds. Ian Thorpe wins three golds in the pool. Wallabies win Tri-Nations Title.

Olympic Games

Olympic Games

There can be little doubt that Australia is one of the cornerstone countries of the Olympic movement. Along with Greece and France, this country has sent a team to every Summer Games since Frenchman Baron de Coubertin resurrected the ancient sporting festival in Athens in 1896. The 2000 Olympic Games in Sydney saw the return of the event to our shores, Melbourne having hosted the 1956 games. This makes Australia one of only five countries to have hosted the world's number one sporting event more than once.

Australia's performances at Olympic level are quite astonishing; especially when one takes into account the cost of sending a team of amateur athletes to the other side of the world. In the early days, when teams travelled by ship, the athletes had to forgo training for anything up to two months while they made the long and arduous journey to Europe and North America.

When the games were revived in 1896—five years before Australia's federation—Australia was represented by Melbourne-born accountant Edwin Flack, who was based in England at the time. Despite the English attempts to claim him as their own, Flack insisted he represented Australia and went on to win the 800 and 1500 m and he also led the inaugural marathon inside the last five miles before collapsing.

Four years later, Australia sent another small team to Paris, and this time tasted success in the sport that would make the country famous: swimming. In the river Seine, Fred Lane claimed first place in both the 200 m freestyle and 200 m obstacle race. Shooter Donald Mackintosh won gold in the live-pigeon event but argument still rages as to whether his event was part of the program or merely an exhibition.

In the ensuing 40 years Australia would win only 12 gold medals, with notable achievements by Sarah 'Fanny' Durack in 1912—the first-ever female swimming gold medallist—and the great Bobby Pearce, who won back-to-back single sculls in Amsterdam, 1928, and in the 1932 Los Angeles Games.

From 1952 onwards, Australia found its place at the Olympics. Not only did Melbourne beat Buenos Aires by one vote to host the 1956 Games, but Australia unleashed a range of champions on the world, women champions in particular. Stars such as Betty Cuthbert, Marjorie Jackson, Dawn Fraser and Shirley Strickland won 13 gold medals between 1952 and

The gymnastics sculpture at the Australian Institute of Sport in Australia's national capital.

RIGHT: *The long journey across Australia of the Olympic Flame was notable for its nationwide spirit of cooperation.*

Australian sports fans are known for their willingness to cheer for all contestants 'game to have a go', regardless of the teams they represent. The photograph shows some of the crowds that lined the route of the women's marathon at the 2000 Olympics in Sydney.

A less-frenetic decade. The low-key opening of the 1956 Olympic Games in Melbourne, Victoria. Australia won 13 gold medals in three sports at what were called the 'friendly Games'.

1964. Since that time Australia has finished in the top 10 on the medal table nine times in 13 attempts, with a best placing of third (in Melbourne), and winning its most gold medals ever (16) and highest total of medals (58) at Sydney 2000.

But it's been in the pool that Australia has asserted its dominance, with only the USA winning more gold medals in Olympic history. Apart from Dawn Fraser, such greats as Murray Rose, David Theile, Kieren Perkins and Susie O'Neill have won golds at successive games, while others such as teenage sensations Shane Gould, who won three gold medals in Munich 1972, and Ian Thorpe, three golds in Sydney, have captured the nation's heart.

In the early days, Australia relied on what seemed a natural propensity for sport, and success was limited to a few disciplines. In Melbourne, 13 gold medals came in just three sports: swimming (eight), athletics (four) and cycling (one). Over the next 16 years, the nation would enjoy gold-medal success in just two other sports: equestrian (two gold medals in 1960) and sailing (one gold in 1960 and two in 1972).

By 1976, Australia could no longer rely solely on its sporting lifestyle to achieve international success. The Eastern Bloc was enabling its athletes to become what amounted to full-time professionals, while the use of drugs was becoming rampant. Not surprisingly, Australia came home empty handed and this result prompted swift reaction from the Commonwealth Government, led by Malcolm Fraser, and the much acclaimed Australian Institute of Sport was created.

Although results were not immediately evident—Australia won two gold medals in Moscow 1980, four in Los Angeles 1984 and three in Seoul 1998 by the 1990s the hundreds of millions of invested dollars

Shirley Strickland was already 23 when she represented Australia at the London Olympics in 1948, where she became the first Australian woman to win an Olympic medal in athletics. A gifted hurdler and sprinter, she won a total of seven Olympic medals and at 31 competed in her third Olympics at Melbourne, winning gold in the 80 m hurdles and the 4 x 100 m relay.

began to pay dividends. After Melbourne, where just three sports yielded gold, Australia had diversified its sports base in a more competitive environment. At the magical Barcelona Games, Australia won seven gold medals in five sports. In Atlanta it was nine golds in six. And with the advantage of home-crowd support, the country won 16 golds in 11 sports at Sydney. Furthermore, they won medals in a total of 20 sports at those 2000 Games.

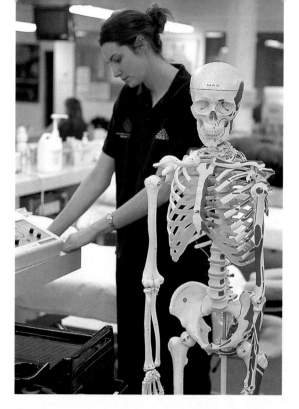

Commonwealth Games

Australia's love for multi-sport competition doesn't end with the Olympics. Beginning life as the Empire Games and first held in 1930 at Hamilton, Canada, the quadrennial Commonwealth Games is arguably more popular in Australia than anywhere else. While some countries have problems convincing their best athletes to attend, Australia has no such trouble; such is the esteem in which this competition held.

Not surprisingly, Australia has also been the most successful country at the Commonwealth Games, with 564 gold medals—77 more than our nearest rival, England—and a total of 1,474 medals in all, 55 more than that country.

Wheelchair basketball at the 2000 Paralympics in Sydney. In common with many other venues at these popular games, the basketball Super Dome was jam-packed for every match.

Paralympic Games

Australia has also embraced the Paralympics since their introduction in 1960, and has been one of the most successful participants. Early records are patchy, but Australia finished second in the medal tally in Atlanta and went one better at home in Sydney. Such a triumph of organisation were those games that the President of the International Paralympic Committee, Dr Robert Steadward, declared them not only the best ever, but unlikely ever to be matched. And to say that the Australian public took the 2000 Paralympics to its heart would be an understatement. The ABC, Australia's public radio and television network and host broadcaster of the games, enjoyed record ratings, while day after day, Homebush Bay was jam-packed with spectators, in particular schoolchildren. Ticket sales were a Paralympic record.

The success of the Sydney Paralympics was due partly to the public recognition of disabled athletes such as Louise Sauvage (track), Priya Cooper (swimming) and David Hall (tennis), for, with the possible exception of the United Kingdom, Australia is the only country in the world where Paralympians are household names. Sauvage's record is phenomenal: winner of eight paralympic gold medals and 11 world championships, winner of the 800 m exhibition races at the Sydney and Atlanta Olympics, not to mention three successive Boston Marathons. Named International Disabled Athlete of the Year in 1999, Sauvage in 1997 won the Australian Institute of Sport's Athlete of the Year award, the first disabled athlete to do so.

It is to be hoped that recent revelations of ring-ins on some Paralympic teams will not mar these games to the extent that the public turns away from them.

Court Sports

Tennis

Australia is the world's most successful tennis nation after the United States. Since Sir Norman Brookes first won Wimbledon in 1907, there has not been a decade in which an Australian has not held one of the four Grand Slam titles. In the 1940s, 1950s and again in the 1960s, Australia dominated the tennis scene, winning more Grand Slam tournaments and Davis Cups than any other country.

Players such as Rod Laver, Margaret Court and Roy Emerson dominated the scene, and after tennis turned professional in 1968, John Newcombe and a young Evonne Goolagong (later Cawley) kept Australia at the forefront of the game. Since Goolagong's last victory at Wimbledon in 1980, successes for Australians have been few and far between, with Pat Cash at Wimbledon in 1987, and Pat Rafter's back-to-back US Opens in 1997–98, the country's only high spots. One of the surprise packets in this patch otherwise barren of successes was the Woodies, Todd Woodbridge and Mark Woodforde. They notched up a record tally of doubles Grand Slams, including six Wimbledons, and Olympic gold and silver medals.

Basketball

Like soccer, basketball suffers because the world's best don't compete here, and although the exodus is not as great, Australia's top four or five players have all gone overseas. While basketball is a very popular sport, the National Basketball League (NBL) has been sagging somewhat in recent years, with the American NBA dominating not only the fans' interest but also the lucrative merchandising market.

The NBL was the boom competition during the 1980s and the results filtered through to the international arena, where Australia finished fourth in three of the four Olympics from 1988. However, it's the women's team that's been the real success story.

While the WNBL might fail to attract substantial sponsorship and crowds, it has acted as one of the world's great nurseries. Australia is the largest foreign presence in the world's premier competition, the American WNBA, and the national team has won bronze and silver medals at the past two Olympics.

The sport has come a long way in 50 years. Barely noticeable in 1950, local club competitions grew stronger in the 1960s, and with the help of imported north Americans, the sport was strong enough to start a national league in 1979. Father–son combination Lindsay and Andrew Gaze have done more for the sport than any. As either player or coach, one or the other has represented Australia at every Olympics since 1960. Andrew also won a NBA Championship ring with the San Antonio Spurs in 1999, one of only two Australians to do so, the other being Luc Longley (Chicago Bulls 1996–98).

Netball

Although not as glamorous as basketball, netball has the highest junior-participant rate among Australian girls. The Australian team dominates the world scene, having won seven of the nine world championships as well as the inaugural Commonwealth Games title. Along with our cricket and rugby teams, the netball team is one of the most revered of all the national sides. Its recent dominance has been so strong that between 1991 and 2000, the team lost just three games.

Few countries can match Australia's efforts in the sporting arenas of the world, both on a relative and absolute scale. While good facilities and a favourable climate have no doubt played an important part, it's the national attitude that has made all the difference: while winning is great, it's giving it your best shot that Australians value—and this is the ultimate reason for their country's sporting pre-eminence.

Hobart's Royal Tennis Court was opened in 1875.

LEFT: Tennis champion Evonne Goolagong, later Evonne Cawley, is arguably one of the two most admired Aboriginal sportswomen to come out of Australia, Cathy Freeman being the other. World champion on both clay and grass at age 19, Goolagong's tennis was described by Rex Bellamy of The Times as 'so beautiful that at times it chilled the blood'.

Jacinta Hamilton in training at the Australian Institute of Sport's basketball facility. Australian women dominate the foreign presence in the USA's WNBA and an Australian team has won medals at the past two Olympics.

PART 2

PLACES IN AUSTRALIA

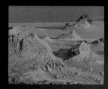

VICTORIA

Merbein • ● **Mildura**
Red Cliffs •

Robinvale •
Murray
Wemen •

Ouyen • Piangil •

Patchewollock • *Lake Tyrrell* Swan Hill •
Sea Lake •

Hopetoun • Barham •
Kerang •
Cohuna •
Birchip • Wycheproof • Gunbower •

Cobram •
Yarrawonga • Rutherglen •
Wodonga ●
Lake Hume

Echucha •
Warracknabeal • Charlton •
Rochester • Kyabram •
Lake Mokoan **Wangaratta** ●

Nhill • Wedderburn • *Ovens* Myrtleford •
Kaniva • Rushworth • **Shepparton** ● *Mt Bogong 1986 m (6514 ft)*
Dimboola • Inglewood • Murchison • Benalla • Bright •
Murtoa • St Arnaud • Euroa • Whitfield • *Mount*
Horsham • *Lake Eppalock* Heathcote • *Waranga Basin* **Bendigo** ● Maldon • *Mt Featbertop 1923 m (6307 ft)* ▲ Hotham •
Lake Lonsdale Maryborough • Castlemaine • Seymour • Mansfield • Mt Buller •
Stawell • Avoca • *Lake Eildon* *Mt Buller 1805 m (5920 ft)*
Halls Gap • Broadford • Yea • Eildon •
Ararat • *River* Daylesford • Kyneton • Dargo •
Dergholm • *Rocklands Reservoir* Creswick • Kilmore •
Beaufort • Woodend • *Goulburn* Licola •
Lake Burrumbeet **Ballarat** ● Ballan • Sunbury • *River* Bai •
Coleraine • Bacchus Marsh • Melton • Healesville • **GREAT DIVIDI**
Casterton • Hamilton • **MELBOURNE** ★ Warburton • *Lake Thompson* Walhalla • Maffra •
Merino • Penshurst • Werribee • Heyfield • *Lake Wellington*
Digby • Lismore • *French I* Warragul • Moe • Sale •
Dartmoor • Macarthur • Mortlake • Cranbourne • Trafalgar • **Traralgon** ●
Nelson • Camperdown • **Geelong** ● Mornington • Morwell ●
Heywood • Terang • Winchelsea • Queenscliff • Korumburra • Yarram •
Warrnambool ● Allansford • Ocean Grove • Sorrento • Rosebud • Leongatha • Seaspray •
Portland • *Portland Bay* Port Fairy • Cobden • Colac • Torquay • Cowes • Wonthaggi •
Cape Bridgewater • Cape Nelson • Gellibrand • Lorne • *Phillip Island* Venus Bay •
Discovery Bay Port Campbell • *Otway Range* *Mornington Peninsula* *Snake I*
Apollo Bay • *Corner Inlet*
Cape Otway • Cape Liptrap • *Wilsons Promontory*
Waratah Bay Tidal River •
South East Point

B A S S   S T R A I T
● Rodondo I ● Hogan I

▲

NORTH

0   50   100   kilometres
0   50   miles

● Curtis I Kent

VICTORIA

The State of Victoria, in the south-east of Australia, offers an enormous range of attractions: you can dine out at one of the many magnificent restaurants of Melbourne, take a drive along the Great Ocean Road and view the rugged western coastline, play a round of golf in the north of the State beside the mighty Murray River or look over the magnificent snow-capped Great Dividing Range from a chalet at a ski resort.

Victoria is a small state, so the ideal way to tour is by road—magnificent beaches, the desert country in the north-west and many of the state's national parks or reserves are all only a day trip from Melbourne. The capital of Victoria, Melbourne, located on Port Phillip Bay, is a vibrant city. It hosts many international events, including the Australian Formula One Grand Prix and the country's biggest horse race, the Melbourne Cup. There is the diverse beach culture of St Kilda, and beautiful parkland along the Yarra River. The city also features an exotic range of excellent restaurants, museums, the Crown Casino, exciting nightlife and world-class sporting venues, plus parks and gardens which can be explored by foot or bicycle. There is a great tramway system for getting around town.

To the north-east of Melbourne are the Yarra Valley and the Dandenong Ranges, home to a number of Victoria's wineries. This region is favoured by Melburnians for quiet retreats. The Dandenong Ranges are full of lush, ferny forests, and a drive along the scenic road to the top of Mount Dandenong offers magnificent mountain scenery. Once at the top, there is a panoramic view of the city of Melbourne and the surrounding area, all the way out to Port Phillip Bay.

Melbourne and much of Central Victoria were built from the profits of the gold rush that swept the area in the mid- to late 1800s. The goldfields region, bordered by Bendigo, Ballarat and Maryborough, is an hour from Melbourne. Bendigo and Ballarat are large towns, and have many attractions, including the goldfields theme park, Sovereign Hill. The small towns of Castlemaine and Maldon, with their wide streets and restored historic buildings (which are now antique and cottage craft shops), will also take you back in time.

After several days of strong cold wind, ice has formed behind this sign to Mount Loch, near Mount Hotham, on the Alpine Highway.

Sovereign Hill in Ballarat is an authentic reconstruction of a nineteenth-century goldmining township.

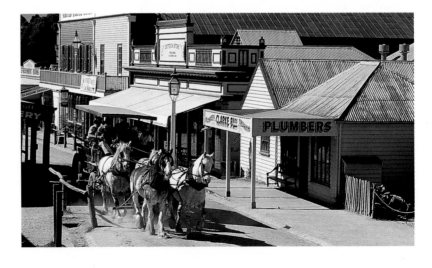

Capital
Melbourne
Area
227 420 sq. km
(87 814 sq. miles)
Proportion of Australia
3%
Population of State
4 660 900
Population Density
20.5 per sq. km
(53.1 per sq. mile)
Population of Capital
3 371 300
Time Zone
10 hours ahead of GMT
Climate
Warm-temperate with
no dry season in east
and drier summers in
west
Highest Point
Mt Bogong 1986 m
(6516 ft)

The Goulburn River starts its journey from the Murray River on the New South Wales border and winds its way down through the centre of the State to Lake Eildon, less than three hours' drive from Melbourne. There is a large irrigation system running off the Goulburn River throughout this region, and the area now supports a prosperous dairy and fruit-growing industry. The waters of the Goulburn also feed into many reservoirs—Lake Nagambie and Lake Eildon in particular are popular with water sports enthusiasts and anglers.

Perched on the extreme western edge of the Great Dividing Range to the west of Melbourne is a series of blue peaks, known as Gariwerd, which forms a striking outline on the horizon. This rugged mass of sandstone pinnacles, part of the Grampians National Park, is very popular with walkers, abseilers and climbers. During spring the whole region is covered in a mosaic of colourful wildflowers; in winter, water tumbles down over the rugged escarpments to waterways below. This region is a haven for wildlife, and many birdwatchers frequent the area, especially in spring.

Winding its way along the west Victorian coastline, the Great Ocean Road—originally built to honour those who served in World War I—offers some of the world's most spectacular coastal scenery, including the famous natural sculptures known as the Twelve Apostles and London Bridge. Sandy beaches nestle between towering cliffs and dolphins and whales can sometimes be seen playing in the roaring seas to the south. The Great Ocean Road leads to some of Victoria's best surfing locations and most popular coastal holiday towns. Many ships have met their end on the rugged western coastline, and the region is often referred to as the 'Shipwreck Coast'. The whole coast from Port Phillip Bay to the border of Victoria and South Australia and beyond is popular with divers, as they can explore many of the wrecks which foundered there.

The peninsula region of South Gippsland, south-east of Melbourne, also has plenty to offer visitors, including the magnificent Wilsons Promontory National Park. This park is one of Victoria's oldest, and features a great diversity of environments—lush rainforests and coastal heathland, granite landscapes and pristine beaches. The park has many walking tracks, of varying lengths and difficulties.

Closer to Melbourne is the nature wonderland of Phillip Island. It is here that you will find one of Victoria's greatest international attractions, the Penguins on Parade. Every evening thousands of penguins swim to the shores of this island to return to their burrows. The island is also home to seals and koalas, and offers excellent surfing and swimming—it is the perfect seaside holiday destination. It is connected to the mainland by a bridge.

Gippsland is a rich dairy farming district and is also rich in coal deposits, which have been mined since the 1800s. Coal Creek, in Korumburra, is a theme park which outlines the history of coalmining in Victoria. Tours of the large power stations in the heart of Gippsland offer an insight into the State's energy system.

Further east, right next to the coast, lies the magnificent lakes district, bordered by the Ninety Mile Beach. Here you can sail in the protected waters of the lakes, or head out to the open sea at Lakes Entrance. A major fishing region, Lakes Entrance is another ideal holiday destination. Croajingolong National Park, in the far south-east of the State, is an important coastal parkland. Cool freshwater streams trickle down the mountains through temperate rainforests, then filter through the sand dunes and merge with the sea. This region is popular with campers, walkers and anglers.

The ubiquitous pied currawong (Strepera graculina).

The Great Dividing Range cuts through the centre of Victoria and is often referred to as the High Country. Here towns nestle in valleys between towering mountains. This is also where the legends of the High Country were made—there are still cattle wandering over the mountains, and cattlemen riding their horses across this vast mountain wilderness.

During the winter months, snow covers the peaks and numerous resorts offer superb skiing, with plenty of ski lifts and excellent accommodation and restaurants. Mount Buller and Mount Baw Baw are only three hours' drive from Melbourne; the larger peaks of Hotham, Falls Creek and Mount Buffalo are further to the north-east.

Melburnians have a special weekend spa retreat less than two hours' drive from town over the Macedon Ranges. The delightful towns of Daylesford and Hepburn Springs are rich in history, and very picturesque, but it is the soothing mineral waters, along with fine dining, excellent wineries and peaceful surroundings, that beckon visitors to this region. Mount Macedon is also a popular weekend retreat, offering stunning views and magnificent old gardens and parks with many walking tracks.

With its beginnings in the High Country to the north-east of the State, the Murray River winds its way along the northern border of Victoria. The Murray provides all sorts of holiday opportunities. For a start, it is home to some of Victoria's best golf courses. Paddle-steamers once transported goods along the river, and though houseboats and ski-boats have now replaced these old vessels, some fine, restored paddle-steamers are still in operation as cruise vessels along the mighty Murray.

The opening of the Great Ocean Road in 1932 greatly increased traffic to the Victorian coastal towns. However, many of the seaside towns, such as Lorne, have remained relatively unspoilt.

At Ninety Mile Beach near Lakes Entrance, the lakes are separated from the ocean by only a thin strip of sand dunes.

Once an inland port, the major town of Echuca lies north of Melbourne on the shores of the Murray. It is one of Victoria's more popular historic tourist towns. Here you can either stay in one of the many hotels or camp along the banks of the river, surrounded by red gum trees and waking to the calls of the Major Mitchell cockatoos.

Proving just how diverse Victoria is, the north-west of the State features a desert oasis that is enormously rich in wildlife and flora—numerous parks and reserves have been created to protect the region's fragile environment. In this area the waters of the Murray River flow out into small streams and creeks and form lakes in the Hattah–Kulkyne National Park, creating a haven for bird life. The Murray–Sunset Park is a different environment again, with undulating sand hills covered in mallee scrub, and heathlands opening up to a series of pink salt lakes.

A complex irrigation system around Swan Hill and Mildura allows the far north-west to produce copious amounts of citrus fruit as well as grapes for sultanas.

Scattered across the State, from the north-west desert country through to the coastal peninsula areas, are the wine regions of Victoria. This State has been producing fine wines since the late 1800s, and today has more than 230 operating wineries. Popular regions include the Yarra Valley, the Mornington and Bellarine peninsulas, the Macedon Ranges and Rutherglen.

At many of the smaller wineries you can talk to the winemakers and sit out under a shady gum tree for a picnic on the premises. The larger vineyards have restaurants, where the menu complements the wines. All the major wine regions have a festival during the year to celebrate their produce.

Victoria is a great holiday destination, and with so many attractions, the most difficult decision for any traveller will be choosing which way to go.

The MacKenzie Falls are one of the spectacular sights along the Wonderland trail in Grampians National Park in central-western Victoria.

MELBOURNE

A mural from Queen Victoria Market—a Melbourne institution that was first built in 1878. Many of the market's buildings have been classified as historic by the National Trust.

Melbourne, Victoria's elegant capital, is truly one of the world's most varied cities, with a lifestyle envied by many. The city is not only the financial focal point of Australia; it is equally renowned for its tree-lined streets and for the delightful parklands and gardens that hug the Yarra River. With beaches and bayside suburbs lining Port Phillip Bay, and the Dandenong Ranges providing a backdrop to the north-east, this picturesque city has much to offer both residents and visitors.

The township of Melbourne was originally settled by graziers, the first being John Batman, who 'purchased' land from the local Indigenous peoples north of Port Phillip Bay. Many other graziers also ventured to the rich river flats of the Yarra River, without permission. Captain William Lonsdale was sent from Sydney to negotiate the land sales in this region. The township was established in 1835, named after the then British Prime Minister Lord Melbourne, and was integrated into New South Wales. It was not until 1851 that Victoria became a separate colony.

The city is set out following a typical nineteenth-century pattern—there is a grid system of streets, all named after early settlers and dignitaries. The main streets leading away from the main railway station, Spencer Street Station, are King, William, Queen, and Elizabeth, then you reach the main shopping area of Swanston Street.

The architecture of Melbourne retains a mix of styles—the ANZ Bank building is in the Gothic style, the Town Hall is art deco, and there are many modern skyscrapers. There are several fine buildings in the city, many of which were financed by the gold rush of the mid- to late 1800s. Examples of such buildings include the Magistrates Court, the Town Hall, the State Library and the Exhibition Buildings, which have been restored and are surrounded by magnificent gardens. There are also some impressive churches, including St Paul's and St Patrick's

cathedrals, both of which have undergone extensive renovations. Como House in Toorak is an elegant Victorian mansion surrounded by superb gardens, and the Block Arcade, built in the 1890s and fully restored, is a wonderful centre for shoppers. One of the more unusual buildings of Melbourne is the Adelphi Hotel, which has a swimming pool that juts out over Flinders Lane, offering swimmers a view of the busy streetscape below.

A great way to get to most of Melbourne's attractions is by taking a free Circle Tram ride. The Circle Trams are a distinctive burgundy colour, not the traditional green of other Melbourne trams, and they circle the city along Flinders, Spencer, LaTrobe and Spring Streets. For visitors, the numerous attractions in the city of Melbourne are perhaps best appreciated on a guided tour, which can be organised through the tourist office in the city. The Yarra River is an integral part of the city and a cruise along the waterway is another lovely way to view the city. For views of the city, try the Rialto Towers Observation Deck, Melbourne's tallest building, which offers a superb 360-degree view of the city and the surrounding area.

The original Government House, which occupied LaTrobe Cottage, and the present-day Government House can both be toured. The Melbourne Stock Exchange also offers tours, and the Bureau of Meteorology's self-guided tour presents an impressive display, which includes interactive television screens. The Old Melbourne Gaol depicts life in a nineteenth-century Australian prison. It is here that Victorian hangings took place, 135 in total, including the infamous bushranger Ned Kelly—death masks made of those hanged can be viewed.

The Old Treasury building, one of the more significant nineteenth-century buildings in Melbourne, underwent a significant restoration in 1994. It features changing exhibitions representing various aspects of Australian history. Built in 1872, the Royal Mint hosts two major displays, one pertaining to the Royal Mint, the other set up by the Royal Historical Society of Melbourne, and providing a comprehensive history of Melbourne.

Melbourne has many parks, used by city dwellers and workers for relaxation, picnicking, or jogging in beautiful surroundings. The Royal Botanic Gardens, established in 1846, are world famous. With large exotic trees and some plants that are now 150 years old, these gardens are among Melbourne's finest. Set on the banks of the Yarra River, they are also home to a number of majestic black swans and flying foxes, or fruit bats. In the 32-ha (79-acre) Fitzroy and Treasury Gardens is a stone building that once stood in Great Ayrton, England. Built in 1755, it was Captain Cook's childhood home. The building was bought in 1933 by Sir Russell Grimwade and rebuilt in the

An aerial view of Melbourne, showing Albert Park in the centre—the site of the Formula One Grand Prix each March.

gardens as a monument to the great explorer. Other beautiful parklands include the Queen Victoria Gardens, which feature a magnificent floral clock 9 m (30 feet) in diameter—more than 7000 plants are used to create this intricate floral display. The clock actually tells the time and is synchronised to chime with the clock on the Town Hall.

The Royal Melbourne Zoological Gardens are on the edge of the city, and with over 3500 animals, the zoo is considered one of the world's finest. During the summer months Melbourne Zoo holds a Twilight Jazz Festival, and patrons bring picnic hampers and enjoy the music in very unusual surroundings. Within an hour's drive of the city there are two other excellent wildlife parks: the Werribee Zoo and the Healesville Sanctuary.

Life is never boring in this city—if there isn't a major sporting event scheduled, then there is probably a festival. Often there are both! A diverse mix of races and cultures sees Melbourne come alive with a variety of exciting and unusual carnivals year round.

The Melbourne Food and Wine Festival runs for approximately three weeks from mid-March, celebrating the diversity of Melbourne, Australia's culinary capital, through 120 outstanding events. This feast of a festival includes the internationally acclaimed Master Class, the Hawkers' Market and the World's Longest Lunch, plus Breakfast Week, Restaurant Week, Chocolate Week and many more delicious events. The Formula One Grand Prix and the Melbourne International Motor Show, both huge and exhilarating events in their own right, coincide with this festival.

There are more festivals in March, including the Yarra Valley Grape Grazing Festival, which involves a number of wineries in the Yarra Valley Region. This region produces some of Australia's best wine, and during the festival food from a selection of restaurants is matched up with wines from the local wineries to create gastronomic delights. Jazz adds to the festival feel of this event.

Festivities head indoors during the winter months, with the

The Brunswick Street Festival takes place in the bohemian inner-city suburb of Fitzroy.

Melbourne International Film Festival and Victoria State Opera season. Spring brings Melburnians outside again for the Royal Melbourne Show and a range of horticultural shows in September. The outdoor tradition flows through to Christmas, and thousands of Melburnians head to the Myer Music Bowl on Christmas Eve for the ever-popular 'Carols By Candlelight' concert.

Melbourne people's love of sport, whether it be football, tennis, car racing or a sport totally foreign to Victoria, such as rugby, is well documented. Many large sporting events are held in Melbourne.

Melbourne is the home of Australian Rules Football, and a visit to Melbourne should include a trip to the Melbourne Cricket Ground (MCG). As well as cricket being played in summer—notably the Boxing Day Test—the Aussie Rules Grand Final is held here on the third Saturday of every September. Tours of the venue are available and include a walk on the hallowed turf of the MCG. During Grand Final week the whole city

The beautiful domed architecture of Flinders Street Railway Station, completed in 1899, was the result of a design competition.

Unlike other Australian cities, Melbourne has retained its popular and efficient tram system that runs along the north–south, east–west grid pattern of Melbourne's roads.

After the strong economic boom of the 1980s, the city of Melbourne has managed to retain the reputation of being Australia's financial centre.

has football fever; it is a great time to visit and there are a number of celebrations in the city.

Every January, Melbourne Park is the venue for the Australian Open, the first Grand Slam tennis event of the year. The main feature of this impressive tennis venue is the centre court roof, which can be opened or closed. With Melbourne's reputation for having four seasons in one day, this has proved very useful. Melbourne Park is also the venue for concerts and productions all through the year, and the outside courts are available for hire.

Melbourne also hosts the first round of the Formula One Grand Prix season each year, in March, and this is another really exciting time to be in Melbourne—the Albert Park Lake area is transformed into an award-winning racetrack and thousands of people join in the festivities, which run over four days. Grand Prix ticket holders have free travel on the Melbourne trams, and after the racing each day the city comes alive as race-goers head towards the restaurants, clubs or the Melbourne International Motor Show.

Horseracing is very popular in Melbourne, and there is excellent racing at the Autumn and Spring Racing carnivals. The Spring Carnival features the Melbourne Cup, Australia's most famous horse race—it is run on the first Tuesday in November, which is a public holiday for Victorians. The festivities that have developed around this horse race are fabulous, and it is an Australian tradition to have a bet on the race, even if you are not a regular punter. Thousands of Melburnians go along on race day and have some fun, with many dressing up in either their Sunday best—including, most importantly, a hat—or fancy dress.

The annual 500cc Motorcycle Grand Prix is held at Phillip Island, to the south of Melbourne. The Australian International Airshow is an exciting biennial event held in Victoria, and features aircraft from all around the world, demonstrating the latest innovations in aviation and aerospace technology. The Airshow is held at the Avalon Airport near Geelong during February.

Melbourne is an ideal destination for shoppers, and has its own fashion festival in summer. In the centre of Melbourne there are a couple of splendid arcades where you can shop in beautiful and historic surroundings: the Block Arcade and the Royal Arcade. Large shopping complexes include Melbourne Central, which features a number of retail outlets, including the Japanese-owned department store Daimaru. This magnificent building has a large glass pyramid roof and shot tower. Nearby are the Myer and David Jones department stores. The Crown Entertainment Complex and Southgate also have an enormous range of exclusive shops, many of them outlets for overseas designer products. In the suburbs, you will find streets which are considered 'the' places to shop for particular things—Chapel Street in South Yarra for fashion, Bridge Road, Richmond, for seconds outlets, High Street, Armadale, for exclusive boutiques and Maling Road, Canterbury, for antiques.

Queen Victoria Market is the place to go for fresh produce and a bargain. It has over 1000 traders offering everything from fresh fruit and seafood through to clothing and leather goods. This historic complex was established in 1878 and is the largest outdoor market in the world.

The city of Melbourne has a large migrant population, and the food and restaurants are influenced by this diversity of cultures: almost any international cuisine is available, and many innovative mixtures are created as well.

Though the central business district of Melbourne features many fine restaurants, the city is traditionally split into cultural sectors: Lygon Street in Carlton for Italian and Richmond for Vietnamese or Greek

The Retro Café is one of the most popular eating places in Brunswick Street, Fitzroy.

the stunning modern $300 million building is an architectural feat in itself. The Museum's priceless collections, which include Aboriginal displays, the famous racehorse Phar Lap, and dinosaur displays, combined with performance, technology and interactive exhibitions, will surely inspire delight and wonder in its visitors.

The Immigration Museum, in the Old Customs House building on Flinders Street, is a contemporary museum that brings Victoria's immigration history to life through voices, images, memories and objects.

The Shrine of Remembrance, which stands proudly between Domain and St Kilda Roads, is, a memorial to the people who served Australia in the wars of the nineteenth and twentieth centuries. It features 42 books of remembrance, which contain the names of 116,000 Victorians who served overseas during World War I. A fascinating feature of the Shrine of Remembrance is the inner sanctuary and the stone of remembrance, which is lit by sunlight precisely at 11 am on 11 November—Remembrance Day—every year.

Scienceworks is a science and technology centre with interactive displays which are very popular with both children and adults alike. This centre is built around an old pumping station in Spotswood and is open every day. The Melbourne Planetarium is also to be found here—it is the only planetarium in the Southern Hemisphere with a state-of-the-art computer system that simulates the experience of moving through the universe.

The Melbourne Maritime Museum has, as its central exhibit, the tall ship *Polly Woodside,* which was built in Belfast in 1885.

When all the sights, sounds, smells and tastes of Melbourne are combined and added to the sheer excitement of its many sporting and arts events and festivals, it's easy to see why Melbourne is such a popular holiday destination for Australian and overseas visitors— and why it is so much loved and enjoyed by those who live there.

food, to name just two. Little Bourke Street is the home of Little China, where you will find superb Chinese cuisine. Melbourne loves to celebrate the Chinese New Year in February, and thousands of people head to the Chinatown precinct to bring in the new year. Large dragons wind their way through the crowd, with firecrackers popping and drums beating in the background.

The suburb of Southgate, an area situated on the banks of the Yarra, features restaurants and the Crown Entertainment Complex. This enormous complex includes the Crown Casino, theatres, a hotel and many shops, clubs and restaurants. On a sunny day in Melbourne you will see people sitting at restaurants on the edge of the Yarra from St Kilda Road all the way to Spencer Street. In the evenings, this part of town comes alive again, with clubs and restaurants open until the early hours.

Melbourne also boasts many fine art galleries, covering a range of styles and types of exhibitions. The main art gallery to see here is the National Gallery of Victoria on St Kilda Road. The gallery's magnificent art collection is made up of paintings, sculptures, drawings and photographs from Australia and overseas. The National Gallery of Victoria is also opening its NGV: Australian Art museum at Federation Square, a magnificent building showcasing the country's finest collection of Australian art.

Also on St Kilda Road is the Victorian Arts Centre, which includes a number of venues for the performing arts. A feature of this centre is the tall spire on the rooftop, which changes colours at night.

The Aboriginal Gallery of Dreamings, in Bourke Street, offers Melburnians and visitors alike the chance to view works of art created by Australia's Indigenous peoples, including dot paintings, boomerangs and didgeridoos. The centre has more than 2500 paintings.

The new Melbourne Museum, next to the Royal Exhibition Buildings, is Australia's largest and the world's most technologically advanced museum—

The Queen Victoria Market is divided into an upper market (selling fruit and vegetables, as well as general wares), and a lower market (specialising in meat, fish, game, gourmet foods, delicatessens and eateries).

ADVENTURE ACTIVITIES

Victoria

Adventure sports are widely followed in Victoria, partly because the state offers such varied terrain. As in New South Wales, the Great Dividing Range is the main focus for walking, climbing, rafting and winter sports such as cross-country skiing and ski touring. However, several other areas also have large tracts of wilderness, including the Grampians, the Otways and the magnificent coastal national parks of Wilsons Promontory and Croajingolong. And even where native bush is absent, travellers can still find adventure: for example, Australia's top climbing area, Mount Arapiles, rises dramatically out of flat wheat country near Horsham in the state's west.

Bushwalking

Even within a 120-km (75-mile) radius of Melbourne, you will find an extraordinary diversity of bushwalking environments, ranging from coastline to grassy alpine plateaus and tall forests of mountain ash; and if you venture further afield, you can hike amid snow-capped peaks in the Australian Alps or through semi-desert in the far north-west—Victoria's own outback. One of the state's most visited national parks is Wilsons Promontory, which has walks of various lengths and levels of difficulty, ranging from tough four-day treks to short outings from the promontory's only settlement, Tidal River. Equally spectacular but less busy coastal walks can be found in Croajingolong National Park in the state's south-east, while the south-west has the Great South-West Walk, an eight-

Mount Arapiles offers around 2000 climbing routes—the highest number for any location in the country. Few serious climbers can resist the challenge of Kachoong, a grade-21 ascent incorporating this spectacular overhang.

to ten-day circuit departing from Portland, with half of the trail running parallel to the coast and much of the remainder following the Glenelg River.

The mountains in the eastern half of the state are ideal for summer walking. In the Alpine National Park, for example, historic bushwalking routes traverse the Wonnangatta Wilderness and the Bogong High Plains. Highlights include the four-day Wonnangatta Horseshoe (a classic crest walk across Mount Howitt and the Crosscut Saw) and the two-day Razor and Viking circuit. Shorter walks on the Mount Buffalo plateau, with its granite tors and views across the farmlands of north-east Victoria, will also give you a feel for the alpine environment.

Walks in the rain-drenched Otways wind through patches of temperate rainforest and tall eucalyptus trees. To the north-west, the dramatic Grampian Mountains feature impressive sandstone escarpments that provide magnificent views across densely wooded valleys, and an extensive network of bushwalking tracks that radiates outward from the mountains' principal settlement, Halls Gap. There is also virtually unlimited potential for off-track hiking.

Rock Climbing

Victoria is also a stronghold of rock climbing in Australia, and one of its most important mountaineering centres is the tiny settlement of Natimuk, near Mount Arapiles. The mountain itself is made of solid sandstone rising up to 200 m (656 feet) high and offers

part of the headwaters of the Murray in the north-east. The Murray Gates (on the Murray itself) also offer challenges; further downstream, the Murray is suitable for family trips in open Canadian canoes. Also at the relaxed end of the scale is the Goulburn River in the Goulburn Valley, where regular stops can be made at local wineries. Perhaps surprisingly, Melbourne's Yarra River also offers good paddling.

Occupying a sheltered valley, Mount Buffalo was the site of the first ski lifts to be built anywhere in Australia. It now offers two chairlifts and four button lifts, as well as 9 km (5.6 miles) of marked cross-country ski trails.

excellent climbs of all standards, ranging from relatively easy ascents to the most difficult in the country.

Mount Arapiles is rivalled for the quality of its climbing by the Grampians. A favourite route here among hard-core climbers is Mount Stapylton, but it is just one of dozens of challenging climbs.

The dramatic granite bluffs and slabs of Wilsons Promontory are also popular, but the principal granite climbing area in the state is the Mount Buffalo plateau. Dotted with enormous outcrops, it is also the site of spectacular Buffalo Gorge, whose North Wall measures 260 m (853 feet) and is one of Victoria's major climbing attractions.

Caving

The country around Buchan and Murrindal, close to the upper reaches of the Snowy River, provides excellent recreational caving. A different kind of subterranean sport can be found across the South Australian border at the volcanic Blue Lake in Mount Gambier; here terrific cave diving takes place in amazingly clear, fresh water.

Mountain Biking

Mountain biking is a widely practised sport in Victoria, and most regional centres have a club, a network of rides and regular competitive events. The sport is especially popular in state forests around Marysville, where there are single tracks as well as downhill courses. There are also good riding areas in the north-east of the state around Bright and Mount Beauty. Elsewhere, the Brisbane Ranges close to Melbourne and Geelong, and Mount Cole near Ararat offer challenging sport.

Canoeing, Kayaking and Rafting

Paddlers have a wide range of waterways to choose from in Victoria. The upper reaches of the Snowy River provide great wilderness trips through the Snowy Gorge. The Mitchell River, which traverses the national park of the same name north of Bairnsdale, is a low-volume waterway that offers interesting but relatively straightforward paddling. Also popular are the Mitta Mitta River in the north-east and the Indi,

Sea Kayaking

With its long coastline, indented with inlets and lagoons and numerous coastal rivers and lakes, Victoria has tremendous potential for sea kayaking and the sport is consequently popular. The bays, beaches and islands of Wilsons Promontory provide all kinds of challenges, while the waterways of Lakes Entrance offer more sheltered paddling. Mallacoota Inlet, close to the New South Wales border, is another popular base and ideally placed for expeditions to the varied coastline and enchanting scenery of Croajingolong National Park to the south.

Winter Sports

Some of Victoria's most popular walking areas become a winter playground for cross-country skiers. When under snow, Mount Buffalo National Park offers beautiful, relatively gentle ski-touring, while in Alpine National Park the backcountry skiing can be as serious and wide-ranging as you want to make it. A variety of short day-trips depart from Falls Creek and Mount Hotham, and extended excursions take in areas such as the Bogong High Plains. There are also several highly technical ski routes, including the traverse of Mount Feathertop. Daytrippers from Melbourne often head for the cross-country ski resort of Lake Mountain which is located less than two hours from the city and has over 70 km (43 miles) of trails.

Hang-gliding and Paragliding

North-eastern Victoria is one of the country's best areas for hang-gliding and paragliding, with the big, grassy hills around Bright offering several schools and ideal conditions for learners. Once you've earned your wings, head for Mount Buffalo, which has a launch ramp at the lip of the Buffalo Gorge and a clear landing area near Porepunkah. The other main centre for these forms of non-powered flight is the area around Torquay and Bells Beach.

Fed by rain and melting snow and ice, the upper reaches of the Murray River supply some of the country's best whitewater kayaking. Highlights include the gorges of Murray Gates, which feature 15 grade-four and five rapids.

SOUTH-WEST VICTORIA

Dramatic and diverse scenery, abundant wildlife, grand regional cities, a veritable cornucopia of fine food and wine and a wealth of historical associations cram into Victoria's south-west. On the coast, steep, forested slopes, soaring cliffs and rolling sand dunes fringe the pounding Southern Ocean.

Melbourne

One of the world's most stunning drives, the Great Ocean Road, winds between Torquay, past the wave-washed stacks of the Twelve Apostles and on across the clifftops to Warrnambool where mother whales winter with their calves. Inland, cones and crater lakes dot a vast volcanic plain which as recently as 6000 years ago shook to the explosive outpourings of a string of volcanoes. Today lush pastures on lava-rich soils support fine-fleeced flocks and prized dairy herds, and proud homesteads remind one of a gracious age of pastoral prosperity.

Different forces were at work further north. The 1850s gold rushes temporarily transformed this area into one of the most densely peopled places on the continent. Fortune-seekers from around the globe streamed onto the goldfields, literally overturning the landscape in a mining frenzy. While clashes between diggers and authorities climaxed in the Eureka Uprising, Australia's best-known civil rebellion, the enormous wealth generated here created the impressive streetscapes of Bendigo, Ballarat and Geelong and made Melbourne the country's financial centre for more than a century. A side benefit of the influx from many lands was the establishment of the wine industry here; today the fertile flats of the Goulburn Valley produce high-quality whites, while further west the Pyrenees and Grampians have an increasing reputation for cool-climate reds.

Known for their wild grandeur, the precipitous east-facing escarpments of the Grampians National Park challenge rock climbers, while bushwalkers take to the gentler western slopes. To the west, surrounded by wheatfields stretching to the horizon, Little Desert National Park preserves a pocket of the Wimmera's original mallee scrub, in spring a wonderland of wildflowers. In Lower Glenelg National Park, to the south, the Glenelg River cuts a spectacular gorge deep into the limestone plain as it wends its way to the sea.

OPPOSITE: The Grampians range is characterised by steep sandstone escarpments and gentle slopes, formed more than 3 million years ago and eroded into the present landforms. The 210 000 hectares (518 900 acres) of National Park provide spectacular bushwalks with Aboriginal rock art, over 200 bird species, endemic wildflowers, and lookout points like this one known as 'The Balconies'.

Sheep in the yard, ready for shearing, near the agricultural town of Casterton.

The Otway Ranges

Tall trees thrive in the Otways' moist climate. Each year, over 1000 mm (39 inches) of rain falls across most of the ranges.

Landmarks such as the Twelve Apostles have made South-West Victoria's coastline famous both nationally and internationally. Less well-known but just as intriguing is the coastal hinterland, which is dominated by the magnificent, rainforest-shrouded Otway Ranges. Extending north-east from Cape Otway parallel to the coast for around 80 km (50 miles) to Anglesea, the Otways start as rolling hills in the south, becoming more rugged as they extend north-east. In places, they drop sharply to the sea, forming an impressive backdrop to the spectacular Great Ocean Road.

This is one of the wettest regions in the country. Moist south-west winds fuel thick clouds that snag and break on the Otways' peaks, dumping most of their liquid cargo on the south-eastern slopes. This high level of rainfall sustains dense stands of blue and mountain grey gum, mountain and alpine ash, and myrtle beech, as well as a lush undergrowth.

The forests of the Otways were heavily logged in the early days of European settlement, but pockets of virgin forest can still be found and regeneration has been swift since large swathes of the range were incorporated in two major reserves, Otway National Park and Angahook–Lorne State Park. Visitors to both areas can view a wide array of wildlife and enjoy exhilarating hiking, camping and 4WD adventures.

The Otways are seldom dry, and winter rains sometimes result in road closures, so off-season travellers should check conditions before they set off. The region can be accessed from the Great Ocean Road, and also from the Princes Highway in the north.

History

The Otways' cool temperate rainforests are similar to those of Tasmania, reflecting the fact that the regions were linked by land until about one million years ago.

Due to the rugged nature of the coastline, the Otways were long viewed only from afar by European mariners, most of whom were sealers and whalers. Cape Otway, near the southernmost tip of Victoria, where the ranges begin, was named in 1800 by Lieutenant James Grant after a fellow sea captain, William Albany Otway, whose surname was also given to the nearby mountain range. Following the foundation of Victoria in 1836 and the consequent increase in sea traffic in Bass Strait, efforts were made to limit the toll of this treacherous coast on passing craft. By 1848, a lighthouse was in place on the tip of Cape Otway.

Workers involved in the construction of the lighthouse were amazed by the region's magnificent tall timbers, and word of these valuable resources spread quickly. By 1852, a timber mill was operating at Apollo Bay and soon huge quantities of wood were being carted off to the goldfields. At one point, 29 sawmills were functioning in an area of 20 square km (7.7 square miles) within present-day Angahook–Lorne State Forest. Farmers followed the loggers and contributed to deforestation by clearing large areas for agriculture. Evidence of these activities can be found throughout the region, including abandoned homesteads, the remains of old horse-drawn tramways and mill sites and the grey stumps of forest giants that fell to the timber-cutter's axe more than 100 years ago.

During the twentieth century, increasing awareness of the forests' ecological and recreational value led to the creation of small forest parks. Two of these

reserves were subsequently incorporated in the larger Angahook–Lorne State Park, and in the mid 1980s Otway National Park was also proclaimed.

Otway National Park

Covering a total of 12,900 ha (31,875 acres), Otway National Park extends approximately 60 km (37 miles) along the coast of South-West Victoria, from just west of Apollo Bay to Princetown, where it merges with Port Campbell National Park. It is divided into two sectors—a narrow coastal strip in the west and a much broader area in the east—and encompasses a remarkable range of habitats.

At the Maits Rest picnic area, visitors can enjoy a 40–50 minute self-guided walk that provides the perfect introduction to the Otway rainforests. Along the trail, look out for animals such as red-necked and swamp wallabies, echidnas and possums. Keen-eyed twitchers may also spot satin bowerbirds and king parrots among a rich array of birds.

East of Glenaire, rivers such as the Aire and the Ford, as well as a cluster of sizeable lakes, offer tranquil waters for boating and canoeing. Platypuses and large numbers of waterbirds make their homes here.

Campers can pitch a tent at the Aire River campground, which has toilets and picnic tables and is particularly popular with local canoeists.

Otway National Park's long stretch of coastline incorporates extensive walking trails. One easy but long walk begins at the Aire River camping area, follows the river and then turns south along the coastline past Point Flinders to reach the lighthouse at Cape Otway. From here, walkers can complete a circuit by following the trail that heads inland. The entire walk takes around eight hours. A shorter—around two hours—but more challenging bushwalk starts at the Shelley Beach picnic area and heads toward the mouth of the Elliott River before looping back to its starting point via the rugged coastline.

At Wreck Beach in the west of the park, you can clamber down a steep flight of steps to view the wrecks of the *Fiji* and the *Marie Gabrielle*. Their anchors are displayed nearby. Further west, a walk from Moonlight Beach to Princetown via Pebble Point will provide glimpses of the Twelve Apostles in nearby Port Campbell National Park.

Excellent camping facilities are available near Johanna Beach and at Blanket Bay near Point Lewis; both sites have picnic tables and toilets.

Laid down 10–20 million years ago, the South-West's limestone cliffs have since been shaped by sea, wind and rain, giving rise to caves, blowholes, and stacks such as the famous Twelve Apostles.

Giant Otway messmates, like this one in Melba Gully Conservation Park near Lavers Hill, once covered much of the ranges.

Angahook–Lorne State Park

Angahook–Lorne may hold a lower status than its better-known neighbour, but it covers a much larger area. Its 21,340 ha (52,730 acres) extend from Cape Patton in the south to Aireys Inlet in the northeast and extend more than 10 km (6 miles) inland at certain points. Here, as in Otway National Park, you'll discover magnificent stands of mountain ash and other forest giants bisected by bubbling streams, impressive waterfalls and fern-filled ravines.

Among Angahook–Lorne's most enjoyable bushwalks is the moderate three-hour return journey from a picnic area outside Allenvale to Sheoak Falls, which plummet 15 m (49 feet), via dramatic Castle Rock Lookout. A shorter, easier trail departs from the Allenvale car park and follows the banks of the St George River. Along the way, walkers enjoy superb views of the ocean and nearby coastline.

Angahook–Lorne has seven coastal camp sites, many of which are suitable for caravans and camper vans, as well as numerous picnic areas.

Exploring by 4WD

The following trek takes you through some of the most spectacular forests in the Otways. It begins on the coast at Aireys Inlet and heads inland through Angahook–Lorne State Park to the top of the ranges before looping back downhill to Wye River on the coast. Most of the tracks described are easy 4WD routes when they are dry, but the frequent wet weather means that they can become challenging or impassable; alternative routes have therefore been given in some cases.

From the main Great Ocean Road on the north side of Aireys Inlet, take the Old Coach Road west, cross Gilbert Street and continue to Painkalac Creek. Here you reach the edge of the forest and the road turns to dirt. Continue straight ahead for just under 1 km (0.6 miles), then turn right onto a track that winds through forest and small farms for about 1.5 km (0.9 miles) to a T-junction.

Turn right onto Gentle Annie Jeep Track. When wet, this road can be slippery. After 3 km (1.9 miles), you pass a camping spot on the right, and at just over the 4-km (2.5-mile) mark you'll see the Ironbark Spur Track, also on the right. Stay on the Gentle Annie Track for another 5 km (3 miles) until it joins the Moggs Creek Track; 2 km (1.2 miles) after that, at a T-junction surrounded by forest, you reach Seaview Road, 15 km (9.3 miles) from the Great Ocean Road.

Seaview Road is a well-formed dirt road that runs along the top of the range through a wide clearing. Birds and black wallabies are often seen grazing on the broad verge. After 4 km (2.5 miles), Seaview Road joins the tarred Deans Marsh Road; turn right here onto the blacktop. (If you want to omit the next section of the trip, you can turn left onto the blacktop off Seaview Road and, at a major road junction 3 km (1.9 miles) south, turn right onto Mount Sabine Road.)

This main road leads west down the range, out of the forest and into farmland. At the 6-km (3.7-mile) mark, turn left onto Pennyroyal Station Road. Just over 2.5 km (1.6 miles) later, you arrive at a crossroads surrounded by farmland where you should turn left onto Pennyroyal Valley Road. If you miss this turn-off, you end up in Deans Marsh, but you can still get onto Pennyroyal Valley Road by turning left near the church.

Initially the valley road is good, but about 2.5 km (1.6 miles) from the crossroads the vegetation closes in and the road crosses a bridge and becomes narrower. Within 50 m (55 yards) of the bridge, turn right onto Dunse Track, which heads into soaring forest. It climbs steeply and the 7 km (4.3 miles) to the top can be hard going in the wet. Just as you get to the summit, you meet another track; veer left here and almost immediately you come to the junction with Mount Sabine Road, 37 km (23 miles) from Aireys Inlet. Turn right.

MOUNT SABINE ROAD SOUTH TO WYE RIVER

Head south on Mount Sabine Road; after about 4.5 km (2.8 miles) you come to a well-defined junction. If you want to experience the best of what the Otways have to offer, turn left here and take the Lorne–Erskine Falls road. Just over 3 km (1.9 miles) from the junction, an access road on the left leads to a car park and a short walking track to the falls. Energetic travellers can take the 2-km (1.2-mile) track that follows the Erskine River downstream to Straw Falls, the Cascades and Splitter Falls. This is a magical area, dotted with ferns, draped in moss and crowded by moisture-loving trees.

Backtrack to the Mount Sabine Road and turn left to head south along the top of the range. About 4 km (2.5 miles) south of the Erskine Falls Road junction you come to the Mount Cowley Track on your left. This leads about 1 km (0.6 miles) to the Mount Cowley fire lookout tower, which has fine views.

Back on Mount Sabine Road and just over 6 km (3.7 miles) from the tower turn-off, you come to a cleared area that was at one time the site of the Curtis Homestead, an excellent spot for camping. Less than 1 km (0.6 miles) past this site you reach Curtis Road. This track is subject to seasonal closure, so it pays to check whether it's open before you set off. If it's closed or you don't want to venture down it, stick to the Mount Sabine Road, head south for another 3.5 km (2.2 miles) from the Curtis Homestead site and turn left onto Wye River Road, a fairly good dirt road that winds downhill for 10 km (6 miles) or so to the coast.

Satin bowerbird (Ptilonorhynchus violaceus).

If you do take Curtis Road, turn right at the track junction about 200 m (220 yards) from the main road. After just under 1 km (0.6 miles) you come to a gate (locked in winter), beyond which the track gets steeper and the thick scrub closes in. About 1 km (0.6 miles) further on, you reach another junction. The right-hand track is a dead end that stops just short of a cliff line and a set of waterfalls. Take the road to the left.

Another 1.5 km (0.9 miles) brings you to the site of Cumberland Station and the remains of a disused forest tramway. Adventurous bushwalkers can search here for a number of waterfalls. The closest is off to the left, just east of north, about 500 m (550 yards) away, at a line of cliffs. Another is off to the right, a little further away, at another line of cliffs.

Curtis Road continues past the tramway, dropping steeply through dense forest before levelling out. Just over 1 km (0.6 miles) later you come to another junction. Turn right here onto Cumberland Track and continue through a wet valley. After about 1 km (0.6 miles), you reach another seasonally closed gate which opens onto the Wye River Road.

The main road takes you directly to the coast; however, if you're in the mood for more challenging off-road driving turn left after 3 km (1.9 miles) onto the Jamieson Track. It passes through a gate (usually locked in winter), then heads downhill. After 1.5 km (0.9 miles), you'll see another road, the Godfrey Track, on the right. Both routes continue downhill for 3 km (1.9 miles) or so to the Great Ocean Road, the Jamieson connecting 1.5 km (0.9 miles) north of the Godfrey, which, in turn, is 1.5 km (0.9 miles) from the Wye River Road junction.

Whichever track you exit from, turn right onto the bitumen and head for Wye River. On reaching the town, you will have travelled approximately 72 km (45 miles) from Aireys Inlet, which is just 35 km (22 miles) away via the Great Ocean Road.

Cape Patton, one of the most dramatic parts of the Great Ocean Road, marks the southern limit of Angahook–Lorne State Park.

Places in
SOUTH-WEST
VICTORIA

AIREYS INLET

Aireys Inlet, a small town, with a population of 675, is on the magnificent and scenic Great Ocean Road, 118 km (73 miles) south-west of Melbourne, and is one of the oldest coastal settlements in this region. Once a base for pirates, it is now a renowned seaside resort, popular for fishing and water sports. Named after John Airey, a settler who came to this area in 1846, the town played an important role on the coast with its Split Point Light-house. Built in 1891 and still in operation, the lighthouse dominates the Great Ocean Road view and is visible to all coming in from the sea. A walking track leads to a clifftop lookout over to the lighthouse which is said to be haunted.

Aireys Inlet is on the eastern boundary of the Angahook–Lorne State Park, a huge parkland which encompasses around 21,340 ha (52,730 acres) of coastal hinterland and fern-filled ravines. It is an ideal area for bushwalking, scenic drives or cool, restful picnics during the spring and summer months. There is a beautiful 12-km (7.5-mile) return walk to Currawong Falls. The Allen Noble Sanctuary on the Great Ocean Road is also an excellent reserve, with plenty of bird life. This area is extremely popular during school holidays and it is best to book accommodation in advance. Many hotels or cottages will only take week-long bookings during the peak holiday season in summer and over Easter.
Map ref: page 339 L8

The city of Anglesea is named after the well known seaside town in Wales.

ANGLESEA

Anglesea has safe, sandy beaches, along with abundant coastal bushland that comes alive with colourful wildflowers in spring. The small seaside town is 168 km (104 miles) south-west of Melbourne at the start of the Great

Ocean Road, a scenic trek that winds around Victoria's western coastline offering superb views of the ocean. With a population of 1975, the town offers all the delights of a seaside resort along with plenty of sandy beaches or grassy knolls on which to sit and take in the scenery.

At the end of the River Reserve Road in town is the Coogaoorah Park. This blends waterways with natural coastal bushland and is an ideal spot for fishing, canoeing and picnics. A series of raised board-walks and platforms allows walkers to view this magnificent wetland without disturbing it. Anglesea is also within easy reach of the mag-nificent Otway National Park and the Angahook–Lorne State Park, both of which offer scenic drives among cool-temperate forests and delightful walks to small fern-lined creeks. Walkers can also delight in the Heathland Cliff Walk, a 3.5 km (2 mile) circuit that takes about one hour to complete. Beginning from the car park at the end of Purnell Street, this walk takes you past massive cliff formations and coastal heathlands, with a viewing platform offering excellent views out to Bass Strait.
Map ref: page 339 L8

APOLLO BAY

Apollo Bay, population 2000, is a seaside resort 189 km (117 miles) south-west of Melbourne on the Great Ocean Road. On the way there you will pass through the pretty villages of Skenes Creek and

The Great Ocean Road leads to Apollo Bay, a major fishing port with a large fish-freezing plant in the town.

Wye River and find many lookouts and viewing platforms affording panoramic views of the coastline and out to Bass Strait. The beautiful rainforests of the Otway Ranges stand tall in the background. Once an important harbour, the sheltered waters have silted up and only smaller vessels are now able to enter the port. The bay and foreshore are the focus of the town, and this magnificent stretch of beach is a haven for beach-lovers, swimmers and surfers. It is also here that the local fishing boats come in with their haul of fresh seafood.

There are two museums in town. The Bass Strait Shell Museum has a huge display of shells from around the world, and information on shipwrecks that have occurred off this treacherous western coastline; the Historical Museum has thousands of photographs showcasing the area's shipping history.

The region lends itself to scenic drives around the coast or inland through the parks. Apollo Bay is within easy reach of the Otway National Park and Cape Otway, the most southerly point on this coastline. A steep, narrow road will take you to Mariners Lookout east of town, where a short walk leads to spectacular views of the township and the coastline. A drive down Barham River Road leads to a 3-km (2-mile) walk through lush forest beside a creek to Mariners Falls. Other falls in the area include Beauchamp and Hopetoun falls. Map ref: page 339 K9

ARARAT

Founded in 1839, Ararat is an important town in a district which is famous for wool and wheat production. Situated 205 km (127 miles) west of Melbourne on the outer edge of the goldfields region of Victoria, near the southeastern ridges of the Grampians National Park, Ararat forms part of the Goldfields Touring Triangle Route which extends to the old goldmining centres of Ballarat and Bendigo.

Horatio Wills was the first settler in this region in 1841, and the first gold

nugget was uncovered in 1854. It was three years later that the big gold rush hit this district, when a large alluvial deposit was found at Canton Lead. By the late 1800s vines had been planted in the area and today there are a number of wineries in this region. The small wine-growing township of Great Western, with the Grampians as a backdrop, is 17 km (11 miles) from Ararat. Best Wines and Seppelts Great Western are the largest wineries in town.

The town of Ararat now has a population of 8300, and boasts many attractions, including a wide variety of sports, from quieter ones such as fishing, bowls and croquet to golf, horse riding, swimming and tennis—plus horseracing, both gallopers and trotters. It is also home to the magnificent Alexandra Gardens, Green Hill Lake, which is popular with water-sports enthusiasts, and One Tree Hill Lookout, which offers spectacular views of the surrounding ranges. Langi Morgala Museum—the name is a word from the local Aboriginal language meaning 'home of yesterday'—displays Aboriginal relics, along with other artefacts from this town's history. Map ref: page 338 G4

AVOCA

This small agricultural and mining town (population 1032) is 182 km (113 miles) north-west of Melbourne, and sits on the banks of the Avoca River, with the nearby Pyrenees Ranges and the rich, fertile soil of the Pyrenees Valley within easy reach. Avoca was named by explorer Major Thomas Mitchell in 1836, and by the 1850s was part of a huge gold rush which extended as far as Maryborough, Ballarat and Stawell. Located near the centre of the Goldfields Touring Triangle Route, Avoca makes an ideal base from which to explore these old goldmining towns.

There are a couple of magnificent bluestone buildings in town, including the chemist shop, which dates back to 1854, and the old bluestone gaol. The Avoca Rock Museum in High Street contains specimens of rocks, gemstones and minerals from all over Australia along with historic

Wine has been produced in Avoca since the 1870s.

photographs and information on Avoca. Nestled in the Pyrenees Valley are a number of excellent wineries, including the Blue Pyrenees Estate, Dalwhinnie, Mount Avoca and Taltarni. The Avoca Wool and Wine Festival is held annually in October. Map ref: page 339 J3

BACCHUS MARSH

A dairy and pastoral township, Bacchus Marsh is only a short drive—53 km (33 miles)—west from Melbourne, and lies in a charming valley between the Lerderderg and Werribee Gorges. The town is named after Captain W.H. Bacchus, who bought a portion of swampland from the area's first settler, Mr K. Clarke. Bacchus built a two-storey brick mansion in 1840 which still stands. Gold was mined in this region many years ago and there are still relics to be found in the State Park, including old machinery.

The most impressive feature of the town, which currently has a population of around 11,000, is the Avenue of Honour, made up of 232 giant elm trees. The trees were planted in 1918 to commemorate servicemen from the local area who fought for Australia in World War I. Adjacent to the railway station in Grant Street is Maddingley Park, which is nearly 10 ha (25 acres) of land—it is a popular place for picnics and other recreational activities.

Outside the town on the road to Melton is the Djerriwarrah Bridge, a spectacular sandstone structure which was built in 1858–59. To the south of Bacchus Marsh is the Werribee Gorge, and to the north lies the Lerderderg State Park, which includes the Lerderderg Gorge. This conservation area boasts the largest single area of eucalypt forest in North-central Victoria, and it is also home to koalas, which live in the large ribbony manna gums. Bacchus Marsh and its surrounding region is popular with gem fossickers, walkers and 4WD owners. Map ref: page 339 M5

The Chinese Gold Discovery Memorial in Ararat remembers Chinese prospectors of the gold rush.

BALLARAT

The large town of Ballarat (population 63,802) is 111 km (69 miles) west of Melbourne. It prospered during the gold rush and is now a major regional centre and a most picturesque tourist town. The city literally glows in autumn when the leaves of its deciduous trees change colour. The botanic gardens near Lake Wendouree are a tranquil spot in this beautiful city.

Ballarat's origins go back to 1837, when William Yuille and his men camped on the edge of the Black Swamp, an area that has since been reclaimed and is now known as Lake Wendouree. Yuille settled here—'Ballarat' is a word in a local Aboriginal language which means 'camping or resting place'. It was not long before the first gold nugget was found by Thomas Hiscock—from the ground near the cemetery in 1851. However, it was not until two years later that two main lodes were found and thousands of miners rushed to the region to try their hand at gold prospecting. Their 'settlement' was a huge tent city.

The Eureka Stockade incident followed in 1854 when there was a major clash over miners' rights and taxes. The miners eventually lined up and simultaneously burnt their licences in a huge campfire. This revolt was led by Peter Lalor under the blue and white Eureka flag, and within days a fight ensued between miners and government

Floral display in the Botanic Gardens in Ballarat.

soldiers. More than 30 people were killed. Sent to trial, the agitators were found not guilty and Lalor went on to become a member of the Victorian Parliament. You will still see the famous flag flying throughout this town today. A Eureka Stockade Memorial sits on the corner of Stawell and Eureka Streets, and an exhibition portraying the event can be found on Eureka Street.

Gold provided a great deal of wealth for this area—it is here that the world's second biggest gold nugget was found. The Welcome Nugget weighed 68,956 grams (2437 ounces) and was found at Bakery Hill in 1858. Without doubt, the biggest attraction is Sovereign Hill, a theme park re-creating the old gold rush days. Its staff members dress in period costume, and it contains realistic stores and banks. It is built on the old Sovereign Hill Quartz Mining Site. There were many Chinese working in the Australian goldfields in the gold rush days. It is said that up to one-third of the population during the 1800s was of Chinese descent—the numerous Chinese graves on McArthur Street certainly seem to reinforce this belief.

The Arch of Victory forms an entrance to the town and to the Avenue of Honour, along which nearly 4000 trees are planted in honour of ex-servicemen. Another feature is the Great Southern Woolshed, on the Western Highway. Based around the wool industry, it features displays of sheep shearing, working sheep dogs in action and an animal nursery. Ballarat Wildlife Park, another

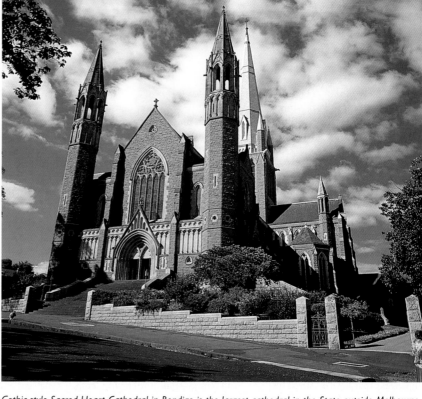

Gothic-style Sacred Heart Cathedral in Bendigo is the largest cathedral in the State outside Melbourne.

popular attraction, is set among 116 ha (287 acres) of scenic peppermint forest where native wildlife such as koalas, kangaroos, emus and wombats can often be seen. South of town is the theme park Kryal Castle, the world's third largest castle which features Gothic architecture. The staff dress as medieval characters and put on shows. The armour, torture chamber, glass-blowing display and stone maze are popular.

Other features of Ballarat include the Ballarat Aviation Museum, which houses a huge collection of vintage and classic aeroplanes, models and memorabilia, and a gold museum which contains a great collection of the alluvial gold nuggets. *See also* Grampians and Pyrenees Wine Region

Map ref: page 339 K5

BENDIGO

Lying on the fertile flats of the Campaspe and Loddon rivers 152 km (94 miles) north-west of Melbourne, this sprawling town (population 70,000) in the heart of Victoria acts as a service centre for much of the outlying area. Gold was discovered in Bendigo in 1851 and the mines around the town went on to produce more than 595 million grams (21 million ounces) of gold, making it one of the richest goldfields in the world. Mining ceased in 1954 when the Central Deborah Gold Mine closed down. The 422-m (1384-foot) deep mine reopened in 1972 and

tours are now conducted to the second of the 17 levels underground; surface tours are also available. The Gold Mining Museum in Eaglehawk has a good collection of artefacts and mining relics.

Along Pall Mall, the main street in town, are numerous historic buildings dating from the nineteenth century, including the Post Office, Law Courts and the impressive Shamrock Hotel, which is still in operation. A quartz fountain, made from over 20 tonnes (20 tons) of the superb stone, was given to the city of Bendigo by the 'Quartz King' George Lansell in 1881. Other superb buildings include the Sacred Heart Cathedral on Wattle Street, believed to be the last Gothic cathedral built in the world.

Nearly as old as the mining industry is the famous Bendigo Pottery, founded in 1857 by Scottish potter George Guthrie. Another of Bendigo's great attractions is the Vintage Talking Tram on which visitors can take an hour-long journey through this historic city. At the depot are a number of vintage trams, many of them restored. Also of interest are the restored Joss House and the Golden Dragon Museum, both of which highlight the contribution of the Chinese to this town.

Off the Loddon Valley Highway in Eaglehawk is Sandhurst Town, which is actually two towns, one representing Bendigo during the gold rush and the other a small country town typical of this region. These two impressive representations are connected via a full-sized

railway. On the outskirts of Bendigo are the Whipstick and Kamarooka Parks, home to the blue eucalyptus. This stunted eucalypt has adapted to the harsh growing conditions of the region and produces excellent eucalyptus oil. Tours of Harland's Eucalyptus Factory are available. The distillery has been operating since 1890 and still produces the popular oil and soaps.
See also Central Victoria Wine Region
Map ref: page 339 M2

BRISBANE RANGES NATIONAL PARK

The Brisbane Ranges National Park is 105 km (65 miles) west of Melbourne and just over one hour's drive away. The park is renowned for its wildflowers and native plants, which are especially prolific in the west of the park on the plateau area. Eucalypt woodlands, with a dense understorey of heaths, are also found on the plateau. During the gold rush years, much of this forest was cut down for mining timbers, building material and firewood. The park is cut by deep gorges and gullies created over the millennia by water eroding the ancient slate and sandstone of the ranges. Visitors will enjoy the abundant flora and bird life, and the pleasant bushwalks and scenic drives.
Map ref: page 339 M6

BROADFORD

Broadford is a town of around 3000 people, and lies approximately 74 km (46 miles) north of Melbourne. Today it services the surrounding pastoral and agricultural industry. However, its past includes a large paper mill—still standing—which dates back to 1890. It is the surrounding areas which attract visitors. Among the standout places are the Tallarook State Forest, to the east, which offers 4WD tracks, camping, and peaceful picnic areas. The State Forest of Mount Disappointment, south-east of Broadford, is named after the towering peak which explorers Hume and Hovell climbed on their journey south in an attempt to view Port Phillip Bay and thus see whether or not they were close to the end of their expedition. Much to their disappointment, a sight of the bay was not possible,

Ruins of the short-lived gold rush days in Brisbane Ranges National Park.

but there is now an excellent panorama of Melbourne and its outer suburbs. Less than 5 km (3 miles) south-west of town is the Mount Piper Education Reserve which, has been set aside in order to protect the local flora and fauna, as there is much cleared grazing land around the region.
Map ref: page 339 P4

CASTERTON

This grazing and agricultural community 371 km (230 miles) west of Melbourne on the Glenelg River lies west of the large country municipality of Hamilton. Explorer Thomas Mitchell passed through this region and was so impressed by its beauty that he named it 'Australia Felix', meaning 'this wonderful land', because it contrasted with the dry, arid country he had recently travelled through. Members of the pioneering Henty family were among the first settlers, taking up land in 1837. The town's name means 'walled city', a reference to the surrounding hills, which give the illusion that the town is enclosed. The town was named after Casterton in Westmoreland, in the north of England, and currently has a population of 2000.

The region boasts natural features such as Baileys Rocks, 30 km (19 miles) north-west of town, which is an outcrop of large green-coloured granite boulders; the Bluff, which offers superb views of the surrounding countryside; and Bilston's Tree, said to be the largest red gum tree in Australia.

The town has other attractions, such as the Historical Museum, housed in the old railway building

on Jackson Street, which has an eclectic assortment of historic items and photographs from this district. On Warrock Road, around 29 km (18 miles) north of town, is Warrock Homestead, where visitors can explore a number of century-old buildings, including a blacksmith's building, stables, woolshed and the old homestead itself.
Map ref: page 338 C5

CASTLEMAINE

Castlemaine is a historic goldmining town in the heart of the former goldmining belt of Central Victoria—122 km (76 miles) north-west of Melbourne—and is a great weekend destination. The town—possibly the archetypal goldmining town of north-western Victoria—was first named both

Forest Creek and Mount Alexander in the 1850s. Later its name was changed to Castlemaine in honour of Viscount Castlemaine. However, it was gold that kept the town prosperous for its first two decades. Herons Creek, south-west of town, is a historic gold digging area which was mined from 1851 to the late 1930s and is now classified by the National Trust.

Castlemaine has a population of 7140. A number of historic buildings made from sandstone mined from local quarries, many of which are now classified by the National Trust, are still standing, and are worth visiting. Buda, one such home, is open for inspection; it was built in 1861 and is set among 2 ha (5 acres) of magnificent gardens. The Castlemaine Market is another interesting building, with an unusual architectural style. It is now used as an art and craft market, and also houses antiques. The town's beautiful botanic gardens were established in 1860 on land that was once a goldmining site.

The beauty of Castlemaine and its surrounding area is probably best appreciated from the Burke and Wills Monument, which stands on Wills Street overlooking the town. This monument was erected in honour of Robert Burke, who served as a policeman in Castlemaine from 1858 to 1860, after which he set off on his exploration of Central Australia.
Map ref: page 339 L3

'Buda', built in 1861 in Castlemaine, was originally the home of jeweller Ernest Leviny.

Watering the vines in the warm, dry climate of the Central Victoria Wine Region.

CENTRAL VICTORIA WINE REGION

The warm climate of Central Victoria's lower regions, the area around Bendigo, Heathcote, Seymour and Rushworth, makes it highly suitable for red wines, particularly shiraz and cabernet.

The Bendigo region, with its undulating hills and eucalypt forests, has a modest annual rainfall of 550 mm (21.5 in) making irrigation a necessity. Since the 1960s, the Bendigo region has become home to many small wineries that produce small quantities of high-quality wine. Of the area's red wines, shiraz occupies the most acreage, closely followed by cabernet sauvignon. The warmer areas produce generous yields, but strong sunshine and low rainfall call for canopy management.

The flat, fertile Goulburn Valley was settled in the 1850s by farmers and graziers. Despite an annual rainfall of only 600 mm (24 in), the Tahbilk Vineyard Proprietary was formed to produce quality wine there from extensive plantings, chiefly of red grapes, in 1860. Phylloxera only partly destroyed the area and some of the original vines still produce fruit. Marsanne grown in commercial quantities is exclusive to the Goulburn Valley. Chateau Tahbilk and Mitchelton produce some of Victoria's best-value and most interesting white wines from it. The patient collector will find aged marsanne a rare treat.

The Central Victorian Mountain Country, a region formerly known as the Strathbogie Ranges stretching east from Seymour, is completely different climatically. At 300–1800 m (984–5905 ft) above sea level, it is influenced by altitude throughout. Rainfall is double that lower down, but frosts are a concern (most vineyards experience snow in winter). The Mountain Country specialises in cooler climate varieties—especially chardonnay, used for both still and sparkling wines. Crisp, fresh, fruity rieslings and gewürztraminers are developing a following.
Map ref: page 339 P2

COLAC

Colac is a provincial centre around 151 km (94 miles) south-west of Melbourne—it is the gateway to the rainforest region of the Otway Ranges. The tall timber logged from these forests has provided residents of Colac (population 12,000) with a thriving timber industry. Other industries include wool, lamb and beef. Rich in farmland, the fertile lands are the result of volcanic activity in the region thousands of years ago. Colac is situated on a volcanic plain that covers much of the Western District of Victoria. The old volcanic headlands surround the town, offer spectacular views of the region.

A major source of recreation is Lake Colac, which is a base for boating, waterskiing and fishing, while magnificent botanic gardens surround the foreshore, providing the perfect picnic location. Lake Corangamite, 25 km (16 miles) north of town, is Victoria's largest lake and home to a wide variety of bird life. Waterfowl can also be found at the Floating Island Reserve, west of Colac, where six islands of separated peat float in a lagoon and offer refuge to wildlife.
Map ref: page 339 J8

DAYLESFORD

Daylesford (population 3500) and the nearby township of Hepburn Springs are popular weekend and holiday destinations, only 110 km (68 miles) north-west of Melbourne. They are set in tranquil scenic countryside on Australia's largest collection of mineral springs. The mineral springs were discovered at the same time as gold was found in the region—in 1854—but after the gold rush was over, the town became known for its mineral spas and the therapeutic qualities these waters possessed. The Hepburn Springs Spa Complex has Australia's only mineral bath facility. You can also head out to the many natural freshwater springs around the town for a tasting of this delightful water, or trek to the blowhole and frolic in the soothing waters in a natural surrounding.

With many wineries in the region, including Sunbury, Macedon, Lancefield and Hanging Rock, together with a wide variety of restaurants, this area is definitely a gourmet getaway. Other attractions of the town include the Lake Daylesford Central Springs Reserve on Wombat Creek, Jubilee Lake, Wombat Hill Gardens, Lavendula Lavender Farm and the Central Highlands Tourist Railway. The Sunday markets, which are very popular with those seeking antiques, bric-a-brac and local produce, are set up beside the tourist railway. The Historical Society Museum has an excellent display of photographs, mining equipment and paraphernalia from the town's past.
Map ref: page 339 L4

DUNOLLY

Sheep were once grazed in this country region—Dunolly is 195 km (121 miles) north-west of Melbourne—by a Scots farmer who took up residence here in 1845. He named the site after his clan's castle in Scotland. However, it was the discovery of gold and the finding in 1869 of the largest gold nugget ever found in this country

An experienced angler 'working the trees', at sunset, on the privately owned Timber Lake near Colac.

Trout are plentiful in Lake Wallace, Edenhope.

that put Dunolly on the map. In fact, more gold nuggets have been found in this district, than in any other Australian goldfield. The 'Welcome Stranger' nugget, as it is known, considered to be the largest nugget ever discovered, weighed 64 kg (2256 ounces) and was dug out from the ground 13 km (8 miles) north-west of the town. The Welcome Stranger Monument on the Goldsborough–Moliagul road marks the site where it was uncovered. The Historical Museum in town features models of famous nuggets and mining equipment, plus Aboriginal relics. The Gold Discovery Information Centre, which houses a replica of the 'Welcome Stranger', is set up in the old courthouse on Market Street, which was built in 1862 and originally used as a town hall. Water sports—on the Laanecoorie Reservoir, 13 km (8 miles) east of Dunolly—are popular recreational activities in this tiny town, with a population of just 720.

Map ref: page 339 K2

EDENHOPE

Edenhope, 401 km (249 miles) west of Melbourne on the shores of Lake Wallace near the Victorian/South Australian border, is one of the oldest grazing towns in Victoria. George and James Hope, pioneers from Scotland, first set up pastoral runs here in 1845, and the area is still mainly sheep and cattle country. William Wallace was the first European to come across Lake Wallace—in 1843. When full, it is 7 m (23 feet) deep. It is a popular venue for boating, waterskiing, swimming, and fishing for trout and redfin. The wetlands around

this lake are an extremely important habitat for waterfowl. Much of the region can be explored through a series of walking tracks.

Edenhope is a small town, with a population of 1000, but it is full of life: annual events include the Henley-on-Lake Wallace Carnival in February, the Edenhope Cup Race Meeting on Labour Day (March) and an annual show in November. Australia's first Aboriginal cricket team, which toured England in the late nineteenth century, trained here, and there is a monument in the town to commemorate this event.

Map ref: page 338 B3

GEELONG

Geelong, 76 km (47 miles) south-west of Melbourne, is Victoria's second largest town. It is really a city in its own right—it has a population of 145,335, and has many outer suburbs, around Corio Bay, on the western side of Port Phillip Bay. The first European settlers in this region were J.H. Cowie and David Stead, who established a property called Cowies Creek. Soon after, in 1840, two pioneering women took up residence at South Corio and the Bellarine Peninsula. Within a year the town boasted many buildings, including a post office and store, and was producing the *Geelong Advertiser,* said to be Australia's oldest morning paper.

The countryside was used for sheep grazing over the next decade until gold was discovered in 1851. Geelong was then an entry point for immigrants hoping to strike it rich on the

goldfields, and a port from which to export the gold. Today Geelong is a large, important regional centre, and the gateway to the Bellarine Peninsula and the western districts of Victoria.

Geelong has a number of features of historical interest. Nestled on the banks of the Barwon River, which runs through the town, is Barwon Grange, an old homestead which dates back to 1856—it has a particularly magnificent veranda. The National Wool Museum display, which is housed in a historic bluestone woolstore, is a fine interpretation of the history of the wool industry in Australia.

As Geelong is on the coast, the sea has also played a major role in the town's history and heritage. The Naval and Military Museum displays a range of records, photographs and wartime relics, along with plenty of information on shipwrecks off the Victorian coastline. The museum is housed in the old Royal Australian Naval College buildings, which were the site of the first Australian submarine base.

Geelong is not short on outdoor recreation opportunities either. Eastern Beach, on the edge of

Corio Bay, is within walking distance of central Geelong and features piers, the Bay City Marina, saltwater swimming pools and lawned parkland. The beach area extends into Eastern Park, a popular recreation area because of its lovely walking tracks.

There are also interesting walks in Geelong, including Bayside Bollard Walk, from Rippleside Park to Limeburners Point along a sealed path. Along its route are a number of large colourful bollards representing characters from Geelong's past. The Heritage Trail explores the city streetscapes, taking in the early history and buildings.

Festivals in the town include the Geelong Gourmet Wine and Food Fair, held on Australia Day every January, the Pako Festa (a food and music festival) and a National Aquatic Festival, both held annually in February. The Bells Beach Surf Carnival is held at Easter, and the Geelong Spring Festival and Geelong Show are in October. The Strawberry Fair and Geelong Speed Trials take place during November. *See also* Port Phillip Bay Wine Region

Map ref: page 339 M7

Fishing boats moored in Geelong's Corio Bay—an arm of Port Phillip Bay.

GRAMPIANS AND PYRENEES WINE REGION

Western Victoria's cool climate has led to it becoming well known for its sparkling wines, especially from such producers as Seppelt in the Grampians. (Seppelt has also planted vineyards in the remote far south-west of Victoria, where the climate is maritime. The area is sparsely planted so far, with the most significant vineyard development at Drumborg.)

The landscape in the Grampians and Pyrenees varies from flat, golden pasture to rugged granite escarpment. The winters are cold and wet, the cool dry summers. Annual average rainfall is around 550 mm (21.5 inches) and vines struggle without supplementary irrigation. Spring frosts are not uncommon and vineyards are deliberately sited on slopes to avoid them.

Premium shiraz from such producers as Mount Langi Ghiran, Dalwhinnie and Seppelt Great Western has earned domestic and international praise. Flavours vary from region to region but are always of juicy berry fruits. Shiraz fans may be surprised by the dominance of chewy black cherry, plum jam and raspberry flavours. Most winemakers use a touch of French oak to complement the fragrant, earthy fruit. Cabernet sauvignon, demonstrating its chameleon-like nature in this difficult climate, is often minty and tinged with eucalyptus, but usually full of purple fruit flavours.

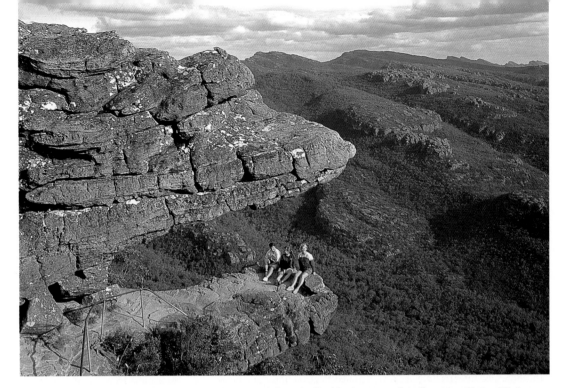

The Balconies (or Jaws of Death), can be reached via a track from the Reed Lookout carpark in Grampians National Park.

Sauvignon blancs from the Pyrenees region are becoming increasingly flavoursome and complex as vignerons learn how best to manage the fruit. A flinty dryness, which is enriched by soft tropical fruit flavours, suggests that this area may become a source of great varietal interest.

Ballarat frequently suffers the coldest temperatures in the State, but regional winemakers here are turning this to their advantage to produce pinot noirs of superb complexity. Recent plantings of sangiovese, pinot grigio and viognier grapes are adding further interest and suggest that the area of the Grampians and Pyrenees has yet to show its breadth.
Map ref: page 339 J5

GRAMPIANS NATIONAL PARK

This park is 260 km (161 miles) west of Melbourne and 25 km (16 miles) south-west of Stawell. The rugged sandstone ranges of the westernmost heights of the Great Divide make up the Grampians National Park, protecting a region rich in native flora, fauna and Aboriginal art sites. A wide variety of soils, topography and localised weather patterns produces a great wealth of botanical species. Eucalypts dominate the forests, while heaths carpet the terrain higher up. In spring, the wildflower display is superb. Animal life is just as varied, and the Grampians are host to mammals both large and small. Kangaroos abound in some areas.

Hundreds of kilometres of vehicle and walking tracks give easy access to some of the State's most spectacular scenery. Just about every outdoor activity can be undertaken, from waterskiing, fishing, hunting, bushwalking and rock-climbing to just enjoying the magnificent panoramas.
See also Grampians and Pyrenees Wine Region
Map ref: page 338 E4

HALLS GAP

Halls Gap, 265 km (165 miles) north-west of Melbourne, is the tourist centre of the Grampians region. Extending for more than 80 km (50 miles) and up to 50 km (31 miles) wide, the Grampians are the beginning of the Great Dividing Range, which extends northwards, eventually ending near Cooktown in Queensland. Thomas Mitchell was the first European to explore this region, in 1836, and not long after that graziers occupied the foothills of the mountains. The gap is named after C. Hall, who set up cattle runs through here. He discovered the mountain pass in 1841 when trying to walk cattle over the range. The Grampians themselves are named after the mountain range in Scotland. Other settlers to the area included goldminers and loggers, whose activities were stopped when the Grampians National Park was formed in 1984.

The main attractions around Halls Gap, itself a town of only 300 people, are the national park

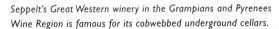

Seppelt's Great Western winery in the Grampians and Pyrenees Wine Region is famous for its cobwebbed underground cellars.

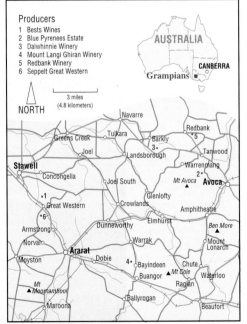

Producers
1 Bests Wines
2 Blue Pyrenees Estate
3 Dalwhinnie Winery
4 Mount Langi Ghiran Winery
5 Redbank Winery
6 Seppelt Great Western

AUSTRALIA
CANBERRA
Grampians

NORTH
3 miles
(4.8 kilometers)

Navarre
Greens Creek Tulkara Redbank
Barkly 5
Joel 3
Landsborough Tanwood
Stawell Warrenmang
Concongella 2
Joel South Mt Avoca Avoca
1 Glenlofty
Great Western Crowlands
6 Amphitheatre
Armstrong Dunneworthy Elmhurst
Norval Warrak Ben More
Ararat Mount Lonarch
Moyston Dobie 4
Bayindeen Chute
Buangor Mt Cole Waterloo
Mt Raglan
Moornambool Ballyrogan Beaufort
Maroona

and the outdoor activities associated with it. Bushwalking, along designated, well-markedtracks, and rock climbing on the rugged peaks are popular with many tourists. Hang gliding is also popular here, as is wildflower study in spring, when the mountain range glows with a mass of brilliant colours. The area is also a haven for bird-watchers. Nearby Lake Bellfield is an ideal spot for sailboats and fishing, while Rocklands Reservoir offers a playground for power boat owners, waterskiers and swimmers.

This region is of great significance to the local Aborigines. The Brambuk Living Cultural Centre houses Aboriginal arts and crafts along with cultural displays and exhibitions. The Brambuk Café allows you to experience true Aboriginal bush tucker.

The Grampians is a diverse region: as well as national parks it also features a number of excellent wineries, including Bests Great Western. The Grampians Gourmet Weekend is an exciting event held in May, offering fine wines, food and entertainment against a backdrop of the rugged Grampians Range. The Halls Gap Wildflower Exhibition is held in spring, and features hundreds of species of flora from the Grampians.
See also Grampians and Pyrenees Wine Region
Map ref: page 338 F3

HAMILTON

Just 312 km (194 miles) west of Melbourne in the heart of the State's west, Hamilton (population 10,131) is the centre of Victoria's fine wool industry and a major regional centre for the small farming communities. Explorer Major Thomas Mitchell came across this grazing land in 1836 and pastoralists soon followed, setting up what is often referred to as 'the wool capital of the world'. During the 1850s, large towns to the east of Hamilton, such as Ararat and Stawell, were involved in Victoria's gold rush, and the grazing land around Hamilton meant that the new settlers of the town could prosper by providing hungry prospectors with food supplies.

At the Big Woolbales in Hamilton, visitors can learn about the wool industry and see sheep being sheared; the Pastoral Museum

houses many pieces of old farm equipment. Another attraction is the Transport Museum, named after Sir Reginald Ansett, who started his career here in the 1930s. Visitors to this country centre can also enjoy walks around Lake Hamilton on the eastern edge of town, where there is an excellent aquatic centre, with playground, swimming area and small boats for hire.

Local wildlife can be seen at the Institute of Rural Learning, which comprises 5 ha (12 acres) of parkland and a series of walking tracks. The elusive eastern barred bandicoot can be found here. Nigretta Falls, north-west of the town, is a magnificent sight when in full flow after rain. Events include Wool Heritage Week and the Sheepvention field days during July, the Garden Expo in October and the Picnic Races in November.
Map ref: page 338 E6

HEATHCOTE

A small grazing and agricultural town with a population of 1725, Heathcote sits on the McIvor Creek not far from the regional centre of Bendigo, about 133 km (83 miles) north of Melbourne. Major Mitchell explored this area and named the creek McIvor after a member of his party—when gold was discovered in 1853 the town was known as McIvor Diggings. With lush forests nearby, the town soon had a timber industry, and with the abundance of heath in the district, the town's name was changed to Heathcote.

The main street is wide and sprawling, featuring small cafés, restaurants, a bakery and basic shops to supply the surrounding farms. Lake Eppalock, to the north, is a popular venue for water sports such as boating and waterskiing. This reservoir was built to irrigate farmland in the nearby region and to the west, and it is also a great place for fishing and camping. A rodeo is held annually at Easter and the Gold 'n' Grapes Festival is held on the weekend before the Melbourne Cup, itself held on the first Tuesday in November.
Map ref: page 339 N3

HORSHAM

With a population of 13,300, Horsham is known as the capital of the Wimmera region of Victoria. It lies 305 km (189 miles) north-west of Melbourne, at the junction of three major highways, the Western, Henty and Wimmera. The first settler to the region was James Darlot, who ventured west and set up a property and homestead in the 1840s after Thomas Mitchell had explored the region. The surrounding town was not well developed until the 1870s. The town's name comes from Darlot's home town in Sussex, England. Horsham and the Wimmera produce a substantial

Nigretta Falls, 15 km (9.3 miles) north-west of Hamilton.

amount of Victoria's wheat, and sheep and wool are the major income earners. On Golfcourse Road is the Wool Factory, a community-based enterprise where disabled workers specialise in the production of fine woollen fabrics. The magnificent botanic gardens on the banks of the Wimmera River were designed in the 1870s but not finished until the 1930s. There are picnic facilities here, along with playgrounds and toilets.

With so many roads leading from this major centre, there are plenty of regions to discover outside of town, including the Grampians Range and the Grampians National Park. There are plenty of walking tracks and natural bushland to explore, and Aboriginal art to see. Nearby Mount Arapiles is popular with climbers, who can be seen making their way to the peak on most weekends. A road also leads to the top where the magnificent views can be enjoyed without expending so much energy. The numerous lakes in the west near Horsham, including Pine Lake, a recreational reserve, are good spots for anglers and for catching yabbies.

To the north of Horsham lies Victoria's desert country and the national parks of Little Desert, Big Desert and Wyperfeld. These offer spectacular desert scenery, colourful wildflowers in spring and delightful camping areas. The Horsham Annual Show is held in late September, the Apex Fishing Competition runs over the Labour Day weekend (March), a Spring Garden Festival takes place in October and the Kannamaroo Festival is in late November.
Map ref: page 338 E2

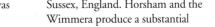

Author Mark Twain noted that 'Horsham sits in a plain which is as level as a floor'.

Wheels from the old Steam Mill in Kyneton (1862).

KILMORE

Originally a supply town for those heading north to the goldfields of Beechworth or Bendigo, little has changed in Kilmore, a small town (population 3500) lying 63 km (39 miles) north of Melbourne. First settled in 1841, it is one of Victoria's oldest inland settlements. The town still services travellers, although visitor numbers dropped when the town was bypassed by the Hume Freeway, which heads north-east towards Seymour. As an alternative route to Bendigo, the Northern Highway offers a chance to look at this historic town.

Some of the town's history is outlined at the Bylands Museum. This museum also houses an extensive display of interesting cable cars and early electric trams, and tram rides through the picturesque

Whitburgh Cottage in Kilmore. The name Kilmore is Gaelic for 'big church'.

surrounding countryside are available on days when the museum is open.

Much of the land around Kilmore is farming land, but the area is also an important region for horseracing. The racecourse in town is the venue for the popular Kilmore Racing Cup and the Kilmore Pacing Cup, two important race meetings on the provincial harness racing calendar. The town also comes alive every year in early December, when the Agricultural Show is held.
Map ref: page 339 P4

KOROIT

Koroit, with a population of 1490, sits on rich agricultural land about 285 km (177 miles) west of Melbourne, near the large regional centre of Warrnambool. The town has a large Irish population, and is most famous for its production of onions and potatoes. Koroit was established in the 1800s—a walk through the streets will reveal a number of historic buildings from that era still in use. Koroit Galleries contains an interesting display of prints and artwork, and the Old Courthouse Inn sells a variety of cottage crafts and gifts.

The most significant feature of the area around Koroit is an extinct volcano in nearby Tower Hill State Game Reserve, which covers about 636 ha (1572 acres) of land. Tower Hill is one of Victoria's most recently active volcanoes and has a large island in the middle. A 16-km (10-mile) walking track takes visitors round the edge of the crater and offers great views into the volcano and out to the Southern Ocean in the distance. Information on the volcano is available at the Natural History Centre, which also has Aboriginal and geological exhibits and information on the history of European settlement in this region. Port Fairy is a beautiful and popular seaside fishing village near Koroit.
Map ref: page 338 F8

KYNETON

The historic township of Kyneton, 85 km (53 miles) north-west of Melbourne, looks like an English town. It is named after Kyneton in England and has more than 30 large ornate buildings classified by the National Trust, as well as hedges and extensive grazing land. Once a supply and stopping point on the way to the goldfields, Kyneton is now a farming community with a population of 3940.

The historic buildings include many bluestone structures that date from the mid-1800s. The museum is housed in a bluestone building that was once the bank. Built in 1855, it is a good representation of the era and contains fine examples of furniture of the period.

In the Steam Mill, which dates from 1862, flour was milled until 1964. It has since been restored and, along with photographs and memorabilia, offers a fine display. Other attractions include two wineries, Knight Granite Hills and Cobaw Ridge, together with parklands such as Blackhill Reserve, and the Lauriston and Upper Coliban Reservoirs. These are popular for trout fishing.

On the banks of the Campaspe River are the botanic gardens, which date from 1866 and have a number of magnificent old trees. Among these are exotic shrubs donated by Ferdinand von Mueller, who was Director of the Melbourne Botanic Gardens when the Kyneton gardens were established.

A daffodil exhibition and the Arts Festival are held in September and the Kyneton Show takes place annually in November.
Map ref: page 339 M4

LERDERDERG STATE PARK

The Lerderderg River, flanked with huge stands of eucalypts, cuts its way through this conservation parkland, which is only an hour from central Melbourne. During the last century the area was worked by gold diggers looking for alluvial gold. Evidence of mining can be found along Byers Back Track and at Tunnel Point, where miners built a tunnel through the solid rock gorge of the Lerderderg River, diverting its flow. The park was originally—in 1963—only a small forest reserve; it has been extended three times, declared a State park, and is now 13,400 ha (33,111 acres).

The region boasts the largest single area of eucalypt forest in north-central Victoria. It is also home to a colony of koalas, who nest in the large ribbony manna gums, their preferred tree. The bird life includes cockatoos, such as the sulphur-crested and gang-gang, and the mighty wedge-tailed eagle.

The magnificent Lerderderg Gorge in the isolated Lerderderg State Park.

The most common eucalypts in the park are the tall, fibrous messmate stringybark found in the mountain foothills, and the red ironbark, easily identified by its goblet-shaped fruit and its dark, thick bark. Close inspection of the ground will reveal wildflowers, bush peas and orchids; the most impressive variety being the large duck orchid.

The isolation of this park makes it ideal for bushwalking. Blackwood Mineral Springs walk will take you past Shaws Lake and onto Sweets Lookout, high above the river—this walk is 3.5 km (2.2 miles) long and takes around 2 hours (return). To see the tunnel, start at O'Briens Crossing and head along Byers Back Track, which follows an old water-race around the valley—this walk is 3 km (1.9 miles) long and also takes around 2 hours (return).

Touring in a 4WD is also popular. Try a drive along the Lerderderg Track, then a walk along Spanish Onion Track down to the cliffs above the Lerderderg River, and then the East Walk, which heads northwest to O'Briens Crossing. Remember to check on seasonal track closures in winter and spring.

The park can be entered from the north via O'Briens Road, off the Greenvale–Trentham road, or from Blackwood, along the Golden Point road. From the south, access is via the Lerderderg Gorge road off the Bacchus Marsh–Gisborne road. There are numerous camp sites along the Lerderderg River, but most have no toilet facilities. The picnic ground at O'Briens Crossing has fireplaces and toilets. Map ref: page 339 M5

LITTLE DESERT NATIONAL PARK

The park runs south of the Western Highway from Dimboola to the South Australian border and is divided into three blocks—western, central and eastern. It is 375 km (233 miles) north-west of Melbourne. The sandy plains that make up much of this park are dominated by mallee and stringybark eucalypts, along with many species of other eucalypts, pines, melaleuca, heaths, banksias and broombush. With dazzling displays of spring wildflowers and the excellent variety of bird life and fauna, this park is a must for nature-lovers. In such a dry landscape, the Wimmera River in the eastern block, with its woodlands of river red gum and black box on the floodplains, gives a different aspect to the surrounding countryside. While much of the park can be explored on foot, sandy tracks, really suited only to 4WDs, criss-cross the park, and in fact the central and western blocks are accessible only to 4WD vehicles. Map ref: page 338 A1

LORNE

Sitting at the foothills of the magnificent Otway Ranges on Loutit Bay 142 km (88 miles) south-west of Melbourne, Lorne has been a popular seaside resort for more than a century. The bay was named after Captain Loutit, who sought shelter in its protected waters in 1841. The town, established in 1871 and named in honour of the Marquis of Lorne, a Scottish peer, now has a population of 1170.

The opening of the Great Ocean Road in 1932 gave a real boost to the town. This road itself is a tourist attraction, winding along the coast from Torquay to near Warrnambool and offering fantastic coastal views. During peak times in summer, the township is very busy—indeed, for much of the year, accommodation must be booked well in advance. However, the town has remained relatively unspoiled, despite its popularity.

Apart from enjoying the sun and surf there are plenty of other things to do in town, including visiting its many craft shops, or looking at the photographic memorabilia in the Historical Society Building on Mountjoy Parade, or visiting the shell museum. And there is also the seafood—seafood here is as fresh as it gets: a small fishing fleet comes in every day with a catch that includes fish and crayfish.

Outside of town Teddy's Lookout offers magnificent views of the coastline. The Erskine Falls tumble over moss-covered rocks at the end of a walk through a glorious fern-lined valley. Lorne is also close to the Otway Ranges and its associated parks, which are ideal for bush-walking, scenic drives and picnics. Map ref: page 339 L8

The Wimmera River, in Little Desert National Park, is a popular camping spot with sites provided for caravans and tents.

Limestone column in Princess Margaret Rose Cave, Lower Glenelg National Park.

LOWER GLENELG NATIONAL PARK

The Glenelg River begins its journey to the sea in the Grampians in western Victoria, 400 km (248 miles) away. The lower reaches of the river are protected within the national park, which also takes in the Glenelg River Gorge. It is possible to launch small boats and canoes at several spots along the river. Other activities are fishing and swimming, while waterskiing is permitted only in designated zones. Numerous vehicle and walking tracks offer many opportunities to view the fauna and flora. There is also a magnificent display of wildflowers during spring in the eastern section of the park.
Map ref: page 338 B7

MACEDON

Macedon, 60 km (37 miles) northwest of Melbourne, is a small town, (population 1800), on the edge of the Great Dividing Range. Mount Macedon, which towers behind, is actually a 1000-m (3281-foot) volcano. The region is heavily forested and often damaged by bushfires. During the summer of 1983 much of Macedon was burnt in the Ash Wednesday fires, but the township remains, and many of the buildings, some which were historic structures, are being restored.

The area has always been forest land—timber was taken from this region and used in the mines during the gold rush. It was when the timber became scarce that orchardists moved to the region and built large mansions surrounded by spectacular gardens. One such property is Ard Choille, set on 98 ha (242 acres). During autumn, the large European trees which dot the landscape around Macedon come alive with warm copper tones.

The Macedon Regional Park encompasses more than 3200 ha (7907 acres) of land which can be used for bushwalking, horse riding and scenic drives. Within the park are the Major Mitchell Lookout and Camel's Hump. The large Memorial Cross, visible from afar, was originally built in honour of World War I soldiers, and was restored during 1996. There are more than 20 km (12 miles) of walking trails in the bush around Macedon.

A large collection of enormous boulders, which were originally formed by lava pushed up from the Earth's surface, forms Hanging Rock, a site which is steeped in much Aboriginal history. It was also the setting for Joan Lindsay's best-selling book and the subsequent film, *Picnic at Hanging Rock*. This is a popular site for harvest picnics and festivals during the year, and for quiet barbecues.
Map ref: page 339 M4

MALDON

Gold was discovered in the Maldon region in 1853 and mined until as recently as the 1930s. The quartz reef goldmines in this area were one of Victoria's richest diggings. At one stage, more than 20,000 men were employed in the diggings. This historic town, 141 km (88 miles) north-west of Melbourne, and 18 km (11.2 miles) north-west of Castlemaine, now has a population of 1300 and has been declared Australia's first 'Notable Town' by the National Trust. The town is also a popular tourist destination.

A stroll down Main Street beneath the line of verandas will take you back to the gold era as you pass antique shops, small quaint retail stores and art galleries. Evidence of the town's heritage is apparent in the large mullock heaps, now covered in grass, outside town, and the Beehive Mine Chimney on Main Street. The Beehive Mine was established in the 1860s and named by a group of Cornish miners, who saw a swarm of bees near the mine. The chimney was built in 1862, and although it fell into disrepair after mining ceased, it has since been fully restored.

Excellent views can be had from Anzac Hill Lookout. Another attraction is the Vintage Railway, which journeys through lush forest from Maldon to Muckleford on the way to Castlemaine, pulled by an authentic steam engine. The railway was originally opened in 1884, during the gold rush, and was in operation for nearly 100 years. The Pioneer Cemetery fascinates many visitors. The Porcupine Township, 3 km (1.9 miles) out of Maldon, recreates an old goldmining town. At Carmen's Tunnel Gold Mine visitors can journey back in time and walk through the tunnel by candlelight.
Map ref: page 339 L3

MARYBOROUGH

Historic Maryborough, 171 km (106 miles) north-west of Melbourne, is surrounded by grazing land in the 'golden triangle' of Victoria, west of Castlemaine.

Dabb's General Store, with its authentically restored shopfront, in Maldon.

Maryborough has been described as 'a railway station with a town attached'.

A thriving industrial town, Maryborough has a population of 7850. The first settlers to the region were three Scottish brothers who set up a run in 1840 to graze their sheep. When gold was discovered at White Hills in 1854, the town became a major supply point for the gold rushes that spread through the centre of Victoria. The town was named by the Gold Commissioner after his home town in Ireland. Mining continued in the region until 1918, after which the town's economic base changed and it became a service and industrial centre.

There are many magnificent old buildings in town, but the most impressive is the Maryborough Railway Station, which is not just a historic site but also a tourist complex. The station has been meticulously restored and is considered one of the finest in Victoria. On what is believed to be one of the longest railway platforms in the Southern Hemisphere is the Maryborough Station Antique Emporium, with antiques, collectables and old wares, as well as an art gallery, a café and markets with country crafts.

Other interesting buildings include a historic bluestone cottage that now houses the Museum of Creative Arts and Sciences. Worsley Cottage, built in 1894 by Arthur Worsley, is the base for the Midlands Historical Society, and features a collection of memorabilia

dating from 1854. Farther afield, the Bristol Hill Lookout Tower in the Bristol Hill Reserve offers spectacular views of the city, and there are Aboriginal drinking wells off Shoreham Drive. The five small wells are formed from granite outcrops and were used by the local Aborigines.

Wineries in the area, including Kangderaar, Newstead and Tipperary Estate, offer tastings and cellar sales. Events include the Maryborough Golden Wattle Festival, in September, and the Maryborough Highland Gathering Championships and Gift, on New Year's Day.
Map ref: page 339 K3

Chateau Tahbilk Winery, near Nagambie.

NAGAMBIE

A large lake in the centre of town is the main feature of Nagambie, a town with a population of 1500 that lies 125 km (78 miles) north of Melbourne. The artificial lake was constructed in 1887, using the plentiful waters of the Goulburn River. The lake is a favourite with waterskiers, while the quieter waters upstream are sought after by canoeists, or anglers trying their luck at landing trout or redfin. Speedboat and waterskiing tournaments as well as rowing regattas are held here throughout the year. Boat hire is also available.

To the north of the town is the Goulburn Weir, which supplies irrigation channels and is linked to the Waranga Basin near Murchison.

This weir was built at around the same time as Lake Nagambie. The surrounding countryside is mainly used for grazing.

The Historical Society and Folk Museum, housed in the old courthouse, contains exhibits illustrating the town's history. There is a Colonial Doll Shop and The Nut House, where Australian nuts and Australian-made products are for sale. There are also several wineries in the region, including Mitchelton Winery and Goulburn Valley. Chateau Tahbilk Winery and Vineyard is housed on a magnificent historic property. The cellars are classified by the National Trust and a visit to this historic property is a must.
See also Central Victoria Wine Region
Map ref: page 339 P2

NELSON

Nelson is a tiny fishing hamlet (population 200) located at the mouth of the Glenelg River in the far south-west of the State, 5 km (3.1 miles) from the border of South Australia and Victoria and 439 km

(273 miles) west of Melbourne. Surrounded by Discovery Bay Coastal Park and Lower Glenelg National Park, it is the natural features around the town that attract visitors.

The Glenelg River flows out into Discovery Bay and anglers are drawn here in the hope of landing bass, southern black bream or Australian salmon. Boating is popular along the estuary and up into the park; canoeing is especially popular, as it is the best way to view the outstanding cliffs of the gorge area of the Glenelg River. Power boats are permitted to use the lower section of the river outside the park area. The Nelson Endeavour River Cruise is another way to view the scenery. This cruise also visits the Princess Margaret Rose Caves with their spectacular stalactites, stalagmites and columns.

The Great South-West Walk, a 250-km (155-mile) trek along the south-west of Victoria, runs through Lower Glenelg Park. This takes about 10 days and should be undertaken only by the fit, and only during the cooler months.
Map ref: page 338 A7

The remote and unspoilt Glenelg River area can be accessed from Nelson.

OCEAN GROVE–
BARWON HEADS

The twin townships of Ocean Grove and Barwon Heads, about 100 km (62 miles) south-west of Melbourne, are at the mouth of the Barwon River where it flows into Bass Strait. With stunning seaside scenery and more than 6 km (4 miles) of sandy beaches, these towns, with a population of 8155, cater for a large number of tourists to the Bellarine Peninsula every summer. Ocean Grove was originally settled in 1854; apart from fishing, leather tanning was a major industry. Bark from the many wattle trees in the area was used in the process.

The major swimming area, Smiths Beach, is frequented by residents and tourists, while the waters off the beach are also popular with surfers, scuba divers, sailors and waterskiers. Other attractions include the Moorfield Wildlife Park, where visitors can feed kangaroos and native birds in a natural setting, and A Maze N Things, which is popular with children. This complex has a large wooden maze along with mini-golf and a puzzle centre. Bushwalkers will delight in the parklands in the Foreshore Reserve and the Nature Reserve, both of which have several walking trails. The foreshore offers magnificent views of the coast and Bass Strait. Local events include the Collendia Cup Ocean Grove Festival in March.
See also Port Phillip Bay Wine Region
Map ref: page 339 M8

The popular Smiths beach at Ocean Grove.

The view from the Grampian Ranges lookout near Penshurst.

PENSHURST

Penshurst lies on the Hamilton Highway between Hamilton and Mortlake in the west of the State, 282 km (175 miles) from Melbourne. It is a small farming town, with a population of 483, and also services the smaller communities in the region. Perched above Penshurst is Mount Rouse, which is 339 m (1112 feet) high and offers commanding views of the countryside and the Grampians district, which lies to the north of the town.

The Grampians are the starting point of the Great Dividing Range. Grampians National Park is popular with bushwalkers, climbers and bird-watchers. During spring the area is covered with wild-flowers. There are also lakes which are popular for water sports and swimming. These include Lake Linlith-gow and Lake Swallow, which are both on Chatsworth Road—yachting, waterskiing and fishing are enjoyed all year. The Penshurst Agricultural Show is held in December.
See also Grampians and Pyrenees Wine Region
Map ref: page 338 E6

PETERBOROUGH

Peterborough, 246 km (153 miles) west of Melbourne, is in the west of the State on the Great Ocean Road. The famous road winds along the coastline from Torquay affording spectacular coastal views of huge cliffs towering above and beaches below. The township, population 210, is at the entrance of Curdies Inlet. The surfing is good, but swimming and windsurfing are the more favoured sports in the relatively safe and protected waters of Curdies Inlet.

The coastline is the major attraction of the area. Along the Great Ocean Road near Peterborough is the Bay of Islands, with an unusual cluster of rocks that have formed small islands. The Bay of Martyrs has a similar group of rock pillars. There are rock formations and rugged cliffs at Crofts Bay and Childers Cove as well. Massacre Bay has a secluded beach area that is popular with anglers. Between Peterborough and Port Campbell the Great Ocean Road offers magnificent views of the natural rock pillars and cliffs of Loch Ard Gorge, London Bridge and the Arch, all of which fall under the protection of the Port Campbell National Park.
Map ref: page 338 G9

POINT LONSDALE

The town of Point Lonsdale, 105 km (65 miles) south-west of Melbourne at the small entrance into Port Phillip Bay, originally served as a signal station from 1854 for ships entering the bay. In 1902 the signal station was replaced by a large lighthouse that is still in service. Point Lonsdale, with a current population of 1740, has always played a major part in Port Phillip's shipping industry.

At Rip View Lookout vessels can be seen sailing in and out of the 'rip', as the treacherous waters of the entrance are known—the rip has taken its toll on shipping over the years. Swimming is best enjoyed on the Front Beach inside Port Phillip Bay; the surf beach is on the Bass Strait side of the head. Walking tracks and a cycling track follow the foreshore right around the head and reserves protect the area. A ferry crosses the bay from the nearby seaside town of Queens-cliff to Sorrento each day. The Marconi Memorial on the Point Lonsdale Road marks the site where the first broadcast was made

The lighthouse at Point Lonsdale, Port Phillip Bay.

to Tasmania in 1906. It is named after the radio equipment supplied by the Marconi Wireless Company.
Map ref: page 339 N8

PORTARLINGTON

The waters of Portarlington are popular for a range of activities, including sailing, snorkelling, safe ocean swimming and excellent surfing, and see the population of Portarlington swell during the summer months from the usual

The Twelve Apostles were once part of a limestone cave system. Gradually the outer limestone wore away creating these stacks.

2565. Situated on the Bellarine Peninsula, 105 km (65 miles) south-west of Melbourne and only 32 km (20 miles) from Geelong, there is also good fishing in the waters of Port Phillip Bay.

The town, named after Lord Arlington in 1851, grew quickly. A steam-powered flour mill was in operation by 1856—this enormous four-storey sandstone building is now classified by the National Trust. It houses historic displays from the area, including displays pertaining to local Aboriginal history.

The Bellarine Peninsula also has a history of winemaking. Near Portarlington is Kilgour Estate, in Bellarine, and Mount Duneed winery is on Feehans Road. The Geelong Gourmet Wine and Food Fair is held on Australia Day in January. *See also* Port Phillip Bay Wine Region
Map ref: page 339 N7

PORT CAMPBELL

Port Campbell, situated near the major attractions of the Great Ocean Road in the south-west of the State—234 km (145 miles) west of Melbourne—is a small crayfishing village. Though Port Campbell has a population of only 200, it plays host to the large number of tourists who visit this coast to view the shipwrecks which it is so renowned for.

On the lengthy voyage to and from England during the 1800s and early 1900s, the ruthless southern coastline of Australia was considered one of the worst stretches of the journey. Many ships met their end along the coastline of what is now the Port Campbell National Park. The most famous is the *Loch Ard*, which was wrecked in 1878, claiming the lives of 52 people. The Loch Ard Gorge is on the stretch of road that runs from Port Campbell east to Princetown, as are a number of other notable clusters of islands off the coastline, such as the Blow Hole, Mutton Bird Island and Elephant Rock. London Bridge is another interesting formation. It was once a double arch resembling London Bridge, but it collapsed in 1990, stranding sightseers, and is now a detached landmass. Without doubt the most spectacular landmark on the whole of the Victorian coastline, and the most photographed, is the Twelve Apostles, offshore stacks which have eroded over the years, with only eight now left standing above the water line.

There are a number of picturesque walks near Port Campbell, including the Port Campbell Discovery Walk, which is 2.5 km (1.6 miles) long. It starts near the Port Campbell beach and takes in some of the delights of the national park. To the north is the township of Timboon, where a 5-km (3.1-mile) walk leads to a magnificent railway trestle bridge.
Map ref: page 339 H9

PORT FAIRY

The fishing town of Port Fairy, 293 km (182 miles) west of Melbourne, is one of the main ports supplying a major share of Victoria's abalone and crayfish catch. Port Fairy is one of the State's oldest ports—many of the buildings date back to the nineteenth century, and more than 50 are now classified by the National Trust. Situated at the mouth of the Moyne River, the town was originally a whaling centre, but fishing and tourism are now its main industries.

The town (population 2505), features many historic buildings, such as Motts Cottage in Sackville Street. The restored stone home of pioneer Charles Mills is on Woodbine Road. The Port Fairy Historical Society, located in the old courthouse, displays photographs and memorabilia. Another interesting walk is along the jetty on the Moyne River, where the fishing fleet docks.

Griffith Island, off the eastern coast of Port Fairy, was once the site of a large whaling station. It is now home to a colony of muttonbirds—they nest on the island in September. The Port Fairy Lighthouse is at the far eastern point of the island. Further afield is Mount Eccles National Park, home to an extinct volcano. Events include the Moyneyana Festival, which is held over January, and the Port Fairy Folk Festival, which features in Labour Day festivities in March.
Map ref: page 338 E8

More than 50 of the old cottages and buildings in Port Fairy have been classified by the National Trust.

PORTLAND

The historic town of Portland, 367 km (228 miles) west of Melbourne, is surrounded by rich grazing land and has a large number of buildings which are classified by the National Trust. Portland was originally established as a whaling and sealing port in the early 1800s because of the deep waters of Portland Bay, but that industry gave way to fishing and grazing when the number of whales decreased in the mid-1800s. Farmers used the port to ship their goods to Melbourne, as this was quicker than travelling by road. The area still relies on grazing and fishing along with tourism, and the town itself now has a population of 11,000. An aluminium smelter has been established in the town and this has helped boost the economy.

Among the classified buildings are the Old Steam Packet Inn, which was built in 1842 using timber from Tasmania and local bluestone, and Burswood, which was built in 1856 and is now a bed and breakfast accommodation house with impressive gardens. In the botanic gardens near Henty Park is a delightful old cottage which has been fully restored and furnished in its original 1857 style.

A walking track from the park circles Fawthrop Lagoon and leads to the vintage car club museum. This wetland, which has been declared a wildlife reserve, is fed by the incoming tide and is home to unusual plant life and numerous birds. Penguins also frequent

Portland—they can be found at Henty Beach on the harbour foreshore. An artificial habitat has been created for these birds which have declined in numbers over the years.

Attractions in the region include the Great South-West Walk, a 250-km (155-mile) trek along the coastline of western Victoria which begins just west of Portland. The walk is divided into 17 separate sections, which vary from 8–22 km (5–14 miles). A more leisurely walk can be enjoyed amid the unique sandstone formations, known as the Petrified Forest, near Cape Bridgewater. Cape Bridgewater is also the site of the last manned lighthouse in Victoria, which is just west of town.

The Portland Show is held in February, and the Dahlia Festival runs over the long weekend in March. The Three Bays Running Marathon takes place in mid-November, and the Surfboat Marathon is held annually in December.
Map ref: page 338 C8

PORT PHILLIP BAY WINE REGION

Geelong and its surrounding area has had a thriving wine industry since the late 1800s, a ready market in Melbourne only 100 km (62 miles) away, and an influx of European settlers. But by the turn of the century a nervous government had reacted to the discovery of phylloxera in the region by eradicating the vineyards, and it was not until the late 1960s that vines were growing there again. However, there are now about 50 vineyards producing wine for local and export markets. Scotchman's Hill, on the beautiful Bellarine Peninsula, and Bannockburn Vineyards are among the better-known producers. Many of the smaller wineries are open for cellar door sales and wine tastings.

As one of Australia's most southerly regions, Geelong enjoys a long ripening period extending

Pelicans are a common sight in Queenscliff waters.

into May, allowing grapes to develop complexity and depth of flavour. Strongly influenced by its proximity to the ocean, the area has scant summer rainfall, chill winds and poor clay soils. When Geelong wine is good, it is very good. Predictably, pinot noir and chardonnay are grown with distinction in the southerly climate. All the cool-climate viticultural tricks are required to protect the slow-ripening fruit. Ironically, low rainfall necessitates irrigation during vine growth.
Map ref: page 339 M7

QUEENSCLIFF

In 1842 Queenscliff was a settlement for the customs house, lighthouse and pilot station at the entrance to Port Phillip Bay, 108 km (67 miles) south-west of Melbourne, on the Bellarine Peninsula. By 1880 it had become a fashionable resort for Melburnians, who would travel to it by steamboat across the bay. Today, while Victoria has many seaside resorts on its shores, none is more elegant than Queenscliff. A short trip on a car ferry from Sorrento takes you to Queenscliff, where grand historic hotels offer superb dining and accommodation. The town's population is 1935.

While it is the grand hotels and magnificent views that attract tourists, there are also plenty of historic attractions to investigate on a visit to today's Queenscliff. The Maritime Museum has recorded the maritime history of the bay and houses artefacts such as the town's old lifeboat. Photographs, maps and records of early life in Queenscliff and the Port Phillip Bay Heads region can be found at the Historical Museum in the centre of town. Fort Queenscliff is one of the largest historic military fortresses in Australia, and has been preserved as a museum.

Every Sunday steam train enthusiasts operate the Bellarine Peninsula Railway, offering visitors a journey from Queenscliff to Lakers Siding 5 km (3 miles) away, or to Drysdale, on the other side of the peninsula. The train is hauled by authentic steam engines which the group has acquired from around Australia, and a journey on it is a must for buffs. See also Port Phillip Bay Wine Region
Map ref: page 339 N7

RUSHWORTH

Gold was discovered in this region in 1853 and this eventually led to the establishment of the town of Rushworth, in the Goulburn Valley—100 km (62 miles) north of Bendigo and 168 km (104 miles) north of Melbourne. At the peak of the gold rush there were 26 mines operating in the area, and more than 40,000 miners; now the town has a population of only 1000. The early name for the area was Nuggety, and the prosperous Nuggety–Whroo goldfields were active until the 1870s. Many of the beautiful historic buildings in the old mining town of Rushworth, including St Paul's Church of England, the Imperial Hotel and the band rotunda, are now classified by the National Trust.

The Waranga Basin, on the outskirts of town, is a huge reservoir which supplies water to the Wimmera and the Mallee in the State's west via more than 350 km (217 miles) of irrigation channels. Built between 1903 and 1905 on a large swamp, it is contained by a large earthen embankment more than 7 km (4.3 miles) long and with a capacity of 410,000 megalitres (108.2 million gallons). The basin

Dairy farms in Portland, such as Gunaoneday Dairy, are open to the public.

Scotchman's Hill vineyard on the Bellarine Peninsula, Port Phillip Bay Wine Region.

is also popular for boating, water-skiing and fishing. The Rushworth State Forest is the largest ironbark forest in the world.
See also Central Victoria Wine Region

Map ref: page 339 P1

ST LEONARDS

A delightful seaside town on the eastern edge of the Bellarine Peninsula, 144 km (89 miles) south-west of Melbourne, St Leonards and its small sister town of Indented Head are popular summer retreats. The two towns feature in Australia's early European exploration expeditions—Matthew Flinders landed in St Leonards in 1802, and a stone cairn in Batman Park at Indented Head indicates the site where John Batman landed during his expedition along the coast in 1835. The area was first settled during the 1850s, when pioneers set up a leather tanning industry using the bark from the wattle trees for tanning the leather. A timber industry was also established, along with fishing (in the waters of Port Phillip Bay), which was lucrative.

St Leonards is a small town now, with a population of just 1023, and close to the popular resort of Queenscliff, where the car ferry sails every day to and from Portsea and Sorrento. It boasts a golf course and a picturesque foreshore—camping is allowed north of the jetty. South of town, on the foreshore past the yacht club, is Edwards Point State Fauna Reserve, which provides a safe habitat for birds including the rare orange-bellied parrot. Vineyards have long been established on the Bellarine Peninsula; Kilgour Estate and Scotchman's Hill, the largest of the wineries on the peninsula, are close to St Leonards.
See also Port Phillip Bay Wine Region

Map ref: page 339 N7

STAWELL

The town of Stawell, 239 km (148 miles) north-west of Melbourne, and 129 km (80 miles) north-west of Ballarat, and with a population today of 6700, was first settled after gold was discovered here in 1853; a huge gold rush that lasted until the 1860s followed. When much of the easily extracted alluvial gold had been recovered and prospectors moved on to easier diggings, Stawell started to establish itself as a farming town. The large Pleasant Creek Quartz Mine was established at this time, and it worked the gold reefs deep down in the ground around Stawell until 1920. Gold has continually been found in the area, and even today there are people mining around Stawell. Stawell is close to the rugged Grampians, which are an ideal area for bushwalking and rock climbing. The Wimmera wheat region and the old goldfield towns of central Victoria can also be easily reached from Stawell.

At Pioneer Lookout and Memorial, on the 'Big Hill'—a goldmining site—is the best place from which to view the town and surrounding area. A memorial was laid here in 1935 to commemorate the pioneers who opened up this region last century. The lookout also indicates the positions of famous mines.

The famous Stawell Gift foot race is held over Easter every year. This event, run by the Stawell Athletic Club, has been conducted since the club was first formed in 1878 and is the oldest professional running race in Australia. The Stawell Gift Hall of Fame in Central Park features videos of events dating back as far as 1927, along with other memorabilia.

Among the town's attractions are the Yabby Farm on the Halls Gap road, which has yabbies and trout for sale. With rod and bait supplied, you can even have a go at catching them yourself. Sisters Rocks are a collection of huge granite boulders on the side of the Western Highway. They are named after the three Levi Sisters, who camped in the area during the gold rush days. Today the boulders are covered in graffiti. Markets are held on the first Sunday of each month at the State Emergency Services Headquarters in Sloane Street. Casper's World in the Miniature Tourist Park, has working models, to scale, of famous buildings such as the Eiffel Tower.
See also Grampians and Pyrenees Wine Region

Map ref: page 338 G3

Central Park on Lower Main Street, Stawell, is where the Stawell Gift has been run since the year 1898.

TORQUAY

The village of Torquay, 98 km (61 miles) south-west of Melbourne, is a surfers' mecca, with long stretches of golden sandy beaches and great waves. The town has a population of 4887, but this number is swelled by the surfers who 'hang out' here during summer. Bells Beach, the famous surf beach where national and international challenges—such as the Bells Easter Classic, a top competition for professional surfers— are held, is near here. The competition was established in 1961. Torquay is also the start of the Great Ocean Road, a magnificent, winding stretch of road that offers superb coastal views and passes through some of the region's more spectacular rainforest areas.

Originally known as Spring Creek, Torquay was named by the Scammell brothers, whose clipper *Joseph Scammell* ran aground on rocks outside the town site in 1891. The Scammells later developed a shipping company here. The name of the town was later changed to Torquay, after the English seaside resort in Devon.

Surfworld, Australia's only surfing museum, is in Surfworld Plaza, which is open every day and features videos, interactive displays and a wave-making tank. You can also buy surfing gear here. Surfing competitions are held from November through to April—the major competitions are held during Easter. The Torquay High Tide Festival is held in early December.

Other attractions in the town include Scammell House, a home that incorporates the deckhouse of the clipper *Joseph Scammell* and, for a spectacular view of the Great Ocean Road and its famous landmarks, a trip through the skies in an authentic Tiger Moth plane.
Map ref: page 339 M8

WARRNAMBOOL

Warrnambool, 265 km (165 miles) west of Melbourne, is on the western coastline of Victoria on the Great Ocean Road. This site was chosen because of its harbour access and it was originally settled by whalers and sealers. Ships from England stopped here on their way to the ports of Melbourne and Sydney, but many met their end on this rugged coastline, and the region is often referred to as the 'Shipwreck Coast'.

Information on the coastline and shipwrecks is available at the Flagstaff Hill Maritime Museum,

Torquay is a popular mecca for surfers, being near both Bells and Jan Juc surfing beaches.

arguably Warrnambool's top attraction. The Flagstaff Hill Maritime Museum uses restored and re-created buildings to depict an early coastal settlement. Features include an operating lighthouse and a number of historic vessels. The *Loch Ard*, one of Australia's better known shipwrecks, lies off the coast along the Great Ocean Road. The *Loch Ard* Peacock, an ornate statue plucked from the wreck, is housed in this museum.

Warrnambool is now a fishing, farming and tourist centre, with a population of 25,500. The town has many magnificent parks and gardens. A fine example of this is the Fletcher Jones clothing factory, surrounded by gardens in which the delightful floral displays are floodlit at night. These gardens are so popular that they are regularly hired out for wedding ceremonies.

Cannon Hill offers panoramic views of the bay and Lake Petrobe. Lake Petrobe Adventure Park provides plenty of fun for the whole family, with a maze, boats, islands and walking tracks. Other attractions include the fairy penguins at Middle Island—a colony of these creatures have made their burrows there. At low tide it is possible to wade across to the island.

The yacht club and the Breakwater Aquarium are at the southwest end of town at Breakwater Rock. The aquarium displays many species of fish found locally, along with a large sea shell collection. Adjacent to the aquarium is Thunder Point Coastal Reserve, with walking tracks leading to fantastic views of the Southern Ocean.

Hopkins Falls, on Hopkins Falls Road, 15 km (9.3 miles) north-east of town, is often referred to as 'Little Niagara'. During summer eels migrate down the river and can be seen falling over the edge. The falls are at their best after heavy rain. Another interesting place to visit is the Tower Hill State Game Reserve, on the Princes Highway west of the town. The reserve is based on an extinct volcano. You can climb to the top of the rim and be rewarded with excellent views of the crater and surrounding countryside.

In early summer, elvers (baby eels) migrate upstream over Hopkins Falls, Warrnambool.

Sunday markets are held every weekend at the showgrounds, the racing carnival is held in May, and the Melbourne to Warrnambool Cycle Classic and the annual show are both held during October.
Map ref: page 338 F8

WEDDERBURN

This town, once one of the State's richest gold producers, but now with a population of only 795, is located on the Calder Highway only 74 km (46 miles) north of the regional centre of Bendigo and 216 km (134 miles) north-west of Melbourne. The township of Wedderburn was originally settled by squatters in the 1840s but from the time gold was first struck here in 1852, the region was inundated with prospectors hoping to find a nugget. Many large nuggets have been found here. While gold was still being mined, swampland surrounding the diggings was reclaimed by a man called Duncan McGregor and an engineer, Carlo Catani. It is suggested that at the peak of this project in 1889, there were more than 500 men involved.

The tawny frogmouth (Podargus strigoides), inhabits the woodlands around Wedderburn.

The dense mallee scrub was difficult to remove, and for many years much of the scrub outside the town was not cleared. As the town grew and these areas were eventually cleared, gold discoveries continued to be made, some as late as the 1950s, when gold nuggets worth $20,000 were found in one resident's backyard. Then, in 1979, the Beggary Lump, an enormous gold nugget valued at $50,000, was discovered. Memorabilia can be seen at the General Store Museum, built in 1910. There is also a coach building and blacksmith's shop here. An annual Gold Dig is held in March.

Seventeen kilometres (11 miles) outside town is the Wychitella Flora and Fauna Reserve, a 3930-ha (9711-acre) park which is believed to have the most concentrated population of mallee fowl. Flora and fauna in the reserve are protected, and gold prospecting is not allowed here.
Map ref: page 339 J1

WINCHELSEA

The small township of Winchelsea (population 1180) sits on the banks of the Barwon River, a large river which flows down towards Geelong before running into the sea at Barwon Heads. Winchelsea is 115 km (71 miles) south-west of Melbourne and 37 km (23 miles) west of Geelong. Originally it was a stopping off point for water and shelter for travellers on the road between the towns of Geelong and Colac, the township is now surrounded by farmland and serves the rural community. The river is good for swimming, and the town is not far from the seaside towns of Barwon Heads and Geelong, where there are beaches and ocean swimming and surfing.

The town features historic bluestone buildings, bridges and shops from the nineteenth century, and magnificent gardens. One notable property is the National Trust property, Barwon Park, on Inverleigh Road 3 km (2 miles) out of town. It is a superb two-storey bluestone mansion which was completed in 1871 by Thomas Austin, a wealthy English grazier who brought animals such as pheasants, quail and foxes to Australia for game sport. He was also responsible for introducing the rabbit, which was later to increase to plague proportions and become a pest throughout Australia; the fox has also caused much destruction and disturbance to native flora and fauna.
Map ref: page 339 K7

The seaside resort of Barwon Heads near Winchelsea is a popular beach, being the closest ocean swimming available to the major city of Geelong.

NORTH-WEST VICTORIA

Red sand plains, tawny wheatfields, lush fruitlands, historic river ports, quiet fishing spots, myriad birdlife, majestic Murray River scenery and a range of activities from waterskiing to 4WD treks—all are found in this 'off the beaten track' part of Victoria.

Melbourne

Wedged into the north-west corner, the Mallee is Victoria's outback—arid and infertile, it is the least populated part of the State. Much of it is now preserved in vast desert parks—Wyperfield and Murray-Sunset national parks and Big Desert Wilderness Park—hauntingly beautiful expanses of dunes, shimmering salt lakes, spinifex and mallee scrub that in spring are transformed into wondrous masses of wildflowers. Animals such as kangaroos, emus and parrots are abundant and the area is also home to the extraordinary mallee fowl, a turkey-sized bird that invests most of its days preparing and maintaining a sophisticated incubating mound for its eggs, but then leaves its newly hatched chicks to fend entirely for themselves.

Wheatfields roll to the horizon on the more fertile plains to the south and east. Here the original vegetation of mallee scrub has been painstakingly removed, most often by way of the mallee roller—in its simplest form a heavy hollow log dragged through the scrub (the enormous roots, which are now highly valued by wood-carvers, were usually burned).

In the north the broad Murray River flows beside dramatic red cliffs of hardened sand, massive river red gums and reedy swamps; waterbirds crowd its banks and a string of overflow lakes. From the mid-1850s until the extension of the railway in the 1880s the Murray River was the major transport link between inland wheat farms and sheep stations and distant southern markets. More than 100 paddle-steamers plied the waters delivering outback produce to railheads at Echuca and Swan Hill, then returning west with supplies. Today tourist cruises operate along the river, although their routes are much curtailed by twentieth-century weirs and water catchments. The city of Mildura, west along the Murray, is the centre of the Sunraysia irrigation area, where marginal mallee lands made fruitful by pumped Murray waters now produces most of the country's dried raisins and sultanas.

OPPOSITE: The paddle-steamer Coonawarra, built in 1894, offers cruises and accommodation on the Murray River, near Mildura.

Huge bales of hay dot the landscape after the harvest in the wheat-belt.

REGIONAL FEATURE

Victoria's Outback

Power is seldom available at camp sites in this region, so travellers requiring night lights will either have to bring their own generator or run a light off the battery in their vehicle.

The north-western corner of Victoria is a wild region of expansive salt flats, sprawling sand dunes and arid scrub. Located just six hours from Melbourne, it is easily accessible yet provides a taste of the kind of arid wilderness found in much more remote parts of the Australian interior. For this reason, it is often referred to as 'Victoria's outback'. A spectacular and surprisingly varied environment, it offers travellers dramatic scenery, challenging hiking and off-road driving, and the chance to view a host of unusual plant and animal species, some of which are unique to the region. Much of Victoria's Outback is encompassed by Murray–Sunset National Park, the second-largest national park in the state.

The southern half of the region is dominated by mallee scrub. The name 'mallee' is an Aboriginal word that refers to the unusual stunted form of these eucalypt trees. Twenty different species of mallees can be found here, many of which live to an age of 500 years. To the north, this vegetation dwindles, giving way to broad swathes of sand and normally dry salt lakes.

A wide range of specially adapted animal species thrives in the arid environment. Most, such as the planigale and native hopping mouse, remain hidden by day, though red and western grey kangaroos are abundant in the northern sector and birdlife, including emus, parrots, wrens and warblers, is plentiful, particularly around floodplains and billabongs. The animal most closely associated with the region is the mallee fowl, a remarkable bird that incubates its eggs in an enormous purpose-built mound of earth.

The principal access route to the region is the Sunraysia Highway, which runs north to Mildura on the New South Wales border. Two main roads branch westward from the Sunraysia: the Mallee Highway, which stretches from Ouyen to the South Australia border and thence to Adelaide, and the Sturt Highway in the far north, which leads directly west to Renmark. Some minor roads are suitable for conventional vehicles, but a 4WD will permit deeper exploration of this fascinating part of the state. Travellers are advised to avoid visiting in the summer months when temperatures, and the risk of bush fires, soar.

Like other robins, the red-capped robin (Petroica goodenovii) builds a cup-shaped nest. Incubation lasts about two weeks.

History

Although Charles Sturt sailed down the Murray River in 1830 and Major Thomas Mitchell passed to the east of here during the 1836 expedition that opened up much of the new colony of Victoria, for the most part early European explorers avoided the immense tangle of sand and scrub that stretched south of the Murray River. The first to venture into the area were cattlemen who drove their herds westward along the banks of the Murray to the new colony of South Australia in the 1840s. Soon afterward, settlers were taking up pastoral leases in the same area. Before the

coming of railways and roads, the river was the major transport artery, and paddle steamers plied up and down the Murray, bringing goods to the settlers and returning to the coast laden with wool.

The present-day farmland areas along the Mallee Highway were declared open for settlement in 1909. Salt harvesting began in the Pink Lakes area in 1916, and in the 1920s construction work began on the locks along the Murray River. Following the introduction of irrigation in the 1930s, much of the land east of Mildura was planted with orchards and vine-

yards. The arid areas away from the river remained unsettled, however. Increasing awareness of their ecological and recreational value led to the Pink Lakes area becoming a national park in the 1970s and the huge Sunset Country National Park (now Murray–Sunset National Park) being dedicated in 1991.

Murray–Sunset National Park

This immense national park covers 633,000 ha (1,564,000 acres) and includes four major wilderness zones. Its most distinctive feature is a group of lakes in the southern end of the park whose distinctive rosy hue forms a striking contrast with the surrounding desert sands and dense mallee scrub, and earned them the name of the Pink Lakes. This is the best base for exploring the area by 4WD, bicycle or on foot. The pleasant campsite at Lake Crosbie is accessible to conventional vehicles and has toilets, fireplaces, picnic tables, gas barbecues, and a limited supply of water. Walkers can follow several pleasant trails around the lakes and view the remnants of the area's salt works and abandoned farming equipment.

Once you leave the environs of the Pink Lakes, you must be entirely self-sufficient and travel in a 4WD vehicle. There are wilderness camping areas at Mopoke, Pheneeys Track, Mount Crozier and Rocket Lake (which can also be accessed via Settlement Track in the north of the park), all of which have toilets, fireplaces and picnic tables.

*The Pink Lakes derive their unusual hue from carotene, a pigment secreted by a species of algae (*Dunaliella salina*) that inhabits adjacent groundwaters. The colour is brightest in spring.*

Along the northern edge of Murray–Sunset National Park, the Murray and Lindsay rivers regularly flood neighbouring plains, creating sizeable billabongs that are inhabited by Murray cod, redfin, golden perch and yabbies.

Murray–Sunset's lakeshores were inhabited by Aboriginal peoples for thousands of years. Signs of their occupation include shell middens, hearths and scar trees.

Exploring by 4WD

Well-prepared 4WD parties can enjoy the full gamut of environments in the area by undertaking the following trek from Ouyen in the south-east to Lock 7 on the Murray River, a distance of 307 km (191 miles).

Head west out of Ouyen on the Mallee Highway towards Pinnaroo, and near the tiny railway siding of Linga, 61 km (38 miles) west of the town, turn north onto the good dirt road leading into Murray–Sunset National Park, 11 km (7 miles) away. After you pass Lake Hardy on your right, continue straight ahead at the next Y-junction for 2 km (1.2 miles) to the camping ground on the southern shore of Lake Crosbie. Roos are common here, as are emus and other birds.

Return to the Y-junction and head west, and after just over 1 km (0.6 miles) turn right onto the Ring Road. Stay on the main Ring Road for nearly 4 km (2.5 miles), then veer left at the next Y-junction onto the Mount Crozier Track. Stretches of soft sand here indicate the start of 4WD-only territory. Most of the surrounding country is covered in mallee scrub, but there are patches of cleared land which are ideal for camping.

About 9 km (5.6 miles) beyond the Ring Road turn-off, you cross Honeymoon Hut Track and come to a Y-junction signposted 'Mount Crozier'. A short distance up this track, 88 km (55 miles) from Ouyen, is the car park for the walking trail to the top of the mountain itself. Although it's not much of a peak, Mount Crozier is the largest hill for many miles and its summit provides impressive views.

MOUNT CROZIER TO CULLULLERAINE

Backtrack to the main road and turn right, continuing westward. At the main Underbool Track some 10 km (6 miles) from the Mount Crozier junction, turn right. You are now on the park's main north–south track, most of which is easy going.

To the west is the biggest wilderness area in the park, the Sunset Wilderness Zone, which can only be explored on foot. If you are travelling early in the morning or late in the evening, you may spot a mallee fowl here as it flits across the track. The distinctive mounds where these birds incubate their eggs are harder to locate and you'd need to do a bit of exploring before you are likely to find one.

Continuing north, you reach Pheneys Track after 25 km (16 miles) and after another 10 km (6 miles) you come to a T-junction, where you should turn right onto the Rocket Lake Rail Track. This track is sometimes called the Nowingi Line Track, after the railway line that was built west from Nowingi on the Calder Highway to Rocket Lake in 1929, to help open the area up for settlement. But the settlers never came, and the line was never opened; it was dismantled soon afterward.

Veer left at the next junction 5 km (3.1 miles) from the Underbool track; 2 km (1.2 miles) later you reach the southern edge of Rocket Lake, 140 km (87 miles) from Ouyen. There are some pleasant camping sites around this

Close encounters with wildlife are common.

remote lake, which is also an excellent spot for birdwatching. The lake was supposedly named by the railway workers: those occupied near the lake fired rockets to let the workers further up the line know when it was time to knock off for the day.

If the lake is dry, you can take the track across it to reach the far side. Otherwise, follow the route around the shore to reach its northern edge. Here, another track heads due north. Nearly 10 km (6 miles) further on, a crossroads, with a small dam on the left, marks the northern boundary of the national park. The east–west track is Settlement Road, which was intended to help open up the area to farming in the 1950s and 1960s. The plan failed, however, and this and other tracks are its only legacy.

Turn left onto Settlement Road and head west for 34 km (21 miles), past numerous sidetracks, to the Yarrara track. Turn right and continue for about 15 km (9.3 miles) to reach Yarrara Forest Reserve. This is the largest remaining stand of belah woodland in Victoria, and it is home to many native birds, such as mallee ringnecks, mulga parrots, fairy wrens, honeyeaters, and robins; in spring, it is carpeted with colourful flowers.

Keep heading north for another 14 km (8.7 miles) or so through rolling wheat country until you reach the main Sturt Highway, then turn right; 10 km east along the bitumen you will come to Cullulleraine, 225 km (140 miles) from Ouyen. Here you will find two caravan parks with camping areas, and a licensed roadhouse where you can obtain supplies and fuel.

CULLULLERAINE TO LINDSAY ISLAND

Head north away from the bitumen, across rolling fields that soon give way to saltbush-studded plains— classic outback scenery. Within 10 km (6 miles), you come to a crossroads. Turn left onto the east–west track, which was once the old stage coach and mail

route from Mildura to Renmark. This road is usually pretty good, but it becomes slippery after even light showers and impassable after heavy rain or flooding.

After 6 km (3.7 miles), you reach Kulnine Station, and nearly 4 km (2.5 miles) after that the track crosses a grid and skirts the river. Some 26 km (16 miles) west of where you turned onto the east–west track you reach Neds Corner, and another 13 km (8 miles) further west you come to the edge of Lake Wallawalla. By now, you are in the northern sector of Murray–Sunset National Park.

The route continues straight through the centre of this lake, which is generally dry. If it is flooded, take the track along the eastern edge, which meets up with the main route 3 km (1.9 miles) west of the lake, just where it veers north. No more than 4 km (2.5 miles) beyond this point, a track on your right leads about 1 km (0.6 miles) to Lindsay Bridge. This is the only access to Lindsay Island.

Between 1847 and 1955, Lindsay Island was used for grazing. During the 1960s, the government planned to build a huge dam in the Chowilla area, downstream in South Australia, which would have flooded all of the island and surrounding country. Bridges were built and the area heavily logged in expectation of this flooding, but the project never got underway.

Popular with anglers and sailors, the island is now one of the wildest parts of the entire state. It is prone to flooding, however, and travellers should check the road conditions locally before venturing into the area.

Continuing across the Lindsay Bridge on the main track, the route heads north, then swings east as it approaches Mullaroo Creek, 10 km (6 miles) from the entrance to Lindsay Island. Cross Mullaroo Bridge, then veer right up toward Lock 7, 82 km (51 miles) from Cullulleraine and 307 km (191 miles) from Ouyen. This is where the trek ends, but the lock, where there are several bush-camping sites, makes a great base for exploring the whole island and, if you are lucky enough to have your own boat, the magnificent Murray River.

The sandy ground of this region favours plants such as the mallees, which put down extensive, multi-branched root systems.

Places in
NORTH-WEST
VICTORIA

COHUNA

This small town (population 2070) is 301 km (187 miles) north of Melbourne, and sits on a branch of the Murray River. It is a popular tourist destination for waterskiers, anglers and boating enthusiasts—nearby Gunbower Island provides the perfect base for these water activities. The Gunbower Island State Forest has magnificent red gum trees. Gunbower Island Wildlife Sanctuary, a part of the State forest, is home to a variety of wildlife, including kangaroos, possums and bird life—these are protected in the sanctuary. Summer brings warm to hot weather, and winter sees the roads in this forest reserve become very slippery, passable by 4WD vehicles only. The barefoot waterskiing championships which are held during April each year are extremely popular with visitors. The region is famous for animal skeletal finds, some of which date back more than 14,000 years.
Map ref: page 341 L8

ECHUCA

Echuca is a word in the local Aboriginal language that means 'meeting of the waters'. This major regional centre was built where the Campaspe and Goulburn rivers meet the Murray, 220 km (137 miles) north

Eastern grey kangaroos (Macropus giganteus).

of Melbourne. Established in 1853, this is one of the oldest river towns in Victoria. An inn was built on the banks of the Murray River by Henry Hopwood, who was an ex-convict. Then a punt was used to ferry passengers across the river—it was from this that the port of Echuca was born. Being on a major route between Victoria and New South Wales, Echuca grew rapidly, with passengers and produce crossing the Murray here. A railway line opened from Bendigo in 1864 and both produce and passengers travelled on the river.

By the 1880s Echuca was Victoria's second largest port. The Echuca Wharf was an impressive sight in those days: by 1884 it had grown to 1.2 km (0.75 miles) long and was built on three different levels to accommodate the different water heights experienced during various seasons. A wood shortage at the turn of the century meant that the paddle-steamers could no longer run as often and the port slowed down. By 1944 the wharf was in disrepair, but it has since been partially restored by the National Trust. They have also protected many other historic buildings in the area. The town's population today is 10,000. The old port is now a museum, and a handful of paddle-

steamers have been done up and returned to their former glory, including the *Emmylou, Canberra* and *Pride of the Murray*.

The Murray River is popular for a variety of water-based activities, including fishing for the massive Murray cod. Houseboats are a great way to explore the river, and can be hired at Echuca from a number of operators. There are many other attractions in town, including the Echuca Historical Society Museum, the World in Wax Museum and the Coach House Carriage Collection, which includes more than 25 restored coaches from around the world. Car lovers will delight in the Holden Motor Museum.

Echuca has several annual festivals and events, including the Southern 80, a waterski race along the Murray which is held on the second weekend in February. The Rich River Festival is run over one week in October, and includes many and varied events.
Map ref: page 341 N9

HATTAH–KULKYNE
NATIONAL PARK

This national park runs east of the Calder Highway between Ouyen and Mildura, and combined with the Murray–Kulkyne Park, the area offers many opportunities for outdoor recreation. The Hattah Lakes system forms the heart of the national park, filling when the Murray River floods. Imposing river red gums line the banks of the Murray River, and red gums, black box, native grasses and water plants are well established around the lakes. The lakes are a haven for birds and

many species breed here. Depending on water levels, canoeing can be an excellent way to survey the lakes, and there are unlimited walking opportunities. There is also a good network of vehicle tracks through the park; they are often very sandy, though, and can become impassable after rain, so they are best suited to 4WDs. Visitors should always carry water with them in this park.
Map ref: page 340 E3

KERANG

There are a number of lakes and swamps in the region around Kerang (population 4030), where the waters from the Loddon River gather. The Middle Lake features one of the largest ibis rookeries in the world—nesting season is particularly popular with birdwatchers,

The Lester Smith Lookout Tower at Kerang.

as thousands of birds arrive to nest between August and April. During the duck season, many hunters descend on the region. Lake Charm is popular for waterskiing and boating activities and the shallower First Lake is the first choice for swimmers.

The town, which is 286 km (178 miles) north of Melbourne, began as an inn next to a bridge which crossed the Loddon River. The inn was built in 1863 by the earliest settler in the region, Woodful Patchell. It was not long after settlement that this Irish farmer started to use the water from the lakes and rivers to irrigate his property. Irrigation has since been widely used throughout the northern regions of Victoria. Farming

Cruises are available on the restored paddle-steamer Emmylou at Echuca.

remains the main industry in the region, although tourism, especially in the summer months, has added to the town's economy.

The town's museum contains artefacts and photographs of the area's history. The Lester Smith Lookout Tower, which used to store the town's water, is now the tourist centre. A climb to the top gives excellent views of the surrounding waterways. There is an annual show held in the first week of October.
Map ref: page 341 K7

MILDURA

Located on the banks of the Murray River in the far north-west of the State—550 km (342 miles) from Melbourne—is Mildura, a town surrounded by hundreds of hectares of farmland in the heart of the Sunraysia region, producing grape vines and citrus fruit. With the constant warm to hot weather, little rain and the plentiful waters of the Murray River, it is a great holiday destination. The name Mildura comes from a word in a local Aboriginal language meaning 'red rock' or 'red earth', which is a description of the deep red soil found in the region.

Pastoralists Hugh and Bushby Jamieson settled in the area in 1847 and, because of the arid land, an irrigation system was set up in the 1880s; this now sees water pumped from the Murray River to provide year-round water for crops. The town has a population of 17,990, and a variety of crops continue to be produced in the area around it, including grapes for sultanas and wine, olives and citrus fruits. The Citrus Shop and Information Centre has plenty of information for visitors about citrus production in the region, and 'Sultana Sam' offers a guided tour of a vineyard.

The heart of the town of Mildura is the Murray River, home to many boats and old paddle-steamers. These huge vessels used to cruise the waters of the Murray picking up loads of wool from sheep stations and shipping them to inland ports. There are still some paddle-steamers using the Murray around Mildura, including the *Melbourne*. This retains its original engine and boiler and operates cruises down to Lock 11—the round trip takes around two hours. The vessel was built in 1912 for the

Victorian government, and was restored in 1965. The *Rothbury* also operates on the Murray, taking visitors to the Golden River Zoo and Trentham Winery.

The Mildura Arts Centre is based around the home of William Chaffey, irrigation pioneer. Built from Murray pine, red gum and red brick, it was completed in 1899. The Centre is an art gallery and theatre, and houses an excellent collection of Australian and European paintings and sculptures.

Further south of town are the Murray–Kulkyne Park and the Hattah–Kulkyne National Park, both of them west of the Murray River. The area is an example of a typical mallee environment, with natural cypress pine woodland and vast areas of mallee scrubland. The Hattah Lakes are a life source for many waterfowl. Both parks have camping areas and sandy 4WD tracks. Visitors should always carry their own water with them in this park.

Events in town include the Mildura Vintage and Arts Festival, which is held annually in March, the Mildura Golf Week in July, Country Music Week in September and the Festival of the Oasis Rose during November. There are also several wineries in the region, including Capagreco and Trentham Estate, and for wine buffs there is

The hot, dry Mediterranean-style climate of Mildura makes it an ideal wine-growing area.

a Sunraysia Wine and Jazz Festival, which takes place annually during the month of November.
See also North-West Victoria Wine Region
Map ref: page 340 E2

NHILL

Located at the halfway point between Melbourne and Adelaide—378 km (235 miles) north-west of Melbourne—Nhill is an important centre for the wheat industry in the Wimmera region. The town was first established in 1877 and wheat soon became the major industry in these vast western plains. Today Nhill has a population of around 1900 and boasts a large wheat silo, which can hold as much as 81,900 cubic m (2.25 million bushels) of the grain.

South of the town of Nhill lies the Little Desert National Park. To the north are the Big Desert Wilderness Park and Wyperfeld National Park. These parks provide great opportunities to drive or walk through mallee scrub—you may even catch a glimpse of the elusive mallee fowl, a bird which builds a large and distinctive mound to incubate its eggs in. Wildflowers bloom throughout the parklands in spring, and the mallee bush is

Massive wheat silos near Nhill.

covered in yellow blooms. Visitors should carry water with them in these parks. Summer is extremely hot in this region, and it is advisable not to travel into these parks during the warmer months.
Map ref: page 340 C10

NORTH-WEST VICTORIA WINE REGION

The north-west corner of Victoria has changed a great deal since a vast irrigation system, using water pumped from the Murray River, was first put in place. Although much of the fruit grown in the irrigation area, which centres on Mildura, is dried and supplies a different market, there are also some soft, fruity, easy-drinking wines produced here on a large scale. Australia's most widely distributed wine, Lindemans Bin 65 Chardonnay, is a perfect example of the style of wine from this region. It is clean, well-made and well-priced. Lindemans Winery, in Karadoc, is the largest and most modern wine-making facility in the country, and all the Leo Buring and Lindemans wines are produced here; although the grapes are sourced from a dozen or more other areas as well. A visit to such huge operations as Lindemans or Mildara Blass, in Merbein, provides a quite different experience from the smaller boutique wineries common in other areas.
Map ref: page 340 E2

OUYEN

Ouyen, 442 km (274 miles) north-west of Melbourne, began as a railway station on the track from Melbourne to Mildura in the early 1900s. It was not until 1910—quite late for settlement by Victoria's standards—that the town was opened up for settlement. Almost immediately sheep farming and wheat production began. Today the town's population is 1335.

The pioneers of this region worked hard removing the mallee scrub, including the large root balls, in an effort to clear the land for wheat production. In town you can see the largest Australian mallee stump, which is kept as a memorial to honour the first settlers. The Local History Resource Centre also pays tribute to the town's heritage.

The Hattah–Kulkyne and Murray–Kulkyne parks are north of town. Stretching as far as the Murray, the parks feature lagoons and waterways that branch off from this large watercourse. Another park worth visiting is the Murray Sunset National Park. It is an area of undulating desert country, mallee scrub and large salt lakes, which are often referred to as the Pink Lakes because they take on a pink hue in overcast weather. These parks offer a chance

Camping facilities are provided at the Wonga Hut site in Wyperfield National Park.

to glimpse the mallee fowl or a number of other birds which inhabit this region, especially along the lagoons of the Murray. Wildflowers are a beautiful sight in spring. The parks are best explored in a 4WD vehicle; camping sites are available, but visitors should carry their own drinking water. Festivals include the Mallee Festival and Vintage Train Trip in March, and the Ouyen Farmers' Festival in November.
See also North-West Victoria Wine Region
Map ref: page 340 E5

RED CLIFFS

Situated only 8 km (5 miles) south of Mildura in the heart of Victoria's Sunraysia country, and 532 km (330 miles) north-west of Melbourne, Red Cliffs has expanded over the years, and is now a suburb of Mildura. This region boasts a true Mediterranean climate, which explains why a visit will reveal endless rows of vineyards and large crops of citrus fruit and olives growing in the red, sandy soil. Named after the vivid red cliffs which form the banks of the nearby Murray, the town was first established in the 1890s, when the Chaffey brothers from Canada selected land in the area with the intention of installing irrigation systems—this had been successfully done in nearby Renmark—to make better use of the copious quantities of water in the Murray River. However, the towering red cliffs were to prove an obstacle for their scheme and the area remained undeveloped for many years. After World War I the region was part of the soldier settlement scheme, and was cleared to make way for farming land. However, the mallee scrub, with its huge

root system, is tough to remove from the soil, and horses and tractors were needed to flatten the land.

Modern technology has meant that water can now easily be pumped up over the imposing cliffs, and this has seen the growth of the town in the latter half of the twentieth century—its population is now 5440. The Red Cliffs Pumping Station—with the Murray River more than 70 m (230 feet) below—irrigates more than 5000 ha (12,355 acres) of land.

Wineries in this area include Lindemans at Karadoc, south of Red Cliffs—an enormous vineyard. The Country Music Festival is held in late September, and the Lunarfest is held in late March.
See also North-West Victoria Wine Region
Map ref: page 340 E2

SEA LAKE

Sea Lake, 333 km (207 miles) north-west of Melbourne, is a wheat-growing and pastoral centre in the Mallee region with a population of 980. Five kilometres (3 miles) north of Sea Lake is a large inland saltwater lake, Lake Tyrell, which is surrounded by masses of saltbush and sand hills. The town of Sea Lake receives its name from this large lake and two other smaller lakes, Washpool and Timboran. Over the years, salt has been mined from the lake, and the main feature of the town is the Cheetham Saltworks, which tourists can visit. There is also a viewing platform at Lake Tyrell which overlooks the lake and surrounding countryside.

To the west of Sea Lake is the desert country of Western Victoria and the Wyperfeld National Park. This park contains a large number of lakes which are connected by Outlet Creek, which runs north–south through the park. The lakes used to fill on a 20-year cycle, but irrigation systems built further north have prevented the lakes and creek system of the Wyperfeld National Park from flourishing. However, it is an interesting region, home to myriad birds, such as the sulphur-crested cockatoo, and native animals such as the kangaroo. Visitors should always carry their own drinking water with them in this park.
Map ref: page 340 G7

The Lindemans Karadoc winery, near Red Cliffs, is the largest winery in the Southern Hemisphere.

The Cobb & Co. coach stop at the Pioneer Settlement Park at Swan Hill.

SWAN HILL

Sitting on the banks of the Murray River, 343 km (213 miles) north-west of Melbourne, is the town of Swan Hill, often referred to as the 'Heart of the Murray'. This large regional centre (with a population of 9600) is surrounded by rich land which produces a variety of crops, including citrus fruits and grapes. A major part of the town's economy is tourism; it has been said that Swan Hill enjoys more sunny days than Queensland's Gold Coast.

Named after the black swans that kept explorer Thomas Mitchell awake when he camped here in 1836, the town was settled in 1840. Farms were soon established, and by 1850 a large port was constructed in town. Paddle-steamers shipped produce along the river. The Pioneer Settlement Park pays tribute to these pioneering days—it comprises 4 ha (10 acres) of buildings, machinery, artefacts and streets which date back to 1830. The park is also the base for the PS *Pyap*, which offers cruises on the Murray River.

Another feature of the town is the Military Expo. With over 5000 rare items, this is the largest collection of military paraphernalia in Australia. Other attractions include the Giant Murray Cod, a tribute to an elusive fish that was once prevalent in these waters: the replica stands more than 11 m (36 feet) tall. On Curlewis Street is a huge Moreton Bay fig tree, believed to be the largest of its type in Australia.

There are a number of parks and sporting facilities in town, including six golf courses, the most favoured being the award-winning Murray Downs Golf Course. Other activities include boating, fishing, swimming and canoeing on the Murray River. South of Swan Hill is Lake Boga, popular for waterskiing, boating and parasailing. There is also a camping area on the foreshore. Wineries in the region include Buller's and Best's, both large-volume producers of Australian wines.
See also North-West Victoria Wine Region
Map ref: page 341 J6

WARRACKNABEAL

Warracknabeal, about 346 km (215 miles) north-west of Melbourne, is now an important service centre for the outlying wheat communities in the Wimmera. It was first settled in 1844, when the Scott brothers set up the Warracknabeal sheep run. Its population today is 2687.

The region suffered a severe drought at the end of the nineteenth century, and it was as a result of this disaster that the Wimmera–Mallee water supply system, which now brings relief to the drought-stricken local farmers in the area, was developed. Apart from sheep, wheat has also contributed to the town's economy, and enormous wheat silos can be seen throughout the region.

The Historical Centre houses a collection of artefacts from former residents, including furniture, a pharmaceutical collection and documents that date back more than 100 years. Visitors can also take a self-guided tour of the town, called the Black Arrow Tour, which passes the National Trust buildings and the old Commercial Hotel, built in 1872. The Yarriambiack Creek, which flows through the town, features a recreational area and a flora and fauna park on its shores. This is an ideal area for walking and picnics.
Map ref: page 340 F9

WYPERFELD NATIONAL PARK

Reached via Hopetoun, or via the small township of Rainbow, the Wyperfeld National Park (450 km [279 miles] north-west of Melbourne) features a series of lakes and rivers—which are normally dry lake beds—connected by Outlet Creek. The park also contains hundreds of species of plants and birdlife. Only after exceptionally heavy rain do the river courses run. The vegetation in the park varies considerably. In the west of the park the sand plains are covered in heath, but mallee dominates the eastern section. Cypress pine woodlands prefer the sand dunes encircling the lakes, and river red gum and black box woodlands cover the floodplains of Outlet Creek and the lakes. This semi-arid environment comes alive in the springtime—wildflowers put on a magnificent display, especially after rain. However, autumn and winter are also good seasons to visit the park. The myriad bird life of the park is another of its major attractions, and birdwatchers will find plenty to occupy their time here. Emus and western grey kangaroos are also plentiful, along with stumpy-tail lizards and sand goannas. Many of the vehicle tracks in the park are suitable only for 4WDs. Visitors should always carry drinking water with them in this park.
Map ref: page 340 C7

Sulphur-crested cockatoo (Cacatua galerita).

In springtime the huge expanses of mallee scrub country in north-west Victoria are transformed into spectacular displays of colourful wildflowers.

SOUTH-EAST VICTORIA

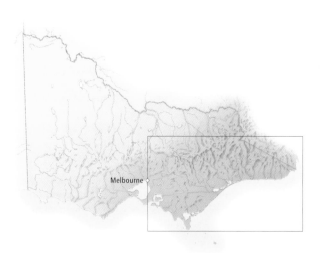

Curving between bay and ocean, Mornington Peninsula combines close proximity to central Melbourne with a range of recreational activities and a wealth of coastal scenery; nearby Phillip Island is famed for its nightly penguin parade.

On the capital's northern edge are the Dandenongs' ferny glades and historic Yarra Valley wineries, while to the south is the windswept granite ruggedness of Wilsons Promontory, a favourite with walkers.

To the north, the State border running ruler-straight from sandy Cape Howe towards the headwaters of the Murray River passes through some of the roughest mountain terrain on the continent. Pastoralists were the first Europeans to tackle these highlands in the 1840s, battling through to the Gippsland coast seeking stock routes and suitable ports. Farmers soon followed, first raising beef cattle, later laying the foundations of Gippsland's fine dairy industry. The old ports which served the coastal traders shipping out produce are now quiet fishing and holiday villages. In the 1850s the discovery of gold sparked a rush to the hills east of Melbourne, giving rise to short-lived boom towns such as picturesque Walhalla. Buried treasure of a different kind—a huge brown coal deposit said to be the largest in the world—underlies Gippsland's LaTrobe Valley, now characterised by open-cut mines and plumes of steam from the Yallourn and Hazelwood power station cooling towers. Cheap power has encouraged secondary industry here, making this one of the most important economic areas in the State.

The coastline of eastern Victoria has changed little since Zachary Hicks, on James Cook's *Endeavour*, made the expedition's first sighting of Australia (the point that now bears his name). Around remote Mallacoota, the vast and wild Croajingolong National Park protects untouched forested slopes, secluded inlets and surf-pounded shores; platypus swim in the creeks, lyrebirds dance in the gullies and waterbirds from pelicans to kingfishers flock to the fish-rich estuaries. To the south-west, Gippsland Lakes Coastal Park and The Lakes National Park take in serene waterways sheltered by Ninety Mile Beach. Nearby Lakes Entrance is a major fishing port, with more than 100 boats in its commercial fleet.

OPPOSITE: High up on the Errinundra Plateau is the largest stand of cool-temperate rainforest in Victoria.

The easily recognisable architecture of Flinders Street Station peers over the trees that line the banks of the Yarra.

REGIONAL FEATURE

Wineries of the South-East

Although the South-East generally has a cool maritime climate, some sheltered valleys are ideal for producing richer red varietals such as cabernet sauvignon.

The De Bortoli vineyards near Dixons Creek, with the winery and dam in the background.

Wine lovers don't have to journey far from Melbourne to sample some of the South-East's finest fare. Indeed two of the state's most renowned winemaking regions lie just a couple of hours from the noise and bustle of the city centre. Yarra Valley, located on the upper reaches of the Yarra River, is one of the state's oldest winemaking regions and one of Australia's success stories, its superior produce, especially its pinot noirs, having gained an exalted international reputation in recent years. The more recently established Mornington Peninsula region, situated on the scenic peninsula of the same name just a couple of hours' drive south of Melbourne, has a shorter and less illustrious history, but is slowly attracting attention both around Australia and overseas with an increasingly impressive range of wines.

Both regions share a cool maritime climate that is particularly suited to producing elegant chardonnays and pinot noirs. Most of the producers are small operations that focus on creating wines of the highest quality, which often appear as very limited releases. The majority of the wineries listed below offer cellar-door tastings, but some sell by mail-order only.

Yarra Valley

The Yarra Valley was the site of Australia's first commercial vineyard, which was established in 1838 by William Ryrie at the Yering cattle station. By 1850, Ryrie had sold his property to an aristocratic young Swiss settler, Paul de Castella, who thought little of the wine-producing potential of the area until one night when his guests drank his last bottle of Pommard. In desperation, he dragged a bottle of Ryrie's previously untouched 'home brew' from the cellar. It was immediately judged 'better than Pommard', which in turn inspired de Castella to re-establish the vineyard.

The famous vineyards of St Hubert's and Yeringberg were also founded at this time, and by the late 1800s wines from the Yarra Valley were already winning gold medals at European wine shows. However, at the end of the century, a combination of economic depression, the threat of phylloxera and the efforts of the temperance movement brought an end to winemaking in the Yarra Valley. The cows moved in and viticulture was all but forgotten.

The first to replant vines was Reg Egan in 1963 at Wantirna Estate, but it was two doctors, John Middleton, at Mount Mary, and Peter McMahon, at Seville Estate, who led the recovery in the Yarra Valley in the early 1960s. The 1970s saw rapid growth and today the region is one of Australia's most successful and diverse wine-producing regions.

The Yarra Valley's soils and climate make it ideal for growing grapes and making premium wine. The warmest vineyards can ripen shiraz and cabernet sauvignon admirably, while the cooler sites produce leaner wines and are better for pinot noir and chardonnay. Along with merlot, these are the predominant grape varieties grown in the valley. Sauvignon blanc, pinot gris, marsanne and roussanne have also been planted recently, but with few promising results as yet.

Some of Australia's first sparkling wine was made from a base wine from the Yarra Valley in the 1880s by Frenchman Auguste d'Argent. Today the area is one of Australia's premium areas for sparkling wines. Recently, it was selected by Champagne houses Moët et Chandon and Devaux as the site for their respective Australian sparkling-wine ventures—Domaine Chandon and Yarrabank.

PRODUCERS

De Bortoli Wines

Established 1987 Owners De Bortoli family Production 150,000 cases Vineyard area more than 130 ha (320 acres)

One of the biggest players in the Yarra Valley, De Bortoli produces excellent wines across its range. The premium products show a lot of new oak, which normally falls into balance with age, whereas the more economical Windy Peak range relies almost exclusively on fruit. De Bortoli's professionally run cellar-door facility carries a total of five labels of varying style and price, and houses a terrific restaurant.

Coldstream Hills

Established 1985 Owners Southcorp Wines Pty Ltd Production 50,000 cases Vineyard area 46 ha (114 acres)

Coldstream Hills was founded by James Halliday, one of Australia's best-known wine writers, to specialise in limited-production, premium-quality pinot noir, chardonnay and cabernet sauvignon/merlot. In 1996, Southcorp acquired the vineyard and the brand, while retaining Halliday as head winemaker. In recent years, the company has added a merlot, sauvignon blanc and pinot gris to Coldstream's portfolio; however, it is the old stalwarts—chardonnay and pinot noir— that continue to be outstanding.

Diamond Valley Vineyards

Established 1976 Owners David and Catherine Lance Production 6000 cases Vineyard area 3.5 ha (8.6 acres)

David Lance is producing some of Australia's best pinot noir. Unfortunately for longtime fans, word has got out and it is increasingly hard to obtain. The Close Planted Pinot Noir is the best, but the Diamond Valley Estate Pinot Noir comes a close second. Bright garnet in color, with a sappy, red-berry flavour, this wine shows a delicate-yet-intense purity of fruit that is instantly alluring and improves significantly following four to six years aging. The Diamond Valley winery is not open to the public and the wines are sold by mail order only.

Producers
1 Coldstream Hills
2 De Bortoli Wines
3 Diamond Valley Vineyards
4 Domaine Chandon
5 Gembrook Hill Vineyard
6 Metier
7 Mount Mary Vineyard
8 Oakridge Estate
9 Seville Estate
10 TarraWarra Estate
11 Yering Station Vineyard
12 Yeringberg

Domaine Chandon

Established 1987 Owners Moët et Chandon Production 120,000 cases Vineyard area 90 ha (225 acres)

Moët et Chandon purchased the Green Point vineyard in the Yarra Valley in 1987 and planted 50 ha (125 acres) with the traditional champagne varieties—pinot noir, chardonnay and pinot meunier. In 1994, they established another 40 ha (100 acres) in the Strathbogie Ranges. Today, reserves of older wines are being built up and the produce is becoming world class, as demonstrated by the elegant 1993 Millennium Reserve, a limited wine released for the year 2000 festivities. Domaine Chandon's production and visitor facilities incorporate the restored historic homestead, which is used for private functions and administration, and the spectacular Riddling Hall and Green Point Reception rooms, which function as the cellar door.

Gembrook Hill Vineyard

Established 1983 Owners Ian and June Marks Production 3000 cases Vineyard area 6 ha (15 acres)

Gembrook Hill doesn't have the high profile of some other producers in the area, but passionate weekend vigneron Ian Marks does make lovely wines. They include a fresh, fruity sauvignon blanc; a complex, toasty chardonnay; and a deceptively light pinot noir that displays sweet fruit, complexity, length and elegance. All three are great food wines and improve with four to five years bottle aging.

Metier

Established 1996 Owner Martin Williams Production 600 cases Vineyard area 8 ha (20 acres)

Owner Martin Williams was Victoria's first Master of Wine and works as a consultant for many Yarra Valley producers. At Metier, he produces a chardonnay and a pinot noir with complex flavors and aromas that would excite any burgundy lover. Produced in tiny quantities, these wines are definitely worth seeking out.

Mount Mary Vineyard

Established 1971 Owners John and Marli Middleton Production 3500 cases Vineyard area 15 ha (37 acres)

Dr John Middleton was one of the founders of the modern Yarra Valley wine industry and has produced some of the best wines in Australia. His intense Cabernets Quintet (a blend of cabernet sauvignon, cabernet franc, merlot, malbec and petit verdot) always lives up to its distinguished reputation, as does his long-living Pinot Noir. Mount Mary wines are available by mail order, at certain exclusive restaurants, and, occasionally, at auctions.

Oakridge Estate

Established 1978 Owners Oakridge Vineyards Ltd Production 30,000 cases Vineyard area 10 ha (25 acres)

Since he took over from his parents in 1990, Michael Zitslaff has seen Oakridge go from strength to strength. He and his team specialise in top-quality cabernet sauvignon, the Reserve Cabernet Sauvignon being one of the area's best. Despite its hefty price tag, the impressive Reserve Merlot also sells out quickly.

Seville Estate

Established 1972 Owners Brokenwood Wines Pty Ltd and Peter McMahon Production 2500 cases Vineyard area 8 ha (20 acres)

Dr Peter McMahon planted his vineyard in 1972 and in 1982 retired from his medical practice to become a full-time winemaker. In 1997, he sold a controlling share of the estate to Brokenwood Wines, but he continues to be involved in the company in a consulting role. Winemaker Alistair Butt maintains the wines' traditional high quality. The Seville Estate Shiraz, for example, is everything you could want from this varietal—rich, with spicy black pepper and ripe savory fruit, wonderful depth, length and complexity.

Tarrawarra Estate

Established 1983 Owner Marc Besen Production 6000 cases Vineyard area 29 ha (72 acres)

Tarrawarra, under the expert supervision of winemaker Clare Halloran, is regarded as one of the top producers of pinot noir in Australia. The Tarrawarra Pinot Noir is powerful yet complex, with excellent structure supporting intense red- and blackberry fruit and brambly characters. The wines are made to last and are at their best with a little age.

Yering Station Vineyard

Established 1838, re-established 1987 Owners Rathbone family Production 15,000 cases Vineyard area 117 ha (290 acres)

The site of Victoria's first winery, Yering Station is still a force to be reckoned with. Winemaker Tom Carson

Antique barrels and water carts are a reminder of the Yarra's relatively long winemaking history.

OPPOSITE: The Domaine Chandon vineyards sit on classic Yarra soils made up of clay and sand loams. Though they occasionally require irrigation, they have produced the region's best red and white wines.

The vineyards at Coldstream Hills occupy an elevated location that results in excellent drainage.

Hot, dry days are a rarity on the Mornington Peninsula, making this a region best suited to cold-climate grape varieties such as chardonnay and pinot noir.

In 1998, Stonier became the first Mornington Peninsula winery to attract investment from a major producer when Petaluma bought a controlling interest in the company.

produces a selection that includes some magnificent wines, such as the Yering Station Reserve Pinot Noir and the complex and delicious pinot and chardonnay in the relatively new Reserve range. Recently, Yering Station entered into a joint venture with the French Champagne producer Devaux to make the elegantly delicious Yarrabank Cuvée. The superb new winery and restaurant have a grandeur that rivals that of the facilities at nearby Domaine Chandon.

Yeringberg

Established 1863 Owner Guill de Pury Production 550 cases Vineyard area 13 ha (32 acres)

Guill de Pury is a direct descendant of Guillaume de Pury, who first established Yeringberg in 1863. The original winery building lay untouched from 1921 until 1969, when Guill de Pury replanted a few acres of vines and began to make wine in the old cellar. These wines are in short supply and were little known until recently. The Yeringberg White reflects the wines of old, with the richness and depth of flavour that come from marsanne and roussanne, while the chardonnay is rich and cheesy and ages gracefully. The savory pinot noir has red cherry and dusty, musty forest-floor characters as well as an elegant structure.

The Mornington Peninsula

Compared with the Yarra Valley, the Mornington Peninsula has a patchy history as a wine region. In the mid-nineteenth century, when the Yarra Valley boasted several well-established vineyards producing good-quality wines, the Mornington Peninsula had only a handful of amateur plots. The depression of the 1890s and the average quality of the wine—not phylloxera, which has never reached the peninsula—spelled the end of these few early enterprises.

The local wine industry only really got underway again in 1974, when Ballieu Myer planted his first vineyard at Elgee Park. Other locals followed his lead, including the Whites at Main Ridge in 1975, the Keffords at Merricks Estate in 1977 and the Stoniers in 1978. A second wave of companies was established in the early 1980s, including Dromana Estate, Moorooduc Estate, Kings Creek, Karina Vineyard and Tanglewood Downs, whose small plantings of around 2 ha (5 acres) were considered huge at the time.

Mornington is a thriving tourist destination and the wineries are often seen as just an attractive adjunct to the peninsula's picturesque landscapes. But winemaking has become a serious business here, and although still very much a boutique winery region, the region now boasts more than 100 vineyards. Moreover, as the vines become better established, quality improves with every vintage.

The area is hilly, so aspect and orientation are all-important. Variations in climate, aspect and soil type distinguish five subregions—Moorooduc Downs, Red Hill, Dromana, Merricks and Main Ridge—whose wines reflect these subtle differences. Generally, however, the region specialises in medium-bodied dry table wines, though it is also beginning to have some success with sparkling wines.

The predominant and most successful grape varieties are chardonnay and pinot noir, with the best pinot noir wines already showing good complexity and structure, and varying in style from elegant and ethereal to huge, rich and impressive. The chardonnays range from crisp, fruit-driven unoaked wines to complex wines exhibiting varying degrees of traditional burgundian winemaking techniques such as fermentation in French oak barrels and extended maturation on lees.

Cabernet sauvignon was originally planted here on the basis of incorrect weather data which suggested that the peninsula was warmer than it is. As a result, growers have had trouble ripening this grape, but when it does mature it is elegant, with cassis and cigar-box aromas that are suggestive of the classic bordeaux style. Such wines tend to enjoy greater popularity abroad than in Australia. Shiraz and sauvignon blanc have been planted successfully at warmer sites, and pinot gris, which does well in the local climate, is currently being touted as the next big thing.

Dromana's visitor facilities include a fine cafe.

PRODUCERS

Dromana Estate Vineyards

Established 1982 Owners Gary and Margaret Crittenden Production 10,300 cases Vineyard area 4.9 ha (12 acres)

Dromana Estate now boasts the largest array of wines on sale on the Mornington Peninsula—from the lower-priced Schinus range through the Dromana Estate range to the Reserve wines. Made exclusively from estate-grown fruit and fermented by natural yeasts, the 1997 Reserve Chardonnay is particularly complex and rich. Dromana also produces a range made from Italian varieties grown in the King Valley, in northern Victoria. Although not strictly Mornington Peninsula wines, they are of outstanding quality, the 'i' label Sangiovese and Nebbiolo representing the most faithful Australian renditions of these varieties.

Main Ridge Estate

Established 1975 Owners Nat and Rosalie White Production 1100 cases Vineyard area 2.4 ha (6 acres)

Pioneers of fine-wine production on the Mornington Peninsula, Nat and Rosalie White have one of the most marginal sites in the region. But skilled viticulture and sensitive winemaking ensure wines of elegance and complexity in all but the most difficult years. The Half Acre Pinot is the finest and most complex of all—never a blockbuster, but, at its best, something more subtle, mysterious and alluring.

Stonier

Established 1978 Owners Petaluma Ltd Production 22,000 cases Vineyard area 61 ha (150 acres)

Brian and Noel Stonier bought this property in 1977 and cannot remember what possessed them to plant vines. It must have been providence, as the winery has flourished over the years. Winemaker since 1987, Tod Dexter was responsible for developing the com-

pany's fruit-driven, easy-drinking pinot noir and chardonnay styles. The richly complex Reserve Chardonnay and Pinot Noir also illustrate his desire to combine maximum fruit integrity with the complexity of extended oak treatment.

T'Gallant Winery

Established 1990 Owners Kevin McCarthy and Kathleen Qualey Production 10,000 cases Vineyard area 10 ha (25 acres)

Movers and shakers on the peninsula, Kevin McCarthy and Kathleen Quealy are also pioneers of pinot gris. They produce two versions, the Tribute Pinot Gris, made in an Alsace style, and a 'pinot grigio' in a crisper, more flinty Italian style. Their other wines include fruit-driven, unoaked chardonnays and the Lyncroft Pinot Noir, which has rich, soft, dark-berry fruit and velvety tannins, and gets better every year.

Tuck's Ridge at Red Hill

Established 1986 Owner Peter Hollick Production 12,000 cases Vineyard area 113 ha (280 acres)

Winemaker Daniel Greene aspires to producing Australia's best pinot noir, and the jump in quality from the 1996 to the 1997 vintage is testimony to his dedication and skills. But credit must also go to vineyard manager Shane Strange, who allows his vines to grow big, believing that their natural vigour will ripen larger crops more efficiently. So far, this unorthodox strategy has proved effective, resulting in pinot noirs that display wonderful complexity and character.

Turramurra

Established 1989 Owners David and Paula Leslie Production 7000 cases Vineyard area 10 ha (25 acres)

Since 1995, David Leslie has been producing pinot noirs, chardonnays and sauvignon blancs that fully deserve the fulsome accolades that they have received. The outstanding 1997 Pinot Noir, which took out the trophy for the best Mornington Peninsula Red Wine awarded by the Australian Sommeliers Association in 1998, displays ripe, dark berry fruit and brambly aromas, subtle hints of truffle and a firm, intense structure on the palate.

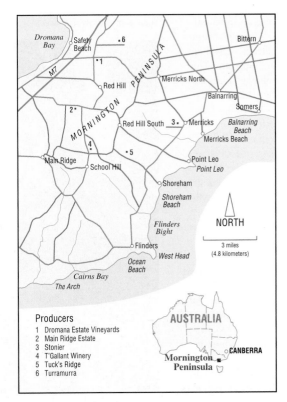

Producers
1 Dromana Estate Vineyards
2 Main Ridge Estate
3 Stonier
4 T'Gallant Winery
5 Tuck's Ridge
6 Turramurra

Places in
SOUTH-EAST
VICTORIA

The Sea Life Centre at the Nobbies, near Cowes, offers guided walks and seal watching.

BAIRNSDALE

Sitting at the southern boundary of the Victorian High Country, 288 km (179 miles) east of Melbourne, and surrounded by the tall timbers of the forestry industry and cleared farmlands, the city of Bairnsdale is a major regional centre, with a population of 10,690. The town's name originated from the Isle of Skye, the birthplace of Archibald McLeod, who established his station— Bernisdale—here in 1844.

The region has plenty of fertile land, and has long supported vegetable farming and cattle and sheep grazing. In the town's early days, much produce was supplied to the goldfields scattered through the hills to the north. Before road transport was viable, the town, sitting as it does on the Mitchell River, was a major port for the river steamers. It is still a major supply point for the region, as well as being a gateway to the High Country to the north and to the splendid lakes system that lies just south of the town on the coast.

The town features galleries, craft shops and museums. The Hillmay House Antique Museum is an 1890s furnished historic home which contains a child's nursery with an excellent display of baby furniture and dolls. The Historical Museum and Resource Centre is a two-storey building housing memorabilia—the grounds are scattered with machinery from bygone eras. St Mary's Roman Catholic Church, in Main Street, was built in 1913 and is noted for its exquisite murals. Paynesville and Lakes

Entrance to the south offer sailing and cruising on the Gippsland Lakes, and the picturesque town of Dargo, nestled in the Victorian Alps, is less than two hours' drive from Bairnsdale.
See also Gippsland Wine Region
Map ref: page 342 E6

BALNARRING

This small township, with a population of 1425, overlooks Westernport Bay. Many Melburnians wanting to escape the city for the beach and the sea have holiday houses here, which they use during the weekends and holiday periods. Situated on the Mornington Peninsula, 80 km (50 miles) south-east of Melbourne, this town is in an ideal position—close to the surf beaches of Point Leo and Somers on the east of the peninsula, and to the bustling seaside resorts of Rosebud and Dromana on the

Snow gum (Eucalyptus pauciflora).

west. The Mornington Peninsula is an area with many fruit farms and wineries, such as Balnarring Vineyard and the Hofferts Balnarring Estate, which are popular with visitors. Both of these wineries are on the Bittern–Dromana road. The markets, such as those at Red Hill and Emu Plains, which are held during the summer and autumn months on varying Saturdays, are also popular.
Map ref: page 337 H6

BAW BAW NATIONAL PARK

This park lies 95 km (59 miles) north of Moe, and is the only Victorian park, apart from the Alpine National Park, with subalpine vegetation, such as the twisted snow gum and the wildflowers that carpet the area in summer. The park has become a base for walkers and cross-country skiers. The busiest time for this park is during winter, when many take on the downhill runs in the village area and others ski cross-country on the many and varied tracks in the park. Fantastic views of the Thomson Dam can be had from the Silvertop Picnic Ground. Wildlife in the park includes the amphibian Baw Baw frog and the rare Leadbeater's possum, as well as numbats, cockatoos and lyrebirds.
Map ref: page 337 N3

BUCHAN

Buchan, a small town—population 400—nestled among cleared rolling farmland and native bushland 361 km (224 miles) east of

Melbourne, is very picturesque, but its main feature for more than a century has been its large cave system, made a reserve in 1897. Formed by underground rivers cutting their way through limestone, it is the stalactites and stalagmites produced by droplets of the dissolved limestone, each with its own individual shape, that give these caves their character. Two caves in the system are open to the public for guided tours: the Fairy and Royal Caves. North of the township, off the Gelantipy Road, is the Shades of Death Cave, which is also open to visitors. A drive north of the town leads into the Alpine and Snowy River regions, which are full of well-equipped camping areas, magnificent scenery, remote unsealed roads and rugged 4WD tracks.
Map ref: page 342 G4

COWES

Cowes is the main town of Phillip Island, a small island which lies at the mouth of Westernport Bay— the town is 150 km (93 miles) south of Melbourne. The island is accessible via a long bridge from the mainland town of San Remo. Cowes was initially a sealing and whaling base, but settlement stepped up in the 1840s when grazing and chicory farming commenced in the area. Now its population is 2400, and the town is a wonderful spot for a summer holiday, with a magnificent foreshore and plenty of restaurants, cafés, guesthouses and shops.

The Phillip Island Heritage Centre features displays of the island's history dating back to the original inhabitants. There are many other attractions here, including the fairy penguin parade: each night these small birds emerge from the ocean onto Summerland Beach to return to their nests. Koalas were introduced onto the island many years ago and now they are abundant. There is also a fur seal colony near the Nobbies, on the far west edge of the island. Visitors can also see, and even touch, native Australian wildlife at the Phillip Island Wildlife Park. The Koala Conservation Centre is a great place to view koalas, from platforms among the treetops.
Map ref: page 337 J6

Sculpture in William Ricketts Sanctuary, the Dandenongs.

CROAJINGOLONG NATIONAL PARK

Situated in the far eastern corner of Victoria, 450 km (279 miles) east of Melbourne, this park stretches for 100 km (62 miles) south along the coast from the New South Wales border. One of Victoria's largest parks, it has a wide diversity of landforms. The vegetation is also varied—there are soft-leaved subtropical species, cool-temperate communities and hardier plants that are resistant to fire and drought. While road travel through the park is restricted, there are numerous dirt tracks giving good access to some interesting places, especially the inlets. At Shipwreck Creek there are some pleasant walks, or you can paddle a canoe on the creek. The Thurra River inlet is set in an unspoilt forest close to the ocean beach. The shallow waters of the river provide safe swimming as well as canoeing, and you can fish along the coast. There are also some good bush and beach walks.
Map ref: page 343 M5

DANDENONG RANGES NATIONAL PARK

The verdant sanctuary of the Dandenong Ranges, only 40 km (25 miles) east of Melbourne, has been a popular picnic ground for Victorians for more than 70 years. This suburban park stretches across three sections of Mount Dandenong. The Ferntree Gully block boasts natural bushland and offers a variety of interesting walks, while the Sherbrooke section includes the tumbling Sherbrooke Falls. The Doongalla section offers spectacular views and rugged bush trails leading down the western side of the mountain. The large tree ferns, the variety of eucalypts, the sounds of the many bellbirds and the spectacular song of the lyrebird are among the natural beauties that will reward visitors to the park.
Map ref: page 337 J3

EMERALD

Tall eucalyptus trees and long-reaching tree ferns surround the aptly named township of Emerald. This small town—with a population of 4054—sits on a scenic hilltop in the Dandenong Ranges, only 54 km (34 miles) east of Melbourne, and is a favourite destination for scenic day drives. Emerald was one of the first towns to be established in the hills of the Dandenongs in 1858, and it now draws a continuous weekend crowd, particularly in summer, when its luxuriant forests offer a cool respite from the heat. Emerald is also the end of the railway line which carries Puffing Billy—a famous Melbourne steam train—through the Dandenongs from Belgrave. The train is a favourite with children and families, who take the

People in Dutch costume celebrating tulip season in Emerald.

scenic journey from Belgrave through the temperate forest and over trestle bridges to Emerald and then back to Belgrave.

Another of the town's attractions is the Emerald Lake Park, an excellent picnic location. It contains a huge lake spreading over more than 50 ha (124 acres). Swimming, paddleboats and a giant water slide are popular attractions here. The park also features many walking tracks and scenic trails, and houses the Emerald Lake Model Railway, one of the largest working small-scale railways in Australia. There is also a kiosk and tearooms, as well as barbecue facilities. Another water source close to town is the Cardinia Reservoir, which is a water storage area for Melbourne and a popular spot for picnics.
Map ref: page 337 J4

The Thurra River winds through Croajingolong National Park, to finally emerge at the rugged south-eastern coast of Victoria.

ERRINUNDRA NATIONAL PARK

High on the Errinundra Plateau in north-eastern Victoria, 463 km (288 miles) from Melbourne, you will find the largest stand of cool-temperate rainforest in the State. Scenic drives and boardwalks help visitors appreciate this priceless beauty. Sitting right in the middle of timber-logging country, this extraordinary park of 25,600 ha (63,258 acres) protects a unique forest, a forest that has not seen fire for over 150 years. With such beauty, it is surprising that the park was not declared until 1988, when conservationists managed to stop efforts to log the ageing forest.

Most of the park is above 1000 m (3281 feet) and is inaccessible during winter, when an abundance of rainfall and snow make the unsealed tracks impassable. With two catchment areas skirting the plateau, spring also sees heavy rain in the park, which helps maintain the spectacular rainforest in the area.

Access to the park is restricted—in wet conditions, closures apply. The main entry is via the Errinundra Road from Club Terrace to the south, or from the Bonang Highway from the east, taking the Errinundra Road. The main roads into the park are unsealed, winding, and should be driven along with caution. They are unsuitable for caravans. There are camping sites at the Gap Scenic Reserve in the north, and on the Bonang River near the intersection of the Bonang Highway and the Gap

Eucalypts and ferns in the dense forest of Errinundra National Park.

Road. Goongerah Camping Area is to the west, off the Bonang Highway, and has toilet facilities.

The interpretation display gives visitors a good insight into the park. The William Baldwin Spencer Trail cuts through the forest; a guide for this trail and many others is available from the park office in Orbost or the information centre at Cann River. Be prepared for wet weather even in the warmer months—bring along a raincoat and a good pair of shoes.
Map ref: page 343 K4

FOSTER

The township of Foster, 180 km (112 miles) south-east of Melbourne, is the gateway to one of Victoria's most popular seaside national parks, Wilsons Promontory National Park. The area of Foster was originally named Stockyard Creek, and was a goldmining

region—there is a museum in town which displays photographs and other memorabilia from the gold-mining days in the 1870s—but by the early 1900s goldmining had given way to dairy farming on the lush, fertile soils of south-west Gippsland. The town's current population is 1107.

There are numerous vantage points where this majestic park area can be viewed, including the Foster North Lookout on the South Gippsland Highway. Mount Nicoll Lookout off the Foster–Fish Creek road is also a superb viewing site, offering uninterrupted views as far as Corner Inlet and Waratah Bay. Wilsons Promontory, or 'the Prom', as it is known, is the southernmost point of the Australian mainland, and features sandy beaches and large rocky outcrops which extend into the ocean waters. It also has myriad bushwalks of varying lengths and degrees of difficulty.

The town, together with thousands of regular and loyal park users, fought off attempts to commercialise the park during 1997.
See also Gippsland Wine Region
Map ref: page 337 N7

GIPPSLAND LAKES COASTAL PARK

The Lakes National Park and the Gippsland Lakes Coastal Park cover the region from Seaspray to Lakes Entrance, and include such natural features as the Ninety Mile Beach and the inland coastal lakes system. The lakes were formed aeons ago, when the sea forced sand onto the shore, creating a series of barriers along the coast. The park is rich in wildlife, and is a popular retreat from the bustling seaside villages that dot the coast. Kangaroos can be seen feeding on the plains along Bartons Hill Track, and seabirds of all kinds are always nearby. Dolphins and seals are regularly spotted searching for food near Barrier Landing, which is accessible only by boat. The region offers fishing, boating, canoeing, swimming, bushwalks, wildlife spotting and, of course, long walks on the beach.
Map ref: page 342 E7

GIPPSLAND WINE REGION

In Victoria's south-eastern corner, Gippsland is the State's most recent area of viticultural rebirth, with current plantings beginning in the 1970s. Like many other areas, Gippsland had a significant table-wine industry in the late nineteenth century that suffered decline for economic and agricultural reasons. More recently, isolation and the scattered nature of the wineries have kept it from achieving recognition.

Cool-climate viticulture is aided by good rainfall, and the cool-climate classics, chardonnay and pinot noir, dominate production here. Spiciness and complexity characterise the fruit flavours. However, rainfall, soils, temperature and terrain vary considerably, reflecting the size of the zone and its proximity to the coast. Wine styles also vary, but production of sparkling wine is negligible. The two founding wineries, Bass Phillip and Nicholson River, are showing the region's potential for great pinot noir and chardonnay.
Map ref: pages 342–43

One of the typical granite outcrops at Wilsons Promontory, on the shores of Whisky Bay, near Foster.

GLENMAGGIE

Sitting on the edge of the Glenmaggie Weir, 228 km (142 miles) east of Melbourne, is the small hamlet of Glenmaggie, named by the McFarlane family, Scottish settlers who ran cattle at the headwaters of the Macalister and Thomson Rivers in the 1840s. The original village of Glenmaggie was established when gold was mined in the vicinity, and while not much of the precious metal was extracted from the Glenmaggie region, the township survived because it also stocked supplies for the mines to the north-east.

A weir was built in 1927 to supply water to the township of Maffra, and also for irrigation purposes. Glenmaggie was flooded when the weir was built and only three buildings—the Anglican church, the Town Hall and Glenmaggie Store—were relocated to their present position. The weir is very popular with waterskiers, swimmers and sailors. Glenmaggie has remained small (population 200); Coongulla, a town on the other side of the weir, houses most of the locals and is the site of most of the area's holiday residences.

This region around Glenmaggie is also a good stepping-off point for those who want to visit the Alpine National Park to the north—the State's largest national park. The Avon Wilderness, where the magnificent Avon River meets the Turton River, is only a short 4WD journey from Glenmaggie.
Map ref: page 342 B6

Camping in the Alpine National Park, north of Glenmaggie.

HEALESVILLE

Nestled in the lush Yarra Valley less than two hours from Melbourne (58 km [36 miles] east of the city) via the Maroondah Highway is Healesville (population 9169). The town has been a popular holiday destination since the beginning of the twentieth century, because of its surrounding forests and beautiful scenery. The town was first settled in 1860 and was named in honour of Sir Richard Heales, the then Premier of Victoria. Timber milling was the main industry, but now much of the region's fine forests have become national parks or catchment areas. The Healesville Sanctuary is a popular tourist attraction. Opened in 1934, it has the largest collection of Australian native species in the world, including snakes, birds, kangaroos, koalas, emus and wombats. The best feature of this park is that the animals roam the grounds among the onlookers.

The Yarra Valley is now one of Australia's premier wine-growing districts, offering world-class vintages. Domaine Chandon, the Australian winery of French champagne manufacturers Möet et Chandon, has a vineyard here. St Huberts Winery in Coldstream, one of the oldest in the region, offers fine wines and food along with a jazz festival on the last Sunday of every month during summer. Other wineries in the area include Coldstream Hills, De Bortoli, Eyton on Yarra and Yarra Ridge, all of which produce excellent wines.

One of outer Melbourne's most scenic drives is along the Black Spur, north of Healesville, which winds across the Great Dividing Range through catchment areas of tall mountain ash trees and broad towering tree ferns. At the end of the range the canopy opens up to reveal the small village of Narbethong and the Black Spur Inn—a delightful pub. There is accommodation here at the inn, as well as at the Hermitage—a National Trust building deep in the mountain range. Another lovely drive north-west of town takes a less well-used road, with large, lush, green tree ferns draping over its edges—to the timber township of Toolangi.

Annual events include the Healesville Show in February, the Grape-Grazing Festival (a wine and food festival) on the first weekend in March, and the Gateway Festival in November.
Map ref: page 337 K2

INVERLOCH

A popular holiday seaside town and fishing port, the small town of Inverloch—population 2100—sits at the mouth of Anderson's Inlet on the Victorian coast, just east of Wonthaggi and only two hours (150 km [93 miles]) south-east of Melbourne.

The coastal strip includes diverse areas. The shoreline has mud flats of mangrove swamps during low tide, or exposed rock pools during high tide. There is a sandy surf beach to the south of Point Norman, outside the inlet on Venus Bay, along with another excellent beach which is more protected and so better for swimming. Windsurfers and sailors use the inlet for safe boating; the yacht club is at Point Hughes, and further along the Esplanade is the angling club. A road stretches all the way along the coast—the foreshore is a reserve, and camping is allowed in designated areas. Nearby,

Scaly-breasted lorikeet
(Trichoglossus chlorolepidotus).

the area around Townsend Bluff and Maher's Landing are popular with birdwatchers.

There are also now many wineries being established in South Gippsland, including the Lyre Bird Hill Winery and the Bass Phillip Winery. The Shell Museum, one of the town's attractions, houses one of the world's largest private shell collections, as well as a large reference library. Shells and handicrafts can also be bought here. The Inverloch Fun Festival is held on the last weekend in January, and the Jazz Festival is on the Labour Day long weekend in March.
See also Gippsland Wine Region
Map ref: page 337 L7

Ninety Mile Beach, in the Lakes National Park, provides good fishing for anglers.

KINGLAKE NATIONAL PARK

This park is 65 km (40 miles) north-east of Melbourne—it is the largest national park near Melbourne. It is on the north-western slopes of the Great Dividing Range, and has many vehicle tracks meandering through eucalypt forests and fern gullies. One of the major attractions is Masons Falls, in the western part of the park. This is reached via one of the park's 24 walking trails. Other tracks lead to panoramic viewpoints. While bushwalking is a popular pastime in this park, visitors can also enjoy some great birdwatching.
Map ref: page 337 J1, J2

KOO-WEE-RUP

Lush green pastures and a good supply of rainfall are what make Koo-wee-rup, 75 km (47 miles) south-east of Melbourne, an important dairy farming and agricultural centre. Situated inland from Westernport Bay, this small township—with a population of 1096—is also a supply stop for tourists travelling along the South Gippsland and Bass highways. The unusual name of this town is a word from a local Aboriginal language meaning 'blackfish swimming'. The area was first settled by Europeans in the 1840s. There was originally much swampland in the region, but it was later drained to make way for grazing land in the 1860s. Thirty years later the railway arrived and after that Koo-wee-rup became a major milk supplier for Melbourne.

Lakes Entrance has the largest inland network of waterways in Australia. It is a major fishing port, and also popular for boating.

Bayles Fauna Park is situated at nearby Bayles, on the South Gippsland Highway, and features a large number of birds and animals native to this region. Tooradin Inlet, on the edge of Westernport Bay, is an excellent picnic location, with a jetty ideal for fishing—many pelicans congregate there. Swamp Observation Tower, east of Tooradin, offers fine views of Westernport Bay and of French Island, which sits in the centre of the bay. The Koo-wee-rup Festival is held in March.
See also Gippsland Wine Region
Map ref: page 337 K5

LAKES ENTRANCE

The town of Lakes Entrance, 324 km (201 miles) east of Melbourne, and the lake system it sits beside have long been popular destinations for holidaymakers.

The town has a population of 4625, and apart from being a tourist resort, also operates one of the largest fishing fleets in Australia, with the Entrance, as it is known, providing access and shelter to the Gippsland Lakes from the Tasman Sea. Many fishing boats operate from the jetty in town, and fresh fish can be purchased from here. The name Lakes Entrance comes from an artificial entrance that was established in 1889—there had always been a natural entrance, but it was unpredictable and did not provide a safe passage.

Five major waterways, including the Tambo and Dargo rivers, find their way to the Gippsland Lakes, which are separated from the ocean by only a narrow stretch of dunes, known as the Ninety Mile Beach. This region forms part of the Gippsland Lakes Coastal Park and the Lakes National Park. There are at least two great ways to explore the waters of the lakes system: on one of the passenger ferries or cruisers, or by hiring a sailing boat and exploring the area yourself. There are plenty of boating craft for rent, including the paddleboats at Cunninghame Arm, near the footbridge. There are also many areas to explore by foot—the footbridge over Cunninghame Arm connects the beach with the Esplanade, and a walking track leads from the centre of town to the entrance itself.

The Ninety Mile Beach offers great views of the coast and is popular with surfers and anglers, while the nearby Nyerimilang Park offers fantastic views of the lakes.

This 178 ha (440 acre) property, which features a homestead built in 1892, is surrounded by semi-formal gardens. They provide a home to birds and wildlife. The park is ideal for picnics.

Other attractions include an antique car and folk museum (at Charma, an 1860s cottage), and a recreation park with water-slides, mini golf and other family activities. The Sea Shell Museum features over 80,000 shells and corals, as well as a large aquarium and model railway. Train buffs should also visit the Stoney Creek Railway Bridge on Colquhoun Road—the trestle bridge was built of local timber in 1916, and is 276 m (906 feet) long and more than 18 m (59 feet) high.

A Sunday market is held at the Mayfair Entertainment Complex, while the Lions Club Fish Tasting is held each year on Good Friday. Other events include a fishing expo in November and a fantastic New Year's Eve fireworks display.
See also Gippsland Wine Region
Map ref: page 342 G6

LEONGATHA

Leongatha—population 4500—is 141 km (88 miles) south-east of Melbourne, and lies at the bottom of the Strzelecki Ranges in South Gippsland, close to Wilsons Promontory. The land at the base of the ranges is dominated by rolling pastures, but the region was once heavily forested with mountain ash trees. The area was cleared for dairy use during the 1870s, and this industry continues today.

Eucalypts, stringy bark and peppermint gums grow in the Kinglake National Park.

Gippsland is home to a number of wineries, including Bass Phillip, on Tosch's Road in Leongatha South, and Lyre Bird Hill, on the Inverloch Road. Other things to do around Leongatha include visiting the Fireling Museum which has an excellent collection of antique lanterns and firearms, some of which are more than 400 years old. The Woorayl Shire Historical Society, housed in the old Mechanics Institute, which is classified by the National Trust, houses memorabilia from the region's past. Moss Vale Park, off the Leongatha–Mirboo North road, lies on the Tarwin River and has around 5 ha (12 acres) of fine English trees; it is the perfect location for a summer picnic. Events in Leongatha include the Daffodil and Rotary Art Festival, which is held in September. *See also* Gippsland Wine Region
Map ref: page 337 M7

MAFFRA

Maffra, 220 km (137 miles) east of Melbourne, took its name from a property belong to an early settler. He had spent time in Mafra in Portugal during the Peninsular Wars and named his run after the town. Maffra is surrounded by rich pastoral land within the irrigation system which feeds off the Macalister River. The town was established in 1875 and is now a service centre to the smaller outlying towns and farms at the base of the Alps. In 1929 the Glenmaggie Weir was established to form the basis for the irrigation system to feed the Maffra region; it was increased in size during the 1950s. The small town of Coongulla grew around the shores of the weir and is now a popular holiday destination for waterskiers and sailors.

The township of Maffra—population 3880—is very picturesque. Maffra was involved in the sugar beet industry between 1890 and 1940, before the irrigation system was built and the dairy industry became the area's main business. The sugar beet venture eventually proved unsuccessful—the history of this undertaking can be found at the Maffra Sugar Beet Museum on River Street. Other attractions include the herb garden on Foster Street and the Wa-De-Lock Vineyard.

There are some small and interesting towns outside Maffra, including Tinamba, which is home to the Schoenmaekers Tavern and the Tinamba Hotel. The tavern offers a genuine Dutch feast, while the atmosphere in the hotel is also a blend of country Australia and Holland. Heading north from Maffra leads you to the alpine country and towns such as Licola which are a great base for bushwalking, 4WD touring or scenic drives. In winter the snow-covered mountains above Maffra are great for cross-country skiing. The Gippsland Harvest Festival is held in March, the Farming Festival in April and the Agricultural Show in October. *See also* Gippsland Wine Region
Map ref: page 342 C6

Black bream caught at Top Lake, Mallacoota.

MALLACOOTA

The tranquil fishing and holiday resort town of Mallacoota (population 960) is perched in the eastern corner of the State, in far east Gippsland, near the border of New South Wales, 531 km (330 miles) east of Melbourne. It is situated at the mouth of a deep inlet of the same name—Mallacoota Inlet—and there is good swimming to be had along Foreshore Reserve.

A whaling port was established here by Ben Boyd and the Imlay Brothers in the 1840s. By the end of the nineteenth century the township was well established as a fishing base. Abalone is still dived for in these waters. In summer tourists come for the boating, fishing, swimming and surfing.

There are many beautiful places to visit nearby, including Shady Gully Walk, which begins in town and leads down through a reserve to Shady Gully. At Bastion Point, which is at the end of Bastion Road, there is a viewing platform which gives outstanding views of the entrance to Mallacoota Inlet, Croajingolong Park, Howe Range and Gabo Island.

Parks in the surrounding area offer excellent bushwalking, scenic drives, birdwatching and 4WD touring. These include Croajingolong National Park, which is an important forest region on the coast and also has superb beaches. Visitors following the Genoa River northward from Mallacoota Inlet will discover the delights of the green timberland regions at the edge of the Great Dividing Range above Genoa. The town's annual events include the Easter Festival of the Great Southern Ocean and the annual Mallacoota Cup soccer weekend in October.
Map ref: page 343 N5

The Macalister Irrigation Scheme, begun in 1929, provides water for the intensive dairy industry around Maffra.

MARLO

This small fishing village, with a population of only 380, lies at the mouth of the Snowy River, along the east coast of the State, 399 km (248 miles) from Melbourne. Here, south of Orbost, the Snowy River flows into a small channel before running out into the Tasman Sea. This is an ideal fishing area, and is much used by anglers wanting to avoid the larger coastal towns.

The town survives on fishing and tourism; one of its great assets is that it is close to the Cape Conran Foreshore Reserve, a picturesque park to the east of town

Sunset fishing in the surf, on the beach at Marlo.

which is ideal for fishing, scuba diving, surfing and bushwalking. Swimming is also popular, but tides and currents can be strong, especially around the mouth of the Snowy River. The best places to swim are Yeerung Beach and Banksia Bluff. Both the Snowy and Yeerung Rivers are suitable for canoeing. Campers can use Banksia Bluff, which has fireplaces and toilets. From Marlo you can also visit the temperate rainforests north of Orbost, by way of gravel roads. The magnificent scenery is well worth the drive.
Map ref: page 343 J6

MOE

The rapidly growing industrial town of Moe is in the heart of the coal-mining region of the LaTrobe Valley in Gippsland, 155 km (96 miles) south-east of Melbourne, at teh gateway to the alpine region. It is situated in the foothills of the High Country. Nearby is the old town of Walhalla, which has been extensively renovated over the past years.

The name of the town comes from the Aboriginal word 'mouay' meaning swamp. Originally the region supported a dairy and pastoral industry, but with brown coal deposits being found under the swamp, the town's interest soon turned to the coal and the energy it produces. The nearby township of Yallourn was actually relocated to enable mining of the coal. Moe now houses coal workers, although there are still many farms in the region—its population today is 16,720.

Old Gippstown sits at the freeway exit to Moe—it has been set up to represent an old pioneer town, and is made up of 30 buildings, which were transported from throughout Gippsland for the display. These authentic homes were then restored on-site; one home is claimed to be that of Angus McMillan, who explored the region and settled here in 1840.

On the way to Walhalla is Moondarra Reservoir, which offers spectacular views from near the spillway and a number of walking tracks. Nearby Blue Rock Lake holds 200,000 megalitres (52.8 million gallons) of water and is popular with residents for swimming, waterskiing and fishing. Walhalla itself is also well worth a visit—there are many old buildings, plus a large old gold-mine and tunnel which are now open for tours. Further north lies the Alpine National Park, a mecca for bushwalkers, 4WD enthusiasts, horse riders and cross-country skiers in winter.
See also Gippsland Wine Region
Map ref: page 337 N5

Horse-drawn tours are popular through the spectacular tulip fields around Monbulk.

MONBULK

Monbulk is a small town, with a population of 3839, in the centre of a large fruit-growing district that has everything from cherries to peaches and strawberries. The rich red soils in the valleys of the Dandenong Ranges and the good rainfall the area experiences combine to provide excellent growing conditions for fruit. In spring the countryside comes alive with blooms destined for the cut flower industry, along with the pink and white blossoms of the cherries and plums.

Nearby Silvan is home to Tesselaar's Tulip Farm, which hosts a magnificent Tulip Festival in

September, when the flowers are in bloom. During spring there are a number of flower shows in the Dandenongs as well as in the neighbouring Yarra Valley region.

Located only 47 km (29 miles) east of Melbourne, this region also boasts a large residential population, with many people choosing to commute to the city and inner suburbs for work, while retaining the picturesque uncrowded lifestyle of the Dandenong Ranges. The town hosts a local market on the third Sunday of every month.
Map ref: page 337 J3

MORNINGTON

Overlooking Port Phillip Bay, Mornington is a seaside resort on the west of the Mornington Peninsula. Only 54 km (34 miles) south of Victoria's capital, it has long been popular with Melburnians during the summer. It has retained its small-town character, despite its popularity. Matthew Flinders was the first European to land in this area, and soon this region, being not far from Melbourne, was settled. Originally the town was known as Schnapper Point, but the name was changed in 1864 to Mornington in honour of the Earl of Mornington.

A unique feature of the town is the number of century-old private changing huts on the beach. These

Nineteenth-century re-creation at the Old Gippstown pioneer township near Moe.

and other historic buildings in the town date back to the 1880s, when the resort first began attracting large crowds from the city.

With white sandy beaches, safe waters for swimming and proximity to the suburbs of Melbourne, it is hardly surprising that this beach and town are so popular. The town's population is 14,150, and its large number of restaurants and cafés attract many visitors. Surfers are catered for further down the peninsula at Portsea or over on the eastern side at Point Leo.

Along the seaward edge of the peninsula, facing the Bass Strait, is the Mornington Peninsula National Park. Port Nepean and the old military fort, which are within the park, were closed to the public for many years; now open, they and the quarantine station and cemetery are among the park's main attractions. Other drawcards for visitors include the wide, sandy beaches and the coastal heathland. The Cape Schanck Lighthouse is situated on the most southern point of the peninsula.

In the centre of Mornington Peninsula there are a number of good vineyards to explore. These include Dromana Estate and Main Ridge Estate. The best way to sample the wines of the district is to visit one of the festivals, such as the Mornington Peninsula Queen's Birthday Wine Weekend held at the Mornington Regional Centre annually in June, or the Mornington Peninsula Carnival of Wine during October/November.
Map ref: page 337 H6

Murray's Lookout at Mount Martha provides an aerial view over Mornington.

MORNINGTON PENINSULA NATIONAL PARK

Port Nepean and the old military fort are now incorporated into this park. This area was formerly known as the Point Nepean National Park, but around 1990 it was amalgamated with the Cape Schanck Coastal Park and now covers a region of craggy headlands and sandy beaches with an abundance of marine life. Game fishing in Victorian waters has become very popular in recent years. Laying berley trails to attract sharks is nothing new, but it has never been done with such success as it has lately in the offshore waters of the Bass Strait beaches and Phillip Island, about 135 km (84 miles) south of Melbourne along the South Gippsland and Bass highways. Threshers, makos, blues, hammerheads, bronze whalers and great whites are all a possibility in this world-class fishery. However, it should be noted that great whites are now protected in most Australian waters.

Anglers don't have to travel a long way offshore for action. In fact, more often than not, the best fish are taken within a kilometre of shore. Between November and May, surface water temperatures in the

The rocky headland at Cape Schank, Mornington Peninsula, often called 'the home of the fur seal'.

stretch of water between Cape Schanck and Cape Paterson reach 21°C (70°F) and higher, attracting schools of bait fish, including barracouta, slimy mackerel, salmon and yakkas (yellowtail). As with many other forms of fishing, a natural progression occurs: the predators follow the prey and it isn't long before reports of shark activity begin to filter through. Always remember, though, that Bass Strait is a dangerous waterway—local knowledge is invaluable. Charter boats and experienced guides are available.

The old Port Nepean Quarantine Station is also included in the Mornington Peninsula National Park area, as well as a historic fort, built in 1882, when attacks from countries such as Russia were feared. Point Nepean can be explored on a tractor-pulled train, and once a month the fort area is opened for cyclists to ride around in the park. Plenty of surfing, swimming, walking and fishing are available on Gunnamatta Beach and Sorrento Back Beach. The park, 95 km (59 miles) south of Melbourne on the eastern side of the entrance to Port Phillip Bay, is open for day-use only.
Map ref: page 336 F6

MORWELL

Coal is the mainstay of Morwell, a town of 17,000 people, set 155 km (96 miles) south-east of Melbourne in the heart of the LaTrobe Valley.

The valley contains one of the world's largest deposits of brown coal. Open-cut mining was established in Morwell in 1916 by the then State Electricity Commission (SEC)—privatisation of government resources sees independent companies operating the State's power supply today. Before the coal industry was developed, dairying was the mainstay of the region. Tours of the open-cut mine, power station and the briquette factory can be organised through the Powerworks Visitors Centre, which also runs spectacular night tours from November through to May.

The building of the Hazelwood Power Station, which opened in 1971, led to the construction of the Hazelwood pondage. This body of water is heated by the power station—it provides warm water for swimming and is very popular with waterskiers.

The Morwell Centenary Rose Garden on Commercial Road is one of Victoria's finest rose gardens. It covers about 1.5 ha (3.7 acres) of landscaped beds containing over 2000 different varieties of roses. The more adventurous might like to head to the Thomson River for whitewater rafting. To the south of the town lies Morwell State Park, which is popular with bushwalkers because of its fern-lined gullies and tall stringybark forests.
See also Gippsland Wine Region
Map ref: page 342 A8

ORBOST

The town of Orbost, 384 km (238 miles) east of Melbourne, sits high in the forested mountains that support its timber industry. Most of the highly prized hardwood from this region is sent to the Brodribb Mill for processing. Much of the area is now protected as parkland—the Rainforest Centre run by the Conservation Department details the intrinsic value of the local temperate rainforests.

The town was first occupied during 1838, and settlers were using the flat swampland by the Snowy River nearby to grow their crops by 1842. Today there are still crops flourishing in these fertile river flats. The town currently has a population of 2515.

North of Orbost the Snowy River National Park offers walking tracks; the Snowy River is also popular with rafters and canoeists. Errinundra National Park, further east, is a plateau with magnificent cool-temperate rainforest. It features raised walking platforms and information boards. The slippery unsealed tracks also provide a challenge for 4WD vehicles.

The Slab Hut Information Centre on the edge of town was built by John Moore in 1872 and provides information on the township of Orbost and the surrounding area. The hut is in parkland which is ideal for picnics. The Snowy River Country Music Festival is held near here in January, and the Orbost Show takes place in March.
Map ref: page 343 H5

The unique, ancient forest in Errinundra National Park, north-east of Orbost, has not experienced bushfires for over 150 years.

PAYNESVILLE

The town of Paynesville (population 2447) sits 306 km (190 miles) east of Melbourne, among the sheltered waters of the McMillan Straits in Gippsland and near the large coastal community of Lakes Entrance. The inland waters of the lakes are protected by dunes and coastal headlands. Large power boats and yachts use the lakes and yacht races are held in summer.

The influence of the boating community is evident in a most unusual church, St Peter by the Lake, built in 1961. Its limestone spire is shaped like a lighthouse, and its pulpit is designed to resemble the bow of a fishing boat. Like a beacon, the cross of the church can be seen by anglers on the lakes, and churchgoers can look out onto Lake Victoria through tall windows behind the altar.

Raymond Island is popular with bushwalkers—access is by car ferry from Paynesville. Rotamah Island lies between the Ninety Mile Beach and Lake Victoria. This island is perfect for bushwalking and bird-watching. Other parkland in the area includes the Lakes National Park and Gippsland Lakes Coastal Park, both of which help protect the fragile seaside environment. A Sunday market is held bi-weekly on the Esplanade with handicrafts and home-made produce for sale, and yachting championships are held during Easter and Christmas. *See also* Gippsland Wine Region
Map ref: page 342 E6

PHILLIP ISLAND

This island, which is connected to the mainland via a long bridge between Newhaven and San Remo, has long been a popular holiday resort for Melburnians—it is only 130 km (81 miles) south of the city. Its attractions have increased recently, with the Phillip Island Race Track hosting rounds of the Motorcycle Grand Prix and the World Superbike Championships.

The first European to see the island was George Bass in 1798. First known as Snapper Island, its name was later changed to honour Governor Phillip. It was used as a military settlement in the early 1800s before farmers moved in during the 1840s. Cowes is the main town on the island. It has safe beaches for swimming, and makes an excellent base for touring the island. The other main towns are Newhaven, Ventnor and Rhyll. Natural features of the island include the Blow Hole, the Nobbies (a large stack of rocks), and magnificent sandy beaches combined with a rugged coastline.

Wildlife has always been an attraction of Phillip Island. The fairy penguin parade is one of Victoria's main attractions, and each evening busloads of tourists venture to Summerland Beach to watch these tiny creatures walk onto the beaches to their burrows. Koalas can also be seen at various locations on the island. For a closer look you can go to the Koala Conservation Centre at Summerland Beach.

Phillip Island also boasts a very large colony of fur seals, at times as many as 6000—more than the human population, which is 4995!—and these can be seen at Seal Rock on the Cowes–Nobbies road. A ferry also runs each day from Cowes to the north of the island, where tourists can have exceptional views of the seals at play.

One of the best fishing spots on Lake King is the McMillan Straits area between Paynesville and Raymond Island.

The Reefworld Marine Aquarium has a tropical aquarium that is home to more than 4000 fish.

The Phillip Island Heritage Centre in Cowes outlines the history of the island, from Aborigines through to the whalers, sealers and farmers. Wineries are a relatively new attraction on the island, but are worth visiting: the Phillip Island Vineyard and Winery is the only permanently netted vineyard in Australia. The nets protect the grapes from birds and from the powerful wind gusts that blow in from Bass Strait.
Map ref: page 337 H7

PORTSEA

Portsea is a small town, with a population of only 750, which is 95 km (59 miles) south of Melbourne. It has long been a favourite holiday destination for Melburnians, especially the wealthy, as is clear from the number of large and expensive homes that grace the area. It is also well known as the place where the then Australian Prime Minister Harold Holt disappeared in 1967 when swimming in the waters off Cheviot Beach.

While Portsea does have some excellent beaches for swimming, the Holt tragedy notwithstanding, it is surfing that is the real attraction for many. The back beach of Portsea has become legendary among surfers. Here you will also find plenty of rock pools to investigate at low tide.

Portsea has always been regarded as the 'fashionable' beach town to be seen at, along with the neighbouring suburb of Sorrento and the strip of coast between these two towns. There are a number of trendy cafés and restaurants to be found here, as well as fish and chip shops that serve up the local catch.

Historic Delgany Country House Hotel, built as a castle in 1920, and now a privately owned guesthouse, is worth a visit. The Mornington Peninsula also has a large number of wineries which are open to the public, mostly on the weekends. The more interesting include Peninsula Estate at Red Hill, where you can listen to jazz while tasting the wines on long weekends, or Hann's Creek Estate at Merricks North, where you can try your hand at a game of boule.

Portsea was named by a settler in the area, James Ford, after an area in Portsmouth, his home town in England. Originally a limeburner settlement, a quarantine station was built in town during 1856 after disease killed more than 80 men who were aboard the ship *Ticonderoga*, which was anchored in the waters of the bay. The area was also the site of a School of Army Health, part of Portsea's Military Area. Tours of the old Quarantine Station Museum and the Army Health Services Museum, both of which are now within the Mornington Peninsula National Park, are available.

Portsea Surf Beach and the surf beaches of Sorrento, Rye and Gunnamatta also form part of the Mornington Peninsula National Park. There are a number of interesting walking tracks, the most popular being the Farnsworth Track, which goes from Portsea to the London Bridge rock formation, taking in heathlands and beach areas and offering excellent coastal views from the clifftops.
Map ref: page 336 F6

POWELLTOWN

The small settlement of Powelltown (population 120) is 85 km (53 miles) east of Melbourne. The town is based on timber, which is found deep in the mountain ash forests on the edge of the Great Dividing Range and across the east of the State, and was named in honour of the Powell timber company, the company that worked the timber processing plant. Mills have been operating in Powelltown for over a century, and one still operates in the town.

In the early 1900s tramlines (with gentle grades) were built, so that the logs could be hauled by teams of horses This was the only means of access into the thick forest. In 1915, steam engines were brought in to haul the logs, and later these were superseded by motorised locomotives. A huge fire ravaged the area in 1939, and unfortunately much of the timber and the infrastructure of the timber industry were destroyed. Logging roads were then built and large trucks were then used to haul the timber. An excellent forestry office in Powelltown has brochures and information on scenic drives and forest walks in the area.

This region lends itself to scenic drives, whether on bitumen or on well-formed gravel roads, with either a conventional vehicle or a 4WD. With a 4WD you can take some of the logging and forestry roads and get a close look at the tall timbers. Other attractions of the area include the Seven Acre Rock, a rocky outcrop offering superb views of the nearby Bunyip State Park, and as far as Western Port Bay on a clear day.

There are also many interesting walks in the forest, such as the 3.6-km (2.2-mile) loop that will take you to the Ada Tree, an enormous mountain ash which is believed to be more than 300 years old. The tree is 76 m (249 feet) tall and has a circumference of 15 m (49 feet)—it dwarfs everything around it. To get to the Ada Tree by car, take the Ada River Road, off the Powelltown–Noojee road.
Map ref: page 337 L3

Cheviot Beach, near Portsea, was named after a ship that was wrecked here in 1887.

The beaches on Phillip Island are popular with both seals and surfers.

ROSEBUD

Rosebud and the neighbouring town of Dromana are on the edge of Port Phillip Bay, 78 km (48 miles) south of Melbourne, and have safe swimming beaches and shady foreshores. The township is named after a vessel which ran aground in this part of the bay in 1851. Many Melburnians remember holidays on the Rosebud Foreshore, where hundreds of caravans and tents merged during the summer months to form a seashore community. Other families built or rented beach houses and would come from Melbourne every

Flathead are commonly caught in Port Phillip Bay near Rosebud.

weekend to enjoy the sun and beach. The district is still popular today, although the seaside town has grown considerably—its population today is 13,275.

The Mornington Peninsula has many attractions for visitors, including the large Mornington Peninsula National Park, on the south-western side of the peninsula, where you will find the surf beaches of Gunnamatta and Sorrento Back Beach. It is also a good area for bushwalking—the Coastal Walk, which stretches from Cape Schanck near the lighthouse to Bushrangers Bay at the southern end of the park, is a scenic trek of 6 km (4 miles). On the third Saturday of every month markets are held on Boneo Road, in nearby Boneo, offering handicrafts and fresh produce.
Map ref: page 336 G6

RYE

Rye (population 7285) is a popular bayside resort on the edge of Port Phillip Bay, 83 km (52 miles) south of Melbourne. It was originally known as White Cliffs because of the limestone deposits from which lime was quarried for use in mortar

in the 1800s. There is a reconstructed lime kiln on the foreshore. Road access was a problem in the early years, and it was not until a port and jetty were built in 1860 that this isolated township began to grow.

Rye has both a back beach and front beach. The front, or Foreshore Reserve, is a sandy stretch frequented by families—it offers safe swimming, camping, a boat ramp and the Rye Jetty. Fishing is popular here, with flathead, snapper, whiting and mullet among the most commonly caught. The back beach is situated in the Mornington Peninsula National Park—it is popular with surfers as it offers a more challenging swim. Australian salmon and mullet can be caught here. Other popular seaside towns near Rye include Sorrento, Rosebud, Dromana and Portsea, while on the other side of the Mornington Peninsula, looking out to Phillip and French Islands, are the quiet beach villages of Somers, Merricks and Hastings.
Map ref: page 336 F6

SALE

Surrounded by pastoral land in the heart of Gippsland, and 220 km (137 miles) south-east of Melbourne, is the regional centre of Sale, with a population of 13,858. It services the outlying farm areas and smaller communities, and also acts as an administrative centre for the offshore oil and gas fields of eastern Victoria. The name Sale comes from a general in the British Army, Sir Robert Sale, who died in battle on the Northwest Frontier Province in India.

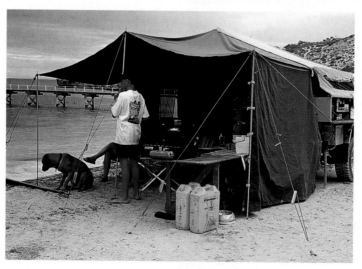

A well-appointed camping trailer on the beach at Rye, complete with mini-kitchen.

Our Lady of Sion Convent in Sale was built between 1892 and 1901.

The town is some 25 km (16 miles) from the coast, but was once connected to the Gippsland Lakes by way of the Thomson and LaTrobe Rivers: a canal was built so that paddle-steamers could carry produce to Lakes Entrance, whence it was shipped to Melbourne. The Sale Canal and port are just off the main highway, at Cullen Park. Further along the canal is the swing bridge, built across the LaTrobe River in 1883. The bridge provided a route across the river to Port Albert, the main port of entry to Gippsland in the mid-1800s. Trade in the town increased with the arrival of the Eastern Railway Line.

There are many features of interest in this old town, including the ornate St Paul's Cathedral, which was originally built in 1885, Bishops Court, the residence of the Bishop of Gippsland, which was constructed in 1885, and the Our Lady of Sion Convent, built between 1892 and 1901. The Bon Accord Tea Rooms are also worth a visit. They are housed in an attractive Victorian homestead surrounded by farmland and lush gardens.

Lake Guthridge, in the centre of town, houses a bird sanctuary. Near Lake Guthridge is the Historical Museum, which displays a history of the town and the region. Sale is also a gateway to the outer Gippsland region and the alpine High Country to the north.
See also Gippsland Wine Region
Map ref: page 342 C7

SNOWY RIVER NATIONAL PARK

This spectacular park, with its splendid river scenery, impressive deep gorges, picturesque forests and diverse vegetation and fauna, protects Victoria's largest forest wilderness, and adjoins Alpine National Park. Numerous vehicle tracks offer opportunities for visitors to explore. The Deddick Trail is suitable for 4WDs only. The Snowy River is also a mecca for canoeists. The southern part of the park is 390 km (242 miles) east of Melbourne.
Map ref: page 343 H3

SORRENTO

Sorrento (population 1160) and the nearby town of Portsea are popular seaside resorts on the Mornington Peninsula. The Sorrento car ferry heads across Port Phillip Bay five times a day to the resort town of Queenscliff. Within easy reach of Melbourne—only 91 km (57 miles) south of the city—this region has long been a favourite summer holiday destination for Melburnians. A drive through Sorrento's tea-tree lined streets will reveal an abundance of stylish holiday homes; the main street features large ornate Victorian hotels which were built in the late 1800s.

The town has several worthwhile historic attractions, including Collins Settlement Historic Site, just off the Nepean Highway on Leggett Ways, where Lieutenant-Colonel David Collins landed and settled in 1803. Because of the lack of drinking water the settlement was abandoned within a year and the group moved on to Hobart. The Nepean Historical Society Museum is in the old Mechanics Institute Hall, which was built in 1876 and is now classified by the National Trust. The Marine Aquarium on St Albans Way where visitors can see the seals being fed, or take a cruise in Port Phillip Bay and swim with dolphins and seals, is also well worth a visit.

Sorrento Beach, on the Nepean Highway, is ideal for swimming, while the back beach, with its tall cliffs, large waves and strong currents, is favoured by surfers. Along the foreshore of Sorrento Beach is parkland with bike paths, picnic facilities, kiosk, toilets and a boat ramp. An interesting walk which allows you to fully enjoy the rugged coastal scenery and superb sandy beaches is Coppins Track, from St Pauls to Sorrento, which was established in 1890 in honour of Queen Victoria's Diamond Jubilee. Meandering along the coastline, it takes in a section of the walking track through the Mornington Peninsula National Park—from London Bridge down to Cape Schanck at Bushrangers Bay in the south.
Map ref: page 336 F6

TRARALGON

Traralgon, 169 km (105 miles) east of Melbourne, has always been a stopping-off place on the way to somewhere else. In the early days it was frequently used by either graziers on their way to the mountain country, or prospectors heading to the goldfields. When the railway arrived in 1877, it became a stopping point on the railway line, which continued on to the east. While today the town itself has a large commercial base, with paper and power industries in the area (and a population of 19,235), it is still also used as a stopover on the way to the Alps or the lakelands of Gippsland. The Tambo Cheese Factory is based in Traralgon, and sells a wide variety of Gippsland cheeses, along with local crafts.

The town has grown significantly over the past few decades, but its history is evident in buildings such as the post office and courthouse, which were both built in 1887. The Traralgon Hotel, with its ornate iron lace work veranda, is classified by the National Trust.

Traralgon is close to the Moondara State Park and reservoir and Baw Baw National Park. Mount Baw Baw is a fascinating mountain, and in winter the slopes are enjoyed by downhill and cross-country skiers, as well as snowboarders.

The nearby Thomson River is an excellent place for whitewater rafting, and the Blue Rock Lake, near Moe, is used for all kinds of water sports. Traralgon is also not far from the historic township of Walhalla, which was a major goldmining town in the 1800s.
See also Gippsland Wine Region
Map ref: page 342 A7

WALHALLA

Nestled in a deep valley on Stringers Creek in Gippsland, 202 km (125 miles) east of Melbourne, Walhalla only just managed to survive the decline of the goldmining era—it is now a tiny historic town, popular with tourists. The small township has only a population of 30—most use the town as a weekend retreat—and is still not supplied with electricity. It is also the start of the well-used Australian Alps Walking Trail, a trail which ends in the Australian Capital Territory, more than 760 km (472 miles) away.

Many buildings in the town have been restored, and there are many ruins to be explored. The rotunda has been standing in the

Cheddar from the Tambo Cheese Factory, Traralgon.

main street since 1896, and is still used during festivals. A small path on the main road leads to an interesting old cemetery terraced on a steep hillside. A visit to the museum, also in the main street, is a great insight into the town's history. Fossicking is still allowed, and the rivers are an excellent playground in summer. The town's Long Tunnel Extended Mine, operational from 1865 until 1911, was the fifth richest in Victoria, bringing in 14 tonnes (14.3 tons) of gold. Guided tours are conducted through the 300-m (984-foot) opening in the hillside.

One of Victoria's most spectacular railway journeys was reborn here in 1994, when the old Walhalla Gold Fields Railway was restored. Now that the Thomson River Trestle Bridge has been fully restored, passengers can cross the bridge and wind their way up through the lush forest of Stringers Creek Gorge. The railway is still being built, and will eventually finish at Happy Creek, where there will be a picnic ground.
See also Gippsland Wine Region
Map ref: page 342 A6

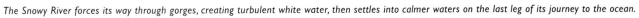

The Snowy River forces its way through gorges, creating turbulent white water, then settles into calmer waters on the last leg of its journey to the ocean.

WARBURTON

Nestled in a lush valley where the Yarra River snakes its way downwards to Port Phillip Bay, and 78 km (48 miles) east of Melbourne, this country town is a delight for day or weekend visits. Gold was discovered here in 1864, and when the gold rush ended the settlers turned to clearing the land. Timber mills were soon scattered through the mountains. Today forestry is still a major industry in Warburton, although tourism is also significant, and has been since the early twentieth century. The town is small, with a population of only 2005.

Warburton has always had a large Seventh Day Adventist community, with Melbourne Adventists moving to the area in 1904 and building a printing works. In 1923 the Sanitarium Health Food Factory was established. Warburton is also home to the Warburton Health Care Centre, which offers therapeutic services for busy city people.

Warburton is the perfect base from which to explore the surrounding ranges, with such interesting places as the historic goldmining towns of Matlock or Woods Point close by, high up in the hills. Tommy Finn's Trout Farm is just outside the town entrance. Here a series of lakes, set among the magnificent ranges, give people

One of a number of trout streams near Warburton.

a better than average chance to catch a trout. Mount Donna Buang is only 6 km (3.7 miles) from the town, and is popular with families from Melbourne seeking a day in the snow. Tobogganing is popular here, as is cross-country skiing at nearby Lake Mountain. The mountain area is also popular with bushwalkers, 4WD owners, mountain and trail bike riders and canoeists.
Map ref: page 337 L3

WARRAGUL

About 100 years ago, the area on which the township of Warragul (population 8910) is situated was mostly swampland, but with hard work and determination, the marshland was filled in, and a successful dairy industry was established on the green fertile flats. The historic centre in the old shire hall outlines the history of the dairy industry in the region. Warragul is 109 km (68 miles) south-east of Melbourne, and is in a rich agricultural area. A Gourmet Deli Trail leads visitors on a gastronomic tour of the region, taking in farms, wineries, fine restaurants and food shops.

The town of Warragul has several attractions, including the old drive-in movie site, now home to the Lillco Garden Railway, which has a miniature railway system, featuring landscaped surroundings and rides on miniature engines. Only 8 km (5 miles) to the east of town is Darnum, home to the Darnum Musical Village, which houses a superb collection of musical instruments.

To the north of Warragul lies the Great Dividing Range and the old timber towns of Noojee and Powelltown, the latter with its trestle bridges and old milling tram tracks, while south of the town is the Mount Worth State Park. Here you will find the Standing Giant, a huge mountain ash which is more than 300 years old. Events include the Gippsland Field Days in March, and the Warragul Springfest in October.
See also Gippsland Wine Region
Map ref: page 337 M5

WILSONS PROMONTORY NATIONAL PARK

With its pristine beaches, spectacular granite rock formations, magical fern gullies and remarkable variety of vegetation and wildlife, Wilsons Promontory National Park, or 'the Prom', as it is usually called, is one of Victoria's most popular parks. Surrounded on three sides by sea, a number of marine parks and reserves also stretch along the coastline. The area has long been a favourite for fishing and boating, not to mention surfing, diving, snorkelling, bushwalking and photography. The shallow waters of Tidal River make this a great place for kids to splash around in; the nearby

The Tidal River in Wilsons Promontory National Park is a popular camping area. Wombat-spotting by torchlight at night is a favourite pastime for visiting children.

The emus in Wilsons Promontory National Park can often be seen crossing or feeding by the main roads through the park.

beaches are ideal for walking, swimming or simply lazing about. There are many walking trails in the park, some of which lead to secluded beaches, or you can hike to the southernmost tip of mainland Australia and visit the lighthouse there. The park is 200 km (124 miles) south-east of Melbourne.
Map ref: page 337 N9

WONTHAGGI

A large commercial and industrial centre in the South Gippsland region of Victoria, Wonthaggi, with a population of 6710, lies 150 km (93 miles) south-east of Melbourne and 2 km (1.2 miles) from the Cape Paterson coastline of Bass Strait. This region is best known for the black coal which was discovered here in 1824 by the explorer William Hovell. It was mined at Cape Paterson from 1859 to 1864. Wonthaggi used to be the main supplier of coal to the Victorian Railways. However, Miners eventually gave up on the operation as transporting the coal was made difficult—ships could not find safe anchorage in Venus Bay.

The coal was left underground until a major strike in the Newcastle coalfields of New South Wales in 1910 led to the Victorian Government encouraging mining to start up in the Wonthaggi coalfield again. Much of the coal was used by the government to keep the State railway system running. Camps, and eventually houses, were set up to support the coalminers and the area grew until the State Coal Mine was closed in

1968. A portion of the coalmine can be viewed today with information available at the Orientation Centre at the East Area Mine.

Wonthaggi is close to the township of Inverloch, which offers plenty of seaside activities such as swimming, surfing, sailboarding and fishing. Wilsons Promontory National Park, with its enormous network of walking tracks and spectacular coastline, is also a pleasant drive from Wonthaggi. The Picnic Races are held here in January, and the Coal Skip Competition takes place during Easter.
See also Gippsland Wine Region
Map ref: page 337 K7

YARRA GLEN

First known as Yarra Flats, the township of Yarra Glen (52 km [32 miles] north-east of Melbourne) is flanked on one side by the Yarra River, which passes the

Picking grapes in a vineyard at Yarra Glen.

town on its way through the river flats of the Yarra Valley to the city and Port Phillip Bay. The area around Yarra Glen is so low that after a heavy downpour of rain the Yarra River rises high enough to cut off the town from the neighbouring towns of Lilydale and Coldstream. Fortunately, this occurs infrequently.

Though the township of Yarra Glen is small, with a population of only 2095, it houses one of the more magnificent hotels in the region, the National Trust classified Yarra Glen Grand Hotel, which is on the main road and has recently been restored. Another local attraction is Gulf Station, on the Melba Highway just out of Yarra Glen. The station was established in the 1850s and is one of the oldest farms in the Yarra Valley region. The whole farm is one of the most complete group of solid timber buildings still to be found standing in Victoria, and houses examples of many of the machines and utensils used in the early pioneering days.

Yarra Glen is at the heart of the winery region of the Yarra Valley—one of Victoria's oldest and most successful wine-growing regions. The Yarra Valley Grape Grazing Festival and the Yarra Glen Show are both held in March.
Map ref: page 337 J2

YARRA JUNCTION

Yarra Junction lies on the edge of the Yarra River at the foot of the Yarra Ranges, 68 km (42 miles) east of Melbourne. There are a couple of theories as to how the town got its name: one is that it is where the Little Yarra and Yarra rivers meet, and the other is that it was named after the junction of the Victorian Railway Line and the smaller 3-foot (91.5-cm) gauge of the Powelltown Tramway.

Along with the neighbouring towns of Warburton, Marysville and Powelltown, Yarra Junction supports a large timber and farming industry, and there were once many sawmills operating nearby. However, now the town's population is reduced to 1120. Much of the region's history is displayed in the Upper Yarra Historical Museum, which is housed in the

Yarra Junction is one of the main sources of fruit for Melbourne.

old railway station. This station was formerly the Lilydale Station, before it was moved to its present location in 1901.

The drive from Lilydale along the Warburton Highway to Yarra Junction offers many spectacular views of the grazing and fruit-growing regions outside Melbourne, along with the magnificent Yarra Valley. Yarra Junction is also home to Yarra Burn Winery, the first winery in the Yarra Valley to manufacture sparkling wines.
Map ref: page 337 K3

NORTH-EAST VICTORIA

This wedge of Victoria is bounded in the north by the Murray River headwaters, and in the south and east by a mighty sweep of the Great Dividing Range—a wild and spectacular place of alpine peaks and grand vistas. On the western edge are the bountiful Goulburn Valley farmlands.

Victoria's high country is the stuff of legends. The first Europeans to venture here were drawn by gold in the 1850s; the diggings were reputedly the toughest, and most lawless in Australia. Nestled between towering slopes the gold towns remain— Omeo, Bright and well-preserved Beechworth (where a horse shod with gold was once ridden through the main street). Banjo Paterson's poem *The Man from Snowy River* immortalises the hardy cattlemen who since the 1850s have brought herds to graze lush spring and summer alpine pastures; the ballad is said to be based on a Corryong stockman and today the town has a museum dedicated to its local hero.

Bushranger Ned Kelly was raised near Benalla and in the late 1870s ranged through this country; clad in his celebrated armour, he made his last stand at Glenrowan. Most of the State's ski resorts are in or on the edge of the sprawling Alpine National Park, which is transformed by winter snows into a vast snowfield offering a range of resorts and international class skiing.

The strong flow of the Goulburn River, as it runs from the western slopes of the Great Dividing Range, was dammed in the 1920s to form Lake Eildon. Popular with anglers and boat enthusiasts, this tree-lined lake feeds an electricity power station and provides a water supply to irrigate the Goulburn Valley, to the north. Centred on the town of Shepparton, the valley is now one of the richest agricultural areas in the State, producing fruit, vegetables and grain as well as beef and dairy cattle. Milawa, just to the east on the 'snow road' between the Hume Highway and the Alps, is famed for its cheeses and mustards. To match the region's fine foods are local wineries providing for every taste, ranging from crisp whites and full-flavoured reds to serious desert wines.

OPPOSITE: A huge red gum in the wetlands of Barmah State Forest.

The sacred kingfisher (Todiramphus sanctus) often hunts in wetland areas for large insects.

The Victorian Alps

The Australian Alps stretch from eastern Victoria into southern New South Wales, forming the highest mountain chain in the Great Dividing Range, the continent's major landform. The Victorian part of the chain is often referred to as the Victorian Alps or, more colloquially, the high country. Once the realm of gold diggers and hardy cattlemen, this is now a playground for many Victorians as well as visitors from further afield, offering spectacular mountain scenery, unusual and varied wildlife and a diverse range of recreational activities. In winter, skiers flock to resorts such as Falls Creek and Mount Buller; in summer, hikers take to the trails, nature lovers come to view birds and wildflowers, and off-road enthusiasts negotiate challenging 4WD routes. Much of the Victorian Alps is now encompassed by the massive Alpine National Park, which stretches from the New South Wales border to the town of Mansfield in the west.

The weather in the Victorian Alps is ever-changing. Snow covers the upper reaches for most of the winter, while summer brings heat to the slopes and particularly the valleys. But snow can also fall in summer months, and even in the space of a day, the weather may switch from extreme heat to freezing cold. Visitors should therefore be prepared for all eventualities and always carry warm clothing as well as adequate food and water. In winter, snow and heavy rain may result in roads being closed at short notice. If travelling at this time, check with a Parks Victoria office for details of track closures before you set off.

History

Aboriginal peoples resided in this mountain region for thousands of years prior to the arrival of Europeans in the early nineteenth century. The first European settlers to explore the area were Englishmen Hamilton Hume and William Hovell, who named the Australian Alps. However, it was not until George McKillop pushed south from Monaro in southern New South Wales to the present site of Omeo that the mountains of Victoria started to yield their secrets.

The first to find a route across the mountains to the southern coast was Angus McMillan, in 1839. Once again, it was the quest for new grazing land by Monaro pastoralists that initiated the journey, with McMillan taking up land for his sponsors on the Tambo River near present-day Ensay. During subsequent expeditions, he opened up a route from the Monaro Plains in New South Wales to the coast at Corner Inlet.

In 1840, Paul Edmund de Strzelecki, a Polish explorer and scientist, was sponsored by the wool baron James Macarthur to find new pastoral country. During his search, he named Australia's highest peak, Mount Kosciuszko—after the Polish patriot Thaddeus Kosciuszko—although he did not climb it. Crossing the Murray River above present-day Corryong, Strzelecki pushed south to the Omeo Plains and from there to Bruthen and the coast.

Following the discovery of gold in the vicinity of the Australian Alps in the mid nineteenth century, hardy prospectors began to comb almost every stream and gully of the Great Divide looking for the precious metal. Many travelled up the Mitta Mitta River and Livingstone Creek to where the town of Omeo now stands, and by 1856 there were more than 600 of them living on the local goldfields.

During the 1850s, German-born botanist Baron Ferdinand von Mueller explored the region extensively and significantly expanded European knowledge of its diverse alpine flora. In 1860, A. W. Howitt was appointed to lead an expedition in search of new goldfields; he explored the Mitchell and the headwaters of the Dargo River, as well as the Wentworth, and found gold on the Crooked River.

In 1864, the government commissioned Angus McMillan to blaze a series of trails through the mountains. In 12 months, over 350 km (217 miles) of track were cut from the Wonnangatta over the Snowy Plains to the top of the range at the Moroka River. Other tracks from Dargo to Harrietville, from the Wellington to the Moroka and from Jordon to Mount Tamboritha were also made.

Loggers and cattlemen were never far behind the prospectors, and stayed on once the gold ran out. It was the cattlemen who created the region's most distinctive heritage. By the late nineteenth century, massive summer cattle drives to the high plains occurred annually. Some of the cattlemen remained on the ranges to tend their herds, living in basic huts, many of which can still be visited today.

During the 1950s, local authorities became more conscious of the ecological significance of the region and imposed limits on stock numbers to control the impact of sheep and horses. Increasing concern over the adverse effects of cattle on the fragile landscape led to these controls being extended, and many grazing licences were withdrawn. Today, only a few cattle owners have access to the high country.

Wildlife

By far the highest mountain range on a relatively flat continent, the Australian Alps form a distinctive ecological zone inhabited by specialised plants and animals, many of which are found nowhere else in the country.

The lower slopes are dominated by eucalypts such as mountain gum and stringybark, the higher slopes by alpine ash, and the area above the snowline by colourful, gnarled snow gums. During spring, as the snow melts, alpine daisies, alpine marsh marigolds and alpine hoveas blossom en masse across the range.

This water channel near Omeo was quarried by Chinese miners and used to wash gold deposits.

OPPOSITE: At 1922 m (6306 feet), Mount Feathertop, in Alpine National Park, is the state's second-highest mountain.

Once endemic to Alpine National Park, the critically endangered brush-tailed rock-wallaby (Petrogale penicillata) is now found only in nearby Snowy River National Park.

These variations in vegetation combined with changeable weather result in an extraordinary diversity of animal life. There are more than 200 species of birds, for example; among the most notable is the noisy gang-gang cockatoo, which migrates here to breed in summer. There are even some emus, though they are rarely spotted. The region's 40 or so mammal species include grey kangaroos, common wombats, echidnas and possums, as well as carnivorous marsupials such as the tiger quoll. They also include several alpine specialists such as the mountain pygmy possum, which was thought to be extinct until 1966 when a live specimen was found, and the now-rare brush-tailed rock-wallaby. Surprisingly, the mountains are also rich in reptiles, with more than 30 species.

Near Mackillop Bridge, the Snowy River separates Alpine National Park from neighbouring Snowy River National Park.

One of the range's most intriguing seasonal inhabitants is the bogong moth. Millions of these large moths migrate to the Alps each year from southern Queensland and northern New South Wales to escape the summer heat. On their arrival in the mountains, they cluster in cool caves and hollows around Mount Bogong. The moths were an important food source for local Aboriginal peoples, who used to congregate here each year to feast on them.

Alpine National Park

Victoria's largest park covers a vast area of 635,580 ha (1,570,518 acres), which encompasses rugged mountains, fast-flowing rivers, huge snowfields, open plains and deep gorges that open out onto wide green valleys. Stretching across much of the range, the park forms a vital protected corridor for the region's flora and fauna.

The idea for a national park in the Australian Alps was first floated by the newly formed Victorian National Parks Association during the 1960s, but it was not until several public inquiries had been held and local people had been persuaded of the idea's merit that the Alpine National Park was finally proclaimed in December 1989.

The park can be divided into six sectors. From west to east, they are: Mount Buller–Stirling, Wonnangatta–Moroka, Mount Hotham–Feathertop, the Bogong High Plains, Wombargo–the Cobberas and Tingaringy. Most of these areas are accessible by road. Mount Buller–Stirling can be reached via Mansfield, along good gravel roads. The Wonnangatta–Moroka area is accessed via Licola, following a well-maintained gravel road, or from Dargo on 4WD tracks. Mount Hotham is serviced by a good bitumen highway—known as the Alpine Road—which runs from Harrietville in the north and from Dargo in the south. The Bogong High Plains are located above Falls Creek at the end of the Mount Beauty Road, a continuation of the Kiewa Valley Highway. The Snowy River Road provides access to the Tingaringy section, and the Benambra and Black Mountain tracks lead into the Cobberas region.

MOUNT BULLER–STIRLING AND LAKE COBBLER

Located only two and a half hours' drive from Melbourne, Mount Buller and Mount Stirling stand atop the Delatite Valley, where the cool streams of the Delatite and King Rivers flow. Mount Stirling offers excellent cross-country skiing and popular walking trails, while Mount Buller caters more for downhill skiers. With many trails surrounding the two mountains and leading up to Lake Cobbler, 4WD touring and cycling are also popular pastimes here.

WONNANGATTA–MOROKA

This section of the park, only 335 km (208 miles) from Melbourne, is much visited and offers a wide range of walking and 4WD tracks, winter ski trails for cross-country enthusiasts, and excellent camping areas, most of which can be reached using conventional vehicles. For many visitors, the main attraction is the Wonnangatta Valley, with its lush valley floor where many pioneers settled last century.

Hidden deep in the mountains at the head of the Wellington River is one of the jewels in the High Country's crown, Lake Tali Karng, which can be viewed from the Sentinel and Echo Point on Rigalls Spur. The descent to the lake is a tough 28-km (17-mile) return trip and should be undertaken only by fit, well-prepared walkers. The trek takes two days, with one night spent camping by the sapphire lake.

Another walking track leads from the popular camping area at Horseyard Flats to dramatic Moroka Gorge, which formed over thousands of years as the Moroka River cut through the range. There are three waterfalls here and, in summer when the water level is low, excellent swimming holes.

Further east, the Moroka Road heads toward the Pinnacles Lookout. You can drive to within 1 km (0.6 miles) of the peak, then take the moderate bush-walking track to the lookout near the fire tower, from where you will enjoy breathtaking views.

MOUNT HOTHAM–FEATHERTOP

Situated in the heart of the national park and incorporating two of the state's highest peaks, Mount Feathertop (1922 m [6306 feet]), and Mount Hotham (1862 m [6109 feet]), this sector receives abundant snowfalls and is best known for its winter sports. While ski tourers range widely across the snowfields, downhill enthusiasts head for the groomed trails of Hotham Heights. Cross-country skiers usually base themselves at nearby Dinner Plain, the more adventurous of them taking the Razorback Trail to Mount Feathertop. This 18-km (11-mile) trek can be completed in a day, though snow camping is possible near Federation Hut below the summit. Come spring, the snow melts, revealing numerous trails that are popular with hikers and cyclists alike, including parts of the Australian Alps Walking Track (see below).

BOGONG HIGH PLAINS

The Bogong High Plains were once an important pasture for cattle, and graziers would drive their herds up here each summer to browse on the lush plains. In the early 1900s, the area became the birthplace of skiing in Victoria and it remains popular with winter-sports enthusiasts. There are unlimited opportunities for cross-country skiers and good downhill facilities at Falls Creek. In summer, visitors can enjoy bushwalking, cycling and horse riding as well as trout fishing at the Rocky Valley Dam and Pretty Valley Pondage.

Popular walks include the moderate 5-km (3-mile) trek from the Rocky Valley Dam to Ropers Lookout, which takes one and a half hours return, or the difficult day hike along the Mount Bogong Staircase,

Snow gums dominate woodlands above the snowline.

which is 16 km (10 miles) return and for the seriously fit only. Another favourite is the return trek from the Bogong High Plains to Wallaces Hut. A picturesque, gentle walk of 2 km (1.2 miles), it takes less than an hour to complete. Built by the Wallace Brothers in 1889 and classified by the National Trust, the hut is the oldest of the historic huts still standing in the park. The woollybutt roof shingles were replaced by galvanised iron in the 1930s.

WOMBARGO–THE COBBERAS

This northern sector abuts Kosciuszko National Park to the north and the Buchan Headwaters Wilderness Area to the south. The only access road suitable for conventional vehicles, the Black Mountain Road, leads to the popular camping areas of Native Dog Flat, Willis on the Snowy River, and the Cobberas Wilderness Area.

The peaks of Mounts Cobberas One and Two are popular bases for walkers, as is Cowombat Flat, site of the wreckage of a DC-3 aircraft that crashed in 1954, killing one crew member.

TINGARINGY

The highest mountain east of the Snowy River, Mount Tingaringy offers commanding views of the Kosciuszko Range and the peaks to the south, near the Snowy River. Most of this sector is classified as wilderness. At the border with New South Wales, it adjoins the Kosciuszko National Park and Byadbo Wilderness Area. Because vehicles and all other mechanical means of transport are banned, the majority of visitors are bushwalkers. They must be well prepared

The Alpine Road crosses the range near Mount Hotham, Victoria's highest settlement.

Bushwalking trails around Mounts Buller and Stirling lead to scenic spots such as Bindaree Falls.

In winter, back roads may become impassable to all vehicles except 4WDs.

and self-sufficient as this is wild country and water can be scarce in summer.

HISTORIC HUTS OF THE HIGH COUNTRY

Scattered throughout Alpine National Park are a number of historic huts built by pioneers who grazed cattle on the high plains during summer. These are now preserved for their historical significance, but can also be used by bushwalkers as temporary or emergency shelters. The most regularly frequented huts include Wallaces Hut on the Bogong High Plains, and Bluff, Bindaree and Craigs huts in the Mount Buller–Stirling sector. Other notable huts are Davies Hut in Wombargo–the Cobbaras and Guys Hut, off the Howitt Road, north of Licola, where you will also find the ruins of the Old Wonnangatta Station.

THE AUSTRALIAN ALPS WALKING TRACK

By far the most impressive of the region's many walking trails is the Australian Alps Walking Track. This spectacular route extends a lengthy 650 km (404 miles) from the old goldmining town of Walhalla in Gippsland, across the Alps and through southern New South Wales, finishing in the Australian Capital Territory at the Namadgi Visitor Centre near Canberra. The track was created in 1968, before the area was declared a national park. It takes more than 10 weeks to complete the entire route, but most walkers tackle it in, or confine themselves to, short sections. Among the most popular is the section that runs from near Falls Creek to Mount Bogong, a distance of 25 km (15.5 miles).

4WD TOURING

In recent years, increasing numbers of visitors have used 4WD vehicles to explore remote and otherwise inaccessible areas of the park, and a good network of suitable roads exists. One of the most popular areas is the Wonnangatta Valley. Zeka Spur Track, the road into Wonnangatta from the Howitt High Plains Road, was once a very challenging track, but it has recently been upgraded and should no longer pose a problem, even for novice drivers. An ideal weekend jaunt would be to camp on the Wellington River outside Licola on Friday night, then travel the 72 km (45 miles) north to the Zeka Spur Track, which winds

downward for 30 km (19 miles) to the valley floor. It should take you three or four hours from Licola along this moderately difficult road. There are camp sites aplenty in the valley, and attractions include the remains of a burnt-out homestead on the banks of Conglomerate Creek and a cemetery perched on the hillside under towering pine trees.

Other interesting 4WD destinations within the national park include Dargo and the Crooked River–Talbotville area, Jacksons Crossing on the Snowy River, and the Deddick Trail. The more adventurous and experienced might like to tackle the Butcher Country Track or the mountain country around Davies Plain in the north. And for experienced off-roaders with time to spare, the challenging Alpine Trek runs for 423 km (263 miles) from Mansfield in the west all the way to Thredbo in New South Wales via Mirimbah, Dargo, Omeo, Sassafras Gap and Tom Groggin. Requiring at least a week, the journey takes

in some of the most spectacular country in the state but also some of the roughest and toughest roads that a 4WD enthusiast is ever likely to encounter, so it's definitely not for the faint of heart.

OTHER ACTIVITIES

The Australian Alps are premium mountain-biking country, with well-formed tracks running alongside deep river gorges, imposing clifftops, large plateaus and verdant valleys. Cyclists should, however, keep in mind that temperatures in the Australian Alps are generally lower than in the rest of the state, with the peaks rarely recording temperatures above 20°C (68°F), even in summer. Restrictions on cycling are in operation in some areas, so check with the park authorities before you hit the trails.

Other popular recreational activities include rafting and canoeing, particularly on the Wellington, Macalister and Snowy Rivers, and horse riding along the mountaintops, an activity that allows visitors to experience this beautiful and historic landscape from the vantage point of the early European settlers.

CAMPING

Bush camping is allowed throughout the park and there are several camping grounds with toilets and fireplaces. For those travelling in conventional vehicles, MacKillop Bridge on the Snowy River in the north-east is an excellent camping area, as are Sheepyard Flat and Lake Cobbler near Mount Buller, Wellington River north of Licola, Anglers Rest north of Omeo and the numerous camping grounds at the top end of the Snowy River Road. Drivers of 4WD vehicles should try areas such as the Wonnangatta Valley, Grant Historical Area, Rams Head at the Cobberas, and Davies Plain. Walkers have the widest choice of sites, with some of the best to be found in the Avon and Buchan Headwaters wilderness zones.

Around 1100 plant species are endemic to Alpine National Park, 12 of which occur nowhere else. Many are alpine specialists.

Places in NORTH-EAST VICTORIA

ALEXANDRA

This small country town (population 2200), is typical of many found in Central Victoria. Much of the surrounding countryside is cleared and utilised for farming. Alexandra is 128 km (79 miles) north-east of Melbourne, near the popular holiday destination of Lake Eildon, with the Lake Eildon National Park offering campers a lakeside camp on the foreshores. This lake is well liked by swimmers, waterskiers and watercraft enthusiasts, including those with houseboats, and anglers also try their luck here, hoping for brown and rainbow trout and redfin. The nearby Goulburn River is one of the State's most important trout fisheries. The town was originally known as Redgate Diggings, during the gold rush days in the late 1800s, but its name was later changed to Alexandra, in honour of the then Princess of Wales. The Timber and Tramway Museum, in Station Street, is housed in the old railway station. This museum displays a range of photographs and artefacts from the pioneer days, when timber was felled in the region. There are also steam engines on display—rides are available on both steam and diesel locomotives.
Map ref: page 344 D8

Carp are abundant in the lakes around Alexandra.

BARMAH STATE FOREST AND BARMAH STATE PARK

The Barmah State Park (21,000 ha [51,891 acres]), the Barmah State Forest (79,000 ha [195,209 acres]), combined with Moira State Park, across the Murray in New South Wales, form the largest red gum forest in the world.

The floodwaters of the Murray River form the wetlands of the Barmah State Park. These are a breeding ground for a wide variety of bird life and fish, and attracted what used to be a large Aboriginal population to the region.

Barmah can be accessed via the Murray Valley Highway from Echuca to the west or Nathalia to the east. During summer and autumn the whole region is available for visitors, but during winter and spring the area floods, and even 4WD vehicles cannot access some areas of the park, so check road conditions before making your travel plans. Camping is allowed at numerous sites throughout the forest, mainly near the Murray River. Because of the fragile wetlands, satisfactory toilet arrangements should be made.

The Dharnya Centre, just outside the township of Barmah, has considerable information on the history of the region and of the Aboriginal people whose home it used to be. The Centre is run by the local Aboriginal people with the help of the Department of Conservation; it also offers accommodation. Kingfisher Cruises operate two-hour cruises on Barmah Lake on Mondays, Wednesdays and Sundays from 12.30 pm.
Map ref: page 344 A2, B2

BEECHWORTH

Nestled among the natural beauty of the Northern Victorian Alps, 275 km (171 miles) north-east of Melbourne, is the historic goldmining town of Beechworth (population 3700). It is history that draws visitors to this town—with more than 30 of its buildings classified by the National Trust; it is currently the best preserved gold town in Victoria.

The town was settled in 1853, and with the discovery of gold there were soon over 8000 gold diggers lining Spring and Reedy creeks. Beechworth Historic Park, with its forests of brittle gum and peppermint, encompasses 1130 ha (2792 acres) of the town and features treasures from the old goldmining days. The self-guided Woolshed Historic Walk, which is in the park, takes around one hour to complete, and goes past diversion tunnels and old mining relics. Other attractions include the restored powder magazine, which was built (of local stone) in the 1850s for the safe storage of the gunpowder used to extract the gold from the ground.

A memorial to the large number of Chinese prospectors who mined this region—the Chinese Burning Towers and Cemetery—stands on Cemetery Road. There you will find the remains of towers, altars and headstones of some of the 1600 Chinese buried there.

Loch Street Museum has a display about Robert Burke, of Burke and Wills fame, who once served as police chief in the district. The gaol cell which held Ned Kelly twice—once when he was young and again, before his execution—is also in Beechworth. Historical browsing, walking, fishing, horse riding and swimming are all on offer in this interesting area.
Map ref: page 344 G4

Benalla is renowned for its roses.

BENALLA

It was the famous explorer Major Thomas Mitchell who first trekked alongside Broken River and camped in 1836 at the site of Benalla; a fountain was later placed in the town gardens in honour of this event. The name was originally Benella, a word from a local Aboriginal language meaning 'musk duck'. Benalla is 198 km (123 miles) north-east of Melbourne, and is the centre of a large agricultural and pastoral area, servicing the surrounding smaller towns and farms. Its population is currently 9200. It is known as the 'Glider Capital of Australia' and these silent fliers can often be seen in the skies above town. The Gliding Club of Benalla offers passenger flights daily. Bushrangers frequented this region and the old courthouse had two visits from the famous Ned Kelly. The Costume and Pioneer Museum in Mair Street houses a magnificent collection of fascinating costumes, including a cummerbund that belonged to Ned Kelly.

An antique carriage in the Harness and Carriage Museum in Beechworth.

The spectacular avenues of deciduous trees in Bright were planted during the 1930s.

In the warmer months you can see where Benalla gets its name 'The City of Roses': the huge trees of the Benalla Gardens offer welcome shade, and hundreds of magnificent roses bloom—not only in the gardens, which were established in 1949, but throughout town. The town's Rose Festival is held every November. The Benalla Art Gallery, situated in the gardens, has a fine collection of Australian artwork and exhibitions, and there is an excellent display of dolls and toys at the Enchantable Collectibles.

Broken River was dammed in 1974, creating a picturesque lake in the centre of town. The lake is popular with swimmers and boating enthusiasts. On the foreshore of the lake is the Ceramic Mural Garden, where potters, helped by local schoolchildren, have decorated more than 1000 ceramic tiles.
Map ref: page 344 E5

BRIGHT

A picturesque country town in the Ovens Valley, 319 km (198 miles) north-east of Melbourne, Bright offers colourful blooms in spring, huge shady trees in the warm summer months, and a kaleidoscope of colour in autumn when the leaves turn amber and fiery red. In winter these leaves fall to the ground, allowing views of the snow-capped mountain tops. Alluvial gold was discovered here in 1853 and the

town's original name was Morses Creek. This was changed in 1862 to Bright, after the English political reformer John Bright. Today the town has a population of 2000, and the timber industry built on the surrounding pine and eucalypt forests, along with a successful tourist industry, is the basis of its prosperity.

Positioned at the gateway to much of the High Country, Bright is frequented by snow skiers in winter, and walkers, mountain bikers, hang gliders and 4WD owners from spring through to autumn. The Bright Autumn and Spring Festivals celebrate the change of seasons.

There are a number of beautiful walks in the region, and the town also has many interesting shops and galleries.
Map ref: page 345 H6

COBRAM

The delightful town of Cobram, 252 km (156 miles) north of Melbourne, sits on the Murray River which snakes its way to South Australia, forming the border between Victoria and New South Wales. It is surrounded by rich fruit-growing and pastoral properties. This area was part of a huge soldier settlement scheme after World War II, and many soldiers established themselves here on dairy and fruit farms in that period. Today the town has a population of 4600, and the region is best known for its holiday activities, which are based on the river. Its New South Wales sister town is Barooga.

Thompsons Beach, near the bridge, is popular for waterskiing, swimming and picnics. Horseshoe Lagoon is another favourite location with swimmers and bushwalkers. Other attractions include the Cobram Matata Deer Farm, on the Benalla–Tocumwal road, where visitors can view red deer. There are also wineries in the region, including Strathkellar Winery.
Map ref: page 344 C2

CORRYONG

Corryong is a small town (population 1274) that lies 435 km (270 miles) north-east of Melbourne. It is the gateway to the Snowy Mountains, and was home to Jack Riley, on whom writer A.B. 'Banjo' Paterson based his famous poem, *The Man from Snowy River*. Riley was buried in the Corryong Cemetery in 1914—his grave, and information on this High Country horseman's life, is still there. The Man from Snowy River Folk Museum contains a replica of a pioneer's hut, as well as old costumes and ski collections. In March the Man from Snowy River Festival is held.

The first settlers to arrive in this region came here in 1837, recognising the potential this fertile land offered for cattle grazing. Three years later the explorer Paul Strzelecki passed through on his way south to Gippsland. Not long afterwards, pastoralists took up cattle runs in this valley, and the High Country cattle tradition still continues here today.

However, it is the majestic mountain country, and the excellent trout fishing in the slow-flowing headwaters of the mighty Murray River and its tributaries, that brings visitors to Corryong today. Corryong is also not far from Australia's highest mountain, Mount Kosciuszcko. Kosciuszcko National Park lies to the north of town, and Victoria's rugged Alps lie to the south.
Map ref: page 345 M4

Cobram is a major dairying area. The Rotary Dairy, on the outskirts of town, is open to the public each day at milking time.

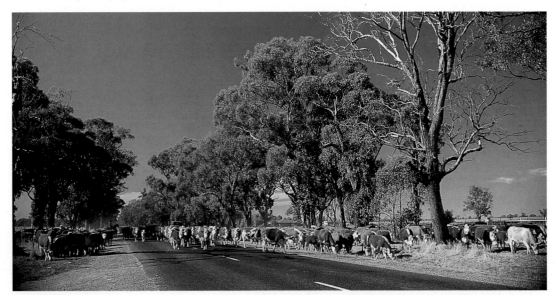

At the foothills of the Alps is the beautiful rolling green landscape of Woods Point near Eildon.

EILDON

Eildon is a small town 136 km (84 miles) north-east of Melbourne, and it sits on one of Melbourne's favourite holiday destinations, Lake Eildon. The town itself is quite small (population 650)—it is the waters of the lake and its 600 km (373 miles) of shoreline that attract visitors.

This region originally supported a timber and mining industry, but between 1915 and 1927 a dam was built; it was 47 m (154 feet) deep and had a storage capacity of 33,700 megalitres (8.9 million gallons). In the 1950s it was decided that this storage system for the Goulburn River was to be extended, and the town of Eildon was established to house the workers for this massive project. A new dam wall, 79 m (259 feet) in height, was erected, and the end result was a massive lake. The lake now holds 3.38 million megalitres (893 million gallons) of water for irrigation—six times the amount of water that is in Sydney Harbour.

Houseboats and other water craft can be hired at the lakeside towns. Fishing is popular, as the lake offers brown and rainbow trout along with redfin. Nearby Lake Eildon National Park and Fraser Inlet are popular with campers, bushwalkers and waterskiers. You will often catch a glimpse of kangaroos here. Events include the Lake Eildon Triathlon in late March, the Navigation Rally for motorbikes in April and the Horseman's Carnival in January.
Map ref: page 344 D8

Wine tastings are available at the Baileys of Glenrowan Winery.

GLENROWAN

Located just off the main highway from Melbourne to Sydney, 221 km (137 miles) from Victoria's capital, Glenrowan is a very small town (population 216) that came to prominence as the place where the notorious bushranger Ned Kelly made his last stand. Ned and his brothers brought havoc to the towns of central Victoria during the 1870s. It was at the Glenrowan Inn that Ned and his gang were besieged and all the members of the gang except Ned were shot. Kelly was later tried for the murder (two years previously) of Constable Thomas Lonigan at Stringybark Creek. He was found guilty, and was hanged on 11 November 1880.

Ned Kelly lives on in Glenrowan, though—a statue of him, wearing his famous metal armour, stands tall, and throughout the town you will find many artefacts and literature relating to the famous bushranger. There are also a number of wineries in this region, extending along the Ovens and King Valleys. These include Auldstone Cellars, Baileys of Glenrowan and HJT Vineyards. Water sports are popular at Lake Mukoan, on the east side of Glenrowan.
See also North-East Wine Region
Map ref: page 344 F5

HARRIETVILLE

A picturesque small town—population 275—at the foot of the Victorian Alps, 344 km (214 miles) north-east of Melbourne, Harrietville sits on the banks of the Ovens River, which runs through the magnificent Ovens Valley. Goldminers were the first settlers here, in 1852, but the rush did not last, and residents took up farming—and, later, tourism. Quiet streets offer country-style fare and hospitality, with a range of accommodation, and small shops for browsing through.

The region around Harrietville is ideal for bushwalking, scenic drives and 4WD touring, with the Alpine National Park presenting plenty of camping opportunities. In summer, a drive to Mount Hotham Village offers commanding views of the blue-toned alpine mountain ranges; in winter, they are capped with brilliant white snow. The town is central to the popular mountain ski resorts of Mount Hotham, Dinner Plain, Mount Buffalo, Mount Beauty and Falls Creek.

Harrietville and the ranges also beckon many anglers, who come here to try their hand at trout fishing. If this fish eludes you in the wild, a visit to the Mountain Fresh Trout and Salmon Farm, or Bright Waters Trout Farm may help to ensure a catch. The town's Market and Fair Day is held in January.
Map ref: page 345 J7

JAMIESON

The tiny country township of Jamieson (population 250) sits at the junction of the Jamieson and Goulburn Rivers near the shores of Lake Eildon, 186 km (116 miles) north-east of Melbourne. Originally a goldmining district, there are many relics and abandoned mines around Jamieson. A scenic drive of the area takes in the neighbouring goldmining townships of Kevington, Woods Point and Gaffneys Creek. There are also many 4WD tracks and walking trails which head up into this rugged country, some which lead to old mine sites; many have great views of the surrounding mountain range. There are still

A hopeful gold prospector tries his luck with a metal detector.

people who head for these hills to try their hand at gold fossicking, but anglers will probably have more luck fishing in the Goulburn River or Lake Eildon, which contains rainbow and brown trout. Lake Eildon is also very popular for water sports, and offers camping on its shores.

North of Jamieson is the Howqua Hills Historic Area, which covers 1300 ha (3212 acres). The Historic Area includes various relics of the goldmining past, including Tunnel Bend, where miners dug a 100-m (3281-foot) tunnel through rock in the 1880s to link the Howqua River with their water race, plus the old water race itself and a brick chimney. A short walk off the main road provides access to the tunnel. The Tunnel Bend Reserve is off the Jamieson–Woods Point road, as are cemeteries at Aberfeldy and mining relics and a cemetery at the historic Woods Point township.

Map ref: page 344 E8

KYABRAM

The irrigation systems channelled through the Goulburn Valley in the north of the State feed the propsperous fruit-growing district of Kyabram. The town is 198 km (123 miles) north of Melbourne, and 40 km (25 miles) north-west of Shepparton, and has a population of 5600. The land here was settled in the 1840s by Mitchell Scobie, and was originally used for grazing and wheat growing. However, the main industry changed with irrigation, which began in the 1890s. Plentiful water, combined with good soils and excellent climate, meant the area was good for fruit growing, especially stone fruits. A fruit-processing plant and cannery were established, providing more employment.

The community-owned Fauna and Waterfowl Park—555 ha (1371 acres)—is situated on Lake Road. There are five ponds with waterbirds—in fact there are over 400 different species of bird life in the park—and mammals living within their own natural environment in the park. Other features include the Stables, also on Lake Road, where renovated horse stables now house a large range of arts and crafts. The Western Gums Egg Experience at the Western Gums Caravan Park has a display of eggs in the Fabergé style, featuring intricate carving and paintings. The Kyabram Show is held in November, as is Market Day, and there is a rodeo in March.

Map ref: page 344 A4

LAKE EILDON NATIONAL PARK

Located on the southern and western shores of Lake Eildon, this park is the result of Fraser National Park combining with the larger Eildon State Park. Visitors to the park will be rewarded by being able to see many different species of native wildlife, including possums and koalas. Bird life is plentiful,

The RSL Memorial Walk in the town park at Kyabram.

with cockatoos, rosellas and miners filling the air with their cries; herons, cormorants, pelicans and ibis, among other water birds, can be found on the lake. The vegetation consists of red box, red stringybark and narrow and broad-leafed peppermints. Canoeing, fishing, boating, windsurfing and swimming are the main attractions of the area, and pleasant bushwalks criss-cross the park. The many forestry tracks in the area to the south of the lake, in the old State park, are popular with owners of 4WD vehicles. The park is 145 km (90 miles) north-east of Melbourne.

Map ref: page 344 E9

MANSFIELD

Mansfield, at the foot of the Victorian Alps and 174 km (108 miles) north-east of Melbourne, is well known as the major gateway to the High Country, and is a popular destination. It first achieved notoriety in 1878, when three policemen were killed by the notorious Kelly Gang at Stringybark Creek. The three men are buried in the Mansfield Cemetery, and there is a monument to them (the Trooper's Monument) in the centre of a roundabout in the town's main street.

Set among some of Victoria's most magnificent mountain scenery, Mansfield (population 2500) is busy in both summer and winter. There is the popular holiday destination of Lake Eildon to the south and the snowfields of Mount Buller and Mount Stirling are not far away. For most of the year the surrounding countryside and mountains are a playground for bushwalkers, 4WD tourers, and campers. It is even possible to take a camel trek and a hot-air balloon ride in this region.

A popular destination near Mansfield is Craigs Hut, which was built on Clear Hills over-looking the valley below for the movie *The Man from Snowy River*. The hut can be reached by 4WD right to the door—if you are travelling by the family car, you will need to walk the last 2 km (1.2 miles). The area is not accessible during winter, as the main Circuit Road is closed.

Mansfield is an ideal starting point for a High Country jaunt in a 4WD vehicle, visiting such places as Matlock, Licola, Wonnangatta Station and Dargo. Another good way to enjoy the scenery is by touring a series of gravel roads in the region, which head through Jamieson and the old goldmining towns of Woods Point and Walhalla.

There are plenty of activities in the area, including bush markets on the Saturday of most long weekends, Mansfield Harvest and Merrijig Rodeo on Labour Day Weekend in March, the High Country Hot Air Balloon Festival in late March, Mansfield High Country Festival in November and the High Cs in the High Country, an open-air concert held at Mount Buller on New Year's Eve.

Map ref: page 344 E7

There are a number of bushwalks through Lake Eildon National Park, varying from energetic five-hour treks, to relaxed one-hour trails.

MARYSVILLE

Deep in the heart of the Yarra Ranges, 93 km (58 miles) east of Melbourne, is the small country town of Marysville (population 650), a popular day and weekend destination with Melburnians.

The township of Marysville was named after Mary Steavenson, the wife of the town's founder, John Steavenson, who first settled here in 1863. Gold was discovered nearby, in the hills around Matlock and Woods Point, and Marysville was a stopping point on the way to and from Melbourne. It also stocked supplies for the prospectors and travellers heading up into the mountain range. Surrounded by tall mountain forest, Marysville has long been a timber town, and a sawmill still exists here today. Other industries in the region include tourism and grazing.

Snow skiing and tobogganing are popular activities at Lake Mountain above the town. Cumberland Scenic Reserve covers 300 ha (741 acres) of mountain bushland including old growth forest. The reserve includes Cumberland Falls and Sovereign View lookout—the lookout gives excellent views over Warburton. Keppels Lookout, on Plains Road, is also well worth a visit—a three-hour walk will reward the energetic with magnificent mountain ash forest scenery and views of the Steavenson River and Marysville. The Wirreanda Festival is held in October, and features a number of activities, including a horse gymkhana, motorcycle rally cross, and a market day.
Map ref: page 344 D9

Steam-driven sawmill at the timber town of Marysville.

Mount Beauty is a photographer's delight during autumn, when the tree-lined streets take on hues of red and gold.

MOUNT BEAUTY

As the name suggests, Mount Beauty is a magnificent country town, situated in the foothills of Mount Bogong in the Upper Kiewa Valley, 350 km (217 miles) north-east of Melbourne. Originally built as an accommodation town for workers on the Kiewa hydro-electricity scheme in the 1940s, the town soon became popular with tourists because of its proximity to the Bogong High Plains and the ski resort of Falls Creek. the town's population is currently 2100.

During winter skiers converge on this picturesque town—they can stock up on supplies, find a bed for the night and hire their ski gear here. Many people also take advantage of the coach-line which ferries skiers to the slopes of Falls Creek. During the rest of the year the area offers magnificent scenery, and there are many bushwalking trails to enable people to see it. The tree-lined roads are great for cycling, especially in autumn, when the roads are edged with golden hues. The large pondage, used for the hydro-electricity scheme, is great for water-based activities such as waterskiing, windsurfing and fishing.

An excellent visitors centre in the town provides information on the hydro-electricity scheme and on the town's history (through an informative museum), and details of attractions in the area. An annual race is held in March to the top of Mount Bogong, and a community market is held on the first Saturday of each month.
Map ref: page 345 J6

MOUNT BUFFALO NATIONAL PARK

Encircled by the Ovens, Buffalo and Buckland rivers, this park offers snow-covered mountaintops in winter and clear, warm days in summer. It is 320 km (199 miles) north-east of Melbourne via the Hume Highway. This rugged park beckons a wide variety of outdoor enthusiasts. Bushwalking is a popular activity after the snow melts—there are more than 90 km (56 miles) of marked tracks in the park. During winter, cross-country skiers are well catered for, and downhill skiers also have many trails to choose from. Anglers will find brown trout in Lake Catani.
Map ref: page 345 H6

MOUNT HOTHAM AND DINNER PLAIN

The small alpine villages of Mount Hotham and Dinner Plain sit right next door to each other—365 km (227 miles) and 370 km (230 miles) north-east of Melbourne respectively—in the snowfields of the Victorian Alps. Their combined population is 370. In winter they are covered in a thick blanket of snow, but when the snow melts in spring, the mountaintop is covered in alpine grass and wildflowers.

Dinner Plain is a small community nestled among the snow gums. Its architecture is uniquely Australian and blends in beautifully with the surrounding scenery. Cross-country skiers use this village as a base, and a shuttle bus operates between the two resorts taking downhill skiers to the chairlifts and slopes of Mount Hotham, which is only 8 km (5 miles) further along the Alpine Road.

Mount Hotham has a large snowfield with many lifts and excellent skiing, for beginners right through to those who play on the black runs. There is also plenty of fun night life on this mountain. The attractions are not restricted to the winter months, as the mountain also attracts bushwalkers, sightseers and rock climbers during summer and spring.

The region is surrounded by the Alpine National Park and is home to a variety of wildlife, including the mountain pygmy possum, once thought to be extinct. The area's best known events are the New Year's Day Celebrations, which include the annual Cattlemen's Horse Race, and the Winter Classic Triathlon, starting on the last weekend in July. Map ref: page 345 J7

MYRTLEFORD

Myrtleford, a delightful old gold town, lies at the junction of the Buffalo and Ovens rivers, 286 km (178 miles) north-east of Melbourne. Surrounded by a large mountain range and with Mount Buffalo looming overhead, the fertile flats of this town are used for cattle-raising and growing crops such as hops, walnuts, tobacco and fruit. Gold was discovered nearby in 1853 which led to the town being surveyed in 1856 by Henry Davidson and then established during 1859. However, it was not until the railway line opened in 1883 that the town really started to grow. The town's population is now 3600.

The Old School Museum provides an insight into the town's heritage. Built in 1870, it contains a restored classroom, kitchen, living room, old printing machinery and memorabilia from World War I. The surrounding mountain ranges offer plenty of attractions for outdoor enthusiasts; Mount Buffalo

Digging a car out after a heavy snowfall in the Alps.

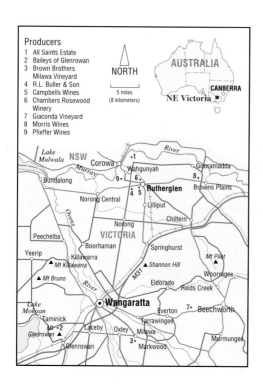

One of the most attractive vineyards in the North-East Wine Region is Boyntons Wines, situated at the foot of Mount Buffalo.

is popular for both snow skiing in winter and bushwalking in summer. Lake Buffalo is also excellent for angling and swimming. A bush market is held in January, and the Tobacco, Hops and Timber Festival is held on Labour Day in March. An annual show features in October and there is a rodeo on Boxing Day. Map ref: page 344 G5

NORTH-EAST WINE REGION

The region around the towns of Corowa and Rutherglen in the north and Glenrowan and Millawa in the south, known as the North-East Victoria Zone, is one of the State's most significant winemaking regions. Growing a remarkably wide variety of grapes, it produces an impressive array of wine styles. These range from outstanding chardonnay to fine shiraz and riesling. However, the region is best known for its distinctively Australian, world-class fortified wines, especially rich muscats and tokays.

As was the case in most of Victoria, it was the 1850s gold rush that created a market for wine in the North-East and funded the development of the necessary infra-structure, most particularly, in this case, the railway between Rutherglen and Melbourne that was to be so vital to export success. Vines were first planted in the Rutherglen area in 1851. As the gold was exhausted, increasing numbers of miners and entrepreneurs began winemaking. By 1870, Rutherglen was the largest vineyard area in the colony.

In the late 1890s, the area benefited from increasing demand for stronger red and fortified wines. However, around the same time phylloxera struck Victoria. In an effort to protect the lucrative North-East, the government forced vineyard eradication in other parts of Victoria. But it was to no avail and most of the region's vineyards were wiped out in 1899.

In the first half of the twentieth century, some local producers managed to continue to sell fortified wines to the United Kingdom while diversifying into sheep farming. Several of the families that continued to make fortifieds, such as the Campbells, Chambers, Morrises and Sutherland Smiths, maintained the aged stocks of muscats and tokays that are the basis of today's highly successful products. However, it was table wines that led the revival of the region's winemaking industry in the mid-1960s, and the area's reds and whites have gained widespread acclaim in recent years. However, at the same time, consumer interest in the opulent fortified wines appears to be waning.

Rutherglen and Glenrowan have a continental climate, with hot days and chilly nights. Spring frosts can be a problem; at about 590 mm (23 inches) per annum, rainfall is low. The King and Ovens valleys, in the foothills of the Great Divide, have higher rainfall, cooler temperatures and more variable soils.

As well as plantings of most major international grape varieties, the North-East has some more specialised produce. When Italian immigrants populated the region after World War II to grow tobacco, they also grew, made and consumed table wine. They continued to purchase wine from Brown Brothers at a time when other Australians had turned away from it; the Brown family repaid the favour by encouraging local growers to develop their vineyards and by contracting their grapes. Hence, the Browns' vineyards at Milawa in the King Valley became a mini-nursery for Italian grape varieties, and nebbiolo, dolcetto, aleatico, moscato, barbera and the Spanish variety graciano still feature in the Brown Brothers range.

Rutherglen has also specialised in durif and shiraz to make its superb vintage ports, and transforms the brown muscat grape into rich, dark muscats that are unique to North-East Victoria. The local version of 'tokay', also a liqueur, is a product of the muscadelle grape; nowhere else in the world is it put to this use.

Many of these products can be sampled at the major wineries, most of which have cellar door sales and offer food. Local festivals include the Winery Walkabout, held in Rutherglen in June, and the Tastes of Rutherglen—a Gourmet Getaway, held every March, involving local wines being paired with fine food in the area's restaurants. Map ref: page 344 F4

Many anglers who come to Omeo for trout fishing use Angler's Rest, north-west of town, as a base.

OMEO

High up in the hills above Bairnsdale, 408 km (253 miles) east of Melbourne, is the tiny (population 274) historic township of Omeo. It is visited by snow skiers on their way to Mount Hotham and Dinner Plain in winter, and owners of 4WD vehicles and horse riders pass through it during much of the year. This is true mountain cattle country: the flats down by the Livingstone and Tambo rivers are also home to the region's main industry—cattle farming. The town

was named by James McFarlane on his journey south; he originally called it 'Omeo B', and it served as a stopping point and cattle station for many years. There are a number of old buildings in town, including the courthouse, which is in the Historical Park (along with a large waterwheel).

Gold was discovered in Omeo during the early 1850s and thousands of prospectors besieged the township. The Omeo diggings, high up in the Alps, were among the roughest in Victoria. Two kilometres (1.2 miles) west of the

town is the Oriental Claims Historical Area, where the Chinese miners worked during the gold rush.

Fishing in the local rivers is popular—as is gold panning in the Livingstone. Snow skiing becomes the focus at the higher towns of Dinner Plain and Mount Hotham in winter. Exploring by 4WD is also popular; it is a good way to visit some of the old goldmining sites and huge stampers that remain as a reminder of the era. The Omeo Show is held in November, the Bush Picnic and Races in March and a Rodeo during Easter.
Map ref: page 345 L8

POREPUNKAH

Set in the picturesque Buckland Valley, where the Ovens and Buckland rivers meet, is the township of Porepunkah, 310 km (193 miles) north-east of Melbourne. The eastern border of the Mount Buffalo National Park lies on the edge of the town; the Alpine National Park is off to the east. The township

owes its start to a gold rush in the 1850s, when many miners came to the Ovens Valley. Eventually the gold petered out and farming became the main industry. The town is small now, with a population of only 385.

With the attractions of the nearby parkland and the beautiful towns of Bright and Mount Beauty, this area is perfect for scenic drives. It is particularly lovely in autumn, when the leaves on the trees turn to shades of copper and gold. Snow skiing is popular at Mount Buffalo in winter, and bushwalking, horse riding, 4WD touring, rock climbing and hang gliding are enjoyed through the rest of the year. Wineries based in the Ovens Valley include Boynton's of Bright, famous for its hospitality and its magnificent views of Mount Buffalo.
Map ref: page 345 H6

RUTHERGLEN

Rutherglen, which lies in the north-east of the State, 277 km (172 miles) from Melbourne, is now the centre of a major wine-producing region, but its origins go back to the gold rush. Gold was first discovered in the 1850s, but Rutherglen's original winemaker, Lindsay Brown, was not smitten with the lust for gold and planted

There is a cluster of vineyards surrounding the town of Rutherglen, with wine-growing country extending south to the Milawa area.

vines in the area instead. The gold fever was not to last, and unfortunately the vineyards also suffered, first through the demise of the gold rush, then because of disease, and finally as a result of the depression years of the 1930s. At this time the fields were ploughed and sheep and cattle grazing took over the land; it was not until the 1970s that the wine industry started to revive in this area.

Wineries to visit include the R.L. Buller and Sons Rutherglen Winery, the Morris Winery, and Campbells Winery. Many of the region's wineries are only a short drive from town—hiring bicycles and pedalling your way around the vineyards is a popular option. Other attractions in Rutherglen, whose population today is 1880, include the old water tower, which is shaped like a wine bottle, and the local museum, housed in the old school building. The main street has several historic buildings, including the old hotel, post office and courthouse, all of which are classified by the National Trust. A Spring Wine and Arts Show is held during September.
See also North-East Wine Region
Map ref: page 344 F3

SEYMOUR

A large farming community and nearby army base support the rural township of Seymour, on the banks of the Goulburn River 101 km (63 miles) north of Melbourne. During 1909 Lord Kitchener declared that Seymour would be a military base, but it was not until World War I that the base was established. Later, in World War II, the base was extended and centred on Pucka-punyal, west of Seymour.

The Royal Australian Armoured Corps Tank Museum at Puckapunyal is home to one of the largest displays of veteran tanks and armament in the Southern Hemisphere. The Royal Australian Corps of Transport Museum complements it, and has a large number of military vehicles from World War I through to the present day, most in operating condition. The town (population 7800) services the military base, and also

caters to the outlying farms and to tourists. Other places of interest in town are the old log gaol, built in 1858, and the Royal Hotel, which dates back to 1849. New Crossing Place, in Emily Street, features a park with bushwalking tracks and is the site of the old Goulburn River punt crossing.

Farming is a big industry in this area, and there are some unconventional farms in the region, including the Capalba Park Alpaca Farm, which has a range of different animals, including alpacas, kangaroos, monkeys, emus, deer, camels and wombats. On sale here are by-products of the emu, such as emu oil. The Spotted Jumbuck, on Highlands Road, features animals such as lambs, sheep and rabbits with uniquely spotted coats, and has sheepskin products and local crafts for sale. Grapes also enjoy the fertile land out on the river flats and the climate—Michelton, Hankin Estate and Somerset Crossing Vineyard are some of the wineries worth visiting.

The Seymour Alternative Farming Expo is a popular event held each year in February. The Agricultural show takes place in October and the Rafting Festival on the Goulburn River is held over the Labour Day weekend in March.
Map ref: page 344 A7

SHEPPARTON

Shepparton, considered the capital of the Goulburn Valley, is 182 km (113 miles) from Melbourne in the State's north, and is set in rich, fertile land, watered by the Goulburn River Irrigation System.

Camel at Capalba Park Alpaca Farm, Seymour.

The International Village Park in Shepparton features country-themed pavilions.

Surrounding the town are 4000 ha (9884 acres) of large orchards within a 10-km (6.2-mile) radius, 4000 ha (9884 acres) of market gardens along the river flats, as well as dairy farms and cattle, all thriving in the warm climate, good soil and excellent water supply Shepparton was originally a crossing point of the Goulburn River in the 1850s, and McGuires Punt was used to ferry passengers and their wares across the river. In 1912 the town began to expand, as the irrigation system was set up and fruit growing and farming became widespread. Because of the freight problems associated with fresh fruit, processing plants and a cannery were established and Shepparton became a strong regional centre. The town's population is now 25,450.

The Shepparton Preserving Co. (SPC), is one of the oldest canneries in Australia—the factory is open to the public for viewing of the processing and canning during the fruit season, which is generally during the warmer months. Visitors can also buy SPC products direct from the factory. Other major factories in the town include Campbells Soups and Australian Country Spinners (Cleckheaton). Shepparton is also home to Furphy's Foundry Museum, where you will find displays of old implements and

memorabilia from the Furphy Foundry, which has been manufacturing cast-iron products, such as the old-fashioned Australian camp ovens, for over a century. John Furphy established the foundry in 1874 and during World War I supplied the military with metal water carts.

Shepparton's history can easily be traced through the Historic Precinct at the corner of Highland and Welsford Streets, where four buildings contain items of the town's heritage which date from 1850 through to 1950. There is also an art gallery on Welsford Street, featuring Australian paintings and ceramics.

Victoria Park, with its 20-ha (49-acre) lake, provides a haven for native wildlife. It is also popular for water sports such as sailboarding, waterskiing and boating. There is a large aquatic centre, which includes a giant waterslide, at the northern end of the lake. Other attractions of the park include picnic areas and a solar-powered telephone. Another unusual and interesting feature of the town is the International Village Park. This 23-ha (57-acre) park has waterways running through it, and a number of pavilions, representing a wide variety of countries, situated beside the waterways.
Map ref: page 344 B4

Vintage aircraft and road transport at the Wangaratta Air World Aviation Museum.

TATURA

A rich agricultural town in the north of Victoria, 169 km (105 miles) from Melbourne, Tatura, like the nearby townships of Shepparton and Rushworth, benefits from the huge irrigation system which was established in the region in the early 1900s. The town was officially gazetted in 1874, and the area was used for grazing sheep, wheat growing and the dairy industry. The region has always been a major producer of quality butter and the dairy industry is still an important contributor. Wheat was produced in large quantities in the late 1800s and the Tatura Wheat Export Movement was set up to export the grain to the United Kingdom. The town now has a population of 2778.

The area has links with the two world wars, as it was the site of four internee camps, and three prisoner-of-war camps (the latter during World War II). The Tatura German Military Cemetery contains the graves of 250 German internees from both world wars. In a program organised by the German government, bodies were exhumed from cemeteries throughout Australia in 1958 and buried here. The Irrigation and Wartime Camps Museum provides considerable insight into the history of both Tatura's camps and its irrigation system. Other attractions of the town include Cussen Park, which has a swamp area that has been set aside as a bird sanctuary. Nearby Lake Bartlett is popular for water sports and features parkland that is perfect for picnicking.
Map ref: page 344 B5

WANGARATTA

Wangaratta, 238 km (148 miles) from Melbourne in the State's north, in close proximity to the wine country, is a large regional centre at the junction of the King and Ovens rivers. The area was first explored by Hume and Hovell in 1824 and was first settled in 1837. The town itself was eventually established in 1849, starting its life as a supply base and stopover for miners in the surrounding goldfields. Woollen mills were set up here in the 1920s and that was when the town started to develop into what it is today—a commercial and agricultural centre with a population of 15,985.

There are several notable historic buildings in town, reminders of the pioneers that first settled here. The impressive Holy Trinity Cathedral took 56 years to build— it was begun in 1909 and not completed until 1965. The main features of this magnificent cathedral are the stained glass windows and the timber belfry—the belfry houses eight bells that were cast in England in 1806 and originally used in a church there. Other historic places of interest include the North-East Historical Society Museum and the Pioneer Cemetery.

The House In Miniatures is also worth a visit. It is a twentieth-century villa, built to scale—2.5 m long, 1.8 m high and 1.6 m wide (8.2 x 5.9 x 5.2 feet)—and took 10 years to construct. It includes furnishings, such as fireplaces with logs, crockery and minute cotton reels in a sewing basket.

Located on the site of an old Aboriginal camp on Ovens Street is the King George Gardens. This English-style garden was established in 1936 and named after King George V, who died while it was being constructed. Two large cannons used in the Crimean War are in the grounds. For aviation buffs, there is the Air World Aviation Museum, which is thought to be Australia's largest collection of antique civil aircraft, that are still in flying condition. There are markets at the Council Carpark every Sunday. The Wangaratta Agricultural Show is held in October, and the Wangaratta Festival of Jazz takes place in November.
Map ref: page 344 F4

WODONGA

Wodonga and its twin city Albury— just across the waters of the Murray River in New South Wales—have combined to become a major service centre. Situated on the Hume Highway between Melbourne and Sydney, 308 km (191 miles) north of Melbourne, these twin towns are used as a major stopover point for travellers on the journey between the two capital cities. Its proximity to Lake Hume and the Murray River, also make this a popular holiday destination.

The explorers Hume and Hovell travelled through this region in 1824 but it was not until the 1830s that sheep runs were taken up in the area. Charles and Paul Huon, who have a lake in town named after them, were the first to take up land. From here the two towns, known collectively as Albury– Wodonga, grew to eventually become Australia's first major decentralised city in 1973.

The city of Wodonga now has a population of 23,640. During the early years of settlement a customs house was established in Wodonga, as it was the only major crossing of the Murray River for many miles. Because of its position it was also an important part of the mail run between the two major capital cities, and also served as

After the inception of an intensive irrigation system in the region, Tatura became an important agricultural centre.

The local government buildings in Wodonga—one of the cities in the Albury–Wodonga twin-city complex.

a cattle market; in fact, at one stage it was the largest cattle market between Melbourne and Sydney.

Stoneleigh Cottage, built in the High Street in 1857 by Paul Huon, is Wodonga's oldest building. The Sumsion Gardens, which include picnic facilities and a playground, overlook Lake Huon and were renovated extensively during the 1950s.

A military camp, which also served as a migrant camp, was established outside the town in 1940. The large Bandiana Military Camp south-east of Wodonga was established in 1942; a large number of army personnel have been stationed here over the last half of the twentieth century. The Royal Australian Army Ordnance Corps Museum is housed at the Bandiana Camp, and displays a large range of tanks, weapons and armoured vehicles.

Across the waters of the Murray, just outside Albury in New South Wales is the Ettamogah Pub, a great tourist attraction as it was designed and built from a cartoon drawn by artist Ken Maynard. This unusual hotel has out-of-square walls and a Chevrolet truck sitting on the uneven roof. The name Ettamogah comes from an Aboriginal word for 'good drinking place'.

East of Wodonga is Lake Hume, a large reservoir used for water sports such as waterskiing, boating, angling and swimming. The Wodonga Show is held four weeks before Easter each year. A community market is held every second Sunday morning, and a Food and Wine Festival is held in September.
Map ref: page 345 H3

YACKANDANDAH

Yackandandah, a town with a population of 700 set 298 km (185 miles) north-east of Melbourne, is a perfect example of an old goldmining town from the nineteenth century. Gold was discovered here in 1852. Because of the significant number of old buildings, the whole town has been classified by the National Trust. Among the most interesting buildings is the Bank of Victoria, which is now a museum.

Many of the others are now used to house art and craft shops and tearooms. On High Street is Ray Riddington's Gallery, which is housed in a store that is nearly 100 years old. Inside is a collection of leather goods, pottery, woodwork and blown-glass items. Wild Thyme features an excellent range of dried

flower arrangements, baskets and handicrafts. The Yackandandah Workshop and Craft Gallery is in the town's old winery, and sells a range of woollen products as well as spinning wheels.

On the Beechworth Road, the Lavender Patch Plant Farm, settled in a picturesque valley, has more than 15 varieties of lavender plants for sale. The farm also sells herbs, toiletries and crafts manufactured from the lavender plant. The farm is open from September through to May. Yackandandah is not far from another significant historic township, Beechworth, which also features extraordinary buildings dating back to the gold rush era.
Map ref: page 345 H4

YARRAWONGA

Yarrawonga, which has a population of 3390, sits beside the Murray where its waters flow into the human-made Lake Mulwala, 263 km

(163 miles) north-east of Melbourne. Lake Mulwala was constructed in the 1930s as storage for the waters of the Murray River, and covers an area of 6000 ha (14,826 acres). The first settler to the region was Elizabeth Hume, sister-in-law of the explorer Hamilton Hume. Elizabeth came here in 1842, and it is believed that because her husband had been killed by bushrangers, she specially designed her homestead so that she had a commanding view of all who approached the house.

The Murray River and the lake are perfect for waterskiing, swimming, boating and sailboarding. The MV *Paradise Queen* is a fine old vessel which offers cruises along the Murray River and around Lake Mulwala, leaving from the Yarrawonga foreshore. There are also river cruises, but in a more modern vessel—the *Lady Murray*—that head along the Murray from Yarrawonga to Corowa. The quieter backwaters are great for fishing, canoeing and birdwatching.

Apart from activities on and around the lake and the river, other attractions of the town include the Pioneer Museum, the Tudor House Clock Museum and Linley Park Animal Farm. The information centre features the Old Yarra Mine Shaft, a simulated mine with many tunnels, one of which includes glow worms, and displays of various minerals and gems. Speedboat races are held in January, and the Yarrawonga Show is held during October. The Red Cross Murray River Marathon starts here on 26 December each year.
Map ref: page 344 E3

Lavender, at Lavender Patch Plant Farm, Yackandandah.

Melbourne City Centre

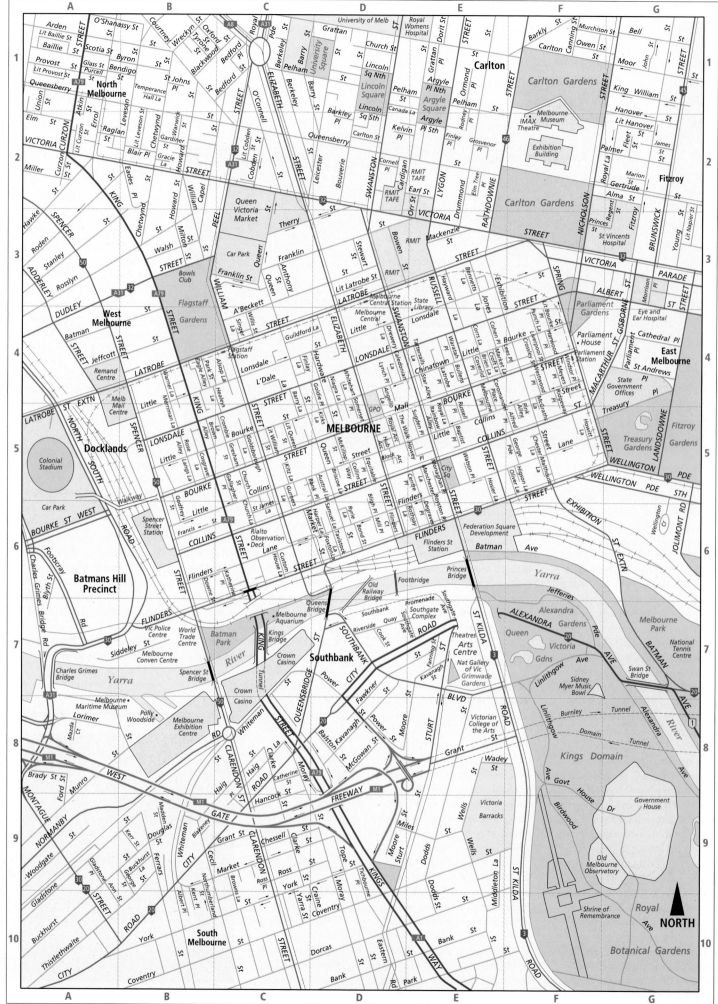

Melbourne Throughroads

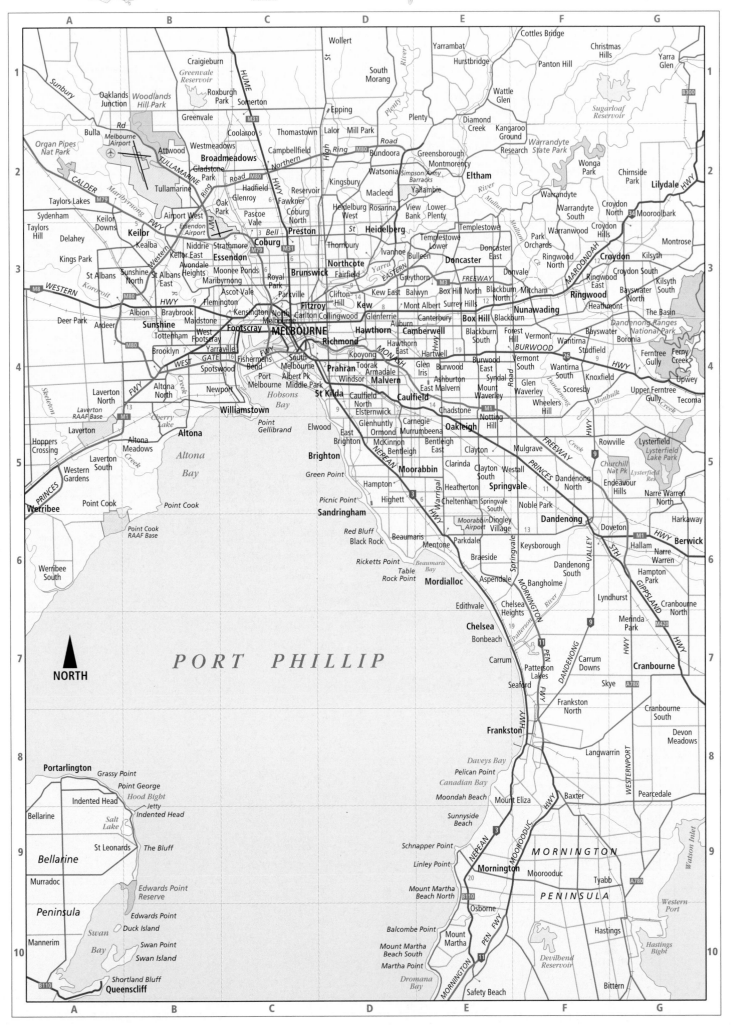

0 2 4 6 8 10
kilometres

PORT PHILLIP

NORTH

A B C D E F G

1 2 3 4 5 6 7 8 9 10

Melbourne and Surrounding Areas

NORTH

BASS STRAIT

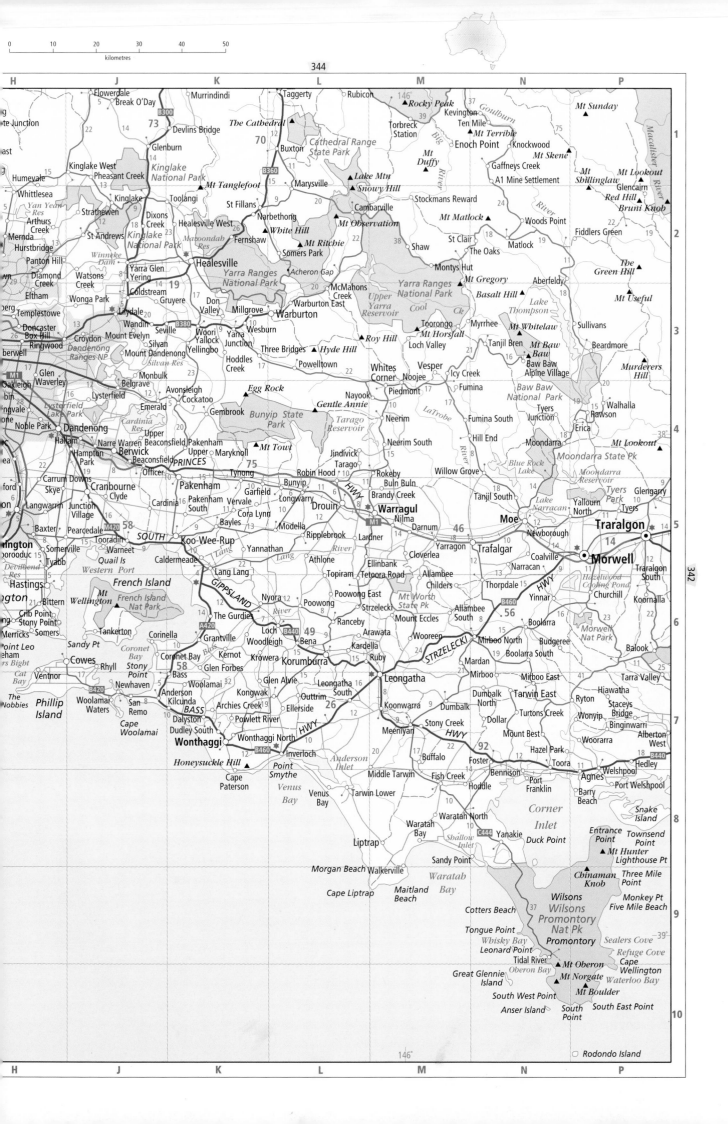

Scale: 0 10 20 30 40 50 kilometres

H J K L M N P

1

Flowerdale
Break O'Day
Murrindindi
Taggerty
Rubicon
Rocky Peak
Mt Sunday
Kevington
Torbreck Station
Ten Mile
Knockwood
Mt Terrible
Enoch Point
Mt Skene
Mt Lookout
Mt Duffy
Gaffneys Creek
A1 Mine Settlement
Mt Shillinglaw
Glencairn
Red Hill
Bruni Knob

2

Kinglake West
Pheasant Creek
Glenburn
Kinglake National Park
Mt Tanglefoot
The Cathedral
Buxton
Cathedral Range State Park
Marysville
Lake Mtn
Snowy Hill
Cambarville
Stockmans Reward
Mt Matlock
Woods Point
Fiddlers Green
Humevale
Whittlesea
Yan Yean Res
Arthurs Creek
Strathewen
St Andrews
Kinglake
Toolangi
St Fillans
Narbethong
White Hill
Fernshaw
Somers Park
Mt Observation
Mt Ritchie
Acheron Gap
Shaw
St Clair
The Oaks
Matlock
The Green Hill

3

Mernda
Hurstbridge
Panton Hill
Diamond Creek
Eltham
Templestowe
Doncaster
Box Hill
Ringwood
Winneke Dam
Watsons Creek
Yarra Glen
Yering
Coldstream
Healesville
Yarra Ranges National Park
McMahons Creek
Warburton East
Upper Yarra Reservoir
Montys Hut
Yarra Ranges National Park
Mt Gregory
Aberfeldy
Basalt Hill
Lake Thompson
Mt Useful
Wonga Park
Lilydale
Gruyere
Don Valley
Millgrove
Warburton
Toorongo
Mt Horsfall
Myrrhee
Mt Whitelaw
Sullivans
Beardmore

4

Croydon
Mount Evelyn
Seville
Woori Yallock
Yarra Junction
Wesburn
Three Bridges
Roy Hill
Loch Valley
Mt Baw Baw
Baw Baw Alpine Village
Murderers Hill
Silvan
Mount Dandenong
Yellingbo
Hoddles Creek
Hyde Hill
Powelltown
Whites Corner
Noojee
Vesper
Icy Creek
Tanjil Bren
Baw Baw National Park
Walhalla
Rawson
Monbulk
Belgrave
Avonsleigh
Cockatoo
Egg Rock
Gentle Annie
Piedmont
Fumina
Tyers Junction
Erica
Glen Waverley
Lysterfield
Emerald
Gembrook
Bunyip State Park
Nayook
Neerim
Fumina South
Hill End
Moondarra
Mt Lookout

5

Dandenong
Narre Warren
Beaconsfield
Pakenham
Mt Towt
Jindivick
Tarago
Neerim South
Moondarra State Pk
Berwick
Beaconsfield Upper
Maryknoll
Robin Hood
Rokeby
Willow Grove
Blue Rock Lake
Moondarra Reservoir
Officer
Tynong
Bunyip
Buln Buln
Tyers Park
Glengarry
Cranbourne
Clyde
Pakenham
Garfield
Longwarry
Drouin
Brandy Creek
Tanjil South
Lake Narracan
Yallourn North
Tyers
Baxter
Pearcedale
Cardinia
Pakenham South
Vervale
Cora Lynn
Bayles
Modella
Warragul
Nilma
Darnum
Moe
Newborough
Traralgon

6

Carrum Downs
Skye
Langwarrin
Junction Village
Koo-Wee-Rup
Yannathan
Ripplebrook
Lardner
Yarragon
Trafalgar
Coalville
Narracan
Morwell
Traralgon South
Somerville
Warneet
Tooradin
Caldermeade
Lang Lang
Athlone
Topiram
Tetoora Road
Ellinbank
Allambee
Childers
Thorpdale
Yinnar
Hazelwood Cooling Pond
Churchill
Koornalla
French Island
Mt Wellington
French Island Nat Park
Nyora
Poowong
Strzelecki
Mt Worth State Pk
Allambee South
Boolarra
Morwell Nat Park
Balook

7

Bittern
Crib Point
Stony Point
Merricks
Somers
Tankerton
Corinella
Grantville
Woodleigh
The Gurdies
Loch
Bena
Ranceby
Arawata
Wooreen
Mirboo North
Boolarra South
Budgeree
Sandy Pt
Cowes
Rhyll
Coronet Bay
Kernot
Krowera
Korumburra
Kardella
Ruby
Mardan
Mirboo
Mirboo East
Tarra Valley
Ventnor
Newhaven
Bass
Woolamai
Glen Forbes
Glen Alvie
Leongatha North
Leongatha
Dumbalk North
Tarwin East
Ryton
Hiawatha
Staceys Bridge
Phillip Island
Anderson
Kilcunda
Kongwak
Archies Creek
Outtrim
Ellerside
Koonwarra
Dumbalk
Turtons Creek
Wonyip
Binginwarri
Alberton West

8

San Remo
Dalyston
Powlett River
Meeniyan
Stony Creek
Dollar
Mount Best
Woorarra
Woolamai Waters
Cape Woolamai
Dudley South
Wonthaggi North
Buffalo
Foster
Hazel Park
Toora
Welshpool
Hedley
Wonthaggi
Inverloch
Anderson Inlet
Middle Tarwin
Fish Creek
Bennison
Port Franklin
Agnes
Port Welshpool
Honeysuckle Hill
Point Smythe
Venus Bay
Tarwin Lower
Hoddle
Barry Beach
Snake Island
Cape Paterson
Venus Bay
Waratah North
Corner Inlet

9

Waratah Bay
Shallow Inlet
Yanakie
Duck Point
Entrance Point
Townsend Point
Mt Hunter
Lighthouse Pt
Liptrap
Sandy Point
Chinaman Knob
Three Mile Point
Morgan Beach
Walkerville
Waratah Bay
Monkey Pt
Five Mile Beach
Cape Liptrap
Maitland Beach
Cotters Beach
Wilsons Promontory Nat Pk
Tongue Point
Whisky Bay
Leonard Point
Promontory
Sealers Cove
Refuge Cove

10

Tidal River
Great Glennie Island
Mt Oberon
Oberon Bay
Mt Norgate
Cape Wellington
Waterloo Bay
South West Point
Mt Boulder
Anser Island
South Point
South East Point
Rodondo Island

H J K L M N P

South-West Victoria

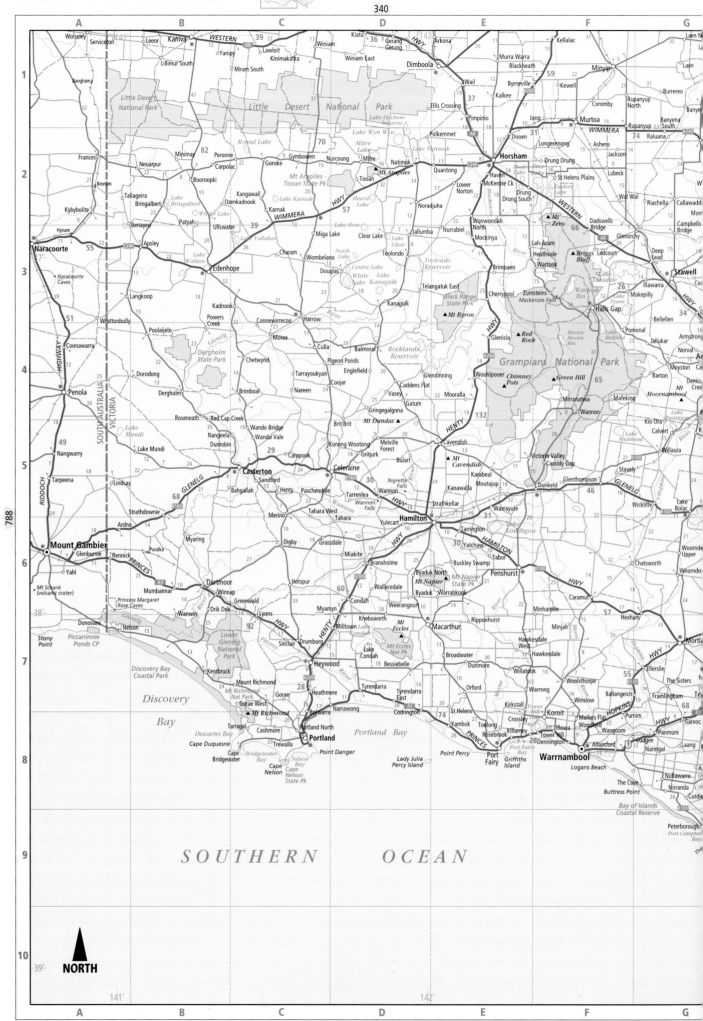

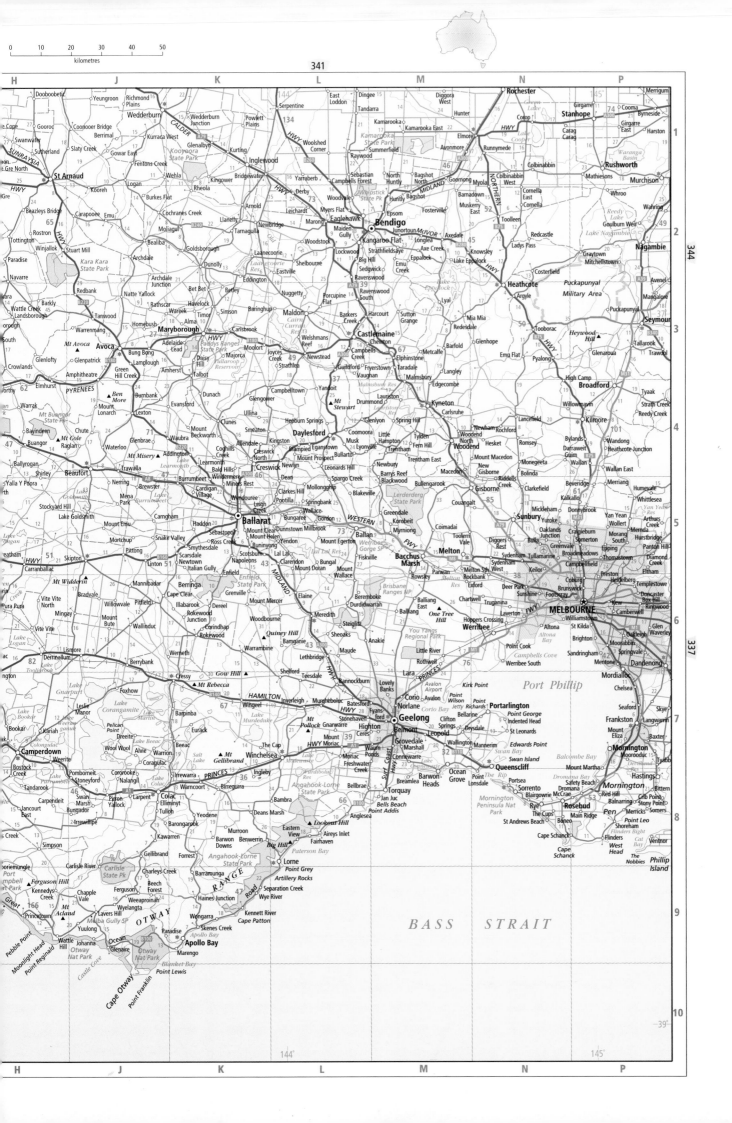

North-West Victoria

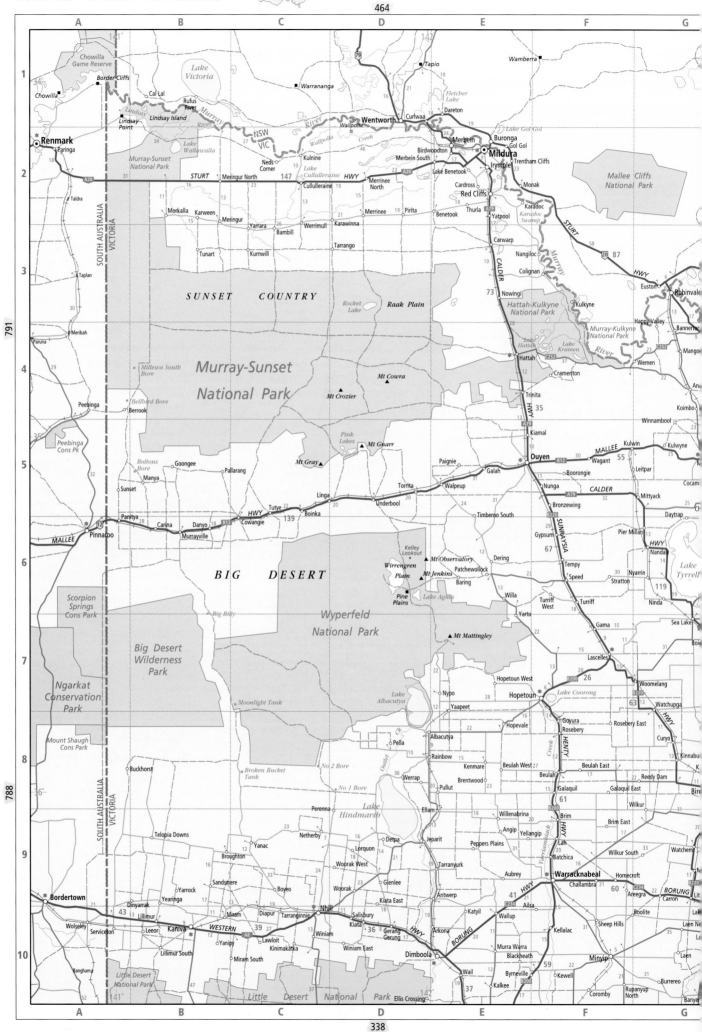

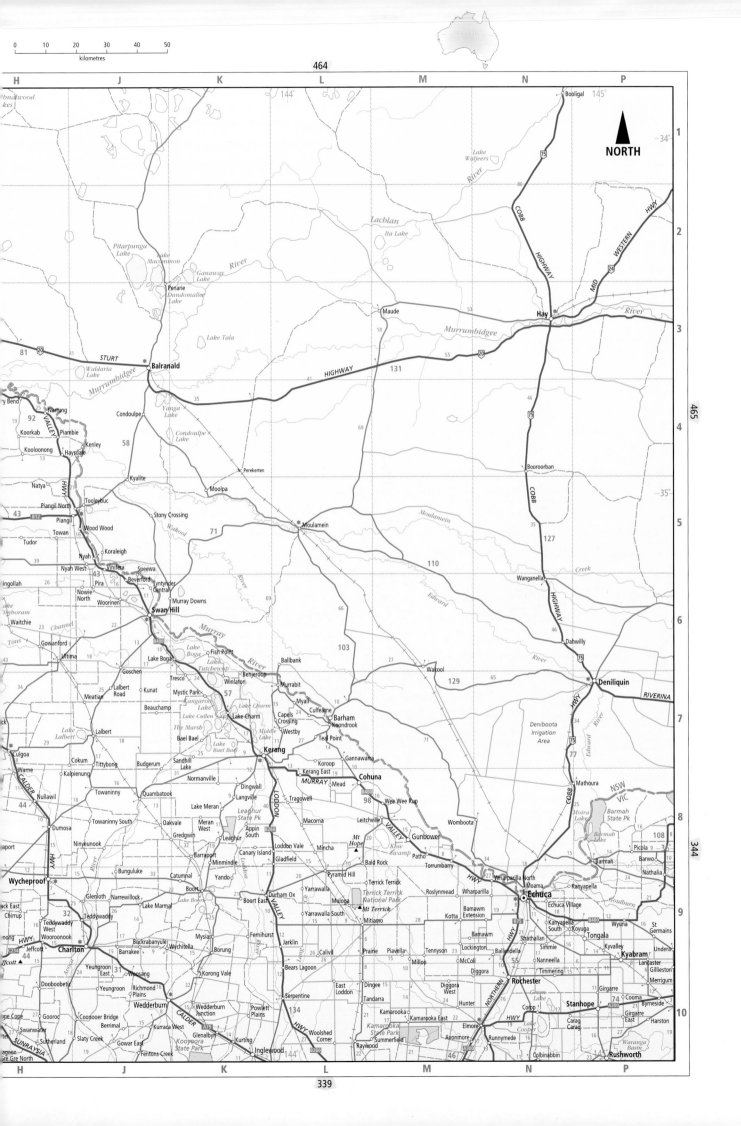

464

339

NORTH

South-East Victoria

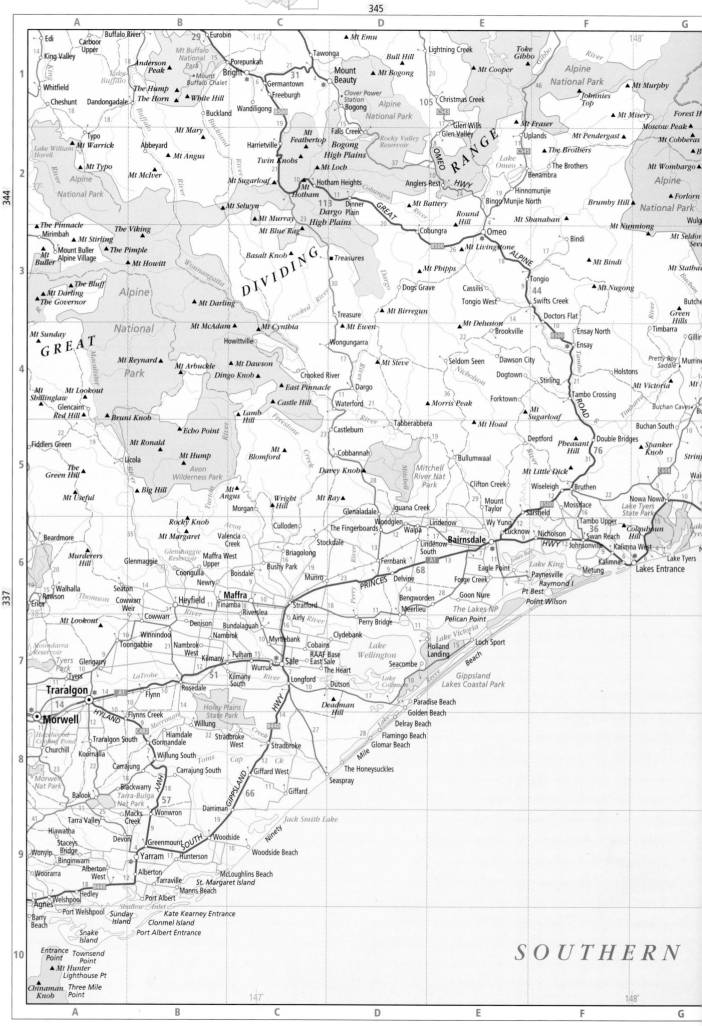

	A	B	C	D	E	F	G

Edi
Carboor Upper
King Valley
Whitfield
Cheshunt
Dandongadale
Typo
Mt Warrick
Abbeyard
Mt Typo
Mt McIver
Mt Angus
The Pinnacle
Mirimbah
Mt Stirling
The Viking
Mount Buller
Alpine Village
Mt Buller
The Pimple
Mt Howitt
The Bluff
Mt Darling
The Governor
Mt Sunday
GREAT
Mt Shillinglaw
Mt Lookout
Glencairn
Red Hill
Bruni Knob
Echo Point
Fiddlers Green
Mt Ronald
Licola
Mt Hump
The Green Hill
Big Hill
Mt Useful

Buffalo River
Eurobin
Mt Buffalo National Park
Porepunkah
Mount Buffalo Chalet
Bright
Germantown
Freeburgh
Wandiligong
Buckland
Mt Mary
Harrietville
Mt Feathertop
Mt Seluyn
Mt Sugarloaf
Mt Hotham
Twin Knobs
Mt Loch
Hotham Heights
Mt Murray
Dargo High Plains
Mt Blue Rag
Basalt Knob
Mt McAdam
Mt Cynthia
Howittville
East Pinnacle
Mt Arbuckle
Dingo Knob
Mt Dawson
Castle Hill
Mt Reynard
Lamb Hill
Mt Blomford
Mt Angus
Morgan
Wright Hill
Culloden

Tawonga
Mount Beauty
Bull Hill
Mt Bogong
Bogong
Falls Creek
Bogong High Plains
Treasures
Treasure
Mt Ewen
Wongungarra
Dargo
Waterford
Crooked River
Mt Steve
Cobbannah
Davey Knob

Lightning Creek
Mt Cooper
Christmas Creek
Glen Wills
Glen Valley
OMEO HWY
Anglers Rest
Mt Battery
Round Hill
Cobungra
Omeo
Mt Livingstone
Tongio West
Treasure
Mt Birregun
Seldom Seen
Dawson City
Dogtown
Stirling
Morris Peak
Mt Hoad
Bullumwaal
Mitchell River Nat Park
Clifton Creek

Toke Gibbo
Alpine National Park
Johnnies Top
Mt Murphy
Mt Misery
Moscow Peak
Forest H
Mt Fraser
Uplands
Mt Pendergast
Mt Cobberas
The Brothers
Benambra
Mt Wombargo
Brumby Hill
Mt Nunniong
Mt Seldon See
Bindi
Tongio
Mt Nugong
Mt Statha
Doctors Flat
Timbarra
Gillir
Ensay North
Ensay
Mt Victoria
Pretty Boy Saddle
Murrin
Holstons
Butche
Green Hills
Mt Sugarloaf
Buchan Caves
Bu
Deptford
Double Bridges
Buchan South
Pheasant Hill
Spanker Knob
Mt Little Dick
String
Wiseleigh
Bruthen
Nowa Nowa
Lake Tyers State Park
Colquhoun Hill
Lake
Tyer

The Honeysuckles
Seaspray
Giffard
Darriman
Wonwron
Greenmount
Woodside
Woodside Beach
Hunterson
Yarram
Alberton West
Alberton
Tarraville
Manns Beach
McLoughlins Beach
St Margaret Island
Port Albert
Jack Smith Lake
Ninety
Mile
Glomar Beach
Flamingo Beach
Delray Beach
Golden Beach
Paradise Beach
Deadman Hill
Gippsland Lakes Coastal Park
Beach
Reeve

Traralgon
Morwell
Churchill
Hazelwood Cooling Pond
Morwell Nat Park
Balook
Tarra-Bulga Nat Park
Macks Creek
Blackwarry
Tarra Valley
Hiawatha
Staceys Bridge
Devon
Binginwarri
Woorarra
Wonyip
Agnes
Barry Beach
Welshpool
Port Welshpool
Sunday Island
Snake Island
Kate Kearney Entrance
Clonmel Island
Port Albert Entrance
Shallow Inlet

Entrance Point
Townsend Point
Mt Hunter
Lighthouse Pt
Chinaman Knob
Three Mile Point

SOUTHERN

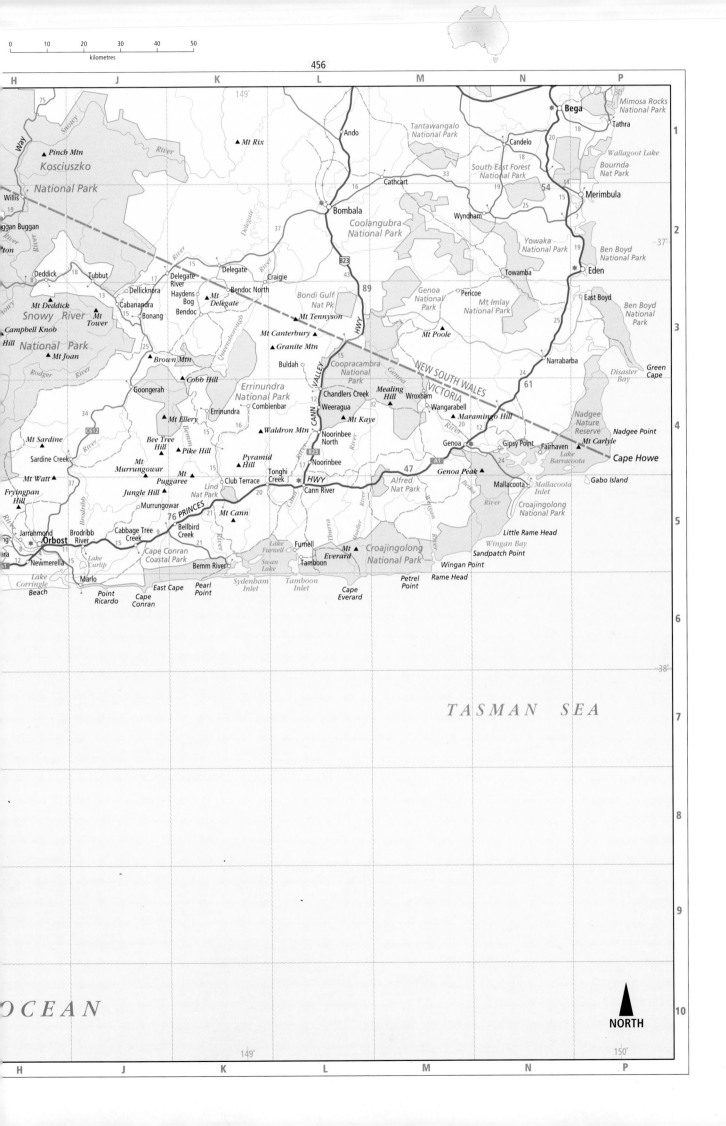

North-East Victoria

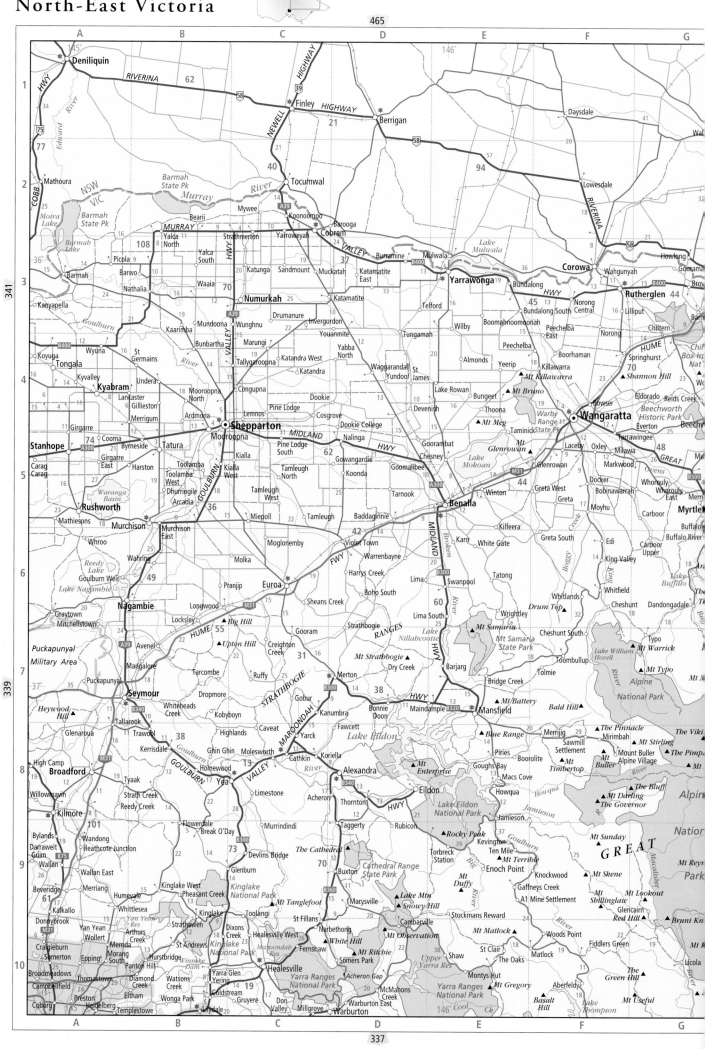

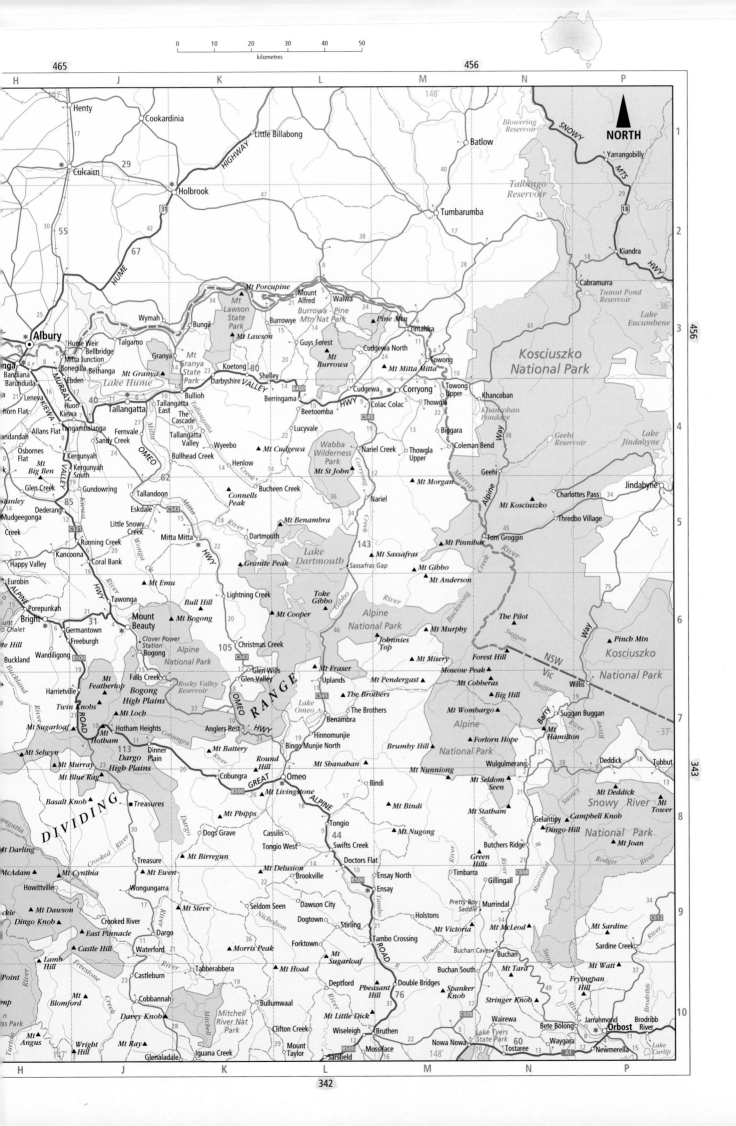

NORTH

0 10 20 30 40 50
kilometres

H J K L M N P

1

Henty
Cookardinia
Little Billabong
Batlow
Blowering Reservoir
SNOWY
Yarrangobilly

29
Culcairn
Holbrook
Tumbarumba
Talbingo Reservoir
MTS
2
Kiandra
HWY

HUME
Cabramurra
Tumut Pond Reservoir
Lake Eucumbene

Mt Porcupine
Mount Alfred
Walwa
Burrowa - Pine Mtn Nat Park
Pine Mtn

3
Wymah
Bungil
Mt Lawson State Park
Burrowye
Tintaldra
Kosciuszko National Park

Albury
Hume Weir
Bellbridge
Talgamo
Mt Lawson
Guys Forest
Cudgewa North
Towong

Granya
Mt Granya State Park
Koetong
Shelley
Cudgewa
Corryong
Towong Upper
Khancoban

Lake Hume
Tallangatta
Darbyshire
Berringama
Colac Colac
Thowgla
Khancoban Pondage

4
Tallangatta East
The Cascade
Lucyvale
Biggara
Geehi Reservoir
Lake Jindabyne

Fernvale
Wyeebo
Mt Cudgewa
Wabba Wilderness Park
Nariel Creek
Thowgla Upper
Coleman Bend
Jindabyne

Bullhead Creek
Henlow
Mt St John
Nariel
Geehi

62
Tallandoon
Bucheen Creek
Charlottes Pass

Connells Peak
Mt Benambra
Dartmouth
Mt Morgan
Mt Kosciuszko
Thredbo Village

5
Mitta Mitta
Lake Dartmouth
143
Mt Sassafras
Sassafras Gap
Mt Gibbo
Tom Groggin

Granite Peak
Mt Pinnibar
Mt Anderson

Mt Emu
Toke Gibbo
Mt Cooper

6
Bright
Mount Beauty
Bull Hill
Mt Bogong
Alpine National Park
Johnnies Top
Mt Murphy
The Pilot
Pinch Mtn
Kosciuszko National Park

Christmas Creek
Mt Misery
Forest Hill
NSW
Vic

7
Falls Creek
Glen Wills
Mt Fraser
Uplands
Moscow Peak
Willis

Mt Feathertop
Glen Valley
The Brothers
Mt Pendergast
Mt Cobberas
Suggan Buggan

Twin Knobs
Bogong High Plains
Lake Omeo
The Brothers
Big Hill
Deddick
Tubbut

Mt Sugarloaf
Mt Loch
Benambra
Mt Wombargo
Barry
Mt Hamilton

Hotham Heights
Anglers Rest
Hinnomunjie
Brumby Hill
Forlorn Hope
Wulgulmerang

8
Mt Hotham
Dinner Plain
Bingo Munjie North
Mt Nunniong
Mt Seldom Seen
Mt Deddick

Mt Selwyn
Dargo High Plains
Round Hill
Mt Shanahan
Mt Statham
Snowy River

Mt Murray
Cobungra
Omeo
Bindi
Mt Tower

Mt Blue Rag
Mt Livingstone
Gelantipy
Campbell Knob
National Park

Basalt Knob
Treasures
Mt Phipps
Mt Bindi
Dingo Hill
Mt Joan

DIVIDING
Dogs Grave
Cassilis
Tongio
Mt Nugong
Butchers Ridge

9
Mt Darling
Treasure
Tongio West
Swifts Creek
Green Hills

Mt Birregun
Mt Delusion
Doctors Flat
Ensay North
Timbarra
Gillingall
Mt Sardine

McAdam
Mt Cynthia
Mt Ewen
Brookville
Ensay
Sardine Creek

Howittville
Wongungarra
Seldom Seen
Dawson City
Mt Victoria
Mt McLeod

Mt Dawson
Mt Steve
Dogtown
Stirling
Mt Tara
Mt Watt

Dingo Knob
Crooked River
Nicholson
Tambo Crossing
Buchan Caves
Buchan
Fryingpan Hill

10
East Pinnacle
Dargo
Forktown
Mt Sugarloaf
Holstons
Buchan South

Castle Hill
Morris Peak
Mt Hoad
Deptford
Pretty Boy Saddle
Murrindal

Lamb Hill
Waterford
Tabberabbera
Double Bridges
Spanker Knob
Stringer Knob

Blomford
Castleburn
Pheasant Hill
Wairewa
Jarrahmond
Brodribb River

Mt Angus
Davey Knob
Cobbannah
Bullumwaal
Mt Little Dick
Nowa Nowa
Bete Bolong
Orbost

Wright Hill
Mt Ray
Mitchell River Nat Park
Clifton Creek
Wiseleigh
Bruthen
Lake Tyers State Park
Tostaree
Waygara
Newmerella

Glenaladale
Iguana Creek
Mount Taylor
Sarsfield
Mossiface
Lake Curlip

H J K L M N P

NEW SOUTH WALES

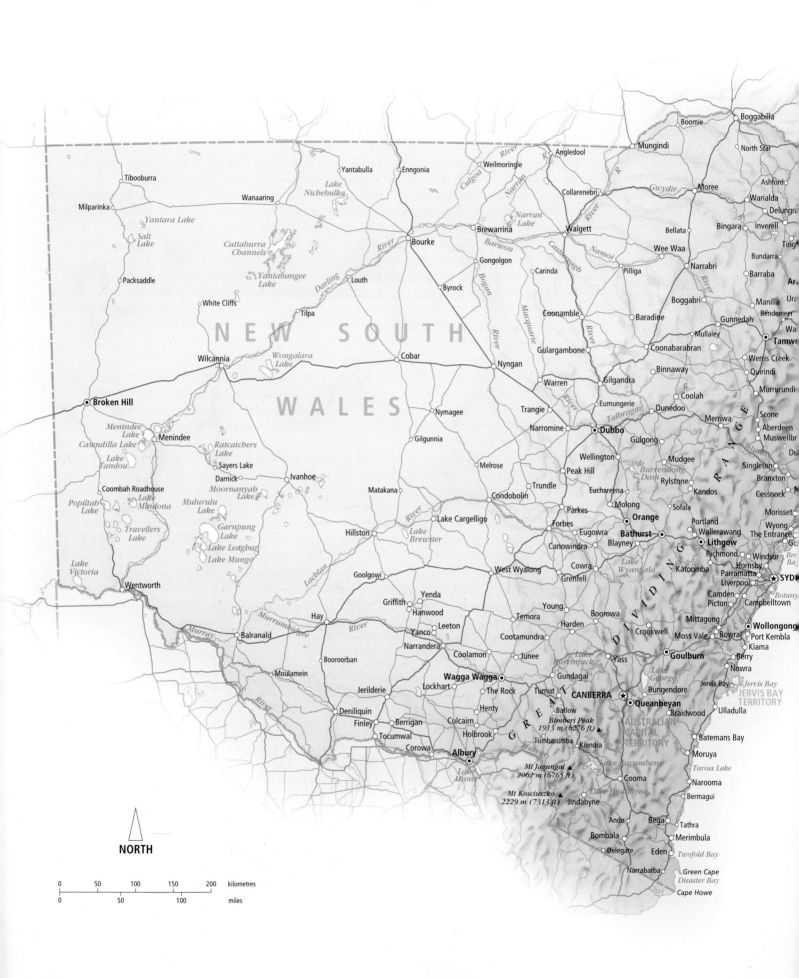

NORTH

| 0 | 50 | 100 | 150 | 200 | kilometres |
| 0 | | 50 | | 100 | miles |

NEW SOUTH WALES

New South Wales encompasses everything from complete sophistication to remote serenity. You can enjoy a café latte in Sydney's cosmopolitan Double Bay one morning and the next day, a billy tea on the banks of the Darling River, leaving civilisation light years behind. Home to Australia's largest city, Sydney, this State offers great diversity, ranging from the snow-covered peaks of the Snowy Mountains to tropical rainforests.

In addition the coast is strung with golden beaches. Then head inland from the coast to the magnificent Great Dividing Range, beyond which are vast wheat plains. Further out is semi-desert, with beacons like the Walls of China, in Mungo National Park, or the placid, tranquil Lake Cawndilla in Kinchega National Park where explorers Burke and Wills had their last taste of 'civilised' living.

New South Wales is over 800,000 sq. km (308,800 square miles) in area, representing more than 10 per cent of the total landmass of Australia. This State has an excellent network of roads throughout that offer easy access to its myriad attractions.

The coastal highway (Highway 1) runs from Timbilica in the south to Tweed Heads in the north (it is the Pacific Highway north from Sydney and the Princes Highway south to Melbourne). From the south are places like Eden, famous as a whale-watching town; with Merimbula, Bega, Narooma and Moruya, they form the 'Sapphire Coast'. Further north is Batemans Bay—gateway to some terrific

hinterland national parks—and Ulladulla, the State's abalone fishing capital. Further on is Nowra, a jumping off point to picturesque Kangaroo Valley or to the sparkling blue waters and dazzling white sands of Jervis Bay. Towards Sydney, the road passes through historic Berry, the city of Wollongong then it cuts through Australia's oldest national park, the Royal, before hitting Sydney's outskirts. Crossing the Sydney Harbour Bridge, the Pacific Highway runs through the city's North Shore until it reaches Wahroonga. From here, the Newcastle Freeway heads north beyond the city of Newcastle.

A bush firefighter from Forbes. In rural areas, volunteers, who are often farmers, provide an essential support service to professional brigades, which have to cover huge areas.

Myall Lakes National Park, near Tea Gardens, has the State's largest string of coastal lakes, fringed by paperbark trees (Melaleuca spp.). It is also an important waterbird habitat.

Jervis Bay on the south coast of New South Wales claims to have the whitest sand in the world. Ideal for swimming, the clear blue waters also offer excellent diving.

Eastern Grey Kangaroos (Macropus giganteus) in Murramurang National Park are often seen on the nearby beaches.

Heading further north you will come to Tenterfield, the town immortalised by Australian singer-songwriter Peter Allen.

To circumnavigate the State, head west, where the Bruxner Highway runs from Lismore to Tenterfield (encompassing some fabulous Great Dividing Range scenery). From Boggabilla the tar gives way to dirt to reach Mungindi and Collarenabri, Walgett and Brewarrina (where you can still see the rocks in the river which the indigenous peoples fashioned into effective fish traps). From Bourke the real adventure of the Outback journey begins—to Wanaaring and through to Milparinka on the Silver City Highway—a distance of some 1330 km (826 miles) from coast to corner. The real Corner Country, however, is to the north of the town of Milparinka in Sturt National Park and Cameron Corner, where a lonely general store sells fuel, drinks and basic foods.

The Silver City Highway runs from Warri Gate on the border, through Tibooburra and Milparinka almost due south through the mining giant of Broken Hill to Wentworth. Initially, the Sturt Highway more or less follows the course of the Murray River, which forms the border between Victoria and New South Wales, but soon peels away to the east to Hay and on through Narrandera to Wagga Wagga. If turning off at Hay, the Cobb Highway takes the traveller south to Deniliquin. From here, you can join the Riverina Highway through the fertile Murrumbidgee Irrigation Area and the towns of Finley, Berrigan and finally Albury. To return to the coast, take the Snowy Mountains and Monaro highways through some spectacular alpine country, which lies thick with snow in winter.

Other highways crisscross the State. The Hume Highway has diversions to Gundagai, where the dog 'sat' on the tuckerbox, and runs through Holbrook. The Gwydir runs from Grafton (famous for its blaze of jacaranda trees) continuing through to the gem-fossickers' paradise of Glen Innes through Warialda, Moree and finally Collarenebri. The Oxley Highway begins on the coast at Wauchope and traverses the Great Divide to reach Walcha. It then runs through to Gunnedah on the Black Soil Plains, Coonabarabran (gateway to the Warrumbungles), Gilgandra and finally arriving in Warren, on the fringes of the Macquarie Marshes, a haven for waterfowl.

Back on the Pacific Highway, the road goes past legendary holiday destinations: Myall Lakes, Bulahdelah Mountain, and on to the North Coast with its recreational meccas like Port Macquarie, Coffs Harbour, Ballina, Byron Bay and, finally, Tweed Heads on the border. The other major route north from Sydney is the New England Highway.

Starting just out of Newcastle, it runs through the wineries and pastoral areas of the Hunter Valley, then the mighty coal-producing districts around Muswellbrook and into the horse stud areas of Scone and Murrurundi. Further north is Tamworth, the country music capital of Australia, which hosts an enormous festival each year, then continue on to Uralla, where bushranger Captain Thunderbolt is buried, then Armidale.

The old goldmining city of Bathurst spawns two major road arteries. The first is the Mitchell Highway, which runs north-west through Orange, Wellington (with its limestone caves), Dubbo (with its massive zoo), the citrus-growing centre of Narromine, Trangie, flood-beleaguered Nyngan, Bourke, Enngonia and finally Barringun, on the Queensland border—just a pub (but what a pub!). The second is the Mid-Western Highway, which spurs south-west through Blayney, historic Carcoar, Cowra, the goldmining town of Grenfell, West Wyalong and across the plain to Hay. Bathurst is also the terminus for the Great Western Highway, which crosses the Blue Mountains.

One of the longest highways is the Newell. It runs from Tocumwal in the south, through historic Jerilderie, Narrandera, West Wyalong, the bushranging district of Forbes, Parkes (with its huge astronomical telescope), Peak Hill, the hub of the West—Dubbo, Gilgandra, Coonabarabran, Narrabri, Moree and, finally to Boggabilla, on the Queensland border.

The Castlereagh links the dry opal fields of New Angledool with Walgett and towns further south like Coonamble, Gulargambone, Gilgandra and Dubbo. The remote Barrier Highway stretches from Nyngan through the copper city of Cobar then Wilcannia to beyond Broken Hill. The Lachlan links the isolated

The old Taralga hotel on the main street, built in 1858.

outposts of Booligal, Hillston and Lake Cargellico with a road that is mainly dirt.

New South Wales has a never-ending diversity of natural and man-made wonders to enjoy. Its World Heritage-listed areas and national parks can be explored on foot, horseback or by 4WD. The beaches and waterways beckon anglers, swimmers, and all watersports enthusiasts alike, while the towns and cities offer both history and a vitality and enthusiasm for the present. New South Wales has it all.

Capital
Sydney
Area
800,640 sq. km
(309,151 sq. miles)
Proportion of Australia
10.4%
Population of State
6,341,600
Population Density
7.9 per sq. km
(20.5 per sq. mile)
Population of Capital
3,986,700
Time Zone
10 hours ahead of GMT
Climate
Warm-temperate with no dry season
Highest Point
Mt Kosciuszko 2229 m
(7313 feet)

Tamworth from Oxley lookout. The city hosts a huge annual country and western festival.

SYDNEY

Sydney is the birthplace of modern Australia. When the First Fleet arrived on 26 January 1788, Governor Phillip faced the task of taking a wilderness and transforming it into a humble imitation of normal eighteenth-century Georgian Britain. Early settlement grew around the Tank Stream, which bubbled from the ground in what is now Hyde Park. Buildings clung to the foreshores of Sydney Cove at that time, but they went no further than the present site of Bridge Street. But by 1794 there were 700 wooden dwellings, plus the brick Government buildings.

Today the Sydney metropolitan area covers around 5000 square km (1930 square miles). Sydney is big, sprawling, brash at times and sensitive at others. Sydney is complex, where the breathtaking beauty of the Opera House and the harbour on a warm summer's day lives side by side with the industrial bleakness of Silverwater. Yet it is Sydney's very diversity that makes it one of the world's great cities.

The most polyglot of all the Australian cities, Sydney is admirably racially tolerant. Though many immigrants band together in suburban enclaves—Vietnamese in Cabramatta, Chinese in Strathfield, and Japanese on the North Shore—Sydneysiders appreciate that their commonality of interests, language and customs initially needs the reinforcement of proximity. The Asian migration has broadened Sydney culturally and, of course, from a culinary perspective, just as the Italians and Greeks did 40 years ago. Someone driving through Campsie, for example, could think they had been teleported to South-East Asia, with shopfronts bearing unfamiliar characters to advertise their trade. Where Greeks and

Italians introduced now-everyday items like garlic and chilli, the Asians have brought with them ingredients such as daikon (Japanese radish), lemongrass and bok choi so now chefs and suburban cooks alike can buy them fresh. As a natural corollary, Sydneysiders have a profusion of choices when eating out: every cuisine in the world is represented from Argentinian to Zulu.

The wonderful climate, more hot than cold, ensures Sydneysiders love outdoor recreation. Weekend barbecues entertaining friends or summers at the beaches that stretch from Palm Beach in the north to Cronulla in the south, are the norm. Sailing—anything from boards to barquentines—in the Harbour, Pittwater or Port Hacking, as well as fishing and golf, are all popular pastimes on Sydney's waterways.

The Central Business District (CBD) is geographically and figuratively Sydney's core. Part of Sydney's appeal is its energy, and much of that has to do with business drive. This city is one of the most important commercial and financial centres of the Pacific Rim. Yet while its more modern skyscrapers are jaggedly angular, preservation orders ensured that the architectural charm and comparative softness of the nineteenth century have remained a part of the cityscape.

Old-style postbox in The Rocks.

Dwarfed by glass, steel and concrete is the Victorian extravagance of the Town Hall and Queen Victoria Building, the neo-Gothic of St Andrew's and St Mary's cathedrals and the colonial genius of Francis Greenway's Macquarie Street buildings. They survive as a restful contrast to the new, encapsulating the ethos of the city itself. Only in The Rocks—that time capsule of Sydney's past, fronting Circular Quay and winding around to Campbell's Cove—is there any sense of architectural homogeneity. Warehouses have become restaurants, brothels are now art galleries, but it is still what Sydney looked like when it was much younger and more cocksure. But instead of larrikins, touts and shady characters, The Rocks is full of tourists, souvenir shops, good pubs and live music. (Other suburbs have retained the grace of the bygone: Glebe, Balmain and Paddington are perhaps the best examples.)

Exploring Sydney from the CBD is like peeling the layers of an onion—from the inside. To the east are the traditional lairs of Sydney's 'elite': Rose Bay, Darling Point, Double Bay; also Bondi—a stronghold of New Zealanders—and Randwick, with its famous racecourse. Closer in is Oxford Street, the mecca of the gay community and scene of the biggest homosexual ritual in the world—the Gay and Lesbian Mardi Gras. It is also famous for its cafés and cheap, imaginative eateries. To the south is Kingsford Smith Airport, and the local suburbs of Mascot and Rockdale. The busiest aerodrome in Australia, it sits on Botany Bay.

Sydney's CBD hugs the harbour, and is flanked by the Royal Botanic Gardens. The city's most famous icons, the Opera House and Harbour Bridge, are visible.

Further on is the Royal National Park, the first to be proclaimed in Australia and the second in the world, which, despite its proximity to the city, still retains rugged areas of natural bushland, natural swimming holes and delightful coastal bushwalks.

Across 'the Coathanger', as the Harbour Bridge is affectionately known, is North Sydney, a secondary business district filled with advertising agencies, funky eateries and smart young things. Directly under the bridge is Luna Park, a famous amusement park, clinging to the harbour foreshores. The outer north and the peninsula hold Sydney's alternative 'prestige' suburbs: Palm Beach, Whale Beach, Turramurra, Pymble and Wahroonga are all sought-after areas. Many are now moving even further out to 'acreages'; large blocks of land on the periphery of the north-western metropolitan area—in suburbs like Dural, Annangrove and Glenorie. But the west is presently the most dynamic player in Sydney's development. As Sydney galloped across the Cumberland Plain, engulfing previously separate entities such as Parramatta, Campbelltown and Liverpool, the outskirts have become integrated. Sydney best epitomises the realisation of the great Australian dream of 'owning your own quarter-acre': home ownership is regarded almost as a birthright. The west also contains some of Sydney's most popular drawcards, such as Australia's Wonderland, great for children, and Eastern Creek Raceway, which hosts international motorsport events.

Sydney has many landmarks, both geographical and cultural: White City is the aspiration of every young tennis player; Taronga Park Zoo flanks the harbour; the Mitchell Library (the best reference source in the country) and Bradley's Head, with gun emplacements that never fired a shot in anger. Then there's Bondi Beach, which every overseas visitor *has* to see, Kings Cross, seedy by day, steamy by night, and Homebush Bay, home of the spectacular Sydney 2000 Olympics. Though it perhaps lacks the international sporting sanctity of Lords in the United Kingdom, the Sydney Cricket Ground is hallowed ground for followers of both the willow and the pigskin, for not only have some of the greatest cricket test matches been played there, but all Rugby League Grand Finals. It is also impossible to omit from a list of Sydney's landmarks the Entertainment Centre, where performers ranging from the world's best rock bands to Julio Iglesias and Australia's own Dame Joan have thrilled audiences for some years now.

All in the one day, there is much on offer: Sydney has karaoke in a Camden club and Rimsky-Korsakov in the Opera House, ice-skating in Ryde and eisteddfods in the Town Hall; there are rages in Rydalmere or romantic dinners in Darlinghurst, at the same time a street party is happening in Padstow while Heidelberg School paintings are viewed in posh Paddington galleries. In this great city, you can get, see or do just about anything your heart desires.

The wake of a ferry winds round the majestic sails of the famous Sydney Opera House. The ferry terminal at Circular Quay is a good starting point for city sights.

Children enjoying face painting at a street festival in the city of Parramatta, which merges with Sydney's western suburbs. Sydney hosts many festivals each year.

Looking westward along Sydney Harbour, the harbour waters peter out into the Parramatta River. The Gladesville Bridge is in the foreground.

Like many other large cities, not all of the city's workforce lives locally. Thanks to improved road networks like the northern expressway, many people commute from as far away as the Central Coast and the Blue Mountains. Ferries are used by Sydneysiders as public transport. A ride across one of the finest natural harbours in the world will take you to Manly, filled with beachside footpath cafés and restaurants. Though not as famous as Bondi Beach, Manly generally has better surfing, and nearby Fairy Bower is very popular with boardriders. On the way across on the ferry you will see Fort Denison, a martello (small, round) tower that was built after an unannounced visit by a fleet of American warships in 1839 prompted concerns that the harbour should have some defences. However, the fort was not completed until 1857, after the Crimean War gave rise to a 'Russian scare'. Before the fort was built, the small island known to the Aborigines as 'Mat-te-wa-ye', a 'favourite rest place', was termed Pinchgut because really troublesome convicts in the First Fleet were put there with very little food. Australia's brutal colonial past is told in the story of convict Francis Morgan, who was condemned to hang there in chains. Three years later, the skeleton still remained on view and the Aboriginals completely avoided the place.

Something else you will see on the ferry ride is the Royal Botanic Gardens, 24 ha (60 acres) of parkland right in the middle of the city, on the foreshores of what used to be called Farm Cove. The Gardens contain a stone wall that marks the site of Australia's first vegetable garden, which was planted at the instigation of Governor Phillip. The Gardens boast huge, old Moreton Bay figs and its national herbarium displays plant specimens collected by botanist Joseph Banks on his voyage of discovery with Captain James Cook in 1770.

Alternatively, you could take a leisurely walk in Hyde Park in the centre of Sydney. One of its most outstanding features is the Archibald Fountain, which has three tableaux, one of which depicts Theseus

Bondi Beach may be Sydney's most famous beach but it is actually one of many beaches strung along the coastline and around the harbour.

slaying the Minotaur. Just across College Street is the Australian Museum, a vast, rambling natural history museum with some excellent hands-on exhibits, and north of Hyde Park is the Art Gallery of New South Wales, an imposing neo-Classical building.

Sydney has some excellent restaurants, and they represent all types of cuisine, many of which have set new standards in food presentation. From intimate eateries to world-class hotel restaurants; from the café to the innovative, trendsetting restaurant; from the informal to the formal, Sydney has it all in the line of eating establishments. Even on weekdays, Darling Harbour and Cockle Bay, to the west of the CBD, throng with crowds eager to shop, eat or simply walk around sightseeing. The aquarium here is one of the greatest in the world while over the other side of the National Trust-classified Pyrmont Bridge is the Powerhouse Museum, exhibiting planes, boats, cars and steam engines and is well worth a look. The Darling Harbour complex itself houses a number of exhibition halls. Abutting Darling Harbour is Chinatown, where visitors can choose from a bewildering array of restaurants or buy specialist ingredients for cooking or herbal medicines. There is also the opportunity to stroll through the Chinese Gardens, incorporating the Garden of Friendship, a gift to Sydney from the people of Quandong Province in China. If sushi is more enticing, just a little further west at Pyrmont are the Sydney Fish Markets, where you can not only buy superb fresh seafood but dine at one of the many seafood restaurants. Many people go there at weekends, order a bottle of wine and sit outside savouring lunch and the harbour views.

Heading west is the Blue Mountains, which, like Bowral and Moss Vale in the Southern Highlands, used to be the summer escape of Sydney's rich. These mountains have a wealth of scenic bushwalking trails, restaurants and gracious old guesthouses. The Paragon Café in Katoomba for example, has been famous for its chocolates since the 1930s, and a little further up from Katoomba at Medlow Bath is the old Hydro Majestic Hotel, which used to be notorious for illicit weekends away. The Blue Mountains' most famous landmark is the Three Sisters, an eroded, sandstone rock formation right at the edge of Katoomba.

Sydney hosts a number of events and festivals. In January, Sydney Festival highlights include Symphony Under the Stars and Opera in the Park. Both events are held in the Domain for free and attract thousands of summer picnickers; at the same time there is the Sydney Fringe Festival based at Bondi. The Gay and Lesbian Mardi Gras is a highlight each March and is televised globally. At Easter it is time for the Royal Easter Show, held at Homebush Bay, and the National Trust Heritage Week. June sees in the Sydney Film Festival and the Darling Harbour Jazz Festival, and July, the International Music Festival. August is the time for the annual City to Surf, a run from the centre of the city to Bondi, raising money for charity. Manly holds its jazz festival in October; in November it is time for the Australian Craft Show. December includes Carols in the Domain, the Sydney to Hobart Yacht Race and of course the New Year's Eve celebrations, which include a spectacular fireworks display that is televised all around the world.

Harry's Cafe de Wheels is a famous pie stall in the inner city suburb of Woolloomooloo. Here you can get a hot pie and mushy peas after partying until 3 a.m.

ADVENTURE ACTIVITIES

New South Wales

RIGHT: Sea kayaking trips in coastal areas may permit participants to observe marine life at close quarters. At Byron Bay in northern New South Wales, for example, kayakers often encounter pods of bottlenose dolphins.

The inhabitants of New South Wales are never far from adventure, for the main focus of outdoor sports here is the Great Dividing Range, which runs parallel and close to the densely populated eastern seaboard for the entire length of the state. Many parts of the Great Dividing Range are rugged enough to have escaped the clearing that occurred as European settlers spread westward from the coast, and today patches of magnificent virgin forest still cloak peaks and escarpments and fill valleys. Although eucalypt forests predominate, alpine heaths cover high peaks in the south, and scattered pockets of subtropical rainforest become more common as you travel northward.

The Great Dividing Range offers almost unlimited challenges for adventurers, including cliffs for rock climbers, vast tracks of bushland for walkers, and scenic fire trails and rugged back roads for mountain bikers. The highest peaks and plateaus of the Snowy Mountains are a winter playground for ski-tourers. The rivers that have carved their way through the ranges offer opportunities for canoeing, kayaking and rafting, while the narrowest gorges provide a venue for the exciting sport of canyoning.

Further west, New South Wales offers entirely different landscapes including semiarid plains and the red-sand deserts and dramatic rockscapes that characterise classic outback country.

Bushwalking

Sydney is an excellent base for bushwalkers, with the state's best-known walking track located on its southern doorstep—the 27-km (16.5-mile) Coast Track in the Royal National Park, which runs from Bundeena to Otford. Beautiful beaches, diverse vegetation and easy access by public transport (train and ferry from the city) contribute to the popularity of this walk, which is one of many in the park.

West of Sydney, the Upper Blue Mountains have the country's most extensive network of bushwalking trails, many of them of historical interest. Bonuses include magnificent cliff-top views, varied wildlife and lush, rainforest-filled gullies. More experienced walkers who prefer navigating through trackless bush should head for wilder areas such as Wollemi National Park to the north and Kanangra Boyd National Park to the south.

Morton National Park, inland from Ulladulla, is also favoured by expert bushwalkers. Indeed, some parts of this park, such as the Castle and Monolith Valley, are so popular that tracks have been formed by usage alone, prompting the park authorities to intervene to prevent erosion. Less experienced walkers will opt for marked tracks such as the one that leads to the top of Pigeon House Mountain, where ladders have been built to provide access to the summit.

Granite tors, alpine lakes, wildflowers, and panoramic views make the Snowy Mountains another favourite area for walkers of all levels of experience. By taking a chairlift from Thredbo then following marked trails, in summer almost anyone can walk to the top of Mount Kosciuszko, Australia's highest peak.

Situated west of the Great Dividing Range, Warrumbungle National Park in central New South Wales features dramatic volcanic peaks and spires, and superb lookouts linked by an extensive network of bushwalking tracks. Further west, you can sample the arid terrain typical of so much of Central Australia at Mutawintji National Park north-east of Broken Hill, where excellent walking tracks follow sandy river beds and skirt rocky ridgetops dotted with caves rich in ancient Aboriginal art.

Rock Climbing

The main focus for rock climbing in New South Wales is the Blue Mountains, where hundreds of kilometres of escarpments offer almost unlimited potential. Overuse led to the closure of the famous Three Sisters formation, but dozens of other cliffs, particularly those around Mount Victoria and Blackheath, provide some of the toughest ascents in the country. Perhaps the most challenging climbs in New South Wales, however, are those on the 300-m (1000-foot) limestone cliffs of Bungonia Gorge near Goulburn, south-west of Sydney. Ascents equally long

In summer, the Nymboida River, which flows north from the Dorrigo Range for about 80 km (50 miles) to the Mitchell River, is one of the state's top whitewater routes, with several grade-four rapids.

and arduous, if not as difficult from a technical point of view, can also be made on the volcanic plugs in Warrumbungle National Park and in Mount Kaputar National Park near Narrabri.

Areas suitable for winter climbing include the cliffs at Thomsons Point near Nowra, and Point Perpendicular, which rises, as the name suggests, sheer from the waters of Jervis Bay. The sea cliffs of Sydney are also popular, although their rock is friable.

A less strenuous form of climbing can be enjoyed on the vast granite slabs of Booroomba Rocks, 20 km (12.5 miles) south of Canberra in the Australian Capital Territory. Although they lie back from the vertical, the slabs offer a challenge because the holds are so tiny. Other granite climbing areas can be found in the New England area in the state's north.

Canyoning

As they make their way down narrow, water-filled crevices, canyoners need to combine the skills of swimming and bushwalking with those of rock climbing and abseiling. With more than 300 deep, narrow clefts in its high sandstone plateau, some of which are up to 100 m (330 feet) deep but only a few metres (10 feet) wide, the Blue Mountains offer the best canyoning in the country. Several Katoomba companies offer guided trips and tuition.

Caving

Jenolan Caves, on the fringe of Kanangra Boyd National Park, form the most famous cave system in the state. Visitor facilities such as lighting, paths and bridges have been incorporated in many of its tunnels and chambers, but there are also numerous adventure caves. However, these, like others in the state, can only be entered with a permit. Serious cavers as well as curious tourists also flock to Wombeyan Caves near Mittagong. Other adventure-caving destinations include Bungonia near Goulburn, Wee Jasper near Yass, and Yarrangobilly in the Snowy Mountains.

Mountain Biking

Among the best mountain-biking areas in the state are the Blue Mountains, where the ride from Woodford to Glenbrook is particularly renowned; the state forests of the South Coast; the New England tablelands in the north; and, in summer, the Snowy Mountains.

Canoeing, Kayaking and Rafting

Coffs Harbour is probably the state's top coastal destination for serious paddlers, being within striking distance of several rivers, including the Nymboida and west-flowing Gwydir—both spectacular wilderness trips with challenging rapids. In southern New South Wales, sections of the Murrumbidgee River and the headwaters of the Murray also offer good paddling, while the Murray–Darling system provides more relaxed, less technical outings.

Sea Kayaking

Popular locations for sea kayaking include the lower reaches of the Hawkesbury River on the northern fringe of Sydney; Yuraygir National Park, north of Coffs Harbour; Jervis Bay on the South Coast; and Port Stephens and Myall Lakes, both situated a short distance north of Newcastle.

Winter Sports

Cross-country skiing in the Snowy Mountains can take you deep into wilderness and far from the long lift queues and noisy après-ski scene. The most famous route is the five-day trip from Kiandra to Kosciuszko, though extended traverses of the Main Range are also popular. Cross-country skiers in Canberra are not only ideally situated for access to the Snowies, but can also take advantage of a magnificent tour located on their doorstep—the journey along the crest of the Brindabella Range.

Mountaineers huddle in an ice cave on Mount Kosciuszko. This is one of the few places in Australia where climbers can hone their snow- and ice-climbing techniques and experience the kinds of conditions they are likely to encounter on much higher peaks overseas.

SOUTH-EAST NEW SOUTH WALES

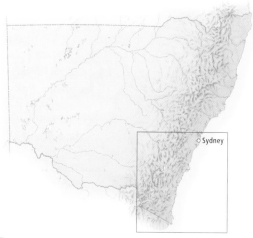

The long, scenic coast of the south-east is surprisingly uncrowded, and never far from wooded foothills and rugged escarpments. The Southern Tablelands, just south-west of Sydney, are known for their historic villages and autumn colour. Inland and to the south, the Great Dividing Range climbs to a vast and wild alpine plateau, most of which is preserved in the mighty Kosciuszko National Park.

Rising gently above the alpine plateau is the blunt peak of Mount Kosciuszko, which is the highest point on the continent. The surrounding national park is the largest in New South Wales and home to the State's acclaimed snowfields and ski resorts. Eucalypt forest covers most of the high country, ranging from towering mountain ash in the lower altitudes to pastel-barked, cold-tolerant snow gums that grow right to the treeline. Above this are herbfields, in summer bright with wildflowers. Walking, horseriding and trout fishing are enjoyed in the warmer months.

The Snowy Mountains Hydro-Electric Scheme dams and diverts the waters of the east-flowing Snowy River west under the mountains. The difference in altitude as the waters fall west is harnessed to generate electricity; the waters feed into the Murray and Tumut rivers, to be used downstream for irrigation. In the 1950s and 1960s construction workers from more than 30 countries, in the main, migrants from postwar Europe, turned the quiet highland town of Cooma into a busy, multicultural centre. The main storage dams—manmade lakes Eucumbene and Jindabyne—are stocked with fish and used for boating and swimming.

The populous Illawarra coastal strip is dominated by Wollongong and Port Kembla, where rich coal seams have fuelled industry for more than a century. First settlers on the forested coast were timber-getters. Prime dairy herds moved onto cleared lands in lush valleys and the south coast centres of Bodalla and Bega are known for their fine cheddars. Further south, Eden is a whale-watching centre. Inland, sandstone cliffs and wilderness are preserved in a string of national parks and reserves. Apples thrive in Batlow's cool climate on the western slopes. Further west, prized merino flocks graze on tawny pastures not far from the nation's capital, Canberra.

OPPOSITE: Sulphur-crested cocktaoos (Cacatua galerita) squawk noisily in a eucalyptus forest in Morton National Park. They are very common in the State's south-east.

The view from Coalcliff, near Wollongong. The coast between Sydney and Wollongong is a string of golden beaches and rolling green hills.

REGIONAL FEATURE

Kosciuszko National Park

In terms of its extent, attractions, activities and grandeur, Kosciuszko National Park is the foremost national park in New South Wales. At 690,000 ha (1,705,000 acres), it is the largest park in the state, extending from the Victorian border all the way to the Brindabella Range west of Canberra, and it encompasses the highest peaks in the land, including Australia's tallest mountain, Mount Kosciuszko, which rises to a height of 2228 m (7310 feet). In winter, the park offers sensational downhill skiing on world-class pistes; in summer, it becomes an idyllic playground for thousands of visitors who flock here to enjoy an almost inexhaustible range of recreational activities.

Mountain grevillea (Grevillea alpina)

Many people travel to Kosciuszko simply to savour the crisp mountain air and expansive views. Some come to investigate the region's rich history, which is evidenced by the many historic huts and homesteads left by pioneering settlers. Others hike along the hundreds of kilometres of walking tracks that lead across peaks and flower-filled meadows, traversing the enormous wilderness areas that account for almost half of the park. Yet others opt to boat, canoe or fish on the numerous lakes and streams, some of which were created during the construction of the Snowy Mountains Hydro-Electric Scheme, Australia's largest power-generating project.

History

Until recently, the Snowy Mountains' harsh winter climate made permanent human occupation impossible. However, it is known that Aboriginal peoples visited the range on a regular basis for thousands of years. Most notably, they travelled here in summer to hunt bogong moths, which migrate annually to the mountains en masse from the plains of north-eastern New South Wales and southern Queensland. Large numbers of Aboriginal peoples from different areas would gather to feast on the moths and celebrate the occasion with elaborate ceremonies.

The first Europeans to venture into the mountains, in the early 1800s, were graziers searching for better grasslands to feed their stock. These pioneers may well have scouted much of the area before the first official exploratory party arrived. It was sponsored by grazier James Macarthur and led by Count Paul Edmund de Strzelecki, a Polish explorer. Strzelecki reached Australia's highest mountain in March 1840 and named it after Polish patriot Tadeusz Kosciuszko. However, he calculated wrongly that nearby Mount Townsend, which he had visited a few days earlier, was the taller peak. There is also a good deal of conjecture as to whether Strzelecki actually climbed either mountain.

In 1859, a minor gold rush at Kiandra brought nearly 10,000 prospectors to the area—among them several Norwegians who are said to have been the first to practise skiing in these mountains—but within a year a lack of gold and the harsh climate had seen off most of these settlers. However, another bounty, in the form of giant stands of timber in the lower valleys of the mountains, soon attracted large numbers of loggers in the late 1800s and early 1900s.

During the first half of the twentieth century, the environmental significance of the Snowy Mountains became more widely recognised and eventually plans were drawn up to protect parts of the range from the continuing degradation caused by summer grazing of sheep and cattle on upper slopes. This resulted in the creation of the Kosciusko State Park in 1944 (the name continued to be misspelt 'Kosciusko' until 1997).

From the late 1940s onward, the region was transformed physically and economically by the massive Snowy Mountains Hydro-Electric Scheme. Employing up to 7000 people, this was an engineering feat of epic proportions. Five rivers were diverted from an easterly to a westerly flow, 145 km (90 miles) of tunnels were bored through solid rock, 17 dams were constructed, 7 power stations established and more than 1600 km (1000 miles) of roads blazed through some of the most rugged terrain in the land. Providing power generation on an enormous scale as well as irrigation for the arid Western Plains, the system altered the entire infrastructure and economy of southern New South Wales and north-eastern Victoria. Some environmentalists have argued, however, that the

OPPOSITE: Melting snow and abundant rain combine to form alpine pools on upland plains.

Created as part of the Snowy Mountains Hydro-Electric Scheme, Lake Eucumbene holds nine times the water of Sydney Harbour.

With the largest vertical drop of any resort in Australia—672 m (2002 feet)—Thredbo caters to skiers of all levels of experience.

damming of the rivers had a catastrophic effect on the ecology of the region's waterways, increasing pest infiltration and siltation and reducing biodiversity. Their concerns were acknowledged recently by an agreement between the New South Wales and Victoria state governments to slowly raise the flow of the Snowy River from 1 per cent of its original level to 28 per cent.

Despite opposition from graziers, a large section of Mount Kosciuszko became a protected area in 1963, which in turn paved the way for the creation of the national park in 1967. Since then, the area under protection has been gradually expanded to its present level so that numerous towns and several ski resorts are now surrounded by tracts of fully protected wilderness.

Activities

The high-altitude plant community is known as the feldmark. Some parts are covered with snow for much of the year; others are exposed to freezing winds.

In winter, when the whole of the range may be covered in snow for up to four months, one pastime becomes the focus of all of the region's activities: skiing. The major ski resorts are located on the eastern flank of Mount Kosciuszko and include Thredbo, Perisher Valley, Blue Cow and Smiggin Holes. These centres offer some of the country's best winter-sports facilities, with many of their pistes now linked to create a vast network of downhill routes and several new runs set aside for the increasingly popular sport of snowboarding. Cross-country skiers can roam even more widely, following numerous trails around Perisher Valley and also in the north of the park around Cabramurra and Mount Selwyn. However, cross-country enthusiasts in particular should be wary of sudden weather changes and always advise someone of their planned route and expected time of return.

The park lends itself to a much greater variety of activities during the rest of the year, when, although the nights can still be chilly, the days are usually clear and sunny. Hiking is the best way to explore the range and appreciate its astonishing scenery, and an extensive network of tracks caters to walkers of all abilities. Routes range from easy one-hour strolls to more challenging day walks and multiday hikes that will test the mettle of even the most experienced bushwalkers. The top of Mount Kosciuszko can be reached via the Summit Walk, which begins at Charlotte Pass, but also connects with other tracks including the Main Range Track and the Kosciuszko Walk, which departs from the top of Thredbo's Crackenback Chairlift.

Detailed bushwalking maps are available from the National Parks and Wildlife Service (NPWS) office in Jindabyne. If you are contemplating an extended, overnight hike, you must be totally self-sufficient and prepared for cold, snowy weather—even in summer. You will also need to carry your own stove and fuel as the lighting of fires in upland areas is severely restricted.

At lower altitudes, there are excellent opportunities for boating, canoeing, swimming and fishing, particularly on tranquil lakes such as Eucumbene, Jindabyne and Tantangara. Trout fishing is another major attraction as the rivers and dams are regularly stocked with brown and rainbow trout from nearby hatcheries (a fishing permit is essential and available from park rangers). Lake Jindabyne is also home to a sizeable population of land-locked salmon, as well as a sprinkling of attractively marked brook trout (actually a char rather than a true trout), and the promise of a 'Jindabyne grand slam'—catching a rainbow trout, a brown trout and a salmon in a

Despite extreme conditions, more than 200 plant species are native to Kosciuszko National Park.

single day—lures many an avid angler. The region's top fishing rivers include the Eucumbene, Thredbo (Crackenback), Snowy, Gungarlin and upper Murrumbidgee, and their respective tributaries.

Among a host of adventure sports on offer locally, whitewater rafting on the Snowy River and trail riding in the high country are particularly popular. Those intrigued by the history of the Hydro-Electric Scheme can join conducted tours to the power stations and dams. Visitors can even head underground, into the networks of caves at Yarrangobilly and Cooleman. Guided and self-guided tours of these systems take in some of the most majestic chambers, tunnels and rock formations in Australia. At Yarrangobilly, there is also a natural hot spa which can be enjoyed year round.

Access

Flights are available from Sydney to Cooma, and from there it's just an hour's drive to the park. However, most visitors travel to the region by car or coach, with the journey from Sydney taking around six hours and the trip from Canberra just two hours.

The main gateway to Kosciuszko is the town of Jindabyne, near the park's eastern boundary, but there are several other access routes. Visitors arriving from western New South Wales can follow the Snowy Mountains Highway through Tumut before entering the park and climbing past Lake Blowering to Kiandra. From there, you can either descend to Adaminaby and head for the ski resorts of Perisher Valley and Thredbo via Jindabyne, or follow the Alpine Way to Cabramurra and Khancoban. Nestled at the foot of towering mountains, Khancoban is the third major

park entry point and the most convenient one for visitors from Albury or Melbourne. From Khancoban, you can follow the Alpine Way past Geehi and Tom Groggin to Thredbo and exit the park near Jindabyne.

In winter, some roads may be closed as a result of snowfalls. During this period, all vehicles must carry snow chains and attach them when advised to do so.

Camping

Kosciuszko offers a wide range of camp sites, but in all areas and at all times of year visitors must be self-sufficient and prepared for adverse weather conditions. The largest camping ground, which caters for tents and caravans, is at Sawpit Creek, on the Thredbo road. It has toilets, hot showers, fireplaces and even cabins for rent (bookings must be made in advance through the NPWS). Other good sites for the car-based camper can be found beside the Murray River at Tom Groggin, near Geehi on the Murray Flats, in the old town site of Ravine or Lobbs Hole below the Yarrangobilly Caves, and at Cooleman Caves on the Long Plain east of Rules Point. Bush camping is permitted throughout the park as long as the location is not in sight of a road or near a watercourse. There are also several old huts scattered across the high country, which can be used in the event of extreme weather.

Commercial camping grounds are located in Jindabyne and Cooma, and there is an enormous range of ski chalets, motels and hotels in both these towns as well as the resorts of Thredbo and Perisher Valley.

Millennia of weathering have reduced enormous blocks of granite to jumbled piles of boulders.

Places in
SOUTH-EAST NEW
SOUTH WALES

Ben Boyd National Park protects fragile coastland from Pambula to Disaster Bay.

ADAMINABY

Adaminaby lies at one end of the looping, circuitous Snowy Mountains Highway on the most exciting section on one of the greatest roads in Australia. Gateway to the Snowy Mountains and 459 km (285 miles) south-west of Sydney, the town is a pleasant hamlet with a population of 300. The main attraction is the nearby Lake Eucumbene, where trout fishing and boating are popular activities—in fact, the site of the original township, 9 km (5.6 miles) south-west of the present one, lies beneath its waters. It was flooded in 1957 under the Snowy Mountains Hydro-Electric Scheme but the original village was moved in its entirety to its present location. The original town sprang up because of its proximity to the former goldmining town Kiandra. Today farming, grazing and tourism are the main industries.

Cross-country skiers taking to the slopes of Mount Selwyn and Blue Cow often stay at Adaminaby. A trip to nearby Providence Portal offers a unique view of water cascading into the lake. Horse riding and Aboriginal cultural tours are other attractions in the area.
Map ref: page 456 B6

ARALUEN

Lying 317 km (197 miles) south-west of Sydney, Araluen is now a mere shell of its glory days in the nineteenth century. Today's tiny population of 100 is far cry from the bustling populous when the valley was home to one of New South Wales' most lucrative goldfields. Sixty years of exploitation followed on from Alexander Waddell's gold discovery in 1851. Poets Henry Kendall and Charles Harpur, and novelist Rolf Boldrewood all spent time there; no doubt at the pub—a great historic hostelry. The Araluen Valley was also a hole-in-the-wall for the Clarke brothers' bushranging gang, who terrorised the area for two years in the 1860s. Nowadays, local industry consists of grazing and fruit growing.

The valley is right in between Deua National Park to the south and Budawang National Park in the north, offering great locations for bushwalking. Araluen is also a base from which to explore the old mining centres of Majors Creek and Captains Flat, and visitors can try their hand at gold panning. These places bear plenty of evidence of their past activity, belying its presence as a quiet naturalists' and painters' paradise.

Reached on 22 km (14 miles) of tar from Braidwood, or on dirt from Captains Flat or Moruya, its name is from an Aboriginal word 'arralyin', meaning 'place of waterlilies'.
Map ref: page 456 E6

BATEMANS BAY

James Cook named Batemans Bay in 1770 after the captain of the *Northumberland*. The town itself was first settled in 1840 and today has a population of around 14,000.

On the coast 297 km (184 miles) south of Sydney, Batemans Bay is situated on the mouth of the Clyde River (known as 'Bhundoo' to the local Aborigines). This river boasts very pure water and consequently the local oysters are excellent, as is the fishing. As befits a town with a strong tourist industry, the weather is near perfect—whether winter or summer. Surfing beaches and quiet backwaters abound, and the local lakes—Durras, Coila and Tuross—are popular for water sports. Lake Coila is also famous for its prawns.

Besides any and all things that are aquatic, including boat hire, Batemans Bay caters for most tastes. Craft lovers are catered for by many local stores and those at nearby Mogo, to the south, also feature Koori crafts. Birdland features a display of exotic birds and Mogo Zoo has a variety of native species. Nearby national parks offer different attractions: Murramarang boasts pretty Pebbly Beach, where kangaroos and wallabies mingle freely with visitors; Budawang, Eurobodalla and Deua have spectacular scenery. Pigeon House Mountain found in Morton National Park is highly regarded among bushwalkers and there are numerous walking trails, including one called the Corn Trail, which follows the same route down the Clyde Mountain that was once used by the early settlers to bring produce to the coast.
Map ref: page 456 E6

BATLOW

Originally known as Reedy Flat, Batlow was named after the surveyor who planned the town. It is 467 km (290 miles) south-west of Sydney and has a population of 1275. Once in the middle of a vast goldmining area, it is now the centre of a fruit industry specialising in pears and apples. Some people argue that Batlow apples are the best found in Australia, and the Big Red Apple Tourist Complex capitalises on this fact. The complex has great views of the Bogan Ranges.

The nearby Blowering Reservoir is used for water sports, while the Hume and Hovell's Lookout commemorates the expedition through the local region by the explorers in 1824. The small ski resort of Mount Selwyn is only an hour's

The view from Batemans Bay at the mouth of the Clyde River.

drive from Batlow. Other local activities include golf, bushwalking, bowls and tennis. The Batlow Show takes place in March. *See also* Tumbarumba Wine Region Map ref: page 456 A5

BEGA

Bega has a population of 4310 and is a major rural business district hub. Slightly inland from the coast, it lies 443 km (275 miles) south of Sydney and it can be reached by following either the Princes or the Snowy Mountains highways.

The area's main industries are dairy farming, timber and tourism, but its most famous product is undoubtedly Bega cheese. Bega cheddar is the number one seller in Australia, grossing some $86 million a year. The factory employs over 100 people and it is worth a visit to see how cheese is made.

Bega is thought to derive its name from the Aboriginal word 'biggah', meaning either 'beautiful' or 'big meeting place'. The town is proud of its history and the new Heritage Centre chronicles the region's past, its ancestors and cultural society. Kameruka Estate, which features beautiful gardens, is National Trust listed and it should not be missed. The Earth Craft Gallery caters for the interests of art and craft lovers.

Being surrounded by national parks, the area is rich in natural beauty. Eastwards, on the coast, are Mimosa Rocks and Bournda. To the north is Mumbulla and in the north-west is Wadbilliga (containing the Brogo Wilderness area). In the south is the South-East Forests National Park.

Four-wheel drive enthusiasts praise the scenery and driving challenge in the Bega hinterland and bushwalking is also a popular activity. Other pursuits in and around the area include fishing, golf and horse riding. Map ref: page 456 E8

BEN BOYD NATIONAL PARK

Extending both north and south of Eden on the Far South Coast, this park protects the superb stretches of rocky coastline on either side of Twofold Bay. There are great surfing beaches, sheltered coves and inlets, sea caves and headlands. At Long Beach the colourful red-

The Surveyor General inn, a Colonial Regency-style sandstone building in Berrima.

and-white rocks have been eroded to form the spectacular columns of the Pinnacles. The coastal heathlands produce spectacular wildflowers in late spring and, further inland, banksia forests give way to dense, tall eucalypts. Some of the access roads can be slippery after rain and are better suited to a 4WD than a conventional vehicle. The ruins of Benjamin Boyd's old whaling station near Twofold Bay, established in the 1840s, are well worth a visit. Map ref: page 456 E9

BERMAGUI

Bermagui is an angler's paradise. Indeed, it achieved international fame back in the 1930s when the American novelist Zane Grey regularly chartered big game boats from here. Anglers seeking to hook a black marlin or yellowfin tuna are almost invariably successful here because the continental shelf is at its closest to the mainland here, so there is great fishing just off the shoreline. Bermagui is situated about 400 km (248 miles) south of Sydney.

Nowadays, this town of 2000 people offers many charter boats for deep-sea fishing and scuba diving trips. The surf beaches are excellent and very popular for water sports. Bushwalking is a favourite pastime at nearby Wallaga Lake—the biggest in New South Wales. This is also a significant breeding area for black swans. Wallaga has special significance for the Yuin Aborigines, and cultural tours are regularly organised by the local Kooris to explain why. (The name 'Bermagui' is the

Aboriginal term for 'canoe with paddles'.) The Bermagui market is held on the last Sunday of each month and features the homemade and the handmade. Other local activities include golf, lawn bowls and indoor bowls. Map ref: page 456 E8

BERRIMA

Like Bathurst, Berrima is steeped in history and is even more popular as a tourist destination because of its proximity to both Sydney and Canberra. It is a small town of just 600 people and is situated 135 km (84 miles) south-west of Sydney in the Southern Highlands.

The quaint and charming feel of the town belies its biggest boasting point: it has Australia's oldest surviving jail (construction began in 1834), now a minor offenders'

institution. In its time, it housed a number of infamous bushrangers.

Berrima also has the oldest continually licensed inn in Australia, the Surveyor-General, named after Sir Thomas Mitchell, who camped on the site in 1829 and proclaimed it an excellent place for a town.

There are many other quaint sandstone Georgian buildings in town, the most notable being Berrima House, built in 1835, the two churches and the Post Office, all dated to 1836.

Situated on the old Hume Highway in the midst of farming and grazing lands, coalmining and cement manufacture are also important local industries. However, there are many artists and artisans who live in Berrima, and it is the arts and crafts that they produce which attract visitors just as much as the history of the town. (On weekends, Berrima can be as crowded as Sydney's George Street during rush hour!)

Although Berrima is extremely popular with cyclists, it lends itself more to the sedentary pursuits, its laid-back ambience encourages easy strolling and browsing, and it has number of coffee shops and restaurants of very high standard.

The Berrima District Museum, located in Market Street, is well worth a visit, plus there are several antique stores in town to tempt collectors. Berkelouw's Books is known to bibliophiles throughout Australia and is just out of town on the old Hume Highway. Map ref: page 456 F3

River fishing is popular in Bermagui and game fishing off the coast.

Crimson rosellas (Platycercus elegans); *common along the south-east coastal strip.*

BERRY

Within easy reach of Sydney—164 km (102 miles) south on the Princes Highway—Berry, which has a population of 1400, is a town with much historic significance. It occupies part of what was a 28,300 ha (69,929 acres) property owned by Alexander Berry in the early nineteenth century.

The National Trust has classified many of Berry's buildings, including the Bunyip Inn, a charming historic guesthouse that dates from 1889 at which time it was a bank building. The Coolangatta Historic Village Resort is housed in cottages once used by convicts.

Originally occupied by Wadi Wadi Aborigines, the district was invaded initially by timber-getters, then dairy farmers. Dairying is still a vital industry. Towards the end of the nineteenth century, settlers planted extended stands of English oaks, elms and beeches, creating a distinctly British feel, which Berry perpetuates today.

Many quaint antique shops, a museum, art galleries and good restaurants draw people to the town, particularly in autumn, when the area's natural beauty complements the other attractions.

The town has a famous doughnut shop—a caravan that is sited on the main street. It has remained unchanged for many years, and is a drawcard as a popular snack spot en route for scenic drives in the Southern Highlands. They cook the doughnuts fresh and the warm cinnamon sugar smell is tempting on a cold winter's day. In spring, try Brango Park Blueberries, Strawberry Fields or the two local wineries. An agricultural show is held every year in February. Local markets are set up in the showground on the first Sunday of each month.
Map ref: page 456 G3

BODALLA

Like Bega, Bodalla is perhaps best known for its cheese, but the town also has important historical links with early Australia. Thomas Sutcliffe Mort, most famous for his pioneer work in exporting frozen meat to Great Britain in huge refrigerated ships, first established Bodalla as a model farm in 1856, and in doing so founded a rural tradition of dairying for the district. (Mort was buried on his property at Bodalla.)

Located on the Princes Highway 349 km (217 miles) south of Sydney, Bodalla is one of the Sapphire Coast group of towns (which includes places such as Bega and Narooma). These town place a great deal of emphasis on tourism and they cater for all manner of guests; despite a population of only 260, Bodalla has art galleries, restaurants and gardens.

Bodalla's proximity to many surf beaches and rivers in the region, that offer numerous water sports, adds to its appeal. There is also some great scenery close at hand. The village of Nerrigundah, famous for its bushrangers, is only a short drive away.
Map ref: page 456 E7

BOMBALA

The tourist brochures describe this town as 'tranquillity in the middle of everything'; indeed it *is* a hidden rural treasure between the Snowy Mountains and the Sapphire Coast. Three hours south of Canberra or 533 km (331 miles) south-west of Sydney, it is home to 1500 people.

Bombala is a stunning blend of the treeless plains of the Monaro district, the rainforests of the Errinundra Plateau and dense native forests. Wildlife is abundant. There are platypuses in the town's river and a quiet visitor on a relaxed evening stroll along the riverbank will perhaps be rewarded with a glimpse of this rather elusive creature. In fact this area has the highest density of platypuses in New South Wales.

Bombala is perhaps the most famous trout fishing centre in the State, and there are many places to stay that are very close to great spots on the river. There are also bushwalks and visitors can fossick for gold. This area is also famous for its vivid jumpers created by the Toorallie Woollen Mill and in January Bombala has a wool and wood festival.
Map ref: page 456 C9

BOWRAL

Just as the expatriate English in the days of the British raj in India left behind the searing summer heat of the plains by escaping to the hill stations, so Sydney's wealthy at the turn of the century would set up in Bowral. Situated in the Southern Highlands, 127 km (79 miles)

The Southern Highlands are renowned for the autumn colour of deciduous species.

south of Sydney, Bowral is home to 7400. It has mild summers but can be bitterly cold in winter. Bowral derives its name from the Aboriginal 'bowrel', which the local tribe bestowed on the giant rock that towers over the town; it is now known as 'The Gib' (after Gibraltar). John Oxley was the first settler in the district, naming his homestead Wingecarribee—perpetuated in the shire name today. Bowral still has a very English ambience about it, with stately homes and magnificent gardens.

While the town attracts Sydneysiders in droves, it is also a magnet for cricket lovers. Although he was born in Cootamundra, Sir Donald Bradman grew up in Bowral, and self-guided Bradman Walk visits some of the town sites associated with the man whom many would argue was the greatest batsman of all. There are also the Bradman Oval and Museum to further commemorate Sir Donald's name. Among other memorabilia, the museum houses the bat he used at Headingly in 1934 to notch up his second highest ever Test score of 304. Bowral has its Tulip Festival every September and there are some great walks in the area.
Map ref: page 456 F3

BRAIDWOOD

Situated on Gillamatong Creek, a tributary of the Shoalhaven River, Braidwood bears the name of pioneer settler Thomas Braidwood Wilson, who also served as surgeon to the convicts. Presently populated by 11,000, Braidwood is a historic gold town classified by the National Trust. It lies 292 km (181 miles) south of Sydney, halfway between Canberra and Batemans Bay, on a superb stretch of the Kings Highway. The road from Braidwood to Batemans Bay over the Clyde Mountain offers spectacular views, but is subject to very heavy fog. Certain buildings 'must' be seen, in particular the Post Office and the Tallagandra Shire Council Chambers, both restored by the Heritage Council. The jail, the infirmary and the Catholic and Presbyterian churches are also worth seeing. This town is also famous as the location for Mick

Jagger's 1969 re-creation of the character of Ned Kelly—a fitting site, as the Clarke Brothers gang of bushrangers used to hole up in the nearby Araluen Valley during the old goldrush days.

Braidwood is nestled right in the Budawang Ranges, and is popular as a base for four-wheel drivers. The terrain is challenging and the scenery diverse. There are three State forests and three national parks nearby to explore. Other local activities include bushwalks, fishing, golf, horseracing, squash, swimming and tennis.

Braidwood has a local arts and crafts centre, a museum, a trout farm and a racecourse. The local rural show is held in February–March, Heritage Week is in April, 'The Quilt Event' is annually in late November and stockhorse events take place in December
Map ref: page 456 E5

BUDAWANG NATIONAL PARK

A true wilderness area with no roads and few bushwalking trails, Budawang National Park is isolated, remote and has very few visitors. It is 16,100 ha (39,783 acres) of extremely rugged yet beautiful terrain. Peace and solitude await the intrepid walker prepared to endure the hardships of wilderness exploration. There are magnificent views from the top of Mount Budawang but they can be obscured by low cloud or rolling thunderstorms. The deep gorges that roll off the steep sides of the three dominating mountains—Currockbilly, Budawang, and the Sugarloaf—are generally impenetrable and give rise to the headwaters of the Yadboro River.

The park is often confused with Morton National Park, which adjoins the northern tip. They are, however, quite different in their topography: Budawang has steep rather than sheer mountainsides and has very lush, wet forests.

This is a park for experienced self-sufficient bushwalkers, well prepared for the arduous walking conditions and capable of reading a compass and topographic map. Proposed walks must be reported

An orchard butterfly in Budawang.

River fishing is accessible to Braidwood, where carp, perch and redfin can be caught.

to the local National Parks and Wildlife Service staff. There is a clearly marked trail to the top of Mount Budawang but it entails a steep climb of about 1 km (0.6 miles) It will take about one hour for the return walk.

There is only one access road to the edge of the park and no vehicle trails within its boundaries. The track ends abruptly at the base of Mount Budawang, where there is a walking trail leading to the top of the mountain and the fire tower lookout. In wet weather this track is impassable to conventional vehicles. There are no designated camping areas or facilities and the high rainfall and extremely cold winters make remote bush camping difficult. Accommodation is available in nearby Braidwood.
Map ref: page 456 E5

BUNDANOON

Being an easy distance—152 km (94 miles) south of Sydney—Bundanoon, together with Bowral, was once a favourite spot in the South-

ern Highlands for Sydney's elite. With streets lined with oaks, elms and poplars, it has retained its genteel charm. Today the town has a population of 2500 and golfers, sightseers, horse riders bushwalkers, and backpackers, make up the weekend clientele at the various coffee shops, restaurants and art nooks. It is also a very popular are for cyclists, who use Bundanoon as a base for the easy runs up to Sutton Forest, Moss Vale and back, which is 33 km (21 miles), or for more arduous exercise through the neighbouring Kangaroo Valley.

Bundanoon is close to Morton National Park, which boasts a labyrinth of bushwalking tracks, spectacular lookouts, deep canyons and cliffs. There is also the Glow Worm Glen (best seen at night) and a Thai Buddhist monastery, which welcomes visitors.

In April Bundanoon celebrates its Gaelic roots by with the Highland Gathering, which features traditional Scottish games, bands and country dances.
Map ref: page 456 F3

Budawang National Park is rich with lush temperate rainforest and rocky gorges.

CAMPBELLTOWN

Campbelltown is really now a suburb of the sprawling city of Sydney—the city centre is 53 km (33 miles) north-east—but originally it was a quiet country village named by Governor Macquarie after his wife's maiden name. Today its population is 150,000 and its dairies supply much of Sydney's milk. The local district also produces poultry and fruit. Architectural landmarks include St Peter's Church (completed in 1824), and Glenalvon and Richmond Villa, two of the original houses. Campbelltown sponsors an annual festival in November: the Festival of Fisher's Ghost. Activities include a big street parade of floats and marching bands, fireworks, and literature and art competitions. The ghost, according to Australian colonial folklore, is that of Frederick Fisher, a Campbelltown farmer who was murdered in 1826 by a fellow ex-convict. Four months later Fisher's 'ghost' was 'seen' by a local man and the subsequent investigation led to Fisher's grave. Fisher's Ghost Creek is a local watercourse perpetuating the legend.

The entrance to Doonkuna winery.

The Campbelltown City Show is second in size only to Sydney's Royal Easter Show. It is held in April. Other activities include bowls, golf and tennis.
Map ref: page 456 G2

CANBERRA DISTRICT WINE REGION

This is the most established and nationally recognised wine region in southern New South Wales. Irrigation is essential here, and there is considerable variation between summer and winter temperatures, more so than in most other Australian districts. The first plantings in 1971 by Dr Edgar Rick at Lake George were later followed by the development of almost another 20 more small vineyards.

The face of the Canberra District is changing, however. What was once little more than an area of hobby farms and amateur winemakers is now also home to a 253 ha (625 acre) vineyard and a 2000 tonne (2200 ton) winery established by BRL Hardy, one of Australia's biggest wine producers. Chardonnay, shiraz, cabernet sauvignon and riesling have done well here and there is some

Brindabella Hills Winery, Canberra District, makers of an award-winning Chardonnay.

support for pinot noir and sauvignon blanc. The Lark Hill Winery in Bungendore produces one of the best pinot noirs from the district. Among other wineries that are well worth a visit are the Brindabella Hills Winery, near Hall; Kyeema Wines at Weetangera; Madew Wines, Lake George, and Pankhurst Wines at Hall.

While not within the ACT, the Murrumbateman area, about 35 km (22 miles) north of Canberra, is part of this general region. Its notable wineries include Clonakilla, Doonkuna Estate, Helm's Wines, Jeir Creek Wines and the Murrumbateman Winery.
Map ref: page 456 C4, D5

CENTRAL TILBA

Central Tilba, 390 km (242 miles) south of Sydney, is perhaps one of the prettiest and most historic towns in the State. A National Trust village of only 100 people, the architecture spans the last years of the nineteenth century and the early years of the twentieth. Its Victorian timber buildings represent an important example of a bygone age and lifestyle. The only constructions still standing are the original weatherboard residences and shops, and the local hotel and general store are particularly evocative of the pioneering days. Many TV commercials have been filmed here, as the only concessions to modernity are the power lines.

The town nestles directly under the sacred 'Gulaga', named Mount Dromedary by Captain James Cook because its peak resembled the camel's back. The area was originally inhabited by the Yuin

tribe (in their language, the word 'tilba' means 'wind'), but the first white settler was Henry Bate, who subdivided the area. The Bate family is synonymous with the history of Tilba. On a sweeping headland overlooking the sea is the grave of politician Jeff Bate, with a headstone bearing a dedication to 'a brave man'. His widow Dame Zara donated the headstone; she was also the widow of drowned Prime Minister Harold Holt.

Gold changed sleepy Tilba into a booming and boisterous place, but the find was short-lived, and peace returned quickly. Dairying replaced digging, and the manufacture of cheese, which still goes on today, became one of this small village's means of survival.

Central Tilba is now totally dedicated to the tourist trade. As such, it has three craft galleries: the Tilba Wood-turning Gallery, Mangrove Craft Gallery and the Gulaga Gallery. Many of the artisans work in the town. There are leatherworkers, wood-turners, jewellers and cheesemakers. Nearby is Tilba's winery, and a deer farm, and both are open to the public.

A festival featuring live music, theatre and exhibitions is held each year on Easter Saturday.
Map ref: page 456 E7

COOMA

In the heart of the Snowy Mountains region, 415 km (258 miles) south of Sydney, the Cooma district boasts gentle country hospitality, crisp, clean air, tranquil riverbanks and waterfalls, forest glades and treeless plains. The townsite was first surveyed in

Little Dromedary rises gently behind the rural town of Central Tilba.

1849. It boomed when gold was discovered at Kiandra in 1860 but declined in the late 1880s. Much later, as headquarters for the famed Snowy Mountains Hydro-Electric Scheme in the 1950s, the town again exploded, with some 10,000 workers billeted around the area. Today the town is home to 8000 people but in winter it throngs with hoardes of holidaymakers or using it as a base or passing through on their way to ski in the numerous Snowy Mountain resorts. In the summer months activities include tennis, horse racing, trout fishing and water sports in nearby lakes Eucumbene and Jindabyne. 'Cooma' is derived from an Aboriginal word 'coombah', meaning either 'big lake' or 'open country'.

Lambie Street, predominantly Georgian in design, is a historic precinct. There is also a statue in town perpetuating the legend of A.B. 'Banjo' Paterson's *Man From Snowy River*. The airliner *Southern Cloud* crashed close to Cooma in 1931, and a memorial was erected to these early aviators.

Cooma also has a number of special events throughout the year. In January, the races and a trade fair are held; March has another race day and in April, Heritage Day. During October/November, Coomafest is held, which features a rock-and-roll picnic, a talent quest and fun run. In November, there are two events—the Snowy Mountains Chainsaw Classic, which also features axemen, and the Snowy Mountains Trout Festival, which has prize money totalling $35,000. Every third Sunday, markets are held at the town's Centennial Park.
Map ref: page 456 C7

DEUA NATIONAL PARK

The 82,926 ha (204,910 acres) of Deua National Park cover the mountains inland from the south coast towns of Narooma and Moruya. Primarily a wilderness park, it is quite accessible and there are great camping spots beside clear rivers, 4WD trails, fabulous walks, caves, diverse flora and a huge range of wildlife.

The park's rugged mountains and valleys were, for a long time, an impenetrable barrier. However, the early settlers of the Monaro

Sulphur-crested cockatoo.

plains needed a stock route directly to the ports at Bega and Eden from where their stock could be shipped to the Sydney market. This led to a stock route being blazed down the steep ridges into the broad valley formed by the Deua River. During the mid-1800s the valley floor was cleared and it became an important feeding area for stock.

Access from the coast is via a network of forestry trails out of Moruya. The few trails that dissect the park have remained open and there are a number of challenging 4WD tracks offering superb views Once in the park, the trails are the domain of the 4WD and the Bendethera, Merricumbene, Mount Dampier and Minuma Trails provide varying degrees of difficulty.

There are established camp sites at the Deua River Camping Area, and the Berlang Camping Area provides picnic and camping

opportunities near the Shoalhaven River. From here it is a 30 minute walk to the Big Hole, the result of a hillside collapsing into an underground limestone cavern, creating a hole 30 m (98 feet) across and 90 m (295 feet) deep.

Deep in the heart of the national park, the Bendethera Valley is possibly one of the best camp sites in New South Wales for those who have 4WD vehicles.

A park for the really adventurous, both amateur and professional speleologists can explore the Wyanbene and Bendethera Caves while remote-country bushwalkers can venture into the rugged southern end of the park.
Map ref: page 456 E6

EDEN

Eden is aptly named. Located on Twofold Bay, 497 km (309 miles) south of Sydney, it features golden sandy beaches and rugged cliffs. What began as a whaling town is now the main port of the south coast and a major commercial fishing centre, with a population of 4000. Chartering boats is very popular with visitors. So is visiting the Killer Whale Museum, which details the history of shore-based whaling as well as featuring local history. It houses the skeleton of

'Old Tom', a killer whale, and it also showcases equipment used in the now-banned whaling industry. Whale-watching is now a particularly popular pastime here. Humpbacks, minke and southern rights as well as the enormous endangered blue whales are regularly sighted off the coast near Eden.

Next to Eden lies the spectacular Ben Boyd National Park, featuring stunning coastal scenery with very rugged cliffs, rock formations and sea caves. The park perpetuates the name of Ben Boyd who established whaling operations in the area in 1842, and built his folly—Boyd Town—across the bay, wanting it to rival Eden. You can also visit the old Davidson Whaling Station. Local beaches are excellent for fishing and water sports. Surfers should try Aslings, while families will enjoy Corcora. There are sea caves to explore at Snug Cove.

In town, there is the McCulloch Campbell Gallery, the Eden Shells Gallery and the Harris Daishowa Chipmill, which is open to visitors by appointment. South of Eden and in the hinterland, there is some fabulous 4WD touring and bushwalking. You can be escorted or pick your own way through to places like Bendethera and Deua National Park.
Map ref: page 456 E9

The coastline near Eden is spectacular and a boat trip during the humpback whale migrating season is sure to offer sightings.

Seven Mile Beach is on the road from Gerringong, a small coastal dairying town between Sydney and Wollongong.

GERRINGONG

The Gerringong area was first settled in the 1820s, initially by cedar-getters but, as the land was cleared dairying became the main industry and remains so today, along with tourism. Just 147 km (91 miles) south of Sydney, Gerringong is a coastal village of 2900 people, where green fields seem to drop into the sea. These impressive views are coupled with the terrific beaches and friendly locals. Seven Mile Beach, where Charles Kings-ford Smith took off in his plane the *Southern Cross* for the flight to New Zealand in 1933, has become part of Seven Mile Beach National Park, which contains a monument to the famous aviator.

Apart from excellent surfing, fishing and bushwalking, there is also Wild Country Park, a local wildlife refuge and home to kangaroos, emus, wombats and many colourful parrot species. You can also visit the Gerringong and District Historical Society. With its primary focus on the dairy indus-try, the museum also has models of early Gerringong and a photo-graphic record of motor racing on Seven Mile Beach in the 1920s.
Map ref: page 456 G3

GOULBURN

Goulburn was named after Henry Goulburn, Under-Secretary for the Colonies at the time explorers James Meehan and Hamilton Hume came through the district in 1818, though John Oxley was the first white man to actually cross the site of the city. For a number of years after Goulburn was gazetted in 1833, it was a garrison town and became a centre for police parties hunting bushrangers. Early experi-ments with farming wheat were supplanted by sheep after the west-ern regions gained supremacy in cereals, and wool is still the pri-mary industry. Goulburn has the distinction of being the last town in the British Empire to be declar-ed a city, in 1864, by being created a bishopric by Royal Letters Patent.

Goulburn is 206 km (128 miles) south of Sydney on the old Hume Highway and is a thriving city of 21,530. It is an important rail centre with many thriving second-ary industries, including textiles, carpets and knitting yarns, in town and around the district. Marulan, 39 km (24 miles) away, has one of the largest limestone quarries in the Southern Hemisphere.

As a historic town, Goulburn has much of interest. In the Gothic Revival style, St Saviour's Cathedral was designed by the famed colonial architect Edmund Blacket and was completed in 1884, with the tower and spire finally added over a cen-tury later. National Trust-classified buildings abound throughout the area, many of which are open to the public. There is also a regional art gallery with a wide range of art and craft forms, often displayed in exhibitions combining the works of local and other artists.

At the other end of the scale is Goulburn's answer to the Coffs Harbour Big Banana and Taree's Big Prawn. It is the Big Merino, a three-storey concrete ram inside which you can see a wool history display and gaze out over Goul-burn and its environs through the eyes of this giant sheep.

Motor racing buffs will be interested in going to Wakefield Park, south-east of the town. It is a privately owned circuit used for many race events. It is favoured by vintage car racing buffs and has been used for many new vehicle releases, inclu-ding the MG-F, which heralded the return of the MG Marque to Australia after an absence of more than 20 years.

Also to the south is Bungonia State Recreation Reserve, which offers bushwalking (steep), caving, climbing, abseiling and canoeing in the spectacular Shoalhaven Gorge, where there are some great views from lookouts for the less adven-turous. Another natural feature in the vicinity is Wombeyan Caves,

The Coolavin Hotel at Goulburn, a rural city that has thrived on wool and stock.

The big merino at Goulburn.

A field fronts Gundagai, a wheat and wool town on the Hume Highway.

with its quite spectacular limestone formations. Visitors to these caves should be careful on the road into the valley, which has nasty switchbacks and blind curves flanking very steep drops. Tarlo National Park, 30 km (19 miles) north of Goulburn, is a refuge for waterbirds, wallabies, long-necked tortoises, platypuses and wombats.

In October, Goulburn has its Lilac City Festival. Other local activities include 4WD touring, fishing, squash and tennis.
Map ref: page 456 D3

GUNDAGAI

The name Gundagai has intriguing origins. It derives from the Aboriginal 'gundabandoobingee', which means either 'going upstream' or, more intriguingly, 'to cut sinews behind the knee with a tomahawk'. Gundagai lies on the Hume Highway 399 km (248 miles) southwest of Sydney. Moved uphill after a disastrous 1852 flood that claimed 98 lives, it now has a population of 4200 and is the centre for a rural economy based on sheep and cattle; wheat, maize lucerne and asparagus are also grown locally.

Gundagai is most famous for the Jack Moses' poem commemorating the bullocky's story of a dog doing its business on a tuckerbox and there is a monument sculpted by Frank Rusconi 8 km (5 miles) to the north of town. Rusconi also sculpted his 'Marble Masterpiece', a miniature replica of the altar of St Maria's Cathedral in Paris. Also

immortalised in bronze are the Rudd Family (Dad, Dave, Mum and Mabel), characters from *On Our Selection* by Steele Rudd.

Gundagai Historical Museum has some interesting folkloric exhibits, such as the saddlecloth that Australia's most famous racehorse Phar Lap wore in the last race before he died. Many of the buildings in town date back over 130 years, and the courthouse saw the trial of bushranger Captain Moonlight. Prince Alfred Bridge is the longest wooden bridge in the Southern Hemisphere.

The town hosts the Dog on the Tuckerbox Festival in November, with a two-day race meeting, which is climaxed by the running of the Snake Gully Cup. There is also country music, some dog sporting events, market stalls and a breakfast at the Dog on the Tuckerbox.

In the area you can also participate in bowls, fishing, golf, squash or have a game of tennis.
Map ref: page 456 A4

GUNNING

Explorer Hamilton Hume first established a station here in 1821, and plans for the town were first approved in 1838. One year later, it was home to 20 horses and 95 people, and included a store and a pub. Now with a population of 500, Gunning boasts antique stores and art and craft shops. It also has a number of historic buildings, including London House, the post office, Royal Hotel and the old

courthouse, which is now a church. The town is 253 km (157 miles) south of Sydney and is situated on the Hume Highway roughly halfway between Goulburn and Yass. There are a variety of scenic walks in the area worth trying and trout fishing is a favoured local pastime. Other activities include tennis and bowls.
Map ref: page 456 C3

HILLTOPS WINE REGION

Yugoslavian immigrants planted vineyards in the Hilltops region, based on Young, at the end of the 1800s, but the region has been producing wine in modern terms for no more than a couple of decades. In 1975, grape-growing was reintroduced to Hilltops in a small way at the Barwang vineyard as part of an overall farm diversification. There were only 13 ha (32 acres) under vine when McWilliam's purchased the property in 1989. They have increased plantings tenfold and established the potential of the region beyond doubt. They have been joined by several growers and a couple of tiny wineries, including the Demondrille Vineyards near Harden. The altitude of Hilltops—more than 460 m (1500 feet) above sea level—is a major factor in wine quality. The dry summer makes irrigation necessary and frost is also a concern. Chardonnay, cabernet sauvignon and especially shiraz have proved most successful to date, but at least one producer, Lindsay's Woodonga Hill in Young, believes there is still potential for other varieties.
Map ref page 456 A2

HUSKISSON

Huskisson lies 196 km (122 miles) south of Sydney on the white beaches and sparkling, clear blue waters of Jervis Bay; it is about a 20-minute drive from the nearest city, Nowra.

The town was most probably named after William Huskisson, who was the Colonial Secretary from 1827 to

1828. At the turn of the century, a major boat-building industry was based in Huskisson, and it produced, among others, the *Lady Denman,* a ferry that plied Sydney Harbour for many years. Today, the ferry occupies pride of place in the Lady Denman Heritage Complex, which is also a more general maritime museum.

These days, fishing and tourism are now the town's main industries, and the population of 1600 often explodes on weekends and holidays, with many people making trips from Sydney or Canberra. There are seasonal whale-watching and year-round dolphin-watching trips that run from Huskisson. Scuba diving is particularly good in the bay with some spectacular underwater caves at Point Perpendicular. Local dive shops sell and hire all scuba-diving equipment, run boat dives and certification courses.

Huskisson is a great base from which to explore the bay, which claims to have the whitest sand in the world. The clear blue waters make it a popular holiday spot for water-sports enthusiasts. Bowls, golf and tennis can also be enjoyed in the area. The town offers plenty of interesting shopping, with an Aboriginal arts and crafts centre and a trading post stocked with antiques and bric-a-brac.
Map ref: page 456 G4

Fishing at Jervis Bay, not far from Huskisson.

Jindabyne is a hub of activity in winter as a stop-off point to several big ski resorts.

JERVIS BAY

Pronounced 'jarvis', Jervis Bay is an extensive inlet and a popular holiday place on the south coast of New South Wales, 208 km (129 miles) south of Sydney. The bay was named in 1791 by Lieutenant Bowen of the transport *Atlantic* in honour of Sir John Jervis, with whom he had served. Later, as the areas inland were settled, the bay was used as a port for small coastal ships that took produce to Sydney and returned with provisions for the local settlers.

Jervis Bay has been the site for some ambitious schemes, none of which came to fruition, but part of the area is still owned by the Commonwealth Government. The Seat of Government Act of 1908 decreed that the capital of the nation should have access to the sea. In the late 1990s, that ownership and what should be done with the land was the subject of heated debate between environmentalists and those who wished to develop the area. Jervis Bay today has a population of around 5000.

Scuba diving is particularly popular in the bay owing to its clear blue waters and spectacular underwater cliffs, caves and quiet sponge gardens. The calm waters make it a special place for a refreshing swim and there are also numerous good bushwalking trails in the region.
Map ref: page 456 G4

JINDABYNE

For skiers, Jindabyne is truly the gateway to the Snowy Mountains. Situated 457 km (284 miles) south of Sydney, it is a good base for a skiing holiday, being just 40 minutes away from the winter playgrounds of Thredbo and Perisher Blue. Jindabyne's cheaper accommodation than that in the on-snow resorts means that this town's usual population of 2000 undergoes an alarming surge from the June long weekend, which heralds the start of the ski season. It is also the last town where you can fuel up, hire snow chains (required by law in Kosciuszko National Park in the snow season), or skis and snowboards on the way to ski resorts.

The original town is now under Lake Jindabyne, flooded as part of the Snowy Mountains Hydro-Electric Scheme in 1966. The surrounding rural district supports sheep and cattle, but Jindabyne's raison d'être is tourism, whether it be for trout seekers who come to cast a line in the lake, bushwalkers, alpine tourists or snow enthusiasts.

In summer, too, Jindabyne still has plenty to offer. Situated in the Snowy Mountains, it offers opportunities for abseiling, gliding and mountain biking. The town is 910 m (2986 feet) above sea level and with a capacity of almost 690,000 gigalitres, the lake gives visitors the chance to sail, windsurf or water-

ski. In the first weekend of December, there is a sailing regatta but be warned, most of the local craft are multi-hulled and are very fast!
Map ref: page 456 B8

KIAMA

The name Kiama is thought to derive from the Aboriginal 'kiaram-a' (meaning 'where the sea makes a noise'). Tourists flock to see the blowhole, which shoots water into the air up to a height of 60 m (197 feet). It was first chronicled by George Bass, who anchored his boat there in 1797. Also popular is the National Trust-classified row of restored timber terrace cottages in Collins Street, which houses craft and antique shops. Others come to trace their lineage in the records of the Family History Centre.

On the Princes Highway, 120 km (75 miles) south of Sydney, Kiama is bordered on one side by

the sea, with an excellent surfing beach, and on the other by the rugged Minamurra Rainforest. A town of 11,300, it now relies on tourism to augment a local economy built on dairying, blue metal mining and fishing. The town has been in existence since 1839.

In June, Kiama hosts an Australian Folk Festival, and in November, a Seaside Festival and Colonial Ball. In December the town lays claim to Australia's largest regional Carols by Candlelight while during February, there's a Jazz Festival. Local activities include bowls, golf, bushwalking, fishing and water sports such as surfing.
Map ref: page 456 G3

MERIMBULA

A very popular holiday destination on the Sapphire Coast, Merimbula lies 476 km (296 miles) south of Sydney and has a population of 4500. The area features clean tidal lakes and all manner of beaches making it a great place for a variety of water sports. It is possible to hire boats locally for some fishing but it isn't necessary as one of the most popular fishing spots is directly off the Merimbula wharf.

Merimbula is close to quite a few national parks, with Bournda National Park being just a short drive away. There is also some good bushwalking in the ancient forests in the foothills of the South Coast Range, where there are some small adjoining towns like Candelo (famous for its arts and crafts) and the pioneering towns of Kameruka and Wyndham are also interesting.

For the children, some fun at the Magic Mountain Complex is a must. Merimbula also has its own aquarium. Other activities that can be taken up here include cycling, bowls, horse riding and tennis.
Map ref: page 456 E9

The coastline around Kiama, just south of Wollongong, with typical grassy hills spilling into the Pacific ocean.

MIMOSA ROCKS NATIONAL PARK

Located on the far south coast of New South Wales, Mimosa Rocks National Park covers an area of about 5000 ha (12,355 acres). It is one of the State's most beautiful coastal parks, with swimming, canoeing, fishing and scuba diving being the main local activities, but it also has superb scenery and some unusual rock formations. It is often very quiet and deserted.

The park lies along a 20 km (12 mile) stretch of coast between the towns of Bermagui and Tathra and it is split into a northern and a southern section with a section of private land running in between. There are several access routes off this road into the various camp sites and picnic areas.

The southern section of the park has some lovely picnic spots at Nelson Beach, Wajurda Point and also Moon Bay, a very protected, sandy beach, ideal for young children. At Bithry Inlet there is a day-visit area and it is possible to canoe on the quiet waters of the inlet.

There are also several quite good camping spots; some are accessible by vehicles while others require you to carry your camping gear a short distance. Many sites have minimal facilities (pit toilets and rubbish bins) or none; for most you will need to bring water. There is one along the Aragunnu Road near the beachfront, where the beach and rock platforms are excellent for fishing and swimming. Others are at Picnic Point, Middle Beach and Gillards Beach, a great place to walk, sunbake or surf.
Map ref: page 456 E8

It is a challenging hike up Pigeon House Mountain, Morton National Park.

MITTAGONG

A town in the Southern Highlands, 123 km (76 miles) south of Sydney, Mittagong was originally intended to become a large industrial centre. Instead, the district is given over to dairying, poultry farming and growing fruit and vegetables, although some industrial activity also contributes to the local economy. 'Mittagong' means either 'little mountain' or 'plenty of native dogs'. The town is home to 5220.

The first white men to traverse the area were led by John Wilson in 1798, but the first land grant was made in 1821 to William Chalker. The nucleus of a village grew in the 1830s. Buildings from the 1860s now provide visitors with sightseeing opportunities. In town are several walking trails and the area is popular with both bushwalkers and 4WD enthusiasts.
Map ref: page 456 F3

MORTON NATIONAL PARK

This vast park stretches south along the Great Dividing Range, from near Moss Vale to where it adjoins the Budawang National Park. The northern portion of the park offers the stunning mountain scenery of Kangaroo Valley and Bundanoon, high sandstone ridges and deep gorges cut by the Shoalhaven River and its tributaries, and the magnificent Fitzroy Falls. The southern section is a rugged wilderness of deep sandstone cliffs and weathered gorges: a bushwalkers' paradise. During spring, wildflowers put on a colourful display. There is a visitor information centre.
Map ref: page 456 E4

Eroded rocks in Mimosa Rocks National Park are remnants of an ancient lava flow.

MORUYA

Moruya is located directly on the Princes Highway, 325 km (202 miles) south of Sydney and this large town is home to some 9000 residents. Although it is actually the smallest of the three major towns on the Eurobodalla coast, it is the administrative head of the entire district. The reasons for this are twofold. The first is because it is in the centre of the shire. The second is because it is one of the oldest towns in the region.

Moruya developed in the 1850s as a gateway to the nearby Araluen and Braidwood goldfields and later it became important as settlers like Thomas Mort developed the local pastoral industries, which are still in operation today.

While the town has a number of historic buildings, Moruya is much better known as a holiday resort.

There are several fantastic surfing beaches like Moruya Heads, Congi, Bingi and that are are only 10 km (6.2 miles) to the east of the town, and the fishing is known to be very good too, particularly on the pretty Deua River or off one of the local coastal headlands. Nearby Deua National Park also offers some challenging 4WD tours and also features many enjoyable bushwalks.

Commercially operated entertainment includes camel trekking, mountain biking or a historic bus tour of an hours' duration that takes in Kiora House, the first homestead built by convicts.

While in town, you can play a game of tennis, have a round of golf, go bowling or go swimming in the town's heated public pool. Moruya has country markets every Saturday morning and an annual rodeo, held at Easter.
Map ref: page 456 E6

A rotunda in Moss Vale amid exotic Southern Highland gardens.

MOSS VALE

A town of around 6100 people, Moss Vale was named in the 1860s after an old resident, Jemmy Moss. Situated high in the picturesque Southern Highlands, 135 km (84 miles) south-west of Sydney, it is surrounded by rolling hills, lush farming areas and quite spectacular scenery. A nearby attraction is Fitzroy Falls, in the 154,000 hectare Morton National Park, where there is a visitor's centre that offers local wildlife information and also notes on the areas bushwalks. A really excellent day trip can be made to Wombeyan Caves, which feature dramatic limestone formations.

In the town, Leighton Gardens exhibit colourful blooms for most of the year. Many of the old buildings in the town have been restored. Tudor House, a preparatory school for boys, welcomes visitors. While there, it is well worth inspecting the memorial fountain and clock tower. Throsby Park is a magnificent colonial mansion that was once owned by the pioneering Throsby family, who lived in it for five generations from the 1830s. Moss Vale has a great golf course.
Map ref: page 456 F3

MURRAMARANG NATIONAL PARK

This park is on the south coast of the State just 300 km (186 miles) south of Sydney or 10 km (6.2 miles) north of Batemans Bay. It follows the coastline from the quiet seaside town of Long Beach all the way to Merry Beach, near the town of Ulladulla. A delightful feature of the park are the wonderfully tame eastern grey kangaroos that coexist with people in many of the small towns and in particular at the very pretty Pebbly Beach.

There are several entrances to the park off the Princes Highway. There are two major entries at the northern end, via Bawley Point or Merry Beach, and in the southern section, enter off the highway near East Lynne to Pebbly Beach and Durras North. The roads through the State Forests to the park are all generally unsealed so caution in wet weather is needed. There are no vehicle tracks in the park itself other than those leading to designated beaches or camping areas. Camping is possible at various locations including Pebbly Beach, South Durras, Depot Beach, Pretty Beach and Merry Beach. Some of these camp sites are commercially operated while the National Parks and Wildlife Service also charges camping fees for its sites. The best walk in the park is to the top of Mount Durras, which offers fabulous views up and down the coast and west to the mountains.
Map ref: page 456 F5

NAROOMA

Popularly called 'Narooma' for many years, it was not until 1972 that the name was officially altered from 'Noorooma' (meaning 'blue water'), the name of an early cattle station. Home to 8100 residents, The town is a tourist resort, one that is renowned for its big-game fishing. Narooma is situated on the Wogonga Inlet and lies 370 km (230 miles) south of Sydney on the Princes Highway. Important industries in the area include sawmilling and oyster farming.

Tuross Lake and Lake Corunna are major attractions, particularly for fishing, and there are many great surfing beaches including Blackfellows Point, Mystery Bay and Bar Beach. Eight kilometres (26 miles) offshore is Montague Island, a flora and fauna reserve.
Map ref: page 456 E7

NOWRA

Nowra is an Aboriginal word meaning 'black cockatoo'. This town has a population of 23,000 and is a bustling centre for the Shoalhaven district, an area given to dairying, vegetable growing and timber milling. The quickest route from Sydney is via the Princes Highway, 179 km (111 miles), but the best way to appreciate the coastal plains on which the city stands is to come by the longer, more scenic route through Kangaroo Valley. Along here is an amazing vista from the Cambewarra Range, which rises around 600 m (1969 feet) above the surrounding countryside.

Tourism is very important to Nowra, and the surrounding area has quite a lot to offer, including both surf and tranquil lakeside beaches, and offshore and riverside fishing. Meroogal, a historic home built in 1886, is open for public inspection, and there is also an excellent historic museum.

Nowra has long been associated with the Navy's Fleet Air arm, and the base, HMAS *Albatross*, is 9 km (5.6 miles) south-west of the town. It contains the Australia Museum of Flight, with a magnificent collection of military aircraft, engines, uniforms and memorabilia. Other local pursuits include fishing, golf, bowls, squash and tennis.
See also South Coast Wine Region
Map ref: page 456 F4

A pig made Robertson famous.

ROBERTSON

Originally known for its potatoes, Robertson shot to fame in the 1990s when the area featured in the Australian hit movie *Babe*. Surrounded by rolling green hills, the town sits high at the crest of Macquarie Pass, and is 143 km (89 miles) south of Sydney, about halfway between the coast and the Southern Highlands. A pretty little village of just 920 residents, Robertson offers many nearby vantage points for spectacular views right down the coast. It can also get very cold in winter, so visitors should choose their timing carefully.

A rather bizarre-looking large reddish-brown concrete mound in the town's centre is actually the Robertson Big Potato, although visitors can be forgiven for not

The coastline at Murramurang National Park, north of Batemans Bay.

seeing an immediate resemblance. Robertson is very close to many natural attractions like Fitzroy Falls in the nearby Morton National Park, which provides bushwalkers with some good walking trails. The local pie shop is quite famous for its tasty pies and it is well worth making this a snack stop on a drive through the Southern Highlands.
Map ref: page 456 F3

SHELLHARBOUR

Shellharbour gets its name from the large number of Aboriginal middens in the area, all listed by the Heritage Commission and regarded as archaeologically significant. In the 1830s Shellharbour was used as a port. By 1855 an embryonic village had formed but with the coming of the railway, its importance declined—until more recently when tourism hit. The town now has 2000 residents.

Just 22 km (14 miles) south of Wollongong, 130 km (81 miles) south of Sydney, Shellharbour is extremely popular with surfers, but there are plenty of other things to do. To the north, surrounded by a 25 km (16 miles) cycleway, Lake Illawarra also affords a chance for waterskiing, paddleboating, sailboarding, canoeing, fishing and prawning; in the town bowls and golf are on offer. To the south is the Marine Aquatic Reserve at Bushrangers Bay, a favoured spot for snorkellers and scuba divers. The rainforest at nearby Macquarie National Park is another attraction and bushwalking is popular here.
Map ref: page 456 G3

SOUTH COAST WINE REGION

Although its climate is not subtropical like the Northern Rivers, the South Coast zone has similar

Winegrowing on the South Coast started in the 1970s.

problems—summer rainfall, high humidity, rot and mildew. Consequently the area's winemakers have been attracted to chambourcin, but chardonnay, shiraz and cabernet sauvignon have all done well in good vintages also. Most of the winemaking is done by contract.

Wineries are a late addition to the South Coast, most dating back no further than the 1970s. Few are household names and fewer aspire to be so, but some—most notably Coolangatta Estate at Shoalhaven Heads and Cambewarra Estate in Cambewarra—are making quality wines. The heart of the area, the beautiful Shoalhaven River region and Nowra, is tourist territory and its wineries would not exist without them. The South Coast area also contains the outlying Sydney region, where Vicary's Winery at Luddenham, has been operating continuously since 1923. The woolshed dances held on Friday and Saturday nights in Vicary's old timber shearing shed are still quite popular.
Map: page 456 F4

TATHRA

Tathra is the smallest of the towns on the Sapphire Coast and is home to 1700 residents. Lying on the coast between

Secluded stretch of Nelson Beach in Mimosa National Park, close to the small coastal town of Tathra.

Bermagui and Merimbula, it requires a detour off the Princes Highway at Bega. Sydney is 461 km (286 miles) to the north.

The town is rich in history and marine tradition. The old timber wharf, which has been restored by the National Trust, now houses a museum in its old cargo shed. It is a mecca for anglers, history lovers and photographers.

Tathra Beach is 3 km (1.9 miles) long. It is patrolled in summer and offers good surfing and it also gives anglers the chance at salmon and tailor. Mogareka Inlet is safer for small children. There is also good scuba diving at Tathra, with local corals, underwater caves and shipwrecks providing plenty of interest and variety. Visitors can also camp and bushwalk at nearby Mimosa Rocks National Park and Bournda State Recreation Area. Other local activities include bowls and tennis.
Map ref: page 456 E8

TUMBARUMBA

Halfway between Sydney and Melbourne in the western foothills of the Snowy Mountains, 507 km (315 miles) south-west of Sydney, Tumbarumba is like Jindabyne on the other side of the range: a good base for skiers in winter. In Tumbarumba's case the local snow venue is Mount Selwyn.

Tourism is only one industry for the district, with fat stock, wool, timber and dairying also contributing to the local economy. In

the 1850s, however, the magnet for people—particularly the Chinese—was gold. However, the rush did not last very long and the population today is only 1600.

Tumbarumba is named after the Tumbarumba Creek run, which in turn borrowed the name from a local Aboriginal dialect. It means 'sounding ground', used to describe the sound of kangaroos bounding over certain areas of the hills.

There are nearby walking tracks, including one named after Hume and Hovell that has picnicking and camping facilities. In designated areas fossicking for gold, sapphires and zircons is permitted. Other alternatives are trail rides or high-country horseback safaris. There is also canoeing and whitewater rafting, mountain biking and 4WD touring, or you can visit the Snowy Mountains hydro-electric power stations. Horseraces have been held in Tumbarumba since 1882. There is a local vineyard, a historic museum and a wool and craft centre. Tumbarumba lies to the west of Kosciuszko National Park and so is a good base from which to explore the national park.

In January Tumbarumba holds its annual rodeo, while February sees the running of the Tumbarumba Cup. In March, it is Showtime and there is a Polocrosse Carnival in May. There is an art show in June and, in November, the Tumbarumba Heritage Week and Street Parade is on.
Map ref: page 456 A6

Causeway on Wadbilliga River in the national park.

TUMBARUMBA WINE REGION

Tumbarumba is the youngest of the southern New South Wales wine regions. Previously the preserve of fly fishers, it is high and remote. Grapes were first planted here in the early 1980s, but there are still only about 405 ha (1000 acres) under vine. BRL Hardy has an interest in Tumbarumba but Southcorp, Australia's largest wine company, is the major presence.

There are a couple of very small wineries here also. Tumbarumba is one of the cooler regions in Australia and most of its grapes go into sparkling wines. Sauvignon blanc is the predominant table wine but chardonnay could become the most prominent white; the pinot noir also has a lot of potential.
Map ref: page 456 A6

TUMUT

A tranquil, pretty town of 6500 with poplar-lined avenues, Tumut is 434 km (270 miles) south-west of Sydney. It owes its name to the Aboriginal 'doomut', or 'quiet resting place by the river'. In 1824 Hume and Hovell passed through this lush valley with its meandering watercourse on their way to Port Phillip Bay. The first settler in the district was a Thomas McAlister, who founded the Darbalara Station in the early 1830s. (This station subsequently produced the Darbalara shorthorn strain of cattle.) By 1887 Tumut was a municipality.

Today, Tumut's economy relies on the area's agricultural and pastoral pursuits but softwood timber milling is also quite an important contributor. The State forests in the district contribute to a certain European ambience in Tumut, particularly around nearby Blowering Dam, where the mountains come down to meet the water. The local residents waterski and sail on Blowering Dam and, of course, come here to fish for trout and perch. Camping is permitted on the foreshores. The area can be explored by 4WD and bushwalking. A canoeing trip on the Tumut and Goobraganda rivers is another possibility, or visitors can opt to go horse riding.

In winter, skiers will find Mount Selwyn easily accessible. Yarrangobilly Caves are nearby and visitors can go on guided or self-guided tours through limestone caverns. You can relax in a thermal pool that stays at a constant 27° C.

Tumut claims it has the oldest horseracing club in New South Wales. The course is set on the banks of the Tumut River and features two magnificent grandstands, built in 1909.

Seven races are held each year in Tumut, with the major event being the Tumut Cup, which is held on Boxing Day. The Festival of the Falling Leaf is held during April and, in October, the town holds the Bogong Fest.
Map ref: page 456 A5

ULLADULLA

Ulladulla owes its name to the Aboriginal word for 'safe harbour'. One of its earliest settlers was the Reverend Thomas Kendall, grandfather of the poet Henry Kendall, who was born there. Though timber was the town's raison d'être in the 1820s, nowadays it is fishing and tourism that maintains the town's prosperity.

Ulladulla (population 9000), situated 246 km (153 miles) south of Sydney on the Princes Highway, has a large fishing fleet. At Easter there is the Blessing of the Fleet, culminating in a fireworks display on the night of Easter Sunday. It is a tradition that originated in Italy. The town also holds a fishing carnival in May.

Ulladulla is also the centre for New South Wales abalone divers, complete with a processing plant on the harbour. Most of the produce is exported to Japan.

Ulladulla's neighbouring towns include Milton, Mollymook and Burrill Lake, all of which are on the eastern side of the Budawang Range. (This is where the Clyde River, with its famous oysters, rises.) Often the towns of Milton and Ulladulla are referred to as a complete entity, but in reality they are actually quite different, with Milton sitting high in the hills and Ulladulla being right on the coast. In Ulladulla, visitors can take part in all kinds of water sports, plus there is also bushwalking, as well as croquet, golf and tennis.

Nearby beaches like Mollymook can be both great for kids and at the same time host surf titles, but if it is too rough there are other spots to swim, including Wairo, Racecourse and Narrawallee. And, of course, the lakes such as Burrill, Cajola and Tabourie are always calm. Ulladulla also offers great fishing for the amateur, and waterskiing for those who want it.

Within easy range are natural attractions such as Pigeon House Mountain, named by James Cook as he sailed up the coast in 1770. Heading south is Murramarang National Park, where the kangaroos on the beach eat out of your hand.
Map ref: page 456 F5

WADBILLIGA NATIONAL PARK

Inland from Narooma on the Far South Coast, the rugged eastern escarpment and plateau of the Great Dividing Range are protected in this park, which almost meets Deua National Park on its northern boundary. The Tuross, Wadbilliga and Brogo rivers rise in these mountains and have carved their wide, deep valleys through the granite of the park; walking tracks to the spectacular Tuross Falls and the Tuross Gorge are recommended for experienced and well-equipped bushwalkers. Although this park is primarily wilderness, it does allow 4WD access via roads from Cobargo and Eurobodalla. You can bush camp at the Cascades.
Map ref: page 456 D7

Vintage cars line Winyard Street, the main street in the town of Tumut.

The stunning coastline at Stanwell Park, near Wollongong, from Bald Hill Lookout.

WOLLONGONG

Known as 'the Gong', Wollongong was incorporated in 1859 as Australia's first country municipality and is now the third largest city in New South Wales. It is 104 km (65 miles) south of Sydney and has a population of over 211, 400.

Navigators Bass and Flinders landed at Lake Illawarra in 1796 and the area was first traversed by Europeans in 1797, when survivors from the wreck of the *Sydney Cove* discovered coal at Coalcliff. For many years, due to the ruggedness of the surrounding ranges, all visits to the district were by sea, but in 1815, on the advice of Aboriginals, explorer and pastoralist Charles Throsby pushed a mob of cattle through to good pasture. Others followed, and cedar-getting became an important industry and a town was planned in 1834. The name Wollongong is thought to be an onomatopoeic attempt by the local Aboriginals to duplicate the sound of waves breaking on the beach.

These days, Wollongong has a reputation of being a 'smog city', largely due to the proximity of Port Kembla—a steel-producing centre since 1928—and as such, considered not worth visiting. Nothing could be further from the truth. The local lighthouse was built in 1872. Illawarra Historical Society Museum has a Victorian parlour. Mount Kembla Village has a pioneer kitchen, blacksmith's shop, original miners' huts and a reconstruction of a tragic mining disaster in 1902.

At Bald Hill Lookout, overlooking Stanwell Park Beach, is a monument to the aviation pioneer Lawrence Hargreaves. It is also a popular spot for hang gliding.

Those who prefer to be more active can also enjoy the many good surfing beaches, foreshore parks, or go prawning, fishing or sailing—there are hire boats available on Lake Illawarra.

As Wollongong is completely ringed by national parks—indeed, there is a chronic shortage of building land into which Wollongong can expand—there are plenty of walking trails in the district. The panoramas from the Illawarra Range, particularly Mount Kiera and Sublime Point, above Austinmere, are simply stunning.
Map ref: page 456 G3

YARRANGOBILLY

This historic village, 497 km (309 miles) south-west of Sydney, is a shadow of what it once was, with only Cotterill's Cottage (named after the family who lived there until the 1950s) and some public facilities still standing. Yarrangobilly is Aboriginal for 'flowing stream'. In winter, the village is frequently covered in snow.

With a tiny population of only 10 people, Yarrangobilly is a great camping and fishing spot, with fascinating spongy tundra-type vegetation. The Yarrangobilly River is chillingly clean. The nearest 'hot running water' accommodation is at Talbingo. Alternatively, stay at Tumut or Adaminaby.

Most people come to the region to visit nearby Yarrangobilly Caves, which were carved by the river out of limestone around 440 million years ago. There are also several good bushwalks around the area.
Map ref: page 456 B6

YASS

Originally called McDougall's Plains by the first Europeans to see the area, explorers Hume and Hovell, the town of Yass was gazetted in 1837. The name means 'running water'.
Nowadays Yass is the centre of a fertile agricultural and pastoral area, with fine Merino wool, and sheep and cattle studs. It has a population of 4840.

Close to the junction of two major highways, the Hume and the Barton, Yass is 292 km (181 miles) south-west of Sydney, and was once thought to be a good site for the proposed Federal capital. Hamilton Hume, who is buried in Yass cemetery in a tomb of his own design, settled in Yass. His house, Cooma Cottage, is listed by the National Trust and is open for inspection.

Yass has always been a rather prosperous town, and its fine old buildings attest to this. (There are still hitching rails along the street.) The museum in Comur Street is worth visiting to see just how Yass made its money in the old days compared with today.

The nearby Gooradigbee River offers excellent trout fishing. Further south is Carey's Cave, with some marvellous limestone formations. Also to the south, Burrinjuck Dam offers a chance to bushwalk, fish, or indulge in water sports. Yass holds its agricultural show in March and a rodeo in November.
Map ref: page 456 C4

YOUNG

The undisputed cherry capital of New South Wales, Young is 378 km (235 miles) south-west of Sydney and has a population of 8500 inhabitants. This town came into being because of a gold rush during the 1860s.

Lambing Flat, as the township was first known, was the site of the infamous anti-Chinese riots. The town was eventually renamed after Sir John Young, who was the Governor of New South Wales between 1861 and 1867.

Today the Young district produces wheat, wool, lucerne and fat lambs. In town, the Lambing Flat Folk Museum and the Burrangong Art Gallery should not be missed. Four kilometres (2.5 miles) south-east of town, the Chinaman's Dam recreation area has picnic and barbecue facilities, a children's playground and several scenic walks.

There are a number of local wineries—Wodonga Hill, Demondrille Vineyard, Hansons Hill Top Winery, Grove Estate Vineyard and Chalkers Crossing Winery—and all of these are open for wine tastings and sales.
See also Hilltops Wine Region
Map ref: page 456 A2

Buddhist temple at Wollongong.

CENTRAL-EAST NEW SOUTH WALES

The coastal strip from Sydney to Newcastle, the birthplace of European Australia, is the most densely populated part of the country. Running further to the north is a sparkling string of lakes and beaches scattered with large and small holiday and fishing towns. Inland, beyond a wide ribbon of adjoining national parks, are the gracious old towns and rolling plains of the central west.

Although now no longer a steel-making centre, the industrial city of Newcastle was built on the powerhouse of coal from the vast reserves that underlie the nearby Hunter Valley. Winemaking in the Hunter dates back from the 1830s; today it is the most-visited wine region in the country, with tastings available from more than 100 wineries. The Mudgee wine area also has a wine history, with its first vines planted in 1858; and a growing reputation for fine foods. Dubbo sits at the junction of the Mitchell, Newell, Golden and Castlereagh highways. Regional centre of the central-west, it is the location of the Western Plains Zoo, the first open-range zoo in Australia and worth spending a day.

The Blue Mountains form a maze of high ridges and blind valleys. They contained early settlement around Sydney until 1813, when a way was found for pastoralists and livestock to spread west onto the inland plains. The convict-built road was opened in 1815; the present highway, with its picturesque towns and villages, follows basically the same route. The discovery of gold near Bathurst in 1851 saw boom towns spring up almost overnight. In the 1870s many were photographed by Beaufoy Merlin (the Holtermann collection), whose images show the crowded streets of gold towns Hill End and Sofala (both now are virtually ghost towns) and the still recognisable shopfronts of Gulgong, childhood haunt of poet Henry Lawson.

Natural landscapes are spectacular. Lakes, inlets, islands, bays and sandy ocean beaches line the coast. Migrating whales are sighted from headlands, and dolphins catch waves with surfers. Fringing the Hawkesbury River is sandstone ridge country famed for its wildflowers. Magnificent parks continue in an almost unbroken line from Sydney's northern outskirts west to Wollemi National Park, where until recently was hidden the Wollemi pine, a survivor from the age of dinosaurs.

OPPOSITE: On Tuggerah Lake, Toukley offers safe swimming and pleasant parklands. You can hire sailboards, paddleboats, surf skis, canoes, jetskis catamarans or kayaks.

Numerous horse, sheep and cattle studs are in the Mudgee district, an area known for its wine and food. Surrounded by hills, it is in the lush Cudgegong River Valley.

REGIONAL FEATURE

The Hunter Valley

Located just two hours north of Sydney, the Hunter Valley is Australia's best-known and most-visited wine region. It was the first area in New South Wales to establish itself as a winemaking centre and pioneered the production of several varietals in Australia, most notably chardonnay. Recently, it has gained an exalted reputation, its sémillons in particular earning a place in the hearts of wine lovers the world over.

The region is divided into the Upper and Lower Hunter. Despite a long history, the Upper Hunter, centred on the towns of Denman and Muswellbrook, has given rise to only a handful of successful winemaking enterprises. The much larger Lower Hunter, which extends north and west from the town of Cessnock, is the site of the majority of the region's wineries and has produced its best wines.

History

The Hunter Valley was settled soon after it was named in 1797, but initially the focus was on coal rather than wine. It wasn't until the 1830s that James Busby, now considered the father of Australian viticulture, and several others planted vines in the Upper Hunter.

Encouraging results led to the founding of the Hunter Valley Viticultural Association in 1847. The Pokolbin and Rothbury subregions, now at the heart of the Lower Hunter, were planted in the 1860s. The late nineteenth century saw the emergence of several famous names. George Wyndham founded the Dalwood vineyards, and, in 1883, Dan Tyrrell made his first wine at the age of 14, beginning an amazing run of 76 consecutive vintages. By 1910, production in the Upper Hunter had ceased temporarily, partly because the region was seen as too difficult to reach.

In 1921, one of Australia's greatest ever winemakers, Maurice O'Shea, began his career in the Lower Hunter, when he took over his family's Mount Pleasant winery and vineyards. He then joined McWilliams in 1932, at a tough time for the local industry. The market had changed and 85 per cent of production was devoted to fortifieds. By the mid 1930s, the area under vines had fallen from 1050 ha (2595 acres) a decade earlier to around half that figure. Undeterred, O'Shea continued to make great table wines, and those he produced in the 1940s and 1950s are still eagerly sought today.

By 1963, the Hunter's wineries were all large enterprises. In that year, however, Dr Max Lake launched Lake's Folly, Australia's first boutique winery, beginning a trend that would transform the industry. The Hunter has produced several other prominent winemakers, including Len Evans, founder of the Rothbury Estate.

Grape Varieties

If there is one grape upon which the Lower Hunter has built its reputation, it is sémillon. Chardonnay is now more extensively planted, but aged Hunter sémillons are justifiably world famous. In time, these great wines pick up toast, honey, butter and lemon characters that are utterly entrancing. Of the other white wines, the verdelho is perhaps the pick of the crop; though the chardonnay is popular, its richness is not to the taste of every palate.

Earthy, leathery flavours dominate Hunter reds, most obviously in the shiraz which is almost as distinctive as the local sémillon. It seems improbable that pinot noir could work in the Hunter, and most agree that it doesn't. However, many of the great O'Shea wines and some of Lindemans' finest Hunter River Burgundies contained a touch of pinot, and many wineries persist in planting this grape.

The Upper Hunter is better suited to white wines, as Penfolds found out the hard way when it moved to the region in 1960 and began planting red varieties. Disappointing results eventually led to it selling out to Rosemount in 1996, the year in which another major winery, Arrowfield, began operating in the Upper Hunter. These few producers have since determined that the conditions are best suited to the production of chardonnay and sémillon.

The Hunter is renowned for its outstanding white wines, especially chardonnay and sémillon.

OPPOSITE: Some viticulturalists believe the Hunter's vineyards are too hot and have inappropriate rainfall patterns for grape growing. Despite this, the region continues to produce great wines.

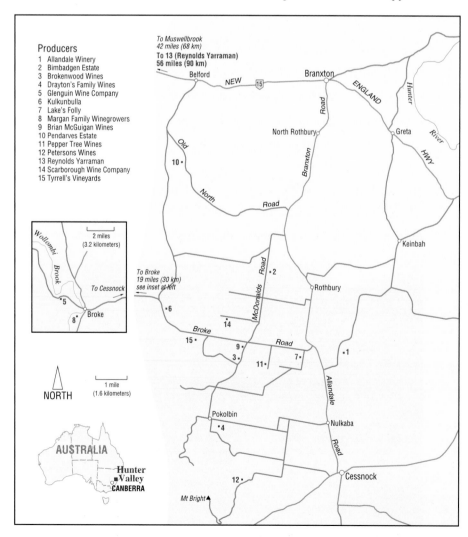

Producers
1 Allandale Winery
2 Bimbadgen Estate
3 Brokenwood Wines
4 Drayton's Family Wines
5 Glenguin Wine Company
6 Kulkunbulla
7 Lake's Folly
8 Margan Family Winegrowers
9 Brian McGuigan Wines
10 Pendarves Estate
11 Pepper Tree Wines
12 Petersons Wines
13 Reynolds Yarraman
14 Scarborough Wine Company
15 Tyrrell's Vineyards

The best vineyards in the Lower Hunter lie at the foot of the volcanic Brokenback Range.

Producers

Allandale Winery, Lower Hunter

*Established 1978 Owners Wally and Julie Atallah
Production 15,000 cases Vineyard area 7 ha (17 acres)*

Allandale was already a famous vineyard in the 1800s, winning worldwide acclaim and operating, much as it does today, by working with selected growers. Now revived, the winery has developed a solid following during winemaker Bill Sneddon's decade-long tenure. The range includes a popular Chardonnay and a selection of excellent wines made with fruit from the Hilltops district. Allandale's mailing list occasionally provides access to older vintages.

Bimbadgen Estate, Lower Hunter

*Established 1972 Owner Mulpha Australia Pty Ltd
Production 50,000 cases Vineyard area 45 ha (111 acres)*

The name of this beautifully sited winery means, rather appropriately, 'lovely views'. Winemaker van de Scheur produces a fairly traditional range but has considerable experience and is one of the industry's lateral thinkers. He has set up several innovative schemes, ranging from wine-tasting events and planting days (which save time and money) to special clubs (which engender loyalty and save on marketing costs).

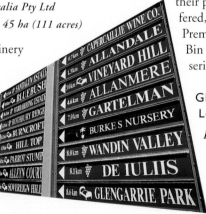

Wine lovers are spoilt for choice in the Hunter.

Brokenwood Wines, Lower Hunter

Established 1970 Owner Private syndicate Production 60,000 cases Vineyard area 57 ha (141 acres)

A flagship winery for the Hunter region, Brokenwood also owns the highly regarded Yarra winery and Seville Estate, and has significant interests in Cowra. It has long sourced fruit from around the nation for its wines, but currently it's a single-vineyard product, the Graveyard Shiraz—drawn from land that was once intended to be a cemetery—that stands out. Now the region's leading shiraz, it is always in demand. The Brokenwood Sémillon, one of the Hunter's most enjoyable versions of this varietal, is also outstanding.

Drayton's Family Wines, Lower Hunter

*Established 1853 Owners Max Drayton and family
Production 100,000 cases Vineyard area 80 ha (198 acres)*

The Draytons have been making wines here for almost 150 years and although they no longer hold the pre-eminent position they once did, high production levels are testimony to the continuing popularity of their products. Several ranges are offered, the most impressive being the Premium—especially the Verdelho and Bin 5555 Shiraz—and the excellent series of Individual Vineyard wines.

Glenguin Wine Company, Lower Hunter

Established Mid 1980s Owner Robin Tedder Production 15,000 cases Vineyard area 15 ha (37 acres)

Winemaker Robin Tedder and his viticulturist brother Andrew have pooled their skills to make this one of the most exciting emerging wineries in the region. The wines all come from individual vineyards, even those made with fruit from Mudgee and Orange. The Mudgee Shiraz is confirmation of that area's promise, but long-term fame is more likely to be achieved with the Hunter Sémillon. These early releases suggest that Glenguin will eventually rate with the best.

Kulkunbulla, Lower Hunter

Established 1996 Owner Kulkunbulla Pty Ltd
Production 2400 cases Vineyard area 6 ha (15 acres)

Originally part of the Brokenback Estate, formerly owned by Rothbury, this small company has made a significant impression in its first few years. Early releases suggest that its future lies with chardonnay, though the sémillons will gain a higher profile in time.

Lake's Folly, Lower Hunter

Established 1963 Owner Peter Fogarty Production 4000 cases Vineyard area 12 ha (30 acres)

Dr Max Lake sold this, the country's first boutique winery, to Perth businessman Peter Fogarty in May 2000; however, his son and winemaker Stephen Lake remains as a consultant. The range consists of a 'Cabernets'—a blend of cabernet sauvignon, petit verdot, shiraz and merlot—and a Chardonnay, both of which benefit from extended cellaring.

Margan Family Winegrowers, Lower Hunter

Established 1997 Owners Andrew and Lisa Margan
Production 20,000 cases Vineyard area 35 ha (87 acres)

Son of the Australian wine writer, Frank Margan, winemaker Andrew learned his craft at Tyrrell's before going it alone with this winery. An advocate of careful selection of varieties for particular sites and of restricting yields, his first releases have been well received, especially the Sémillon and Shiraz.

Brian McGuigan Wines, Lower Hunter

Established 1967 Owner Brian McGuigan Wines Ltd
Production 620,000 cases Vineyard area 1280 ha (3,163 acres)

One of the wine industry's great salesmen, Brian McGuigan did much to pave the way for Australian producers in the tough American market during his time at Wyndham Estate. More recently, he has turned his winery into a tourist stop that also includes a restaurant, cafe, bakery and cheese company.

Pendarves Estate, Lower Hunter

Established 1986 Owners Philip and Belinda Norrie
Production 5500 cases Vineyard area 20 ha (49 acres)

Philip Norrie's vineyards are situated on an outcrop of limestone that is unique in the Hunter. As well as producing standard Hunter varieties, he has joined several other winemakers in championing verdelho and other unusual varieties such as chambourcin.

Pepper Tree Wines, Lower Hunter

Established 1983 Owner Pepper Tree Wines Pty Ltd
Production 75,000 cases Vineyard area 60 ha (148 acres)

The Pepper Tree winery forms part of an attractive complex incorporating Roberts Restaurant and the Convent Guesthouse. The company has a significant interest in Coonawarra's Parker Estate and multi-regional blends are a speciality. Winemaker Chris Cameron has pinned his hopes on his fine merlot, aiming to make it Australia's best.

Petersons Wines, Lower Hunter

Established 1981 Owner Colin Peterson Production 15,000 cases Vineyard area 16 ha (40 acres)

Originally founded by Colin Peterson's father, Ian, this small winery has attracted a sizeable following, particularly for its Chardonnay and Back Block reds. Many of the super-premium wines are only available to cellar-door visitors. The associated Peterson House, opened in 1993, specialises in premium sparkling wine.

Reynolds Yarraman, Upper Hunter

Established 1968 Owners Jon and Jane Reynolds
Production 15,000 cases Vineyard area 60 ha (148 acres)

Winemaker Jon Reynolds had a successful career with Houghtons and Wyndham before taking over the old Horderns Wybong Estate, which dated back to 1837. Since then, he has made some wonderful wines, most notably the Sémillon. His range made with fruit from the Orange district is also highly recommended.

Scarborough Wine Company, Lower Hunter

Established 1987 Owners Ian and Merrelea Scarborough
Production 10,000 cases Vineyard area 12 ha (30 acres)

This winery, which has a sensational view, is planted on one of the few patches of terra rossa in the Hunter Valley. Former contract winemaker Ian Scarborough produces one of the region's best chardonnays, and also makes small amounts of pinot noir in some years. A second chardonnay is produced for export markets.

Tyrrell's Vineyards, Lower Hunter

Established 1858 Owners Murray and Bruce Tyrrell
Production 750,000 cases Vineyard area 507 ha (205 acres)

Edward Tyrrell planted the first vines on this estate in 1858. In 1883, at age 14, Dan Tyrrell took over the winemaking and worked 76 consecutive vintages before passing the reins to nephew Murray. Shiraz and sémillon (especially the Vat 1) are the stars here, but the pioneering Vat 47 Chardonnay is also one of Australia's finest. The Long Flat commercial wines are also extremely popular.

The bottling plant at Tyrrell's Vineyards in the Lower Hunter.

Antique wine presses are on display in the Golden Grape Estate wine museum near Pokolbin in the Lower Hunter.

Places in
CENTRAL-EAST NEW SOUTH WALES

BARRINGTON TOPS NATIONAL PARK

Both Barrington Tops and Gloucester Tops form a high plateau on the Great Dividing Range between Scone and Gloucester on the Mid North Coast. It is an area of very high rainfall and sudden, dramatic weather changes—storms and even snowstorms. The park obtained a World Heritage listing for its quite magnificent and diverse vegetation, which ranges from snow gums and heathlands at the higher altitudes to cool-temperate rainforest with the deciduous Antarctic beeches in more sheltered gullies and subtropical rainforest in the lower valleys.
Map ref: page 459 J3

BATHURST

Marking the very end of the Great Western Highway out of Sydney, about 200 km (124 miles) to the east, Bathurst is a city for history buffs. Being this country's oldest

inland city, Bathurst has some truly magnificent buildings reflecting its early heritage: the Court House in particular is one example. Governor Macquarie named Bathurst after the then Secretary of State for the Colonies, Earl Bathurst. Gold was discovered in 1851 at Summer Hill Creek, about 50 km (31 miles) to the north-west, and the resulting rush saw nearby towns like Ophir, Rockley, Sofala and O'Connell spring up almost overnight. The news of easy wealth also brought bushrangers such as Frank Gardiner, Johnny Gilbert, Ben Hall, Vane and O'Meally into the area.

In 1862, Cobb and Co established its first service in New South Wales, with Bathurst as the headquarters. Charles Darwin visited Bathurst in 1836, and a plaque in Machattie Park commemorates the event. More recently, J.B. Chifley, who took over from John Curtin as Labor Prime Minister after Curtin's death in 1945, was born in Bathurst in 1885, and was also buried

in the Bathurst Cemetery in 1951. The house that he grew up in is located in Busby Street.

Today Bathurst has a population of 31,000. It is home to the Mount Panorama racing circuit, site of 'the Great Race' watched by millions of Australians every year. Bathurst is situated on the Macquarie River, which is a mecca for canoeists who often use the nearby Bridle Track to access local camping places such as Bruinbun. The convict-built Bridle Track is a spectacular drive in itself, ending up at the historic old goldmining town of Hill End.

Nearby Mountain View is a picturesque cherry, sheep and cattle property and wildlife refuge. This is an old goldmining area and there is also a museum and relics and you can try your luck fossicking for sapphires and gold, go fishing for trout or ride horses. There is accommodation available here and also at Yarrabin, a 400 ha (988 acre) sheep-grazing and wildlife refuge.
Map ref: page 458 D7

BELMONT

Belmont, a quiet town on the eastern shore of Lake Macquarie, is 155 km (96 miles) north of Sydney. The home of the famous Australian artist, Sir William Dobell (open to the public) is situated at nearby Wangi Wangi; Belmont is otherwise an almost culture-free zone. Home to 6250, sport's the name of the game here, with swimming, fishing and sailing being the most popular activities. Belmont is, in fact, a huge yachting centre on Lake Macquarie.
Map ref: page 459 J6

BLAYNEY

Blayney (population 2610) is 235 km (146 miles) west of Sydney and is in the centre of a rich agricultural district producing wool, fat lambs, wheat, vegetables and fruit. There are also many sheep, cattle, horse and pig studs in the area, but for many years Blayney has been most famous for its abattoir.

Visitors, however, will no doubt be more interested in this town's many arts and crafts shops, and its proximity to the delightful historic village of Carcoar. The local residents enjoy Carcoar Dam during the summer months for various water sports and horse riding is also popular. Also be aware that Blayney can be extremely cold during the winter.
Map ref: page 458 C8

Sail Point at Belmont.

BLUE MOUNTAINS NATIONAL PARK

Being only about 100 km (62 miles) west of the Sydney Harbour Bridge, the Blue Mountains National Park has the highest number of visitors of any New South Wales park. The raw beauty of its towering sandstone cliffs and very deep gorges are the result of this continual weathering action. These very same features formed a natural barrier to the early settlers. However, in 1813 Blaxland, Wentworth and Lawson found a route through and behind them a rough road was cut through the thick, scrubby bush to the rich plains to the west—the present day Great Western highway. There is an alternative route, along the Bells Line of Road, which forms the park's northern boundary.

The development of the Blue Mountains area was hastened when oil shale seams were discovered in the Wolgan Valley in the 1860s. The Great Western Railway, built a little later, in 1868, ensured the scenic beauty of the mountains was within reach of Sydney residents. so the entire region became a big tourist attraction.

As early as the 1890s, reserves were established to protect the natural areas within the mountains. The Blue Mountains National Park was proclaimed in 1959.

Around the major towns of Katoomba, Leura and Blackheath there are accessible lookouts and superb picnic locations. Both the Scenic Railway, with its near vertical drop, and the Skyway cable car that stretches across deep, fern-filled gullies, provide breathtaking

Barrington Tops National Park offers many walks through World-heritage rainforest.

The rugged sandstone escarpments of the Blue Mountains were a formidable natural barrier for early explorers.

views. The most famous attraction in the mountains is the rock formation known as the Three Sisters, which is situated in Katoomba. There are viewing platforms, walks to the base of the rock formations and an information and souvenir shop as well as places to eat.

There are also very good lookouts off the Bells Line of Road at Pierces Pass, Mount Banks. At Mount Tomah there is the excellent High Country botanical garden.

More active pursuits in this area include bushwalking deep in the Grose Valley, abseiling off the sheer sandstone cliffs or canyoning and whitewater rafting. Bushwalking is particularly popular and the park has many wonderful well-known trails. The best time is in spring for the wildflowers as winters can be bitterly cold and snow can fall. Some walks are easy and include scenic lookouts; others extend into deep river valleys and require peak fitness or an overnight camp.

Much of the Blue Mountains is wilderness, but Newnes and the Newnes State Forest, on the southern fringe of the Wollemi National Park, offer other interesting places to explore by 4WD. There is some camping in the park but the southern section is much more remote and walkers must be very fit and well-equipped. Also, despite their clean and fresh appearance, streams in the Blue Mountains are polluted and all water should be boiled.
Map ref: page 458 F9

BOOTI BOOTI NATIONAL PARK

This small park, on a narrow strip of land between the Pacific Ocean and Wallis Lake in the beautiful Myall Lakes district of the Mid North Coast, is 10 km (6.2 miles) south of Forster. The area is justly renowned for great surfing beaches, sailing and windsurfing opportunities on the saltwater lake, as well as for its fishing.
Map ref: page 459 L4

BRISBANE WATER NATIONAL PARK

Set in the very rugged sandstone country in the lower reaches of the Hawkesbury River, about an hour's drive—50 km (31 miles)—north of Sydney and just to the west of Gosford, this park is a real boating paradise. Covering some 11,300 ha (27,922 acres), it features peaceful bays and mangrove-fringed inlets for fishing, broad reaches for water-skiing, plus many deep gorges with rainforest and heavily timbered slopes. The main attractions are the many hundreds of kilometres of walking trails through superbly scenic terrain and some of the best Aboriginal art in the Sydney district. The Great North Walk from Sydney to Newcastle dissects the park and involves an overnight walk but there are also a number of shorter walks leading off the main track. There is basic bush camping without any facilities, and no 4WD tracks. The Somersby Falls area has some picnic facilities and there is a walking trail to the falls. The focal point of the park is at Girrakool on the main road from Calga where there are picnic facilities and a number of walking trails.
Map ref: page 459 H7

BULAHDELAH

On the Pacific Highway, 261 km (162 miles) to the north of Sydney, Bulahdelah (population 1100) is the main aquatic gateway to the splendours of Myall Lakes. It is surrounded by water, bush and mountain scenery. The word 'Bulahdelah' has seen 13 different spellings since the original 'boola-deela', which comes from Kattang, the language of the Worimi, the ancestral inhabitants of the Great Lakes. It means 'place beneath the mountain where the two rivers meet'; the two rivers being the Myall and the Crawford.

Since the early nineteenth century, the area has been a supplier of high quality hardwood, and numerous local State forests still supply the industry. The forests also house a diverse range of flora and fauna, including 275 species of birds, 45 species of mammals and 41 species of reptiles and frogs. There are some particularly rare animals in this list, including the golden-tipped bat, yellow-bellied glider, sooty owl and the nocturnal tiger quoll. On Bulahdelah Mountain alone, there are 16 different species of orchid.

The many things to see in and around Bulahdelah include visiting the historic Court House, the old inn which was a staging post for Cobb and Co, or the Bulahdelah Steam Logging Railway. Then there is the Mungo Brush and the old trestle bridge. And of course, there's the Grandis (*Eucalyptus grandis*), which is the tallest tree in the State. Hiring a houseboat to explore the lakes system is a popular activity, as are the many water sports with boats for hire. You can also go bushwalking, birdwatching, fishing and horse riding.
Map ref: page 459 L4

Springtime is the ideal bushwalking season in Brisbane Water National Park.

Cessnock is a peaceful country town in the heart of the Hunter Valley vineyards.

CANOWINDRA

Even newsreaders often pronounce Canowindra phonetically, not as it should be: 'Ca-nown-dra'. Its name comes from an Aboriginal term for 'home'. Sited about 300 km (187 miles) west of Sydney, the town is the service centre for a district that produces mainly lucerne, wheat, wool and fat lambs.

Canowindra, which has a population of 1720, is most famous as the hot-air ballooning capital of New South Wales, a title the town can still rightly claim. The best time to go aloft is during the calm hours of dawn, between the months of April and October, when the winds are at their lowest. Canowindra's historic claim to fame is that the town was taken over for three days by bushrangers Ben Hall and Frank Gardiner, holding the population in Robinson's Hotel (now called the Royal) and forcing them to party. The group also included the town's policeman!

More recently, fossil scientist Dr Alex Ritchie has been responsible for spreading Canowindra's name all over the world. Dr Ritchie has

researched a vast fossil find. Local stone beds contain thousands of fossils of Late Devonian fish (about 360 million years old) of over 100 different species. Hailed as one of the world's greatest fossil discoveries, the locals, with some government aid, are building an 'Age of Fishes' Museum, which will draw even more tourism into the district. An entire industry, including a website, has sprung up locally because of this exciting palaeontological discovery.
Map ref: page 458 B8

CESSNOCK

Like Lithgow, Cessnock suffers the stigma of being a coalmining town, but it has much to offer the tourist. Being a reasonably close 266 km (165 miles) north of Sydney, right in the heart of the Hunter Valley, it is a long day trip from the city.

Cessnock was named after Cessnock Castle in Scotland by the pioneer Scots settler John Campbell, who received a land grant of 2560 acres in 1826 from Governor Darling. His estate was subdivided in 1853 and a village developed. In

1856 coal was discovered and by the turn of the century this had brought prosperity to the district and the security of employment.

Running parallel with mining ventures was wine production. Today, Hunter Valley wines are regarded as being among the best in Australia—particularly its reds.

The Cessnock area was once a favourite haunt of bushrangers as it was close to Sydney but backed onto wild bush. Today the area encompasses over 20 towns and villages, with many descendants of the pioneer settlers of 150 years ago among the 17,500 residents. Free settlers and ticket-of-leave convicts became graziers, timber-getters, miners and grape-growers. Now, while the coal is still important, local industries include cattle breeding, dairying, mixed farming, timber milling, pottery and also clothing manufacture.

There is a lot to do in Cessnock. It is a very strong racing town, with both harness and greyhound events occurring on a regular basis, with the Dr Jurds Jungle Juice Cup held during July. Also well worth a visit is the historic twin-gabled timber building of Marthaville, which is on the Wollombi Road at Cessnock. It was the home of George Brown, a man of many talents. In his day he was builder, sawmiller, prospector, magistrate, coroner, councillor and vigneron! Built back in the 1880s, Marthaville is now home to many local art and craft exhibitions.

The biggest drawcard here is, of course, tours of the wineries, all of which have cellar door sales. Some of these wineries have been in the

same families since the first vines were planted, and the upper Hunter has some superb views as you journey from one vineyard to the other. Four-wheel drivers will also find plenty to do in the nearby Watagan Mountains, and people with cars will have much to see on scenic drives throughout the district. There are also opportunities to participate in bowls, golf, horse riding, swimming, tennis and hot-air ballooning.
See also Hunter Valley Wine Region
Map ref: page 459 H6

COWRA

Cowra (population 9200) takes its name from an Aboriginal word meaning 'rocks', no doubt because of the granite outcrops that overlook the town, which is 307 km (191 miles) west of Sydney.

In the early days, the Wiradjuri people moved along the Lachlan River from Forbes to Goolagong and onto Cowra where they split into three clans, one that moved to Carcoar, another went to Reids Flat, and the third remained in Cowra—the Erambie Aboriginal Reserve was declared there in 1891.

The district chiefly produces fat lambs, cattle, wool, wheat, lucerne, asparagus and also other vegetables. There are a number of secondary industries as well.

Although the Cowra district is rich in colonial history, it is somewhat dwarfed by the Japanese prisoner of war breakout of 1944, in which four Australian guards were killed and 247 prisoners lost their lives. The Japanese dead are

The Japanese Gardens in Cowra were created in memory of their prisoners of war.

Cattle farming is an important industry around Cowra.

buried in a separate cemetery, suitably marked, on the outskirts of town. Rather than creating lasting racial enmity, this event has actually made Cowra one of the most tolerant towns in New South Wales. Its calendar of events and festivals now mirrors those of Japan's, and its Japanese gardens, designed by Ken Nakajima, are based on the Imperial Gardens in Kyoto. Visitors can also see Australia's World Peace Bell, a replica of the one housed in the UN Building in New York.

Less well known is that Cowra also housed European migrants after World War II. In 1948, the first arrived and were housed in the World War II army base. Three thousand people from East European countries, including Poland, Czechoslovakia, Estonia, Latvia and Germany, arrived. The men were sent to work on projects like the Snowy Mountains Scheme while the women and children stayed in camp, where they were taught English. The migrants had a tremendous impact on Cowra. The women worked as domestics, cooks and fruit pickers. Many set up businesses. Edgell's was a major employer. Hundreds of children were educated and many moved on to illustrious careers. A reunion was held in Cowra in 1998.

There is much to see in Cowra. The museum is an interactive war, rural and rail experience, and it has over 8000 exhibits, including one of Australia's largest operating model railways. The Bellevue Nature Reserve and Observatory is a scenic lookout and nearby Conimbla National Park offers some rustic camping, bushwalks and

birdwatching. For water sports, head to Wyangala Dam or you can try horse riding at one of the areas many properties. Stargazing at the Darby's Falls Observatory can reveal the secrets of the stars. A craft shop is in town, while the bridge over the Lachlan River has pylons adorned with Aboriginal art. Cowra holds a Moon Viewing at the Japanese Gardens in April and then in May Japanese Children's Day is observed with activities and games. Also in May, Cowra hosts the largest dog show in New South Wales: the Kennel Club Championship Dog Show. July sees the Cowra Picnic Races and Wine Show; August, Japanese Bon (food) Day, with folk dancing and a special dinner; September the Agricultural Show. October is a big month, with both the Japan Cowra Cup Races and the delightful Sakura Matsuri (cherry blossom festival), featuring Japanese tea ceremonies, pottery, kite flying, martial arts and calligraphy demonstrations. Finally, in November, there is the Cowra Chardonnay Festival.
See also Cowra Wine Region
Map ref: page 458 B9

COWRA WINE REGION

Vines were first planted in Cowra, part of the greater Central Ranges wine region, in 1973, with chardonnay by far the predominant grape variety grown here.

Fruit grown in the region was widely used by wine producers such as Petaluma in the Adelaide Hills, Rothbury Estate in the Hunter Valley, Richmond Grove in the Barossa and Brokenwood and Hungerford Hill, which are both in the Hunter Valley.

Cowra Estate is the local winery with the highest profile, though as with the others, its wines are made outside the district. The increase in interest in the district has allowed the establishment of grape crushing facilities and it probably will not be long before the first winery is well-established. Cowra is considerably warmer than most people imagine, being much warmer than both the Hunter Valley and Mudgee districts, although humidity is low. It has proved to be a good source of dependable commercial whites that are excellent value.
Map ref: page 458 B9

CROWDY HEAD

Crowdy Head, 373 km (232 miles) north of Sydney, is very popular for just-caught prawns from the local fish co-op and also for sightseeing at the Crowdy Head lighthouse, which takes in sweeping views that extend from Cape Hawke all the way to Middle Brother Mountain. The place is home to 170 people but it boasts an excellent surf club and is a great place for many water sports. There are some very long stretches of Crowdy Bay National Park to explore either by bushwalking or by 4WD. Just to the north is Diamond Head, a craggy headland of unsurpassed beauty that provides a haven for campers, wildflower enthusiasts (in spring), and scuba divers and boardriders.
Map ref: page 459 M3

Crowdy Head is abundant in wildlife and offers rock pool exploration, birdwatching and spectacular headland bushwalks.

A concrete bridge over Wallis Lake links the twin towns of Forster and Tuncurry.

DENMAN

Six vineyards and some spectacular scenery surround the traditional rural town of Denman, which is about 300 km (186 miles) north of Sydney, has is home to 800. The Upper Hunter is a beautiful part of the State, with rolling pastures, rich farmland and rugged scrub-covered mountains. The area is well known for its wines: Rose-mount has been in operation here since the 1850s and other notable wineries include Arrowfield, Horse-shoe Vineyard and Inglewood. Like Scone, Denman is also a centre for horse breeding and has a number of magnificent horse studs.
See also Hunter Valley Wine Region
Map ref: page 458 G4

DUBBO

Dubbo, the 'Hub of the West', is 404 km (251 miles) west of Sydney and is the only city in the area. Proclaimed in 1966, John Oxley first visited the area in 1818 on his way to the Macquarie Marshes. In 1824 the first pastoralists arrived, followed, in 1833, by Robert Dul-hunty who took up a property he called Dubbo (the name has many interpretations, from 'red earth' to 'foggy' to 'head covering' and 'pos-sum-fur head-covering'). In 1841, recognising that Dubbo was an important stopping place on the stock route to Victoria, Frenchman Jean Serisier opened a store on the banks of the Macquarie River. Eight years later, in 1849, a village was proclaimed.

Nowadays, it is a thriving city of 36,430 inhabitants and the area produces wheat, wool, fat lambs, dairy cattle, poultry, vegetables and fruit. Secondary industries include the abattoir, a flour mill, several timber mills, a joinery, a brick and pipe works, clothing and an air engine works.

Dubbo is perhaps most famous for the Western Plains Zoo, the first open-range zoo in Australia. Just outside of town, on the Peak Hill Road, the zoo covers 300 ha (741 acres) and houses a terrific variety of animals; it is maybe best known for its endangered black rhino breeding program. You can drive the 6 km (3.7 mile) track, hire a bike or even walk.

Dubbo Military Museum has wheelchair access and guided tours. This private collection of World War II memorabilia includes guns, planes, tanks, vehicles, uniforms and documents. There are over 50 major exhibits.

Old Dubbo Jail is also worth a look. It has been faithfully restored after being closed down in 1966. The gallows, which were dismant-led early in the twentieth century, have been re-erected. Seven men were hanged on these gallows in the period 1877–1904, the last of whom was a Chinese, Ah Chick, who killed a Peak Hill grazier. The most notorious to die was Jacky Underwood, a participant in the Breelong massacres of 1900, with Jimmy Governor (which was much later immortalised in Thomas Ken-eally's book *The Chant of Jimmie Blacksmith*).

Dubbo hosts a three-day jazz festival in August. Other activities in and around Dubbo include fish-ing, bowling, tennis and a variety of water sports.
Map ref: page 458 B4

DUNGOG

Birthplace of the famed cricketer Doug Walters, Dungog means 'a clear hill' or 'a thickly wooded hill'. It nestles in the Williams River Val-ley, 241 km (150 miles) north of Sydney. The town was firmly est-ablished by the 1840s. In the mid-1800s a military guard of horse-troopers was stationed here to protect the area against bush-rangers. Its population is 3425.

The Gringai were the local tribe and the first white settlers were timber-getters. When timber was king, it had to be freighted to Clarence Town, then head of navigation for the Williams River.

Now the local economy relies on dairying, grazing, forestry and, to a lesser extent, poultry and deer farming, hydroponics and tourism. It is an excellent base for exploring the Barrington Tops National Park, which has excellent bushwalks. Horse riding, cycling, birdwatching, 4WD tours, fishing and water sports are also popular here. Dungog's annual Agricultural Show is held each year in November.
Map ref: page 459 J4

FORSTER

Forster and its twin town Tuncurry are linked by one of the longest pre-stressed concrete bridges in the Southern Hemisphere. Forster, which has a population of 18,000, sits on a narrow strip of land that lies between Wallis Lake (one of the Myall Lakes) and the Pacific Ocean. It is 326 km (202 miles) north of Sydney and is renowned for its great beaches and its fishing, especially flathead, bream, tailor and whiting. Ten kilometres (6.2 miles) from the town is Booti Booti National Park, which offers quite a dramatic range of scenery that varies from tropical rainforest to beaches. Besides water sports, you can go bowling, play golf or spend some time in Forster's many art and craft galleries.

The Australian International Ironman Triathlon is in April; June has a country music festival and a national sports fishing convention. August offers a dramafest and in September is the Great Lakes Life-style and Leisure Expo. Australia Day celebrations are also big.
Map ref: page 459 L4

Each October, jacaranda blossoms carpet the streets in Dungog.

The grandstand at Gloucester oval is dwarfed by the sharply rising peaks of the Bucketts Hills in the background.

GILGANDRA

Situated on the Castlereagh River, 448 km (278 miles) north-west of Sydney, 'Gilgandra' derives from the Aboriginal word for 'long waterhole'. Its European origins began in the 1830s with settlers grazing their flocks by the river. It was also once called 'the windmill town' because of the plethora of windmills that brought up water from the Great Artesian Basin. However, these have mostly gone as the town now uses mains water. The population is presently 5160.

Gilgandra was also the scene of the first 'Coo-ee' (the traditional bushman's cry for help) army recruitment march of 1915, after the Gallipoli disaster. This set an example to the rest of Australia and many other similar marches followed nationwide.

Gilgandra Observatory has been operating for 22 years, giving the public a chance to view the night skies through a 2-metre-long (6.5 feet) telescope with a 31 cm (1 foot) diameter mirror. Open every night, the observatory also houses a good collection of meteorites, rocks and fossils. It is surrounded by a rather delightful garden that features well over 80 varieties of roses. Gilgandra Flora Reserve has an excellent display of wildflowers in spring.

The Gilgandra Coo-ee Festival is held in October and features a variety of activities highlighted by a street parade, stalls, the Australian Coo-ee Calling Championships, a country music quest, a bushman's relay, goat races and the Gilgandra Gift footraces. Other things to do locally include bowls, swimming (pool), golf and tennis.
Map ref: page 458 B2

GLOUCESTER

Flanked on the east by the Mograni Range, Gloucester (population 2600) is bounded to the west by a range of unusual-looking monolithic hills called the Bucketts. The name derives from the Aboriginal word 'buccans', which means 'big rocks', also commemorated by Bucketts Way, the road that leads into the town from the south via Raymond Terrace. The town is 279 km (173 miles) north of Sydney.

Other major access routes are from Nabiac, on the Pacific Highway to the east, from Walcha to the north—which involves some dirt sections—and from the west across the Barrington Tops from Scone, which is also largely unsealed.

The first white man in the district was Surveyor Henry Dangar, early in 1826, but by the early 1830s, a number of farms were established along the Barrington River. The town is now the centre of a rich dairying, cattle-raising and mixed-farming district. Bowls, bushwalking, fishing, golf, squash, tennis and water sports can all be enjoyed in and around Gloucester.
Map ref: page 459 K3

GOSFORD

Gosford is located between Newcastle and Sydney, which is 88 km (55 miles) south, in a region called the Central Coast. It is a favourite tourist and holiday destination.

Planned in 1839, the town was named by Governor Gipps after the second Earl of Gosford, with whom he had served on a commission of inquiry in Canada. Initially, the town grew in tandem with East Gosford, a private township of tea merchant Samuel Peek, but the two were amalgamated into a municipality in 1886, and Gosford Shire was declared in 1947.

Thanks to an efficient railway service and the Sydney–Newcastle Expressway, hundreds of Gosford residents (population is 42,190) commute to Sydney, making it a satellite town. Local industries include growing vegetables, citrus fruit, passionfruit and dairying, poultry farming, mixed farming and timber. A fine sandstone is quarried close to town and numerous secondary industries support a buoyant economy.

The whole area is a tourist playground, but Gosford is particularly famous for its water sports. The fishing is excellent, and the area is a surfer's paradise. For boardriders, MacMasters, Avoca and Forresters Beaches are legendary, while bodysurfers and families may prefer Copacabana, Terrigal, Killcare or Wamberal. There is a beach in the area to suit everybody. Scuba divers also love the crystal-clear waters of the Central Coast, with plenty of wrecks to explore off Terrigal.

Henry Kendall's cottage, where the poet lived in the 1870s, is now a colonial museum. The Australian Reptile Park regularly 'milks' spider and snake venom to supply antivenines around the world. Nearby Old Sydney Town is a realistic re-creation to scale of Sydney as it was in 1810, including the Tank Stream, Sydney Cove, Government House and soldiers' huts.

About 9 km (5.6 miles) south-west of Gosford is Brisbane Water National Park, which offers panoramic views from 100-metre-high (328 feet) cliffs overlooking the Hawkesbury River. It comes alive with Christmas bells and waratahs during November and December and offers many bushwalks. There is also Aboriginal art carved into sandstone boulders and rockfaces.

In town itself, the courthouse and prison are the oldest buildings on the Central Coast. Other activities available are bowls, squash and tennis.
Map ref: page 459 H7

Waterskiing on Brisbane Waters is a popular activity in the Gosford region.

Spring waratahs in the Blue Mountains near Hartley.

GULGONG

The Town on the Ten Dollar Note has become The Town on the Old Ten Dollar Note. Gulgong, which is 303 km (188 miles) north-west of Sydney, has made much use of its appearance on the currency—which featured a couple of shop-fronts from the gold-rush days, frozen in time by the photography of Henry Beaufoy Merlin, from the collection of Bernard Holtermann.

Just like Hill End, Gulgong (the name means 'deep waterhole') owes its existence solely to the discovery of gold in 1866. By 1872, Gulgong and its satellite villages boasted a population of 20,000, which was a mix of Greeks, Italians, Bulgarians, Scots, Irish, Chinese, Americans, English, Canadians and, of course, native-born Australians. A rowdy, boisterous town in those days, it incited a visiting English clergy-man to proclaim 'Why man, there's nothing like it … Gulgong is the hub of the world!'

Nowadays Gulgong is a far more sober and quiet country town of around 2250 residents, and is one of the best-preserved gold-rush towns in all of New South Wales. It features winding, narrow streets, a good number of National Trust-classified buildings and hitching posts on the paths.

The Pioneers' Museum, which has been converted from an old bakery and produce store, has probably the best collection of Australiana in the country. Cover-ing half a hectare (1.2 acres), this place is a must for history lovers. The Prince of Wales Opera House remains unchanged from the gold-

rush days. It has supposedly seen some very famous performers such as Lily Langtry, Lola Montez and Dame Nellie Melba sing here, but some definites are boxer Les Darcy, William Morris Hughes (who delivered a rather fiery oration on the necessity of conscription in World War I) and, more recently, the pianist Roger Woodward. The Henry Lawson Centre has a quite magnificent collection of Lawson memorabilia including paintings, books and poems. Alhough he was born in Grenfell, Lawson moved to the area with his family while still a boy, and many of his writings allude to Gulgong. The Henry Lawson Birthday Celebrations are held in June.

To the north-east of Gulgong is the immense Ulan Coal Mine, which has the longest conveyor belt in the Southern Hemisphere. It is open for public inspection.

Gulgong also has a craft shop with fetching pieces made from local woods and clays. The Pratt's Winery is 2 km (1.2 miles) outside of town on the Mudgee road. Gul-gong is also within easy reach of the many wineries in and around the Mudgee area. For the active, there is golf and bowls.
See also Mudgee Wine Region
Map ref: page 458 D4

HARTLEY

The protected historic site of Hart-ley reflects the simplicity of life in the mid-1800s. It is situated on the Great Western Highway, 123 km (76 miles) west of Sydney and just below Victoria Pass. Once a thriv-ing settlement it went into decline when the railway bypassed it, and today the township has fewer than 200 residents. Historic buildings include two churches, three old inns and private homes. Of the churches, only St John's Anglican is still in regular use, but the other, St Bernard's, is still sanctified.

The Court House was the scene of trials of hundreds of convicts and is now a museum, brought vividly to life by tape recordings based on actual trial transcripts. Guided tours are available from National Parks and Wildlife Service and there is very good bushwalking and 4WD touring in the area. Near-by are the spectacular Jenolan Caves.
Map ref: page 458 E8

Kanangra wildflowers.

HILL END

There are three different ways into Hill End, 276 km (171 miles) west of Sydney, a former gold-rush town that has been an official Historic Site since 1967. The most pictur-esque route is via the Bridle Track, from Kelso, just out of Bathurst. This convict-built road winds beside the Macquarie River and

features some spectacular views. An alternative is an equally wind-ing road from Sofala, the other goldmining town, and the third option is to come in from Mudgee via yet another gold town—Har-graves. All of these roads are dirt and warrant extreme care.

Like Gulgong, Hill End owes its existence solely to the discovery of gold. In 1851, the first gold strike was made and in its heyday the population was in excess of 20,000. By 1873, Hill End had 53 hotels and shops catering to every need and appetite.

Hill End's biggest find was the famous Holtermann Nugget, a massive conglomerate of reef gold 1.5 m (5 feet) high and 0.5 m (1.6 feet) across. It weigh-ed 236 kg (520 pounds) and had a gold content of over 8.5 kg (19 pounds). As with all boom towns, by the time gold finally ran out in 1895, Hill End had become a ghost town.

Today the population of the town is only 200 and it is administered by the National Parks and Wildlife Service. Visitors can go fossicking for gold and the area is particularly good for 4WD tour-ing. Throughout the town are plaques that mark the sites where significant buildings once stood. There is a general store that is still in operation and the Royal Hotel, which was built in 1872, is still serving cold beer.
Map ref: page 458 D6

KANANGRA–BOYD NATIONAL PARK

This park is located west of Sydney, in the Blue Mountains near Jenolan Caves. Famous for its rugged terrain and wild-erness areas, the park occupies the south-west corner of the group of parks that protect the Blue Mountains and the Hawkesbury. With sand-stone cliffs and gorges, caves, waterfalls and panoramic views, this is a park for experienced, well-equipped bush-

An old bushman's hut in the rugged terrain of Kanangra–Boyd National Park.

Cahill's Lookout is just off Cliff Drive in Katoomba. It overlooks Megalong Valley to the west.

The Edge Maxvision Cinema has a six-storey high screen showing Blue Mountains views as well as feature films.

Katoomba's markets are on the first and third Saturdays each month; the Blue Mountains Folk Festiva is in March. The Winter Magic Festival in June is part of Yulefest, from June up until August right through the district. There is plenty to do at other times, including bowling, golf, horse riding, swimming, tennis or you can go 4WD touring.
Map ref: page 458 F8

walkers, and there is a labyrinth of tracks. Frequent snowfalls during winter and sudden thunderstorms in summer mean that you need to carry appropriate clothing at all times. The vegetation is mainly eucalypt forest, with heathlands on exposed ridges and rainforest in sheltered gullies.
Map ref: page 458 E9

KATOOMBA

Originally called 'Crushers' after a local quarry, in 1877 this coalmining area was given the Aboriginal name—'Katoomba', which means 'falling water' or 'falling together of many streams'. It is now the administrative centre of the Blue Mountains, and is also the gateway to some spectacular scenery.

Being only 104 km (65 miles) west of Sydney, Katoomba (population 8500) and its environs attract some three million visitors each year. Most of them will visit Echo Point and the Three Sisters, known in Aboriginal mythology as Mennhi, Wimlah and Gunnedoo. These have recently been incorporated into the Blue Mountains National Park, a move that will doubtless stop rock climbers from further eroding the geologically fragile sandstone formations.

Fitter visitors can try descending the Giant Stairway. This is almost 1000 steps that lead down to the floor of the Jamieson Valley. They are quite steep. However, there are many easier bushwalks that lead along the edge of the escarpments

that rise above the Jamieson and Grose Valleys, overlooking the many spectacular natural attractions such as the Ruined Castle and Mount Solitary.

For the less active, there is the Scenic Railway, which was originally designed to take coalminers 250 m (820 feet) down the cliff-face and reputedly the steepest in the world. Alternatively, the nearby Skyway cable car offers superb views over the Katoomba Falls and the valley floor.

Other spots well worth seeing include the oldest pub in the Blue Mountains, the Carrington Hotel. It was built in 1880 as a temporary home to the rich, the famous and the royal. Another icon in the area is the Paragon Café, which offers a most delectable array of mouthwatering chocolates guaranteed to tempt the tastebuds of even the most fastidious health fanatic.

The explorers' Tree —a blaze tree marked by the early explorers, Blaxland, Wentworth and Lawson, the first explorers to find a way through the mountains to the fertile western plains—is on the road just west of Katoomba township and marks the start of the Six-foot Track, a three-day walk through the Megalong Valley to Jenolan Caves.

KU-RING-GAI CHASE NATIONAL PARK

Located in the northern suburbs of Sydney, this park has magnificent views across Broken Bay to Palm Beach and Brisbane Water National Park. Some of the sandstone caves and shelters have Aboriginal engravings and drawings, and the Garigal Aboriginal Heritage Walk takes you to a selection of these. Naturally enough, the park is popular at weekends, and there is a marvellous range of bushwalking tracks along creeks and ridgelines. There are also picnic facilities, and boat ramps at Cottage Point and Akuna Bay.
Map ref: page 459 J8

LEURA

'Leura' is Aboriginal for 'lava', and while the Blue Mountains are mostly sandstone, volcanic rocks do occur in the area. Of all the mountain villages, Leura (population 3800) is the most prestigious, as some of the grand houses in the district are found here. Leura Mall is charming and olde worlde, with coffee shops, restaurants and art galleries, all in heritage colours.

Leura is 107 km (67 miles) west of Sydney and a close neighbour to Katoomba. Along Cliff Drive are the Leura Cascades, a great spot for family picnics or barbecues. The drive also offers access to many beautiful waterfalls, like Leura, Linda, Lila and Bridal Veil Falls, and, like Katoomba, is right on the national park border, where there are some spectacular bushwalks.

Most visitors come to see the gardens and mansions. Everglades Gardens is owned by the National Trust and was designed by Danish landscaper, Paul Sorenson. Nearby Leuralla, another grand home, also houses the largest collection of toys, dolls, teddy bears and model railways in Australia.

The view from Sublime Point is also worth seeing, while the active can play golf at Fairmont Resort, or the equally famous Leura Golf Club, with fine greens and traps.

Leura Fair and the Garden Festival are held in October each year, while the local markets are on the first Sunday of each month.
Map ref: page 458 F8

Akuna Bay marina is a boating haven off Cowan Creek deep in Ku-Ring-Gai Chase National Park.

LITHGOW

Lithgow is a town of 13,500 inhabitants and is situated in the heart of the Blue Mountains, 143 km (89 miles) west of Sydney. Although a coal town since 1841, it has a lot to offer the visitor in things to see and do. Named after William Lithgow, a New South Wales Auditor-General, the town was the birthplace of Olympic runner Marjorie Jackson—the 'Lithgow Flash'.

Blast Furnace Park is a monument to the town's industrial history. The first iron and steel cast in Australia were produced here in 1886, when William Sandford established a blast furnace. Production ran until 1928, when the industry moved to Port Kembla.

Eskbank House is a historic house with period furniture, a blacksmith's forge, a coach-house and a display of Lithgow pottery. Australia's oldest commercial pottery, it was established in 1833.

The Small Arms Museum in Methven Street commemorates an era in Lithgow's history. It has one of Australia's most comprehensive collections of machine guns, rifles and related items. Lithgow State Mine Railway Heritage Park is on the site of the former Lithgow Power Station and colliery.

There are also a number of national parks in the area, such as Blue Mountains and Wollemi, and there is the old mining town of Newnes, which is close to the famous glowworm tunnel. But Lithgow's greatest tourist attraction continues to be the Zig Zag Railway. The first rail link to the western region of New South Wales, it traversed spectacular mountain scenery, where one engine pulled and yet another pushed up some terrifying grades. Now the return journey covers 12 km (8 miles) and is very popular family entertainment.

Leura's local markets are held every second month on the first Saturday in the month. Other year-round activities include bushwalking, 4WD touring and golf.
Map ref: page 458 E7

LORD HOWE ISLAND

Lord Howe Island lies off the east coast of Australia, 700 km (435 miles) north-east of Sydney. It is roughly crescent-shaped, and about 11 km (6.8 miles) long and 1.5 km (0.9 miles) wide. The island resulted from a volcanic eruption from a submarine ridge that runs between the South Island of New Zealand and the Chesterfield Reefs. It was first sighted in 1788 by Henry Lidgbird Ball, commander of HMS *Supply*, who named it after the first lord of the British Admiralty, Richard Howe.

Thick tropical vegetation and isolation made attempts at early settlement fairly unsuccessful, but by 1851 the population consisted of 16 people who had become entirely self-sufficient. They traded fresh produce with ships, primarily whalers, but far a more profitable trade was in kentia palms, which later became one of the most popular palms in the world. Lord Howe is the only place in the world where the kentia palm grows naturally.

In 1981, 70 per cent of the island was made a Permanent Park Reserve and a year later, the island was placed on the World Heritage List. Today the island is home to 320 residents and visitor numbers are strictly regulated. There are only a few cars on the island and visitors either hire bicycles or walk. It offers some wonderful nature experiences including birdwatching, scuba diving and snorkelling, coral viewing, cycling, fishing, mountain climbing, walking, and a variety of water sports.
Map ref: see map of Australia, page 23

MAITLAND

Older than Melbourne and 16 years younger than Sydney, Maitland (population 50,000) lies along the banks of the Hunter River, 191 km (119 miles) north of Sydney. Originally called Wallis's Plains, it was renamed in the 1820s after Sir Frederick Lewis Maitland, Admiral of the Fleet, to whom Napoleon surrendered in 1815.

Maitland's imposing architecture is a reminder that in the nineteenth century this city rivalled Sydney. Many of Maitland's heritage-protected buildings date back to the

Historic St Mary's Rectory in Maitland.

1820s. Significant places of interest abound. Walka Water Works was constructed between 1882 and 1887 to provide Newcastle with a more hygienic and reliable source of fresh water. Classified by the National Trust, historic features are the pumphouse and the sandstone reservoir wall. This is a popular recreation area.

Grossman House (1862) and Brough House (1870), of classic Georgian design, form a unit with St Mary's Anglican Church and Rectory (1867 and 1881). Maitland Heritage Mall is noted for its rotunda, fountain and 1860 drawing of the town inlaid in the pavement. The Black Boy statue, erected more than 135 years ago, was originally a hitching post for horse-drawn vehicles.

Windermere House, believed to be the oldest homestead in the Hunter Valley, was built by convicts in 1821 and has historic photographs and equipment.

To the south are the Watagan Mountains, which offer hang gliding, rock climbing and terrific 4WD touring; to the north are the famed Barringtons, where you can self-drive or take 4WD tours. In town, Maitland is a great place to shop for antiques or arts and crafts.

The Hunter's biggest family market day is held at Maitland Showground on the first Sunday of each month (excluding January) and on the first and third Sunday

Visitor numbers are strictly limited on World Heritage-listed Lord Howe. The island has the world's southernmost coral reefs.

in November and December. The Maitland Rockin' celebrates Elvis's birthday in January, and April is Heritage Month, when the city also celebrates the Hunter Valley Steamfest. The Maitland Garden Ramble is held in September.
Map ref: page 459 J5

MERRIWA

Merriwa is in the Upper Hunter, 348 km (216 miles) north-west of Sydney. It is the centre of an agricultural and cattle-raising district and the town has a population of 1100. The Old Stone Cottage dates from 1847 and is now the local history museum. The post office dates from 1880, while the Anglican church was built in 1899. To the south-west is a designated gem fossicking area and a little further on is Goulburn River National Park, which features bushwalks on wide sandy riverbanks under some lovely orange cliffs. Here visitors are likely to see some wombats, eastern grey kangaroos and emus.
Map ref: page 458 F4

MOLONG

Molong (population 1565) is a centre for a rural economy based on fine wool and wheat, cattle, fat lambs, orchards and vineyards. It gets its name from the Aboriginal word meaning 'place of rocks'. A government stockyard was established at Molong in 1828, and in 1845, a copper mine was opened.

Molong is 291 km (181 miles) west of Sydney and the road into town from Orange is lined with

pretty poplar trees. The grave of Yuranigh, Sir Thomas Mitchell's Aboriginal guide, is just outside Molong. There are several historic buildings in the town, including a museum. The State sheepdog trials are held here in March. Visitors can also participate in swimming, fishing, bowls, golf and tennis.
Map ref: page 458 B6

MORPETH

Morpeth's earliest name was Green Hills, and there has been a settlement here since 1834. On the Hunter River, the town became the Hunter Valley's busiest port until 1850, when the railway arrived. The town is 199 km (124 miles) north of Sydney.

Several buildings in the town are National Trust classified, most notably Closebourne House, which was built by Edward Charles Close. Other buildings worth inspecting include the old Commercial Bank, the courthouse, police station and Roman Catholic church.

Morpeth has many antique and bric-a-brac shops. It has been a suburb of Maitland since 1944 and today the population is 1120. The town hosts a jazz festival in May.
Map ref: page 459 J5

MOUNT WILSON

In the 1860s, Mount Wilson was subdivided into 62 portions and was put up for auction in 1870. There was little interest as the area was regarded as almost inaccessible. With the opening of Bell railway station in 1875, however, the land around here sold very quickly.

The bridge over the Hunter River at Morpeth, once an important river port.

Mount Wilson is still a rustic mountain village of only 100 residents where Sydney's wealthy have their country retreats. It is famous for its cool-climate gardens, which are popular with daytrippers from Sydney, 140 km (87 miles) southeast. Some are open all year round; others in spring and autumn.

Unlike most of the Blue Mountains, which are predominantly sandstone, Mount Wilson is capped with volcanic rock, so plant growth is luxuriant, with one area, for obvious reasons, being known as the Cathedral of Ferns.

Visitors can enjoy English-style Devonshire teas, or buy antiques or crafts from the tiny stores. The Mount Tomah Botanic Gardens, on the Bells Line of Road before the Mount Wilson turn-off, is also spectacularly beautiful and worth visiting. There are also plenty of interesting walks in the area.
Map ref: page 458 F8

MUDGEE

Mudgee's name comes from the Aboriginal word 'moothi'—'a nest in the hills'. It was established in 1838, making it the second oldest town west of the Great Dividing Range (after Bathurst). The area was initially explored by James Blackman and William Lawson; the first settlers were the Cox brothers.

Mudgee was settled 14 years before Melbourne, and the town was considered to be so well laid out that surveyor Robert Hoddle followed the same principles when asked to survey the City of Melbourne. For many years the only mode of travel from Wallerawang, near Lithgow, was by Cobb and Co coach. Relics of the coaching days can still be seen on the Lithgow–Mudgee road. Mudgee is 271 km (168 miles) north-west of Sydney

and is cradled in an upland valley of the Cudgegong River (a tributary of the Macquarie), which runs through rich lucerne flats and fertile grazing country and alongside vine-clad red soil slopes. All this contributes to making Mudgee (population 8200) the centre of a wool- and wheat-growing district. Nowadays Mudgee is renowned for its wines. Though the industry has been extant in the area for almost 150 years, in the 1950s Mudgee was famous for its fortified wines. Now, over 20 vineyards in the region produce rich, full-flavoured reds, and some good chardonnays.

Some of the nearby attractions include Munghorn Gap—34 km (21 miles) north of the town—the second oldest declared nature reserve in New South Wales. It features great bird life, including satin bowerbirds, superb lyrebirds, wonga pigeons and gang gang cockatoos. There are walking trails, a picnic area, and caves to explore.

Wollemi National Park is also close by. Covering 450,000 ha (1,111,950 acres), it is the State's largest wilderness area. Within it are wonderful Aboriginal carvings, cave drawings, hand stencils and grinding grooves.

Frog Rock is a natural rock formation by the side of the Cassilis road, in the shape of a crouching frog. Hands on the Rock, closer to Gulgong, has stencilled Aboriginal hands from hundreds of years ago. To the south-east, Windamere Dam provides some great opportunities to fish, sail, swim and canoe.

From July to September, Mudgee opens its gardens for viewing and the Garden Expo is held in October. Mudgee Small Farm Field Days is on in July and September sees the Rotary Art Show, and the Mudgee Wine Fest.
Map ref: page 458 D5

Merriwa is an agricultural town in the Upper Hunter Valley region.

Pristine white sand dunes surround Myall Lakes, a natural fresh–brackish water system with over 40 km (25 miles) of beaches.

MUDGEE WINE REGION

One of Australia's oldest and best known viticultural regions, the Mudgee area is part of the Central Ranges wine region, which lies about 300 km (185 miles) inland in an area west to north-west of Sydney. German settlers planted the first vines in Mudgee in 1858 and the story from then on is somewhat familiar. More vine plantings followed and soon there were more than 50 vineyards supporting a thriving wine industry. The 1872 gold rush drew more people but the depression of 1893 virtually destroyed viticulture in the region. However, a few hardy souls persisted, notably one of the original families, the Roths, at their Craigmoor winery.

There was little else until the late 1960s revival, led by vigneron Bob Roberts, whose Huntington Estate soon established a reputation for excellent wines and has since become known for hosting an exceptional annual music festival.

Huntington Estate was followed a year later by Botobolar, where Gil Wahlquist established one of the first vineyards in Australia to use organic growing methods, a practice that has been continued by subsequent owners. Montrose began in 1974 with winemaker Carlo Corino, a native of Italy's Piedmont. Not surprisingly, Montrose led the way in Australia with plantings of barbera, sangiovese and even nebbiolo.

Few of the several small wineries that followed built a reputation to match that of Huntington Estate and they suffered the indignity of seeing most of the grapes they produced head east to be made into some of the Hunter's more celebrated wines. This trend stopped when larger producers moved into the region. Orlando–Wyndham relocated winemaking from the Hunter to Mudgee and now owns Montrose and Craigmoor, and Mildara Blass followed suit with Half Mile Creek. But the winery most likely to bring Mudgee to

A Mudgee region winery sign.

the attention of the world is Rosemount Estate with its delightful Mountain Blue Shiraz Cabernet and the new Hill of Gold range, represented by a chardonnay, a cabernet sauvignon and an excellent shiraz. These wines have now shown that Mudgee fruit can make first-class wines.

Although close to the Hunter Valley as the crow flies, the two districts are separated by the Great Dividing Range, giving Mudgee a cooler, drier climate. Most vineyards rely on irrigation. Cabernet sauvignon has been particularly successful in the region and shiraz has done well. There are also some significant plantings of chardonnay.
Map ref: page 458 D5

MURRURUNDI

Now the centre for a cattle, sheep and horse breeding district, Murrurundi is a historic town with many of is fine old buildings being classified by the National Trust. The Royal Hotel was built in 1863 on land purchased by the surveyor Henry Dangar. Apart from one small difference—that it originally had wooden pillars to support the veranda—the pub is exactly the same as it was when the Cobb and Co coaches drew up. Today Murrurundi has a population of 2345 and it is found 347 km (216 miles) north-west of Sydney.

Just a 30 minute drive out of Murrurundi, on the Isis River, are the Timor Caves. Most of the caves are accessible to the public, although some—with a very high carbon dioxide content—have been

sealed up for preservation. The most famous is Main Cave, which bears the signature of Fred Ward (Captain Thunderbolt), the bushranger.

Also not far from the town is the enormous Wallabadah Rock. According to some sources, only Uluru (Ayers Rock) in the Northern Territory and Mount Augustus in Western Australia are bigger monoliths. It is 61 ha (151 acres) around the base and is 950 m (3117 feet) high. It is on private property, so permission from the council is required to inspect it.
Map ref: page 458 G2

MUSWELLBROOK

Originally called 'Muscle Brook' (and still pronounced that way), Muswellbrook has a population of 11,080 and is both a coalmining town as well as the centre of an important pastoral and dairying area. The town is 281 km (175 miles) north of Sydney.

The Muswellbrook Mine is estimated to have 170 million tonnes of coal reserve. Operating both as an open-cut and an underground mine, it produces about 2.2 million tonnes of coal a year.

The Muswellbrook area is part of the Hunter Valley wine region and some of its best wines come from the region's vineyards. It is part of the Upper Hunter horse stud scene and its race meetings are important local events.

Nearby Wollemi National Park is a particular favourite with bushwalkers. The Spring Wine Festival is held in October.
See also Hunter Valley Wine Region
Map ref: page 458 G4

MYALL LAKES
NATIONAL PARK

Two-thirds of the area of this magnificent park consists of a series of shallow, connected coastal lakes, separated from the Pacific Ocean by high sand dunes. It is the largest coastal lake system in New South Wales. There is a diversity of vegetation here, which varies from rainforest, heath and paperbark swamps to dry sclerophyll forests and it is believed that the Grandis, a superb 76 m flooded gum, is the tallest tree in the State. It can be seen by taking Stoney Creek Road from either the Lakes Way or the Old Pacific Highway. There are also many species of threatened animals found here.

The park is particularly popular, especially in school holidays. The tranquil lakes provide wonderful opportunities for safe swimming, fishing, sailing, windsurfing and canoeing, while the ocean beaches offer excellent surf as well as beach fishing. The park is located 230 km (143 miles) north of Sydney and is accessed via Tea Gardens.
Map ref: page 459 M5

NELSON BAY

Nelson Bay is a much-loved tourist resort on the south-eastern shores of Port Stephens, and lies 224 km (139 miles) north of Sydney. In the 1800s it was home to a group of Chinese fishermen who caught and salted fish for shipment to China. While commercial fishing is still quite an important industry in the area, today the tourist dollar is equally important. The town has a population of 5500, which grows exponentially on summer week-ends in and more so during school holidays or on long weekends.

Nelson Bay is in a 'blue water wonderland', with an abundance of beaches and wildlife, good fishing (on the beach and offshore game fishing), scuba diving in the marine reserves off Fly and Halifax points, and cycling tracks along the shore-line. The bay has a group of resi-dent bottlenose dolphins and boat operators offer trips to sight the dolphins. Other pursuits include bowls, golf, tennis, water sports and whale watching in season. *See also* Northern Rivers Wine Region

Map ref: page 459 K5

NEWCASTLE

The largest non-capital city in Aus-tralia, Newcastle is 173 km (107 miles) north of Sydney and it has a population of 500,000. It covers the sixth largest urban area: from

Catherine Hill Bay in the south to Nelson Bay in the north and out to Cessnock in the west. Newcastle has a reputation as being a dirty, brawling industrial city, but it is well served with modern air-con-ditioned shopping centres, plenty of activities and much to see. Some of the city's finest Victorian and Edwardian buildings can be found in the Hunter Mall, established in the 1980s. Tourism will increase as industry grinds inexorably to a halt, to be relocated elsewhere. The city started out badly, being a penal settlement for convicts who had transgressed while serving their original sentences. Its reputation even then was 'unsavoury'. The convicts were employed as cedar-getters, miners and lime-burners.

In 1797, the site of the city of Newcastle was discovered by Lieu-tenant John Shortland, looking for escaped convicts who had stolen a government boat, the *Cumberland*. He sailed up the coast as far as Nel-

The town hall in Newcastle is one of many fine old sandstone buildings in this city.

son Bay, and on the return journey, hugging the shore to make sure the convicts had not landed, noticed a small island a short distance from the mainland. He christened it 'The Nob' (now known as Nobbys). The island had obscured an opening to a fine harbour, and as he climbed a hill (now Fort Scratchley) to get a better view of the river and surrounding district, he noticed a seam of coal protrud-ing from the ground, so he named the river the 'Coal River'. For-tunately for wine-makers who came later, the name was changed to the Hun-ter River in 1804, in honour of the then Governor of New South Wales. (Coal Valley chardonnay does not exactly have a good marketing ring to it.)

On the instigation of potential settlers, the penal settlement was moved to Port Macquarie and sur-veyor Henry Dangar was commissioned to supervise and design the layout of New-castle. Those free settlers who had taken over all the convict cottages resisted this, and it explains the some-what chaotic layout of modern-day Newcastle. Early

industries included coal and timber, later followed by shipbuilding, salt manufacture and copper smelting. This was then supplanted by iron smelting and a steelworks.

Newcastle has had its share of natural disasters, most significant of which was the 1989 earthquake, which destroyed buildings and claimed human lives. These days, the city is completely recovered, and seems to have more civic pride than ever before.

Of historical interest is Fort Scratchley, which was the site of a Japanese submarine attack in 1942 and is now home to the Newcastle Region Maritime Museum. In the centre of the city, the Newcastle Regional Museum is a must for everyone. It contains Supernova, which has Newcastle's Science and Technology exhibits.

On a hill just south of the city is an obelisk, which was erected in 1847 when sailors complained that the demolition of an old landmark windmill interrupted the correct plotting of their bearings.

Newcastle is close to one of the greatest 4WD beaches found in Australia, Stockton—a long, rather treacherous sand trap even for the experienced driver. Stockton Beach can have the worst sand conditions in Australia, especially when it has been hot, dry and windy. It is also a favourite location of fishermen, who run customised 4WDs with wide sand tyres and, usually, V8 engines. Permits are required for four-wheel driving and these are available from the pie shop, 1 km (0.6 miles) north of the Ladis Lane entrance to the beach.

Map ref: page 459 J6

Little Beach at Nelson Bay in Port Stephens, which is just north of Newcastle.

NORTHERN RIVERS WINE REGION

Grape-growing in New South Wales began soon after the arrival of the First Fleet in 1788, with vines planted near what is now Circular Quay in Sydney Harbour, but most people would consider the lush subtropics of northern New South Wales an unlikely place to find grapes. However, grapes there are, and several wineries to go with them—some of the State's earliest vineyards were in the Northern Rivers zone. Colonial surveyor Henry Fancourt White planted the first in 1837, and within three decades there were 30 or so more. After a period of decline, grape-growing was revived at Hastings River by the Cassegrain family in the 1980s. This winery is the largest producer, followed by Bob's Farm at Port Stephens.

Irrigation is unnecessary but the significant rainfall and very high humidity can be a problem. This is one reason the Cassegrains turned to chambourcin, a grape that is highly resistant to mildew and produces a wine of intense colour and flavour. A French hybrid developed in the nineteenth century, chambourcin is no longer found in its original home and, being a hybrid, it is not allowed to be re-imported there. Both the chardonnay and sémillon have been successful in some vintages.
Map ref: page 459 M2

Winery sign near Orange.

NUNDLE

Located at the foot of the Great Dividing Range, 423 km (263 miles) northwest of Sydney, Nundle (population 350) is a good place for quiet walks along the banks of the Peel River or for the beauty of the local mountains.

The town sprang up in the gold rush of the 1850s, and visitors can still pick up a little colour with the pan. Prospectors last century took out more than 1.5 million dollars in alluvial gold, but it is thought there is still a great deal of the yellow metal left. In fact, Nundle is a fossicker's dream, with not just gold but also quartz crystals and other semi-precious stones filling out the wish list. Equipment can be hired.

While the historical museum will take hours to see properly, the more active are also catered for with trout in well-stocked streams, and sailing, swimming and fishing are possible at nearby Chifley Dam.

The Hanging Rock picnic and camping area (not the famous one, in Victoria, near Mount Macedon), and Sheba Dams, have some great bushwalks. Other local activities include tennis, bowls and forest drives.
Map ref: page 459 H2

ORANGE

The location in which the midwestern city of Orange stands was originally known as Blackman's Swamp, after the chief constable of Bathurst, who in 1818 had accompanied explorer John Oxley into the region. Situated 257 km

Apples growing in the country town of Orange.

(160 miles) west of Sydney and just 14 km (9 miles) north-east of Mount Canobolas—an extinct volcano and the highest peak—1395 m (4577 feet) between the Blue Mountains and the Indian Ocean, Orange was named by Thomas Mitchell. This man had fought in the Peninsular War with the Prince of Orange, who later became the King of Holland.

Orange (population 37,000) is now the centre for a fertile, productive district that raises sheep, cattle and pigs, and grows wheat, potatoes and peas plus other crops. Apple and cherry growing, forestry and dairying also play a part in the region's economy.

The city has also grown from a rich mining history. In the 1850s, gold was discovered at nearby Ophir and Lucknow, and regional museums display mining relics, as well as demonstrating what life was like back in the 1880s. Country mansions and historic homes will delight history buffs who might like to try the sign-posted Heritage Trail, which winds through the city. Now, the boom could be on again. Cadia Goldmine—an open-cut gold and copper mine some 25 km (16 miles) from Orange—is operational and should bring new prosperity to what is an already affluent district.

Orange is justifiably proud of being a sophisticated, cosmopolitan and cultural town. Two of Australia's foremost poets were born here. The first of these was A.B. 'Banjo' Paterson, and a monument marking the site of his home is located just outside the town. An annual festival celebrates the poet's life in Orange. The

Pruning vines at Cassegrain Vineyard, Northern Rivers region. This winery cultivates Australia's most northerly pinot noir vines.

second was Kenneth Slessor, who spent his early years here before later moving to Sydney.

The area has a growing cottage industry in unusual culinary produce, such as venison and pickled walnuts, and the town has some good restaurants. Orange's parks and gardens will also delight the visitor. Cook Park is the most acclaimed. It has a begonia house, a sunken rose garden and huge, ancient trees. The Orange Botanic Gardens feature a historic church, a billabong and native trees.

Mount Canobolas is an absolute must when visiting Orange. Often snowcapped in winter, it has bushwalking trails, lookouts and picnic spots. Visitors can glimpse blacktail wallabies, wombats and many varieties of birds. At the base of the mountain is Lake Canobolas with a picnic spot and swimming hole. Other activities include bowls, golf and motocross.

See also Orange Wine Region
Map ref: page 458 C7

Canola crops near Orange, an important farming district, flower in spring and the seeds are later harvested for their nutritious oil.

ORANGE WINE REGION

The region around Orange, at an altitude between 600 and 900 m (2000 and 3000 feet) above sea level, is well known, in spite of its name, for its apples. Centred on Mount Canobolas, it is also part of the greater Central Ranges wine region and has proved very successful for grape growing. The climate varies from the very cool slopes of Mount Canobolas to the much warmer, neighbouring lower districts. Night temperatures during the growing season can be very cool and, because most of the rain falls in winter and spring, irrigation

is needed. Wind makes careful site selection imperative but doing so reduces the risk of spring frosts. The two largest producers here are Bloodwood and Brangayne, both close to the town of Orange. The chardonnay from this area has some lovely fruit flavours, while its shiraz is elegant and spicy.
Map ref: page 458 C7

PATERSON

Paterson is located 207 km (129 miles) north of Sydney and it is named after William Paterson, the Lieutenant Governor of New South Wales from 1801 to 1809.

It was in 1801 that he explored the Hunter River and discovered its two main tributaries, which Governor King named the Paterson and the William Rivers. First European settlement along the banks of the Paterson was in 1820. Now, with the river trade gone, Paterson is a

delightful, placid town of 200 inhabitants, with most of its buildings classified by the National Trust. Some of the more notable are: Annadale, a historic residence built in 1839 for Major Edward Johnstone, the local magistrate; the Paterson Tavern (1845), formerly the Commercial Hotel; St Paul's Church and cemetery (1845); the Paterson Court House Museum (1860), which fulfilled its legal function for over 100 years and became a museum in 1974; and St Ann's (1846), the oldest Presbyterian church in Australia still in use.

Not all the classified buildings are nineteenth century: the Paterson School of Arts was built in 1935 and was used as a community hall and movie hall in the 1950s. A quiet stroll through Paterson's streets, largely unchanged since the late 1800s, is very rewarding, and while some of the private residences are obviously not open to the public, commercial buildings such as the hotels are. Paterson is close to Tocal Agricultural College.
Map ref: page 459 J5

PENRITH

Penrith, 54 km (34 miles) west of Sydney's CBD, is one of Sydney's fastest-growing areas. Though agriculture and animal raising are still carried on in the district, Penrith is losing its semi-rural appearance. A town of 172,000 it has its own personality: a bustling, thriving one.

Say 'Penrith' to any Sydneysider and two images immediately spring to mind. First is Penrith Panthers, reputedly the world's largest club,

headquarters of the football club of the same name. Set on over 80 ha (198 acres), Panthers has an amazing glut of activities, including cable waterskiing, mini-car racing, waterslides, swimming pools, a tennis complex and a lake where it is possible to windsurf, canoe or have fun with paddleboats. Inside the building there are six restaurants and such a vast array of poker machines that it makes Las Vegas appear deficient. The second is the Head of the River, the annual rowing competition between the major Sydney boys' private schools. The stretch of the Nepean River used for this contest is so well suited to the sport that Penrith was the host city to the canoe and rowing events for the Sydney 2000 Olympics.

Penrith was named by Governor Macquarie after a town found in Cumberland in England. The Aboriginal name for the area was 'mulgoa', now the name of a suburb in Sydney's outer west, which is very close to Penrith.

The first European to see this section of the Nepean valley was Captain Watkin Tench back in 1879; also the explorers Blaxland, Wentworth and Lawson crossed the Nepean at Emu Ford on their way to the Blue Mountains.

The town began growing after William Cox built the road over the Blue Mountains, and it later experienced a boom when the g old rushes began, as it was the last staging post before the western plains. Bowls, squash and tennis are also possible in Penrith.
Map ref: page 458 G8

Paterson has many historic buildings, which date from 1826 to the early 1900s.

PORT MACQUARIE

Named after Governor Macquarie by explorer John Oxley in 1818, 'Port' has had an interesting and varied history. On Oxley's return to Sydney, some 425 km (264 miles) south, Macquarie thought the place suitable as a penal settlement for those convicted of crimes in New South Wales. The convicts could be used here to cut down timber and ship it back to Sydney, as timber supplies from the then penal settlement of Newcastle were becoming scarce. So, in October 1821, there were 102 people living in Port Macquarie, plus their military guard. In 1823, the first sugarcane to be cultivated in Australia was planted here but by 1830 an influx of free settlers saw the penal settlement come to an end.

Old Royal Hotel at Port Macquarie, rebuilt in 1880.

Today Port Macquarie has a population 39,000 and services a district where dairying, timber-getting, fishing and oyster farming are the principal industries, but it is also a town where the tourist is king. With two major shopping centres and more than 60 local restaurants ranging from five star to fish and chips, Port is perfect for holidays, or for the transient visitor to restock and revitalise. Located at the mouth of the Hastings River, the town has 85 km (53 miles) of coastline stretching both north and south. With good surf, secluded rock pools and sand dunes, visitors can indulge in any water-based activity, from hiring a jetski to chartering a deep-sea fishing boat.

The area caters for ecotourism, with a range of tours through the river systems, rainforest and wilderness locations. Alternatively, camel safaris along the beach or overnight camping by a lagoon are possible, or you can try a river cruise which visits the oyster farm, the canal system and Settlement Point.

For families, there is Peppermint Park, full of outdoor activities, with barbecue facilities. Fantasy World has ghosts, castles and dragons, and train rides. It also has a barbecue and picnic area.

Sea Acres has a treetop rainforest walkway while nearby Wauchope has Timbertown, a re-creation of life in the pioneering days.

Being one of the oldest towns in the State, Port Macquarie offers plenty for the history buff. On the corner of Clarence and Hay Streets is the courthouse, with its high-pitched roof and sweeping veranda. Built in 1868, it originally had a lockup and even a post office.

There are guided tours daily in the school holidays. Tacking Point Lighthouse, erected in 1879, is also worth a visit. There are plenty of other activities including surfing, swimming, golf and tennis. The Port Festival is held at the end of September/beginning of October.
Map ref: page 459 M2

QUIRINDI

The district surrounding Quirindi, 383 km (238 miles) north-west of Sydney, is part of the fertile Liverpool Plains and it produces wool, grain and seed crops, vegetables, lucerne, lambs, cattle, pigs, poultry, and dairy products. Thomas Mitchell, in 1831, referred to the area as 'Cuerindi', thought to be an Aboriginal word for 'nest in the hills'. Squatters had already moved in by the 1820s and the town was proclaimed in 1856. Today the town is home to 3100.

One of the first towns in New South Wales where polo was played, Quirindi continues its equine love affair with a polo meeting in August, as well as the Quirindi Rodeo, held the second weekend in March, and regular race meetings. The Turf Club has been in existence for over 50 years and considers its racecourse to be the 'showcourse of country racing'. There is also a small folklore museum housed in a historic cottage. Other things to do include golf, horse riding, and tennis.
Map ref: page 458 G2

RAYMOND TERRACE

Governor Macquarie visited Raymond Terrace, 201 km (125 miles) north of Sydney, in 1812 and 1818. It was known even then by that name. The village was gazetted in 1837 and the courthouse, built in 1838, is still in use.

By the 1840s, the town was really booming, being at that time a busy centre where wool, transported by road from the New England district, was shipped to Sydney via the river. These days, agriculture and dairying are the primary industries, but the area supports a number of productive secondary industries.

Situated on the Pacific Highway, Raymond Terrace (population 9250) is always busy, but visitors can escape from the traffic and noise to take the Heritage Walk and wander around the historic buildings of the town. There is the courthouse, the first homestead, Irrawang (built in 1830) and the Anglican church and its rectory. Some 8 km (5 miles) out of town

is Sketchley Pioneer Cottage and at nearby Williamtown, the RAAF has an aircraft museum.

Raymond Terrace is a good base for 4WD touring and for anglers who want to spend extended time on nearby Stockton Beach, just past Williamtown. Bowls, golf and swimming are other local activities.
Map ref: page 459 J5

RICHMOND

In 1789 Governor Phillip climbed a hill just near the junction of the Hawkesbury and Grose rivers and named it Richmond Hill. In the next ten years, farmers grew wheat on the lowlands by the river, often suffering disastrously due to flooding. In 1810, Governor Macquarie founded Richmond, 60 km (37 miles) north-west of Sydney, one of five Hawkesbury River towns that would be above the high-water mark (or so the theory went). The schoolhouse (1813) was the first building, also used as a church. These days vegetables and corn are grown on the river flats and dairy cows are raised. The RAAF has a base here from where it conducts pilot training, usually in Hercules transports, and the University of Western Sydney's campus is just south of the town. The population today is 9200.

Visits to the local cemeteries are useful for those interested in Australian history. William Cox, the early roadbuilder, for example, is buried here in the grounds of St Peter's Church, which was built in 1841. Richmond Estate, where connoisseurs can taste and purchase fine wines, is close by.
Map ref: page 458 G8

Main street, Raymond Terrace, with buildings from the mid-to-late 1800s.

Fishing boats on the Hunter River at Raymond Terrace prepare for departure.

ROYAL NATIONAL PARK

Gazetted in 1879, this national park is the oldest in Australia and the second oldest in the world. Just 32 km (20 miles) south of Sydney, bordered by the Pacific Ocean and the shores of Port Hacking, it is an area of quiet beaches and bays, with headlands and sea caves carved out of the sandstone; inland, there are creeks, waterfalls and clear rock-pools. Banksia heathlands cover the stony ground, making glorious displays of wildflowers in spring, while open forest and rainforest are found further from the coast. A range of walking tracks lead to isolated beaches, or follow tree-lined streams. Bush camping (with a permit) on some of the walking tracks is possible.

Map ref: page 459 H9

RYLSTONE

A picturesque town with many historic buildings, Rylstone is 241 km (150 miles) north-west of Sydney. A small town of 200, it was first surveyed in 1842. A counter lunch at a local pub can have you believing that you are back in those days.

Many visitors come to see the Aboriginal paintings on sandstone overhangs not far from the town centre. Rylstone's proximity to Lake Windamere also has great tourist appeal. Lake Windamere offers all sorts of water sports, with a large picnic area and many boat ramps. It is popular with anglers.

Using Rylstone as a base, the visitor is in striking distance of all of Mudgee's wineries, or by heading north-east through Wollemi and Goulburn River national parks, the vineyards of the Hunter. (The latter is a very pretty drive, but the roads are narrow and wind up and down the mountain ranges, so it is wise to exercise some care.)

Map ref: page 458 E5

SCONE

'The Horse Capital of Australia', Scone is 306 km (190 miles) north-west of Sydney. It is surrounded by rich pastoral country in the Upper Hunter Valley. There are a total of 65 horse studs found in this area, a veritable honour roll, with 'Arrow-field', 'Alabama', 'Segenhoe' and 'Wakefield' being merely the tip of the top. Some studs are open to the public on certain days during the Scone Horse Festival in May. For horse lovers, the Australian Stock Horse Museum in Kelly Street is also worth visiting. Scone holds its Horse Festival in May. Besides horse studs and some noted sheep stations, the district also produces some fine wines—the vineyard of Birnam Wood is the latest addition to the viticultural register.

Scone is a wealthy town of 4500 with all modern conveniences, and there is much of interest around the town. Twenty kilometres (12 miles) to the north, up the New England Highway, is the Burning Mountain, a burning coal seam that is believed to have been alight for 1000 years. The Aboriginals called it 'the Stone Woman of Fire'.

Closer to town, Middlebrook Station is a working property with displays of shearing and mustering and is owned by the Henderson family. Groups of ten or more people can take in morning tea, lunch or afternoon tea in an old, now-converted shearing shed.

On the other side of town, on the Gundy road, is the Belltrees historic homestead, which also welcomes visitors. This property has a shearing shed, stables, a chapel and museum, and it has been in the White family for seven generations. Further out are the old gold-mining areas at Moonan Brook and Moonan Flat, where there is a very good pub.

Keeping on the same road you will eventually come to the famed Barrington Tops. It is a magnificent drive into the Tops from Moonan Flat, climbing constantly, with some superb views over the entire Upper Hunter Valley. The road, however, is dirt and it is very corrugated, so care must be taken at all times. At the top of the climb there is a large dingo gate that must be opened—and closed! The variation in altitude from valley floor to top of the range is so great that you can see subtropical rain-forest, the native deciduous Antarctic beeches and snow gums all in the same day. (The Tops is actually the highest range in Australia after the Snowy Mountains.)

Once on the plateau, visitors can make use of many walking tracks, or, by arrangement with the National Parks and Wildlife Service, 4WD trails. Polblue Swamp is most unusual: it is a large sphagnum moss swamp bisected by channels of icy cold water. There are duckboard walking paths that ensure visitors can appreciate the beauty without damaging this unique environment. From there, it is down the other side to Gloucester, but note there is no fuel between Moonan Flat and Gloucester, a distance of 65 km (40 miles).

Further to the south of the town is pretty Glenbawn Dam—Scone's aquatic playground. Twice the size of Sydney Harbour, the Lake Glenbawn State Recreation Area offers sweeping views, boating, fishing, water sports, bushwalking, golf, horse riding and has both picnic and barbecue facilities. Cottages, cabins and camp sites are available for those who want to stay there for longer than a day.

Other local activities in and around the Scone region include golf, hockey, polo and polocrosse.

Map ref: page 458 G3

The rich rural landscape around Scone in the Upper Hunter Valley has fostered many horse studs in the area.

Quambi Museum in historic Stroud.

SINGLETON

On the New England Highway in the Hunter Valley, 234 km (145 miles) north of Sydney, Singleton is an elegant old town with historic buildings and old-style rose gardens. European settlement dates back to the early 1800s, but before that the district was home to the Wanuaruah people. The first white man to arrive was John Howe, chief constable of Windsor. Benjamin Singleton, a member of his party, settled there on a grant of land and in 1836 subdivided part of his land as the town of Singleton. He put his residence near a ford across the Hunter and the town grew up around him. Coal has been mined in the district since 1870.

Now Singleton has a population of 22,000 and services both the miners and a district producing milk and cheese, fat lambs, beef cattle, wool, stock feed, fruit and vegetables. There are also a number of wineries in the area. Singleton boasts the Southern Hemisphere's largest sundial and visitors should also inspect the gardens at the historic house, Townhead. Nearby Lake St Clair, formed by the Glennies Creek Dam in 1983, is 26 km (16 miles) from Singleton via the Bridgeman Road. The recreation area has free electric barbecues, hot-water showers, and toilet facilities. Overnight camping is permitted, and there is also a boat ramp. Canoeing, sailing, sailboarding, swimming and fishing are popular pastimes. There are plenty of good opportunities to go bushwalking as well, as Wollemi, Barrington Tops and Yengo national parks are within easy striking distance. In Scone, golf and tennis are also on offer.
Map ref: page 459 H5

SOFALA

In the Turon River Valley, Sofala is the oldest gold town in Australia. Situated 243 km (151 miles) north-west of Sydney, it was settled three weeks after the strike at Ophir, and the population very quickly swelled to around 40,000.

Sofala is a little different today with only 100 residents, but with its weathered buildings and picturesque setting, it is well worth a visit. You can still get a cold beer at the Royal Hotel, and do a little fossicking as well and the area is great for 4WD touring.

The surrounding district grows superfine wool, and most of the properties have relics and remnants of the old days. One, Chesleigh Homestead, contains 7 km (4.4 miles) of the original Cobb and Co coach road to Hill End. It also has extensive underground mines, alluvial diggings, water-races (used to sluice river gravel to search for gold), old shanties and hectares of land with history to explore. The 1400 ha property has 3 km (1.9 miles) of river frontage, horses, tennis courts, games room, gold-fossicking equipment, fishing tackle, a swimming pool and spa. It takes house guests.
Map ref: page 458 D6

SPRINGWOOD

On his way to Bathurst in 1815, Governor Macquarie was impressed by 'a pretty wooded Plain near a Spring of very good fresh Water'. He called the place 'Spring-Wood'. Today Springwood is a residential centre and tourist resort of 7100. It is 72 km (45 miles) west of Sydney in the lower Blue Mountains, 310 m (1017 feet) above sea level.

Most people who come to Springwood are bushwalkers, and there are a number of tracks, ranging from easy to sweaty, in close proximity to the village. More sedentary folk may like to browse through the antique stores or visit the Local History Centre and community art gallery. These are both housed in Braemar, a National Trust Federation home. Springwood railway station is also a listed property. The grave of Sir Henry Parkes, Father of Federation and after whom the town of Parkes was named, is in Springwood cemetery.
Map ref: page 458 G8

STROUD

In 1826, the Australian Agricultural Company purchased 400,000 ha (988,400 acres) of land in the Port Stephens area and proceeded to develop Stroud, which is 163 km (101 miles) north of Sydney, as a company headquarters. Built by convicts, Stroud's construction was overseen by Sir Edward Parry, a former Arctic explorer. His wife supervised the construction of St John's Anglican Church, a Gothic Revival structure made from the clay bricks of the area. Another building using the same materials, also convict-built, was the Australian Inn, the first pub in Stroud and, like the church, it was erected in 1833.

In 1918, Alfred Bowen bought the inn, which by then was a rather dilapidated remnant of its glorious past—and he painstakingly demolished it brick by brick. Using those same materials—bricks, fireplaces, cedar doors and skirting boards—he then built Chalford House, which remained in the Bowen family until 1996, when it was bought by the current owners. It is now once again opened to travellers.

Stroud today is home to 500 people and is full of history and classified buildings … and one unusual event. Every year, it holds an international brick-throwing contest between four centres named Stroud: one here, one in England, one in Canada and one in the United States.
Map ref: page 459 K4

Pelicans are common in many coastal towns.

SYDNEY HARBOUR NATIONAL PARK

This must surely be one of the most outstanding national parks in the world. Scattered around what is possibly the most beautiful harbour in the land is a series of national parks that together protect a number of headlands.

Access to the various parks is very easy, with major roads leading to all areas, and even government bus routes pass by many parks. There are several excellent walking trails around parts of the foreshore, each of these provide unsurpassed views over the spectacular harbour.

The area is dotted with historic fortresses and gun emplacements and this adds to the interest of the park. The park also includes North Head and its Quarantine Station, where various tours can be taken

Sofala township was once a booming gold town but is now a small, sleepy village.

Sydney Harbour National Park flanks much of the shoreline of this busy city's harbour and includes five harbour islands.

(including spooky ghost tours by night) and Dobroyd Point, all near Manly; Middle Head to Bradleys Head and, on the southern side of the harbour, Nielsen Park and South Head. There are also a number of harbour islands included in the park and tours to these can be arranged through National Parks and Wildlife Service (NPWS).
Map ref: page 453 G5

TAREE

'Taree' is a diminutive of the Aboriginal word 'tareebit' that described a particular figtree, which grows in the Manning Valley. Found 333 km (207 miles) north of Sydney, Taree stands on an old grant of land made to William Wynter, the first permanent settler on the Manning, who moved to the area in about 1831. In the early 1850s, Henry Flett, Wynter's son-in-law, laid out a private town.

Now Taree has a population of 17,500 and is the commercial and industrial centre of a district given chiefly to dairying, timber cutting, mixed farming and fishing. It offers much to the tourist: river cruises, horse riding, fishing, golf, horse and greyhound racing, squash, tennis and 4WD touring, but its appeal lies in nearby attractions.

Crowdy Bay National Park is just 35 km (22 miles) to the north and this area is noted for its fishing and surfing. Diamond Head is the main camping area inside the park, with barbecue and toilets, but be

warned as visitors must bring in their own water—something that holds true for the entire 6000 ha (14,826 acres) reserve of coastal plains. There are good walking trails in the park as well. Australian author Kylie Tennant wrote the novel *The Man on the Headland* in a self-built hut on Diamond Head.

Boorganna Nature Reserve, the second one to be declared in the State, covers 396 ha (979 acres) and is just over 6 km (3.7 miles) west of town. It features a walking track through rainforest.

Five kilometres (3.1 miles) south of town is Kiwarrack State Forest, which is perfect for car touring, as it offers a magnificent scenic drive. The best spots to stop and have a look are at the Pines Picnic Area and also Breakneck Lookout. All up, it is an easy 16 km (10 mile) drive through the forest.

Another area worth visiting is Coopernook State Forest, which offers spectacular views of the Manning Valley. Middle Brother Forest has several walking trails, one of which passes the two largest blackbutt trees in the State—'Bird Tree' and 'Benaroon'.

The Taree aquatic festival is held every year in April and June is busy with the town hosting its annual Envirofair and also The Taree City Festival (biannual). The Agricultural Expo is on in July; in August there is the Gold Cup Racing Carnival and in October, the Taree Show and Trade festival.
Map ref: page 459 L3

TERRIGAL

Terrigal translates as 'place of little birds'. Just 98 km (61 miles) north of Sydney, this town and tourist resort of 8000 people is on on the Central Coast of New South Wales and stands on the same stretch of surfing beach as the adjoining town of Wamberal.

Nearby lagoons around Terrigal are shark-free so they attract many visitors for swimming, boating, fishing, prawning and many other water-based activities.

Jutting into the ocean just south of Terrigal is a rather impressive headland called the Skillion and a hefty walk to the top reveals great coastal views. Bouddi National Park, a great place for bushwalkers, campers and anglers, is also close.
Map ref: page 459 J7

THE ENTRANCE

The Entrance has a population of 22,000 and it gets its name from its position on the waterway that allows water to enter Tuggerah Lake from the Tasman Sea.

One of the first settlers here was farmer Thomas Cade Batley, who built a house on Homestead Hill in 1836. Dairying later became the major industry but inevitably it caved in to tourism for this pretty seaside holiday town.

Situated about halfway between Sydney and Newcastle—103 km (64 miles) north of Sydney—the principal weekend attractions are boating, fishing (both lake and ocean), prawning, swimming and waterskiing. It has clean beaches and a number of very pleasant picnic spots along the lakeside. Visitors can also take a pleasant cruise on Tuggerah Lake.
Map ref: page 459 J7

TOORAWEENAH

Like Coonamble and Coonabarabran, rustic little Tooraweenah, with only 100 inhabitants, is yet another gateway to the magical Warrumbungles. It is located 488 km (303 miles) north-west of Sydney. Visitors can take gliding flights over the countryside with the Warrumbungle Gliding Club on weekends and there are many scenic drives in the area, including one that has sections of unsealed road leading into the Warrumbungle National Park, which offers some of the State's best bushwalks, excellent camping facilities and has a population of resident koalas.
Map ref: page 458 B2

Taree is near many natural attractions: national parks, reserves and forests.

TOUKLEY

Toukley is very popular with the sailing fraternity. It is also quite a hit with families who like the safe swimming the lake provides, with surf beaches also easily accessible.

Situated between Budgewoi and Tuggerah on the Central Coast, 110 km (68 miles) north of Sydney, Toukley is a favourite prawning spot and water sports are popular. It has a population of 7125. The nearby Munmorah State Recreation Park and Red Gum Forest will appeal to bushwalkers.
Map ref: page 459 J7

WAUCHOPE

Wauchope (which is pronounced 'war-hope', not 'watch-a-pee', as for its namesake the Northern Territory), is the timber town of New South Wales. It is 422 km (262 miles) north of Sydney and has a population of 4690. It is also the centre of a cattle, dairying and mixed farming district. It was named after an early settler, Captain Robert Wauch.

The town's major attraction is Timbertown, a replica of an old timber town, where visitors can return to the bygone days of horse-drawn wagons, steam trains, bullock teams and woodcutters.

Mount Seaview, which is 55 km (34 miles) west of Wauchope, has some excellent 4WD driving. There are also organised safaris for those who do not have a 4WD vehicle.
Map ref: page 459 M2

The Hawkesbury River near Wisemans Ferry is visited for water sports and bush scenery in an easy day-trip from Sydney.

WELLINGTON

Explorer John Oxley named the Wellington Valley after his hero, Arthur Wellesley, Duke of Wellington, who defeated Bonaparte at the Battle of Waterloo. Oxley journeyed down the Macquarie River in 1818 in search of the fabled inland sea, and on the basis of his report, a penal settlement was established in the district in 1823, under the command of Lieutenant Percy Simpson. The settlement did not last long, as pioneers soon came into the area to set up properties. Gold was discovered at Wellington in 1849 at a place called Mitchell's Creek. Gold was also found at Ironbarks, today known as Stuart Town, so it is a place worth trying your hand at some fossicking.

Home to 6000, Wellington is 354 km (220 miles) north-west of Sydney and is the service centre for a rich agricultural district of 4000 sq. km (1544 square miles) that produces wool, wheat, sheep and cattle, with some market gardening and dairying on the fertile flats of the Bell and Macquarie Rivers.

The Wellington Caves are the main attraction. While they are less extensive than Jenolan, they boast the world's largest stalagmite—at 15 m (49 feet) high and 32 m (105 feet) around the base. Resembling the Virgin Mary, this cave is called Cathedral Cave. Another cave also open to the public, the Gaden Cave, is smaller but has more exquisite formations. Bone Cave has fossilised skeletons of animals that roamed the Wellington Valley millions of years ago and is reserved for scientific study. It is thought that George Ranken discovered the caves in 1830, when he accidentally fell into one!

Burrendong Dam offers water sports and fishing. Built originally to mitigate flood damage, the dam supplies irrigation water to places as far west as Warren. It backs up the Cudgegong River for 26 km (16 miles) and the Macquarie for 35 km (22 miles). It is also home to an arboretum for native plant life. Other pursuits around town include bowls, golf and tennis. In November, Wellington hosts the Balloon and Bentleys Festival and the Formula One boat Races are held each December.
Map ref: page 458 B5

WINDSOR

Windsor was one of five town sites selected by Governor Macquarie and originally developed to provide a safe haven when the Hawkesbury flooded—which was fairly often. At first called Green Hills, Macquarie changed the name because of a supposed similarity with the English town of Windsor.

Windsor is 54 km (34 miles) west of Sydney and has population of 1870. The town has some fine colonial architecture; St Matthew's Anglican Church being the oldest Anglican church in Australia.

Other places to go that are near to Windsor include the Australian Pioneer Village, where the oldest timber dwelling in Australia, Rose Cottage, is located. A blacksmith displays his trade on certain days, and there are also some barbecue and picnic spots and a lake with paddleboats. Cattai National Park, 14 km (9 miles) to the north-east, also has activities that will be of

E.J. Davidson, a poet in Timbertown, a historic village reconstruction near Wauchope.

interest to the young, such as canoe hire. The town is a great place for antique or art and craft and shopping, and it is a popular stop-off point en route to exploring the Blue Mountains region.

Windsor has a craft market each Sunday in the Mall. It is also the scene of three famous 'Bridge to Bridge' races. One for powerboats is held in May; another, for canoes, is in October, and the third, for waterskiers, is in November.
Map ref: page 458 G8

WINGHAM

Known as 'the friendly town', Wingham, 345 km (220 miles) north of Sydney, is also the oldest town on the Manning River and was built around an English-style village green. This is surrounded by 13 buildings including two pubs, the post office and courthouse, all of which are National Trust classified as historically significant. The museum displays Aboriginal activist Jimmy Governor's cell.

The town has a population of 4900 and dairying and timber-getting are the biggest local industries. Nearby Wingham Brush is one of the few subtropical floodplain rainforests left in the State. It is now a major maternity site for the grey-headed flying fox. There are walks through the forest and you can have lunch there at one of the picnic sites or on the riverbank. Facilities are provided. Wingham also makes a good starting point for the Bulga Forest Drive, which features Ellenborough Falls, at 160 m (525 feet), the longest single-drop falls in Australia. Bulga has bushwalking and camping areas.

Wingham holds a rodeo in January and its Agricultural Show in March and the Manning Valley Beef Week is held in April–May.
Map ref: page 459 L3

Sunnyside Ridge lookout in Wollemi National Park in the northern Blue Mountains.

WISEMANS FERRY

Wisemans Ferry, 66 km (41 miles) north-west of Sydney (population 400), is named after Solomon Wiseman, an ex-convict who ran a ferry service over the Hawkesbury River and later established an inn here. Described by the local clergyman as a man 'deeply read in the corruption of human nature', Wiseman is believed to have killed his wife by pushing her down the steps of the inn while arguing over beer. Her ghost is said to haunt the hotel, which still stands. The river is very popular for water sports. Nearby Dharug National Park contains a wealth of indigenous rock engravings, some of which are up to 8000 years old. The convict-built Old Northern Road forms the park's western boundary. A feat of engineering, the road is open to cyclists and walkers and the park has some excellent bushwalks.
Map ref: page 459 H7

WOLLEMI NATIONAL PARK

A huge park west of Sydney in the Blue Mountains, it stretches from the Bells Line of Road, where it abuts the Blue Mountains National Park, north to the Hunter Valley. Much is designated wilderness, with some of the most rugged mountain country in Australia—sheer cliffs and ridges, cool rivers, deep canyons and ancient vegetation. This is excellent country for experienced bushwalkers but, because it is so remote, you need to be well prepared. From Bells Line of Road it is possible to reach the old train tunnels of the Newnes mining area, visiting the canyons of Deep Pass and the rock gardens of the Lost City on the way. Camping with basic facilities is available at Newnes and Wheeney Creek.
Map ref: page 458 F5

WOLLOMBI

Wollombi (population 500) is a very pretty little village only 127 km (79 miles) north-west of Sydney. Just south-west of Cessnock, it is reached via dirt roads. There is a small museum and some noteworthy colonial buildings, including St John's Anglican Church, the post office and the courthouse. The Endeavour Museum contains some very interesting relics of the local area's social history, and a local brew, Dr Jurd's Jungle Juice, is worth trying. Once, Wollombi holds a village fair in June and a folk festival in September. Nearby national parks offer plenty of bushwalking.
Map ref: page 459 H6

WOY WOY

Originally known as Webbs Flat after the first European in the area, James Webb, who arrived in 1834, the name was conferred in 1888. Woy Woy means 'deep water' and the town relies almost entirely on tourism for its community income, although being within commuting distance of Sydney—100 km (62 miles) south—a number of city workers live in here. The population is 12,200.

These days, fishing, boating and swimming—along with the beautiful scenery—attract large numbers of visitors. There are also several important national parks in the area, including Brisbane Water, which features the Bulgandry Aboriginal rock carvings and has an abundance of wildflowers, bushwalks and bird life. The wreck of the *Maitland* is found within Bouddi National Park, which offers good bushwalking, swimming and fishing areas. Near the entrance to the park, the Marie Byles Lookout has great views right down to Sydney. In November Woy Woy celebrates the Oyster and Wine Festival.
Map ref: page 459 H7

Strangler fig (Ficus watkinsiana), Wingham Brush.

WYONG

A popular tourist resort on the Central Coast, Wyong was founded on timber-getting in the 1840s and 1850s. The name means 'place of running water'. Chief industries are timber milling, dairying, poultry farming and citrus fruit. It is only 109 km (68 miles) north of Sydney, which makes it an easy day trip from the city.

The District Museum has some interesting relics of early logging days, as well as material relating to early ferry services across the nearby lakes, a system that stretches from Lake Munmorah in the north to Killarney Vale in the south, and also Budgewoi and Tuggerah Lake, the largest, which offers access to the sea at The Entrance.

The Wyong hinterland is quite popular with bushwalkers and campers. To the north, there are some State forests that also offer fun for drivers of 4WDs and feature some superb lookouts, which are appreciated by photographers.

Around Wyong you can go fishing, greyhound racing, trotting or try various water sports. Wyong has a population of 3200.
Map ref: page 459 J7

NORTH-EAST NEW SOUTH WALES

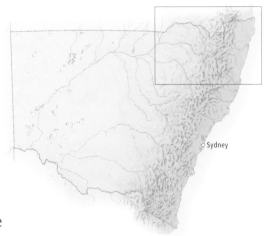

Always popular with holidaymakers, the north coast of New South Wales offers the winning combination of fine surf beaches, fast-flowing rivers and unspoilt mountain wilderness. Straddling the Great Dividing Range are the high grasslands and prosperous sheep properties of the vast New England Tableland. Further out to the west are the fertile black soils of the Liverpool Plains.

The coastal strip from Coffs Harbour north through Byron Bay claims the best climate in the country—sunny, but not too humid. Subtropical plants such as sugar cane and bananas thrive, while Grafton is known for its magnificent jacaranda trees. Beaches are wide and sandy and the waters are famed for prolific hauls of prawns and fish. Inland, the many rivers that rise in the mountains cut spectacular gorges as they rush through dense eucalypt and subtropical rainforest to lush coastal lowlands. A massive amount of timber, including sought-after cedar ('red gold') was cut from the region; Wauchope, just inland from Port Macquarie, features a working replica of an old timber town.

Because of its elevation, the New England Tableland has mild summers and cool winters; most rain falls on the eastern edge, so the tops and western slopes are considerably drier than the coast. Pastoral holdings here date from the 1830s and today the district is known for its merino flocks. Regional centres include the university and cathedral city of Armidale; Uralla, best known as the burial place of bushranger Captain Thunderbolt, and Tenterfield, birthplace of Federation (Henry Parkes delivered a very impassioned

speech here in 1889) and Peter Allen, who later immortalised his hometown in song.

The rich Liverpool Plains support sheep and horse studs, wheat and cotton growing and mixed farming. Country music capital Tamworth is the major centre; famous poet Dorothea Mackellar was born in Gunnedah, to the north-west, now surrounded by vast, flat fields of wheat and cotton. Cotton crops follow the Namoi River Valley further west to Narrabri and Wee Waa, and cotton also grows around Moree, to the north. Evidence of past volcanic upheavals can be seen in the basalt spires and domes of Mount Warning in the far north, and Mount Kaputar and the striking Warrumbungles in the west.

OPPOSITE: The lighthouse on South Solitary Island became automated in 1975. The original brass and prism glass lantern is in the museum at nearby Coffs Harbour.

Colourful murals adorn the Nimbin Hotel. Nimbin developed as a centre for alternative living after the 1973 Aquarius Festival.

REGIONAL FEATURE

Big River Country

The large wedge of northern coastal New South Wales centred on Grafton and bounded by the Gibraltar Range and its national parks in the west, Bundjalung National Park in the north and Yuraygir National Park in the south is known as Big River Country, in recognition of the mighty Clarence River system, its main aquatic artery. Rising high in the rugged mountain rainforests of the Great Dividing Range along the New South Wales–Queensland border, and fed by tributaries flowing in from as far afield as Glen Innes, Guyra and Ebor, the Clarence remains one of the last great untamed and un-dammed rivers of south-eastern Australia.

Big River Country encompasses a remarkable array of environments, ranging from undeveloped beaches and coastal woodlands to pristine waterways and rugged, bush-clad mountains. Such diversity creates abundant opportunities for leisure activities, most notably fishing on rivers, lakes and the coast, and bushwalking in several superb national parks.

The Clarence River valley can be regarded as defining the southern boundary of the east coast's true subtropical zone. Sugar cane and bananas thrive here, and tropical fish such as fork-tailed catfish, tarpon (ox-eye herring) and mangrove jack are occasionally caught alongside more familiar species including Australian bass, bream, whiting and flathead.

History

Long inhabited by Aboriginal peoples, the region was first sighted by a European in 1799, when Matthew Flinders moored near Yamba. However, Flinders failed to realise that a major river system lay a short distance inland and it was only when convict Richard Craig escaped from the Moreton Bay penal colony in 1831 that a non-indigenous person finally set eyes on the Clarence River valley. Craig subsequently made his way to Sydney where he described what he called 'the big river' and its immense stands of red cedar trees to local merchants. In return for a pardon and a reward of £100, he led a party of cedar cutters back to the area, and they were soon followed by other loggers, surveyors and pastoralists.

In 1839, the river was renamed after the Duke of Clarence and in 1851 the town of Grafton was established. By then, the valley had become the centre of several thriving industries. Logging and dairy and beef farming led the way but were soon rivalled by the sugar industry, which was established in the 1870s. Today, sugar production is the valley's principal economic activity. On the lower reaches of the river, however, the most important industries are prawn trawling and fishing, although in recent years tourism has become increasingly significant in coastal towns such as Yamba.

Bundjalung National Park

Situated on the northern side of the mouth of the Clarence River, this 17,738-ha (43,830-acre) wilderness is an idyllic coastal hideaway incorporating tranquil rivers, flower-filled meadows and 38 km (24 miles) of expansive, sandy beaches. Prior to white settlement, this was the territory of the Bundjalung Aboriginal people. Today, the only signs of their formerly widespread presence are numerous middens scattered along the banks of the Evans River.

Bundjalung is a birdwatcher's paradise. Hundreds of honeyeaters feed on the nectar of the park's abundant banksias, and colourful species such as the superb and variegated fairy wrens are commonly seen around camp sites. Along the coast, silver gulls, terns and oystercatchers forage on the sand, while ospreys, white-breasted sea-eagles and brahminy kites patrol the skies. Egrets, spoonbills, herons and ducks are also spotted regularly, mainly around the inland swamps. Botanists will delight in the park's vivid displays of wildflowers. In early spring, the heathland's myriad blooms include purple irises, yellow waxflowers, white daisies and pink boronia.

Bundjalung is easily reached by turning off the Pacific Highway at the national park sign approximately 3 km (1.9 miles) south of Woodburn. The first 5 km (3.1 miles) of this road is bitumen, the last 13 km (8 miles) unsealed and sometimes heavily corrugated in places. However, conventional vehicles, including caravans, should have no trouble negotiating the route if they proceed slowly.

Four-wheel-drive vehicles are permitted on the beach between the Black Rocks Rest Area in the centre of the park and Shark Bay, 12 km (7.5 miles) to the south. To avoid possible mishaps, drive on the sand only during the hour or two prior to and following low tide. Avoid driving in or near the dunes as several varieties of native birds nest here.

There is no charge for camping within the park, and sites do not need to be booked in advance. Facilities at the Black Rocks Rest Area include pit toilets, picnic tables, firewood and fireplaces. Visitors looking for a more comfortable site should try the Woody Head camping ground on the park's southern boundary, where amenities include hot showers, toilets, washing tubs and a small kiosk. Drinking water is not available within the park and should therefore be carried at all times.

Yuraygir National Park

This park on the southern side of the Clarence encompasses the largest stretch of undeveloped coastline in eastern Australia. Magnificent beaches provide opportunities for angling, surfing and walking, and visitors can also canoe and fish on inland lakes and rivers.

Casting from a canoe is the best way to fish for bass on the upper reaches of the Clarence River.

OPPOSITE: *Close to the coast, the Clarence's meandering path has formed several sizeable islands.*

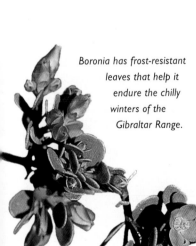

Boronia has frost-resistant leaves that help it endure the chilly winters of the Gibraltar Range.

There are several ways into Yuraygir. From Yamba, you can take the road south to Angourie, where you'll find excellent walks and some of the best surfing in Australia. East of Grafton, roads lead to the popular resorts of Minnie Water and Diggers Rest, as well as the settlement of Wooli. At the southern end of the park, Station Creek lies just a short distance from the Princes Highway. There are campsites at most of these places (fees apply) and a number of commercial camping grounds, motels, hotels and caravan parks can be found in adjacent towns and resorts.

Fishing

Despite years of intensive commercial activity by trawlers, netters and trappers, the Clarence River estuary and the adjacent coastline continue to provide varied and productive fishing. The town of Yamba offers the most convenient access to the lower reaches of the Clarence, its numerous ramps allowing anglers to either fish within the estuary system or head off-shore. Iluka also has a number of ramps, and smaller boats can be launched near the hotel as well as up-stream at an old ferry approach near the power lines.

Breakwalls at the river's entrance and in its lower reaches make excellent land-based platforms for anglers targeting tailor, mulloway (jewfish), bream, blackfish, flathead and whiting, and Yamba's famous Middle Wall is one of the best-known fishing hot spots in the entire region. Where the North and South walls extend offshore from the river mouth, they also offer access to migratory pelagic species including tuna, mackerel, kingfish and cobia, as well as sharks and mulloway, especially after floods.

The extensive sand flats within the estuary system are top spots for whiting, bream and flathead, as well as crabs and prawns in season. Good catches of dusky flathead and other species can be taken by drift fishing all the way up the river to well beyond Harwood and at least as far as Maclean and Lawrence at times.

Among the many fine rock- and beach-fishing locations are Woody Head, Iluka Bluff, Little Bluff

Paperbark and cypress swamps are distinctive habitats within Bundjalung National Park.

and Frasers Reef on the northern side of the river mouth, and, on the south side, Flat Rock, Green Point and Angourie Point as well as several more remote (and therefore quieter) rock platforms within Yuraygir National Park. Tailor, bream, mulloway, drummer, groper and other species can be taken from the headlands, along with big surface fish including Spanish mackerel, longtail tuna, mackerel tuna, yellowtail kingfish and cobia. The beaches in-between are likely to yield whiting, bream, tailor, flathead, dart and the occasional big mulloway or jewfish.

Shelley Head, in Yuraygir National Park, is a particularly good rock-fishing spot accessible via walking trails from either Angourie Point or Red Cliff. The turn-off to Red Cliff is located at Maclean, on the Pacific Highway. This same road leads to nearby Brooms Head and the beautiful Sandon River. Brooms Head is a small village with a caravan park and store. It offers good beach and rock fishing, especially for tailor, and reef fishing offshore. With due care, it is possible to beach-launch a boat here. The

Sandon River lies south of Brooms Head and marks the end of this particular coastal road, with the Sandon's southern shores being reached via Minnie Waters to the south, along a 4WD track. The Sandon has a boat ramp that provides access to prolific reefs offshore and to the river's small estuary. Whiting, bream and flathead are the major targets in the estuary, along with the occasional mangrove jack taken around the rock bar further upstream.

ANGLING UPRIVER

The highest tributaries of the Clarence hold scattered, marginal populations of introduced trout, but as the branches of this mighty river tumble from the high escarpments and merge, native species predominate. First and foremost among these—in terms of both size and importance—is the once-threatened and still-protected east coast or Clarence River cod.

A kissing cousin of the western Murray cod—a species from which it developed in the relatively recent evolutionary past—the east coast cod is a strikingly attractive, highly territorial species capable of reaching perhaps 40 kg (88 pounds) in exceptional cases, though it is more commonly found in the 1- to 10-kg (2.2- to 22-pound) range.

East coast cod numbers declined dramatically during the twentieth century until rescued from the brink of extinction in the 1980s. Today, thanks to their protected status and careful restocking of depleted stretches of various rivers, east coast cod populations are rising, and in the not-too-distant future limited sport fishing (on a purely catch-and-release basis) for this challenging, hard-fighting species could even be reintroduced. Meanwhile, any angler accidentally hooking one of these magnificent native fish should carefully unhook it and return it quickly to the water.

Other notable fish species in the freshwater reaches of the Clarence system include eel-tailed catfish, Australian bass, Nepean herring, eels and the occasional golden perch or yellowbelly (possibly escapees from farm dams). Of these, it is the Australian bass that attract the greatest interest from anglers. The rugged Clarence Gorge, a short distance upstream from Copmanhurst, acts as an effective natural

Washpool National Park's highly fertile, mainly volcanic soils have given rise to a thick covering of forest broken only by scattered rock outcrops and pinnacles.

The settlements of Yamba and Iluka flank the narrow entrance to the Clarence River estuary.

The mountain brushtail possum (Trichosurus caninus) replaces the common brushtail possum in upland forests. It can be distinguished from its more widespread cousin by its heavier body and much smaller ears.

barrier to the free movement of bass for years at a time. Occasionally, however, it is inundated by massive flooding, allowing fish of all sizes to move in both directions and thereby maintaining a healthy population of bass above the gorge in rivers such as the Mann, Nymboida and the upper Clarence. Access to these regions can be difficult because much of the land fringing the Clarence is private. However, adventurous anglers who launch canoes at Jackadgery or Cangai are likely to enjoy exceptional sport.

More accessible and consistent bass fishing is available downstream from the Clarence Gorge, near Fine Flower and Copmanhurst, as well as in lower tributaries of the Clarence such as the Orara, Coldstream and Esk rivers and Sportsmans Creek. In these tributaries, bass are often caught along with other brackish water species including estuary perch, bream, flathead and the occasional ox-eye herring (tarpon) and mangrove jack.

Washpool National Park

Several of the Clarence's tributaries begin high in the Gibraltar Range, which forms the western boundary of the Big River Country. This is a wild region of majestic, rugged peaks and lush, dense rainforests. Mountain streams tumble through boulder-strewn gorges, their banks lined with delicate ferns and mosses. In the forest canopy, huge bird's-nest and staghorn ferns cling precariously to the branches of ancient, giant trees, occasionally crashing to the ground with a mighty thud when their weight becomes too much for their host to bear. On the leaf-littered rainforest floor, fungi of every imaginable shape and size decorate the rotting timber.

Three contiguous national parks—Washpool, Gibraltar Range and Nymboida—preserve an enormous swathe of this astonishing wilderness; all enjoy World Heritage status as part of the Central Eastern Rainforest Reserves area, which was declared in 1994.

The most accessible of the Gibraltar Range national parks, Washpool National Park protects 27,700 ha (68,450 acres) including the largest area of old-growth, warm-temperate rainforest in New South Wales. A large proportion of the national park consists of an elevated, trackless plateau that in some places rises as high as 1200 m (4000 feet) above sea level. Numerous species of trees, shrubs and flowering plants clothe its ridges and steep slopes, including the world's largest remaining stand of coachwood.

Wildlife is abundant in Washpool. More than 260 species of birds have been recorded including currawongs, eastern yellow robins, scrub wrens, fantails, Lewin honeyeaters, crimson rosellas and king parrots. Sharp-eyed travellers might also catch a glimpse of the elusive lyrebird foraging around forest edges. The most intriguing of the park's feathered inhabitants, however, is the satin bowerbird. After constructing an elaborate bower out of fine twigs, the glossy, dark blue male tries to attract a female by placing small blue objects such as straws, feathers and pen tops around the bower. Single-minded in his devotion to this task, he collects these items from any available source, including tents and picnic sites.

Most native mammal species are nocturnal, but several can be seen around camp sites including three species of possums. The thick-set mountain brush-tailed possums are the most regularly encountered as they often scavenge around picnic tables. Ringtail possums are more elusive, but, with the aid of a good torch, may be spotted high in the trees beside the walking tracks. The much smaller sugar-gliders are more difficult to locate, but, again, using a torch may help you locate one of these charming creatures. Near the park entrance, koalas and greater gliders can sometimes be sighted in the tops of tall eucalypts.

Washpool's walking trails range from a pleasant one-hour stroll along the banks of Coombadjha Creek to demanding three-day hikes through remote wilderness. Anyone attempting these extended treks into the park's interior should be reasonably fit and fully equipped for emergencies. A compass, topographic maps and wet-weather gear are essential.

Though remote, the park is accessible to conventional vehicles and roads are generally well maintained. Caravans and trailers should have no trouble negotiating the track into Bellbird Camping Area, but should not attempt the steep descent into the walk-in camp sites at Coombadjha Camping Area.

Bellbird Camping Area is the park's main camping ground; it has picnic tables, fireplaces, firewood and toilets, and a large shelter shed where visitors can cook during wet weather. Washpool National Park is a region of high rainfall, and showers or thunderstorms are likely at any time of year.

Gibraltar Range National Park

Abutting the southern boundary of Washpool, Gibraltar Range National Park covers 17,273 ha (42,682 acres) of rugged granite peaks, rainforest, heathlands and towering eucalypts. Wildlife is particularly prolific here, with eastern grey kangaroos, red-necked wallabies and swamp wallabies spotted regularly in various parts of the park. Rarer species include the endangered parma wallaby and the seldom-seen tiger quoll. The rich array of birds includes king parrots, eastern yellow robins, rufous fantails, a multitude of honeyeaters, and the magnificent wedge-tailed eagle. At certain times of the year, rangers lead night walks in search of nocturnal mammal species such as the greater glider, squirrel glider, sugar glider, brush-tailed possum and short-nosed bandicoot.

There is a camping area at Mulligan's Hut, 10 km (6 miles) inside the park along the Gwydir Highway. One of the most interesting trails here is the 5-km (3.1-mile) return hike to Dandahra Falls; however, the last part of the track is very steep and should therefore only be attempted by fit walkers.

Nymboida National Park

With no walking trails, no major roads and few other facilities for visitors, Nymboida is the least accessible of the Gibraltar Range national parks. However, it offers superb whitewater rafting as well as exhilarating wilderness experiences for self-sufficient and well-prepared canoeists and bushwalkers.

Nymboida's 19,000 ha (47,000 acres) of almost impenetrable forest are centred on the steep-sided Mann River valley. At the eastern end of the park, the Mann meets the Nymboida River forming a raging torrent that plummets through deep, forest-clad valleys. Several local tour operators run thrilling trips down these dramatic waterways.

Adventurous visitors can venture into the national park in a canoe from Buccarumbi or on foot from Jackadgery. Vehicle access is difficult, with only two rough 4WD tracks penetrating the park. One leads through Ramornie State Forest to Ramornie Forest Camping Area; the other leaves the Gwydir Highway at Glen Innes and follows the Narlala Road and Cooraldooral Fire Trail to the Mann River.

Canoeists tackling the upper reaches of the Clarence should be prepared to portage through boulder-strewn narrows.

Places in
NORTH-EAST
NEW SOUTH WALES

ALSTONVILLE

Alstonville's population is 3678 and the town is located on the Bruxner Highway, which runs between Ballina and Tenterfield and eventually to Boggabilla in the central north-west. It is located 791 km (491 miles) north of Sydney.

Originally this area was involved in timber-getting but these days the local industries consist mainly of macadamia nut farms and avocado and propagation plus a variety of other, sometimes

Roasted Alstonville macadamias.

unusual tropical fruit. There are many unique nurseries in the area, which supply plants nationwide.

Alstonville is essentially a central point for nature-based excursions in the region, such as Bundjalung National Park, which lies to the south; to the north are the twin parks of Nightcap and Mount Jerusalem. An agricultural show is held in late October. Other pursuits in town include swimming, squash, bowls and tennis.

Map ref: page 461 P3

ARMIDALE

Almost halfway between Sydney and Brisbane, 566 km (352 miles) north of Sydney, Armidale is one of the prettiest, stateliest rural cities in New South Wales. The area where this city of 23,500 now stands was originally home to the Anaiwan Aboriginals for 10,000 years and an Aboriginal painting site can be found at Mount Yarrowyck, 30 km (19 miles) west of Armidale. The first settler here was William Dumaresq, who took up land in 1835; another four years later the Commissioner of Crown Land, G.J. Macdonald, established a head station. He named it Armidale, after his father's estate in Scotland.

Gazetted in 1849, Armidale is now the principal city of New England. The area is known for its high-grade fine wool and also as the source for bloodlines for several noted sheep studs. However timber processing, dairying and the production of stone fruits and potatoes also feature.

A ricketty cottage garden fence captures the country charm of Armidale.

At 200 m (656 feet) high, Bald Rock is the largest granitic monolith in Australia.

The city is renowned as an educational and ecclesiastical centre. The town has two cathedrals—St Mary's (Roman Catholic) and St Peter's (Anglican)—and the town is host to not only New England University and the Armidale Technical College and TAFE, but also several exclusive private schools.

Thirty-five of Armidale's buildings are National Trust classified, and there are two historic homesteads: Saumarez, to the south, and Booloominbah, within the grounds of the University of New England. One of many museums worth a visit is the New England Regional Arts Museum.

There is a heritage walk that runs for 3 km (1.9 miles) around town, or you can visit the Aboriginal Cultural Centre and Keeping Place. Armidale hosts the New England Wool Expo in May, an Autumn Festival in March, and Town and Country garden tours are held in the first weekend in November.

Less than two hours' drive from Armidale is New England National Park, which is on the World Heritage List. Nearby are four other

national parks: Oxley Wild Rivers; Guy Fawkes; Cathedral Rock and Dorrigo. Nearby natural attractions include Wollomombi Falls, Ebor Falls and Hillgrove Gorge.

Local activities around Armidale include abseiling, canoeing, bushwalking, fishing, horse riding, golf, squash, tennis and gliding.

Map ref: page 461 J8

BALD ROCK NATIONAL PARK

Hugging the Queensland border, Bald Rock National Park, 5451 ha (13,469 acres), is tucked away in thickly forested country 29 km (18 miles) north of Tenterfield. The park's centrepiece, the dome-shaped granite monolith of Bald Rock, is one of Australia's best-kept secrets. This huge dome, weathered in stripes of grey, brown and pink, rises high above the surrounding eucalypt forest and rainforest.

Smaller outcrops of rock are also scattered throughout the park. The park has two walking tracks, both of which lead to the summit, with magnificent views west and north across the border to Girraween

National Park and east to the Pacific. Both tracks are shaded most of the way to the base of the rock by stands of eucalypts, mainly stringy-bark and New England blackbutt. Accessible to conventional vehicles, the park has a camping area with basic facilities (barbecues, tables and pit toilets) and is a pleasant place to visit at most times of the year, although the winters are quite often bitterly cold.

Map ref: page 461 K3

BALLINA

Ballina (population 12,500) sits at the estuary of the Richmond River, 789 km (490 miles) north of Sydney. It is now the heart of a thriving fishing industry. Originally the first white residents were cedar-getters but farmers and graziers took up when they left. Now tourism is an important local industry. With ready access to surf beaches, Ballina is a magnet for beach-lovers.

There is plenty to do around Ballina, including the usual water sports of surfing, sailing and scuba diving, plus whitewater rafting on the upper reaches of the Richmond River. There is even a 'Skirmish'

adventure park. Other activities include abseiling, mountain biking, climbing, hang-gliding, horse riding, parachuting and skydiving.

Slightly less taxing activities are golf, bushwalking, bowls, camel trekking, fossicking for gold, 4WD touring in the hinterland or whale-watching in spring and autumn.

For lovers of Australian kitsch, a visit to the Big Prawn is a must, but you can also visit a 'castle' (a family fun attraction), inspect the naval museum, the opal and gem museum, or go to a tea-tree or macadamia nut plantation. Ballina holds its Southern Cross Arts and Craft Festival in September.

Map ref: page 461 P3

BANGALOW

Bangalow is a rustic, quaint village set in the Byron Bay hinterland, 820 km (509 miles) north of Sydney. This town of 700 has many art, craft and antique shops and is a regional centre for the dairy industry, and fruit and vegetable production. There is a fine second-hand bookshop, called Uncle Pete's Books, in Byron Street. An excellent walking track leaves from town and winds its way along the banks of Byron Creek. Bangalow makes a good base from which to explore other areas by car. Rural markets are held in Bangalow on the last Saturday of each month.

Map ref: page 461 P2

BARRABA

Barraba is the centre for a pastoral area producing high-grade fine wool, and is 532 km (330 miles) north-west of Sydney. Earlier, asbestos mining at nearby Woods Reef augmented the area's economy, but the mining has ceased and the population is now 2280.

A monument in the town commemorates Allan Cunningham's crossing of the Manilla River in 1827; Thomas Mitchell is also associated with the area. Barraba is also close to two magnificent national parks: Mount Kaputar to the west, and the tiny Warrabah Park to the south-east. Mount Kaputar in particular is worth a visit, reserving almost 37,000 ha (91,427 acres) of forest-clad mountains and volcanic peaks. Its diverse conditions provide habitats for an immense variety of wildlife including koalas,

walleroos, kangaroos, gliders, possums, wedge-tailed eagles, honeyeaters, parrots and treecreepers. The Barrabor Festival is held annually on the first weekend in November.

Map ref: page 461 G7

BELLINGEN

Bellingen is a beautiful town, located on the Bellinger River only 40 km (25 miles) from the major coastal centre of Coffs Harbour; 568 km (353 miles) north of Sydney. It marks the beginning of a spectacular drive over the Great Dividing Range to Dorrigo. Home to 11,420, the town was originally called 'Boat Harbour', and it was once the backwater from where red cedar was floated down to the mouth of the Bellinger River (first encountered by timber-getters in 1841).

Farmers followed the sawyers and the area is now a prosperous district with a strong agricultural heritage. Dairy farming and the production of pigs, maize and fruit are the predominant industries. A far more recent venture, Advanced Wind Technologies specialises in energy-producing windmills.

Bellingen is more for the contemplative, artistically inclined visitor than the active adventure-seeker, abounding in art and craft

The Macadamia Castle, near Ballina.

shops and upmarket coffee and tea-houses and it is a terrific place to come to unwind. Another sedentary pursuit is to explore Mac's House of Rocks, which features lapidary work, opals and other gemstones.

For the active, however, all is not lost: there is canoeing, golf and swimming. The rugged Dorrigo National Park is in the north-west, while Bongil Bongil National Park is on the coast, just south of Sawtell. Bellingen holds a jazz festival in August each year and holds its markets on the third Saturday of every month.

Map ref: page 461 M8

Musicians enjoying a jam session in Bangalow, an arty north coast town.

BOGGABRI

Boggabri (population 1000) derives its name from an Aboriginal
dialect, meaning 'place of creeks'.
The town is 555 km (345 miles)
north-west of Sydney in the centre
of a rural district that produces
wool, wheat, fat lambs and cattle.
The district also has an important
connection with horses. Many of
the members of the First Australian
Light Horse came from Boggabri,
mainly due to the efforts of Lieutenant-Colonel Ken Mackay, who
travelled throughout New South
Wales in 1897 seeking the best
horsemen. Two local geographical
features—Barbers Pinnacle and
Barbers Lagoon—owe their names
to an escaped convict known as
'the Barber', who lived with the
local Aboriginal tribe for many
years. Some 20 km (12.5 miles)
to the north is Leard State Forest,
which is a prime gemstone
fossicking location.
Boggabri holds
its annual pic-
nic races each
year in July.
Map ref: page
460 E8

Rainforest skink, Border Ranges.

BORDER RANGES NATIONAL PARK

With its dramatic setting on the
rim of an extinct volcano, with
Mount Warning the remnant core,
this is one of the most scenic parks
in New South Wales. Abutting the
Queensland border, the park forms
part of a World Heritage-listed area
to preserve its cool-temperate and
subtropical rainforests, and numerous rare plant and animal species.
The Tweed Ranges scenic drive
makes a large loop through the
park, and there are excellent walks
along the way; do not miss the
Antarctic beech trees in the rainforest walk at Bar Mountain and
The Pinnacle walk with its breathtaking views across the Tweed
Valley to Mount Warning. Roads
in the park are gravel and steeply
graded, and a 4WD vehicle would
be more useful in wet conditions.
Map ref: page 461 N2

BRUNSWICK HEADS

Captain Rous was the very first
European to journey across the
Brunswick River
in 1828 and he
named it after
Queen Caro-
line of Bruns-
wick, wife of
King George IV.
Today, the small
seaside town of
Brunswick Heads
(population 1600) maintains a
maritime connection with the tidy
commercial fishing fleet moored in
the harbour. Situated 842 km (523
miles) north of Sydney, Brunswick
is a good spot for beach and river
water sports but it is most famous
for its fishing and its fish. Many
pundits claim that the North

The fishing fleet at Brunswick Heads, a quiet seaside village on the north coast.

One of the many local surf shops in Byron Bay, a New Age and surfing mecca.

Coast's best seafood is available at
Fins, on the riverfront. The town
has a good art gallery, and tennis,
bowls and golf are also on offer.
Brunswick Heads Nature Reserve
with local flora and fauna is well
worth a look. The Brunswick
Heads Festival of Fish and Chips
is held in January.
Map ref: page 461 P2

BYRON BAY

Once an unspoilt backwater on
the State's north coast, Byron Bay
is now a mix of cultures and lifestyles (including the alternative).
Situated 832 km (517 miles) north
of Sydney, Byron has a year-round
subtropical climate, with summer
temperatures dominated by a cooling onshore breeze. Such an idyllic
climate explains its presently burgeoning population—currently
around 7000—and its attraction
as a holiday destination.

Named by Captain Cook after a
pillar of the English establishment,
sailor Sir John Byron (who was also
the grandfather of the famed poet),
Byron Bay now is very international. Local restaurants embrace almost
every national cuisine, and there
are services with origins from all
over the globe, like tarot readings,
shiatsu massage and tai chi. Cape
Byron, which is the easternmost
point of Australia, is a great spot
from which to watch migrating
whales and frolicking dolphins.

Byron Bay has several good surf
beaches, and the breaks are famous
worldwide. Watego's Beach, with
its white sands and crystal waters,
has a break that is popular with
bodysurfers and boogie boarders,
is directly under the Cape Byron
lighthouse. The crystal-clear waters
are popular with snorkellers and
divers. There are also some great
drives in the Byron hinterland,
with spectacular views to the coast.

Regular events at Byron include
the famed East Coast Blues Festival
in June, the Writers' Festival in
early August and the Byron Food
Fest in the first week October. The
Byron Bay Classic (surfing) is held
during the Easter weekend.
Map ref: page 461 P2

CASINO

Casino derives its name from the
fact that in the 1840s Henry Clay
and George Stapleton, two early
settlers, called their station Cassino
[sic], after the town in southern
Italy. Timber-getting (especially
cedar) and cattle raising were the
principal early industries, but to
some extent these have given way
to dairying and pig raising. Casino
is now also an important air, rail
and road junction for north coast
tourist traffic. It is a bustling, busy
place with a population of 13,000
and has a large variety of clubs,
restaurants and sports venues, including golf and tennis.

Straddling the Richmond River,
741 km (460 miles) north of Sydney, the town has a large milk-
products factory and a meatworks
that is one of the biggest of its
kind in the Southern Hemisphere.

Casino also houses the north
coast headquarters of the Forestry
Commission. Local anglers have
success in Cook's Weir and in the
river. For history and culture buffs,
there are totemic Aboriginal rock
carvings on the Tenterfield road.
There is also a museum in town.

Known as the Beef Capital, between May and June Casino holds Beef Week—from 7 to 9 a.m., the town's butchers set up barbecues in the main street. The entertainment is extremely varied and includes a milking competition, comedy, several live bands, fashion parades, a street parade, street performers, art exhibitions, a cattle auction and a talent quest.

Map ref: page 461 N3

COFFS HARBOUR

Thought to be a corruption of Korff's Harbour, Coffs owes its name to John Korff, a cedar-getter in the 1850s. Originally two towns (the other was called Coffs Harbour Jetty) which gradually merged, Coffs is one of Australia's major timber ports. On the mid-north coast 1582 km (361 miles) north of Sydney it is also now that area's commercial centre. The CSIRO assessed it to have one of the best climates in the country—more hours of sunshine than areas further south and less humidity than places further north. This feature has been a contributory factor for Coffs Harbour's population of 60,000 and its popularity as a holiday resort.

Regarded by many sailors as one of New South Wales' safest all-weather ports, until the lighthouse was built in 1878, Coffs was shunned by captains as being too dangerous. Not surprisingly, the town now has a yacht club, a refurbished marina and a large commercial fishing fleet. Other

industries in the region include banana growing, dairying, engineering and sawmilling.

Coffs Promenade is a popular attraction, with numerous specialty shops and restaurants. There is also a beautiful botanic garden with a mangrove boardwalk. Some more enticements in the area include art, crafts and antique shops.

For families, there is the zoo, the Big Banana Theme Park, the Butterfly House and the Plaster Fun House. Coffs Harbour Jetty Foreshores makes an ideal picnic spot, with great views over the beaches, which are great for surfing, swimming or fishing.

Active people can enjoy golf, horse riding or whitewater rafting on the nearby Nymboida River. Those with 4WD vehicles can explore the rugged hinterland but there are 4WD adventure safaris for those without a 4WD. On Sundays, markets are held at the jetty.

Map ref: page 461 N7

COONABARABRAN

Coonabarabran (the name means 'an inquisitive person') started life in 1860, the first buildings being a courthouse and prison (restored in 1967 and still in use), and today the town is home to 3800. It was at Coonabarabran that Australia's only Chinese bushranger, Sam Poo, shot and wounded a police constable. He was tracked down, captured and hanged.

On the Newell Highway, 454 km (282 miles) north-west of Sydney, Coonabarabran is the

Coffs Harbour marina, where fishing charters and whale-watching cruises depart.

closest centre to the famed Warrumbungles. This sharp volcanic plateau literally erupts from the surrounding plains. It covers over 21,000 ha (51,891 acres) and is under supervision of the National Parks and Wildlife Service. The park is full of kangaroos, koalas, emus and an abundance of bird life. A walk over the Grand Hightops is unforgettable, and though it takes 4–6 hours, it is accessible with children.

White Gum Lookout and Gurianama walks are suitable for prams and wheelchairs. There is a powered camp site at the park with an amenities block, cleared sites and electric barbecues.

Visitors have many opportunities in the Coonabarabran area. They can take a scenic helicopter flight over the 'bungles, or go on an eco-tour with Coonabarabran Country

Tours, or gain some appreciation of Aboriginal life with Milton Judd's Aboriginal Site Tours.

Siding Springs Observatory, 24 km (15 miles) to the west, has the Southern Hemisphere's largest optical telescope. Crystal Kingdom is within easy walking distance of the main shopping centre and Shea's Miniland has life-size animated dinosaurs and a fantasy Stone Age train that takes visitors through natural bush settings and the exhibits. It is 9 km (5.6 miles) from Coonabarabran on the Warrumbungle road and has barbecues and picnic settings, 'Paddle-O-Saurus' boats, a bush puppet theatre, a museum and a waterslide.

Map ref: page 460 C10

Sidings Spring Observatory near Coonabarabran, where night skies are often clear.

Coffs Harbour's walk-in banana.

THE BIG BANANA
COFFS HARBOUR

protecting a vast area of rainforest. The park has good, established walking trails that entice you to enjoy and observe the rainforest and its prolific bird life. The major attraction of the 7885 ha (19,484 acres) park is the Skywalk and the Walk With Birds, which provide easy access into the treetop canopy to observe this unique ecosystem at close quarters and offer impressive viewing points. The Rainforest Visitors' Centre houses a 50-seat video theatrette featuring the history and ecology of rainforests in the State, and has a shop and displays. From here, two walks lead into the rainforest: the Lyrebird Walk and the Wonga Walk, the latter being over 5 km (3.1 miles) long but well worth the effort. From the Never Never picnic area there are other short walks. There are no camping facilities but bush camping is permitted.

Map ref: page 461 M7

The thundering waters of Dangar Falls in Dorrigo National Park, a World Heritage listed park.

COONAMBLE

A pleasant rural town situated on the inland plains in north-eastern New South Wales, Coonamble, with a population of 3125, is in the natural centre of a very rich and productive pastoral district. Wool, wheat, fat lambs and beef cattle are the principal products.

The town lies 562 km (349 miles) north-west of Sydney, in the artesian belt and has a reticulated supply of bore water. It takes its name from the initial run in the area, Koonamble. The site of the town was established in 1817 and it became a watering place for stockmen.

Coonamble is in fairly close proximity to the spectacular Warrumbungle National Park, the Pilliga Scrub and the famed Macquarie Marshes. For the bird enthusiast, the Marshes offer an experience that is rarely duplicated anywhere in Australia. You can also go fishing, boating or swimming at nearby Warrana Weir.

Coonamble is also big on horse-racing, and has six annual meetings. The Wool Festival Gold Cup is held in association with the Coonamble Festival each October, and is one of the richest inland one-day race meetings in Australia. The Coonamble Show is in May.

Map ref: page 460 A9

DORRIGO

As graziers moved east from Armidale in search of more pastures in the 1840s, they discovered rich volcanic soils around what became Ebor and Dorrigo, but the credit for the original European discovery of the Dorrigo Plateau goes to an escapee from Moreton Bay Penal Settlement, Richard Craig. He recognised the potential of vast stands of red cedar, and others soon followed into what became known as the 'Don Dorrigo Scrub'. (The name commemorates the Spanish general Don Dorrigo but, coincidentally, is Aboriginal for 'stringybark'.) Nowadays, the local district is famed for its potatoes, but dairying, beef cattle and timber are other important resources.

Dorrigo is 599 km (372 miles) north of Sydney and has a population of 1200. It is a historic town with many older buildings refurbished and restored to their original appearance; the Dorrigo Hotel is National Trust listed. The town has one of the few bakeries in Australia that still uses a wood-fired oven, and the local paper is still printed in town on the original presses.

The town stands at the entrance to Dorrigo National Park, perhaps Australia's most accessible rainforest. Also near Dorrigo are Dangar Falls and Griffiths Lookout, and the

Waterfall Way, which features great vistas and stunning plant life, ranging from gigantic trees, clinging vines, plus numerous staghorns, elkhorns and bird's-nest ferns.

Dorrigo has a thriving arts and crafts movement, from wood-turning to woolcraft. There is also is the Steam Railway and Museum, with 57 locomotives, 300 carriages and wagons, and thousands of smaller exhibits. It is the largest collection of railway memorabilia in the Southern Hemisphere.

Map ref: page 461 M7

DORRIGO NATIONAL PARK

Located 600 km (373 miles) north of Sydney on the Great Dividing Range near Dorrigo, this park has attained World Heritage Listing,

EVANS HEAD

A popular destination, Evans Head (population 2800) has sweeping beaches and exudes an idyllic holiday torpor. Located 767 km (476 miles) north of Sydney, it was known as 'Gummingar' by local Aboriginals, and there are a number of important indigenous sites in the area, including Goanna Headland. These days, the primary industry is fishing and delicious prawns are also netted locally.

Close by are the Broadwater and Bundjalung National Parks. The Broadwater has unspoilt beaches, great for fishing or water sports, and a heathland that becomes a colour fest in spring. In June, there is the Evinrude Seafarer Fishing Classic, in August, the Seafood Carnival and, over the New Year,

The Warrumbungles form the backdrop to the Coonamble district.

Gunnedah as seen from Porcupine Lookout.

the Great Eastern Fly-in. Local markets are held regularly. Tennis and bowls can be played in town.

Map ref: page 461 P4

GLEN INNES

Glen Innes is 667 km (414 miles) north of Sydney and its population is 6000. Long before Europeans reached the Northern Tablelands, the Nugumbul tribe migrated there seasonally. They called the place 'Eehrindi', which means 'wild strawberry'. John Oxley was the first white explorer to visit the Glen Innes district in 1818; 36 years later the town was proclaimed and named after Major Innes, principal landowner in the district.

In 1872, the discovery of tin at Vegetable Creek (known today as Emmaville) caused a population explosion, and other minerals and gems that followed in the wake were antimony, gold, bismuth, molybdenite, sapphires and emeralds. Glen Innes still produces top-quality sapphires and is popular with fossickers. Besides mining, current local industries include dairying, raising beef and sheep, mixed farming and also vegetable growing. The town has beautiful parks, some of which line Rocky Ponds Creek. It also boasts some well-cared-for nineteenth-century buildings, one of which contains the Land of the Beardies Folk Museum. (The area is known as 'Land

of the Beardies' after two early stockmen who sported long beards.)

Fishing and golf are local recreational pursuits and nearby Gibraltar Range National Park has a range of bushwalks. In Centennial Parklands' Martins Lookout are the Australian Standing Stones, a sculptural group dedicated to the contribution made to Australia by people of Celtic origin.

Glen Innes commemorates its Celtic background with two festivals: the Australian Celtic Festival in May and the Land of the Beardies Festival in November. Other festivals are the Minerama in March, an annual gem and mineral fest, and the Emmaville Gem Fest and Swap Meet, which is held in September.

Map ref: page 461 J5

GRAFTON

'The Jacaranda City', Grafton is famous for its 7000 trees, graceful old buildings, beautiful parks and its mighty river, the Clarence. The city is 667 km (414 miles) north of Sydney. As with Dorrigo, escaped convict Richard Craig was the first white man in the district. For a pardon and £100 he brought a party of cedar-getters back to the area. They were followed later by pastoralists. The town was proclaimed in 1851 and named after the Duke of Grafton by his grandson, Governor Fitzroy. City status was conferred in 1885 and the population of Grafton today is 18,500.

The list of buildings classified by the National Trust ranges from the serene (Christ Church Cathedral) to the infamous (Grafton Jail). Grafton council has purchased and restored many fine old homesteads, like Schaeffer House—which now houses exhibits belonging to the Clarence River Historical Society —and Prentice House, now the regional art gallery. There are a number of craft galleries, art studios and antique shops in town, or visitors can take a drive up to Ulmarra, 12 km (7.5 miles) north

of Grafton, which has been classified by the National Trust and also has craft, bric-a-brac and antique stores. Alumy Creek School has displays showing what schooldays were like at the turn of the century.

Visitors can also take a boat to Susan Island, home to the largest flying fox colony in the Southern Hemisphere. Cruisers and houseboats are available for hire to explore the Clarence River's islands and river towns. Other local activities include canoeing, fishing, gliding, horse riding, greyhound racing, golf, bowls and tennis.

The annual Jazz Festival is held at Easter, while in July visitors can lay a few bets at the Racing Carnival, especially on the Grafton Cup, reputedly the richest horserace in rural Australia. (The Grafton Jockey Club is one of the oldest in the country.) October sees Grafton's most famous occasion, the Jacaranda Festival, which was first held in 1935 and the Bridge to Bridge Ski Race on the Clarence. If you are around in November, the Sailing Classic is on. Community markets are held on the last Saturday of each month.

Map ref: page 461 M5

GUNNEDAH

Right in the heart of the wheat belt, Gunnedah is built on a hillside overlooking the Namoi and Mooki Rivers, 515 km (320 miles) north of Sydney. The name means 'many white stones', and the site of the town was originally the principal crossing place on the Namoi, hence a major centre for teamsters. First settled by Europeans in 1834, and today home to 10,000 residents, it

is the birthplace of the poet Dorothea Mackellar. There is a life-size bronze memorial to her in Anzac Park, while yet another memorial honours a great Aboriginal warrior and the leader of the Gunnedarr people, Combo Gunnerah. He was immortalised by Ion L. Idriess in his book *Red Chief*.

Housing the archives of the local historical society, the Water Tower Museum was originally the town's water reservoir, built in 1908. Other historic buildings include the Town Hall, Courthouse, the Catholic convent, Brunton's Flour Mill and Cohen's Bridge. The Rural Museum has many items on display ranging from shovels to steam engines and purportedly has the largest gun display in northern New South Wales.

Lake Keepit is only a half-hour drive from Gunnedah, and it is the town's playground for water sports, fishing and bushwalking. The Lake Keepit Soaring Club organises joy-flights over the dam. Further off the beaten track, 4WD touring is possible near Gunnedah, but as the surrounding country largely consists of black-soil plains, when it becomes wet, even 4WDs and tractors get stuck!

In January, Gunnedah hosts the Tomato Festival and Australia Day celebrations. In April, there's the Gunnedah Show and Rodeo and Campdraft; in May, the Spinners and Weavers Expo, and an eisteddfod; in June, the Gold Cup Horse Races and the Lake Keepit Sailing Regatta; and in August, Gunnedah's most famous event: the 'Agquip' agricultural field days. Tennis or bowls can be played in town.

Map ref: page 460 F9

Grafton is best known for its stunning jacaranda display during October.

INVERELL

Known as 'the Meeting Place of the Swans' or 'the Sapphire City', Inverell is situated on Gwydir Highway, 733 km (455 miles) north of Sydney. The first commercial venture was in 1863, when Colin and Rosanna Ross started a general store for the settlers moving into the district. (Nearby Ross Hills carries on their family name.) The man who gave the town its Gaelic name was Alexander Campbell, a Scot who established a property in 1835—Inverell—in the district.

Today a town of 10,000, the old way of life is perpetuated at Inverell Pioneer Village. A collection of authentic buildings from the area, the village includes Goonoowigall school, Paddy's Pub, The Grove homestead, a blacksmith's hut and miner's hut, Oakwood Hall (a printer's shop) and Gooda Cottage, which houses an excellent collection of gemstones. Good gemstones —including diamonds, sapphires and zircons—have long been found in the area, along with tin, bauxite and silver. Fossicking areas abound and equipment can be hired.

Buildings in town worth a visit include the Court House, which was completed in 1887. Nearby is the Town Hall and just around the corner is the Arts and Crafts Gallery, which holds local and visiting exhibitions and sells fine examples of ceramics, woodwork, painting and needlework. The most recent building is the Bicentennial Memorial, which has three courtyards: one devoted to the Tertiary Period and Aboriginal tribal culture; the second, to the period from 1788 to 1888, and the third from 1888 to 1988 and beyond.

Kempsey is famous for its Akubra-brand hats.

The Lake Inverell Reserve is an aquatic sanctuary covering 100 ha (247 acres) and is home to a large variety of waterbirds, platypuses, wallabies and black swans. The area is great for bushwalking and fishing. Copeton Dam has a 939 ha (2320 acres) recreation area offers whitewater rafting below the dam and, on the eastern foreshores near Tingha, bushwalks include the old mining settlement (but take care in the diggings). Gwydir Ranch Park is a recreation area close to the river but the dam is accessible only by 4WD. It is private property, but visits can easily be arranged.

Wildlife abounds at Goonoowigall Wilderness Reserve and the marked tracks provide peaceful walks by cool rapids and huge granite outcrops. Remains of some old Chinese earth ovens and mines can be found here.

Commanding views of the town and the surrounding district can be observed from the McIlveen Park lookout, west of town. Also worth a visit are Morris' Honey Farm and the Bottle Museum. The Draught Horse Centre shows visitors the five different breeds of draught horse that played a role Australian pioneering. Gilgai winery, at an elevation of 760 m (2494 feet), is one of the highest vineyards in Australia. Green Valley Farm provides unusual fun rides and has a native and exotic zoo and beautiful gardens. The famous Smith's Museum from Tingha is housed here and features a rare collection of gems and minerals from around the world. Also worth seeing are the Ashford Limestone Caves and Macintyre Falls.

In town, tennis, golf and bowls are possible. Inverell's Hobby Market is held on the first Sunday of each month and the Sapphire City market on the third Sunday. The Great Inland Fishing Festival is held in January and Australia Day celebrations take place in the Pioneer Village. In February, there is the Inverell Show. The Grafton–Inverell Cycling Classic is held in September, and the Sapphire City Floral Festival in October. The year concludes

Macadamia nuts are native to Australia and Lismore has many plantations.

with both the Venetia Carnival and the Inverell Cup Racing Carnival.
Map ref: page 461 H6

KEMPSEY

Named after the Valley of Kempsey in Worcestershire, England, Kempsey began life in the early 1830s. In 1836 Enoch Rudder, who later subdivided his land to create a village, operated a punt service across the Macleay River.

Kempsey is 463 km (288 miles) north of Sydney and the town has a population of 9050. The area's economic base is timber-getting and dairying, though some light industry exists, including the world-famous Akubra hat factory.

Tourism is important, and the area has many and varied activities on offer, including scenic flights, skydiving, fishing, cycling, 4WD touring, horse riding, horseracing and water sports.

History buffs will enjoy the Macleay River Historical Society Museum and Settler's Cottage as well as Kempsey's numerous nineteenth-century buildings.

In March, the town holds the Festival of the River. This embraces water sports, street theatre, line-dancing and an art exhibition. During July, a round of the Australian Off Road Racing Championship is held; in August, Festival of the River and in September, another Country Music Festival; in October, the Truck Show, and in November, a Classic Bike Rally.
Map ref: page 461 M9

KYOGLE

This 'Gateway to the Rainforest' takes its name from an early cattle run, which in turn borrowed from the Aboriginal 'kauiou-gal', which means brush turkey, or bustard. Situated on the headwaters of the Richmond River, 796 km (494 miles) north of Sydney, the town is nestled between the McPherson, Tweed and Richmond Ranges.

Kyogle is adjacent to the spectacular World Heritage listed Border Ranges National Park, which has many marvellous bushwalks that range from 50 m (164 feet) to 10 km (6.2 miles). The spectacular three-hour-return walk to The Pinnacle offers panoramic views over the Tweed Valley.

Once reliant on timber for its existence (first cedar, then hoop pine), Kyogle is home to 4000 and is the centre of a rich agricultural and dairying district, with Norply (a ply timber mill) employing much of the town's workforce. There are many Heritage buildings and some homesteads date back to the early 1800s. Amateur anthropologists will be fascinated by the large number of Aboriginal sites.

You can swim, camp or fish at nearby Toonumbar Dam; in town there is the option to play bowls or tennis but as the average annual rainfall is 1100 mm (43 inches), bring your umbrella! There is a rodeo held in July, an agricultural show in October, and in November, a golf tournament.
Map ref: page 461 N2

LISMORE

Though the Aboriginal name for the area was 'Tuckurimba', this very rich agricultural centre, 821 km (510 miles) north of Sydney, took its name from the property named Lismore, owned by an early station owner, William Wilson.

One of the most densely populated rural areas in Australia (currently 27,250) dairying, pig farming, bacon curing, banana growing, sugar cane, sawmilling and engineering are the dominant local industries. Early pastoral efforts centred on sheep, but the area made them prone to liver fluke, footrot and catarrh. For humans, however, the subtropical climate is excellent, with mild to warm temperatures all year and a really good rainfall.

The original inhabitants had a fairly wide-ranging territory, travelling as far as the Bunya Mountains in Queensland for their annual bunya nut food crop. Aboriginal relics can be seen at the Richmond River Historical Society Museum.

Lismore is in the centre of an area known as 'The Big Scrub'. Visitors can take an indoor rainforest walk, and Wilsons Park still has residual rainforest, indicating what the country was like before the cedar-getters moved in. Visitors can also take a river cruise or visit Macadamia Magic, a processing plant and tourist complex. Other activities are bowls, squash, tennis golf, swimming and waterskiing.

Festivals include the Trinity Arts Festival and Gem Festival (May), the Lantern Festival (June), the Lismore Cup Race Day and Garden Week (September) and the Northern Rivers Folk Festival and North Coast National Show (October). Map ref: page 461 N3

MACKSVILLE

Originally called 'Macks Village' after two early Scots settlers, Macksville (population 2800) lies at the junction of Taylors Arm Creek and the Bowra River, where they become the Nambucca River. This fertile district, 519 km (322 miles) north of Sydney, supports vegetables, maize, bananas, timbergetting and dairying.

Local activities include 4WD touring, golf, horseracing and water sports, with picnicking and fishing on the banks of the Nambucca River being popular local pastimes. North of the bridge there are barbecues and tables. At Taylors Arm, 20 km (12.5 miles) upriver, is the Cosmopolitan, reputedly the original 'pub with no beer' immortalised by Slim Dusty on the only 78 rpm record to go gold in Australia. Macksville hosts a number of festivals, with both the Nambucca Country Music Festival and the Agricultural Show held in April; the Autumn Orchid Show and the annual Trek to the Pub with No Beer are on in May; the Eungai Art and Craft Show is in July, and the annual Flower Show, in September. Map ref: page 461 M8

MACLEAN

Maclean (population 3000) was originally known as Rocky Mouth and it was established in the early 1860s by Scots pioneers. Situated on the confluence of the north and south arms of the Clarence River, the town is 703 km (437 miles) north of Sydney and is the commercial centre of an area where sugar cane, fishing and timbergetting are the important industries. Maclean has several historic buildings, including Stone Cottage and the Bicentennial Museum. To celebrate its Scottish heritage, a Highland gathering is held in town over Easter. Map ref: page 461 N5

MOREE

Situated on the Mehi River, 705 km (438 miles) north-west of Sydney, Moree derives its name from an Aboriginal word meaning either 'waterhole' or 'rising sun'.

A sheep station first took up the name Moree in 1848. The explorer Allan Cunningham was the first European through the area—in 1827—and Sir Thomas Mitchell followed later, in 1832.

The village of Moree was later established—in 1852—when the Brands family opened a general store and, later on, a pub.

The town's main claim to fame are its artesian mineral spas, which are much sought after by sufferers of arthritis and rheumatism. These were sunk in 1895, and so popular were they that by 1900, the town had its own brewery.

Moree (population 10,000) was home to the first pecan nut farm in Australia (1966) but it has been far better known as the centre for an important cotton-growing industry since the 1960s. The Moree Art Gallery houses an extensive collection of Aboriginal art and the Mary Brand Park is named after one of the town's founders. Map ref: page 460 E5

Bananas are big business around Macksville and much of the north coast region.

The fertile river flats of the Clarence River near Maclean. Shifting silt has formed islands in the lower reaches of the river.

Mount Kaputar's Nandewar Range.

MOUNT KAPUTAR NATIONAL PARK

This park is inland, in the north-west of this region, about 30 km (19 miles) from Narrabri. The peaks of Mount Kaputar and Coryah are dominant. At 1520 m (4987 feet) and 1400 m (4593 feet) respectively, they are among the highest in the State. The Nandewar Range was formed by volcanic action 18 million years ago and the basaltic peaks are all that remain of this ancient landscape. Great walking trails, which vary greatly in length and difficulty, lead to lookouts and unusual rock formations like Sawn Rocks—oddly shaped, organ-pipe formations of basalt rock. Scenery varies from high altitude vegetation to snow gum forests and bare larval flow rock with commanding views. The park's many different animals include kangaroos, marsupial mice, gliders, possums, and the elusive koala. Above are eagles and kites; on the blossoms are brightly coloured parrots. There are huts and camp sites with hot showers and wood barbecues at Dawsons Spring.
Map ref: page 460 E7

Bananas, avocados, pineapples and macadamias are cultivated in Mullumbimby.

MULLUMBIMBY

Proclaimed a village in 1888, Mullumbimby's dairying and agricultural industries developed rapidly after the opening of the railway in 1894. Nowadays the area around the town produces dairy products, cattle, bananas, pigs, pineapples, avocados and timber. Tourism has also become an important part of the local economy. The town is 842 km (523 miles) north of Sydney (population 2500) and has an art gallery and heritage park, and it is set in a beautiful, lush environment, making it perfect for scenic drives and walks. Wanganie Gorge and Rainforest are popular destinations, along with Nightcap National Park and Tuntable Falls. Mullumbimby has its annual show in October.
Map ref: page 461 P2

MURWILLUMBAH

About 30 km (19 miles) from the mouth of the Tweed River, Murwillumbah (or 'Murbah', as it is known to the locals) is 874 km (543 miles) north of Sydney.

Home to 7200, the town is in a rich agricultural district growing sugar cane and bananas and raising dairy cattle. The name 'Murwillumbah' means either 'good camping ground' or 'place of many possums'. Always at the mercy of floods, this town has been damaged numerous times. The local historical society has many photographs that document the floods, and also images of the disastrous fire of 1907. Murwillumbah is close to four World

Rowing on the Tweed River at Murwillumbah, with Mount Warning behind.

Heritage-listed national parks. Mount Warning National Park is situated around an eroded volcanic plug, named by James Cook in 1770. A walk to the top of Mount Warning (first achieved in 1868) takes an average, fit adult about 4–5 hours for the return trip and affords stupendous views.

Nightcap National Park takes in Terania Creek, site of massive anti-logging demonstrations in the late 1970s. The subtropical rainforests are home to endangered species. Then there is the Border Ranges National Park, which is 38 km (24 miles) west of Murwillumbah.

Finally, there is lush Lamington National Park, which is just over the border in Queensland. Other pursuits around Murwillumbah include tennis, golf and bowls or you can go swimming.
Map ref: page 461 P1

NAMBUCCA HEADS

Popular both as a stopover and a holiday destination, Nambucca Heads (population 6000) is 532 km (330 miles) north of Sydney. Its history is based around boat-building, agriculture and timber-getting. It was here that shipwright John Campbell Stewart built many boats including the *Royal Tar*, which in 1876 was the largest ship built in New South Wales. In 1893 and 1894, this ship transported members of the socialist, teetotal New Australia Association to Paraguay to build new lives over there.

The Copenhagen Mill and Ship-yard foreshore walk allows visitors to see how huge logs supported the keels of ships being built a hundred years ago. The Vee Wall Breakwater on the beach not only ensures safe water for small boats, sailboards and swimmers, it also provides a very colourful outdoor gallery for graffiti artists, who have decorated the rocks with their musings.

Water sports and fishing are very popular in Nambucca; you can also go fishing, 4WD touring, watch the horseraces and play bowls, golf or tennis. Markets are held monthly, every second Sunday. In April both the Nambucca Country Music Festival and the local agricultural show are held; in Easter there is a Quilt exhibition. During May, the annual 'Trek to the Pub with No Beer' (at Taylors Arm) takes place.
Map ref: page 461 N8

NARRABRI

'Nurruby' Station was taken up in 1834, and the town of Narrabri— 608 km (378 miles) north-west of Sydney—was surveyed some 25 years later. Today it is the cotton capital of Australia with a population of 7300. Visitors during April–June will see everything covered by the 'snow' of white cotton. Several buildings in town date from the late nineteenth century, including the post office.

Just west of town, at Culgoora, is the Australia Telescope, which links to others in western New South Wales. Mount Kaputar National Park lies 53 km (33 miles) to the east. Mount Kaputar is the remnant of an 18-million-year-old volcano, and has slopes covered by open forest and savanna woodland. This park is particularly

Beech trees in the New England area.

The long breakwater at Nambucca Heads is covered in colourful graffiti.

popular with rockclimbers, however, there are also a number of short wilderness walks.

Horseracing is popular, and the town boasts a very good racecourse; other pastimes are golf, bowls and tennis. Narrabri has an agricultural show in April, Farmcraft Field Day in last weekend in May, and holds a spring festival in October.
Map ref: page 460 E7

NEW ENGLAND NATIONAL PARK

Rugged mountain scenery, swift-flowing streams, lush rainforests and a wide variety of animal life make New England National Park one of the most important areas of biodiversity in New South Wales. The park was placed on the World Heritage List in 1986. It is 85 km (53 miles) east of Armidale and covers 30,068 ha (74,298 acres). Most of this park is a trackless wilderness that has been penetrated by only a few small groups of well-equipped bushwalkers. Excellent panoramic views to the north, south and east can be had from Point Lookout, which, at 1564 m (5131 feet) above sea level, is the highest point in the park.

Vegetation in New England is extremely rich and varied, and botanists have identified more than 500 different species of plants. One of the most interesting is the Antarctic beech, which grows just below the often mist-shrouded escarpment at altitudes above 1200 m (3937 feet). More than 100 species of birds have been seen in the park including king parrots, crimson rosellas, honeyeaters, fly-

catchers and the superb lyrebird. Visitors who wish to pitch a tent can camp at Thungutti Rest Area just inside the park entrance but another camping ground, better suited to caravans, is located at Styx River, 2 km (1.2 miles) from the park boundary. Visiting the park is possible throughout the year, although winters are cold.
Map ref: page 461 L8

NIGHTCAP NATIONAL PARK

Nightcap National Park is 34 km (21 miles) north of Lismore and covers 4945 ha (12,219 acres). It takes its name from the spectacular Nightcap Range, which rises in places to 900 m (2953 feet) above sea level. Its southern boundary borders Whian Whian State Forest, which is also good for hiking and birdwatching. Protesters Falls in the Terania Creek section of the park was the site, in the late 1970s, of one of the biggest conservation battles in New South Wales. A combination of good soils and the highest recorded rainfall in New South Wales has enabled huge brush box, blackbutt and flooded gum to flourish in the wet sclerophyll forest that borders the rainforest. The almost constant damp

conditions in the forest allow an incredible array of colourful fungi to grow on the tops and sides of fallen branches strewn across the forest floor. Bird life is prolific and includes uncommon species such as Albert's lyrebirds, regent bowerbirds and wompoo pigeons.

The park can be visited throughout the year but January–March can be very wet. There is a small area for overnight camping (one night only) at Terania Creek.
Map ref: page 461 N2

NIMBIN

Nimbin lies north-west of Lismore, just outside the foothills of Nightcap National Park, 847 km (526 miles) north of Sydney. Prior to European settlement, it was a place of 'men's business' and male initiation for the Bundjalung tribe.

In 1973 the Australian Union of Students chose it as the location for the Aquarius Festival, and Nimbin's fate was sealed. It became a focus for alternative lifestyles and, more significantly, the environmental movement. The boost in the population (now 1270) saved a town in decline.

Shop facades still display the original psychedelic murals that were all a part of the 'flower power' of the 1970s, and Nimbin's Museum—devoted to social history— follows a Rainbow Snake through eight rooms, tracing in chronological order: Aboriginal culture, the pioneer days and the hippy era. (The latter includes displays like Kombi vans rescued from lantana bushes, decorated with original 1970s murals.) There is no entry fee, just a voluntary donation.

Nimbin is an interesting living social document for those who did not experience the culture of free love and Jefferson Airplane. To the northern end of the Nimbin Valley lies Nimbin Rocks, an escarpment covered with forest and containing caves inhabited by bentwing bats.
Map ref: page 461 N2

Street art in Nimbin, where alternative lifestylers revived a declining dairy town.

Squirrel glider (Petaurus norfolcensis).

NYMBOIDA

Nymboida, 683 km (424 miles) north of Sydney, houses an important power station that supplies electricity right up to the Queensland border. However, it is for whitewater rafting that this tiny town of 350 and its river are most famous. The Nymboida river offers some of the best, most adrenalin-pumping rafting available in Australia, with rapids like the Devil's Cauldron living up to its name.

The Nymboida Cup canoeing contest is held here every September. Those of more gentle inclination can, however, take a slow, ambling bushwalk or relax beside the river enjoying live music at the Nymboida Coaching Station—a reference to the old days when Nymboida was a stopover on the Cobb and Co route from Grafton to Armidale. Nymboida is close to the Nymboi–Binderay National Park, which contains part of the Nymboida and Little Nymboida Rivers and the recreational spots of Cod Hole and the Junction. These embrace areas of rainforest and old-growth forests. There are no defined tracks, but experienced and well-equipped bushwalkers will revel in the conditions.
Map ref: page 461 M6

OXLEY WILD RIVERS NATIONAL PARK

This park, south-west of Armidale, preserves a number of river gorges that are generally inaccessible. Fortunately, some of the most dramatic features—the waterfalls that tumble off the escarpment into the wild gorges—are found at the edge of the escarpment where the access is easy. The park covers an area of more than 111,000 ha (274,281 acres), making it one of the largest in the State. It has many boundaries with up to 10 separate river gorges being included in the park. These gorges are separated by farming and forestry land on the higher plateaus.

The park can be accessed from many different points. Turn-offs along the road between Armidale and Kempsey lead to several spectacular waterfalls. Close to the Oxley Highway near Walcha is Apsley Falls. The lookouts over Wollomombi, Apsley, Dangars and Tia falls are all easily accessed by vehicle with easy, short walking tracks to the viewing platforms.

The more adventurous bushwalker will find that exploring the deep gullies on foot brings even more excellent rewards: clean, running streams, an enormous variety of bird life and native animals such as wallabies. Canoeing is possible on the rivers, especially at Georges Junction where the access is easiest. There are many beautiful camping opportunities beside the wild rivers and remote camping is permitted anywhere in the park except at designated picnic areas. But as most of the deep river gorges have no vehicle access you will need to backpack in all your own camping equipment.
Map ref: page 461 K8

South West Rocks is a favourite holiday destination.

SAWTELL

For centuries Aboriginals hunted and fished on the waterway known now as Bonville Creek, at Sawtell, 580 km (360 miles) north of Sydney. Then came the cedar-getters in 1863, and slowly, more Europeans followed. A village was proclaimed in 1923 and named after Oswald Sawtell, a landowner. Now Sawtell (population 6500), just 6 km (3.7 miles) south of Coffs Harbour, is a thriving holiday centre featuring a rustic village atmosphere with tree-lined streets. It has a fully restored cinema, shops, cafés and restaurants, a million-dollar RSL club and on the first Saturday of each month, Sawtell has street markets.

There are plenty of sports, too. Besides beach swimming, there are alternatives in a safe rockpool and sandy creeks. Sawtell has an 18-hole golf course and facilities for bowls, croquet and tennis. Anglers can choose between beach, rock and estuary fishing, and there are boat ramps at Bonville Creek and Boambee Creek. In June Sawtell celebrates with an annual Jazz and Blues Festival and in December there is the big Street Party.
Map ref: page 461 N7

SOUTH WEST ROCKS

Situated 498 km (309 miles) north of Sydney, South West Rocks (population 3100) is the largest seaside town in the Macleay Valley. It boasts a variety of really beautiful beaches, some suitable for families, some for surfing. It also has a rich history. Trial Bay Jail, for example, was first occupied in 1886, and was used to intern 500 German prisoners in World War I.

Smoky Cape Lighthouse, the highest in New South Wales, has terrific views and is well worth seeing. Before the lighthouse was built, several ships were wrecked locally, including the *Koodooloo*, its rusting remains visible off Main

Apsley Gorge, one of ten river gorges found in the rugged Oxley Wild Rivers National Park, much of which is inaccessible.

Beach. A fully restored boatman's cottage provides tourist information, history and local art and crafts. There is an aquarium, and visitors can charter boats. The area is also extremely popular for scuba diving. Nearby Arakoon State Recreation Area and Hat Head National Park are good for bushwalking. The town also has facilities for fishing, bowls, golf, squash and tennis.
Map ref: page 461 N9

TAMWORTH

Tamworth, 440 km (273 miles) north of Sydney, was named after the Staffordshire town represented by the then British Prime Minister Robert Peel. John Oxley was the first white explorer in the district in 1818. By 1830 squatters had moved in but they were dispossessed in 1834 when the Australian Agricultural Company was granted two massive holdings, the larger of which took in the site of Tamworth.

The town was gazetted in 1850. The discovery of gold at nearby Nundle further stimulated growth in Tamworth, which was an important coaching station. Sometimes called 'The City of Light', Tamworth was the first town in Australia to have electric street lighting. At the centennial celebrations for this event in 1988, the Power Station became a museum.

Proclaimed a city in 1946, today Tamworth has 36,000 residents and it is famous Australia-wide for its annual Country Music Festival, an 11-day event featuring every branch of 'country', from ballads to

Supplies from Tenterfield's saddlery, immortalised in Peter Allen's song.

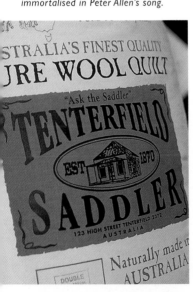

Tamworth holds the world's longest line-dance record, won during its annual country music festival, which is held in January.

bluegrass and bush poetry. There is a harmonica championship, guitar workshops and a big street parade. This event regularly attracts around 30,000 visitors. As a result of the festival, the Gallery of Stars (a waxworks of the Country and Western famous) and the Hands Of Stone Corner (handprints) have been set up in the city.

Calala Cottage is a townhouse built in 1875 for Philip Gidley King, the first Mayor of Tamworth. ('Calala', incidentally, means 'place of battle' and was the Aboriginals' name for the Peel River.)

The Art Gallery has works by Hans Heysen and Julian Ashton, and an excellent collection of Australian silver and ivory figurines. There are also many natural attractions in the area, including Warabah National Park and Sheba Dams Reserve. Keepit State Recreation Area, with its availability of water sports, is 57 km (35 miles) to the south. Other local activities are bowls, clay target shooting, horse riding, squash and tennis.
Map ref: page 460 G9

TENTERFIELD

Tenterfield began in the 1840s, when a resident gave the name to his property. Around 758 km (471 miles) north of Sydney, it is now the centre of a cattle-raising district which also produces wool, maize and cold-climate fruits.

Tenterfield (population 3400) is justifiably proud of its history, and there are two historic walks. One such walk takes in the Post Office (1881), with its Italianate façade, clock tower and metal mansard roof, and passes the School of Arts where, on 24 October 1889, Henry Parkes made an impassioned speech that started the impetus for independence and culminated in Federation on 1 January 1901. Next is St Stephen's Church (1884), where the social event of 1903 was the marriage of Alice Walker to A.B. 'Banjo' Paterson, and the Technical College (1870), which was used by Cobb and Co. as a change station for horses.

Then there is the Tenterfield Saddlery, immortalised by Peter Allen in a song about his grandfather, George Woolnough, and family. Built in 1860 of hand-cut blue granite, it is the town's most popular tourist destination.

The building that housed the Tenterfield *Star* is another feature. *The Star* was first published in 1870; one of its editors, Major J.F. Thomas, defended 'Breaker' Morant at his court martial in South Africa during the Boer War.

A second walk takes in the old Salisbury House, built for Isaac Whereat, who had been first mate on Nelson's flagship *Victory* before he came to Australia.

There are natural attractions in the town's vicinity. Bluff Rock—a

huge piece of granite 10 km (6.2 miles) south on the New England Highway—commemorates a dark page in the district's history. Following attacks by Aboriginals on shepherds and sheep, the hands at Bolivia Station attacked them at Pye's Creek, drove them toward Bluff Rock, then, legend has it, threw them over.

Woollool Woolloolni, also close to town, has been declared an Aboriginal Place. This 370 ha (914 acre) reserve has a huge mushroom-shaped rock that is sacred to the Aboriginals, who now run cultural tours there. A 4WD is needed to get to the site. Ghost Gully, an unusual example of erosion, and the famous Bald Rock National Park is only 29 km (18 miles) to the north. Sport lovers can play bowls, golf or tennis, or swim.
Map ref: page 461 K3

TINGHA

Almost 30 km (19 miles) east of Inverell and 721 km (448 miles) north-west of Sydney, Tingha (with a population of 850) is well known to gem fossickers, with sapphires, zircons and quartz crystals there for the taking. Smith's Mining and Natural History Museum is situated on the banks of Copes Creek and boasts a good New England gemstone and mineral collection, antiques and artefacts.
Map ref: page 461 H6

An old hotel at Uralla harks back to its heyday as a goldrush town.

TWEED HEADS

Tweed Heads is the bustling, busy, and sometimes frantic northern-most town on the New South Wales coast, 907 km (563 miles) north of Sydney.

John Oxley named the Tweed River after one of the members of his 1823 expedition in the *Mermaid.* However, the original name of the settlement was 'Cooloon'.

Tweed Heads shares its main street with its twin Queensland town, Coolangatta. Both towns are at the mouth of the Tweed River. In the days when poker machines were illegal in Queensland but not in New South Wales, large clubs sprang up in Tweed Heads to cater for Queenslanders who would have a flutter and then head back across the border. This gave rise to far better restaurants and nightclubs than one would expect for a town of only 6000. Tweed Heads has excellent surfing beaches (not as crowded as on the nearby Gold Coast) and boats are for hire to fish in the Tweed estuary or on Cobaki Lakes. River cruises are popular. Other options include tennis, golf and bowls.
Map ref: page 461 P1

URALLA

Situated on the New England Highway between Tamworth and Armidale, Uralla is 544 km (338 miles) north-west of Sydney. A town of 2400, it is surrounded by a district producing fine merino wool, cold-climate fruits and oats. A gold rush in 1852 created a tent city that in turn became a village. This was gazetted in 1855. (Fos-

sickers may still find a little 'colour' at the old Rocky River diggings.) Uralla is perhaps best known for having a celebrity in its cemetery. In 1870, the gentleman bushranger Fred Ward, otherwise known as Captain Thunderbolt, was killed in a shoot-out with the police at Kentucky Creek. Flowers are still put on his grave even today. Prospective visitors should be warned that at a height of 1017 m (3337 feet) above sea level, Uralla can be bitterly cold in winter.
Map ref: page 461 J8

URUNGA

Situated where the estuaries of the Kalang and Bellinger Rivers combine, Urunga is only 32 km (20 miles) south of Coffs Harbour;

554 km (344 miles) north of Sydney. Its name translates as 'long white beach'. The first Europeans to see the region were the crew of the *Northumberland,* captained by William Wright, when the ship entered the estuary in 1841.

The basis for the town's existence was cedar-getting, sawmilling and shipbuilding, but now this town of 2700 is popular for its fishing and its beautiful river, ocean and mountain setting. A broad lagoon provides safe swimming for children and is great for sailboarding and gentle boating.
Map ref: page 461 N8

WALCHA

Walcha's name is an Aboriginal term for the sun. When Hamilton Sempell carved out a station in the upper Apsley Valley in 1832, he called it Wolka and this is actually how the town's name is correctly pronounced. John Oxley, the first European in the district, preceded Sempell by 16 years.

Now the district produces mostly fine merino wool, cattle and hardwood. This is rugged country, as visits to nearby Oxley Wild Rivers and Werrikimbe National Parks will attest, but besides bushwalking and 4WD touring, there are many things to do in town. The home of Abraham Nivison is the oldest surviving in New England, and there are several historic sites, including a pioneer cottage and

museum complex where visitors can experience what life was like back in the town's early days.

Walcha is 456 km (283 miles) north-west of Sydney on the Oxley Highway between Port Macquarie and Bendemeer—one of the best 'driver's roads' in the State. The present population is 1750.
Map ref: page 461 J9

WARIALDA

'A place of wild honey' in Aboriginal lexicon, Warialda is located on the Gwydir Highway between Inverell and Moree, 681 km (423 miles) north-west of Sydney and has a population of 1440. It is the centre of a rich pastoral, agricultural and stud cattle area and the University of New England has a research station nearby. Most come to try their luck at gem fossicking, to bushwalk or to watch the horse-races. Cuddell Animal Kingdom is popular with children.
Map ref: page 460 F5

WARRUMBUNGLE NATIONAL PARK

This park is 27 km (17 miles) west of Coonabarabran in central New South Wales. Volcanic activity over millions of years, followed by the erosion of less durable rocks, has produced the dramatic landforms and scenery of the Warrumbungle Range. Remnants of ancient volcanic plugs tower way above the

The sharp, flat spire of the Breadknife pierces through the treetops in Warrumbungle National Park.

The Racecourse Trail in Werrikimbe National Park, New England region.

forested slopes, the most distinctive and widely photographed of these is the tall, thin, jagged spire of the sharp-looking Breadknife.

Bushwalking and mountain climbing are the main activities in the park; there is a good range of walking tracks, from an easy nature walk of 1 km (0.6 miles) to more challenging walks and climbs to lookouts with spectacular views. The Blackman camping ground has good facilities; Pincham and Wambelong have basic facilities. A camping permit is required and is obtainable in advance or from the visitor centre. Note that this is a low rainfall area, so always carry sufficient water for your needs while within the park.
Map ref: page 460 C10

WEE WAA

In the 1840s two squatters called Campbell and Ryan ran a station in the area called Weeawaa, which is thought to be Aboriginal for 'fire thrown away'. Today Wee Waa is a town of 2000 and is famous for its cotton, wool, meat, wheat and other cereals. There are two wineries—the Historic Cuttabri Wine Shanty and the Cubbaroo Cellars. Boating and fishing are possible.

Drivers who prefer tarred roads will find Wee Waa, 650 km (404 miles) west of Sydney, is the end of the line. Further west is Burren Junction's artesian spa.

The more adventurous traveller can experience the Pilliga Scrub by cutting west-southwest, or by heading west through Burren to the opal fields north of Walgett. Wee Waa has several festivals, including the Cotton Festival in March, the

Agricultural Show in April and there are also free guided cotton tours from April to July.
Map ref: page 460 D7

WERRIKIMBE NATIONAL PARK

On the eastern slopes of the New England Tablelands, 90 km (56 miles) north-west of Port Macquarie, lies this World Heritage-listed park. Three rivers, the Hastings, Forbes and Kunderang Brook, rise in these mountains and tumble down in cascades and waterfalls, through deep rugged gorges and steep-sided valleys on their way to the coast.

With its range of varying altitudes, Werrikimbe National Park protects a great diversity of flora, from the subtropical rainforest gullies of Cobcrofts Brush, right through temperate rainforest with some fine Antarctic beech trees, to snow gums, and alpine heaths and swamps. The area is teeming with wildlife, in particular, kangaroos and wallabies.

The gravel roads must be avoided during bouts of wet weather as they become very slippery; winter snowfalls do sometimes occur, so be prepared for very cold weather. There is great camping (with basic facilities) at Cobcrofts and Mooraback on the western side of the park and Brushy Mountain on the eastern edge.
Map ref: page 461 L10

WOOLGOOLGA

Woolgoolga describes itself as 'the Missing Piece of Paradise' and is known to the locals as 'Woopi'.

It derives its formal name from landowner Thomas Small, who in 1874 called his place Weelgoolga, the name thought to be used by the Yaggir people to describe the area in general and lilly pilly trees in particular. Banana and vegetable growing—and tourism—are now the main industries. A town of 4000 inhabitants, it is 608 km (378 miles) north of Sydney and as you approach it up the Pacific Highway from Coffs Harbour, the first visible landmark is the Guru Nanak Sikh Temple, perched high on the crest of a hill. This is a massive, imposing building erected by the Punjabi Sikhs whose ancestors had originally been brought to Australia as labourers on the canefields of Queensland, but moved south to become banana planters. This was the first Sikh temple built in Australia, and the town also has the Raj Mahal Indian Cultural Centre, an Indian theme park.

Woolgoolga looks out to sea and the Solitary Island Marine Reserve, one of the most significant group of islands on the New South Wales coast. It is popular with scuba divers and snorkellers because of the tremendous array of marine life, with schools of pelagic fish, rays, turtles, clownfish and numerous varieties of coral. There are good, local surfing beaches and fishing spots, together with great views from the headland over tiny neighbouring villages like Red Rock, Emerald Beach and Corindi and the coastline itself. Bushwalks in nearby forests like Wedding Bells and Woolgoolga Creek Flora Reserve reveal striking examples of hoop pine and silver quandong.
Map ref: page 461 N7

WOOLI

The coastal village of Wooli, 695 km (432 miles) north of Sydney, is located on a peninsula with the Wooli River on one side and Solitary Island Marine Reserve on the other. Behind it is Yuragir National Park. Wooli has 460 residents and a burgeoning oyster industry. It is proud of the fact that the river waters are completely surrounded by the national park, creating exceptionally clean water completely untainted by industry.

The marine park is a favourite for anglers and scuba divers, and boats can be chartered for fishing, diving, whale and dolphin watching or scenic cruises.
Map ref: page 461 N6

YAMBA

The largest resort town in the Clarence Valley, 715 km (444 miles) north of Sydney, Yamba translates as 'edible shellfish'. The earliest European contact with the area occurred in 1799, when Matthew Flinders moored near the estuary, but it was 1861 before the town was surveyed. Yamba (population 4500) is noted for its fishing and mild climate, and its surf beach is regarded as one of the safest.

For those interested in history, the Story House Museum contains a photographic display of early life in the town. For the more active, Yamba offers sea, lake and river fishing, and boats are available for hire. At Brushgrove, 35 km (22 miles) to the south-west, you can also hire houseboats. Daily passen-

Yamba is the place to sample seafood.

ger ferries run to Iluka, and there are also river cruises. Good fishing and prawning is available at Lake Wooloweyah, and the superb Yuraygir National Park, with its sand ridges and banksia heath, is close by for bushwalking. At Angourie, 5 km (3.1 miles) to the south is a freshwater pool, known as the Blue Pool. Only 50 m (164 feet) from the ocean, it is a favourite spot with families for picnics and swimming. Yamba holds a community market on the last Sunday of each month and in September–October the Family Fishing Festival takes place ending with a Seafood Expo.
Map ref: page 461 N5

NORTH-WEST NEW SOUTH WALES

Far horizons, stony plains, mountains of ore, vast fields of snowy cotton and the snaking lifeline of the Darling, Australia's longest river, characterise these wide brown lands. Here a winter downpour can turn the red desert into a riot of rapidly blooming wildflowers. Now speed is of the essence—before the water evaporates, plants must flower and set seed, then lie dormant until the next deluge.

Aboriginal groups lived lightly on the land, in times of drought retreating to the banks of the Darling or gathering at hidden waterholes in the fastness of Mutawintji. Mutawintji, Mount Gunderbooka and Mount Grenfell hold galleries of their rock art.

Watercourses winding west deceived early Europeans into believing they flowed to an inland sea. Explorers Charles Sturt and later the unlucky Burke and Wills crossed the dry plains west of the Darling in fruitless searches, discovering nothing but sandhills and salt lakes. It was challenging country for the pastoralists who spread onto it in the late 1880s. The enormous Sturt National Park in the 'Corner' (where three States meet), domain of the majestic red kangaroo, is made up of several former sheep stations. The dingo-proof fence following the State borders here was designed to keep wild dogs away from the flocks of New South Wales.

The largest population centre is found in the mining city of Broken Hill, location of both the School of the Air and Royal Flying Doctor bases and source of more than one third of the world's silver. Mineral wealth has also been dug from the copper mines of Cobar and the opal seams of White Cliffs and Lightning Ridge. Many towns found along the Darling are former inland ports—Bourke and Brewarrina in the north, Wilcannia and Menindee downstream. Riverboats then were dependent on the Darling's uncertain flow, and often waited months for floodwaters to flush them south. Now the Darling's waters are channelled into the permanent storage system of the Kinchega Lakes in order to provide a secure and reliable water supply for Broken Hill. The lakes are also a mecca for inland waterbirds and are popular year-round for fishing and boating.

OPPOSITE: The Darling River, near Bourke, is one of Australia's grand rivers, bringing life to the dry and desolate outback towns of New South Wales.

The Silverton Hotel and the stark, dry outback landscape surrounding it has become famous in several feature films.

REGIONAL FEATURE

Corner Country

The country west of the Darling River is considered by many to be the beginning of the real outback. On this immense sweep of saltbush, sand dunes and gibber plains which stretches toward the famous Corner Post where the boundaries of Queensland, South Australia and New South Wales meet, a few remote homesteads and small bush settlements are the only signs of human habitation in an otherwise harsh and intimidating landscape. Here, the red kangaroo, emu and wedge-tailed eagle reign supreme, the heat shimmers almost continuously off the burnt red rock, and the mulga bushes whistle in the steady breeze. In most respects, this country remains just as it was when the first European explorers arrived more than 150 years ago.

Although visitor facilities in the Corner Country are limited, two important national parks—Sturt and Mutawintji—offer a wide range of activities as well as fascinating insights into the region's history and ecology. Furthermore, well-prepared and experienced off-road travellers can enjoy a wide range of exciting 4WD tours through some of the most spectacular outback scenery on the continent.

The Corner is an especially remote and hostile environment. Travel in summer is best avoided as the flies are intolerable, the heat unbearable, and the risk of dehydration very real. Autumn through to spring is much more appropriate, but travellers arriving in winter should be prepared for cold nights.

Although many of the area's roads are dirt tracks, most can, with care, be travelled in a normal family car. However, a 4WD vehicle is safer and will allow wider exploration. On all trips, travellers should carry extra water, food supplies and basic vehicle spares.

Australia's largest bird of prey, the wedge-tailed eagle (Aquila audax) is often seen soaring on thermals over hills and jump-ups, scanning the ground for prey.

OPPOSITE: Mutawintji National Park, which encompasses more than 300 significant Aboriginal rock-art sites, was returned to its traditional owners in 1998 and is now managed by Mutawintji Local Aboriginal Land Council.

Patrolled regularly by boundary riders, the Corner's dingo fence protects the 7.6 million sheep that roam the Western Division from dingoes and wild dogs.

History

For thousands of years before Europeans arrived, Aboriginal peoples lived in large numbers along the Darling and Murray Rivers and their tributaries, and, in smaller concentrations, in the desert country to the north. Europeans first reached this area in the early nineteenth century when Charles Sturt and Hamilton Hume discovered the Darling River in 1829 and followed it downstream to its junction with the Warrego. Sturt surmised that the Darling entered the Murray. Disagreeing, Thomas Mitchell set out from near present-day Bourke in 1835 to prove that it didn't, but eventually had to acknowledge that Sturt was correct.

In 1844, Sturt set off again to search for a great inland sea which, he believed, lay at the heart of the continent. From Adelaide, he and his party travelled via the Murray and the Darling to a place close to present-day Menindee. From there, they travelled north to a well-watered spot Sturt called Depot Glen. With no other water sources for hundreds of miles, this became their prison for five months, until rain allowed them to move on. Establishing another camp at Fort Grey, Sturt led several reconnaissance trips into the surrounding desert, during which he discovered and named Cooper Creek, Strzelecki Creek and Eyre Creek, but found no trace of an inland sea.

By the time the Burke and Wills expedition passed this way in 1860, pastoralists had settled in the area and paddle steamers plied both the Murray and the Darling. Burke's party planned to head north, using rockholes at Mutawintji as a major supply point before pushing on to Cooper Creek. As is well known, the expedition ended in disaster; indeed, the bushmen who were sent out to find the party did more to open up this country than the explorers ever did.

Silver, lead and zinc were first discovered here in 1875 at Thackaringa, south-west of present-day Broken Hill, and then in 1881 at Umberumberka where a settlement was soon established. Named Silverton, it grew into an important town, but declined quickly as its ore ran out. Shortly afterward, however, the main lode at Broken Hill was discovered.

Gold was found at granite diggings near present-day Tibooburra in 1880, but the small pickings and harsh conditions brought this brief rush to an end around 1890. By then, however, significant numbers of pastoralists had already settled in the area.

In the 1880s, the state governments began to build enormous fences along their boundaries to keep out rabbits. Some of these have been adapted to keep dingoes out of grazing lands in New South Wales. The longest fence now stretches more than 5000 km (3100 miles) from southern Queensland to the Gulf of Carpentaria. Regularly damaged by animals and engulfed by shifting sands, the Corner's fences are maintained by the Wild Dog Destruction Board.

Sturt National Park

Covering 310,000 ha (766,000 acres) along the Queensland and South Australia borders, Sturt National Park protects the Corner itself and some of the most desolate but impressive country in the region. Although the park's major attraction is the vastness of its outback scenery, it offers much else besides. Visitors will encounter some of the continent's most impressive concentrations of wildlife, including huge kangaroo and emu populations, and come across historical sites including the remnants of the explorers' camps at Depot Glen and Fort Grey and pastoralists' stations such as Olive Downs and Mount Wood.

EXPLORING THE PARK

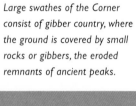

Large swathes of the Corner consist of gibber country, where the ground is covered by small rocks or gibbers, the eroded remnants of ancient peaks.

Information on the park is available locally from the National Parks and Wildlife Service (NPWS) office in Tibooburra. Make sure you pick up a leaflet on the excellent self-guided drive tour, which loops for 110 km (68 miles) via Mount Wood and Olive Downs, and provides a fine introduction to the park's landscapes and wildlife. In particular, it takes in magnificent examples of Sturt's most distinctive landforms—long, flat-topped hills known as 'jump-ups'.

Near the park entrance, a short trail leads from Dead Horse Gully camp site through granite boulders and beefwood trees, and offers fine views of nearby abandoned goldfields. At Mount Wood and Olive Downs, short tracks lead to the tops of jump-ups, providing panoramic vistas.

ACCESS AND CAMPING

Sturt National Park lies 330 km (205 miles) north of Broken Hill along the Silver City Highway, which is partiallly sealed. There is also an unsealed road from Bourke and Wanaaring. Both routes are impassable after rain, so check conditions locally before you set off.

Despite its isolation, the park caters well for visitors, with three excellent camp sites, all providing water, toilets and barbecues. These are located at Dead Horse Gully, 1 km (0.6 miles) from Tibooburra; just outside the old homestead of Olive Downs; and near Fort Grey on the western fringe of the park. A small camping fee applies and should be deposited in the honesty tins provided at all sites.

Abundant in semiarid regions, the emu (Dromaius novaehollandiae) is nomadic, moving on when supplies of food and water dwindle.

Mutawintji National Park

Located 130 km (85 miles) north-east of Broken Hill, Mutawintji National Park also protects splendid outback scenery—here dominated by imposing sandstone outcrops—but is best known for its magnificent Aboriginal rock art. Paintings, stencils and engravings scattered throughout the Byngnano Range constitute a fascinating record of the rich culture that thrived here prior to European settlement.

The most important assemblage of rock art is located at Mutawintji Historic Site in the west of the park, which was placed under permanent protection in 1967, before the surrounding area became a national park in the 1970s. Visitors to the historic site must be accompanied by an accredited guide. To get the best out of a visit to Mutawintji, join one of the regular tours run by the NPWS and usually led by an Aboriginal guide. Contact the NPWS office in Broken Hill for more information.

EXPLORING THE PARK

Visitors can explore other parts of the park at their leisure. At Homestead Creek, a number of excellent walking trails offer insights into local Aboriginal history. The Thaakaltjika Mingkana Walk, which leads to a cave decorated by Aboriginal paintings, is only 20 minutes return and wheelchair accessible. The 30-minute Rockholes Loop takes in Aboriginal engravings and views of the Rockholes, Homestead Gorge and the Byngnano Range.

A more challenging walking track, the three-hour Homestead Walk wends past craggy cliffs around Homestead Creek then heads into enchanting Homestead Gorge. The three-hour Byngnano Walk affords spectacular views of the gorges along the range, but should be attempted by fit walkers only.

Look for euros and rock-wallabies among the boulders and red and western grey kangaroos in open areas. Shinglebacks and bearded dragons often bask on rocks, while birds, including emus and fairy martins, frequent the park's many waterholes.

ACCESS AND CAMPING

It takes about two hours to drive to the park from Broken Hill along a dry gravel road. This route frequently becomes impassable to all vehicles after rain. Roads also connect Mutawintji with White Cliffs and Tibooburra. Within the park, a dirt road leads to the walking tracks and to Mutawintji Historic Site.

There is a pleasant camping ground at Homestead Creek which sits amid shady river red gums and has firewood, toilets and bore water (but no drinking water). The site operates on a first-come, first-served basis and a small fee applies.

The Trek to the Corner

This challenging 1171-km (727-mile) 4WD expedition from Broken Hill takes in all the major sights of the Corner. The starting point is the Silver City's main thoroughfare, Argent Street. Head east here and follow the signs for Tibooburra and Mutawintji. About 3 km (1.9 miles) from the town centre, turn onto the Silver City Highway.

After 55 km (34 miles), you'll see the turn-off to Mutawintji National Park and White Cliffs on the right. Another 61 km (38 miles) further on, you'll come to the side road to Mutawintji, which is 9 km

When threatened, the inland bearded dragon (Pogona vitticeps) responds by opening its mouth and thrusting out its spine-covered throat or 'beard'.

Most roads in the Corner are un-fenced so drivers must keep an eye out for wandering stock, es-pecially around dawn and dusk.

(5.6 miles) away. Try to plan your visit to the park to coincide with one of the excellent NPWS guided tours of its superb rock art.

When you are ready to move on from Mutawintji, return to the White Cliffs road and head north. Drive 26 km (16 miles), turn right, then turn right again after another 48 km (30 miles). At a major junction 23 km (14 miles) further on, or 213 km (132 miles) from Broken Hill, you join the main White Cliffs–Tibooburra road. Turn right here and after 42 km (26 miles) you reach White Cliffs. At the second crossroads, turn right to reach the town centre.

Founded in 1890, White Cliffs was the first commercially viable opal field in Australia and by 1899 its population had grown to 4500. To avoid the heat, miners built dwellings underground. Eventually, there were also underground hotels and eating houses, as well as dozens of underground grog shanties. By all accounts, it was a wild place.

Although more tranquil today, White Cliffs still has the feel of a pioneer town. Its permanent population of 100 or so swells in the winter months when hopeful prospectors return to continue their search for the stones that may make their fortune.

There are two hotels in the town as well as a camping ground at the Opal Pioneer Reserve. The pub can also supply fuel, while the general store opposite has fuel and supplies.

WHITE CLIFFS TO TIBOOBURRA

Return the way you entered the town and at the road junction 42 km (26 miles) from White Cliffs drive straight ahead. When you meet the main Broken Hill–Tibooburra road, or Silver City Highway, at a T-junction 134 km (83 miles) from White Cliffs, turn right. Soon afterward, the scenery begins to change. Sand ridges become prominent and about 12 km (8 miles) from the road junction lakes are visible both sides of the road—Cobham and Green Lakes to the left, Salt Lake to the right. Cobham and Green are freshwater lakes and when they have water in them the birdlife can be superb.

You reach the Wanaaring road junction 67 km (42 miles) north of the White Cliffs road junction; 5 km (3.1 miles) beyond this point a turn-off to the left leads to Milparinka. Staying on the main road, you reach the town of Tibooburra after 42 km (26 miles), having travelled 461 km (286 miles).

Tibooburra is a delightful bush town, situated amid low, rocky hills—its name actually comes from an Aboriginal term thought to mean 'heap of boulders', and the early gold prospectors knew it as 'the Granites'. The town has two notable hotels, the Family and, almost directly opposite, the Tibooburra, both of which have cold beers and basic but comfortable accommodation. The Family is famous for the colourful murals on its wall, which were painted by some well-known bush artists, including Clifton Pugh. Tibooburra also has a caravan park and a couple of stores and service stations.

It's a good idea to stop in at the NPWS headquarters in the main street to check road conditions and collect information on Sturt National Park.

TO THE CORNER POST

Head north out of town on the Silver City Highway and take the turn-off 19 km (12 miles) north of the town to the Jump-up Loop Road. The loop heads 12 km (8 miles) west to the ruins of Mount King Homestead and then north along the edge of Connia Creek for 25 km (16 miles) to Olive Downs Homestead, passing through rolling, stony hill country cut by red-gum-lined creeks. Along the way, a few jump-ups provide fine vantage points offering impressive views of the surrounding country.

About 2 km (1.2 miles) south of Olive Downs Homestead, now a ranger base, you'll find a camping area. At the T-junction further on, near the old shearers' quarters, turn left. Head toward the homestead, turn right through the gate and then head north, away from the buildings. This track heads north toward the border, then swings south-west past some tanks and yards to meet with the main track from Tibooburra at Binerah Well, 33 km (21 miles) from Olive Downs.

Turn right at this T-junction and head north again for 15 km (9 miles) toward Binerah Downs, just south of Toona House Gate on the New South Wales–Queensland border fence. Keep a lookout for a track on the left-hand side, just south of the airstrip on your right, which is marked with a sign, 'MW 162'. Turn left here (but not hard left).

The track heads almost due west and traverses some spectacular sand-ridge country before joining the main Cameron Corner–Tibooburra road just north of Fort Grey Homestead. Turn right here, then after 8 km (5 miles) turn left and continue westward for 18 km (11 miles) to the Dog Fence.

Drive through the large gate, close it and turn right. The Corner Post, where the three states meet, is about 150 m (165 yards) north of the gate. The boundaries were originally surveyed and marked by James Cameron in 1880, and their intersection is also known as Cameron's Corner. The present post, however, dates from 1969. Nearby is the Corner Store, where you can get a cold beer, snacks and fuel, and a camping area. You have now travelled about 169 km (105 miles) from Tibooburra.

THE ROAD SOUTH

Retrace your steps through the gate, then drive 29 km (18 miles) to Fort Grey, where you'll find a small, pleasant camp site to the east of the homestead, close to the lake where Sturt and his men camped during their 1844–45 ordeal. The tree the explorer blazed still stands to the south-east of the normally dry lake bed.

Continue south-east on the main road, which crosses the usually dry bed of Frome Swamp before exiting the park north of Waka Homestead. About 64 km (40 miles) from Waka, turn right at the junction. About 7 km (4.4 miles) south, this station track enters Gum Vale Gorge and follows the creek bed for a short distance. About 1 km (0.6 miles) into the gorge, a track on the left heads along another dry creek bed for 7.5 km (4.7 miles) to an old gold mining and battery site. This is an interesting spot to explore and a picturesque place to have lunch.

Backtrack to Gum Vale Gorge, turn left and head west to exit the gorge. Veer left at the Y-junction 4 km (2.5 miles) from the gorge and head south, sticking to the main station track which initially follows the headwaters of Evelyn Creek. At the T-junction 8 km (5 miles) further on, turn left toward Milparinka. Less than 7 km (4.4 miles) along the road, turn left toward Mount Poole Homestead and Depot Glen. All the land from here on is privately owned, so visitors should stick to the tracks and historic sites.

Less than 2 km (1.2 miles) further north, as you approach Preservation Creek, a track on the right leads 1 km (0.6 miles) through a gate to the edge of the creek and a small cemetery. Here you'll find the grave of James Poole, Sturt's second-in-command, who died as he set off for Adelaide. A tree blazed by Sturt's men stands nearby; the adjacent monument was placed here by Sir Sidney Kidman, who owned this property at the turn of the century. The other graves are those of station owners and workers.

Just past the turn-off to the cemetery, a track leads upstream to Depot Glen. Here, gums line the creek and corellas career overhead—it's a scene that has changed little since Sturt's day and a tranquil spot at which to contemplate the heroism of those early explorers.

The summit of Mount Poole can be reached via a track that turns left off the cemetery track. It heads across the creek and through a gate, then meets with a station track that comes from the homestead; here you need to turn right. A short distance further on, the track veers left and heads across lightly rolling gibber country to a small parking area. A short walk takes you to the top of the hill with its fine views and a cairn built by Sturt's men.

Backtrack to the main road and turn left. At the road junction 12 km (7.5 miles) further on, head to the right. After less than 1 km (0.6 miles) you reach the Albert Hotel, the heart and soul of modern-day Milparinka. The town was founded following the discovery of gold in 1881 at Mount Brown, and before long was catering for over 2000 prospectors. Although several buildings still stand, only the hotel is inhabited. It offers cold beer, good meals and basic accommodation as well as fuel.

Return to the main road junction, turn right and cross Evelyn Creek. About 1 km (0.6 miles) further on, turn right onto the Silver City Highway. From here, it's an easy four-hour drive back to Broken Hill, by which time you will have driven 1171 km (727 miles).

The landscape of Sturt National Park is characterised by low granite hills. Aboriginal peoples quarried these rocks to obtain material for blades and tools.

Places in
NORTH-WEST
NEW SOUTH WALES

An abandoned mine at Broken Hill, a massive mining town known as the Silver City.

BOURKE

Of all the towns in New South Wales, Bourke must have the most legendary folkloric reputation. Self-proclaimed as 'The Gateway to the Outback', this town of 10,000 has long been synonymous as the last outpost of civilisation. Expressions like 'back o' Bourke' merely scratch the surface of the rich cultural history of a town. 'Bourke shower' (a dust storm) 'No work in Bourke', and many other catchphrases also make it part of Australian linguistic heritage. Then there is Bourke's literary heritage: Henry Lawson made the Carriers Arms (a Cobb and Co staging station) home for quite some time in 1892. Thomas Mitchell built Fort Bourke here in 1835—a wooden palisade against the warlike local Aboriginal tribes. Bourke was the highest town on the Darling River from which wool could be shipped downstream in the halcyon days of riverboat trade.

From Sydney, Bourke is reached via the Mitchell Highway, which, after Nyngan, becomes hedged by relentless grey-green scrub and red earth, a journey totalling some 778 km (483 miles). Despite the dry surroundings, Bourke is incredibly verdant, as it is irrigated for citrus and cotton crops and you can also go fishing. But it is still an Outback town, an outpost, a frontier marker. Fishing on the Darling River is a major attraction but even if you are not an angler, every Aus-

tralian should see Bourke at least once. There are several local festivals worth seeing. The Bourke Mateship Festival, held since 1992 in September, features water sports, paddleboats, art and historical exhibitions, an old-time ball and damper cooking, while the Back O'Bourke Stampede, which is essentially a professional bull-riding contest and rodeo, is held in October. The Bong Bong Races are held in November.
Map ref: page 463 K4

BREWARRINA

Known as 'Bree' to locals, Brewarrina lies on the Barwon River, 783 km (486 miles) north-west of Sydney or 100 km (62 miles) east of Bourke. Brewarrina (population 1250) is in the centre of a vast pastoral district that extends up to the Queensland border. Back in the old days it was famous for the size of the wool clip loaded at the paddle-steamer wharf. As the river was shallow here, it was also originally the site of a stock crossing.

The name derives from an Aboriginal word meaning 'the fisheries', and even today, you can see the old Aboriginal fish traps in the river. Made from partially submerged boulders, the traps consist of funnels used to drive the fish into the shallow holding ponds.

Like most Outback New South Wales country towns, Brewarrina has had its share of racial tensions

over the years. Last century, it was the scene of the infamous Breakfast Creek massacre. However, local residents are actively working to promote mutual understanding, and the Aboriginal Cultural Museum provides insight into the local Aboriginal history.

In terms of European culture, there is the Settlers' Museum. On the eastern edge of town there is a milk bar that is a relic from the 1950s and it is worth dropping in for a milkshake.

Fishing is good here, both in the Barwon River and also at nearby Narran Lake, 40 km (25 miles) east, and perch, cod and freshwater catfish are the prizes. The town also holds the Outback Surf Boat Classic, which is on in September.
Map ref: page 463 M3

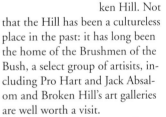
Silver Perch caught in the Barwon River.

BROKEN HILL

Almost all the streets of Broken Hill have names relating back to its mining operations or ores— a legacy of what made the Silver City the only sizeable town in the far west of New South Wales. It is 1163 km (101 miles) north-west of Sydney and has a population of 21,560. In 1883 German-born boundary rider and part-time prospector Charles Rasp found what he thought were tin samples on a rise that explorer Charles Sturt had described in his diary as 'a broken hill'. Rasp formed a syndicate to mine the ore, which turned out to be extremely rich

silver–lead–zinc, and Broken Hill Proprietary Ltd (BHP) was born. More than a third of the world's silver has come from Broken Hill, but now the ore is finally running out, and the townsfolk, all of whom in one way or another have been dependent on the mine for their livelihood, are turning to tourism.

Signs of the times consist of some large boards in the streets that note sites of interest such as historic buildings, including the Town Hall and Post Office. An air of cosmopolitanism has started to pervade Broken Hill. Not that the Hill has been a cultureless place in the past: it has long been the home of the Brushmen of the Bush, a select group of artists, including Pro Hart and Jack Absalom and Broken Hill's art galleries are well worth a visit.

Apart from Pro Hart's Gallery, there is the Living Desert Sculpture Park, where sculptors from all over the world created massive works from Wilcannia sandstone. These are sited to be visible for over 100 km (62 miles) and represent an arcing flow from the Pinnacle Hills to Fred Hollows' grave at Bourke.

Broken Hill affords all the customary diversions of any large city. But the most fascinating activity that it offers is its mine tour.

A 23 km (14 mile) drive out to Silverton—a historic town in its own right—is well worth the small effort, and if you head beyond the town, you will see the plains where the action shots for *Mad Max* were

A rock sculpture in the Living Desert Sculpture Park at Broken Hill.

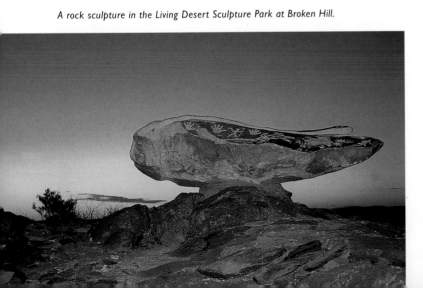

staged. Broken Hill also makes a very civilised base for visiting some of the other fascinating Outback locations like Menindee, Kinchega and Sturt National Parks, or the very isolated Mootwingee National Park. The Barrier Ranges also offer good 4WD touring but if you are uncertain about your cross-country skills, there are a number of 4WD tour operators in the Hill. Broken Hill's Outback and All That Jazz Festival is held early in March.

Map ref: page 462 B8

COBAR

At 704 km (437 miles) north-west of Sydney, Cobar sits pretty much in isolation in western New South Wales. Most people arriving in Cobar come into town by the Barrier Highway from Nyngan or Wilcannia but the more adventurous may prefer to take the dirt from either Bourke or Louth to the north or Lake Cargellico, Hillston or Condobolin to the south.

Cobar derives its name from the Aboriginal 'coburra', which means 'burnt earth used as body decoration' and it is this coloured earth that is Cobar's raison d'être. In 1870, three men drilling for water found some red-coloured stones, which they showed to a Cornishwoman living on Priory Station. She recognised them as copper ore and so the mining boom began. What started as a tent city soon had a population of 10,000 and, at one point in time, the Great Cobar copper mine was reputed to be the largest in the world.

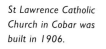

St Lawrence Catholic Church in Cobar was built in 1906.

Dead trees haunt the eerie lakes of Kinchega National Park, which supports a spectacular array of birdlife.

Today the population of Cobar is a still strong 6000 people.

Several of the buildings from those halcyon days still remain standing. These include the Great Western Hotel, which claims to have the longest veranda found in Australia. Cobar also experienced a revival in the 1960s, when mining giant CSA ran a water pipeline 135 km (84 miles) from Nyngan directly into the town.

Cobar now has tree-lined streets and is literally an oasis in predominantly semi-arid, dusty country.

The Great Cobar Outback Heritage Centre is a local museum that is well worth visiting. It is housed in the Great Cobar Copper Mine's Edwardian administration building (1910 and has wheelchair access, souvenirs, refreshments and guided tours of the museum and its surrounds. It covers all aspects of this town's industrial, pastoral and Aboriginal history. There are also some interpretive signs to guide visitors through the grounds and there is an amazing collection of mining and transport artefacts.

A rather interesting and unusual excursion is to participate in one of the underground mine tours. For those who have a more cultural bent, the work of local artists is on display at the Gloria Gallery.

An alternative is to explore some rather interesting Aboriginal cave paintings about 40 km (25 miles) out on the Wilcannia road (Barrier Highway); inspections are made by arrangement with the local owners. For the more sport-inclined, local pursuits include golf, bowls and swimming.

Map ref: page 463 K7

KINCHEGA NATIONAL PARK

This is an arid park with unique inland water features. Covering an area of 44,000 ha (108,724 acres), it is located 110 km (68 miles) south-east of Broken Hill.

There is access to the park along a tar-sealed road from Broken Hill but all the other gravel roads found within the area become impassable after even just a little rain. The town of Menindee is located just outside the park boundary.

Kinchega contains the historic Kinchega Homestead where many artefacts of the bygone wool industry remain. Visitors to the park can follow the tourist drive, which marks the points of interest.

Descriptive brochures on these points are available from the information office at Kinchega. The Darling River on the park's boundary provides many fishing opportunities and there are delightful camp sites among the river red gums. There are two major lakes within the Park—Menindee and Cawndilla. These lakes teem with bird life, which makes this place a birdwatcher's delight. Be warned, however, that in summer the temperature is very high and the area is best avoided at this time.

Map ref: page 462 C9

An operating opal mine at Lightning Ridge.

LIGHTNING RIDGE

Thirty years ago, Lightning Ridge consisted of a general store and the tiny, spartan Diggers' Rest Hotel. The access roads were all unsealed, and if it rained—an extremely rare occurrence—you got out quickly unless you wanted to be trapped by mud for weeks. The town is near the Queensland border, 760 km (472 miles) north-west of Sydney and it is home to 7000 people.

These days sealed roads enable adventurous visitors—who are keen to see the only place in the world where black opal is found—to come in droves. The Diggers' Rest has a long bar, carpets on the floors and even pool tables. The massive Lightning Ridge Bowling Club now dominates the town. Its 3600 members enjoy fine dining, including fresh seafood flown in daily. With both a synthetic green and a more recently added natural one, the club hosts the Black Opal Classic tournament every October. Players from all over the country come to test their skills, attracted by the $25,000 in prize money.

Mining methods have changed over the years too. Whereas in the old days, prospectors used picks and buckets to bring the ore to the surface, now they use jack-hammers and massive industrial vacuum cleaners. There are also open-cut operations on the fields.

You can, of course, buy opal in Lightning Ridge, but there are plenty of other things to do. You can fossick in the mullock heaps (a practice known as 'noodling'), visit the cactus nursery, take a joy flight or soak away tired muscles in the hot mineral baths.

There are under-ground mine tours, or you can watch a master lapidarist fashion opal into jewellery. The Bottle House Museum features collections of bottles, mining relics and minerals and is worth a visit as is the Bush Moozeum just out of town at Simm's Hill. The Goondee Aboriginal Keeping Place features artefacts and there are also educational tours. Lightning Ridge is purportedly the fastest growing town in north-western New South Wales. More than 50 different nationalities are represented around the opal fields, which is where most of the population lives. Some may be rich, but their accommodation remains fairly primitive by city standards. Visitors, however, are well catered for and can play golf and tennis or go horse riding or swimming. In July, the town hosts the Gem and Opal Festival; while over Easter, there are the Great Goat Races; in June a Pistol Shoot is held.
Map ref: page 463 P2

MENINDEE

Menindee was the first town built on the banks of the Darling River, lying among the overflow lakes that form the Menindee Lakes Storage. In 1849, river navigation pioneer Francis Cadell established a store at a spot named in 1835 by the explorer Thomas Mitchell as 'Laidley's Chain of Ponds'. Burke and Wills stayed in Maiden's Hotel before venturing off for their date with destiny. One of their Afghan camel drivers is buried just outside town and historic markers abound throughout the town. Today the town has a population of 980. It is located 1133 km (704 miles) north-west of Sydney.

The local lakes provide important breeding grounds for many species of birds. The wreck of the paddle-steamer *Providence* is worth seeing, and fishing for perch or cod is possible along the river.

Kinchega National Park is very close to town, with its multiple Aboriginal sites in a landscape of grey soil plains and red sandridges. It houses the original Kinchega Station woolshed, which in its time saw six million sheep shorn. Quite a number of species of waterfowl live in the overflow lakes and the Darling. Mungo National Park is a little further to the south-west. It is World-Heritage listed, representing a remarkable record of Aboriginal life dating back 40,000 years. There is an abundance of wildlife and bird life here also, plus the visually stunning Walls of China, a 30 km (19 miles) crescent dune of orange, grey and white earth. Around Menindee there are particularly good spots for fishing, 4WD touring and a variety of water sports.
Map ref: page 462 C9

NARROMINE

Established by William O'Neill in 1878, Narromine, 444 km (276 miles) west of Sydney, is almost the geographic centre of New South Wales. The town lies on the Macquarie River—its fertile flats fed by irrigation from Burrendong Dam. Narromine is famous for its wheat, wool, citrus fruits, prime lambs, vegetables and cotton.

Narromine's main non-pastoral claim to fame is its association with flying. Besides having the oldest country aero club in Australia, Narromine was also the landing place for Ross and Keith Smith on their 1920 record-breaking flight from England to Australia. A memorial stone and plaque where their Vickers Vimy came to rest is on the golf course, not far from the clubhouse, and the Aero

The sandy landscape and rocky outcrops of Mungo National Park, which is possible to see in a day trip from Menindee.

Club's visitors' book reveals quite a pageant of Australian aeronautical history: Charles Kingsford Smith, Charles Ulm, Nancy Bird as well as others. Today, Narromine is home to 3390 and continues its lengthy love affair with flying: it is known as the gliding capital of New South Wales and the Australian Gliding Championships are held here.

Narromine has also produced a number of sporting champions, including Olympic sprinter Melissa Gainsford-Taylor and world champion clay target shooter, Kevin Heywood. So it is not surprising that many sports can be enjoyed locally, including bushwalking, golf, horseracing, polo and polocrosse, tennis and some water sports.
Map ref: page 463 P8

NYNGAN

When Sir Thomas Mitchell journeyed through this outer western district in 1835—571 km (355 miles) north-west of Sydney— he recorded the name 'nyingan', which he took to

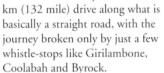
Nyngan rides on the sheep's back.

be 'long pond of water'. Over the years, Nyngan (which presently has a population of 2500) has had its fair share of water, the most recent disastrous floods being in 1990 and 1997. The local district is mostly pastoral, with a number of famous sheep studs in the area. Early stations often had to be abandoned due to conflict with the local Aboriginals, but these days Nyngan is fairly free of racial tension. Reminders of those early days, and the days before European settlement, can be found on several carved trees in the district, fashioned by the Bogan-gal Aboriginal tribe to commemorate important events.

A social history museum, 'The Story of Nyngan', in Pangee Street, concentrates on the flooding, but it also covers many other aspects of the town's history. It is chiefly an audiovisual museum, housed in the old railway refreshment room.

Nyngan's copious reserves of water also supply the copper town of Cobar. North of Nyngan is a series of creeks flowing from the Macquarie River into the Bogan

River. These creeks are a magnet to inland anglers, attracted by the prospect of catching golden perch, catfish and cod. Bird life is very common all along the rivers. The wetlands of the Macquarie Marshes, with their abundance of bird life, are 80 km (50 miles) away to the north-east. The area hosts a number of waterskiing carnivals each year. Other annual events include the Sheepdog Trials and Expo in August and the Nyngan Show in May.

Also in the district is the grave and memorial marker of Mitchell's botanist, Richard Cunningham, who became lost during one of his forays in search of specimens and was killed by Aboriginals.

Situated on the Mitchell Highway, Nyngan is the gateway to many legendary Outback towns, with Cobar, Wilcannia and Broken Hill off to the west along the Barrier Highway, and Bourke to the north-west.

Bourke is at the very end of a 212 km (132 mile) drive along what is basically a straight road, with the journey broken only by just a few whistle-stops like Girilambone, Coolabah and Byrock.

The Nyngan district has much to offer the adventurous visitor, but tourists should be warned that the summer months can be extremely hot. However there is plenty to do

The radio telescope at Parkes was used to relay messages for the first moon mission.

year-round, including bowls, golf, squash tennis and water sports plus it is a great place for birdwatching.
Map ref: page 463 M7

PARKES

Goldmining was the original industry in the Parkes district. In 1862, reef gold was found around Parkes and was worked for about five years, and then a little later, important finds of alluvial gold were made. The settlement that formed was known as Bushman's, after a mine called Bushman's Lead, but the name was changed in 1873 to honour statesman Sir Henry Parkes (then just plain Mr

Parkes). Now a town of 10,000, the Parkes district, produces wheat, wool, fat lambs, cattle and pigs, and the town itself, 359 km (223 miles) west of Sydney, is an important wheat storage centre.

Many people come to Parkes to inspect the CSIRO radio telescope, with its 64 m (210 feet) diameter saucer-shaped antenna. The telescope was made famous recently in the movie *The Dish*. It is sited in the Parkes region because it is a very low radio-interference zone and the area normally has low wind speed. The Visitors Centre, which is open daily, has an excellent audiovisual presentation on how the telescope works.

Other attractions in the Parkes area include the Henry Parkes Historical Museum (in Clarinda Street, named after the Father of Federation's first wife, Clarinda Varney), which features relics and items from the pioneering and goldmining days. Pioneer Park boasts a collection of historic agricultural implements and machinery and the Motor Museum on Craft Corner has 18 cars displayed.

The Parkes Show is held during August while each October long weekend, several hundred people converge on Parkes for an antique motorbike rally. The town has a swimming pool and there are some good local walks.
Map ref: page 463 P10

An old shed at Pioneer Park at Parkes displays an array of early farm vehicles.

The dusty landscape of outback town Silverton makes it popular with film-makers.

SILVERTON

Originally known as Umber-umberka, Silverton, 1186 km (737 miles) north-west of Sydney, acquired its current name in 1880 following the discovery of rich silver–lead ore. In 1883, extensive rushes again occurred and the town was surveyed, but the rich finds at Broken Hill, 25 km (16 miles) to the south-east, attracted the miners and from housing a population of 3000, Silverton quickly declined. The final straw was the closure of the Silverton Tramway—a private railway linking Broken Hill with Cockburn, South Australia, via Silverton—in 1970. Today the population is only 50.

With its red earth, blazing blue sky and a harsh, unyielding landscape, Silverton is very popular with film-makers. *Mad Max II*, *A Town Like Alice* and *Razorback* were all shot here. Visitors should see the vast Mundi Mundi Plains, where the amazing chase scenes in *Mad Max* were filmed.

Silverton has many historic buildings, including the old jail and the museum. The town is full of artists and galleries. Visitors can ride camels, go underground at nearby Day Dream Mine, which opened in 1885, picnic at Umber-umberka Reservoir or camp at Penrose Park. There is also a two-hour walking trail, which winds through creeks, valleys and the town itself. The Visitors' Centre is a tiny schoolhouse where Dame Mary Gilmour, the poet, was at one time a local teacher.
Map ref: page 462 A8

TIBOOBURRA

Thought to mean 'heap of granite rock', Tibooburra is in the extreme north-west of the State, 1311 km (814 miles) north-west of Sydney, in a very dry area where some wool is produced. This remote township can be the hottest in Australia on most summer days—it is what the Outback is all about. Tibooburra is a 'ghost town' of the late 1800s: another boomer and crasher with only 130 residents remaining. (Just as with Arltunga in the Northern Territory, water became far more valuable than gold in the extremely harsh conditions.) Now, two pubs and a smattering of shops service the surrounding countryside. The town has the only hospital in the area, which is linked to the Royal Flying Doctor Service.

Many of the historic buildings are built from the local granite, including Braybrooks' House, the Family Hotel (which has a 24-hour liquor licence), and the Tibooburra Hotel. The Mount Stuart Aboriginal Artefact Collection is also worth seeing.

Sturt National Park starts at Tibooburra and covers 310,634 ha (767,577 acres) of eroded cliff-rimmed mesas and gibber plains. Temperatures can reach 50° C (122° F) in summer, so potential visitors should reconsider! During winter, however, it can be cold at night, but beautiful during the day. At the very extreme of the State, in the park, is Cameron Corner, the junction of the borders of Queensland, New South Wales and South Australia. Here there is the longest fence in the world. Five thousand kilometres in length (3105 miles), it theoretically keeps Queensland dingoes out of sheep country and is known colloquially as the 'dog fence'. On the New South Wales Labour Day weekend, Tibooburra has a famous gymkhana and rodeo.
Map ref: page 462 C2

TRANGIE

Trangie (Aboriginal for 'quick') derives its name from the old Trangie Station, which was first owned by J.C. Ryrie. The first settler, however, was John Campbell, who came from Dubbo in 1883, setting up a farm and a pub—the Swinging Gate. Trangie's subsequent growth resulted from it becoming a staging centre for Cobb and Co on the route from Dubbo to Bourke. The town was also well-used by teamsters who carried goods into (and wool out of) stations like Panjee, Emereran and The Overflow.

The construction of Burrendong Dam was a boon to Trangie landholders. With an average district rainfall of only 457 mm (18 inches), the irrigation schemes saw Trangie

The landscape around Tibooburra is dry and desolate with some distinctive and ancient boulder-strewn plains.

Tibooburra stages a rodeo on the October long weekend.

facing a new prosperity, forever banishing images of aridity with a maze of irrigation channels and a range of different crops. Cotton is now the economic base. The town is 478 km (297 miles) north-west from Sydney and has a population of 1000.

Map ref: page 463 P8

WALGETT

Torn by strained racial relations for many years, Walgett has still much to offer the visitor. Its name means 'meeting of the waters', presumably because the town stands near the junction of the Barwon and Namoi Rivers, 679 km (422 miles) north-west of Sydney. The name Walgett was first used in 1838 by the station owner John Campbell for his property.

The explorer Sturt originally came through the area in 1829, and found what he described as 'an unbroken sheet of water, which was evidently very deep and literally crowded with pelicans and other wildfowl'. Today Walgett rides on the sheep's back, with cotton as an extra crop.

Presently home to around 2300 inhabitants, Walgett is the gateway to the major opal fields found at Lightning Ridge, Angledool, Glengarry and, most recently, Grawin Tanks. The Grawin was actually a boom field in the 1920s, particularly when 'The Light of the World' —an opal that was as big as a fist and weighed 450 grams—was dug out on Richard's Hill. (It is now in the United States.) The Grawin has recently experienced a renaissance, but whereas the old-time miners used a pick, shovel and a bucket,

now it is done with jackhammers and giant vacuum cleaners. Burren Junction is about 100 km (62 miles) east of Walgett over a bad dirt road. It boasts a superb hot artesian bath, open 24 hours a day. On the other side of town, about 100 km (62 miles) to the west, is Narran Lake, which is one of the largest yet least-known lakes in Australia, and it abounds in native animal and bird life. The best way to see it is by plane, which can be arranged through the Walgett Aero Club. The area is also great for a fossicking or 4WD tour.

Map ref: page 463 P4

WARREN

There is a bit of confusion over where Warren derived its name. It is believed that it comes from one of the following Aboriginal words: 'warrien' (a large root); 'wurren' (strong), or 'wurrena' (level and flat). The first Europeans in the region were explorers John Oxley, in 1818, and Charles Sturt, ten years later. Oxley made his journey during a very wet period and was unable to penetrate the Macquarie Marshes, to the north-west of the present town. When Sturt came through, it was much drier, and he managed to ascertain that the Macquarie River, far from feeding a vast inland sea, actually fed into the Darling River. The country around Warren was taken up initially by William Lawson (he was a son of the explorer who first blazed a way over the rugged Blue Mountains with Wentworth and Blaxland), and Thomas Readford in 1845. The first 'town' building was not erected until 1850.

Warren is situated 533 km (331 miles) west of Sydney and has these days has a population of 2600. It is the centre of a vast pastoral district that services legendary sheep studs like Haddon Rig and Mumblebone. The construction of the Burrendong Dam brought with it a guaranteed supply of water so pastoralists were then able to branch out into crops like cotton, forage crops and grain sorghum.

Sometimes described as 'the Randwick of the West', Warren's showground and racecourse complex is one of the best in the State, with facilities for racing, trotting, rodeos and a variety of other equestrian activities.

The Macquarie River offers some excellent fishing along its banks, and some good catches of yellowbelly, cod, freshwater bream and catfish are almost surefire.

Warren's main attraction, however, is the Macquarie Marshes. Whereas these marshes defeated Oxley and other early explorers who followed, they are a delight for today's visitors. This is the largest wildfowl breeding area in eastern Australia. As many as 120 different species of birds have been observed in this area. The Warren Show is held in May. Other local activities include tennis, golf, bowls and water sports.

Map ref: page 463 P7

WHITE CLIFFS

Like its opal-mining equivalent, Coober Pedy in South Australia, White Cliffs is a town that has seen humans turn into moles because of the extreme heat: they all live underground, choosing to dig their

Pelican in Narran Lake near Walgett.

houses into the earth rather than erect them. The average temperature in summer is 35° C (95° F) and in winter, 17° C (63° F).

White Cliffs opal field is 1063 km (660 miles) west of Sydney and was established in 1884, which makes it the oldest in Australia. The town reached its peak in the early 1900s, with between 4500 and 5000 miners searching for the elusive 'colour'.

The population is dramatically less today, with only 255 residents, but opal mining still goes on, with jewelled opal 'pineapples' being a unique local find. The opalised skeleton of a plesiosaur was discovered in 1976 and is on display in the town.

White Cliffs is also the site of Australia's first solar power station, which opened in 1983. There are also several historic buildings in town worth inspecting, including the old police station and the post office. Tourists should be warned that summer is not the best time to visit White Cliffs.

Map ref: page 462 E5

WILCANNIA

Located on the junction of the Darling and Paroo Rivers, Wilcannia was once known as 'the Queen City of the West' as it was then the third largest inland port in Australia when the paddle-steamers plied back and forth to Adelaide. They carried wool one way and then turned in the other direction with supplies for the town.

The first riverboat was taken by the inland waterway legend Francis Cadell to Mount Murchison Station in 1859. The following year a post office was established and in 1866, the first store.

By the 1870s, Wilcannia— 962 km (597 miles) to the west of Sydney—was an important coaching station for travellers to the western goldfields. Although today there are only 900 residents, Wilcannia is still the centre for a vast wool district. The town is situated in the hottest part of the State and suffers from very unpredictable rainfall. There is a self-guided tour that takes in some of Wilcannia's historic sandstone buildings. The town is a good jumping off point for outback exploration or for fishing in the rivers.

Map ref: page 462 E7

SOUTH-WEST NEW SOUTH WALES

Wool and wheat hold sway in the sprawling lands of south-western New South Wales. Stretching west from the foothills of the Great Dividing Range, the region broadens into the ordered green fields of the Murrumbidgee Irrigation Area, then, as it heads further west, flattens into semi-arid plains, red sand and saltbush. Meandering through this is a network of mighty rivers.

○ Sydney

These rivers are the Darling, Murrumbidgee, Lachlan and wide brown Murray; red gum forests line the banks and their marshes and overflow lakes are gathering places for many thousands of waterbirds. The rivers also draw anglers hoping to hook a Murray cod, Australia's largest and most sought-after freshwater fish.

The Newell Highway runs north–south through the region, from the wheatfields fringing the radio-telescope town of Parkes, through the Riverina town of Narrandera to the Murray. Further west, the Cobb Highway runs north–south through the town of Hay. At the junction of two east–west highways, Hay sits beside a crossing over the Murrumbidgee and was once a Cobb and Co depot and river port. This is sheep stud and wool country, location of the great nineteenth century stations and legendary shearing sheds: Tarwong, Willandra and One Tree Plain.

Global warming at the end of the last Ice Age transformed the then fertile land with brimming freshwater lakes into the parched plains, billabongs and claypans of today. Evidence of this remarkable story of climatic change is preserved in the Willandra Lakes World Heritage Region, it includes Mungo

Lake where the bone-dry sands hold a record of Aboriginal life stretching back for at least 40,000 years. When explorer John Oxley gazed from the Cocoparra Ranges over the 'desolate plains' bordering the Murrumbidgee he despaired that they 'would never again be visited by civilised man'. Now made lush by diverted river waters, some of these lands are among the most productive in the country, growing rice and citrus, vine and stone fruits. Several towns in the area, including Griffith and nearby Leeton, were designed by the architect for Canberra, Walter Burley Griffin. The region's largest population centres are the cities of Wagga Wagga and Albury.

OPPOSITE: The eerie and barren landscape of Mungo National Park has clues to Australia's earliest inhabitants.

Auctioneers in bright pink shirts vie with the farmers at the stockyard sales in Wagga Wagga. Sheep farming is a vital industry in this part of the State.

Also known as the pink cockatoo, the Major Mitchell cockatoo (Cacatua leadbeateri) is named after the surveyor and explorer Sir Thomas Mitchell. Widespread in arid parts of the interior, it normally nests in a tree hollow.

OPPOSITE: The scattered mounds and pinnacles that line the former shore of Lake Mungo are the remains of a huge sand dune.

REGIONAL FEATURE

Mungo National Park

Like many so-called lakes of the immense, arid Australian interior, Lake Mungo, the central feature of Mungo National Park, 110 km (68 miles) north-east of Mildura, seldom holds a drop of water. Yet, up to 15,000 years ago it was part of an enormous system of freshwater lakes linked by Willandra Creek, then a major tributary of the Lachlan River. This system was rich in aquatic life and supported an abundance of terrestrial plants and animals as well as thriving Aboriginal communities. Evidence of this early human occupation of the continent was first discovered here in the 1960s. At that time, the finds were considered the most important archaeological discoveries yet made in Australia and led to UNESCO declaring the national park and the surrounding area the Willandra Lakes World Heritage Region in 1981.

Today, visitors to 28,000-ha (69,200-acre) Mungo National Park can learn about these and other fascinating archaeological discoveries while investigating the area's recent history and intriguing flora and fauna.

History

When the lakes of the Willandra system were full, Aboriginal peoples lived on their shores in large numbers, fishing for cod, perch and mussels, hunting for kangaroos and wallabies, and gathering emu eggs. Even after the lakes dried up, approximately 15,000 to 18,000 years ago, smaller groups continued to inhabit the area, gradually adapting to the more arid conditions. Some of their descendants still live in the area and a number are involved in managing the park.

Europeans arrived in the mid-nineteenth century but settled sparsely, finding the arid land useful only for grazing sheep. One group of settlers established the huge Gol Gol sheep station, on the site of which Mungo National Park is located, and, in 1869, built the Mungo Woolshed, which can still be seen near the park entrance. In 1922, Gol Gol was subdivided into smaller blocks, including Mungo and Zanci stations. Concerns over the impact of sheep on the fragile environment eventually led to Mungo Station being acquired by the National Parks and Wildlife Service (NPWS) in 1978 and a park being proclaimed in 1979.

By then, the hugely significant archaeological digs were already underway. Among the first finds to cause excitement in the scientific community was the unearthing, in 1969, of the bones of a young woman, referred to by the scientists as 'Mungo I', who had clearly been cremated during some kind of ceremony. Subsequently dated to 25,500 years ago, these bones are still the earliest evidence of human cremation ever discovered. An equally exciting find made a short time afterward—the ochre-decorated remains of a young man, later dubbed 'Mungo III' and dated to 30,000 years ago—provided what was then some of the earliest evidence of burial ceremonies. These and other discoveries made at Mungo constitute the longest record of continuous human habitation ever found in Australia, which dates back at least 40,000 years.

Intriguing palaeontological evidence retrieved at Mungo also revealed that the region was once home to giant marsupials, including a kangaroo that stood 3 m (10 feet) tall and a wombat the size of a rhino. Measurements taken in Mungo's ancient hearths, meanwhile, have resulted in benchmark studies that show that our planet experienced significant changes in its magnetism around 30,000 years ago.

Exploring the Park

The visitor centre, located at the park entrance, provides a comprehensive introduction to the archaeological and palaeontological significance of the lake as well as the area's pastoral heritage and ecological treasures. Suitably briefed, visitors can then depart on a 70-km (44-mile) self-guided drive, which heads initially across the lake to the dramatic landform known as the Walls of China. This was originally a crescent shaped sand dune, or lunette, that ran the full length of the lake's eastern shore. After the water evaporated, it slowly solidified. It was then carved into the unusual shapes present today by thousands of years of weathering. This, in turn, revealed and continues to expose sediments rich in fossils, bones and middens.

The next section of the drive, which is one-way, takes you over the Walls of China into mallee country. The road then circles back to the north-eastern side of the lunette, returning to the park entrance via the north-western corner of the park.

Visitors can stretch their legs on three short walks. The 1-km (0.6-mile) Grassland Walk departs from the main camp site near the visitor centre. It provides a fine introduction to the park's flora, which is dominated by belah (casuarina), bluebush and mallee, and its rich fauna, which includes red and western grey kangaroos, bats and echidnas, reptiles such as geckos, dragons and shinglebacks, and emus, Major Mitchell cockatoos and orange and white-fronted chats. The Foreshore Walk follows the western edge of the lake bed, while a 0.5-km (0.3-mile) walk into the mallee branches off the eastern side of the drive tour.

Access and Accommodation

The road to Mungo is unsealed but normally open to conventional vehicles; check conditions locally before you set off and stock up with fuel and supplies as none are available in the park.

There are camp sites near the park entrance and at Belah Camp, both of which have basic facilities. It is also possible to stay at the old shearers' quarters (book through the NPWS) or at the independently operated Mungo Lodge, located just outside the park.

Places in
SOUTH-WEST
NEW SOUTH WALES

The Magpie's Nest vineyard in the Big Rivers wine region, near Wagga Wagga.

ALBURY

Situated right on the banks of the Murray River 583 km (362 miles) south-west of Sydney, Albury and its twin town Wodonga represent a huge regional growth centre. They are both on the Hume Highway, the main road between Sydney and Melbourne. Founded near the spot where Hume and Hovell first came across the Murray on their journey to Port Phillip in 1824, the town site was named after a small village in Surrey, England.

Though initially slow to grow (just three years after gazetting, the population had grown to seven), Albury became significant as a port for the paddle-steamers plying up and down the river. The thriving local wine industry can trace its roots back to the German settlers who first arrived in 1840.

An energetic rural city, the population today is 59,000. A stroll around town will reveal fascinating insights into the town's history, as the architecture dates from the late nineteenth century in many places. Albury is also home to the Charles

View of Albury from the war memorial.

Sturt University. This region has quite a large array of manufacturing enterprises, including woollen and newsprint mills.

The famous Ettamogah Pub, immortalised in the cartoons and comics of the same name, is only 15 km (9.3 miles) to the north. Water sports and fishing can be enjoyed on Lake Hume, 12 km (7.5 miles) from town, and the *Cumberoona*, a paddle-steamer replica from the 1880s, plies up and down the river. You can even get some wind in your face with an Iron Horse Motorcycle Tour.
Map ref: page 465 M8

BALRANALD

Balranald (population 1450) lies on the Murrumbidgee River, some 130 km (81 miles) west of Hay and 889 km (552 miles) south-west of Sydney. Further west is Mallee Cliffs National Park, and to the north-west is the unique Mungo National Park. The town's links with history include Charles Sturt (who visited the region in 1830), Thomas Mitchell, and Burke and Wills. The town was a busy river port in the mid-nineteenth century. The Homebush Hotel was established in 1878.

One hundred kilometres (62 miles) north of Balranald is Boree Plains, a 51,000 ha (126,021 acre) sheep and cattle station that adjoins Mungo National Park, and which offers accommodation in the shearers' quarters and camping. You can hire a 4WD, visit the School of the Air classroom in a 100-year-old train carriage, and see mallee fowl, kangaroos and emus close up. Golf, fishing and swimming are also possible here.
Map ref: page 464 F5

BAROOGA

Along the picturesque Murray Valley Highway west from Albury, turning north-west at Cobram, is the holiday town of Barooga, on the banks of the Murray River, 711 km (442 miles) south-west of Sydney. A town of 1000, it boasts excellent river beaches and very pretty countryside where the local industries include citrus and grape-growing. Seppelts has a winery in the district, and there is also a good golf course with very reasonable rates. Visitors can loll around or swim off the sandy beaches by the Murray River, or go and visit the Dalveile Gallery with its antique oil lamp collection, or take a stroll through Barooga's Botanical Gardens. Just across the Murray River, in Victoria, is Cobram, Barooga's sister town.
Map ref: page 465 K8

A Murray cod from Barooga.

BERRIGAN

Situated on the Riverina Highway just between Albury and Deniliquin, Berrigan, which has a population of 1000, boasts a number of old buildings that date as far

back as the 1880s. Berrigan is 726 km (451 miles) south-west of Sydney and it lies in the middle of rich agricultural lands, but has long been synonymous with horseracing: historic Kilfenora Stables are quite close to the racecourse. The course and the racing club have been going since the 1890s, and these days the town holds five meets each year, with the major of these being the Berrigan Gold Cup. Also offered are golf and tennis.
Map: page 465 K7

BIG RIVERS WINE REGION

Big Rivers is a very hot, dry region centred around Wagga Wagga and Griffith in the Riverina area and could not have become a top wine-producing area without irrigation.

Ironically, irrigation is also the source of Big Rivers' poor reputation domestically—that of a soulless mass producer of bulk wines. But where growers are prepared to restrict their yields through canopy management, pruning and by minimising irrigation, the quality of the wine has been improved greatly. Big Rivers is now one of the heroes of the Australian wine industry. It is now producing some surprisingly good wines, although its old reputation is proving hard to shed. A lot of its wine does end up in the ubiquitous casks, but it also produces much 'sunshine in a bottle'—the flavourful, great-value wines that sell so well both in Australia and on the export market. Most Big Rivers producers make huge quantities

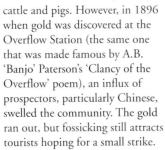

The Wagga Wagga Winery restaurant.

of wine but sprinkled among these mega-establishments are several smaller, rarely encountered wineries. Sémillon is the most widely planted grape but chardonnay plantings are increasing. Shiraz is by far the dominant red variety.

Many of the original Big Rivers growers were returned servicemen from the First World War or Italian immigrants who moved to the area after both world wars. But it was the McWilliam family who really pioneered viticulture in the area, at Hanwood, in 1912. The prevalent style produced was of fortifieds to match the national taste at that time. The McWilliam clan also pioneered the move to premium table wines, but the good climate ensures that Big Rivers will continue to remain an important source of the fortified material.

Where Big Rivers has stunned both the critics and the public alike, has been with its excellent botrytis sémillons. Pioneered in 1982 by the de Bortoli family, in Bilbul, these luscious, concentrated dessert-style wines are world class and have catapulted the district to the attention of wine lovers around the world. Noble One (the incredibly successful first vintage from 1982) in particular, and the subsequent Black Noble changed public perception of both de Bortoli and the Riverina forever.

Under Brian Croser's direction, the Charles Sturt University Winery (formerly the Riverina College of Advanced Education) now not only produces some of Australia's best and brightest winemakers, but is also a well-respected source of wine. The cellar door is located on campus, just 8 km (5 miles) out of Wagga Wagga.
Map ref: page 465 K4, N6

CONDOBOLIN

Regarded as the geographic centre of New South Wales, 'Condo' is situated on the Lachlan River on red soil plains, 467 km (290 miles) west of Sydney. A town of just 3500 residents, its name derives from the Aboriginal word for 'hop bush'. The surrounding rural district survives on its wool, wheat, cattle and pigs. However, in 1896 when gold was discovered at the Overflow Station (the same one that was made famous by A.B. 'Banjo' Paterson's 'Clancy of the Overflow' poem), an influx of prospectors, particularly Chinese, swelled the community. The gold ran out, but fossicking still attracts tourists hoping for a small strike.

Lake Condobolin Recreation Area is popular for water sports and fishing, and the town also has facilities for bowls, golf and tennis. One of the very last Aboriginal chiefs of the area is buried about 40 km (25 miles) out of town.
Map ref: page 465 M1

COOLAMON

Coolamon (population 1360) lies in the centre of a rich wheat and fat lamb district 30 km (19 miles) north-west of Wagga Wagga (between Junee and Mandera), 521 km (324 miles) south-west of Sydney. When the railway arrived in 1881, the town was laid out on the original Coolemon Holes run, but the spelling soon changed to more closely reflect the Aboriginal word 'coolamon', meaning a hollowed-out piece of wood suitable for carrying water or food.

Known as 'the turkey capital' as large numbers of these birds are produced in the district, it is also famous for its museums, antique shops and historic buildings that abound throughout the area.

The Ardlethan Walking Track is close by. A racing town, special events during the year include the Anzac Day Races, the Pacers' Cup and the South-west and Riverina Pacers' Derby. Coolamon has a number of festivals. In March, there's the Vintage Tractor Pull; in August, the Agricultural Show; in September, a Hootenanny (folk festival) and the biannual Canola Festival is in October.
Map ref: page 465 M5

COOTAMUNDRA

Cootamundra means 'turtles', 'low flying' or 'a marsh'. It is 427 km (265 miles) south-west of Sydney and home to 6400. Like Bowral, Cootamundra is tied up with cricketer Sir Donald Bradman. He was born here in 1908 and 'Bradman Cottage' has been restored and converted into a museum full of cricketing memorabilia. It is open to the public seven days a week between 8.30 a.m. and 4.30 p.m. (At the time of Bradman's birth, it was a local midwife's hospital.) Sir Donald's grandparents are buried in Cootamundra cemetery.

First settled in the 1830s, today the town is a major rail junction for the western and Riverina lines. It is also an important stock-selling centre and the surrounding district supports grazing, agriculture and mixed farming, plus there is much secondary industry in the town.

This is the home of the Cootamundra wattle *(Acacia baileyana),* one of the best known of all cultivated acacias. August is a the best time to visit, when the fun of the Wattle Time Festival takes place. Cootamundra is also a big racing town, with harness and gallopers.
Map ref: page 465 P5

A pretty purple carpet of Paterson's curse belies the nature of this plant, a pest for graziers in the Cootamundra district.

FORBES

On the banks of the Lachlan River, situated 371 km (230 miles) west of Sydney, Forbes commemorates the name of the first Chief Justice of New South Wales, Francis Forbes, who did a great deal to ensure that trial by jury was introduced to the colony.

John Oxley was the first explorer to track the Forbes region in 1817, but it was gold that drew the large numbers of eager prospectors (over 30,000) to the district in 1861. For the next four years, the town was a magnet not only to honest people, but also to bushrangers like Ben Hall and Frank Gardiner. Hall was buried in the Forbes cemetery after being shot by troopers (at age 27) at Bogan Gate to the north. Yet another celebrity in the graveyard is Ned Kelly's sister Kate.

When the gold ran out at the end of the 1860s, Forbes reverted to being an agricultural and pastoral centre. Nowadays, the town has 9000 residents and the local industries include wool, fat lambs, beef cattle, poultry and pigs, as well as wheat, fruit, wine grapes, lucerne and dairy products.

Forbes is rich in history. The Albion Hotel was originally a Cobb and Co depot—tunnels used to transport the gold to and from the banks that still exist

The Council building in Forbes. The town's grand Victorian architecture reflects the optimism of the gold boom days.

COROWA

Corowa sits on the Murray River, 636 km (395 miles) south-west of Sydney, and is the centre of a prosperous district growing wool, cereal crops, fat stock and wine grapes. Corowa's secondary industries include wine-making, timber milling, and the processing of malt and stock feed.

The town's name is of Aboriginal origin and it means a pine that exudes gum for affixing spearheads. Corowa (population 5200) was surveyed in 1857 and marked an important crossing place for stock. Later, miners used it in the rush to the Victorian goldfields.

Federation was vital to Corowa; when New South Wales and Victoria were separate colonies, customs posts were stationed at every crossing point along the Murray River. Federation gave much easier access to the Victorian markets. The Federation Museum has documents and memorabilia relating to that event on display.

There are delightful bushwalks in the hinterland, and the river provides good opportunities for birdwatching river cruising, swimming and fishing. Corowa claims to have the world's largest bowling club; but there is also a golf course and tennis courts.
Map ref: page 465 L8

DENILIQUIN

Situated on the Edward River in south-west New South Wales, 789 km (490 miles) south-west of Sydney, Deniliquin (population 8500) lies at the junction of the Cobb and Riverina highways. With more sunshine per year than Queensland's Gold Coast, the town is the third largest in the Riverina district and centre of the renowned Riverina sheep-breeding and wool-growing industry.

Benjamin Boyd established Deniliquin in 1845 as a personal holding. In 1849, a town was given the name 'Sandhills', but two years later was gazetted as 'Deniliquin', a corruption of the name 'Denilakoon', a leader of the local Aboriginal tribe who was 2 m (6.6 feet) tall and immensely powerful.

In the early days, the town was a busy crossing point for livestock, and agriculture was already the base for Deniliquin's economy. Today it is surrounded by highly developed farms and grazing land. Irrigation made the land more reliable and enabled extensions of crops. Rice is now an integral part of all this, along with wheat, barley, oats, oil seeds and lucerne.

Historical attractions include Peppin Heritage Centre and the Courthouse; others are the Edward River Island Sanctuary, the Barmah Forest and the Lawson Syphon, an irrigation marvel. Deniliquin has beautiful parks, gardens, waterways and forests and many sporting facilities, such as clay-target shooting, golf, bowls, tennis and squash. It has the Sun Festival in January, a jazz festival at Easter and World Record Ute Muster in October.
Map ref: page 465 H7

The Edward River near Deniliquin; popular for swimming, waterskiing and fishing.

beneath the building, and the look-out tower can be seen on the roof. The Lachlan Vintage Village re-creates the community as it was in the nineteenth century, with early buildings reconstructed on site and displays of goldmining and early machinery. Included are Ben Hall's cottage and also the home of the poet Henry Lawson.

In the Historical Museum in Cross Street are relics of the bush-ranging days; the museum itself began life as Osborne Hall, a dance hall which was attached to the Os-borne Hotel. All facets of Forbes' history, from Aboriginal lifestyle and artefacts to furniture, photo-graphs, clothing, household items and machinery are all on display. A great deal of the museum's space is devoted to Ben Hall.

South of the town, on the New-ell Highway, is Gum Swamp, which has a specially constructed hide for viewing waterbirds. There are two wineries on the outskirts of town: Sandhills Wineyard and Lachlan Valley Wines. Forbes also has a great racecourse, a bowling green, squash and tennis courts, and a golf course. Other activities include fishing, gold panning and water sports. The town hosts a five-day jazz festival in January.
Map ref: page 465 P2

GRENFELL

Grenfell is an agricultural and pas-toral centre 363 km (225 miles) west of Sydney. It was first settled by graziers in the 4650s.

The area really boomed with the discovery of gold at Emu Creek on John Woods' 'Brundah' run in 1866 and the area is still good for fos-sicking. The town was marked out a year later, and named after J.G. Grenfell, district Gold Com-missioner, who had been recently shot by bushrangers at Narromine. In its heyday, Grenfell boasted 30 pubs. Today the town is home to just 2500 people.

The town's main claim to histor-ical fame is that Henry Lawson was born on the diggings there, at One Mile, and a monument marks the spot. Also born in Grenfell was the cricketer Stan McCabe, a superb batsman, first-class fieldsman and useful medium-pace bowler. His family lived here for some time and a museum in Camp Street has some unusual cricket photos.

An ingenious display of oranges heralds Griffith's annual spring festival, which celebrates gardens in this irrigation area.

Weddin Mountains National Park is 19 km (12 miles) to the south. It has some walking trails winding through wild vegetation and native animals are readily seen. Its best-known attraction is Ben Hall's Cave, used by the bushrang-ing gang as a refuge. The cave was also used as a base for forays to pillage the Gundagai–Yass Cobb and Co run. O'Brien's Lookout, on the Cowra road, provides some good views right over the town and the old gold diggings.

First held in 1958, the Henry Lawson Festival of the Arts is cele-brated over the Queen's Birthday weekend in June each year.
Map ref: page 465 P3

GRIFFITH

Griffith is 615 km (382 miles) south-west of Sydney and is a com-paratively modern town, designed in 1914 by Walter Burley Griffin, the architect who also designed the city of Canberra.

The town is named after Sir Arthur Griffith, who was the first Minister for Public Works in the New South Wales government. Thanks to irrigation (pioneered by the McCaughey brothers), what was once largely barren land now supports a thriving agricultural economy and the town's present population is 15,000.

Many varieties of vegetables, fruit, grapes, rice, wheat and cotton are produced, plus sheep and wool.

The local wine industry went under a transformation recently. While years ago Griffith's wines were regarded as inferior, it now produces some first-rate wines, including those of De Bortoli, McWilliams Hanwood (known for its port) and Miranda. There are 15 local vineyards in all.

The Murrumbidgee River pro-vides plenty of opportunities for fishing and water sports, while golf and bowls are both possible in town. The view from Scenic Hill shows what lushness irrigation has brought the surrounding country-side. Pioneer Park Museum is to the north of the town, as is Coco-parra National Park.

Griffith holds the Festival of Griffith in Easter and the colourful Festival of Gardens in October. *See also* Big Rivers Wine Region
Map ref: page 465 K4

Volunteer bush firefighters provide a vital service in rural areas.

The rarity of a passing motorist ensures a friendly wave on the monotonous stretch of the Sturt Highway across the Hay Plain.

HAY

Originally known as Lang's Crossing, Hay was once a Murrumbidgee sheep fording point. Charles Sturt passed by on his way down the river in 1829, and in 1858, Francis Cadell—the legendary riverboat identity responsible for opening up much of both the Murrumbidgee and the Darling Rivers—opened a store here. The town was named in 1859 after local politician and pastoralist, Sir John Hay.

Today, Hay (population 2930) is an essential service centre for a vast pastoral area. The major crop is wool, but there are several world-famous sheep studs in the area. At the junction of three highways—Sturt, Midwestern and Cobb—and midway between Sydney and Adelaide, Hay is a welcome sight

An abandoned hotel at One Tree, near Hay.

for travellers journeying from Sydney—758 km (471 miles) to the north-east. It appears after the long drive across the Hay Plain from West Wyalong—surely the most boring drive in New South Wales. An old saying pertinent to the district is 'The three hottest places in New South Wales are Hay, Hell and Booligal—in that order'. Booligal is the next stop north on the Cobb Highway, 78 km (48 miles) away. Hay Gaol Museum was built in 1878 and houses an impressive collection of local memorabilia. Hay also houses *Sunbeam,* the original Cobb and Co coach that served Hay on the Deniliquin–Hay–Wilcannia run until 1901. Also around Hay, Ruberto's Winery is open to visitors. Hay hosts the Australian Hang-liding National Championships in January and the Bush Week Festival is held in March.
Map ref: page 465 H5

HENTY

Named after the Henty family of pioneer pastoralists, this town was originally called Doodle Cooma. It is 542 km (337 miles) south-west of Sydney.

For 32 years this town of only 100 people has hosted one of the most important agribusiness events to be held in Australia: the Henty Machinery Field Days. This special local event is to commemorate the unveiling of a harvester-header at the 1914 Henty Agricultural Show by local farmer Headlie Taylor. The Taylor Header subsequently revolutionised grain farming and is regarded by many to be the single greatest contribution to the grain industry. (An original header is on display in a special building in Henty Park.) Henty Machinery Field Days showcase over 200 million dollars' worth of farming equipment and technology. Held in September over three days, the event regularly attracts over 50,000 visitors, who also come to see the fashion, crafts and cooking displays. Just to the west of the town is a memorial plaque for a Sergeant Smyth, who was shot dead there by 'Mad' Dog Morgan.
Map ref: page 465 M7

HOLBROOK

Changing the names of towns was a popular pastime during World War I (particularly in South Australia, which had a high proportion of early German immigrants). In New South Wales, Germanton was rechristened 'Holbrook' after a Victoria Cross-winning British submarine commander. A replica of Commander Holbrook's submarine is visible from the highway as you drive through town. Holbrook (population 1330) is halfway between Sydney and Melbourne on the Hume Highway—516 km (320 miles) south of Sydney.

In the nineteenth century, Germanton was an important staging post on the Cobb and Co Melbourne–Sydney run, and the main street has many buildings from that era, including the Woolpack Inn. Built in 1895, almost 80 years later it was turned into a museum, with 22 rooms housing turn-of-the-century fashions, furniture and artefacts. The racecourse has been in use since the end of the nineteenth century and the major event held is the Commander Holbrook Cup, which is on Anzac Day.
Map ref: page 465 N7

JERILDERIE

A town in the Riverina district, Jerilderie lies 692 km (430 miles) south-west of Sydney, on vast surrounding plains noted for merino studs, the production of wool, fat lambs, cattle and wheat.

Jerilderie means 'a reedy place' and the town houses a small community of 1000 that is proud of its place in Australian history. Today it provides many sporting facilities and amenities not found in towns of similar size, such as golf, horseracing, bowls, tennis and water sports.

The Ned Kelly Post Office was the original telegraph station sabotaged by the Kelly gang in 1879, who robbed the Bank of New South Wales of more than £2000. The bank is in Powell Street, named after the 1850s founder of the town, John Caractacus Powell. The Willows houses local archives and items of farming and historic significance. The home of John Monash, one of Australia's greatest generals, can also be found here.
Map ref: page 465 K6

The Commercial Hotel in Junee, an important wheat and canola-farming district.

JUNEE

Aboriginal for 'speak to me', Junee (population 5000) calls itself the Rail and Jail Town. The 'Rail' is easy to explain, as Junee is quite an important train centre on the Riverina line. In 1945 the largest circular railway locomotive roundhouse in the Southern Hemisphere was opened here, with a 32 m (105 foot) turntable and 42 repair bays. The 'Jail' refers to a high-tech, privately owned and operated local correctional centre.

Junee is situated on the Murrumbidgee River about halfway between Sydney and Melbourne on the Olympic Way—446 km (277 miles) south-west of Sydney.

It is the centre of a grazing and agricultural district, though gold was mined in the area during the nineteenth century at Old Junee, Junee Reefs and Illabo.

Nowadays, the district is the largest producer of canola in the State. Junee also has the largest

The Sharfield grain silo near Junee.

wheat terminal in the entire Southern Hemisphere, and it has a storage capacity of a whopping 153,000 tonnes (168,606 tons).

Other agricultural activities in the district include ostrich and deer farming; and the local sporting activities include golf, swimming, horseracing, bowls and tennis.

'Jewnee Run', which was established in 1845, was the original property in the district. In 1876, Christopher Crawley built what is currently the Hotel Junee, and another 18 years later he erected Monte Cristo Homestead. This is now an award-winning tourist attraction; it has been faithfully restored and boasts a very impressive collection of antiques and horse-drawn carriages.

In February, the town hosts a Pro Rodeo; in March, there is a Billycart Derby; in April, a Vintage and Veteran Car Rally; June offers the Kennel Club Championships; September has the Monte Cristo Charity Ball and in October, there is the Agricultural Show.
Map ref: page 465 N5

LEETON

Named after C.A. Lee, Minister for Public Works when the Murrumbidgee Irrigation Area (MIA) was being developed, Leeton was the first of many Riverina towns to be designed by the architect Walter Burley Griffin, in 1912.

Leeton (population 7000) is 560 km (348 miles) south-west of Sydney and is the administrative centre for the MIA, with many Government departments based there. The local economy relies predominantly on agriculture, with the town housing major food-processing organisations, such as the Ricegrowers Cooperative, Leeton Citrus Juices and a stock-killing centre. (In 1940, the Letona cannery—another important local employer since 1914— established a record of canning 419,609 tins of fruit in one day.)

Visitors can inspect the Quelch juice factory, visit a sheep-milking farm, see the historic Hydro Hotel, built in 1919, or call in at the old Whitton Court House Museum.

Two local wineries—Toorak and Lillypilly Estate—are open for tastings, and just 2 km (1.2 miles) out of town is Fivebough Swamp, a waterfowl sanctuary. Harness racing, gliding and hot-air ballooning are popular tourist attractions, with bowls, golf and water sports also on offer. Leeton holds the SunRice Festival during Easter in even-numbered years.
Map ref: page 465 L5

MOAMA

Moama (population 6000) is the twin of the Victorian town of Echuca, which lies directly across the Murray River, 864 km (537 miles) south of Sydney, connected to Echuca by a bridge. Originally called Maidens Punt, the town was renamed in 1851 after the Aboriginal name for the area. These two towns represent a monument to the paddle-steamer days, as taking a gentle river cruise will indicate. Horseshoe Lagoon is a reserve near the bridge consisting of 16 ha (40 acres) of natural bushland. Here visitors can take in the local history of Old Moama Wharf, and the recently restored Moama slipway, or simply enjoy the tranquility and the abundant bird life. Other area activities include canoeing, fishing, river cruising or swimming.
Map ref: page 465 H8

NARRANDERA

One of the Riverina's earliest settlements, Narrandera (population 5000) was proclaimed in 1863, taking its name from an early pastoral holding. (The name means 'place of lizards'.) The town is 584 km (363 miles) south-west of Sydney and is the centre for an economy that is based on wheat, wool, oats, barley, lucerne, fruit, beef cattle, fat lambs, and poultry.

Narrandera is on the Murrumbidgee River, which, together with nearby Lake Talbot, means there is an abundance of water and wildlife, all of which are great for fishing, water sports, bushwalking and horse riding. Narrandera's Race Club has a long history, dating back to 1879, and hosts five major meets each year. The town also has art galleries and antique shops, a bowling green and golf course.

Many of the town's buildings have been classified and are being used as restaurants or galleries. The Parkside Cottage Museum is also of interest.
Map ref: page 465 L5

Fishing for Murray cod in the Murray River at Moama.

Anglers enjoy the peace and tranquility at Albert Lake, which is close to Wagga Wagga, a thriving Murrumbidgee city.

attractions for children include a miniature world of railways, mini-golf and there is also an extensive foreshore playground and family picnic area with free barbecues. The magnificent sandy beaches, surrounded by red gum forests, have been popular with tourists for over a century. Festivals include the Tocumwal Easter Extravaganza and the Tocumwal Angling Classic in January. Other local activities include horseracing, horse riding, bowls and golf.

Map ref: page 465 J7

WAGGA WAGGA

Wagga Wagga (population 58,700) is more commonly known simply as 'Wagga' (which means 'crow' in the language of the Wiradjuri, the largest Aboriginal tribe in New South Wales, who first settled in the area). The city is situated on the Murrumbidgee River, 486 km (302 miles) south-west of Sydney, with Cootamundra and Temora to the north, Narrandera to the west, Albury to the south and Tumut in the east. It forms the hub of a vast district that supports the production of wheat, fat lambs, the dairy industry and mixed farming.

Settlers beat the explorers to this district: Charles Sturt was almost ten years behind the land-seekers when he came through in 1829. Robert Holt Best founded the Wagga Wagga run in 1832. Now the city is a vital business, agricultural, educational and industrial centre, one of the bigger settlements in the southern region.

History buffs can participate in the three National Trust walks, passing by buildings that date from 1865. Other attractions are the zoo, art gallery, botanic gardens and Historical Museum. With prolific parks and gardens, including a formal Shakespearian garden, the city can be a visual delight in spring.

Sports enthusiasts will find golf, tennis, fishing, bushwalking, bowls, croquet and water sports as well as greyhound racing, horseracing and trotting are all available.

Olive oil made in Wagga Wagga.

TEMORA

With a name that is believed to be of Celtic rather than Aboriginal origin, Temora services the Riverina's wheat district. It is 458 km (284 miles) south-west of Sydney and has a population of 5900.

The first white settlers came to the region in the 1850s and 1860s, carving themselves huge runs, but the population remained fairly small until the Temora Goldfield was proclaimed in 1880, bringing 20,000 people into the district. There were some great finds here, including the Mother Shipton nugget, and there is a facsimile of it in the town's Rock and Mineral Museum. This museum is found inside the award-winning Temora Rural Museum. It also features Temora greenstone, a stone much sought after by lapidaries.

Another special exhibit is the Paragon Gold Project, near town. Given all this, the Temora region is particularly good for fossicking and attracts many keen collectors.

During World War II, over 10,000 RAAF personnel passed through training at Temora, and with one of the most fog-free landing strips in the State, it continues with its aviation traditions today through civilian training, gliding and also skydiving. Temora holds its annual show in September and the Temora Rural Museum Annual Exhibition is on in the second Saturday of March. Regular markets are held every last Saturday of the month bar December and January.

Map ref: page 465 N4

THE ROCK

The name of this town says what this place is all about—a giant outcrop some 363 m (1191 feet) high. The Rock has 850 inhabitants and is located 32 km (20 miles) south-west of Wagga or 511 km (317 miles) south-west of Sydney. It is surrounded by some quite distinct scenery that is particularly appealing to photographers.

The bird life here is also varied and attracts many birdwatchers. Walking trails run through the Rock Nature Reserve, culminating at the summit. The Rock Show is held the third Saturday in October.

Map ref: page 465 M6

TOCUMWAL

The Aboriginal name Tocumwal translates as 'a bottomless pit in the river' and water sports and fishing are popular here. Situated on the Murray River 727 km (451 miles) south-west of Sydney, the town has a long association with aviation. In World War II, it had the biggest airstrip in the Southern Hemisphere and there are still two gliding and flying schools here. The Sportavia Soaring Centre encompasses all types of flying activities.

Founded in 1862, Tocumwal (population 2000) is a historic town, with many fine examples of colonial architecture listed by the National Trust. There are four historic pubs, open gardens, display gardens, working woodturners, art studios, an emu farm, antiques and wineries. Some

Music lovers can enjoy the orchestral concerts, which are held at the city's outdoor music bowl and entertainment centre.

Charles Sturt University even has its own winery, which is open for tastings and sales. Festivals include the Summer School of Strings in January, the Wagga Wagga Gold Cup in April–May and the Golden Gown Awards in June. In September there is the Jazz Festival, the Riverina Antique Fair and the City to Lake Fun Run, followed in October by the Garden and Leisure Festival.

See also Big Rivers Wine Region
Map ref: page 465 N6

WENTWORTH

Near the junction of the Murray and Darling Rivers, Wentworth is just over 30 km (19 miles) west of Mildura and 1076 km (668 miles) south-west of Sydney. Named after William Charles Wentworth, in the 1850s it was an important river transport centre for wool and provisions. Now, the town has a population of 1400 and is the centre for a fruit and wool district. The first residence went up in 1851. St John's Anglican Church (built in 1871) is only one of many buildings in town of interest to historians. The Buronga Winery and the Cod River Aquarium are worth a visit. A relic of the old days of Wentworth, the paddle-steamer

The Buronga Winery, in the Wentworth region.

Hiring a houseboat at Wentworth is a relaxing way to enjoy the Darling River.

Ruby is moored at a wharf. Visitors can hire houseboats to explore the river systems and catch their own dinner in the process.
Map ref: page 464 C4

WEST WYALONG

On the Mid-Western Highway, West Wyalong is the last real outpost of civilisation before Hay, 260 km (161 miles) away and is 524 km (325 miles) west of Sydney. Now the commercial hub of a lucrative wool, wheat and mixed farming area, West Wyalong (population 3700) owes its existence to a gold strike in 1893. The original strike had been made at Wyalong, a few kilometres to the northeast, but when it ran out and the 'main camp' proved to have more water, West Wyalong came into being. Though one of the richest fields in New South Wales in its day, mining ceased in 1914. Like Gulgong, the town retains images of its former days of glory in its narrow, winding streets and some architectural remnants. The District Museum has a scale model of a working goldmine, and the Aboriginal Art Centre holds some fascinating artefacts from Central Australia.

East of West Wyalong is Weddin Mountains National Park. Camping is possible in the national park, but you have to bring your own water. Birdwatchers and bushwalkers be warned that there are few tracks in the park, so they should take care.

For squatters taking up land in the western district, the Weddin Mountains marked the beginning of the plains, known as the Bland, or the Levels. In the 1850s and 1860s, bushrangers used them as a base from which they emerged to steal horses from squatters or gold from the coaches. The father of one bushranger, John O'Meally, ran a pub somewhere up in the ranges, but after Frank Gardiner robbed the Eugowra gold escort of £14,000 in 1862, troopers looking for him set fire to O'Meally's pub and burnt it to the ground. The money was never found.
Map ref: page 465 M3

WILLANDRA NATIONAL PARK

In the late 1880s, Big Willandra Station was a famous Merino stud which occupied 290,000 ha (796,590 acres) of the flat red sandplains of central western New South Wales. Over the years, settlement led to subdivision, and the final leasehold was resumed in 1972 to form Willandra National Park.

The old homestead, woolshed, stables and other station buildings were later added to the park. Willandra Creek forms the northern boundary of the park, and Willandra Billabong attracts many species of waterbirds. Trees such as black box and coolibahs line the banks of the creek and waterhole; away from water, the semi-arid sandplains are sparsely covered with saltbush and native grasses. Emus and kangaroos are abundant here.

It is possible to stay in the old homestead, however bookings are essential. There is also a camp site near the homestead. Fees apply.
Map ref: page 465 J2

YANCO

Home to 700 residents, Yanco is 607 km (377 miles) south-west of Sydney, near Leeton. The Yanco Powerhouse Museum in town was originally built in 1913 to supply power to the Murrumbidgee Irrigation Area (MIA) but was closed down in 1957, when hydro-electricity from the Snowy Mountains Scheme became available.

The building is five storeys high and is made entirely of concrete. It now displays farm machinery and items of local history and also has a theatrette seating 60.

On Yanko Station, Samuel McCaughey first experimented with the irrigation procedures that led to the creation of the MIA. Although his mansion is now an agricultural high school, it is open to the public. There are extensive red gum forests along the Murrumbidgee where there are scenic drives leading to some pleasant fishing and swimming spots.
Map ref: page 465 L5

An emu rouses campers at Willandra.

Sydney City Centre

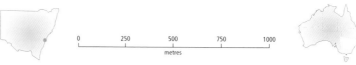

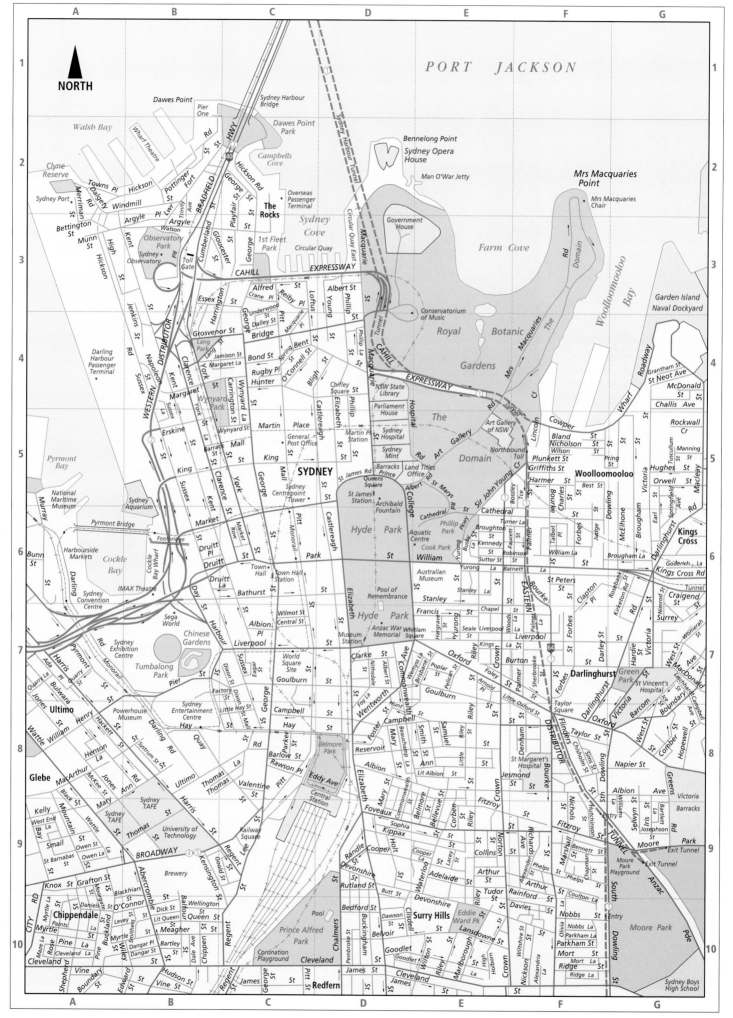

Sydney Throughroads

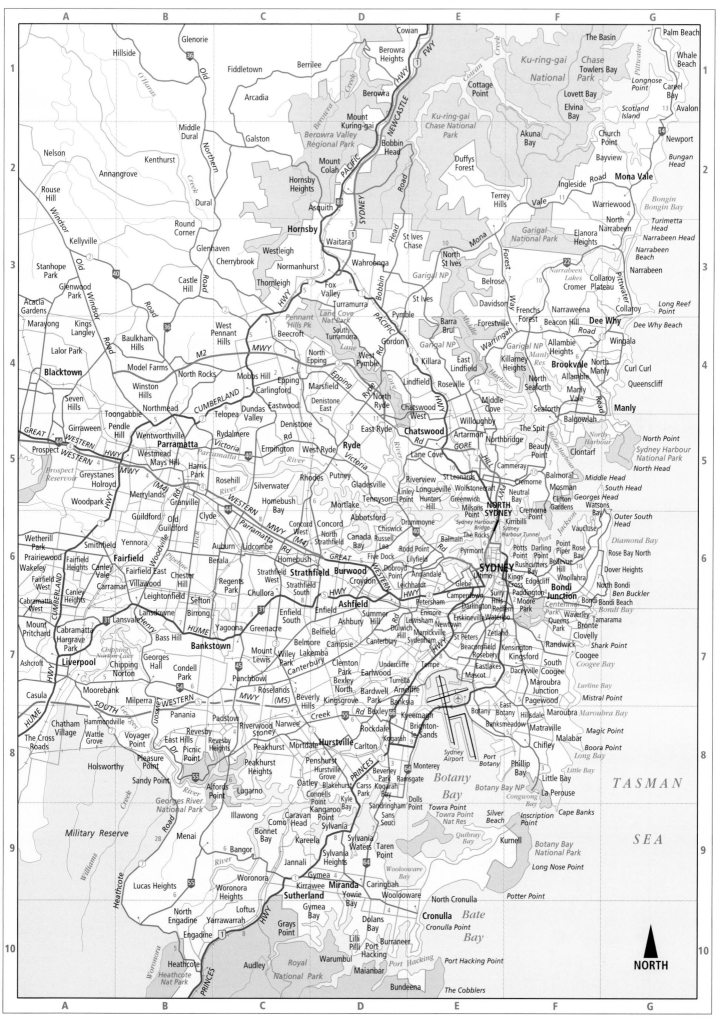

kilometres
0   2   4   6   8

A **B** **C** **D** **E** **F** **G**

Hillside

Glenorie

Fiddletown

Berrilee

Cowan

Berowra Heights

The Basin

Palm Beach

Whale Beach

Ku-ring-gai Chase National Park

Towlers Bay

Longnose Point

Carcel Bay

Avalon

Newport

Nelson

Middle Dural

Arcadia

Galston

Mount Kuring-gai

Berowra

Bobbin Head

Duffys Forest

Lovett Bay

Elvina Bay

Church Point

Akuna Bay

Bayview

Bungan Head

Mona Vale

Annangrove

Kenthurst

Berowra Valley Regional Park

Mount Colah

Ku-ring-gai Chase National Park

Terrey Hills

Ingleside

Warriewood

Narrabeen Head

Rouse Hill

Dural

Hornsby Heights

North St Ives

North Narrabeen

Narrabeen Beach

Narrabeen

Stanhope Park

Round Corner

Glenhaven

Westleigh

Normanhurst

Wahroonga

St Ives Chase

St Ives

Belrose

Davidson

Collaroy Plateau

Cromer

Collaroy

Blacktown

Parramatta

Fairfield

Liverpool

Bankstown

Strathfield

Burwood

Ashfield

SYDNEY

NORTH SYDNEY

Chatswood

Manly

Brookvale

Dee Why

Hurstville

Sutherland

Miranda

Cronulla

Botany Bay

TASMAN

SEA

Bate Bay

NORTH

Sydney and Surrounding Areas

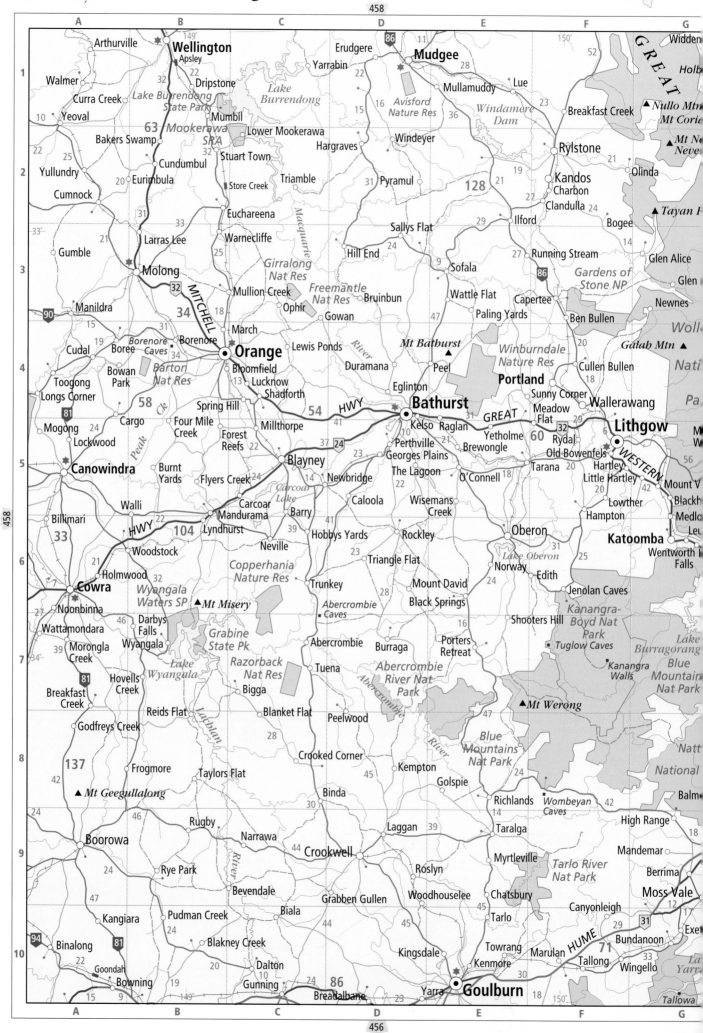

Row labels (top and bottom): A B C D E F G

Column labels (left and right): 1 2 3 4 5 6 7 8 9 10

458 (left margin)

Arthurville, Wellington, Apsley, Erudgere, Yarrabin, Mudgee, 86, 11, 28, Widden, GREAT

Walmer, Dripstone, Mullamuddy, Lue, Holb, Nullo Mtn, Mt Coric

Curra Creek, 32, 22, Lake Burrendong State Park, Lake Burrendong, 15, 16, Avisford Nature Res, 36, 23, Breakfast Creek, 52, Mt Ne Neve

Yeoval, 10, Mumbil, Windeyer, Windamere Dam, Rylstone, Tayan

Bakers Swamp, 63, Mookerawa SRA, Lower Mookerawa, Hargraves, 21, Olinda

Yullundry, Cundumbul, 32, Stuart Town, Triamble, Pyramul, 31, 128, 19, 27, Kandos, Charbon, Clandulla, 24, Bogee

Cumnock, Eurimbula, 20, Store Creek, Euchareena, Sallys Flat, 29, Ilford, Glen Alice

Gumble, Larras Lee, 21, 33, Warnecliffe, 25, Girralong Nat Res, Hill End, 24, 9, Sofala, 27, Running Stream, Glen, Newnes

Molong, Mullion Creek, Freemantle Nat Res, Bruinbun, Wattle Flat, Capertee, Gardens of Stone NP, Woll

Manildra, 90, 34, 18, Ophir, Gowan, 47, Paling Yards, Ben Bullen, Nati, Pa

Cudal, 15, Borenore Caves, Borenore, March, Lewis Ponds, River, Mt Bathurst, Winburndale Nature Res, 20, Galah Mtn

Boree, 19, Orange, Bloomfield, Duramana, Peel, Cullen Bullen, 18

Toogong, Bowan Park, Barton Nat Res, Lucknow, Eglinton, Portland, Sunny Corner, Wallerawang

Longs Corner, 58, Shadforth, HWY, Bathurst, GREAT, Meadow Flat, 32, 29, Lithgow

Mogong, 81, Cargo, Spring Hill, Millthorpe, 54, 41, Kelso, Raglan, 31, Yetholme, Brewongle, 60, Rydal, Old Bowenfels, Hartley, WESTERN

Lockwood, 24, Four Mile Creek, Forest Reefs, 37, 24, Perthville, 21, Tarana, 20, Little Hartley, Mount V

Canowindra, Burnt Yards, Flyers Creek, 24, Blayney, 22, Georges Plains, The Lagoon, O'Connell, 18, Lowther, Hampton, Blackh, Medlo, Leu

Billimari, 33, Walli, Carcoar Lake, 14, Newbridge, Caloola, Wisemans Creek, Oberon, Katoomba, Wentworth Falls

Mandurama, 22, 104, Carcoar, Barry, 41, Hobbys Yards, Rockley, 31, Lake Oberon, 25

Woodstock, Lyndhurst, 39, 23, Mount David, Norway, Edith, Jenolan Caves, Kanangra-Boyd Nat Park

Holmwood, 21, 32, Neville, Triangle Flat, 28, Black Springs, 24, Shooters Hill, Tuglow Caves, Kanangra Walls, Lake Burragorang

Cowra, Copperhania Nature Res, Trunkey, Abercrombie Caves, Porters Retreat, 16, Blue Mountains Nat Park, Mt Werong

Noonbinna, 27, Wyangala Waters SP, Mt Misery, Abercrombie, Burraga, 47, Kanangra Walls

Wattamondara, 46, Darbys Falls, Grabine State Pk, Tuena, Abercrombie River Nat Park, River, National

Morongla Creek, 39, Wyangala, Razorback Nat Res, Bigga, 34, Hovells Creek, Lake Wyangala, Blanket Flat, Peelwood, 47, Balm

Breakfast Creek, 81, Reids Flat, Lachlan, Crooked Corner, Kempton, Golspie, Richlands, Wombeyan Caves, 42, High Range, 18

Godfreys Creek, 137, Frogmore, Taylors Flat, 28, Binda, 45, 24, Natt

Mt Geegullalong, 42, Rugby, Narrawa, Crookwell, 44, Laggan, 39, Taralga, Myrtleville, Tarlo River Nat Park, Mandemar, Berrima, Moss Vale

Boorowa, 46, Rye Park, 24, Bevendale, Roslyn, Woodhouselee, Chatsbury, Canyonleigh, 31

Kangiara, 47, Pudman Creek, Biala, Grabben Gullen, Tarlo, 45, 29, Bundanoon, Exet, La Yarr

Binalong, 94, 81, Blakney Creek, 24, 44, Kingsdale, Towrang, Marulan, HUME, 71, Wingello, 33

Goondah, 22, Bowning, 19, Dalton, 10, Gunning, 24, 86, Breadalbane, 23, Yarra, Goulburn, Kenmore, Tallong, 18, 150, Tallowa

94, 15, 9, 149, 23

0 10 20 30 40 50
kilometres

New South Wales

H J K L M N P

1

mi Creek Glen Gallic Doyles Creek 30 Maison Dieu Glendon Brook Vacy Martins Creek Clarence Town 26 152° Allworth Limeburners Creek 22 Mungo Brush
10 Warkworth Redbournberry Paterson Wallaroo Nat Res Karuah 88
Mt Wambo ▲ 11 Bulga Belford 15 Branxton Greta 22 Woodville 22 Seaham 21 1 Tea Gardens Hawks Nest
Singleton Hunter River Swan Bay Port Stephens Soldiers Point Shoal Bay
16 43 Rutherford Wallalong 17 Swan Bay 51 Nelson Bay
37 Broke Rothbury Maitland Morpeth Grahamstown Lake Boat Harbour
▲ Kindarun Mtn Yellow Rock Abermain 28 Metford Raymond Terrace Williamtown Anna Bay Tomaree Nat Pk
Cessnock Kurri Kurri 37 Beresfield Sandgate
27 69 31 30 Bellbird 27 Pelaw Main 19 Fern Bay Newcastle Bight

2

Putty Paxton Kearsley Kitchener 37 Wallsend Stockton
Mt Yengo ▲ Ellalong Broadmeadow Newcastle
Wollombi Brunkerville Boolaroo 18 Charlestown Port Hunter
Yengo Laguna Warners Bay Toronto
23 Watagans Nat Pk 23 Redhead
National Bucketty Cooranbong Dora Creek Belmont
Park Cedar Brush Creek Morisset Lake Macquarie
RANGE 19 1 Gwandalan Swansea
Colo Heights Dooralong Wyee 46 Catherine Hill Bay

3

River Kulnura Yarramalong 85 Doyalson Lake Munmorah
St Albans Jilliby Budgewoi
27 Central Mangrove Wyong Noraville
Popran NP Peats Tuggerah Norah Head
Wisemans Ferry Ridge 21 Ourimbah Tuggerah Lake
Dharug Nat Pk 19 Calga Gosford The Entrance
Stanley Park Maroota Kariong Terrigal
t Irvine Marramarra Nat Park Woy Woy
ilpin 40 28 44 Brooklyn Bouddi NP
rrajong Cattai Berowra Waters Umina Killcare

4

5

Richmond Windsor Brooklyn Broken Bay
Box Hill 88 Palm Beach
Londonderry Cranebrook Hornsby Ku-ring-gai Chase NP
Springwood Blaxland Parklea Mona Vale
Penrith 32 HWY Blacktown Terrey Hills Narrabeen Long Reef Point
34 St Marys 31 Pymble 28 Manly
Erskine Park 14 Chatswood TASMAN
Kemps Creek Parramatta North Sydney Port Jackson
Warragamba 23 SYDNEY SEA
Bringelly Bankstown Bondi Junction
Bents Basin SRA Liverpool Hurstville
Verombi Eagle Vale Como 55 Botany
Narellan Sutherland Caringbah Botany Bay
Camden Heathcote Cronulla Port Hacking
89 Campbelltown Bundeena

6

7

icton Dharawal SRA 18 Waterfall Royal National Park
Appin 104 69 Helensburgh
oor Wilton Lake Cataract Stanwell Park Coalcliff
Buxton 47 Lake Cordeaux 31 1
Bargo Lake Avon Thirroul
Yanderra Corrimal
Yerrinbool Balgownie
Imerton Wollongong Red Point
gong Unanderra 18
Dapto Port Kembla Lake Illawarra
angaloon 61 Shellharbour
48 21 Albion Park Bass Point
Robertson 75 Minnamurra
Jamberoo Kiama
Kangaroo Valley Budderoo NP Werri Beach
Berry HWY Gerringong
ers Brush 17 42 Gerroa

8

9

10

151° 152°

▲ NORTH

South-East New South Wales

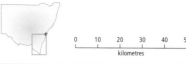

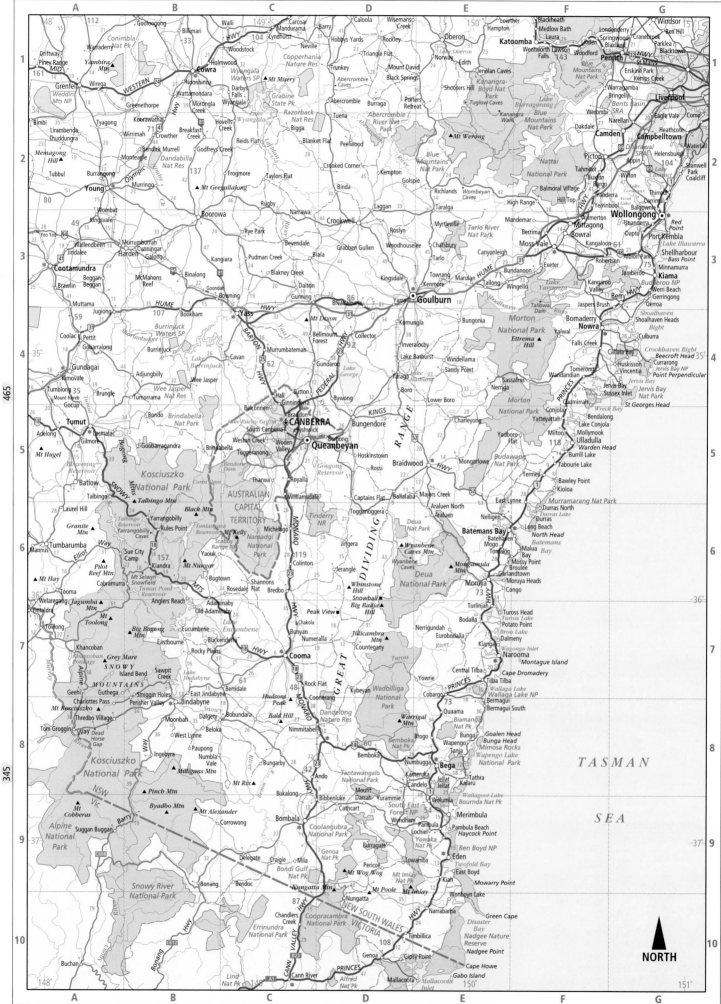

Canberra to the Snowy Mountains

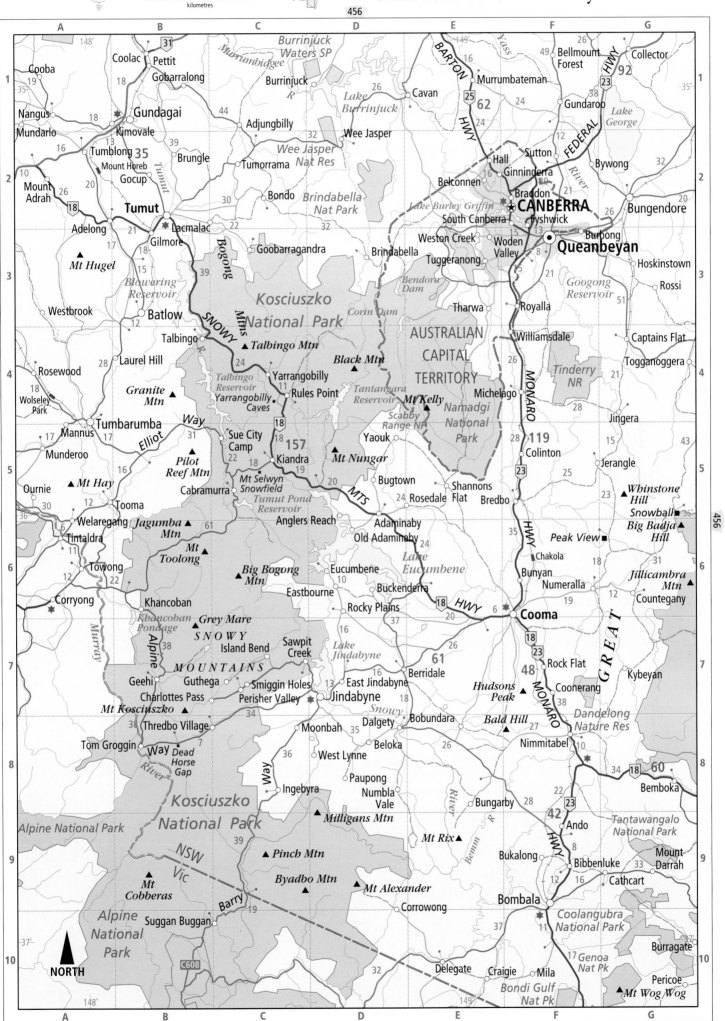

NEW SOUTH WALES

0   10   20   30
kilometres

NORTH

AUSTRALIAN CAPITAL TERRITORY

Kosciuszko National Park

SNOWY MOUNTAINS

Alpine National Park

Central-East New South Wales

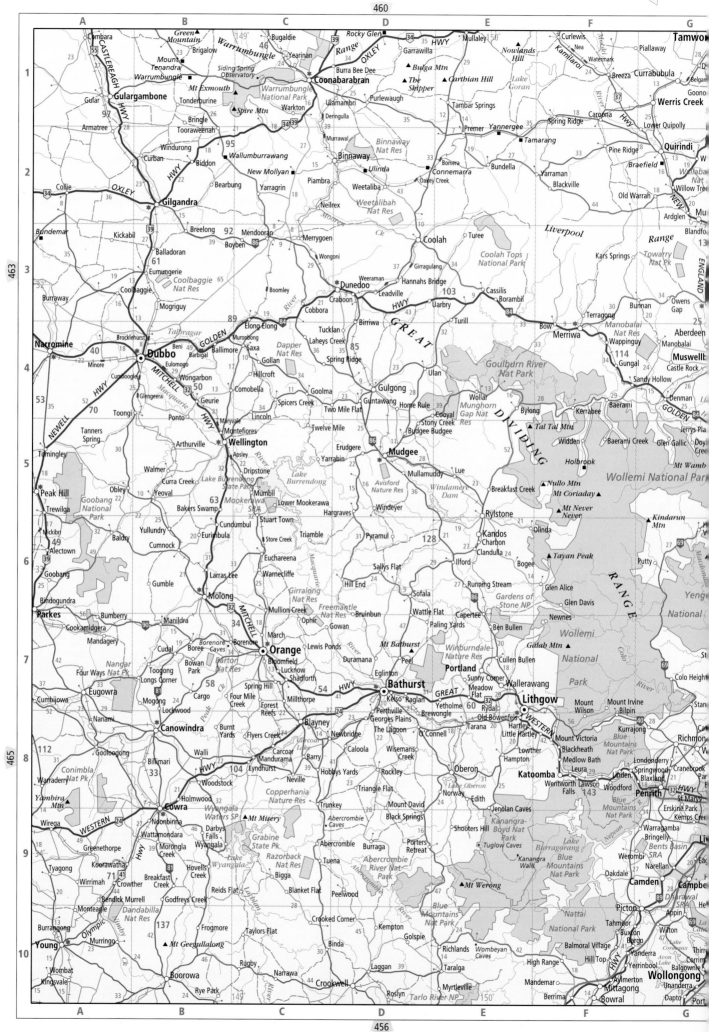

kilometres

0 10 20 30 40 50

NORTH

Aberbaldie
ore
ngowan
Glen Morrison
Weabonga
23
Woolomin
affe
Niangala
Ogunbil
32
owling Alley Point
Hanging Rock Nat Pk
undle
amura
29
Back River Nat Res
Barry
Gulph Mtn
Ellerston
Moonan Flat 39
Woolooma
trees
Mt Barrington
Davis Creek
Mt Royal Nat Pk
berwell
Singleton
Belford
Branxton
Greta
43 Rutherford
Rothbury
36
Cessnock
Bellbird
Paxton
Ellalong
Wollombi
Watagans Nat Pk
laguna
ucketty
19
nura
27
Central Mangrove
NP
Calga
Kariong
Woy Woy
Brisbane Water NP
Brooklyn
Terrey Hills
North Sydney
ta
SYDNEY
Bondi Junction
rstville
Botany
aringbah
Cronulla
Bundeena
Royal ional Park

Brackendale
Mt Sugarloaf
Mummel Gulf Nat Pk
Rlamukka
Nowendoc
Barakee Nat Res
174
Bralga Tops
Mernot Nat Res
63
Woko National Park
Polblue Cons Res
Upper Bowman
Rawdon Vale
Barrington Tops National Park
Gloucester Tops
Mt Royal
Chichester
Salisbury
Underbank
Chichester Dam
Carrow Brook
Halton
Munni
Bandon Grove
St Clair
Allynbrook
Gresford
Tyraman
Wallarobba
Glendon Brook
Vacy
Martins Creek
Paterson
Redbournberry
Abermain
Kearsley
Kitchener
Brunkerville
Kurri Kurri
Pelaw Main
Broadmeadow
Warners Bay
Toronto
Cooranbong
Cedar Brush Creek
Morisset
Dora Creek
Wyee
Dooralong
Yarramalong
Jilliby
Wyong
Tuggerah
Ourimbah
The Entrance
Gosford

TASMAN SEA

Oxley Wild Rivers NP
34
152
Kangaroo Flat
Mt Werrikimbe
Werrikimbe Nat Pk
Yarrowitch
Myrtle Scrub
Mount Seaview
Mt Seaview
Doyles River Nat Pk
Raffles Peak
Nowendoc
Dingo Tops Nat Park
Bulga
Elands
Mooral Creek
Number One
Bobin
Apple Tree Flat
Bretti Nat Res
Bretti
Tibbuc
Mount George
Rookhurst
Wingham
Kimbriki
Tinonee
Barrington
Burrell Creek
Rainbow Flat
Copeland
Krambach
Nabiac
Dyers Crossing
Forbesdale
Gloucester
Stratford
Craven Nat Res
Craven
Wards River
Little Myall River NP
Coolongolook
Wootton
Markwell
Bandon Grove
Main Creek
Fosterton
Stroud Road
Boolambayte
Bulahdelah
Dungog
Stroud
Booral
Girvan
Nerong
Bombah Point
Brookfield
Allworth
Clarence Town
Limeburners Creek
Mungo Brush
The Broadwater
Karuah
Seaham
Wallalong
Swan Bay
Soldiers Point
Tea Gardens
Hawks Nest
Shoal Bay
Nelson Bay
Boat Harbour
Anna Bay
Tomaree Nat Pk
Maitland
Morpeth
Metford
Beresfield
Raymond Terrace
Sandgate
Williamtown
Fern Bay
Stockton
Wallsend
Newcastle
Charlestown
Redhead
Belmont
Swansea
Gwandalan
Lake Macquarie
Catherine Hill Bay
Lake Munmorah
Budgewoi
Noraville
Norah Head
Tuggerah Lake

Kemps Pinnacle
Mt Banda Banda
Willi Willi Nat Pk
Kumbatine Nat Pk
Upper Rollands Plains
Forbes River
Kindee
Pappinbarra
Bellangry
Beechwood
Ellenborough
Bagnoo
Byabarra
Herons Creek
Comboyne
Lorne
Central Lansdowne
Lansdowne
Coopernook
Moorland
Taree
Killawarra
Johnock
Old Bar
Wallabi Point
Khappinghat Nat Res
Diamond Beach
Hallidays Point
Failford
Tuncurry
Forster
Forster Keys
Coomba
Wallis Lake
Wallingat Nat Res
Elizabeth Beach
Pacific Palms
Blueys Beach
Boolambayte
Bungwahl
Seal Rocks
Sugarloaf Bay
Smiths Lake
Myall Lakes National Park
Broughton Island

South Kempsey
Hat Head NP
Kundabung
Crescent Head
Maria River Nat Pk
Limeburners Creek Nat Res
Point Plomer
Saltwater Lake
Telegraph Point
Blackmans Point
Port Macquarie
Tacking Point
Lake Innes
Lake Innes Nat Res
Bonny Hills
North Haven
Laurieton
Watson Taylor Lake
Johns River
Coralville
Crowdy Bay National Park
Crowdy Head
Harrington
Manning Point
Farquhar Inlet

SOUTH PACIFIC OCEAN

-32°
-33°
-34°

152° 153°

North-East New South Wales

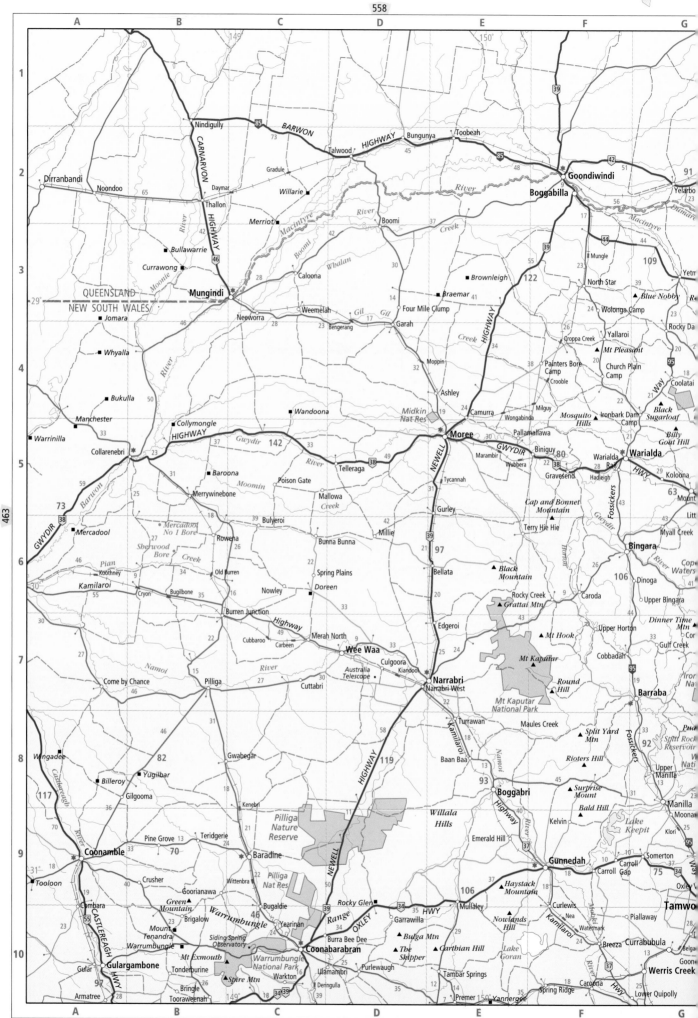

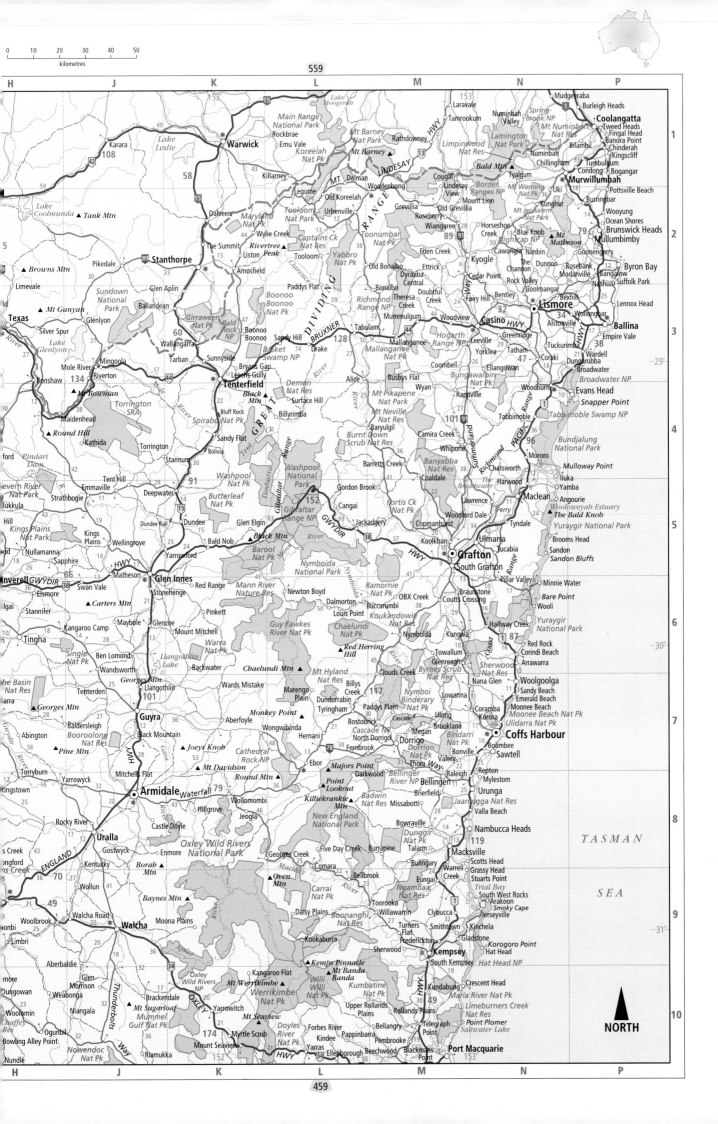

North-West New South Wales

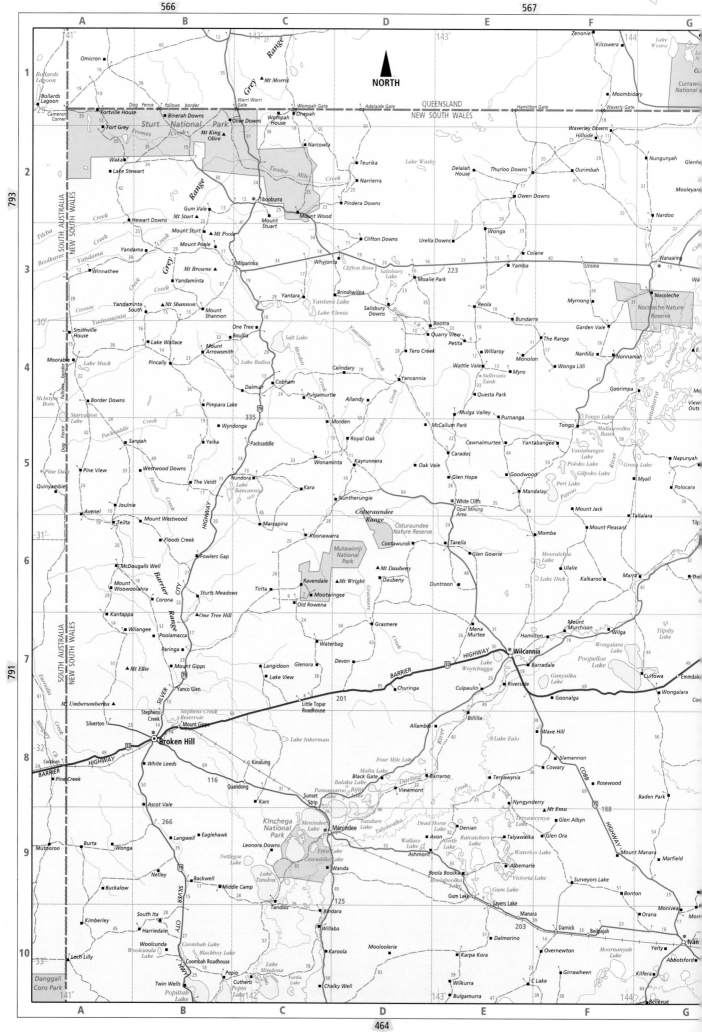

New
South
Wales

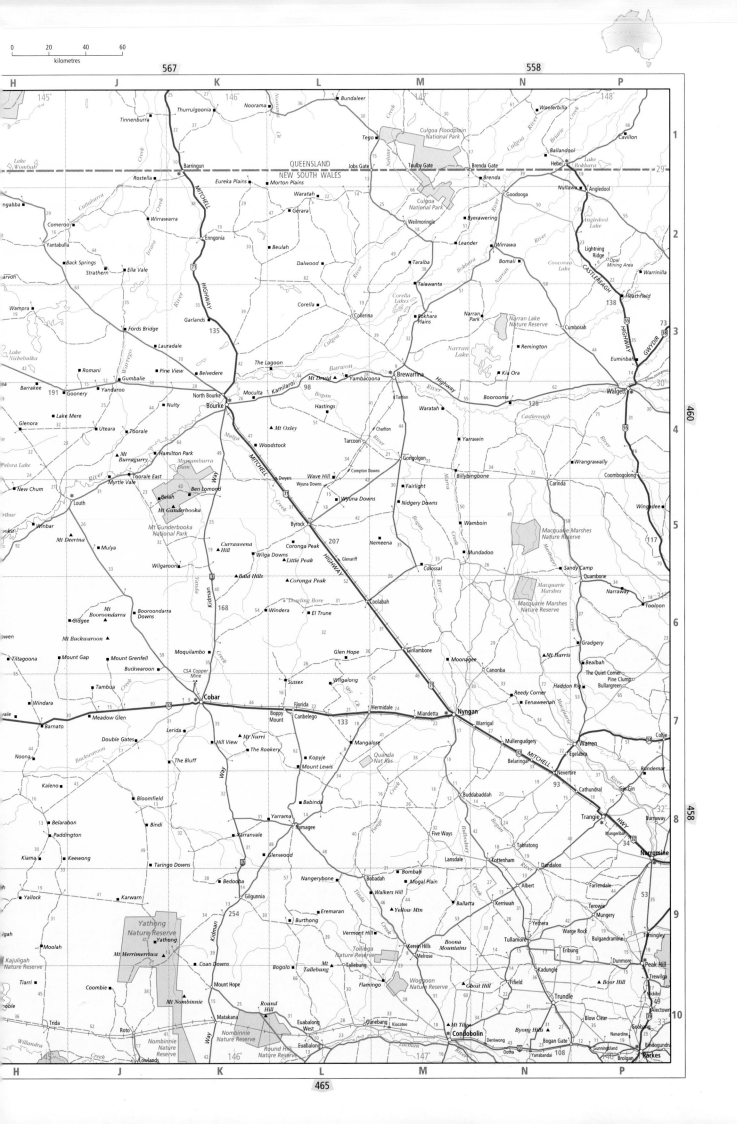

NEW
SOUTH
WALES

0 20 40 60
kilometres

H   J   K   L   M   N   P

QUEENSLAND
NEW SOUTH WALES

Thurrulgoonia
Tinnenburra
Noorama
Bundaleer
Woolerbilla
Cavillon

Culgoa floodplain
National Park
Ballandool
Lake
Bokhara

Tego
Hebel
Angledool

Barringun
Jobs Gate
Toulby Gate
Brenda Gate
Nullawa
Angledool
Lake

Rostella
Eureka Plains
Morton Plains
Brenda
Goodooga

Comeroo
Wirrawarra
Waratah
Gerara
Weilmoringle
Byerawering
Leander
Wirrawa
Lightning
Ridge
Opal
Mining Area

Yantabulla
Enngonia
Beulah
Dalwood
Taralba
Bomali
Coocoran
Lake
Warrinilla

Back Springs
Strathern
Ella Vale
Corella
Talawanta
Narran
Park
Heathfield

Wampra
Gumbalie
Pine View
Belvedere
The Lagoon
Collerina
Corella
Lakes
Pokhara
Plains
Narran Lake
Nature Reserve
Cumborah
Euminbah

Fords Bridge
Lauradale
Barwon
Mt Druid
Yambacoona
Brewarrina
Kia Ora
Remington

Romani
Yandaroo
Moculta
North Bourke
Kamilaroi
Bogan
Tarrion
Waratah
Borooma
Walgett

Goonery
Bourke
Hastings
Charlton
Yarrawin
GWYDIR

Glenora
Lake Mere
Nulty
Woodstock
Tarcoon
Gongolgon
Billybingbone
Carinda
Coombogolong

New Chum
Uteara
Toorale
Mt Oxley
Wave Hill
Compton Downs
Fairlight
Wamboin
Wingadee

Louth
Mt
Burragurry
Hamilton Park
Myrramburra
Dam
Dwyers
Wyuna Downs
Wyuna Downs
Nidgery Downs
Mundadoo
Macquarie Marshes
Nature Reserve
Narraway

Winbar
Toorale East
Myrtle Vale
Belah
Ben Lomond
Byrock
Coronga Peak
Nemeena
Colossal
Sandy Camp
Quambone
Tooloon

Mt Deerina
Mulya
Mt Gunderbooka
Curraweena
Hill
Wilga Downs
Little Peak
Glenariff
Macquarie
Marshes
Macquarie Marshes
Nature Reserve

Mt Gunderbooka
National Park
Wilgaroon
Bald Hills
Coronga Peak
Dowling Bore
Loolabah
Gradgery
Bealbah

Mt
Booroondarra
Gidgee
Booroondarra
Downs
Windera
El Trune
Glen Hope
Girilambone
Moonagee
Mt Harris
The Quiet Corner
Pine Clump
Bullargreen

Mt Buckwaroon
Mount Gap
Mount Grenfell
Moquilambo
Wilgalong
Canonba
Reedy Corner
Haddon Rig

Tiltagoona
Buckwaroon
CSA Copper
Mine
Sussex
Florida
Hermidale
Miandetta
Nyngan
Eenaweenah

Windara
Tambua
Cobar
Boppy
Mount
Canbelego
Warrigal
Warren
Collie

Barnato
Meadow Glen
Lerida
Hill View
Mt Nurri
Mangalore
Mullengudgery
Egelabra
Bandemar

Noona
Double Gates
The Bluff
The Rookery
Kopyje
Mount Lewis
Quanda
Nat Res
Belaringar
Nevertire
Gin Gin
Cathundral

Kaleno
Bloomfield
Babinda
Five Ways
Buddabaddah
Trangie
Burraway

Belarabon
Bindi
Yarrama
Nymagee
Tabratong
Mungeribar
Narromine

Paddington
Tarranvale
Lansdale
Tottenham
Dandaloo

Kiama
Keewong
Taringo Downs
Glenwood
Bombah
Albert
Farrendale
Terowie
Mungery

Yallock
Karwarn
Bedooba
Nangerybone
Bobadah
Mogal Plain
Kerriwah
Warge Rock
Bulgandramine

Gilgunnia
Walkers Hill
Ballatta
Yethera
Bulgandra

Yathong
Nature Reserve
Yathong
Eremaran
Burthong
Yellow Mtn
Tullamore
Eribung
Dunmore
Tomingley

Mt Merrimerriwa
Coan Downs
Vermont Hill
Kereen Hills
Melrose
Boona
Mountains
Kadungle
Peak Hill
Trewilga

Tiarri
Coombie
Tollinga
Nature Reserve
Mt
Tallebung
Tallebung
Woggoon
Nature Reserve
Ghost Hill
Fifield
Trundle
Boor Hill

Moolah
Mount Hope
Bogolo
Flamingo
Kiacatoo
Blow Clear
Gobhang

Tarri
Trida
Roto
Matakana
Round
Hill
Euabalong
West
Gunebang
Mt Tilga
Byong Hills
Bogan Gate
Brolgan
Parkes

Nombinnie
Nature Reserve
Round Hill
Nature Reserve
Euabalong
Condobolin
Derriwong
Oxley
Nanardine
Gunningbland

South-West New South Wales

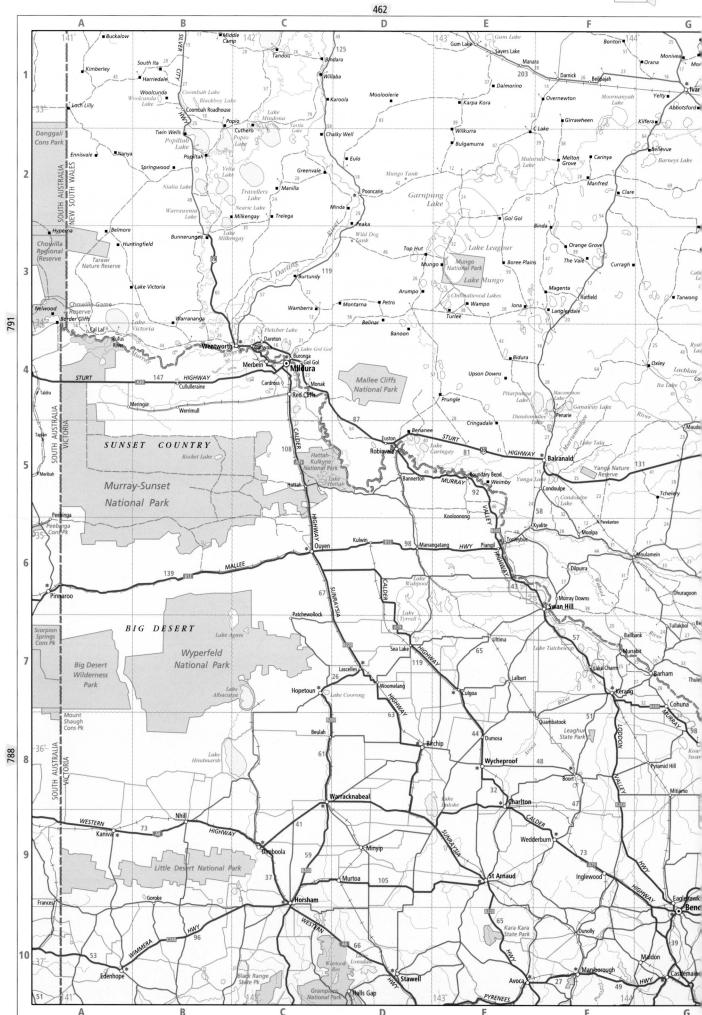

New
South
Wales

SOUTH AUSTRALIA
NEW SOUTH WALES

791

788

SOUTH AUSTRALIA
VICTORIA

A B C D E F G

340 341

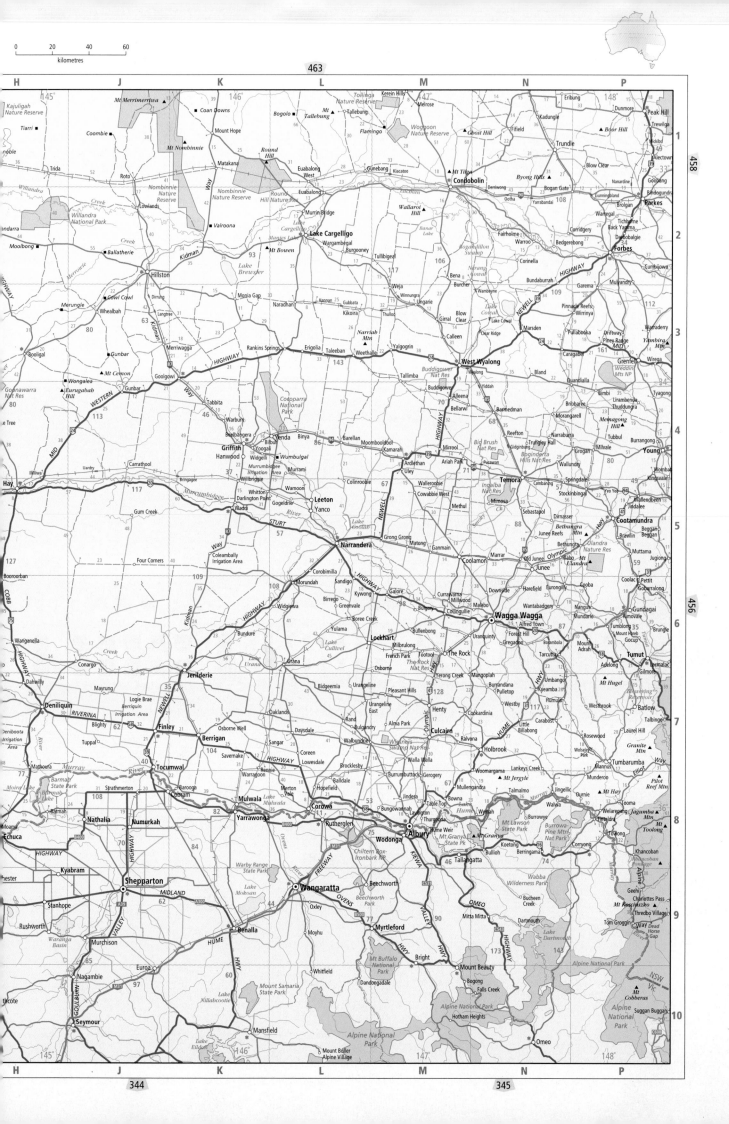

NEW
SOUTH
WALES

0 20 40 60
kilometres

AUSTRALIAN
CAPITAL
TERRITORY

AUSTRALIAN CAPITAL TERRITORY

The Bungendore Rodeo in full swing. This small town, established in 1837, is about 30 minutes' drive from Canberra. It is a popular spot for visitors, with arts and crafts and antiques shops, restored historic buildings that are still in use, and wineries.

Section 125 of the Commonwealth Constitution Act of 1900 provided that the seat of Australian government should lie in Commonwealth Territory. Nine years of prolonged political debate preceded the choice of Canberra as the nation's capital, with 2,330 sq. km (899 sq. miles) ceded by New South Wales to make the surrounding Australian Capital Territory.

The ACT is approximately halfway between Sydney and Melbourne. The primary road routes in are the Monaro Highway (which heads almost straight north from Cooma), the Barton Highway (which comes in from the north-west just out of Yass), and the Federal Highway (which travels alongside most of the western shore of Lake George and originates just south-west of Goulburn). The enigma of Lake George is that its waters regularly recede, for no apparent reason, then fill again, often without the benefit of heavy rains.

A great way to view the ACT is by hot air balloon—watch the sun come up over the Brindabella Ranges in the fresh air and with minimal traffic, then look down and see the design of the city of Canberra. There is a Balloon Fiesta each year, which is part of the National Multicultural Festival. Those wanting something a little more daring can try tandem skydiving or whitewater rafting; courses are

available on the Murrumbidgee, Cotter and Goodradigbee Rivers, at all levels of experience.

Over 40 per cent of the ACT is taken up by Namadgi National Park, the most northerly alpine environment in Australia. Though devoted mainly to wilderness areas, the park allows horse riding in designated areas and its streams attract trout anglers. There are also picnic and camping areas along the main access roads and the visitors' centre on Naas Road provides not only information on the park but has audiovisuals and hands-on displays. The Australian National Botanic Gardens promise sightings of kangaroos, amazing native plants, a rainforest gully and many peaceful picnic spots.

Another park worth visiting in the adjoining area is Brindabella, which has some terrific 4WD tracks which eventually lead the visitor out of the park and through to Yarrangobilly Caves. Drivers should be aware, however, that local farmers have been known to block access to the more rugged areas. Magnificent mountain scenery and old cattlemen's huts, however, more than make up for any inconvenience.

Europeans first explored the region in 1821, when explorer/surgeon Charles Throsby Smith came as far as Black Mountain, where Telstra's 195 m (640 feet) tower now stands. Famous botanist Allan Cunningham followed, and the area was named Limestone Plains and regarded as suitable for pastoral pursuits. In 1824, the first European settler, Joshua Moore, arrived to set up his property 'Canberry', and the following year, wealthy Sydney merchant Robert Campbell blazed out another property, which he called 'Duntroon'. It is now, of course, Australia's most famous military college, and has been since 1910.

What is less well known is that the Australian Capital Territory has an adjunct at Jervis Bay. The

Duntroon House, now part of the Royal Military College, but originally the homestead of Robert Campbell and his family, early settlers in the region. The property was a sheep station before its life as a military college.

same Act which proclaimed the need for an independent capital also demanded that the Federal Government have access to the sea, so an area of 5 sq. km (1.9 sq. miles)—later increased to 72.5 sq. km (28 sq. miles)—was also ceded by the NSW government to the federal government. Throughout most of its history, Jervis Bay has been the preserve of the Royal Australian Navy, and in the late 1990s there was bitter debate about its future.

History buffs should make time to visit Lanyon, some 30 km (19 miles) south of Canberra. Lanyon preserves life as it was in a nineteenth century homestead, and is classified by the National Trust. There are many original Sidney Nolan paintings in the house, including some of the well-known 'Ned Kelly' series, plus an Aboriginal canoe tree, rambling gardens and fascinating outbuildings. Further south, on the banks of the Murrumbidgee River, is Cuppacumbalong homestead, which has a private cemetery, a craft centre, a restaurant and pleasant areas for picnicking and swimming.

Other places worth visiting include Cockington Green, a miniature English village 9 km (6 miles) north of Canberra on the Barton Highway; the Gininderra Falls, which features craft and art galleries, shops and a restaurant, and is popular with abseilers; the National Dinosaur Museum (directly opposite); and Bywong Mining Town, a re-creation of late 1880s mining settlements, which is off the Gundaroo Road. Though somewhat overshadowed by other

radio telescopes such as the one at Parkes, Mount Stromlo Observatory was one of the first in Australia.

At Tidbinbilla, about 40 km (25 miles) south of Canberra, is the Canberra Deep Space Communications Complex, which has models of spacecraft and some exciting audiovisual displays, and helps command, track and record results from various NASA space projects.

Visitors coming this far should also take in the Tidbinbilla Nature Reserve, where kangaroos and koalas can be easily viewed and there are good picnic and BBQ facilities. Corin Forest Recreation Area, with its 1 km (0.6 mile) alpine slide and interesting bushwalks, and Cotter Dam Reserve, with river swimming, a children's playground and picnic and camping areas, are two popular spots for local people, as well as visitors.

One out-of-the-way monument that is rarely alluded to in any tourist information can be found on a dirt track that spurs off the Canberra–Queanbeyan road. It commemorates a disastrous 1940 plane crash in which top-ranking Air Force officers, Cabinet ministers and civil servants lost their lives. Coming in the darkest days of World War II, the crash could not have occurred at a worse time.

The ACT is one of the country's major tourist areas—it has varied countryside, historic dwellings, museums and wildlife parks to explore, as well as being home to some of the nation's most historically important buildings, and the seat of government.

The Brindabella Ranges, seen from the Mount Ainslie Lookout in Canberra. The region was evocatively written about by Miles Franklin, author of My Brilliant Career, *who was raised here.*

Capital
Canberra
Area
2360 sq. km
(1465.5 sq. miles)
Proportion of Australia
0.03%
Population of Territory
308 057
Populaton density
130.7 per sq. km
(338.5 per sq. mile)
Population of capital
307 732
Time Zone
10 hours ahead of GMT
Climate
Warm-temperate with no dry season
Highest Point
Bimberi Peak,
1913 m (6277 ft)

CANBERRA

Captain Clint Verhagen and Warrant Officer (2nd class) Andrew Russell. The Royal Military College is the officer training school for the Australian Defence Force. The College aims to teach its students 'how to think, not what to think'.

Canberra's CBD, as seen from the Mount Ainslie Lookout. Canberra is small, far from the coast and the country's major population centres, and planned—these factors have allowed it to remain in tune with its environment.

Supposedly an indigenous word for 'meeting place', Canberra is the seat of Australia's federal government. In contrast to most Australian cities and towns, the national capital is a fully planned city. It enjoys four very distinct seasons, with flowering blossoms in spring followed by hot, dry summers; the rich tapestry of autumn colours then appears, itself to be replaced by crisp, cool winters. Winters often see light snowfalls, and heavy fogs regularly close the airport. Today's Canberra is modern and stylish, and offers many attractions—restaurants, wineries, shopping, entertainment, art galleries, museums, parklands, national monuments and family attractions are all within easy reach of the 'bush capital'. It boasts modern infrastructure and services, technology parks, a sophisticated tertiary education sector and thriving business and industry, all in a city that works in harmony with its natural surroundings.

Canberra's genesis lies in bitter and hostile dispute. Prior to Federation in 1901, intercolonial controversy raged over the site of the new nation's capital. Ultimately, the Yass–Canberra site was agreed on. While Melbourne became the temporary capital (a situation which persisted until 1927), an international competition was announced for the design of Canberra, and once again, controversy raged. Objections to the terms and conditions set by the

Royal Institute of British Architects meant that Empire architects boycotted the competition, and first prize went to American Walter Burley Griffin. His plan used free-flowing lines, in sharp contrast to the other entries, and envisaged a city surrounded by national parks, bushland and mountain ranges. However, nothing ran smoothly. Committees changed Burley Griffin's design, incorporating elements of the other entries, and it was not until 1915 that this unharmonious scheme was rejected. Burley Griffin continued to fight over design changes with the government, and his employment was terminated in 1920, long before construction was completed. Canberra grew slowly. Though construction had begun in 1911, World War I interrupted proceedings. The politicians moved to Canberra in 1927, but the huge, lumbering public service remained behind in Melbourne until well after World War II. Development was much quicker after 1955, with Canberra rapidly becoming Australia's largest inland city. The Molonglo River was not dammed until 1964, creating Lake Burley Griffin, the centrepiece of the city.

The best way to gain an appreciation of the design of Canberra is to visit any of the lookouts on the surrounding hills. Telstra Tower, on Black Mountain, is 195 m (640 feet) high and has viewing galleries and a revolving restaurant. The recently opened CSIRO

The new Parliament House was designed by a team led by Aldo Giurgola, of Mitchell/Giurgola and Thorp. It has several outstanding features: an 81 metre (266 feet) flagmast; the Foyer, with its 48 marble-clad columns, rather like a eucalypt forest; Australian timber, used throughout the building; and over 3000 works of Australian art.

Discovery Centre, at the base of Black Mountain, showcases Australia's scientific achievements and discoveries. The centre is of particular benefit to schoolchildren, as it has interactive displays and allows direct contact with researchers and laboratories. On the summit of Mount Pleasant are memorials to the Australian Artillery and Armoured Corps. Red Hill overlooks Parliament House, southern Canberra and the Woden Valley, and from Mount Ainslie visitors can see central Canberra and Lake Burley Griffin, which has a shoreline of over 35 km (22 miles), complete with cycling and walking tracks.

On the southern foreshore of the lake is the National Gallery of Australia, which houses a collection of over 95,000 works—an excellent collection of Aboriginal and Torres Strait Islander art (some of which has successfully toured international galleries), and works by modern and postmodern artists, including a number of Australians, such as Arthur Boyd, Tom Roberts, Arthur Streeton, Sidney Nolan and Brett Whiteley. It also hosts a long-running series of outstanding feature exhibitions. In the grounds, sculptures by such luminaries as Auguste Rodin, Henry Moore and the Tiwi people of Melville and Bathurst Islands blend with the natural environment; the gallery's restaurant is situated in an artificial fog sculpture by Japanese artist Fujiko Nakaya. The National Gallery is connected to the High Court by a footbridge. With its lofty public gallery—seven storeys high—and murals by Jan Senbergs, Australia's final court of appeal should definitely be put on the visiting list. Also on the foreshore is the National Library of Australia, opened in 1968. An eclectic building designed in neo-Classical style, the library contains more than 5 million books, as well as photographs, documents, newspapers and periodicals. It is the country's largest reference library, and runs behind-the-scenes tours that show how the collection is stored and displayed; it also has exhibitions drawn from rare and significant collections. Its exterior features 44 square columns of Carrara marble, and inside are Aubusson tapestries (made from Australian wool). It also contains stained glass windows by Australian artist Leonard French.

Between the National Library and High Court is Questacon, the National Science and Technology Centre, with interactive displays and DIY experiments for would-be scientists aged 8 to 80. Experience an earthquake, take a photograph of your own shadow, witness the formation of a tornado or a lightning bolt, or enjoy Sideshow, an interactive exhibit which explains the science behind the fun of the fairground. Further south is the Canberra Railway Museum, which boasts Australia's oldest working steam locomotive, the 1210, built in 1878. Australia's biggest steam engine, the 256 tonne (282 tons) Bayer-Garrett 6029, is also on display, alongside vintage carriages, rail motors and other railway memorabilia.

The nation's newest and perhaps most important museum is the National Museum of Australia, which features ground-breaking displays on indigenous Australians, settlers, pioneers and ordinary people. Or

Parliament House is a popular excursion for Australian schoolchildren—they can watch proceedings in the House of Representatives and the Senate, and they can learn a great deal of history from the art and gardens of Parliament House itself.

Sunset over the National Library. This image shows clearly why Canberra is known as the 'bush capital': no matter how sophisticated government or business or national institutions become, the reality of the rural world, is only ever a paddock or two away.

The Royal Australian Mint was opened in 1965—it was commissioned to produce Australia's decimal currency. The Mint has since struck coins for several other countries, and also makes medals, medallions, seals and tokens. Here a quality control officer checks a coin in the Proofing Hall—the Mint was the first in the world to gain international ISO 9002 accreditation.

take a step back in time and experience the country's film and sound heritage at ScreenSound Australia, an art deco building holding a huge collection of radio, film and television records dating back as far as the 1880s. Artefacts and supporting documents supplement the collection of over one million items. The nation's passion for sport is explained and explored at the Australian Institute of Sport, which is around 10 minutes from the city, in the suburb of Bruce. This is where Australia's elite athletes train and prepare for events such as the Olympic Games. There are tours with athletes through the world-class facilities, or visitors can test their abilities at Sportex, an interactive sports exhibition.

On the lake itself are three landmarks: the Captain Cook Memorial Jet, a 140 m (459 feet) water jet known irreverently to Canberrans as 'the Royal Flush'; the Carillon, a three-column belltower that was a gift from the British Government to mark Canberra's Jubilee; and the refurbished National Capital Exhibition on Regatta Point, where visitors can learn about the city's planning and building history since the 1820s. Lake Burley Griffin is set in parklands, including Commonwealth Park and Weston Park. You can hire bicycles to cycle round the lake, or you can take a sightseeing cruise. Paddle-boats, windsurfers and sailing boats can also be hired.

Burley Griffin designed Canberra as a centre of politics. The crown of his plan consists of a triangle formed by Kings, Constitution and Commonwealth Avenues, with the apex dominated by Capital Hill and Parliament House. The new Parliament House, finished in 1988, is built into the top of the hill, so that the building merges into its surroundings—with the result that a grass walkway exists on the roof!—and beautifully demonstrates the culture and creativity of the Australian people. It contains fine paintings and artefacts, and is well worth a visit.

The old Parliament House, where federal Parliament sat from 1927 until 1988, has not been wasted—it now houses the National Portrait Gallery. Here the faces of famous Australians are preserved in photographs, etchings, prints, paintings and sculptures. The Gallery also has a constant rotation of temporary exhibits. There are many other fine galleries in Canberra, too, including the Canberra Museum and Art Gallery, the Beaver Galleries, the Solander Gallery, the Aboriginal Dreamings Gallery, the Yarralumla Gallery and the Chapman Gallery.

One of the most popular attractions in Canberra is the Australian War Memorial, at the end of Anzac Parade. It houses a huge collection of relics, models and paintings commemorating the sacrifices of Australians in all theatres of war, plus the Bradbury Aircraft Hall and the new Anzac Hall. Children have a chance to relate to the experience of war by following the World War II trail, and there is an interactive centre with costumes and replicas as well. The War Memorial is a grand structure, and a visit is a moving experience. It also houses the Pool of Remembrance and the Tomb of the Unknown Soldier.

One of the early homesteads—Yarralumla—is now the official residence of the Governor-General; the Prime Minister's Lodge is on the corner of Adelaide Avenue and National Circuit. The Royal Australian Mint, which presses all Australian coin and also prints notes, is in Deakin—visitors can mint their own coin and view a collection of early Australian coins. Canberra is also home to Australia's best-known military school, Duntroon Royal Military College. The Officers' Mess at Duntroon is actually the old stone homestead of the Campbell family, early pioneers in the district. Robert Campbell is commemorated in a stained glass window in the Church of St John the Baptist, near Anzac Park. The graveyard there offers the visitor an insight into the area's early history, as does the adjacent schoolhouse, which has been converted into a museum. Other relics are kept in Blundell's Cottage, built in 1835 by the Campbell family on the northern shore of the lake.

For those who like their sightseeing made easy, there is the Canberra Explorer bus service, which runs every hour seven days a week on a 25 km (16 miles) route around the city. There are 19 stops, and passengers can get off and rejoin the tour at any time.

Canberra also has a thriving restaurant and café scene—very good and very diverse, with cuisines ranging from contemporary Australian to Asian, Mediterranean and the even more exotic Turkish and Russian all available. There are over 300 restaurants to choose from, and diners should also sample some local wine. Though the district's viticulture does not yet have the reputation of New South Wales' famous Hunter Valley or Mudgee, the climate in this area is similar to that of Bordeaux, and the local wine, based on cool-climate grapes, naturally, has a distinct style. There are 22 or so wineries in the area, including Clonakilla, Helm Wines, Lark Hill, Doonkuna and Brindabella. Some of these, including BRL Hardy's Kamberra complex at the city's racecourse, have cellar door and function centres. Madew Winery is building a million-dollar cellar door and restaurant at its Lake George facility.

There are many other family-oriented activities in or near Canberra. There is the Gold Creek Village, which includes a historic schoolhouse and residence built in 1883 or, if you seek more nature-based activities, you can feed some of the more than 500 species of native and exotic birds at the Bird Walk Atrium. There are also the giant skeletons, skulls and fossils of the National Dinosaur Museum, and real live pythons at the Australian Reptile Centre, plus the National Aquarium and Wildlife Park, where visitors can hand-feed native animals and view fish from the Great Barrier Reef.

Nearby Hall has a market fostering home produce and folk art, held on the first Sunday of every month; Bungendore, another nearby town, has been totally classified by the National Trust. Its village square has a historic re-creation of the tale of a local bushranger of the 1850s.

Canberra hosts a number of festivals and events, the most famous of which is probably Floriade, held in September, when the gardens and parks provide visitors with stunning views of flowers and plants. However, the event that brings the most 'heads' and tourist dollars to Canberra is vastly different—almost counterculture—to the city's normally staid, white collar existence. Every December, just after Christmas, Canberra throbs to the roar of V8 engines as the Street Machine Summernats are held. This is an event featuring what used to be called 'hot rods'—modified and heavily accessorised saloon cars, usually Holdens and Fords. There are wet T-shirt competitions, no T-shirt competitions, 'burn-outs' and what could be called concourses d'inelegances. It is rowdy Australian fun. Young fun. Summernats is an experience no one should miss. January sees the Canberra World Cup Showjumping; February the Royal Show, the Multicultural Festival and St Valentine's Jazz Festival; March is horseracing, the Canberra Festival and the PGA Seniors Golf; April the Anzac Day Parade and Service at the War Memorial, and the ACT and Australian Science Festivals. Other notable events are the Festival of Contemporary Arts in October and the Canberra Rally in November.

This statue of two acrobats is located, appropriately, outside the indoor arena at the Australian Institute of Sport. The AIS trains athletes from all over Australia in a live-in environment, using cutting-edge training equipment, nutritional and psychological advice, and career assistance— athlete places at the AIS are hotly contested.

The National Gallery of Australia is not just a place to look at paintings—it runs a tour service, and is committed to art history research. It also has an expanding loan, transfer and exchange program with other galleries, so that more of its acquisitions can be seen by more people.

REGIONAL FEATURE

Lakes and Streams of the Capital

Even a juvenile Murray cod (Maccullochella peeli) makes an impressive catch. Trolling with a deep-diving plug, bladed spinner, metal spoon or spinnerbait works well on this species.

Although the Australian Capital Territory is noted for its picturesque location in the foothills of the Great Dividing Range, it comes as a surprise to many visitors to learn that this seat of government is also a varied and productive angling destination. Within the territory's boundaries lie several large, well-stocked lakes, as well as numerous streams holding sizeable populations of brown and rainbow trout.

The major fishing lakes are located within metropolitan Canberra, allowing visitors to base themselves in the city and still get an early start each day. Trout anglers may have to travel a little further afield, but the rewards will more than justify the effort required.

Urban Lakes

The main fishing lakes are Lake Burley Griffin in the city centre, Lake Ginninderra in the northern suburb of Belconnen, and Lake Tuggeranong in the southern suburb of Tuggeranong. Over the years, these three bodies of water have earned a sound reputation as productive fisheries for both native and introduced species. Regulations prevent the use of petrol-powered vessels on their waters, but canoes and electrically powered watercraft are allowed.

The largest and oldest of the Canberra lakes, Burley Griffin was filled in 1964 as a result of the damming of the Molonglo River. Between 1981 and 1995, it was stocked with a variety of fish species including more than 100,000 Murray cod and 150,000 golden perch or yellowbelly. Brown and rainbow trout and silver perch were introduced more recently, but their numbers have gradually declined as those of the native freshwater fish have grown. Predominant among the latter is the golden perch, which grows to an aver-

age size of between 1.5 and 2.5 kg (3.3 and 5.5 pounds) and in some cases reaches 4 kg (8.8 pounds). It can be fished with lures or natural bait. Medium-to-large deep-diving lures in sharply contrasting colours work best, while the most effective baits include live yabbies and wood, bardi and witchetty grubs.

Lake Burley Griffin also has substantial populations of carp and redfin. Although not highly prized by anglers, these species offer a decent introduction to fishing and are targeted by experienced anglers using fly- or coarse-fishing tackle. To the surprise of many, Lake Burley Griffin also yields large Murray cod, with regular reports of specimens in the 10- to 25-kg (22- to 55-pound) range occurring every summer. Any deep-diving, strong-swimming lure or plug will attract this species, but anglers who are serious about Murray cod should think big, both in terms of lure and line.

Lake Ginninderra was created in 1976 by the damming of Ginninderra Creek, and between 1981 and 1995 was stocked with nearly 60,000 Murray cod and 150,000 golden perch. The latter species is now the most abundant of the more desirable fish and can be caught using lures or baits. Deep-diving lures in small-to-medium sizes are best and, again, contrasting colours work well. The best natural baits include scrub worms, grubs and yabbies.

Murray cod ranging from about 6 to 15 kg (13 to 33 pounds) seem to be caught more frequently in Ginninderra than in Burley Griffin. Many are taken using baits such as simple garden worms and large wood or bardi grubs. For the angler with an electrically powered boat, trolling lures along the edge of the weed beds works well for both Murray cod and golden perch.

Lake Tuggeranong is the most recently constructed of the capital's lakes. It got off to a bad start, with little return from stocking programs and early pollution problems resulting from the construction of a large shopping mall on its shores. However, it has started to yield some respectable, albeit limited, catches of both golden perch and Murray cod. It also hosts large carp and redfin populations.

Trout Streams

The principal trout-fishing rivers within the territory are the Gudgenby and the Cotter, both of which flow into the Murrumbidgee River. The Gudgenby River traverses the mountainous and spectacular southern part of the territory. Its higher sections, which are characterised by swirling rapids and deep plunge pools, contain significant populations of rainbow trout. In the lower reaches, where the river is slower and narrower, the weed beds and undercut banks conceal some respectable brown trout.

The accessibility of Canberra's lakes makes them highly attractive to anglers. Among the few drawbacks is poor water clarity, especially after heavy rain.

The Cotter River flows through subalpine terrain in the higher country and pine plantations at lower elevations. The entire river is virtually free of development and is very picturesque. However, only certain sections are open to fishing; for example, all three dams along the waterway—the Cotter, Bendora and Corin—are out of bounds for anglers.

The short section of the river extending from immediately below Cotter Dam to where it joins the Murrumbidgee is easily accessible and dotted with attractive public camp sites and picnic grounds. Until recently, it offered good trout fishing, but unfortunately carp have now infested the area and, as a result, trout numbers have declined. However, after heavy rain some trout come over the dam wall, providing fair but short-lived sport, especially in the large pool immediately beneath the dam wall.

Upstream from Cotter Dam, between the confluence of Pierces Creek and just below Bendora Dam, more than 20 km (12.5 miles) of the river can be fished, although seasonal closures apply. This stretch of water yields small- to medium-sized rainbow trout and, in the early season (October), some respectable rainbows which have not yet made their way back downstream to the Cotter Dam.

The most accessible part of this stretch is Vanitys Crossing, but even here there is little room for casting from the banks and most anglers prefer to wade along the river. Wider exploration of this part of the Cotter

requires a 4WD vehicle or a long hike. If you are considering either of these options, make sure you obtain a good-quality 1:25,000 topographic map, as the area is a maze of forestry and fire trails. Hikers should be aware that the terrain is quite steep and the vegetation dense; however, the rewards include spectacular scenery and lightly fished waters.

The quality of fishing here is largely determined by the level of flow, which is regulated at Bendora Dam. High or rising levels offer the best conditions. Trout require remarkably little cover in these shallow waters, so experienced fly and lure casters usually fish their way up the river looking for sheltered spots and investigating them thoroughly. Lure casters should stick with small, shallow-to medium-depth lures or the ever-popular bladed spinners. Fly fishers should opt for basic patterns such as Royal Wulff or Red Tag. Nymphing is also productive. You can keep your options open by using a larger Wulff pattern with a small nymph under a 20-cm (8-inch) dropper.

This part of the Cotter River also hosts small populations of Macquarie perch, river blackfish and trout cod. All are protected species and, if caught, must be returned unharmed to the river.

Other notable trout streams lie just outside the Australian Capital Territory, within easy reach of Canberra. These include the Gooradigbee to the west and the Queanbeyan to the east, with the former offering the region's best fishing for quality trout.

Even narrow upland tributaries like this one are likely to hold significant populations of brown and rainbow trout, although the fish will probably be of a modest size.

Reaching some of the territory's streams may require a 4WD or hiking through rugged bush. Using a canoe is an excellent way to access quieter stretches.

Canberra City Centre

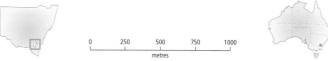

0   250   500   750   1000
metres

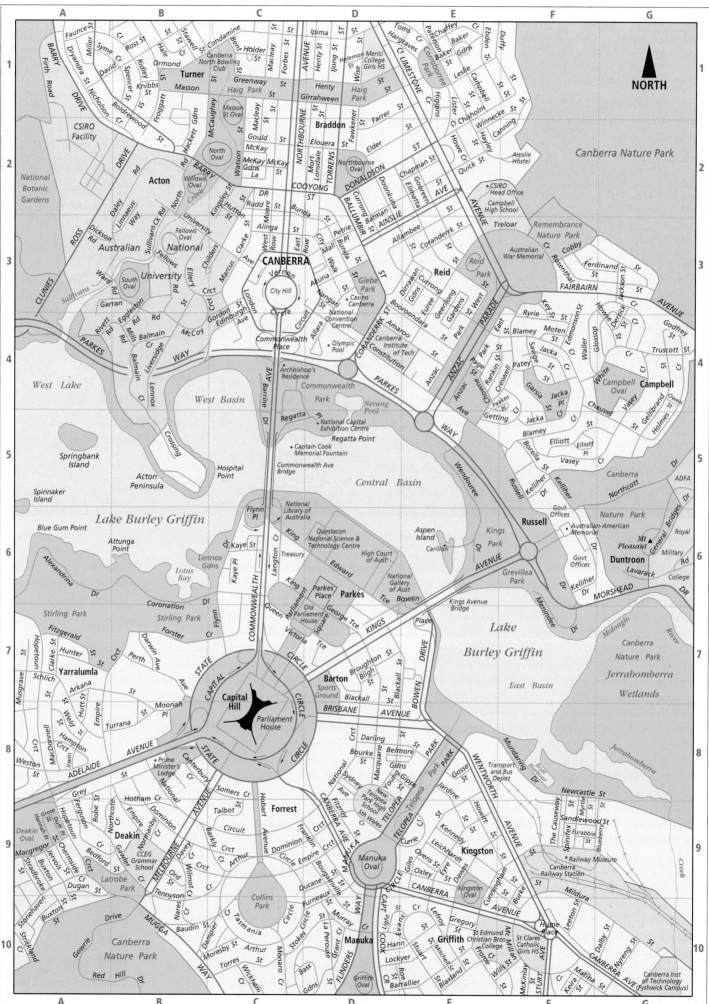

NORTH

AUSTRALIAN CAPITAL TERRITORY

Australian Capital Territory

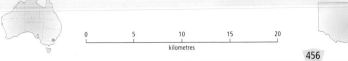

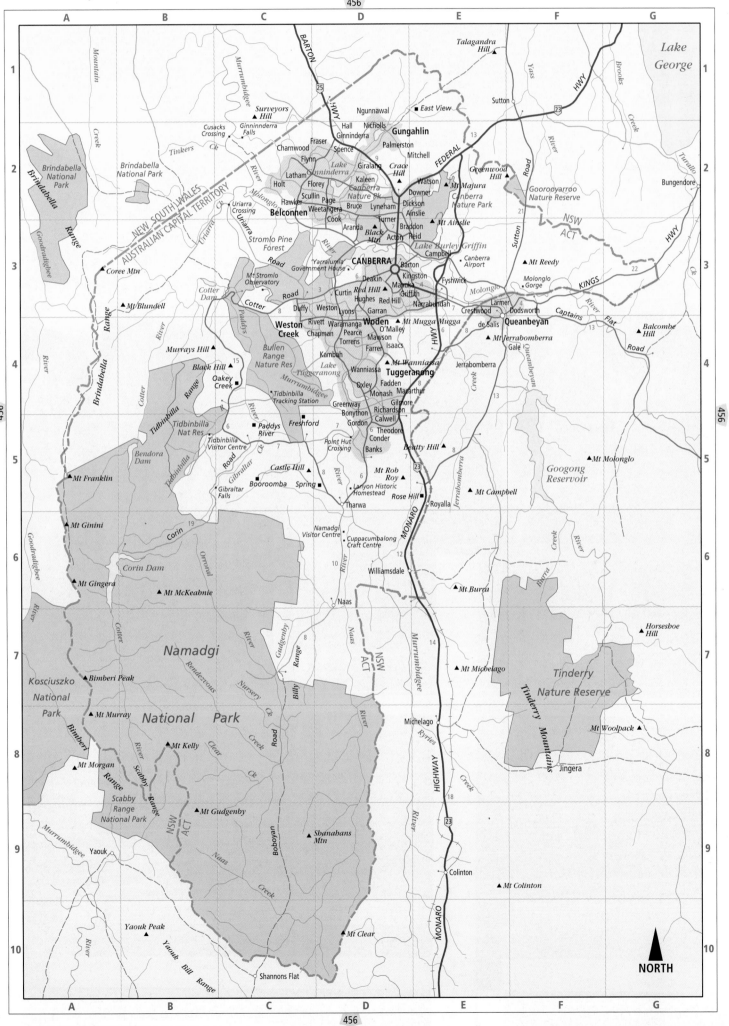

0 5 10 15 20
kilometres

Lake George

Talagandra Hill

BARTON HWY

Sutton

Ngunnawal · East View

Surveyors Hill

Cusacks Crossing

Ginninderra Falls

Hall · Nicholls
Ginninderra · **Gungahlin**
Fraser · Spence · Palmerston
Charnwood · Mitchell
Flynn

Giralang · Crace Hill

Greenwood Hill

Latham · Kaleen
Holt · Florey
Scullin · Page
Hawker · Bruce
Cook · Weetangera

Watson · Mt Majura
Downer
Canberra Nature Park
Dickson
Ainslie

Gooroyarroo Nature Reserve

Belconnen

Lake Ginninderra
Canberra Nature Pk

Lyneham
Aranda · Furner
Black Mtn · Braddon
Acton · Reid · Mt Ainslie

NSW ACT

Uriarra Crossing
Uriarra

Stromlo Pine Forest

Cotter Road

CANBERRA

Lake Burley Griffin

Barton
Campbell · Canberra Airport

Mt Reedy

Yarralumla Government House

Deakin · Kingston
6 · Manuka
Curtin · Red Hill · Griffith
3 · Hughes · Narrabundah
Duffy · Weston · Lyons · Garran

Fyshwick

Molonglo Gorge · Molonglo

KINGS

Mt Stromlo Observatory

Cotter Dam

Paddy's River

Cotter Road
8

Crestwood · Dodsworth
Larmer
de Salis

Captains Flat Road

Weston Creek
Rivett · Waramanga
Chapman · Pearce
Torrens

Woden · Mt Mugga Mugga
O'Malley
Mawson
Farrer · Isaacs

Mt Jerrabomberra
Gale

Queanbeyan

Balcombe Hill

Murrays Hill

Black Hill
15
Oakey Creek

Bullen Range Nature Res

Kambah
Wanniassa · Mt Wanniassa
Tuggeranong

Jerrabomberra

Lake Tuggeranong
Oxley · Fadden
Monash · Macarthur

13

Tidbinbilla Nat Res

Tidbinbilla Tracking Station

Greenway · Gilmore
Bonython · Richardson
Gordon · Calwell

Mt Molonglo

Paddys River
Freshford

Theodore
Conder

Googong Reservoir

Mt Franklin

Tidbinbilla Visitor Centre

6

7

Point Hut Crossing
Banks

Beatty Hill

Mt Campbell

Gibraltar Road

Castle Hill
Booroomba
Gibraltar Falls
Spring

8 · Mt Rob Roy

Lanyon Historic Homestead

Rose Hill · Royalla

Mt Ginini

Corin
19

Tharwa

Namadgi Visitor Centre

MONARO

Horseshoe Hill

Corin Dam

Mt Gingera

Mt McKeabnie

Cuppacumbalong Craft Centre

10

Williamsdale

Mt Burra

Tinderry Nature Reserve

Namadgi

Naas

12

Tinderry Mountains

Mt Woolpack

Kosciuszko National Park

Bimberi Peak

Mt Michelago

Michelago

National Park

Mt Murray

Ryries Creek

Jingera

Bimberi Range

Mt Kelly

Scabby Range

NSW ACT

Mt Morgan

Mt Gudgenby

Scabby Range National Park

Shanahans Mtn

Yaouk

HIGHWAY

18

Colinton

Mt Colinton

Yaouk Peak

Yaouk Bill Range

Mt Clear

Shannons Flat

MONARO

NORTH

AUSTRALIAN CAPITAL TERRITORY

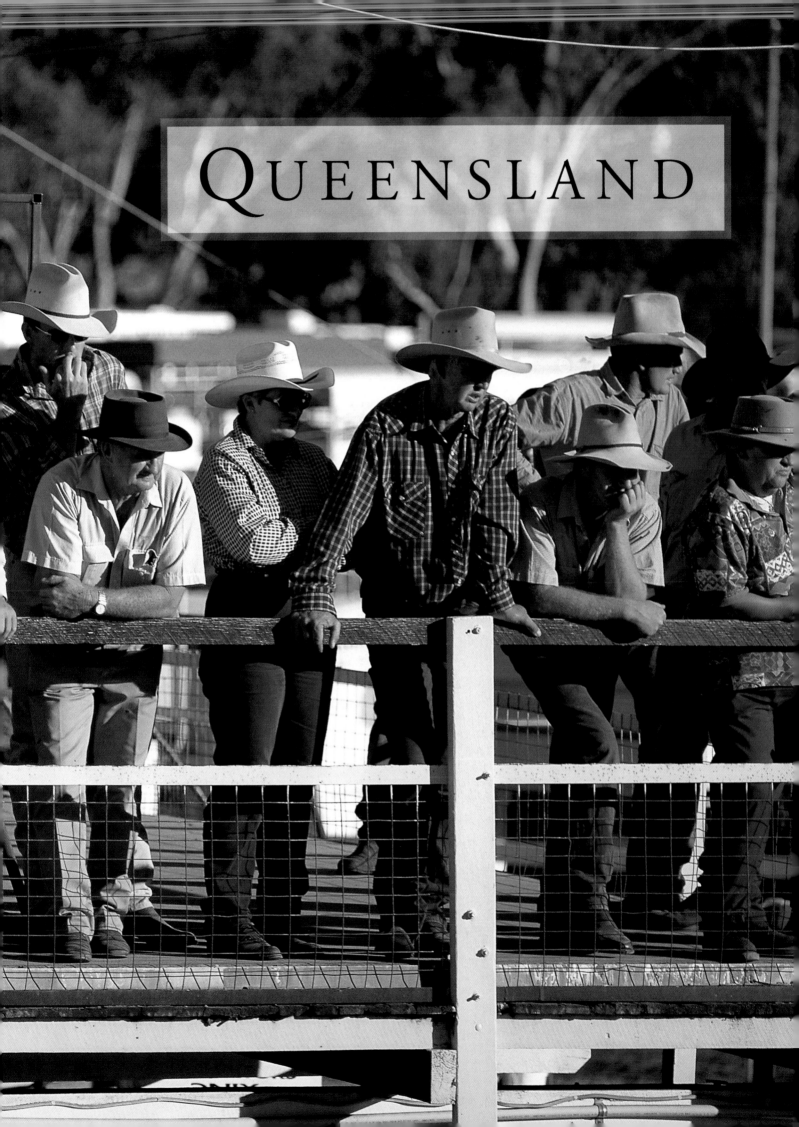

QUEENSLAND

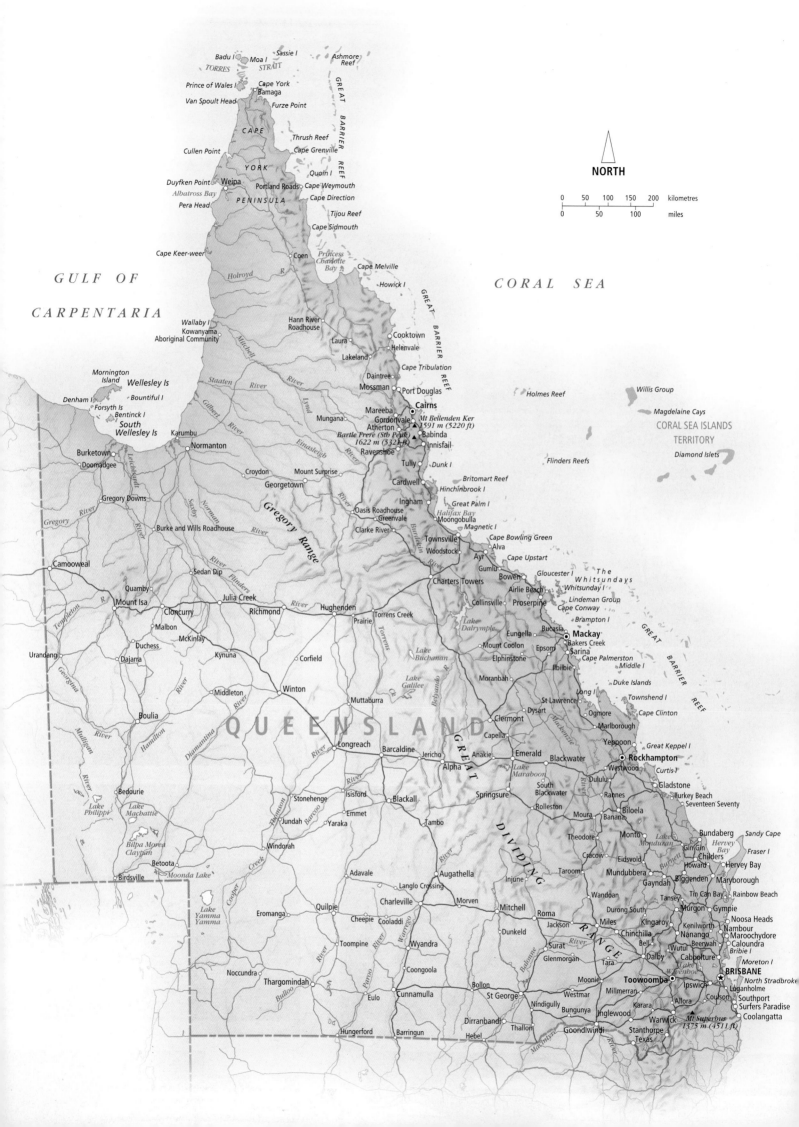

NORTH

0 50 100 150 200 kilometres
0 50 100 miles

GULF OF
CARPENTARIA

CORAL SEA

TORRES *STRAIT*
Badu I   Moa I   Sassie I   Ashmore Reef
Prince of Wales I
Bamaga
Cape York
Van Spoult Head
Furze Point

C A P E
Thrush Reef
Cullen Point
Cape Grenville
Y O R K
Quoin I
Cape Weymouth
Duyfken Point   Weipa
Portland Roads
Albatross Bay
Cape Direction
Pera Head
P E N I N S U L A
Tijou Reef
Cape Sidmouth

GREAT BARRIER REEF

Cape Keer-weer
Princess Charlotte Bay
Cape Melville
Coen
Howick I

Mornington Island
Wallaby I
Hann River Roadhouse
Cooktown
Kowanyama Aboriginal Community
Laura
Helenvale
Lakeland
Cape Tribulation
Denham I
Forsyth Is
Bountiful I
Daintree
Bentinck I
Mossman
Port Douglas
South Wellesley Is
Karumbu
Cairns
Mareeba   Mt Bellenden Ker 1591 m (5220 ft)
Burketown
Normanton
Mungana   Gordonvale
Atherton   Babinda
Doomadgee
Bartle Frere (Sth Peak) 1622 m (5321 ft)
Innisfail
Croydon
Ravenshoe
Gregory Downs
Mount Surprise
Tully   Dunk I
Georgetown

Holmes Reef
Willis Group

Magdelaine Cays
CORAL SEA ISLANDS TERRITORY
Diamond Islets
Flinders Reefs

Gregory River
Burke and Wills Roadhouse
Cardwell
Britomart Reef
Ingham   Hinchinbrook I
Oasis Roadhouse   Great Palm I
Greenvale   Halifax Bay
Moongobulla
Clarke River   Magnetic I
Camooweal
Townsville
Woodstock   Cape Bowling Green
Sedan Dip   Ayr   Alva
Quamby   Gumlu   Cape Upstart
Mount Isa   Julia Creek   Charters Towers
Bowen   Gloucester I   The Whitsundays
Cloncurry   Richmond   Hughenden   Collinsville   Airlie Beach   Whitsunday I
Malbon   Torrens Creek   Proserpine   Lindeman Group
McKinlay   Prairie   Cape Conway
Duchess   Brampton I
Dajarra
Urandangi
Bucasia
Eungella   Mackay
Mount Coolon   Bakers Creek
Epsom   Sarina
Elphinstone   Cape Palmerston
Ilbilbie   Middle I
Moranbah
Duke Islands

Boulia   Middleton   Winton   Muttaburra   Corfield
Long I
St Lawrence   Townshend I
Dysart   Ogmore   Cape Clinton
Clermont   Marlborough
Capella   Yeppoon   Great Keppel I
Longreach   Barcaldine   Jericho   Anakie   Emerald   Rockhampton
Alpha   Blackwater   Westwood   Curtis I
Lake Maraboon   Gladstone
Springsure   Dululu   Turkey Beach
South Blackwater   Raunes   Seventeen Seventy
Rolleston   Biloela
Moura   Banana
Bedourie   Stonehenge   Isisford   Blackall
Theodore   Monto   Bundaberg   Sandy Cape
Emmet   Tambo
Jundah   Yaraka   Cracow   Eidsvold   Gin Gin   Hervey Bay   Fraser I
Windorah
Taroom   Mundubbera   Childers
Betoota   Adavale   Augathella   Injune   Gayndah   Howard   Hervey Bay
Birdsville   Langlo Crossing   Morven   Wandoan   Tansey   Biggenden   Maryborough
Charleville   Mitchell   Roma   Durong South   Tin Can Bay   Rainbow Beach
Quilpie   Jackson   Kingaroy   Murgon   Gympie
Cheepie   Cooladdi   Dunkeld   Miles   Chinchilla   Nanango   Noosa Heads
Toompine   Wyandra   Surat   Bell   Kenilworth   Nambour
Coongoola   Glenmorgan   Tara   Wutul   Beerwah   Maroochydore
Noccundra   Moonie   Dalby   Cabolture   Caloundra
Thargomindah   Cunnamulla   Bollon   Millmerran   Toowoomba   Bribie I
Eulo   St George   Westmar   Ipswich   BRISBANE   Moreton I
Nindigully   Allora   Loganholme   North Stradbroke
Dirranbandi   Karara   Coulson   Southport
Hungerford   Barringun   Thallon   Goondiwindi   Inglewood   Warwick   Surfers Paradise
Hebel   Bungunya   Stanthorpe   Mt Superbus 1375 m (4511 ft)   Coolangatta
Texas

QUEENSLAND
GREAT DIVIDING RANGE

QUEENSLAND

Queensland is a big State—the second-largest in Australia. From Coolangatta, on the New South Wales border, to the tip of Cape York it is 3000 km (1863 miles). From the Northern Territory border in the west to Sandy Cape in the east, the distance is more than 1350 km (838 miles). Queensland's infrastructure is thus necessarily huge, with a network of over 176,635 km (109,690 miles) of roads.

There is also 9357 km (5811 miles) of rail, ten major airports, including two international ones—Brisbane and Cairns—and 15 major ports. Geographically, Queensland can be divided into four main regions, all running from north to south. First there is the rich, fertile coastal strip, with reliable rainfall and good weather—this is where 60 per cent of the population lives. In the far north this section is tropical, with high rainfall, and access is difficult, with lush rainforests coming right down to the sea in places. Further south, the rainfall is not as reliable, but there are sections of subtropical rainforest as far south as the New South Wales border and Lamington National Park.

Next there is the Great Dividing Range, a mountain system running right through the State from north to south. To the west of the range is the third main region, the rolling, timbered tablelands typified by the Atherton Tablelands and the Darling Downs. These consist generally of volcanic, black soil that is particularly fertile and highly productive. Finally, in the west are the grasslands that make up more than half the State. This is grazing country; it has a very unreliable rainfall and droughts are not unusual. It is also the country of waving plains of Mitchell

grass in Australia's vast natural grasslands. A major part of it is also mulga country, with forests of near impenetrable mulga trees. The mulga is a lifesaver, though, as it sustains stock through droughts.

Queensland has the fastest growing population in Australia: in 1938, the population was just one million, in 1974 it reached two million, and by March 1992 it was three million. It is anticipated that the population will increase to between 4.1 and 4.3 million by the year 2011. In common with most other developed regions, Queensland is experiencing a 'greying' of the population, with increasing median ages and a higher proportion of people in the 65 years and over age-group. This trend is expected to accelerate during this century.

Surf-lifesaver competes in a surfski event at Caloundra on the Sunshine Coast. These volunteers rescued over 10,000 swimmers in Australia in the 1999–2000 season.

The Gold Coast lives up to its name as the afternoon sun hits the high-rise strip on the State's most famous beach at Surfers Paradise.

Overlooking the town and waterways of Noosa Heads, where
the buildings cannot be built
higher than the trees. Great
Sandy National Park and World
Heritage-listed Fraser Island
are easily accessible from this
holiday town.

Queensland is also rich in history. It is in this State 'Banjo' Paterson wrote the words of Australia's unofficial national anthem, *Waltzing Matilda*. It is also the birthplace of the Australian Labor Party, which began as a result of the shearers' strike. QANTAS (Queensland and Northern Territory Aerial Services), one of the world's leading international airlines, was conceived, born and took to the air here. John Flynn, the visionary who started the Royal Flying Doctor Service, the world's first medical service of its kind, was a Queenslander.

The State had a fairly inauspicious beginning—Brisbane was selected as the site of a convict penal colony. For

a while, the settlement was for convicts only, but as free settlers started to arrive, the penal settlement was abandoned. The population increased dramatically as the rich farming land of the Darling Downs was opened up. In 1859, the colony of Queensland was declared. It relied almost entirely on farming, including sugar cane in the northern areas. Around 1867, the discovery of gold at Gympie revived the colony's falling fortunes. More goldfields opened around Charters Towers and Palmer River.

The sugar farmers, who were using forced labour ('Kanakas') brought in from the Pacific Islands to work their properties, considered seceding when this practice

A group of workers take a break
at the end of a day's labour at
Neilsen's quarry near the south-
eastern town of Beaudesert.

Capital
Brisbane
Area
1,730,650 sq. km
(668,256 sq. miles)
Proportion of Australia
22.5%
Population of State
3,456,300
Population Density
2.0 per sq. km
(5.2 per sq. mile)
Population of Capital
1,574,600
Time Zone
10 hours ahead of GMT
Climate
Warm-temperate in the
south and tropical in
north; wet along the
coast with semi-arid
and desert inland
Highest Point
Mount Bartle Frere
1622 m (5322 feet)

fell into disfavour, with the approach of Federation near the end of the nineteenth century. The move to secede was unsuccessful, and in 1904 indentured labour was banned.

Queensland is blessed with a great climate worthy of its popular name—the Sunshine State. Stretching along the coastline are myriad islands, with North and South Stradbroke, Moreton and Fraser Islands in the south, all easily reached from Brisbane. Further north are Great Keppel, Heron, the Whitsunday group, Magnetic Island (off Townsville), Dunk, Hinchinbrook, Lizard and Green Islands, to name just a few. Add to that the eighth wonder of the world, the Great Barrier Reef, which parallels the Queensland coast for almost its entire length, and it's clear why people in their millions make this State their holiday destination. International visitors may appear to have the higher profile, and their numbers are steadily increasing, but most of the visitors who come to Queensland are still from within Australia.

The Great Barrier Reef, the greatest single tourist attraction in Queensland, is a wonderland of coral atolls, reefs and islands; indeed it is the world's largest and the most famous coral formation and is so large that it is the only natural structure visible from space. The entire reef is now protected as part of a World Heritage Park. The reef has its problems, though, with natural phenomena such as cyclones, or predators such as the crown of thorns starfish, which at odd times multiply and causes severe damage to sections of reef. Visitors and scientists come from all over the world to study and admire this magnificent and beautiful marine paradise.

Inland Queensland also has much to offer. From Carnarvon Gorge National Park to the Gulf Country and the wilderness of Cape York, and all the historic cities and towns in between, there is an endless variety of sights and sounds to delight the visitor.

The economy of Queensland has always relied on agriculture and mining, but during the course of the twenty-first century tourism will become increasingly important. The ratios between the three industries may vary from time to time, but a sound economic future for the State is assured. The coastal strip, with the bulk of the population and its endless attractions, will continue to claim most of the attention, and the tourists, but the sparsely populated hinterland, for the foreseeable future, will provide the basis of the State's substantial and growing mining and agriculture economy.

LEFT: Bottle shop billboard advertising prices for XXXX and VB, two very popular brands of beer. Beer is Queensland's most popular alcoholic beverage, accounting for 55% of liquor sales.

Homestead in Tabinga, near Kingaroy, which was built in 1846 by the Haly brothers in the traditional Queenslander style.

BRISBANE

Brisbane has a much more relaxed attitude and a far more casual atmosphere than its southern cousins. Maybe the city has retained a 'little bit of country'. With all its dramatic growth, both skywards and outwards, the people of Brisbane get things done without having to resort to a hectic pace. Perhaps it is a by-product of the superb climate.

Brisbane River was named by John Oxley after Thomas Brisbane, the governor of New South Wales, in 1823. In about 1824, the city started life—as a penal colony. At one time it was the largest penal colony on the Australian mainland, with over 1000 convicts. At that time free settlers were not allowed to come within 80 km (50 miles) of the settlement. But slowly the free settlers moved in, and in 1839 the penal settlement closed. Queensland became a separate colony in 1859, with Brisbane as its capital.

Brisbane's character is moulded by the river around which it is built, and though the skyline has changed greatly since the 1960s, when the tallest

Fishing in Moreton Bay, just off the coast of Brisbane, is an easy weekend escape for city dwellers. Dolphins visit the the bay, which is ringed by huge sand islands.

Brisbane from a hot air balloon. This city has undergone a boom and many new buildings have sprung up since the city hosted World Expo in 1988.

building was the Town Hall, at 91 m (299 feet) above street level, the central business district has remained mainly within the loop of the river. Seven bridges cross the Brisbane River—the newest and longest is the Gateway; the best known and the prettiest is the Story Bridge, designed by Dr John Bradfield, the man who designed the Sydney Harbour Bridge.

The river is also a busy thoroughfare. Ferries carry passengers from bank to bank while motorised gondolas and large coal ferries go about their business. Paddle-steamers and cruise boats are a great way to see the river, day and night. Visitors have an unrestricted view of the city while they float past the Cultural Centre, the Maritime Museum, the University of Queensland, the Botanic Gardens and Newstead House. This low-set stately house in Newstead Park was built in 1846, and is the oldest surviving homestead in the city. Much of the administration of the growing colony of Queensland was carried out from this house. Walter Hill, the Colonial Botanist, laid the foundations for the gardens and was instrumental in introducing the distinctive and colourful jacaranda and poinciana trees to the city.

Brisbane is an outdoor city—its average minimum and maximum temperatures are 15° C (59° F) and 25° C (77° F). On weekends the city comes alive with people, at the botanic gardens, the riverside markets and at South Bank Parklands on the river overlooking the city. South Bank has restaurants and cafés, buskers and wandering performers, a beach and a swimming lagoon, the Wildlife Sanctuary, and barbecue and picnic areas. Next door is the Queensland Cultural Centre, which incorporates the Queensland Museum, Queensland Art Gallery and Queensland Performing Arts Complex. Brisbane also has restaurants offering cuisines from all around the world. The Queen Street Mall has outdoor cafés and eating places and a relaxed atmosphere. For late night entertainment, there are plenty of nightclubs and bars.

Brisbane is also fascinating for history lovers with sandstone dominant in many of Brisbane's more imposing buildings. The National Bank has tall Corinthian columns and pilasters of limestone with an ornate interior bathed in natural light from the leadlight dome, an extravagant example of the Victorian period. The Treasury Building is considered the finest example of Italian Renaissance architecture in the Southern Hemisphere. The building was reopened in 1995 as the Treasury Casino, with the exterior left untouched. The latest addition to Brisbane's list of impressive sandstone buildings is the University of Queensland, with its central core of sandstone buildings set around a cloistered court.

The Observatory in Wickham Terrace, just north of the city centre, was built by convict labour in 1828 as a windmill. It failed dismally at this, and was used instead as a convict-powered treadmill to grind grain.

When free settlers took over Brisbane, the convicts were sent to one of Moreton Bay's most beautiful islands, St Helena. This prison existed from 1867 to 1932 and was constructed by its residents. There are day trips by launch to tour the ruins.

Brisbane is also the heart of a dynamic and exciting tourist region. North of the city are the Glasshouse Mountains and the subtropical valleys of the Caboolture Shire, along with the beaches of Bribie Island and the Sunshine Coast. Fraser Island is about two hours' drive from Brisbane. The ever-popular Gold Coast, with its theme parks, surfing and swimming beaches, is barely an hour away, and can now can be reached by electric train to Nerang and Robina. Moreton Bay and the islands of the Bay are a stone's throw away, and there are wineries at nearby Mount Tamborine and Mount Cotton.

At the Australian Woolshed there are sheep-shearing demonstrations, cows to be milked and baby lambs to be bottle-fed. Visit Lone Pine Sanctuary to cuddle some of Australia's unique animals and birds. The Alma Park Zoo has an abundance of native animals plus some non-natives. The Brisbane Forest Park is a 26,500 ha (65,482 acres) area of natural bushland, with camping and picnic areas, yet it is only about 6 km (3.7 miles) from the city centre, making bushland easily accessible for city folk.

The choices in accommodation range from five-star luxury hotels to the more economical hotels, hostels and caravan parks. The CBD has excellent choices, many with views of the river and the city. The inner western suburbs towards the airport have a great range of hotels, motels and holiday apartments, which are generally at lower rates than those right in the city centre.

The major festival held each September in Brisbane is what used to be called the Warana Festival but is now called the Brisbane Festival. This is a significant arts festival with plays, shows and exhibitions mainly centred around the Performing Arts Complex and its three superb theatres at the Queensland Cultural Centre down on the river bank. The Springhill Festival is generally held around the middle of September and is a gathering of arts and crafts in a very relaxed market-style setting.

The War Memorial Shrine in Anzac Square, Ann Street, was built in 1930. A bronze statue commemorates the Boer War.

'Fiesta Tropicale', a mobile performing arts group, entertains at the riverside markets in Brisbane's South Bank Parklands.

ADVENTURE ACTIVITIES

Queensland

Queenslanders market their homeland as 'Beautiful one day, perfect the next', and this slogan could apply equally to the state's adventure activities. The almost unlimited scope for outdoor pursuits is mainly a result of Queensland's remarkable range of landforms and environments, many of which have been recognised by UNESCO World Heritage listing. The most notable of these are the Great Barrier Reef and the ancient rainforests that extend from Cape York all the way to the New South Wales border. Others include spectacular remnants of volcanic landscapes such as the Undara lava tubes and Glasshouse Mountains, the deserts and plains of the interior, the savanna and swamps of the Gulf Country, the famous fossil fields of Riversleigh and remote oases such as Lawn Hill National Park.

Adventurers heading to the Sunshine State should keep in mind the region's seasonal weather patterns when planning their itineraries. In particular, the Wet Season that affects the far north can upset many well-laid plans, turning relaxed river trips, for example, into life-threatening undertakings. Tropical cyclones are another threat, with associated sea surges swamping boats along the coast, winds toppling trees and heavy rain swelling rivers. Even Queensland's renowned high levels of sunshine are not without their dangers and all travellers should make sure they have adequate sun protection and sufficient water.

Located about one hour's drive south of Cairns, the Tully River incorporates more than 40 grade-four rapids, making it one of the state's top rafting rivers.

Bushwalking

Walking through rainforest is one of the finest experiences that Queensland has to offer and, fortunately, opportunities for such outings abound. Options range from long trails through the cooler subtropical rainforests of places such as Lamington National Park in the Gold Coast Hinterland to short strolls along boardwalks in tracts of true tropical rainforest in areas such as Daintree National Park in the state's far north and Eungella National Park, inland from Mackay.

Most bushwalking tracks in the north of the state are limited to a few kilometres (a couple of miles) in length, though in some parks such as Eungella National Park several short walks can be linked together to create a rewarding day trip. One of the few multiday trails is the Thorsborne Trail, a five-day hike along the east coast of Hinchinbrook Island, Australia's largest island national park. This is one of the best bushwalks in the country.

A popular inland destination for bushwalkers is Carnarvon Gorge National Park in Central Queensland. Here, the enjoyable and demanding Battleship Spur Walk, which requires two or three days, follows a sometimes rough track that takes in a fine cross-section of the park's varied environments.

Brisbanites are fortunate in that their city lies close to several national parks with excellent walking

trails. One group of such parks to the south occupies a crescent of bush-clad volcanic peaks and ridges on the New South Wales border known as the Scenic Rim. It includes the Lamington and Springbrook national parks, whose lush, shady rainforests offer a cool refuge in summer, and Mount Barney National Park, whose more sparsely vegetated ridges are popular among walkers during the cooler months.

Rock Climbing

Although there is no shortage of peaks and cliffs in Queensland, it's still something of a challenge for climbers to find rock faces that are not overgrown with lush foliage or too exposed to the fierce tropical sun. Queensland's best-known rock formations are the Glasshouse Mountains, a group of volcanic plugs that rises dramatically from the lowlands bordering the Sunshine Coast. Although many of the cliff faces here are loose and therefore dangerous, there are several safe but challenging climbs.

The most popular climbing area in Queensland, however, is Frog Buttress, a relatively small cliff near Boonah, south of Ipswich. For less strenuous outings, Brisbane-based climbers travel to the granite boulders and slabs of Girraween National Park near the New South Wales border. In the north of the state, Townsville climbers have established many exciting routes on nearby Mount Stuart.

Caving

Sometimes just getting to a cave in Queensland is an adventure in itself. Camooweal Caves, for example, within the national park of the same name, lie beyond Mount Isa at the end of a rough road only 13 km (8 miles) from the Northern Territory border. More accessible is Chillagoe–Mungana Caves National Park, 200 km (124 miles) inland from Cairns, where guided tours of the magnificent limestone system are available. Cave tours are also on offer at Capricorn Caverns, which is situated on private property in the hills north of Rockhampton. Nearby are Cammoo Caves and the caves of Mount Etna, where recently a conservation battle was fought to prevent mining and preserve ghost-bat habitat.

For an exhilarating adventure that combines caving and bushwalking, head to the Undara lava tubes—the largest lava tubes in the world, at 160 km (100 miles) in length—in Undara Volcanic National Park, 261 km (162 miles) south-west of Cairns.

Mountain Biking

The coastal ranges of Queensland make for great mountain biking. The sport is particularly popular in Brisbane, where favourite destinations include Daisy Hill and a purpose-made course at Kooralbin. Nerang State Forest is popular with Gold Coast riders and further north good touring can be enjoyed in Crediton State Forest, inland from Mackay.

Mountain biking in Cape York can be an enthralling experience, though cyclists need to be aware of the danger of a crocodile attack when fording rivers. Cairns, especially the area around Smithfield, is a centre for downhill cycling.

Canoeing, Kayaking and Rafting

Close to the state capital, the Brisbane River offers enjoyable kayaking in its upper reaches. To the north, a pleasant and relaxing paddling holiday can be enjoyed on the tannin-stained Upper Noosa River, which passes through part of Cooloola–Great Sandy National Park. Higher volumes of water in the rivers of the far north create excellent conditions for whitewater rafting. Among the waterways popular with commercial rafting operators are the Tully, North Johnstone and Russell rivers.

Sea Kayaking

In many ways, Queensland is ideal for sea kayaking. The water is never very cold and there is a diverse range of coastal environments to explore. However, in the northern half of the state kayakers run the risk of encountering deadly box jellyfish and cyclones during summer, and crocodiles throughout the year.

One of the best places to sea kayak is Hinchinbrook Island, halfway between Townsville and Cairns, where there are beautiful beaches and waterfalls, and you can enjoy spectacular views of the rugged island from the water. Cape York is ideal for extended sea-kayaking expeditions, with the most challenging options involving an island-hop through the Torres Strait Islands to Papua New Guinea. Less difficult but equally rewarding are kayaking tours of the Whitsunday Islands and, further south, Fraser and Morton islands.

National parks such as Sundown, situated 250 km (155 miles) south-west of Brisbane, are a mecca for lovers of wilderness. The park has no marked trails but bushwalkers can navigate by following the Severn River.

Donna Cave is one of three caves open to the public in Chillagoe-Mungana Caves National Park. The entire system covers an area roughly 6 km (3.7 miles) wide and 60 km (37 km) long, and includes about 650 chambers.

SOUTH-EAST QUEENSLAND

Fine sandy beaches fringe this lush coastal strip, and offshore is a string of easily accessible islands. The jagged blue spires of the Glasshouse Mountains, thus named in 1770 by James Cook because their glistening, rain-washed walls reminded him of the glass furnaces of his native Yorkshire, are the eroded remnants of slow lava flows, which millions of years ago solidified in the vents of ancient volcanoes.

More than half the State's population live in the expanding cities and towns of the Gold Coast, south of the capital, and the Sunshine Coast, to the north. Inland, prosperous country towns dot the black-soil plains of the Darling Downs, one of the continent's great food bowls, before arable lands give way in the west to arid and sparsely settled cattle country.

For 4WD enthusiasts, a long highway of empty beaches stretches from the sophisticated resort centre of Noosa Heads and on the rainforest-covered Fraser Island. Nearby Hervey Bay is host every winter to migrating whales, while its seagrass pastures sustain a precious population of endangered dugongs. Deep within the dramatic canyon of Carnarvon Gorge, north of Roma, are luxuriant fern glades, moss gardens and rare, slow-growing cycads; extensive galleries of Aboriginal rock art cover the walls of sandstone overhangs. Drought-resistant bottle trees rise above briga-low scrub and parched grass in the wide dry lands to the west. Centres in this region have varied claims to fame: Roma is the 'Gateway to the Outback';

Charleville is the birthplace of the airline, QANTAS; Kingaroy is the 'Peanut Capital'; the Darling Downs, where author Steele Rudd once farmed, provided inspiration for his characters Dad and Dave; Warwick is the 'Rose and Rodeo City' (for its horse studs and floral emblem); Toowoomba, with more than 100 ha (247 acres) of parks and gardens, is the 'Garden City'; Gympie styles itself as the 'City that Saved Queensland' because the 1867 gold discovery here rescued an economically ailing colony; and the old river port of Maryborough, with its elegant, historic buildings, is known as the 'Heritage City'.

OPPOSITE: The coral trout (Plectropoma maculatum) is a predatory reef fish of tropical waters. The trout will strike savagely at all types of cast, jigged and trolled lures, and dive powerfully toward the sea bed when hooked.

Rowers preparing for a race at Caloundra, on the Sunshine Coast, a holiday town with 13 km (8 miles) of surf beaches just 96 km (60 miles) from Brisbane.

REGIONAL FEATURE

Fraser Island

Studies have shown that the rate of advancement of sandblows such as the one that borders Lake Wabby is between 40 and 90 cm (16 and 35 inches) a year.

First-time visitors to Fraser Island often struggle to find the right words to describe the appeal of this magical mound of sand off the southern coast of Queensland. For some, the enchantment lies in its diversity: Fraser's habitats range from luxuriant sub-tropical rainforest to melaleuca swamps, eucalypt forests, heaths, mangroves, beaches and freshwater lakes. For others, it owes much to its fascinating and highly visible wildlife: the island is home to more than 230 species of birds, numerous reptiles and the purest strain of dingo in Australia; in addition, migrating whales and other marine life are regularly spotted off its shores. Yet other visitors delight in the bewildering choice of recreational activities, including fantastic fishing in both surf and calm marine waters, idyllic swimming in pristine rivers and lakes and superb bushwalking. The simple fact that Fraser has something for almost everyone goes some way to explaining why the island has become one of the country's most popular travel destinations.

Measuring 123 km (76 miles) from north to south, and 25 km (15.5 miles) across at its widest point, Fraser is the biggest sand island in the world. It is part of the Great Sandy Region, which formed over the course of at least one million years as rivers washed eroded rock fragments to the coast. Slowly, the grains of sand and gravel piled up, forming beaches, dunes and, in the case of Fraser, a large island. Seeds carried by birds and ocean currents then germinated in Fraser's sands, creating a layer of vegetation that helped stabilise the dunes and, in turn, allowed further life to flourish. These processes continue today.

History

The Aboriginal Butchulla people are thought to have inhabited Fraser Island, which they named *K'gari*, for more than 5000 years. Nourished by the island's abundant supplies of food, their population rose to a relatively high level. It has been estimated that when Europeans first arrived in the early nineteenth century nearly 2000 Butchulla were living on the island. Soon after this, however, the Aboriginal population was decimated by imported diseases, the effects of alcohol, and violent attacks perpetrated by settlers. Tragically, by the end of the nineteenth century, the population was down to 150 or so, and in 1905, the few survivors were transported to mainland Aboriginal reserves as far away as Cairns.

Captain James Cook was the first European to provide a written record of the island, in 1770, and he supplied names for Sandy Cape, Indian Head and Seventy-Five-Mile Beach.

Often found scavenging at camp sites, the lace monitor (Varanus varius) can grow to a length of 2 m (6.5 feet) and weigh up to 14 kg (31 pounds).

Nineteen years later, Matthew Flinders sailed by in his ship, the *Norfolk*. He then returned to skirt the shores of what became known as Great Sandy Island in 1802, aboard the *Investigator*.

The island's present name derives from a notorious incident that occurred in 1836. On 13 May, a ship called the *Stirling Castle* struck a coral reef off Rockhampton. The captain, James Fraser, and his pregnant wife Eliza, managed to escape in a longboat with 16 other passengers and crew. With dwindling fresh water and virtually no food available, they beached on Great Sandy Island. The entire party was quickly rounded up by members of the Butchulla tribe, who then held Mrs Fraser captive for nearly seven weeks. During that time Captain Fraser and several of the crew died; the rest of the crew managed to escape and walk south toward Moreton Bay. Mrs Fraser was eventually rescued by a government search party, and within ten years of her escape, the island was being referred to as Fraser Island.

In the early 1860s, loggers arrived on the island to harvest its trees, a practice that continued until 1992. During the first 70 years of operations, bullock drays hauled the timber out of the forests to loading points on the coast. Giant satinay (turpentine) trees were especially sought-after for their straight trunks and resistance to marine borers. In the late nineteenth century, many of the largest specimens were sent to Egypt for use in the construction of the Suez Canal.

During World War II, Fraser became a base for the famous Z Force commando units. Thousands of soldiers trained on the island, preparing themselves in the rainforests and on the mangrove-lined coast for similar conditions on Pacific Islands. After the war, mining companies arrived to exploit the high levels of rutile and zircon in the island's sand. Sandmining operations began in 1971 and continued until 1976 when the Commonwealth Government withdrew export licences in response to growing concerns about the environmental impact of mining.

Fraser Island–Great Sandy National Park

Fraser Island is now part of Great Sandy National Park, which also includes the Cooloola region on the mainland. In addition, the entire island, apart from a few freehold areas, is managed by the Queensland Parks and Wildlife Service (QPWS) as a Recreational Area. The international ecological significance of Fraser was recognised in 1992, when the island was declared a World Heritage area by UNESCO.

These reserves protect a landscape that is continually being refashioned by shifting sands. On the eastern side of the landmass in particular, tides slowly form and reform sandbars, gutters and bays, and wind creates huge sandblows. The east coast is also noted for its richly coloured sands. Their hues, ranging from yellow through orange and rusty red to brown, are the result of thousands of years of weathering of iron-rich minerals in the sands.

Inland, a range of sand-adapted vegetation blooms on the dunes, including grasses, eucalypt and banksia woodland, and subtropical rainforest. This blanket of green is studded with more than 40 perched lakes—rain-fed lakes that form in the dunes when the sand mixes with organic debris and peat to form an impermeable base. Fraser's perched lakes contain some of the purest drinking water found anywhere in the world, even though some of it is stained the colour of tea by tannin from plants. Rain and underground springs also fuel a number of pristine streams that flow to the coasts. The biggest is Eli Creek, which runs onto the eastern beach south of the *Maheno* wreck.

ACTIVITIES

A 4WD vehicle is essential if you want to explore the island fully. The eastern beach is the island's main thoroughfare, but should only be driven within two hours either side of low tide, when the sand is firm. The inland tracks are narrow, so keep your speed down and watch for oncoming traffic. During prolonged dry spells, some of these tracks may be very sandy and therefore difficult to negotiate. Always carry a spade to dig yourself out of soft sand and bogs, and deflate your tyres to around 175 kPa (25 psi); you may even have to drop them back to 140 kPa (20 psi) to deal with very soft sand.

For more than 70 years, visitors have been travelling to Fraser Island to enjoy its excellent and varied fishing. At the height of the season each year, between July and October, hundreds of anglers gather on the east coast beaches to fish huge schools of tailor then migrating up the coast. Other fish found off the eastern shore include silver bream, jewfish and golden trevally. In the calm waters on the western side of the island, whiting, flathead and bream can be caught throughout the year. Plenty of bait can be gathered on Fraser by digging for bloodworms, pumping up yabbies from sandflats at low tide, and gathering pipis. Fishing or collecting bait in lakes or streams is not permitted.

The golden colour of Fraser's sandblows results from a thin layer of iron oxide that coats the white sand grains.

The Maheno was wrecked off Fraser Island in 1935. Despite intense efforts on the part of its Japanese owners to refloat it, its rusting hulk remains embedded in an east-coast sandbank.

Bushwalkers can hike for miles along the magnificent beaches and also explore numerous delightful forest trails in the interior. The 6-km (3.7-mile) Lake Birrabeen to Central Station walk, which takes about two and a half hours, meanders through varied vegetation, including banksia heathland, eucalypt woodland and, near Central Station, subtropical rainforest. You can explore this last habitat more fully on a short walking track at Central Station (requiring 25 minutes each way), which follows crystal-clear Wanggoolba Creek through towering stands of brush box, hoop pine, white beech, ribbonwood and strangler figs. Often, you will be accompanied by conspicuous rainforest birds such as the eastern yellow robin and rufous fantail, and you may also come across less common bird species such as the noisy pitta, emerald dove, white-headed pigeon and wompoo pigeon.

Wherever you travel on the island, you will almost certainly see dingoes. Indeed, Fraser Island is probably the best place on the continent to see these wild animals at close quarters. In most other parts of the country, they have interbred with domestic dogs, but the dingoes on Fraser remain a relatively pure strain. If you do encounter a dingo, keep your distance and do not be tempted to offer it any tidbits. Feeding these animals interferes with their natural hunting instinct, leading them to depend on scraps and handouts. In turn, they lose their natural fear of humans and can become aggressive.

ACCESS AND ACCOMMODATION

Fraser is approximately 250 km (155 miles) north of Brisbane and can be accessed from the mainland by vehicular barge or ferry, passenger launch, aircraft or

camping is permitted in most areas unless signs indicate otherwise. Cabins can be rented at Happy Valley, Eurong, and Dilli Village; Fraser is also the site of one of Australia's leading luxury ecoresorts, Kingfisher Bay, situated on the north-east side of the island.

Wooden tracks have been laid at various points along the east coast to limit degradation of fragile sand dunes by vehicles.

The Fraser Island Trek

This trek travels the entire east coast of Fraser, while a detour permits exploration of the interior. The main route starts at Hook Point on the southern tip of the island. From here, a road leads inland to Dilli Village, a distance of around 23 km (14 miles). If you arrive around low tide, you can cut across to the eastern beach via tracks at the 7-km (4.4-mile) and 13-km (8-mile) points. When the tide is at its lowest, the beach is up to 100 m (110 yards) wide. Even if conditions are good, however, you should take your time and watch out for rock bars and creeks.

Dilli Village, located just off the main beach, has a camp site and holiday units (which must be booked in advance). From here you can detour inland—see the Southern Lakes Drive section below—or continue up the main beach to Eurong, a distance of 10 km (6 miles). This small settlement has accommodation, a general store and fuel station. Nearby is the Eurong QPWS Information Centre.

Heading north from Eurong, take the detour off the beach after 3 km (1.9 miles) to avoid One Tree Rocks. Just beyond the rocks, a walking trail leads to Lake Wabby, the deepest lake on the island. This trail measures about 2.5 km (1.6 miles) each way and crosses a large sandblow. A side road 1 km (0.6 miles) further north leads to another trail to the lake.

Five kilometres (3.1 miles) further up the main beach, take the inland bypass around

private boat. Barge services operate regularly from Inskip Point, near Rainbow Beach, to Hook Point; from River Heads to Wanggoolba Creek and Kingfisher Bay; and from Hervey Bay to Moon Point. There are airstrips at Toby's Gap, Wanggoolba Creek and Orchid Beach. A number of commercial tour operators also run day trips and multiday camping safaris to the island. If you don't have your own 4WD, you can hire one at Hervey Bay, Rainbow Beach, the Sunshine Coast and Brisbane. All vehicles must carry an access permit, available from QPWS offices.

There are QPWS camp sites at Lake Boomanjin, Central Station, Lake Allom, Waddy Point, Wathumba, Lake McKenzie and Dundubara. Facilities include toilets, picnic tables and showers (except at Lake Allom). Dilli Village and Dundubara are the only sites suitable for caravans or camper trailers. Beach

More than 300,000 visitors a year now travel to Fraser Island, many embarking from the vehicle barges that ply the short crossing from Inskip Point to Hook Point.

Poyungan Rocks. About 5.5 km (3.4 miles) beyond the rocks, at Rainbow Gorge, a walking track leads through dramatic, multihued sandstone formations.

Continuing north, take the bypass at Yidney Rocks to Happy Valley, the island's largest settlement. It offers a range of accommodation and a store with food and fuel. From Happy Valley, it's 6 km (3.7 miles) to Eli Creek. This crystal-clear stream is one of Fraser's most delightful features, offering excellent swimming and picturesque picnic spots. About 3 km (1.9 miles) further north, the rusting wreck of the *Maheno* sits in the middle of the beach. This ocean liner was blown ashore during a cyclone in 1935, as it was being towed to Japan to be scrapped.

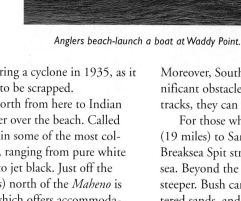
Anglers beach-launch a boat at Waddy Point.

For much of the run north from here to Indian Head, imposing cliffs tower over the beach. Called the Cathedrals, they contain some of the most colourful sands on the island, ranging from pure white through reds and yellows to jet black. Just off the beach and 6 km (3.7 miles) north of the *Maheno* is Cathedral Beach Resort, which offers accommodation, camping and a general store with food and fuel.

QPWS rangers are located at Dundubara, 6.5 km (4 miles) further north, 76.5 km (47.5 miles) from Hook Point. From here, it is nearly 20 km (12.5 miles) to the great basalt promontory known as Indian Head. The top of the headland provides magnificent views, and the waters below are thought to offer the best fishing on the island. On the northern side is a short stretch of beach that is popular with swimmers and picnickers. Continuing along the main beach track, you soon come to Middle Rocks, where a boardwalk leads to the Aquarium or Champagne Pools. These natural rock pools make fine swimming holes, but watch for waves breaking over the rocks.

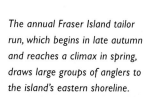
The annual Fraser Island tailor run, which begins in late autumn and reaches a climax in spring, draws large groups of anglers to the island's eastern shoreline.

Just beyond the next headland, at Waddy Point, there is a pleasant camp site among the coastal banksias, as well as a QPWS ranger station. You have now travelled 103 km (64 miles) from Hook Point. Orchid Beach, just a couple of kilometres (1.9 miles) further north, once housed a resort, but now has only a general store providing limited food and fuel.

The long run north from Waddy Point to Sandy Cape and its lighthouse traverses a remote area of the island and is undertaken by relatively few visitors. The area inland is closed to vehicles and, on the main beach, the sand soon gets softer. Moreover, South and North Ngkala Rocks pose significant obstacles and although both have bypass tracks, they can be hard to negotiate.

For those who do venture northward, it's 31 km (19 miles) to Sandy Cape, where a sandbar known as Breaksea Spit stretches for 30 km (18.5 miles) out to sea. Beyond the cape, the beach narrows and becomes steeper. Bush camping is permitted here on the sheltered sands, and there's a walking track to Sandy Cape Lighthouse, 8 km (5 miles) south of the cape itself, where the beach track ends.

THE SOUTHERN LAKES DRIVE

This sidetrip from Dilli Village on the east coast takes in many of the highlights of Fraser's interior. From the northern edge of the village, head inland, turn right at all the minor track junctions and then turn right again at the major track junction 7 km (4.4 miles) from the beach. Just over 3 km (1.9 miles) beyond this turn-off lies Lake Boomanjin, the world's largest perched lake. A good camp site with toilets, fireplaces and cold showers is located among the trees here.

Heading north from Lake Boomanjin, you pass Lake Benaroon and its bush camping area and then, after 11 km (7 miles), come to the shores of Lake Birrabeen. With its clear turquoise waters and white sands, this is a lovely spot for a picnic and a swim.

Continue another 3 km (1.9 miles) to a road junction, where either track will take you to Central Station, less than 6 km (3.7 miles) away. This was once the heart of logging operations on the island. Today, there is an excellent camping area with toilets, showers, fireplaces and rubbish disposal, as well as a QPWS ranger station. Make sure you take a walk along enchanting Wanggoolba Creek. Next, head toward Eurong and after about 1 km (0.6 miles) turn left, or north, to Pile Valley, 2 km (1.2 miles) away. Take some time here to explore and admire the rainforest's magnificent giant satinay trees.

Turn left at the next couple of junctions and just over 5 km (3.1 miles) from Pile Valley you come to Lake McKenzie, 37 km (23 miles) from Dilli Village.

Lake McKenzie is perhaps the island's picturesque lake, with its perfect white sand and searingly blue water meeting beneath an exquisite backdrop of thick, verdant forest. Nearby, a good camp site has toilets, showers and fireplaces.

From the lake, return to the main road and turn left. Continue straight ahead at the first crossroads. About 3 km (1.9 miles) further on, you come to a major crossroads where you should turn right. After another 11.5 km (7 miles), a track on the right leads a short distance to Lake Wabby Lookout car park and a trail to the lake itself. The walk downhill is easy but the return seems twice as steep, although the trees here at least provide some shelter from the often-fierce sun. The deepest lake on Fraser Island, Wabby is slowly being engulfed by a vast sandblow which has formed a huge, steep dune at the water's edge.

The main road continues to wind through thick forest, then reaches the junction with Smith Road after 2 km (1.2 miles). Turn right here and you will soon reach the top of a hill where a car park on the left provides access to a lookout over the immense Stonetool Sandblow. Like many other sandblows on the island, Stonetool is being driven slowly inland by the prevailing south-easterly winds.

From the lookout, the main track drops steeply down the hill. This was once a terror strip for drivers, before a series of chained wooden rails was laid down to prevent vehicles bogging in the soft sand. Beyond this slope, and just under 20 km (12.5 miles) from Lake McKenzie, you return to the eastern beach, about 6 km (3.7 miles) north of Eurong. From there you can retrace your steps southward to Dilli Village and your starting point at the island's southern tip.

Indian Head was named in 1770 by Captain James Cook after he sighted a group of indigenous Butchulla people on its summit.

Places in SOUTH-EAST QUEENSLAND

BEAUDESERT

Beaudesert is a small town with a population of 4120 and is 69 km (43 miles) south of Brisbane. It was named after a station near Mudgee in New South Wales, although the name can be also traced back to Britain. Originally settled in the 1840s, the district is a rich agricultural, beef and dairying producer, using the water of the Logan and Albert Rivers for irrigation. The Beaudesert Blue is a prized pumpkin that bears the name of the town.

Boys Town, established in the early 1960s and based on the US organisation that aims to reintegrate young offenders, is located on the outskirts of the town. The Beaudesert racecourse holds a race meeting each year in support of this very worthy establishment.

Jubilee Park is home to a museum which contains an 1875 slab hut that illustrates early building techniques. There are many national parks in the area, including Lamington National Park, which is on the New South Wales border.
Map ref: page 559 M8

BILOELA

Biloela comes from an Aboriginal word for 'white cockatoo' and although it is the main service centre for an agricultural area producing grain and cotton, it is probably more widely known for coal from the Callide open-cut mine. The town has a population of 6180 and is situated south-west of Rockhampton in the fertile Callide Valley, which is at the junction of the Dawson and Burnett Highways, 570 km (354 miles) to the north of Brisbane.

Advance Australia Fair is a rural theme park that acts as a living museum of the district's industries. Greycliffe, an old homestead in Biloela, is open to the public, as is the Callide Power Station and also the cotton ginnery. Nearby Callide Dam is very popular for sailing, swimming and other water sports. Cania Gorge National Park, with its spectacular sandstone cliffs, is not very far away.
Map ref: page 559 HI

Sulphur-crested cockatoo (Cacatua galerita)

BOONAH

Boonah (population 6970) is 100 km (62 miles) south-west of Brisbane, and is the centre of an agricultural region in the Fassifern Valley that forms a part of the 'Valleys of the Scenic Rim'. Initially the area relied on dairying, pigs and timber; now its mainstay is beef cattle and cultivated crops such as potatoes and carrots. It was also the railhead for the rail line out from Ipswich until the trains stopped running back in 1964.

The region was initially opened up by explorer and botanist Allan Cunningham, and it was originally named Blumbergville, after the Blumberg brothers, who opened the first store. The town's name was changed to Boonah in 1887. Moogerah Dam is close by and is very popular with both anglers and waterskiers.
Map ref: page 559 M8

BRIBIE ISLAND

Bribie, as it is generally referred to by the locals, is just 51 km (32 miles) long and 7 km (4 miles) wide and is joined to the mainland by a bridge that crosses Pumiceston Passage. It is 60 km (37 miles)

north of Brisbane, and has a population of 10,740. Located at the mainland end of the bridge, a monument honours the last of Bribie's Aboriginals, Kalma-Kutha, who died in 1897. Less than a hundred years before her death, the island had been home to about 600 Aboriginals living in substantial huts. The first European to explore Bribie was Matthew Flinders, who

Fishing boats and dinghies on Bribie Island.

visited in 1799 and named Point Skirmish after an altercation with the local people.

Bribie is a water paradise, and offers fishing and surfing on its open beaches, and safe boating on the calm waters of Pumiceston Passage. The northern end of the island, and its beaches, are protected in Bribie Island National Park. In spring it is a picture of pink boronia, wattle, bottlebrush and other wildflowers.
Map ref: page 559 N6

BUNDABERG

Bundaberg (population 54,821) is at the centre of a major sugar-producing area with timber, beef and avocadoes also grown here. Yet is best known for its rum: 'Bundy' is the most widely known liquor in Australia (tours of the distillery are conducted each day).

Bundaberg is a city of tree-lined streets, parks and gardens, located some 368 km (229 miles) north of Brisbane and 15 km (9 miles) from the coast, on the banks of the Burnett River. The streets are ribbons of colour when the poincianas flower in spring. Bundaberg is also a tourist centre.

A rural property in the Beaudesert area, featuring a classic tin and timber Queenslander-style farmhouse.

For a start, it is the southernmost gateway to the Great Barrier Reef, and in particular to the 'two ladies of the reef', Lady Elliott and Lady Musgrave Islands. Both these magnificent islands are true coral cays which visitors can stay on or explore on a day cruise.

Between mid-August and October Bundaberg becomes a whale-watching town, as the humpback whales pass close to the coast. The nearby townships of Elliott Heads, Bargara, Innes Park and Burnett Heads—all on the coast and no more than 15 km (9 miles) from Bundaberg—are all highly sought after as holiday destinations, and boast some of the most pristine beaches in Australia.

Just north of Bargara is the Mon Repos Environmental Park, site of one of the Southern Hemisphere's most significant turtle rookeries. Between November and January each year loggerheads, leatherback and the rarer flatback turtles leave the ocean to nest here.

Bundaberg is also the birthplace of the pioneer aviator Bert Hinkler. His ambition for flying was fuelled by his studies of the ibis on the area's lagoons and in the Bundaberg Botanical Gardens. In 1928 he completed the very first solo flight from England to Australia. During 1983–84, Hinkler's house was moved from England to the Hinkler House Memorial Museum and relocated to the Bundaberg Botanical Gardens.

Map ref: page 559 L2

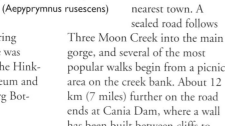

Rufous bettong
(Aepyprymnus rusescens)

BUNYA MOUNTAINS NATIONAL PARK

Set amidst cool mountain forests, and only four hours west of Brisbane, this park is the ideal place to escape the city's humid summers. It has the largest stand of bunya pines in the world. Aboriginals from the Waka Waka tribe used to collect the tasty nuts which grew at the top of the trees. But axemen in search of valuable timber entered the area in the mid-1870s and soon most of the trees had gone. The park has beautiful waterfalls and abundant wildlife.

Map ref: page 559 K6

CANIA GORGE NATIONAL PARK

Cania Gorge National Park, about 500 km (311 miles) north of Brisbane, is sometimes described as a smaller Carnarvon Gorge. Like Carnarvon, it has spectacular sandstone cliffs, caves and rock formations, plus a dammed lake for water sports.

Cania Gorge National Park is mostly very thick bush, with some pockets of rainforest, and is cut by creeks. The park is 26 km (16 miles) from Monto, the nearest town. A sealed road follows Three Moon Creek into the main gorge, and several of the most popular walks begin from a picnic area on the creek bank. About 12 km (7 miles) further on the road ends at Cania Dam, where a wall has been built between cliffs to block the creek—this provides irrigation water for the district, and makes waterskiing, swimming, sailing, canoeing and fishing all possible. Other activities include bushwalking, rock climbing, gold panning in the creeks and fossicking for semi-precious stones in the gorge area. Camping is not allowed anywhere in this park.

Map ref: page 559 J1

CARNARVON NATIONAL PARK

The Carnarvon National Park encompasses 251,000 ha (620,221 acres) of the rugged, isolated Consuelo Tableland, a plateau of the Great Dividing Range in central Queensland, and guards one of Australia's most spectacular natural gems: Carnarvon Gorge.

The original visitors to this scenic wonderland, the Aboriginals, have long since vanished, but their unique artistry remains. Over 50

The Amphitheatre in Carnarvon National Park is known for its acoustic qualities.

Aboriginal sites have been identified, and most of these are decorated with engravings and paintings, with stencils being the predominant form. Cathedral Cave, one of the largest Aboriginal rock-art sites so far discovered, is about 10 km (6 miles) from the camping ground. Another is 500 m (1641 feet) off the main track at the 'Art Gallery', dated at over 4000 years old.

The park is 720 km (447 miles) north-west of Brisbane and while Carnarvon Gorge occupies only a small fraction of the entire park, it is certainly the most scenic and easily accessible section. The gorge is over 30 km (19 miles) long and follows the twisting course of the creek, with walls rising vertically 200 m (656 feet). A diversity of plant life can be found in the park and wildlife is abundant, including the elusive platypus, which may be seen at dusk in Carnarvon Creek.

Map ref: page 558 D2

Bunya pines are the distinctive vegetation of Bunya Mountains National Park.

Wills Street in Charleville, a town hit hard by drought and flood in the past century.

CHARLEVILLE

Charleville (population 3400) is a very well-known town of western Queensland, 744 km (462 miles) west of Brisbane. It is the centre of a rich pastoral district, and in 1922 it was at one end of the first regular flight service by the Australian airline, QANTAS (Queensland and Northern Territory Aerial Services), which ran between Charleville and Cloncurry.

Charleville also prides itself on being at the heart of the mulga country. Mulga or, to give it its Aboriginal name, 'Booga Woongaroo', is a lifesaving tree. In times of drought, when the graziers and landowners talk about being out 'cutting mulga', it means that the drought is especially bad as all the feed is burnt and useless and only the mulga survives to feed the sheep and cattle.

At the end of the nineteenth century, Charleville was a thriving community. It had ten pubs, and up to 500 bullock teams passed through the town during the wool season. Cobb and Co moved their coach-building factory here from Bathurst, New South Wales, in 1893 and continued building 'the tall ships of Charleville', as the coaches became known, until 1920, when lack of demand forced the closure of the factory.

The Stiger Vortex guns located south of the town are an indication of the desperation of the schemes devised to break the drought of 1902. These tall cones were filled with gunpowder, which was fired into the air in the hope of making rain. The plan was not successful. In contrast to that drought, the massive rains of April 1990 almost completely devastated Charleville, but with typical country resilience, the town has slowly recovered.

Charleville is home to a base for the Royal Flying Doctor Service, the Charleville School of Distance Education and a pastoral research laboratory. In September the Booga Woongaroo Festival is held.
Map ref: page 558 A5

CHILDERS

Childers is 311 km (193 miles) north of Brisbane, and has a population of 1500. It is a sugar town as well as a National Trust town. Even though a 1902 fire destroyed much of the town, many impressive Victorian buildings remain—these are listed by the National Trust. The major crop, sugar cane, has been grown in the area since the 1870s, but now avocadoes and vegetables are also produced, using irrigation water from the Monduran Dam.

A visit to the Pharmaceutical Museum, which still has its original cedar fixtures, a 1906 cash register and leather-bound prescription books, is a must. At the Isis sugar mill you can see raw cane turned into familiar white sugar crystals. There is also a historic walk that leads through the town.
Map ref: page 559 L2

CHINCHILLA

The name of this town is said to come from the Aboriginal word 'jinchilla', meaning 'cypress pine'. Chinchilla is 293 km (182 miles) west of Brisbane, and has a population of 6020. The district relies on timber, grazing and grain growing, and it is also known as the polocrosse (a hybrid of polo and lacrosse) centre of Queensland.

This area contains one of the world's largest known deposits of petrified wood, reputed to be 140–180 million years old. You can fossick for the wood around Baking Board and Magic Stone, where you might also come across gemstones such as agate and jasper.

The Folk Museum and Sawmill are also worth a visit. Boonarga, east of Chinchilla, has a memorial to the *Cactoblastis* moth, the insect that was imported to eliminate the prickly pear plague in a successful biological control program. In 1925 over a quarter of a million hectares (over 617,750 acres) were inundated by prickly pear, but within ten years the larvae of this moth had completely eradicated it.
Map ref: page 559 J5

Female figbird (Sphecotheres viridis) *feeding her young in the D'Aguilar Range National Park rainforest just outside Brisbane.*

A pair of 1 kilo (2.2 pound) bass, caught in Somerset Dam, near Esk.

D'AGUILAR RANGE NATIONAL PARK (WITHIN BRISBANE FOREST PARK)

The D'Aguilar Range overlooks Brisbane from the north-west, and its ridges provide views over the city and out across Moreton Bay. Just 30 minutes' drive from Brisbane's centre, it has the closest rainforest to the city and offers a quiet, cool escape from the city.

One of the easiest areas for walking and camping is between Bellbird Grove and Camp Mountain in the south-eastern corner of the park. Rangers recommend late August and September as a good season to walk or camp in the park, particularly for the wildflowers. Wildlife is also a major attraction. Wrens, flycatchers, finches and other small, colourful birds flit through the undergrowth all day, while colourful parrots can be seen feeding in taller trees morning and afternoon. After dark, possums can be spotted (by torch) in the trees.
Map ref: page 559 M7

ESK

Esk (population 1175) is the administrative centre for the shire of the same name. It is an attractive town, set in the mountains of the upper Brisbane Valley, 98 km (61 miles) west of Brisbane. It has broad streets lined with the typical country Queensland buildings of the late nineteenth and early twentieth centuries. The two-storey timber Club Hotel is a classic example, with wide verandas and cast-iron railings on each floor. Descendants of the fallow deer that were given to Queensland by Queen Victoria

in 1873 can be seen at times in the Brisbane Valley. Lake Wivenhoe, Somerset Dam and Atkinson Dam all have excellent facilities and provide venues for many water sports, including rowing, boating, waterskiing and swimming. The nearby historical homesteads of Bellevue and Caboonbah are well worth a visit.
Map ref: page 559 L6

GIN GIN

Gin Gin (population 1200) is a pretty town on the Bruce Highway at the turn-off to Bundaberg, 366 km (227 miles) north of Brisbane. Some of the earliest settlements of the Burnett Valley were around Gin Gin. Gregory Blaxland, one of the team that crossed the Blue Mountains— the mountain barrier to the west of Sydney— settled in Gin Gin around 1842. Another resident was the infamous James McPherson, Queensland's only bushranger, known as the 'Wild Scotsman', who held up the Royal Mail on several occasions. In March, the Wild Scotsman Bushranger Festival is held.

Attractions in town include the Historical Museum, the Curra-

jong Gardens and the Moonara Craft Spinning Inn. East of Gin Gin, on the Bundaberg road, are the Mystery Craters. These strange sandstone formations were probably made by meteors. Nearby is Haig Dam, a great spot for the boating and fishing enthusiast.
Map ref: page 559 L2

GIRRAWEEN NATIONAL PARK

Girraween National Park is about 260 km (161 miles) by road from Brisbane, and 26 km (16 miles) south of the nearest town, Stanthorpe. It is dominated by granite domes, tors and boulders.

Bald Rock Creek is one of the park's best features, which has rocky rapids and deep waterholes, one near the main picnic ground and another delightful rock pool

further just a bit further down the creek. These are great places to do some exploration. Walking is the main activity in the park. Trails vary in length from 600 m (1967 feet) to 7.5 km (4.7 miles) and they lead to The Pyramid, Castle Rock, Sphinx and Turtle Rocks, and Mount Norman.

This region can be very hot during the day in summer, but winter temperatures can plunge to –8° C (28° F). Many bushwalkers prefer the more pleasant, cool weather of autumn and spring. Spring also has a marvellous wildflower display: thick flowering heath and a wide variety of flowering shrubs, such as wattles, pea flowers, mint bushes, daisies and rockroses.
See also The Granite Belt Wine Region
Map ref: page 559 L9

Girraween National Park is scattered with enormous granite boulders and domes.

GOLD COAST

It was only in 1996 that the Gold Coast and Albert Shires were amalgamated to form the second-largest council in Queensland—the Gold Coast City Council. The Gold Coast is 66 km (41 miles) south of Brisbane, and stretches from Beenleigh in the north, taking in South Stradbroke Island, right down to the Queensland/New South Wales border and the towns of Coolangatta and Tweed Heads. The Gold Coast region has one of the highest growth rates in Australia, something like four times the national average, and lays claim to being the tourist capital of Australia, with a million overseas and several million Australian visitors a year—its own population is 334,000.

With a climate providing more than 300 days of sunshine per year, some of the best surfing and swimming beaches in Australia patrolled by the largest body of lifesavers in the country, many exciting theme parks, and a lush hinterland of national parks, mountain hideaways and spectacular views, it is no wonder the area draws visitors like a magnet.

The building boom from the 1960s to the 1980s saw Surfers Paradise, in particular, go from a relatively small holiday community

Preparing cotton bales for transport at Goondiwindi, centre of a vast rural district.

to a bustling, busy and glittering strip of high-rise buildings. At the same time, developers have turned vast areas of the Gold Coast into a maze of canals and expensive residential subdivisions.

Probably the greatest attraction, particularly for families, is the area's theme parks. You can visit Movie World to gain insights into moviemaking, stunts and pyrotechnics; Sea World for sea lion and shark shows; Dreamworld for its action rides and the white tigers on Tiger Island; Wet'n'Wild for spectacular water rides and twisters; and Cable Ski World for waterskiing, bungee jumping and go-cart racing. Parks and sanctuaries where visitors can

'talk to the animals' include Fleay's Wildlife Park, the Currumbin Bird Sanctuary, Paradise Country, Royal Pines, Pioneer Plantation, Tropical Fruit World and Aussie Country Down Under.

For the golf enthusiast the Gold Coast is a paradise, with a choice of about 60 courses, some designed by international golfing greats.

For a complete change of pace, spend a few days exploring the hinterland, which offers spectacular views, bushwalking, camping and even abseiling. Lamington National Park is Australia's largest reserve of subtropical rainforest, with some 160 km (99 miles) of great walking tracks. Near O'Reilly's Rainforest

Guesthouse is Australia's first tree-top walkway, where visitors can stroll into the forest canopy some 16 m (52 feet) above the ground. Springbrook and Tamborine National Parks offer some spectacular scenery, waterfalls, rock pools and a huge array of flora and fauna. The hinterland is dotted with guesthouses, restaurants, craft galleries and farm-type resorts offering a new style of Gold Coast holiday.

For the shopper the Gold Coast is also heaven, as the area has some of the biggest shopping centres in the Southern Hemisphere, offering goods ranging from the ultimate in resort wear and accessories to artworks and antiques.

Map ref: page 559 P8

GOONDIWINDI

The same river red gums that Allan Cunningham saw when he came through this area in 1827 still line the banks of the Macintyre River. When Queensland became a separate colony in 1854 a customs house was built on the ferry crossing here, because the river forms the border between New South Wales and Queensland. This building still stands today, and houses a fascinating collection of memorabilia put together by the Historical Society. The name Goondiwindi

Aerial view of Surfers Paradise, on Queensland's Gold Coast. As well as hosting the Indy car races, the Gold Coast is home to a multitude of wildlife parks and theme parks.

(pronounced Gundawindy), is said to come from the Aboriginal word 'goonawinna', which officially means 'resting place of the birds'.

Goondiwindi is a very modern, prosperous town, the commercial, service and recreation centre for a vast area producing some of Australia's best wool, wheat, beef cattle and cotton. It is 360 km (224 miles) west of Brisbane, and has a population of 5000. In a good season, the Waggamba Shire is rated with the best of Australia's primary producing regions.

The town's hero is Gunsynd, 'The Goondiwindi Grey', a race-horse owned by a local syndicate; it won 29 races and became one of the best loved racehorses in racing history. A statue of it now stands in Apex Park near the Border Bridge. Goondiwindi Botanic Gardens, which is set on 25 ha (62 acres) of land, is being developed to house inland plants that cannot survive in coastal climates. This is a wonderful community project offering great family recreation—sweeping lawns, barbecue areas and a 5 ha (12 acres) lake encircling a bird-nesting island. Boobera Lagoon, a permanent deep-water lagoon on the river, is a wildlife sanctuary and a great waterskiing venue. Goondiwindi's annual spring festival takes place each year in October.
Map ref: page 559 H9

GYMPIE

Gympie is 161 km (100 miles) north of Brisbane, and has a population of 11,825. It is the town reputed to have saved the young colony of Queensland from bankruptcy back in the 1860s. Drought had devastated the colony's farms, but then James Nash discovered gold in 1867 and the rush was on.

The town's name comes from 'gimpi gimpi'—the Aboriginal name for a stinging nettle bush that covered the banks of the Mary River. When the gold ran out—around 1925—dairy farming, fruit and vegetable production, and Forestry Department plantations took over; these continue to be the region's chief industries.

Gympie is the main entrance into the delights of Cooloola Beach, Great Sandy National Park and Fraser Island, but it has attractions of its own as well. At the Deep Creek Gold Fossicking Park you

The town park in Gympie, a town where fossicking for gold can yield some finds.

can explore an old goldmining site and pick, shovel or pan to find your own gold, for instance.

Incidentally, Mary Street, the main street, meanders through the town, mainly because the road still follows the old bullock route. Even though rebuilding has eliminated the greatest kinks, it still has a case of the 'wanders'. On the northern side of town is a timber museum which has timber exhibits and also displays some of the early timber-cutting techniques and a fully working steam-driven sawmill.

On the Brisbane Road, adjacent to Lake Alford, is a goldmining museum, the main attraction being a simple four-room timber cottage that was once the home of the first Labor prime minister of Australia, Andrew Fisher. Another interesting building is the original retort house of the Scottish Gympie Gold Mining Company, where gold was extracted from quartz.

The Gympie Country Music Muster, which is held in August, is a must for all country music fans, while the Goldrush Festival takes place during October.
Map ref: page 559 M4

HERVEY BAY

Hervey Bay—291 km (181 miles) north of Brisbane—is a very large expanse of water protected by the bulk of Fraser Island. It was named by James Cook in 1770, after Captain Hervey, who later became the Earl of Bristol.

Hervey Bay is also the collective name given to the scattered seaside resorts that dot the southern shore of the bay, and these include Gatakers Bay, Urangan, Toogoom and

Torquay, and the inland town of Howard. The population of the area is 42,300.

Hervey Bay is an aquatic paradise, and caters for all sports and pastimes. Boating and fishing enthusiasts have a choice of jetty, reef, beach and estuary, and may even indulge in some game fishing.

Because the bay is protected, it has little or no surf, and provides safe swimming. Hervey Bay is an ideal spot for diving, featuring coral and artificial reefs teeming with marine life. Neptune's Reefworld at Urangan with its coral reefs and fish life exhibits will no doubt appeal to snorkellers as much as it does to divers. There is a ferry to Fraser Island from Urangan.

Over recent years, the region has become famous as the playground for those gentle giants of the sea, the humpback whales. From August to October families of these majestic creatures stop in the bay to rest and play. They are on their return journey to the Antarctic

after calving in the northern waters. Thousands of whale-watchers now come each year to catch a glimpse of the playful humpbacks, with a breach sighting—a whale throwing itself out of the water—the ultimate treat. To celebrate the whales' return, Hervey Bay stages a Whale Festival for two weeks each year during August. The Blessing of the Fleet, an illuminated procession of floats, is the highlight of this exciting fortnight.

To learn about the early settlement of Hervey Bay and Fraser Island, visit the Hervey Bay Historical Museum at Pialba, or go to Woody Island National Park, with its ruined lighthouse, graves and buildings. Brooklyn House in Howard is a gracious Queensland-style timber home which was built in 1870 predominantly of cedar and beech and has since been lovingly restored to its former glory. The house is still a family home and offers guided tours and scrumptious Devonshire teas.
Map ref: page 559 M3

INJUNE

Injune is a small cattle and timber town with a population of 395. It is 570 km (354 miles) north-west of Brisbane and around 90 km (56 miles) north of Roma, making it the southern entrance to Carnarvon Gorge National Park. The gorge brings many visitors to the area, and plays a large part in the economy of the town. Lonesome National Park, a small park north-east of Injune, has some spectacular views from the plateau of the Dawson and Arcadia river valleys.
Map ref: page 558 E4

Seabirds flocking at Woody Island National Park, near Hervey Bay.

The technical college in Ipswich is from the Victorian era.

IPSWICH

Ipswich is Queensland's oldest provincial city, a mere 40 km (25 miles) west of Brisbane, with a population of 131,514. In 1827 it was called Limestone Hills, because of the limestone that was mined by the convicts, but its name was later changed by Governor Brisbane. Ipswich has large deposits of coal and has become a major industrial centre—Brisbane aside, it has the State's most diversified manufacturing base. It was an important river port for produce until the railway arrived here in 1876.

Ipswich has many examples of the classical timber Queensland home and also fine nineteenth century buildings, among them the Civic Group, which consists of the Town Hall, Post Office and Bank of Australasia. The Amberley Air Force Base, south of the city, is the largest RAAF base in Australia and also the home of the F1-11 fighter bomber. Rosewood, a small village south of Amberley, has a charming church built in the early 1900s that is said to be the largest wooden church in the South Pacific.
Map ref: page 559 M7

KINGAROY

Dominated by enormous peanut silos—and the home of Queensland's former premier Joh Bjelke-Petersen—the town of Kingaroy, 209 km (130 miles) north-west of Brisbane, is the peanut capital of Australia. The town has a population of 11,590, and services the productive South Burnett district. It has also earned a name as the nation's baked bean capital, with 75 per cent of Australia's navy bean crop grown in the region. An Abo-

riginal word for red ant, 'kinkerroy', gave the town its name. Kingaroy had a slow start until the railway opened in 1904, followed, in 1924, by the first major peanut plantings.

The Peanut Heritage Museum located in the town's old powerhouse is the only peanut museum in Australia, and it is well worth a visit. The Peanut Van in Kingaroy Street has been operating for 25 years, and has 12 flavours of peanut to choose from. The Peanut Festival is in early March; the Taabinga Music Festival is in October. *See also* South Burnett Wine Region
Map ref: page 559 L5

LAMINGTON NATIONAL PARK

Dominant on the skyline behind the Gold Coast beaches are the green peaks and plateaus of the border ranges. Here Lamington National Park protects magnificent subtropical rainforest that rises to more than 1100 m (3609 feet).

The two main starting points for exploring Lamington National Park are Binna Burra and Green Mountains (also known as O'Reilly's because of the well-known guesthouse), each about an hour-and-a-half's drive from Brisbane or an hour from the Gold Coast. Binna Burra is well known for its long-established accommodation lodge. For a visit to Lamington National Park, three items are absolutely essential: a raincoat, insect repellent and a good bird identification book. This splendid rainforest retreat is overrun with birds. The repellent is for the abundant leeches. Of course the raincoat is needed for the rain that gives rainforest its name.

At both Binna Burra and Green Mountains, pademelons graze the lawns early and late in the day, while spotlighting with a torch in the forest at night will reveal possums, bandicoots, frogs and geckos.
Map ref: page 559 N8

MAIN RANGE NATIONAL PARK

This park, south-west of Brisbane, takes in the peaks and ramparts of the Great Dividing Range and it stretches approximately 55 km (34 miles) north and south of Cunninghams Gap. Roads and walking tracks cut through rainforest and eucalypts to lookouts with spectacular views.

The park includes the historic Spicers Gap, which took drays laden with Darling Downs produce to the port of Brisbane. You can still follow the pioneers' route by going through Spicers Gap (part by 4WD, part only on foot) and search out historic relics along the way. The major feature of the park is the Governor's Chair, a rocky bluff providing views south to the Border Ranges and north towards Brisbane, with Moogerah Dam and surrounding hills far below. The southern end of the park also has some delightful features,

Regent bowerbird (Sericulus chrysocephalus)

including Queen Mary Falls, which are near the small town of Killarney, about 34 km (21 miles) from Warwick.
Map ref: page 559 L8

MARYBOROUGH

Maryborough, 250 km (155 miles) north of Brisbane, is one of the oldest cities in Queensland, having been first settled in 1843. It developed as a port to service the influx of free settlers. When steam-driven machinery was introduced, timber such as kauri was harvested from the extensive forests and the region provided most of Queensland with timber. Around 1860 sugar cane was first planted—this industry is still one of the region's major activities. Maryborough's population today is 25,527.

Many European immigrants arrived in the town during the second half of the nineteenth century. The splendid old houses, mostly built of local timber and reflecting the classic timber Queenslander design, have given Maryborough its reputation as one of the most beautiful historic towns in Queensland. This can best be appreciated by following the Heritage Walk, which takes in 28 historic buildings in the central business district. There is also a driving tour, which takes in a total of nearly 80 buildings and historic sites.

Each Thursday is Heritage Market Day, highlighted by the firing of the 'Time Cannon' at 1 p.m. and attended by the Town Crier. The Maryborough Heritage City

Mustering cattle across a river in the Main Range National Park.

Queenslander in Maryborough—being raised on stilts with a wrap-around veranda and wide eaves help cool the house.

Festival is held in early September, and the Maryborough Masters Games are in late September.
Map ref: page 559 M3

MILLMERRAN

The local Aboriginals once used this place as a lookout, and the Aboriginal words for 'eye' ('meel') and 'to look out' ('merran') gave the town its name. The region has a history of producing excellent wool, but the future may bring new industries—extensive coal deposits were discovered nearby in the 1970s. Millmerran is 208 km (129 miles) south-west of Brisbane and has a population of 3127. The oldest building in the shire, All Saints Chapel, dates back to 1877 and is in the nearby township of Yandilla. Originally erected as a private chapel, it has been an Anglican church since the early 1900s.
Map ref: page 559 K8

MITCHELL

Mitchell (population 1300) is situated on the Warrego Highway on the banks of the Maranoa River between Roma and Charleville, 567 km (352 miles) west of Brisbane. The town is named for the explorer Thomas Mitchell, who passed through the area in 1845. Mitchell is the southern gateway to the Mount Moffat section of Carnarvon National Park. The park has no facilities here, so visitors must be self-sufficient. Mitchell is also the birthplace of Australia's shortest-serving prime minister, Francis Forde, who led the nation for just 6 days in 1945. A monument near Arrest Creek records the arrest of the 'last of the

bushrangers', Patrick and James Kenniff, who murdered two men at Lethbridge Pocket in 1902.
Map ref: page 558 D5

MUNDUBBERA

Mundubbera (population 2299) is the citrus centre of Queensland, noted for its mandarins. Among its many citrus orchards is the Gold Mile Orchard, the largest in the Southern Hemisphere. The Big Mandarin acts as the town's information centre and as a window for the citrus industry. Beef cattle, grain, peanuts, dairying and timber also feature. The town is east of Maryborough, near where the Boyne, Auburn and Burnett Rivers meet, 363 km (225 miles) north-west of Brisbane. There are two claims for the origin of the name, one proposing it came from the Aboriginal words for 'foot' and 'step', after the footholds cut into the area's tall trees, while the other cites an Aboriginal word meaning 'meeting of the waters'.
Map ref: page 559 K3

NAMBOUR

Nambour, 98 km (61 miles) north of Brisbane, gets its name from an Aboriginal word meaning 'red-flowering tea-tree'. It is the administrative centre for the Maroochy Shire and is primarily a sugar town, but there is also dairying, timber, bananas, pineapples and citrus fruit grown in the district. The shire is one of the fastest-growing in the State and the population is expected to exceed 100,000 in the near future—Nambour's population today is 22,746. With more than a quarter of the population over 50,

the Sunshine Coast University of the Third Age has become popular, and has more than 1200 students.

The Sunshine Plantation, which is just south of Nambour, has an enormous fibreglass pineapple as its emblem, one of the local landmarks, and on its 12 ha (30 acres) produces some 60 varieties of tropical fruits, nuts and spices. The plantation is open to visitors, with a train ride around the property being the highlight.
Map ref: page 559 M5

NANANGO

Nanango has a population of 8321 resident and is located 185 km (115 miles) north-west of Brisbane. The town of Nanango initially sprang up around a single general store, but the area really boomed when gold was discovered in the 1860s at what was later to become known as Seven Mile Diggings.

The name 'Nanango' originally comes from the area's first sheep run, which was established back in 1842. Nowadays beef cattle have replaced the sheep, plus the area is also being cultivated with crops of beans and grain.

The Boondooma Dam is a good local recreational area which offers camping sites as well as some picnic facilities. It is a good site for anglers, as the dam is stocked with perch and bass. Also nearby is the National Trust-listed Boondooma Homestead, an old stone house constructed during the mid-nineteenth century. Another attraction well worth a visit is the Nanango Astronomical Observatory—it runs on solar power, a world first.
Map ref: page 559 L5

The Auburn River descends into rock pools in rugged Auburn River National Park.

NOOSA HEADS

Noosa Heads has a population of 11,690 and it is located at the most northerly point of the Sunshine Coast, 144 km (89 miles) north of Brisbane. It is one of Australia's most enticing resort destinations. The sophisticated cafés, boutiques, hotels and restaurants have given the area a cosmopolitan air, and strict building laws have ensured that no building is higher than the trees. The name Noosa is said to derive from an Aboriginal term for 'shade' or 'shadow'. Noosa Heads is the southern entry point to the Cooloola Section of the Great Sandy National Park, Cooloola Beach and Rainbow Beach, the departure point for Fraser Island.

During the nineteenth century loggers cut timber such as kauri, hoop pine, and cypress from up-river forests and floated it down to the mills at Tewantin. The ruins of their camps can still be seen along the river.

The northerly aspect of the ocean beach ensures excellent waves, making it popular with surfers. Many anglers consider the section of the river known as the Narrows to be the best fishing spot on the east coast, particularly for the elusive bass. The Everglades, not far from Lake Cootharaba, is also popular, particularly with nature lovers. The Festival of Waters is held around the end of August to early September.
Map ref: page 559 N5

ROMA

Roma, 480 km (298 miles) west of Brisbane, is the 'Gateway to the Outback' and the commercial centre of the Maranoa District, which produces wool, wheat, citrus fruit, timber and beef. Its population is 6775.

The town is named after Lady Diamantina Roma Bowen, who was the wife of the first governor of Queensland, George Bowen. Back in 1859, when Queensland separated from New South Wales and became a colony in its own right, Roma was the first settlement to be gazetted.

In 1863 a Mr S. Bassett planted a vineyard at Roma; it is still operating as 'Romavilla', and is the oldest as well as one of the largest vineyards in the State. Memorial Avenue, with its 93 bottle trees, with each one being dedicated to a man lost in World War I, extends from the cenotaph to the railway station.

The Big Rig, one of the best-preserved oil drilling rigs of its era, is on display near Roma's Information Centre, east of the town, and will form the centrepiece of the proposed National Oil and Gas Museum, which will be located here.
See also South-East Queensland Wine Region
Map ref: page 558 E5

Pale-headed Rosella
(Platycercus adscitus)

ST GEORGE

St George is a small town (population 2500) 569 km (353 miles) south-west of Brisbane, and is on the banks of the Balonne River. The site received its name on St George's Day, 23 April 1846, when the explorer Thomas Mitchell crossed the Balonne. Now three major highways lead to the town.

The heavily irrigated district produces much of Queensland's cotton crop. Other crops include grain, sunflowers and grapes and, of course, sheep and cattle. The water for all this comes from the E.J. Beardmore Dam, not from the annual rainfall, which is less than 500 mm (19.5 inches). This dam not only supplies water for crops and stock, but also provides some excellent fishing for yellowbelly; the dam and the river have led to St George being known as the 'inland fishing capital'.

Birdwatchers will delight in the diverse bird life among the white gums along the river banks. Rosehill Aviaries, 64 km (40 miles) west of St George, houses the most

Oyster Rocks are part of the headland in Noosa National Park; this 430 ha (1063 acres) parcel of bushland is a welcome respite in the highly urbanised Sunshine Coast.

comprehensive collection of Australian parrots in the world—there are more than 60 species, housed in some 80 aviaries, totalling more than 600 birds.

Map ref: page 558 E8

SOUTH BURNETT WINE REGION

In a few short years, the wine industry has done a lot for the local economy of the Burnett Valley, near Kingaroy. There are now well over 200 ha (500 acres) planted to a variety of grapes, and more are going in all the time.

Many observers remain sceptical, because the fertility of the region suggests that high yields may be difficult to obtain. Rain during harvest and the possibility of hail are also potential problems. But initial results have exceeded all but the wildest predictions, and there are many smiling and relieved winemakers in Burnett. In time, the region may be as famous for its wines as it has been for its peanuts and pumpkin scones.

Three wineries that offer cellar-door tastings and other facilities are Crane winery and Stuart Range Estate, both near Kingaroy, and Barambah Ridge Winery and Vineyards, in Redgate, which is near Murgon. The size of the new Clovely Estate's operation in Burnett is not insignificant by any standards, but it is massive for Queensland. Its three labels, in ascending order of quality, are Fifth Row, Left Field and Clovely Estate. Much of the production will be exported.

Map ref: page 559 L5

SOUTH-EAST QUEENSLAND WINE REGION

Queensland's oenological history began around 1850, with German settlers in the Toowoomba district west of Brisbane, but the number of vineyards soon declined. The State's oldest continuously operating winery, Romavilla, is at Roma, nearly 500 km (315 miles) north-west of Brisbane. Now, in the south-east of the State, completely new viticultural locales such as Mount Tamborine and Mount Cotton are being developed. When Mount Tamborine Vineyards and Winery, just an hour's drive from Brisbane, was planted in 1998, very few people expected that it

The rugged nature and difficult terrain of Sundown National Park make it one of the State's least accessible national parks.

would soon rank as Queensland's most successful winery in terms of annual tonnage crushed. Mount Tamborine's vineyards provide only a small percentage of the grapes for its winery, the rest being sourced from vineyards throughout Australia. Its sparkling wines are popular, but spend little time on lees. Its fortifieds have been well received. Its best red is a Padthaway shiraz.

The Mount Cotton Winery, which is on the outskirts of Brisbane, was developed as part of a tourist complex where visitors can observe all stages of the production of sparkling wine. The new winery is state-of-the-art. Chambourcin has been planted in the hot and humid surrounding vineyards, and 20 different varieties of this grape have been planted at company's Ballandean vineyards.

Map ref: pages 559 F5; 557 D4, D5

The medal-winning Mount Tamborine vineyard produces 125,000 cases per year.

STANTHORPE

Stanthorpe is 219 km (136 miles) south-west of Brisbane, and has a population of 10,601. At 811 m (2661 feet) above sea level, this town is one of the highest in the State, and it consistently records Queensland's lowest temperature. The mild summers grant the area a virtual monopoly on the growing of stone fruit. Grapes and wine are also produced, and wineries are now Stanthorpe's leading tourist attraction. All offer tastings and sales.

Stanthorpe had a late start—it was not until the discovery of tin that a hastily planned township developed at the Quart Pot crossing, which had previously merely been the site of an inn catering for passing traffic. Tin also gave the settlement its name: 'stannum' is the Latin word for 'tin'.

Within a short distance of Stanthorpe are several national parks, notably Girraween and Sundown. The Granite Belt Spring Wine Festival in October sees the town booked out as visitors come from all over to join in the festivities. *See also* The Granite Belt Wine Region

Map ref: page 559 L9

SUNDOWN NATIONAL PARK

Sundown National Park, 250 km (155 miles) south-west of Brisbane, was created in the late 1970s from parts of three large sheep stations which, over time, had become uneconomic to run. Copper, tin and arsenic were once mined in the Red Rock area in the north of Sundown, but very little wealth was gained from the low-grade ore. Sundown's most striking feature is the Severn River. At most times of the year it is a series of large rocky waterholes in its upper reaches, but after prolonged heavy rain it becomes a raging torrent. Walking along the banks of the river or up one of the many narrow gorges is recommended. Sundown's rugged terrain—steep gullies, eroded ridge tops, gorges and creek flats—makes the park a mecca for wilderness seekers. The park has a wide range of vegetation, including eucalypts, white box and cypress, and animals such as kangaroos and wallabies are quite commonly seen. *See also* The Granite Belt Wine Region

Map ref: page 559 K9

Surf-lifesavers competing in a sprint event at Caloundra on the Sunshine Coast.

SUNSHINE COAST

The Sunshine Coast is the name given to the coastal region that stretches from Bribie Island and Caloundra in the south to Noosa Heads and beyond in the north, and all this just an hour's drive— 85 km (53 miles)—north of Brisbane. The Sunshine Coast has 150 km (93 miles) of perfect surfing beaches, tropical fruit plantations and larger-than-life tourist attractions. The area is experiencing growth both in its tourism industry and in its population (currently 166,000), but is taking a low-key approach to its expansion, avoiding the high-rise buildings that distinguish the Gold Coast, which is just to the south of Brisbane.

The Glasshouse Mountains, named by James Cook in 1770 because they appeared to be inside a glasshouse, are weirdly beautiful, and are the first landmark visitors see when travelling up from Brisbane. Inland is Nambour, one of the prettiest sugar towns in southeast Queensland. Buderim, located on a plateau between the Blackall Range and the coast, is noted for its beautiful homes and gardens. Australia's only ginger factory, and the world's largest, is at Yandina, 9 km (6 miles) north of Nambour. Eumundi's brewery can be toured and the Saturday market at Eumundi is one of the coast's best.

The Blackall Range and the popular villages of Monteville, Flaxton and Mapleton are all craft and art orientated, and are well worth visiting any day of the week. Mapleton and Kondilla national parks, with their dramatic waterfalls and walking tracks, are a pleasant contrast to the coastal regions. The Sunshine Coast has plenty to offer the surfer, from Moffat Beach at Caloundra to Alexandra Headland at Maroochydore, to Coolum and Peregian Beaches, and to the near-perfect conditions of Laguna Bay at Noosa.
Map ref: page 559 N5

TAMBO

Tambo (population 592), on the banks of the Barcoo River and 861 km (535 miles) north-west of Brisbane, has perhaps the best grazing land in western Queensland. It also has some of the oldest buildings in this part of Queensland, and some of the most unusual. McLeod's House, once a part of the Live and Let Live Hotel, has unusual foundations—a bed of logs laid on the ground, instead of stumps.

Another building of note is the Old Post Office Museum, which is where the Tambo Teddies are manufactured. This cottage industry has grown enormously— in 1996 the ten thousandth Tambo Teddy was made. All Tambo Teddies are individuals, and each has a name.

Take note of the bottle trees in the town, in particular the enormous one in Edward Street, on the site of the first Catholic church in town.

The Salvator Rosa Section of Carnarvon National Park, 120 km (75 miles) east of Tambo, is part of the history of the area and also has some wonderful natural attractions. A 4WD vehicle is needed to drive through this park.
Map ref: page 558 A2

TAROOM

Taroom is a small town which has a population of 2981 and is located 464 km (288 miles) north-west of Brisbane on the Dawson River. Like so many other towns, it was first settled by sheep farmers. The sheep have now been replaced by beef, wheat and sorghum. The name of the town comes from an Aboriginal word 'taroom'—'wild lime tree'—which the Aboriginals used for perfume and as a food. The town has a mixed history. Its darkest hour was in 1857: eleven Europeans were killed by Aboriginals at Hornet Bank Homestead, and in the aftermath the local Jiman tribe was decimated, with 300 Aboriginals indiscriminately killed. On the other hand, the

Like its American namesake, the Texas countryside is good for cattle grazing.

town boasts a coolibah tree on which the explorer Ludwig Leichhardt carved his initials, during his expedition to Darwin in 1844. The tree now stands on the main street of Taroom. The Isla Gorge National Park is 50 km (31 miles) north of Taroom; at the 14 km (9 miles) mark, keep an eye out for the rare *Livistona* palms, which are visible from the highway.
Map ref: page 558 G3

TEXAS

Texas (population 900) is a small town on the Dumaresq River, 312 km (194 miles) south-west of Brisbane, where it forms the border with New South Wales. Tobacco crops once surrounded the town but these have given way to other products, such as lucerne, wool, cattle and timber.

The McDougall brothers established a station in the area in about 1840. They later had a bitter dispute with a claim-jumper, one they likened to a US border war, so they named their property 'Texas'. The town developed in the mid-1880s. A feedlot, south of Texas, established some years ago, has grown to be the biggest in the Southern Hemisphere. This has provided much-needed employment for the town as well as a ready market for many of the grain and lucerne crops. Tours of the feedlot can be made.
Map ref: page 559 J10

THE GRANITE BELT WINE REGION

The granite belt on the New South Wales border and on the western edge of the Great Dividing Range, is perhaps more widely known for its two great National Parks, Girraween and Sundown, than it is for wine, despite the fact that grapes were first planted there in back in the 1860s. With several wineries within less than 10 km (6 miles) out of Ballandean, including Robinsons, Ballandean Estate, Bungawarra and Granite Ridge, and several more along the New England Highway through Glen Aplin to Stanthorpe and beyond, there is plenty to attract visitors.

Conditions in this huge State are extremely varied. The Granite Belt, at 700 to 1000 m (2300 to 3300 ft) above sea level, is one of the highest wine regions in Australia. This area normally has temperatures that are 5–10° C (9–18° F) cooler than in the coastal districts, and snow is not unknown. Even though the Granite Belt is well established, it is too early to identify the varieties that will be most successful there. Cabernet sauvignon and shiraz dominate, and merlot is showing much potential, but pinot noir is

less successful. There is also some interest in red Italian varieties, and chambourcin's ability to withstand rain and humidity has given it a following outside the Belt. Sémillon and chardonnay are by far the most successful whites in this area.

New plantings across Queensland—in established regions such as the Granite Belt, districts like Toowoomba and the Burnett that haven't seen vineyards for decades, and completely new viticultural locales such as Mount Tamborine and Mount Cotton—will soon lead to Queensland's wine production exceeding that of Tasmania.
Map ref: page 559 L9

TOOWOOMBA

Toowoomba is Queensland's largest inland city, with a population of 90,563, and it marks the start of the Darling Downs. Perched on the edge of the Great Dividing Range —125 km (78 miles) west of Brisbane—at an elevation of 800 m (2625 feet), and with over 1000 ha (2471 acres) of parks and gardens, Toowoomba has quite deservedly earned the title of the Garden City of Queensland. Its prosperity is

based to a large extent on the fertile soil of the Darling Downs.

Allan Cunningham first sighted the Downs in 1827, and he was soon followed by squatters; by the 1900s intensive agriculture had taken over. The Downs is a prolific producer of all types of grain crops, and in good years two crops can be harvested. In recent years, cotton has been more extensively grown.

The first settlement started at Drayton, around a store, a pub and a blacksmith's shop. A lack of water prompted many of the town's residents to move to 'The Swamp', as Toowoomba was first called. There are any number of theories as to where the name originated, but Thomas Alford, one of the early settlers in the region, named his house 'Toowoomba', and by the 1860s this had become the town's name.

When the railway arrived in 1867, the position of Toowoomba as the commercial and service centre for the Downs was assured. Around this time many of the city's finest buildings were constructed. The city has many reminders of its colourful past, including the magnificently restored City Hall, the impressive Empire Theatre, and the Royal Bulls Head Inn at

Drayton, now a museum operated by the National Trust. The Cobb and Co Museum houses Australia's largest collection of horse-drawn carriages and is the national centre for the research and conservation of Australia's horse-drawn vehicles.

The University of Southern Queensland is based in Toowoomba, and some of its schools date back to the nineteenth century.

Heritage walks and tourist drives are laid out around the city and its outskirts and provide an insight into the history and beauty of this country-style inland city. Toowoomba celebrates the coming of spring with the Carnival of Flowers, held in the last full week of September. A major attraction of this festival is the number of private residences that open their gardens to the public. The owners work for months to prepare for the home garden competition.
See also The Granite Belt Wine Region
Map ref: page 559 L7

WARWICK

Warwick is the second-largest city on the Darling Downs—with a population of 11,300—and it is in the southern region, on the banks

Flowerbeds in Toowoomba's botanical gardens.

of the Condamine River, 164 km (102 miles) south-west of Brisbane. Patrick Leslie set up a sheep station on the Condamine River back in 1847. The red rose is Warwick's floral emblem, and the Australian Rough Riders Association is based in the town, which has become known as the Rose and Rodeo City. The Rose and Rodeo Festival is held in late October, and since 1929, only war and severe drought have stopped the annual rodeo.

St Mary's Church and the Town Hall, built out of the excellent local sandstone, are worth a visit. The area around Warwick is also popular among fossickers, with gold, silver, agate, shell fossils and petrified wood being some of the treasures found in the region. People come from all around the world for the annual Rock Swap Festival, which is held over Easter.
Map ref: page 559 L8

The rope and tie event at the rodeo in Warwick, the oldest and best-known rodeo in Australia.

CENTRAL-EAST QUEENSLAND

In addition to the great natural wonder of the Great Barrier Reef, this region also boasts a string of idyllic islands, opalescent waters, dazzling sands and forested ranges. Manicured rows of bright green sugar cane add further colour to the coastal plain, while to the west, cattle stations sprawl across lands rich in gems, minerals and precious ores.

Agnes Water, in the south of the region, claims the title of Queensland's most northerly surf beach. Beyond here the rolling waves of the Pacific are muted by the coral rampart of the Great Barrier Reef, more than 200 kilometres offshore in the south, but sweeping closer as the coast stretches north. Within the calm waters between the outer reef (which lines the edge of the continental shelf) and the mainland are a myriad of low-lying coral atolls, cays and smaller reefs. The Whitsunday Passage, by contrast, is dotted with more than 70 'high' islands, both large and small; which rise abruptly from sparkling waters; rugged, rainforested and with fringing coral reefs, they are the peaks of a former coastal range submerged by rising sea levels.

The Fitzroy Basin and central tablelands were opened up to pastoralists by Ludwig Leichhardt who on his successful 1844 trek through here reported 'luxuriant grasses and herbs'. The city of Rockhampton began life in the 1850s as a river port for the area's cattle industry. Leichhardt also noted seeing coal—today huge open-cut operations mine Blackwater's thick seams. Further

west along the Capricorn Highway (named for the Tropic that it roughly follows) is the world's largest sapphire deposit, centred on Anakie; fossickers can collect a licence from nearby Emerald, named not for the gemstone, but for the colour of its pastures after rain. Clermont, in the centre of the region, is the State's oldest inland town. Further west is rugged sandstone country and dry plains, where stock rely on the reservoir of the great artesian basin for water. Charters Towers, in the northwestern corner, was once the centre of a thriving goldfield; called 'the World' by its residents—it had a stock exchange which never closed (the restored exchange building now houses a shopping arcade).

OPPOSITE: The Great Barrier Reef is made up of 2900 individual reefs and is home to many species. There are 1500 fish species, 400 corals, 4000 molluscs, 500 seaweeds and 215 species of birds.

Blackheath Thornburgh College, established in 1919, is one of several fine boarding schools in historic Charters Towers.

REGIONAL FEATURE

The Whitsunday Islands

Narrow-barred Spanish mackerel (Scomberomus commerson) normally weigh in at between 2 and 20 kg (4.4 and 44 pounds), although 55-kg (121-pound) specimens have been reported.

Vivid images of the Whitsunday Islands adorn billboards, magazines and travel agents' windows throughout Australia—and for good reason. This archipelago of more than 70 islands, located just off the Queensland coast between Bowen and Mackay, epitomises the kind of tropical haven we all dream of escaping to at least once in a while. Forest-clad slopes drop steeply to white-sand beaches, gleaming yachts drift across transparent turquoise waters, multihued birds dart through dense forests, shoals of brightly coloured fish shimmer over fringing reefs, and idyllic camp sites and bush cabins nestle in the shade of picture-postcard palms. This enchanting environment could so easily, like many others in Australia, have been ruined by settlement and overdevelopment, particularly given its tourism potential. But although several well-known resorts hug the islands' shores, they occupy only a small percentage of the total land area—only eight of the 70-odd islands are inhabited—and there is little that mars the magnificent scenery. Furthermore, the entire archipelago is now protected by several national parks, including Lindeman Islands National Park, Molle Islands National Park and Whitsunday Islands National Park, which protects 32 islands, including the largest, Whitsunday Island.

History

Part of the Cumberland and Northumberland island groups, the Whitsundays are continental islands, which means they were once part of the mainland. Indeed, until the end of the last ice age, when sea levels rose, the islands visible today were the peaks of a large coastal mountain range.

For thousands of years, Aboriginal peoples lived on some of the larger islands, such as Whitsunday, Hook and Lindeman, and traded with mainland peoples. The islanders had an abundance of resources

Usually seen on warm days near water, dragonflies have excellent vision and catch most of their insect prey on the wing. They also eat tadpoles and small fish.

at their disposal, including fish, crabs, dugong, wallabies, birds, yams and wild fruits, and lived well.

The European connection with the Whitsundays began on 3 June 1770, when James Cook sailed through the archipelago on his first voyage up the Queensland coast. Cook noted that the islands abounded in good, safe anchorages, and named them the 'Whitsundays' after the day on which they were first sighted (although, as it transpired, he was a day out, having forgotten to adjust his calendar when crossing what is now known as the International Dateline).

Over the next 100 years, many other mariners landed on the islands to replenish their supplies, but commercial exploitation of the archipelago's rich stocks of timber, fish and wildlife didn't get underway until the latter part of the nineteenth century. Then, settlers from the mainland established small sawmills on a number of the islands to cut hoop pine, while others started hunting dugongs for their oil and gathering trochus shells for the mother-of-pearl button industry.

Small-scale exploitation of these resources continued in the early twentieth century, when parts of the islands were leased to incomers, some of whom introduced sheep. At the beginning of the 1930s, several far-sighted residents began to build accommodation for tourists, giving rise to the industry that dominates the local economy today. Around the same time, state governments started to set aside large areas of the islands as reserves, ensuring that future generations would enjoy the Whitsundays' relatively pristine character.

Exploring the Whitsundays

The idea of swimming among the thousands of tropical fish and coral species that inhabit the adjacent Great Barrier Reef Marine Park is what draws the majority of visitors to the Whitsundays. Many of the islands have their own fringing reefs, allowing visitors to snorkel, dive and even reef-walk directly offshore. The clearest waters are usually to be found off the northern islands such as Hook, Langford, Border and

An aerial view of the south-eastern end of Whitsunday Island. Whitehaven Beach is on the far side of the peninsula.

Hayman is the most northerly island in the Whitsunday Group. Its resort, which occupies about one-fifth of the island, offers luxurious accommodation and a wide range of activities.

The sometimes deafening sound made by cicadas comes only from the males. It is produced inside the insect's abdomen by flexible membranes called tympanal organs.

Deloraine, though even there conditions may not be as good as on the outer Barrier Reef. Divers keen to explore further afield can, however, join organised tours to the outer reefs departing from some resorts and from Airlie Beach on the mainland.

The abundance and variety of coral and fish inhabiting the reefs is staggering; it's easy for snorkellers and divers to become spellbound when they first enter this amazing underwater world. But remember that currents around some of the islands are strong, so make sure you don't drift too far. For added safety, always swim with at least one other person. Take care not to damage fragile coral, and protect your feet with sturdy shoes when reef-walking.

Visitors can walk and rock-hop for miles along the beaches of the Whitsundays, but many of the islands also have marked bushwalking tracks that provide access to the heavily forested inland areas. On Whitsunday Island, a 1-km (0.6-mile) trail connects Dugong Beach and Sawmill Beach. At the end of Whitehaven Beach, one of the longest—6 km (3.7 miles)—and prettiest beaches in the archipelago (indeed, it was recently selected as Australia's most beautiful beach by a TV travel program), a trail follows a boardwalk around Hill Inlet and up to an impressive lookout at Tongue Point. Long Island has 13 km (8 miles) of graded trails, including the 3.5-km (2.2-mile) Circuit Track, which provides superb views of the Whitsunday Passage and other islands to the east. Even more expansive panoramas are available at the top of Mount Jeffreys on South Molle Island, reached via a 3-km (1.9-mile) return hike. The Spion Kop track, also on South Molle,

Red emperor inhabit deep waters.

provides a fine introduction to the islands' varied habitats, including rainforest, eucalypt forest and heathland, and takes in a flying fox colony as well as relics of Aboriginal occupation. Lindeman Island also has several trails, including the 8.5-km (5.3-mile) Loop Walk, which traverses open woodlands and rainforest, and climbs to a number of rewarding viewpoints.

Bushwalks like these provide extra opportunities for viewing the archipelago's captivating wildlife. There are relatively few mammals, though a group of rock wallabies lives on Whitsunday Island and there are a few colonies of flying foxes. Reptiles, however, are abundant, including green tree snakes, green tree frogs and Gould's goannas. These large lizards are particularly common near camp sites because they have realised that areas frequented by humans provide rich pickings. Take care not to leave out any food that may attract goannas, as some snacks may be harmful and all will blunt the reptile's natural hunting instinct.

Birdlife is prolific both in the forests and along the shores. Scan the trees for colourful forest kingfishers and parrots such as black cockatoos and rainbow lorikeets. On the beach, watch for ospreys and sea eagles spiralling in thermals and a wide variety seabirds scouring the shoreline. At night, the silence is often broken by the loud *book-book* call of the southern boobook or the mournful wailings of an eastern curlew searching for its mate. Green turtles and dolphins are regularly spotted in shallow water and humpback whales pass by during their migration from Antarctica to the tropics in June, returning south between late August and late October.

Fishing

For anglers, the Whitsundays offer a multitude of options. You can set up camp on one of the islands, tour in your own craft or charter a boat from Airlie Beach, Shute Harbour or Conway Beach, all of which offer fully equipped yachts, available with or without experienced crews. To be consistently successful when fishing in this area, you may need to venture onto the more exposed eastern coasts of the islands, and to troll a lure, drop a jig or soak a bait well away from the most popular anchorages and cruising grounds.

On the bottom-fishing front, species such as coral trout plus various emperors and cod can still be found in reasonable numbers. Top spots include Langford Island and its reef system, Hook Passage, Mackerel Bay, the eastern side of Hook Island, parts of the reef surrounding Deloraine Island, and the waters around Cid Island. The major pelagic species are mackerel (school, spotted and Spanish), queenfish, several kinds of trevally, cobia, black kingfish and various tunas. There are also reasonable numbers of small marlin and big sailfish to the north and east of the islands, particularly in late winter and spring.

The Spanish mackerel run along this coast traditionally hits its peak between July and October, although a few decent mackerel are caught in almost any month. The same is true of queenfish, tuna and cobia. Productive areas for these surface fish tend to be located on the east coasts of the outer islands. The waters around Langford, Deloraine and Haslewood

Starfish come in myriad colours.

islands, in Solway Pass and even around South Molle Island are particularly good for trolling, lure casting, jigging, and 'floater' fishing with lightly baited weights.

Access and Camping

Unless you arrive in your own boat, the easiest way to visit the Whitsunday Islands is to book a package with a tour operator. Options range from luxury resorts to multiday yacht tours. For independent travellers and campers, water taxis and various types of power and sail boats operate out of Airlie Beach, transporting visitors to and from numerous locations on the islands, including remote camp sites.

Camping in this unspoiled environment is hard to beat. Whitsunday Island has the best facilities, with the largest site at Dugong Beach on the west coast, and another sizeable site at Sawmill Beach, a popular anchorage. At Joe's Beach, a smaller, more secluded camp site is conveniently located for snorkeling on an adjacent reef. There is also a fine bush-camping site at Geographers Beach on Henning Island. Other islands with good facilities include North Molle (Cockatoo Beach) and Thomas Island (Sea Eagle Beach).

Permits are required for national park sites and are available from Queensland Parks and Wildlife Service offices. Campers must take their own drinking water to all islands except Whitsunday and North Molle, along with adequate food and two days' emergency rations in case bad weather delays their return. Fires are banned, so you will also need a gas stove if you wish to cook. A medical kit including vinegar for treating marine stings should be carried too.

Although the white-bellied sea eagle (Haliaeetus leucogaster) remains common around the Australian coastline, its numbers have declined where nesting grounds have been disturbed by urban and tourist developments.

Abundant along the north-east coast, the rainbow lorikeet (Trichoglossus haematodus) roosts and often travels in large flocks. It feeds mainly on nectar from eucalypts and banksias.

Places in
CENTRAL-EAST
QUEENSLAND

Round Hill Head near Seventeen Seventy, a distinctive landmark just north of Agnes Water.

AGNES WATER

Agnes Water (population 120) is situated 491 km (305 miles) north of Brisbane, on 5 km (3.1 miles) of curving white sand believed to be the most northerly surfing beach in Australia. The great weather and quiet, get-away-from-it-all location make it a perfect holiday spot. Just 6 km (3.7 miles) north of Agnes Water is the the town Seventeen Seventy, named after Cook made his second landfall in Australia. The locals consider that reason enough to claim the town as the rightful birthplace of Queensland.

Eurimbula National Park, covering the area where Joseph Banks collected plant specimens, is about 14 km (9 miles) from Agnes Water. There is a camping ground at Bustard Beach but campers need to be self-sufficient and bring water. Mount Colosseum National Park is accessed some 6 km (3.7 miles) out of Miriam Vale—this park is also undeveloped, so visitors must be self-sufficient here too.
Map ref: page 561 L10

Airlie Beach is the main jumping off point for the Whitsunday Islands.

AIRLIE BEACH

Airlie Beach, 1122 km (697 miles) north of Brisbane, is the gateway to the Whitsunday Islands. In 1987 Airlie Beach, Shute Harbour and Cannonvale were incorporated into the new town of Whitsunday. In the 1960s, Airlie Beach consisted of a single shop and a small group of holiday shacks. The 1970s and 1980s then saw an influx of residents with a corresponding growth in visitors. The trend has continued, and the completion of Lake Proserpine, a dam on the Proserpine River, will ensure a plentiful water supply for agriculture and the growing population. The local population—now 1440 —and visitors are well catered for by restaurants and top-quality holiday accommodation.

The tropical island resorts of Hayman, Hamilton, Daydream and South Molle, to name a few of the 74 islands that are just off the coast of Whitsunday and which lie inside the Great Barrier Reef, are only some of the attractions of the area. Sunshine, blue water and sandy beaches are the theme of the Whitsundays. Here you can hire a yacht and cruise the clear waters between the islands; take a seaplane out to the Great Barrier Reef for a snorkel; or try your skills at sea kayaking. On shore, the nearby Conway National Park, known for butterflies, is also worth a visit.

The calm, protected waters lend themselves to a variety of boating events, and these include the Hamilton Island Race Week in August, the Great Whitsunday Fun Race in September, the Grand Prix Series for 18-foot (5.5 m) skiffs, and the Hayman Big Boat Race.
Map ref: page 226 F2

ANAKIE

Anakie (population 400) is situated 939 km (583 miles) north-west of Brisbane, in probably the world's largest known sapphire deposit, which covers some 216 sq. km (83 sq. miles). Rubies and even the occasional diamond have also been found in the gemfields.

The word Anakie comes from an Aboriginal word meaning 'twin peaks'. The two satellite towns of Sapphire and Rubyvale, just north of Anakie, grew to cater for miners. The gemfield became commercially productive in the 1890s, and today most of the sapphires are sent over to Thailand for cutting.

The world's most valuable black sapphire was discovered in Anakie in 1935. Cut as the President's Heads Sapphire, it is now in the Smithsonian Institute in Washington DC. In August Anakie holds its Gemfest Festival.
Map ref: page 226 E9

AYR

Ayr (population 8300) is a sugar town in what is now, mainly due to irrigation, Australia's most productive sugarcane-growing area. Rice growing is also a major industry in the vicinity of the town.

Ayr is located 1276 km (792 miles) north of Brisbane and it was named after the birthplace in Scotland of the Queensland premier of the early 1880s. It was almost completely rebuilt after a rather disastrous cyclone in 1903. The town also suffered severe damage in the cyclone of 1959.

Home Hill, situated some 7 km (4 miles) to the south, is Ayr's sister town; the two towns are linked by the bridge over the Burdekin River. This is often referred to as the 'Silver Link'. The Ayr Nature Display houses one of the major collections of butterflies, shells, rocks and native fauna found in Australia.
Map ref: page 226 D1

BLACKWATER

From the late nineteenth century to the 1960s, Blackwater—823 km (511 miles) north-west of Brisbane —was originally a service centre for beef cattle. Then in 1962, a 7 m (23 feet) thick coal seam was discovered 20 km (12 miles) south-west of the town and, by the late 1960s, three mining companies were operating in the area.

Branch lines to Blackwater gave direct rail access to the power station and also to Gladstone; now the town is the coal capital of Queensland and has a population of 8000. Blackwater Mine, an open-cut operation just to the south of Blackwater, produces coking coal, which is exported.

Blackwater has an International Flag Display, consisting of 36 flags, representing the different nationalities that established the town between 1965 and 1970. It is the largest flag display in the world except for the United Nations Building in New York. Blackdown Tableland National Park, to the south, has spectacular cliffs and gorges and good bushwalks.
Map ref: page 561 F9

BOWEN

Bowen was the first settlement in North Queensland, founded in 1861 and it is named after George Bowen, Queensland's first governor. It It is 1162 km (722 miles) north of Brisbane, and has a population of 13,400.

Bowen is the mango capital of Queensland.

Bowen is widely known for its produce, in particular its mangoes and tomatoes: indeed, this district is often referred to as the market garden of Queensland. Bowen claims to have the best climate in Australia, with an average of eight hours of sunshine daily, and this undoubtedly accounts for the district's incredibly high production rate. Bowen also supports a major fishing fleet, and the beef industry is also flourishing.

The high, white stacks of salt, visible from the main road on the approach into town, are the result of evaporating the water from the saltwater ponds. North of the town is Abbot Point, the most northerly coal shipping port in Australia. Here coal from the Collinsville and Newlands fields is loaded from a jetty that extends almost 3 km (1.9 miles) into the sea.

Bowen is also renowned as the home of the oldest licence-holder in North Queensland, the North Australian Hotel, which first opened its doors in 1862. A set of murals, scattered throughout the town, depict the town's history.
Map ref: page 560 E2

CHARTERS TOWERS

Back in its 'golden years', between 1872 and 1916, the locals called Charters Towers 'The World'. At that time it had its own stock exchange (which was open around the clock, seven days a week), something like 100 gold mines, the same number of pubs and taverns and a population around the 30,000 mark so, for the residents, it certainly was their world.

Gold brought prosperity, and many grand buildings were constructed—indeed, Charters Towers is home to more National Trust properties than any other place in Queensland. The classical Victorian style features wide verandas and cast-iron lattice work. The old Venus gold treatment plant and stock exchange have been restored and are open for viewing. The old Civic Club, which was built by a group of businessmen around 1900, is another striking building that is worth a visit.

The last mine was closed in 1926, but with modern extraction methods many of the older mine dumps are being reworked. Charters Towers is 1367 km (849 miles) north of Brisbane, and has a population today of 9650. It is now the centre of a thriving beef industry, and cotton, tobacco, citrus trees, grapes and vegetables flourish on the fertile river flats. Charters Towers is also renowned for its boarding schools, which cater mainly for students from Papua New Guinea, the Torres Strait Islands and northern Australia.
Map ref: page 560 B2

Charters Towers has many buildings from late-nineteenth century gold-rush days.

CLERMONT

Clermont, 1000 km (621 miles) north-west of Brisbane, is the oldest inland settlement in northern Queensland and, again, it was the discovery of gold in the 1870s that started the boom. These days the town has a population of 2800, and the region breeds cattle and sheep and produces timber, wheat, sorghum and safflower.

Clermont has a rather chequered history. In 1870 and again in 1916 the Wolfgang and Sandy Creeks flooded the town, causing major loss of life. After these floods the town's houses, shops, school and even the two-storey hotel were hauled to their current site up and onto higher ground.

Tours of the Blair Athol coalfields, which contain the world's largest deposit of steaming coal, are conducted nearby. Copperfield, a deserted copper mining town, is located 6 km (3.7 miles) southwest of Clermont; a single chimney, rusted machinery and a cemetery are the only reminders of the long-gone boom days. The Clermont rodeo is held in September.
Map ref: page 560 D7

EMERALD

Emerald (population 13,300) is 896 km (556 miles) north-west of Brisbane, and is the hub of the Central Highlands and the centre for cattle, agriculture and tourism. It is also the centre for a major irrigation scheme based on water from Lake Maraboon, one of Queensland's largest water storages. There is only one old building in Emerald, as between 1936 and 1968, four devastating fires destroyed all but the railway station. The timber station was built in 1901, and is classified by the National Trust; it still services the Central Highlands area. Outside the town hall there is a 250 million-year-old fossilised tree, given to Emerald by BHP after it was found in 1979 during bridge building for the Gregory Mine. Nearby Lake Maraboon is a magnificent recreation area with a background of parks and mountains. The Pioneer Village and Museum is another must, as it depicts early life in the highlands. The town's cotton ginnery and the Gregory Mine are also open for tours.
Map ref: page 560 E8

A farmer with his dogs, working his property in eastern Queensland's agricultural region.

EUNGELLA NATIONAL PARK

This park, in the mountain ranges north-west of Mackay, protects a mix of tropical and subtropical rainforest, and is one of Queensland's most spectacular parks, with cloud-shrouded peaks, deep gorges and lush rainforest. Much of it is rugged and inaccessible, but the southern section, adjacent to the access road, is popular with campers and day visitors. The park can

The king orchid (Dendrobium rex) *is found in Eungella National Park.*

provide a special treat for visitors lucky enough to see one of the shy resident platypus in the creek by the camping area. Eungella National Park is adjacent to the town of Eungella, which is about 80 km (50 miles) west of Mackay.

The most popular activity in the park is bushwalking. The northern section is for experienced, well-prepared walkers only; the southern section around Broken River has a number of walking tracks. Back on the other side of Eungella township, a road turns off north towards Finch Hatton Gorge, which is also worth seeing and more walking tracks start here.
Map ref: page 560 F3

GEMFIELDS RESERVE

This reserve in western central Queensland, covering an area of 9000 ha (22,239 acres), is in an area famous for sapphires—it has produced world-class gems, some of them found by fossickers. The reserve is set aside for fossicking; licences are available on the fields or from the Department of Minerals and Energy at Emerald. The

gateway to the Gemfields is the township of Anakie, on the Capricorn Highway 42 km (26 miles) west of Emerald. Other towns on the fields are Sapphire and Rubyvale, respectively 10 and 18 km (6.2 and 11 miles) directly north of Anakie, and The Willows, about 37 km (23 miles) to the southwest. To avoid the extremes of heat and wet, the best time to visit is between March and October.
Map ref: page 560 E9

GLADSTONE

Gladstone is 545 km (338 miles) north of Brisbane. The key to its industrial growth is its excellent harbour, supported by the natural resources needed by industry—land, water, transport, coal, limestone and electricity.

Gladstone's growth from the time the Port Curtis pastoral district was proclaimed in 1854 to the 1960s was fairly slow, although it expanded rapidly after World War II when the port became a bulk-handling facility for coal from the vast Callide and Blackwater fields and for grain from inland Queensland. The building of the alumina plant in the 1960s and 1970s signalled an unprecedented growth rate. In the 1970s, Gladstone was

a small community of some 6000 people with a meatworks and some port trade. Today, the population is 37,500 and it is an area of giants, having the world's largest alumina plant, the State's largest power station and the State's busiest port, handling more tonnage than even Sydney, and soon to have Australia's largest aluminium smelter. Yet this industrial growth has not been at the expense of quality of life here.

Gladstone is also a tourist town, as it is the departure point for the southern section of the Great Barrier Reef. Charter boats cater for all, mainly servicing Heron Island (the most southerly resort island on the reef), and the uninhabited Masthead Island and North-West Islands, where campers are welcome provided they have permits.

There are also attractions in Gladstone itself. Gladstone Tondoon Botanic Garden is one of Australia's totally native botanic gardens, specialising in plants of the Port Curtis and Far North Queensland regions. The gardens extend over 55 ha (136 acres) and are located about 8 km (5 miles) from the city. Nearby Lake Awoonga has had its capacity increased over the years to service the power station and aluminium smelter, and the Lake Awoonga Recreation

With its fringing reef, Heron Island, off Gladstone, is a scuba diver's paradise.

Park has water-sports, magnificent scenery, family picnic area and even a tree-top restaurant.

A walk from the Auckland Park Waterfall—floodlit at night—up the 111 steps to Victoria Park gives panoramic views of the harbour and the islands. The major festival is the Harbour Festival, held over ten days at Easter time and timed to coincide with the finish of the Brisbane to Gladstone Yacht Race.
Map ref: page 561 K9

MACKAY

Mackay, 975 km (605 miles) north of Brisbane, started life as a port for the export of wool and tallow from the hinterland's cattle and sheep. Around 1865 the first sugar cane was planted, and by the mid-1880s there were 30 sugar mills processing the cane. Mackay then became the leading sugar district in Australia—a position it still holds as producer of a third of Australia's entire sugar harvest.

Between 1863 and 1906, most labourers in the cane fields were South Sea islanders who worked as indentured labourers. When the government later prohibited non-European immigration, hundreds of Greeks, Italians, Scandinavians, Spaniards and Maltese flocked to Queensland, and to the sugar industry in particular.

Today Mackay has a population of 58,641, and is a rich mix of nationalities. Just north of Mackay is one of the best artificial harbours

Sugar cane crops are burnt to remove leaves and weeds prior to harvest in June–December.

on the east coast—it also boasts the world's largest sugar terminal. To the south is Hay Point, one of the biggest coal-loading complexes in the world, with an annual capacity of 50 million tonnes (55.1 million tons). During the crushing season (July–November) there are tours of Farleigh Mill, a working sugar mill, and Polstone Sugar Cane Farm.

Mackay's heritage walk takes in the Police Station, the Court House and Commonwealth Bank, buildings that are all over 100 years old and listed with the National Trust. Greenmount Homestead, 18 km (11 miles) west of Mackay, houses possessions of the Cook family, the original European settlers in the region. West of the town is Eungella National Park; to the north is Cape Hillsborough National Park, which has rainforest that runs down to the beach and rocky headlands. Mackay is also a base for cruises that take visitors out to Brampton, Lindeman and Hamilton Islands and beyond to the Great Barrier Reef and the spectacular Whitsunday Islands.
Map ref: page 560 G4

MOUNT MORGAN

Driving into Mount Morgan (population 3164) is like going back in time. This former gold and copper mining town, 671 km (417 miles) north of Brisbane and a 30-minute drive south-west of Rockhampton,

is now quiet and peaceful after a hundred years of mining. The result of all this mining is the awe-inspiring 300 m (984 feet) deep crater. The town has so much history and so many fine buildings that the National Trust of Queensland and the Australian Heritage Commission have listed the entire town as a historic site.

Places not to miss include the Coronation Light in Anzac Park, built in 1902 to celebrate the coronation of King Edward VII, and the Mafeking Bell, cast at the mine at Mount Morgan from English pennies donated by children to celebrate the relief of Mafeking, South Africa, during the Boer War. It is outside the Scout Hut in Dee Street. Visitors can also take rides

behind one of the fully restored Hunslett locomotives that were purchased in 1904 and used at the mine until 1947. Not far out of town is the Big Dam, which is worth a trip for the water sports, a picnic or as a quiet spot for anglers to dangle their lines.
Map ref: page 561 J9

PROSERPINE

Proserpine is 30 km (19 miles) from Whitsunday and 1097 km (681 miles) north of Brisbane, and is the departure point for Airlie Beach, Shute Harbour and the Whitsunday Islands. This productive valley was named after Proserpina, the Roman goddess of fertility, and supports a very prosperous sugar industry. The population of the town is 3100. A visit to the folk museum which displays clothing and furniture of early pioneers is a must. Also worth a look is the wildlife sanctuary, which features a reptile house and a walk-through aviary. At the nearby aquarium you can watch colourful tropical fish being fed. There is also a very pleasant hike to Cedar Creek, in the rainforest-clad hills just behind Proserpine itself.
Map ref: page 560 F2

Carpet python (Morelia spilota).

North Keppel Island is a national park off the coast just north of Rockhampton.

ROCKHAMPTON

Driving into Rockhampton from the south, visitors cross the Tropic of Capricorn, which is marked by a huge metal sundial known as the 'The Capricorn Spire'. This region is the heartland of Australia's premium beef cattle industry, and recent estimates have calculated that the Fitzroy Basin beef herds number more than 2.5 million. The human population of the town is 65,000.

Rockhampton is 633 km (393 miles) north of Brisbane, and grew up around the spot where, in 1855, Colin Archer, who had sailed up the Fitzroy River as far as he could, bringing supplies to his property Gracemere, unloaded his cargo. A stroll around the Quay Street Historical Precinct will show you a number of outstanding buildings, including the city's second customs house, the former offices of the Mount Morgan Gold Mining Company, the Criterion Hotel, the former Queensland National Bank building and the former Union Bank of Australia building.

There is plenty to do and see on the whole Capricorn Coast. A short distance from Rockhampton, on the coast, is Yeppoon, the stepping-off place for visits to Great Keppel Island. Byfield State Forest, north of Yeppoon, is a pleasant, secluded rainforest environment; at Cooberrie Park Flora and Fauna Centre you can cuddle a koala or feed a kangaroo; at Koorana Crocodile Farm, feeding and cuddling are not recommended! Emu Park, down the coast from Yeppoon, has a 12 m (39 feet) high structure of pipes in the shape of a large sail, which commemorates James Cook's voyage in the *Endeavour*. North of Rockhampton are the Cammoo Caves and the Capricorn Taverns. Both cave systems are worth exploring, particularly the Cathedral cave in the Capricorn Taverns.

There are many festivals, rural shows and carnivals in and around Rockhampton. Central Queensland University's Multicultural Fair, held in August, and Rockhampton's Family Festival, in September, are two that should not be missed.
Map ref: page 561 J8

NORTH QUEENSLAND

Sugar is king on the fertile strip east of the ranges; here tropical beaches and offshore islands offer some of the Great Barrier Reef's finest scenery and resorts. Beef cattle rule on the inland plains, where stock routes and development roads link far-flung stations and isolated communities in some of Australia's wildest and most remote country; this is also the location of the fossil beds of Riversleigh, Australia's richest palaeontological site.

To the north-west are the renowned barramundi fishing grounds of the Gulf. The busy port of Townsville is the administrative, business, cultural and industrial centre of northern Queensland, and a major jumping off point for visitors to the reef. From here the Bruce Highway winds north through spectacular scenery—wide, palm-fringed beaches, towering rainforest and mist-shrouded ranges. The narrow-gauge lines that frequently cross the highway haul the sugar cane harvest into processing mills.

Offshore is a string of nearly 30 tropical islands, once a coastal mountain range, but cut off by rising sea levels at the end of the last Ice Age. The island peaks include lofty Hinchinbrook, Queensland's largest island, with forested slopes and pristine beaches preserved in a magnificent national park. The spectacular view across Hinchinbrook Channel—from just north of Ingham—takes in glossy green mangrove forest, rugged island and distant blue waters. This stretch of coast has one of the highest rainfalls in the country; Tully, which is completely surrounded by the lush greenery of sugar cane fields, is Australia's wettest town, and the constantly replenished racing waters of the nearby Tully River make it one of the best white-water rafting destinations known.

Immense cattle stations are scattered across the vast inland plains and flood-prone grasslands that reach to the southern shores of the Gulf. The first European to cross these wild lands was explorer Ludwig Leichhardt, in 1844, and later, in 1861, the explorers Burke and Wills. Settlements are small, few and far between. Burketown (named for explorer Robert Burke), the oldest, dates from 1861. The discovery of gold, and later silver, saw an influx of miners from the 1880s; the Gulflander train still runs once a week between Normanton and Croydon on a railway line laid then to carry ore from inland mines all the way to the coast.

OPPOSITE: *Aerial view of Normanton, near the coast on the Gulf of Carpentaria, in the heart of Queensland cattle country.*

Bedarra Island is the country's most expensive resort, featuring unspoilt rainforest, hidden caves, secluded beaches—and a well-stocked open bar.

REGIONAL FEATURE

Gulf Country

The Gulf of Carpentaria is a vast, relatively shallow body of warm, often turbid tropical water separating Queensland's Cape York Peninsula from Arnhem Land in the Northern Territory. Along its southern shore lies some of the wildest country in Australia, which is characterised by savannah and mangrove forests, swamps and mud flats, and maze-like river systems that are home to large populations of freshwater and saltwater crocodiles. Little changed since the first European explorers arrived in the middle of the nineteenth century, this region is sparsely populated, with only a few isolated settlements and cattle stations studding the wilderness. It's this relatively unspoilt, undeveloped character, however, that attracts a wide range of visitors, whether it be 4WD enthusiasts seeking off-road adventures, travellers tracing the footsteps of explorers and pioneers, or keen anglers drawn by the productive waterways.

Travelling in the Gulf Country is not to be undertaken lightly. Many roads are 4WD only, and may be impassable from late November until May, when cyclones and severe tropical storms occur regularly. Even during the dry season, you should make sure you have a well-equipped 4WD vehicle and carry ample fuel, water and food, as well as basic medical supplies. Always remember, too, that this is croc territory and the dangerous saltwater species is abundant on the shores of the gulf, in estuaries and along rivers—often well above the tidal limits. Take heed of all warning signs, camp at least 50 m (55 yards) from water, and avoid swimming in deep rivers. When fishing, stay well back from the water's edge, don't stand on logs over deep pools, and dispose of fish offal and other refuse far from your camp.

The Norman River and nearby Normanton were both named after Captain W.H. Norman who led a sea search for the missing explorers Burke and Wills in 1861.

History

The Gulf of Carpentaria became the site of the first recorded visit to Australia by a European explorer in 1606, when Dutch navigator William Jansz landed briefly on the eastern shore. He was followed by his compatriots Jan Carstensz, who sailed around the gulf in 1623, and Abel Tasman, who in 1644 followed the coastline from the Torres Strait southward round the entire gulf and then west to the Kimberley.

For the next 150 or so years, no other European sail broke the horizon until Matthew Flinders voyaged south from Torres Strait in November 1802, careening his leaking ship, the *Investigator*, on the shores of Sweers Island, just north of present-day Burketown. In 1841, John Stokes, in the *Beagle*, mapped the southern shores of the gulf, naming the Flinders River and the Albert River among other places. He rowed a whaleboat up the Albert River for more than 80 km (50 miles), reaching what he called 'the Plains of Promise', where he envisaged 'tapering spires rising from the many Christian hamlets that [would] ultimately stud this country'. He was clearly an optimist.

The first land-based European explorer to pass through this region was Ludwig Leichhardt. He and his party traversed the region en route from Moreton Bay to the remote outpost of Port Essington in the

Northern Territory in 1845, following the southern shore of the gulf from the Mitchell River on Cape York westward to the Roper River.

In 1855, Augustus Gregory travelled across the Top End from the Victoria River in the Northern Territory via the gulf to Moreton Bay on the east coast. His route followed the shore of the gulf from Roper Bar in the west to the Gilbert River in the east. Six years later, Burke and Wills reached a point just south of the coast, near present-day Normanton, where mangroves blocked their route to the sea. Dismayed, they returned south to Cooper Creek and their tragic fate. Search parties sent to look for them, including those led by McKinlay, Landsborough and Walker, travelled east and then south-east across the Gulf Country from the Albert River, where Burketown now stands, to the Pacific coast.

Burke's efforts were subsequently commemorated by the renaming of Carpentaria Township (originally settled in 1861) as Burketown in 1865. Burketown suffered some severe blows in its early days, including an epidemic of a tropical disease (possibly dengue,

typhoid or yellow fever) that decimated the population and forced some survivors to relocate to Normanton. However, even the slow growth of such centres encouraged others to settle and explore the region.

In 1872, D'Arcy Uhr, a former Burketown police magistrate, drove a herd of 400 cattle across the plains to the Top End despite strong resistance from local Aboriginal peoples. Soon after, Nat Buchanan drove 1200 head from central Queensland to a property near Darwin. In 1878, Buchanan set off again, this time with 20,000 head, which he drove all the way across the gulf, establishing a major stock route that would subsequently be used by other pioneer pastoralists such as the Durack and McDonald families.

Towns such as Normanton and Burketown continued to develop as service centres for the areas's thriving cattle industry, but were also boosted by the discovery of gold near Croydon in the 1880s. This led to the construction of the famous and still-operational Gulflander Railway between Croydon and Normanton and the erection of many grand buildings in both these towns. Though gold mining

The shoreline of Mornington Island. Mornington was named in 1802 by Matthew Flinders, after the Earl of Mornington, then Governor-General of India.

continues today on a small scale, Croydon is now a ghost town and the beef cattle industry, along with Karumba's busy fishing port, is once again the focus of the region's economic activity.

The Gulf Track

This 4WD tour takes you from Normanton, the gulf's largest settlement, along the coastal plains to Burketown. From there, travellers can either continue west to the Northern Territory or follow a loop south and east to return to Normanton. About half of the loop tour is sealed, but the road along the gulf and into the Northern Territory is rough going in places and a 4WD is definitely recommended.

NORMANTON TO BURKETOWN

Located on the Norman River, Normanton has a population of around 1200. Throughout the dry season, this number is swelled by visitors, many of whom use the town as a base for exploring and fishing the extensive tracts of low, marshy land and winding waterways nearby. Normanton has a good deal of character, with a number of classified historic buildings, including the shire offices and the railway station. Accommodation is available at a couple of hotels and at the local caravan park.

The Little Bynoe River near Burke and Wills' Camp 119. It was the explorers' last camp site before they reached the edge of the gulf on 11 February 1861.

Leaving Normanton, head south toward Cloncurry, and about 5 km (3.1 miles) from the Purple Pub, at a major road junction, veer right onto the dirt toward Burketown. For the most part, this is a reasonably good road, though immediately after the Wet it may be chopped up and late in the dry season it can become corrugated and incorporate long, deep stretches of bulldust—and you ain't seen deep bulldust until you've seen Gulf Country bulldust! Take great care, too, at creek and river crossings.

About 37 km (23 miles) from Normanton, and just before you get to the causeway across the Little Bynoe River, a track on the left leads 2 km (1.2 miles) to the site of Burke and Wills' Camp 119. Though it looks a little forlorn today, the ring of trees blazed by Burke still stands, and a number of monuments testify to the fact that this was the most northerly of the explorers' camps. Just north of this point, Burke and Wills were prevented from reaching the sea by an impenetrable barrier of mangroves. All they could do was taste the salty water and observe the rise and fall of the tide before returning southward.

If you plan to camp in this area, follow any of the tracks west from the monument and within 1 km (0.6 miles) you will come to the banks of the Little Bynoe where there are some pleasant sites. Don't forget that estuarine crocodiles inhabit these streams.

Returning to the main road, you cross the Little Bynoe and then, less than 3 km (1.9 miles) later, the Bynoe River. Another 3 km (1.9 miles) takes you to the Flinders River and its causeway. Cattle are common around these crossings early and late in the day, so drive carefully. On either side of the road here, a sea of golden grass stretches as far as the eye can see.

The Inverleigh Homestead turn-off is 71 km (44 miles) from Normanton, then another 73 km (45 miles) of dust needs to pass under the wheels before you reach the sidetrack to Wernadinga Homestead. Approximately 11 km (7 miles) west of the Wernadinga Homestead track junction you come to the Alexandra River. If the river is flowing, take the crossing slowly, as there are a number of deep holes in the riverbed. Once you reach the western bank, you will see a stock gate which may be open or closed. Pass through it and leave it as you found it.

Just beyond the gate, and 156 km (97 miles) west of Normanton, you come to a junction with the main Cloncurry–Burketown Road. Veer right here, and less than 2 km (1.2 miles) along the road turn onto the long and winding causeway across the Leichhardt River. The route passes close to a tree-shaded, sandy island that is probably the best camp site between Normanton and Burketown. A short distance downstream from the causeway, you'll find Leichhardt Falls. In summer, these 12-m (40-foot) cascades are a seething mass of water and spray; during the Dry, they slow to a trickle, but still constitute an impressive enough sight to warrant the walk.

Just beyond the island, you cross the main stream via a small concrete bridge where a somewhat puzzling sign on the upstream side says, in woven wrought-iron letters, 'God is'. A little further on, the road climbs the western bank of the stream and then, after another 1 km (0.6 miles), a track on the left leads to Floraville Homestead. If you turn left here and keep left at the next two minor track junctions, you end up about 1.5 km (0.9 miles) from the main road, at the monument to Frederick Walker. Walker led one of the parties that searched for Burke and Wills in 1861. Although he didn't find the explorers, he did discover their most northerly camp site, Camp 119. Later, while living in Burketown, Walker contracted the fever that nearly wiped out the whole town, and eventually he died at this remote and lonely spot.

Most of the creek crossings on the route from the Leichhardt River to Burketown are bitumen causeways, with the road in-between varying from a narrow dirt track to a well-graded road. Near Harris Creek, 57 km (35 miles) beyond the Leichhardt River, the bitumen begins and leads all the way to Burketown, 230 km (142 miles) from Normanton.

BURKETOWN AND BEYOND

Once one of Australia's most unruly towns, where nearly everyone carried a gun, Burketown is now one of its friendliest. As well as warm hospitality, you'll find accommodation and cold drinks at the local pub, the Albert Hotel/Motel; the general store supplies

Many of the Gulf Country's rock outcrops are surmounted by what look like piles of boulders. These formed as sedimentary layers were cracked and eroded by temperature changes, rain and wind.

basic food requirements and fuel. Turning left at the pub will take you to the local tourist office, and a camping ground just opposite.

There are a few historic sites in and around the town, including a tree blazed by the explorer William Landsborough, a cemetery and the historic wharf and post office. But it's the town's setting that usually delights visitors, offering dramatic views across the immense, flat plains toward the coast and, at night, a vast canopy of unbelievably bright stars.

If you are in the region in September or October and up early in the day, you may be lucky enough to see a unique weather phenomenon known as a 'Morning Glory'—a long tube of cloud that rolls in from the gulf. Such formations can reach incredible sizes, extending in a sweeping arc for hundreds of kilometres, and have a depth of 1000 m (3280 feet) or more. At times, they form as low as 50 m (164 feet) above the ground—an astonishing sight.

Leaving Burketown on the main road heading south-west, you reach a turn-off after 5 km (3.1 miles) which leads to Escott Lodge, 13 km (8 miles) away. This 225,000-ha (556,000-acre) cattle station caters for travellers with self-contained rooms, a camping ground, licensed restaurant, flights to nearby points of interest including the offshore islands, and boat hire. It also has fuel and basic supplies and a number of pleasant riverside camp sites (accessible by 4WD only). Escott is well known in fishing circles as a top spot for barramundi, so with a little luck you might also catch a magnificent feed.

Back on the main road and heading south, you reach a fork in the road 25 km (15.5 miles) from Burketown. From here, you can head west to the Northern Territory. The first part of this route takes you across the Gregory and Nicholson rivers and along a fairly rough road through scrubby vegetation to Hell's Gate Roadhouse. Named after the nearby limestone outcrop which, in the old days, was seen as the entrance to the even wilder and therefore more dangerous country to the west, the roadhouse has accommodation, meals, fuel and supplies. Nearby are some

The freshwater crocodile (Crocodylus johnstoni) *can be distinguished from its fearsome saltwater relative by its narrower snout and smaller build.*

spectacular escarpments and tranquil lagoons that are home to multitudes of waterbirds. From Hell's Gate, it's another 50 km (31 miles) to Wollongorang Station just across the state border, and, beyond that, a demanding 266-km (165-mile) drive to the next sizeable settlement, Borroloola. A sealed road leads from there to the Stuart Highway.

The other fork takes you to Gregory Downs, 92 km (57 miles) due south. The Gregory Downs Hotel, an old Cobb & Co staging post, has accommodation, food, fuel and supplies, and there are pleasant camp sites by the river. From here, you can venture west into Lawn Hill National Park (see p. 528), a remote but beautiful reserve that protects a dramatic swathe of country cut by the majestic Lawn Hill Gorge, where 60-m (200-foot) cliffs rise above a palm-fringed river. The World-Heritage-listed Riversleigh fossil deposits are also located nearby.

From Gregory Downs, take the Wills Developmental Road south-east to the Burke and Wills Roadhouse, 144 km (89 miles) away. Here you can join the Matilda Highway, which runs all the way from the New South Wales–Queensland border to the Gulf of Carpentaria (see p. 532). It's an easy drive through scrub and then coastal plains to return to your departure point at Normanton, where you complete a round trip of approximately 675 km (419 miles).

Fishing

Though the ocean bed here is for the most part mud, silt or sand with just a few outcrops of rock or coral, the Gulf of Carpentaria is nevertheless an extremely fertile body of water. It is particularly famous for its abundant prawns, which, in turn, attract large numbers of fish. But its richness also has much to do with the remarkable number of major waterways that drain into it, especially in the east and south where slow-moving rivers and streams meander in great muddy braids across the plains to the warm, shallow sea.

This combination of diverse marine life and varied habitats makes the gulf one of the country's top fishing destinations and ensures that a steady stream of anglers is prepared to undertake the long journey to its shores. Travel to the area is easiest during the dry season, but unfortunately this is the least productive time for anglers, especially those on the hunt for barramundi. Since travel during the peak of the wet season is potentially hazardous, the best option is to visit immediately after or before the Wet.

Northern saratoga (Scleropages jardini) respond most readily to lure-casting with spoons, spinners, plugs, small minnows and poppers.

The towns of Normanton and Burketown both make good bases for fishing expeditions. At Normanton, anglers can simply drop a line in the Norman River, or they can launch a boat near the wharf in order to explore further afield. Good barramundi fishing is available in the lower reaches of rivers such as the Flinders, Norman, Saxby and Carron, particularly from late March or April until June and again in October and November (check the current closed seasons before fishing). Upstream you'll also find sooty grunter (black bream), fork-tailed catfish and saratoga.

Around Burketown, the maze of waterways formed by the Gregory, Nicholson and Alexandra river systems could keep you busy for a lifetime. The barramundi fishing is particularly good here, and

higher up the rivers, sooty grunter, catfish, archer fish and freshwater long tom are prolific. Some waterways also hold pockets of northern saratoga.

On the lower reaches of the rivers, mangrove jacks, estuary cod, threadfin salmon and small queenfish are abundant, along with trevally, fork-tailed catfish, sharks, rays and sawfish. Mud crabs are also prolific.

Offshore, there is excellent fishing around the islands of Mornington, Bentinck, Denham, Forsyth, Sydney, Bountiful and Sweers. Mornington, the largest of the islands, is noted for barramundi, cod of several species, mangrove jacks, barracuda, mackerel, queenfish, cobia, prolific numbers of trevally and a wide variety of reef species. It is also one of the most reliable and productive areas in Australia for catching (or at least hooking!) the spectacular and highly prized giant herring or 'ladyfish'. Mornington and Sweers both have fishing lodges—Birri Fishing Resort on the former and Sweers Island Resort—and both islands can be reached easily by air from Burketown.

The plains along the edge of the Gulf of Carpentaria are often inundated for much of the Wet. In summer, their smooth surfaces make for relatively easy driving.

Places in
NORTH
QUEENSLAND

ATHERTON

Atherton (population 10,200) is 1727 km (1072 miles) north of Brisbane. It sits on the Atherton Tableland between Cairns and Innisfail and is 760 m (2494 feet) above sea level. It is the centre of a rich agricultural district, where maize is the main crop.

The town was named after John Atherton, who settled in the area around 1877. The town's beginnings were as a camp for timbergetters seeking elusive cedar trees. Later, the European and Chinese pioneers arrived, drawn to the area by the promise of gold and tin. They stayed, and laid the foundations of the rich agricultural industry; they also established the beef and dairy herds.

The Chinese built a joss house in 1900 which has been classified by the National Trust. Atherton's old post office houses a gallery, museum, visitor's centre and tearooms. US Flying Fortresses were based in the area during World War II. Crystal Caves, located in Main Street, houses a unique underground cave museum with some quite fascinating giant crystal formations, fossils and fluorescent minerals from around the world.

There is a walking track to the top of Hallorans Hill, where there are splendid views of the town and surrounding area. To the north-east of the town is the Tinnaroo Falls Dam, where you can swim or fish. Millaa Millaa Falls, which is in the south, is also attractive. For a different experience, take a steam train ride to Herberton. The Railco Steam Railways is a non-profit organisation, staffed mainly by volunteers, and operates the only full-sized steam locomotives in North Queensland. Two major festivals are held in Atherton each year: the Maize Festival is on in September and the Tableland Folk Festival is held in October.
Map ref: page 563 L6

BURKETOWN

Burketown is a small town with a population 210 and is located on the Gulf of Carpentaria, 2093 km (1300 miles) north-west of Brisbane. It is the oldest town on the Gulf, being first settled in 1861, when pastoralists opened up enormous cattle runs in the region.

With wetlands to the north and drier grasslands to the south, the area continues to support a substantial beef industry. From its early days, Burketown was considered wild and lawless, somewhat akin to the cowboy towns of the American Wild West.

Barramundi from a waterhole near Burketown.

The town was originally known as Carpentaria Township, but it was later renamed after the explorer Robert Burke, who crossed the region in 1861 during his ill-fated expedition from Melbourne to the Gulf. Burketown hosts the World Barramundi Championship over Easter, and also the Gregory Canoe Race, which is in May. Races and rodeos are held in July.
Map ref: page 562 C7

CARDWELL

Cardwell is 1523 km (946 miles) north of Brisbane, sandwiched between the ocean and the mountains. With the highest rainfall in Australia, the rich hinterland yields a great variety of produce, including beef, sugar cane, tea and bananas. One of the first northern towns to be settled, Cardwell was once the only port between Bowen and Somerset, at the tip of Cape York, but the rapid growth of Townsville put an end to further development. Cardwell today has a population of 8850, and is a popular fishing and holiday town. It is within easy reach of its main attraction, Hinchinbrook Island, Australia's largest island national park.
Map ref: page 563 M7

CHILLAGOE

Chillagoe is an extremely tiny town (population 220) situated on the Burke Development Road, 209 km south-west of Cairns and 1899 km (1179 miles) north-west of Brisbane. It was once a major mining town, but these days relies almost solely on the tourist dollar. In the early 1900s a large proportion of the lead, silver and copper mined in Queensland came from around Chillagoe. The mines also yielded gold, tin, zinc, fluorspar, wolfram and molybdenum. Mining is now confined to one quarry, which crushes limestone, although a recent discovery of rare blue marble deposits may again bring Chillagoe to the attention of world markets. An excellent museum displays the old copper smelters. Another local attraction is the Chillagoe–Mungana Caves National Park, which are 8 km (5 miles) south of the town. This park is noted for its splendid limestone caves. In May crowds pour into Chillagoe for the annual rodeo and races.
Map ref: page 563 K6

GEORGETOWN

Georgetown, 1955 km (1214 miles) north-west of Brisbane, started life as a gold town serving the booming Etheridge Goldfields. Its population today is 340—very much reduced from the 3000 in the heady days of the 1870s.

The area now supports cattle-raising but mining is still booming. The Kidston Gold Mine was reopened in 1985 and is now one of Australia's major producers, delivering up to 6 tonnes (6.6 tons) of the valuable metal each year. Georgetown is quite naturally a favourite with fossickers but not just for the gold—gem collectors will enjoy the Agate Creek Mineral Reserve, as it contains some of the world's best quality coloured agates and it is located just south of the town. The nearby Tallaroo Hot Springs are also worth seeing.

Eastern yellow robin
(Eopsaltria australis)

Being positioned at a major road intersection, the town is also a popular stop for the massive beef road trains that ply the lonely highways. The small town of Forsayth, 40 km (25 miles) south of Georgetown, is the terminus for trains from Cairns; the Cairns–Forsayth rail journey only takes 24 hours!
Map ref: page 563 H7

The Atherton to Herberton steam train is run by a group of railway enthusiasts.

HINCHINBROOK ISLAND NATIONAL PARK

This is Australia's largest island national park, rugged and richly vegetated, about halfway between Townsville and Cairns. The island cannot be reached by vehicle and its tracks are wide enough only for walkers. The backbone of the island is a chain of rugged granite peaks in the south, giving way to lesser peaks in the north-west, and offset by the eastern sandy beaches and the western mangrove swamps.

The highest point on the island is Mount Bowen, 1142 m (3747 feet); its spectacular north face drops in cliffs and rocky forested slopes almost to sea level. Bush-walking and camping are popular on the island and there are a number of tracks. A boardwalk along one of Missionary Bay's southern creeks provides a path through dense mangroves. Then a track leads through a sandy area and over dunes to the open eastern beach at Ramsay Bay. From here, a 32 km (20 mile) track (Thorsborne Trail) runs down the eastern side of the island, sometimes paralleling the beach, sometimes winding inland. Map ref: page 563 M8

INGHAM

The climate and soil in the region around Ingham—1471 km (913 miles) north of Brisbane—were perfectly suited to sugar cane, which was introduced back in the early 1870s. The town has a population of 5700, and continues to prosper from its sugar production; the region produces some three million tonnes (3.3 million tons) of sugar cane a year. The town's other claim to fame is that the ballad *Pub with No Beer* is said to have its origins here, at Lee's pub. From all accounts, in 1942, after the Battle of the Coral Sea, the Americans drank the pub dry in celebration of the victory.

The nearby Wallaman Falls National Park is a popular spot with visitors, and the Jourama Falls National Park, south of the town, has an attractive picnic and camping ground beside Waterview Creek and its waterfalls.

The region has a strong Italian and Spanish Basque background, illustrated by the ornate family mausoleums in the Ingham cemet-

The coastline on the eastern side of Hinchinbrook Island—the only way around this island is by bushwalking.

ery—the Italian Festival, held in May, is a major event celebrating this heritage. The Maraka Festival, which takes place each October, highlights the sugar industry. Map ref: page 563 M8

INNISFAIL

Innisfail is 1614 km (1002 miles) north of Brisbane, and has a population of 8150. Its economy is primarily based on sugar, although tea, fishing, timber and dairying also play a big role. Fishing, particularly, is a very important industry here, and prawn trawlers, line fishing boats and mackerel boats can often be seen anchored in the Johnstone River.

Like Ingham, the character of the district was established with the influx of migrants, mainly Italian, after World War I. The town and the area have retained

A roadside trailer selling tea at an Innisfail tea plantation.

that very cosmopolitan mix ever since. Many Chinese settled in the area, and the Joss House they built still stands in Ernest Street. In the 1950s, Dr Alan Maruff started growing tea commercially at Nerada, west of Innisfail, and over the years the production of tea from the Nerada Plantation has continued to increase. Tours of the plantation are conducted.

At Mena Creek, south of Innisfail, are the ruins of Paronella Park, a Spanish-style castle that was built by a migrant named José Paronella. There are also walks through rainforest and stands of bamboo and kauri pine to Mena Creek and Teresa Falls. Mount Bartle Frere, north of the town, is the highest mountain in Queensland; a hiking track leads to the top and offers some magnificent views of the surrounding region. Map ref: page 563 M6

KARUMBA

Karumba, situated at the northern end of the Matilda Highway, 2125 km (1320 miles) north-west of Brisbane, was named after a local Aboriginal tribe. Eight kilometres (5 miles) from the town is Karumba Point, the only stretch of beach in the Central Savanna that can be accessed by road. The sunsets from this beach are exceptionally beautiful. Karumba is a small town (population 620), and is considered by many to be extremely friendly, casual and laid-back, perhaps a bit rough around the edges, but a great town to visit and stay awhile.

The only Queensland port in the Gulf of Carpentaria, Karumba is a major stop for the prawn trawlers operating in the Gulf and the Arafura Sea, and is one of Australia's largest prawn processing centres. The Empire Flying Boats used Karumba for repairs and refuelling on their way to Britain from Australia. It was also a base for the flying-boat Catalinas during World War II—the old slipway is still used today as a boat ramp.

Anglers know Karumba because of the barramundi in its wetlands, which extend for 30 km (19 miles) towards Normanton. In 1992, a group of anglers formed the Gulf Barramundi Restocking Association. They spawn fingerlings to replenish stocks in the Gulf rivers. The Barraball is held at the end of each year, and people come from all over to celebrate the end of yet another barramundi fishing season. Map ref: page 562 E6

LAWN HILL NATIONAL PARK

This spectacular oasis in arid far north-western Queensland boasts a beautiful creek lined by lush tropical vegetation winding through a gorge of multicoloured sandstone. This park has been progressively enlarged, and it is now one of Queensland's largest. A notable inclusion in 1992 was the Riversleigh Section, protecting this area's internationally significant fossil deposits. The enormous Lawn Hill Creek, fed by numerous springs, flows through fissures in the Constance Range, with walls of orange, red and grey sandstone falling 60 m (197 feet) to the pools and waterholes. Rainforest vegetation in this oasis includes cabbage palms, figs and the prominent dark green, broad-leaved Leichhardt trees.

Among the large numbers of birds and other animals are wallaroos, the rare rock ringtail possum and fairy martins. The creek itself is home to crocodiles, but they are the harmless freshwater variety. The upper and middle sections of the gorge also offer a chance to go for a swim or do some boating.
Map ref: page 562 A8

Magnetic Island with its many bays and beaches is only a ferry ride from Townsville.

MAGNETIC ISLAND

Magnetic Island is 8 km (5 miles) and about 20 minutes by fast ferry from Townsville, and 1379 km (856 miles) north of Brisbane. Captain Cook named the island in June 1770 when his 'compass would not travis well when near it'. Just over 2000 people live on this beautiful island, which has more than half its 5184 ha (12,810 acres) protected as national park. There

is a host of activities to satisfy visitors here, including water sports such as snorkelling, scuba diving, waterskiing and swimming and, of course, fishing. Wildlife abounds on the island, particularly koalas, which are numerous and roam freely. For the birdwatchers, some 160 species have been recorded on Magnetic.

There are 23 bays and beaches all around Magnetic Island, and buses run regularly between the

towns. Bicycles, mopeds or minimokes can be hired. There are also 24 km (15 miles) of walking tracks, and tours of animal reserves and trips to the Great Barrier Reef. All budgets are catered for with the range of accommodation available and the shopping facilities and eating establishments are excellent.
Map ref: page 563 N9

MISSION BEACH

Mission Beach is 1608 km (999 miles) north of Brisbane, and has a population of 3525. Fourteen kilometres (9 miles) of coastline and wide, white sandy beaches met by rainforest make up the Mission Beach area, which includes the settlements of Bingal Bay, Garners Beach, Narragon Beach, Clump Point and Wongaling Beach. The Cutten brothers established a farming industry here in the 1880s, growing pineapples, tea and coffee. Now, sugar cane and bananas dominate the region's agriculture. In 1912 an Aboriginal mission was established on what is now South Mission Beach, hence the name. Tourism is a growth industry in North Queensland and Mission

Lawn Hill National Park with Lawn Hill Creek and its sandstone gorge has been a site of Aboriginal occupation for at least 35,000 years.

The commercial centre of Townsville crowds around Ross Creek, with the city's international port on Cleveland Bay.

Beach attracts a fairly large share of visitors. From Clump Point you can take a day trip to Dunk Island, just 4 km (2.5 miles) away. Dunk is also the access point, by water taxi, to Bedarra Island, famous for its very exclusive resorts.
Map ref: page 563 M7

NORMANTON

Normanton (population 1150) is 2053 km (1275 miles) north of Brisbane, on the Norman River, 80 km (50 miles) from the coast. It is the administrative centre for the Carpentaria Shire. The explorer Ludwig Leichhardt and the Burke and Wills expedition passed through this area, in 1844 and 1861 respectively.

Normanton began life as a cattle port but later boomed during the goldmining at Croydon and the copper and silver mining at Cloncurry. It was around that time, between 1888 and 1891, that the unusual railway line was constructed between Normanton and Croydon. The famous railmotor, known as the Gulflander, leaves the grand old station at Normanton every Wednesday on its leisurely trip to Croydon, 152 km (94 miles) away. The trip takes over four hours, stays overnight in Croydon and then the train makes its unhurried way back to Normanton. The sleepers are of a hollow steel construction that can be filled with mud, sand, or whatever, making ballast unnecessary on the track. Amazingly, 95 per cent of the track is still the original and is in surprisingly good condition.

There are several landmarks in and around the town that are all worth a visit. In the Carpentaria Shire Council Park is a replica of 'Krys, the Savanna King', the largest recorded saltwater crocodile

taken in Australia. It measured 8.6 m (28 feet) and was shot in the Norman River in 1958 by Krystina Pawloski. The National Hotel—or Purple Pub, as it is better known—was built in the early 1900s and has survived floods (boats were hitched to the veranda in 1974), and also a fire, to become a major attraction. Camp 119, the last camp of Burke and Wills just before they reached the Gulf of Carpentaria, is found on the road to Burketown, on the banks of the Little Bynoe River. The Normanton Barra Classic fishing competition is held on the weekend before Easter and it is followed by the World Barramundi Championship at Burketown, held over Easter.
Map ref: page 562 E7

TOWNSVILLE

Townsville is 1363 km (846 miles) north of Brisbane. It is a thriving international port and Australia's largest tropical city, with a population of 124,925. It lays claim to having 320 days of sunshine a year and to receiving three-quarters of its annual rainfall in the wet season, between October and March. Cyclones also feature in the city's sultry tropical climate.

The small settlement on Cleveland Bay at the mouth of Ross Creek had a slow start, and it was not until John Melton Black persuaded Robert Towns, from Sydney, to invest in a boiling-down works for the cattle industry that there was some growth. Thousands of labourers from the South Pacific worked the sugar and cotton fields and the coffee plantations. Copper was found at Einasleigh in 1866, and the discovery of gold at Cape River, Ravenswood and Charters Towers soon followed, establishing

Townsville as a regional centre. Other factors in the city's growth were the railway from the west, which terminated at Townsville, and the region's first meat-freezing works, established in 1892 at Ross River. During World War II, Townsville was a major staging base for US and Australian troops, due mainly to its strategic position near the South Pacific region. In 1942, the town was bombed three times by Japanese aircraft, but no damage was done.

There are many historic buildings in Townsville, particularly around the waterfront park area. The typical Queenslander, high-set on stilts, of timber construction and with verandas, is very common.

Townsville is the northern centre for higher education, being the home of James Cook University, formerly the University College of Townsville, which specialises in marine biology, and of the Great Barrier Reef Marine Park Authority and also the Australian Institute of Marine Science. The city is also home to the North Queensland Cowboys rugby league team.

In 1986 the city of Thuringowa was officially declared; it shares a common boundary with Townsville, and the two are promoted as twin cities. Thuringowa is the fastest growing city in Queensland and currently it has a total population of around 40,000 living in an area of 1872 sq. km (723 sq. miles), and a growth rate exceeding 6 per cent per annum.

The Townsville Town Common Environmental Park is a refuge for brolgas, jabirus and also other wetland birds during the

wet season. They move out when the swamps dry up and crack. The Great Barrier Reef Wonderland, with its walk-through underwater tunnel, giving a great all-round view of the coral and the fish, is well worth a visit.
Map ref: page 563 N9

TULLY

Tully has a population of 3100 and lies south of Innisfail—and 1565 km (972 miles) north of Brisbane—in one of Australia's highest rainfall areas. Tully was originally a pastoral area known as Banyan. When the town was surveyed it was named Tully after a member of Dalrymple's 1864 expedition.

The town supports a thriving sugar cane, tea and banana growing area. The Tully Sugar Mill was constructed in 1925, the last of the sugar mills built in Queensland. The mill has an assigned area of 24,000 ha (59,304 acres), from which an annual crop of some two million tonnes (2.2 million tons) is harvested between June and November each year. Twenty-nine harvesters are employed. The cane travels over 200 km (124 miles) of light gauge rail to the mill for crushing. Some 230,000 tonnes (253,460 tons) of sugar results, and this is exported through the bulk sugar terminal, which is at nearby Mourilyan Harbour.

During the crushing season, from June to December, the mill is open for tours. The Kareeya Power Station, on the wild Tully River, is also open to the public. For thrill-seekers, the Tully River is famous for its whitewater rafting and it is well worth taking a day trip.
Map ref: page 563 M7

Whitewater rafting guide at Tully River.

OUTBACK QUEENSLAND

The semi-arid rolling downs, now covered in knee-high Mitchell grass, once formed the bed of a shallow inland sea. Fossilised bones of the huge dinosaurs that once roamed here have been uncovered, with *Muttaburrasaurus* named after a local town, and dinosaur footprints pit a now rock-hard mudflat near Winton. This is now sheep and cattle country steeped in history, from the landmark shearers' strike to fame as home of 'Waltzing Matilda'.

Brisbane

Emus and grazing red and grey kangaroos are frequently sighted from the roads and brolgas congregate around marshes during the spring breeding season. The large Diamantina Gate National Park is centred on the well-watered areas of the enormous Diamantina River floodplain.

Luckless explorers Burke and Wills trudged through here in 1860 and 1861; reports of pastures brought back William Landsborough, searching for them, led to a scramble for pastures around what is now the cattle centre of Hughenden. Crossing the region is the Matilda Highway, named for the song composed by Banjo Paterson at Dagworth Station; now Australia's unofficial national anthem, it had its first public airing in Winton in 1895. Winton was also the birthplace, in 1920, of the airline QANTAS; Cloncurry, to the north, pioneered the Royal Flying Doctor service. In 1891 striking shearers gathered in Barcaldine's main street under a stately ghost gum in meetings that led ultimately to the formation of the Australian Labor Party; still standing, the gum is now known as 'The Tree of Knowledge'. Away to the north is Camooweal, Queensland's westernmost town, which arose at the junction of historic stock routes and is now a stopping point for road trains carrying beef from surrounding stations. In Longreach the Stockman's Hall of Fame honours the pioneers of the inland in a purpose-built corrugated iron, sandstone and timber structure housing a range of exhibits and interactive displays.

Also in the region is Mount Isa, the State's most important mining centre, with its rich reserves of copper, lead, silver and zinc. Smelter chimneys tower above the city; below is the country's largest underground mine. Mount Isa's multicultural population is made up of more than 50 nationalities, including Australia's largest Finnish community.

OPPOSITE: The ranges around Mount Isa, a major mining town and service centre in the Queensland outback. This city administers an area about the size of Switzerland.

A road train driver at Hughenden inspects his rig. These enormous trucks—one can weigh as much as 115 tonnes (127 tons)—ply the outback transporting livestock.

REGIONAL FEATURE

The Matilda Highway

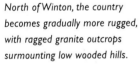

The sculpture outside this hotel in Winton was created for the town's centenary. Its subject refers to the settlement's original name of Pelican Water Hole.

The Matilda Highway is a tourist route, made up of a number of shorter roads, that leads from the New South Wales–Queensland border to the Gulf of Carpentaria. It's a terrific way to travel the length of the state and takes in some of the country's most important outback towns, majestic scenery and fascinating historic sites. Although the entire route is sealed, a 4WD is useful for exploring side roads.

From the Border to Longreach

The trek starts at the border town of Barringun (see South-West Queensland map), which has fuel and basic accommodation, including a camp site. The road north from here is bordered in some places by sweeping grasslands, in others by thick scrub. After 119 km (74 miles), you come to Cunnamulla, a service centre for the local pastoral industry.

Continuing north for 194 km (121 miles) takes you to Charleville (see South-East Queensland map), one of the biggest outback towns in Queensland. Situated, like Cunnamulla, on the Warrego River, Charleville was first settled in the 1860s. In 1893, it became a base for the American company of Cobb & Co, which continued to construct its famous stagecoaches here until 1920. Just a couple of years later, Qantas began its first regular air services between Charleville and Cloncurry, further north.

The road follows the Warrego River for another 84 km (52 miles) to Augathella, which has a hotel, motel and caravan park; then, 116 km (72 miles) further north, you come to Tambo. This is one of the region's oldest towns, having been settled in 1863, and the rich grazing land that first attracted settlers is still the lifeblood of the area. Tambo is a good base from which to head 120 km (75 miles) east and explore the remote Salvator Rosa section of Carnarvon National Park.

North of Winton, the country becomes gradually more rugged, with ragged granite outcrops surmounting low wooded hills.

About 57 km (35 miles) north of Tambo, you cross the Barcoo River, one of the major tributaries of Cooper Creek. There is a pleasant camp site here on the northern bank, away from the road.

Continuing north for 40 km (25 miles), you reach Blackall, home of star shearer Jackie Howe. In 1892, he clipped 321 sheep in 8 hours using hand shears—a record that still stands today and wasn't beaten by mechanical shears until the 1950s! Blackall is the centre of a rich pastoral region widely regarded as the state's premier merino sheep and cattle-stud area.

About an hour's drive and 107 km (67 miles) north of Blackall is Barcaldine. This town was the focus of the 1891 shearers' strike, which was the catalyst for the foundation of the Australian Labor Party. The Australian Workers' Heritage Centre, opened in 1991, commemorates those fraught days with an interesting photographic exhibition and museum.

Head west from Barcaldine for 80 km (50 miles) to the village of Ilfracombe, then travel another 27 km (17 miles) to the thriving township of Longreach on the scenic Thomson River. A fascinating town, Longreach has an excellent range of sights, services and accommodation, and merits at least an overnight stay. Its Stockman's Hall of Fame is one of the nation's best museums and a vivid reminder of the achievements of the pioneers who opened up this country.

The Longreach region was first explored by Augustus Gregory in 1858 and, although the area was settled in the 1870s, the town wasn't gazetted until 1887. The railway arrived in 1892 and in the early twentieth century the flourishing sheep industry brought the area great wealth. In 1922, Longreach became the headquarters of Australia's first airline, Qantas, following the company's maiden flight between Longreach and Winton in February 1921. Between 1922 and 1930, Qantas built seven aircraft here—the first planes to be constructed in Australia.

Longreach to Karumba

For much of the 174 km (108 miles) from Longreach to Winton, the road runs arrow-straight, with the vast grasslands broken by only by widely scattered outcrops. About 120 km (75 miles) north of Longreach, Lorraine Station offers accommodation and camping. Guests can also participate in the daily activities of this 30,000-ha (74,000-acre) working property.

Winton, situated 174 km (108 miles) north of Longreach, was founded in 1875. It holds the honour of having been the site of the first public recital of Banjo Paterson's famous song 'Waltzing Matilda', in 1895, and the first Qantas board meeting, in 1921. The town also boasts its fair share of historic architecture and a fine museum.

A signpost 145 km (90 miles) north of Winton points to Combo Waterhole, the billabong that in-

The flat, grassy plains that line the highway near Longreach are used mainly for grazing sheep. The area is thought to have about 800,000 sheep and 20,000 beef cattle.

spired 'Waltzing Matilda'. About 20 km (12.5 miles) further north, the famous Blue Heeler Hotel is the first sight to greet you as you enter Kynuna, and you'll always find a warm welcome and cold beer here.

Another famous watering hole is one of the highlights of McKinlay, 75 km (47 miles) beyond Kyuna. Reached by way of a sidetrack, the Walkabout Creek Hotel, which featured in the *Crocodile Dundee* films, has fuel—some of the cheapest around—drinks, food, cabins and a camp site.

By the time you reach the junction with the Flinders Highway, 14 km (8.5 miles) east of Cloncurry and 91 km (57 miles) from McKinlay, you are travelling through scraggy hills. Birthplace of the Royal Flying Doctor Service in 1928, the 'Curry is an important service centre for the local beef and mining industries. The surrounding country, with numerous small settlements tucked into rugged, picturesque ranges, is well worth exploring.

Leaving Cloncurry, turn off the main Flinders Highway onto the narrower Burke Developmental Road. When you pass the historic pub at Quamby, 43 km (26.5 miles) further north, you are still in rolling range country, but 137 km (85 miles) later, when you reach the Burke and Wills Roadhouse (see North Queensland map), the scenery has changed to flat scrub. Fuel, basic supplies, and accommodation are available at the roadhouse.

The scrub comes to an end after 80 km (50 miles), at the Bang Bang Jump-up, where the road drops to the Gulf Plains. Continue across the plains to Normanton, 194 km (121 miles) north of the Burke and Wills

Roadhouse and 374 km (232 miles) from Cloncurry. Normanton is the shire headquarters and an important service centre with several interesting historic buildings.

Head north out of the town across the river. At a major junction 29 km (18 miles) further on, the bitumen swings west and leads 40 km (25 miles) across flood plains to Karumba. A small but significant fishing port, it has a hotel and caravan park, fuel, basic foodstuffs and almost anything you need for fishing. When you come to a halt here on the shores of the Gulf of Carpentaria, you will have travelled a total of 1786 km (1109 miles) from your departure point on the New South Wales border.

Enormous road trains regularly make the long journey from outback centres to east-coast cities. Each vehicle can weigh up to 140 tonnes (154 tons) and measure 53 m (174 feet) in length.

Places in
OUTBACK
QUEENSLAND

BARCALDINE

Barcaldine—1066 km (662 miles) north-west of Brisbane and with a population of 1730—is known as the Garden City of the West and is the centre of a major wool-growing and cattle-raising district.

The town was established in 1886 as the terminus of the Rockhampton railway. Cobb and Co coaches set out from the town across the State up until 1914. In 1887 artesian water was located, giving Barcaldine a ready source of water. The town's citrus orchards attest to the efficacy of the bore water; however, it made the locally brewed beer totally undrinkable!

The agricultural district surrounding Barcaldine is cattle country.

Barcaldine is famous as the strike headquarters for the six-month shearers' strike in 1891. Over 1000 shearers camped in and around the town and their march in May 1891 was Australia's very first May Day march. From this turbulent period the Australian Workers Party was created, which eventually became the Australian Labor Party.

The 'Tree of Knowledge', a large gum tree that is now at least 200 years old, is where the striking shearers gathered for their meetings. This tree is now the focal point of a garden area, which features a monument shaped as shearing blades bearing the names of the 13 men who were jailed as a result of the shearers' strike.

Mad Micks Hoppers and Huts Funny Farm in Pine Street is worth a visit. Enjoy billy tea and damper, then see relics of outback history, including a bush shearing shed, a slab-style Cobb and Co changeover station, an art gallery and a marvellous antique doll display.
Map ref: page 565 N9

BLACKALL

This district was originally explored by Thomas Mitchell in the mid-nineteenth century, as he followed the Barcoo River. Blackall, which was named after the second governor of Queensland, Samuel Wensley Blackall, is 959 km (596 miles) north-west of Brisbane and has a population of 2000.

The town has also a reputation for producing some of the best sheep and cattle in Queensland. In 1885 the State's first artesian bore in was sunk here, but unfortunately the water was undrinkable.

Shearer Jacky Howe set the world record for hand-shearing in Blackall in 1892, by shearing 321 sheep in under eight hours. In the same year he set a machine-shearing record of 237 in eight hours at Barcaldine Station. His machine shearing record was not broken until 1950.

The steam-driven Blackall Wool Scour, 5 km (3.1 miles) north of town, was built in 1908. It is a rare link to the past, as it is the only remaining example of the 52 steam-driven wool scours that were built in Australia. In September the Spring Time Affair is held; this is followed in October by the annual rodeo.
Map ref: page 565 N10

Barcaldine is on the Landsborough Highway, part of a route known as the Matilda Highway.

BOULIA

Boulia, 1593 km (989 miles) north-west of Brisbane, is the centre of a massive shire that has a human population of only 520 people but there are more than five times as many sheep and cattle. Burke and Wills passed through the area in 1860 and named the Burke River and Wills Creek. The town is on the edge of the Simpson Desert, and the Red Stump in the main street warns travellers of the dangers of travel in this desolate place. This is the area where the eerie 'Min Min' light can be seen. The light, described as resembling a car headlight or a luminous football, seems to be especially visible in the area around the Min Min Hotel, which burnt down in the early twentieth century. None of the explanations suggested has been accepted by the hundreds who have seen this light.
Map ref: page 564 D7

CAMOOWEAL

It is worth noting that Camooweal, is some 200 km (124 miles) north-west of Mount Isa but it comes under the same city council. This

Vivid white salt pans in the Simpson Desert, which is adjacent to Boulia.

must be one of the largest city council areas in the world, with part of the Barkly Highway as its main street. It has a population of 200 and is 1989 km (1235 miles) north-west of Brisbane. The town's claim to fame today is that it is the last town before the Northern Territory border. However, in the old droving days it was the main dipping centre for cattle crossing the State border. The Shire Hall, built in 1922–23 and extended in 1938, is classified by the National Trust.

The Camooweal Caves National Park has some of the biggest and least explored limestone caves in Australia. Cavers need to be experienced and well-equipped and all caving is restricted to the dry season as the caves fill with water in the wet season. During the day, the caves are home to roosting bats and owls, plus other birds and animals escaping the heat.
Map ref: page 564 A1

CLONCURRY

Cloncurry is 1689 km (1049 miles) north-west of Brisbane, and has a population of 3900. The Cloncurry Shire is mainly cattle country, although mining still plays a major part in the economy; during World War I Cloncurry was Australia's biggest producer of copper. The explorer Robert Burke named the

An old steam tractor in the Mary Kathleen Memorial Park in Cloncurry.

Cloncurry River after his cousin Lady Elizabeth Cloncurry, and later the town was named after the river. As late as 1974, 22 carat straw gold was discovered in the area. This type of gold, occurring near the surface, looks like lengths of wire and is very rare. The only other place it has ever been found is in South Africa.

Cloncurry has the reputation of being extremely hot—in 1889 a temperature of 124° F (51.1° C) was recorded here. This has never been known to have been exceeded anywhere else in Australia.

The town is proud to lay claim to some important firsts in the areas of aviation, health and education. The first commercial flight of the fledgling airline QANTAS (Queensland and Northern Territory Aerial Services) was between Winton and Cloncurry in 1920. The Royal Flying Doctor Service's (RFDS) first base was set up in Cloncurry in 1928.

This unique Australian service was the brainchild of a Presbyterian minister, John Flynn, and it now spreads a mantle of safety between Derby in Western Australia, Cairns in Queensland, Broken Hill in New South Wales and Port Augusta in South Australia. In 1960 the first Queensland lesson of the School of the Air was broadcast, using the RFDS radio network. This service is now known as the School of Distance Education.

There is much to see around Cloncurry. Just a few kilometres down the Landsborough Highway is McKinlay, home of the Walk-about Creek Hotel, made famous in the film *Crocodile Dundee*. The

Cloncurry/Mary Kathleen Memorial Park in McIlwraith Street includes buildings moved there from the abandoned uranium mining town of Mary Kathleen. John Flynn Place, incorporating the Fred McKay Art Gallery and the RFDS Museum, pays tribute to a man who saw a need and filled it despite enormous odds.

The Gidgee Inn, built by the Pearson family, is an example of recycling and outback ingenuity. Rammed earth walls, corrugated iron, recycled hardwood and jarrah logs reclaimed from the old railway bridge in Cloncurry all contribute to this distinctive motel. You can take a quiet walk through the Afghan Cemetery in Henry Street or the Chinese Cemetery on the Flinders Highway, where the remains of some hundreds of

Chinese miners are buried. There is a memorial to Burke and Wills located some 43 km (27 miles) west of Cloncurry, found on the banks of the Corella River.
Map ref: page 564 E3

HUGHENDEN

Hughenden (population 1900) lies 250 km (155 miles) east of Charters Towers and 1610 km (1000 miles) north-west of Brisbane, at the junction of the Townsville–Mount Isa railway line, and on the banks of the Flinders River.

The centre of local government for the enormous Flinders Shire, Hughenden is surrounded by cattle and sheep country. The area was named by Ernest Henry when he drove his cattle into the Jardine Valley in 1863—he named his cattle station Hughenden, after his grandfather's English manor.

In more recent years, Hughenden has become quite famous for the almost complete fossil dinosaur skeleton that was unearthed nearby at Roseberry Downs.

The Porcupine Gorge National Park, which is located some 60 km (37 miles) north of the town, is an interesting place that resembles a small-scale Grand Canyon.

About 40 km (25 miles) north of Porcupine Gorge are the famed Cheviot Hills, where high-quality peridot gemstones can be found. Brazil is the only other place on Earth where this unique and rare stone has been discovered.
Map ref: page 565 L3

Grand Hotel in Hughenden: a complete dinosaur skeleton was unearthed nearby.

The pub made famous in the film Crocodile Dundee, near Kynuna.

JULIA CREEK

Even though Julia Creek (population 602) is the administrative centre for the McKinley Shire, a shire of 41,000 sq. km (15,826 sq. miles), it is fairly isolated, being 550 km (342 miles) from Townsville, 250 km (155 miles) from Mount Isa (on the Flinders Highway) and 1686 km (1047 miles) north-west of Brisbane.

The district has quite massive shale oil deposits that contain the rare element vanadium, which is used in the production of high-quality steel. If an economical way to extract the vanadium can be devised, Julia Creek may one day become a booming mining town. There are four bores all within 2 km (1.2 miles) of the town, but the water is hot, and most houses have installed special systems to cool it.

The Julia Creek Dirt and Dust Triathlon weekend, part of the Saucony Adventure Series, is generally held around May—the town then plays host to upwards of 500 triathletes from around the world.
Map ref: page 564 G3

The Australian Stockman's Hall of fame in Longreach tells the story of pioneers.

KYNUNA

Kynuna is a small, remote town (population 85) almost midway between Winton and Cloncurry, on the old Diamantina stock route. It is 1509 km (937 miles) north-west of Brisbane. The Blue Heeler Hotel is well known in the district and the flashing tongue of the blue heeler dog in the pub's neon sign is a very welcome sight after a hot day. Twelve kilometres (7 miles) south of the town is the Combo Waterhole, reputed to be the billabong that A.B. 'Banjo' Paterson wrote about in *Waltzing Matilda*. Just up the road, towards Cloncurry, is the small town of McKinlay, home of another famous watering hole: the Walkabout Creek Hotel, which was made famous in *Crocodile Dundee*.
Map ref: page 564 G5

LONGREACH

Longreach is a large town (population 4452) 1173 km (728 miles) north-west of Brisbane. It is the centre of the region's pastoral industry, its commercial and administrative base, and a major tourist attraction in its own right.

Although semi-arid, the country around Longreach is excellent for grazing; it is at the centre of Mitchell grass country—the only natural grasslands in Australia. It has been said that Longreach has had a greater influence on Australian life than any other town or city, certainly far beyond what one would expect of a town of its remote location and small size.

Mount Isa's highly developed railway services Australia's largest underground mine.

The town was named after a 9 km (6 mile) reach of the Thomson River. The rapid expansion of the town of Longreach in the early twentieth century was largely due to the wool industry, but this was followed in the 1920s by a boost of a different nature—flying.

The establishment of QANTAS (Queensland and Northern Territory Aerial Services), and the building of the first hangar in Longreach, were the beginning. Between 1926 and 1927, seven DH 50 biplanes were built in this hangar. Not only is QANTAS the second longest-serving airline in the world, it is the only airline to build its own aircraft. This historic hangar now houses a fascinating display.

The Australian Stockman's Hall of Fame and Outback Heritage Centre were officially opened by Queen Elizabeth II in 1988. It pays tribute to the early pioneers, the stockmen, the women, the ringers, the Aboriginals and all the other people who pioneered

and worked in outback Australia. The Outback Muster and Drovers' Reunion is the most important annual occasion at the Stockman's Hall of Fame. Bush poetry, yarn telling, music, novelty events and book launches all form a part of this major festival.

Also in Longreach are the Longreach School of Distance Education, with students spread over an area twice the size of Victoria, and Pamela's Dolls and Crafts, with over 1500 dolls and a fascinating collection of outback memorabilia.
Map ref: page 565 L8

MOUNT ISA

There are some interesting statistics attributed to Mount Isa, not the least being that it is the site of Australia's largest underground mine. The city is 1804 km (1120 miles) north-west of Brisbane, and it administers an area the size of Switzerland—about 50,000 sq. km (19,300 sq. miles).

Were it not for the towns of Mount Isa (population 24,100) and Cloncurry (population 3900), though, this vast area would be almost unpopulated. A remarkable statistic from 1973 is that there

were more than 2.5 vehicles per resident. The enormous mine at Mount Isa is the basis of Queensland's mining industry, and has an annual output of 11 million tonnes (12.12 million tons) of ore.

This is one of the few areas in the world where the four minerals —copper, lead, silver and zinc— are found in close proximity. The area around Mount Isa is a fossicker's dream, with occasional finds of the prized Maltese crosses. In such

a hot and isolated region, those who live in Mount Isa—the population is made up of over 50 nationalities—have made their city a modern inland oasis, which contrasts sharply with the surrounding hot and dusty outback.

Lake Moondarra, an artificial lake 20 km (12 miles) north of the town, and Lake Julius, a further 80 km (50 miles) away, are great spots to cool off from the heat. Lake Julius is noted for its fishing

and water sports. The Riversleigh Fossils Interpretive Centre and the Royal Flying Doctor Service base are both worth a visit. The city hosts the Gregory River Canoe Race in May, and the Rodeo and Mardi Gras is in August.
Map ref: page 564 C3

MUTTABURRA

Muttaburra may be just a small town (the population is only 200) but it is most famous for something big. It is well known by palaeontologists as the place that *Muttaburrasaurus,* a famous dinosaur fossil, was first discovered. The town is in sheep and cattle country, 119 km (74 miles) north of Longreach, 152 km (94 miles) north of Barcaldine and 1217 km (756 miles) north-west of the state capital.

Lake Dunn, or as the residents call it, 'The Lake', is a remarkable inland waterway 3 km (1.9 miles) long and 1.6 km (1 mile) wide. It is home to more than 80 species of birds, and is perfect for water sports and picnics. Lake Galilee, a saltwater lake some 40 km (25 miles) long which is a wildlife sanctuary, is worth visiting if it has water— check with Tourist Information. Aramac, 95 km (59 miles) south, is

also worth a visit, even if it is just to see the statue of the white bull, a replica of a bull in the herd stolen and driven to South Australia by Harry Redford.
Map ref: page 565 M7

Centenary sculpture of the poet A.B. 'Banjo' Paterson, in Winton.

WINTON

Winton was first known as Pelican Waterhole but this was, apparently, too long and cumbersome to hand-frank onto stamps, so the postmaster decided to rename the town Winton, after his birthplace in Bournemouth in England.

Winton is 1345 km (835 miles) north-west of Brisbane, and has a population of 1667. Located as it is on two major highways and being the terminus for the railways from Townsville and Rockhampton, the town is the major road and rail centre for most of western Queensland. It is here that the massive road trains arriving from the Gulf country bring the cattle which are then loaded onto the trains.

Winton also has historic links to QANTAS (Queensland and Northern Territory Aerial Services). The first board meeting of QANTAS was held in the Winton Club in 1920 and the first registered office of the company was opened in the town in the same year. A.B. 'Banjo' Paterson wrote the words to Australia's unofficial national anthem, *Waltzing Matilda,* when he visited Dagworth Station near Winton in 1895, and gave the first reading of the poem at Winton's North Gregory Hotel.

The Waltzing Matilda Centre was opened in early 1998 and commemorates the song and Australian bush poets. The Bronze Swagman Award is an annual presentation for bush verse.
Map ref: page 565 J6

Muttaburra is most famous for its dinosaur but the town survives mainly on income derived from cattle raising.

SOUTH-WEST QUEENSLAND

The Mitchell Highway, named for explorer Thomas Mitchell who spied out the surrounding prime pastoral country, runs along the eastern edge of this region. To the west, grassy downs give way to wide horizons and dry mulga woodlands. In the south is the confusing web of frequently changing and often dry watercourses known as Channel Country, where explorers Burke and Wills perished. Opal fields dot the centre here and there.

Beneath all of this is the extraordinary reservoir of the Great Artesian Basin. The entire region is rich in outback history and Australian iconic images.

Remote Birdsville, on the edge of the fearsome Simpson Desert, before Federation, was a centre for collecting tax on trade into Queensland along the Birdsville Track. It is now famous for its annual raceday when spectators arrive in a swarm of light aircraft. The tiny settlement of Bedourie, surrounded by arid lands and next stop north on the 'Track' has lent its name to the wry expression 'Bedourie shower'—a dust storm. In the south-eastern corner is Cunnamulla, which is located on the Mitchell Highway; Cunnamulla is also the southernmost town on the Mathilda Highway which runs all the way to the Gulf. Meandering through the Channel Country are sluggish rivers with names famous in folksong—Diamantina, Barcoo, Cooper and Paroo.

When filled by floods from upstream, the Channel Country rivers spill over their banks to form broad marshes that quickly fill with birdlife; the pastures left as the waters recede are reputedly the best for cattle-fattening on the continent and the reason legendary beef industry families—the Kidmans and the Duraks—established stations in the area. West of the grasslands, the vegetation consists mainly of drab-looking mulga wattle, with some occasional clumps of silver-leafed ironbark, kurrajong and cypress pine. Although visually uninteresting, mulga will sustain stock through drought times and when drenched by infrequent rains, it bursts into colourful and fragrant bloom.

The 'Dig Tree' on the banks of Cooper Creek close to the South Australian border, in 1861 witnessed the tragic twists and turns of fate that resulted in the deaths from starvation of explorers Burke and Wills.

OPPOSITE: Working with cattle in a holding yard. Cattle raising is a big industry in south-west Queensland, which has a large proportion of the State's 10,444,000 meat cattle.

The three-lined knob-tailed gecko (Nepfrurus levis) is a nocturnal lizard that shelters in burrows during the day. Living in a wide range of arid and semi-arid habitats, it forages at night in open woodland, scrub, spinifex sand-plains and dunes.

The Adventure Way

Encounters with road trains on outback roads can be hazardous. Pull over to allow these massive vehicles to pass, and never attempt to overtake one unless you can see the road is clear for about 1 km (0.6 mile) ahead.

The Adventure Way is a series of roads that leads from Cunnamulla across the Grey Range to the remote river-braided flatlands of the south-western corner of Queensland and onward to Innamincka in South Australia. Most of the route runs along the sealed Bulloo Developmental Road, but further west there are some unsealed roads and for this reason a 4WD vehicle is recommended. The Adventure Way makes a terrific, scenic shortcut for those heading west from Brisbane to the deserts of Central Australia.

Cunnamulla to Noccundra

Currawinya National Park encompasses an area of 151,300 ha (373,860 acres) but has almost no facilities. Visitors must therefore be entirely self-sufficient.

Cunnamulla, on the junction of the Balonne and Mitchell Highways, lies 794 km (493 miles) west of Brisbane along good bitumen highways. Situated on the Warrego River, Cunnamulla was founded in the late 1860s, about five years after the region was first settled and large pastoral leases taken up. Today, it has

a population of around 1700 and is an important service centre and railhead for the area, which supports sheep, some cattle, and recently introduced angora goat herds. Offering several motels, a caravan park and well-equipped stores, the town is a good stopover for anyone travelling west along the Adventure Way or north or south on the Matilda Highway.

Heading west out of Cunnamulla, it's an easy run on the bitumen for 67 km (41.5 miles) through lightly wooded cattle country to the small township of Eulo, on the banks of the Paroo River. Eulo has a pub, the Eulo Queen Hotel, and a general store where you can obtain fuel and food. There's also a caravan park with basic amenities for campers. The town is best known for the Yowah Opal Fields to the north-west, and as the home of the World Lizard Racing Championships, held in late August or early September each year. A detour of 68 km (42 miles) to the south will take you to remote Currawinya National Park. It incorporates some of the country's largest inland freshwater lakes, which draw huge numbers of birds, especially during the dry season when other sources of water fail.

Continuing for 133 km (83 miles) west takes you to Thargomindah, the shire centre and the last town of significant size you will pass through on this route. It has a number of fuel outlets, a couple of general stores and, of course, a pub, the Bulloo River, which has lodgings. The Oasis Motel also has accommodation and there is a local caravan park.

Another 119 km (74 miles) to the west, you come to the turn-off for Noccundra, which is situated 19 km (12 miles) south of the junction and a total of 338 km (210 miles) west of Cunnamulla. Established in the 1880s and planned as a sizeable town, Noccundra failed to develop, and its pub, the locally famous Noccundra Hotel, is all that remains of the settlement. Nevertheless, the hotel is a fun place to stop for a beer, stock up with fuel, and find out about conditions on the roads ahead. There's also a camping area and a few rooms for those wanting accommodation. Additional camp sites are located along the nearby Wilson River, which is popular with local fishermen.

Noccundra to Innamincka

Returning to the main road junction, turn left and drive another 7 km (4.4 miles) to a major Y-junction, where you should veer left. The right fork leads to Durham Downs, 133 km (83 miles) away, before rejoining the main road. This alternative route may be preferable if Cooper Creek is running high (see below).

The main road, still blacktop, continues west to the Jackson Oil Field, 43 km (26.5 miles) from the Noccundra turn-off. Pumping and refining equipment lines the route and all the land here is private. For the next 32 km (20 miles), the Adventure Way traverses rolling gibber country, passing scattered oil

A widespread wetland bird often found on outback seasonal lakes, the Australasian little grebe (Tachybaptus novaehollandiae) builds a floating nest from water-weeds then ties it to reeds to prevent it being swept away.

wells and pumps, until suddenly the bitumen gives out near the Naccowlah Oil Field. Soon after, you begin to cross the wide flood plain of Cooper Creek and then, some distance on, the main channel. If the river is in flood—and it happens up here much more often than further west at Innamincka—the road could be cut or very wet. Check before you leave Noccundra, and if you hear that this route is under water, take the alternative route via Durham Downs, where there is an easier crossing.

Once past the main channel, the road climbs onto higher ground, leaving the flood-prone country be-hind. About 40 km (25 miles) west of the Cooper Creek crossing, it meets up with the Nappa Merrie–Karmona–Durham Downs road. Then it swings west across stony desert country for 75 km (47 miles) or so to another junction. Straight ahead, but out of sight, is Nappa Merrie Homestead and, just beyond it, the famous Burke and Wills 'Dig Tree', where a tragic misunderstanding sealed the explorers' fate.

To reach Innamincka, turn left and stay on the main road, which, about 6 km (3.7 miles) later, crosses the Burke and Wills Bridge over the Cooper, here confined, more or less, to one main channel. About 4 km (2.5 miles) south of the bridge, you come to a major road junction. Continuing straight ahead will take you to Tibooburra in New South Wales. That route leads for 111 km (70 miles) via Orientos Homestead to Santos Homestead, and then a further 58 km (36 miles) to the main Noccundra–Tibooburra road, near Naryilco Homestead. From there, another 103 km (64 miles) via Warri Gate on the Queensland–New South Wales border will take you all the way to Tibooburra.

To continue to Innamincka, 46 km (29 miles) from here, turn right. For most of the way, the road traverses gibber country, but in places you pass an impressive sand ridge or two. Arriving in Innamincka, Cooper Creek is on your right and the pub and the general store are on your left. You are now 246 km (153 miles) west of the Noccundra pub turn-off and 565 km (350 miles) from Cunnamulla.

The national parks office here can provide information on trips into the surrounding desert. The magical Coongie Lakes lie 112 km (70 miles) to the north-west. To the south-west, the Strzelecki Track leads across the bleak Strzelecki Desert for 431 km (268 miles) to Lyndhurst at the northern edge of South Australia's Flinders Ranges.

Travellers can try their luck fos-sicking for opals at Yowah near Cunnamulla. An important source of these precious stones, Yowah holds an Opal Festival in August.

Places in SOUTH-WEST QUEENSLAND

BIRDSVILLE

Birdsville, of all Australian towns, most typifies the outback: the hazards and perils of travelling in this very dry continent and the heat, harshness, remoteness and rugged beauty of the land. The town is tiny, with a population of only 100, and sits on the eastern edge of the Simpson Desert, in the extreme south-western corner of Queensland, 170 km (106 miles) from Poeppels Corner (which joins three States) and 1573 km (977 miles) west of Brisbane.

The Diamatina River near Birdsville.

The famous Birdsville Track starts here and runs 536 km (333 miles) to Marree, in South Australia. The track can be travelled at most times by conventional vehicles, but it should be treated with respect: it can be extremely treacherous, especially during the wet season (October to March).

Diamantina Crossing, as Birdsville was first known, was at the junction of a number of stock routes from west and central Queensland to Adelaide. There was a border customs post here—it closed after Federation. In 1923 one of Birdsville's hotels became a hospital of the Australian Inland

Mission and there is still a medical station in the town. The Annual Birdsville Races are held in September, and the population explodes briefly to between 5000 and 7000. All proceeds from the race meeting go to the Royal Flying Doctor Service and Birdsville Hospital. The only remaining hostelry, the historic 1885 Birdsville Hotel, does a roaring trade during race week.

The water supply is drawn from a 280 m (919 feet) deep artesian bore. The water is so hot when it reaches the surface that it is put into holding ponds to cool before being pumped around the town.

About 8 km (5 miles) north of town, on the Bedourie road, is a small stand of one of Australia's rarest trees, the waddy-wood (*Acacia peuce*). Only three stands of these trees are known in Australia. The trees are very slow growing, very prickly—particularly when small—and the wood is extremely hard.
Map ref: page 566 C4

CUNNAMULLA

This is the southernmost town on the Matilda Highway, which winds through western Queensland from here, near the New South Wales border, to Karumba on the Gulf of Carpentaria. Cunnamulla is located 848 km (527 miles) west of Brisbane and is the major town in the Paroo Shire, which produces cattle, sheep and wool, and has a population of 1630. It is on the Warrego River, famous for its Murray cod and golden perch. Currawinya National Park, about 90 km

Murray cod caught in Cunnamulla's Warrego River.

(56 miles) from Cunnamulla, is one of the most remote parks in the State. The Cunnamulla–Eulo Festival of Opals, held in August/September, is a lively event, with a Sandhill Digging Championship and a Dingo Derby; it ends with the World Lizard Racing Championships, which are held in Eulo.
Map ref: page 567 P8

CURRAWINYA NATIONAL PARK

One of Queensland's largest national parks, Currawinya, is found in semi-arid mulga country, yet ironically it provides the most extensive waterbird habitat inland found in eastern Australia.

The park is well and truly in the outback: it lies just south-west of Cunnamulla and to the north of Hungerford, on the New South Wales border. However, the Paroo, the major river in the region, borders or flows through most of the eastern section of the park. It has long, deep waterholes that have never been known to dry up.

Other creeks, lakes and lagoons also seasonally carry large quantities of water. Access to the park is via Cunnamulla and Eulo, Thargomindah or Bourke. All tracks within the park are unsealed and 4WD vehicles are recommended.

Currawinya's most fascinating feature is its two lakes which, even though only kilometres apart, are

Setting up camp in Currawinya National Park, a mecca for dedicated birdwatchers.

entirely different. Lake Numalla is a large freshwater lake covering more than 2200 ha (5436 acres). However, after rain, hundreds of small lakes, swamps and claypans form a mosaic through the dunes here. The other, Wyara, is much larger and is a salt lake.

These lakes support an incredible array of waterbirds, with each lake catering for completely different communities of birds.

The striking beauty and contrast of the countryside itself together with the wildlife—especially the great variety of bird life—are certainly the main attractions to be found around Currawinya.
Map ref: page 567 L9

EULO

Eulo is a very tiny town that is located some 68 km (42 miles) west of Cunnamulla and 918 km (570 miles) west of Brisbane. Even though the population is small (only 90!), the place literally hums —with bees. For many years beekeepers have been coming to Eulo —some from as far away as Dubbo in New South Wales—during the winter to gather the pollen and honey from the yapunyah trees. The yapunyah honey has a taste all its own, one unique to the outback.

Also in the area are the opal fields of Yowal and Duck Creek— they are just a short distance away and there is a fossicking field set aside for visitors. The Cunnamulla– Eulo Festival of Opals, held in August/September each year, culminates on a Sunday at Eulo with the World Lizard Racing Championships. A specially constructed track is used and the day normally starts with a lizard auction, followed by a five-race program. There are special conservation guidelines for lizards entered in this race.

In what must be a first, Eulo boasts a granite memorial to a racing cockroach called Destructo, which was brought to an untimely end by being accidentally squashed underfoot by an excited punter.

A visit to Palm Grove, surely Australia's remotest winery, is very interesting; you can sample their date wine and other date products.
Map ref: page 567 N8

Raw Queensland opal. Both Eulo and Quilpie are in the heart of opal country.

QUILPIE

This part of western Queensland is the land of opal. Quilpie (population 734) is 953 km (592 miles) west of Brisbane and right in the middle of opal country. It is also the centre for the area's beef and sheep properties. The late Des Burton, a Quilpie chemist, is credited with having the boulder opal recognised on world markets. A visit to the town's Catholic church is a must, for the altar, lectern and font are covered with brilliant opal slabs made and donated by Des Burton. Duck Creek and Sheep Station Creek are the places to visit for opal fossicking. There are 800 ha (1977 acres) in which to fossick, but permits are required for both fossicking and camping. Permits are best obtained from the courthouse in Cunnamulla. Visitors coming from Brisbane way should try the 'opal byway' loop: from Charleville, go south-west to Eulo via Cunnamulla, then take a smaller detour to Yowal and on to Quilpie via Toompine.
Map ref: page 567 L5

THARGOMINDAH

Right on the edge of a desert, Thargomindah, 1014 km (630 miles) west of Brisbane (population 280), originally serviced local cattle stations such as Bulloo Downs and Durham Downs and later was a stopover for Darling River wool steamers from Bourke. Gazetted in 1874, it was the first town to have reticulated bore water and hydro-electricity. Using outback ingenuity, the pressure of the artesian water was harnessed to drive a water turbine to power a generator. The press proclaimed it one of three major centres of electricity: Paris, London and Thargomindah! It supplied the town's electricity from 1893 until 1951. Nearby Lake Bindegolly is an important waterbird breeding site for darters, ducks and others.
Map ref: page 567 L8

Outback architecture: corrugated iron and snipped tin window detail.

CAIRNS AND CAPE YORK

Huge, tropical and remote, the great triangle of Cape York combines tropical rainforest, pristine beaches and the Great Barrier Reef with its high eastern coast and rugged escarpments, and sweeping savanna and isolated cattle stations to the west of the Great Dividing Range. Unfolding vistas of tropical sea and rainforest-clad hills make the journey from Cairns to the World Heritage-listed Daintree one of the most amazing in the country.

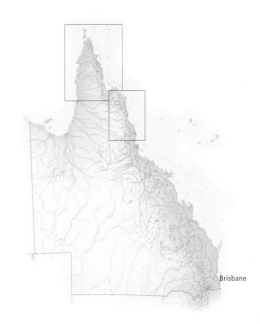

Beyond here, extraordinarily varied landscapes and the challenge of reaching the most northern point of mainland Australia attract 4WD adventurers from around the world. Cairns, with an international airport, is a major tourist centre, and the resort town of Port Douglas is very popular.

The steep coastal range, which in places rises sheer from the sea, is the result of a massive upthrusting of the ocean floor between 60 and 200 million years ago. Rainfall here is heavy, arriving mainly in a monsoonal deluge between December and April (the Wet), and the peaks are almost permanently mist-shrouded. The dense vegetation on the slopes of the Daintree is recognised as the oldest continually surviving rainforest community on the planet. While eastern-flowing rivers tumble swiftly to the sea; those heading west wind between avenues of forest and, when flood-swollen, spill in a shallow sea across the sparsely vegetated plains of the Carpentaria Basin. By the end of the dry season (around October), bushfires often sweep across these now-parched lands.

The region's rich resources have sustained Aboriginal people for more than 30,000 years. Sandstone escarpments near Laura, west of Cooktown, shelter fabulous galleries of their rock paintings, in one of the richest bodies of rock art in the world. The 1870s discovery of gold around the Palmer River drew more than 20,000 goldseekers, many of them Chinese, to mine in difficult tropical conditions. Cooktown, Cairns and Port Douglas grew to service the fields. The hill town of Kuranda, west of Cairns, lies at the end of one of the country's most scenic rail journeys; in its steep climb to the edge of the Atherton tableland, the tiny train crosses the face of Stoney Creek Falls and passes through fifteen hand-cut tunnels.

OPPOSITE: A lone yacht moors off a sandy atoll in the Great Barrier Reef. The reef stretches for 2300 km (1428 miles) and its area is greater than that of the United Kingdom.

Children doing their schoolwork outdoors in Kuranda, a small town north-west of Cairns.

Daintree National Park

One hundred million years ago, when Australia was still part of the supercontinent of Gondwana, the landmass was cloaked with dense tropical rainforest, and it was in these forests that most of the continent's modern-day life forms originally evolved. Following Australia's separation from Gondwana and its long voyage northward into warmer climes, this covering of forest dwindled, and most plants and animals were forced to adapt to more arid environments. Today, only pockets of tropical rainforest survive in Australia. Such habitats are vitally important, not only because they are extraordinarily rich in plant and animal life, but also because they harbour irreplaceable evidence of the early evolution of Australian wildlife, in the form of hundreds of relict species.

Of the true tropical rainforests remaining in Australia, the vast majority are encompassed by the Wet Tropics World Heritage Area, a ribbon of reserves that runs down the north-east coast of Queensland from Cooktown to Townsville. The richest, most diverse forest is coastal lowland rainforest and the largest remaining tract of this kind is protected by 76,000-ha (187,800-acre) Daintree National Park, centred on the river of the same name, which flows from the Great Dividing Range near Mossman and reaches the sea about 100 km (62 miles) north of Cairns.

History

The indigenous inhabitants of this region are the Kuku Yalanji people, who developed, over millennia, a detailed knowledge of the rainforest environment and its cycles. Traditionally, they organised their lifestyle around seasonal changes and the availability of different resources. Prior to the wet season, for example, they would relocate to the drier upland areas, returning to the coast in winter to hunt and gather in the forest and fish from dugout canoes along the rivers and coast. The Kuku Yalanji put rainforest plants to a remarkably wide variety of uses, ranging from food to building materials, tools and medicines. Today, tours led by Aboriginal guides demonstrate the extent of this knowledge and its continuing usefulness.

The Kuku Yalanji called the famous Daintree landmark now known as Cape Tribulation *Kulki*. The English name was coined by the first European to record a visit to these shores, James Cook. Cook's ship, the *Endeavour*, was holed on a reef just north of the cape in 1770, prompting the wry name and forcing him to careen the ship in a bay to the north— the site of present-day Cooktown.

European settlers were lured to the region in the mid-nineteenth century by rich stands of cedar and by the discovery of gold and tin in the tablelands. Both Cairns and Port Douglas initially developed as ports for the goldfields. As supplies of minerals petered out in the early twentieth century, increasing

A tropical species, the common queenfish (Scomberoides commersonnianus) can be targeted with live or dead bait, lures or flies. When using lures, speed of trolling and movement are all-important.

The Daintree is near the northern limit of the range of the eastern water dragon (Physignathus lesuerii). Fossils indicate that this species has changed little in 20 million years.

numbers of settlers took advantage of the warm, humid climate to grow sugar and tropical fruits. These products continue to play an important role in the local economy, though tourism has more recently become its mainstay, with resorts in and around the towns of Cairns and Port Douglas—gateways to the Great Barrier Reef and the Daintree—attracting millions of visitors from all over the world.

Rainforest Ecosystems

Because it ranges from sea level to more than 1300 m (4265 feet), Daintree National Park encompasses diverse habitats. Mountains and plateaus lie to the west, ocean to the east; in-between are coastal mangroves, heaths, rivers and swamps. But it is rainforest that dominates. Viewed from within, the thick forest canopy virtually blocks out the sunlight, resulting in nutrient-deficient, shallow soils. In response, many rainforest trees have developed giant flanged roots, known as buttresses, that reach out across the forest floor for a firmer hold. Clumps of cycads and palms cluster in clearings, curtains of vines and creepers hang from host trees, almost every branch is festooned with ferns, fungi and mosses. Many of the plants are relict species that have grown in these forests for tens of millions of years. Among them is the highest concentration of primitive flowering plants on Earth.

Such plant diversity results in a corresponding variety of animal life. Birds abound, ranging from robins and honeyeaters to riflebirds, bowerbirds and vividly hued kingfishers and parrots. There are at least

At Cape Tribulation, rainforest reaches right down to the shoreline, with beach almonds and beach pandanus fringing the dazzlingly white sands.

Frequently sighted along the Daintree River, the saltwater crocodile (Crocodylus porosus) may appear sluggish but can move rapidly over short distances. Take great care on river banks and do not swim in local waterways.

The Daintree Valley is home to around 250 kinds of birds and passengers on river cruises can expect to see up to 50 species during a single outing.

six species of pigeons, the largest and most impressive of which is the colourful wompoo fruit-dove, which spends most of its time in the canopy; others include the superb fruit dove and the pied imperial pigeon.

Light scratching sounds in the leaf litter usually indicate the presence of chowchillas. Measuring about 28 cm (11 inches), these conspicuous birds, with their dark brown backs and white-and-orange neck and chest markings, are found only in the Wet Tropics. Other native ground dwellers include the large brush turkey and the slightly smaller orange-footed scrub-fowl, which builds one of the biggest nests in the world.

But the Daintree's most distinctive avian inhabitant is the cassowary, a huge flightless bird, often standing up to 2 m (6.5 feet) tall, with black plumage and a brilliant blue-and-red featherless neck and head, topped by an impressive casque. Cassowaries are occasionally spotted on rainforest trails, but if you do encounter one, don't get too close: they are notoriously temperamental and can inflict serious injury with the sharp claws on their powerful legs. Sadly, cassowary numbers have plummeted in recent years, mainly as a result of habitat destruction but also as a result of collisions with passing cars. Always drive slowly and carefully when passing through cassowary country.

Reptiles include snakes, frilled lizards and forest dragons. Mammals, being mostly nocturnal, are harder to spot, but by day you may come across red-legged pademelons, native rats and musky rat-kangaroos. Among the rarest residents are the Herbert River ringtail possum, a beautiful brown-and-white creature found only above 300 m (1000 feet), and the Bennett's tree-kangaroo, which is confined mainly to the rainforests between the Daintree River and Cooktown, and is more often heard rustling foliage than seen.

Rainbow bee-eater (Merops ornatus)

Exploring the Park

Daintree National Park is divided into three parts: the 56,500-ha (138,376-acre) Mossman Gorge Section, 80 km (50 miles) north-west of Cairns; the 16,959-ha (41,906-acre) Cape Tribulation Section, 104 km (65 miles) north of Cairns; and tiny Snapper Island, just off Cape Kimberley.

MOSSMAN GORGE SECTION

The Mossman Gorge Section, located 5 km (3.1 miles) from the town of Mossman, the most northerly of Queensland's sugar towns, is the park's largest tract of wilderness. However, most of it is undeveloped and therefore out of reach to all but the most experienced, energetic and well-prepared bushwalkers. The only readily accessible part of the park is the exquisite gorge, where the river swirls through a jumble of giant granite boulders and a short 2.7-km (1.7-mile) circuit trail provides a fine introduction to the Daintree's rainforests.

At the nearby Mossman Gorge Aboriginal Community, Kuku Yalanji Dreamtime Walks offer guided tours of the gorge, during which you will learn about the indigenous peoples' relationship with the rainforest and about the techniques they developed over many thousands of years for identifying, gathering and adapting a wide range of rainforest resources.

CAPE TRIBULATION SECTION

To reach the Cape Tribulation Section of the park, head north from Mossman toward the delightful hamlet of Daintree, then take the turn-off to Cape Tribulation. This road leads for 5 km (3.1 miles) to the ferry across the Daintree River, which operates between 6 a.m. and midnight daily. From the northern side of the river, a mainly sealed road leads all the way to Cape Tribulation itself, the park's most famous landmark, 34 km (21 miles) away. The drive is delightful, the rainforest closing in on the road in places to form a narrow, verdant tunnel.

Cape Tribulation is idyllic, the tropical rainforest sweeping right down to stunning white-sand beaches and their fringing reefs. It's worth spending at least one night in the area to enjoy the stupendous scenery and the wide range of activities including swimming, walking and birdwatching. There are several comfortable lodges dotted around the adjacent forest, and Masons Store has fuel and food supplies.

The most accessible of Cape Tribulation's beaches is Myall Beach. A four-hour return bushwalk leads from here to Emmagen Creek on the northern side of the cape, providing sweeping views of rainforest-clad hills and beautiful coastline. (Walkers should start this trip on the outgoing tide so they can skirt around

the rocks at Emmagen Beach.) Further south, at Oliver Creek, near Noah Beach, the Marrdja Boardwalk wends for 1400 m (0.9 miles) through mangroves and ancient rainforest plants such as zamia palms, cycads and ribbonwoods.

Remember that swimming off Cape Tribulation's beaches is only possible between October and April because box jellyfish (also known as marine stingers) are present and can inflict a lethal sting. And never swim anywhere near the mouth of a saltwater creek or in the Daintree or Bloomfield Rivers as estuarine crocodiles inhabit these places.

The road beyond Cape Tribulation, which leads to the park's northern boundary and onward to Cooktown, is for 4WD vehicles only and may be closed after even light falls of rain; check the road conditions locally before you set off. The drive to the Bloomfield River on the northern edge of the park is spectacular, climbing steeply up hill and down dale as it traverses the Great Dividing Range.

SNAPPER ISLAND

Located off the mouth of the Daintree River, Snapper Island can only be reached by private boat. It has limited camp sites with no facilities, and visitors must take their own water. Its attractions include bushwalks, diving and snorkeling on adjacent reefs, and a sense of remoteness and tranquility.

Boating and Fishing

Guided wildlife cruises regularly explore the Daintree River, allowing passengers close-up views of forest and riverine dwellers, including the area's fearsome saltwater crocodiles. You can also launch your own boat at the town of Daintree (next to the caravan park) or downstream beside the ferry crossing. At the Daintree ferry launching ramp, small aluminium dinghies with outboard motors are available for hire. Other boat ramps in and around the park include Rocky Point, Coopers Creek and, on the Mossman River, Cooya Beach and Newell Beach. The northern end of Newell Beach provides access to Saltwater Creek.

Despite a drastic decline in fish stocks in recent decades, the Daintree offers satisyfing shore-based, estuarine and offshore fishing. Among the most commonly caught species are barramundi, mangrove jack, fingermark, javelin fish (grunter), pikey bream, trevally, queenfish, barracuda, estuary cod, black jewfish, archerfish, tarpon (ox-eye herring), snub-nosed dart and tripletail. Further upstream, you'll also find sooty grunter and jungle perch.

Live-bait fishing and lure casting are the most productive ways of working the lower Daintree River, although trolling and dead baiting can also produce results. Hot spots include Stewart Creek, Virgil Island, the stretch just downstream of the ferry crossing, South Arm, Broadwater and Ballast Heap.

Off the coast, there are numerous coral reefs holding significant numbers of tropical-reef and open-ocean species such as coral trout, wrasse, emperor,

sea perch, sweetlip, giant trevally, jobfish, tuna, mackerel, marlin and sailfish. The best time of year to fish the Daintree River and its adjacent coral reefs is during the warmer months, from late September until February or March each year; the hot, extremely wet weather at that time can, however, make travel difficult. Restrictions on fishing apply and vary throughout the region; enquire at a Queensland Parks and Wildlife Service office before you head off.

Camping

There are no camping facilities in the Mossman Gorge Section, though bush camping—with a permit—is allowed in remote areas. In the Cape Tribulation section, the main camp site is at Noah Beach; it has toilets, showers and drinking water. Snapper Island also has a small site. Campfires are prohibited in the park, and only fuel stoves should be used. As well as the national park sites, there are a number of private camping areas, hostels and holiday units nearby.

The Daintree's rainforests are home to 3000 plant species from 210 families—17 per cent of all of Australia's plant species. Over 700 of these plants are found only in this region.

Places in
CAPE YORK AND CAIRNS

BAMAGA

Bamaga is the most northerly town in Queensland—it is just 33 km (20 miles) south of the tip of Cape York but 2688 km (1669 miles) north of Brisbane. The area was settled by islanders from Saibai in the Torres Strait in 1948, and was named after one of the islanders' leaders. The town (population 815) has an Aboriginal Council.

Jackey Jackey Airfield, an important staging point for aircraft during World War II, is named after the Aborigine who accompanied Edmund Kennedy on the ill-fated 1848 Cape York expedition. Of the three survivors of that expedition, Jackey Jackey was the only one to reach the tip and the waiting ship.

Travelling to the tip is less hazardous these days and travellers can now enjoy a remote holiday at the wilderness lodge that is located within walking distance of the most northerly point of Australia.
Map ref: page 568 C2

CAIRNS

Cairns, 1703 km (1058 miles) north of Brisbane, is the perfect starting point for exploring Far North Queensland. The coastal attractions include the magnificent Great Barrier Reef and, further north, the tropical beaches of the

Marlin Coast. Inland you will find the rainforests and plains of the Atherton Tableland and the Gulf savanna. To the north lie the lush Daintree National Park and the varied wet-tropics landscape of Cape York.

The city itself mixes grand colonial architecture, old pubs and high-set Queenslander style homes with modern shopping malls and apartment blocks. In the early days Cairns and Port Douglas were great rivals but in 1924, when the railway line from Brisbane was terminated at Cairns, Cairns then became the major city in North Queensland. It has grown at a phenomenal rate since 1979, with many new suburbs appearing as if by magic—its population is now 101,000.

The city is a major tourist destination for overseas travellers, especially since the opening of the Cairns International Airport. It is also a popular holiday destination for Australians wanting to experience this part of their own country. Accommodation ranges from the luxury island resorts and five star hotels to rainforest retreats, family units, camping and caravan parks to backpacker hostels. There is a stunning array of things to see and

A wide range of fresh fruit and vegetables can be bought at Rusty's Markets in Cairns.

do in Cairns. Explore the deserted mining towns and the small isolated communities that still service the mining and pastoral industries. Take a trip out to the Great Barrier Reef for snorkelling, scuba diving, swimming or just admiring the myriad life forms and fascinating colours of the coral.

The Kuranda Scenic Rail ride up the range west of Cairns goes through tunnels, over bridged ravines and past the Barron Gorge waterfalls, arriving at the station of Kuranda, reputed to be the prettiest railway station in the country. The Kuranda markets are famous for their variety and quality. Also, there is a 7.5 km (4.7 miles) trip to Kuranda on the Skyrail, the world's longest gondola cableway, which rides above the World Heritage rainforest canopy, with spectacular views of the Coral Sea beaches, cane fields and the mountains.

Other activities include white-water rafting down the Tully River, a thrilling hot-air balloon flight at sunrise, a 4WD safari through the rugged outback country, or a Tiger Moth or helicopter sightseeing ride over spectacular waterfalls and rainforests. The Australian Woolshed puts on shearing and working sheep dog demonstrations, and Barron Gorge Power Station, an underground hydro-electric power station, is open for tours.

The future of Cairns seems well assured, with the tourist industry continuing to grow, the $100 million Sherga RAAF Base near Weipa

currently under construction, the multi-million dollar Tully Millstream hydro-electric scheme and the possibility of the Cape York Space Station project finally becoming a reality. Cairns' main annual festival, 'Fun in the Sun', is held every year in October.
Map ref: page 569 D7

Seisia jetty, to the north of Bamaga, the closest town to the tip of Cape York.

COOKTOWN

Cooktown, 1930 km (1199 miles) north of Brisbane, was founded as a port for the Palmer River goldfields, more than a century after Captain James Cook spent 48 days on the banks of the river that bears his ship's name, *Endeavour*, repairing the vessel after it had been damaged on a coral reef off Cape Tribulation, to the south.

In the mid-1870s Cooktown was Queensland's third busiest port. As the gold started to run out, tin was discovered nearby and the town continued to prosper as a port for the Burns Philp Company's island trade and as an access point for traders into Papua New Guinea. Nowadays Cooktown is a tourist town (population 1300), and the gateway to Cape York.

A visit to the Lion's Den Inn is a must. It is an old pub on the coast road from Cape Tribulation. It has heaps of character and there are good camping spots behind the pub towards the creek. Cooktown also has many fine buildings from the gold rush era, notably the Bank of New South Wales, an imposing building with wooden counters and the old gold scales are also on display.

The Captain Cook Historical Museum is housed in what was initially a school. It was built in 1888 and run by Irish nuns, and now it displays 200 years of Cooktown's fascinating history. The Chinese Joss House is part of the legacy left by the thousands of Chinese who flocked to this area during the gold rush years, many are buried in the Cooktown cemetery.

Beautiful Lizard Island, northeast of Cooktown, is remembered partly as the scene of a long-ago tragedy: Mary Watson, her small son and her Chinese servant were attacked by Aborigines and fled the island in an iron tank. All three died of thirst on an uninhabited island 18 km (11 miles) off the mainland. Mary is buried in the Cooktown cemetery and there is a monument to her in the town. In June the town puts on the Cooktown Discovery Festival and re-enacts Cook's landing.
Map ref: page 569 C3

A tour boat plies the crocodile-inhabited waters of the Daintree River, near Daintree.

DAINTREE

Daintree is quite a small village, with a population of just 150, and is tucked away on a bend of the Daintree River, 1801 km (1118 miles) north of Brisbane.

Some 11 km (7 miles) before the town, a ferry takes cars across the river. From there the road is sealed to Cape Tribulation, but from there on this road is unsealed, so 4WD vehicles are recommended, especially after rain as the road can become very muddy.

This particular part of the far north Queensland coast is generally referred to as the Reef and Rainforest Coast, as the massive, lush tropical rainforest sweeps right down onto the beaches to meet the stunning Great Barrier Reef.

Daintree was once the heart of a thriving timber industry that was then based around the prized red cedar. Now, tourism is increasingly becoming the main industry for this tropical town.

Take a leisurely cruise on the Daintree River and maybe catch a glimpse of that creature of the dinosaur age—the saltwater crocodile. But beware, these crocodiles are dangerous and can and will eat people if given the chance, so do not swim in the area without seeking local advice on safe places. The bird life in the area is extremely varied and quite spectacular. The Daintree Village Timber Museum tells the story of the days of the early timber-getters.
Map ref: page 569 C5

The outer suburbs of Cairns edge into the tropical forests of the Macalister and Lamb ranges in this rapidly expanding city.

Riding a bucking bull at the annual rodeo in Mareeba.

MAREEBA

Mareeba (population 17,310) is situated 1759 km (1092 miles) north of Brisbane, at the point where the Barron River and Granite Creek meet—the name is derived from an Aboriginal word that means 'meeting of the waters' or 'place to meet'.

The first thing visitors notice on entering Mareeba is its massive concrete water tower. The town is the hub of Australia's main tobacco-growing region but cash crops such as pineapples and mangoes are also grown in the area.

All around the district are signposts marking the camp sites where US and Australian servicemen were based during World War II. It was from the airfield south of Mareeba that Allied aircraft flew many missions in the Battle of the Coral Sea. A walk through Granite Gorge, to the south of the town, allows visitors to experience the mass of grey granite boulders which were produced by volcanic action many centuries ago. In July the town hosts the Rodeo Festival.
Map ref: page 569 D8

PORT DOUGLAS

The old fishing village of Port Douglas, 1759 km (1092 miles) north of Brisbane, is now one of the leading tourist towns of Far North Queensland. This is due mainly to its proximity to the reef and the rainforest (it is the closest town to the Great Barrier Reef), and its superb year-round climate. All this natural beauty is supported by numerous restaurants and shops, luxury hotels and resorts and historic Queenslander buildings.

Back in the gold rush days of the Hodgkinson River during the 1880s, Port Douglas boomed, and the town became a major shipping port for sugar. Its decline, and its losing battle with Cairns as the major northern port, started in 1885, when the decision was made to build a railway line from the inland mining regions to Cairns. The cyclone of 1911 that destroyed most of the buildings compounded the population slide. The decline was complete when the railway line from Brisbane terminated at Cairns in 1924. By the early 1980s, however, tourism meant Port Douglas' population began to increase and today its population is 2100.

Port Douglas is a great base for exploring the region. You can take day tours to the reef, join a 4WD safari, ride the Bally Hooley sugar train, and travel along the coast to the Daintree and Cape Tribulation rainforests. The Low Isles, on the reef, lie just offshore Port Douglas.

The region is also a known fishing ground for mighty black marlin; Dickson Inlet is best for smaller challenges such as coral trout, red emperor or barramundi. Don't miss the award-winning Rainforest Habitat, which gives a taste of life in the rainforest. The Port Douglas Reef and Rainforest Festival is held each May.
Map ref: page 569 D6

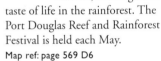

Cane toads races are held in Port Douglas.

Port Douglas is the closest point to the Great Barrier Reef, which starts 37 km (23 miles) offshore. It is a two-hour trip to the deeper outer reef by wavepiercing catarmaran.

THURSDAY ISLAND

Thursday Island (population 4000), lies just off very the tip of the Cape York Peninsula and 2738 km (1700 miles) north-west of Brisbane and is Australia's most northerly settlement. It forms the administrative centre for the 14 inhabited islands of the Torres Strait and it is largely populated by Torres Strait islanders. Access is by ferry or plane services from Bamaga on the mainland.

Thursday Island has a fine natural harbour in Port Kennedy, and visitors will notice the profusion of small aluminium boats, known as 'tinnies'. Fishing is very much a favourite activity of the islanders.

View of Thursday Island (foreground), looking towards the neighbouring Prince of Wales Island, in Torres Strait just north of Cape York.

Thursday Island was a major base for the pearling fleets in the early days, and many Japanese pearl fishermen are buried in the local cemetery. The island was later subjected to experiments in tropical farming that failed, including a cultured pearl industry and green turtle farming. Today there are conducted tours of the island, which include a visit Green Hill Fort, built in 1892 during the Russian invasion scare, and Quetta Rock, the site of the sinking of the SS *Quetta* in February 1890. 'The Coming of the Light' Festival is held each year in July.

Map ref: page 568 C2

WEIPA

Weipa (population 2359) is a fairly isolated town on the eastern coastline of the Gulf of Carpentaria, and it is located 2507 km (1557 miles) north-west of Brisbane.

It is the site of the world's largest and richest bauxite deposit. Bauxite is the raw material for aluminium and is extracted by the open-cut method. The bulk of the output, after washing and grading, is then shipped to the smelter located in Gladstone. Kaolin, a fine white clay used in paper manufacturing, is also mined in the area. The white kaolin mounds contrast strongly with the vibrant red bauxite.

The town of Weipa North accommodates hundreds of miners. It was built in the 1960s by the Queensland Government and the mining company Comalco. Napranum, formerly known as Weipa South, is where most of the area's Aboriginal community is based.

Weipa is a major supply point for visitors to Cape York, and there are some fine fishing spots north of the town. Sherga, a major strategic air base, has been under construction for some years and is located south of the town.

Map ref: page 568 B6

Brisbane City Centre

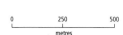

metres

0 250 500

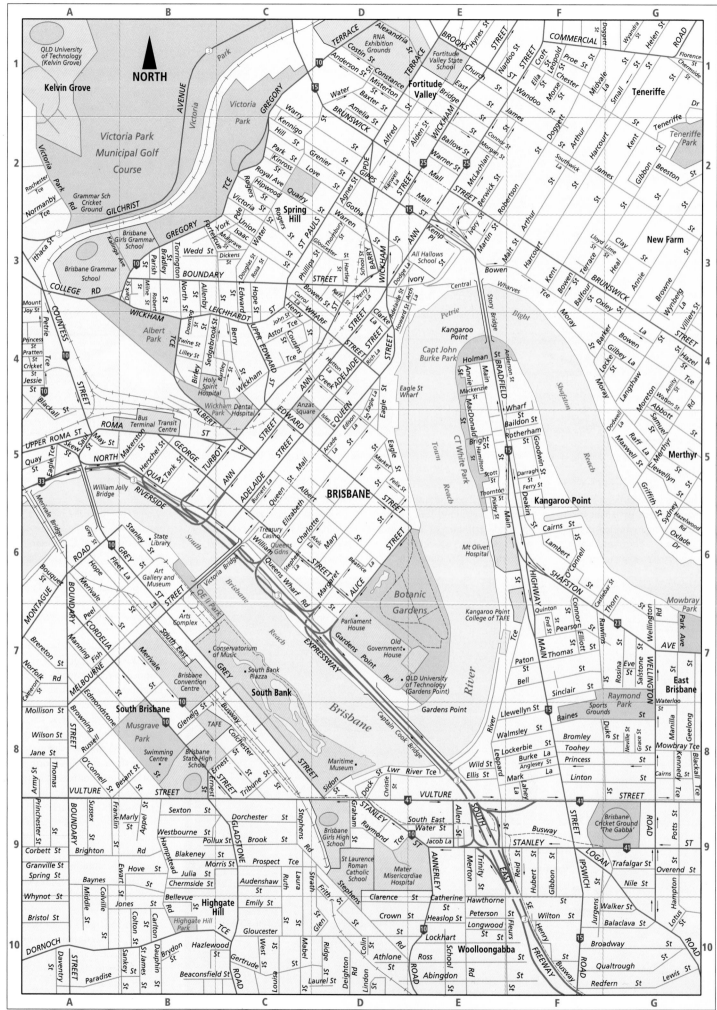

NORTH

QLD University of Technology (Kelvin Grove)

Kelvin Grove

Victoria Park

Victoria Park Municipal Golf Course

Fortitude Valley

Teneriffe

Teneriffe Park

Spring Hill

New Farm

Brisbane Girls Grammar School

Brisbane Grammar School

Albert Park

Holy Spirit Hospital

Wickham Park

Wickham Dental Hospital

Anzac Square

Bus Terminal Transit Centre

William Jolly Bridge

BRISBANE

Kangaroo Point

Capt John Burke Park

Kangaroo Point

Eagle St Wharf

Mt Olivet Hospital

Merthyr

State Library

Art Gallery and Museum

Arts Complex

Treasury Casino

Queens Gdns

South Bank

South Brisbane

Brisbane Convention Centre

South Bank Plazza

Conservatorium of Music

Swimming Centre

Brisbane State High School

Maritime Museum

Botanic Gardens

Parliament House

Old Government House

Gardens Point

QLD University of Technology (Gardens Point)

Kangaroo Point College of TAFE

East Brisbane

Mowbray Park

Raymond Park

Sports Grounds

Musgrave Park

Highgate Hill

Highgate Hill Park

Brisbane Girls High School

St Laurence Roman Catholic School

Mater Misericordiae Hospital

Brisbane Cricket Ground 'The Gabba'

Woolloongabba

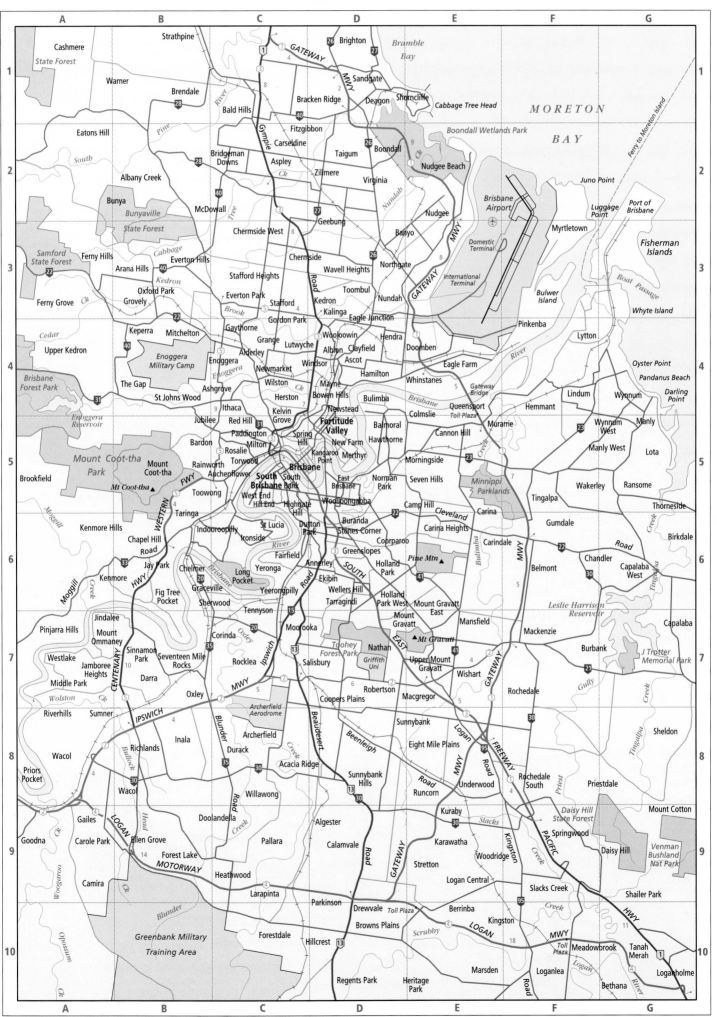

Brisbane and Surrounding Areas

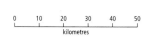

0 10 20 30 40 50
kilometres

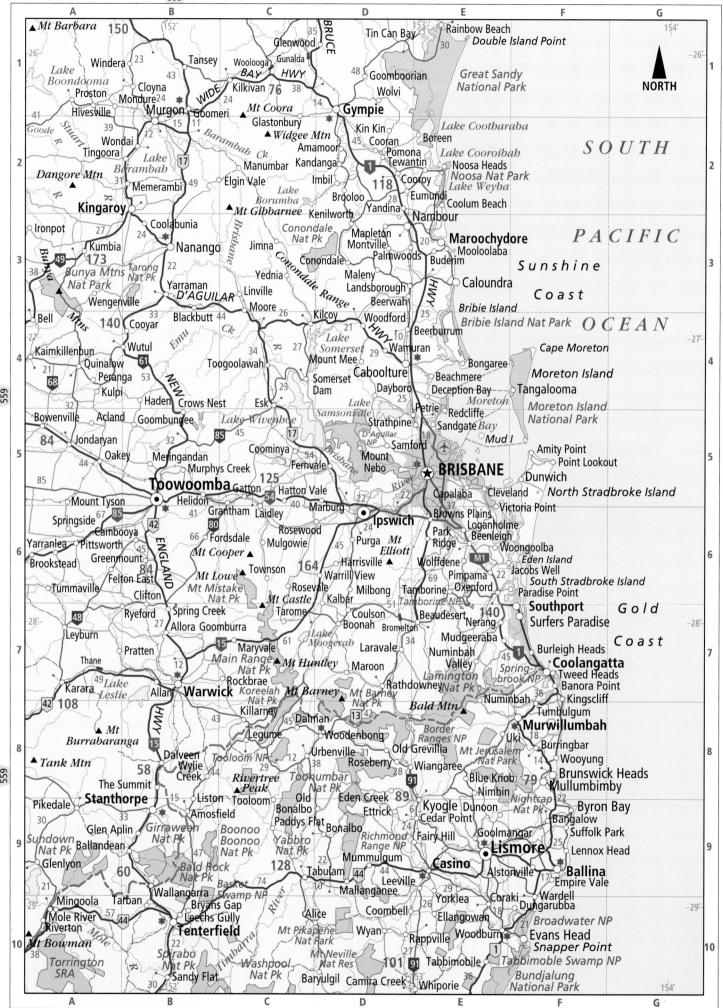

Queensland

Gold Coast and Surrounding Areas

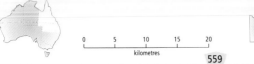

kilometres

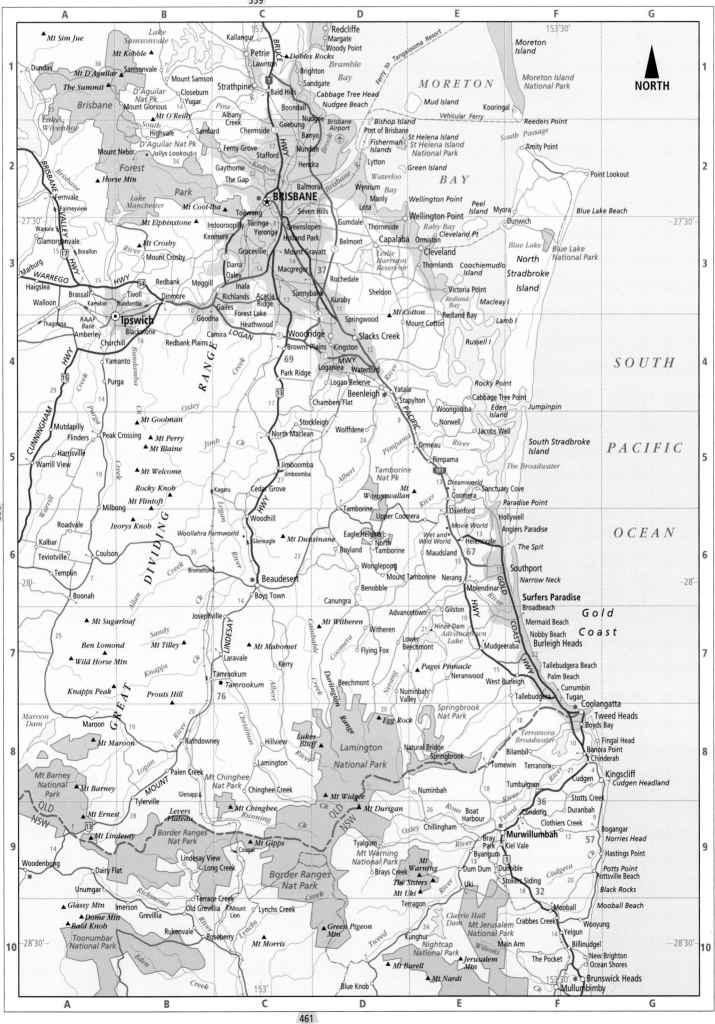

NORTH

Q U E E N S L A N D

S O U T H

P A C I F I C

O C E A N

M O R E T O N

B A Y

Gold
Coast

South-East Queensland

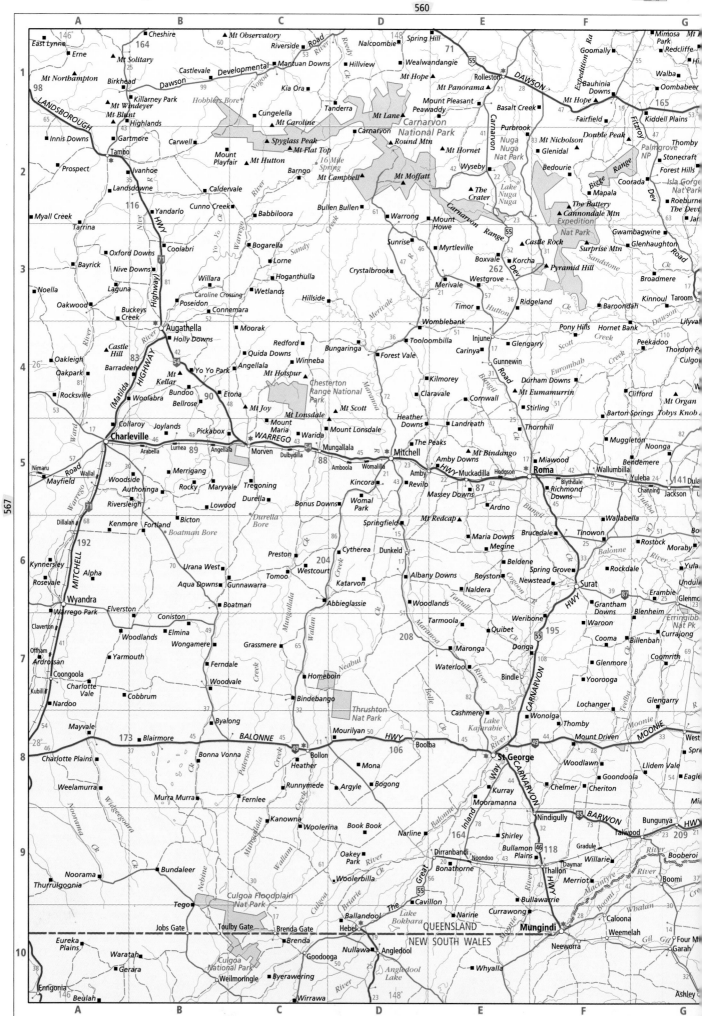

Central-East Queensland

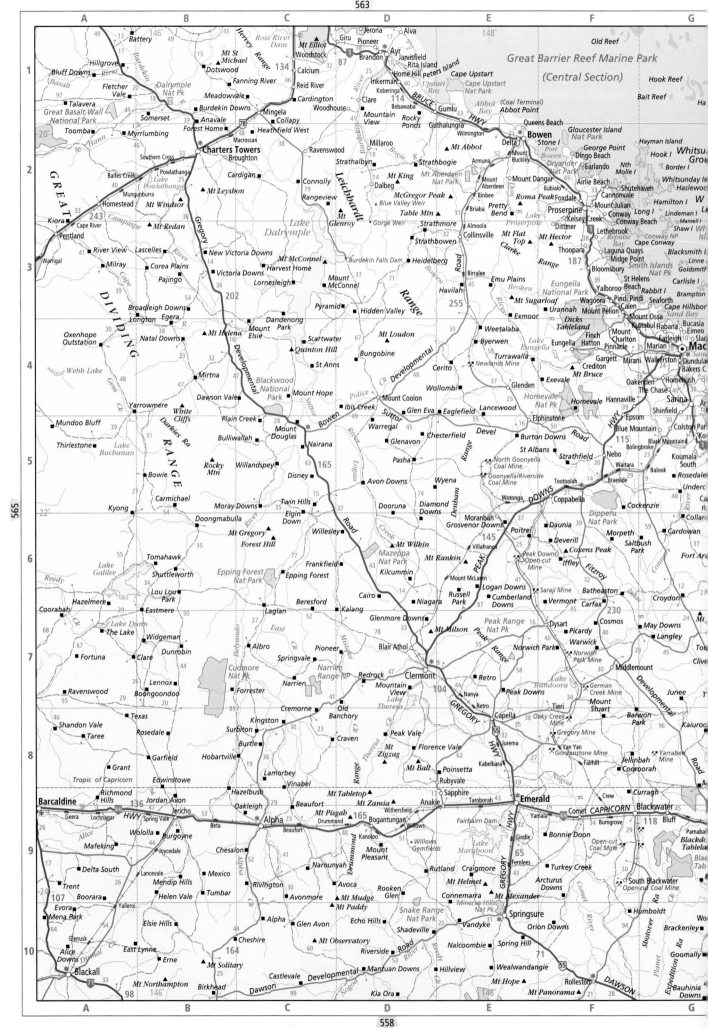

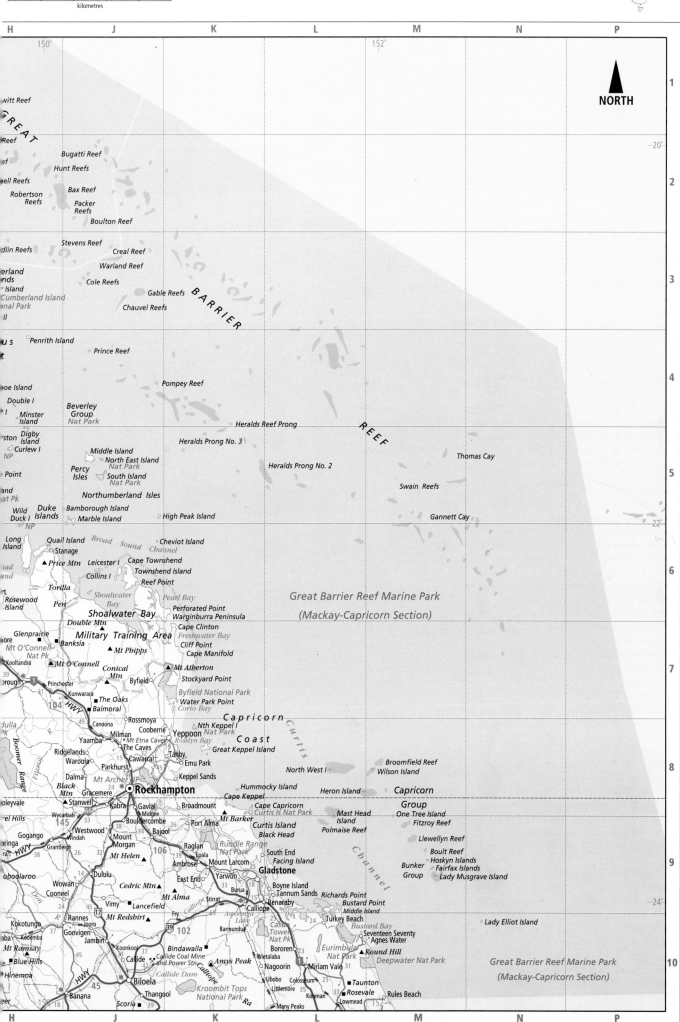

NORTH

QUEENSLAND

0 20 40 60 80 100
kilometres

150°

witt Reef

GREAT

Reef

ef

Bugatti Reef

Hunt Reefs

well Reefs

Robertson
Reefs

Bax Reef

Packer
Reefs

Boulton Reef

dlin Reefs

Stevens Reef

erland
nds

Creal Reef

Warland Reef

Island

Cumberland Island
nal Park

Cole Reefs

Gable Reefs

BARRIER

ll

Chauvel Reefs

u s

Penrith Island

t

Prince Reef

oe Island

Pompey Reef

Double I

Beverley
Group
Nat Park

I

Minster
Island

Digby
Island

Curlew I

NP

Middle Island

North East Island
Nat Park

Heralds Reef Prong

REEF

Point

Percy
Isles

South Island
Nat Park

Heralds Prong No. 3

Heralds Prong No. 2

Thomas Cay

and

at Pk

Northumberland Isles

Swain Reefs

Wild
Duck I

NP

Duke
Islands

Bamborough Island

Marble Island

High Peak Island

Gannett Cay

Long
Island

oad

nd

Quail Island

Stanage

Price Mtn

Collins I

Leicester I

Broad Sound
Channel

Cheviot Island

Cape Townshend

Townshend Island

Reef Point

Great Barrier Reef Marine Park

(Mackay-Capricorn Section)

Torilla

Pen

Rosewood
Island

Shoalwater
Bay

Pearl Bay

Perforated Point

Warginburra Peninsula

Shoalwater Bay

Glenprairie

ore

Mt O'Connell
Nat Pk

Kooltandra

Double Mtn

Banksia

Mt O'Connell

Military Training Area

Mt Phipps

Cape Clinton

Freshwater Bay

Cliff Point

Cape Manifold

brough

Conical
Mtn

Byfield

Mt Atherton

Stockyard Point

Princhester

Kunwarara

The Oaks

Byfield National Park

Water Park Point

39

104

HWY

Balmoral

Corio Bay

Capricorn

Curtis

ulla

Canonna

Rossmoya

Cooberrie

Nth Keppel I
Nat Park

Coast

Boomer

Range

oad
nd

49

Yaamba

Ridgelands

Milman

Mt Etna Caves

The Caves

Yeppoon

Rosslyn Bay

Great Keppel Island

Waroula

Parkhurst

Cawarral

Tanby

Emu Park

North West I

Broomfield Reef

Wilson Island

Dalma

Black
Mtn

Mt Archer NP

Gracemere

Keppel Sands

Hummocky Island

Heron Island

Capricorn

Rockhampton

Cape Keppel

Group

oleyvale

Stanwell

Wycarbah

Kabra

Gavial

Midgee

Broadmount

Cape Capricorn

Curtis Is Nat Park

Mast Head
Island

One Tree Island

el Hills

145

66

33

Boulcombe

38

Port Alma

Mt Barker

Fitzroy Reef

Gogango

aringa

Grantleigh

HWY

Windah

Westwood

Mount
Morgan

26

Bajool

Raglan

Epala

Rundle Range
Nat Park

Curtis Island

Black Head

Polmaise Reef

Llewellyn Reef

Boult Reef

106

38

Mt Helen

Ambrose

Mount Larcom

35

South End

Facing Island

Hoskyn Islands

Bunker

Fairfax Islands

oboolaroo

14

Dulula

Wowan

Cedric Mtn

East End

Yarwun

Burua

Gladstone

Boyne Island

Group

Lady Musgrave Island

Cooneel

Mt Alma

Tannum Sands

Richards Point

24

45

Vimy

Lancefield

Stirrat

Benaraby

Bustard Point

Middle Island

Kokotungo

Rannes

Jooro

Mt Redshirt

Fry

65

Calliope

Turkey Beach

Lady Elliot Island

Goovigen

Jambin

Barmundu

24

Castle
Tower
Nat Pk

Bustard Bay

aba

Mt Ramsay

Kodemba

Koonkool

37

Bindawalla

Wietalaba

Bororen

Eurimbula
Nat Park

Seventeen Seventy

Agnes Water

Blue Hills

45

Calide

Callide Coal Mine
and Power Stn

Nagoorin

Round Hill

Deepwater Nat Park

Great Barrier Reef Marine Park

Hinemoa

HWY

45

Biloela

Callide Dam

Ubobo

Colosseum

Miriam Vale

31

(Mackay-Capricorn Section)

Banana

Thangool

Kroombit Tops
National Park

Amys Peak

Littlemore

Kotenan

25

Taunton

Rosevale

Rules Beach

18

Scoria

Ra

Many Peaks

Lowmead

North Queensland

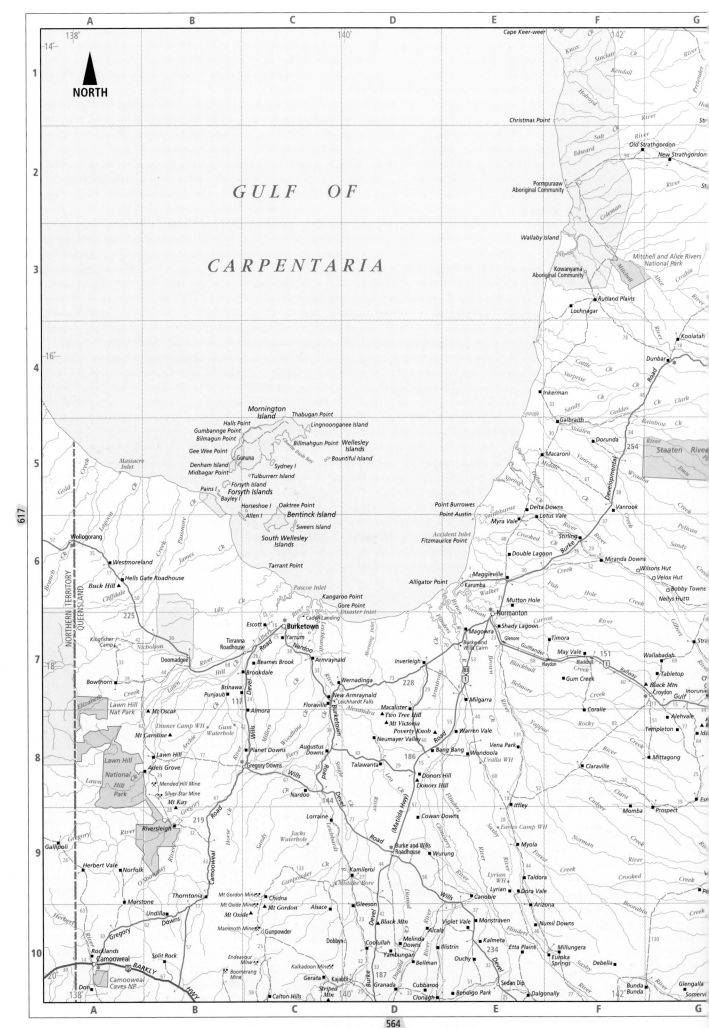

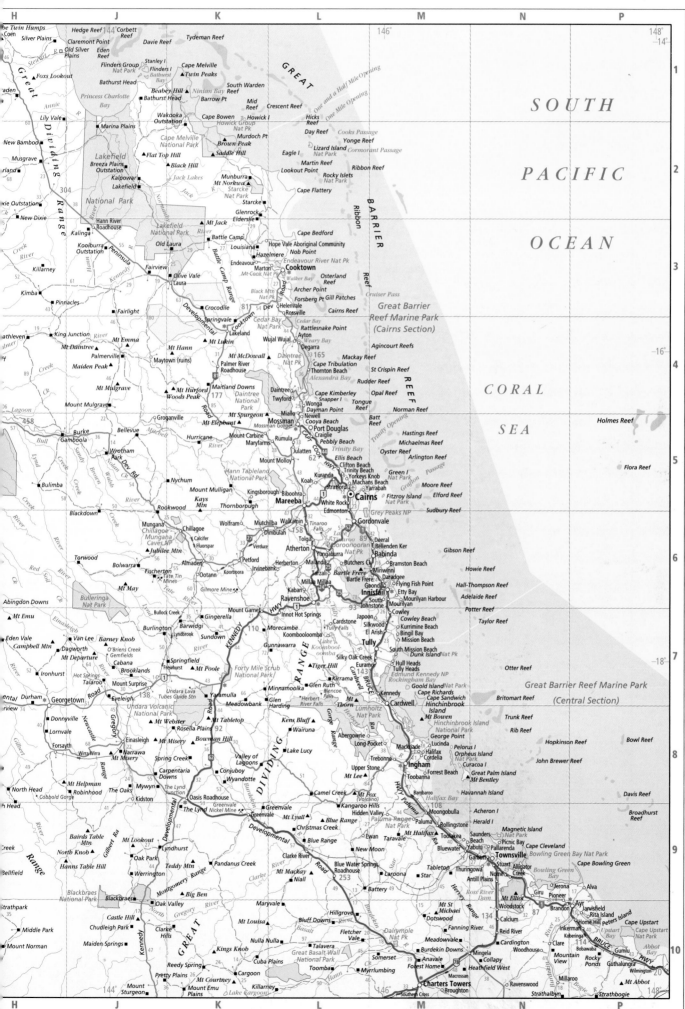

Outback Queensland

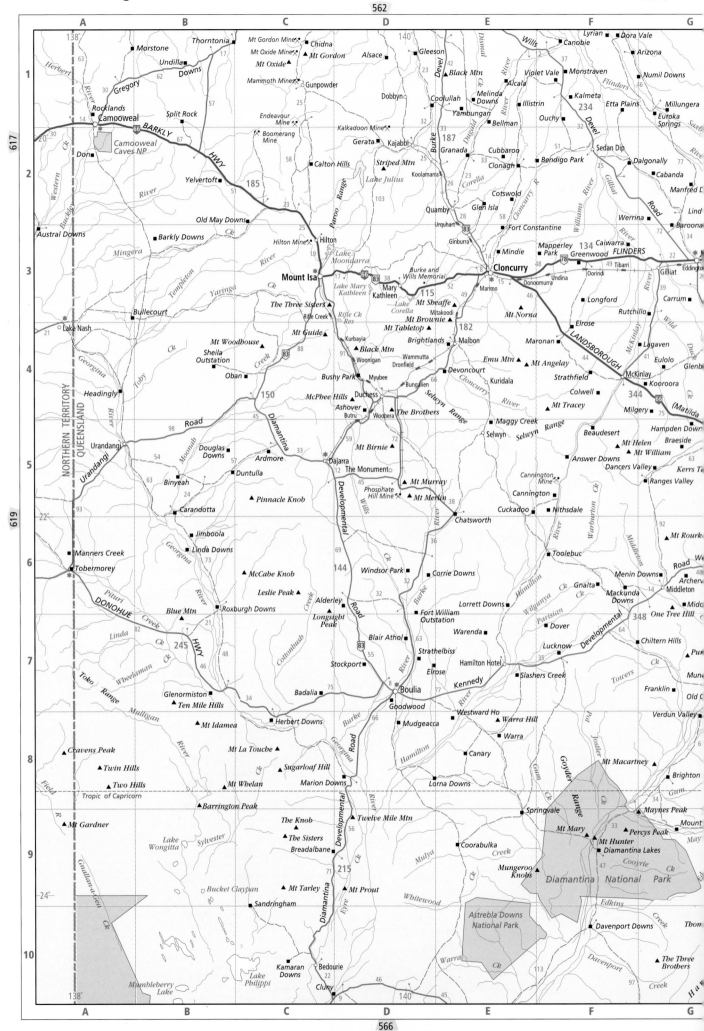

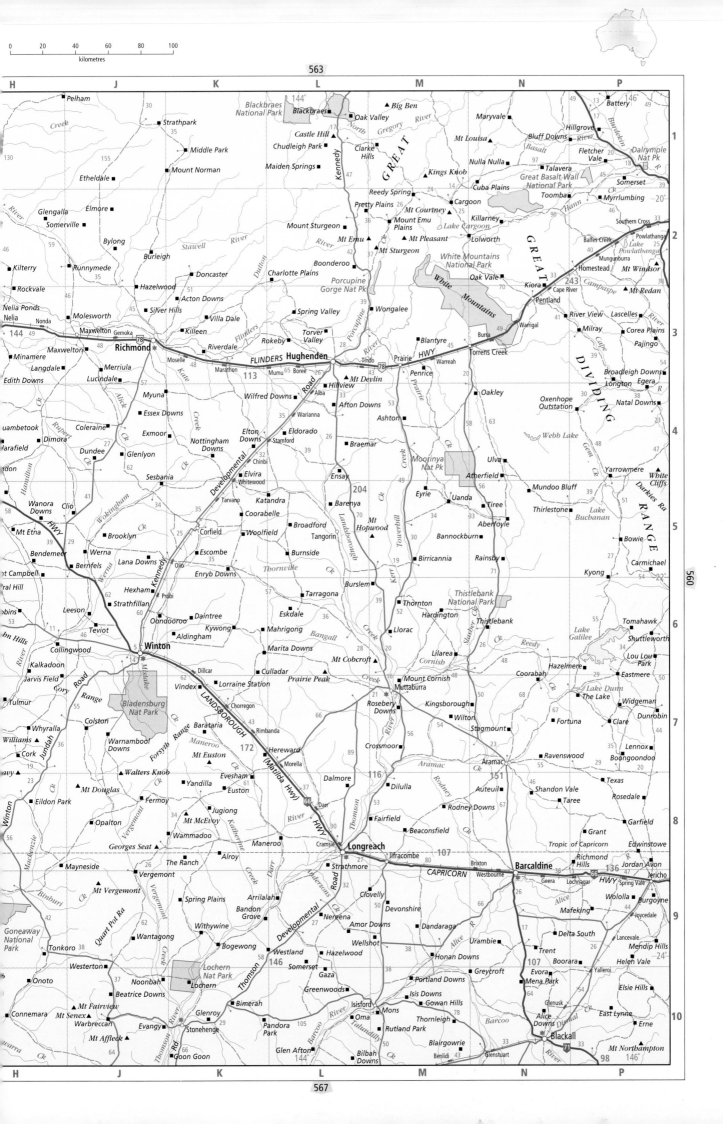

565

QUEENSLAND

560

Scale bar:
0 20 40 60 80 100
kilometres

Grid labels (top): H J K L M N P
Grid labels (side): 1 2 3 4 5 6 7 8 9 10

Place names and features:

Pelham
Strathpark
Middle Park
Mount Norman
Etheldale
Glengalla
Somerville
Elmore
Bylong
Burleigh
Kilterry
Runnymede
Hazelwood
Doncaster
Rockvale
Nelia Ponds
Nelia
Molesworth
Maxwelton
Gemoka
Richmond
Minamere
Maxwelton
Merriula
Langdale
Lucindale
Edith Downs
Myuna
Coleraine
Essex Downs
Exmoor
Nottingham Downs
Elton Downs
Eldorado
Stamford
Warianna
Dimora
Dundee
Glenlyon
Sesbania
Tarvano
Chinbi
Elvira
Whitewood
Katandra
Coorabelle
Woolfield
Broadford
Tangorin
Burnside
Wanora Downs
Clio
Brooklyn
Werna
Lana Downs
Olio
Escombe
Enryb Downs
Mt Etna
Bendemeer
Bernfels
Hexham
Prubi
Strathfillan
Leeson
Teviot
Oondooroo
Daintree
Kywong
Aldingham
Collingwood
Winton
Dillcar
Lorraine Station
Vindex
Chorregon
Rimbanda
Baratria
Kalkadoon
Jarvis Field
Tulmur
Colston
Warnambool Downs
Mt Euston
Hereward
Morella
Crossmoor
Whyralla
Williams
Cork
Jundah
Walters Knob
Yandilla
Evesham
Euston
Dalmore
Dilulla
Mt Douglas
Fermoy
Jugiong
Mt McEvoy
Wammadoo
Maneroo
Cramsie
Longreach
Eildon Park
Opalton
Vergemont
Georges Seat
Alroy
Ilfracombe
Mayneside
The Ranch
Strathmore
Vergemont
Mt Vergemont
Spring Plains
Arrilalah
Clovelly
Devonshire
Binburi
Bandon Grove
Nereena
Amor Downs
Dandaraga
Withywine
Bogewong
Westland
Somerset
Hazelwood
Wellshot
Honan Downs
Urambie
Tonkoro
Noonbah
Lochern
Gaza
Greenwoods
Portland Downs
Greycroft
Westerton
Onoto
Beatrice Downs
Bimerah
Isisford
Isis Downs
Gowan Hills
Mt Fairview
Mt Senex
Connemara
Warbreccan
Evangy
Glenroy
Pandora Park
Oma
Mons
Thornleigh
Mt Affleck
Stonehenge
Goon Goon
Glen Afton
Bilbah Downs
Benlidi
Rutland Park
Blairgowrie
Glenstuart
Blackall
Mt Northampton
Erne
East Lynne
Elsie Hills
Helen Vale
Yalleroi
Mendip Hills
Lancevale
Boorara
Evora
Mena Park
Trent
Delta South
Joycedale
Wololla
Burgoyne
Mafeking
Spring Vale
Jericho
Jordan Avon
Edwinstowe
Garfield
Grant
Richmond Hills
Barcaldine
Westbourne
Brixton
Geera
Lochnagar
Rosedale
Taree
Shandon Vale
Auteuil
Rodney Downs
Beaconsfield
Fairfield
Ravenswood
Texas
Boongoondoo
Lennox
Clare
Dunrobin
Widgeman
Fortuna
The Lake
Stagmount
Wilton
Kingsborough
Rosebery Downs
Muttaburra
Mount Cornish
Lilarea
Hazelmere
Coorabah
Eastmere
Lou Lou Park
Shuttleworth
Tomahawk
Lake Galilee
Lake Dunn
Reedy
Aramac
Thistlebank
Thistlebank National Park
Hardington
Llorac
Thornton
Burslem
Tarragona
Eskdale
Mahrigong
Marita Downs
Mt Cobcroft
Prairie Peak
Culladar
Kyong
Carmichael
Bowie
White Cliffs
Yarrowmere
Mundoo Bluff
Thirlestone
Lake Buchanan
Bannockburn
Aberfoyle
Tiree
Uanda
Rainsby
Birricannia
Mt Hopwood
Tangorin
Barenya
Ensay
Ulva
Atherfield
Eyrie
Braemar
Ashton
Oakley
Afton Downs
Warianna
Hillview
Mt Devlin
Alba
Boree
Mumu
Marathon
Moseble
Riverdale
Killeen
Rokeby
Torver Valley
Spring Valley
Villa Dale
Silver Hills
Acton Downs
Wongalee
Porcupine Gorge Nat Pk
Charlotte Plains
Boonderoo
Mount Sturgeon
Mt Emu
Mt Sturgeon
Mt Pleasant
Blantyre
Prairie
Penrice
Warreah
Tindo
Hughenden
Richmond
FLINDERS HWY
Hillview
White Mountains National Park
Oak Vale
Kiora
Pentland
Burra
Warrigal
Torrens Creek
River View
Milray
Corea Plains
Pajingo
Broadleigh Downs
Longton
Egera
Natal Downs
Oxenhope Outstation
Webb Lake
Gem Ck
Darkies Ra
GREAT DIVIDING RANGE
Homestead
Mt Windsor
Mungunburra
Lake Powlathanga
Powlathanga
Balfes Creek
Southern Cross
Mt Redan
Campaspe
Cape River
Lolworth
Killarney
Lake Cargoon
Toomba
Talavera
Myrrlumbing
Somerset
Fletcher Vale
Dalrymple Nat Pk
Battery
Hillgrove
Bluff Downs
Nulla Nulla
Cuba Plains
Kings Knob
Maryvale
Mt Louisa
Big Ben
Oak Valley
Castle Hill
Clarke Hills
Chudleigh Park
Maiden Springs
Blackbraes
Blackbraes National Park
North Gregory River
GREAT
Kennedy
Reedy Spring
Pretty Plains
Mt Courtney
Cargoon
Mount Emu Plains
Stawell River
Dutton
Flinders River
Hamilton River
Rupert Ck
Alick Ck
Wokingham Ck
Kennedy Developmental Road
Landsborough (Matilda Hwy)
Thomson River
Darr River
Thornville Ck
Bangall Ck
Kerr Ck
Towerhill Ck
Cornish Creek
Slasher Ck
Rodney Ck
Aramac Ck
Thomson River
Barcoo River
Alice River
Talundilly
Quart Pot Ra
Vergemont Ck
Forsyth Range
Maneroo
Gory Range
Mistake Range
Bladensburg Nat Park
Bladensburg National Park
Lochern Nat Park
Goneaway National Park
TROPIC OF CAPRICORN
CAPRICORN HWY
Wantagong
Mackenzie Ck
Katherine Ck
Andersons Ck
Landsborough River
Mt Etna

Numbers along roads (selected):
130 155 30 35
46 59 35
144 49 48 113
57 62
46 45 51
41 35 26 34 25
39 29 62 60 5 14 62
11 46 53
155 43 172
36 19 23 34 61
146 58 42
26 62 37
56 38 64 66
243 49 45 33 90 39 20
13 49 97
40 25 38 33
41 39 54
30 23
48 47 51
27 54
35 29 20
44
67 46 55 136 65 47
26 44
17 26
78 80 107 27
151 67 23 50 54
68 26 48
71
34
204 70 49 30 19 16 21 52 26 10 50
55 107 54 64 98 33 146 43

Route markers: 78, 78 (Flinders Hwy), 66 (Landsborough/Matilda Hwy), 71 (Blackall), 65

144° (top), 146° (top right), 144° (bottom left), 146° (bottom right)
−20°, −22°, −24°

South-West Queensland

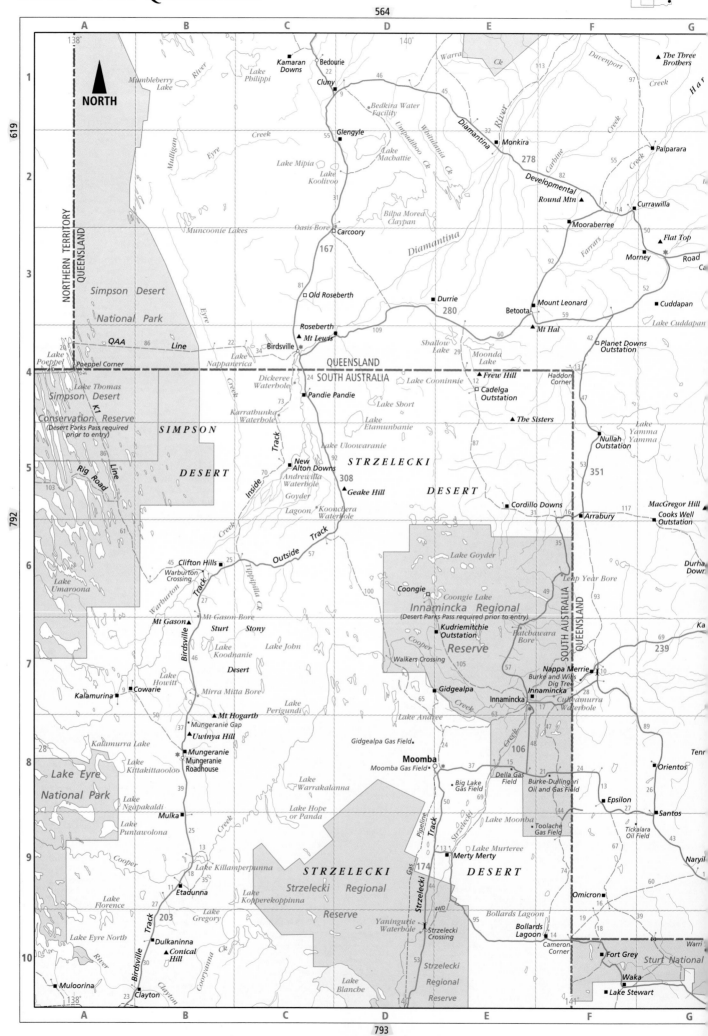

NORTH

A B C D E F G

619

792

QUEENSLAND

NORTHERN TERRITORY

QUEENSLAND

138°

140°

144°

Mumbleberry Lake

Lake Philippi

Kamaran Downs

Bedourie

Cluny

Bedkira Water Facility

Glengyle

Lake Mipia

Lake Koolivoo

Lake Machattie

Bilpa Morea Claypan

Mulligan

Eyre

Creek

River

Muncoonie Lakes

Oasis Bore

Carcoory

Simpson Desert

National Park

Old Roseberth

Roseberth

Mt Lewis

Birdsville

QAA Line

Lake Poeppel

Poeppel Corner

Lake Nappanerica

Dickeree Waterhole

Pandie Pandie

Karrathunka Waterhole

Simpson Desert Conservation Reserve
(Desert Parks Pass required prior to entry)

Lake Thomas

K1

Rig Road

Line

SIMPSON

DESERT

Inside

Track

Goyder

Lagoon

New Alton Downs

Andrewilla Waterhole

Koonchera Waterhole

Geake Hill

STRZELECKI

DESERT

Lake Uloowaranie

Clifton Hills

Warburton Crossing

Warburton

Birdsville

Track

Outside Track

Tirrawuarra Ck

Mt Gason Bore

Mt Gason

Sturt Stony

Desert

Lake Koodnanie

Lake John

Lake Umaroona

Lake Howitt

Kalamurina

Cowarie

Mirra Mitta Bore

Mt Hogarth

Uwinya Hill

Mungerie Gap

Mungeranie

Mungeranie Roadhouse

Kalamurra Lake

Lake Kittakittaooloo

Lake Eyre National Park

Lake Ngapakaldi

Lake Puntawolona

Mulka

Cooper

Creek

Lake Perigundi

Lake Warrakalanna

Lake Hope or Panda

STRZELECKI

Strzelecki Regional

Reserve

Lake Killamperpunna

Lake Kopperekoppinna

Lake Florence

Etadunna

Lake Gregory

Cooryanna Ck

Yaningurie Waterhole

Strzelecki Crossing

Muloorina

Birdsville Track

Clayton River

Clayton

Dulkaninna

Conical Hill

Lake Eyre North

Lake Blanche

Strzelecki Regional Reserve

REGIONAL

DESERT

Diamantina

Warra Ck

The Three Brothers

Davenport Creek

Har

Monkira

Palparara

Developmental

Round Mtn

Currawilla

Mooraberree

Morney

Flat Top

Road

Durrie

Mount Leonard

Betoota

Mt Hal

Cuddapan

Lake Cuddapan

Planet Downs Outstation

Frew Hill

Haddon Corner

Cadelga Outstation

QUEENSLAND

SOUTH AUSTRALIA

Shallow Lake

Moonda Lake

Lake Cooninnie

Lake Short

Lake Etamunbanie

The Sisters

Nullah Outstation

Lake Yamma Yamma

Cordillo Downs

Arrabury

MacGregor Hill

Cooks Well Outstation

Durham Down

Lake Goyder

Innamincka Regional
(Desert Parks Pass required prior to entry)

Coongie

Coongie Lake

Leap Year Bore

SOUTH AUSTRALIA

QUEENSLAND

Kudriemitchie Outstation

Reserve

Cooper

Walkers Crossing

Gidgealpa

Nappa Merrie

Burke and Wills Dig Tree

Innamincka

Cullyamurra Waterhole

Patchawara Bore

Ka

Lake Andree

Gidgealpa Gas Field

Moomba

Moomba Gas Field

Big Lake Gas Field

Della Gas Field

Burke-Dullingari Oil and Gas Field

Orientos

Epsilon

Santos

Gas

Pipeline

Strzelecki

Track

Lake Moomba

Toolache Gas Field

Tickalara Oil Field

Merty Merty

Lake Murteree

Omicron

Naryil

DESERT

Bollards Lagoon

Bollards Lagoon

Cameron Corner

Tenr

Fort Grey

Sturt National

Waka

Lake Stewart

113

97

278

82

32

45

46

9

55

31

167

81

280

109

24

73

92

70

308

57

100

25

45

27

46

50

37

28

39

25

13

18

35

11

27

203

23

59

60

14

278

55

50

52

29

13

47

87

53

351

31

16

117

35

49

93

105

57

65

63

10

28

17

24

48

106

37

15

21

24

50

69

44

95

13

13

26

27

43

74

60

67

19

39

16

18

14

53

239

Ka

89

90

138°

140°

144°

1 2 3 4 5 6 7 8 9 10

A B C D E F G

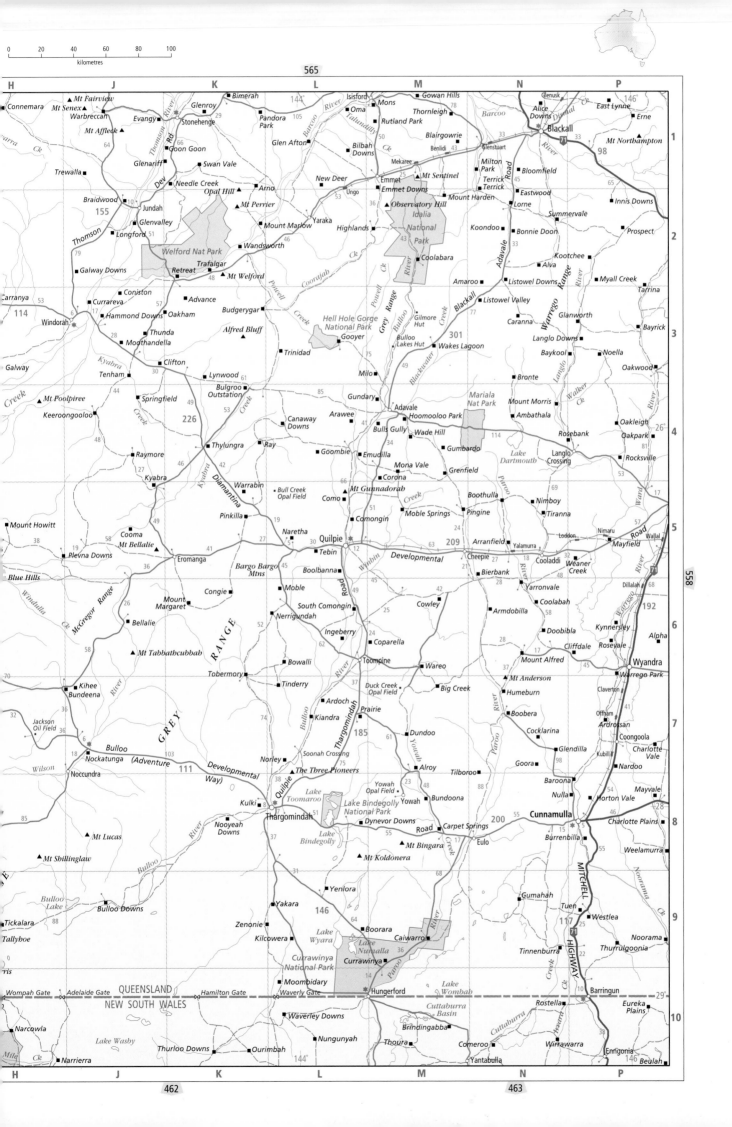

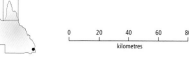

Cape York

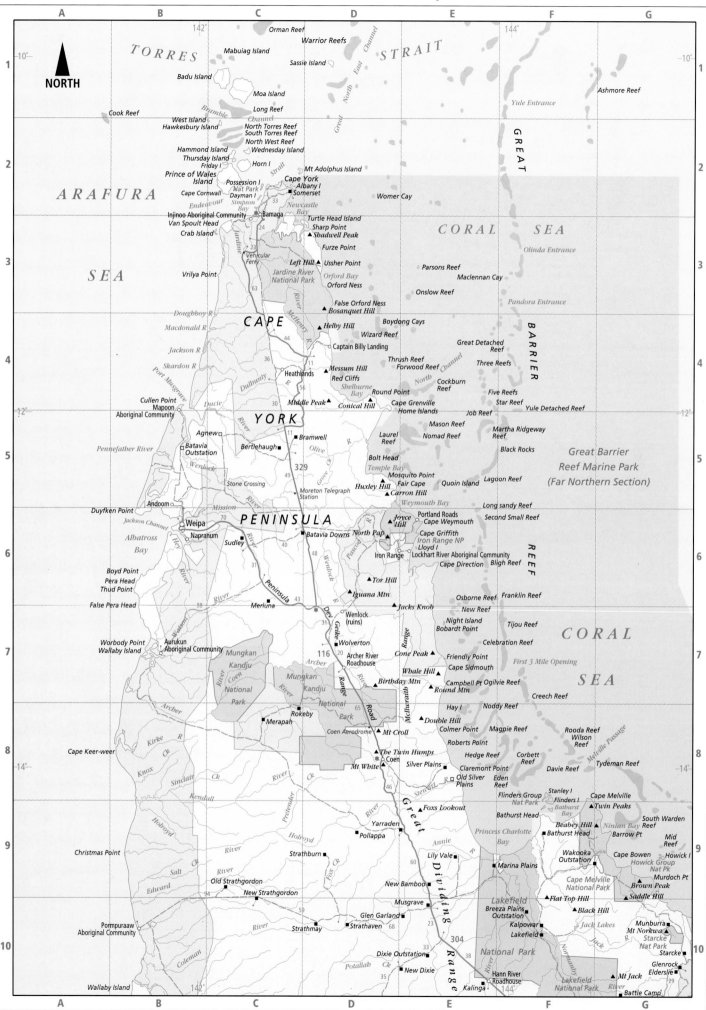

Cairns and Surrounding Areas

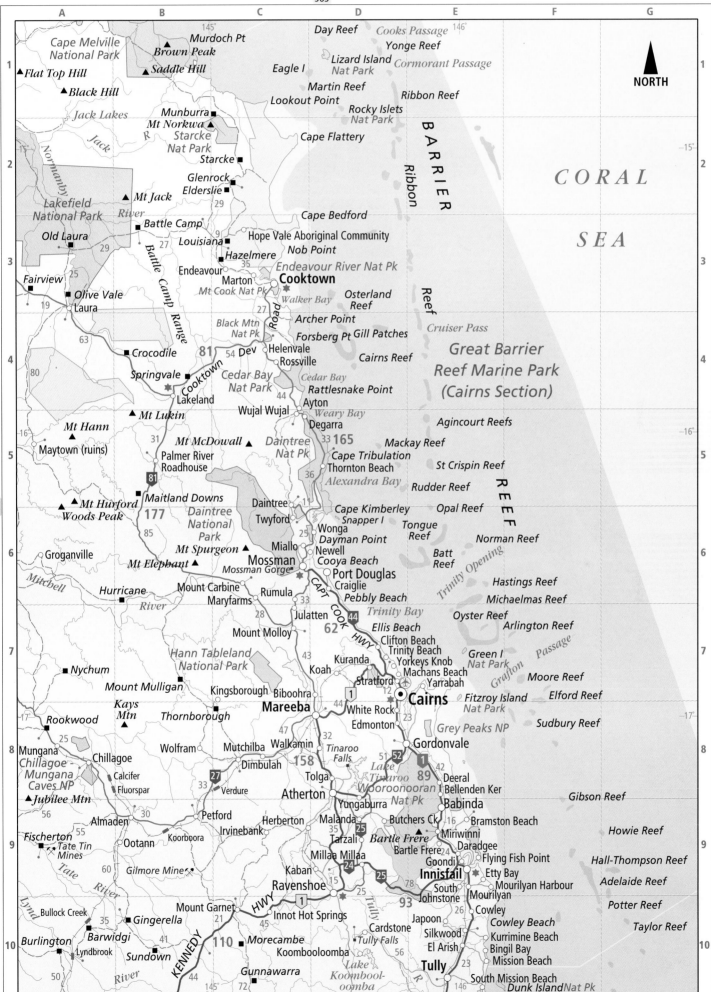

Scale 0 10 20 30 40 50 kilometres

NORTH

Cape Melville National Park
▲ Flat Top Hill
▲ Black Hill
Jack Lakes
▲ Murdoch Pt
▲ Brown Peak
▲ Saddle Hill
Munburra
Mt Norkwa ▲
Starcke Nat Park
Starcke
Glenrock
Elderslie
▲ Mt Jack
Battle Camp
Louisiana
Hazelmere
Endeavour
Marton
Day Reef
Cooks Passage
Yonge Reef
Eagle I
Lizard Island Nat Park
Cormorant Passage
Martin Reef
Lookout Point
Ribbon Reef
Rocky Islets Nat Park
Cape Flattery
Cape Bedford
Hope Vale Aboriginal Community
Nob Point
Endeavour River Nat Pk

Lakefield National Park
Old Laura
Fairview
▲ Mt Jack
▲ Olive Vale
Laura
Crocodile
Springvale
Lakeland
▲ Mt Lukin
▲ Mt Hann
Maytown (ruins)
▲ Mt Hurford
Woods Peak
Maitland Downs
Palmer River Roadhouse
Daintree National Park
Groganville
▲ Mt Spurgeon
▲ Mt Elephant
Hurricane
Mount Carbine
Maryfarms
Rumula
Julatten
Mount Molloy
Nychum
Hann Tableland National Park
Mount Mulligan
Kays Mtn
Thornborough
Kingsborough
Biboohra
Rookwood
Mareeba
Mungana
Chillagoe-Mungana Caves NP
Chillagoe
Calcifer
Fluorspar
▲ Jubilee Mtn
Almaden
Petford
Verdure
Wolfram
Mutchilba
Dimbulah
Walkamin
Tinaroo Falls
Atherton
Tolga
Herberton
Irvinebank
Koorboora
Malanda
Yungaburra
Fischerton
Tate Tin Mines
Ootann
Gilmore Mine
Tarzali
Kaban
Ravenshoe
Millaa Millaa
Bullock Creek
Gingerella
Mount Garnet
Innot Hot Springs
Burlington
Lyndbrook
Barwidgi
Sundown
Morecambe
Koombooloomba
Gunnawarra
Lake Koomboolomba
Tully Falls
Cardstone

Cooktown
Mt Cook Nat Pk
Walker Bay
Osterland Reef
Archer Point
Forsberg Pt
Gill Patches
Cairns Reef
Black Mtn Nat Pk
Helenvale
Rossville
Cedar Bay Nat Park
Cedar Bay
Rattlesnake Point
Ayton
Wujal Wujal
Weary Bay
Degarra
Mt McDowall
Daintree Nat Pk
Cape Tribulation
Thornton Beach
Alexandra Bay
Daintree
Twyford
Cape Kimberley
Snapper I
Wonga
Dayman Point
Miallo
Newell
Cooya Beach
Mossman
Mossman Gorge
Port Douglas
Craiglie
Pebbly Beach
Trinity Bay
Ellis Beach
Clifton Beach
Trinity Beach
Yorkeys Knob
Kuranda
Koah
Machans Beach
Stratford
Yarrabah
Cairns
White Rock
Edmonton
Gordonvale
Wolfram
Deeral
Bellenden Ker
Wooroonooran Nat Pk
Babinda
Butchers Ck
Bramston Beach
Miriwinni
Bartle Frere
Daradgee
Goondi
Flying Fish Point
Innisfail
Etty Bay
Mourilyan
Mourilyan Harbour
South Johnstone
Cowley
Japoon
Cowley Beach
Silkwood
Kurrimine Beach
El Arish
Bingil Bay
Mission Beach
Tully
South Mission Beach
Dunk Island Nat Pk

CORAL SEA

Great Barrier Reef Marine Park (Cairns Section)

Agincourt Reefs
Mackay Reef
St Crispin Reef
Rudder Reef
Opal Reef
Tongue Reef
Norman Reef
Batt Reef
Hastings Reef
Michaelmas Reef
Oyster Reef
Arlington Reef
Green I Nat Park
Moore Reef
Fitzroy Island Nat Park
Elford Reef
Grey Peaks NP
Sudbury Reef
Gibson Reef
Howie Reef
Hall-Thompson Reef
Adelaide Reef
Potter Reef
Taylor Reef
Cruiser Pass
Trinity Opening
Grafton Passage

BARRIER REEF
Ribbon Reef

QUEENSLAND

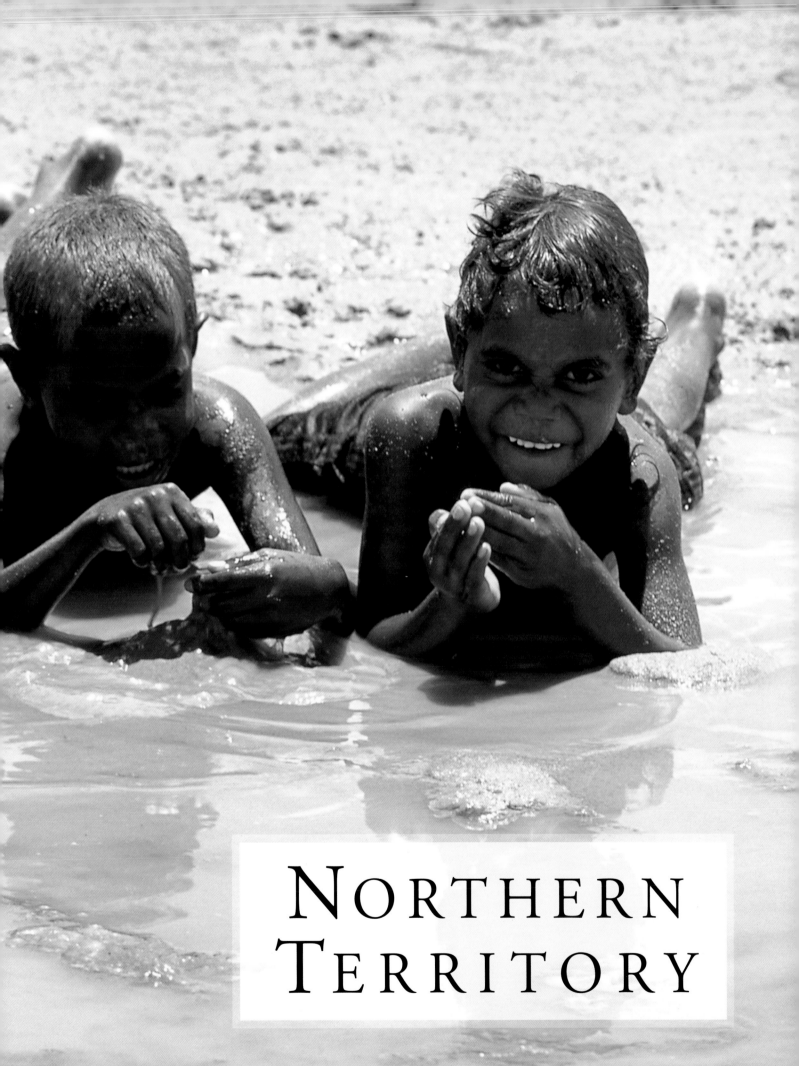

NORTHERN TERRITORY

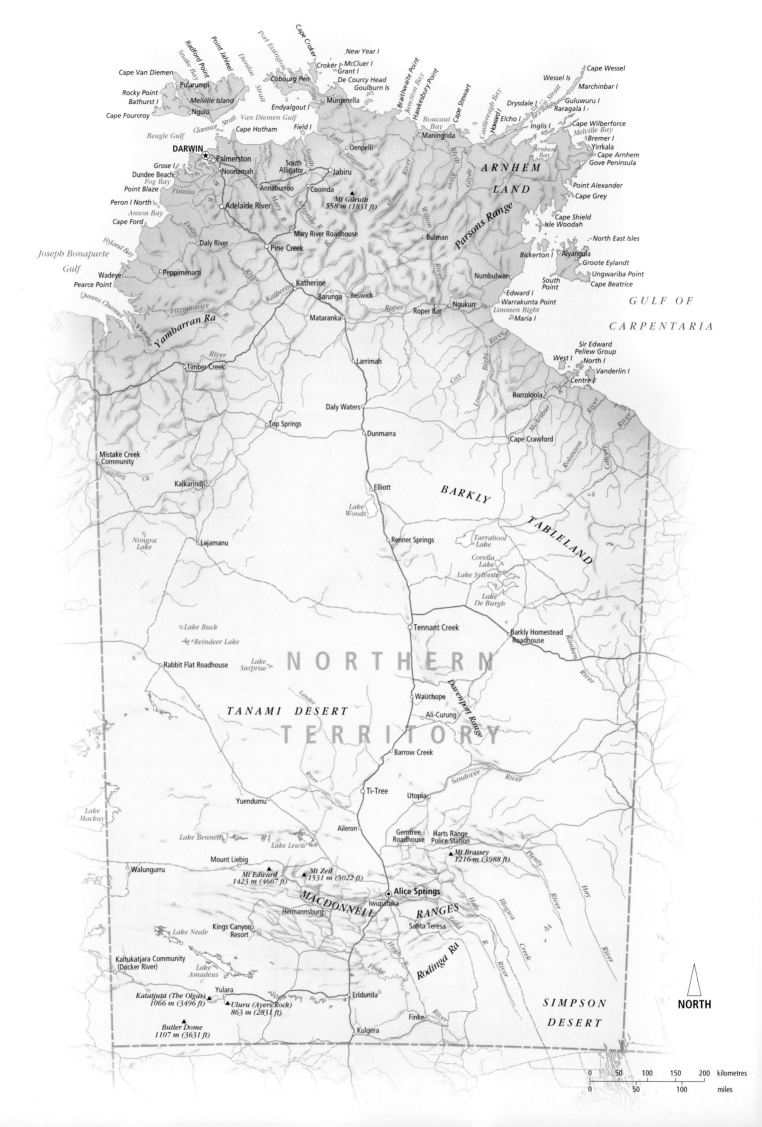

Cape Van Diemen
Radford Point
Point Jahleel
Snake Bay
Pularumpi
Rocky Point
Bathurst I
Cape Fourcroy
Melville Island
Nguiu
Cape Croker
New Year I
Croker I
McCluer I
Grant I
De Courcy Head
Goulburn Is
Braithwaite Point
Hawkesbury Point
Junction Bay
Cape Stewart
Howard I
Castlereagh Bay
Cape Wessel
Wessel Is
Marchinbar I
Drysdale I
Guluwuru
Raragala I
Elcho I
Inglis I
Cape Wilberforce
Melville Bay
Bremer I
Yirrkala
Cape Arnhem
Gove Peninsula

Cobourg Pen
Dundas Strait
Port Essington
Endyalgout I
Murgenella
Cabourg Pen
Clarence Strait
Van Diemen Gulf
Field I
East Alligator R.
Oenpelli
Maningrida
Blyth River
Glyde R.
Arnhem Bay

Beagle Gulf
DARWIN
Palmerston
Noonamah
Grose I
Dundee Beach
Fog Bay
Point Blaze
Finniss R.
Peron I North
Anson Bay
Cape Ford

South Alligator
Jabiru
Mt Gilruth
558 m (1831 ft)
ARNHEM
LAND
Parsons Range
Point Alexander
Cape Grey

Joseph Bonaparte
Gulf

Hyland Bay
Wadeye
Pearce Point
Queens Channel

Annaburroo
Cooinda
Adelaide River
Mary R.
Daly River
Mary River Roadhouse
Pine Creek

Mann River
Wilton River
Bulman

Cape Shield
Isle Woodah
North East Isles
Bickerton I
Alyangula
Groote Eylandt
Ungwariba Point
Cape Beatrice

Peppimenarti
Daly River
Katherine
Barunga
Beswick
Mataranka

Numbulwar
South Point

GULF OF
CARPENTARIA

Fitzmaurice R.
Yambarran Ra
Victoria River
Timber Creek

Roper River
Roper Bar
Ngukurr
Edward I
Warrakunta Point
Limmen Bight
Maria I

Larrimah

Cox R.
Limmen Bight R.
Sir Edward
Pellew Group
West I
North I
Vanderlin I
Centre I

Daly Waters
Dunmarra

Borroloola

Top Springs

Lake
Woods

Elliott

BARKLY
TABLELAND

Cape Crawford

Robinson R.
McArthur R.
Calvert R.

Mistake Creek
Community
Stirling Ck

Kalkarindji

Renner Springs

Tarrabool
Lake
Corella
Lake
Lake Sylvester
Lake
De Burgh

Rankin R.

Lajamanu

Nongra
Lake

Lake Buck
Reindeer Lake

Lake
Surprise

Tennant Creek

Barkly Homestead
Roadhouse

Rabbit Flat Roadhouse

NORTHERN

Davenport Range
Wauchope
Ali-Curung

TANAMI DESERT

Lander River

TERRITORY

Barrow Creek

Lake
Mackay

Yuendumu

Ti-Tree

Sandover River

Utopia

Lake Neale

Lake Amadeus

Lake Bennett

Lake Lewis

Mount Liebig

Walungurru

Mt Edward
1423 m (4667 ft)

Aileron

Gemtree
Roadhouse

Harts Range
Police Station

Mt Brassey
1216 m (3988 ft)

Mt Zeil
1531 m (5022 ft)

Alice Springs
Iwupataka

MACDONNELL
Hermannsburg

RANGES
Santa Teresa

Plenty River

Hay River

Kaltukatjara Community
(Docker River)

Kings Canyon
Resort

Rodinga Ra

Hale R.
Todd R.
Illogwa Creek

Hugh R.
Finke R.

Katatjuta (The Olgas)
1066 m (3496 ft)
Yulara

Uluru (Ayers Rock)
863 m (2831 ft)

Erldunda

SIMPSON

Butler Dome
1107 m (3631 ft)

Finke
Kulgera

DESERT

NORTH

0   50   100   150   200 kilometres

0   50   100 miles

NORTHERN TERRITORY

The Northern Territory—the Outback, Australia's last frontier. Even the official name has a wild, romantic ring to it. For a hundred years the Territory has attracted adventurers, incurable romantics and pioneers—tough cattlemen, rough-around-the-edges crocodile shooters, desperate gold hunters, and hardened businessmen wanting to take a gamble on the trucking game, running a store, or looking for diamonds, oil or gas.

For many the reality is not so far from the dream. While there are no buffalo or crocodile shooters travelling the Territory any more, there are still tall, whippet-like young men and women riding horses, cracking whips and wheeling cattle through the dust, and older, more weather-beaten souls behind the wheels of three-dog (trailers) semis, or sitting in the air-conditioned cabs of graders or dump trucks in a mine somewhere. But now in their spare time they sit down in air-conditioned houses to play computer games, watch videos, and drink a beer—you no longer have to be 'tough' to live in the Territory.

The Northern Territory takes up about one-sixth of Australia, covering almost 1.4 million sq. km (521,000 sq. miles), but is home to fewer than 180,000 people. Half of those live in the Darwin metro region and a big percentage of the rest live in Alice Springs, Katherine, Tennant Creek, Nhulunbuy and Yulara. A sprinkling of other towns and Aboriginal communities leaves the greater part of the state to very few people. Around 23 per cent of the total population is Aboriginal, and more than 50 per cent of the Territory is classed as Aboriginal land—reserve, community land, pastoral land or freehold.

The distances between habitations are extreme in the Territory. Even on the Stuart Highway, where a big percentage of the towns are situated, there are over 200 km (124 miles) between them. On the lesser bituminised roads, you may well travel twice that distance between dwellings. Once onto the dirt, 400 km (248 miles) between points of civilisation is not uncommon.

The Ghan railway, established in 1929 to travel between Alice Springs and Adelaide, was named after the pioneer Afghan camel drivers who traversed the same route.

The 37,530 sq. km (14,261 sq. mile) Tanami Desert varies from yellow to red in its colouration. The plains are covered in spinifex grasses and low shrubs.

The mammoth 'three dog' trailers, or road trains, that haul goods through the Territory can be more than 50 m (164 feet) long, and 2.5 m (8 feet) wide.

Capital
Darwin
Area
1,349,130 sq. km
(520,940 sq. miles)
Proportion of Australia
17.5%
Population of Territory
190,000
Population Density
0.14 per sq. km
(0.36 per sq. mile)
Population of Capital
86,600
Time Zone
9.5 hours ahead of GMT
Climate
Tropical north with two seasons: wet and dry; subtropical in south ranging from semi-arid to desert
Highest Point
Mt Zeil 1,531 m
(5,023 ft)

The road network is pretty good. The great ribbon of the Stuart Highway cuts right through the centre, from the Northern Territory/South Australia border all the way north to Darwin. Do not expect dual lanes, but it is a good road. The Barkly Highway comes in from Queensland, across the billiard table flatness and golden grasses of the Barkly Tablelands, meeting the Stuart at Three Ways, and the Victoria Highway heads west from Katherine, as part of Highway 1, into Western Australia. Add the Kakadu Highway, the Roper, the Table-lands, and the Lasseter Highway out to Uluru (Ayers Rock), and you have all the main bituminised roads. Even on these highways, the blacktop can be just one lane wide—you will need to drop a set of wheels into the dirt when passing another vehicle. If a road train is approaching, do not expect it to move off the bitumen.

Most of the rest of the blacktop goes out to tourist attractions—to Litchfield National Park, around the southern edge of the West MacDonnell Ranges and to Kings Canyon. The Territory prides itself in the fact that 90 per cent of the major tourist attractions are accessible by conventional vehicles.

Much of the road network and the blacktop is a result of the planned expansion and upgrading of the beef road network of the 1970s. Before then most of the roads, even the highways, were dirt; only the Stuart between Alice and Darwin was blacktop, a hangover from World War II. The Stuart Highway

The Northern Territory flag features the Territorial colours and emblem, together with the Southern Cross.

owes its existence to John McDouall Stuart, who in the early 1860s led a number of expeditions north from South Australia and finally crossed the continent in 1862. The Overland Telegraph line followed his route and a track sprang up beside this ribbon of wire, dotted with signs of civilisation in the form of repeater stations—Alice Springs, Tennant Creek, Elliott, Katherine and others.

Until 1911 the Northern Territory was part of South Australia, then the federal government took over for a while. Between 1926 and 1931 the Territory was divided in two, with Northern Australia being looked after by Darwin, and Central Australia being administered from Alice. In 1931 the federal government took control again. It was not until 1978 that the Territory was finally granted self-government, although not full Statehood. Many decisions, much to most Territorians' grief, are still made in far-away Canberra.

Stretching from the arid interior north into the tropics, the Territory has extremes in climate and vegetation. Around Alice Springs the country is dry, with sand ridges and sand plains, cut here and there with low rocky ranges covered in arid landscape vegetation. The weather varies from hot, dry summers, with the occasional storm, to drier, cooler winters. In summer, temperatures of 45°C (104°F) are not uncommon, and winter day temperatures are a mild 15–23°C (59–73°F).

Rainfall varies, with September being the driest month (an average of 10 mm [4 inches]), and February the wettest (an average of 50 mm [2 inches]) of rain.

In the Top End the climate is tropical, with two distinct seasons, the Dry from May to November, and the Wet. Most of Darwin's 1500 mm (59 inches) of rain falls during the Wet, especially in the first three months of the year, with virtually no rainfall in June, July and August. The temperature range is rather static, with maximum temperatures in the low thirties (around 90°F) nearly all the time, and minimums in the mid twenties (around 77°F). In the three driest months already mentioned, the minimum temperatures are around 20°C (68°F). Some people find the Wet's high humidity almost unbearable—the month before the Wet is the worst.

It is no wonder that the Dry is the most popular time to visit the Centre and the Top End of the Northern Territory, but during the Dry you see a drier, tamer country than you would see in summer. With a good road network and air-conditioned cars and motels, it may pay to see the Territory when most other travellers are not there. Certainly the Wet shows a more verdant countryside, a landscape that is more subject to the vagaries of the weather; you will capture a wilder side of the Territory then—one that is closer to its reputation.

The hotel in Grove Hill, 20 km (12 miles) north-east of Hayes, on the old north–south road, was originally built from recycled materials obtained from the mines and railway in the area.

Over millions of years, floodwaters have eroded the soft sandstone at the base of Kings Canyon, causing huge slabs to shear from the walls, widening the canyon.

DARWIN

Following the destruction of Darwin by Cyclone Tracy in 1974, a new, modernised and commercial city was developed in place of the original capital.

The tropical climate of Darwin make the city's lush 34 ha (84 acre) Botanical Gardens a popular attraction.

The most cosmopolitan of Australian cities, Darwin is Australia's only tropical capital. It is closer to much of Asia than it is to much of southern Australia—Jakarta is closer than Brisbane, and Singapore is closer than Hobart.

The city sits on the eastern shore of Port Darwin, a convoluted inlet on the Beagle Gulf, itself an inlet of the Timor Sea. The centre of the city and the port are on a wide isthmus of land between Frances Bay and Fannie Bay, and most of the suburbs are either directly to the north, or spread along the Stuart Highway. There are just under 100,000 people in the greater metro area, making Darwin the smallest capital city in Australia—but what it lacks in population, it makes up for in variety.

There are more than 50 ethnic groups in the city, and a large number of these have been here almost from the very first days of settlement. Aboriginal people have been living here for 40,000 years or more, of course, and Darwin is home to a vibrant Aboriginal culture, with Aboriginal language, art and craft, dance and music an everyday affair. And

Macassan *bêche-de-mer* fishermen from the islands of modern-day Indonesia have probably been sailing this coast for the last few hundred years.

In the 1500s Dutch navigators discovered the Great South Land, and in 1644 Abel Tasman sailed and mapped much of the north-west coast and the Gulf of Carpentaria. Port Darwin was named and mapped by John Stokes and John Wickham on the *Beagle* in 1839. Charles Darwin and his ship were not yet famous—it was another 20 years before he wrote *On the Origin of Species*.

Britain tried to establish a base in northern Australia, but failed—at Port Essington on the Cobourg Peninsula, which lasted just over 10 years, from 1838, and also at Escape Cliff, near the mouth of the Adelaide River, begun in 1863 and abandoned four years later. In 1869 Port Darwin (which was officially called Palmerston but the name never caught on) was established.

A year later the construction of the Overland Telegraph line between Darwin and Adelaide began. This was the real start of the city. With the discovery of gold at Pine Creek 200 km (124 miles) south of Darwin, over 7000 Chinese and a handful of Europeans streamed through on their way to the diggings. A railway line south to the fields brought more workers from India and Malaya, and the port also attracted pearlers, with their crews of Japanese and islanders—by the early 1900s the port was more Asian than European.

During World War II Darwin was Australia's front line, suffering greatly from Japanese bombing raids, and becoming the headquarters for the Allied effort to the north. During the late 1940s to the early 1960s Darwin was a frontier town, with crocodile shooters, buffalo shooters, pioneer cattlemen and other 'wild west' characters calling it home. In 1974 Cyclone Tracy devastated the city of Darwin, killing 64 people and injuring thousands. It led to the rebirth of the city, with a huge redevelopment occurring soon afterwards.

There is a host of things to do in and around the city. For those who enjoy looking into the past there are the old Town Hall and Government House (1883), the Court House and Police Station (1884) and Hotel Darwin, originally called the Palmerston (1883). A wander around the Fannie Bay Gaol, which was in use from 1883 until 1979, gives visitors an insight into conditions endured by prisoners here. There are also many reminders of World War II, including the Oil Storage Tunnels (some open to the public), the anti-submarine boom net tower and the East Point gun emplacements.

The Museum and Art Gallery of the Northern Territory is a must, with displays covering just about every aspect of the Territory's history and art. The

The Asian-style Mindil Beach Sunset Markets take place every week during the dry season, and are a Darwin institution.

Australian Aviation Centre has an impressive display of Territory aviation history and is dominated by a USAF B52 bomber. There are also the Australian Pearling Exhibition, the Indo-Pacific Marine facility (both at the Wharf Precinct), and Lyons Cottage, built in 1925 to house Australian Telegraph Company workers, which has a marvellous collection of old photographs.

For those who love local markets, try the Mindil Beach Sunset Market, with its local and regional handicrafts and food stalls, and the Parap Market. Darwin's oldest market is the Rapid Creek Markets, held every Sunday morning—food lovers will be overwhelmed by the choices. There is a wide variety of restaurants in the city, including many kinds of Asian restaurants, plus Mongolian, Greek, Latin American and Australian (with buffalo, camel, barra, mud crabs and more on the menu).

The city is also a fine base from which to explore the Top End. The Darwin Crocodile Farm and the Territory Wildlife Park, and the Windows on the Wetlands, are on the Arnhem Highway, 60 km (37 miles) south-east of Darwin. A little further along the highway are the jumping crocodiles of the Adelaide River. If you want to see a croc up close, this is the spot! There are also the Marrakai and Fogg Dam Conservation Reserves with their water birds, and the Wildman and Shady Camp Reserves, which are well-known fishing spots. Offshore are the Tiwi Aboriginal islands of Bathurst and Melville. There is a great cultural experience to be had on the islands; tours run from Darwin regularly.

The fishing in Darwin is brilliant. There are plenty of places to throw a line in and you can catch barra almost everywhere. Close to the port there are wrecks that act as artificial reefs, and around these you will find barra, cod, black jewfish, tuna, queenfish and Spanish mackerel.

Special annual events that take place in Darwin include the Hummingbird Corroboree Park Challenge fishing competition at Easter, the Back to the Bush Annual Campdraft and Rodeo in July, the Royal Darwin Show in July, the Darwin Cup Carnival in July, the Darwin Rodeo and Country Music Concert in August, the famous Darwin Beer Can Regatta and the Festival of Darwin in August/September. The Darwin Symphony Orchestra also performs at many special evening concerts.

Darwin Harbour is popular with pleasure-seekers and boating fanatics. However, swimming is not recommended between October and May, due to the presence of box jellyfish.

ADVENTURE ACTIVITIES

Northern Territory

RIGHT: *Located south of the Lasseter Highway, the main road to Uluru, Mount Conner rises 344 m (1129 feet) above the surrounding plains. The climb to the top is steep but straightforward and requires two to three hours.*

Renowned for its outback scenery, Aboriginal culture, the great landmarks of Uluru and Kata Tjuta, and the wetlands of Kakadu, the Northern Territory is an enticing but daunting adventure-travel destination. Services are often few and far between, with many towns consisting of little more than a cluster of houses, a shop and a pub, and extreme weather can turn even a short outing into an ordeal. It is for these reasons that some of the Territory's parks impose strict regulations on visitors. At Uluru–Kata Tjuta, for example, walking is not permitted away from approved tracks and camping is not allowed anywhere within the park. Other national parks have less rigid rules but do request that visitors make their plans known to rangers. Despite these restrictions, however, well-prepared travellers can take advantage of a wide range of adventure activities and almost unlimited potential for wilderness exploration.

Bushwalking

The Northern Territory offers numerous unique bushwalking experiences, both in the Red Centre and in the Top End. The former's arid climate creates an environment that is surprisingly rich in fauna and flora, and its ancient rocks seem like the bones of the earth. A good introduction to desert walking is the Larapinta Trail, which runs through the West MacDonnell Ranges from the outskirts of Alice Springs. The initial 62 km (38.5 miles) of the trail take four to five days; a second 42-km (26-mile) section to the west requires another four days of hiking. Eventually, the trail will run for an uninterrupted 220 km (137 miles) through the ranges, from Alice Springs all the way to Mount Sonder.

Though much shorter, the walks in Uluru–Kata Tjuta are equally fascinating. The most rewarding is the Base Walk, a 9.4-km (5.8-mile) circuit of Uluru, which takes in spectacular rock formations and Aboriginal sacred sites. At Kata Tjuta (the Olgas) the half-day Valley of the Winds Walk provides a terrific tour of the giant conglomerate domes.

In Kakadu, there are numerous short walking trails, many of which are to or along watercourses, often allowing hikers to enjoy a swim at a waterhole en route. One enjoyable day-walk circuit leads over the top of Nourlangie Rock, one of the park's major Aboriginal art sites. Longer walks are possible between other tourist havens such as Jim Jim Falls, Twin Falls and Koolpin Gorge, but the scarcity of water and potential navigation difficulties—iron deposits in the rocks have been known to play havoc with magnetic compasses—mean that they are for experienced and self-sufficient walkers only. Permits must be obtained well in advance for all off-track walks.

Nitmiluk National Park, centred on Katherine Gorge, also has several interesting tracks. Perhaps the best outing is the hike from the visitor centre to the eighth gorge, which takes a day, followed by a paddle down the river on air mattresses through the series of gorges. Hikers can exit from the gorge system at various points, via gullies that drop down from the southern plateau. The most interesting of these is Butterfly Gorge, which shelters a pocket of rainforest inhabited by hundreds of butterflies. The other major walk at Nitmiluk is the tough, five-day, 66-km (41-mile) hike to Edith Falls. Walkers spend each night at a

After a hard day's adventuring, there's no better way to unwind than a long soak in the thermal pools at Mataranka, south of Katherine. The water in the pools stays at a constant temperature of 34°C (93°F).

riverside camp site, so water is not a problem provided you carry enough during the day and don't lose sight of the triangular blue markers that identify the trail.

Another waterside walk can be enjoyed at Redbank Gorge in the West MacDonnell Ranges. This involves an easy stroll along a sandy riverbed, followed by a more arduous clamber through the gorge itself, across piles of boulders and a series of rock pools usually filled with surprisingly cold water. Although taxing, the return trip can be accomplished in a few hours. In Watarrka National Park, the highlight for bushwalkers is the Giles Track, a dramatic two-day, 22-km (13.5-mile) walk from Kathleen Springs to Kings Canyon.

Rock Climbing and Caving

There's no shortage of accessible rock in the Territory, but the intense heat can be a major obstacle. Despite this, Alice-Springs-based climbers think nothing of driving 200 km (124 miles) to Glen Helen Gorge for a weekend's climbing, a spot that at least offers the opportunity for a post-climb swim in the river at the base of the cliffs. Technical rock climbing is not allowed in Uluru–Kata Tjuta National Park.

Cutta Cutta Caves Nature Park southeast of Katherine has several caves which can be explored on guided tours.

Mountain Biking

Technical mountain biking is not a widely practised sport in the Northern Territory, due to a shortage of suitable single track. However, there are some eroded 4WD trails in the MacDonnell Ranges which offer fun riding. Great mountain-bike touring trips are possible on backroads in the Top End as well as the Centre, but participants should be wary of the dangers of heat exhaustion and dehydration.

Canoeing, Kayaking and Rafting

At Nitmiluk National Park during the Dry season, visitors can hire canoes to explore the Katherine River's magnificent system of 13 gorges. Most of these gorges are separated by rocky sections, some of which may require short portages.

For more adventurous paddlers, exciting hard-core river trips are available in various parts of the Top End. These are not difficult journeys from a technical point of view, but require that paddlers are totally self-sufficient and aware of the dangers posed by estuarine or saltwater crocodiles. Local advice should be sought in advance of any trip.

Sea Kayaking

Although much of the Northern Territory's coast consists of uninspiring mudflats and mangroves, there are some glorious stretches of shoreline and magnificent beaches, especially around the Gulf of Carpentaria. Self-sufficiency, experience and meticulous planning are prerequisites for all trips and paddlers should always be on the lookout for saltwater crocodiles, even on short outings and especially around river mouths. Keep in mind also that permission to enter certain areas may need to be obtained from the traditional Aboriginal owners.

For a good weekend kayak trip from Darwin, head west across Port Darwin to Mandorah and explore the coastline of the Cox Peninsula.

Exploring the Devils Marbles Conservation Reserve involves some walking and a certain amount of scrambling and climbing. The rocks are the eroded remains of a 1.5-billion-year-old granite intrusion.

THE TOP END

From Aboriginal art to unique wetlands—the Top End of the Northern Territory is an area of tremendous cultural and natural significance. Much of the region is inaccessible by road and during the Wet season, from October to March, even the roads become impassable. Beef cattle, buffalo and tourism have all played their part in the fortunes of the Territory. It's frontier country—rugged terrain, vast distances and crocodiles—but its rewards outweigh the dangers.

Darwin, founded in 1869 after numerous attempts had been made to establish settlements elsewhere in the Top End, is a good stepping off point for some of the fine national parks in the region.

South of Darwin is Litchfield National Park offering spectacular year-round waterfalls and good swimming. To the east of Darwin is Kakadu National Park, a World Heritage area, where magnificent Aboriginal rock art galleries can be found. In Kakadu National Park the cliffs of the Arnhem Land Escarpment descend to the coastal floodplains, which support millions of migratory birds including magpie geese and whistling ducks. Brolgas and jabirus (Australia's only type of stork) feed in the shallows and barramundi inhabit the East Alligator River.

South of Kakadu National Park, and accessible by road from the city of Katherine, is Nitmiluk (Katherine Gorge) National Park. Here you can take a boat trip along the Katherine River to see the colourful sandstone walls of the gorge. Wallabies, dingoes, echidnas and freshwater crocodiles are some of the larger kinds of animals that live in the park.

The stony ridges sustain bloodwood and Darwin stringybark eucalyptus trees as well as a variety of grasses. Edith Falls is a lovely swimming spot in the park.

Katherine is at the junction of the Victoria Highway, leading to Kununurra in north-east Western Australia, and the Stuart Highway, the main north–south route. Along the Victoria Highway are the Keep River and the Gregory National Parks, which both have important Aboriginal sites.

South of Katherine, near the junction of the Stuart Highway and the Roper River Highway that heads east to the Gulf country, is Elsey National Park, where the warm springs of Mataranka provide a shady oasis.

OPPOSITE: The normally tranquil waters of the Katherine River, in Nitmiluk National Park, become a raging torrent of brown water during the Wet season.

A school teacher broadcasts a lesson over the radio to the children in the 'world's largest classroom'— the School of the Air.

REGIONAL FEATURE

Kakadu National Park

Allosyncarpia ternata *is a medium-sized tree found only in the Top End. Within its limited range, however, it occupies a variety of habitats including monsoon rainforest, upland savanna and more exposed, rocky areas of the Arnhem Land Plateau.*

OPPOSITE: *From the top of the escarpment at Ubirr, visitors can enjoy a 360-degree panorama that takes in the surrounding flood plains, Arnhem Land and dark patches of rainforest.*

*Abundant on the floodplains of Arnhem Land, the agile wallaby (*Macropus agilis*) moves to higher ground during the Wet then returns to the flatlands when waters subside to feed on flourishing plants.*

Kakadu National Park is one of Australia's largest national parks and unquestionably one of the continent's most significant ecological treasures. Dominated by the majestic Arnhem Land escarpment, an almost unbroken wall of sandstone that runs for 500 km (310 miles) along its eastern side, Kakadu encompasses immense tracts of savanna woodland, seasonal wetlands, an entire river system (the South Alligator), spectacular waterfalls, paperbark swamps, mangroves and coastal mudflats. These varied habitats are in turn home to an astounding range of wildlife. Here you'll find more than 1600 plant species, 64 mammal species (more than one-quarter of Australia's total), 128 kinds of reptiles including both the saltwater and freshwater crocodile, and 274 species of birds. In addition, Kakadu protects an estimated 7000 Aboriginal art sites, including several that date back more than 18,000 years, as well as thousands of other archaeological sites, which have yielded some of the earliest evidence of the human colonisation of the continent.

Kakadu draws visitors from around Australia and, indeed, all around the world, at a rate of well over 200,000 people every year. Most come in the dry season, from April to October, when the climate is almost perfect for travelling. For the few who come during the Wet and are prepared to put up with the heat and humidity, the rewards can be even greater—the waterfalls flow strongly, the billabongs are full, the area is lush and green. In contrast, by late in the dry season, much of the bushland is tinder dry and grass fires, lit in the park as part of its management control system, often blacken large areas. However, roads to some of the more remote attractions may be flooded and impassable during the Wet.

At all times of year, visitors to Kakadu should remember that dangerous estuarine, or saltwater, crocodiles inhabit many of the park's waterways. Take great care near all rivers and pools—despite their name, salt-water crocodiles also inhabit fresh water—and heed all warning signs. Many of the popular swimming holes are safe, but, if in doubt, check with park rangers.

History

Current estimates suggest that Aboriginal peoples first reached this area approximately 50,000 years ago. The word 'Kakadu' derives from the name of one of the area's earliest inhabitants, the Gagudju people. Their longstanding association with the area is reflected in the park's magnificent paintings and engravings. This rock art also records the visits of Macassan voyagers who travelled to the area from present-day Indonesia, well before Europeans arrived in the seventeenth century, to fish, gather trepangs and search for pearls. It also depicts encounters with Dutch and, later, British, sailors, who are shown along with their ships, axes and firearms.

Following European settlement of Australia, the East Alligator, South Alligator and West Alligator Rivers were first sighted and named in 1818 by British surveyor Phillip Parker King, who mistook the many crocodiles he saw on the riverbanks for alligators. In 1845, Ludwig Leichhardt led the first land-based expedition to the area during his epic 15-month trek from Moreton Bay in Queensland to Port Essington near present-day Darwin, and was the first European to describe the Arnhem Land escarpment.

The Kakadu region was little settled or developed during the following century. Uranium was discovered near the South Alligator River in 1886, but it wasn't until the mid-twentieth century that settlers realised what it was. In 1969, uranium deposits were found at the site of the present-day Ranger Mine, fuelling interest in the exploitation of what was clearly a valuable and extensive resource.

Kakadu National Park was proclaimed in 1979 and soon afterward expanded to its present size of 19,804 sq. km (7700 square miles). In 1981, its international cultural and ecological significance was recognised by UNESCO, which declared it a World Heritage Area. Today, one-third of the park remains the property of its traditional Aboriginal owners but is leased on a long-term basis to Parks Australia. The traditional owners also hold a majority of seats on the park's board of management.

When the national park was set up, pre-existing mineral leases at Ranger, Jabiluka and Koongarra—all located within the park boundaries—were maintained and the areas excluded from park titles. The Ranger Uranium Mine began operations in 1980, and permission for the commencement of uranium mining at Jabiluka was given in 1982 and reconfirmed in 1991. Since then, however, the area's traditional owners and conservationists have opposed mining development at Jabiluka, claiming that it will endanger park

A great egret (Ardea alba) forages among water lilies. These birds were once widely hunted for the long plumes they develop during the breeding season, which were used to decorate ladies' hats.

Also known as the policeman bird, the jabiru (Ephippiorhyncus asiaticus) is Australia's only stork.

ecosystems and sacred sites. UNESCO has also warned that the project may infringe World Heritage values. Despite this opposition, the federal government asserts that no damage will be incurred and plans to push ahead with the proposed mine.

Exploring the Park

By far the best place to start any tour of Kakadu is the Bowali Visitor Centre on the Kakadu Highway near Jabiru. The centre's excellent exhibits provide a wealth of information on the park's treasures; in addition, there are displays of Aboriginal arts and crafts, and a range of locally produced souvenirs is offered for sale. Guided walks to many of the major art sites depart from here daily, and you can also pick up maps and other information on the park's wide range of bushwalking trails and 4WD tracks.

The nearby town of Jabiru is Kakadu's residential hub. It was originally built for workers from the Ranger Uranium Mine, but is now also home to many park staff as well as people employed in the tourism industry. Jabiru offers a wide range of services including fuel, supplies, a post office, supermarket and accommodation, most notably at the distinctive Crocodile Hotel, which is built in the shape of an enormous saltwater crocodilex, the totem of the

Gagudju people. Their legends recount how an ancestral being called Ginga emerged from the sea at the beginning of the Dreamtime and created the region's rocky outcrops. One day, however, Ginga caught fire and had to rush to the river to cool off; as he reached the water, he turned into a crocodile.

At Jabiru Airport, 6 km (3.7 miles) east of the town, visitors can arrange scenic flights over Kakadu, the Arnhem Land escarpment and the adjacent plateau, which is Aboriginal land. Tours of the nearby Ranger Uranium Mine are also conducted regularly.

For a fabulous introduction to the park's wetland habitats and fauna, head south to Yellow Waters, a magnificent billabong on the South Alligator River. A boardwalk here extends several hundred metres along the edge of the picturesque waterway, providing many fine vantage points, but regular boat cruises offer even better views of the startling array of wildlife. Enormous flocks of magpie geese and wandering whistling ducks throng the waters and fill the air with their cries. Comb-crested jacanas stride over pools, stepping daintily from one lily pad to another. Haughty jabirus and brolgas forage along the shore, and massive saltwater crocodiles bask in the sun on the banks with one eye on passing prey.

A short distance from Yellow Waters is the Warradjan Aboriginal Cultural Centre, which provides intriguing insights into local Aboriginal culture through its displays of indigenous artefacts and locally produced artworks, many of which are for sale.

IN THE GALLERIES

Opportunities to visit Aboriginal rock-art sites abound in Kakadu. One of the most accessible and impressive is Ubirr, situated about 40 km (25 miles) north-east of Jabiru and 3 km (1.9 miles) north of the Border Store where the road crosses the East Alligator River and enters Arnhem Land. From the car park, a 1-km (0.6-mile) circuit trail leads to the main sites. A wide range of artistic styles is on display, including stick-like Mimi figures—some estimated to be up to 20,000 years old—and the more recent (less than 3000 years old) and highly striking 'X-ray' paintings. Beyond the main gallery, a steep path leads to the top of the rocky escarpment, from where you can enjoy splendid views of the surrounding floodplains and billabongs and the Arnhem Land escarpment.

The upstream picnic area near the Border Store is the departure point for Bardedjilidji Sandstone Walk. A 2.5-km (1.6-mile) stroll, the trail wanders through tall, tropical grasses, past giant termite mounds, pandanus, fig and native peach trees, as well as oddly shaped sandstone outcrops and rocky overhangs concealing fine examples of Aboriginal art.

The artistic treasures found around Ubirr are rivalled by those at Nourlangie Rock, 19 km (12 miles) south of the Bowali Visitor Centre. The highlight here is the Anbangbang rock shelter, which has been used by Aboriginal peoples for at least 20,000 years and features many paintings of animals such as wallabies. The shelter and other galleries are reached via a gentle loop trail of 1.5 km (0.9 miles), most of which is accessible to wheelchairs. Interpretive signs along the track provide an informative commentary on many of the images and their origins.

The paintings in the Anbangbang shelter depict mythical figures such as Namonjok, a dangerous spirit, and Namarrgon, the Lightning Man. Many were painted by Nayombolmi, also known as Barramundi Charlie, in 1964. In many cases, he simply traced over existing, much earlier works. Such repainting is a traditional and accepted practice in Aboriginal culture, but can only be carried out by local, authorised artists.

On the western side of Nourlangie Rock, an easy 3.4-km (2.1-mile) hike—allow between one and a half and two hours—takes you through open woodlands to one of the most interesting art sites in Kakadu, Nanguluwur Gallery. Paintings on its walls illustrate various aspects of the daily lives of local peoples, from ancient to modern times. Evidence found here, such as the remains of fish, shellfish, turtles and wallabies, suggests that the gallery was also used as a living and eating area over thousands of years.

To the north of Nourlangie is Koongarra Saddle, from where there is a pleasant 3 km (1.9-mile) walk to the crystal-clear Gubara Pools. Another, longer bushwalk links Nourlangie and Nanguluwur art sites. It involves some fairly strenuous climbing, so you need to be quite fit and should allow between six and eight hours for the return hike. It is also important

Extremely long toes allow the comb-crested jacana (Irediparra gallinacea) to walk across the surface of billabongs using water lilies as stepping stones.

The sandstone escarpment that bisects Kakadu is the western edge of the Arnhem Land Plateau. Almost entirely Aboriginal land, it covers approximately 100,000 sq. km (38,600 square miles).

Up to 1300 mm (51 inches) of rain fall on Kakadu during the wet season, swelling rivers and billabongs and flooding flatlands.

Barramundi are the main target for anglers in Kakadu and some monster fish are taken in waterways such as the South Alligator River, especially in April and May.

that you register your departure with the park rangers and sign in again on your return. A trail map is available from the visitor centre.

FALLING WATERS

Kakadu's many dramatic waterfalls are at their best during the wet season when torrents of water thunder over the Arnhem Land escarpment. However, they are also harder to reach at this time of year and most travellers opt to visit them early in the Dry—though, be warned, by the end of the dry season many of the falls are reduced to a mere trickle.

The most impressive of the park's cascades are Jim Jim and Twin Falls. The former is reached via a rough, 60-km (37-mile) track that branches off the Kakadu Highway 37 km (23 miles) south of the visitor centre. This road was intended to provide 2WD access, but when reopened after the Wet it quickly deteriorates into corrugations and long stretches of thick bulldust and can be hazardous even in a 4WD. At the end of the road, a short track leads through forest to the rocks at the bottom of the falls. It's a spectacular scene, with the waters plummeting 200 m (656 feet) into the creek below. The pool at the bottom tends to be chilly but is a great place to cool off or enjoy an invigorating swim during warmer weather.

Jim Jim has a camp site with toilets barbecues and tables, and it's a good idea to use this as your base for a day trip to nearby Twin Falls. It is reached via a sandy 10-km (6-mile) track that is slow and winding and will take about an hour to drive in a 4WD vehicle. The track ends at one a white sandy beach by a creek; from here, you have to take to the water, either swimming or paddling on an inflatable mattress for

about 1 km (0.6 miles) past sheer rock faces, before scrambling across a pile of boulders to the base of the falls. This is an enchanting spot with a lovely sandy beach and a huge, clear, natural splash pool. The falls themselves are only about half the height of Jim Jim, but equally impressive in their own way.

About 50 km (31 miles) south of the turn-off to Jim Jim, another dirt track leads for 12 km (7.5 miles) to Barramundi Falls. This small waterfall tumbles down the escarpment into a large, clear pool. Short trails lead to several idyllic swimming spots with narrow, sandy beaches. The pool is home to freshwater crocodiles, but these pose no danger to humans unless provoked. Camping is allowed here, at a site called Maguk, but there are no facilities.

Another delightful waterfall, Gunlom Falls, is located 37 km (23 miles) from the park's southern entrance station and reached via an unsealed road that is, however, negotiable in a conventional vehicle. It ends at a pretty, grassy picnic area, from where it's a short, wheelchair-accessible, 100-m (110-yard) stroll to the large, sandy bottomed pool at the base of the falls—a terrific picnic and swimming spot, especially suited to children. When Waterfall Creek is in flood, the 70-m (230-foot) falls are a truly impressive sight.

Several walking trails begin at the foot of Gunlom Falls. Highly recommended for those of reasonable fitness is the climb to the top of the cascade, which takes about half an hour each way. The rewards include a splendid panorama that takes in much of the escarpment, a broad sweep of the plains and a bird's-eye view of the pandanus-lined pool far below. Ludwig Leichhardt is reputed to have stood on this very spot during his overland journey in 1845.

Those keen to savour the scenery here can pitch a tent at the adjacent camp site, which has good facilities. About 23 km (14 miles) south of Gunlom Falls, on the upper reaches of the South Alligator River, is the Gimbat picnic area, named after the adjacent Old Gimbat Station Homestead. Also nearby is Coronation Hill, which became a major source of controversy in the late 1980s when BHP proposed mining gold and platinum here. The traditional owners of this land, the Jawoyn people, were strongly opposed to the proposal as they considered Coronation Hill a sacred site, guarded by the spirit Bula, and had had registered it as such in 1985. They also regarded the area as 'sickness country' and believed that if the earth here were disturbed, illness would overcome all who subsequently entered the area. Following an investigation, the federal government placed a 50-year ban on mining here; its decision was influenced by the concerns of indigenous inhabitants but also by suggestions that cyanide residue from mining operations could leak into the South Alligator River floodplain and destroy the delicately balanced ecosystems.

LAND'S END

Only one track in the park provides access to the park's northern boundary on the shores of Van Diemen

Gulf and its intriguing coastal environments. Suitable for 4WD vehicles only, it departs from the left-hand side of the Arnhem Highway, about 18 km (11 miles) from the western entrance station and winds for 12 km (7.5 miles) through eucalypt forest traversed by occasional sand ridges to Two Mile Hole. There is a shady camp site here beside the waterhole, but no facilities; furthermore, water from the billabong should be boiled before use. There is also boat access and good fishing, particularly for barramundi. Another 26 km (16 miles), first through forest and then across open plains, takes you to Four Mile Hole, another scenic site that is also a popular fishing spot. It has only basic facilities and offers little shade to protect you from the fierce sun. Saltwater crocodiles are common in and around these waterholes, so do not swim in them, and be alert on their banks.

The track then continues across plains and mangrove swamps for another 43 km (26.5 miles) to the head of the West Alligator River and the shore of Van Diemen Gulf. Though sandflies can be a nuisance, the mangrove swamps constitute a fascinating habitat that is rich in birds and aquatic life.

Access and Camping

Kakadu National Park is an easy two-and-a-half hour drive from Darwin along the sealed Arnhem Highway. A short distance beyond the park's western boundary, you come to the main entrance station, which is staffed by park rangers during office hours. An entrance fee applies and your permit is then valid for 14 days (or multiple entries to the park within the 14-day period). To reach the park from the south, turn off the Stuart Highway 90 km (56 miles) north of Katherine at Pine Creek. From there, it's 59 km (37 miles) to the park boundary; 6 km (3.7 miles) further on you reach the southern entrance station where you can obtain your 14-day permit, maps and information on the park.

Kakadu offers some superb camping experiences, often at picturesque sites located near escarpments, waterfalls and billabongs. Two caravan parks, at Jabiru and Cooinda, offer a full range of facilities, while the formal camping areas at Merl (near Ubirr), Muirella Park (between Jabiru and Yellow Waters), Mardugal (near Yellow Waters) and Gunlom Falls can also accommodate caravans and have showers, flushing toilets and water, as well as facilities for the disabled. At all these sites, a camping fee is charged and usually collected on the spot by park rangers. A free camping area with pit toilets only, which is also suitable for caravans, is located at Malabanjbanjdju, 13 km (8 miles) south of Jabiru.

Throughout the park you'll also find a number of other, less developed camping areas, most of which have toilets and barbecues, but no showers, as well as some more remote camping grounds with no facilities at all. Your national park permit allows you to camp at these spots at no extra charge.

It is estimated that Kakadu has between 5000 and 6000 crocodiles. The saltwater or estuarine crocodile (Crocodylus porosus) is the world's largest living reptile.

Places in
THE TOP END

ADELAIDE RIVER

Just over an hour's drive south of Darwin, 119 km (74 miles) from the city, the township of Adelaide River (population 370), on a stream of the same name, is a popular stopover for travellers. Back in the early 1880s the town site was an overnight stop for miners heading to the Pine Creek goldfields; it remained a stopping point when the rail arrived later that same decade. There is a lot to see and do in town today—there are several museums, such as the Motor Cycle Haven and the Adelaide River Railway Station, as well as a number of World War II sites, including the War Cemetery and the large ammunition depot at Snake Gully.

The township played an important role for Australia during World War II: after the bombing raid on Darwin in February 1942, Adelaide River became the centre of military activity as the Australian and US headquarters were relocated there, along with camps, hospitals, airfields and army supply depots.

The town offers easy access to the delights of Litchfield National Park and the Daly River and there is good fishing in the nearby streams and rivers. Annual events include the Adelaide River Show, rodeo, campdraft and gymkhana, which are held in June, along with the Country Race Meeting and the Country Music Festival.
Map ref: page 614 D5

BATCHELOR

The small township of Batchelor (population 650) is 14 km (9 miles) off the Stuart Highway—106 km (66 miles) south of Darwin—and was once the main town for Rum Jungle, Australia's first uranium mine and one of the largest economic influences on the Top End's development at that time. Uranium was discovered in the area in 1949, and in 1952 the township of Batchelor was established to service the nearby mine site. Today, apart from a couple of deep, jungle-clad, human-made lakes, little remains of this mining venture.

The inimitable bushman's hat; an icon of the Outback.

The Adelaide River Railway Station Museum, Adelaide River.

The area had been first settled by Europeans in the late 1800s, and up until the 1940s had seen a steady and varying stream of tin miners, Chinese market gardeners and copper prospectors. During World War II the town was an important base and was bombed by the Japanese.

Since the closing of the mine in 1963 and the cessation of ore processing in 1971, the town of Batchelor has been a lot quieter. The town's lush green surroundings remain largely unspoilt. Today it is the site of a TAFE college specialising in Aboriginal tourism, and of an export abattoir. But its big attraction these days is its proximity to Litchfield National Park—it is a 25 minute drive to Florence Falls, one of the highlights of the park. The town also offers the closest accommodation to the park.
Map ref: page 614 D5

CUTTA CUTTA CAVES NATURE PARK

These ancient limestone caves, up to 15 m (49 feet) deep, are managed as a commercial venture and are open to the public seven days a week. Guided tours of the caves are conducted every day and a short walking trail takes people through a typical tropical woodland. Recently the Tindal Cave was added to the complex. The caves are home to orange horseshoe bats and brown tree snakes. Picnic tables and toilets are provided. May to October is the best time to visit the caves. The park is 30 km (19 miles) south of Katherine, just off the Stuart Highway.
Map ref: page 614 F8

DALY RIVER

South-west of Adelaide River, 232 km (144 miles) south of Darwin, is the small riverside community of Daly River (population 150). A Jesuit mission opened here in 1885, and for a time copper was mined nearby. A government-run smelter operated in the area in the early 1900s. For tourists this is for all intents and purposes the end of the road—to the west is the Daly River/Port Keats Aboriginal Land Trust.

There is great fishing to be found in the Daly River for barramundi, threadfin salmon, catfish and sooty

4WD vehicles crossing the Daly River, 232 km (144 miles) south-west of Darwin—'the end of the road'.

grunter. For the travelling angler there are a number of fishing lodges, and boats for hire. Aboriginal arts and crafts are available at the Aboriginal art centre, and the area is richly endowed with native flora and fauna. Other attractions in the area include the old Jesuit mission and mine sites. Annual events include the Northern Territory Barra Nationals in April, and the Northern Territory Barramundi Classic in May.

Map ref: page 614 C6

ELSEY NATIONAL PARK

The headwaters of the Roper River near the township of Mataranka on the Stuart Highway provide tranquil spots for canoeing, swimming and fishing. There are a few good walks through the monsoon forests along the Roper, especially one to Elsey Falls. The park has camping and caravan facilities. The Mataranka thermal pool on the Waterhouse River is the other popular feature of this park. Situated near Mataranka Homestead, a commercial venture within the park where a replica of the old Elsey Homestead (of *We of the Never Never* fame) has been built, the warm waters attract many visitors during winter.

Map ref: page 614 G8

Bark humpies near the replica of the old Elsey Homestead, Elsey National Park.

GREGORY NATIONAL PARK

This park, 160 km (99 miles) south-west of Katherine on the Victoria Highway, was named after the explorer A.C. Gregory, who trekked through this country in 1855. It features magnificent gorges and important Aboriginal cultural and art sites, and protects the plant and animal communities of this fragile area, which is part tropical, part semi-arid. The park has a diversity of flora, with heathlands, spinifex, melaleuca forests, nutwood, turpentine and giant boab trees in abundance; flowering eucalypts dominate other areas of the park. Feral donkeys, wild pigs, brumbies and stray cattle compete with the native animals, and both saltwater and freshwater crocodiles inhabit the creeks and billabongs. The area is very rich in bird life.

The eastern (smaller) section of the park has a number of attractions, including Joe's Creek Walk, which takes visitors up to the face of the escarpment, and the Escarpment Lookout, which gives good views from the top of the Stokes Range east up to the entrance of the Victoria Gorge. There are camping areas at Limestone Gorge and near the Bullita Homestead.

Map ref: page 614 D10

GURIG NATIONAL PARK AND COBOURG MARINE PARK

The remote Gurig National Park lies 570 km (354 miles) east and north of Darwin. Permits are required to enter, and only 15 vehicles are allowed in the park at one time. Bookings are essential. The road is sealed up to the East Alligator River crossing and from

there it deteriorates. The last 70 km (43 miles) into Black Point on Cobourg Peninsula is sandy and corrugated. This national park is the traditional home of four clans of Aboriginal people who today live within the boundaries of the park. The camping area is at Smith Point, only about 100 m (328 feet) from a sandy white beach. Here you can swim (but keep an eye out for crocodiles), walk along the beach, and watch turtles lay their eggs at night. Fishing for certain species of fish is permitted within the

A secluded beach at the remote Cobourg Marine Park.

Cobourg Marine Park, and you can also join a tour by boat to explore the ruins of the Victoria Settlement at Port Essington, which was abandoned in 1848.

Map ref: page 614 E2
(Cobourg Marine Park 614 E1)

The spectacular yet fragile ecosystem of Gregory National Park, 60 km (99 miles) south-west of Katherine.

The wetlands near Jabiru, in Kakadu National Park.

JABIRU

Surrounded by the World Heritage and internationally acclaimed Kakadu National Park, and the subject of a fair amount of contro-versy, Jabiru—254 km (158 miles) east of Darwin—is a mining town which was established in 1981 to house the workers for the uranium mines of Ranger, Jabiluka and Koongarra. It makes a fine base from which to explore the sur-rounding park; other nearby resorts, with camping grounds, are at Cooinda to the south, or on the banks of the South Alligator River to the west.

The town has a population of 1735. It is a modern, sparkling clean mining community that has all the services a traveller requires. The surrounding national park offers some of the finest Aboriginal art sites imaginable, fantastic barra fishing, as well as spectacular scen-ery and incredible bird life. Annual events include the Kakadu Barra Bash in March, the Oenpelli Open Day in August, and the Jabiru Wind Festival in August/September.
Map ref: page 614 G4

KATHERINE

Katherine is a bustling community on the southern bank of the Kath-erine River and astride the Stuart Highway, at its junction with the Victoria Highway, the main route to the west. It is 321 km (199 miles) south-east of Darwin. This major Top End town (population of 11,200) services an area the size of the State of Victoria, and has

a multicultural mix which enhances its 'Outback' image. In recent years the town has become a major military centre, with the RAAF Base Tindal, and army units and training areas, close by.

The river was named by John McDouall Stuart in 1862, and nine years later the Overland Telegraph line crossed this major permanent stream at Knotts Crossing, where a store was soon established, selling grog by the gallon! In 1876 Spring-vale became the first lease to be taken up in the Northern Territory; the homestead, 100 m (328 feet) from the river, was built three years later. It was the focal point for much of the activity—business

and social—in the area for the next few years. The homestead and surrounds, a short distance to the west of the town, are now an idyllic camping ground and resort, with the home-stead housing a fine display of memorabilia. A post office was established in 1883 and that same year the gold rush to Halls Creek in Western Australia saw many hopefuls pass through the town.

In 1902 Mrs Aeneas Gunn stayed in Katherine, at the Sportsman's Arms Hotel, on her way to Elsey Station, 60 km (37 miles) to the south. Her book, *We of the Never Never*, has become a classic. The railway from Darwin arrived on the north side of the Katherine River, at what became known as Emungalan, in 1917, but it was another six years before the bridge across the river was completed. This ensured the town's growing importance as a railhead for the expanding Vestey's cattle empire—Vestey's and others were shipping thousands of head of cattle to the recently established Vestey's Freezing Works in Darwin.

In World War II the town came under army control, as most of the civilians had been evacuated south, a process that was hurried along when the Japanese bombed the

Katherine airfield in March 1942. This bombing led to the road, which was really just a track, south to Alice Springs being rapidly up-graded to bitumen. After the war a meatworks was established in town, and Katherine became a centre for the rapidly expanding roadtrain network. In 1963 the Katherine Gorge National Park was proclaimed, setting the town on course to becoming a major tourist centre.

Today Katherine offers travellers all they require. The town itself has many places of interest, including the historic Springvale Homestead, the Katherine School of the Air, the Katherine Railway Museum and Gallery and the Katherine Museum. The Katherine Hot Springs, and the Katherine Low Level (a small park along the river), are pleasant spots to swim and have a picnic, just on the edge of town.

The major attraction of the town and the area is Katherine Gorge, which lies within the Nitmiluk National Park, 32 km (20 miles) east of town. You can camp out in the park, go on a cruise (which should not be missed), go canoeing, swimming or bushwalking. It really is a spec-tacular place, with a number of gorges separated by rock bars and rapids. Accessed north of Kath-erine, but still within the park, is Edith Falls, another very pleasant swimming and walking area.

One of the thirteen huge sandstone gorges to be found in Nitmiluk (Katherine Gorge) National Park.

F-18 jet and ground crew at the military base RAAF Base Tindal.

Further north of the town, and west of the small settlement of Pine Creek, is the Umbrawarra Gorge Nature Park, while a little further on is the Tjuwaliyn (Douglas Hot Springs) Nature Park, one of the real delights of the region. About 120 km (75 miles) north-west of Katherine is the recently proclaimed Flora River National Park, which has some spectacular stretches of river backed up behind tall, natural limestone barriers called turfa dams. The river is spring fed and there is good fishing, excellent canoeing, boating and walking along this delightful rainforest-shrouded waterway. South of the town is the Cutta Cutta Caves Nature Park, with its weirdly shaped rock formations and underground caves.

Annual events in Katherine itself include the Red Cross Canoe Marathon and horseracing in June, the Katherine Show and the Katherine Campdraft and Rodeo in July. July is also the time for the Australian Red Cross Triathlon (swim, cycle, run) in the beautiful Nitmiluk National Park.
Map ref: page 614 F8

KEEP RIVER NATIONAL PARK

This park, 48 km (30 miles) east of Kununurra, is not far from the Northern Territory/Western Australia border and is only a short distance from the Victoria Highway. It offers red sandstone cliffs, spectacular sweeping views and giant boab trees along the banks of the Keep River. In the Wet, the river is a raging torrent, but during the Dry you can walk along the river bed to view the wealth of Aboriginal rock art in caves and rock shelters and on the walls of the gorge. Some of the rock formations resemble the Bungle Bungles in Western Australia. Camping and picnic facilities and walking tracks are available. There are also several sacred sites in the park, which are fenced off and signposted; visitors are asked not to venture into these.
Map ref: page 614 A10

LITCHFIELD NATIONAL PARK

This park, with its magnetic termite mounds, rainforest pockets and waterfalls splashing down from the plateau into crystal-clear pools, is only two hours' drive from Darwin, via the town of Batchelor. On the perimeter of the park are a motel and caravan parks; there are bush camping and unpowered caravan sites in the park. Walking tracks lead to several lookouts with spectacular views. Highlights of the

The rocky red sandstone cliffs at Nigli Gap in Keep River National Park.

park are the Florence, Tolmer, Wangi and Sandy Creek Falls, an area of spectacular eroded sandstone formations called the Lost City, Blyth Homestead, a magnetic termite plain and the Reynolds River.
Map ref: page 614 D5

MATARANKA

Situated 110 km (68 miles) south of Katherine and 427 km (265 miles) south of Darwin, Mataranka is known as the capital of the Never Never Country, as it was near here, at Elsey Station, that Mrs Aeneas 'Jeannie' Gunn lived, and later wrote her acclaimed novel, *We of the Never Never*. The town (population 245) is located on the main north–south highway, and boasts a small number of shops and the Never Never Museum, which houses a good display concerning the area's early history.

Just a couple of kilometres south of the township is the turn-off to Mataranka Homestead, which was established in 1916 as an experimental station for sheep and horses. The homestead is the centre of activities for the surrounding Elsey National Park and offers accommodation and camping. Near the homestead is a replica of the original hand-hewn timber Elsey homestead—the original Elsey homestead, along with the graves of

There is a great interest in sport in indigenous outback communities.

many of the characters in the book, is about 22 km (14 miles) south of the present-day township.

The thermal pool, which has been the main attraction here for generations, is close to the main Mataranka Homestead, but is included in the park. The pool, which is surrounded by rainforest, is a constant 34°C (93°F), and flows at something like 30 million litres (8 million gallons) a day. The Roper River, which has its source not far from the homestead, picks up the water from the thermal pool and flows through the park. A good road skirts the southern edge of the river, giving access to pleasant picnic grounds and a small camping ground. A walking trail leads from here about 3 km (1.9 miles) to Mataranka Falls.

Annual events to look out for include the Australia Day Cricket Match in January, the Back to the Never Never Festival in May, and the Mataranka Bushman's Festival, which includes a campdraft, night rodeo, and gymkhana, in August.
Map ref: page 614 G8

An aerial viewpoint of the gorges at Nitmiluk (Katherine Gorge) National Park.

NHULUNBUY

There are only two ways to reach the modern mining town of Nhulunbuy (population 3500), located on the Gove Peninsula in northeastern Arnhem Land, 1042 km (647 miles) east of Darwin. You can either fly, or you can take a long 4WD trip via Katherine and then the Mainoru Road north-east to Nhulunbuy. You need a permit to drive this route; these can be obtained from the Northern Land Council in Darwin, Katherine or Nhulunbuy. Access is only possible via this route from late April to November—in the Wet, rains close the roads. There are designated camping areas along the way and the total distance from Katherine is 700 km (435 miles), the last fuel being at Bulman. No other supplies are available, so be prepared.

Nhulunbuy was originally established as a service centre for the very large bauxite mine nearby, owned and operated by mining giant, Nabalco. The adventurous traveller who gets to this town will find an almost tourist-free area, undiscovered by the masses, with several kinds of attractions. If you are into fishing or diving, you will certainly enjoy the surrounding coast and islands. Boats can be hired for fishing and you will catch barra, mangrove jack, Spanish mackerel, queenfish and a lot more. The town is surrounded by

Aboriginal land, and there are a number of art and craft galleries and museums, including Yirrkala Arts and Crafts and Nambara Arts and Crafts, in town. There are also tours to outlying Aboriginal communities, and there are Aboriginal guides who will take you on food-gathering trips. Tours of the mine and the alumina plant are available.
Map ref: page 615 M4

NITMILUK (KATHERINE GORGE) NATIONAL PARK

Over millions of years the Katherine River has cut through the sandstone plateau to form a series of 13 gorges, though most visitors see only the lower two. Nitmiluk is part of the traditional land of the

Jawoyn people; they have now been granted title to the park, which is leased to the Northern Territory Conservation Commission, and managed jointly by the Jawoyn and the Commission. Katherine Gorge is one of the great natural wonders of the north. Abundant bird and fish life, as well as crocodiles, inhabit this area. The gorge is 32 km (20 miles) from Katherine along a sealed road. Tour boat cruises operate on the Katherine River and canoes can be hired. The park has more than 100 km (62 miles) of walking tracks that meander across the rocky tops of the escarpment to the edge of the gorge. For overnight jaunts you need to register with the ranger. Scenic flights, swimming and photography also attract visitors.

The Edith Falls section of the park is 45 km (28 miles) north from Katherine along the Stuart Highway and 20 km (12 miles) in, along a sealed road. This small waterfall tumbles over a series of ridges and through a number of pools to a large pool fringed by monsoon forest. The pool is safe for swimming, and there are pleasant walks along the river bank.

There are camping grounds near Katherine Gorge—a boat ramp is located nearby (10 hp motors

are the maximum allowed), and there is some excellent fishing in the waters below the gorge and in the first gorge itself. There is also a camping ground at Edith Falls, plus several bush camping areas along walking trails.
Map ref: page 614 F7

PINE CREEK

Pine Creek is 230 km (143 miles) south of Darwin, and has a population of 610. The area around the town was the scene of extensive mining in the 1870s and 1880s—one of the largest open-cut gold mines in the Territory was in operation here until 1995—and the region is rich with historic sites, such as Grove Hill and Mount Wells. The railway station was built in 1888 and is now a historical display of the North Australia Railway, while nearby one can view an 1877 steam engine with carriages which were used on the railway from 1880 to 1943. The museum is housed in the original mining warden's house and has a display about the Overland Telegraph line and the mining years. The Miners Park houses machinery used on the old mines. The Northern Goldfields Loop, a marked, well-maintained dirt road, starts outside Pine Creek and leads north to just beyond Hayes Creek. This is an alternative route to Darwin.

North-west of the town, via a good dirt road, is Tjuwaliyn (Douglas Hot Springs) Nature Park. You can camp here—the nearby Douglas Daly Park offers good camping and accommodation. A little further on, past Tjuwaliyn, on a route which is now really a 4WD track, is Butterfly Gorge. You need to be a little active to take the walk through the riverine forest to the pool at the mouth of the gorge, but it is well worth the effort.

To the west of Pine Creek is the less visited but peaceful and picturesque Umbrawarra Gorge Nature Park, and closer to town is the Copperfield Recreation Reserve, a pleasant spot for a swim, picnic or even to camp for a while. The town is a good jumping-off point for Kakadu National Park via the Kakadu Highway. Highlights of the town include the annual Pioneer Goldrush Weekend and Horse Races in May.
Map ref: page 614 E6

The proprietor of the general store at Pine Creek on the Stuart Highway.

TIMBER CREEK

Located less than 100 km (62 miles) west of the Victoria River Road-house and 602 km (374 miles) south of Darwin, on the Victoria Highway and alongside the mighty Victoria River, is the tiny historic town of Timber Creek (population 150). Originally established as a police post in the late 1800s, the town, nestled in an open woodland setting, now services the cattle properties of the surrounding region, as well as catering for passing travellers. It is also a good base from which to explore the spectacular Gregory National Park, and anglers will find it hard to drag themselves away from the great fishing on offer in the river. For something a little more tranquil, you can put your own boat in the river and cruise this wide waterway, or join a river cruise past magnificent rugged gorges and dramatic landscapes.

The town has various services available, along with a general store that can supply most needs. If you are passing through in September, join in the fun and activities of the Timber Creek Races, with a camp-draft, races, gymkhana and a ball.
Map ref: page 614 C10

VICTORIA RIVER CROSSING

The Victoria Highway, as it heads west from Katherine, is one of the most scenic routes in the Territory, passing through a variety of beautiful country, none more spectacular than the rugged escarpment country around the Victoria River Crossing. The Victoria River, thought by the first European explorers to lead to an inland sea, makes a modest start south-west of Kalkarindji and wanders north to the sea through the Victoria River District. The river was named and navigated by Captain Wickham in the Beagle in 1839, but it was to be another 17 years before Augustus Gregory landed at the mouth of this river for his explorations inland.

Victoria River Crossing is little more than a roadhouse (which has been described as 'the flashiest pub in the scrub'), motel and caravan park—population 10—located on the western edge of the Victoria River, 522 km (324 miles) south-west of Darwin. The eastern section of the Gregory National Park surrounds this small hamlet. There is some good fishing in the river, and a lot of crocodiles! West of the Crossing a road south to the

A healthy-sized barramundi caught in the waters of the Victoria River.

famous Victoria River Downs station leads through the spectacular Jasper Gorge. A little downstream from the Crossing is the original crossing point, while further west is Kuwang Lookout.
Map ref: page 614 D9

WILDMAN RESERVE

This reserve takes in a significant proportion of the extensive Mary River Wetlands. Located 170 km (106 miles) from Darwin off the Arnhem Highway, it provides excellent opportunities for visitors to experience a tropical wetland environment. Roads in the Wildman Reserve are gravel, but they are suitable for conventional vehicles except during the wet season, when flooding may cause road closures.

Fishing is extremely popular in the area, particularly at Shady Camp and North Rockhole, where the highly sought-after barramundi are regularly caught. There are boat ramp facilities as well as toilets, picnic and camping facilities at each location. However, bring all the supplies you might need, including own drinking water and insect repellent. There are two private wilderness lodges in the reserve which offer full accommodation and fishing tours.

Couzens Lookout is an excellent vantage point to view the Mary River and extensive areas of attractive red waterlilies. Walking and birdwatching are popular activities here, as there are huge numbers of water birds to be found along the waterways and billabongs. Be very wary of saltwater crocodiles throughout this region.

Located at Beatrice Hill, around 60 km (37 miles) from Darwin between the turn-offs to Fogg Dam and Wildman Reserve, is the Window on the Wetlands Visitor Centre. This complex was set up to give visitors an overview of the Northern Territory's wetlands. The complex has displays, computer touch screens and a video room, providing historic background, plus details of local wildlife, seasonal changes, and much more. The best time to visit the area is from May to October.
Map ref: page 614 E4

The rugged escarpment country around Victoria River Crossing, along the Victoria Highway west of Katherine.

CENTRAL NORTHERN TERRITORY

The Stuart Highway runs like a spine through the arid country of the central Northern Territory. It is named for the explorer John McDouall Stuart who, after several attempts, finally crossed the continent from south to north in 1862. West of the highway is the vast Tanami Desert, which stretches to Western Australia. The highway itself runs through the Barkly Tableland. Some of the sparsely populated land supports vast cattle stations; much of it is managed by Aboriginal land trusts.

Nearly 600 kilometres (373 miles) south of Darwin, near the junction of the Stuart Highway and the Carpentaria High-way, which heads east to Borroloola and the Gulf of Carpentaria, is Daly Waters, which has the oldest pub in the Territory. Named by Stuart like many of the towns along the Stuart Highway, it assumed importance in the 1870s as a repeater station for the Over-land Telegraph line. It was also a watering hole for stockmen driving cattle from Queensland to the Kimberley. In the 1930s it served as a refuelling stop for QANTAS.

Further south, Three Ways Roadhouse marks the junction of the Stuart Highway and the Barkly Highway, the main route between the Northern Territory and Queensland. Almost 200 kilo-metres (124 miles) east down the Barkly Highway is the Barkly Home-stead Roadhouse, a welcome supply point between Three Ways and Camooweal in Queensland.

John McDouall Stuart named Tennant Creek on one of his exped-itions in 1860. Now the town is the main regional centre for the Barkly Tableland. When gold was first discovered there in the 1930s, the area became the focal point of Australia's last big goldrush. Mining is still underway in the area, but the boom is over.

South of Tennant Creek, on the Stuart Highway, are the Devils Marbles. These huge orange-red spherical granite boulders are spectacular at sunset. East of the Devils Marbles is the Davenport Range National Park. The Davenport Range straddles a tran-sition zone between the flora and fauna of the tropical north and the arid centre. The park, one of the newest in the territory, is surrounded by four cattle stations and is rich in Aboriginal, mining and pastoral history.

OPPOSITE: The Barkly Tableland is almost perfectly flat with virtually no rocks or trees—its grey-brown soil covered in tufts of Mitchell grass.

The rises and rocky outcrops of the Tanami Desert are low lying, due to the very high degree of erosion over millions of years.

The Davenport Range

Situated south-east of Tennant Creek and north-east of Alice Springs, the Davenport Range extends for approximately 90 km (56 miles) down the eastern side of the Northern Territory. A biological interzone between the tropical woodland savannas of the Top End and the arid Red Centre, it is home to an intriguing mix of flora and fauna, and has a fascinating ancient and recent human history. Much of the area is now protected by the Proposed Davenport Range National Park, which encompasses 1120 sq. km (432 square miles) between the Davenport Range and the Murchison Range. Little developed and with no sealed roads, it offers adventurous travellers a complete wilderness experience.

History

The Davenport Range is the boundary between the traditional lands of the Warumungu, Alyawarre and Kaytetye peoples. It has yielded numerous archaeological finds, including artefacts that indicate the presence of another, earlier people, and several small flint quarries that date back thousands of years.

The first Europeans to come to the area were Christian missionaries in the late nineteenth century. They were followed by pastoralists, then miners searching for gold, copper, tin, scheelite and wolfram along the tributaries of the Frew River and especially Hatches Creek. For some time, there was a flurry of activity in the area. Wolfram, used in the hardening of steel and most notably in armaments, was much in demand in the early twentieth century, and by 1938 around 200 men were working in mines. That year, however, a severe drought and soaring summer temperatures resulted in the main water supply almost drying up. Forced to endure appalling conditions, the miners threatened to abandon the area until the Australian Inland Mission provided them with a pedal-powered wireless so that in an emergency they could call up the doctor at Tennant Creek using morse code. Mining then continued through the 1950s, but went into decline soon afterward and had ceased by 1968.

In March 1993, the Northern Territory government decided to create a new national park in the area. The concept was debated and developed for the next few years, then the park was finally opened to the public in 1996. However, at the time of writing it has not yet been officially proclaimed, mainly as a result of unresolved native title issues.

Davenport Range National Park

The main attractions in the park for both wildlife and visitors are the Frew River and Lenee and Whistleduck creeks. In an otherwise semiarid environment, these waterways and their many, almost permanent waterholes are a lifeline for a surprisingly wide range of animals, including 105 species of birds (this is a prime nesting area for budgerigars), desert mice, antechinuses, dunnarts, spectacled hare-wallabies, northern nailtail wallabies, black-footed wallabies, euros, kangaroos and dingoes. The waters also support seven species of fish, and small inland crabs.

The park's main camp site is at the Old Police Station Waterhole on the Frew River. When full, the waterhole is more than 1 km (0.6 miles) long, about 100 m (110 yards) wide and deep enough for swimming. It only rarely dries up, though its depth fluctuates depending on recent rainfall.

Magnificent river red gums line the banks and couch grass has spread under the trees creating a delightful camping ground. From the comfort of your tent, you can often observe budgerigars nesting in the hollow branches overhead; mudlarks, crowned babblers, short-billed corellas, darters, teal ducks, wood ducks and red-backed kingfishers also abound. Local mammals are more reclusive, although some may be located at night with the aid of a spotlight.

There is another developed camping ground at Whistleduck Creek and there are two basic camp sites on the Frew River. At all these sites, swimming is possible when the waterholes are full and you can even launch a canoe at the Old Police Station Waterhole. There is also plenty of scope for bushwalking, though as yet there are no marked trails. Popular outings include following the Frew River or climbing from the Old Police Station Waterhole to the top of the range, where you'll enjoy superb views of the outback.

The national park is bounded by four pastoral stations and the Anurrente Aboriginal Land Trust. Part of one of the access roads crosses the land trust but is open to the public. Park authorities have been consulting with the Anurrente regarding further developments in this area. The owners of Kurundi Station, which forms the park's northern border, are currently considering a private tourism development.

A major issue for park management has been the eradication of introduced species, such as cats, donkeys and horses, and the removal of stock. To this end, the northern and southern boundaries of the park have now been fenced.

Access

Because the Proposed Davenport Range National Park is remote and unstaffed, visitors must be well prepared and carry all necessary supplies, first-aid equipment and vehicle spares. The best time to visit is between March and September when the days are pleasantly warm, the nights cool, and the waterholes usually full. Fuel and limited food are available at Epenarra and Kurundi homesteads.

All roads leading into the park are gravel and a high-clearance vehicle, preferably 4WD, is recommended. There are four main points of entry. The most-travelled route runs from Bonney Well on the Stuart Highway, 86 km (53 miles) south of Tennant

Creek, to the turn-off to Whistleduck Creek, 68 km (42 miles) to the east, and onward from there to Epenarra Station, a total distance of 120 km (75 miles). Another route leads to Epenarra from the Barkly Homestead Roadhouse on the Barkly Highway in Queensland, and covers 121 km (75 miles).

From Epenarra, it is 35 km (21.5 miles) to the right-hand turn-off to the Old Police Station Waterhole, and another 9.6 km (6 miles) to the waterhole itself. If you remain on the main road at the turn-off and continue for 29 km (18 miles) toward Hatches Creek, you will come to another access road to the Old Police Station Waterhole. Though rough, this 4WD route, known as the Frew River Loop Track, presents an enjoyable diversion for experienced off-road drivers and should take about an hour to negotiate. It leads to a couple of basic camp sites that will appeal to travellers seeking solitude.

A third access road to the national park leaves the Stuart Highway 43 km (26.5 miles) north of Barrow Creek and travels for 123 km (76 miles) via Murray Downs Homestead to the Old Police Station Waterhole turn-off. You can also reach the park from Alice Springs, travelling via the Stuart and Sandover highways and then turning off at Ammaroo Station—a trip of approximately 500 km (311 miles).

Although it occasionally consumes small mammals, reptiles and insects, the collared sparrowhawk (Accipiter cirrhocephalus) feeds mainly on small birds, which it often seizes in mid-air.

Located just off the road linking Kurundi and Epenarra homesteads, Cloughs Lookout offers magnificent 360-degree views of the surrounding country.

Places in
CENTRAL
NORTHERN
TERRITORY

The Daly Waters pub; the oldest hotel in the Territory.

BARKLY HOMESTEAD

Barkly Homestead, around 210 km (130 miles) east of Tennant Creek and 1158 km (719 miles) south-east of Darwin, is located on the Barkly Highway close to its junction with the north–south Tablelands Highway, which leads to Cape Crawford and Borroloola on the Gulf. This small roadhouse (population 10), the only sign of habitation on the flat grassy plains of the Barkly Tableland, is the only supply point between Three Ways on the Stuart Highway and Camooweal in Queensland, a distance of 450 km (279 miles). The road-house will meet most of a traveller's requirements, and even features a five-hole golf course!
Map ref: page 617 L8

BORROLOOLA

Set on the banks of the McArthur River, 80 km (50 miles) inland from the muddy waters of the Gulf of Carpentaria and 976 km (606 miles) south-east of Darwin,

Borroloola has a rich historical past. The town was established as a port in 1885 for the mining camps inland and the pastoral properties on the Barkly Tablelands to the south. It was a wild town, with sly-grog shops, and horse and cattle stealing commonplace, inhabited by, as one government official described the locals, 'the scum of the earth'. Today its population is 1450, and it serves the fishing and mining industries, along with the surrounding pastoral properties.

The Heritage Walk, which winds its way through the old town past grave sites, old buildings, and along the McArthur River, is a good way to explore the town. The old Police Station, now an excellent museum, was constructed in 1886, and is the oldest surviving example of an outpost police station in the Northern Territory.

Fishing is the prime attraction of this region, with the river and

the Sir Edward Pellew Group of islands just offshore being the main drawcards. Borroloola is also a good stepping-off point for those 4WD tourers heading east across the Gulf Track to Queensland. Cape Crawford, 116 km (72 miles) south-west of Borroloola, is little more than the Heartbreak Hotel/ Motel at the junction of the Carpentaria and Tablelands Highways. This small settlement is a base for seeing the amazing Lost City rock formations, which are only accessible via helicopter.

The premium social event in the area is the Heartbreak Bush Ball, which takes place in October. The Borroloola Fishing Classic is held in April, and attracts fishing people from all over the Territory and north Queensland. The Borroloola Rodeo, which includes bush races and campdrafting, attracts the crowds annually in August.
Map ref: page 617 M1

DALY WATERS

Located just off the Stuart Highway, 595 km (369 miles) south of Darwin, the small hamlet of Daly Waters (population 25) has been, almost right from the time of first settlement, nothing more than a pub; it was named by John McDouall Stuart in 1862, and in 1871 became the site of a repeater station for the Overland Telegraph line—its only other claim to fame.

Licensed in 1893, the Daly Waters pub is the oldest hotel in the Territory. It was originally a watering hole for the stockmen on the long cattle drive across the Territory from Queensland to the Kimberley in Western Australia. In 1926 it was a refuelling point for the London to Sydney Air Race, and in the 1930s it was an important stopover for QANTAS— the passengers were given a meal at the pub. During World War II, the airstrip was a refuelling point for the bombers flying north, and today the old aerodrome hangar has been restored by the National Trust and is a museum.

Just to the south of the old town, on the main highway, is the turn-off to Borroloola, and at the junction of these two highways is the Hi-Way Inn. The Daly Waters Rodeo, Campdraft and Gymkhana is held every September.
Map ref: page 616 G2

DEVILS MARBLES
CONSERVATION RESERVE

This pile of huge rounded granite boulders is an awesome sight next to the Stuart Highway 90 km (56 miles) south of Tennant Creek. The boulders are the result of exposure and weathering over millions of years. Visitors can wander through the boulders for a chance at that quintessential photograph. This is an Aboriginal sacred site, and visitors are asked to respect the cultural heritage of the area. The reserve has picnic tables, toilets, camping facilities and unpowered caravan sites.
Map ref: page 617 H9

ELLIOTT

Situated approximately halfway between Alice Springs and Darwin—740 km (460 miles) south of the capital—on the Stuart

These orange-red granite boulders are known as the Devils Marbles, and Karlukarlu to the Kaytej people.

The Stuart Highway. There are three main highways through the Northern Territory: the Barkly, the Victoria and the Stuart.

Highway is the small township of Elliott (population 430). Like many towns and hamlets on this route north, the town started out as a repeater station on the Overland Telegraph line. During World War II it became a major stopping point and an interim camp for the large numbers of troops and supplies heading north, at which time the road was upgraded from a two-wheel track to bitumen. The town is named after a Captain Elliott, who was the officer in charge of the interim camp.

Heading further north it is about 100 km (62 miles) to the roadhouse at Dunmarra and another 45 km (28 miles) to the Hi-Way Inn at Daly Waters. South, on the long run to Tennant Creek, the only signs of habitation are Renner Springs (92 km [57 miles] south) and Three Ways (226 km [140 miles] south), the latter being just 24 km (15 miles) north of Tennant Creek.
Map ref: page 617 H4

KALKARINGI

Located on the banks of the Victoria River, 779 km (484 miles) south-west of Darwin and 170 km (106 miles) south-west of Top Springs on the Buchanan Highway, the small township of Kalkaringi (population 150) was once known as Wave Hill, and was an outpost of law and order since its early days. It still has a police station, along with a caravan park, a supermarket and a service station that dispenses limited supplies, fuel and take-away food. It is also the spot where the bitumen runs out: to the west the road is all dirt. Travellers use the route through Kalkaringi as they head west to the West Australian border; the other

major road junction is just east of town, with the Lajamanu Road, which leads south to the Tanami Road and Rabbit Flat.
Map ref: page 616 D4

RABBIT FLAT ROADHOUSE

The isolated Rabbit Flat Roadhouse is located on the Tanami Road in the Tanami Desert, 1161 km (721 miles) south-west of Darwin. Travellers use this road for access between Halls Creek in Western Australia and Alice Springs in the Territory. The road is reasonable, although it really is 4WD country. Travellers should be prepared for crossing this harsh region.

The Rabbit Flat Roadhouse (population 2) is a little oasis in the surrounding desert. It has limited trading days, being open only between 7 am and 10 pm, four days a week: closed Tuesday, Wednesday and Thursday. The roadhouse dispenses fuel (diesel, petrol), beer, soft drinks and take-away food, and payment is cash only.
Map ref: page 616 B9

TENNANT CREEK

Tennant Creek, on the Stuart Highway 994 km (617 miles) south of Darwin, is the main regional centre for the Barkly Tablelands, and is just over 500 km (311 miles) from Alice Springs. It is also 25 km (16 miles) south of the road junction and roadhouse known as Three Ways, from where you can continue north to Darwin or turn east to Queensland and Mount Isa.

The creek was discovered and named in 1860 by John McDouall Stuart on his trek across the continent, and in 1872 it became the site for a repeater station on the Overland Telegraph line. The town

sprang up a few kilometres to the south of the station. Gold was discovered in the area in 1930, and Australia's last great gold rush began. It turned out to be the third richest goldfield in Australia; mining is still carried out, but the boom years have gone.

Today, Tennant Creek (population 3500) is a friendly community with modern amenities. Its strategic position on the Stuart Highway and a variety of attractions make it a popular stop for travellers. Much of the town's history can be seen at Battery Hill, home of the Tennant Creek gold stamping battery and mining museum. Several mines, including the Burnt Shirt Mine and the Golden Forty (or Noble's Nob) Open Cut Mine, once the richest gold-mine in Australia, can be toured. There is also a historic walk to some of the notable relics of those golden days. Other buildings of interest include the Overland Telegraph Station, and the old Australian

Bush thick-knee
(Burhinus magnirostris)

Inland Mission, built in 1932. Tuxworth Fulwood House was constructed as an army hospital in 1942, and today houses photographs and displays of early mining life, plus machinery and equipment. Aboriginal culture is very strong in Tennant Creek, and you can view a number of murals here, watch art and craft being made, purchase items at the local art and craft centre or go on a bush tucker tour.

North of Tennant Creek is the Attack Creek Historical Reserve. The creek got its name following an incident between John McDouall Stuart and local Waramunga Aborigines. Stuart was forced to retreat to South Australia, before finally crossing the continent in 1862. Mary Ann Dam, 5 km (3 miles) north of town, is a human-made lake suitable for small boats and canoes, an ideal spot for a swim and a picnic. The Pebbles, 17 km (11 miles) to the north of town, is an extensive area of granite boulders that are miniatures of the Devils Marbles. Just to the north of the small outpost and hotel of Wauchope 115 km (71 miles) to the south, are the Devils Marbles. A stop-over in Wauchope is definitely worthwhile.

The Northern Territory Street Circuit Go-Kart Grand Prix is held in April; the Tennant Creek Art Award and Tennant Creek Cup are in May; the Tennant Creek District Show is in July; and the Spring Flower Show and Goldrush Folk Festival are held every August.
Map ref: page 617 H8

Mural by Aboriginal artists at the Lands Council building, Tennant Creek.

SOUTHERN NORTHERN TERRITORY

The Red Centre is the mythical heartland of Australia. Here, in the midst of arid desert are treasures of nature and Aboriginal culture. The famous monolith Uluru (Ayers Rock) displays its amazing changing colours at sunrise and sunset. Not far from Uluru is Kata Tjuta (the Olgas), a group of smaller dome-like conglomerate monoliths. Yulara is the well-organised service centre for the Uluru–Kata Tjuta National Park.

Some 450 kilometres (279 miles) north-east of Uluru is the Red Centre's largest town, Alice Springs. Indeed, it seems that all roads in the region head more or less to the Alice. Founded with the Overland Telegraph line in 1872, the Alice straddles the usually dry Todd River. It is surrounded by the MacDonnell Ranges, where there are several wonderful national parks. Close to the Alice, various gaps in the ranges—Emily Gap, Jessie Gap and Simpson's Gap—provide picturesque picnic spots.

East of Alice Springs, Trephina Gorge National Park offers good walking along dry creeks fringed with river red gums and the chance to spot rock wallabies. Further east along the Ross River Highway is Ruby Gap National Park, and south of the Ross River Homestead is N'Dhala Gorge Nature Park where you might be able to spot some of the ancient Aboriginal rock carvings.

To the west of Alice Springs, the West MacDonnell National Park incorporates some spectacular chasms and gorges including Standley Chasm and Ormiston Gorge on Namatjira Drive. Larapinta Drive passes through the Hermannsburg Aboriginal settlement, established by German Lutheran missionaries in the nineteenth century.

South of Hermannsburg is the Finke Gorge National Park and to the east of Finke Gorge is the Watarrka (Kings Canyon) National Park. These parks feature a stunning and unique variety of flora—relics from when the region was part of the wet tropics, including the MacDonnell Ranges cycad and the red cabbage palm. Mammals such as red kangaroos, rock wallabies and dingoes inhabit in the parks. There are also venomous king and western brown snakes and harmless pythons. Myriad plant life, including river red gums, ghost gums, spinifex, mulga and acacias provide habitats for hundreds of different varieties of birds.

OPPOSITE: The distinctive red colouration of the rocky escarpment in Watarrka National Park is due to the presence of iron oxide.

Artist Alicia Entata at work at the Ntaria Arts Centre, Hermannsburg.

REGIONAL FEATURE

Uluru–Kata Tjuta National Park

Many desert plant species have adapted to both fire and drought. Trees such as the desert oak (Allocasuarina decaisneana), for instance, are protected from fire by their extremely thick bark.

The Red Centre's most prominent landforms, Uluru (Ayers Rock) and Kata Tjuta (the Olgas), have long since assumed the status of national icons. Considered sacred sites by the region's traditional inhabitants, they have also acquired a mantle of myth and mystery for more recent settlers, becoming one of the country's major tourist drawcards and a place of pilgrimage for huge numbers of visitors from all parts of Australia and from overseas.

The two sites are now protected by Uluru–Kata Tjuta National Park, which covers 1325 sq. km (512 square miles). Managed jointly by the traditional Aboriginal owners and the federal government, the park was declared a World Heritage Area in 1987 and subsequently an International Biosphere Reserve.

Geological Origins

Uluru and Kata Tjuta have their origins in major tectonic events that took place around 600 million years ago. Movements of plates in the earth's crust thrust layers of rock upward, forming a towering mountain chain known as the Petermann Ranges. Subsequent weathering washed huge amounts of rocks and sand down these mountains and onto the plains. Some of this material compacted and solidified, forming the rocks that now constitute Uluru and Kata Tjuta. Despite further uplifting and weathering, only the tips of these formations are visible today; indeed, it is thought that they may extend as much as 6 km (3.7 miles) beneath the surface.

Average annual rainfall at Uluru is about 220 mm (8.6 inches). Most falls in short but torrential downpours that form dramatic cascades along the Rock's flank.

Above ground, Uluru rises 340 m (1115 feet) from the surrounding desert, and Kata Tjuta reaches 600 m (1970 feet). It is believed that the 36 individual domes of Kata Tjuta may once have been a single dome many times the size of Uluru. Rain, wind and alternate heating and cooling caused the rock to expand and contract, and crack into smaller sections which were subsequently worn smooth by further erosion. The effects of this process can also be seen on the surface of Uluru, where parts of the rock are flaking and occasionally fall to the ground.

History

Archaeological evidence gathered to date suggests that Aboriginal peoples have lived in this part of Australia for at least 22,000 years. Collectively, the area's traditional inhabitants are known as the Anangu (meaning 'we people'), but they include three separate groups: the Yankunytjatjara, Pitjantjatjara and Ngaanyatjara. The network of language, kinship and religious connections that unites the Anangu community extends over an enormous territory, linking them with other Aboriginal peoples as far afield as Kings Canyon, Papunya, Port Hedland, Kalgoorlie, Ceduna, Yalata, Maralinga and Alice Springs.

Fundamental to the Anangu way of life is the Tjukurpa, a body of knowledge, religious beliefs and law that provides explanations for the origins of all living things and of the features of the landscape. It explains, for example, how Uluru was formed during the creation period (also known as the Tjukurpa) when a large, flat sandhill turned to stone. Soon after this event, the Kuniya, or carpet snake people, camped at the base of the rock. One day, the Liru, venomous snake men, attacked the Kuniya camp. Kulikudgeri, a fierce Liru fighter, slew a young warrior; in response, the warrior's mother struck Kulikudgeri on the nose with a digging stick, killing him. According to the Tjukurpa, events such as these left their mark on the landscape, and on walks around Uluru today Aboriginal guides will point out many features connected with these stories, including the aforementioned digging stick, Ngaltawadi.

The area's original inhabitants led a nomadic existence, retreating to permanent water sources during dry spells, then fanning out across the desert following rains. During these sorties, they would often renew contact with other groups and visit remote sacred sites. Their diet varied according to the season and the availability of different foods but comprised a wide variety of plants including bush tomato, quandong, tubers and yams, as well as game such as kangaroos, wallabies, lizards and birds.

The first European explorer to reach this remote region was Ernest Giles, who in 1872, during his attempt to cross the western half of the continent, coined the name of Mount Olga for Kata Tjuta, after the European Queen of Württemberg. He was followed, in 1873, by William Gosse who gave Uluru its English name in honour of the then Chief Secretary of South Australia, Henry Ayers.

Over the next 50 years, very little European exploration of this south-western corner of Central Australia took place. However, following Harold Lasseter's reports at the end of the nineteenth century of an enormous reef of gold in the Petermann Ranges, prospectors began to scour the area. Soon after, pastoralists arrived in increasing numbers. They showed little respect for the rights of the traditional inhabitants, who continued to follow their nomadic lifestyle while settlers attempted to enclose and place stock on large areas of land. As a result, clashes between Europeans and the Anangu became more frequent and violent. The incomers also brought diseases, such as smallpox, that decimated Aboriginal populations.

In the mid-twentieth century, a government-sponsored process of assimilation forced many Aboriginal people to take up residence in reservations or at missions, or seek employment on cattle stations. This, and the misguided practice of removing children of mixed descent from Aboriginal communities and placing them with white foster families or in government children's homes, soon had a devastating effect on traditional Aboriginal culture.

The first tourists arrived at Uluru and Kata Tjuta in the late 1940s and by the mid 1970s more than 50,000 visitors a year were tramping around the area, inadvertently desecrating sacred sites, much to the dismay of the Anangu. In 1976, the Northern Territory's Aboriginal Land Rights Act paved the way for indigenous peoples to claim traditional lands, and the Anangu subsequently sought ownership of their territory. After nine years of legal battles, the Anangu and the Uluru–Kata Tjuta Land Trust were awarded freehold title to their lands on 26 October 1985. They immediately agreed to lease the area encompassing Uluru and Kata Tjuta back to the Commonwealth

The rock that makes up Uluru has a much finer texture than the coarse conglomerate of Kata Tjuta. Uluru is mainly arkose, a smooth sandstone formed under immense pressure and rich in fine grains of feldspar and quartz.

Government as a national park. Today, the park is managed on a cooperative basis by Environment Australia and the traditional owners.

Flora and Fauna

Rainfall in the Red Centre is low and erratic, and the temperature generally high, though it can fall below freezing on winter nights. In such an extreme environment, where water and food supplies are highly unreliable, plants and animals have to develop ingenious adaptations to survive. Some plant species, such as yellow-top daisies, golden everlastings and purple mulla mullas, bloom only after rains, their seeds lying dormant in the sand at other times. Certain kinds of frogs, known as burrowing frogs, sit out periods of drought deep underground, wrapped in a water-filled cocoon of shed skin; when the rains come, they tunnel out to feed and breed.

Many animal species are nocturnal, and some diurnal species emerge only very early or late in the day when the desert heat is less fierce. Visitors are therefore likely to see only a small proportion of the area's wildlife. Among the most visible animals are birds such as crested pigeons, budgerigars, butcherbirds and wedge-tailed eagles, and mammals such as

euros and dingoes. In total, over 400 plant species, 22 species of mammals, 150 different bird groups and many reptiles and frogs have been recorded in the park.

The Anangu's long experience of the desert environment gave them a profound knowledge of its rhythms and idiosyncrasies. This enabled them to harvest efficiently an enormous range of natural resources. As well as passing this knowledge on to the next generation of Anangu, today's elders generously teach visitors about local flora and fauna on guided walks.

Exploring the Park

Many visitors rush around Uluru and Kata Tjuta, attempting to see everything in a day or two. This is a mistake as the park's main sites are widely scattered and, furthermore, this is an environment that repays careful study. The best place to begin your visit is at the Uluru–Kata Tjuta Cultural Centre, where informative displays provide fascinating insights into the lifestyle and beliefs of the Anangu peoples as well as the region's ecology. You can also book tours, guided walks and other activities here, and purchase a wide range of books, arts and crafts. Numerous organised tours also depart from Ayers Rock Resort at Yulara, including helicopter and plane flights, motorcycle tours and nature tours. For more information, contact the Visitor Centre at the resort.

ULURU

Even a brief introduction to Anangu culture should deter most visitors from attempting the once-popular climb to the summit of Uluru. The path to the top follows a sacred route taken by ancestral beings during the creation period or Tjukurpa; it is also a steep and arduous hike. For both cultural reasons and safety concerns, the Anangu would prefer that visitors remain at ground level. Those who do insist on scaling the Rock should bear in mind that several people have died during the two-hour-return climb. Carry plenty of water and use the safety chain that lines most of the route. Never attempt the trip if you suffer from a heart condition, respiratory problems or vertigo.

Many of Uluru's most interesting features can be seen from walking tracks around its edge. For a comprehensive investigation, take the Base Walk, a 9.4-km (5.8-mile) circuit of the monolith which requires around four hours to complete. It provides a bewildering variety of perspectives on this magnificent landform, taking in caves, waterholes, spectacular rock formations and historic rock art. The walk is particularly rewarding in the company of an Anangu guide, who will explain how various topographical features relate to Tjukurpa stories and demonstrate how desert resources were used to make foods, implements and medicines. Guided tours are also available on several shorter tracks such as the Mala Walk, a 2-km (1.2-mile), wheelchair accessible route which takes about an hour, and the Liru Walk, which extends from the Cultural Centre to the Rock, a distance of 2 km (1.2 miles), requiring about half an hour each way.

At the end of the day, most visitors head for the sunset viewing area to watch one of nature's great spectacles—Uluru slowly changing colour, from orange to deep red then violet and purple, as the setting sun is reflected off stone and sand.

KATA TJUTA

Though less visited than its famous neighbour, Kata Tjuta—which means 'many heads'—is an equally impressive sight. Its 36 domes of all shapes and sizes create a maze of valleys and give the formation an everchanging appearance as you move around it. For the local Anangu people, this landmark is the home of Wanambi, a mythical snake with large teeth, a thick mane and a long beard; most Tjukurpa stories about Kata Tjuta are, however, kept secret.

Visitors can explore the domes and gullies by following two main walking tracks. The longer Valley of the Winds Walk, which is 6 km (3.7 miles) long and requires at least three hours to complete, winds through the domes to the Karu and Karingana lookouts, both of which provide magnificent views of the surrounding country. (On very hot days, the track may be closed for safety reasons.) A shorter track of about 2 km (1.2 miles), the Olga Gorge Walk, leads to a thicket of spearwood vines at the end of majestic, steep-sided Olga Gorge.

Access and Facilities

Flights are available from all capital cities to the airport at Yulara. By road, it is 465 km (283 miles) from Alice Springs along the sealed Stuart and Lasseter Highways. All the roads within the park are sealed. Drivers can also follow a scenic backroad from Alice Springs via Larapinta Drive and the Mereenie Loop Road. This route is open to conventional vehicles, but approximately 200 km (124 miles) of it is unsealed.

There are no accommodation or camping facilities within the national park, but five establishments at Yulara (Ayers Rock Resort) provide accommodation ranging from luxury suites to budget rooms. In addition, there is a large camping ground with tent sites, van sites and airconditioned cabins. Yulara also has a variety of eateries, an entertainment centre, and a shopping mall with a bank, newsagency, post office, travel agency, gift shop, photo supplies shop and supermarket.

VISITOR ETIQUETTE

It is important to remember that Uluru and Kata Tjuta are areas of special cultural and religous significance to Aboriginal people and include sacred sites that are open to men or women only or are off-limits to all but initiated Anangu. Notices posted around the base of Uluru, and elsewhere, clearly mark areas closed to the general public and visitors should respect the wishes of the Anangu by obeying these signs.

Although many of the sites in the park are highly photogenic, the Anangu do not like themselves or their sacred areas to be photographed. Do not take pictures of local people without first asking their permission, and conform with all signs requesting that you refrain from photographing particular sites. If in doubt, obtain guidelines from any of the visitor centres or from hotel reception areas.

Ernest Giles described Kata Tjuta's domes as 'composed of untold masses of round stones of all kinds and size, mixed as plums in a pudding and set in vast and rounded shapes upon the ground'.

Places in
SOUTHERN
NORTHERN
TERRITORY

ALICE SPRINGS

Located almost in the centre of the continent, 1513 km (940 miles) south of Darwin, Alice Springs (population 27,520) is to many the epitome of the 'Red Centre', gaining international fame as one of the places to visit in Australia. The town is located at the very foot of

An Outback camel safari.

the rugged MacDonnell Ranges, near Heavitree Gap, where the Todd River has cut its way through this rocky barrier to give access through the range. It began life as a repeater station on the Overland Telegraph line in 1871. The station took its name from the spring, or waterhole, in the bed of the Todd River, close to the original telegraph station, which was named by Superintendent of Telegraphs, Charles Todd, after his wife, Alice. The location was near a regularly used ceremonial ground of the Arrernte Aboriginal clan. The station buildings, the first European buildings in Central Australia, are now an excellent museum and picnic spot—they are a short distance north of the town centre.

Initially the town was called Stuart, after the great explorer who blazed a way north across the continent in 1860–61; while his route passed through another gap in the range a little to the west, it is on

A cosmopolitan cafe in Todd Mall, Alice Springs.

the whole his route that the telegraph line and the original railway line followed. Cattle stations were taken up in this region in the 1870s and there was soon a police station as well. In 1887 gold was found at Arltunga, 130 km (81 miles) east of the telegraph station. At its height, this small outpost supported over 400 people, making it the biggest enclave of Europeans in the Centre; most of them followed the telegraph line to Alice before pushing into the more remote, harsh country further east.

Between 1926 and 1931 the separate territory of Central Australia was formed, and its administrative centre was Alice. In 1929 the railway finally arrived from the south—the name of the town was officially changed to Alice Springs soon after. As a railhead, the town grew as a major supply centre, not only to the outlying cattle stations but also to the rest of the Territory. During World War II the Stuart Highway

north to Darwin was bituminised as part of the war effort to supply the thousands of troops in the Top End. In the 1950s a novel by Neville Shute, *A Town Like Alice*, along with the subsequent film and television program, brought wide acclaim to this remote town, and really started the tourist industry on which much of the town now bases its economy.

The town and its surrounds have much to offer. In the centre of Alice Springs are the historic buildings of the old town gaol (1909), Adelaide House (1926), designed by the Reverend John Flynn (founder of the Royal Flying Doctor Service, which was established here in 1939 and still operates from near here), and the old Hartley Street School (1930), the first school in the region. Within a few kilometres of town are the buildings and

pleasant surrounds of the old Telegraph Station, the Strehlow Research Centre with its great Aboriginal cultural display, the stunning displays of the Alice Springs Desert Park, the Transport Heritage Centre and the Central Australian Museum, to name just a few.

The area is also well endowed with natural attractions; the West MacDonnell National Park incorporates such well-known attractions as Standley Chasm, Simpson's Gap, Ormiston Gorge and Pound and Redbank Gorge. In the eastern MacDonnells are Trephina Gorge, N'Dhala Gorge, the Ross River homestead, and the historic site of the Arltunga goldfields. Further afield are such international attractions as Rainbow Valley, Uluru (Ayers Rock), Kings Canyon and the Simpson Desert. You can enjoy camel rides, horse rides, balloon trips and 4WD excursions in and around the local area, as well as Aboriginal cultural tours that take in bush food, art or Dreaming trails.

The Alice also has a good range of restaurants and cuisines. You can share your dinner with a camel, take a balloon ride to breakfast, or enjoy the friendship of a bush gourmet barbecue. The Overlander Steakhouse, like a number of eating places in the town, has buffalo, kangaroo, emu, crocodile, camel, barramundi and more traditional fare on the menu.

There is an absolute host of annual events: Heritage Week in April; the Central Australian

The dust flies at the Alice Springs Rodeo, a popular event which takes place annually in August.

Country Music Festival in April/May; the Bangtail Muster, which incorporates a parade of floats down the Todd Mall, in May; the Finke Desert Race, Australia's fastest desert race for motorcycles and vehicles, in June; the Alice Springs Show and the famous Lions Camel Cup in July; the Central Australian Aboriginal Art and Craft Exhibition in July/ August; the Alice Springs Rodeo, also in August; the Henley-On-Todd, the world-famous waterless regatta where 'boats' are run down the sandy bed of the Todd, in September; the International Cultural Festival in October; and the Corkwood Festival in November.

Map ref: page 619 H6

ARLTUNGA HISTORICAL RESERVE

In 1887 gold was discovered near Arltunga, and suddenly Central Australia's first gold rush had begun. Many of the fortune seekers were already in the area, as they had rushed up to the 'ruby' fields at Ruby Gap (the rubies turned out to be semi-precious garnets). Some miners pushed their barrows 600 km (373 miles) from the Oodnadatta railhead in South Australia to reach the Arltunga field. Later a government battery was established at Arltunga—the town was actually larger than the outpost of Alice Springs for a while. Today there is a visitor centre with a small museum, slide shows and a working two-stamp battery. Adjacent to the historical reserve there is a fossicking reserve, and with the right permits you can even try your luck at fossicking for an elusive gold nugget, and explore some of the old mines in the area—the best place to stop if you want to fossick is the Arltunga Hotel. Arltunga lies 110 km (68 miles) east of Alice Springs along the Ross Highway.

Map ref: page 619 J6

CHAMBERS PILLAR HISTORICAL RESERVE

This reserve lies 163 km (101 miles) south of Alice Springs along the Old South Road; en route you pass the Ewaninga rock carvings. The road is sandy and corrugated in places, with river and dune crossings, and the drive takes you through some picturesque country along the fringe

Sunset illuminates the magnificent sandstone monolith of Chambers Pillar Historical Reserve.

of the Simpson Desert. John McDouall Stuart, in 1860, was the first European to sight this solitary sandstone pillar which, including its 25 m (82 feet) high pedestal, stands 58 m (190 feet) above the dune landscape, and he named it after James Chambers, one of his expedition sponsors. The monolith was formed from sandstone sediments laid down under a shallow sea around 400 million years ago. Until the advent of the railway line, subsequent explorers and overlanders all used Chambers Pillar as a landmark on their journeys through the Centre, and carved their names in the soft sandstone rock face.

Map ref: page 619 H8

EWANINGA CONSERVATION RESERVE

A small reserve protects the low hills of Ewaninga, which are covered in petroglyphs. So ancient are these intriguing rock carvings that their meanings are not known by the traditional owners of the land. The reserve lies 25 km (16 miles) south of Alice Springs along the Old South Road, in red sand plain country. It is open to the public. A walking track from the car park with interpretive signs has been provided so that visitors may get an insight into the way people lived in this area so long ago. This reserve is for day use only.

Map ref: page 619 H6

FINKE GORGE NATIONAL PARK

This park was established to protect the incredible gorges which the Finke River and its tributary, the Palm River, have carved through the ancient mountains of central Australia. In these gorges the red rock walls have eroded to incredible shapes. The spectacular Palm Valley is home to 2000 red cabbage palms, which are unique to this area, remnants of an era when this region was part of the wet tropics.

Palm Valley is 138 km (86 miles) west of Alice Springs along Larapinta Drive; past the Hermannsburg Community you turn left (south—the last 16 km [10 miles] along the bed of the Finke River is for 4WD vehicles only). It is an easy drive, however, and very picturesque. Two pleasant walks lead visitors through the valley. There are other walks along the way, as well as picnic areas. There is a camping area, 4 km (2.5 miles) back from the car park.

Map ref: page 618 F7

Much of the road in Palm Valley, Finke Gorge National Park, is for 4WD vehicles only.

Tropic of Capricorn marker, near Gemtree, north of Alice Springs.

GEMTREE

Located 1513 km (940 miles) south of Darwin and 140 km (87 miles) north-east of Alice Springs on the Plenty Highway, Gemtree (population 10), as its name suggests, was established purely to look after the growing number of people who come to this part of the Harts Range to look for gemstones. These are some of the richest gem fields in Australia, and contain beryl, garnets, iolite and zircons. The caravan park in Gemtree runs regular tours of the fields, and fossicking equipment can be hired here, and stones can be cut and polished. Basic supplies and fuel are also available. The Plenty Highway, which continues east towards Queensland, becomes a dirt road a short distance beyond Gemtree.
Map ref: page 619 H4

JERVOIS HOMESTEAD

Jervois Station (population 15) is 356 km (221 miles) east of Alice Springs and 1715 km (1065 miles) south-east of Darwin. It is one of the newest properties in Central Australia, being originally purchased by the Broad family in the early 1960s. The homestead is on the Plenty Highway, and although there is bituminused road from Alice Springs east to Gemtree, from Gemtree to the Queensland border the road is graded and unsealed—therefore a 4WD vehicle is recommended.

The homestead store carries limited supplies for travellers. It also has fuel, as well as shower and toilet facilities. It is open during daylight hours, seven days a week. A unique feature of the homestead, worthy of an inspection, is the huge rocket-proof shelter which was built during the 1960s. This was to serve as protection from any wayward Blue Streak rockets—these were being launched from Woomera in South Australia during that period.
Map ref: page 619 L5

KULGERA

A small settlement (population 25) on the Stuart Highway, just 20 km (12 miles) north of the Northern Territory/South Australia border, Kulgera is little more than a short wayside stop for travellers. It is 1762 km (1094 miles) south of Darwin, 278 km (173 miles) south of Alice Springs and 156 km (97 miles) north of Marla in South Australia. The little town is surrounded by stark rocky outcrops, some as high as 600 m (1969 feet), but there is little else to attract the traveller here.

A dirt road heads east from the blacktop at Kulgera to the small settlement of Finke, where adventurous travellers can either head north to Alice Springs along the Old Ghan Line or travel south-east into the Simpson Desert. To the south, just before the South Australian border, another sandy track heads west to Mulga Park homestead and then north on to Curtin Springs, on the main road that leads to Uluru (Ayers Rock).
Map ref: page 618 G9

Many old homesteads, such as this one in Kulgera, have been turned into museums.

N'DHALA GORGE NATURE PARK

Just 8 km (5 miles) from Ross River Homestead and 88 km (55 miles) from Alice Springs, N'Dhala Gorge is of great cultural significance to the Eastern Arrernte Aboriginal clan. Around 6000 petroglyphs (rock carvings) have been recorded in the gorge—one can only wonder at the unknown history of these magnificent yet mysterious works of art. The track from Ross River Homestead, for 4WD vehicles only, winds along the picturesque river bed and through a valley where great forces of nature have twisted the rock ledges. The park has picnic tables, a bush toilet and limited camping facilities.
Map ref: page 619 J6

ROSS RIVER

The Ross River Homestead (population 20) is 88 km (55 miles) east of Alice Springs and 1592 km (989 miles) south of Darwin. This historic homestead is also a tourist destination that offers travellers a chance to experience the East MacDonnell Ranges. There is plenty to do, including bushwalking; those with a 4WD can enjoy N'Dhala Gorge to the south, Trephina Gorge to the north, or Ruby Gap Nature Park and the Arltunga Historical

Reserve to the east. Gold was discovered at Arltunga in 1887, as were garnets, the latter first being reported as rubies, which started a rush into the area.
Map ref: page 619 J6

TILMOUTH WELL

Along the formed, unsealed road known as the Tanami Road, Tilmouth Well (population 8)

Aboriginal petroglyphs in N'Dhala Gorge National Park.

is 1667 km (1035 miles) south of Darwin, and 195 km (121 miles) north-west of Alice Springs, on Napperby Station. Tilmouth Well is one of the larger working cattle stations in Central Australia, and has been set up with a restaurant and bar, swimming pool, barbecue, green lawns, golf course and clay shooting range. There are also bushwalking trips and a bore run.

The roadhouse also supplies travellers with limited grocery supplies, hardware, car accessories, take-away food, ice and alcohol, as well as fuel. Basic mechanical repairs, tyres and tyre repairs are also available here, and major credit cards are accepted. Four wheel drives are recommended for travelling along the Tanami Road—caravans and conventional trailers are not.
Map ref: page 618 F4

TNORALA (GOSSE BLUFF) CONSERVATION RESERVE

Thundering through the stratosphere at an unbelievable speed, a piece of cosmic rock, possibly a comet, about 600 m (1969 feet) across, collided with the Earth right in the centre of Australia.

The Royal Flying Doctor Service has been serving the Outback since 1939.

The continent was at that time still part of the supercontinent known as Gondwanaland, and it is very likely that no living thing witnessed this momentous event. About 130 million years later the early Aboriginal Australians named this crater Tnorala, and wove their totemic Dreamtime stories about the place into the fabric of their culture. In 1872 the explorer Ernest Giles saw this crater from a distance; thinking that it might be a row of hills, he named it Gosse Bluff, after P.H. Gosse, a friend and a member of the Royal Society. Today Tnorala Conservation Reserve (4759 ha [11759 acres])

has been handed back to its Aboriginal owners, who manage it in conjunction with the Parks and Wildlife Commission of the Northern Territory.

You should first check with the Parks and Wildlife Commission regarding the need for permits to access Tnorala Conservation Reserve. The best access to Tnorala is via Namatjira Drive and Tylers Pass, west of Alice Springs. This road is sealed for 130 km (81 miles) to Glen Helen, then there are around 68 km (42 miles) of formed gravel road, which can be corrugated at times. The view from Tylers Pass is magnificent, and worth a look Access by 4WD vehicle is recommended. There is a picnic area with pit toilets, but lighting fires, pets and camping are not allowed in the reserve.
Map ref: page 618 F6

TREPHINA GORGE NATURE PARK

Two gorges dissect the East MacDonnell Ranges: Trephina, which has a wide vista, and John Hayes Rockhole, which has a narrow aperture carved out through time by the flow of water. Access to Trephina is possible by conventional vehicle, but to get to John Hayes Rockhole a high clearance 4WD vehicle is required. Trephina Gorge Nature Park is noted for its massive quartzite cliffs and its sandy creeks lined with river red gums. The waterholes attract a diversity of bird life as well as marsupials and macropods such as black-footed rock wallabies.

Like many other gorges in the Eastern MacDonnell Ranges, Trephina offers excellent bush-walking tracks and a chance to view the surrounding ranges and some of the more elusive rock wallabies that inhabit this area. Camping sites are

provided, with tables, free wood, free gas barbecue and drinking water, at Trephina Bluff and Trephina Gorge. At John Hayes Rockhole there are picnic tables and toilets but no drinking water. From Trephina Gorge there are two very pleasant one-hour return walking tracks: the Trephina Gorge Walk and the Panorama Walk. A longer ridge-top walking track has also been made for the more experienced walker. This walk links Trephina Gorge with John Hayes Rockhole and you should allow 6½ hours one way. Along these walks you may see a wide range of bush food such as the native fig or the very tasty wild passionfruit.

The park lies 85 km (53 miles) east of Alice Springs along the Ross Highway. When you have turned off onto the Trephina Gorge access road, look out for the side road that leads to the biggest ghost gum tree in Central Australia.
Map ref: page 619 H6

A sandy creek lined with eucalyptus trees runs through the awesome quartzite cliffs of Trephina Gorge, in Trephina Gorge Nature Park.

Mertens' water monitor
(Varanus mertensi)

WATARRKA (KINGS CANYON) NATIONAL PARK

The magnificent Kings Canyon, with sheer sandstone cliffs to 270 m (886 feet) high, is in this park. Set in the western end of the George Gill Range, north of Yulara and 302 km (188 miles) south-west of Alice Springs, the canyon, with its permanent waterholes and lush vegetation of cycads, palms, ferns and desert oaks, is in sharp contrast to the spinifex and stunted bushes of the surrounding arid hills. A range of fauna shares this oasis, including rock wallabies and

euros in the gorges, parrots, honey-eaters, native pigeons and birds of prey, and giant peren-ties (goannas) and other lizards and snakes. There are a number of walks, including two construc-ted walking tracks in the canyon area: one along the creek and one around the rim of the canyon. All camping and accom-modation is provided by commercial operators in the actual park.
Map ref: page 618 D7

WEST MACDONNELL NATIONAL PARK

West of Alice Springs, the parallel ridges of the MacDonnell Ranges con-tain an amazing array of canyons, cliffs and ridges, ancient hills and valleys, permanent waterholes and sandy creek beds. The West MacDonnell National Park incorporates a number of smaller parks and reserves. Some of the places worth visiting are: Ellery

Dramatic Heavitree quartzite rock of Glen Helen Gorge, West MacDonnell National Park.

Creek Big Hole, a large permanent waterhole just 90 km (56 miles) west of Alice Springs along Namatjira Drive; the Ochre Pits, where for thousands of years the local Arrernte people collected ochre for ceremonial purposes; Ormiston Gorge, which offers

perhaps the most striking scenery and brilliant colours in the West MacDonnells; Redbank Gorge; Serpentine Chalet, a small bush camping area; Serpentine Gorge; Simpsons Gap; Glen Helen Gorge and Standley Chasm.
Map ref: page 618 F5

The majestic sheer sandstone rock face of Kings Canyon in Watarrka (Kings Canyon) National Park, proclaimed in 1984, rises to 270 m (886 feet).

Darwin City Centre

NORTHERN TERRITORY

Darwin Throughroads

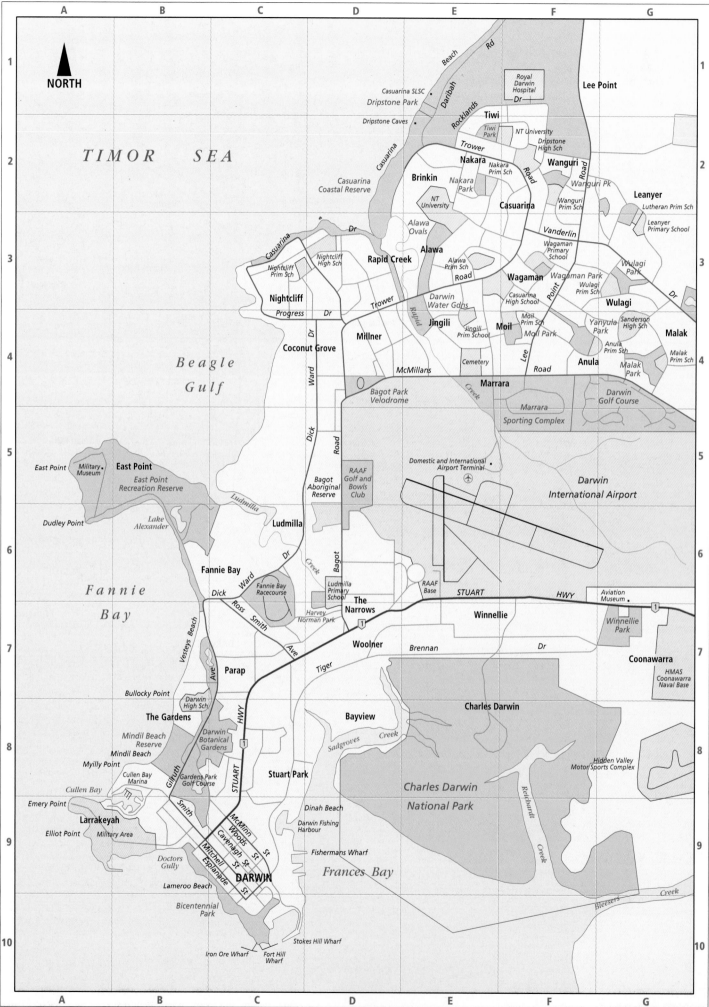

NORTH

0   500   1000
metres

TIMOR SEA

Beagle Gulf

Fannie Bay

Beach Rd
Casuarina SLSC
Dripstone Park
Dripstone Caves

Royal Darwin Hospital
Dr
Lee Point

Daribah
Rocklands
Casuarina

Tiwi
Tiwi Park
NT University
Dripstone High Sch

Casuarina Coastal Reserve

Trower

Nakara
Nakara Prim Sch
Wanguri
Road
Wanguri Pk
Leanyer
Lutheran Prim Sch

Brinkin
Nakara Park
Wanguri Prim Sch

NT University
Casuarina
Leanyer Primary School

Dr
Casuarina

Nightcliff High Sch
Nightcliff Prim Sch

Alawa Ovals

Vanderlin
Wagaman Primary School
Wulagi Park

Rapid Creek

Alawa
Alawa Prim Sch
Road
Wagaman
Wagaman Park
Wulagi Prim Sch
Wulagi

Nightcliff
Progress Dr

Trower

Rapid
Darwin Water Gdns
Casuarina High School
Sanderson High Sch

Millner
Jingili
Jingili Prim School
Moil
Moil Prim Sch
Moil Park
Yanyula Park
Malak

Coconut Grove
Ward Dr

McMillans
Cemetery
Anula Prim Sch
Anula
Malak Prim Sch
Malak Park

Dick
Road

Marrara

East Point
Military Museum
East Point
East Point Recreation Reserve

Bagot Park Velodrome

Marrara Sporting Complex
Darwin Golf Course

Dudley Point
Lake Alexander

Ludmilla

Ludmilla

Bagot Aboriginal Reserve

RAAF Golf and Bowls Club

Domestic and International Airport Terminal

Darwin International Airport

Fannie Bay
Fannie Bay Racecourse

Ward Dr
Creek
Bagot

Ludmilla Primary School

RAAF Base
STUART HWY
Aviation Museum

Dick
Ross Smith

Harvey Norman Park

The Narrows

Winnellie
Winnellie Park

Vesteys Beach Ave

Parap
Ave
Smith Ave
Tiger

Woolner
Brennan
Dr
Coonawarra
HMAS Coonawarra Naval Base

Bullocky Point
Darwin High Sch

Bayview
Charles Darwin

The Gardens
HWY

Mindil Beach Reserve
Darwin Botanical Gardens
Sadgroves Creek

Hidden Valley Motor Sports Complex

Mindil Beach
Myilly Point

Cullen Bay Marina
Gardens Park Golf Course
Stuart Park

Charles Darwin National Park
Reichardt Creek

Cullen Bay
Gilruth

Emery Point
Larrakeyah
Smith

Dinah Beach

Elliot Point
Military Area
McMinn St
Woods St
Cavenagh St
Mitchell St
Esplanade

Darwin Fishing Harbour

Doctors Gully
Fishermans Wharf

Lameroo Beach
DARWIN
Frances Bay

Bicentennial Park

Bleesers Creek

Iron Ore Wharf
Fort Hill Wharf
Stokes Hill Wharf

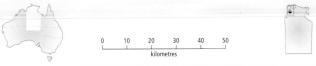

Darwin and Surrounding Areas

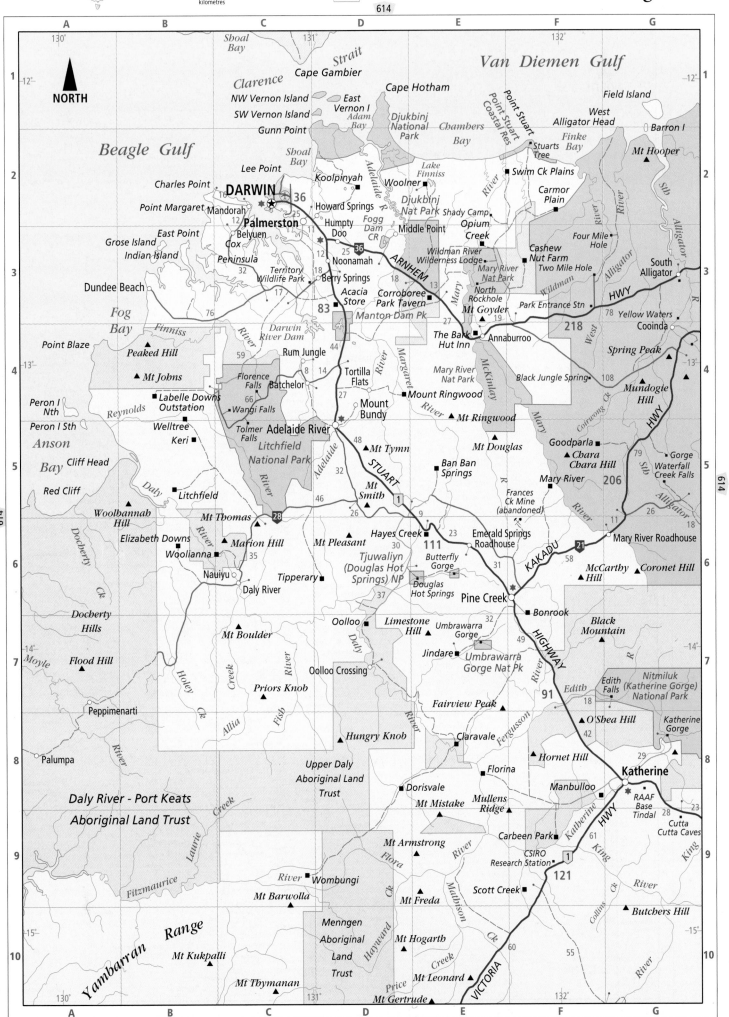

NORTH

kilometres
0 10 20 30 40 50

Beagle Gulf

Clarence Strait

Shoal Bay

Cape Gambier

Cape Hotham

Van Diemen Gulf

NW Vernon Island
SW Vernon Island

East Vernon I
Adam Bay

Djukbinj National Park

Chambers Bay

Point Stuart
Point Stuart Coastal Res

Field Island

West Alligator Head

Barron I

Finke Bay

Mt Hooper

Gunn Point

Shoal Bay

Stuarts Tree

Lee Point

Charles Point

DARWIN

36

Koolpinyah

Woolner

Lake Finniss

Swim Ck Plains

Carmor Plain

Point Margaret
Mandorah

Palmerston

Howard Springs

Humpty Doo

Djukbinj Nat Park

Shady Camp

Opium Creek

Four Mile Hole

Belyuen
Cox

Noonamah

Fogg Dam CR

Middle Point

Wildman River Wilderness Lodge

Cashew Nut Farm

Two Mile Hole

South Alligator

East Point
Grose Island
Indian Island

Peninsula

Berry Springs

Acacia Store

Corroboree Park Tavern

Mary River Nat Park

North Rockhole

Mt Goyder

Park Entrance Stn

HWY

Dundee Beach

Territory Wildlife Park

83

Manton Dam Pk

13

218

78 Yellow Waters

Fog Bay

Darwin River Dam

Rum Jungle

The Bark Hut Inn

Annaburroo

Cooinda

Point Blaze

Peaked Hill

Florence Falls

Batchelor

Tortilla Flats

Margaret River

Mary River Nat Park

McKinlay

Black Jungle Spring

108

Spring Peak

Mt Johns

Labelle Downs Outstation

Wangi Falls

66

Mount Ringwood

Mundogie Hill

Peron I Nth

Welltree
Keri

Tolmer Falls

Adelaide River

Mount Bundy

Mt Ringwood

Mt Douglas

Goodparla

Chara Chara Hill

Gorge Waterfall Creek Falls

Peron I Sth

Reynolds

Mt Tymn

48

Ban Ban Springs

79

Anson Bay

Cliff Head

Litchfield

Litchfield National Park

32

Mt Smith

STUART

Mary River

206

Red Cliff

Woolbannah Hill

Mt Thomas

28

46

26

9

Frances Ck Mine (abandoned)

11

18

Elizabeth Downs
Woolianna

Marion Hill

35

Mt Pleasant

Hayes Creek

111

23

Emerald Springs Roadhouse

Mary River Roadhouse

McCarthy Hill

Coronet Hill

Nauiyu

Tipperary

Tjuwaliyn (Douglas Hot Springs) NP

Butterfly Gorge

31

KAKADU

21

58

Daly River

Pine Creek

Bonrook

Black Mountain

Docherty Hills

Mt Boulder

Oolloo

Limestone Hill

Umbrawarra Gorge

32

49

HIGHWAY

Flood Hill

Moyle

Oolloo Crossing

Jindare

Umbrawarra Gorge Nat Pk

Edith Falls

91

Edith

18

Nitmiluk (Katherine Gorge) National Park

Peppimenarti

Priors Knob

Fairview Peak

O'Shea Hill

Katherine Gorge

42

Palumpa

Hungry Knob

Claravale

Hornet Hill

29

Katherine

Daly River - Port Keats Aboriginal Land Trust

Upper Daly Aboriginal Land Trust

Florina

Manbulloo

RAAF Base Tindal

28

Dorisvale

Mt Mistake

Mullens Ridge

HWY

61

Cutta Cutta Caves

Mt Armstrong

Carbeen Park

23

CSIRO Research Station

1

Wombungi

Mt Barwolla

Flora River

Mt Freda

121

60

Butchers Hill

Yambarran Range

Mt Kukpalli

Menngen Aboriginal Land Trust

Mt Hogarth

55

Mt Thymanan

Mt Leonard

VICTORIA

Mt Gertrude

NORTHERN TERRITORY

The Top End, Northern Territory

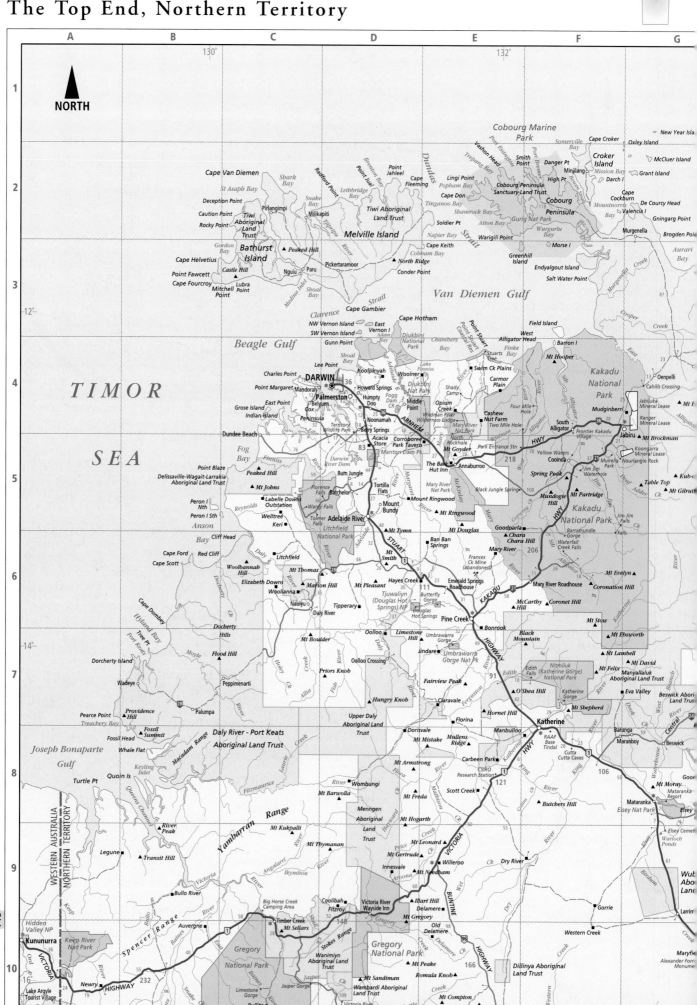

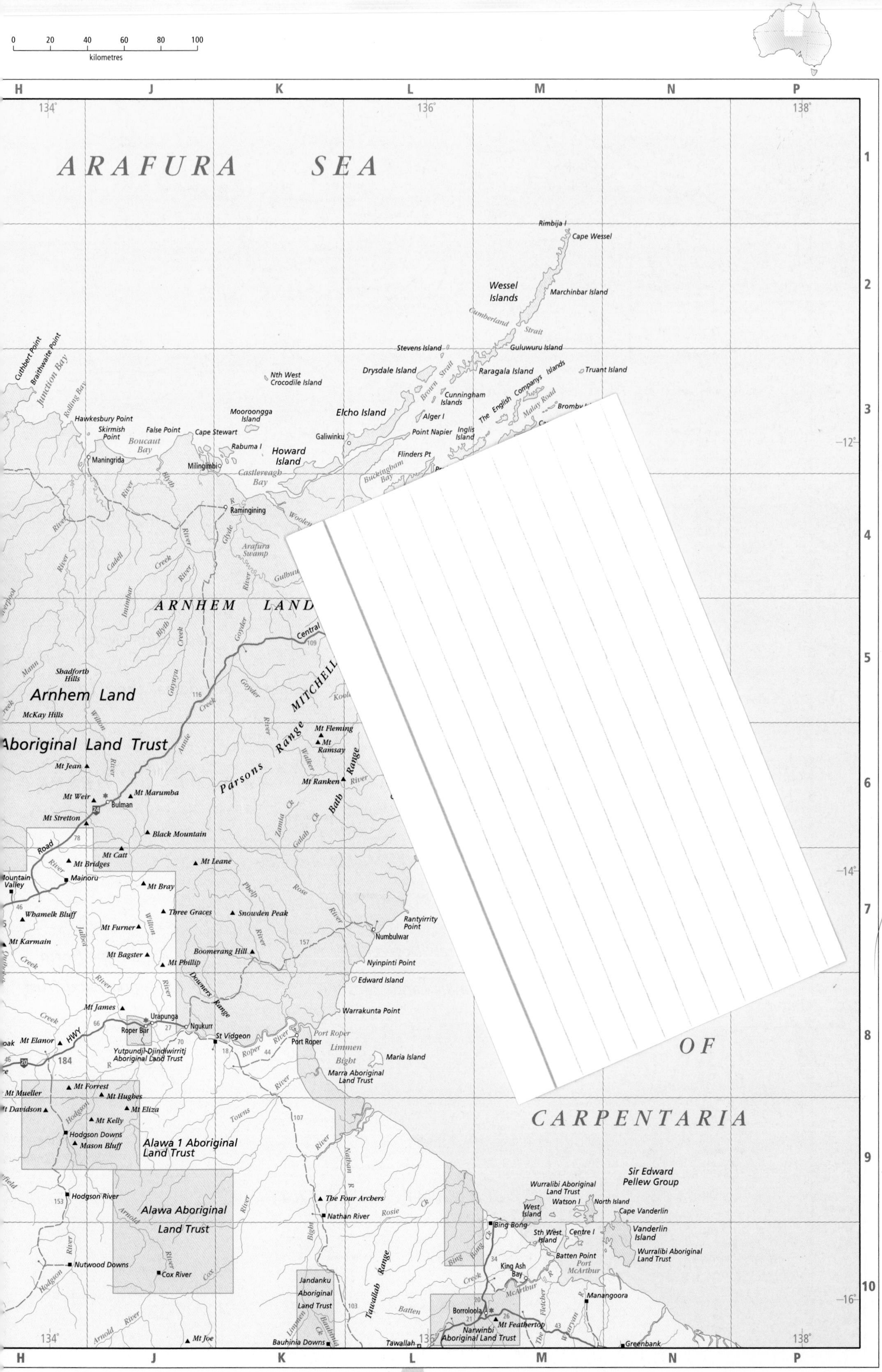

0 20 40 60 80 100
kilometres

134° 136° 138°

1

A R A F U R A S E A

Rimbija I
Cape Wessel

*Wessel
Islands*

2

Cumberland Strait

Stevens Island
Guluwuru Island
Cuthbert Point
Braithwaite Point
Junction Bay
Rolling Bay
Nth West
Crocodile Island
Drysdale Island
Raragala Island
Truant Island

3

Hawkesbury Point
Skirmish Point
False Point
Cape Stewart
Mooroongga Island
Elcho Island
Cunningham Islands
Alger I
The English Companys Islands
Bromby I
Boucaut Bay
Galiwinku
Point Napier
Inglis Island
Malay Road
Maningrida
Rabuma I
Howard Island
Flinders Pt
−12°
Milingimbi
Castlereagh Bay
Buckingham Bay

4

Ramingining
Arafura Swamp
Gulbut

A R N H E M   L A N D

Central
109

5

Sbadforth Hills
Arnhem Land
116
MITCHELL
Kook
McKay Hills
Mt Fleming
Mt Ramsay

Aboriginal Land Trust
Parsons Range
Mt Ranken
Mt Jean

6

Mt Weir
Bulman
Mt Marumba
Road
78
Mt Stretton
Black Mountain
Mt Catt
Mt Bridges
Mt Leane
Mountain Valley
Mainoru
−14°

7

Mt Bray
46
Whamelk Bluff
Three Graces
Snowden Peak
Mt Furner
Rose River
Rantyirrity Point
Mt Karmain
157
Numbulwar
Mt Bagster
Boomerang Hill
Mt Phillip
Nyinpinti Point
Edward Island

8

Mt James
Urapunga
Warrakunta Point
66
Ngukurr
HWY
St Vidgeon
Port Roper
Mt Elanor
27
Roper Bar
70
Port Roper
Limmen
46
20
184
18
Roper
44
Bight
Maria Island
Yutpundji-Djindiwirritj Aboriginal Land Trust
Marra Aboriginal Land Trust

O F

9

Mt Mueller
Mt Forrest
Mt Hughes
Mt Davidson
Mt Kelly
Mt Eliza
107
Hodgson Downs
Alawa 1 Aboriginal Land Trust
Mason Bluff
Sir Edward Pellew Group
Wurralibi Aboriginal Land Trust
Watson I
North Island
West Island
Cape Vanderlin
153
Hodgson River
The Four Archers
Alawa Aboriginal Land Trust
Nathan River
Bing Bong
Vanderlin Island
Sth West Island
Centre I
Wurralibi Aboriginal Land Trust
Batten Point
Port McArthur

10

Nutwood Downs
Cox River
Jandanku Aboriginal Land Trust
103
34
King Ash Bay
Manangoora
60
−16°
Borroloola
21
26
Mt Feathertop
43
Greenbank
Mt Joe
Bauhinia Downs
Tawallah
Narwinbi Aboriginal Land Trust

134° 136° 138°

C A R P E N T A R I A

Central Northern Territory

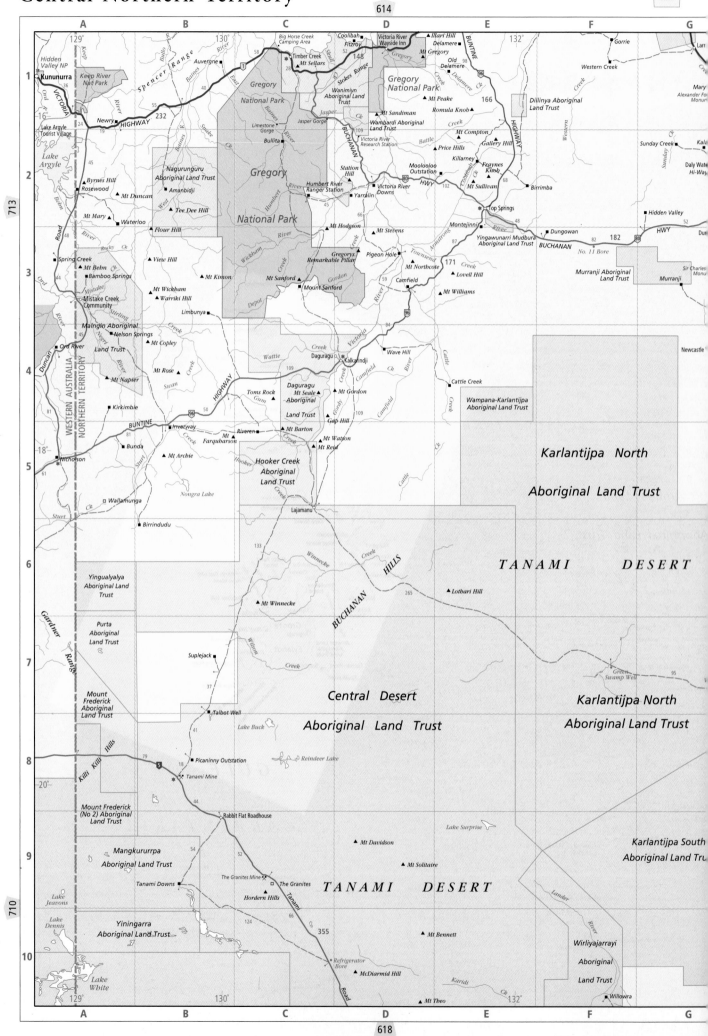

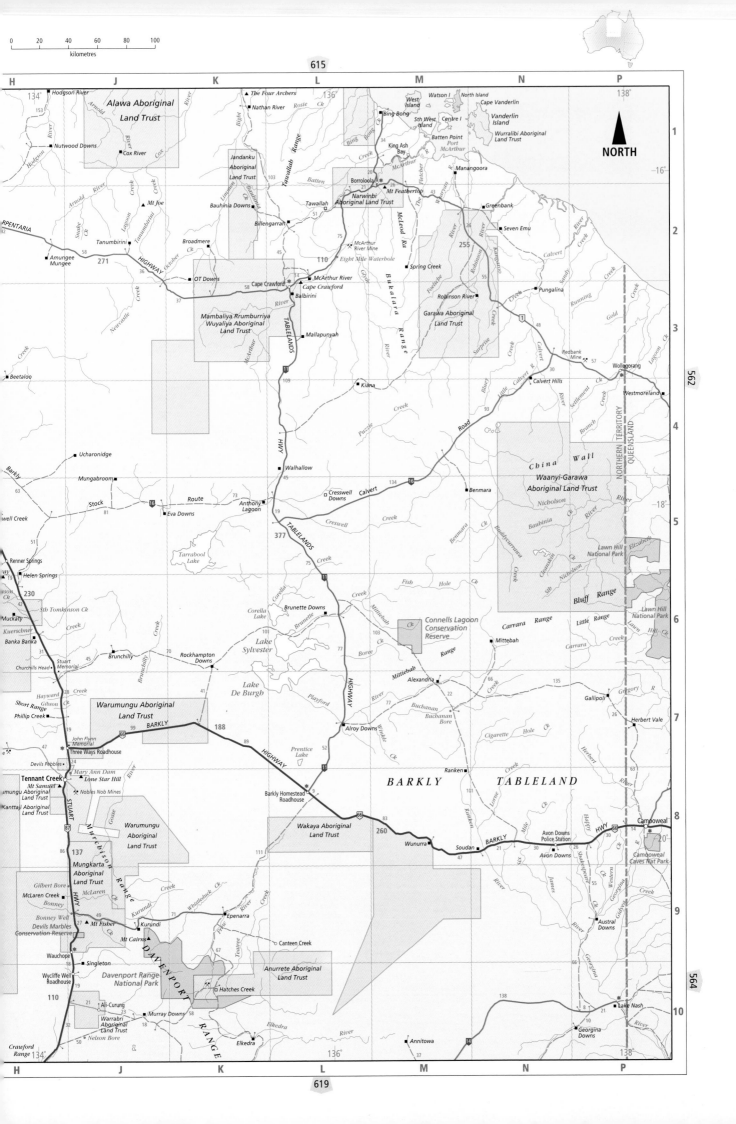

Southern Northern Territory

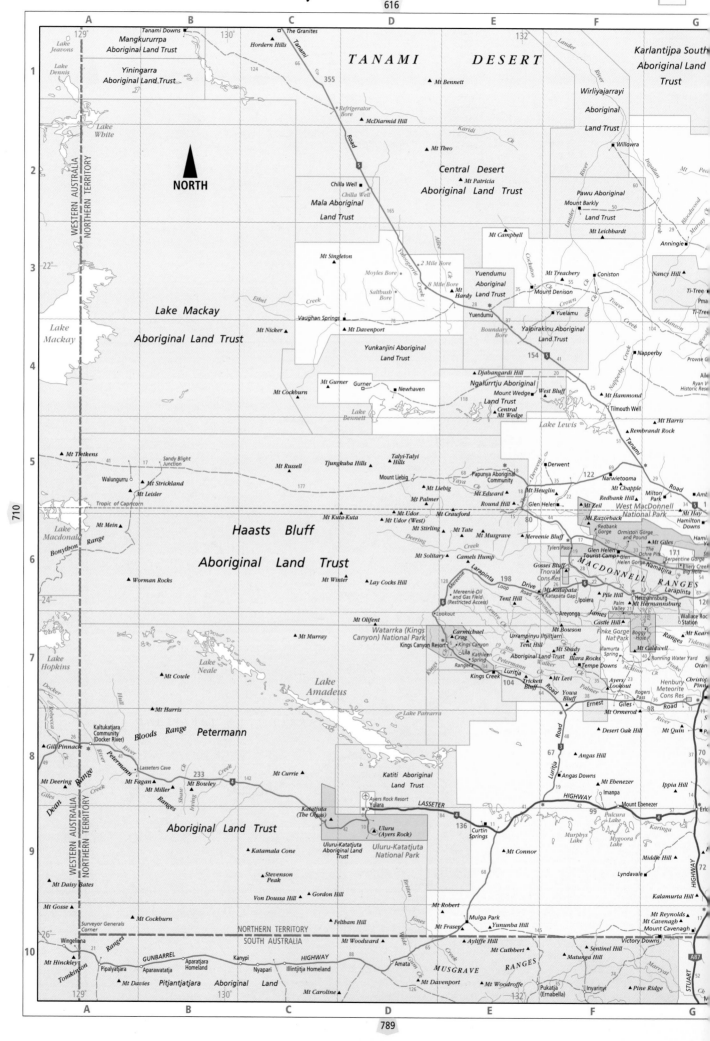

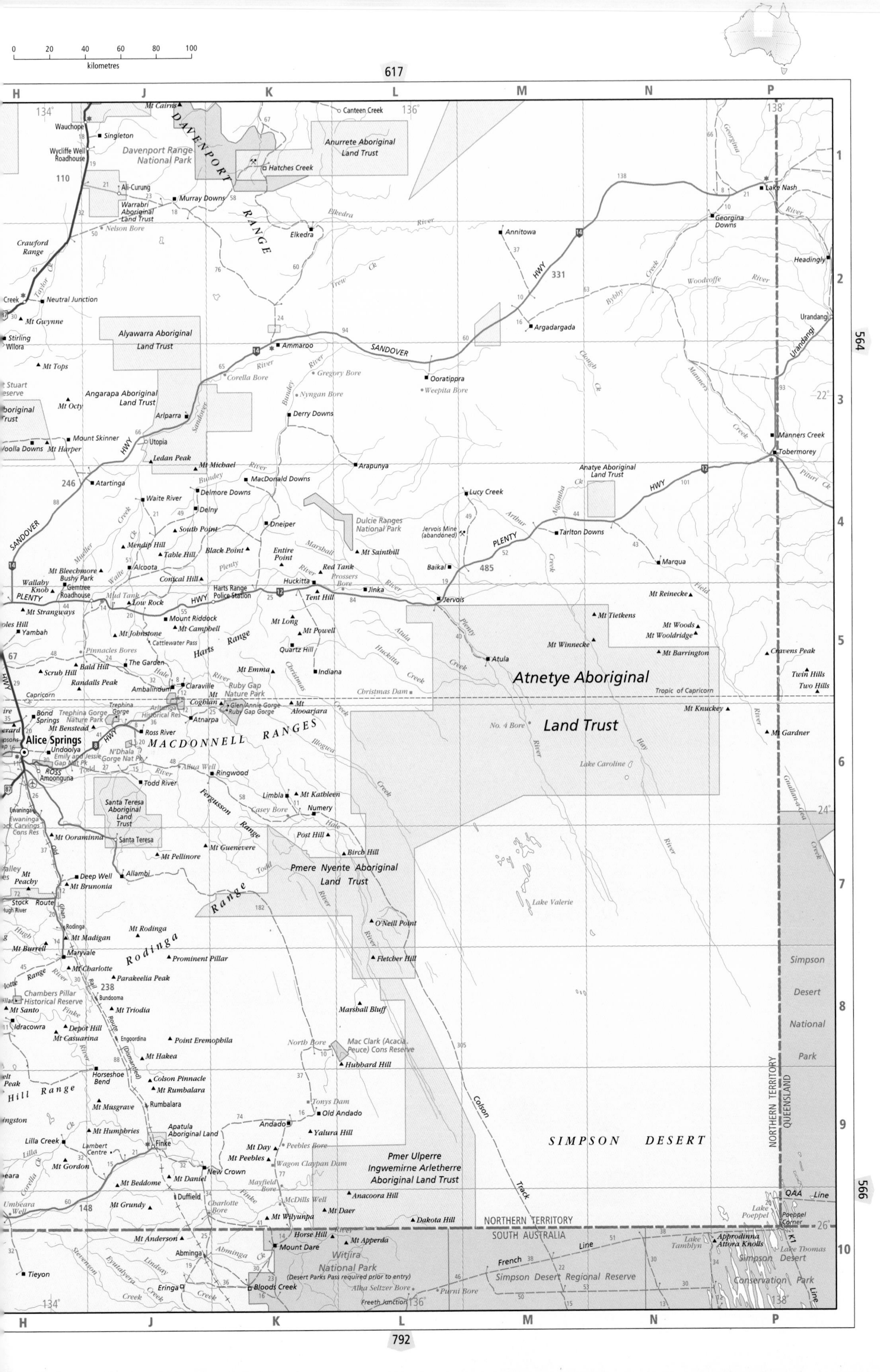

0 20 40 60 80 100
kilometres
617
H J K L M N P
1 2 3 4 5 6 7 8 9 10
134° 136° 138°
22° 24° 26°
564
566
792
Mt Cairns
Wauchope
Singleton
Wycliffe Well Roadhouse
Davenport Range National Park
DAVENPORT RANGE
Canteen Creek
Anurrete Aboriginal Land Trust
Hatches Creek
Ali-Curung
Warrabri Aboriginal Land Trust
Murray Downs
Nelson Bore
Crawford Range
Elkedra
Elkedra River
Lake Nash
Georgina Downs
Georgina River
Annitowa
HWY
331
Headingly
Creek
Neutral Junction
Taylor Ck
Trew Ck
Bybby Creek
Woodroffe River
Urandangi
Mt Gwynne
Stirling
Wilora
Alyawarra Aboriginal Land Trust
Ammaroo
SANDOVER
Argadargada
Mt Tops
Corella Bore
Gregory Bore
Ooratippra
Weepita Bore
Nyngan Bore
Angarapa Aboriginal Land Trust
Mt Octy
Arlparra
Derry Downs
Bundey River
Cloughs Ck
Manners Creek
Mount Skinner
Utopia
Woolla Downs
Mt Harper
Ledan Peak
Mt Michael
Arapunya
Anatye Aboriginal Land Trust
Tobermorey
Pituri Ck
Atartinga
MacDonald Downs
Delmore Downs
Waite River
Lucy Creek
Delny
Dulcie Ranges National Park
Dneiper
South Point
Jervois Mine (abandoned)
PLENTY
Tarlton Downs
Mendip Hill
Table Hill
Black Point
Entire Point
Marshall
Mt Saintbill
Arthur Creek
Algamba
Mt Bleechmore
Alcoota
Red Tank
Baikal
485
Marqua
Wallaby Knob
Bushy Park
Gemtree Roadhouse
Conical Hill
Harts Range Police Station
Huckitta
Prossers Bore
Jinka
Jervois
Mt Reinecke
Field
Mud Tank
Low Rock
Tent Hill
Mt Strangways
Mount Riddock
Mt Campbell
Mt Long
Mt Powell
Mt Tietkens
Mt Woods
Mt Wooldridge
Yambah
Mt Johnstone
Cattlewater Pass
Harts Range
Quartz Hill
Atula
Huckitta Creek
Mt Winnecke
Mt Barrington
Cravens Peak
Pinnacles Bores
Bald Hill
The Garden
Scrub Hill
Mt Emma
Indiana
Christmas Creek
Atnetye Aboriginal Land Trust
Twin Hills
Two Hills
Randalls Peak
Hale River
Claraville
Ruby Gap Nature Park
Christmas Dam
Tropic of Capricorn
Capricorn
Ambalindum
Arltunga Historical Res
Cogbian
Glen Annie Gorge
Ruby Gap Gorge
Mt Alooarjara
Mt Knuckey
Bond Springs
Trephina Gorge Nature Park
Atnarpa
No. 4 Bore
Mt Benstead
Ross River
Mt Gardner
Alice Springs
MACDONNELL RANGES
Illogwa Creek
Undoolya
Emily and Jessie Gap Nat Pk
N'Dhala Gorge Nat Pk
Lake Caroline
ROSS
Amoonguna
Todd River
Ringwood
Todd River
Fergusson Range
Limbla
Mt Kathleen
Numery
Ewaninga Rock Carvings Cons Res
Santa Teresa Aboriginal Land Trust
Casey Bore
Hale
Post Hill
Mt Ooraminna
Santa Teresa
Mt Guenevere
Birch Hill
Mt Pellinore
Pmere Nyente Aboriginal Land Trust
Todd
Deep Well
Allambi
Mt Peachy
Mt Brunonia
Stock Route
Range
Lake Valerie
O'Neill Point
Rodinga
Mt Rodinga
Mt Madigan
Mt Burrell
Maryvale
Rodinga
Prominent Pillar
Fletcher Hill
Simpson Desert National Park
Mt Charlotte
Parakeelia Peak
238
Chambers Pillar Historical Reserve
Bundooma
Mt Santo
Mt Triodia
Marshall Bluff
Idracowra
Depot Hill
Mt Casuarina
Engoordina
Point Eremophila
North Bore
Mac Clark (Acacia Peuce) Cons Reserve
Hubbard Hill
Mt Hakea
Horseshoe Bend
Colson Pinnacle
Mt Rumbalara
Rumbalara
Hill Range
Mt Musgrave
Tonys Dam
Old Andado
Colson Track
NORTHERN TERRITORY
QUEENSLAND
Mt Humphries
Apatula Aboriginal Land
Andado
Yalura Hill
Lilla Creek
Finke
Lambert Centre
Mt Day
Peebles Bore
SIMPSON DESERT
Mt Peebles
Wagon Claypan Dam
Pmer Ulperre Ingwemirne Arletherre Aboriginal Land Trust
Mt Gordon
New Crown
Mt Daniel
Mayfield Bore
Mt Beddome
Duffield
McDills Well
Anacoora Hill
QAA Line
Umbeara Well
148
Mt Grundy
Charlotte Bore
Mt Daer
Mt Wilyunpa
Dakota Hill
Lake Poeppel
Poeppel Corner
NORTHERN TERRITORY
SOUTH AUSTRALIA
Mt Anderson
Horse Hill
Mt Apperda
Approdinna Attora Knolls
Mount Dare
Abminga
Abminga Ck
Witjira National Park
(Desert Parks Pass required prior to entry)
French Line
Lake Tamblyn
Lake Thomas
Simpson Desert Conservation Park
Tieyon
Simpson Desert Regional Reserve
Eringa
Bloods Creek
Alka Seltzer Bore
Purni Bore
Freeth Junction
K1 Line
Stevenson Creek
Eyntalyera Creek
Lindsay Creek

NORTHERN TERRITORY

WESTERN
AUSTRALIA

NORTH

0   50   100   150   200   kilometres
0   50   100   miles

KIMBERLEY

Joseph Bonaparte Gulf
Cape Londonderry
Bonaparte Archipelago
Admiralty Gulf
Bigge I
Kalumburu
Port Warrender
Cambridge Gulf
Brunswick Bay
Augustus I
Kuri Bay
Wyndham
Ord
Kununurra
Buccaneer Archipelago
Mt Hann 779 m (2556 ft)
Lake Argyle
Lake Argyle Tourist Village
Collier Bay
Cape Leveque
Lombadina Mission
Pender Bay
King Sound
Derby
Mt Wells 983 m (3224 ft)
Warmun (Turkey Creek)
Cape Baskerville
Willare Bridge Roadhouse
King Leopold Ranges
Broome
Roebuck Roadhouse
Fitzroy Crossing
Halls Creek
Roebuck Bay
Cape Latouche Treville
La Grange Bay
La Grange Aboriginal Community (Bidyadanga)
Fitzroy River
Billiluna
Balgo

GREAT   SANDY

Eighty
Mile
Beach

DESERT

Lake Gregory

Spit Point
Pardoo Roadhouse
Port Hedland
Lake Wills

Dampier Archipelago
Montebello Is
Barrow I
Dampier
Karratha
Roebourne
Marble Bar
Percival Lakes
Tobin Lake
Lake Auld
Lake Mackay

Mt Herbert 366 m (1200 ft)
Nullagine
Gregory Range
Oakover River

North West Cape
Exmouth
Onslow
Fortescue
Pannawonica
PILBARA
Auski Roadhouse
Hamersley Range
Tom Price
River
Mt Mebarry 1253 m (4111 ft)
Newman
Capricorn Roadhouse

GIBSON DESERT
Kiwirrkurra
Lake MacDonald

Exmouth Gulf
Coral Bay
Ashburton
Paraburdoo
Lake Disappointment
Lake Hopkins

Minilya Roadhouse
Kennedy Range
Kumarina Roadhouse
LITTLE SANDY DESERT
Giles Meteorological Station

Cape Cuvier
Point Quobba
Lake MacLeod
Gascoyne
River
Bernier I
Dorre I
Carnarvon
Gascoyne Junction
W E S T E R N
Lake Carnegie
Warburton
Wingelinna

Shark Bay
Cape Inscription
Dirk Hartog I
Murchison
River
Denham
A U S T R A L I A

Steep Point
Overlander Roadhouse
Wiluna
Lake Way
Lake Wells
GREAT VICTORIA

Murchison Roadhouse
Meekatharra
DESERT

Cue
Lake Austin
Leinster
Lake Thistle

Kalbarri
Galena
Mount Magnet
Sandstone
Lake Noondie
Leonora
Laverton
Lake Rason

Yalgoo
Lake Ballard
Lake Carey
Lake Minigwal

Geraldton
Northern Gully
Greenough
Morawa
Paynes Find
Lake Moore
Menzies

Dongara
Mullewa

Eneabba
Carnamah
Lake Barlee
NULLARBOR PLAIN

Jurien
Wubin
Bonnie Rock
Badgingarra
Kalgoorlie
Boulder

Moora
Bindi Bindi
Coolgardie
Lancelin
Wongan Hills
Nungarin
Southern Cross
Kambalda
Lake Lefroy

Bindoon
Goomalling
Merredin
Lake Cowan
Madura Hotel
Eucla

Wanneroo
Cunderdin
Bruce Rock
Balladonia
Caiguna

Northam
York
Narembeen
PERTH
Midland
Beverley
Norseman

Rottnest I
Armadale
Brookton
Corrigin
Fremantle
Serpentine
Wickepin
Rockingham
Pinjarra
Lake Hope
Salmon Gums

Mandurah
Waroona
Narrogin
Lake Grace
Lake King
Great Australian Bight

Myalup Beach
Collie
Wagin
Ravensthorpe
Gibson
Mt Arid 357 m (1171 ft)
Point Dempster

Bunbury
Boyup Brook
Katanning
Hopetoun
Esperance
Cape Pasley
Cape Arid

Cape Naturaliste
Dunsborough
Busselton
Gnowangerup
Archipelago of the Recherche

Margaret River
Bridgetown
Cranbrook
Bremer Bay

Augusta
Pemberton
Mount Barker
Flinders Bay
Denmark
Cheyne Beach
Walpole
Albany

WESTERN AUSTRALIA

Many West Australians will think nothing of journeying a thousand kilometres (620 miles) for a few days' fishing. First impressions of the State for visitors are daunting—it is over 1400 km (870 miles) from the border at Eucla to the State capital, yet the same distance north from Perth will only reach Onslow on the mid-north coast, with another 1800 km (1120 miles) to get to the northernmost settlements of the State at Kununurra and Wyndham.

Taking up over a massive 2.5 million sq. km (965,000 sq. miles), Western Australia is by far the largest State in Australia, occupying more than a third of the mainland. It has enough attractions and plenty of delights to keep the most jaded traveller happy and contented. The State also has a sense of newness—almost rawness—about it, a vitality that transcends its boom-and-bust mineral-based economy, and an open, friendly, independent, outdoor lifestyle; it feels different from the rest of Australia.

With a population of about 1.8 million people—over 1.2 million of which live in Perth—the State is very sparsely populated. Over 90 per cent of the population lives in the more temperate south-west, so once you head inland, there are only a handful of towns that have more than a thousand people, and all those towns owe their livelihood and prosperity to mining.

In the south-west of the State, the Mediterranean climate and relatively high rainfall mean prosperous farming land, forests of tall trees, and delightful rivers and streams; there is a lushness and verdancy here not found anywhere else in Western Australia.

This area is, in the main, rolling hills and plains, but two mountain ranges—the Stirling and the Porongurup—have created a unique habitat, complete with their own flora and, to a lesser degree, some unique fauna. The Darling Ranges behind Perth are little more than a line of hills bordering what was once a swampy sand plain.

Vast areas of the State are uninhabited, with much of it being classed as semi-desert or desert. The Great Victoria, Gibson, Little Sandy and the Great Sandy deserts stretch from near the southern coast all the way to the north-west coast north of Port Hedland, and to the southern edges of the Kimberley, making up two-thirds of the State.

Timber—from the jarrah and karri hardwood forests—is the mainstay of Manjimup, in south-west Western Australia, but ecotourism and other agricultural products—potato, cauliflower, apple and grapes for wine—are growing in importance.

Rottnest Island, today Perth's favourite playground. The island has had a chequered history—it has been a farming settlement, an Aboriginal prison, a pilot station for Fremantle, an internment camp and a military post.

Ships being loaded with livestock for export at Fremantle. The harbour here was made accessible to large ships only in the 1890s, by Charles Yelverton O'Connor, who blasted away the sand bar at the mouth of the Swan River.

BELOW: Wine tasting at Cape Mentelle, Margaret River. The winery was founded in 1970, and now crushes around 700 tonnes of grapes annually. The grapes are either organic, or grown with low chemical input.

Capital
Perth
Area
2,529,880 sq. km
(976,863 sq. miles)
Proportion of Australia
32.9%
Population of State
1,831,400
Population Density
0.72 per sq. km
(1.87 per sq. mile)
Population of Capital
1,341,900
Time Zone
8 hours ahead of GMT
Climate
Warm-temperate in the south-west with hot, dry summers and mild, wet winters; tropical in the north with wet summers
Highest Point
Mount Meharry 1253 m
(4111 feet)

But it would be quite wrong to write this desert country off as uninteresting and always the same. Here, in this vastness, subtle changes take place continually; nothing is the same for long. Vast stretches of spinifex country eventually give way to mallee and mulga, changing yet again to gentle desert oak-dotted plains, or low, red-raw rocky ranges marked by the occasional vivid ghost gum.

Among this desert and semi-desert country are the two other 'mountainous' regions of Western Australia: the tallest in the state is Mount Meharry, in the Pilbara region, reaching just 1253 m (4111 feet). In the far north of the state is the rugged Kimberley region, whose highest peak, at 983 m (3225 feet), lies within the King Leopold Ranges.

If there is variety in these desert lands, then the coast offers a real kaleidoscope of habitats, experiences and images. The coastline stretches for over 15,000 km (9315 miles), from Eucla across the west-

ern half of the cliff-lined Great Australian Bight, to Esperance and onwards, past hundreds of rocky headlands interspersed with bays of glistening white beaches and turquoise blue water, to Cape Leeuwin. Here the cool waters of the Southern Ocean meet the warmer waters of the Indian Ocean, and it is this ocean that laps the shores of Western Australia all the way north to its meeting with the Timor Sea and the Northern Territory border. Long stretches of sand intermingle with lines of cliffs, small bays, islands and reefs, including the Ningaloo Reef, the second-longest fringing coral reef in Australia (and one more readily accessible than Queensland's Great Barrier Reef).

North of Broome, heading along the Kimberley coast, the sea and ocean mix in a virtual battleground, and roaring tides and raging currents have carved great rents into the coast, leaving the coastline littered with dozens of islands and reefs. It is one of the most dangerous coasts in the world, as well as being one of the most spectacular.

The climate is as varied as the land. The south has hot, dry summers and mild, wet winters—Perth has the mildest climate of any Australian capital, with average summer maximums of about 30°C (86°F) and winter minimums of around 8°C (46°F).

The desert country has very hot, dry summers, with the temperatures often in the high forties (those over 117°F), and mild, dry winters, with temperatures in the mid-twenties (around 77°F). Marble Bar, in the north-west of the State, is recognised as the hottest place in Australia.

The tropics have two seasons: the Wet and the Dry. The Wet is in summer—hot, muggy, and, of course, wet. The temperature is often 30°C (86°F) or more, and the humidity is high. Occasionally there are tropical cyclones along the coast, and when these move inland they can bring heavy rain to a large area of the state. The Wet means road closures—any dirt roads can stay closed for weeks as they become mud bogs. The Dry, or winter, is mild and sunny. This is the better time to visit the north of the State.

The road network through the south-west of the State is well maintained, and in the main it is bitumen capped, but away from settled areas bitumen is reserved for major highways and towns. Only two highways make it to the border in a bitumen state: the Eyre Highway in the south across the Nullarbor, and the Victoria Highway in the north, east of Kununurra. The others are dirt, and in some cases very rough dirt.

Once north of either Geraldton (on the coast) or Meekatharra (inland), the only roads that are blacktop are the main North West Coastal Highway, the Great Northern Highway, and a couple of major roads to Tom Price and Exmouth. You will have to travel on gravel roads to experience the delights of the Pilbara, the Gascoyne or the Kimberley—once away from the major mining towns, the roads and tracks are really 4WD standard only.

Many of Western Australia's wildlife species have evolved slightly differently from those found in the eastern states. Some of its species, including the state emblem, the numbat, are found only in this state.

Western Australia offers the visitor vast expanses of natural beauty which have a diverse range of landscape, flora and fauna. The hugeness of the state and its seasonal differences mean a number of visits—perhaps at varying times of the year—are the best way to experience all the delights of Western Australia.

WESTERN TIME ZONE

TURN BACK CLOCKS

45 min

LEFT: Sign for the Western Time Zone, on the Eyre Highway. Western Australia is two hours behind Eastern Standard Time— an indication of the enormous size of Australia's landmass.

The much photographed beach at Point Ann, in the Fitzgerald River National Park. Point Ann was the start of the rabbit-proof fence, which was built in 1904 and 1905 and went as far north as Meekatharra.

PERTH

Street lamp in Perth. There was gas street lighting in central Perth until the 1920s, though other nearby areas, such as Subiaco, Claremont and Fremantle, had local electricity supply services from as early as the early 1900s. Commercial electricity generation began in Perth in 1888.

London Court, in Perth. This popular shopping arcade was built in 1937, as an Elizabethan-style arcade. It runs from St George's Terrace to Hay Street Mall, and is best known for its replica of Westminster Abbey's Big Ben clockface. At the Hay Street end, four knights come out to fight every quarter hour, and at the St George end St George and the dragon do battle.

On the northern bank of the Swan River, Perth is the fourth biggest city in Australia. It has a population of over 1.2 million and is arguably Australia's most modern city—the mining boom of the 1970s and 1980s transformed its skyline, and everything on the streets beneath it.

The city and its greater metropolitan area sprawls over more than 5700 sq. km (2200 sq. miles) of undulating sand plain, from Rockingham on the south coast, north for 55 km (34 miles) to the coastal suburbs of Burns Beach and Mindarie. Inland the metropolitan area stretches to the rolling hills of the Darling Ranges and the city of Armadale, and along the Swan River north and east to Upper Swan and Brigadoon.

Vast areas within this region have been kept as open land, and much of the Swan River frontage is open to the public. The beaches and the surf are thought by the locals to be the best of any Australian capital. The southern beaches in the lee of Garden Island offer calmer waters, and the Swan River has many bays and areas to swim in. Offshore there are a number of islands, including Rottnest Island.

Britain's fear of a French or Dutch colony being established on this far west coast of Australia led in 1826 to the push for a colony in Western Australia. In that year Albany was established, and the following year Captain James Stirling arrived here to explore the Swan River. Britain agreed to support another colony, but only in a minimal way, and Australia's first free settlers, without convict labour, arrived with Captain Fremantle on 2 May 1829. Stirling, the colony's first Lieutenant-Governor, arrived in June and headed inland to find a site for the settlement; in 12 August the foundation of Perth was declared.

For the first few decades growth was slow, and there was a huge shortage of labour. Convicts arrived in 1850 to help bolster the workforce, but even after

another 20 years, by which time the transportation of convicts to Australia had ceased, the population of the city was still less than 5000. In the 1870s the Overland Telegraph line between Adelaide and Perth was completed, and during the following decade a number of railways around the city and further afield were built—all this helped the settlement to grow.

That slow growth at least allowed the city to be laid out to a plan. The surveyor, John Septimus Roe, laid out his main boulevard, St George Terrace, along the flat land parallel to the river; Hay and Murray Streets, which were to be the retail sector of the city, were on hillier ground, but parallel to the main boulevard. Other streets ran at right angles to these, forming what was, and still is, the heart of the city.

The Government Legislative Council of Western Australia was formed in 1832 and the old legislative building was erected four years later. That same year, Perth's oldest surviving building, the Courthouse, was built. Other early buildings include the Old Perth Boys' School (1854), the Bishop's House (1859), the Wesley Uniting Church (1870), and the former Government Printers Office (1879).

Mount Eliza, which blocked the city's expansion to the west, is today Kings Park, one of the jewels in Perth's crown. The 400 ha (988 acres) of park and bushland provide many fine panoramas of the city and the river, and are a showcase for Western Australia's vast floral wealth and colourful bird life. A couple of roads wind through the park, and there are also walking and bike paths, plus some lovely picnic areas and playgrounds.

Perth's, and Western Australia's, fortunes changed when gold was discovered. First it was far away in the Kimberley and the Pilbara, then the finds grew closer and richer, until almost unbelievable discoveries occurred at Coolgardie and Kalgoorlie during the 1890s. The population of the State rocketed, and by the turn of the nineteenth century the city had over 29,000 people. Many of Perth's finer old buildings date from this boom period: the refurbished commercial buildings along King Street, the Central Government Building (1874–1902), His Majesty's Theatre (1904) and the Perth Mint (1898).

Perth's fortunes waned during the 1920s and 1930s and did not really revive until after World War II. The next mineral boom began

in the 1960s and 1970s, when iron ore, oil and natural gas were discovered and developed, and Perth grew into the city it is today—modern, cosmopolitan, egalitarian and friendly.

Northbridge, on the northern side of the city, has a strong migrant heritage, and comes to life at night—it has one of the highest concentrations of restaurants anywhere in Australia. There are a number of riverside restaurants in South Perth, Crawley and Nedlands, as well as down at Fremantle and if you want to partake in food and a little flutter, there is always the Burswood Casino.

Fremantle, Perth's port, is a part of the Perth experience. It became a city in its own right by 1929, and survived the building demolitions of the 1890s and the 1960s to emerge in 1987, when it was the host city for the America's Cup sailing challenge, as a city rich in heritage and character. 'Freo', as nearly everyone calls it, is home to a 500-strong fishing fleet and a vast number of yachts and pleasure craft.

Over 150 buildings in the port, including The Round House (built in 1831 and Western Australia's oldest public building), the Esplanade Hotel (1890s) and the Fremantle Prison (which was built by convict labour and used from 1855 to 1991) are classified by the National Trust. The National Trust Fremantle Markets, established in 1897, are still open every weekend, and have just about everything on offer, from bric-a-brac and fashions to fresh produce. Yet another good spot to visit is the Fremantle Arts Centre and History Museum, housed in a magnifi-

cent building constructed by convicts in the 1860s to be the colony's first lunatic asylum. The WA Maritime Museum contains a first-class international exhibit about the many early Dutch wrecks that litter the coastline of Western Australia.

If you enjoy fine food, alfresco cafés, or even quirky beers such as 'Dogbolter' or 'Redback', then Freo is definitely the place for you. South Terrace is known as the cappuccino strip, while on Victoria Quay, the E Shed Markets have an international food court and offer some particularly good seafood restaurants.

As you would expect, there are plenty of good fishing opportunities both in and around Perth and Fremantle, with estuary fishing in the Swan and Canning Rivers, throughout the port area and also off the beaches, where you can catch a variety of different fish such as tailor, garfish, flathead, whiting, mulloway and tommy ruff.

The Perth Royal Show is held each year during September/October, and the Kings Park Wildflower Festival is around the same time. In late October, Perth hosts the Australian round of the FIA World Rally Championships; the Highland Games are held at Armadale in November/December, and there are Australia Day Celebrations in January. Fremantle hosts the Sardine Festival in January, and the Fremantle Festival in November.

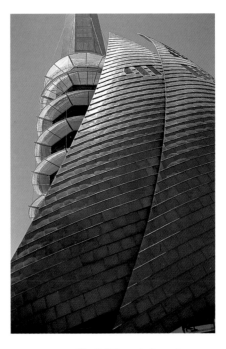

The Bell Tower, in Barrack Square. The bells themselves are from St Martin-in-the-Fields in London, and were a bicentennial gift to Western Australia in 1988.

The skyline of Perth's CBD. Today the city is an attractive and tasteful combination of colonial and modern architecture.

ADVENTURE ACTIVITIES

Western Australia

Adventure travellers keen to experience Western Australia's wide range of activities must be prepared to cover a good deal of ground. For although the state has plenty of appropriate venues, including rivers, mountains and caves, they tend to be separated by enormous stretches of outback. Travelling through the immense arid lands of Western Australia can, however, be thought of as an adventure in itself, one that makes your arrival in places like the Kimberley or the Pilbara all the more exciting.

The Kimberley alone could supply a lifetime of thrills, with its vast plateaus and myriad gorges offering endless challenges for walkers, river runners, climbers and cavers alike. Similar opportunities abound in the Pilbara. Self-sufficiency and high-level bush skills are essential in these areas and in other remote parts of Western Australia, where emergency services may be a long way away.

Only in the south-west of the state will you find an impressive array of adventure-sports locations within a relatively small, densely populated area. The proximity of delightful beaches, wineries, historic towns and other more general tourist attractions make this an especially enjoyable region to explore.

Bushwalking

Pride of place among Western Australian walking routes goes to the Bibbulmun Track, a 963-km (598-mile) path from Kalamunda, inland from Perth, to Albany, on the south coast. It follows a series of interconnected bush corridors, passing through many of the varieties of forest that occur in this corner of the state, as well as rural landscapes. Rather than walking the full length of the track, most people tackle the Bibbulmun in sections, a day or weekend at a time.

Other extended hikes in the south include the Cape to Cape Walk, a coastal walk running the full length of Leeuwin–Naturaliste National Park, and the famous Ridge Walk in Stirling Ranges National Park, a three-day excursion that includes ascents of three peaks over 1000 m (3300 feet). The Stirlings also offer several great day walks such as the climbs up Bluff Knoll, Mount Hassell and Mount Talyuberlup.

Further north, near Exmouth, there are coastal tracks in Cape Range National Park. Inland, the Hamersley Ranges in the Pilbara provide excellent opportunities for experiencing the outback environment. The most impressive walks here run through deep, water-filled gorges which provide welcome shelter from the often-extreme heat. Gorge walks are also a feature of other parts of the north, such as Kalbarri National Park near the west coast and many parts of the Kimberley. However, the Kimberley's gorges can be as much of a curse as a blessing, for many routes that appear feasible on a map turn out to be blocked by impassable canyons. (Of course, this is just the kind of thing that gives the area unparalleled appeal for hard-core adventurers.) Another of the north's challenges is the day trip to the summit of Mount Augustus, or Burringurrah as it is known to the traditional inhabitants, in Mount Augustus National Park, where wonderful views and intriguing Aboriginal art provide further interest.

With exquisite beaches and the southernmost coral reefs in the world, Rottnest Island is an ideal destination for snorkellers, who can view several shipwrecks as well as colourful gardens of coral and thriving and varied marine life.

Canoeing, Kayaking and Rafting

Western Australia is a dry state, but it does have some navigable rivers with reliable water levels. The Avon River, for example, which flows to Perth, offers good paddling, including some rapids, and is the site of the annual 135-km (84-mile) Avon Challenge. More technical paddling can be enjoyed on the Murray River where it cuts through the ranges near Dwellingup. Other destinations in the south-west include the Warren, Deep and Blackwater Rivers. Trips to rivers in the north of the state, such as the Ord, Fitzroy and Murchison, require careful planning, not only because of the length of the rivers but also because of the difficulties involved in getting on and off the water in remote locations.

LEFT: The cliffs and gorges of Kalbarri National Park consist mainly of layers of sandstone which formed from sediments laid down on tidal flats more than 400 million years ago.

Rock Climbing

An abundance of exciting climbing is available in Western Australia, but the most popular destinations are a long way apart. The greatest concentration is in the south and south-west; among the most enjoyable venues are the sea-cliffs of West Cape Howe, the Gap and Willyabrup. The granite domes of the Porongurup Ranges also offer good sport, while greater challenges can be found on Bluff Knoll in the Stirling Ranges.

The Western Australian outback contains countless cliffs, but often the rock is very unstable and the climate too hot for comfortable climbing. One area that is a long way from Perth but gaining popularity among climbers is Kalbarri National Park, which offers high-quality climbing and is conveniently situated close to Kalbarri township.

Caving

The south-west is also the focus of caving in Western Australia, with Leeuwin–Naturaliste National Park being the most popular destination. It has an extraordinary system, part of which can be viewed on guided tours and part of which is set aside for adventure caving. In the far north-west, spelunkers are drawn to the caves in the limestone hills of Cape Range National Park. Other destinations include the Nullarbor and the little-explored caves of the Kimberley.

Mountain Biking

Mountain biking is popular in the southern part of the state, from Perth east to Esperance. Elsewhere, the heat and lack of shade is oppressive, and back roads are often either very rocky or sandy, neither of which makes for enjoyable cycling. Perth-based cyclists head for the hills near Midland and the downhill and cross-country trails around Dwellingup, 80 km (50 miles) to the south. There is a highly active mountain biking club at Bunbury, which makes the most of the varied terrain in the forests of the south-west.

Sea Kayaking

There is enormous potential for sea kayaking in Western Australia and the sport is just starting to take off there. One of the most convenient destinations for a weekend outing is Rottnest Island, which can be reached in two to three hours from Perth; other islands, such as Garden, Bird, Seal and Penguin islands, are even closer.

In the north, on the Pilbara Coast, the 42 islands of the Dampier Archipelago constitute a sea-kayaker's paradise, with the some islands just 2 nautical miles offshore. The Kimberley coast provides perhaps the ultimate challenge, with 400 km (250 miles) of remote and barren coastline punctuated by tidal whirlpools. To add to the excitement, the scarcity of fresh water makes it necessary to paddle up estuaries—the hunting grounds of estuarine crocodiles—to look for creeks. A much more relaxed time can be enjoyed at Ningaloo Reef, off Exmouth, one of the richest aquatic environments in the country, which is inhabited by dolphins, turtles, dugongs and myriads of fish, including the area's famous whale sharks.

Sea kayakers pass a small sea-bird colony off Trigg Beach in Perth's northern suburbs. The city's river-mouth location means that water-based adventure activities are readily accessible.

SOUTH-WEST WESTERN AUSTRALIA

The south-west is the most fertile corner of this vast and mineral-rich State. Originally settled in the 1820s by the English, European forays into the region began much earlier. By the mid-1600s the Dutch had mapped the west coast. Numerous wrecks of Dutch East India Company ships, which enlisted the aid of the Roaring Forties westerly winds in their journey to Java, lie along the coast.

Perth ○

Perth nestles on the banks of the Swan River, 19 km (12 miles) inland from the clear turquoise waters of the Indian Ocean and the historic port of Fremantle. The State capital is at the centre of a network of roads that lead north (the Brand and Great Northern Highways), east (the Eastern Highway), south-east (the Albany Highway) and south (the Bussel Highway).

Black swans, western grey kangaroos, western brush wallabies, quokkas, and a variety of reptiles and birds inhabit this region. During the migratory season, whales can be seen from Cape Naturaliste at the northern tip of Leeuwin–Naturaliste National Park and from the Walpole-Nornalup National Park on the south coast. Dolphins might join you for a swim at the gorgeous beaches near Dunsborough or Margaret River, an area famous for its beautiful vineyards as well as its limestone caves and exceptional surfing.

Magnificent karri, jarrah and marri forests tower in the area around Walpole, Denmark and Pemberton and during spring, from September to November, a stunning variety of wildflowers are in bloom. About 65 km (40 miles) north of Albany, on the south coast, are the jagged peaks of the Stirling

Range while a trip of about 40 km (25 miles) south of the Stirlings takes you to the granite mounds of the Porongurup Range.

Further east, on the Southern Ocean, lies Esperance near Cape Le Grand National Park and the islands of the Recherche Archipelago. Hundreds of kilometres north of Esperance are the goldfields that boomed during the 1890s. Norseman, at the junction of the Eyre and Eastern Highways, is the gateway to the west for travellers who have crossed the Nullarbor from the east. North of Norseman—and about 600 km (373 miles) east of Perth—is Kalgoorlie, with its ornate early nineteenth century buildings and rich mining history.

OPPOSITE: Albany's Town Hall. The building was built in 1887, the late Victorian period, and is Classical revival in style.

The famous Elephant Rocks, at William Bay National Park. These granite rocks provide shelter for a small swimming beach.

REGIONAL FEATURE

The Leeuwin–Naturaliste Coast

Located 261 km (162 miles) south of Perth, the Leeuwin–Naturaliste Coast is one of the most scenic and fascinating parts of Western Australia. Extending for 120 km (75 miles) between the 'two capes'—Cape Naturaliste in the north and Cape Leeuwin (the state's most south-westerly point) in the south—and forming the western side of a broad peninsula, it offers picturesque coastal and forest scenery, excellent fishing, swimming and bushwalking, and extraordinary geological formations. It is also the site of one of the country's most prestigious wine regions, which surrounds and is named after the town of Margaret River. Other local attractions include cheese factories, galleries, and studios making crafts ranging from gumnut ornaments to jewellery and furniture.

Wine producers in the Margaret River area face many challenges, including porous soils and strong, salty, spring winds that inhibit vine growth and in turn keep yields low.

History

The peninsula is underpinned by a long granite formation, known as the Leeuwin–Naturaliste Ridge, which formed around 600 million years ago and today lies about 40 km (25 miles) from the sea. The area between the ridge and the ocean was once under water but gradually filled with debris and sediments. It is now capped by limestone and sand dunes, and swathed in jarrah, banksia and melaleuca woodlands broken by heathland, swamps and caves.

Aboriginal occupation of the area dates back to around 40,000 years ago; evidence includes bones, tools and other artefacts found at numerous sites. The earliest evidence of a European visit to the area is a reference, in 1622, to 'Leeuwin's Land' in the log of the Dutch East India Company ship *Leeuwin*. A second reference was made by another Dutch mariner, J. P. Poereboom, who, in 1685, anchored in a bay thought to be present-day Flinders Bay. Many other explorers followed the Dutch, including Matthew Flinders himself, who named Cape Leeuwin in 1801, and French mariner Nicolas Baudin, travelling on the *Géographe*, who christened Hamelin Bay, Cape Naturaliste and Geographe Bay.

The region remained sparsely inhabited until the early 1920s, when British immigrants were encouraged to settle here under the Group Settlement Scheme. The dairy, beef and timber industries soon became, and remain, the economic backbone of the region. However, tourism has become increasingly significant over the past 25 years, with the magnificent scenery, thriving wine industry, and sporting and cultural events such as the annual Margaret River Classic surfing competition and the outdoor concert at the Leeuwin Estate winery gaining national and international recognition.

Brookland Valley Vineyard is one of many Margaret River wineries that have attracted significant investment from major wine companies in recent years.

Leeuwin–Naturaliste National Park

Most of this magnificent coastline is incorporated in Leeuwin–Naturaliste National Park. Covering an area of 19,700 ha (48,700 acres), it consists of a long thin strip of protected land running along the shoreline, broken at one or two points by private holdings. In places, it also extends some way inland. The sealed Caves Road runs parallel to the coast and provides access to most sections of the park. Some side roads are unsealed but usually in good condition and suitable for 2WD vehicles. Additional information on the park is available from the CALM offices at Bussellton and Margaret River, and rangers are stationed at Yallingup, Cowarump Bay, Boranup and Augusta.

PARK ACTIVITIES

Leeuwin–Naturaliste is a bushwalker's delight, offering a wide range of treks. The demanding Cape to Cape Walk wends its way for 140 km (87 miles) along the entire coast, but can be tackled in separate sections. Experienced walkers seeking a challenging day walk should try the 20-km (12.5-mile) track from Cosy Corner to Skippy Rock. Soft sand and narrow rock platforms make this a fairly arduous hike, but the scenery en route is superb.

There are also established bushwalking trails at Cape Naturaliste (a moderate one-and-a-half-hour walk through a cluster of limestone rock pinnacles to a dramatic lookout from where you may spot whales), Bunker Bay (an easy one-hour walk through heathland to coastal lookouts) and Ellensbrook Homestead (an easy, wheelchair-accessible, 2-km [1.2-mile] stroll to enchanting Meekadareebee Falls). Brochures and track maps are available from the CALM offices at Bussellton and Margaret River.

With the warm Leeuwin Current running offshore, the fishing from the beach, off rocks, and over reefs in small boats is excellent year-round. Good catches of skippy, tandan, snapper, whiting, school and gummy sharks, and flathead are regularly made, and during late summer and early autumn Australian salmon migrate up the coast to the Perth area and back again. Abalone and crayfish can be caught in a number of bays, but licences are required.

The coastline also offers numerous great diving spots, particularly in protected bays and around the islands and reefs. At Hamelin Bay, a dive trail takes in four of the fourteen shipwrecks known in the area. Sailing and windsurfing are also popular pastimes at various points along the coast.

SOUTH-WESTERN WILDLIFE

The national park's animal inhabitants include western grey kangaroos, brushtail possums, honey possums and fat-tailed dunnarts. Around 200 species of

When it opened in 1896, Cape Leeuwin lighthouse had the world's largest kerosene wick lamp which was visible for 40 km (25 miles). The lamp was converted to electricity in 1982.

birds have been recorded, including the wedge-tailed eagle, various kites, the red-tailed tropic bird and a wide range of seabirds. Wildflowers are particularly colourful around headlands and in low heath areas in spring and early summer. Acacias, orchids, coastal daisy bush, cocky's tongue, banksias and one-sided bottlebrush are among the most notable plant species.

The migration of both humpback and southern right whales can be observed from the coast at certain times of the year. Both species pass by in July on their way to their northern breeding grounds and then again as they return southward between October and November. The best vantage points are Cape Leeuwin, Cape Naturaliste, Gracetown Lookout at Cowaramup Bay, and around Sugarloaf Rock. Southern right

whales are often seen lazing in shallow bays, which offer refuges in which they can breed at a safe distance from the predators that inhabit deeper waters.

GOING UNDERGROUND

Beneath the dunes, heaths and forests of the park lies an extraordinary assemblage of underground caves and passageways. It includes more than 360 caves, ranging from narrow tunnels to enormous caverns measuring 14 km (9 miles) in length, many of which are decorated with spectacular stalagmites and stalactites. Over the years, fossils of long-extinct marsupial lions, Tasmanian tigers, koalas, and even a gigantic wombat-like creature the size of a horse (dated to around 37,000 years ago) have been found in these passages, which are now considered among the oldest and most valuable archaeological sites in Australia.

Visitors can join guided tours of four of the most spectacular caves—Yallingup Cave, to the north of the park, Mammoth and Lake Caves in Boranup Forest, and Jewel Cave in the south close to Augusta. In addition, two 'adventure caves' in Boranup Forest are open to experienced groups of cavers.

EXPLORING THE PARK

By taking several detours off the Caves Road, visitors can sample the diversity of scenery and activities on offer. At the northern tip of the peninsula, a sealed sidetrack leads from Dunsborough to the Cape Naturaliste lighthouse. Built in 1903, this is an excellent vantage point from which to view the cape and Geographe Bay to the east. A 4WD track leads from the lighthouse to the shore, where there is good surfing and fishing, and a 3-km (1.9-mile) walking trail connects the lighthouse with Bunker Bay, a picturesque spot where you'll find toilets and picnic tables. On the western side of the headland is Sugarloaf Rock, a pyramid-shaped rock located on a rough, exposed section of coastline. Watch out for dangerous waves when walking on the rocky shoreline.

Returning to Dunsborough and heading south along Caves Road, the next point of interest is the small town of Yallingup, a popular holiday destination, particularly among surfers keen to tackle the shore's huge, rolling swells. A caravan park and wide range of other accommodation are available here.

The next detour off Caves Road, Smiths Beach, is another popular surfing spot and also good for swimming and fishing. A caravan park and other accommodation are located near the beach, and there is a protected boat ramp. Nearby Canal Rocks consists of several chains of rocks that extend into the ocean from the headland, forming natural canals. A walkway and bridge lead to the rocks, allowing visitors to view the channels and the waves surging through them. This is a good fishing spot, but too dangerous for swimming.

Further south, the Cowaramup Road leads to Gracetown and scenic Cowaramup Bay. Just before you reach the town, look for the viewpoint on the right, which offers a superb panorama of the coast-

Located on the Cape to Cape Walk, north of Moses Rock car park, Quininup Falls flows freely in winter but dries up between mid-spring and late autumn.

line. The fishing is good here, and when the swells are right the surfing is superb. The town offers picnic facilities, toilets and a caravan park.

Prevelly Park, at the mouth of the Margaret River, is located just outside the park, but is nevertheless worth a detour. The area is famous for its superb surfing, with the annual Margaret River Classic attracting competitors from all over the world. Visitors can view the coast—and watch the surfers—from adjacent headlands. Canoeing is also a popular pastime here, and there is abundant birdlife along the pristine Margaret River. Ellensbrook Homestead, near the mouth of the river, is an interesting historic property managed by the National Trust and open to the public. It was built in 1857 by Alfred Bussell for himself and his young wife, Ellen.

Continuing south from Margaret River, the Caves Road enters the Boranup Forest. Covering 3200 ha (7900 acres), this is the largest karri forest growing in limestone sands. Much of Boranup was clear-felled between 1882 and 1913, but the karri trees have since regenerated and some stand up to 60 m (200 feet) high. A pleasant detour along Boranup Drive through majestic karris leads to the Boranup camping area, which has barbecues, tables and toilet facilities, but no water. This is a terrific spot for viewing the area's diverse wildlife and plant life. Birds are abundant and there are several spectacular multiheaded grasstrees, some standing over 5 m (16 feet) high, with more than 15 heads. After dark, campers often spot brush-tail possums foraging in the trees.

South of the forest, a side road leads to Hamelin Bay. Set behind Hamelin Island and the surrounding reef, this pretty stretch of coastline offers excellent swimming, diving and snorkelling. The beach is ideal for walking, and climbing to the headland provides magnificent views. A caravan park is located right beside the beach and there is also a boat ramp. Last century, Hamelin Bay was a port serving the local timber industry, and in its heyday it had a jetty and heavy moorings for ships. The rotting stumps of the jetty can still be seen in the water, and the camping ground stands on the site of the former timber yard.

Near Hardy Inlet, the Caves Road links up with the Bussell Highway which leads southward to the town of Augusta. From here, a road swings south-west along the coast to Cape Leeuwin, where the Indian and Southern Oceans meet. The impressive Leeuwin Lighthouse, which began operations in 1896, crowns the rugged promontory. In 1895, during the construction of the lighthouse, a spring was tapped to supply the workers, the water being diverted along a wooden channel to a wooden

Dramatic formations line many of the park's 360 caves.

water wheel. This rudimentary system was used until 1928; since then, salt deposits have steadily encrusted the wheel, encasing it in crystals.

Margaret River Wine Region

In little more than 30 years, the small farming community of Margaret River has become a flourishing centre for an internationally recognised wine industry. A key factor in this development has been the ability of the region's wineries to consistently produce top-quality wines. Although Margaret River is responsible for only about 1 percent of Australia's overall production, its wines make up as much as 20 percent of the premium market. Margaret River chardonnay and cabernet sauvignon are now particularly highly regarded, with the region producing many of Australia's best examples, and the delicious sémillon/sauvignon blanc blends are also popular on restaurant wine lists throughout Australia and overseas.

Although winemaking in Western Australia dates back almost to the beginning of European settlement, the first vineyards at Margaret River were small plots planted by European immigrants in the early twentieth century. In 1955, the distinguished American viticulturist, Professor Harold Olmo, from the University of California at Davis, spent eight months at the University of Western Australia studying the wine industry in the Swan Valley. He suggested in an aside that Margaret River might also prove to be suitable for growing premium grapes. That remark spawned a paper on Margaret River's viticultural potential by University of Western Australia agronomist Dr John Gladstones, which in turn served as a catalyst for the establishment of wineries.

The following are among the region's top producers. With the exception of Moss Wood, all offer cellar-door tastings and sales.

The lush vegetation found along inland waterways in Leeuwin–Naturaliste National Park contrasts with the drier heathlands that predominate on the coast.

Hay Shed Hill's name derives from the fact that prior to becoming a winery it was a dairy farm whose property included a hay shed situated on a prominent rise.

Decommissioned wine barrels have been turned into a decorative feature outside the winery at Brookland Valley Vineyard.

PRODUCERS

AMBERLEY ESTATE

Established 1986 Owners Syndicate Production 60,000 cases Vineyard area 78 acres (32 ha)

Although Amberley Estate has always aimed first and foremost for commercial success, it has, at the same time, managed to produce wines of exemplary quality. Its Sémillon Sauvignon Blanc is one of the region's better examples, and the Shiraz and Cabernet Merlot consistently have good varietal definition, smooth texture and abundant flavour. A restaurant on the estate offers sumptuous food and picturesque views of the surrounding countryside.

BROOKLAND VALLEY VINEYARD

Established 1984 Owners BRL Hardy and the Jones and Poynton families Production 7500 cases Vineyard area 20 ha (49 ha)

Brookland first came to attention with its tropically fruited Sauvignon Blanc and then the powerful, full-flavoured Chardonnay. Recent expansion has resulted in two regional wines being introduced (a white and red under the Verse 1 label) and the construction of a new winery (which is due to open in 2001). The winery's charming Flutes Café occupies an idyllic position overlooking the estate gardens.

CAPE MENTELLE

Established 1970 Owners Veuve Clicquot and David Hohnen Production 65,000 cases Vineyard area 120 ha (297 acres)

The Cape Mentelle vineyard was one of the region's first, and its fine wines have ensured it remains at the forefront of local production. Most notably, the winery won Australia's most prestigious award, the Jimmy Watson Trophy, in consecutive years with its 1982 and 1983 Cabernet Sauvignons. Co-owner Hohnen and winemaker John Durham have steadily refined the reds and produced some impressive whites, especially the powerful and complex Chardonnay and classy Sémillon/Sauvignon Blanc.

CULLEN

Established 1971 Owners the Cullen family Production 16,000 cases Vineyard area 28 ha (69 acres)

Cullen was the third winery established in Margaret River and since then has always been among the industry's leaders. In recent years, winemaker Vanya Cullen has transformed the family business into one of Australia's foremost boutique wineries. The complex, classically structured, velvety Cabernet/Merlot is Australia's best, the Chardonnay is among the nation's most impressive, and the wood-aged Sauvignon Blanc/Sémillon has an enthusiastic following for its beautifully integrated oak and ripe, juicy flavors. The restaurant highlights local produce and has a veranda offering sweeping views of the vineyard.

DEVIL'S LAIR WINES

Established 1981 Owners Southcorp Production 25,000 cases Vineyard area 35 ha (87 acres)

Named after the nearby cave in which the fossilised remains of a Tasmanian tiger were discovered, Devil's Lair was the first Margaret River winery to be taken over by a major Australian company, but has retained its distinctive identity. The Cabernet and especially the Chardonnay continue to go from strength to strength, and the Fifth Leg wines (one white and one red) are high-quality regional blends.

HAY SHED HILL VINEYARD

Established 1973 Owners Liz and Barry Morrison Production 17,000 cases Vineyard area 18 ha (45 acres)

Hay Shed Hill has a smallish state-of-the-art winery and stylish cellar-door outlet, and markets its wines with flair. The Sauvignon Blanc, Sémillon and Chardonnay all show good varietal definition and are clean, fresh and flavoursome, while the Pinot Noir and Cabernet are the most appealing of the reds.

LEEUWIN ESTATE

Established 1969 Owners Horgan family Production 35,000 cases Vineyard area 95 ha (235 acres)

The reputation of this showcase winery rests on the quality of its Art Series Chardonnay, widely held to be the best produced in Australia. Since the first release in 1980, this opulent, full-flavoured, complex white has aged more gracefully than any other Australian chardonnay. The Prelude Chardonnay and the Art Series Cabernet Sauvignon are also highly regarded. The winery has an outstanding restaurant and is the venue for an annual open-air classical concert that attracts renowned international performers.

MOSS WOOD

Established 1969 Owners Keith and Clare Mugford Production 5500 cases Vineyard area 8.5 ha (21 acres)

Moss Wood is one of Australia's finest boutique wineries and its vineyard one of the country's most distinguished viticultural sites. The Cabernet is recognised as one of the best produced in Australia, while the Chardonnay and Sémillon are also highly sought after. Moss Wood is not open to the public but enthusiasts are welcome by appointment.

PIERRO

Established 1980 Owner Mike Peterkin Production 9000 cases Vineyard area 21 acres (8.5 ha)

Pierro first came to notice with the intense, pristine flavours of its outstanding Chardonnay. The Sémillon/Sauvignon Blanc is also excellent, and the Pinot Noir and Cabernets seem to improve with each vintage. A new winery was recently constructed on the property.

VASSE FELIX

Established 1967 Owners Heytesbury Holdings Production 55,000 cases Vineyard area 34 ha (84 acres)

Incorporating one of the region's earliest vineyards, Vasse Felix has been among Western Australia's outstanding wineries for the past decade. Both the Shiraz and the Noble Riesling are the finest examples of these varietals produced in the state, and the Sémillon and Cabernet are among Margaret River's best. The winery's impressive restaurant pairs the estate wines with innovative cuisine.

VOYAGER ESTATE

Established 1978 Owner Michael Wright Production 27,000 cases Vineyard area 74 ha (183 acres)

This estate has produced increasingly complex and interesting wines in recent years, with the Chardonnay outstanding and the Sémillon and the reserve wines under the Tom Price label also impressive. The winery's manicured lawns, lavish rose gardens, restaurant and stunning Cape Dutch architecture ensure a memorable visit.

CHATEAU XANADU

Established 1977 Owners Chateau Xanadu Wines Ltd Production 47,000 cases Vineyard area 135 ha (334 acres)

Xanadu had already gained a reputation for its white wines in the 1980s and dramatically raised the quality of its reds in the 1990s. The cabernets (especially the Reserve) are among the region's best, while the oak-matured Sémillon, the Chardonnay and the Sémillon/Sauvignon Blanc are all highly recommended.

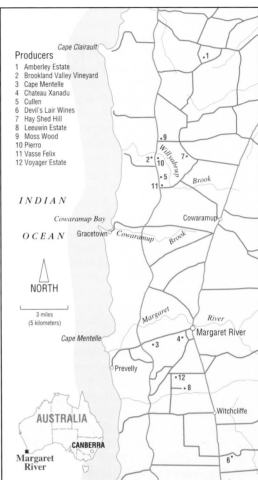

The cellar door at Vasse Felix. The opening of a new winery in 1999 has helped Vasse Felix raise production levels yet maintain quality.

Places in
SOUTH-WEST
WESTERN AUSTRALIA

ALBANY

Albany, 417 km (258 miles) south-east of Perth, is one of Western Australia's top tourist destinations. It is the State's most historically significant town and its oldest settlement. The first European visitor, Captain Vancouver, claimed the area for Britain in 1791. Other early visitors included the French explorer Bruni d'Entrecasteaux, who arrived in the same year, and Matthew Flinders, who came here about 10 years later. Britain took formal possession in 1826, sending the ship *Amity*, with troops and convicts, to form a colony.

Originally called Frederickstown, in 1832 the first governor of the new Swan River Colony, Governor Stirling, was the man who changed its name to Albany. The town's perfect natural harbour helped make it a major port, and from the 1850s steamers from England and naval ships operating in the Indian Ocean used Albany as a coaling station. This continued until the turn of the nineteenth century, when Fremantle was established.

Since the early 1800s seals and whales had been hunted here, and in the 1840s a land-based whaling

station was established at Albany. Initially hunting southern right whales, in later years the station hunted sperm whales. It was the last whaling station in Australian waters, finally closing its slipway in 1978. Today, the rich marine life along the coast is a major tourist attraction, with the southern right whales arriving in the waters off Albany between July and October. Seals can often be seen along the coast and off nearby islands.

The town lost a lot of its importance as Fremantle developed, but it has evolved into an important business and supply centre for the local fishing fleet and processing operation—in particular the meat processing plant and the sawmilling interests in the surrounding region—and Albany now has a population of 30,000 and services the many farms in the district.

In the town itself there are over 50 historic buildings, many of which are now museums, display galleries or restaurants. Patrick Taylor's Cottage, built in 1833, is now a museum. The Old Gaol, built in 1851, is also a museum.

The whaling museum, Whaleworld, details the whales and the whaling operation that at one time

The Old Farm, Strawberry Hill, is the site of the first farm in the Albany district.

flourished here. The Old Farm, on Strawberry Hill, built in the 1830s, was the first farm in the region, and one of the oldest in the State. The National Trust took it over in 1963 and it is now furnished in various styles, each one representing a different era.

There are a number of national parks and reserves in the area, including Torndirrup National Park, just outside town. The coastline is spectacular—a day trip to view the Gap, the Blowholes, Natural Bridge and Jimmy Newhills Harbour is a must. A little further to the east is Two Peoples Bay Nature Reserve, an important bird and animal habitat, while about 70 km (43 miles) inland is the outstanding botanical environment of the

Stirling Ranges National Park. Over a thousand species of plants exist here—the best time of year to visit to see the floral display is between August and November. There are magnificent wildflower displays all around Albany during this time.

Fishing from beach or boat can be excellent, especially for salmon, tarwhine, shark, queen snapper, tommy ruff, groper and whiting. The protected waters of Oyster Harbour are good for garfish, whiting and flounder. Surfing and diving are also popular—a wreck has been sunk in the Sound to create an artificial reef, and this is now a decent dive site.

A variety of cultural, social and sporting events are held in Albany throughout the year, including two Wildflowers Festivals, in September and October, and the Agricultural Show and the Summer Street Fair are both on in November.
See also Great Southern Wine Region
Map ref: page 706 F10

AUGUSTA

Augusta is a small town—it has a population of 550—and is located 325 km (202 miles) south of Perth, on the more protected eastern side of the promontory that ends at Cape Leeuwin. This is at the far south-western tip of the State, where the waters of the Indian and Southern oceans clash. The Blackwood and Scott Rivers form Hardy Inlet, and much of the town stretches along its shores and also along those of Flinders Bay.

Misery Beach, 20 km (12.5 miles) south of Albany, is a well-known fishing spot for herring, whiting, silver bream and salmon.

The first settlers arrived here in 1830, making it the State's third-oldest settlement. A monument to the *Emily Taylor*, the ship that brought the first Europeans here, stands on the shores of the bay.

About a kilometre further south, near Barrack Point, there is a whaling memorial and a whale rescue information shelter. It was here that in 1986 the world's most successful whale-saving operation was carried out, when over 100 stranded false killer whales were returned to the sea.

The Augusta Historical Museum is located in the heart of town and has information on the town's early days, and details on the Leeuwin Lighthouse and the many shipwrecks that dot the coast. The area's history is also quite closely aligned with the timber industry—jarrah, marri and karri were all cut here—and the museum has an excellent display on the period during the 1880s that brought the town to prominence.

The area is richly endowed with natural attractions, including the spectacular Leeuwin–Naturaliste National Park, where you can picnic, bushwalk and camp. Hamelin Bay, 17 km (11 miles) north of the town and on the west coast within the park, is another magnificent spot, and is popular with campers, divers, surfers and anglers.

There are more than 300 caves found in this area and Jewel Cave is one of the most popular of these. Heading further north, towards the small hamlet of Margaret River, there are several other well-known caves well worth a visit, including Lake and Mammoth Caves, while the more adventurous and more experienced cavers can explore the Moondyne Cave system.
Map ref: page 706 B8

BEVERLEY

This small town in the Avon River valley, 127 km (79 miles) east of Perth, was once one of the major towns in the area. Settled in the

Karri forests grow throughout the region around Albany, once a major timber town.

1830s, it wasn't until the Great Southern Railway passed through that the town took on any real importance or substance. After the last passenger train made its last call in 1975, the town went back to being a quiet village of just 760 residents, which services the local mixed farms in the valley.

There are a number of fine old historic buildings in and around the town itself, such as the old police station, courthouse and railway station, and there is also a very good Aeronautical Museum that traces the development of aviation in Western Australia.

Less than 50 km (31 miles) south of the town are the Yenyening Lakes, which are very popular among the locals for sailing, swimming and waterskiing. For walkers, the nearby County Peak makes for a very pleasant interlude. Visitors and locals can join in the family fun at the Beverley Duck Races, which are held each September on the Avon River; an Arts and Gallery Purchase Exhibition is held around Easter.
Map ref: page 706 D5

BREMER BAY

This small holiday resort of only 190 people is 594 km (369 miles) south-east of Perth, at the mouth of the Bremer River, on the horseshoe-shaped bay of the same name. It is one of the best fishing spots on the south coast, and good catches of salmon, whiting, tommy ruff, trevally and queen snapper are common around the bay; you can add groper to that list if you are fishing from the rocks. There are also good diving and surfing spots right along the coast.

Matthew Flinders first sailed this coast in 1801–02, and sealers and whalers no doubt sheltered in the protected waters of the bay. Edward John Eyre passed through here on his epic crossing of the Bight in 1841, and the area was slowly opened up by pioneer pastoralists. Gold and other minerals were found in the surrounding region, but nothing ever really boomed, leaving the area generally untouched for today's nature-lover.

The town is one of two places (the other being Hopetoun) that gives conventional vehicles access to the Fitzgerald River National Park, with its spectacular scenery and an amazing floral display from late winter through to spring. Over 1800 plant species, with 80 or so endemic, are found in this park, which was declared a World Biosphere Reserve in 1978 because of its virgin bush and the variety of its plant life. Within the park, on the banks of the Gairdner River, is the 1858 cottage of Quaalup Homestead, established by an early settler. It contains a good display of memorabilia and is furnished in the style of the day. There is a self-contained guesthouse and a camping ground at the same spot. Wellstead Homestead, west of town, was established around the same time and is still owned by members of the family that established it.
Map ref: page 706 H9

Market gardeners picking cauliflowers on one of the mixed farms in the south-west valleys.

BRIDGETOWN

Situated in scenic surroundings on the Blackwood River, 274 km (170 miles) south of Perth, Bridgetown is a small town (population 1520) that is the commercial centre for its region, a region which produces apples and stone fruits. The district is also an important timber area, with jarrah forests and pine plantations. Some tin mining is carried out around the area, but the region

A Bridgetown hotel, built in 1884.

is known first and foremost for the natural beauty of its lush, rolling hills, its rivers and forests, and its magnificent displays of wildflowers —it is considered by many to be one of the prettiest parts found anywhere in Western Australia.

The region was first settled in the 1850s, and there are a number of places to visit that date from those early days. The home of the

first settler, John Blechynden, is on the banks of the Blackwood River, while to the north-east, just out of Boyup Brook, is a tree blazed by the 1840 explorer, A.C. Gregory.

There are galleries and museums to stroll through and those people interested in craft markets should visit the River Markets, which are held every second Sunday at the Blackwood River Park.

Scenic drives in and around the area worth a try include the Geegeelup Heritage Trail, a 52 km (32 miles) loop taking in the historic towns of Bridgetown and Greenbushes. You can also take a walk or a picnic through the Bridgetown Jarrah Park, which is 20 km (12 miles) from the town.

A number of annual events are held in Bridgetown and these include the Greenbushes Dry Land Regatta, which is on during March, the Blackwood Marathon, which is in October, and then there is the Blues Festival in November, and the local show, in late November.
Map ref: page 706 C8

BUNBURY

This city on the south-west coast of Western Australia, 184 km (114 miles) south of Perth is the region's major port. It is centred right on a deep-water harbour where there are bulk storage and handling facilities. Those extensive facilities testify to the fact that inland lies some of Western Australia's richest agricultural land; the whole area is also rich in minerals. Ilmenite, rutile and zircon were discovered in the sands along the coast and have

Myalup Beach, 45 km (28 miles) from Bunbury, offers good fishing and hang-gliding.

been heavily exploited since the 1950s, while bauxite, used in the production of aluminium, has also been found nearby. The timber industry has always been important to Bunbury, with two-thirds of the State's hardwood forests found in the region, while woodchip, a contentious export, is also serviced by the port at Bunbury.

The first European sighting was that of French explorer Captain de Freycinet, on the *Geographe* in 1803. In 1829, the then governor in charge of the new Swan River Colony sent a detachment south to look for good land. They explored the estuary and the two rivers, the Collie and the Preston, that now carry their names. However, it was not until a Lieutenant Bunbury arrived in 1836 that real development took place. The early settlers traded with the sealers and whalers who anchored in the bay. When the government placed a handling charge on the sealers and whalers they moved, and Bunbury nearly died, staying subdued until the railway arrived in 1891.

Now it is the major city in the south-west, with a population of 28,000, and acts as the region's administration and business centre. In recent years, the area around the port has seen a lot of improvement, and Bunbury combines city and country in a pleasant blend, making it a popular place to live and visit, and an ideal base for touring the beautiful south-west.

Around the town there is quite a number of art and craft galleries with a fine range of local craft, including some delightful woodcraft made from local West Australian timbers. There is also King Cottage Museum, a five-room cottage built in the 1880s that houses a good display of colonial artefacts. Bunbury's St Mark's Anglican Church is the second oldest in the State.

Wild dolphins regularly visit the beach along Koombana Bay and have become a major attraction in their own right, prompting the building of the Dolphin Discovery Centre nearby. The beaches, bays and inlets close to town offer quite a range of safe swimming and surfing beaches, ideal for boat cruising, yachting, fishing and crabbing.

The surrounding forests have a number of pleasant scenic drives and you can also drive and walk through the Tuart Forest, one of the finest stands of tuart found in the State, and unique to the south-west. The *Leschenault Lady* is a vintage steam train that once hauled logs from the forests—it now takes people on a very pleasant day trip through those same forests to the towns dotting the coast and inland.

Just to the north of Bunbury, on the long arm of the Leschenault Estuary, is the pleasant hamlet of Australind. A scenic drive along the inlet can be quite delightful; the town has a number of historic buildings, and a fine gemstone collection housed in Henton

New housing development around the south-west's major port at Bunbury.

Mount Arid in Cape Arid National Park, an area explored by the French in 1792.

its length. To see marine life up close, visit the Oceanarium; if you are into diving or snorkelling, the jetty offers one of the best dives around. The amount of marine life in, on, and around the pylons has to be seen to be believed.

For those who enjoy browsing through local markets, the Vasse and the Railway Markets are held regularly. There are also plenty of art and craft galleries to visit as well as many old buildings, such as the Old Butter Factory, Newton House and the Court House.

Special events in this town include the Busselton Antique Fair and Collectors' Exhibition and the Busselton Beach Festival, all in January, the Wildflower and Craft Exhibition in September, and the Agricultural Show in November.
Map ref: page 706 B7

CAPE ARID NATIONAL PARK

This park, 80 km (50 miles) northeast of Perth, is famous for its magnificent beaches and headlands. In the northern section is Mount Ragged, the highest peak of the Russell Range, which reaches 594 m (1949 feet) in height. The granite hills and pools of permanent water provide habitats for a number of rare plants and animals; and a variety of ferns and orchids grow all around Mount Ragged. Bird life here is prolific, with the rare Cape Barren goose a regular visitor, and flocks of the endangered ground

parrots survive here. During the winter months, migrating southern right whales can be spotted close inshore while on the beaches seals can be seen dozing lazily. Bush-walking is also popular in this park, and coastal fishing is good all year.
Map ref: page 707 P7

CAPE LE GRAND NATIONAL PARK

Cape Le Grand National Park lies about 40 km (25 miles) east of Esperance and is renowned for its sandy beaches, beautiful bays and stunning, rocky headlands.

The most spectacular feature is a chain of massive outcrops of granite and gneiss in the southwest corner: Mount Le Grand, at 352 m (1155 feet), Frenchman

Peak, which is 262 m (860 feet) high and the smaller 180 m (591 feet) Mississippi Hill. Heathland, banksia and paperbarks, as well as several species of mallee, grow in the park, and mammals and birds abound. Fishing and boating are also popular activities in this park.
Map ref: page 707 M8

CERVANTES

A two-masted American whaling ship gave its name to a small island when it was wrecked there in the early 1800s, and that, in turn, gave its name to the small fishing village that sprang up on the nearby coast. Today this small fishing town has a population of 900 and it is most popular with beach-lovers and anglers, many of whom make the 243 km (151 miles) trip north from Perth just for a weekend.

The town's beaches are ideal for swimming, boating and especially sailboarding. So good and predictable are the winds that a round of the World Cup Slalom Sailboarding Championships is held in Cervantes each year in December.

Nambung National Park almost surrounds the town, and its major drawcard, the Pinnacles, are 29 km (18 miles) to the south. Here thousands of limestone pillars, standing up to 4 m (13 feet) tall, dot the barren landscape. A one-way loop drive takes visitors, in conventional vehicles, through the heart of this unique region.

A bit further north is Jurien Bay, another enjoyable fishing village, and inland are a number of other, not so well known but still very interesting, national parks.
Map ref: page 706 B2

Cottage, built in 1883. Annual events in Bunbury include the Agricultural Show in March and Art Extraordinaire in August.
See also Geographe Wine Region
Map ref: page 706 B7

BUSSELTON

This seaside town has a population of 18,500 and sits 236 km (147 miles) south of Perth, on the shores of Geographe Bay, a lovely bay of calm waters, long beaches and sheltered coves, ideal for water-based activities. The primary industries of dairy and beef cattle, sheep, fruit and vegetable markets, and forestry have supported the region very well; the relatively new venture of wine-making is now finally gaining some headway.

In 1801 a French sailor named Vasse drowned in what is today known as Geographe Bay. A small river bears his name. The first pioneers in the region were the Bussell brothers in 1832, and a town soon developed around the timber and dairying industries, plus the necessity to ship produce from all the districts around the bay.

The Busselton Jetty, all 2 km (1.6 miles) of it, is the longest wooden jetty in the Southern Hemisphere. Today it is a major landmark, and train rides are conducted daily along

Le Grand Beach in Cape Le Grand National Park, home to honey possums, kangaroos and seals.

COLLIE

This coalmining town (population 9500) is centred on the State's only coalfield, 206 km (128 miles) south of Perth. It is picturesque, with lovely parks and gardens, and is surrounded by heavily timbered jarrah forests and the Collie River Valley in the Darling Range.

The town was established in 1883, when a shepherd discovered coal here, nearly 60 years after the river had been named by a visiting naval surgeon, Dr Alexander Collie.

Quokka
(Setonix brachyurus)

Places of interest include the Historical and Mining Museum, the Muja Power Station (which has tours), and the scenic Collie River. A couple of nearby dams, Wellington and Harris, offer some very pleasant picnic areas, and Honeymoon Pool is a delightful camping and picnic spot.

Special events held here include the Country and Western Roundup in March, the Griffin Festival in May, the Collie to Donnybrook Cycle Race in August and the Collie Show in November.

Map ref: page 706 C7

COOLGARDIE

Located at the junction of the Great Eastern Highway, the Coolgardie–Esperance Highway and the main road to Kalgoorlie and the goldfield towns further north, 554 km (344 miles) east of Perth,

Coolgardie today is a small town, with a population of only 1200— more a service town for the passing traffic than anything else. Once it was the boom town on the newly discovered goldfields: during the 1890s it had a population of over 15,000 very thirsty miners, more than 20 hotels for them to slake their thirst in, three breweries to keep the pubs supplied and six banks to process the thousands of ounces of gold that were found.

The architecture of the main street, part of the Great Eastern Highway, is reminiscent of those early days, and there are many old buildings gracing the roadway. The wide streets are lined with a variety of styles, from corrugated iron and wood homes to some grand old stone buildings.

The Marble Bar Hotel is one of the pubs still standing, and dates back to the turn of the nineteenth century. One of the largest buildings on the main thoroughfare, the Wardens Court Building, was erected in 1898 using local stone and it now houses the Mining Registrar's Office, the Tourist Bureau as well as the Goldfields Exhibition, an excellent display of photos, life-size models and old memorabilia from the gold-rush days.

The Railway Station Museum, built in 1896, also has a fine display relating to transport, and the Ben Prior's Open Air Museum features machinery and mining equipment from the early days.

Legendary outback eccentricity on display at a home in Coolgardie.

Bluff Knoll in Stirling Range National Park, can be accessed from Cranbrook.

The main annual events are the Coolgardie Day Celebrations, in September, and the Metal Detecting Championships, which are are held during October.

Map ref: page 707 L3

CRANBROOK

This picturesque town (population 320), Cranbrook is situated among rolling hills 328 km (204 miles) south-east of Perth, just off the Albany Highway. This town is a wheat and sheep farming centre but for most travellers it is also the gateway to the spectacular nearby Stirling Ranges. The town was declared in 1899, and was initially a watering point on the Great Southern Railway. Early on it was an important centre for the extraction of sandalwood, which was exported to China for use in temples, but today the area is better known for its vineyards, wool production and wildflowers. From Sukey Hill

Lookout, 5 km (3 miles) out of town, you get a fine view of the surrounding area, including salt lakes, undulating farmland and the Stirling Ranges. The main annual event of the year is the Wildflower Show, which is held around late September/early October.

Map ref: page 706 E8

DENMARK

The township of Denmark, with a population of 4500, nestles along the idyllic banks of the Denmark River, 470 km (292 miles) southeast of Perth, and is surrounded by picturesque hinterlands and forests. There are a number of scenic drives from Denmark, such as the Scotsdale and Mount Shadforth Scenic Drives, which give some superb panoramic vistas of both the ocean, which is nearby, and the encircling landscape. During the wildflower season, the scene becomes a kaleidoscope of beautiful colours.

There are wineries too numerous to mention that are open for cellar tastings and wine sales, and for something a little different, try the Bartholomew's Meadery, which produces mead, a fortified drink made from honey. Bridgart's Farm (for its seasonal produce), Mount Romance Emu Farm, and Pentland Alpaca Stud and Tourist Farm are all worth a visit.

Denmark also makes a terrific base from which to explore the nearby coastal scenery and the William Bay National Park, with its spectacularly beautiful, yet very rugged coastline. There are plenty of fabulous beaches to visit, with one of the most popular spots on the coast being Peaceful Bay. The more tranquil waters around Wilson Inlet are alive with bird life and there is a variety of boat cruises available on the Inlet.

For history buffs there is the Historical Museum, while art and craft enthusiasts will find plenty of galleries to wander through. The Art and Craft Markets, which are held in December, January and Easter are a highlight, as is the Denmark Country Show in March. *See also* Great Southern Wine Region

Map ref: page 706 E10

D'ENTRECASTEAUX NATIONAL PARK

Stretching about 130 km (81 miles) along Western Australia's southern coastline, D'Entrecasteaux National Park covers some 115,000 ha (284,165 acres) of diverse and mainly untouched country. It is renowned for its huge sand dunes, limestone cliffs and long, white, sandy beaches. Inland there are lakes, wetlands, the Shannon, Donnelly and Warren Rivers, areas of heathland and tracts of tall karri and jarrah forest. Wildlife here includes a small number of quokkas, chuditch, brush-tailed, ringtail and pygmy possums, wallabies and bandicoots, and southern right whales, which follow this coastline during their migration.

D'Entrecasteaux National Park protects a pristine, diverse and isolated coastline.

In 1990 archaeological studies carried out in Lake Jasper, in the park's northern sector, found Aboriginal artefacts, trees and grasstree stumps that were deep under water, and ancient camp sites dating from 40,000 years ago, when the Minang people lived in this region.

The park has several highlights. The picturesque Donnelly Boat Landing picnic and camping site (with barbecue and toilet facilities as well as a boat launching ramp) has good fishing and swimming. A lovely stretch of water, with some spectacular limestone cliffs and a beautiful beach, leads 11 km (7 miles) to the river mouth.

Yeagarup Lake is a pleasant spot, and has barbecues and also toilet facilities. From here you can walk into the Yeagarup Dunes. A 4WD-only track leads from the lake to the coast; it is about 10 km (6 miles) long, and the drive will take about 30 minutes.

Mount Chudalup is a granite outcrop 188 m (617 feet) high, with good views to the coast. A quite steep, 1 km (0.6 miles) walking and climbing track leads to the summit, the return journey taking about one-and-a-half hours. There are barbecue and picnic facilities at the car park. Windy Harbour (conventional vehicle access) and Salmon Beach (4WD only) are good for photography, swimming (be careful of rips at Salmon Beach) and fishing. There are caravan park facilities and a small settlement at Windy Harbour. Broke Inlet is an extensive shallow lake, and the area around is good for walking as well as birdwatching and fishing.

There are several conventional vehicle trails leading off the Vasse Highway, Windy Harbour Road and South Western Highway to the park's main features. There are also 4WD tracks going to various sections of the park and to the coast. There are a few designated camping areas with basic facilities, but there are also many appealing bush camping spots, particularly for 4WD enthusiasts. No supplies are available in the park—bring all your requirements, including water. The nearest fuel and supplies are available at Pemberton, Northcliffe and Walpole, so stock up here prior to your departure.

Map ref: page 706 B9

The emerald green waters of Green's Pool (pictured), Elephant Rocks or Madfish Bay are accessible to the west of Denmark.

DONNYBROOK

First settled in 1842 by a group of Irishmen, Donnybrook—219 km (136 miles) south of Perth—today it has a population of 4000 people. It is most noted for its quality fruit and vegetables; sheep, dairy cattle and timber also play an important part in the region's economy. Back in the 1880s, however, Donnybrook was a goldmining centre, albeit one that was short-lived.

Well worth a visit is the historic Anchor and Hope Inn, built in 1862 as a coaching inn, and now restored to its original glory. Also of interest is the old Goldfields Orchard and Cider Factory, where you can have a go at gold panning and fishing. For canoeists, there is a canoe course, Trigwell Place, on the Preston River, where there are also barbecue and picnic facilities. If you are in the area at Easter, join in the activities of the Apple Festival. *See also* Geographe Wine Region
Map ref: page 706 C7

DROVERS CAVE NATIONAL PARK

Lying on Western Australia's coastal limestone belt, this park takes its name from the drovers' stock route that passed through here during the 1800s. When the railway line was opened in 1894, the trail was largely reclaimed by the bush. In 1955 a petroleum exploration company rediscovered many of the caves and sinkholes in the region. The park

The entrance to Stockyard Gully Cave in Drovers Cave National Park.

Farming pears at Sunnyhills Orchard, Donnybrook.

was officially declared in 1972 to help protect the caves, the fossil deposits of prehistoric mammals and the area's plant life.

The park is quite small—about 2681 ha (6625 acres)—and is still a wilderness area. It has only one main track—a single-lane, sandy 4WD-only trail—leading in a north–south direction through its centre. While the whole limestone area here is riddled with sinkholes, caves, crevices and numerous rock depressions, the trail itself leads to the most interesting ones.

Driving into the park from the south, Drover's Cave is the first to be reached. The cave is located about 50 m (164 feet) off the track on the right-hand side. It is suitable for exploration only by experienced speleologists. Those wanting to explore the cave should contact the ranger. A further 1 km (0.6 miles) north is Hastings Cave. This cave is open to the public, but a great deal of care is needed—huge beehives hang like curtains over the entrance to the cave. The main track ends at Moorbe Cave. It once housed a small operation to mine bat droppings, and evidence of that operation—timber structures and the old train-track rails—is still there. Visitors can climb a couple of hundred metres (around 656 feet) down into this cave system, but only experienced cavers should venture to proceed further.

Wildflowers are another delightful feature of the park—there are several different varieties of banksia and wattles, as well as parrot bush, smokebush, one-sided bottlebrush, purple flag, curry flowers, native violets, and the twining old man's beard also grows here.

Bushwalking in the park is fairly restricted because of the very dense scrub and because the sinkholes and limestone crevices and cavities are quite dangerous. While camping is not prohibited, there are no nice, easily accessible sites; it would be better to bush camp outside the park, or to arrange accommodation at nearby Jurien. There are no facilities so you must take in all supplies, including water and a good tick repellent. Access to the park is off the Jurien Road. The turn north into the park is 5 km (3 miles) east of Jurien.
Map ref: page 706 B1

DWELLINGUP

This small town (population 455) was ravaged by fire in 1961, and again 10 years later, the last time leaving only the hotel, a few houses and outbuildings still standing. Situated deep in the heart of forest country, 119 km (74 miles) south of Perth, Dwellingup has always been a forestry town, right from its founding at the turn of the nineteenth century. In 1918 it became a base for the management of and research into the local jarrah forests. The many roads through the forest give people a chance to view these magnificent trees, some of which are over 40 m (131 feet) in height, up close. To learn more about the timber and associated industries, visit the Forest Heritage Centre in town, which details the resources and also the conservation efforts that have gone into the surrounding forests.

The Dwellingup History and Visitor Centre is a good place to start your touring. From here you can head out to several pleasant picnic and walking spots, including Scarp Pool, Nanga Mill and Pool, Island Pool, Marrinup Falls, and Oakley Dam and Falls. The Lane Pool Reserve, east of the town, is a 50,000 ha (123,550 acres) reserve which is situated along the Murray River, where trout, marron and freshwater cobbler can be caught.

A seal at the jetty in Esperance, while common in the region, still attracts onlookers.

The Bibbulmun long-distance walking trail passes through this reserve, and bushwalkers can join it from here for a day or even longer. For a more unusual outing, take a ride on the Hotham Valley Tourist Railway, which runs on the original 1910 line between Dwellingup and Pinjarra through farmland and jarrah forest, making a pleasant trip for steam buffs. A special event held every year here is the Dwellingup Log Chop, which is on in February.

Map ref: page 706 C6

ESPERANCE

Esperance is 743 km (461 miles) south-east of Perth, situated on a coast that has near-perfect white sandy beaches, azure water, and rocky headlands—all sheltered by the islands of the Recherche Archipelago, which stretch across the bay and along the coast. Long considered a summer holiday town by the people of the inland goldfields, Esperance (population 9500) has much to attract the visitor.

This coast was first sighted by Dutch mariners in 1627, and then by George Vancouver in 1791. A year later the French arrived, giving their names to many of the islands

Quoin Head in Fitzgerald River National Park, which has 1784 different plant species, 75 of which are endemic.

and headlands along the coast. In 1841 Edward John Eyre passed through, and it was at tranquil Rossiter Bay, east of present-day Esperance, that Eyre met Captain Rossiter of the French whaling ship *Mississippi*, and secured some badly needed supplies. However, it was to be more than another 20 years before pioneer settlers made their way to this coast. In the 1890s the town became an important port for the goldfields, but its importance waned when the Perth to Kalgoorlie railway line was opened in 1896. The area remained extremely poor farming land until the 1950s, when it was discovered that the soil was missing trace elements— since then the surrounding area has been transformed into a productive farming region.

The town has a rich heritage—the Museum Village and the Esperance Municipal Museum help preserve that, while the Old Cannery Arts and Crafts Centre houses workshops, exhibitions and the Society of Artists, with many locally made products for sale.

The town is centrally situated to a number of excellent parks and reserves, the best known being those along the coast to the east, consisting of Cape Le Grand National Park, and further

afield, Cape Arid National Park. Magnificent white sandy beaches, delightful bays and islands and bulky granite outcrops, many of them rolling in a graceful arc into the blue waters of the Southern Ocean, make this an outstanding coastal area. Offshore the sea is dotted with dozens of islands, and the fishing, diving, surfing and sailboarding can be superb.

Further east again is the long strip of protected land along the cliff-lined coast, the Nuytsland Nature Reserve, which includes the historic Israelite Bay Telegraph Station. Built in 1877, the station was an essential link in the communication network that once stretched along this coast, and linked Perth to the rest of the country.

To the west of Esperance is the much smaller Stokes National Park, while inland there is the small Peak Charles National Park and the much bigger Dundas Nature Reserve. The wildflowers are a great attraction during the spring months in all these parks, particularly at Cape Le Grand, with over 200 species being recorded. The Wildflower Society conducts guided walks from September to November from the Helms Arboretum.

In recent years, from July to November, there have been regular sightings of southern right whales

Freckled monitor (Varanus tristis orientalis)

along the coast, as they rest in the sheltered bays to calve. They have become another drawcard to the town and the area. Annual events and festivities include the Agricultural Show in October and the Sailboard Classic, which is held in late December/early January.

Map ref: page 707 M8

FITZGERALD RIVER NATIONAL PARK

This 329,039 ha (813,044 acres) park lies on the south coast right in between the towns of Bremer Bay and Hopetoun. It is particularly important botanically as a World Biosphere Reserve. Access is restricted to either end of the park, in an effort to control the spread of dieback disease.

From the east, the scenic Hamersley Drive gives access to Four Mile, Barrens, Mylies and West beaches. Many of the tracks are 4WD only. The landscape varies from protected beaches, sea cliffs, steep ranges and extensive plains to river systems emptying into the ocean via broad estuaries. There is an abundance of flora and fauna. The extensive coastline features whale-watching from August to November, excellent bushwalking, and some very good fishing (note that fishing regulations apply).

Map ref: page 707 H8

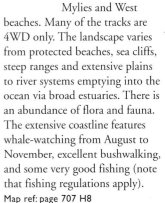

View of Mount Barker, which is located in the Great Southern Wine Region.

GEOGRAPHE WINE REGION

Newly formed Geographe covers a very wide and diverse region from Capel to the Ferguson Valley in the Bunbury hinterland, the farming lands of Donnybrook and the dairy country around Harvey. Vineyards are being planted at an astonishing rate by farmers seeking to diversify, by large companies searching for cheaper vineyard land, and also by major investment groups keen to take advantage of the tax concessions and Western Australia's potential for exporting its wines.

There are fertile, brown loamy soils on the coastal strip from Capel to Harvey. Temperatures in the warm, sunny growing season are moderated by the sea and by the early sea breezes during summer. The area is perhaps best suited to merlot, chardonnay and verdelho. Its major winery is the long-established Capel Vale, which draws grapes from many parts of Western Australia.

In the Ferguson Valley and the hills behind Harvey, vineyards have been planted between 250 and 300 m (800 and 1000 feet) above sea level. These receive about 10 per cent more rainfall and have a more moderate climate than on the flat. The soil

is granitic gravel over clay loam, which retains water better than the alluvial sands nearer the coast. The best-suited grape varieties appear to be shiraz, chardonnay, sémillon and sauvignon blanc.

Donnybrook is on a continuation of the Darling Scarp, with fruit trees on the valley flats and vineyards on the gently undulating slopes. The fertile soils contain decomposed granite and ironstone gravel. It is a warm area for growing grapes, with hotter peaks and colder troughs than areas closer to the coast and some believe it is most ideally suited to the production of medium-priced dry reds.

A few of the larger producers here include Capel Vale Wines, which has won an extensive export market, Killerby Vineyards, noted for its classy chardonnays, and Chestnut Grove Wines, which has recently built its own winery in order to maintain greater control over the winemaking process.
Map ref: page 706 B6–B7

GREAT SOUTHERN WINE REGION

Great Southern is Australia's largest, and Western Australia's coolest, viticultural region. It consists of five subregions centred around Mount Barker, with Denmark,

Frankland, Albany and the Porongurups about a half-hour drive away. While the climate of both Denmark and Albany are moderated by the sea, Frankland and Mount Barker experience more continental conditions. In particular, the greater temperature variability inland means that although average mean temperatures are lower, there are more extreme high readings. Fortunately, these tend to occur before ripening, so fruit quality is not adversely affected. Rainfall, too, tends to be more variable farther inland. Soils tend to be either loams derived from granite and gneissic rocks or gravelly sandy loams.

Given the size of the region, it is not surprising that certain subregions suit some varieties better than others. Mount Barker has been particularly successful with riesling, cabernet sauvignon, pinot noir and shiraz; Denmark with chardonnay and pinot noir; Frankland with riesling, cabernets and shiraz; Albany with chardonnay and pinot noir; and the Porongurups with riesling.

Sailors' tools from whaling ships.

The past decade has seen some really significant changes. Many growers are seeking greater control over wine production by having their own wineries. From mature vineyards such as Forest Hill at Mount Barker, Westfield (which is leased to Houghton) and Alkoomi at Frankland, Bouverie and Wyjup (leased to Plantagenet) and Windy Hill (leased to Goundrey), the quality of fruit is quite impressive.

Great Southern is becoming an increasingly more important producer of some premium wines, and its best wines are quite stunningly good. However, this region's relative isolation, lack of world-class tourist infrastructure and the part-time nature of much of the wine industry has meant that its growth and international exposure has been comparatively less impressive than that of Margaret River.
Map ref: page 706 E10–F10

HOPETOUN

This small town, with a population of only 400, is situated right on the southern coast of Western Australia, 605 km (376 miles) southeast of Perth. It flourished as a port for the inland goldfields early in the twentieth century; previously it was known as Mary Anne Harbour, and during this time it served early settlers and sealing and whaling ships. The town was declared in 1901 at which time its name was changed to Hopetoun. Today it features a substantial jetty and breakwaters on a lovely bay.

This delightful spot offers a very wide range of fishing opportunities in close proximity to the town— from the beach, off the rocks or the jetty, offshore and also in the landlocked Culham Inlet and nearby rivers. To the west, and easily accessible from Hopetoun, is the large Fitzgerald River National Park, where nearly 1800 species of plants flourish along a wild, untamed coastline. A number of walking tracks in the park, at East Mount Barrens and No Tree Hill, are excellent ways to experience this reserve. Dunn's Swamp, 5 km (3 miles) north of the town, is a

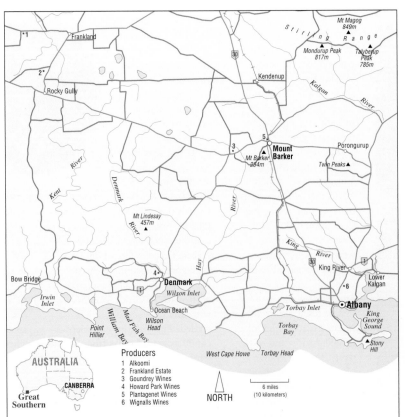

Producers
1 Alkoomi
2 Frankland Estate
3 Goundrey Wines
4 Howard Park Wines
5 Plantagenet Wines
6 Wignalls Wines

6 miles
(10 kilometers)

NORTH

peaceful spot, and is ideal for going bushwalking or birdwatching. The town's main festivities occur during the Summer Festival, when a host of activities take place, including concerts, fishing competitions and a variety of exhibitions.
Map ref: page 707 J8

HYDEN

This tiny town (population 190) is 346 km (215 miles) south-east of Perth, in the heart of the wheat belt. European pioneers first came to this semi-arid area in search of sandalwood, but settlement only occurred in the 1920s. The town is best known for the rock formation called Wave Rock. Located about 4 km (2.4 miles) from town, this granite rock has the appearance of a breaking wave, with the overhang more than 15 m (49 feet) high. A low retaining wall above the lip of the wave is a man-made scar, built in the 1950s to channel water directly into Hyden's reservoir.

The town and the surrounding area have a number of other attractions, including Mulka's Cave, the Gnamma Holes, the collection of the region's memorabilia at the Pioneer Town, a wildlife park (adjacent to the caravan park), and a seasonal display of native orchids—the best in the State and some of them extremely rare—that burst from the ground June–August.
Map ref: page 706 G5

JOHN FORREST NATIONAL PARK

Sheltered in the Darling Range Escarpment just 26 km (16 miles) east of Perth, this park—2676 ha (6612 acres)—was established in 1898, and is the nation's second oldest. Initially known as Greenmount National Park, its name was changed to John Forrest National

North Head at Jurien Bay, where the waters are protected by offshore reefs.

Park in 1947 to honour one of Western Australia's explorers and a State premier (1890–1901).

Most of the park's attractions are found along its many walking trails, most of which are quite easy. These trails lead to park features such as the Hovea Falls, which is 2 km (1.2 miles) return (allow an hour); Gauging Weir, which is only 500 m (1641 feet) return (allow 20 minutes) and National Park Falls, which is 3 km (1.9 miles) return—allow an hour-and-a-half. All of the falls generally flow in winter and spring. The trail along Jane Brook to Rocky Pool is a 7 km (4.3 miles) return walk, and will take around 3 hours. The John Forrest Heritage Trail—around 5 km (3.1 miles) each way (mostly quite easy walking)—retraces part of the old eastern railway line, including the Swan View Tunnel, which was built back in the 1890s.

Mountain bike riding is especially popular in the park. There are a series of trails, from the really challenging to the very easy. No competitive riding is allowed and riders are asked to keep off walking trails. There are also trails for horse riders. These meander through sections of bushland well away from the crowd. Horses must keep to designated tracks and not eat or trample the vegetation.

There are a number of pleasant picnic spots in the park—all of these have barbecues, tables and toilet facilities, including disabled access—plus centrally located tea rooms, an attractive pool area nearby, a tavern and restaurant, and shelter areas at various points.

The park is set in a beautiful jarrah forest, which is still largely in its natural state. Each year during spring, thousands of people come

to this park just for the wildflowers alone—there are orchids, kangaroo paw, melaleucas, bottlebrush and wattles. Over 100 species of birds have been recorded, plus 23 species of native mammals and more than 20 species of reptiles.

Access to the park is by a sealed road up the Darling Escarpment, 10 km (6 miles) from the Perth suburb of Midland. There are three entrances that lead off the Great Eastern Highway. Bush camping is permitted here, but an application must be made to the park ranger. Water is available in the park's main facilities area.
Map ref: page 706 C4

JURIEN

The crayfishing fleet that operates out of this large protected bay, and tourism, are the main employers in this very small town (population 130), which is 240 km (149 miles) north of Perth.

The tourism in this area centres around the coast, the offshore reefs, and the great fishing and diving that can be enjoyed here. The old jetties are available for the public to fish and swim from, and there is equally good fishing and swimming off the many beaches. Jurien is well serviced with boat ramps and boat anglers can expect to catch jewfish, baldchin, mackerel and snapper. The area is popular with divers and is also good for sailboarding.

Only a few kilometres inland (about 2 miles) is the Drovers Cave National Park, and a little further on is the larger Lesueur National Park. The former park has a range of limestone caves, and the latter is one of the finest wildflower areas in Western Australia.
Map ref: page 706 A1

Grasstrees and cycads in the jarrah forest in John Forrest National Park.

Kalgoorlie's first hotel, the Exchange, built in 1893, evolved from a tin shed.

KALGOORLIE

When Paddy Hannan struck gold here—593 km (368 miles) east of Perth— in 1893, he found the last great goldfield in Australia—and the largest. It changed the history of Western Australia. Within a month of his discovery hundreds of miners were on the field, and two years later the town, originally known as Hannans, was home to 6000 people, with over another 1000 in nearby Boulder. By 1902, after the swelling population of the goldfields had ensured that Western Australia stayed within the newly founded Commonwealth, the number reached over 30,000— today's population is 33,000.

Since then the fortunes of this great historic town have ridden the roller-coaster ride of fluctuating gold prices. The 'Golden Mile', one of the richest ore bodies on Earth, yielded most of the early great mines. It has more recently been turned into a gigantic open-cut mine, the Superpit, in the vital quest for the elusive metal.

The 1970s nickel boom brought added prosperity and action to the town, so a nickel smelter was built. While nickel and gold remain the mainstay of the economy, the twin towns of Kalgoorlie and Boulder are important service centres for the outlying pastoral properties and a growing tourist trade. In the early days lack of water was a huge problem on the field; this was later solved by the construction of the Mundaring–Kalgoorlie Pipeline, a technical feat that many said could not be accomplished.

There are many buildings dating from the late 1800s still to be seen in 'Kal', as the locals call town— they include those along Hannan Street in Kalgoorlie and Burt Street in Boulder, the towns' main streets. The town halls in both Kalgoorlie and Boulder are excellent. There are also several museums, including the Goldfields War Museum, the School of Mines Museum, the Museum of the Goldfields, and the Historical Society Display. The last of these is a very fine photographic collection of the area and is housed in the Boulder Railway Station.

Hannans North is one of the original mines, and tours of both above- and underground workings are run daily. The Golden Mile Superpit Lookout offers expansive views of this vast working and is open each day, blasting permitting.

There is more to see and do around the town, including trying your luck at the Boorara Fossicking Area, 18 km (11 miles) out. The Kanowna Heritage trail is a 22 km (14 miles) trip, or try boarding an old steam-powered rattler for the hour-long run on the Loopline Railway. During March, have a go at the Western Australia Gold Panning Championships, or enjoy the Kalgoorlie–Boulder Community Fair, also held in March. There is also the Spring Festival in September, including the world two-up championships.
Map ref: page 707 L2

Gold nuggets: the origin of Kalgoorlie wealth.

KAMBALDA

Kambalda, 635 km (394 miles) east of Perth, is a town reborn. First settled when gold was discovered in 1897, the town, then called Red Hill, was abandoned and forgotten when the gold ran out 10 years later. In the mid-1960s, though, vast deposits of nickel were found, and by 1967 a treatment plant and modern town was in operation at this site. Its population today is 3500.

On Lake Lefroy, a vast, flat salt pan of over 500 sq. km (193 sq. miles) just to the south-east of the town, land yachts race nearly every Sunday. The Red Hill Lookout, John Hill Viewpoint and Defiance Open Cut Lookout all give quite different views of the vast mining operation carried out in Kambalda.
Map ref: page 707 L3

KATANNING

Located in the heart of one of the most prosperous agricultural regions in the State, 287 km (178 miles) south-east of Perth, Katanning (population 5100) is known for its annual stud Merino sales, and also as a major producer of cereal grains.

Before the Europeans came, the natural springs in the area were a meeting place for the local Aboriginals, and the name of the town is said to come from their term for 'a place to meet'. The first Europeans came in 1835, and within 5 years much of the land was taken up by sheep properties. The first flour mill started in 1891 and still stands—it was also the site of the first electric power plant in Western Australia, which supplied not only the mill but also the street lighting. The tourist office is in the Old Mill, which has been completely restored. The town has a couple of other old buildings, including the Anglican church, built last century, and the King George Hostel, built in the early 1900s to house men working at the Old Mill.

Lake Dumbleyung, north of the town, is famous as the site for Donald Campbell's successful world record water speed attempt in his boat *Bluebird* in 1964. It is now a popular spot for water activities as well as a sanctuary for bird life.

In the early 1970s a strong Muslim community settled here and each July has the Islamic Celebrations, while in October there is the annual Art Prize, the Agricultural Show and also the Great Southern Cycling Classic.
Map ref: page 706 E7

The view from Red Hill overlooking Kambalda, a mining town that started with gold and now yields its wealth in nickel.

Breakaways Ridge National Park is a day-trip from the service centre of Lake King.

LAKE KING

The first white explorer through this area was J.S. Roe in 1848, but it was not until settlement of the area, in the late 1920s, that the town of Lake King was finally established. This small community (population 150), located 465 km (289 miles) south-east of Perth on the edge of the wheat belt, is a service centre for the surrounding farms. Located 130 km (81 miles) south of Wave Rock and 70 km (43 miles) north of Ravensthorpe, the town's major claim to fame is the profusion of wildflowers that erupt here each spring. The town also acts as an access point for the sandy track that goes west through the Frank Hann and Peak Charles National Parks; it then meets the main Norseman–Esperance road, 155 km (96 miles) north of the coastal town of Esperance.
Map ref: page 707 H6

LANCELIN

This town lies 127 km (79 miles) to the north of Perth and is the sailboard mecca of Western Australia. Its long stretches of white sandy beach are also ideal for a swim, while the offshore reefs and breaks make it *the* place to practise sailboarding. A couple of close inshore islands provide a well-protected anchorage, as well as adding to the area's attractions for divers and anglers. The town is small (population 400), but is also a major commercial rock lobster centre—amateur anglers will also find plenty of spots to cast a line.

Off the beach you can catch tailor, mulloway and shark; offshore, silver trevally, samson fish, mulloway, Westralian jewfish and snapper.

The extensive bare dunes just out of town are the perfect location for the off-road enthusiast, while a run north along a sandy 4WD track, just behind the first line of dunes, takes you to some excellent swimming, fishing and diving spots. Special events include the Ocean Classic Windsurfing competition in January and sand dune buggy racing at Easter.
Map ref: page 706 B3

LESUEUR NATIONAL PARK

An important area for flora conservation in southern Western Australia, Lesueur National Park was gazetted in 1992 after a proposal to mine coal and construct a power station in the area was defeated. The variety of landforms has produced an enormous diversity of flora in this region.

The many mammals include bats, echidnas, dunnarts, honey possums and kangaroos. Bird life is also very prolific, and Lesueur is thought to be the only place where four different species of fairy wren are known to occur together. The salt lakes are also important refuges for several resident and migratory wading birds. Walking is the best way to explore the park, but you must carry water, as there are no facilities or designated camping areas. A good tick repellent is also strongly recommended. Access to the park is by 4WD only.
Map ref: page 706 B1

MANDURAH

Mandurah is a very popular year-round holiday resort, largely due to its proximity to Perth, which is only 83 km (52 miles) away—about an hour's drive south. The town is set on a maze of waterways on the expansive Harvey Estuary and Peel Inlet.

The area around Mandurah was originally settled in the 1830s by Thomas Peel, who took up a vast spread of land in the immediate area. His enterprise failed, and he died penniless 35 years later. The town, though, has thrived, and now has a population of 47,000. Today there are a large number of accommodation houses, numerous places to eat and a good range of entertainment in the town and the surrounding area, so there is always something to do.

There are also plenty of fishing opportunities here, with one of the easiest spots, especially for children, being the old road bridge in the heart of town, where you stand a good chance of catching tailor, mulloway, whiting, garfish and tarwhine. Other spots to try are the jetties, beaches, estuary and inlet, while offshore the fishing is good for Westralian jewfish, snapper and King George whiting. Crabbing is also a popular pastime.

There are many events and festivities held in Mandurah throughout the year, and these include the Crab Festival, which is in February, and the Art and Craft Festival in March. Blessing the Fleet is held in October, a fishing competition in November and the Mandurah Community Fair in December.
Map ref: page 706 B5

MANJIMUP

The imposing timber arches you drive under as you enter this town at its northern and southern entrances are a good indicator of what this area is best known for—tall timber. Many of the tourist attractions are timber-related, and a visit to the Manjimup Regional Timber Park is a must. Here you can take a close look at the State's only timber museum, along with Bunnings' Age of Steam Museum, the Historical Hamlet and a display of vintage machinery. For a first-hand look at the timber industry, the Forest Industries Federation runs guided tours into the forest. For a closer, awe-inspiring look at the giants of the forest, take a drive out to the Four Aces and see the four massive, towering karri trees, each believed to be hundreds of years old.

Manjimup (population 500) is situated 310 km (193 miles) south of Perth and there are a number of wineries in the area open for cellar tasting and wine sales, or you can enjoy a picnic or barbecue in the orchard at Fontanini's Nut Farm— in season you can pick your own chestnuts, walnuts and fruit.

The region around Manjimup also abounds with many walking trails through the magnificent karri forests, or you can cool off at Fontys Pool and enjoy a picnic in its lovely gardens. Another must for visitors is the colourful, dazzling display of flowers in the region during the wildflower season in spring. The town's Agricultural Show is held in March.
See also Pemberton Wine Region
Map ref: page 706 C8

Fishing at Mandurah Beach, where mulloway and tailor catches are likely.

MARGARET RIVER

Originally founded on dairy cattle and timber, this town—282 km (175 miles) south of Perth and with a population of 7000—has become more recently renowned as the centre of an excellent wine-producing area and a great holiday spot. While the wineries are major drawcards, swimming and fishing are also favourite pastimes. This is cave country, too, and Mammoth and Lake Caves, near Margaret River, are open for guided tours daily. The town also boasts many fine old buildings, such as Ellens-brook Homestead, which was built in 1851, and the Old Settlement Craft Village, are both well worth a visit. Events not to be missed are the Margaret River Wine and Food Festival, the Agricultural Show, and the Surf Classic, all in November.
Map ref: page 706 A8

A museum is now in the old convict-built police station at Mount Barker.

MERREDIN

The largest centre in the eastern wheat belt, Merredin is situated on the Great Eastern Highway beside the Perth–Kalgoorlie railway line, 258 km (160 miles) east of Perth. Once an important stop for those en route to the goldfields, today Merredin (population 3520) has services and facilities for travellers and for the surrounding pastoral properties, which mainly produce wheat, wool and pigs.

Its early history began when the goldfields were discovered in Cool-gardie in 1892; this then led to the construction of a railway link that reached Merredin a year later. The railway played an important part in the town's history, and much of that era's heritage is on display in the Railway Museum located in the

Cape Mentelle Winery, near Margaret River. Cape Mentelle's Cabernet Sauvignon and Chardonnay are award-winning.

station, which was built in 1893. A walk around the Merredin Park Heritage Trail is a great way to discover more about the town. Yet another interesting building is the Cummins Theatre (1928), built from pressed brick.

Special events and festivals held during the year include the Vintage Fair and Country Music Festival, which are both held in September/ October, and the Central Wheat Belt Games in October.
Map ref: page 706 F3

MOUNT BARKER

One of Western Australia's earliest settlements, Mount Barker is a small town (population 1600) 367 km (228 miles) south-east of Perth, along the Albany Highway, in a region of diverse ecological features and natural attractions. It is also a rich agricultural area, and

while sheep and cattle still play a significant role, the newer enter-prises of viticulture and wildflowers are also finding a market.

Some of the original buildings are well preserved, such as the St Werburgh's Chapel (1872), the Grain Mill (1842) and the Old Police Station, built by convicts in 1868 and now a museum. There are also a number of art and craft galleries, while outdoor enthusiasts will enjoy the natural beauty of the nearby Stirling Range and Porong-urup National Parks, both of which are famous for their resplendent array of wildflowers during spring. Special events include the Mount Barker Wine Festival in January, the Machinery Field Day in March and the Great Southern Wine Festival in October.
See also Great Southern Wine Region
Map ref: page 706 E9

Many properties around Merredin produce wool; these bales are ready for export.

MUNDARING

Nestled in the Darling Range, Mundaring—34 km (21 miles) east of Perth—was once the name of a vineyard owned by the Jacob family, originally established by the Gugeri family in 1882.

The vineyards, however, were not to be the town's claim to fame, and between 1898 and 1902 the Mundaring Weir and Number 1 pumping station were designed and built to supply water to the goldfields in Kalgoorlie, 550 km (342 miles) away. The water pipe-line finally reached Kalgoorlie in 1903, and the weir continues to supply this water under the Great Southern Towns and Goldfields Water Supply Scheme.

There is a very pleasant picnic area right at the weir, and a visit to the C.Y. O'Connor Historical Museum (named after Charles O'Connor who designed the weir) will also be of interest. There is another museum nearby in the Old Mahogany Inn, built in 1837. Other attractions include the Mun-daring Arts Centre, the hillside gar-den of the Lavender Path and its tearooms, and the Community Sculpture Park, which has a display of interactive sculptures, an amphi-theatre and a walking trail.

For the outdoor enthusiast, a drive to the Hills Forest, which has many walking trails that pass right through ancient jarrah forests—as well as a nature-based activity cen-tre—is a must, as is a trip to the nearby John Forrest National Park.
See also Perth Hills Wine Region
Map ref: page 706 C4

NAMBUNG NATIONAL PARK

The centrepiece of Nambung National Park is the Pinnacles, about 150,000 unusually shaped limestone columns. They have been sculpted into weird forms: some look like tombstones, others are round and pointed; still others are sharp and jagged. Ranging from a few centimetres up to nearly 5 m (16 feet) high, the pinnacles were formed by the interaction of water, quartz, sand and limestone, and are estimated to be between 10,000 and 30,000 years old—quite young in geological terms.

There is a one-way loop track of about 5 km (3 miles) through the Pinnacles area, which is suitable for conventional vehicles but not for caravans. From the Ranger Station there is a 500 m (1641 feet) loop walk that passes hundreds of pinnacles, and also takes in a splendid lookout. The white and red sand deserts, and the Painted Desert, are spectacular areas worth exploring —inform the ranger before setting out on foot, though, and always carry drinking water. On the coast, Kangaroo Point and Hangover Bay, both popular fishing spots, have toilets and picnic facilities (there are also gas barbecues and a shelter at Hangover Bay). The beautiful beaches along this section of the coastline are ideal for swimming and also for walking.

This park is home to a wide variety of plants, including acacias, myrtles, casuarinas and banksias; the wildflowers bloom in spring. There are also emus and grey kangaroos, and a variety of reptiles, including bobtail skinks and snakes. Over 90 species of birds have been recorded here.

The main northern road into the park, leading from Cervantes, and the tracks to Kangaroo Point and Hangover Bay, are all suitable for conventional vehicles, but the last 6 km (4 miles) into the Pinnacles can be corrugated. For a great 4WD experience, come into the park from Lancelin, on the coast some 70 km (43 miles) away, along a sandy (including some beach sections) trail with some rough, rocky sections—allow 3 hours for this. The trail passes through the small fishing villages of Grey and Wedge Island along the way. This route allows a 4WD experience, plus a return to the city via the sealed Brand Highway, or vice versa.

This is a day-visit park only; there are no camp sites. Open fires are not permitted, but there are free gas barbecues supplied. Cervantes—17 km (11 miles) from the Pinnacles—has a variety of motel and caravan park facilities, as well as fuel and other supplies.
Map ref: page 706 A2

NANNUP

Graziers were the first European settlers into the region in the mid-1850s, and today this historic town (population 600) is still part of a farming district, with dairy farm-

Pinnacles, Nambung National Park. Dutch explorers thought they were the remains of a lost city.

ing and fruit growing, along with timber, playing important roles. The town is situated 294 km (183 miles) to the south of Perth, and has much charm and character, with many original buildings still in use. You can walk along the Nannup Heritage Trail, or take a variety of scenic drives in the picturesque surrounding countryside. You can also sample some of the local wines produced at Oldfields Donnelly River Wines.

The Blackwood River is quite a pleasant place do do some canoeing, and birdwatchers in particular will delight in the purpose-built Blackwood Billabong Bird Hide. Special events for Nannup include the Music Festival in March, the Daffodil Display in August, and Wildflower Display, while Discovery Week is in September.
Map ref: page 706 C8

NARROGIN

Situated within the heart of the State's richest farming land, 196 km (122 miles) south-east of Perth, Narrogin is a major railway junction and the largest service centre in the region, with a population of 4500, and it meets the needs of the surrounding agricultural industries of sheep- and pig-raising and cereal growing. Although the first settlers moved into the area in the 1860s, development was slow until the Great Southern Railway reached Narrogin in the 1880s. With the building of the Hordern Hotel beside the railway line, the settlement grew and the town site was declared in 1897. Those interested in the town's heritage and history will enjoy the Heritage Trails, of both the township and the district, while the old Court House Museum (1893) has displays of the pioneer days. If you enjoyed *A Fortunate Life* by Albert Facey, you can visit his house here.

Bird- and nature-lovers will delight in a trip to the Dryandra State Forest, where there is an abundance of fauna and flora and some great bush-walks, with a profusion of wildflowers in spring.

Annual festivals and events include the Central South Eisteddfod in May, the Agricultural Show and Spring Festival in October and the Rev Heads Weekend in November.
Map ref: page 706 E6

The water pipeline from the weir in Mundaring runs all the way to the goldfields town of Kalgoorlie, a distance of 550 km (342 miles).

The library at the Benedictine Monastery at New Norcia .

NEW NORCIA

Founded by the Benedictine monk, Dom Rosendo Salvado, in March 1846, this small, historic township (population 140) is 129 km (80 miles) north-east of Perth, on the Victoria Plains, along the Great Northern Highway. Originally a small self-sufficient village was built here by the monks around their church, and now, New Norcia with its extraordinary buildings and olive trees, has a definite Spanish feel about it. While the monks continue with their ecclesiastic work, visitors will find much to interest them architecturally, historically and spiritually, in this unique settlement.

The self-guided walk along the New Norcia Heritage Trail takes you past many of the town's landmarks, such as the (still operating) flour mill built in 1879 and the ornate structure of St Gertrude's College, built in the early 1900s. Also well worth a visit is the Museum and Art Gallery, where you can also purchase a wide range of local goods from the shop, many produced by the monks themselves, including their famous bread and olive oil. If you are in the region in July, you can visit the Olive School and Olive Symposium, and in August you could take part in (or simply watch) the Avon Descent.
Map ref: page 706 C3

NORSEMAN

Known as 'The Golden Gate to the Western State', the goldmining town of Norseman (population 1100) is located some 724 km (450 miles) east of Perth, at the junction of the Eyre and Eastern Highways, 207 km (129 miles) south of Coolgardie. It is said that a horse made the first discovery, stumbling over a large gold nugget in the 1890s. Today Norseman's quartz reef is the richest in Australia. Those interested in mining and those early gold rush days will enjoy a visit to the Historical and Geological Collection, which is exhibited in the School of Mines.

Gem fossickers can scratch around on the gemstone leases north and east of town, while gold seekers and those interested in old mining sites should take a drive on the Dundas Coach Road Heritage Trail. There are also a number of interesting geological sites—such as the Salt Lakes, Dundas Rocks and Mount Jimberlana—and a pleasant swimming spot at Bromus Dam.

Norseman is also an important quarantine checkpoint for travellers from the eastern States. Annual events include the CWA (Country Women's Association) Art and Craft Expo in August/September and the Gala Day in December.
Map ref: page 707 M5

NORTHAM

Set astride the Avon River in the heart of the valley of the same name, 95 km (59 miles) east of Perth, Northam is the largest town in the region, with a population of 7500. First settled in 1836, the area did not develop until 1886, when Northam was linked to Perth by rail—this important part of the town's heritage is displayed in the old Railway Station Museum.

There are a number of other attractions in the town, including Austwide Sheepskin Products, the largest sheepskin tannery in Australia, and the pedestrian suspension bridge, which offers visitors a good chance to see the large colony of regal white swans as they gracefully glide up and down the Avon River.

There are several art and craft outlets to browse through, and if you are looking for something a little more exhilarating, there is hot-air ballooning, to give you a bird's-eye view of the area. Festivals and events include the Avon Descent White Water Classic and River Festival in August, the

Peel Estate winery in the Perth Hills Wine Region.

Agricultural Show in September and the Avon Valley Country Music Festival in November.
Map ref: page 706 D4

PEMBERTON

Pemberton is a small town (population 900) 344 km (214 miles) south of Perth, and has a splendid, picture-postcard setting, surrounded by lofty forests of karri, jarrah and marri. The Karri Visitor's Centre should not be missed, and there is a unique ride through the timber on the 1907 replica Pemberton Tramway. To get a bird's-eye view of the forest, you can climb 60 m (197 feet) up the trunk of the Gloucester Tree, to the highest fire lookout in a tree in the world.

Trout anglers will find plenty of waterways and dams to cast a line in, while wine-lovers are well catered for with a number of wineries in the area. For craft enthusiasts there are a number of excellent woodcraft galleries on hand.
See also Pemberton Wine Region
Map ref: page 706 C9

PEMBERTON WINE REGION

The viticultural potential of the area around the timber towns of Pemberton and Manjimup was first mooted by Dr John Gladstones in a 1977 research paper that drew attention to its similarities with Burgundy. The Manjimup area has moderately fertile, lateritic gravelly sands and gravelly loams. It is ideal for grape growing, having a comparable climate to Bordeaux. It has similar mean temperatures and almost identical sunshine hours, although with heavier rainfall, more temperature variability and less relative humidity.

The transition from the marri forests to karri about halfway between Manjimup and Pemberton marks a climatic change as well as a shift in soil type. The climate of Pemberton is cooler, with lower temperatures and fewer sunshine hours, more rainfall and greater relative humidity. Although gravelly loams are found on some of the higher slopes of Pemberton, the soil generally changes to more fertile loams that are associated

Council workers and contractors work on a new roundabout in Norseman, an old gold town and good gem fossicking location.

The old railway station at Northam (1884) is now a museum of railway history and local artefacts.

with vigorous growth. There is still debate about which grape varieties best suit the area.

The stars of the region to date have been winemakers who have established their reputations elsewhere. Moss Wood founder Bill Pannell and his son Dan have established Picardy, convinced that the area will produce outstanding pinot and chardonnay. Their best wine so far is a stunning velvety merlot cabernet, while the Picardy Shiraz pushes the boundaries for the variety. John Kosovich's Bronzewing Chardonnay (Westfield) has been outstanding, while John Brocksopp (Leeuwin Estate) has produced tiny quantities of a fruity roussane and a fine, medium bodied shiraz with clear varietal definition. Keith Mugford makes a fine, taut chardonnay and a spicy, savory pinot from the Lefroy Brook vineyard that is sold under the Moss Wood label.
Map ref: page 706 C8–C9

PERTH HILLS WINE REGION

The wineries in these picturesque rolling hills, stretching from the Bickley Valley north to Mundaring, enjoy sweeping views of the capital city of Perth. They have mainly appeared in the past 30 years. In terms of the wines produced, the area has not been particularly exciting until very recently. Now, its merlots and sparkling white wines have begun to be noticed.

The area exudes warmth and charm and comes alive at the weekends. This is true boutique wine

country, populated by growers and winemakers in love with their lifestyle and what they are able to grow and create. Visitors are made welcome at these mainly homestead affairs, and there is a strong sense of promise for the future.

Among the larger winery operations are Baldivis Estate, Hainault Vineyard and Peel Estate Wines. Try to sample Hainault's outstanding 100 per cent pinot sparkling wine called Tallus, and the Peel Estate's spicy shiraz. The quality wines from this area represent very good value for money at this time.
Map ref: page 706 C4

PINJARRA

Straddling the South Western Highway and alongside the Murray River, 96 km (60 miles) south of Perth, Pinjarra, with a population of 3390, is one of the oldest towns in the State. The first Europeans arrived in the early 1830s. It did not take long for these original farmers to begin producing bountiful harvests in the fertile land-

scape. They called the region Pinjarrup, from the Aboriginal word meaning 'place of swamps'. The surrounding Murray District is rich in agriculture and history. It has a diverse range of landscapes, with a maze of waterways, undulating grazing pastures and verdant jarrah forests.

There are plenty of attractions both in and around Pinjarra for visitors. The many fine old and restored buildings in town, reminders of a past era, can be admired by walking the Pinjarra Heritage Trail, past buildings such as the Edenvale residence, St John's Church (1861), the Original School House (1862), the Post Office (1880s) and the Old Blythewood Homestead.

Cooper's Mill, built in 1843 to grind wheat and corn, is somewhat unusual—it can only be reached by boat, and is one of only two wind-driven mills still standing in Western Australia.

For flower-lovers, a stroll around the Heritage Rose Garden, which features 364 old-fashioned roses, is

a must; the surrounding area is a patchwork of colourful wildflowers during the season. The nearby Alcoa Refinery conducts tours of the mine site and refinery. Special events not to miss, if you are in the area, are the Old Blythewood Music Evening in February, the Pinjarra Festival and the Rotary Art Exhibition and Sale, both in June, and the Lions Rodeo and the Murray Arts & Crafts Open Day and Teddy Bears' Picnic, both happening in November.
Map ref: page 706 C5

ROCKINGHAM

This once peaceful seafront village on Cockburn Sound, 47 km (29 miles) south of Perth, was one of Western Australia's earliest settlements; by the turn of the nineteenth century the port was one of the busiest in the State, loading timber from Jarrahdale for shipping to England. Times got quieter when the port of Fremantle took its place, and the town again took on a sleepy facade.

Its delightful settings and surrounds, though, were slowly being discovered by travellers, and it soon became a popular tourist destination, the sheltered waters of Cockburn Sound and Mangles Bay ideal for water sports, and for fishing—anglers can expect catches of tommy ruff, tailor, snapper, mulloway and trevally. The town's population today is 66,000.

While the beaches are popular, away from the water, nature-lovers and birdwatchers will enjoy the Karnup Nature Reserve, or the Lake Richmond–Anne Mueller Environmental Walk, with diverse bird and floral species. For history buffs there are the Rockingham Museum and the Granary, and a walk along the Old Rockingham Heritage Trail leads past notable landmarks pertaining to the early settlement in East Rockingham.

There are also wineries to visit, and art and craft outlets to browse through, and market devotees will not want to miss the Sunday markets. Annual events include the Navy Open Day in October/ November, and Baldivis Fair and the Spring Festival in November.
Map ref: page 706 B5

Checking the vines at Salitage Wines, the largest in the Pemberton Wine Region.

SHANNON NATIONAL PARK

Located some 358 km (222 miles) south of Perth in Western Australia's spectacular southern forest region, Shannon National Park— 53,500 ha (132,199 acres)—is largely a virgin wilderness area of untouched forests, wetlands, sand dunes and swamps.

Shannon is in the middle of the south-west's tall timber country, but this park has a great deal more to offer than just tall trees. Based around the old abandoned timber town of Shannon (now a camping ground), the national park contains what many describe as a kaleidoscope of 'ecotypes': it has both old growth and regrowth karri forests as well as biologically rich heathlands and wetlands. Some of the forest areas here have never been touched and so, like some sections of the Southern River basin, they are still in a pristine state.

The whole Shannon area is a bushwalker's delight. The Bibulmun Track, Western Australia's premier bushwalking trail (from Perth to Walpole) leads through the park. Other trails include the Shannon Dam Trail, which is 3.5 km (2.2 miles) long and winds through towering karri and marri trees, thickets and swamp area. This is mostly an easy trail—the first 1.5 km (0.9 mile) is suitable for wheelchairs. The Rocks Loop Trail is 5.5 km (3.4 miles); it climbs through rocky outcrops to a lookout over the Shannon town site. Only an average degree of fitness is needed; allow 2 hours for the walk.

There are also many old logging trails that are ideal for walking— ask the ranger for a map. Swimming and canoeing are popular in the Shannon Dam, particularly in

summer; trout fishing is also very popular in the Shannon Dam and River, and there is a golf course at the old Shannon town site. The main camp ground has barbecues, hot showers and toilet facilities. Backpack bush camping is allowed throughout the park. Make sure you always carry water.

The old town site of Shannon is 53 km (33 miles) south of Manjimup, but you can also purchase your fuel and supplies at Quininup, which is only 20 km (12 miles) away. The park's main areas are accessible by conventional vehicle. The best time to visit the area is from October to May.
Map ref: page 706 D9

Memorial to the pioneers of Southern Cross.

SOUTHERN CROSS

Gold was discovered here in 1888 by two prospectors who, at the time, were more interested in finding water. The town is 366 km (227 miles) east of Perth, and received its name from the fact that they used the stars of the Southern Cross to find their way. A number of mines

were developed in the area; however, the finds were to be overshadowed by the gold discovered further east a few years later. While some mining is still carried on, the town is now quite well known as the centre for a rich agricultural area, with a profusion of colourful wildflowers in spring.

Southern Cross' current population is 1500. Reminders of the days of gold are preserved in the Old Court House (1892), which is now the local museum, at the old cemetery, and also in the Mining Registrar's office.

Wimmera Hill, on the highway just west of the town, was the site of the first major gold discovery in Western Australia and gives good views over the town and surrounding farmland. Koolyanobbing, 50 km (31 miles) north from Southern Cross, is a 'modern' ghost town, having closed down in 1983 after less than 30 years in existence.

Hope's Hill, which is just 6 km (3.6 miles) from town, is the now desolate site of what was a booming gold town of the 1890s; Mount Palmer, another rich gold town of that era, is now nothing more than a pleasant picnic area. Frog Rock, 34 km (21 miles) south of Southern Cross, is a popular place for wildflowers and a good picnic spot.

The annual King of the Cross Two Day Enduro motocross championship in August is well worth a visit, as it draws many competitors from far and wide.
Map ref: page 707 H3

STIRLING RANGE NATIONAL PARK

Bluff Knoll, the highest peak in the Stirling Range, rises 1073 m (3521 feet) above sea level and is typical of the rugged peaks of this area, with sheer cliffs and breathtaking views. The climate is variable: in winter (June–August) it is cold and wet, and higher in the ranges even spring is unpredictable.

Sudden cold changes can bring rain or hail, even snow. The best time to visit is late spring and early summer, when the days are warming up and the wildflowers are in bloom. Birds found here include western rosellas, splendid wrens, red-capped parrots and golden whistlers, while wedge-tailed eagles can be sighted riding the thermals. Common here, but seldom seen, are western grey kangaroos, blackglove wallabies, emus, quokkas and honey and pygmy possums. The park is 330 km (205 miles) southeast of Perth, north of Albany.
Map ref: page 706 F9

From a distance, the Stirling Range takes on a blue hue; it rises abruptly from the surrounding plains to 750 m (2461 feet).

Sandalford Wines blends most of its wines from fruit grown in several regions.

some sections are narrower and lower—watch your head. The trail ends 100 m (328 feet) or so into Cook's Cave. Only experienced cavers (speleologists) should proceed beyond this point. In winter there is often water flowing along the creek bed—the caves can fill to the ceiling and are then dangerous. In summer, the creek bed is usually dry. Watch out for the nesting owls as well as stalagmites and stalactites in the caves, and for bees and their honeycomb veils that are found around the cave entrances.

Wildflowers flourish in the area, particularly the colourful *Banksia sphaerocarpa*. There are also some large, ancient species of *Macrozamia*—cycads—which are believed to be over 1000 years old.

Access from the sealed Jurien Road is via Cockleshell Gully and Grover Roads to Gould Simpson Road (4WD only). Camping is not allowed in the park. There are no facilities—you need to bring your own drinking water (and tick repellent). Just outside the southern section of the park, off Grover Road, there is a bush camp site at Three Springs. The nearby town of Jurien has a full range of accommodation including hotels, motels and caravan parks.

Map ref: page 706 A1

STOKES NATIONAL PARK

Located west of Esperance, this park protects Stokes Inlet and the surrounding lakes, plus beautiful beaches, rugged headlands, sand dunes and low hills. Vegetation ranges from heaths to yate, swamp yate and paperbarks, which have formed a low, dense forest that is home to numerous species of waterbirds.

Stokes Inlet is popular for boating and canoeing, but visitors should take care, as there are extensive shallow areas and rock outcrops. Fishing in the inlet and along the beaches can land Australian salmon, black bream, mullet and King George whiting. A 'heritage trail' bushwalk is an easy 45 minutes, and it offers some excellent views of the inlet and also the surrounding area.

Map ref: page 707 K8

STOCKYARD GULLY NATIONAL PARK

A series of caves linked by an ancient watercourse that carved its way underground through rolling limestone hills, is the significant feature of this small national park in the hinterland of Jurien Bay, 280 km (174 miles) north of Perth. It is a wilderness area of 2000 ha (4942 acres) and is accessible only by 4WD. The Stockyard Gully Cave area was on the Old North Road, which ran between Perth and the Geraldton region. In the late 1800s the trail was busy, taking sheep and cattle to Perth and transporting farm equipment and supplies north by bullock dray and camel. Stockyard Gully provided good feed and water for sheep and cattle along the route.

Bring a torch, because the main highlight of a visit here is a walk along a sandy creek bed through three underground caves linked by open sections of creek bed. From the car park the trail leads along the creek bed to Stockman's Cave. Turn off your torch about 100 m (328 feet) in and listen for the bats. The cave is around 300 m (984 feet) long. Middle Cave, a much shorter cave, is next, followed by Cook's Cave. The caverns are up to 10 m (33 feet) wide in parts and 5 or 6 m (16 to 20 feet) high, but

SWAN VALLEY WINE REGION

Olive Farm (1830) is thought to be Australia's oldest continuous winery still in use, and it was established within a year of the founding of the Swan River Colony at Perth. Two of the State's largest companies, Houghton (1859, owned by BRL Hardy) and the independent Sandalford (1840) planted vines in the Swan Valley soon after.

Until the 1960s, most Western Australian vineyards were concentrated in this particular region, although some inland plantings were at one time attempted. Family vineyards that were developed in Swan Valley and the surrounding

Kangaroo paw (Anigozanthos species).

district by Slav migrants during the 1920s and 1930s produced fortified and table wines for local consumption. These vineyards still exist today and they offer some modestly priced wines of very good to reasonable quality that can be purchased at the cellar door.

Because of the threat of phylloxera, the import of vine materials was banned in Western Australia until the late 1950s, so many of the classic varieties were not available to growers. But during the 1970s, with strict quarantine measures still in force, varieties such as chardonnay, sémillon, sauvignon blanc, cabernet franc, merlot and pinot noir were released. This, together with modern technological developments—the more widespread use of stainless steel, better refrigeration and the use of more expensive oak—have led to substantial improvements in quality of table wine produced. Houghton's very popular White Burgundy contains a considerable proportion of chenin blanc, a wine that does particularly well here.

Swan Valley has a hot Mediterranean climate. Compared with other Australian wine regions, it has the highest mean January temperature, 24.3° C (75.7° F), lowest summer rainfall, 107 mm (4.2 inches), lowest relative humidity, 47 percent, and the most sunshine hours, 9.7. The valley is a flat, alluvial plain of deep loamy soils with very good moisture retention.

Map ref: page 706 C4

TOODYAY

The small, pleasant town of Toodyay is home to 800, and is 98 km (61 miles) north-east of Perth on the banks of the Avon River. It was one of the first inland towns in the State, and has many fine old buildings dating from the 1860s, when the town was moved from its original flood-prone position to its present site. Because of the wealth of old buildings, the whole town has been classified by the National Trust. Places of interest include Connors Mill (1870), the third steam-powered flour mill to grace the town and now the tourist centre. The old jail currently houses a museum.

Toodyay offers plenty of other attractions, including the Coorinja Winery, some rather pleasant picnic areas at Reservoir Lookout and Drummond's Park, and Duidgee Park on the banks of the Avon. The Avon Valley National Park nearby is a wealth of wildflowers in spring. The Moondyne Colonial and Convict Festival is held in May, the Avon Descent passes through in August, the Highland Games and Festival of the Celts are in September, and the Toodyay Festival and Agricultural Show are in October.
Map ref: page 706 D4

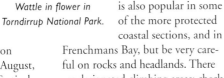

Wattle in flower in Torndirrup National Park.

TORNDIRRUP NATIONAL PARK

Located just 10 km (6 miles) south of Albany right on the edge of the Southern Ocean, this picturesque national park contains some sections of coastline which are the roughest in Western Australia. The park, situated across Princess Royal Harbour from Albany, is small, just 3906 ha (9652 acres), but is one of the State's most visited parks, with around 250,000 visitors each year.

The area is a delight for bushwalking, both cross-country and around the park's many spectacular bays and headlands. There are both short and long walks with good trails. Do not miss the Gap, the Natural Bridge, the Blowholes, Stony Hill and Salmon Holes—all are extremely dramatic and picturesque places. The area is a photographer's delight, so take plenty of film. The heathlands give a colourful wildflower display in spring. Fishing is also popular in some of the more protected coastal sections, and in Frenchmans Bay, but be very careful on rocks and headlands. There are designated climbing areas: check with the ranger. There are good sealed roads, suitable for conventional vehicles, leading to all main areas. Camping is not allowed in the park, but there are a number of nice places to have a picnic where you can enjoy the spectacular views. Other nearby attractions—just outside the park boundaries—are the old Quarantine Station and also the Whaleworld Museum.
Map ref: page 706 F10

Summer is the best season for fishing Walpole Inlet.

WALPOLE

Nestled around Walpole Inlet, 431 km (268 miles) south-east of Perth, and surrounded by extraordinary red tingle and karri forests, Walpole is both a picturesque and a quiet small town (population 450), making it a great holiday destination. The Tree Top Walk in the Valley of the Giants is truly unrivalled. Here, a walkway that is 420 m (1378 feet) long has been erected in the tingle forest canopy, at times 40 m (131 feet) above the ground, and this breathtaking experience, accessible for children, wheelchairs and the elderly, should not be missed. On the water, the Walpole and Nornalup Inlets can be explored by houseboat or ferry, and the Thurlby Herbal Farm makes a pleasant outing. Naturelovers will find the wildflowers in springtime, especially in the surrounding Walpole–Nornalup National Park, a delight. Annual events include the Easter Sunday Market Day and the Orchid Show in October.
Map ref: page 706 D10

WALPOLE–NORNALUP NATIONAL PARK

Surrounding the Walpole and Nornalup inlets on the south coast, this park contains forests of gigantic karri and unique tingle trees. The Frankland River and the Deep River flow through it and empty into sheltered inlets. The park also offers 40 km (25 miles) of truly magnificent coastline, from Irwin Inlet in the east to Mandalay Beach in the west. The rugged Nuyts Wilderness has been isolated so that visitors can enjoy its wild pristine environment. No vehicles, pets or fires are allowed here, and the access is via a small footbridge across Deep River near Tinglewood Lodge. An absolute must-see is the Valley of the Giants, where a 400 m (1312 feet) walking track traverses the forest of karri and tingle trees. Scenic drives display the grandeur of the park—waterfalls, mountains, forests, rivers and the wild ocean beaches. Canoeing is popular on the rivers, there are several boat-launching facilities, and fishing is always good in the inlets and the rivers or from the beach. The park is located 430 km (267 miles) to the south of Perth and 121 km (75 miles) west of Albany.
Map ref: page 706 D10

WILLIAM BAY NATIONAL PARK

William Bay National Park is off the South Coast Highway about 14 km (9 miles) west of Denmark. It includes 10 km (6 miles) of coastline, sandy beaches, low headlands and sand dunes, plus heathland. Seepages and permanent streams in the heathland support scattered groves of peppermint trees, and on the sheltered side of Tower Hill there is a spectacular stand of gigantic karri trees.

Along the coast between Greens Pool and Madfish Bay a series of granite boulders and rock shelves extend about 100 m (328 feet) out to sea, dramatically reducing the heavy seas of the Southern Ocean and forming protected pools and channels for swimming. The viewing platform overlooking Greens Pool is designed for easy access by the disabled. The beaches and headlands of the park offer good fishing, swimming and interesting walking. No camping is allowed anywhere in the park.
Map ref: page 707 E10

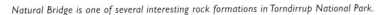

Natural Bridge is one of several interesting rock formations in Torndirrup National Park.

Gigantic karri and tingle trees line the tree-top walk in the valley of the giants near Walpole.

YALLINGUP

Situated on a spectacular stretch of coastline, 266 km (165 miles) south of Perth, and surrounded by the Leeuwin–Naturaliste National Park, Yallingup makes a terrific place to explore Cape Naturaliste, including its extraordinary cave systems. It is a tiny town, with a population of just 100 people but there are many things to do in and around this region.

Drinkers can savour the local wines, or watch ales being brewed at the Bootleg Winery or Abbey Vale Vineyard. Local flower farms in the area specialise in fresh and dried flowers; there is also quite a range of galleries to visit.

Surfers will revel in the excellent waves along Yallingup beach, and the whole area is a real magnet for anglers and divers. The Malibu Surfing Competition is held in Yallingup in December.

Map ref: page 706 A7

YANCHEP

Originally this town was called Two Rocks; the more modern and catchy 'Yanchep Sun City' gained wider acclaim as the base for one of the America's Cup's yachting challenges. Today Yanchep, a tiny town (population 500) 57 km (35 miles) north of Perth, is one of Perth's most popular tourist destinations and recreational areas, catering for those who love to go boating, fishing, diving, surfing and sailboarding.

Lagoon Beach is one such spot, while if you want to get away from the beach scene you can do some pleasant walking in the nearby Yanchep National Park. This small park is home to a number of native mammals, including western grey kangaroos and bandicoots, and a host of waterbirds. There are also a number of caves in the area as well as in the park, which are worth a look, as are the several lakes. Row-boats are a good way to enjoy the calm waters of Lake McNess. The Yaberoo Budjara Heritage Trail is a great bushwalking trail that extends for 28 km (17 miles) north of Joondalup and right along the chain of coastal lakes that makes this part of Western Australia so picturesque. Yanchep has a Golf Fest each year during September.

Map ref: page 706 B4

YANCHEP NATIONAL PARK

Established in 1905, Yanchep is one of Western Australia's very oldest parks and perhaps one of the most popular for day trips from Perth.

Located only 51 km (32 miles) north of the city, it has a rather picturesque setting around Loch McNess, with plenty of grassy, shaded areas, ideal for picnics. There are a number of very easy walking trails, providing opportunities for birdwatching and photography of wildlife, World War II bunkers and the scenic lake and bushland. Near one of the main car parks there is a koala sanctuary, where visitors can see the animals at close range. Rowboats and paddle-boats are also available for hire, but camping is not allowed.

Map ref: page 706 B4

YORK

York is situated 94 km (58 miles) east of Perth in the Avon Valley, and it is Western Australia's most historic town as well as its first inland town.

Settled in 1830, the town was proclaimed the following year, with wool being the main produce. The town was originally a convict depot in the 1850s, and when gold was later discovered at nearby Yilgarn in 1889, York got another good boost to its prosperity. It current population is 3000.

The town is particularly popular for weekend trips for people from Perth, and it has much to offer the visitor. Balladong Farm, established in 1831, was the oldest farm found in Western Australia and it is now a working museum, and children can feed the farm animals here. The Residency, where the resident magistrate was based, dates back to 1843 and is now a museum. The York Motor Museum houses one of the finest collections of vintage cars, motorcycles and horse-drawn vehicles found in Australia and it is well worth a visit. The old two-storey railway station, built in 1886 and one of the few remaining two-storey station buildings in Australia, houses a historic railway collection. The Sandalwood Press in York is Western Australia's only working printing museum.

The picturesque Avon Park, which is located right alongside the Avon River, has a very pleasant picnic area, while the Mount Brown Lookout, just east of town, offers a 360-degree panorama of the surrounding countryside.

Town events in York include the Earth Care Festival in March, Heritage Week, which runs over Easter, the Antique Collectors Fair in April, York Sports in June, the Veteran Car Rally and Daffodil Festival, both in August, the Agricultural Show and the York Jazz Festival, both in September, the York Arts and Crafts Award, held in October and the York Rose Festival, which is in November.

Map ref: page 706 D4

Classing a merino fleece. Fine wool is York's main produce.

CENTRAL-WEST WESTERN AUSTRALIA

Fishing, swimming, wildlife, wildflowers and stories of shipwrecks are just a few of the attractions of the coast north of Perth. Home to an array of bird and animal life it is one of the most renowned wildflower regions in the state. Denham, situated on the Peron Peninsula, is Australia's westernmost town. Geraldton, further north, offers fine beaches, good fishing and offshore islands and reefs.

Perth

The Murchison River winds its way through ancient rock gorges to the sea at Kalbarri National Park. The sand plain around the gorges supports a prolific variety of heathland plants and ends abruptly in colourful cliffs that have been sculpted by the pounding surf of the Indian Ocean. Native mammals and a rich diversity of birds and reptiles inhabit the park.

Dugongs, whales and stromatolites, a form of life that has existed for 3000 million years, as well as the famous dolphins inhabit the waters of Shark Bay, near Monkey Mia. Inland from Shark Bay are some of the oldest dated rocks yet found on the Earth's crust.

In 1616, the Dutch explorer Dirk Hartog sailed into Shark Bay but it was not until the 1870s that Europeans eventually occupied the area permanently when settlers and sheep arrived from York in England. Carnarvon, which is located at the mouth of the Gascoyne River, is still an important agricultural centre. Prawning has replaced whaling as Carnarvon's main maritime industry.

The history and present fortunes of the interior are closely tied up with mining. Early in the 1890s gold was discovered at Mount Magnet, inland from Geraldton.

Later in the 1890s the first gold claims were pegged at Leonora, further to the east. While wool and transport form part of Leonora's lifeline, it is still a goldmining centre. Yet another old goldmining town—Wiluna—stands at the junction of the Canning Stock Route (heading north), the Gunbarrel Highway (heading east), and the roads to Leonora (south) and Meekatharra (east).

Near the mining centre of Meekatharra is the world's largest monolith, Mount Augustus, which, although less well known, is more than double the size of Uluru (Ayers Rock). Rain permitting, the inland region is ablaze with wildflowers from July to September.

OPPOSITE: Dolphins and dugongs swim in the waters off François Peron National Park. The park is home to Project Eden, which aims to eliminate feral animals and reintroduce several native animals that have become rare.

Canning's Cairn, in the Durba Hills, on the Canning Stock Route. Canning built the cairn to serve as a landmark, and indeed there is a great vew of the entire area from the spot.

REGIONAL FEATURE

Shark Bay

Bordering the most westerly point on the Australian mainland, Shark Bay is one of the most ecologically important regions on the continent. Its warm, shallow waters are rich in fish and sea grasses, which in turn support an extraordinary array of marine mammals, including the world-famous bottlenose dolphins of Monkey Mia. In addition, the bay's gently sloping shores are home to one of the world's few existing colonies of stromatolites—rock-like mounds formed by algae that may be the oldest living things on Earth—and a beach made entirely of fossilised shells, while further inland, red sand dunes and semiarid scrub shelter marsupials, abundant reptiles and hundreds of species of colourful wildflowers. The international significance of the bay was acknowledged in 1991 when it was declared a World Heritage area by UNESCO.

Shark Bay is shaped like a tilted W, with Dirk Hartog Island forming the upper part of the left-hand arm and the narrow Peron Peninsula neatly dividing the bay into halves. The surrounding land is arid and sparsely inhabited. The small seaside town of Denham (Australia's most westerly town), the fishing hamlet turned tourist resort of Monkey Mia and the salt-mining centre of Useless Loop are the region's only sizeable settlements.

The shoreline near Denham. Shallow waters and excellent visibility mean that even from land visitors may spot dolphins, dugongs, turtles and manta rays.

History

Dirk Hartog Island occupies an important place in the European history of Australia. It was here, in 1616, that Dutch explorer, Dirk (or Dirck) Hartog, came ashore and nailed a pewter plate to a wooden post; in doing so, he became the first European to set foot on the west coast of Australia and only the second traveller to record a visit to the continent. Hartog's plate was found in 1696 by his compatriot William de Vlamingh while he was charting Australia's western coastline. De Vlamingh took the plate back to Holland, replacing it with one of his own. Three years later, English mariner William Dampier, who had visited the area briefly in 1688, spent a short time moored in the adjacent bay. Noting an abundance of sharks, he named it 'Shark's Bay'. Dampier was, however, unimpressed with the seemingly barren land and for some time his negative reports did much to deter other mariners from exploring the continent further.

In the late eighteenth century the French laid claim to the west coast, and in 1801 a French scientific expedition led by Nicolas Baudin visited the area aboard the *Géographe*. The ship's zoologist, François Péron, made important studies of local plants and animals, and recorded a number of encounters with Aboriginal peoples. His pioneering endeavours are commemorated in the names of both the Peron Peninsula and Francois Peron National Park.

In 1850, Shark Bay became the site of Australia's first pearling base, well before the discovery of even richer pearl beds off Broome, further north. Soon afterward, fishermen and pastoralists

began to settle in the area, and a fish-canning operation was opened in Monkey Mia in 1912. Pearling and fishing are still significant activities in the region, but it is tourism that has allowed Denham and Monkey Mia to prosper, especially since a sealed road to the towns was completed in 1985.

Shark Bay Marine Park

The region's most important reserve is Shark Bay Marine Park, which covers 23,000 sq. km (8900 sq. miles) of ocean and seashore and is a vital refuge for large numbers of sea- and land-based plants and animals. Most significantly, the reserve encompasses the world's largest seagrass meadows, which are home to the greatest number of seagrass species in any one area. These meadows provide sustenance for huge colonies of sea mammals, including approximately 6000 turtles and 10,000 dugongs—around ten percent of the world dugong population. Also known as sea cows, dugongs can grow to 3 m (10 feet) in length and live for up to 70 years. Their nearest ocean-going relatives are the manatees of the Caribbean, though they are also related to elephants.

Shark Bay is located where warm tropical waters overlap with more temperate southern ocean; as a result, it harbours an unusual mix of tropical and temperate fish species, including colourful angelfish, butterflyfish and wrasse as well as the more muted southern species such as mulloway and tailor. The bay is also home to manta rays and, as its name indicates, sharks, including tiger sharks. Humpback whales and whale sharks swim along the coast during their annual migrations, but seldom enter the bay.

Shark Bay's best-known inhabitants, however, are the bottlenose dolphins that visit the shores of Monkey Mia almost every day to feed and interact with human visitors. These remarkable encounters date from the 1960s when a local woman, Ninni Watts, began feeding dolphins during fishing trips. The dolphins quickly learned to follow Ninni back to Monkey Mia and were soon turning up on a regular basis in search of handouts. Word about the phenomenon spread, attracting growing numbers of curious nature-lovers and marine biologists from all over the world. In the 1970s, a dolphin protection group was set up to safeguard the animals and during the

following decade a small visitor centre was opened. The area became a reserve managed by the Department of Conservation and Land Management in the mid-1990s; more recently, a new interpretive centre has been constructed and visitor facilities upgraded.

Today, the feeding and viewing of Monkey Mia's bottlenose dolphins is strictly controlled by rangers to make sure that the animals are neither harmed nor overfed. By limiting the amount of food provided to the dolphins—strict fines are imposed on anyone caught feeding them elsewhere—park authorities aim to prevent the dolphins becoming dependent on humans.

Shark Bay's abundant marine life is often visible from shores and headlands around the bay, and a wide range of nature-watching tours is now available, including boat trips and flights over the seagrass beds. However, the reserve's treasures are not confined to the open ocean. At Hamelin Pool, you can view the world's largest group of stromatolites. These strange, bulbous forms were created over thousands of years by microscopic creatures called cyanobacteria. Able to survive only in heavily saline water, cyanobacteria secrete a mucus that traps sediment, thereby forming and slowly enlarging the rock-like mounds. The stromatolites of Hamelin Pool are about 3500 years old; however, fossilised versions found in north-west Australia indicate that cyanobacteria existed there around 3.5 billion years ago. That makes these tiny creatures, now found in only a few locations around the world, Earth's earliest known life form.

Near Shell Beach you'll come across another rarity— one of only two beaches in the world made up entirely of fossilised shells. The shells, which are 10 m (33 feet) deep in places, are the remains of cardiid cockles, small shellfish which, like the cyanobacteria, thrive in Shark Bay's salty water. The weight of the shells has compressed the lower layers into sedimentary rock. At different points along the beach, this rock has been quarried and used by local people as building material. You can see structures made of shelly limestone blocks in and around Denham.

Sizeable coral reefs lie just off the east coast of Dirk Hartog Island and diving trips can be arranged for groups of visitors.

Monkey Mia's dolphins are never fed more than one-third of their daily food requirements. This ensures that the animals retain their natural hunting instincts.

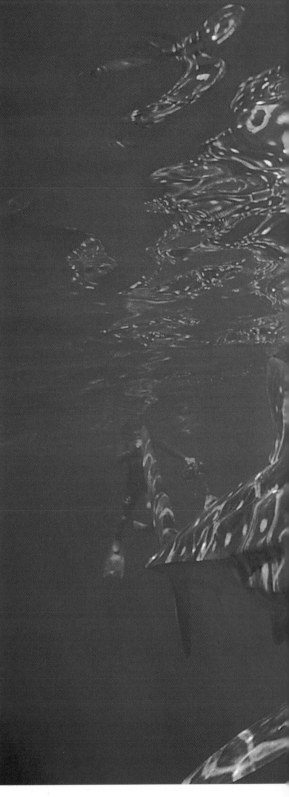

Francois Peron National Park

Formerly a sheep station, the northern third of the Peron Peninsula was purchased by the Western Australian government and opened as a national park in 1990. Its 52,000 ha (128,500 acres) include scrub, sand dunes and distinctive gypsum claypans known as birridas. Once landlocked saltwater lakes, these pans are now mostly dry, although a couple have been breached by the sea, forming wide, shallow lagoons. The vegetation includes a typical range of arid-country species such as wattles, hakeas, grevilleas and myrtles, as well as the ubiquitous and distinctive Shark Bay daisy creeper, with its purple flowers.

More than 100 species of birds have been recorded here, including fairy wrens, finches, grass wrens and wedgebills. The park's 98 species of reptiles include the bizarre and appropriately named thorny devil, a small lizard covered in prominent spines, which spends most of its time guzzling its daily intake of several thousand ants. Euros and other small wallabies are common, as are numerous species of rodents.

Many of the Peron Peninsula's original animal inhabitants were displaced by species introduced by European settlers such as cats, goats, rabbits and foxes. In an effort to redress this ecological setback, park authorities recently set up Project Eden. This aims to eliminate feral animals and reintroduce several of the now rare and endangered species which once thrived here, such as the red-tailed phascogale, banded hare-wallaby and bilby.

The old sheep-station homestead and its outbuildings are open to the public and, with the aid of informative signs, provide a fascinating insight into the lives of early European settlers. The homestead also features an old hot-water artesian bore, which is still in operation. The water is pumped up from 390 m (1280 feet) below the ground to a specially built hot tub and shallow splash pool. Visitors are free to make use of the tub and pool during their visit.

Conventional vehicles can travel as far as the homestead, but other roads in the national park are suitable only for 4WD vehicles. Campers can pitch a tent at several official sites, some of which occupy idyllic positions on the shores of the bay.

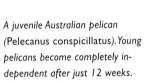

A juvenile Australian pelican (Pelecanus conspicillatus). Young pelicans become completely independent after just 12 weeks.

Fishing

Although Shark Bay's status as a marine park means that a range of restrictions apply to fishing (check with the park authorities before you set off), it is still the case that few other destinations in Australia offer the same fascinating mix of angling opportunities in such pristine and strikingly beautiful surroundings.

Even the more accessible waters around Monkey Mia and Denham boast enough snapper, mulloway, trevally, barracuda and cobia to keep anglers happy for days. But the most productive and exciting areas lie further afield, particularly in the shallow inshore waters at the southern end of the bay, where many line-class records, including tailor weighing more than 7 kg (15.4 pounds), have been taken.

The remote headland of Steep Point on the western arm of the bay offers some of the best land-based fishing in the country, with fish as large as marlin, sailfish and sharks being hooked here on a regular basis. There is also consistent action on big Spanish mackerel, shark mackerel, cobia, tuna, trevally and smaller sharks, as well as bottom and midwater species such as mulloway, pink snapper, nor'westers, baldchin groper (wrasse) and cod. Nearby, South Passage and Useless Loop, located just inside the bay, are most famous for their amazing runs of big pink snapper, which are taken in numbers by boat fishers and, to a lesser extent, shore and jetty anglers.

Angling opportunities also abound on Dirk Hartog Island. These range from sedately casting a line for abundant sand whiting and flathead on the shallow flats immediately in front of the island's comfortable lodge to the adrenalin-charged pursuit of giant tailor, snapper and Spanish mackerel from the high, wave-battered western cliffs. Offshore, on the many reefs, gravel beds and sand patches, pink snapper are present in extraordinary numbers, along with more tailor, some big bluebone or baldchin groper (wrasse) and seasonal runs of Spanish mackerel, shark mackerel and cobia. Further offshore again, you'll encounter tuna, wahoo, marlin and the occasional sailfish, as well as plenty of the toothsome critters for which Shark Bay was first named.

To the north-west of Shark Bay, Bernier and Dorre islands turn on some superb mackerel fishing at times, and have great, almost untapped potential for marlin, sharks, cobia, wahoo and the like.

The whale shark (Rhincodon typus) is the world's biggest fish, growing to a length of 12 m (39 feet). Despite its size, the whale shark poses no threat to humans, and divers often paddle alongside these massive creatures when they visit north-western waters between March and May.

Places in
CENTRAL-WEST
WESTERN AUSTRALIA

BURRINGURRAH (MOUNT AUGUSTUS) NATIONAL PARK

Mount Augustus is the biggest rock in the world, almost twice the size of Uluru. To the Wadjeri tribe, the Aboriginal people who inhabited this region, Mount Augustus was known as Burringurrah. They made many rock engravings here, and a large number of stone tools have also been discovered. Water draining from the rock and then seeping underground supports stands of white-barked river gums, and mulga, myall, gidgi and other wattles are scattered across the plains. A circuit drive of 49 km (30 miles) provides access to all points of interest in the park.
Map ref: page 708 F2

CARNARVON

Carnarvon, the tropical gateway to the north, is located 905 km (562 miles) north of Perth, on the southern side of the mouth of the Gascoyne River. Most of its port facilities are located on Babbage Island, which is just offshore and connected to the mainland by a causeway, and at South Carnarvon near Mangrove Point.

The Dutch explorer Dirk Hartog sailed along this coast in 1616, landing on an island that now bears his name, just a short distance south in Shark Bay. Soon followed William Dampier, who left unimpressed. It was not until the explorer George Grey visited Shark Bay that any land exploration was carried out. His 1839 expedition resulted in a number of places around this region being named, including the Gascoyne River, which he discovered and named after a friend.

The town was gazetted in 1883, seven years after the first settlers drove sheep north from York to take up land in the district. It became an important port as the vast pastoral holdings produced large quantities of wool. The One-Mile Jetty juts out from Babbage Island

nearly 1.5 km (1 mile), and was built in 1904 to service the growing trade with the town and the hinterland. Nearby is the Lighthouse Keeper's Cottage, which was built around the same time and is now a museum. The wide streets of Carnarvon are also a legacy of these early years, when camel trains had to be able to make a turn in the main street.

In 1950 a whaling station was based here. This was eventually closed down in 1962, and today this building is the prawning factory, and tours are conducted there during the winter months. The town has also seen some high-tech industries established, including the satellite tracking station used by OTC, the former overseas arm of Telstra, Radio Australia and a NASA tracking station. All of these have closed, and the prominent dish of the station is now used as a pedestal for a fine viewing platform. The town is now an important agricultural centre, with a

population of 7000, and bananas and exotic fruits grown on a number of nearby plantations. A rich prawn and scallop fishery is also based in Carnarvon, and 65 km (40 miles) north is the Lake Macleod Salt Mine.

Carnarvon is a fine base from which to explore the surrounding area, and the coast is well known for its many attractions and great fishing. Offshore there are the long thin islands of Bernier and Dorre, while further south are the bays, inlets, rugged bluffs and headlands of Shark Bay and its marine park. If you are into surfing, Three-Mile Beach is considered by many to have the best left-hand break in the world. Inland are the Rocky Pools on the Gascoyne River, and further afield there are a number of semi-desert parks and reserves. The major celebration of the year is the Carnarvon Festival, held in August.
Map ref: page 708 B2

CARNEGIE HOMESTEAD

Located on the western end of the famous Gunbarrel Highway, 1296 km (805 miles) north-east of Perth, Carnegie Homestead (population 6) offers an important refuelling point for travellers who venture along these lonely dirt roads. Located nearly 350 km (217 miles)

Scrimshaw: whaler's art on whale teeth.

east of the nearest town, Wiluna, Carnegie is first and foremost a sheep station covering a vast area of this semi-desert scrub country.

Although inhospitable country, this area saw a flurry of explorers in the late nineteenth century. John Forrest passed through in 1874, and Ernest Giles journeyed to the north in 1876. David Carnegie, and another expedition led by Lawrence Wells, both heading for Halls Creek, passed through this region in late 1896/early 1897.

For those travelling east, this is the last homestead and the last spot for fuel before Warburton Aboriginal Community, nearly 500 km (311 miles) away. To the east of Carnegie is Mungali Claypan Nature Reserve, and a little further on is the Gibson Desert Nature Reserve, centred around a track junction called Everard Junction.
Map ref: page 709 N4

CUE

The glory days of Cue, 'Queen of the Murchison', once the site of the richest goldfields in Western Australia, are long gone. Today all that remains in this small town (population 250) 646 km (401 miles) north-east of Perth are the fine buildings that were built in the 1890s. The main street is classified by the National Trust, as are a number of other buildings, including the primary school, the Masonic Lodge and the old jail.

Extensive mining was carried out at the turn of the nineteenth century, including at the nearby Big Bell and Day Dawn mines. Today's mining activity depends on the current price of gold, but still

One of Carnavon's industries—satellite tracking—is now a tourist attraction.

The area around Denham is a model for environmentalists—native fauna is thriving as introduced species are being removed.

there are many prospectors willing to try their luck in and around these old mine sites. Keep in mind, you do require a Miner's Right, and need to check areas for mining leases before prospecting for any gold. Walga Rock, which is 50 km (31 miles) south of Cue, is a large monolith that warrants a visit; during spring the wildflowers alone are worth the trip.

Map ref: page 708 G6

Denham

The World Heritage-listed Shark Bay, a huge gulf on the Indian Ocean coast of Western Australia, is cut neatly into two by the long finger of the Peron Peninsula. On the peninsula's western shore, and 830 km (515 miles) north of Perth, is the small seaside town of Denham (population 700), the most westerly town in Australia; and the town which was once the centre of Western Australian pearling.

Dirk Hartog Island, directly offshore, was the site of the first European landfall in Australia, in 1616. The first pioneers arrived in the area in the 1860s, bringing their sheep to the freshwater soaks along the coast. They were followed by the pearlers and sandalwood harvesters. In 1898 the town was gazetted, and named after Captain Henry Denham, who had charted the bay 30 years earlier. On his trip he blazed a rock at Eagle Bluff—a section of this rock collapsed into the sea, but it has now been recovered and relocated at the Pioneer

Park, a couple of hundred metres back from the jetty.

A salt mine across the water at Useless Loop, the dolphins at Monkey Mia and the World Heritage listing of Shark Bay represent the town's more recent history. The François Peron National Park was proclaimed in 1990 and takes up much of the peninsula north of the town. The original Peron Homestead can be reached by normal car, but trips further north, to Cape Peron, require a 4WD.

The Department of Conservation and Land Management (CALM) has instigated Project Eden, which plans to eradicate all the feral cats and foxes from the peninsula, north from the narrow isthmus—about 25 km (16 miles) south of Denham—and make the park and intervening area a haven for rare native animals. So far the plan is working, and a number of endangered animals have been successfully released there.

The town has safe swimming beaches and is an excellent spot to dangle a line: anglers can expect to catch salmon, whiting and flathead from the beach or jetty.

Outside the protection of the bay and from the cliffs of Steep Point, the most westerly point on the mainland, you can have some great action with cobia, tuna, Spanish mackerel and more. The major event of the year, the Shark Bay Fishing Fiesta, a fishing competition, gets under way in the first week of August.

Map ref: page 708 B4

Dongara

While the township of Dongara (population 2500) is located on the Brand Highway on the banks of the Irwin River, 357 km (222 miles) north of Perth, its port is located 3 km (1.8 miles) away at Port Denison. These twin towns act as the centre for the Irwin Shire, a mixed farming district which gained prominence through the discovery of oil and natural gas in the 1960s—these have been piped to Perth since 1970. The fishing boat harbour at Port Denison, one of the largest in the State, is the base for the crayfishing fleet, which during the lobster season—December to June—is busy bringing catches back to the town's local processing factory.

The area was first explored by George Grey in 1839, and in 1846 Augustus Gregory discovered a coal seam here. Settlement followed Gregory's report of good land, coal and other minerals, and the district was soon a rich wheat producer, with a flour mill operating by 1859. Russ Cottage, built during the 1870s and home to the Dent family, has been restored to its original style, while the old police station houses the tourist centre and historic display.

The nearby coast is popular with anglers, divers and sailboarders, and the town makes an ideal base from which to explore the surrounding countryside.

Ellendale Pool, a pleasant swimming and picnic area, the beautiful Coalseam Conservation Park with its wildflowers, the Burma Road and the Yardanogo Nature Reserves are just some of the area's attractions.

The tourist centre can provide visitors with up-to-date information on the best wildflower displays as well as on the enjoyable 1.6 km (1 mile) walk along the Dongara Heritage Trail. Annual events include the Batavia Coast Craft Market Day and the Lions Market Day, both in April, and the Blessing of the Fleet in November.

Map ref: page 708 C9

Shark Bay is a popular diving area. Denham is located on the shores of Shark Bay.

GASCOYNE JUNCTION

If you are heading to the Burringurrah (Mount Augustus) National Park, it is more than likely that you will drive through the tiny town of Gascoyne Junction (population 35), and while there might not be much to keep you here, it is the last place to buy a cold beer this side of Meekatharra. The Junction, located 1065 km (661 miles) north of Perth on the southern side of the Gascoyne River, is the centre of the desert merino fine wool industry, and its small and only pub is an original relic of the old droving days. It also doubles as a general store for the town's residents and passing travellers.

The Kennedy Ranges National Park can be reached by a reasonable dirt road from Gascoyne Junction. This large park of rugged breakaway and gorge country has a number of walking trails and basic camping sites. Winter and spring are the best times to visit—wildflowers can be profuse. Gemstone and mineral specimen prospectors may find petrified wood, opalite, chalcedony and many other kinds of semi-precious stones in places around the town.

Rocky Pool, 54 km (34 miles) from town on the main road to Carnarvon—and located right on the Gascoyne River—is a popular spot for swimming, fishing and camping. The Junction Race meet

is held at Gascoyne Junction in the middle of July and is a great occasion if you are in the area.
Map ref: page 708 D3

GERALDTON

A year-round holiday climate just 423 km (265 miles)—five hours' drive—north of Perth, makes Geraldton (population 31,000) one of the most popular places in the State, especially in winter. Good beaches, offshore islands and reefs, an inland ablaze with wildflowers in spring, and an interesting history that dates back to the first European contact with Australia, 370 years ago, along with good facilities in and around the town, make the town a great destination.

The islands of the Abrolhos, which lie 100 km (62 miles) offshore, were the scene in 1629 of one of the greatest shipwrecks and mutinies in Australian history. Here the Dutch ship *Batavia* was wrecked, and in the months that followed, a drama of mutiny, murder, survival and rescue were played out on the islands and nearby mainland.

George Grey, on his walk back to Perth after being wrecked at the mouth of the Murchison River in 1839, was the first to bring back good reports of the area. The first British ship anchored here in 1841, naming it Champion Bay after the ship; the name was changed to

St Francis Xavier Cathedral at Geraldton was designed by J.C. Hawes.

Geraldton when the town was surveyed 10 years later. Miners and pioneer pastoralists opened up this region, and today the area is rich farming land, with market gardens along the river being fed from an all-year underground stream, and with the port as the major base for the crayfishing fleet which operates from Geraldton.

There are plenty of fishing opportunities in and around Geraldton. The harbour is home to tommy ruff and garfish, while further offshore the reefs produce pink snapper, baldchin tuskfish,

Westralian jewfish, sweetlip and mackerel; off the beaches you can catch tailor, mulloway and whiting. Diving and surfing are popular, and fishing and diving trips to the Abrolhos Islands are available.

Annual events and festivities include the Geraldton Windsurfing Classic in January, the Batavia Seafood Festival in February, the Batavia Coast Fishing Classic in April and the Festival of Geraldton held in October.
Map ref: page 708 C8

KALBARRI

Located at the mouth of the Murchison River, 590 km (366 miles) north of Perth, Kalbarri has grown from virtually nothing in 1950 to a pleasant seaside town with a population of 1200, and offering all amenities.

The rocky wild coast north and south of the town has claimed many ships, dating back to the first Europeans known to have ventured this way. In 1629, two suspected mutineers were marooned on this coast near Wittecarra Gully, just south of the town, making them the unintended first Europeans to settle on the continent. In 1712 the *Zuytdorp* was wrecked along the cliffs that now bear that ship's name, and in 1839 George Grey's ship was wrecked at the mouth of the river he named the Murchison, when he was exploring the coast. His forced march south along the coast to Perth resulted in much of

The coast between Dongara and Geraldton. Fishing is both an important industry in its own right and a drawcard for tourists.

the region being opened up to pioneer pastoralists.

Kalbarri National Park, with its stunning river gorges, is right on the doorstep of the town. There is also a beautiful bird park, Rainbow Jungle, just south of Kalbarri; and the Kalbarri Wildflower Centre, covering 16 ha (40 acres) of undisturbed bush, is also close to town.

There is good surfing, sailboarding and diving in the area, and whale watching is becoming more common as the whales have begun to return to the region.

The coast also provides fabulous fishing, and while the boat fishing is excellent, fishing from the rocks, beach or in the river is more rewarding. Coral trout, mulloway, snapper, tailor, Spanish mackerel and more may be caught at such places as Chinaman's Rock, Red Bluff, Rainbow Valley and Pot Alley Gorge. The annual Blessing of the Fleet is held each November.
Map ref: page 708 C7

The North West Coastal Highway passes just to the east of Kalbarri National Park on its way from Geraldton to Carnavon.

KALBARRI NATIONAL PARK

Kalbarri National Park, on the west coast north of Geraldton, is a paradise for walkers, with magnificent scenery along the coast and in the river gorges. The park covers 186,000 sq. km (71,796 sq. miles), and through its heart flows the Murchison River. The river has created some 85 km (53 miles) of spectacular red and white banded gorges. A number of unsealed roads give good access to the gorge country, at such places as the Loop, Nature's Window and the Z Bend. The lookouts, Hawks Head and Ross Graham, give fine river views.

The wettest months are June and July, and after that the wildflowers, for which the area is famous, begin to bloom. These cooler months are the best time to explore the park. The spring wildflower display in the park is magnificent, with over 500 species on show; the park is also home to 170 species of birds and a number of mammals. Along the coastline are some dramatic rock formations, and the views from the cliffs are stunning. There is excellent fishing along the rock platforms and beaches, and in the estuary.

The nearby town and fishing port of Kalbarri is good base for visitors—travel companies here can arrange canoeing, rock climbing, abseiling, camel trekking, and other activities, through the park and along the coast.
Map ref: page 708 C6

KENNEDY RANGE NATIONAL PARK

The Kennedy Range, an eroded plateau in the outback of Western Australia, is located about 800 km (497 miles) north of Perth and 160 km (99 miles) east of Carnarvon. It is breakaway country on a large scale; the range is nearly 200 km (124 miles) long and, in parts, up to 25 km (16 miles) across. The park is 141,660 ha (350,042 acres) in area.

The elaborate branched gorges and towering sandstone cliffs rise up like battlements over 100 m (328 feet) high from the flat surrounding plain. This mass of craggy, white–orange, brown and even black cliff faces are a remnant of the land surface that elsewhere has been eroded away.

There are a number of activities to be enjoyed by visitors here, including walking, photography, exploring the canyons and gorges,

wildflowers in spring, birdwatching, and outback camping. Gemstones can be found here, as well as ancient marine fossils embedded in rocks around the range.

Early morning light on the east face of the range is particularly spectacular for photographers. The main access is from the east side of the range north of Gascoyne Junction. These roads are gravel (quite suitable for conventional vehicles) but can be slippery, or even closed, after heavy rain. Access into the western side of the range, which also includes some spectacular breakaway country, is strictly 4WD through private station properties—travellers must get the appropriate permission first.

There are basic camping facilities in the National Park, such as pit toilets and wood barbecues. Wood is scarce, so bring your own or gas cooking equipment. There is no drinking water, and the nearest fuel and supplies are at Gascoyne Junction, 60 km (37 miles) away. The whole area can be extremely hot in summer: temperatures of 45°C (113°F) plus are common, so the best time to visit is between May and October. The area is remote and travellers must be totally self-sufficient.
Map ref: page 708 D2

Kalbarri, Geraldton and Dongara all have good conditions for sailboarding.

Sons of Gwalia gold mine, at Leonora. The company produces around 400,000 ounces of gold per year from its several Western Australian mines.

LAVERTON

Laverton (population 1020) is situated 361 km (224 miles) north of Kalgoorlie and 935 km (581 miles) north-east of Perth, on the road to Warburton, and services both the mining and grazing industries surrounding it. Sandalwooders came early to the area, to gather this valuable timber, but it was not until the discovery of gold in 1896 that the town became established, with the field becoming one of the richest in Western Australia. The town was originally named 'British Flag', after the first mineral lease; by 1901 there were a number of large mines in the area and a population of about 3500. In time, however, the gold pickings became lean and the town declined, reviving again only with the discovery of nickel at nearby Windarra in 1969. That led to the infamous Poseidon share rise and fall where some investors won millions, while others lost everything. The mining site is silent today and its original buildings now house a visitors' centre, while a heritage trail takes walkers around the mine and old processing site.

The town now has an increasing number of tourists who stop to use its services and prepare for the trip across the Great Victoria Desert to Uluru (Ayers Rock) and on to Alice Springs. Two permits are required to travel this road. Applications should be made to the

Aboriginal Affairs Planning Authority in Perth, and the Central Land Council in Alice Springs.

To get a good view of Laverton and its surrounds, take the short climb up Billy Goat Hill. Those who love to explore around old mining fields and towns will find several in the Laverton district including Burtville, Gladiator, Heffernans and Just in Time. The Mines Department has a large-scale map available for travellers to get the most out of their explorations.
Map ref: page 709 N8

LEONORA

The once flourishing goldmining town of Leonora (population 1500) is 830 km (515 miles) north-east of Perth and 237 km (147 miles) north of Kalgoorlie, and leaves a unique impression on visitors with its many vestiges of a past era. The explorer John Forrest first wandered through this area in 1869 with a party searching for the lost Leichhardt Expedition. He named Mount Leonora in honour of the wife of the then West Australian governor. He was not, however,

too impressed with the countryside. In 1896 the first gold claims were pegged at Leonora—and at its twin town Gwalia (the Gaelic name for Wales)—and in those busy, hardworking times it soon became the largest centre in the north-eastern goldfields.

Today it still maintains that role and is the railhead for copper from the northern copper mines and nickel from Leinster. Gold continues to play an exciting and important part in Leonora's future, while the surrounding pastoral

Breeding plumage of the cattle egret (Bubulcus ibis).

industry produces a substantial wool clip during good years. While once you could have journeyed around town in the State's first electric trams, today you will have to walk along the Gwalia Heritage Trail to experience the town's history first-hand. There are plenty of buildings dating back to the 1890s to admire, and for those who want to learn more about the town's past, visits to both the Gwalia Historical Museum and Historical Gallery are a must.
Map ref: page 709 L8

MEEKATHARRA

The township of Meekatharra is found on the Great Northern Highway, 196 km (122 miles) north of Mount Magnet and 763 km (474 miles) north of Perth, and is part of Western Australia's Outback Mid-West region. It is an area that is transformed during the wildflower season—from July to September—with the countryside becoming a mass of beautiful colour from plants such as everlasting daisies.

The town has had a new lease of life in the last 15 or so years as more and more mines have opened up. The town is once again a major service centre for the outlying mines and vast pastoral holdings, and has a population today of 1000. Many old buildings still exist, including the Old Courthouse (1912), which is classified by the National Trust, and there are old mining ghost towns to explore and fossick around throughout the local area.

Meekatharra is also the closest town to Mount Augustus, the world's largest monolith, more than twice as big as Uluru (Ayers Rock). The rock is protected by the surrounding Burringurrah National Park, which is also home to a number of rare plants. The special event of the year in Meekatharra is the horseracing, in October.
Map ref: page 709 H5

MENZIES

The town of Menzies is located 132 km (82 miles) north of Kalgoorlie and 687 km (427 miles) east of Perth on the road to Leonora. The town began with the discovery of gold in 1894 and the opening of the nearby Lady Shenton Mine. At its peak in 1905, this once-bustling town had a population of over 10,000, and included 13 hotels and 3 breweries. Visitors today will find it a lot quieter— the population now is 350—the historical buildings, made from local stone, the only tangible reminders of its booming past history.

Buildings of note include the Town Hall and Shire Offices, built in 1896, and the Railway Station, which is now renovated. The old cemetery is also a place to wander round and try to imagine what hardships and isolation those early miners had to endure. Nearby attractions include the Coongarrie National Park and the ghost towns of Kookynie and Niagara.
Map ref: page 709 L9

MORAWA

Morawa, a small town with a population of 1200, is situated 179 km (111 miles) from Geraldton and 395 km (245 miles) north of Perth, in the State's mid-west. Many tourists flock to this area during the wildflower season, which is usually from July to October, as the countryside is covered with colourful blooms; plants such as everlasting and wreath flowers, wild pomegranates and native orchids form a veritable multicoloured carpet.

The primary agriculture of the region is cereal farming. Sheep, pig and cattle raising, together with

Wreath flowers (Leschenaultia macrantha) are common around Morawa in spring.

newer markets for emu, ostrich and marron, are also important.

History buffs will enjoy a wander through the police station and jail, and a walk along the Hawes Heritage Trail. Nearby scenic spots include Koolanooka Springs and Bilya Rock. The major annual event is the Morawa Music and Art Spectacular in October.
Map ref: page 708 E9

MOUNT MAGNET

Situated on the Great Northern Highway, 247 km (153 miles) east of Geraldton and 566 km (351 miles) north of Perth, Mount Magnet is the oldest surviving gold settlement of the Murchison field. Pastoralists ventured into the area with their sheep in the late 1870s, and the rush for gold began in 1891, when the first rich diggings were discovered; the township of Mount Magnet was proclaimed soon after. The town is small now (population 620), but it is still the service centre for the surrounding goldmining operations and pastoral properties, and tourists will find plenty to see in an overnight stop.

There are heritage walks and drives which will take you past notable relics of the gold rush era, as well as historic buildings and sites, such as the Post Office and Shire Building (1898) and the Old School House (1896). The Historical Society Museum has a remarkable collection of memorabilia. The nearby scenic spectacle of the Granites is a great place to explore, and wildflowers are prolific in August and September. Annual events include the race meetings

in February and May and the gymkhana in October.
Map ref: page 708 G7

MULLEWA

Situated 99 km (61 miles) east of Geraldton and 521 km (324 miles) north of Perth, in the Northern Midlands, Mullewa (population 900) is in the midst of wildflower country and surrounded by sheep and wheat farms.

An outing to the Jack Murray Wildlife Sanctuary, and a visit to the small but delightful church of Our Lady of Mount Carmel would be of interest to visitors. Architecturally a mixture of Byzantine, Romanesque, Greek Orthodox and Spanish styles, the priesthouse, now a museum, gives an insight

into the life of Monsignor John Hawes, an extraordinary architect, stonemason and carpenter. This church was the culmination of his achievements. Nearby is the stone-pitched Tenindewa Pioneer Well, as well as a natural glacier bed, which is a great place for wildflowers. Major annual events are the Wildflower Show in August and the Mullewa Agricultural Show in September.
Map ref: page 708 D8

WILUNA

Located at the junction of the 4WD Gunbarrel Highway to the east, the long and arduous 4WD trek of the Canning Stock Route to the north, and the main dirt road west to Meekatharra or south to Leonora, and 946 km (587 miles) north-east of Perth, Wiluna is a service town for the surrounding and more remote sheep and cattle properties, mining camps and Aboriginal communities. Gold was discovered here in 1896 and the mine soon became the largest in Australia. However, when the mine closed in 1947 the town declined. Today mining activities are still carried on close to the town, but the current population (300) is far short of the 10,000 that once lived here. The town has two fuel outlets, but they are sometimes out of one or more fuels, so it is worth ringing to check in advance of a planned stop.
Map ref: page 709 K5

View from Ullaring Rock, near Menzies, where sandalwood now provides industry.

CENTRAL-EAST AND SOUTH-EAST WESTERN AUSTRALIA

Vast expanses of sparsely populated arid lands characterise the Central-East and South-East of Western Australia. Nineteenth-century explorers traversed this inhospitable mulga, mallee and desert country in their efforts to find pastoral and farming land. The land did not yield their desire but after heavy rain even the desert comes alive with wildflowers.

The Eyre Highway crosses the Nullarbor Plain closely hugging the Great Australian Bight. Near the historic telegraph town of Eucla, 11 km (7 miles) from the South Australian border, there are lookouts affording views of the Bunda Cliffs, which plunge precipitously into the Southern Ocean. Sand dunes cover and uncover the remains of the Overland Telegraph Line near Eucla. Seals, whales and albatrosses can be seen from Eucla National Park. The vegetation here is mostly mallee scrub and heathlands.

Further west, via Nuytsland Nature Reserve and the Eyre Bird Observatory turn-off, the highway veers from the coast. North of the Eyre Highway is the famous straight stretch of railway track through the spinifex country on the journey between Sydney and Perth. North of the railway line, a few unsealed highways and stock routes dot the numerous deserts

There are several nature reserves in the Great Victoria Desert—including the Great Victoria Desert Nature Reserve, the Plumbridge Lakes Nature Reserve and the Yeo Lake Nature Reserve—all of which are accessible by 4WD vehicle.

North is Warburton, an important Aboriginal population centre in the Warburton Ranges It lies on the unsealed road popularly known as the Gunbarrel Highway, the route through the Aboriginal lands of central Australia between Western Australia and the Northern Territory. Aboriginal land stretches throughout this region—through the Gibson Desert to the Great Sandy and Tanami Deserts. The Gibson Desert was named by Ernest Giles who led an expedition westwards from Alice Springs in 1874. The death of one of his companions, Alf Gibson, forced the party to abandon its journey, which wasn't successfully completed until 1875.

OPPOSITE: Sand plains at Eucla. Temperatures are a little lower, and rainfall is a little higher, around Eucla than on the rest of the Nullarbor.

Wildflowers at Eucla. Mallee is the typical vegetation of the thin strip of the Eucla coast—the escarpment above is a karst area.

REGIONAL FEATURE

The Gunbarrel Highway

At the heart of the vast, arid interior of south-eastern Western Australia lies the Gibson Desert. Covering 156,000 sq. km (60,200 square miles), this desolate but fascinating region encompasses gibber plains, rocky outcrops, and long, parallel sand ridges, and is one of the wildest and most sparsely populated parts of Australia. Travellers can, however, explore its dramatic landscapes, view its surprisingly varied flora and fauna, and follow in the footsteps of early European explorers by driving the historic Gunbarrel Highway, one of the country's major 4WD tracks.

The route runs for 1409 km (875 miles) from Yulara near Uluru in the Northern Territory to Wiluna in Western Australia. As it traverses extremely remote country, travellers must have a robust 4WD vehicle and carry plenty of food and water. Separate permits are required for passing through Aboriginal lands in the Northern Territory and in Western Australia; these should be obtained before departure from the Central Land Council in Alice Springs and the Aboriginal Affairs Department in Perth. Travellers should also register with the police at their departure point and again upon arrival at their destination. The journey from Yulara to Wiluna normally takes three to four days.

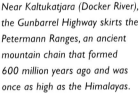

Near Kaltukatjara (Docker River), the Gunbarrel Highway skirts the Petermann Ranges, an ancient mountain chain that formed 600 million years ago and was once as high as the Himalayas.

History

The Gibson Desert has been home to traditionally nomadic Aboriginal peoples for thousands of years. But it wasn't until 1874 that the region was visited by a European, Ernest Giles, who led an expedition westward from the Overland Telegraph station near present-day Alice Springs. Giles named the desert in memory of one of his companions, Alf Gibson, whose death forced the party to abandon its journey. The following year, Giles managed to travel all the way across the continent to the west coast, but passed further south, through an area he named the Great Victoria Desert. On his return journey a few months later, however, he succeeded in crossing the Gibson Desert.

Giles was followed into the region by other exploratory parties, including, in 1891, the Elder Scientific Exploring Expedition, which reached the Everard Ranges, and, in 1896, the Calvert Scientific Expedition, led by Lawrence Wells, which journeyed east out of Wiluna, around the northern side of Lake Carnegie.

In 1897, explorer David Carnegie led a small party into the region from the goldfields, passing north of present-day Leonora and then skirting Mount Everard before heading for Halls Creek in

the Kimberley. Returning south, he passed further to the east, close to Thryptomene Hill, where he named Lake Breaden after one of his men. He also named McPhersons Pillar, a spectacular rock pinnacle in the north of the Gibson Desert Nature Reserve.

In 1930, an expedition entered the desert from Alice Springs in search of a huge reef of gold that had supposedly been found by Harold Lasseter. After a series of disagreements, the party members split up and headed their different ways. Lasseter claimed he had found his gold reef again west of the present-day Giles Meteorological Station, near Lake Christopher, but he died on the return journey and despite several subsequent searches, no one else has ever located it.

Following World War II, the Australian government allowed Britain to begin testing nuclear and ballistic missiles in southern Central Australia. An army surveyor, Len Beadell, was given the task of choosing and planning several test sites and constructing roads across the vast, arid interior. Between 1955 and 1964, he and his Gunbarrel Road Construction Party opened up more than 2.5 million sq. km (965,000 square miles) of desert country and graded over 6500 km (4000 miles) of roads. The most important of these roads was the Gunbarrel Highway, which became the first route to link Central Australia with the west. Following its completion in 1958, Beadell was awarded the British Empire Medal in recognition of his work.

Yulara to Warakurna

Before you set off along the Gunbarrel Highway, make sure you stock up on fuel, food and water at Yulara as there are no other reliable sources of supplies for quite some distance. Leaving Yulara, turn right 8 km (5 miles) from the village and head towards Kata Tjuta on the sealed road. On the far side of the domes, 44 km (27 miles) from Yulara, you'll come to a junction, where you should turn left. The bitumen soon gives way to dirt, but for the most part the road west to Kaltukatjara (Docker River) is fairly good, with only the creek crossings and the occasional washaway causing problems. You cross Irving Creek 84 km (52 miles) west of the Kata Tjuta turn-off, and Shaw Creek, 26 km (16 miles) further on.

The Hull River, 190 km (118 miles) from Yulara, marks the turn-off to Lasseter's Cave, where the prospector holed up for several weeks and waited vainly for help. Follow the track leading south just before the normally dry stream and you will come to a parking area. From here, it's just a short walk to the cave and a plaque commemorating Lasseter's exploits. Though there are no facilities, camping is permitted and the shady gum trees create a pleasant picnic spot.

As you approach Kaltukatjara, the country becomes more dramatic, with weeping desert oaks standing out starkly against the purple-tinged backdrop of the Petermann Ranges. The Aboriginal community at Kaltukatjara, 234 km (145 miles) west of Yulara, offers limited fuel and supplies at the general store, but few other services for travellers.

After another 26 km (16 miles), you'll pass the intersection with the Sandy Blight Junction road. Soon afterward, you enter an area of magnificent desert ranges, which Giles named Schwerin Mural Crescent. At the T-junction 75 km (46.6 miles) west of Kaltukatjara, turn right onto the original route of the Gunbarrel Highway. Left leads south along the original route, but that section is now closed to travellers.

Warakurna Roadhouse, 28 km (17 miles) further on and 337 km (209 miles) from Yulara, is the first reliable source of supplies, offering fuel and food as well as a small, well-established camping ground. The nearby Giles Weather Station, which was originally set up to monitor weather conditions on the Woomera Rocket Range and now plays an important role in the country's national meteorological network, can be visited by prior arrangement.

Like many desert plants, Sturt's desert pea (Swainsona formosa) only flowers after heavy rain, when each plant may carpet an area of up to 2 m (6 feet) in diameter.

In 1931, Harold Lasseter was stranded for weeks in this cave near the Hull River while returning from the gold reef he claimed to have located years earlier. His body was later found a short distance away at Irving Creek.

Warakurna to Carnegie

Leaving Warakurna, travellers have two options. One is to follow the original Gunbarrel Highway, which swings off to the right, 16 km (10 miles) west of the roadhouse. This rougher, distinctly 4WD route leads along the southern ramparts of the Rawlinson Ranges, passing a couple of trees marked by Len Beadell, then veers south to Jackie Junction. From there, it heads west across the Todd Range, past Mount Samuel (on top of which there is a lookout), to the junction with the Heather Highway, 370 km (230 miles) from Warakurna. If you take this route, make sure you have a robust vehicle and enough fuel to reach Carnegie.

The other option involves heading southward, or left, at the junction 16 km (10 miles) west of Warakurna toward to Warburton. This road is wide and straight and is usually very good, although at times it can be a mass of corrugations. Warburton, an important Aboriginal community, offers fuel and other basic services and has a pleasant camping ground. You'll also find some excellent locally made Aboriginal arts and crafts for sale here.

At Steptoes Turn-off, 40 km (25 miles) southwest of Warburton, turn right onto the Heather Highway. Road conditions tend to deteriorate a little here, but should pose no major problems. The country also changes, to rolling, gibber-covered, spinifex plains, and the panoramas are extensive.

At the next junction, 47 km (29 miles) west, follow the Heather Highway north. From this point on, the road becomes more of a track and is often washed out after rain. The Heather Highway meets the original Gunbarrel 39 km (24 miles) further north.

A tree located 11 km (7 miles) west of this junction is marked with one of the aluminium plaques left by Len Beadell. Just west of the tree, a track leads less than 1 km (0.6 miles) south to a water bore topped with a hand pump. This water isn't great, but it could save your life in an emergency.

Continuing west past Thryptomene Hill, you come to Camp Beadell, 64 km (40 miles) west of the T-junction of the Gunbarrel and Heather highways. The flat top of Mount Beadell, 6 km (3.7 miles) further on, is the site of a monument to the surveyor and offers sweeping views of the surrounding country.

A short distance beyond Mount Beadell, you enter the Gibson Desert Nature Reserve. The reserve's 19,000 sq. km (7350 square miles) encompass several ranges of low, eroded peaks, including the Browne, Young and Alfred and Marie ranges, as well as a number of salt lakes and pans, the largest of which is Lake Newell in the east. Since the reserve's dedication in 1977, the Department of Conservation and Land Management (CALM) of Western Australia has carried out a number of surveys that have identified important populations of rare or endangered native animals. Sadly, the lesser stick-nest rat has slipped into oblivion—its demise almost certainly due to predation from the feral cats and foxes that roam this arid environment—but other animals such as the long-tailed dunnart have a secure stronghold in the Young Range. Other small marsupials present in the park include the mulgara, the wongai ningaui, the spinifex-hopping mouse and the bilby.

At Everard Junction, 57 km (35 miles) north of Mount Beadell, the Gunbarrel Highway intersects with the northbound Gary Highway, another of Len Beadell's roads. The Gary provides access to the north-western corner of the nature reserve, which consists mainly of undulating sand country. Near the reserve's northern border lies Lake Cohen, an ephemeral fresh-water lake which, when it has water, throngs with the sounds of hundreds, sometimes thousands, of nesting birds. This is also a popular camp site, though there are no facilities here or anywhere else in the reserve.

Continuing westward on the Gunbarrel Highway, you leave the nature reserve about 30 km (19 miles) west of Everard Junction. After 2 km (1.2 miles), you reach the junction of the Hunt Oil Road. On the south side of the road is the Geraldton Historical Society Bore can be used to obtain water in an emergency.

Between here and Mangkili Claypan, 55 km (34 miles) further west, the track improves. You enter the small Mangkili Claypan Nature Reserve just before the road crosses the pan's normally dead, dry heart. If there is water in the claypan, take the tracks that run around the edge. On the other side, the road crosses the north–south Eagle Highway, then passes through rocky country. Parts of the track are often washed away here, so take care. About 80 km (50 miles) west of the claypan, you enter sandhill country.

Carnegie Station, 152 km (95 miles) west of Mangkili Claypan and 492 km (306 miles) west of Warburton, supplies petrol and diesel fuel, food and drinks, and has camping, cooking and dining facilities. Emergency repairs are also available.

Carnegie to Wiluna

Although the Gunbarrel officially ends at Carnegie, the fun doesn't really stop until you get to Wiluna, and that's another 350 km (217 miles) away.

About 30 km (19 miles) west of Carnegie, a track heads off to the right to Glenayle Station Homestead and the Canning Stock Route. Another 54 km (34 miles) westward, the road crosses a small, dry

creek bed and immediately afterward, on the right, there's a camping area known as Harry Johnson Water. To the south, just out of sight, is the vast, white expanse of salt-encrusted Lake Carnegie.

At the western end of the lake, the road swings south, passing a couple of turn-offs before heading west again. Old mine works and other signs of prospecting activities become more common as you near the end of the track at the remote town of Wiluna, 266 km (165 miles) from Harry Johnson Water, and 1409 km (875 miles) from Yulara.

Many parts of the Gunbarrel Highway are corrugated. Driving at around 80 kph (50 miles per hour) should help reduce vibrations as at this speed cars tend to skip across the depressions.

Hummock grasses (Triodia spp.), commonly known as spinifex, are among the few plants hardy enough to survive in arid areas such as the Gibson Desert.

Places in
CENTRAL-EAST
AND SOUTH-EAST
WESTERN AUSTRALIA

Balladonia Homestead is 28 km (17.4 miles) east of Balladonia.

BALLADONIA

The tiny township of Balladonia (population 20) is located 939 km (583 miles) east of Perth, 193 km (120 miles) east of Norseman, and 182 km (113 miles) to the west of Cocklebiddy, on the Eyre Highway. Between the tiny settlement of Caiguna in the west and Balladonia is one of the longest straight stretches of bitumen in the world, running 145 km (90 miles) in length.

Once the site of a telegraph station, today Balladonia consists of only a hotel/motel and a service station. The site of the nearby Balladonia Station Homestead was selected back in 1879 by the

Ponton brothers and John Sharp for their sheep station—rock from the surrounding granite outcrops was used to build the original homestead in 1880, as well as the fences. The gallery of oil paintings at the homestead will be of interest to visitors as the paintings depict Balladonia's history.
Map ref: page 711 A8

COCKLEBIDDY

This place is hardly worth a mention, apart from the fact that on most journeys across the Nullarbor, between the towns of Ceduna in South Australia and Norseman in Western Australia—and 1164 km (723 miles) east of Perth—this is one of the few places travellers can actually stop for fuel, refreshments and accommodation. Travellers tend to find Cocklebiddy (with a population of only 7) to be one of the most expensive places for fuel on the Nullarbor. But then there are no bargains anywhere on the entire Nullarbor crossing!

Just to the north-west of this small hamlet are the Cocklebiddy Caves, one of a number of subterranean caverns under the surface of

the Nullarbor. A number of cave diving records have been set in this area, but a major rainstorm caused a large cave-in a few years ago that trapped a caving team for several days, and it is still considered too unsafe to explore.

To the south, and closer to the coast, is the Eyre Bird Observatory, one of four major bird study bases around Australia. This complex is reached via a track that turns off the main highway 17 km (11 miles) east of the motel complex at Cocklebiddy. Accommodation and nature-based courses are run from the Observatory, but space is limited, so call beforehand.
Map ref: page 711 D8

EUCLA

Now best known as a truck stop for the passing parade of motorists making the run across the Nullarbor from Perth to the eastern States, or vice versa, Eucla is just 11 km (7 miles) from the West Australian side of the border, 1438 km (893 miles) east of Perth, close to a great escarpment that overlooks the flat coastal plain and the band of mobile white dunes along the coast itself. It is a popular spot to stop and refuel or even stay overnight.

Close to the beach and a mere 4 km (2.5 miles) away are the relics of the old Overland Telegraph line repeater station, connecting Western Australia with the rest of Australia. This station was once the busiest on the whole line: the base was staffed with both West and South Australians, since two morse code systems were used. In 1929 the station was abandoned and shifting sands now cover and uncover its remains.

A town was proclaimed here in 1885 but it never actually eventuated. The Bunda Cliffs, plunging 90 m (295 feet) into the sea, can be viewed from a couple of lookouts near the present-day hamlet of Eucla (population 45). The Eucla National Park takes in a vast sea of mallee, heathland and scrub, inland from the cliffs of the Great Australian Bight.
Map ref: page 711 G7

Cocklebiddy Caves—more than 100 m (328 feet) below ground—includes some of the longest underwater caves in the world.

The Old Telegraph Station, in Eucla National Park, almost hidden in the sand dunes.

Quarantine checkpoint at Eucla: disease control is essential in agriculture.

of Eucla and 1377 km (855 miles) east of Perth, along on the Eyre Highway, and the place was named after the original homestead. Although it is generally considered to be just a stopover for travellers crossing the Nullarbor, the region around here is actually quite a well-known meteorite site—the shattered fragments of a huge meteor that plummeted to Earth here during the Ice Age are strewn over a 60 km (37 miles) area, making this one of the largest meteor sites found in the world. Of interest also is a bird and animal sanctuary which is located at the rear of the Mundrabilla motel.
Map ref: page 711 E7

with its fuel and supplies is a popular and necessary stop when heading on through Western Australia to Uluru or Alice Springs. However, it is not open 24 hours a day. The main route is from the south from Laverton—a rougher 4WD route follows the original Gunbarrel Highway to Carnegie Homestead and Wiluna. Two permits are required to travel these roads—apply to the Aboriginal Affairs Planning Authority in Perth, and the Central Land Council in Alice Springs. The Aboriginal community itself is out of bounds for travellers, but artefacts can sometimes be bought from the store.
Map ref: page 710 D10

GIBSON DESERT NATURE RESERVE

This desert was named after Alfred Gibson who died of thirst on the expedition led by Ernest Giles in 1874. An arid region of spinifex, sandhills and *Triodia* desert grass, it is home to the rare bilby and the golden bandicoot. It is accessed via the Gunbarrel Highway.
Map ref: page 710 C8

MUNDRABILLA

The first Europeans to settle in this very remote and desolate area were Thomas and William Kennedy, who established the Mundrabilla Homestead in the early 1870s.

The motel and service station complex is all that is located out here, with its total resident population of only eight Mundrabilla is located 66 km (41 miles) west

WARBURTON

Located on the Gunbarrel Highway, 1536 km (954 miles) northeast of Perth, Warburton is an important Aboriginal community, with a population of 450. It is nearly 700 km (435 miles) northeast of Leonora and 560 km (348 miles) west of Uluru (Ayers Rock).

The road is dirt for all its length and can be rough, so the roadhouse

Emus (Dromaius novaehollandiae) drinking. Emu farming is an ecologically sustainable business, and emu oil may have health benefits.

WOLF CREEK METEOR CRATER RESERVE

Just 30 km (19 miles) south of Halls Creek, the Wolf Creek crater abuts the Great Sandy Desert, punctuating an otherwise flat spinifex landscape. The world's second largest confirmed meteorite crater, it measures 853 m (2799 feet) across and is 46 m (151 feet) deep. The near-symmetrical circle left by the impact indicates the meteor came almost straight down, creating an explosion equivalent to that of an atomic bomb. It was not discovered until 1947. A 4WD is essential.
Map ref: page 710 E1

THE KIMBERLEY

In the far north of the State, the Kimberley has been called Australia's last frontier. Huge tides swirl around a rugged coastline; during the Wet season, temperatures soar, rivers flood and roads become impassable. Nevertheless, the area's attractions—aqua water and white sands of the Indian Ocean coastline, the gorges on the Gibb River Road track, the ancient domes of the Bungle Bungles and the enticing Buccaneer Archipelago—draw many visitors.

The reefs and islands of the archipelago protect the entrance to King Sound where William Dampier anchored in 1688. Huge 12-metre (39-foot) tides here are the largest in Australia. On the mudflats of King Sound, is the town of Derby, which became a major port after gold was discovered in 1885 at Halls Creek, precipitating Western Australia's first goldrush. Pastoralists were the first white settlers to arrive in the Kimberley in the 1870s and the cattle industry is still a very important one to the region's economy.

Lying east of Halls Creek on the Great Northern Highway is Fitzroy Crossing, a good access point for the Devonian Reef National Parks —Geike and Windjana gorges and Tunnel Creek. North-east of Halls Creek is Purnululu National Park, site of the famous striped domes of the Bungle Bungle Ranges. The 350-million-year-old structures of Purnululu have been sacred to the Kimberley Aboriginals for thousands of years, containing many burial sites and rock art.

North of the Bungle Bungles is Kununurra, a town founded in the 1960s at the centre of the Ord

River scheme. The Ord River scheme was an ambitious project designed to alleviate the problem of too much water in the Wet season and not enough water in the Dry. One of its results is the massive Lake Argyle, created by the Ord River Dam.

Wyndham, a town to the north-east of Kununurra, was originally a port servicing the goldfields of Halls Creek. It is still an outlet for the beef industry. North-east of Wyndham is the remote Drysdale River National Park where important Aboriginal art and rainforest plants can be found.

OPPOSITE: Windjana Gorge. The riverbank soil suits Leichhardt trees, native figs and cadjeputs, which then provide shelter for waterbirds, a colony of fruit bats and corellas. Freshwater crocodiles can often be seen in the pools.

Sunset over the Derby jetty at low tide. Derby was never a great site for a port, being subject to rips and whirlpools and tidal variations of up to 11.3 m (37 feet).

The Gibb River Road

The Kimberley was one of the first parts of the continent to form, about 1.5 billion years ago. During subsequent periods, it was covered by ocean, which laid down layers of sediments clearly visible in many parts of the plateau today.

The Gibb River Road is an unsealed track that runs from Highway 1 near Kununurra through the heart of the Kimberley Plateau to the coastal town of Derby on King Sound. Originally established as a beef road linking remote cattle stations to the ports of Derby and Wyndham and now one of Australia's top 4WD routes, it traverses majestic terrain and provides access to scenic waterfalls and delightful hidden gorges. Idyllic camp sites line the route and concealed among the rocky bluffs are superb examples of Aboriginal rock art.

The 710-km (441-mile) road is rough in places and very remote. A 4WD is recommended and travellers should make sure that their vehicle is in good

mechanical order and that they have plentiful supplies of fuel, food and water. The plateau's rocky terrain is particularly hard on tyres, so always carry at least two spares. As the road is unfenced and passes through large swathes of pastoral country, drivers should be alert for wandering stock and wildlife, especially around dawn and dusk. The route becomes impassable during the wet season, so plan to travel between April and October.

A number of cattle stations along the Gibb River Road have opened their properties up to tourism, offering camping grounds and other kinds of accommodation. Most of the land along the route is private

the Cockburn Range. From the river, it's 6 km (3.7 miles) to the turn-off, on the right, to Emma Gorge. Part of El Questro Station, and located just 1 km (0.6 miles) from the road, the gorge is a delightful spot. Accommodation in tented cabins is available at Emma Gorge Resort, but no camping is permitted. Even if you decide not to stay overnight, you can still, for a small charge, walk to the gorge and enjoy a refreshing swim there. The resort also has a bar, large swimming pool, shop and restaurant.

The entrance to El Questro Station itself lies another 10 km (6 miles) along the Gibb River Road. The homestead, 17 km (11 miles) south of the main road, offers a range of accommodation, from luxurious suites to budget rooms, as well as pleasant, secluded camping sites. You can enjoy a rejuvenating soak in the thermal pools at Zebedee Springs, and, if you have a small boat or canoe, explore picturesque Chamberlain Gorge. Other outdoor activities available here include bushwalking, birdwatching, fishing, camel rides, helicopter trips and 4WD tours. The station also has a general store and fuel.

Continuing west on the Gibb River Road for 4.5 km (2.8 miles) from the El Questro turn-off, you come to Fish Hole, a picturesque camping spot with permanent water, which is marked by a distinctive group of boab trees. About 20 km (12 miles) beyond Fish Hole, you reach the wide Pentecost River, which is tidal downstream and freshwater upstream. A causeway leads across the river and is normally free of water, except at the beginning of the dry season. The fishing downstream can be productive, but saltwater crocodiles are common here, so be very careful.

Just before the crossing, there is a track on the right that meanders northward for some distance, following the river and leading to a number of camp sites. It then loops around the Cockburn Range and veers north again, eventually reaching the outskirts of Wyndham, some 80 km (50 miles) from the Gibb River Road junction. The track is very rough in places, but the route might appeal to experienced off-road drivers looking for a challenging detour.

After crossing the Pentecost River, the next major junction is the track to Home Valley Homestead, 8 km (5 miles) further on, on the right. This working cattle station is one of three in the Kimberley run by the hospitable Sinnamon family. Home Valley offers

property, so travellers should pitch tents only where provision has been made for camping. No special permits are required to travel this route.

Kununurra to Kalumburu Junction

Head west out of Kununurra along the Victoria Highway (Highway 1) in the direction of Wyndham. At the junction with the Great Northern Highway, approximately 45 km (28 miles) from Kununurra, turn right and drive toward Wyndham for 8 km (5 miles). When you reach the Gibb River Road junction, turn left onto the dirt track.

You encounter your first river, the King River, at the 17-km (11-mile) mark, but the watercourse is normally dry and easily crossed. The surrounding country is dominated by the dramatic red bluffs of

El Questro Homestead occupies a dramatic position on a clifftop high above the Chamberlain River.

Eateries, shops and even barbecues are few and far between on the Gibb River Road, so travellers should carry cooking equipment such as pots and a fire grate.

accommodation, meals, a station store, fuel, tyres and mechanical repairs, as well as an agreeable waterside camping ground with excellent amenities. Fishing, boating, swimming and canoeing can also be enjoyed here, and the Sinnamons organise various activities, including barramundi fishing, horse riding, scenic flights and 4WD treks, many of which take visitors into remote and normally inaccessible areas.

Beyond the turn-off to Home Valley, the Gibb River Road offers dramatic views, especially in the evening light, of the Cockburn Range and the Pentecost and Durack rivers. You cross Bindoola Creek 19 km (12 miles) further on and then again another 18 km (11 miles) along the road. Both crossings are dry for most of the year and problem-free.

After a steep climb up Gregorys Jump Up, it's only another 3 km (1.9 miles) to the right-hand turn-off to the Durack River Homestead, a total distance of 57 km (35 miles) from the Home Valley track junction. This station is also run by the Sinnamon family, and at the homestead on the Durack River, less than 1 km (0.6 miles) off the main road, accommodation, meals, fuel, tyres and repairs are

all on offer. There is also a small store, and campers can pitch a tent at nearby Jacks Waterhole, where there are even flush toilets and hot showers. This picturesque spot is ideal for boating, swimming, canoeing and fishing. Tours into the surrounding wilderness are operated from the homestead to local points of interest such as Oomaloo Falls, Mosquito Hills, Karunjie Station and Edith and Netapus pools.

Continuing along the Gibb River Road, you cross Bamboo Creek after 10 km (6 miles). The creek has near-permanent water, and there is a reasonable camp site nearby, which can be reached by taking the track on the right just before the crossing.

A further 12 km (7 miles) brings you to the left-hand turn-off to Karunjie Homestead. If you wish to visit this, the third of the three properties operated by the Sinnamon family, you will need to book beforehand by contacting Home Valley Station. Accommodation is available and you can participate in the station's activities or join one of the tours into the rugged and as yet untamed surroundings. The station is also a top spot for fishing and birdwatching.

The Durack River lies another 5 km (3.1 miles) along the Gibb River Road. At the crossing there are a number of tracks on both sides of the banks which lead to fine camping areas with good, permanent water.

After another 20 km (12 miles), you come to the track into Ellenbrae Station, on the right. Accommodation is also available here, with all meals if required, and there is a pleasant camping ground with good facilities, including the use of a communal kitchen. The station shop offers limited supplies and an interesting range of local arts and crafts; fuel may also be available, but it is best to check with the station in advance. If you have time, you can hike into the surrounding bush, and if you have your own canoe you can enjoy a paddle along the river, where the birdlife is prolific. The nearest camp site is just a few kilometres further along the main road, at Dawn Creek, which normally has water in it. There's also another site 24 km (15 miles) from Dawn Creek, beside Campbell Creek, where a right-hand track leads down to a pleasant, shady spot by the river.

The next crossing, Russ Creek, lies just 20 km (12 miles) further west, and once again a track on the right just before the waterway leads to a riverside camp site. From here, it's another 22 km (14 miles) to the junction with the Kalumburu Road, a rough, 4WD-only track that leads to the Mitchell Plateau and the Kalumburu Aboriginal community. To continue on the Gibb River Road, turn left. At this point, you will have travelled a total of 291 km (181 miles) from Kununurra.

Kalumburu Junction to Derby

On the right-hand side of the road, 40 km (25 miles) from the Kalumburu Road junction is the track to Gibb River Station. There are no facilities or fuel here, however. Over the next 20 km (12 miles), you cross a number of creeks, including Bryce, Mistake, Hann and Snake, but none offers a decent spot to pitch a tent. Indeed, it's not until you reach Mount Elizabeth Homestead, 30 km (19 miles) down a side-track off the right-hand side of the main road, 70 km (44 miles) from the Kalumburu Road junction, that you'll find a camping area with any facilities.

Mount Elizabeth Station is operated by the Lacy family whose ancestors were the first Europeans to settle in this part of Australia. Like a number of other stations in the Kimberley, Mount Elizabeth successfully combines tourism with cattle grazing. Accommodation at the homestead (which must be booked in advance) and meals are available, as well as a camping ground with flush toilets and hot showers. The family also operates a tour company called Bushtrack Safaris, which specialises in birdwatching, botany, bushwalking, Aboriginal art, fishing and photographic tours of the surrounding region.

Continuing along the Gibb River Road for 9 km (5.6 miles) brings you to another worthwhile detour. A track on the right leads to a parking area 4 km (2.5 miles) from the main road, and from this point it's a short walk to the Barnett River Gorge. As well as a pleasant swimming hole, there are some good camp sites here, and if you explore the gorge you may come across some interesting Aboriginal rock art.

The Barnett River itself crosses the Gibb River Road 27 km (17 miles) from the track junction. The next major point of interest is the Mount Barnett Roadhouse, 6 km (3.7 miles) beyond the river, on the right. It has toilet and shower facilities, a good range of supplies, fuel and a workshop that can carry out most mechanical repairs. The roadhouse is also the entry point to beautiful Manning Gorge. Beside the tranquil, clear, cool waters of Lower Manning Gorge, there's a delightful camp site with basic facilities. If you plan to camp here, you must first purchase a

*Found only in north-west Australia, the boab (*Adansonia gregorii*) is closely related to the baobab trees of Madagascar. The boab's bulbous trunk can grow to about 25 m (82 feet) in diameter.*

Dating back 1500 years, Wandjina art is the most distinctive style of rock art in the Kimberley. It is characterised by images of spirit beings, or Wandjina, with large eyes, no mouth and a halo-like shape around their head.

Many rock faces contain dramatic evidence of the awesome forces that fashioned the Kimberley Plateau. Once horizontal, these sedimentary layers have at some point been buckled and tilted.

permit at the roadhouse. This is a great spot for swimming and canoeing, though the area of navigable water is small; there is also plenty of birdlife around the water. An easy walk (one hour each way) leads to Upper Manning Gorge, where you will be rewarded with a panoramic view of a huge pool surrounded by high cliffs. There is a fair amount of Aboriginal art around the gorge, much of it concealed under rocky overhangs and therefore hard to find.

If you can tear yourself away from this exquisite gorge, you'll soon find another, just 15 km (9 miles) further along the Gibb River Road. Galvans Gorge, located just 1 km (0.6 miles) off the main road, has a waterfall and a large main pool where you can enjoy a swim. On the adjacent cliff face, there is an impressive example of Aboriginal rock art.

Returning to the Gibb River Road, you soon begin to climb up the flank of the Phillips Range, and from the highest part of the road there are magnificent views to the north. Another delightful gorge awaits you 17 km (11 miles) from Galvans Gorge and 32 km (20 miles) from Mount Barnett Roadhouse. Located 5 km (3.1 miles) from the main road, beside a car park and camping area, Adcock Gorge is an idyllic spot with an enchanting pool.

Continuing along the Gibb River Road, you cross Billy Goat Springs and pass the turn-off to Beverley Springs Homestead before reaching the left-hand track into Mount House Homestead at the 20-km (12-mile) mark. For those looking for supplies, the homestead has fuel, tyres and batteries, and a store where food can be purchased. Accommodation is also available, but must be booked in advance.

If you are looking for another place to cool off, take the right-hand track to Surprise Springs, about 15.5 km (10 miles) west of the turn-off to Mount House. After 8 km (5 miles), you'll come to a small camping area, and from there it's a short walk to a waterfall and a large, inviting pool.

About 21 km (13 miles) past the turn-off to Mount House, the Gibb River Road crosses Grave Creek, then another 3 km (1.9 miles) brings you to Saddlers Springs crossing, where water normally covers part of the road. Just 1 km (0.6 miles) up the road is the Imintji Aboriginal community, where some fuel and supplies are available and camping is permitted. Another 9 km (5.6 miles) takes you into King Leopold Range Conservation Park and the right-hand turn-off to Bell Gorge. This is one of the

most spectacular gorges in the Kimberley and well worth the rather slow 30-km (19-mile) drive required to reach it. Along the way, the track skirts the King Leopold Ranges, and leads past the old Silent Grove Homestead, once an outstation of Mount Hart Station and now the site of a camping ground and seasonal ranger station. It then follows Bell Creek, passing some pleasant, shady camping spots, and ending at a large boab tree that has a bell carved into its trunk. A short hike from here leads to a wondrous vista of terraced waterfalls and gorges, formed over thousands of years as Bell Creek gradually carved its way through the Isdell Range. Parrots and budgerigars are common here and you may even spot a dingo.

Back on the Gibb River Road, the route continues southwestward; 3 km (1.9 miles) from the turn-off to Bell Gorge, the road crosses Bell Creek, where a small camp site can be found on the right, before the crossing. Soon after, the road begins to climb the King Leopold Ranges and you encounter a short stretch of bitumen. Pull over near the top of the hill to admire the view to the north.

The next 10 km (6 miles) crosses a number of minor creeks with small camping spots. The best of these is at Dog Chain Creek, 21 km (13 miles) from the turn-off to Bell Gorge. A couple of kilometres (1.2 miles) further on, you come to the left-hand junction with the Millie Windie Road. Two hundred metres or so (220 yards) along this road, a rough 7-km (4.4-mile) track branches off south to the Lennard River Gorge. From the car park, walk down the hill to the gorge rim, then follow the trail down to the water. The gorge measures 5 km (3.1 miles) in length, and its sheer cliffs are an impressive sight.

Returning to the Gibb River Road, after 7 km (4.4 miles) you reach the turn-off, on the right, to Mount Hart Homestead. Nestled in the folds of the King Leopold Ranges, 50 km (31 miles) from the main road and still within the conservation park, the homestead is something of an oasis, offering comfortable accommodation and hearty meals. There are no camping facilities, however; the nearest camp site is on the Gibb River Road, just beyond the turn-off to Mount Hart, at Apex Creek.

About 1.5 km (0.9 miles) beyond Apex Creek, you reach beautiful Inglis Gap. Stop at the small parking area on the left and enjoy the wonderful views of the surrounding plains and ranges.

Leaving the conservation park and continuing along the Gibb River Road, you pass the track to Napier Downs Homestead, 56 km (35 miles) from the turn-off to Mount Hart. Just beyond this junction, the sheer, rugged battlements of the Napier Range rear up on either side of the road as you pass through Yammera Gap. Formed under ocean as a massive barrier reef during the Devonian period (408–360 million years ago), the Napier Range is rich in fossils and has yielded the remains of marine creatures, extinct reptiles and giant mammals.

Another 9 km (5.6 miles) further on, you cross a bridge over the Lennard River. Just beyond the bridge,

to the right, there's a small camping spot. Less than 1 km (0.6 miles) past the crossing, and about 65 km (40 miles) from the Mount Hart Track junction, a good dirt road on the left leads to the so-called Devonian Reef national parks of Windjana Gorge and Tunnel Creek, and the Great Northern Highway 123 km (76 miles) away. If you have some spare time, these parks are well worth the diversion.

The Gibb River Road continues through flat pastoral country, reaching the next road junction after another 45 km (28 miles). The right-hand track here leads to Kimberley Downs Homestead. About 40 km (25 miles) beyond this junction, another track on the right runs for 6 km (3.7 miles) to Meda Station and the May River. The river is a popular spot with locals and the fishing is good, but be warned that estuarine crocodiles inhabit the area.

The Gibb River Road meets the Great Northern Highway 34 km (21 miles) from the May River turn-off. Head to the right here and, after 7 km (4.4 miles) of sealed road, you will reach the town of Derby, having driven a total of 710 km (441 miles) from Kununurra.

Helicopters allow anglers to explore otherwise inaccessible waterways. Catfish, mangrove jack, threadfin salmon and bream are sought year-round, but between March and December barramundi become the main quarry.

Places in
THE KIMBERLEY

China Wall, at Halls Creek, is a quartz vein that has intruded into softer sandstone.

DERBY

Derby (population 5000) is located on King Sound, near the mouth of the Fitzroy River, just 220 km (137 miles) north of Broome, with the town of Wyndham some 914 km (568 miles) away via Highway 1, and just over 690 km (428 miles) by the Gibb River Road. It is 2509 km (1558 miles) north of Perth. While Aboriginals inhabited this area well before the coming of the Europeans, it was Alexander Forrest, blazing his way through this region in 1879, who started the land rush that saw Europeans quickly taking up the land along the Fitzroy River in huge pastoral properties. Derby was proclaimed officially in 1883, and with the discovery of gold at far away Halls Creek in 1885, it was not long before it became a major port.

The cattle industry still plays a major role in Derby's economy, but mineral wealth, tourism and a number of defence establishments are today changing the face of the town. It has also become the gateway to the magnificent gorge country of the central Kimberley, as well as to the maze of islands that dot the Kimberley's rugged coastline. There are a number of historic attractions to interest the visitor, such as the Pigeon Heritage

Mudskippers on the Derby foreshore.

Trail, the Boab Prison Tree—a giant, hollowed-out boab tree with a girth of 14 m (46 feet)—and the Old Derby Gaol and Police Yard, both built in the 1880s.

Anglers will not be able to resist casting a line from the jetty; there is also a boat ramp that gives access to the sea. While the fishing here is good, even spectacular, the tides and currents must be watched—Derby has the second-highest tidal range in the world, at 11 m (36 feet). There are quite a few special events and festivals during the year: Kingtide Day in March, the Boab Festival in July, the Kimberley Arts Festival in September, and the fun and frivolity of cockroach-racing, seed-spitting, stubby-sipping and frog-racing events held at the Spinifex Hotel on Boxing Day.
Map ref: page 712 E7

DRYSDALE RIVER NATIONAL PARK

This is Western Australia's most northerly park, in the north of the Kimberley. It is a wilderness park, and provides great opportunities for walking and nature observation —there are no facilities, nor are there any authorised vehicle tracks. The rivers and creeks contain many steep-sided gorges, cliffs and several magnificent waterfalls, the largest being Morgan Falls and Solea Falls.

There are also remnant pockets of rainforest along the 48 km (30 miles) of the Carson Escarpment and in some gorges, such as Worriga Gorge. The bird and animal life is diverse: short-eared rock wallabies, sugar gliders, purple-crowned fairy wrens, Gouldian finches and grey and peregrine falcons, plus many species of reptiles, frogs, and freshwater fish.

The best time to visit Drysdale River National Park is during the Dry season, which is from May to October, as most rivers of the Kimberley are in flood during the Wet. A 4WD vehicle is essential here—the only way into the park is via station tracks. Visitors must obtain permission from the stations before using these tracks.
Map ref: page 713 K3

FITZROY CROSSING

Fitzroy Crossing is a small settlement (population 1200) located on Highway 1, some 255 km (140 miles) east of Derby, 290 km (180 miles) west of Halls Creek, and 2696 km (1674 miles) north of Perth. Once a sleepy little hamlet on the banks of the mighty Fitzroy River, it began life as a watering hole for travellers stranded by floods at the crossing of the river. With the construction of a bridge across the Fitzroy in 1974, a new town grew up to the south.

This is cattle country, and the town services the outlying stations; it also has all the important facilities (fuel, stores and repairs) for travellers. There are a number of things to see and do in and around the town. The Crossing Inn, built by Joseph Blythe in the 1890s as a shanty inn and trading store, is located near the old town site and river ford, and still offers travellers a cold beer. At the old town site you can see other reminders of the past, too, such as the former post office and police station.

A visit to the nearby Geikie Gorge National Park, where the Fitzroy River flows through a striking slash in the range, is not to be missed. There are a number of walking trails, as well as boat tours, operated by the Department of Conservation and Land Management (CALM), which take visitors for a cruise up the best section of the gorge. Freshwater fishing in the Fitzroy River can be rewarding, with catches of barramundi and sooty grunter available. Annual

events in the area include the Fitzroy Valley Rodeo, held in June.
Map ref: page 713 H9

HALLS CREEK

Halls Creek is situated 2989 km (1856 miles) north of Perth in the East Kimberley. It was the site of Western Australia's first gold rush, which began in 1886.

Today, the town has a population of 3000 and is headquarters for the vast Halls Creek Shire, as well as a major service centre for the surrounding pastoral district. Tourism and mining are becoming increasingly important in this region. The town is located on the Northern Highway, quite close to its junction with the Tanami Road to Alice Springs, and right at the junction of the Northern Highway and the Duncan Highway, which leads in an easterly direction to Katherine via Wave Hill.

Places of interest include Old Halls Creek, the site of the original township, and old gold mines of the Ruby Queen Mine and Bradley Mines. Other attractions include the China Wall, Palm Springs and Sawpit Gorge, and the horseracing and rodeo, which run in August.
Map ref: page 713 L9

KALUMBURU

Kalumburu is an Aboriginal community in situated in the far north of Western Australia—3170 km (1969 miles) north of Perth—with a population of 600. This community was established in 1932 when a mission was set up here by

Benedictine monks, who had also started a mission at nearby Pago 24 years earlier. The township was bombed by the Japanese during World War II and the place was near-abandoned from then until after the war, when both the missionaries and the Aboriginal people returned. Today the community runs its own affairs, and the mission maintains a school and church area. The town can provide basic requirements, and the mission can supply limited fuel.

You need a permit to stay on the Aboriginal community lands—this can be arranged at the community office. Camping and fishing are allowed at many places along the coast north of the township, and the fishing is nothing short of fantastic. Visits to the nearby Drysdale River National Park can be arranged from here but you must be self-sufficient to visit this remote park and carry all your own supplies. Map ref: page 713 K2

KUNUNURRA

The 'green' capital of the north, 3345 km (2077 miles) north-east of Perth, Kununurra owes its existence and its verdant looks to the great man-made lakes that lie close by. Established when the Ord River Scheme was first built in 1961, the town slumbered for many years, as a number of different ideas were tried to make the hugely expensive irrigation scheme work. Finally,

more than 30 years after it was finished, the scheme looks like fulfilling most of its early promise, with a large variety of crops, especially sugar, now being grown over the very flat and fertile plains of the lower Ord River.

This area was first explored by Alexander Forrest during his 1875 expedition, the expedition which opened up the Kimberley for pastoral development. The famous Durack family established their cattle empire over much of the land that was to be resumed and flooded when the Ord River dam was built in the 1960s. In recent years diamond finds south of the town and oil and gas discoveries in the Timor Sea have seen the town take on a new vitality. It now has a population of 5500, and is well serviced, with all that travellers in this vast region, far from a major capital city, might require.

Just on the east side of town is the Mirima National Park, which has as its heart the Hidden Valley. The rock formations here are spectacular, and a number of walking trails in the park give a visitor tantalising glimpses of the natural wonders of the area.

On the other side of town is Lake Kununurra, the smaller of the two dams on the Ord and used as a regulating dam for the irrigation areas nearby. The waters of the dam are a very popular swimming, boating and waterskiing area, while the backwater, locally known as the

Anglers land two trevally off the Kimberley coast—fishing is a big attraction here.

'Everglades', is a real birdwatcher's delight. It is also a great spot to enjoy a little canoeing.

The main dam on the Ord is some 70 km (43 miles) away, and holds back the waters of Lake Argyle, the largest man-made lake in Australia. The lake is popular for boating, fishing and swimming, and there is a small camping and accommodation resort for visitors. The river, from below the dam wall to Lake Kununurra, is a popular stretch of water with both small-boat owners and canoeists. The irrigation area is also worth a look, while more natural delights can be found at Valentine's Rock Pool, Black Rock Falls or Middle Springs. Point Spring Nature Reserve, a small area of rainforest

about 50 km (31 miles) north of the town, is an idyllic picnic spot and home for many bird species.

There is a good choice of fish and a variety of fishing spots in and around Kununurra, with catches of black bream, sooty grunter, catfish, and of course barramundi, to excite and entice the most inexperienced anglers. The most popular fishing spots include Ivanhoe Crossing, Bullocks Crossing, Fords Beach and Valentine's Creek.

There are a number of festivals and events held each year in Kununurra, such as the Dam to Dam Dinghy Race in June, Ord Tiki Day and the Agricultural Show in July, and rodeos, race meetings and art exhibitions in August. Map ref: page 713 N5

Lake Argyle, near Kununurra is nine times the size of Sydney Harbour. The lake and its shores now provide a habitat for at least 60 bird species, and for other animals.

MIRIMA (HIDDEN VALLEY) NATIONAL PARK

Located just 2 km (1.2 miles) from Kununurra in the East Kimberley region of Western Australia, Hidden Valley National Park—only 1800 ha (4448 acres)—is a mass of twisted valleys and many eroded sandstone gorges within a broken, strangely sculpted range.

With permanent waterholes and plenty of shelter, this was once a popular meeting place and corroboree ground for the Miriuwung people. There are rock paintings and engravings, and grooves in the rocks above Lily Pool—where the Aboriginals once sharpened their hunting axes and spears.

Today this is the Kimberley's most visited national park. The area is a photographer's delight, particularly in the early morning and late afternoon, when the richness of the sun's rays bring out the deep textures in this eroded landscape. There is also much bird and animal life, and the unusual-shaped boab trees also grow here, clinging to the cliff walls.

There are many walking trails throughout the valleys and leading into the hilltops—most are short, between 500 m (1641 feet) and 1 km (0.6 mile) and quite easy, although care is needed with loose, brittle rocks along the tracks. The ridge-top trails also involve climbing over some crumbly rock faces. Allow 1 hour return for the main Didbagirring climb trail. There is also an easy nature trail that is about a kilometre (0.6 mile) long.

Mirima has often been referred to as the 'Mini Bungle Bungles', as it has sections where the rock formations resemble the beehive shapes for which the Bungle Bungles have become famous, although Mirima's are not as spectacular.

There are picnic facilities, tables, toilets and an information shelter, but camping is not allowed in the park. The Hidden Valley Caravan Park—one of a number in Kununurra—is adjacent to the park. The best time to visit is mid-year, between May and October.
Map ref: page 713 N4

MOUNT BARNETT

Originally Mount Barnett was the name given to the surrounding cattle station, but it now refers more to the roadhouse situated on the Gibb River Road, 2809 km (1744 miles) north of Perth. The station and roadhouse are owned by the Kupungarri Aboriginal community (population 250), which has a large housing estate on the opposite side of the main road, a little to the south of the roadhouse. Situated over 300 km (186 miles) north-east of Derby and 400 km (248 miles) south-west of Kununurra, Mount Barnett has for many years been a favoured spot where travellers have stopped, refuelled and refreshed as they journey along the Gibb River Road.

The camping area down on the Barnett River, just below the Lower Manning Gorge, is pleasant, and the swimming hole is delightful. There is a good day walk to the Upper Manning Gorge and a number of Aboriginal art sites close by.

Hidden Valley (Mirima) has sandstone landforms that are 360 million years old.

The camping ground makes a good base from which to explore some of the other gorges, found through the ranges to the south.
Map ref: page 713 J6

PURNULULU (BUNGLE BUNGLE) NATIONAL PARK

Located in the far northern Kimberley region, Purnululu National Park was declared in 1987, and was established to protect the spectacular Bungle Bungle Range. The best time to visit is from May to September; the park is closed from 1 January to 31 March each year. This park is definitely 4WD only and good ground clearance is vital as Spring Creek Track, the only access into the park, has jagged rocks, bulldust, soaks and creeks which are often impassable until well into the Dry.

The Bungle Bungle Range is around 360 million years old; it has been home to the Aboriginal people for at least 20,000 years, and contains many sacred sites and galleries of rock art. The distinctive beehive domes with their striped orange-and-black bands are the remnants of an ancient sandstone plateau. Wind and water have carved deep gorges and sheer-sided chasms, and in some sections the strange towers stand alone.

Bushwalking is the main activity around these parts, because any exploration into the Bungle Bungles must be done on foot. The park is 109 km (68 miles) north of Halls Creek and 250 km (155 miles) south of Kununurra.
Map ref: page 713 N7

Manning Gorge in the Kimberley—near Mount Barnett. The falls on the Upper Manning are at their best between May and July.

WINDJANA GORGE, TUNNEL CREEK AND GEIKIE GORGE NATIONAL PARKS

These three parks in the Kimberley are also known as the Devonian Reef National Parks, as the geology of this region provides an idea of life 350 million years ago, before the existence of reptiles and well before mammals evolved.

Much of the area was, at that time, covered by a vast inland sea, and in the warm shallow water there was an immense coral reef. At Windjana Gorge, Tunnel Creek and Geikie Gorge, floodwaters have, over millennia, deeply eroded the ranges and exposed layers of fossils and a cross-section of the limestone strata of the ancient reef. The best time to visit the area is between May and September, the Dry, when the days are clear and hot and the nights are cool.

Windjana Gorge
The Lennard River has cut through the limestone range to form a very large gorge. It is flooded during the Wet season, but in the Dry season, the river forms large pools and tall Leichhardt trees, native figs and paperbarks grow all along the banks. The area is a drawcard for birdwatchers as it is home to many species of birds, and freshwater crocodiles are often seen basking on the banks. Windjana is 145 km (90 miles) from Derby and 150 km (95 miles) from Fitzroy Crossing.
Map ref: page 712 G8

Aerial view of Wyndham Port, which today handles live cattle exports, plus raw sugar and molasses produced at Kununurra.

Tunnel Creek
This park preserves a cavern or tunnel 750 m (2461 feet) long, carved out of the limestone by water seeping through it over thousands of years. The tunnel height varies from 3–12 m (10–39 feet) and it is about 15 m (49 feet) wide. In one section the roof has fallen in, leaving an opening to the top of the range. Tunnel Creek is 180 km (112 miles) from Derby and 115 km (71 miles) from Fitzroy Crossing.
Map ref: page 713 H8

Domes and conical peaks of the Bungle Bungle Range in Purnululu National Park.

Geikie Gorge
Situated where two ranges—the Oscar and Geikie ranges—meet, this gorge was formed by the mighty Fitzroy River carving a canyon 30 m (98 feet) deep through the limestone. The Aboriginal people from this region operate a boat tour of Geikie Gorge, which gives visitors a unique perspective on the park, its plants and animals. The riverbanks are a wildlife sanctuary, and apart from a permitted area along the west bank, no one is allowed within 200 m (656 feet) of either bank. The park is 16 km (10 miles) from Fitzroy Crossing and around 280 km (174 miles) from the coastal town of Derby.
Map ref: page 713 J9

WYNDHAM

The northernmost town in Western Australia—3355 km (2083 miles) north of Perth—Wyndham sits beside the muddy grey waters of the Cambridge Gulf. It is the administrative centre for the East Kimberley Shire, and has a population of 1550, but has lost much of its importance to the 'new' town of Kununurra, 100 km (62 miles) to the south-east.

Phillip Parker King surveyed this coast in 1818, naming the great gulf that the town is located on, while the port came into exist-ence when gold was discovered at Halls Creek in 1886. The town also became an important outlet for the beef industry that grew up in the Kimberley, and a large jetty was built here in the 1890s to handle the ever-increasing cargo. A meatworks, which was started in 1919, closed down in 1985.

During World War II the town was bombed by the Japanese and today there are two main parts to it. The 'Old Port' is located close to the old meatworks and marks the site of the original town before the bombing, while the newer part of town is 5 km (3 miles) away on slightly higher ground.

One of the best views possible, which offers a fine panorama of the gulf and the five rivers that flow into it, is seen from the top of the Bastion at Five Rivers Lookout. Just south of town is the Parry Lagoons Nature Reserve, one of the finest bird habitats and bird-watching areas in the State. Other attractions include Moochalabra Dam and the nearby Aboriginal art sites, the pioneer cemeteries, both close to town, the Prison Tree and the Grotto. The local museum and tourist information centre is located down at the Old Port. Annual events held in the town include the Wyndham Cup Horse Race, which is on during August.
Map ref: page 713 M4

THE PILBARA

Geologically, the Pilbara is an ancient area. The rock mass of the Western Plateau, jutting out into the Indian Ocean, appears to have been stable for 600 million years. The north-west coast offers great fishing and the Ningaloo Marine Park, south of Exmouth, attracts divers from all over the world. Heading further inland, spectacular coloured rocky ranges are laced with gorges and rock pools.

Perth

While the Pilbara has supported sheep and cattle, mining is its mainstay. The port at Dampier was built in 1966 to shift huge amounts of iron ore being extracted from the region. When Dampier became too large, Hamersley Iron founded the town of Karratha, now the largest town in the Pilbara. Roebourne, near Karratha, was first settled in 1866 and was an important centre at that time for the pastoral industry.

Inland from Roebourne is the Millstream-Chichester National Park. The land is mostly dry and inhospitable but the porous rock that lies beneath the bed of the Fortescue River absorbs the rain and this underground water feeds the pools of the Millstream oasis as well as the towns in the region.

Further inland, the Karijini National Park is situated between the mining centres of Wittenoom, Newman, Paraburdoo and Tom Price. Some of the gorges that are found in the northern section of this vast park support lush vegetation. When the sun can penetrate into the chasms, the rock walls here blaze red and purple. Elsewhere in the park's more desolate areas, spinifex is the dominant vegetation, and the rocks are red, black and brown.

North of Karijini is Port Hedland, which was originally a centre for the pastoral and pearling industries, but now an important port for the shipping of iron ore and salt. The historic pearling town of Broome is 604 km (375 miles) north-east of Port Hedland, along the Great Northern Highway. Broome's pearling heyday was in the early 1900s; now it is largely a tourist centre and a good base for exploring the beaches and Aboriginal communities of the Dampier Peninsula to the north. South-east of Port Hedland is the historic mining town of Marble Bar, named for a huge band of jasper, which is located about 5 km (3.1 miles) from the town.

OPPOSITE: An open cut mine at Tom Price. The town was named after Thomas Moore Price, vice-president of the US giant Kaiser Steel, and a major supporter of the development of the mineral resources of the Pilbara.

The jetty at Broome. While Broome is still involved with pearls, it now depends on other industries—beef cattle and tourism, primarily— for its economic viability.

REGIONAL FEATURE

The Coral Coast

Located on the western edge of the Pilbara, the Coral Coast is named after the spectacular fringing reefs that run parallel to the shoreline of the remote and rugged North West Cape Peninsula. Protected by the Ningaloo Marine Park, these coral systems are home to an extraordinary array of marine life and are regularly visited by the largest fish species in the world, the whale shark. Inland, the North West Cape Peninsula is crowned by the Cape Range, a long, low chain of limestone hills that conceals caves, canyons, and ancient marine fossils, and harbours a fascinating array of rare and intriguing wildlife.

History

The first recorded landing of a European on the Coral Coast occurred in 1618 when Captain Jacobz stepped ashore from his ship, the *Mauritius*. Other explorers passed this way soon afterwards, including Francisco Pelsaert, captain of the unfortunate *Batavia*, in 1619, but it wasn't until Lieutenant Phillip Parker King sailed these waters in 1818 that the coast was mapped with any degree of accuracy. Despite King's efforts, the jagged reefs continued to claim passing craft, belonging mainly to whalers and pearlers, and at least 30 shipwrecks were recorded.

Small numbers of pastoralists began to occupy land on the cape in the 1880s, and in 1912 the Vlamingh Head Lighthouse was constructed at the peninsula's northern tip. During World War II, Exmouth Gulf was used as a submarine refuelling base, and in the 1950s the Cape Range became the focus of a search for oil, which resulted in the construction of several roads. Overall, however, the region developed little until 1967, when the town of Exmouth was founded as a service centre for the US–Australia Harold E. Holt Naval Communication Base. More recently, tourism has become the mainstay of the local economy, encouraging the growth of visitor facilities at Exmouth in the north and Coral Bay in the south, and the coast's natural wonders now draw travellers from all over the world.

Ningaloo Marine Park

Ningaloo Marine Park encompasses 4000 sq km (1544 square miles) of ocean extending from the tip of North West Cape to Amherst Point, south of Coral Bay. Its major feature, Ningaloo Reef, is the second-largest coral reef in Australia, one of the planet's biggest fringing reefs, and one of only two reefs in the world located on a western coast. For most of its length, it runs parallel to the cape, about 1 km (0.6 miles) out to sea, but in places it lies just 100 m (330 feet) offshore, allowing even novice divers and snorkellers to experience its myriad wonders. These include 250 species of coral and more than 500 species of fish.

For divers the world over, however, the reef's main attraction is the chance to swim with whale sharks, the largest fish in the sea. Groups of up to 12 of these enormous but harmless creatures, each measuring up to 12 m (40 feet) in length, visit the reef almost daily between March and June to feed on plankton. Scuba divers and snorkellers can not only view the animals at close quarters but also swim alongside them as they float majestically across the reefs. This is a truly awe-inspiring experience and Ningaloo is the only place on Earth where such an encounter is virtually guaranteed.

Most of the fish species found on Ningaloo Reef belong to a small number of families including the damselfish, butterflyfish, wrasses, angelfish and parrotfish.

Between May and November, enormous manta rays also visit the reef to feed on plankton, and humpback whales frequent the park's waters between June and November before returning to the Antarctic for the summer breeding season. Ningaloo is also home to significant populations of dugongs and green, hawksbill and loggerhead turtles, with hundreds of turtles coming ashore to lay eggs at places like Turquoise Bay between October and February.

Cape Range National Park

Founded in 1969, Cape Range National Park covers 50,581 ha (124,985 acres) on the western side of the North West Cape Peninsula. Encompassing rocky plateaus and canyons, spinifex plains, coastal dunes and beautiful beaches, the park is home to a fascinating range of wildlife. Notable mammals include red kangaroos and euros (also known as hill wallaroos) and, in more rugged areas, significant populations of rare black-striped rock-wallabies. More than 154 species of birds have also been recorded here.

A road runs down the western side of the national park from Exmouth to Coral Bay, while the Shothole Canyon and Charles Knife roads provide access to the eastern side. The best place to begin a visit is at the Milyering Information Centre, just inside the northern boundary on the coastal road, where you can obtain information, trail maps and camping permits. Several excellent and picturesque camping

Vlamingh Head Lighthouse was staffed until 1967, when radio transmitters at the nearby Harold E. Holt naval base replaced the light as a warning system.

grounds are dotted along the coast, the largest of which is located in the most famous of the park's many gorges, Yardie Creek Gorge.

Walking tracks allow visitors to explore the varied landscapes and scout for wildlife. The most popular track leads 2 km (1.2 miles) inland along the northern side of Yardie Creek, a return trip of about an hour. In the early morning or evening, you may spy elusive black-striped rock-wallabies on the southern cliffs of the gorge. Look out too for birds of prey such as the white-bellied sea-eagle, brahminy kite, osprey and spotted harrier. The creek itself is a fascinating environment, being inhabited by both freshwater fish and saltwater species such as cod, stingrays, snovel-nose sharks and mullet. The saltwater species enter the creek when the mouth is open to the sea; when their return route is cut off they gradually acclimatise to the rising proportion of fresh water.

On the eastern side of Cape Range, the 7-km (4.4-mile) Lightfoot Trail is a beauty. Beginning at the end of Charles Knife Road and marked by rock cairns, it traverses rugged terrain and provides excellent views of the surrounding country; walkers should allow between two and three hours for the hike. Another trail of about 10 km (6.2 miles) leaves from the car park near the Thomas Carter Lookout and heads north to the picnic area at the end of the Shothole Canyon Road—a trip of about three hours.

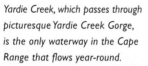

Yardie Creek, which passes through picturesque Yardie Creek Gorge, is the only waterway in the Cape Range that flows year-round.

Visitors can explore Yardie Creek by boat, too. Private boats without motors are permitted on the creek, and Yardie Creek Tours operate cruises on most days during the tourist season. At Mangrove Bay, a specially constructed hide allows visitors to observe wildlife frequenting the beach.

The Coral Coast Trek

This drive tour entails a circuit of the entire North West Cape Peninsula, taking in Exmouth Gulf, Cape Range National Park and the shores of Ningaloo Marine Park. It departs from the North West Coastal Highway at Minilya Roadhouse, 142 km (88 miles) north of Carnarvon. A 4WD vehicle is essential for the section south of Yardie Creek. Travellers should allow at least three days for the round trip.

At the signposted turn-off located 8 km (5 miles) north of the roadhouse, turn left in the direction of Exmouth. The road from here to Exmouth is good and for most of the way traverses rolling sandplains covered with spinifex, native grasses, bluebush and hundreds of other plant species.

Lyndon River, 26 km (16 miles) north of the road junction, is forded via a low causeway that is sometimes flooded. The river is a fairly short stretch of water, but it does attract birdlife and other animals. You cross the Tropic of Capricorn 12 km (7.5 miles)

further on, then reach the road to Coral Bay, 86 km (53 miles) north of Minilya. Keep heading north past the turn-off to Ningaloo Homestead, 39 km (24 miles) away. Looking east from here, you should be able to see the low peaks of the Giralia Range.

Not long after passing the Burkett Road junction, 138 km (86 miles) from Minilya, you will have your first views of Exmouth Gulf, and the Cape Range to the left. After another 64 km (40 miles), you reach the turn-off to the Charles Knife Road. Built in the 1950s by oil exploration teams and fairly well maintained, the track climbs along a razorback ridge to an old wellhead near the top of the range. Along the way, you have excellent views back to the coast and across the rugged gorge country. A second road leading into the range, the Shothole Canyon Road, branches off the main highway 7 km (4.4 miles) further north, passing through a steep-sided canyon before arriving at a pleasant picnic spot.

Continuing north, the main highway runs parallel to the sparkling blue waters of Exmouth Gulf, and numerous sidetracks lead down to pristine beaches. Exmouth is located 225 km (140 miles) from Minilya and offers a wide range of services. It's also a good place to book a diving trip or charter a fishing boat.

TO YARDIE CREEK

Heading north from Exmouth, turn left at the 11-km (7-mile) mark onto the road signposted as the 'Cape Range Tourist Way/Yardie Creek Road'. Less than 16 km (10 miles) from Exmouth, a good dirt road heads east to the coast, providing access to a number of attractive beaches, the most popular of which is the Mildura Wreck beach, the northernmost point on North West Cape. The remains of the *Mildura*, which ran aground in 1907 while carrying cattle from the Kimberley, sit a short distance offshore.

About 2 km (1.2 miles) past the Cape Range–Yardie Creek junction, or 18 km (11 miles) from Exmouth, the pleasant Lighthouse Caravan Park is located on the left-hand side of the road. Less than 1 km (0.6 miles) further on, a road leads off to the left up the hill to the Vlamingh Head Lighthouse, from where you can fine views of the coastline.

The rugged Cape Range rises to 314 m (1030 feet).

Returning to the main road and heading south, you come to the turn-off for Yardie Creek Homestead, 33 km (21 miles) from Exmouth, which offers accommodation, meals and basic supplies. The entrance to Cape Range National Park is 40 km (25 miles) from Exmouth and the visitor centre is at Milyering, 11 km (7 miles) beyond the park entrance. At Mandu Mandu, some 14 km (9 miles) south of the visitor centre, the fringing reef is so close to shore that it is almost on the beach. Yardie Creek, the most visited site in the park, is further south, 87 km (54 miles) from Exmouth.

YARDIE CREEK TO CORAL BAY

Heading south from Yardie Creek, you exit the park after 8 km (5 miles). About 22 km (14 miles) further on, you reach a track that leads 12 km (7.5 miles) west to Point Edgar and the ruins of the old whaling station at Norwegian Bay. The station operated between 1913 and 1929 and then again between 1949 and 1957, harvesting mainly humpback whales. The Norwegian Bay track continues along the coast, then crosses a region of very mobile sand dunes before rejoining the main access track.

From the junction, it is another 15 km (9 miles) through sand dunes to Ningaloo Station shearing shed. About 1 km (0.6 miles) south of the shed, you meet a station track. Turn left here for Coral Bay (right leads to Ningaloo Homestead). The track skirts a few sand ridges before passing through a gate and continuing east. At the junction about 8 km (5 miles) from the shearing shed, take the track that veers south and is signposted 'Coral Bay 54 km'. Approximately 41 km (26 miles) from the shearing shed, you'll see a bay and a pleasant campsite. This is probably the best camping spot between Ningaloo Homestead and Coral Bay.

About 57 km (35 miles) from the Ningaloo shearing shed, you'll see Cardabia Homestead to the right; just past this point you meet a major track. Less than 2 km (1.2 miles) further on, you are back on the bitumen. Turn right for Coral Bay and after 5 km (3 miles) of blacktop you'll be in the heart of this small town, 108 km (67 miles) from Yardie Creek and a total of 195 km (121 miles) from Exmouth. From here, you can return to the North West Coastal Highway and Minilya Roadhouse.

The beaches north of Ningaloo Homestead are ideal for snorkelling, with warm, shallow waters, and reefs located just offshore.

Places in
THE PILBARA

BROOME

This subtropical town 2356 km (1463 miles) north of Perth has a fascinating history, and a cosmopolitan feel which originates from its early pearling days. Although pearling still plays an important role in Broome's economy, the town is now one of Western Australia's most popular tourist destinations, with the beautiful Cable Beach a major drawcard. Broome's population is 11,150.

Aboriginal people lived along this coast for thousands of years,

Broome's streets reflect its Japanese, Malay and Chinese pearling heritage.

and the Malays and Macassans sailed the coastline well before the coming of Europeans; the first European to visit was William Dampier, in 1688. In 1821 the British sent Phillip Parker King to survey the coast; he named Roebuck Bay. By the 1870s pearling was a major activity along the Kimberley coast, with about 80 boats working from Cossack, near Roebourne, and by 1880 a settlement had grown up right near the mouth of Dampier Creek. In 1883 the township of Broome was officially proclaimed. Pastoralists soon arrived, opening up the inland. Then in 1889 Broome was connected to the Overland Telegraph line from the south. Also, a submarine telegraph cable was laid between Broome and Banjawangie in Indonesia.

Between 1900 and 1914 Broome was at its peak. World War I saw the trade in pearl shell suspended and, sadly, the town never again rose to its prewar heights, although pearling did resume after the war. With the demise of markets for mother-of-pearl shell after World War II, the cultured pearl industry was born and it still thrives today.

There are plenty of things to see and do in Broome. A visit to the Japanese and Pioneer Cemeteries and the Historical Society Museum gives an insight into the harsh life people endured in the town's early days. Chinatown is a veritable hive of business, centred on the pearling industry, and this area features a number of fine old buildings and also the Sun Pictures movie house, possibly the world's oldest open-air picture garden. Visitors can wander through the pearl emporiums, then drive out to the Willie Creek Pearl Farm and learn all about how the cultured pearls are grown.

Cable Beach, which was named after the submarine cable, has miles of clean white sand, turquoise blue sea, and safe swimming. Vehicles

Gantheaume Point, just south of Broome. Dinosaur footprints were discovered here in 1935.

are permitted to drive along the beach north of the boat ramp— this is also a nude bathing area. Nearby is the Malcolm Douglas Crocodile Park, where visitors can see mature crocodiles and other reptiles at close quarters and in their natural habitat.

Anglers will find plenty of places to drop a line here, including Crab Creek, Barred Creek, Willie Creek, Fisherman's Bend and Prices Point. Gamefishing is also becoming a major attraction; the Sailfish Fly Rod Challenge is held in June, and the Broome Gamefish Tournament competition is in July—both are 'tag and release' events.

Just outside town is the Broome Bird Observatory. This is a research base and is one of the world's top wader-bird-viewing locations and it is certainly worth visiting. Guided tours and ornithological courses are run here and there are many beach, mangrove, plain and bushland excursions and walks. Accommodation as well as caravan/camping facilities are also available.

The Dampier Peninsula, north of Broome, features a great coastline, secluded bays, spectacular red pindan cliffs (especially during the warm glow of early evening light), and some great fishing, as well as a good variety of bird and animal life. Access is pretty good, but it is 4WD country. A number of Aboriginal communities that live on the Peninsula have opened their doors to travellers, as have one or two cattle stations.

There are several special events held in Broome, including the O-Bon Festival in August while the Shinju Matsuri (Festival of the Pearl) is in August/ September. Accommodation is always short at this time of year, so book ahead.

Map ref: page 715 N1

Roebuck Bay near Broome was named after Dampier's ship—he failed to find freshwater here.

CORAL BAY

This small village (population 300), situated 1145 km (711 miles) north of Perth on the 'Coral Coast' south of Exmouth and the Cape Range National Park, is on the edge of the Ningaloo Marine Park.

The park protects the reef of the same name, the longest coral reef in Western Australia, and the second longest in Australia after Queensland's Great Barrier Reef. However, the Ningaloo reef is much closer to shore and more readily accessible, so it is a place to be enjoyed by the whole family.

Whether you are into fishing from shore or boat, diving, swimming or just relaxing, this place has it all. Coral Bay is the southern gateway to the park, and it has a wide range of accommodation and facilities are located here, all within an easy walk of the beach.

Children and adults can swim among a mass of tropical fish just metres from the shore at Coral Bay, while the more adventurous can head off on a snorkel or scuba dive with the local dive operator. If you are in the area at the right time of the year you might even get the chance to snorkel with the giant but harmless whale sharks. The sailing and boating are fantastic, and the well-equipped angler and diver have much of the coast to explore; a number of sanctuaries have been established along the coast and for the most part these

exclude any fishing. Anglers and divers should check with the local tourist outlet or ask the Fisheries Department for bag limits and for areas where you can fish and dive.
Map ref: page 714 B9

COSSACK

Located at the mouth of the Harding River, 1587 km (986 miles) north of Perth, Cossack has had a chequered past since it was founded in 1863—it was then called Tien Tien, after the boat that landed the first settlers there. It soon became the major port for the area and was the base for a large pearling fleet that operated from the port. It was named Cossack in 1873, after the warship of the same name which brought the governor of the day to the port for a visit.

During the late 1880s the port was busy, as gold prospectors went through the area to the new, rich finds of the Pilbara. Many of the town's fine buildings date from this time, but over the following decade the town went into decline as the port silted up and the growing demand for port facilities saw nearby Port Sampson take over as the major town in the region.

By the 1930s less than a dozen buildings remained in Cossack and another 20 years later the town was abandoned—it population today is a tiny 3. In 1979 restoration work was begun, and in the early 1990s the Heritage Council of Western

Australia took over control of the town, continuing with extensive restoration work to the present day.

Apart from the faithfully restored buildings in the town there is a museum with a wonderful display of early Cossack memorabilia, an art gallery, home to the annual art awards, tearooms located in the old Customs House, and a large stone warehouse, which now has on display a selection of Aboriginal art and local products.

A wide safe beach will win over the children, and there is good fishing from the wharf, along the beaches or among the mangroves in the river. You can expect to catch barra, mangrove jack, bream, threadfin salmon and mackerel. Blue swimmer and mud crabs can also be also found along the shoreline. The annual Cossack Art Ball and Art Award both take place every year in July.
Map ref: page 714 F5

DAMPIER

The port of Dampier, 1573 km (977 miles) north of Perth is the focus of much of the activity in the north-west, including the massive North-West Shelf Project, situated on the nearby Burrup Peninsula. The port really got its start when

*Red kangaroo
(Macropus giganteus)*

Hamersley Iron built the ore-loading facility in 1966. Today it has a population of 1900 and it is the biggest tonnage port in Australia—over 1500 ships load a total of over 60 million tonnes of iron ore here annually, from mines as far away as Tom Price, Paraburdoo, Brockman, and the new mine at Marandoo. Large quantities of salt, gas and condensate also pass through the port.

The town takes its name from the nearby Dampier Archipelago, a group of 42 islands first visited and named by William Dampier in 1688. Its major attractions and recreational activities centre around these islands, which have a fascinating history of shipwrecks, whaling, pearling and farming. Nowadays the islands are mainly reserves.

On the Burrup Peninsula there is one of the best collections of Aboriginal rock engravings—there could hardly be a more spectacular setting for this ancient art.

The diving around the coast is good, and the fishing fantastic. You can expect to catch a good range of fish, from big tuna, coral trout, red emperor, giant trevally, cobia and more. The annual Dampier Classic and Game Fishing Classic are held on the first weekend in August.
Map ref: page 714 F5

Dampier is a boating paradise; it is thought to have more boats per head than any other Australian town.

EXMOUTH

Exmouth lies 1272 km (790 miles) to the north of Perth, near the top end of North West Cape. This town did not actually come into being until 1967, when a support town was required for the US–Australian Naval Communication Base which was established nearby.

It was not the first time that the strategic position of the Cape had been used—during World War II, Exmouth Gulf, lying within the protection of the Cape, had been a resupply base for submarines operating in the Indian Ocean.

Exmouth (population 2600) is a fine base for fishing and diving enthusiasts, and there are a number of boat ramps close by, giving easy access to the waters of the Indian Ocean or to the calmer waters of Exmouth Gulf.

In the Gulf you can throw a line in for whiting and bream, offshore you can expect to catch queenfish, marlin tuna, and sailfish, and along the reefs you can look for snapper, cobia, barracuda, cod, mackerel, wahoo, spangled emperor and giant trevally. In the mangrove creeks along the shoreline of the Cape you are likely to find mangrove jack and tarwhine. Fishing is permitted in the waters of the Ningaloo Reef Marine Park, but there are bag limits and other regulations that apply to the area.

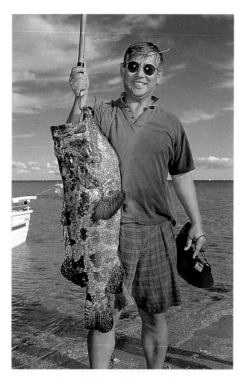

*A large potato cod (*Epinephelus tukula*) taken from the ocean near Exmouth.*

In more recent years the town and the nearby coral reefs of the Ningaloo Marine Park have become a worldwide mecca for divers wanting to swim with giant whale sharks. This is the only place in the world where it can be virtually guaranteed that a trip out for the day will result in a swim with these gentle plankton-eating giants. The peak time for the whale sharks is from March to June; the humpback whales begin to appear in the winter months, as do the huge schools of manta rays. The turtle nesting season, when hundreds of hawksbill, green and loggerhead turtles come up onto the beaches at night, runs from November to January.

There are a couple of major fishing competitions and these include the Billfish Bonanza in April and the Ultralight Tackle Gamefishing Competition in August, while other festivities include the Arts and Crafts Show in July and the Festival of Trees in November.
Map ref: page 714 C7

KARIJINI (HAMERSLEY RANGE) NATIONAL PARK

Karijini is part of the Hamersley Range in the Pilbara region, 310 km (193 miles) from Roebourne and 285 km (177 miles) from Port Hedland. The best time to visit is May–October; the Wet is a time of thunderstorms, cyclones, and temperatures over 40°C (104°F). The mountains and escarpments have been eroded to form a series of magnificent gorges and very deep, narrow chasms. This is rugged and ancient land—indeed the spectacular banded-iron formation of the gorge dates back more than 2500 million years. Wildflowers vary with the season and rainfall; in the cooler months you may see yellow flowering sennas and acacias, and purple mulla-mullas. The area is also rich in bird life and fauna.
Map ref: page 715 H9

KARLAMILYI (RUDALL RIVER) NATIONAL PARK

Situated 420 km (261 miles) east of Marble Bar in Western Australia's Great and Little Sandy Deserts, Karlamilyi National Park is about as remote and lonely as any spot in Australia. The Martu people have lived in this area for thousands of years. Two sizeable Aboriginal communities continue to live within the park boundaries, largely following their own traditions, with little outside influence. There are 28 registered Aboriginal sites, including rock art areas, in the park.

Proclaimed in 1977, the park, 156,459 ha (386,610 acres), took its English name from William Rudall, a government surveyor who explored this area between 1896 and 1898. Karlamilyi is little changed today.

This is strictly 4WD country—tracks in the park are unmaintained, corrugated, sandy and, in some sections, quite slow and rocky. If you want to walk in the park, be prepared—there are no marked trails. Do not walk alone and always carry water with you.

Much of the park is red sand dunes and spinifex—there are even some salt lake sections. Its real appeal is the breakaway country in the Broadhurst Range—very tall, colourful cliffs, valleys, sandstone and quartzite plateaus, eroded pinnacle shapes, and picturesque waterholes. The best of these is Desert Queens Baths, a series of rockpools cradled by tall, orange–red gorge walls.

Karijini National Park. Karijini is the Panyjima, Innawonga and the Kurrama peoples'—the traditional owners'—name for the area.

Bands of jasper—first thought to be marble—at Marble Bar. Jasper is a highly coloured cryptocrystalline variety of quartz.

MARBLE BAR

Marble Bar is famous as the hottest locality in Australia and during the 1920s recorded 160 days in a row over hundred degrees on the old Farenheit scale (38°C). The town is 1980 km (1230 miles) north of Perth and just over 200 km (124 miles) from Port Hedland—the last 58 km (36 miles) are un-sealed, but the road is still pretty good, most of the time.

Gold was discovered in the region in the 1890s but by the early 1900s the gold had petered out and the miners left. In 1936 there was another major find, and this was worked until 1955. Marble Bar shares with the goldfields town of Nullagine the distinction of being on 'Mad Man's Track', a frontier track which lured prospectors eager to find their fortune, so thousands headed this way during the boom days. Today, the town's population of 360 make a living from tin and manganese, and from the occasional tourists who come to this historic, remote settlement.

Worth seeing is the 'marble bar', really a band of jasper, across the Coongan River, about 5 km (3 miles) from town; also Chinaman's Pool, a popular swimming spot; and Coppins Gap, a little further out but also a good place to have a swim. In town there are a number of old stone buildings dating from the 1880s. The Iron-clad Hotel, named after the iron-clad battleships of the American Civil War, is worthy of some time as well. The Marble Bar Cup and Ball is usually held in June or July.
Map ref: page 715 J6

At the end of a slow, rough trail, about 18 km (11 miles) off the park's main track, is the camp site near the entrance to the gorge—allow around one-and-a-half hours each way. Access to the baths is via a relatively easy unmarked trail up the creek bed, around 1 km (0.6 mile) from the car park—about half an hour each way. Along the Rudall River, which generally flows only after cyclonic downpours, are several waterholes that make ideal camp sites—Tjingkula-tjatjarra ('Jarra') Pool, is one.

Access from the north is via the Telfer Gold Mine (Newcrest Mining)—you must get permission to use this road. From the south, travel northeast from Newman via the Tallawanna Track, which leads past the southern park boundary. Access into the Aboriginal communities is not encouraged. It is advisable to travel with a minimum of two vehicles in this area, and with radio contact. The nearest supplies are at Newman and Marble Bar—you will need to be totally self-sufficient for the entire return trip.
Map ref: page 715 N8

KARRATHA

The Pilbara's largest and also probably its best-serviced town, Karratha, is located 1553 km (964 miles) north of Perth and a short distance off the North West Coastal Highway, and has a large selection of facilities, accommodation and there are plenty of interesting things to see and to do here.

Only 20 km (12 miles) outside of Karratha is the major Western Australian port of Dampier and its massive ore-loading facilities. The name 'Karratha' derives from a word in a local Aboriginal language that means 'good country', and it was the name of the first station property in the area, which was taken up in the 1860s.

The present-day town was established by Hamersley Iron Pty Ltd when Dampier outgrew its available land, and with the continual development that has been occurring in the area, the town is sure to grow even bigger. Its current population is 8350. While Karratha is mainly used by visitors as a base for exploring the surrounding area, as

well as the coast and the islands, there are also many inland delights, such as the Millstream–Chichester National Park and also the gorges found around Wittenoom.

The Karratha Festival is held on the second weekend each year in June, and the FeNaCING Weekend Festival is held on the first weekend in August.
Map ref: page 714 F5

Cleaverville, north of Karratha, is popular with 4WD and fishing holidaymakers.

MILLSTREAM–CHICHESTER NATIONAL PARK

Millstream is an oasis of green in this park of the central Pilbara. In the north is the Chichester Range, with its rocky peaks, gorges and hidden rock pools, sloping gradually down to the plains of the Fortescue River; then the land rises again to the bulk of the Hamersley Range. The Millstream oasis on the Fortescue River is a series of deep spring-fed pools surrounded by palm trees and eucalypts. Most plants here flower after the winter rains, so the best wildflower display is June to August. The Millstream palm is unique to this area, and the date palms here were planted in the nineteenth century by Afghan camel drivers. A variety of birds and mammals can also be seen. Activities at Millstream include swimming in waterholes at Deep Reach and Crossing Pool, and boating (no power boats are allowed).

Map ref: page 714 F6

Deep Reach Cliffs, in Millstream–Chichester National Park. The traditional owners of this region are the Yinjibarndi people.

NEWMAN

Located in the heart of the Pilbara, 1180 km (733 miles) north of Perth, Newman is a modern mining town, with a population of 2000, built to service the workers and their families who live close to Mount Whaleback, the largest single open-cut iron ore mine in the world. It is the administrative centre of the East Pilbara Shire—the largest shire in Australia, and the only shire to completely split

Remote bush road between Newman and Karlamilyi (Rudall River) National Park.

the State, with an area bigger than the State of Victoria, or of Italy.

Being such an important centre it has a large range of facilities and everything a traveller could require. The town takes its name from the nearby Mount Newman, which was named in 1896 after the local explorer, Aubrey Newman. In 1957 a massive iron ore deposit was discovered at Mount Whaleback. Things to see around town include the BHP Iron Ore Silver Jubilee

Museum Gallery, with its magnificent leadlight window depicting the Pilbara landscape, and also the Mining and Pastoral Museum. A tour of the local mining operation is sure to impress by its sheer size and the massive equipment being used. Ophthalmia Dam, 15 km (9 miles) north of town, supplies the town with water, and has a pleasant picnic area on its banks, and Radio Hill Lookout takes in expansive views of the whole region as well as the town site.

The Newman Waterhole Circuit is a very pleasant 4WD day trip that takes in a number of waterholes and also some Aboriginal art sites. You will be surprised at the diversity of bird life and plants on this trip, as well as by the sheer grandeur of the gorges and waterholes. Maps are available from the local tourist centre.

Karijini National Park, to the north-west of the town, takes in a large area of rugged range and gorge country that is well worth exploring. Newman is also a jumping-off point for the remote Karlamilyi (Rudall River) National Park and the Canning Stock Route, but both areas are the domain of the well-equipped and experienced four-wheel driver.

Map ref: page 715 J9

ONSLOW

The original town site for Onslow was established in 1885, at the former mouth of the Ashburton River, as a port for the surrounding sheep stations and also as a centre to supply goods and services to the pearling and mining industries. A deeper port with better facilities was needed, however, and most of the buildings, along with the residents, were moved during 1925 to the new town site along the coast at Beadon Bay, 1404 km (872 miles) north of Perth.

The vestiges of the old town site still remain as a stark reminder of yesteryear. Although it is small (the town's population is 800) and isolated, and set in a harsh climate, Onslow is a very green town, with plenty of shady trees. Mining and pastoral properties of sheep and cattle are the town's lifeblood, yet tourism is also beginning to play an important role.

Onslow has had its share of historic events and misfortunes. Cyclones have devastated the town on numerous occasions, forcing the closure of the port in 1963, and during World War II its airfield was bombed by the Japanese. For a look back into the town's history, visit the Shell Museum and the

Onslow Goods Shed Museum. There are also some excellent fishing opportunities both along the coast and offshore, with the most popular spots being Beadon Creek and Four Mile Creek, where you can fish for mangrove jack, bream and estuary cod.
Map ref: page 714 D7

PORT HEDLAND

Port Hedland is situated 1779 km (1105 miles) north of Perth and it was originally just a quiet country town. The first settlers here took up land for cattle grazing in 1863. Times have certainly changed here, though, and the Port Hedland of today (population 15,000) is a very busy administrative centre and port, servicing not only the mining community but also the surrounding cattle stations.

Originally named Mangrove Harbour in 1863, the port became a busy base and thoroughfare for pearling luggers in the 1870s, and then the gold prospectors, when colour was found at Marble Bar. The town site was not officially gazetted until 1896, and its first jetty was built a few years later. A second jetty was completed in 1911, and a rail link between Port Hedland and Marble Bar was also built to help with the movement of people and goods.

While the extraction of tin, gold, copper and manganese over the years brought prosperity to the region, it was the discovery of the astounding rich body of iron ore in the 1960s in the hinterland that led to the huge development of Port Hedland and its surrounds. The accompanying explosion in population required the building of a new satellite city—South Hedland; a deep-water port was also needed as the world's biggest ore carriers constantly use the port.

Much of what relates to mining here is on a really massive scale: the machinery is huge, and the BHP Iron Ore Railroad carries the world's longest regularly scheduled trains, bringing the ore from outlying mining sites into the port.

No visit to Port Hedland would be complete without a tour of the BHP iron ore facilities at Nelson Point. Another important mineral extracted from the land is salt, and the large expanses of white conical towers waiting for shipment overseas stand out starkly against the barren red landscape.

Port Hedland has four Heritage Trails. These trails take visitors past many of the town's historical landmarks, giving an insight into its early days. Other notable relics are the Pioneers and Pearlers Cemetery, the Don Rhodes Mining Museum, the Police Station and Jail (1903), the Court House (1900), Olde St Matthews Church Art Gallery and Exhibition Centre, Pretty Pool and the Redbank

Bridge Lookout. Day outings from Port Hedland, for those with a 4WD vehicle, can lead to such attractions as the Ord Ranges, Poonthune Pool and Whim Creek, which is the site of one of the oldest pubs in the Pilbara. Extended forays that are worth considering include trips to Marble Bar and Nullagine, the Newman Waterhole Circuit, Millstream–Chichester National Park, Karijini National Park and also Eighty Mile Beach.

Some well-known but isolated fishing and camping spots are accessible by 4WD, such as Tichilla, Pardoo Station, Twelve Mile Creek and Cape Keraudren.

Closer to Port Hedland, the harbour is an excellent fishing area, with chances of landing black jewfish and Spanish mackerel, while Spoil Bank, a sand spit just west of the jetty, is the spot for threadfin salmon. Those with a boat will find endless places to fish, not only offshore, but along the mangrove-lined coast, where you can catch queenfish and barramundi; the mangrove crabs here are plentiful, and reputed to be the biggest in Australia. If you find yourself in the region be-

The spectacular Hamersley Ranges stretch for 400 km (248 miles) through the Pilbara region.

tween September and April, you may see flatback turtles nesting on the town beaches; if you arrive here between June and October, you may see the humpback whales pass by on their annual migration.

This busy community runs several events during the year, including Heritage Week in April, the Music Festival in September, while the Beerfest and the Port Hedland Art Awards are both in October.
Map ref: page 715 H5

Port Hedland's solar salt industry, begun in 1965, has production capacity of more than 3 million tonnes (3.3 m tons) per year.

Wittenoom gorge walls are only a short drive from the old town centre.

ROEBOURNE

Located on the North West Coastal Highway right at the junction of the road to Wickham, Cossack and Point Samson, 1577 km (979 miles) north of Perth, Roebourne can boast of being the oldest town on the north-west coast. Named after the State's first surveyor-general, John Roe, the town was settled in 1866, the area having been explored just five years earlier.

Many pioneers took up pastoral leases in the area and the town became the administrative centre for the region until the railway line was built between Marble Bar and Port Hedland. With the building of the railway, the town declined, until the 1960s, when the iron-ore boom ensured its future. Its population today is 1695.

A walk or drive around the town reveals many old buildings dating from the 1880s, with the old jail now the town's tourist bureau and museum. The 52 km (32 miles) Emma Withnell Heritage Trail commences in the heart of Roebourne and takes travellers out to historic Cossack, on to Wickham —built during the 1970s for the ever-expanding workforce of the iron-ore industry—and then to Point Samson, the old port for the area and a tranquil seaside town with excellent beaches and good fishing. The annual events in town include the Roebourne Royal Show in June, and the Roebourne Cup and Ball in July.
Map ref: page 714 F6

SANDFIRE

A small oasis on the long run north from Port Hedland to Broome and the Kimberley—and 2070 km (1285 miles) north of Perth— Sandfire originated in the 1970s when a fuel truck broke down here and suddenly found itself dispensing petrol to passing motorists. It was a lonely and hard life for much of the time, but this small haven (population 20) is still an important one for travellers. It can provide all the basic requirements of travellers as well as a cold drink, meals and accommodation.

Access to the Eighty Mile Beach is possible near here, and there is a small caravan and camping park just a little further south, at the Nallal Downs homestead. The beach is a good fishing spot and a well-known locality for the shells that are washed up on the beach in incredible numbers. Further north, about 160 km (99 miles) south of Broome, is Port Smith, which also has a camping and caravan park.
Map ref: page 715 L4

TOM PRICE

The town of Tom Price is 1632 km (1013 miles) north of Perth and it was built at the base of Mount Nameless after the discovery of the huge iron deposit at nearby Mount Tom Price in the 1960s; it takes its name from a minerals expert and surveyor for the US-based Kaiser Steel Corporation who was an enthusiastic supporter of the development of the iron ore potential of the Pilbara. This discovery, of what is probably the largest iron ore body ever found, was the trigger for the establishment of Hamersley Iron Pty Ltd, and for the construction of the mine, the port of Dampier and the railway between the two towns.

The town has a population of 3560, and is now the administrative centre for the surrounding Ashburton Shire. It is also close to the gorges and rugged ranges of Karijini National Park, and because of the natural attractions of the area and the vast mine workings, it is a popular stopover for visitors travelling through the Pilbara. Annual events here include the Tom Price Nameless Festival in August.
Map ref: page 714 G8

WITTENOOM

Wittenoom lies about 1660 km (1030 miles) north of Perth. This little town has refused to die completely, even though it has been officially abandoned and declared uninhabitable—its population is now only 25. It was declared uninhabitable because of the blue asbestos, which was mined here from the 1930s through to 1966, when the mines closed for economic reasons. The health hazards of this mineral, an insidious cancer caused by the asbestos fibres that easily float through the air when disturbed—and then into people's lungs—are quite well known.

The town is located quite close to some magnificent gorges which are readily accessible to normal vehicles; a 4WD will give access to others. Many of the gorges have magnificent waterfalls when the rivers flow after heavy rain. Fortescue Falls are especially noteworthy. The attractions of the town itself include the original town site and the natural pool—called Town Pool—in Wittenoom Gorge, the old asbestos mine located in Vampire Gorge, and the vast Karijini National Park. A road from the old town leads south into the park and another gorge, Hancock Gorge. The Fortescue River, which can be reached by a good dirt road north of the town, has many fine waterholes and patches of palm and paperbark forests.
Map ref: page 715 H8

Wittenoom Gorge is famous for Tiger Eye, a gemstone with 'stripes' of brown, yellow and red.

Perth City Centre

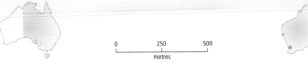

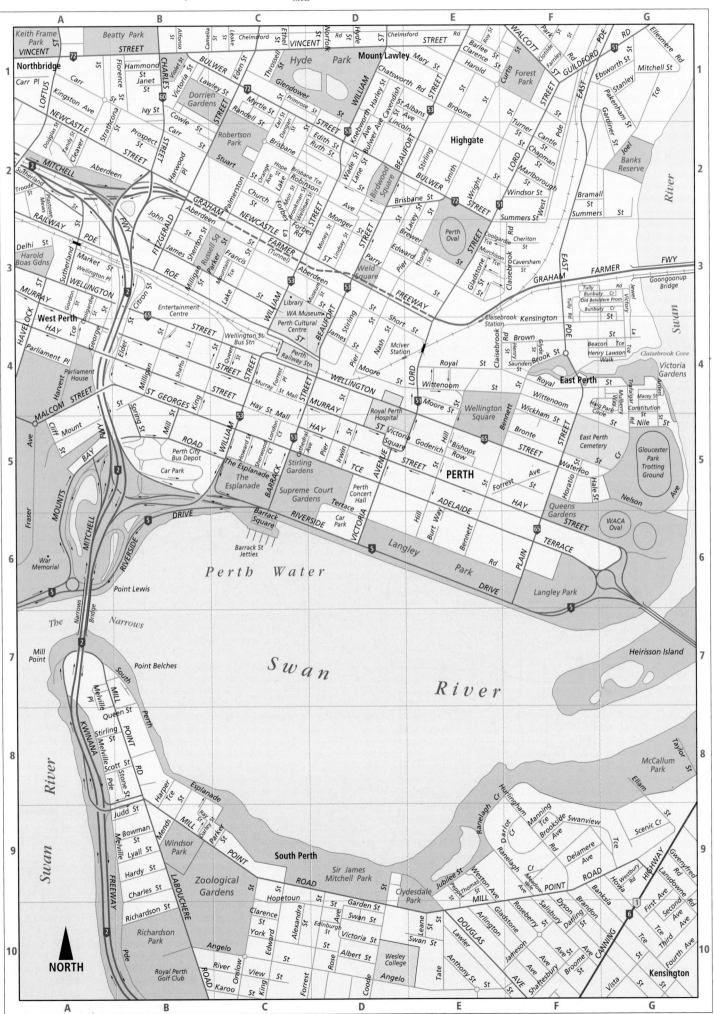

Perth Throughroads

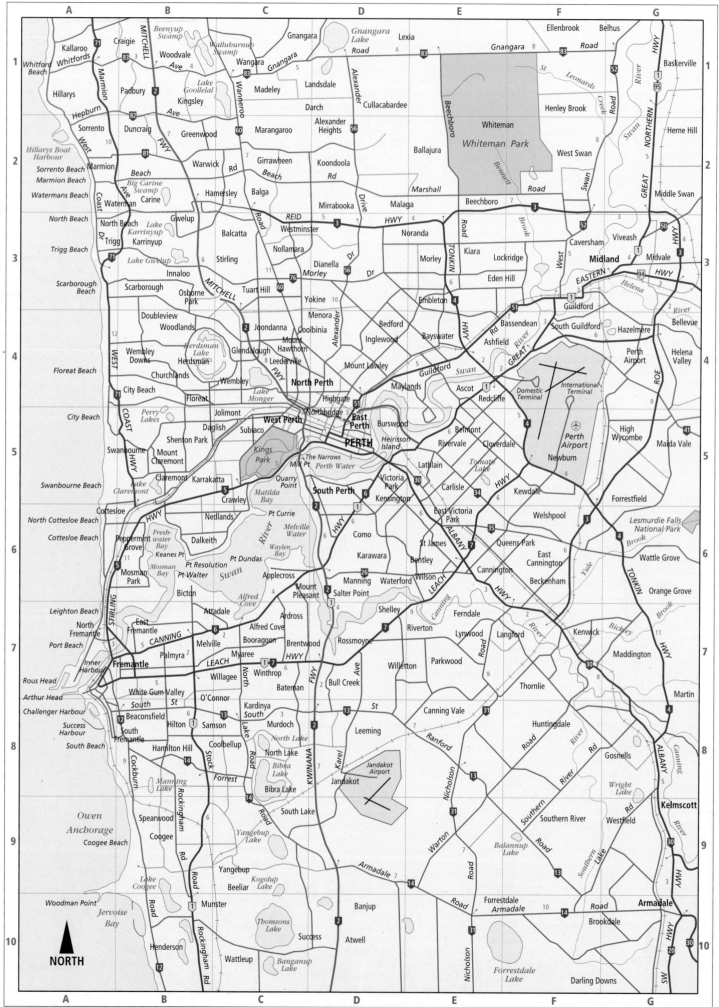

NORTH

Perth and Surrounding Areas

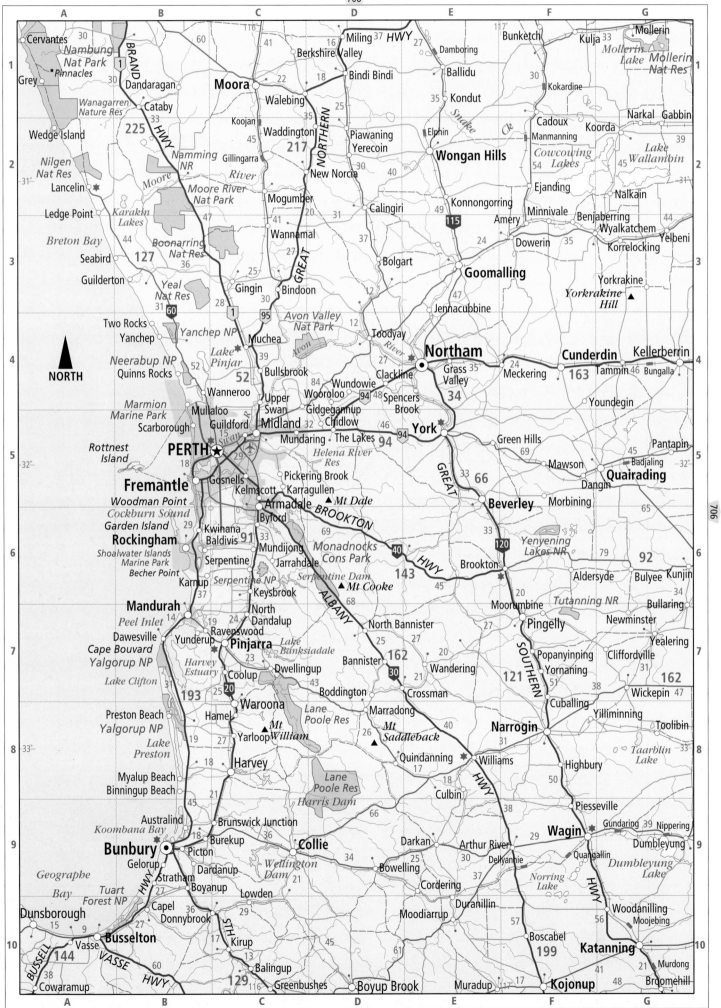

WESTERN AUSTRALIA

South-West Western Australia

6

BARREN ROCK

Known Barren Reef
CILT MANNAR

GN 78 G

1 9 0 Km

94 km?

SIA DWEEP D
u = inhabited

LR 36 IS
12 Atoll
3 reef
5 banks

largest Kutch
17 Omile
735 Om?
23 N 69 E

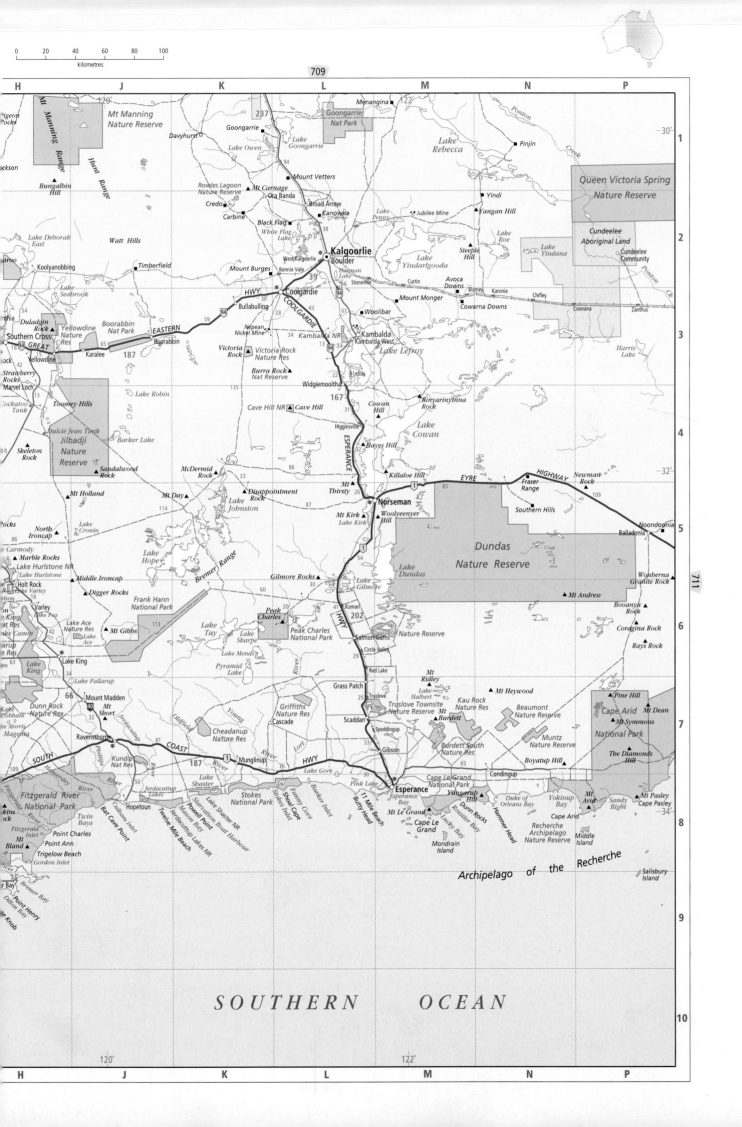

kilometres

0 20 40 60 80 100

H   J   K   L   M   N   P

WESTERN AUSTRALIA

Mt Manning
Nature Reserve

Mt Manning Range

Hunt Range

Watt Hills

Bungalbin Hill

Lake Deborah East

Koolyanobbing

Lake Seabrook

Timberfield

Duladgin Rock

Southern Cross

Yellowdine
Nature Res

GREAT

Yellowdine

Karalee

Boorabbin Nat Park

EASTERN

Boorabbin

187

HWY

Bullabulling

Coolgardie

COOLGARDIE

Strawberry Rocks

Marvel Loch

Cockatoo Tank

Toomey Hills

Lake Robin

Dulcie Jean Tank

Jilbadji
Nature
Reserve

Barker Lake

Sandalwood Rock

Skeleton Rock

McDermid Rock

Mt Day

Disappointment Rock

Lake Johnston

Mt Holland

North Ironcap

Lake Cronin

Carmody

Marble Rocks

Lake Hurlstone NR

Lake Hurlstone

Middle Ironcap

Digger Rocks

Holt Rock

Lake Varley

Varley

Lake Fox

Lake Ace
Nature Res

Lake Ace

Mt Gibbs

Frank Hann
National Park

Bremer Range

Lake Hope

Lake Tay

Lake Sharpe

Lake Mends

Peak Charles

Peak Charles
National Park

Lake
King

Lake King

Lake Pallarup

Mount Madden

Mt Short

Ravensthorpe

Dunn Rock
Nature Res

Pyramid Lake

Young River

Oldfield River

Griffiths
Nature Res

Cascade

Cheadanup
Nature Res

SOUTH

COAST

Munglinup

187

HWY

Kundip
Nat Res

Phillips River

Jerdacuttup

Lake Gore

Lake Shaster

Lake Shaster NR

Stokes
National Park

Hopetoun

Jerdacuttup Lakes

Jerdacuttup Lakes NR

Powell Point

Mason Bay

Twelve Mile Beach

Culham Inlet

Fitzgerald River
National Park

Point Charles

Point Ann

Trigelow Beach

Gordon Inlet

Bremer Bay

Point Henry

Twin Bays

Bat Cave Point

Starvation Boat Harbour

Stokes Inlet

Fanny Cove

Shoal Cape

Barker Inlet

SOUTHERN   OCEAN

Goongarrie

Davyhurst

Lake Owen

Lake Goongarrie

94

Rowles Lagoon
Nature Reserve

Mt Carnage

Ora Banda

Credo

Carbine

Black Flag

White Flag Lake

Mount Vetters

Broad Arrow

Kanowna

Kalgoorlie

Boulder

West Kalgoorlie

Mount Burges

Bonnie Vale

39

Hannan Lake

Coolgardie

30

59

94

28

43

Nepean
Nickel Mine

34

Victoria Rock

Victoria Rock
Nature Res

Burra Rock
Nat Reserve

135

Cave Hill NR

Cave Hill

Kambalda NR

Kambalda

Kambalda West

13

94

23

Lefroy

Widgiemooltha

22

167

31

Higginsville

ESPERANCE

Hayes Hill

32

Mt Thirsty

26

Norseman

Mt Kirk

Lake Kirk

Woolyeenyer Hill

1

54

Gilmore Rocks

Lake Gilmore

60

20

Kumarl

41

HWY

202

Salmon Gums

Circle Valley

29

Red Lake

Grass Patch

25

Truslove

Scaddan

Speddingup

53

Gibson

76

River

Lort River

30

65

Pink Lake

Esperance

Esperance Bay

11 Mile Beach

Burty Head

Mt Le Grand

Cape Le Grand

Cape Le Grand
National Park

Yungarup Hill

Dunn Rocks

Rossiter Bay

Lucky Bay

Mondrain Island

Duke of
Orleans Bay

Hammer Head

Recherche
Archipelago
Nature Reserve

Middle Island

Archipelago   of   the   Recherche

Salisbury Island

Menangina

Goongarrie
Nat Park

Lake Rebecca

Pinjin

Queen Victoria Spring
Nature Reserve

Jubilee Mine

Yindi

Yangan Hill

Cundeelee
Aboriginal Land

Cundeelee
Community

Lake Penny

Steeple Hill

Lake Roe

Lake Yindana

Lake Yindarlgooda

Curtin

Stoneville

Mount Monger

Avoca Downs

Blamey

Karonie

Cowarna Downs

Chifley

Coonana

Zanthus

Woolibar

61

Kambalda

Lake Lefroy

Harris Lake

Biryarinytinna Rock

Cowan Hill

Lake Cowan

Killaloe Hill

EYRE

HIGHWAY

Fraser Range

Newman Rock

Southern Hills

109

Noondoonia

Balladonia

Wonberna
Granite Rock

Dundas
Nature Reserve

Mt Andrew

Booanya Rock

Coragina Rock

Rays Rock

Mt Ridley

Lake Halbert

Mt Heywood

Kau Rock
Nature Res

Pine Hill

Cape Arid

Mt Dean

Mt Symmons

Mt Burdett

Truslove Townsite
Nature Reserve

Beaumont
Nature Reserve

Muntz
Nature Reserve

Cape Arid
National Park

The Diamonds Hill

Burdett South
Nature Res

Boyatup Hill

Condingup

Mt Arid

Sandy Bight

Mt Pasley

Cape Pasley

Yokinup Bay

Cape Arid

Central-West Western Australia

WESTERN
AUSTRALIA

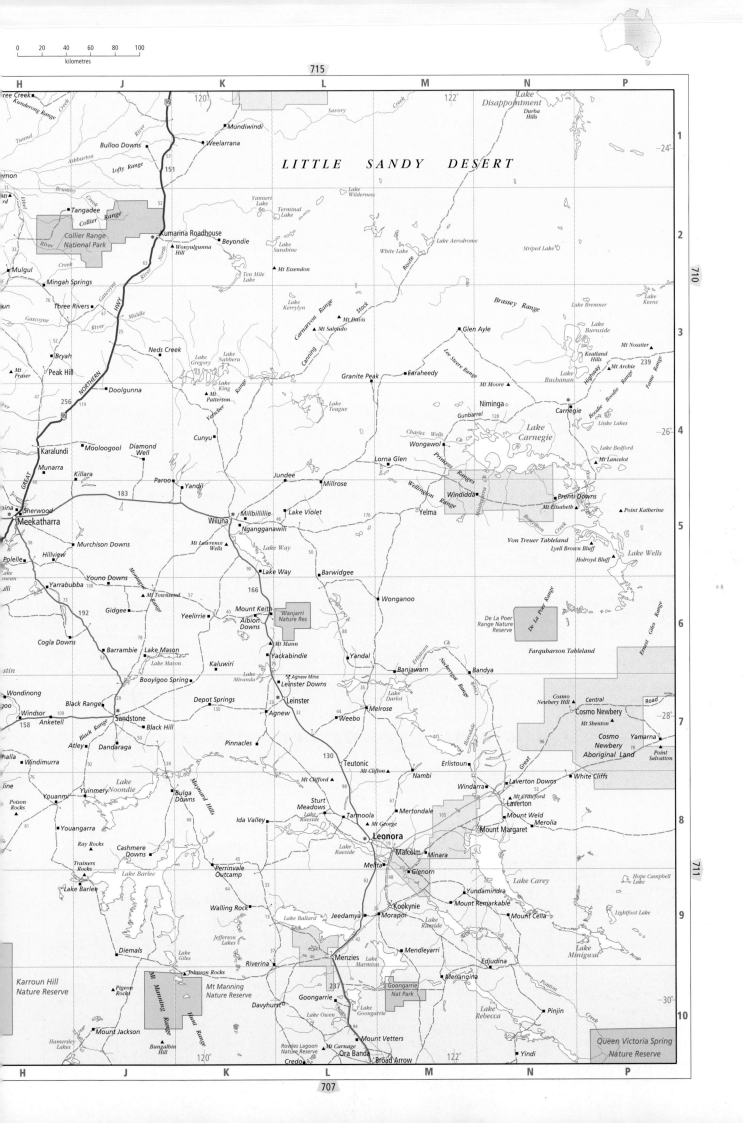

Central-East Western Australia

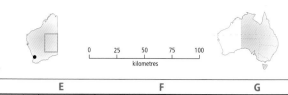

0 25 50 75 100
kilometres

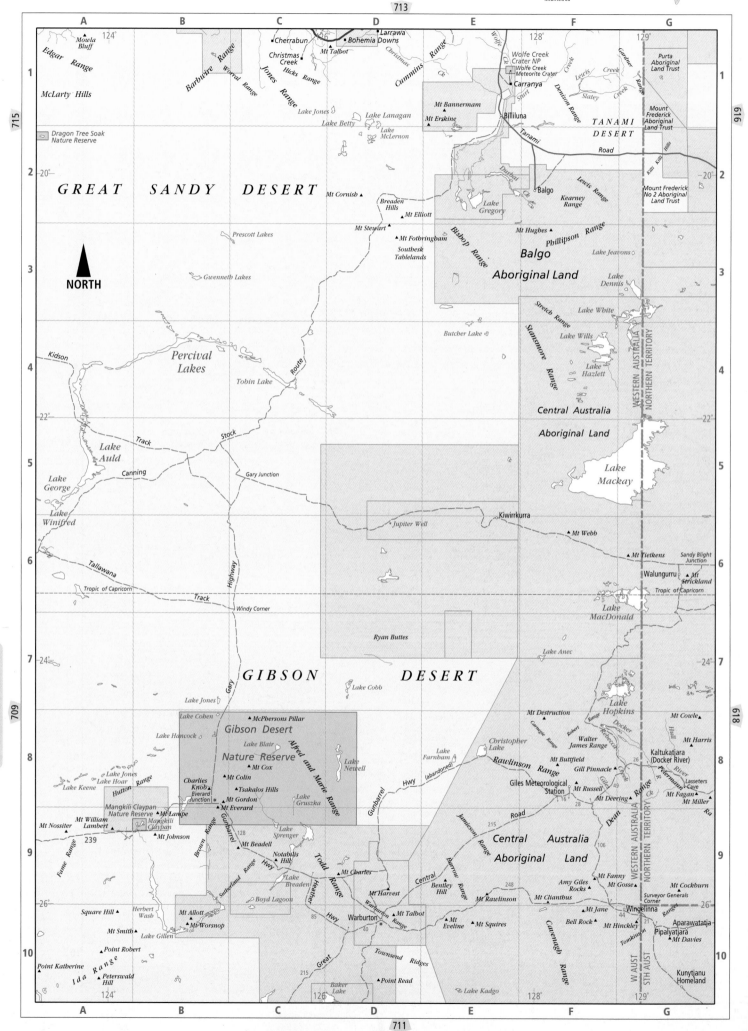

GREAT SANDY DESERT

Edgar Range
Mowla Bluff
124°
McLarty Hills

Dragon Tree Soak
Nature Reserve

Barbwire Range
Worral Range
Jones Range
Hicks Range
Cherrabun
Christmas Creek
Mt Talbot
Bohemia Downs
Larrawa
Cummins Range
Christmas Ck
Wolfe Creek Crater NP
Wolfe Creek Meteorite Crater
Carranya
Purta Aboriginal Land Trust
Mount Frederick Aboriginal Land Trust

Lake Jones
Lake Lanagan
Lake Betty
Lake McLernon
Mt Bannermam
Mt Erskine
Billiluna
Mt Cornish
Breaden Hills
Mt Elliott
Durkal Ck
Lake Gregory
Balgo
Kearney Range
Lewis Range
Phillipson Range
TANAMI DESERT
Tanami Road
Kimi Kim Hills
Mount Frederick No 2 Aboriginal Land Trust

20°

Prescott Lakes
Mt Stewart
Mt Fothringbam
Southbesk Tablelands
Bishop Range
Balgo Aboriginal Land
Mt Hughes
Lake Jeavons

NORTH

Gwenneth Lakes
Lake Dennis

Stretch Range
Lake White
Stansmore Range
Lake Wills
Lake Hazlett

Percival Lakes
Kidson
Tobin Lake
Route
Butcher Lake

Central Australia Aboriginal Land

22°

Track
Stock
Gary Junction
Lake Auld
Canning
Lake George
Lake Winifred

Lake Mackay

WESTERN AUSTRALIA
NORTHERN TERRITORY

Jupiter Well
Kiwirrkurra
Mt Webb
Mt Tietkens
Sandy Blight Junction
Walungurru
Mt Strickland

Tallawana
Tropic of Capricorn
Highway
Track
Windy Corner
Lake MacDonald
Tropic of Capricorn

Ryan Buttes
Lake Anec

24°
GIBSON   DESERT
Lake Cobb

Lake Jones
Lake Coben
McPhersons Pillar
Gibson Desert
Lake Blair
Nature Reserve
Lake Newell
Alfred and Marie Range
Lake Farnham
Christopher Lake
Mt Destruction
Carnegie Range
Robert Range
Docker
Lake Hopkins
Mt Cowle
Mt Harris
Kaltukatjara (Docker River)
Lasseters Cave

Lake Hancock
Mt Cox
Charlies Knob
Everard Junction
Mt Colin
Tsakalos Hills
Mt Gordon
Mt Everard
Lake Gruszka
Gunbarrel Hwy (abandoned)
Rawlinson Range
Walter James Range
Mt Buttfield
Gill Pinnacle
Giles Meteorological Station
Mt Russell
Mt Deering
Petermann Range
Mt Fagan
Mt Miller

Lake Keene
Lake Jones
Lake Hoar
Hutton Range
Mangkili Claypan Nature Reserve
Mt Lampe
Mangkili Claypan
Brown Range
Gunbarrel
Lake Sprenger
Gunbarrel Hwy
Mt Beadell
Notabilis Hill
Todd Range
Heather Range
Gunbarrel Hwy
Jameson Range
Barrow Range
Central Range
Bentley Hill
Amy Giles Rocks
Mt Fanny
Mt Gosse
Mt Cockburn
Surveyor Generals Corner

Mt Nossiter
Mt William Lambert
Mt Johnson
239
Fanne Range

Central Australia Aboriginal Land

26°
Square Hill
Herbert Wash
Mt Smith
Lake Gillen
Point Robert
Peterswald Hill
Mt Allott
Mt Wornsop
Boyd Lagoon
Subotland Range
Lake Breaden
Mt Charles
Mt Harvest
Warburton
Warburton Range
Mt Talbot
Mt Eveline
Mt Squires
Mt Rawlinson
Mt Clianthus
Amy Giles Rocks
Bell Rock
Mt Jane
Wingellina
Aparawatatja
Pipalyatjara
Mt Davies
Kunytjanu Homeland

Point Katherine
Ida Range
124°
Townsend Ridges
Baker Lake
Point Read
Lake Kadgo
128°
Cavenagh Range
Tomkinson Range
129°
W AUST
STH AUST

South-East Western Australia

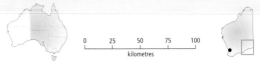

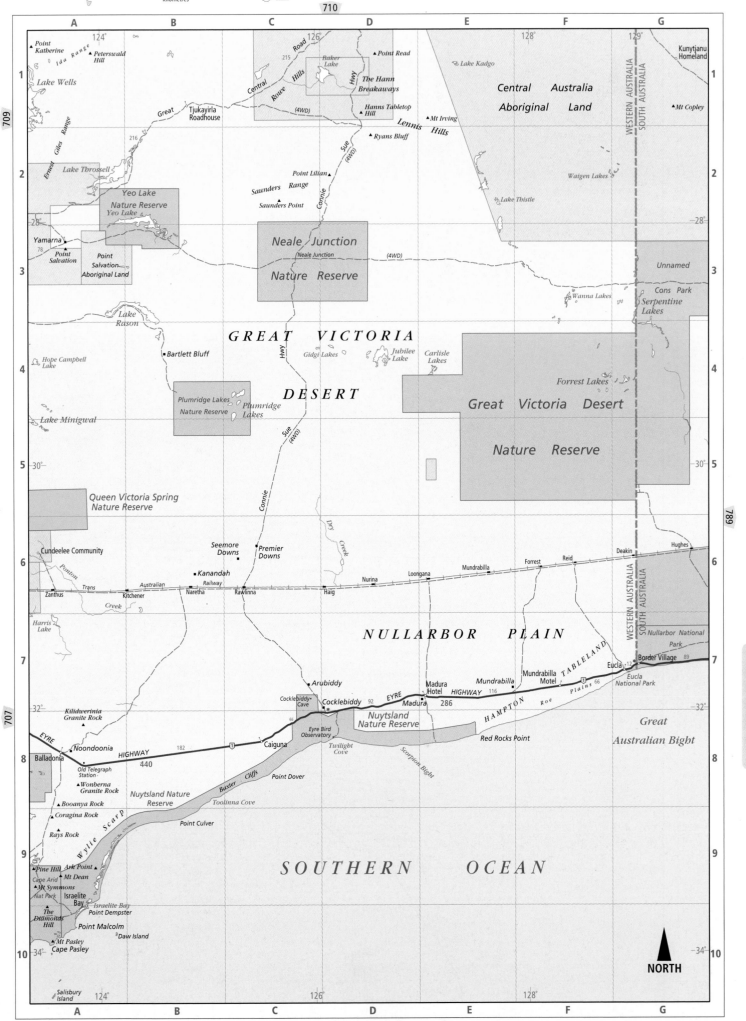

0   25   50   75   100
kilometres

SOUTHERN   OCEAN

NORTH

The Kimberley, Western Australia

NORTH

INDIAN OCEAN

122°

14°

124°

Bona

Mar

Coronation
Islands

Cape Brev

Heywood Islands

Darcy Island
Champagny Island

Brunswic
Bay

Augustus Island

Cape L

Camden Sound

Adele Island

Deception Bay

Hall Point

Kuri Bay

Kunmun
Aboriginal

16°

Wedge Hill
Mt Methuen

George
Water

Buccaneer Archipelago

Montgomery
Islands

Bathurst I

Cockatoo I
Koolan Island

Doubtful Bay

Yampi Sound

Koolan

Wood
Islands

Eagle
Bay

Collier
Bay

Mt L
Watcott Inlet

Goose Channel

Cape Leveque

Sunday I

Strickland Bay

Wotjalum
Aboriginal Land

Yule Entrance

One Arm Point

Cone Bay

McLarty Range

Lombadina Mission

Thomas Bay

Cygnet Bay

Pt Usborne

Mt Disaster

Military
Training Area

Lombadina Point

Willie Pt

Compass Hill

Lombadina Point

Cape Borda

Cunningham Pt

Oobagooma

Pender Bay

King

Emeriau Point

Robinson

River

Mou

Lacepede Islands

Beagle Bay

Cornambie Point

Sound

Sandy Point

Disaster
Bay

Pt Torment

Alexander

Ck

Beagle Bay

Beagle Bay
Aboriginal Land

Stokes Bay

Cape Baskerville

Barker

Carnot Bay

Christine Pt

Meda

Nap
Dow

Country Downs

North Cliffs

Derby

Cape Bertholet

Mt Raible

Fraser

River

Meda

Kimberley
Downs

River

Coulomb Point

Mt Jowlaenga

Mowanjum
Community

James Price Point

Mount Jowlaenga

Point Coulomb
Nat Reserve

4WD

4WD

117

Quondong Point

Yeeda

HWY

RAAF Base
Curtin

Devonian
Con

Cape Boileau

Kilto

Ck

40

30

Willare Bridge
Roadhouse

41

Blina

Drew

56

NORTHERN

Roebuck
Roadhouse

221

NORTHERN

259

53

29

Cable Beach

19

Manguel Creek

Udialla

Camballin

Ellendale

Broome

Roebuck
Plains

Mount Anderson

Liveringa

Calwynyardah

Gantheaume Point

Fitzroy

Paradise

Entrance Point

45

Myroodah

Roebuck Bay

GREAT

Luluigui

Mt

Thangoo

1

Frome Rocks

Nerrima

Bush Point

Creek

River

Cape Villaret

Dampier
Downs

Mt Arthur

Noon

Ecobeach

90

Moulamen
Hill

Cape Latouche Treville

Barnhill

Port Smith

Gourdon Bay

Gregory

Port Smith

Sandy Lake

Babrongan Tower

Mowla Bluff

Kalyeeda

False Cape Bossut

La Grange Bay

La Grange Aboriginal Community
(Bidyadanga)

Mt Collins

Mt Jarlemai

Mt James

Mt Tue

Cape Bossut

Admiral Bay

Geoffroy Bay

Frazier
Downs

Mowla Bluff

Cape Jaubert

Desault Bay

Edgar Range

Cape Missiessy

Nita Downs

122°

124°

TIMOR SEA

Cape Londonderry
Cape Talbot
Sir Graham
Moore Islands
Lesueur Island
Cape Bougainville
Parry Harbour
Cape Ruthieres
Cassini Island
Cape Bernier
Gibson Point
Napier
Broome
Bay
Barton Plains
Pago
Cone Mtn 24
pelago
Montesquieu
Islands
Kalumburu
Cape Voltaire
Borda
Island
Kalumburu Aboriginal Land
Cape Onslow
Admiralty
Port Warrender
Bigge Pt
Gulf
Carson River
Cape St Lambert
Joseph Bonaparte
Surveyors
Pool
Mt Conner
Buckle Head
Admirality Gulf
Aboriginal Land
Crystal Head
Mt Reid
Thurburn Bluff
Gulf
Mitchell Falls
Theda
River
Mt McMillan
Cape Dussejour
Lacrosse Island
Quoin
Island
Mt Anderson
Donkins Hill
Couchman Range
Foster Range
Drysdale River National Park
Mt Nicholls
Dome Hill
Ord River
Nature Res
Turtle Point
Queens Channel
Mitchell River
Oombulgurri Aboriginal Land
Mt Carty
Cambridge
Gulf
River Peak
Enid Falls
Viotti Peak
Elephant Hill
Prince Regent
orge Basin
ature Reserve
Mt York
Mt Bradshaw
KIMBERLEY
Mt Mongona
Forrest
River
Oombulgurri
Mt Connection
Adolphus
Island
Parry Lagoons
Nature Res
Legune
Transit
Hill
King
Cascade
Woodhouse R
Drysdale River
Mt Hann
Mulligan Ranges
Wyndham
Carlton Hill
pong Pyramid
Mt Hann
Mt Dorothy
Mt Lawley
Home Valley
Ivanhoe
Mirima
(Hidden
Valley)
Nat Pk
Keep River
Nat Park
Mt Jameson
Drysdale River
Jacks Waterhole
Durack River
Grotto
Kununurra
Caroline Ranges
Ellenbrae
94
Pentecost Range
Emma
Gorge
Lake
Kununurra
393
El Questro
Mt Lacy
Mount
Elizabeth
Mt Throssell
Newry HWY
Gibb River
Karunjie
(Pentecost Downs)
Dunham
Lake Argyle
Tourist Village
Rosewood
Amanbidji
Mt Duncan
Barnett River
Gorge
108
Chapman
Glen Hill
Mt Duncan
Manning River
Gorge
Mount
Barnett
Doon Doon
Tee Dee Hill
Waterloo
Flour Hill
Galvans Gorge
Pompeys
Pilar
Lissadell
Beverley
Springs
Adcock Gorge
Argyle
Diamond Mine
Spring Creek
Mt Bebn
Bamboo Springs
Phillips Range
Bow River
Mt Parker
Mistake Creek Community
Silent Grove
Mount House
Mt Lush
Mabel Downs
368
Warmun
(Turkey Creek)
Osmond Valley
Malngin Aboriginal
Land Trust
Nelson Springs
Mt Frank
Pastoral
Tableland
Mt Remarkable
Texas Downs
Osmond Range
Leopold
Bedford Downs
Purnululu Nat Pk
Mt Bebn
Mt Broome
Mt Ord
Glenroy
Mt Wells
Mt Ranford
Bungle Bungle
Ranges
Ord River
Mt Napier
Millie Windie
Pittard Bluff
Mornington
Mt Leake
King
Springvale Hill
Springvale
Alice Downs
Kirkimbie
Tunnel Creek
Nat Park
Narrie Range
Lansdowne
Mt Laptz
Turner
Turner Hill
Bunda
Leopold Downs
Mt Frederick
Conical Peak
Nicholson
96 HWY
Brooking
Gorge CP
Mt Winifred
Nicholson
Brooking Springs
Geikie Gorge NP
Mt Cummings
Mt Amburst
Sophie Downs
Flora Valley
Windoo Hill
Wallamunga
Fitzroy Crossing
Fossil Downs
Muludja Community
Mt Ball
Halls Creek
China Wall
Birrindudu
Gogo
Mount
Amhurst
Koongie
Park
Quanbun
Lamboo
Saw
Tooth Gorge
Duncan
Gordon
Downs
Yingualyalya
Aboriginal Land
Trust
Old Cherrabun
Mount Pierre
Louisa Downs
Margaret
River
Ruby Plains
Dukes Dome
Larrawa
Mt Dockrell
McClintock Range
Purta
Aboriginal Land
Trust
Cherrabun
Casey Falls
Bohemia Downs
293
Christmas
Creek
Mt Talbot
Wolfe Creek
Crater NP
Wolfe Creek
Meteorite Crater

The Pilbara, Western Australia

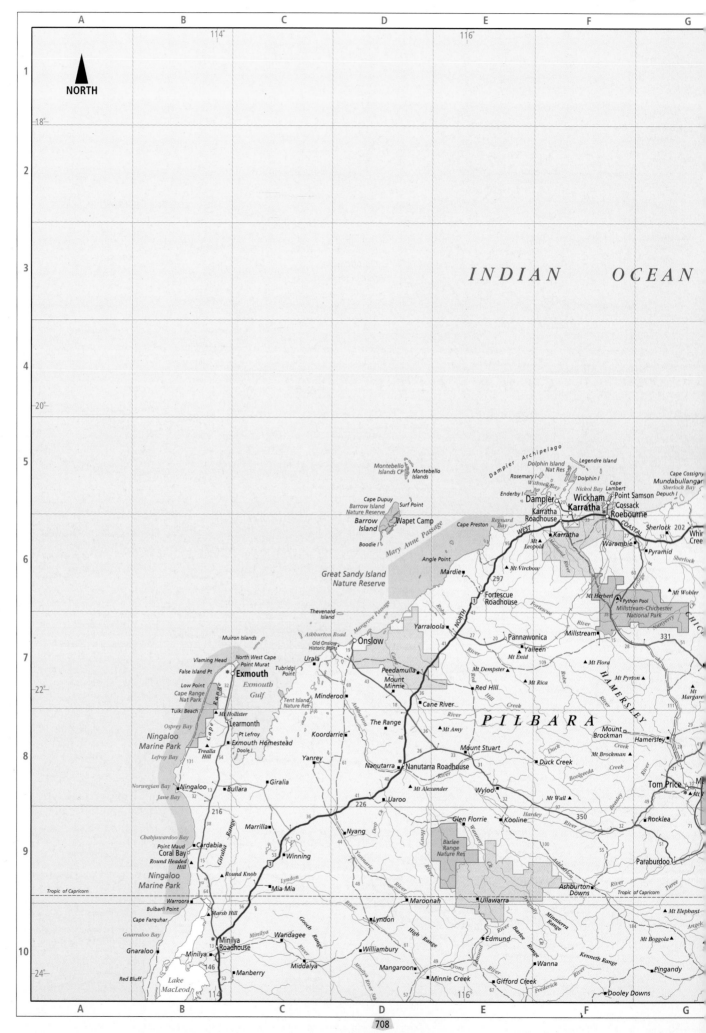

0 20 40 60 80 100
kilometres

H J K L M N **P**

120°

1

Rowley Shoals
Marine Park

Point Coulomb
Nat Reserve
James Price Point
Quondong Point
Cape Boileau
122°

▲ Mt Jowlaenga
Mount
Jowlaenga

Mowanjum
Community

■ Kilto Ck
56

NORTHERN 221
40

Yeeda

1 HWY

Willare Bridge
Roadhouse

Roebuck
Roadhouse
19

Manguel Creek
■

Udialla
■

−18

Cable Beach

Broome
Gantheaume Point
Entrance Point

Roebuck
Plains

Roebuck Bay

GREAT

Frome Rocks ▲

2

Thangoo
Bush Point

Cape Villaret
Ecobeach
Gourdon Bay
Cape Latouche Treville
Port Smith
False Cape Bossut
La Grange Bay
Cape Bossut

Banhill
Port Smith

La Grange Aboriginal Community
(Bidyadanga)

Dampier
Downs

Sandy Lake

Babrongan Tower ▲
Mowla Bluff
■

Mt Collins
■

3

Admiral Bay
Geoffroy Bay
Cape Jaubert
Desault Bay
Cape Missiessy

Frazier
Downs
■

Edgar Range

Nita Downs
■

Anna Plains
■
319
150

Shovel Lake

McLarty Hills

4

Mile

Eighty Mile Beach
Mandora
45

Beach HWY

Sandfire Roadhouse

Eighty

NORTHERN
49

Dragon Tree Soak
Nature Reserve

−20°

Poissonnier Point
Breaker Inlet
Cape Keraudren

44
291

Kidson

Track

5

Spit Point

edland

Pardoo

Pardoo
Roadhouse
50

De Grey

GREAT
53
20
30

1

Strelley
45
1393

Carlindi
■

Muccan
■

Yarrie
■

Callawa
■

De Grey River

Oakover

Isabella Range

Gregory Range

6

42

Indee
■

Wallareenya
■

Tabba Tabba
■

Lalla Rookh
■

57

Coongan
■

Eginbah
■

Bamboo Creek
(abandoned)

Warrawagine
■

124

Strelley River

Marble Bar
Comet Mine

Rippon
■

Mount Edgar
■

Hills Rd

Carawine
Gorge

Yilgalong Creek

Woodie and Nifty
Minesite

Private

Lake
Waukarlycarly

Kidson

7

262

95

Yule

Woodstock
■

Hillside
■

26

Corunna
Downs
■
103

Nullagine

Road

Paterson Range

Throssell Range

Telfer Mine

8

96

Mulga Downs
■

RANGE

Bamboo
Springs
■

Nullagine
41

4WD

Oakover River

Coolbro

Mt Isdell ▲
Creek

Rudall River

Lake
Dora

National Park

Lake
Blanche

Eva Broadhurst Lake

Lake
George

ttenoom

Auski Roadhouse

42

Fortescue

Bonnie
Downs
■

River

Noreena Downs
■
58

Mt Divide ▲

Mt Hodgson ▲

Broadhurst Range

Rudall

Mt Connaughton ▲

Lake
Winifred

9

Yampire
Gorge
Fortescue
Falls

35
63

Marillana
■

78

Roy Hill
■
37

Balfour
Downs
■

Tallawana

Track

Harbutt Range

Juna Downs
■

Mt
Mebarry ▲

GE
36

Ethel Creek
■

Jigalong

Billinnooka
■
61

Walgunya
■

Jigalong
■

Robertson Range

McKay Range

Runton Range

207

126

Kalgan Ck

East

Opthalmia
Mt Newman ▲
Range

Carawinilla Creek

Robertson
Range

Emu Lake

Tropic of Capricorn

10

Turee Creek
■

Prairie Downs
■

Newman

Capricorn
Roadhouse
42

Sylvania
■

Jigalong
Aboriginal
Land

Savory Creek

Lake
Disappointment

Durba
Hills

−24°

Tunnel

Mundiwindi
■

Bulloo Downs
■

Weelarrana
■

57
151

Lofty Range

LITTLE SANDY DESERT

120°

122°

H J K L M N **P**

WESTERN
AUSTRALIA

SOUTH AUSTRALIA

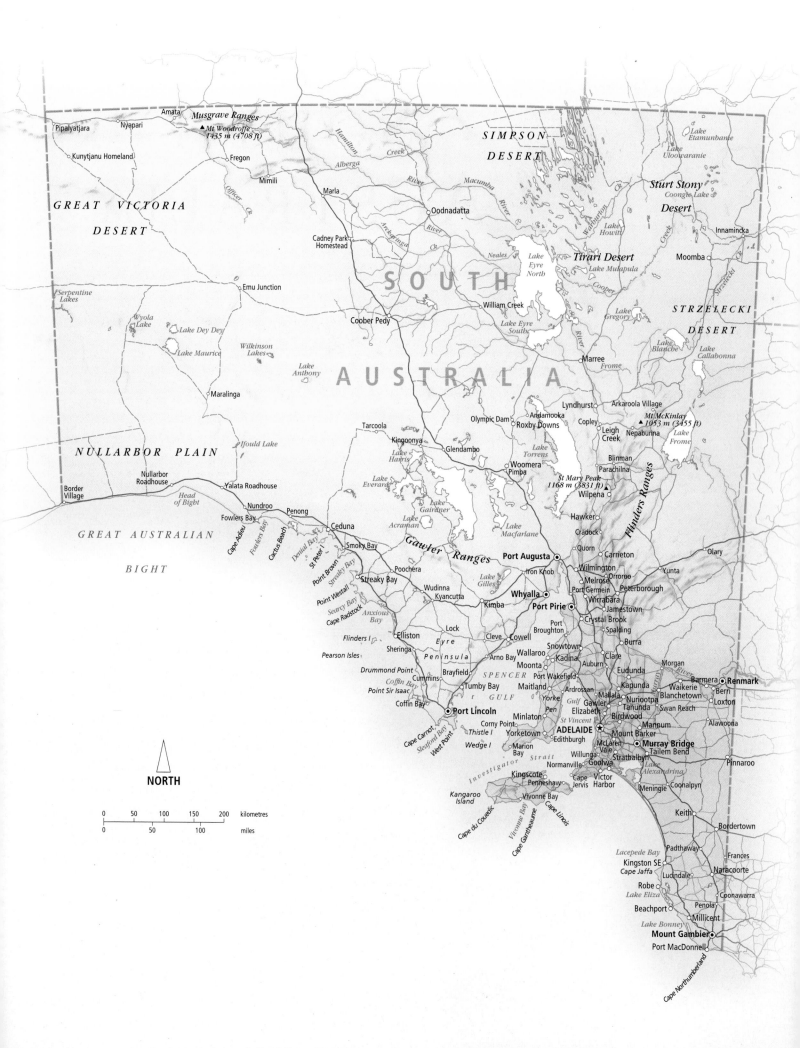

SOUTH AUSTRALIA

When most people think of South Australia, they picture Adelaide, its fine elegant capital, or the wine-growing regions of the Barossa Valley or the Coonawarra, or perhaps the spine of mountains that is the Flinders Ranges, the great expanse of shifting sand of the desert or the flatness of the Nullarbor Plain. All these are most definitely worth visiting, but the state has much more to offer than these.

Most of South Australia's 1.4 million population live in Adelaide; the remainder of people mostly live in and around the coast. Less than one per cent of the population lives in the arid areas north of Port Augusta, which is just 315 km (196 miles) from Adelaide.

South Australia has land borders with every other mainland state, the only state to do so. Taking up 983,480 sq. km (379,623 sq. miles), the State occupies about one-eighth of the total land mass of Australia. More than 80 per cent of South Australia receives less than 250 mm (9.75 inches) of rain a year, making it the driest state in the driest continent on Earth—anywhere away from the more luxuriant south-east of the state is semi-arid to desert.

Much of the state is also flat, with more than 80 per cent less than 250 m (820 feet) in height. Only the Mount Lofty Ranges and their more spectacular continuation, the Flinders Ranges, can really boast mountains of any sort—the highest peak, St Mary Peak, in the heart of the Flinders, tops out at just

1170 m (3839 feet). The rugged and imposing Flinders cut right into the heart of the State, beginning their trail north in the more well-watered part of the state around Gladstone and ending up surrounded by stark desert country at Mount Hopeless, just south of the Strzelecki Track.

The lower section of the Murray River is the only major river in South Australia. It enters from the east, where it has formed the boundary between New South Wales and Victoria, winds its way west to the foothills of the eastern edge of the Mount Lofty Ranges and then turns south. It follows a slow, tortuous path through Lake Alexandrina and Lake Albert, forming the long arm of the Coorong in the process.

The Victorian-style dome of the historic Adelaide Arcade building in Grenfell Street.

A wide valley and yellow cliffs characterise the landscape along most of the length of the Murray River.

Capital
Adelaide
Area
983,480 sq. km
(379,751 sq. miles)
Proportion of Australia
12.8%
Population of State
1,487,300
Population Density
1.5 per sq. km (3.9 per
sq. mile)
Population of Capital
1,088,300
Time Zone
9.5 hours ahead of GMT
Climate
Warm-temperate in the
south-east with hot, dry
summers and mild, wet
winters; to the west
and inland is semi-arid
and desert
Highest Point
Mount Woodroffe
1435 m (4708 ft)

Other rivers in the State are short, small or ephemeral. The only exception is in the far north, where the streams of inland Australia flow towards Lake Eyre, whose catchment area covers around 25 per cent of the Australian continent, most of it in South Australia. However, rarely do these streams reach the lake. These rivers offer long, coolibah-shrouded waterholes along their lengths. In many parts of the north-east they are the only surface water to be found for hundreds of kilometres.

The long, indented coastline of South Australia is very spectacular, offering a diversity of landscapes, from sweeping beaches to sheer, rugged cliffs, to small, protected bays. There are also many offshore islands, the biggest being Kangaroo Island (the third-biggest island off the Australian mainland after Tasmania and Melville).

Deciding where to go in South Australia will depend on the time of year. Adelaide's mid-summer average maximum temperature is around 29°C (84°F); mid-winter's maximum is around 15°C (59°F). The south of the state is cooler all year round and late spring, summer and early autumn are the best times to visit. Summer is delightful along the coast, but if you want to see the ever-growing population of whales that visit the coast, go in winter. Winter is also, by far, the best time to visit the far north of the state—the Simpson Desert, one of the great 4WD journeys, is a crowded thoroughfare! For those visiting the Flinders Ranges, the best time is late winter and early spring, when the wildflowers bloom.

The road network also varies depending on which area of the state you are in. Major highways cut through the state from east to west, converging on

The State flag is a British Blue Ensign featuring the state emblem of a white-bellied piping shrike.

Adelaide from Broken Hill in New South Wales, from Mildura and Ouyen in northern Victoria and from Horsham and Portland in central and southern Victoria. The latter is the main road link to Melbourne. From the west and the north come the two great highways that lead, respectively, from Perth (the Eyre Highway) and Darwin (the Stuart Highway) and converge at Port Augusta before heading south to Adelaide.

These are the only bitumen routes through these areas. The Eyre Highway cuts across the Nullarbor Plain close to the spectacular coastline of the Great Australian Bight, and the Stuart Highway runs through the heart of the state, past the opal-mining centre of Coober Pedy to the Northern Territory border south of Alice Springs. Both these routes are devoid of habitation for hundreds of kilometres—it pays to stop at each and every lonely and remote roadhouse to revive.

The rest of the South Australian road network—in the far south, through the Murraylands, around Adelaide and throughout the Yorke Peninsula and Eyre Peninsula—is, for the most part, extensive, with much of it bitumen. The dirt roads are, in the main, very good, but for those not used to travelling on such surfaces the smoothness can be seductive, so take care—a slight dusting of dirt on an otherwise hard clay or limestone bed can sometimes make it easy to lose control.

In the Flinders Ranges the bitumen only goes as far north as Wilpena; the road along the western flank of the range is bitumen to Lyndhurst. North of here are the well-known outback routes of the Strzelecki, Birdsville and Oodnadatta Tracks—all dirt. These long, dusty dirt tracks, while not as bad as they used to be, can be a little daunting in the normal family car; they are much easier with a 4WD. Elsewhere in the far north and north-west of the state the routes are not suitable for normal cars.

From desert landscapes to beautiful coastlines, opal mining town to festival city, world-class wineries to fabulous national parks, South Australia has something that will appeal to each and every visitor.

Steel vats and wooden barrels outside the Charles Melton winery in the Barossa Valley.

Granite Island at Victor Harbor is home to many fairy penguins, and tours are available to watch them at sunset. The island is joined to the South Australian mainland by a causeway 630 m (2067 feet) long.

The former copper-mining town of Burra is nestled in the Bald Hills Range in central-eastern South Australia.

ADELAIDE

The historic Glenelg tram is a popular tourist ride in Adelaide, travelling between the heart of the city and the popular seaside suburb of Glenelg.

The Adelaide Festival Centre in Elder Park on the banks of the Torrens, is considered to house some of the finest perfomance space in the world.

Australia's fifth-largest city, Adelaide, owes much of its charm to the man who first designed its layout—Colonel William Light. He also selected the city's location—10 km (6.2 miles) from its port— Port Adelaide. His plan was simple: a rectangular grid pattern centred around five squares—the largest and central one being Victoria Square—and bordered by the River Torrens to the north. North of the Torrens he planned North Adelaide, laid out around a single square, Wellington Square. His thoroughfares were wide and tree lined, with the widest and grandest (King William Street) running north–south, linking North Adelaide and Adelaide. Around the city's peri- meter he planned a vast area of parklands, nearly 1000 ha (2471 acres) in all, and along North Terrace, just south of the Torrens, he placed Government House. 'Light's Vision', a bronze figure of Light over- looking the city he planned, stands on Montefiore Hill.

To the founding forefathers' credit, the plan has essentially remained intact. Located about halfway along the eastern shores of the Gulf St Vincent, Adelaide and its metropolitan area now stretch for about 80 km (50 miles), from the beachside suburb of Aldinga north-east to Gawler. For nearly the whole length of this area, the Mount Lofty Ranges form a backdrop of low hills and deep valleys. The suburbs have crowded up to the ranges and even climbed

their flanks in some places, but for the most part the scene is a natural green one, the city protected by a string of parks and reserves.

The city, named after Queen Adelaide, was founded as the colony of South Australia and was proclaimed in 1836. During the 1840s the city, carried by copper discoveries at Kapunda and Burra, began to take shape. The first churches, the Holy Trinity Anglican Church and Christ Church, were built; Government House and the Adelaide Gaol were both begun in 1840, and Old Parliament House, now restored as a museum, was built in the 1850s. The Supreme Court was built in 1868, and the suburban railway to Glenelg was opened in 1873. In 1872 the Overland Telegraph line between Adel- aide and Darwin was completed, connecting the city to London via the telegraph. During those early years other villages sprang up nearby. Unley, Prospect, Hindmarsh and a dozen others began as wayside stops and watering points, later becoming suburbs— the city now covers nearly 2000 sq. km (772 sq. miles).

Today, driving along King William Street towards the Torrens, the layout of this city is immediately evident. Past the Adelaide Oval, considered by many one of the finest-looking traditional cricket grounds in the world, you cross the Torrens River to arrive at North Terrace. (For children, a trip on *Popeye*, a launch

Adelaide is the only major metropolis in the world to have its city centre completely surrounded by parkland.

that plies the river from near the Festival Centre to the Adelaide Zoo, is a great outing.) This tree-lined boulevard has many fine buildings: Government House, the State Library, the South Australian Museum, the Art Gallery of South Australia (which contains the largest collection of Aboriginal artefacts in the world) and Adelaide University. A little further along, past the Royal Adelaide Hospital, are the Botanical Gardens and the State Herbarium, begun in 1855. These gardens include the oldest glasshouse in an Australian botanical garden, and the only Museum of Economic Botany; the Conservatory contains a tropical rainforest. To the west of King William Street is Parliament House, completed in 1939; a little further along, in what once was the Adelaide Railway Station, is the Adelaide Casino.

Cruises and seafood are available at Fishermen's Wharf.

Continuing along King William Street you come to Rundle and Hindley Streets—the former is the shopping heart of Adelaide, the latter is the night spot centre—then the Town Hall. A little further south is Victoria Square, with lawns and a fountain, the terminus for the Glenelg tram, and the clock tower of the GPO. King William Street continues to South Terrace, where gardens and parks, including the rose garden and conservatory and the Himeji Gardens (a traditional Japanese garden), make up the southern perimeter of the city proper.

Being so close to the Barossa Valley and the wineries of the Vales to the south, it is no wonder that Adelaide boasts more restaurants per capita than any other city in Australia. Hindley and Rundle Streets in the heart of the city, Gouger Street, close to Victoria Square, and O'Connell and Melbourne Streets in North Adelaide are the best places to go.

Glenelg, on the coast just 10 km (6.2 miles) from the city centre, and a city in its own right, is the summer playground for Adelaide residents and visitors—the largest amusement park in the state, and many restaurants, are here. Port Adelaide, 25 minutes

west of the city, is home to the South Australian Maritime Museum, the Historic Military Vehicles Museum, and the South Australian Historical Aviation Museum, among others. Here you can also cruise on an old sailing ketch, or take a steam train ride along the old Semaphore Railway.

The beaches south of Port Adelaide (including Glenelg) are ideal places to swim and many have a jetty where kids and adults can dangle a line. Further south the beaches are even better; surfers love the breaks in and around Christies Beach, Moana and Seaford. For divers there are the reefs and marine sanctuaries at Port Noarlunga or at Aldinga.

The nearby Mount Lofty Ranges offer other nature experiences— seeing native animals close up at Cleland Wildlife Park, picnics and day bushwalks at Belair National Park, and rock climbing at Morialta Falls Conservation Park.

Any mention of Adelaide must include reference to its major international festival, the Adelaide Festival, held in March; artists from around the world come to perform here. There are a host of other festivals and events, including the Adelaide Fringe Festival in February, the Oakbank Racing Carnival in April, the Royal Adelaide Show in late August/early September, and the International Rose Festival in October. In the Adelaide Hills, the Barossa Valley or down along the Fleurieu Peninsula there are many other festivals.

For the history buff there are the Mortlock Library of historical material, the Migration and Settlement Museum and the South Australian Police Museum, and the SA Theatre Museum, a magnificent complex of halls and theatres.

Adelaide is often referred to as the 'city of churches' due to the large number of churches and, some think, because of a perceived serenity about the city.

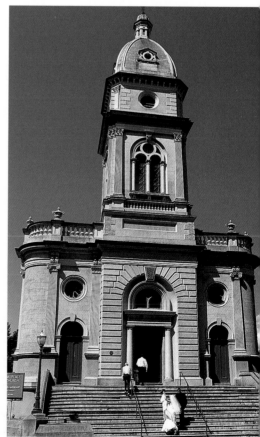

Koonalda Cave in Nullarbor National Park contains some of the earliest evidence of Aboriginal art, dating back 15–20,000 years.

RIGHT: Murray River National Park, which occupies three separate areas of flood plain along the Murray near Renmark, offers stress-free paddling on the river and its tranquil backwaters.

Most of the bushwalking trails on Kangaroo Island traverse coastal heathland, allowing walkers to observe the abundant marine life as well as terrestrial animals.

South Australia

South Australia is the country's driest state, which means that outdoor activities require careful planning. Not only is drinking water hard to come by, but also dense forests and woodlands that might provide shade and shelter from winds are scarce. In summer, temperatures soar, particularly in the north of the state, so travellers should save more arduous undertakings for the winter months.

South Australia's major landforms include the series of rugged mountain ranges that runs north from Adelaide culminating in the Flinders and Gammon ranges; these provide plenty of challenges for walkers, cyclists and climbers. In the south-east, the vast lagoons of the Coorong and the 650 km (404 miles) of the Murray River that wend from the border with New South Wales and Victoria to the sea are favoured by canoeists and kayakers. Caving is also popular in South Australia, perhaps because it provides escape from the heat and glare, but also because the state has the best cave diving and some of the best dry caving in the country.

Bushwalking

The Flinders Ranges are the most popular walking destination in South Australia, offering a variety of options and experiences in several different national parks. Only three hours from Adelaide, in the southern Flinders, is Mount Remarkable National Park. Here, the camping area at Mambray Creek is the starting point for several good day walks as well as multiday excursions. The central Flinders Ranges,

located four and a half hours from Adelaide and mostly encompassed by Flinders Ranges National Park, feature some of the state's most spectacular scenery, which is best appreciated on foot. The most prominent feature is Wilpena Pound, an immense natural amphitheatre ringed by peaks and crisscrossed by marked trails of varying lengths and difficulties. One of the most strenuous hikes here is to the summit of St Marys Peak. Other, gentler walks explore woodlands, gorges and rock art.

Both Mount Remarkable National Park and Flinders Ranges National Park are traversed by the 1500-km (930-mile) Heysen Trail, which begins at Cape Jervis south of Adelaide and winds up in Parachilna Gorge, just north of Wilpena Pound. Nearer Adelaide, the trail runs along the Mount Lofty Ranges and through the picturesque Barossa Valley.

Experienced hikers seeking a challenge should investigate off-track walking in the Gammon Ranges, at the northern end of the Flinders. This is a serious undertaking as water supplies can be unpredictable and the area's maze of valleys and gorges can make navigation difficult.

At the opposite end of the scale of difficulty, and the state, are the walking tracks in Flinders Chase National Park on Kangaroo Island. Here, where the climate is far more temperate, gentle marked trails pass through tall eucalypt forest and take in dramatic coastal scenery.

Rock Climbing

The best rock climbing in the state is found on the cliffs of Moonarie, on the outside of Wilpena Pound in the Flinders Ranges. Such is the quality of the sport on

these imposing rock walls that many climbers regularly travel here from interstate. Closer to Adelaide, climbers frequent the much smaller rock faces of Onkararinga Gorge and Morialta.

Caving

Among the state's most notable caves is the extensive limestone system under the Nullarbor Plain. Centred mainly on Ceduna, it is closed to the general public but can be explored by experienced cavers who have obtained a permit from the national park authorities. In the south of the state, the flooded caves of Mount Gambier are a venue for cave diving, a particularly dangerous form of caving. Nearby is the town of Naracoorte and the Naracoorte Caves Conservation Park, where tunnels and chambers are open to tourists as well as adventure cavers.

Mountain Biking

Due to the roughness of many of the state's back roads, mountain biking is a particularly popular style of cycling in South Australia. Favoured destinations include the Adelaide Hills and other parts of the Mount Lofty Ranges, the Fleurieu Peninsula, the Barossa Valley, the Flinders Ranges and Kangaroo Island. Mountain biking is not permitted in national parks or conservation areas, however.

The most famous cycling route in South Australia is the Mawson Trail, which stretches for 800 km (497 miles) from the heart of Adelaide to Blinman in the Flinders Ranges. Following pre-existing 4WD tracks and dirt roads for much of the way, it includes many challenging hills and some technical sections, most notably in the northern half.

Canoeing, Kayaking and Rafting

As a dry state, South Australia has no whitewater rivers, but there is plenty of scope for canoe touring, particularly on the Murray River and its tributaries. Chowilla and Ral Ral Creeks, which flow into the Murray close to the border with New South Wales and Victoria, are good locations for this kind of backwater exploration. Similar but more popular is the two-day paddle along Katarapko Creek near Loxton, which passes through dense stands of red gums thronging with birdlife. The Glenelg River on the South Australia–Victoria border is another scenic waterway favoured by canoeists.

The major event on South Australia's canoeing calendar is the Red Cross Murray Marathon from Yarawonga to Swan Hill, which covers a distance of 500 km (310 miles). Lasting five days, it draws entrants from all over Australia.

Sea Kayaking

Sea kayakers interested in birds should make for the Coorong, a vast saltwater lagoon that extends 145 km (90 miles) south-east from the mouth of the Murray River. At the river mouth are Lake Alexandrina and its offshoot, Lake Albert; both offer plenty of scope for sea kayaking in sheltered waters. Other favourite destinations include the mangrove inlets of Port Adelaide and the coast north of Cape Jervis, at the tip of the Fleurieu Peninsula.

Further west, two national parks at the southern end of the Eyre Peninsula offer great sea kayaking. Coffin Bay National Park encompasses a T-shaped peninsula. On its north-eastern side is a large, sheltered bay with a convoluted coastline that is ideal for exploring by sea kayak; the exposed southern and western shores will entice more adventurous paddlers. Lincoln National Park, to the east, which protects the Jussieu Peninsula, also has a scenic, complex coastline of beaches, cliffs and bays, as well as the added attraction of several adjacent islands.

One of the highlights of Moonarie, on the outer wall of Wilpena Pound in the Flinders Ranges, is the Great Wall, a sheer sandstone cliff face, 50 m (164 feet) high.

SOUTH-EAST SOUTH AUSTRALIA

Australia's greatest river, the Murray, as well as forming the border between New South Wales and Victoria, reaches the end of its journey in this corner of South Australia, giving life to a flourishing agricultural industry irrigated by its waters. Majestic river red gums line the banks despite its heavy use by locals and tourists for canoeing, waterskiing, houseboating, camping and fishing.

The Murray ends near the sea, at Lake Alexandrina, a permanent freshwater lake, and Lake Albert. Running from the mouth of the Murray to the east for almost 145 km (90 miles) is the Coorong, a narrow saltwater lagoon, home to many species of water birds and campers during the summer.

To the south of the Adelaide Hills lies the Fleurieu Peninsula, which was named by the French explorer Nicholas Baudin in 1802, who was attempting to chart the coast in the opposite direction to Flinders whom he met in Encounter Bay. A mere 13 km (8 miles) across from Cape Jervis at the tip of the peninsula lies Kangaroo Island, the third-largest of Australia's offshore islands. Due to the absence of dingoes, foxes and rabbits, the island provides sanctuary for some native animals which are endangered on the mainland.

From Kingston south and east to the Victorian border is one of South Australia's most productive agricultural regions. The largest population centre is Mount Gambier, renowned for its dairy products. There are a number of extinct volcanic craters in the area, some of which are now lakes, the most well known being Blue Lake because of its deep blue colour at certain times of the year.

To the north of Mount Gambier is the Naracoorte Caves Conservation Park, which has a World Heritage listing, due to significant fossil deposits. The Bat Cave is home to hundreds of thousands of common bent wing bats during summer. Their departure for feeding in the evenings is an amazing sight. Further inland are the Ngarat Group of Conservation Parks, popular with 4WD enthusiasts. The undulating sand dunes, covered for the most part with mallee, are spectacular in spring when the wildflowers attract not only birds but bees as well.

OPPOSITE: Oak barrels at Katnook winery in the Coonawarra— Australia's prime red wine producing area.

Kangaroo Island was cut off from the mainland by rising sea levels around 9500 years ago.

Coonawarra and the Limestone Coast

Situated close to the Victorian border, Coonawarra is known throughout Australia and the rest of the world for its elegant yet richly flavoured wines, particularly its superb cabernet sauvignons. Remarkably, this widespread fame rests on a relatively tiny strip of paprika-colored soil—known as terra rossa—measuring only about 20 km (12.5 miles) in length and 1.5 km (0.9 miles) in width, narrowing at each end, and varying in depth from just a few centimetres to 1 m (an inch or so to about 3 feet). Lying on top of quick-draining limestone and a high water table, this thin loam generates exceptional grape development and characters, and has been the source of many great Australian wines in recent decades.

The region around Coonawarra, which includes several other promising winegrowing districts, including Padthaway, Mount Gambier, Mount Benson and Robe subregions, is known as the Limestone Coast, a name that derives from the area's geological origins and make-up. The land here originally formed from sediments deposited on the floor of an ocean which, a million years or so ago, extended to the Naracoorte Ranges. Following the last ice age, the sea withdrew, leaving the limestone high and dry and Coonawarra 150 km (93 miles) from the coastline.

The terra rossa soil formed from a mixture of clay, organic materials and minerals that was deposited on the limestone. Its deep russet-red colour derives from oxidation of exposed iron-rich particles. Patches of this soil are found throughout the region, though nowhere in such concentration as in Coonawarra.

It's not only the area's soil that is conducive to winemaking. Regular, generous cloud cover and mild temperatures allow grapes to ripen slowly and develop sweet, full-fruit flavours, without loss of acidity. With no major mountain barrier in the region, the Limestone Coast's climate is generally maritime, although areas further north and inland experience less rain and more sunshine than those on the coast.

Early Development

The first person to exploit the viticultural potential of the Limestone Coast was John Riddoch, who planted vines—largely shiraz and cabernet sauvignon—at Coonawarra in 1890. He then built the limestone winery that still stands on Wynns Coonawarra Estate today. In the early twentieth century, however, Coonawarra remained a minor wine-producer compared to other South Australian vineyard regions. Furthermore, despite the quality of the area's production, a vine-pull scheme was introduced in the 1930s as a result of disastrous sales of its table wines, and two-thirds of the vines were sacrificed to dairy, orchards and livestock. The decline continued until 1951, when David Wynn and his father Samuel purchased the remains of the original Riddoch property, a demonstration of their faith in the viticultural potential of Coonawarra at a time when others were dismissing it. Since then, Wynn's has been joined by other, now-famous brand names, including Lindeman, Brand and Redman, all of which have helped develop the area and, in turn, have reaped the benefits of its high-calibre grapes.

Coonawarra was originally best-known for its shiraz, but recently cabernet sauvignon has come to dominate red-wine production.

The use of specially imported French oak barrels has helped Coonawarra winemakers develop complex white wines, especially chardonnays and rieslings.

The Padthaway subregion, 53 miles (85 km) north of Coonawarra, was first planted by Seppelt in 1963. The suitability of its soil and climate for grape growing were soon evident, though, somewhat surprisingly, conditions seemed to favour white varieties (notably chardonnay) rather than reds. Hardys and Lindemans have invested here too, and the area continues to be characterized by large companies growing fruit for use in various products. Although it remains less famous than Coonawarra, Padthaway produces far more grapes.

Located less than 30 km (18.5 miles) from the coast, Mount Gambier is the state's southernmost viti-cultural subregion and its potential remains untested. There are five small producers here, and chardonnay and cabernet sauvignon are the dominant varieties. Closer to the coast, Mount Benson is one of Australia's newest wine areas. Lindemans planted experimental vines here in 1978, and Southcorp is a major investor, along with Cellarmaster Wines and, more recently, M. Chapoutier & Co, a major French producer.

Wine Styles

Throughout the first half of the twentieth century, when shiraz was the dominant red grape in Australia and fortified the dominant style, Coonawarra managed to retain small plantings of cabernet sauvignon, the variety that has recently become its forte. Coonawarra cabernet has a distinctive perfume and complexity that derive from its cool climate and terra rossa; it also displays the rich blackcurrant, plum, cassis and chocolate characters that are typical of the variety, frequently tinged with hints of mint and eucalyptus.

Although now something of a bridesmaid to ca-bernet sauvignon, shiraz from the Limestone Coast has a distinguished history and continues to display a powerfully spicy character. The local riesling is also surprisingly good; it is made in a fruity and fragrant style by only a small number of producers, most notably Wynns and Hollick. Some winemakers, es-pecially Rymill and Katnook Estate, envisage a great

Padthaway Estate Vineyards. Although it is so close to the acclaimed red wine region of Coonawarra, the Padthaway area produces excellent white wines.

future for sauvignon blanc in the region. Chardonnay has enjoyed mixed fortunes in Coonawarra, but has become one of the star performers at Padthaway, where it makes elegant but fruity still wines as well as complex sparkling wines. Producers in the Mount Benson and Robe subregions are still experimenting with different grape varieties, but some recently released shiraz has been surprisingly lush.

Producers

Most of Coonawarra's producers are located just off the Riddoch Highway, which runs north to south between Naracoorte and Mount Gambier. The hub of the winemaking region is Penola, a charming village featuring many beautifully restored stone and weatherboard early settlers' cottages. Most of the winemakers listed below welcome visitors and offer cellar-door tastings and sales.

The vintage usually takes place in April, though it can go on until June. Rain is a threat during this period, with wet weather often commencing early in winter.

Bowen Estate, Coonawarra

Established 1972 Owners Doug and Joy Bowen Production 15,000 cases Vineyard area 25 ha (62 acres)

Doug Bowen purchased and planted his plot of terra rossa in 1972. Since then, his family-owned and managed estate has a gained a deserved reputation for wines that display the excellent quality that can be obtained when Coonawarra fruit is carefully tended, hand pruned and sensitively handled. Bowen wines have layers of intense flavour, a lush feel in the mouth, and remarkable length, and will further reward those who have the patience to cellar them carefully.

Katnook Estate, Coonawarra

Established 1890s Owner Wingara Wine Group Production 60,000 cases Vineyard area 240 ha (593 acres)

The name of this estate derives from the name of the property built here by John Riddoch in the 1860s, and both Riddoch's homestead and the woolshed where he made his second vintage constitute part of the modern winery complex. The Katnook brand wasn't actually established until 1979, but it now features some of Coonawarra's most intensely flavoured and painstakingly crafted wines. A recent Jimmy Watson trophy for the 1997 Shiraz is an indication of their calibre. Among the most notable offerings is Odyssey, a wine of huge flavour and structure coupled with fine balance and complexity, which is made from the top 1 per cent of hand-selected cabernet fruit.

Lindemans, Coonawarra

Established 1908 Owner Southcorp Wines Production 9000 cases Vineyard area 100 ha (247 acres)

British immigrant and Australian viticultural pioneer Dr Henry John Lindeman planted his Cawarra vineyards in the Hunter Valley of New South Wales in 1843; today, his name is one of national wine-maker Southcorp's most successful brands. The Lindemans Coonawarra trio of Pyrus, Limestone Ridge and St George, the brand's flagship wines, are crafted from premium Coonawarra fruit and made only in great vintages. St George is one of Australia's classic single-vineyard cabernets and shows rich plums, chocolate and smoky wood on the palate.

Padthaway Estate, Padthaway

Established 1979 Owners Dale Baker and Ian Gray Production 6000 cases Vineyard area 50 ha (124 acres)

Until recently, this vineyard was the Padthaway area's sole viticultural attraction. It is located on the site of a former sheep property belonging to early settler Robert Lawson, and the gracious homestead, built in 1882, remained the Lawson family residence until 1980, when it was sold for use as luxury accommodation. Among Padthaway's most notable successes are its sparkling wines, which demonstrate the area's potential for cool-climate white grapes.

Redman Winery, Coonawarra

Established 1966 Owners Redman family Production 20,000 cases Vineyard area 30 ha (74 acres)

Bill Redman started work in the Riddoch vineyards in 1901—the year of John Riddoch's death. In 1908, he purchased 16.2 ha (40 acres) of Riddoch vines and established a winery. A contract with Tolleys allowed him to sell much of his 'burgundy' to the British market, until the 1920s when Tolleys cancelled the contract because the quality of Redman's Coonawarra reds made it hard for them to sell their other wines. In 1954, the Redman family company adopted the business name Rouge Homme, and their wines were subsequently marketed under that label. However, after Lindemans bought Rouge Homme in 1965, Owen Redman purchased 6.5 ha (16 acres) of aged shiraz vines from a colleague and produced his first shiraz under the Redman Winery label with fruit from the 1966 vintage. Redman's red wines—the family has never made whites—have a characteristic leafy edge, and are gutsy and tannic.

Rouge Homme Winery, Coonawarra

Established 1954 Owner Southcorp Wines Production 73,000 cases Vineyard area 200 ha (494 acres)

Originally founded by the Redman family, this winery was acquired by Lindeman's in 1965. The wines are always of Coonawarra origin and of consistently good quality, offering value for money and something for all tastes. The Richardson's Red Block, which boasts a Jimmy Watson Trophy, is a blend of classic bordeaux varieties; it has all the fruit intensity and tannic strength expected of wine from established Coonawarra vines, tinged with an intriguing spiciness as well as green vegetal flavours.

Rymill Coonawarra Wines, Coonawarra

Established 1974 Owner Peter Rymill Production 50,000 cases Vineyard area 160 ha (395 acres)

Perhaps the closest thing Coonawarra has to a château, the Rymill winery, opened in 1990, is a masterpiece of modern design. Picturesque vine plantings and distant red gums can be seen from its upper-level balconies, and the ultra-modern, stainless steel winery can be viewed from an internal platform. The wines are made to express unique regional characters and to complement food. The sauvignon blanc suggests that this variety has great potential in the area.

Wynns Coonawarra Estate, Coonawarra

Established 1891 Owners Southcorp Wines Production 380,000 cases Vineyard area 800 (1976 acres)

No visit to Coonawarra is complete without a pilgrimage to this historic limestone building. The region's first winery, it was completed by John Riddoch in 1896 and, even at that time, was extremely well equipped, boasting cool basement storage rooms, a steam-

powered crusher, and cooling coils for the stone-fermenting tanks. After the death of its visionary founder in 1901, the property entered a gradual decline halted only when it was purchased by Samuel Wynn and his son David for £22,000 in 1951. Today, the classic shiraz beloved by many as Wynns Hermitage remains a benchmark, and the black label Cabernet Sauvignon is collected every year by aficionados. The premium John Riddoch Cabernet Sauvignon and Michael Shiraz are made only in exceptional years.

Zema Estate, Coonawarra

Established 1982 Owners Demetrio and Francesca Zema Production 10,000 cases Vineyard area 50 ha (124 acres)

In the 1960s, when he was a painter at nearby Penola, Demetrio Zema made small batches of wine at home and dreamed of owning a vineyard and winery on terra rossa. His dream came true in 1982, and now the entire Zema family contributes to the winemaking process at this estate. The Zemas have retained traditional practices, favouring dryland viticulture, hand pruning, and part-barrel fermentation. The results are superb—rich, fruit flavours with earthy aromas and robust tannins. The family hand-selects its best fruit to produce small quantities of the Family Selection Cabernet Sauvignon, which like most Zema wines, represents great value for money.

A vineyard at Wynn's, with the historic winery in the background. The company's shiraz and cabernet wines have gained an international reputation for their quality and potential for ageing.

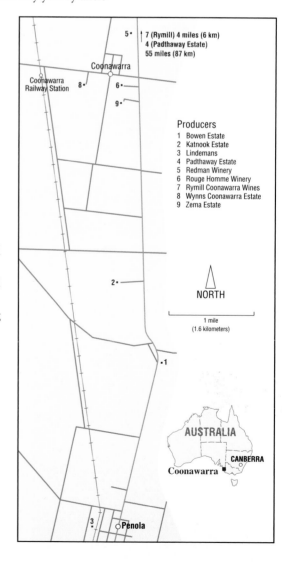

Places in
SOUTH-EAST
SOUTH AUSTRALIA

AMERICAN RIVER

A pleasant base from which to explore Kangaroo Island—the town of American River is 140 km (87 miles) south-west of Adelaide, on Kangaroo Island—American River received its name when an American ship sailed into the wide river mouth in 1803 and stayed while some of its crew built a small schooner, the *Independence,* from local timber. Today it is a small, quiet beachside resort, with a population of 260. The tranquil waters of the river and Eastern Cove add to the serenity. The river flows into Pelican Lagoon and its conservation park. With five small islands, the park is an aquatic reserve. Fish breed here, and it is also an important refuge for water birds, particularly pelicans. They make instant friends with the anglers who fish from the wharf or the waters of Eastern Cove.

On an evening walk around the town you will often see wallabies, possums and other nocturnal animals, while during the day the foreshore is an excellent place for birdwatching. There is also good canoeing and boating in the protected waterways. A major feature of the town is the colourful carpet of small freesias that bloom around the end of August.

Map ref: page **788 B3**

Antique farm equipment at Clayton Farm, Bordertown.

BORDERTOWN

Situated on the Dukes Highway just west of the South Australia–Victoria border, 281 km (175 miles) south-east of Adelaide in the Tatiara (a word in an Aboriginal language meaning 'the good country') district, Bordertown is a major service centre for those travelling between Adelaide and Melbourne, as well as for the rich cereal growing and sheep grazing areas that surround it.

Bordertown came into prominence during the gold rush days of the 1850s, when gold was taken by horseback from the Victorian diggings to Adelaide. South of the town is the rich wine-growing area of the Coonawarra, while to the north is the mallee scrubland of the Ngarkat Group of Conservation Parks, which are popular for touring and camping. The town's population today is 2200.

A 40-km (25-mile) historic drive starts near the Bordertown Civic Centre and takes you to 11 heritage sites. Just 10 km (6.2 miles) from town is the historic township of Mundulla, with its National Trust hotel and museum. The bird life at the nearby Moot-Yang-Gunya Swamp and at the Poocher Swamp closer to Bordertown is varied.

Robert 'Bob' Hawke, Prime Minister of Australia during the 1980s, was born here in 1929—there are tours of Hawke House, his childhood home. Those interested in old machinery will not want to miss the Clayton Farm Vintage Field Day held in April. Other festivities include the Concert Band and Fiesta in September.

Map ref: page **788 C10**

Surf fisherman on Younghusband Peninsula, Coorong National Park.

CANUNDA NATIONAL PARK

Canunda National Park is the largest coastal park in this region, taking up 9358 ha (23,124 acres). It is dominated by large sand dunes and rugged limestone cliffs. In the north of the park, close to Southend, there are a number of short walking trails. The Khyber Pass Walk, to a spectacular area of sand dunes, starts at a car park on the Bevilaqua Ford track. From the Cape Buffon lighthouse the Seaspray Walk takes visitors along the edge of the cliffs for about 1.5 km (0.9 miles). The Seaview Walk is a 4-km (2.5-mile) extension to the Seaspray Walk (about 2 hours return). In fact, you can walk for a couple of hours along the cliffs, all the way to McIntyre Beach. The Jetty Walk and the Coola Outstation Walk are two other short walks that can be accessed from Southend. At the Southend end of McIntyre Beach there is a large shell midden, where the original inhabitants of the area gathered to feast. There are a number of these middens along the coast. For the keen angler the coast can provide good catches of salmon, mulloway, flathead and the occasional shark.

Visitors may sight some of the world's rarest birds, including the orange-bellied parrot and the hooded plover, as well as those magnificent birds of prey, the white-bellied sea-eagle and the swamp harrier. Penguins and seals are also regular visitors, as are much larger sea mammals, including the southern right whale and the minke whale, which pass by on their migrations to and from Antarctica; dolphins are also often seen in the bays.

Stumpy-tailed lizard (Tilinqua rugosa).

Access by conventional vehicles is limited to Cape Buffon and Boozy Gully in the north of the park (via Southend), and to Oil Rig Square in the central section of the park (via Millicent). For those with a 4WD vehicle the whole park is accessible—just follow the orange marker posts from Southend to Carpenter Rocks. This route can be challenging—you need to deflate your tyres to 110 kPa (around 16 psi) to get through. It is important to make sure you stick to the track.

A permit, available from the ranger, is required to camp in the park. There are camping spots close to Southend. Oil Rig Square has water and toilets, but it can be a very exposed site. Number Two Rocks, in the southern section of the park, also has toilets. There are caravan parks in Millicent, Southend and Carpenter Rocks.

Map ref: page **788 F8**

COORONG NATIONAL PARK

This beautiful part of South Australia protects ancient shifting dune formations, tranquil waterways and marshlands, with the pounding surf of the Southern Ocean crashing

Cape Spencer Lighthouse, Innes National Park.

against 60 km (37 miles) of coastline from the mouth of the Murray River south. Having reached the end of its journey, the Murray seldom gains access to the sea, and its sluggish and silted waters fan out into Lake Alexandrina and Lake Albert and down into the shallow Coorong, creating wetland environments and breeding grounds for bird life. Popular activities here include beachcombing, fishing, photography, birdwatching, bushwalking, canoeing and boating. The park is 210 km (130 miles) south-east of Adelaide.

Map ref: page 788 B6

FLINDERS CHASE NATIONAL PARK

This park occupies the entire western end of Kangaroo Island. The area is a major sanctuary for a wide variety of native animals, there being no dingoes or introduced predators on the island. The scenery here is striking and spectacular. High rocky cliffs drop into a wild and rugged ocean. The constant battering of the Southern Ocean's swell and nature's elements have carved into the limestone and ironstone formations, creating the most sensational geological configurations, such as those at Remarkable Rocks. Here groups of graphic orange granite boulders seem to balance precariously on a smooth granite dome. The park is also rich in flora, and in spring the heathland flowers are a riot of colour, competing with native orchids and other flowering shrubs. At Rocky River camping area the wildlife is very much 'at hand', with wallabies, emus and koalas easily seen. Scenic spots not to be missed are the Admirals Arch, a natural arch below

the Cape du Couedic lighthouse, Weirs Cove, where supplies were loaded for the lighthouse, and Cape Borda and its historic lighthouse settlement. The park is 210 km (130 miles) south-west of Adelaide and 100 km (62 miles) west of Kingscote (on Kangaroo Island).

Map ref: page 788 B1

GOOLWA

Goolwa is located 82 km (51 miles) south of Adelaide, close to the mouth of the Murray River, where a barrage across the Goolwa Channel is part of a series of human-made barriers to stop salt water entering the great freshwater expanse of Lake Alexandrina and the river itself. Once an important inland port that linked the Murray River trade with the ocean port of Port Elliot, the town is now more a tourism and holiday centre—its population today is 3000. The paddle-steamers tied up to the wharf are a vivid reminder of days gone by, and are an excellent way to see the river; the *Captain Sturt* is the only Mississippi paddleboat on display in Australia.

A free car ferry operates across to Hindmarsh Island—a tranquil holiday retreat and dairy farming community. Captain Charles Sturt landed here on his epic trip down and back up the Murray River in 1829–30. At the southern end of the island are the sand-filled channels which lead to the Murray Mouth and on to the open ocean. These have always proven to be a barrier to the sea.

The Coorong, one of Australia's great water bird habitats, lies on the eastern side of the mouth and

is now protected in the long sweep of the Coorong National Park. Cruises from Goolwa take in the river mouth and the delights of the Coorong. The town's railway station is a base for a number of steam trains that operate between Goolwa and nearby Port Elliot, as well as Mount Barker, further inland. The Armfield Slip still features the building of wooden boats, and a wooden boat festival is held here each year. Other annual events in the area include the Goolwa to Milang Sailing Classic in February, and the 'Markets on the Wharf', held on one weekend each month between December and March.

Map ref: page 788 A5

INNES NATIONAL PARK

The first glimpse of the coast as you head towards the tip of Yorke Peninsula, once seen, is never forgotten. The striking coastline, with its rocky cliffs and extrusive headlands, is broken by beautiful sandy beaches and secluded coves, with a number of offshore islands in a shimmering sea. The park was originally established to protect the rare western whipbird and its habitat of dense heath and mallee scrub, which is the most prevalent flora. Gravel roads circle the park, leading to idyllic sheltered bays and scenic lookouts; the area is a favourite destination for campers, anglers, divers, surfers, nature lovers and birdwatchers—ospreys can be seen flying and, at times,

nesting on rocky pinnacles along the coast. Pondalowie is a popular camping spot. The park is 300 km (186 miles) west of Adelaide.

Map ref: page 788 A2

KEITH

Located in the centre of a rich farming area, 236 km (147 miles) south-east of Adelaide, Keith (population 1180) is on the Dukes Highway in the region once called 'The 90-Mile Desert'. Originally settled in the 1840s, it was not until after World War II that it was discovered that the 'desert' was short of trace elements in the soil. With the addition of those minerals the land was soon cultivated. To the north of the town is a series of reserves, the largest of which is the Ngarkat Conservation Park. The main street, Heritage Street, has a fine collection of historic buildings. Annual events include the Country Music Festival in March and Horse Trials in April.

Map ref: page 788 C9

The Sir Richard Peninsula at Goolwa, separates the sea from the Goolwa Channel.

KINGSCOTE

The 'capital' of Kangaroo Island, Kingscote—120 km (75 miles) south-west of Adelaide—is the largest town on this island, with a population of 1450. It is the island's trade centre and is serviced by regular flights from Adelaide as well as the daily Sealink passenger and vehicle ferry from Cape Jervis, 110 km (68 miles) south of Adelaide. Established in 1836 as the first 'official' settlement in the then new colony of South Australia, Kingscote is situated on Nepean Bay, with the sweep of cliffs leading south to the mouth of Cygnet River, where the surrounding swampland is home to a multitude of bird life. To the north the cliffs descend to Reeves Point, the most famous heritage site in South Australia, where the first settlement was located, while out in Nepean Bay are the Beatrice Island and Busby Islet Conservation Parks.

Kangaroo Island is the third-largest island off the Australian mainland, being smaller only than Tasmania and Melville Island in the Northern Territory. Intensive farming on Kangaroo Island became possible after the discovery that the soil only lacked trace minerals. The island is a popular

The giant lobster known as 'Larry', Kingston S.E.

tourist destination, with fine beaches and great fishing, diving and surfing. Much of the island is protected in national parks.

The Hope Cottage Folk Museum, operated by the National Trust, is housed in one of the island's most historic homes. The surrounding grounds have a number of features of interest, including the reconstructed light from the Cape Willoughby Lighthouse. There is a eucalyptus oil distilling plant and yacca gum is also produced, both relics from earlier times. In the cliffs in the front of the town little penguins nest, and tours are run by the National Parks and Wildlife Service. Nearby, on the northern side of the wharf area, pelicans are fed daily.

Map ref: page 788 B3

KINGSTON S.E.

Kingston S.E. (population 1430) is located on the shores of Lacepede Bay, just to the south of the Coorong National Park, 305 km (189 miles) south-east of Adelaide. The S.E., for south-east, is to avoid confusion with Kingston-on-Murray, another town in South Australia. As you approach this fishing and tourist destination you will either come past the very large lobster known as 'Larry' on the Princes Highway, or via the old Cape Jaffa Lighthouse, erected on the foreshore. The town is an important fishing port, especially for crayfish—or lobster. Snapper, shark, salmon, whiting and garfish are also caught regularly. Lacepede Bay is considered by the locals to be the safest area of water in the State and is ideal for swimming, windsurfing and sailing.

The area was first settled in the 1850s, but not before some survivors from the shipwrecked *Maria* were massacred by Aboriginals in 1840. The town was proclaimed in 1866, the same year the post office and police station were built. The famous lighthouse was built on Margaret Brock Reef, just off Cape Jaffa, a few kilometres south of Kingston, in 1870. Cape Jaffa today is a small holiday and fishing community, ideal for those who want to get away from it all. In January in Kingston S.E. there is the Lions Surf Fishing Competition, and the annual show is in October.

Map ref: page 788 D7

LITTLE DIP CONSERVATION PARK

This park is part of a group of parks which stretches from the South Australian–Victorian border north-west towards Kingston S.E., and includes the Canunda National Park. The parks preserve a coastal wilderness of complex dune systems and low trees further inland. The region also encompasses numerous inland fresh and saltwater lagoons and lakes which

provide a sanctuary for large numbers of waders and water birds. Vehicle access tracks are limited; there are designated 4WD only tracks that follow the coastline and meander through the sand dunes. Fishing enthusiasts will find plenty of places for good beach fishing, but swimming is not recommended as all the beaches along this coastline are dangerous, with strong tides, rips and undertows. While the wildlife is not abundant, sometimes you will be lucky enough to see a seal resting on the beach. The bird life is prolific—there have been 200 species of birds recorded, including many migratory waders. The park is 410 km (255 miles) from Adelaide.

Map ref: page 788 E7

MILLICENT

Located astride the Princes Highway, north-west of Mount Gambier and 411 km (255 miles) south-east of Adelaide, Millicent is a busy commercial centre, with a population of 5120, servicing the rich

The Shell Gardens at Millicent.

surrounding farming land. It is also a gateway to Canunda National Park, which stretches along the rugged windswept coast.

The area was first settled in 1851 and the surrounding swamps were drained in a huge scheme that started in 1863 and continued into the 1900s. Nearly 1500 km (932 miles) of drains were built, along with 500 bridges. In the very early 1900s pine plantations were established and two paper mills were later constructed south of the town.

The Millicent National Trust Museum is recognised as one of the most significant regional museums in South Australia. It has many

Seals are occasional visitors along the coastline in Little Dip Conservation Park.

award-winning displays, including a fully equipped blacksmith's shop and a shipwreck room containing artefacts from wrecks along the nearby coast. Also worth a visit are the Millicent Shell Gardens, the local art gallery, and the town's many pleasant parks and gardens, including the Memorial Garden with its rotunda.

The nearby Canunda National Park offers camping and 4WD touring along the beach (some prior experience is necessary). Fishing and surfing are also popular there. The Tantanoola Caves Conservation Park is just a short drive south of Millicent and guided tours are available of these unique limestone caves. A number of nearby lakes, including the Lake McIntyre Reserve, are well-known bird habitats.

Map ref: page 788 F9

There are several crater lakes near Mount Gambier, including Blue Lake, with an average depth of 77 m (252 feet).

MOUNT GAMBIER

Mount Gambier, 462 km (287 miles) south-east of Adelaide, is the south-east's unofficial capital, with a population of 21,260, and is a well-known tourist focal point, as well as an industry and business centre. Set in pleasant rolling hills, the area produces fat lambs, fine cheeses, dairy products, wool and wheat. Apart from the rich farmland, the region is home to the largest softwood timber milling industry in Australia. There are many plantation forests of radiata pine and the occasional large timber mill. The district is also famous for its Mount Gambier limestone, which is used as a building material all over southern Australia.

The town is located at the base of Mount Gambier, which is the highest point of an extinct volcanic crater that has, as its heart, a number of lakes, including Valley Lake and Browne Lake. There is a very pleasant picnic area here, and a steep walk to Centenary Tower on top of the peak, with views of the surrounding countryside. There are walking trails and boardwalks on the shore and a profusion of bird life around the lake. Nearby is Blue Lake, the deepest of the lakes near the city, set in another extinct volcano. It turns a deep cobalt blue in November before changing back to grey in late summer.

Mount Gambier was the first part of South Australia to be named in 1800 by Lieutenant James Grant, sailing by in the *Lady*

Nelson, but it was not until 1839 that settlement began. That was a couple of years before the explorer Thomas Mitchell arrived, only to find that George Henty was already working the area. The town was surveyed in 1861 and the railway arrived in 1879. The poet Adam Lindsay Gordon served here with the mounted police in the 1850s and gained lasting fame, not only for his poetry, but also by jumping a horse over a wooden fence onto a ledge on the very lip of the Blue Lake crater.

Much of the surrounding area is limestone: the Cave Gardens in the centre of the city are a very pleasant example. Umpherstone Cave has been planted with terraced gardens and is floodlit at night; Engelbrecht Cave is open to the public, as well as to divers. Piccaninnie Ponds and Ewen Ponds, which are both closer to the coast, have crystal-clear water bubbling up from deep underground, and are excellent for snorkelling or diving. Mount Schank, further south, is another extinct volcano, and was also named as the *Lady Nelson* sailed the coast. A walking trail climbs this peak, and continues into the crater itself.

The city is a well-known sporting location, and regularly hosts a number of national and State events, including shooting and tennis. Annual events in town include the Country Music Festival

in February, the Blue Lake Festival in March, Field Days in April and the Eisteddfod in August.

Map ref: page 788 F10

NARACOORTE

Located in the south-east of the State, 346 km (215 miles) from Adelaide, Naracoorte owes its fame mostly to the caves that are nearby. The largest and most significant of the 60-plus caves along the Cave Range is the Victoria Fossil Cave. First discovered in 1894, it won worldwide acclaim when in 1969 an amazing diversity of fossils was found. In all, over 93 species of animal fossils have been found, including many that are extinct, such as a marsupial lion, a large echidna, a giant tree-browsing kangaroo and a hippo-size wombat. A modern interpretive centre recaptures the pre-historic landscape. A number of caves contained within the Naracoorte Caves Conservation Park are open to the public.

The area was first settled in the 1840s, when it was known as Mosquito Plain. The

railway arrived in 1876, and several buildings from this era still grace the town. Today the town has a population of 4720, and is a major service centre for the rich agricultural area that surrounds it and produces fat lambs, wool and cattle.

Bool Lagoon, 17 km (10.5 miles) south of the town, is a vast wetland that is alive with birds. Over 155 species, including brolgas, Cape Barren geese and numerous species of ducks and waders, use this reserve. There are boardwalks and hides for watching the birds. Calendar events include the Swap Meet and Three Day Equestrian Event in May, and the Underground Music Festival in October.

Map ref: page 788 E9

The Victorian mansion Struan House, Naracoorte.

The view from Red Bluff Nature Reserve, Ngarkat Conservation Park.

NGARKAT GROUP OF CONSERVATION PARKS

The park takes in the Ngarkat, Scorpion Springs, Mount Rescue and Mount Shaugh Conservation Parks and is considered a significant wilderness area, linking with Victoria's Big Desert region. Its landscape of disordered, undulating sandhills is covered in a mantle of mallee eucalypts; heath blankets the plains between the dunes. In the few places where surface soaks provide water there are larger trees. The wildflowers in spring attract not only birds and bees, but also apiarists. The parks are also home to some unusual animals, such as the ningau, silky mouse and pygmy mouse, along with the more common echidnas and western grey kangaroos. This region can get extremely hot during the summer months. Ngarkat Conservation Park is 300 km (186 miles) south-east of Adelaide.
Map ref: page 788 B9

PENOLA

Penola lays claim to being the gateway to the famous wine-growing area of the Coonawarra, one of Australia's premium red wine growing regions. Wynns Coonawarra

Estate winery, the Padthaway winery, Haselgrove, and more than a dozen others have wine-tasting, cellar door sales and tours, so it is easy to enjoy the results of this great grape-growing region.

The town itself, 397 km (247 miles) south-east of Adelaide and with a population of 1150, is historic, being on the crossroads of traffic travelling between Adelaide and Melbourne, including the carts and drays that headed further south in earlier days. It was the first town in the south-east, established in 1850, six years after the first settlers arrived. There is a good collection of heritage buildings, including John Riddoch's magnificent 1880s mansion, and Yallum Park, said by some to be Australia's best-preserved Victorian house. The first vines in the area were planted on this property. The former post office, which built in 1865, houses the National Trust Museum.

Sister Mary MacKillop, the nun who founded the Sisters of St Joseph and started a small school for poor children in Penola, is commemorated by a signposted, wide-ranging tourist drive and by a display housed in the school house she had built in 1867. The town is also famous for a number of poets and writers who found inspiration here, amongst them Adam Lindsay Gordon and Will Ogilvie. A short distance out of town, on the road to Robe, is the Penola Conservation Park; the Greenrise Recreation Ground, close to town, is a peaceful venue for boating, fishing or a picnic. Penola Founders Day is celebrated in April, the annual festival is in June and the Penola Show is in October.
Map ref: page 788 E10

PORT MACDONNELL

The most southerly port in South Australia, 490 km (304 miles) south-east of Adelaide, this was once the second-busiest port in the State, loading wool and wheat for Melbourne and Adelaide. Today it is a quiet seaside port, with a population of only 680, but still with the biggest

crayfishing fleet in the State. Reminders of the old days are the historic 1862 customs house, and the 1882 lighthouse and local courthouse. The Maritime Museum gives a good indication of how dangerous this coast once was to the sailing ships that transported the goods which made the port busy.

The cottage of poet Adam Lindsay Gordon is in the nearby Dingley Dell Conservation Park, and the Piccaninnie Ponds and Ewen Ponds Conservation Parks are a short distance away along the coast. To the north is Mount Schank, with its walking trails, and to the east, just across the border in Victoria, is Lower Glenelg National Park and the tranquil waters of the Glenelg River. But it is the coast around Port MacDonnell that is the main attraction for visitors—surfers and anglers love its wild, windswept nature. Summer activities include the Bayside Festival, held in January.
Map ref: page 788 G9

ROBE

Settled along the shores of Guichen Bay, just 130 km (81 miles) north of Mount Gambier and 350 km (217 miles) south-east of Adelaide, Robe is a charming seaside village that reminds visitors of yester-year—the town has many fine old buildings, including the Customs House, Robe House and the Caledonian Inn. Aboriginals were the

earliest known inhabitants, but pioneer settlers followed in the footsteps of the early explorers and by 1846 Robe had become South Australia's third most important port, exporting wool and horses. From the mid-1800s it saw a rabble of gold seekers, including 16,500 Chinese, pass through on their way to the Victorian goldfields. The port is somewhat quieter today—its population is 730—with professional crayfish and shark fishing fleets operating out of the sheltered anchorage.

Water-based activities, especially fishing, are popular pastimes here. Dropping a line at the breakwater

Wynns Coonawarra Estate is the only winery in the Penola area dating from the nineteenth century.

Robe has many secluded beaches, some with 4WD dune and beach tracks.

or jetty could hook you garfish, mullet and trevally; the bay yields delicious King George whiting. The nearby Little Dip Conservation Park protects a rugged, windswept, imposing limestone coastline and sand dune range just south of Robe; a trip along the park's 4WD dune and beach tracks is definitely a driving challenge. Behind the dunes are a number of lakes, and with such a varied range of habitats and vegetation, it is no wonder that this area is home to a wide variety of flora and fauna, with bird life being especially prolific.

Map ref: page 788 E7

SEAL BAY CONSERVATION PARK

Seal Bay, Kangaroo Island, 190 km (118 miles) south of Adelaide, must be one of the best places in the world to see sea lions and fur seals at close quarters. The wide white beach of Seal Bay plays host to dozens of these animals, which are surprisingly tolerant of humans. Often, if you are lucky, a young seal will approach you as you sit on the beach—a great experience! Guided tours with a ranger are a highlight of any trip to Kangaroo Island. Access to other beaches and bays along the coast from Seal Bay is totally prohibited, and there is no swimming, boating or fishing are allowed in the adjoining aquatic reserve. Picnic shelters, gas barbecues and toilets are provided

at the Bales Bay visitor area at the eastern end of Seal Bay. Camping is not allowed. The best time to visit is during spring and summer.

Map ref: page 352 B3

TAILEM BEND

Located near the junction of the Duke, Ouyen and Princes Highways, 26 km (16 miles) south of Murray Bridge and 106 km (66 miles) east of Adelaide, Tailem Bend (population 1600) is close to the last great bend of the Murray River. Proclaimed in 1887, the town is laid out atop the lofty east bank of the river and is a major road and railway junction, with railway workshops and marshalling yards. It also provides many necessary services for the surrounding mixed farming communities.

The town's interesting colonial history has been re-created in the pioneer village at Old Tailem Town, a few kilometres north,

Seal Bay has a large colony of Australian sea lions. Ranger-guided tours are available.

where you can saunter around the many exhibits and buildings that capture the atmosphere of bygone days. A ferry from Tailem Bend takes vehicles across the river to Jervois. From there it is just an 11-km (6.8-mile) drive to Wellington, at the junction of the river and Lake Alexandrina.

Map ref: page 788 A7

VICTOR HARBOR

Situated along the wide, sandy shore of Encounter Bay, 81 km (50 miles) south of Adelaide, this often breathtakingly beautiful part of South Australia has long been a very popular holiday destination. Named after HMS *Victor* by its commander in 1837, Victor Harbor's beginnings in the early 1830s were a somewhat gruesome affair, with hardy pioneers harvesting whales and seals from the surrounding waters. By 1837 a whaling station had been established on Granite Island, just offshore, to process the catches. The island is now connected to the mainland by a causeway.

The first permanent settlers did not arrive until 1839 and Victor Harbor soon became an important trading port, initially because of the whaling station, and later as a shipping port for wool and other primary industries developing along the Murray. By World War I the port had lost its importance; today, Victor Harbor's population is 5950 and it is mainly a holiday and retirement town.

The town boasts a number of historic homes and buildings, including the railway station, St Augustine's Church (1869), the

Anchorage Guesthouse, built early this century, and the 1890s mansion, Adare. Most visitors to Victor cross the causeway to Granite Island—some take a ride across on the famous horse-drawn trams. Alternatively, a chairlift goes to the high point in the centre of the island for a bird's-eye view of the surrounding bay, other islands and the nearby mainland. The Penguin Interpretive Centre, on Granite Island, is worth a visit, and there are fairy penguin walks.

The Cockle Train, a restored steam train, runs between Victor and Goolwa, recalling the days when steam was king and Victor and Goolwa were part of the rich Murray River trade. Nature lovers will enjoy the wildlife of the nearby Urimbirra Wildlife Park or the

The antique horse-drawn tram in Victor Harbor.

native plants and trees in the Nangawooka Flora Park. Further afield are a number of other parks, including the Newland Head Conservation Park.

Victor Harbor is one of the State's most popular fishing destinations, and keen anglers can cast a line from the jetties, rocks, around the bay, or in the nearby streams, all with more than a good chance of catching salmon and mulloway; garfish, whiting, and Australian salmon are common around the bay. The town also attracts artists and photographers. Their works are exhibited at the Rotary Art Show, held in January. Other annual events are the Apex Easter Craft Fair and the start of the whale season in June—when the coast is crammed with people watching the whales. The Folk Festival is in October.

Map ref: page 788 B5

WESTERN
SOUTH AUSTRALIA

The vast western plains of South Australia seem feature-less and inhospitable to most visitors. Indeed, much of the inland requires a permit for entry as it is either Aboriginal land or part of the Woomera and Maralinga Prohibited Areas. The Nullarbor Plain, the largest single slab of lime-stone in the world, is a daunting barrier between eastern and western Australia.

Far below its surface is a labyrinth of sub-terranean caverns and rivers. There are a number of caves accessed by sinkholes, which usually support local wildlife, within the Nullarbor National Park and Nullarbor Regional Reserve. Most of these are not open to the public because of their immense palaeontological significance, but it is pos-sible to join a licensed tour operator at Ceduna to inspect some of them. Further along the Eyre Highway, the main route for travellers crossing the Nullarbor, is the tiny town of Penong. It is mostly recognised as the turnoff to reputedly one of the best surfing locations in Australia, Cactus Beach. Yalata appears on most maps just as a roadhouse but the village is well-known for the interesting range of Aboriginal artefacts available there.

An Unnamed Conservation Park, surrounded by land owned by the original inhabitants—the Pitjant-jatjara and Tjarutja people—is an arid land sanctuary. Its parallel ridges of sand and sparse covering of scrub are home to a range of animals adapted to the harsh con-ditions, such as the spinifex hopping mouse and the long-tailed dunnart, both of which are nocturnal and so escape the blistering conditions. The Great Victoria Desert, of which this park is a part, in the north-western corner of the State, is home to Gould's goanna one of a number of moni-tors which inhabit the deserts of Australia.

Woomera Prohibited Area contains rocket ranges used by the British Government (and others) from the 1950s to the 1970s to test rockets and other missiles. It covers a vast area of the state's north-west. Maralinga was the site of British nuclear tests around the same time. Many Australian servicemen participated in these tests.

OPPOSITE: The jetty at Denial Bay, near Ceduna is a popular fishing spot. Bullock drays were once driven here to load up the ships in port.

The coastline around Ceduna is noted for its breath-taking scenery and clifftop walks.

REGIONAL FEATURE

The Nullarbor Plain

Since the Eyre Highway was finally sealed in 1976, the drive across the Nullarbor has been easier and safer. However, wandering wildlife and driver fatigue are still significant hazards.

OPPOSITE: The Nullarbor's uniformity can be disorienting for bushwalkers, so be careful not to stray far from tracks or roads, and always carry plenty of water.

At first glance, the stark scenery of the Nullarbor Plain seems to offer little to waylay the passing traveller. The ribbon of tar that is the Eyre Highway stretches ruler-straight to the horizon; on either side of the road, dull coloured saltbush and bluebush spread across a level, light brown land, blurring into a distant shimmering haze. The region's name—derived from a Latin phrase *nulla arbor*, meaning 'no trees'— seems entirely appropriate.

But those prepared to pause a while and look a little closer will find that there is more to this seemingly barren environment than meets the eye. Take any track off the highway to the south, for example, and you soon find yourself atop spectacular 60-m (200-foot) cliffs, looking down on the torrid shore of the Southern Ocean, where seals and sea lions sprawl on rocks and, from time to time, majestic southern right whales surface in bays. Spend time exploring the desert and you will discover fascinating, arid-adapted flora and fauna. At night, vast, untarnished skies reveal a mesmerising display of stars, and you can drift off to sleep pondering the fact that the ground beneath you conceals some of the largest systems of limestone caves in Australia.

History

The Nullarbor Plain stretches 300 km (186 miles) west of the Western Australia–South Australia border and 250 km (155 miles) to the east. It is the world's largest semiarid limestone landscape and originally formed from sediments on the floor of a shallow ocean between 50 and 70 million years ago. Around 23 to 25 million years ago, the entire region was lifted above sea level by tectonic plate movements. Little geological activity has occurred since then, with the result that the plain remains flat and featureless. Even the action of irregular rains has failed to leave a trace on the surface, as water soaks rapidly into the porous rock. Underground, it's a different story, however: here, variations in the hardness of the limestone layers mean that rainwater has slowly carved great channels, chambers and caves, even subterranean lakes.

In recent years, the Nullarbor's cave systems have been extensively explored by cave-divers, yielding evidence of early Aboriginal occupation of the region. Much of this evidence is in the form of artworks pressed into the soft walls of underground caves and passages. Koonalda Cave in the northern central section of the park, for example, has long been recognised as one of Australia's most significant prehistoric art sites, with some of the earliest-known Aboriginal engravings. Located 80 m (260 feet) undergound and measuring 45 m (150 feet) in height, Koonalda was used by Aboriginal peoples from at least 24,000 years ago as a source of water and stone, and as a ceremonial site.

Over the centuries, the descendants of these early Aboriginal inhabitants had to adapt to increasingly arid conditions as the continent's climate changed. They developed a nomadic hunter-gatherer lifestyle, moving from one water source to another as rains came and went. Throughout this time, the underground pools provided emergency supplies.

To European settlers, unaware of this subterranean source, the Nullarbor presented a seemingly insurmountable barrier to travel and settlement, and it wasn't until 1841 that the plain was finally crossed, from east to west, by John Eyre, during an arduous five-month journey. Pioneer graziers soon followed the explorer's route into the Nullarbor, discovered the underground water supplies and used them to support their stock, a practice that continues today in some areas.

A telegraph line was strung across the plain in 1877, but it wasn't until World War II that a road was constructed and it wasn't sealed until 1976. The Trans Australian Railway line dates back to 1907 when surveyors began plotting its route between existing railheads at Kalgoorlie and Port Augusta. Work on the line commenced in 1912 and the first train completed the east–west journey in October 1917. Today, the famous Indian–Pacific service traverses the centre of the Nullarbor Plain during its epic three-day journey across the continent. The journey includes a section of track on the Nullarbor that, at 478 km (297 miles), is the longest stretch of straight railway in the world.

Nullarbor National Park and National Reserve

Along the coast on the South Australian side of the border, most of the Nullarbor is public land. Nullarbor National Park runs from the state boundary to the Nullarbor Roadhouse and approximately 20 km (12.5 miles) inland, while Nullarbor Regional Reserve extends from the park's northern boundary eastward along the northern edge of Yalata Aboriginal Land to Yellabinna Regional Reserve, and north to the Trans Australian Railway Line. Together, the national park and reserve encompass 2,873,000 ha (70,992,000 acres) of undeveloped wilderness.

Lake MacDonnell, near Penong, produces large amounts of salt, which are harvested regularly, and is also Australia's most important source of gypsum.

The Nullarbor Plain ends abruptly at the sheer sea cliffs that flank the Great Australian Bight. Clearly visible rock layers indicate the different kinds of sediments that were laid down over millennia.

their young. Probably the best spot for viewing these magnificent creatures is Head of Bight, located just to the east of the national park on Yalata Aboriginal Land. A permit is required and can be obtained from Yalata Roadhouse or Nullarbor Roadhouse, where you can also arrange guided tours, including helicopter flights.

Inland, where the only reliable source of water lies deep underground, wildlife keeps a low profile. Plant cover is sparse, and consists mainly of drought-resistant bluebush and saltbush, though there are clumps of mallee and she-oaks nearer the edges of the plain. Smaller native mammals, which were once common here—at least 32 species were present at one time—have almost vanished as a result of competition with and predation by introduced species such as cats, foxes and rabbits. However, western grey and red kangaroos are common, especially after local rain, and dingoes roam widely across the plain. This is also the last great stronghold of the southern hairy-nosed wombat, which usually emerges at night to feed on dry grasses, retreating to a cool burrow during the day.

There is no public access to the Nullarbor's extensive cave systems, but cavers can apply for permission to visit the miles of tunnels and passageways. Prospective visitors must demonstrate experience and skill, and usually visit in the company of a park ranger.

Those travelling in a 4WD can take an interesting, though long, detour off the Eyre Highway into the interior, a journey that conveys a strong sense of the Nullarbor's vastness and allows you to view country that is more typical of the plain than the land fringing the highway. At Yalata, follow the road north across Ifould Lake for 142 km (88 miles) to Ooldea on the railway line. Cross the railway and follow it west to Watson, where you return to the south side of the line. Continue past O'Malley and Fisher stations to Cook, where fuel may be available (check in advance). Turn left here and drive 104 km (65 miles) south to rejoin the Eyre Highway 44 km (27 miles) west of the Nullarbor Roadhouse.

Fishing

The Nullarbor coast is renowned as a happy hunting ground for anglers. Productive surf beaches begin just a few kilometres west of Ceduna, and the fishing improves toward Head of Bight. As a rule of thumb, mulloway (jewfish) is the target in summer and salmon in winter, though there are some areas and times of the year when the two can be targeted together.

Mulloway usually move in to feed along the shoreline gutters almost as soon as the inshore Bight waters begin to warm with the onset of summer. At this time of year, there are few other parts of Australia where big mulloway are taken at such impressive sizes and with such regularity—catches vary in size from school fish up to 40-kg (88-pound) giants, but 20 kg (44 pounds) is a fair average. Scotts Beach, near Fowlers Bay, is regarded as the first serious mulloway area beyond Ceduna. It has produced hundreds of monster catches over the years and is without doubt

Although visitor facilities are limited, the park and reserve ensure that this remarkable landscape is accessible to the public and that its wildlife and landforms receive continued protection. Travellers can explore the hauntingly bleak interior via 4WD tracks on the northern side of the Eyre Highway. To the south, numerous side roads lead to coastal lookouts and short walking trails which provide magnificent views, although the steep cliffs mean that there are few places where you can actually descend to the seashore.

Wildlife watching is the Nullarbor's most rewarding activity. The coastal cliffs, which run for 200 km (124 miles)—forming the world's longest stretch of coastline without a natural harbour—provide bird's-eye views of marine mammals including whales, seals and sea lions. Southern right whales congregate along the Bight in winter and spring to calve and nurse the most convenient place for uninitiated anglers to start their quest. Other renowned mulloway-fishing beaches include Tuckamore, the Dog Fence, Yalata and Twin Rocks, but these are more remote and reaching them requires a 4WD.

Mulloway tackle for these beaches needs to be robust and well assembled, as sharks and the occasional big snapper are also likely when conditions are favourable. A 3- to 3.6-m (10- to 12-foot) fast taper surf rod is ideal and the reel, regardless of style, must hold at least 400 m (1300 feet) of the chosen line class. Most serious mulloway chasers opt for 12- to 15-kg (26- to 33-pound) line, which provides the necessary 'grunt' if a truly big fish grabs the bait and bolts for the horizon. Extra strong hooks in the 6/0 to 8/0 range are mandatory, as is 30- to 40-kg (66- to 88-pound) monofilament trace material and a range of surf sinkers of up to 170 g (6 ounces). Surf conditions can often be turbulent, which calls for either star or grapnel sinkers to ensure the bait stays on the hook.

Live bait is the best option when fishing mulloway here, and most experienced anglers set aside a day to catch bait before venturing onto the beach. This can be a tricky business as ideal fish are hard to obtain in summer. Occasionally, it is possible to berley a school of yellow-eye mullet or juvenile salmon within casting range, and bigger salmon can sometimes be found in small, isolated pockets around rocky headlands and near inshore reefs.

In winter and spring, the coastal waters virtually teem with salmon, and just about all the beaches between Ceduna and the Western Australia border hold salmon schools from May through to the end of September. An average fish would weigh 3.5 kg (7.7 pounds), but plenty of salmon above 5 kg (11 pounds) are taken each year, and these really pull hard in heavy surf, providing excellent sport. Both lures and bait will take the salmon, with fresh West Australian pilchards the best option. Quality 6- to 8-kg (13- to 18-pound) surf tackle is all that is required, and long casts are the exception rather than the rule. Most of the better gutters run quite close to the beach—so close, in fact, that saltwater fly fishing for salmon is practical in many areas.

Access and Camping

Venturing onto the Nullarbor Plain requires thorough preparation and caution. Although the Eyre Highway is now entirely sealed, services along this route are few and very far between. Furthermore, there are no accessible sources of fresh water, so anyone contemplating camping must carry their own substantial supplies. All travellers should also carry plentiful fuel and food, a well-stocked first-aid kit and spares for their vehicle, which should be in good repair.

Although most parts of the Nullarbor are accessible from the Eyre Highway, many of the best beaches lie on Aboriginal-owned land. Visiting these areas requires a permit, which can be obtained in Ceduna or from the Yalata or Nullarbor roadhouses.

Accommodation and camping are available at the Nullarbor and Yalata roadhouses, and at Nundroo and Penong (no camping) in the east. Bush camping is possible at any number of places, but permits are required for camping in Nullarbor National Park and Nullarbor Regional Reserve; contact National Parks and Wildlife South Australia for details.

Between November and March, the waters of the Bight yield huge mulloway (Argyrosomus hololepidotus), which are often caught in deep gutters close to the shore.

TOP: A small wheatgrowing centre on the eastern edge of the Nullarbor, Penong is surrounded by numerous windmills that pump water to the surface from underground aquifers.

Enormous white-sand dunes line Cactus Beach, a favourite destination among surfers, who flock here to test their skills on its one left- and two right-turning breaks.

Places in
WESTERN
SOUTH AUSTRALIA

CACTUS BEACH

Cactus Beach, 21 km (13 miles) south of Penong, is famed for its surf. The offshore reefs which shape the three excellent breaks here (Cactus, Castles and Caves) are also feeding grounds for salmon, turtles, stingrays and seals—all prey of white pointer sharks for which, since a fatal attack on a board-rider in 2000,

The OTC (Overseas Telecommunications Commission) centre, Ceduna.

Cactus is now notorious. Reached by an unsealed white lime road, the beach curves between the roaring, unpolluted waves of the Southern Ocean and pale, rolling sandhills. Just inland are tidal salt lakes.
Map ref: page 789 F10

CEDUNA

The largest town in the far west of the state, 795 km (494 miles) west of Adelaide, Ceduna, with nearby Thevenard—a deep-sea port just 4 km (2.4 miles) away—services a hinterland of cereal-producing land and a fishing fleet that chases fish, abalone, and crayfish. Grain, salt and gypsum are stored for export in the huge silos and stockpiles that dominate the skyline of Thevenard.

For many travellers Ceduna is the last town of any note before the Nullarbor, or the first of any size

after driving from Western Australia. The town's name is said to come from a word in an Aboriginal language— 'chedoona', which means 'a resting place'; an apt name indeed for a place at one end of the Nullarbor.

Matthew Flinders came this way in 1802, naming the larger, outer bay Denial Bay; the French explorer, Nicholas Baudin, named the smaller bay, on which Ceduna is located, Murat Bay. The original township was established in the 1840s at Denial Bay, 13 km (8 miles) west of present-day Ceduna and on the western side of the bay. Ceduna was proclaimed in 1901 and soon grew into the major port it is today. Its population now is 4050. The original McKenzie Landing, at the bay, and the McKenzie Ruins, on the road to Davenport Creek, are heritage listed.

The present-day jetty at Denial Bay, which is only a third of its former length, is excellent for fishing and crabbing. The surrounding waters are also gaining acclaim as an oyster-growing area.

Named its white snout, the white pointer shark can be found in waters off Cactus Beach.

Apart from the swimming, fishing, diving, surfing, or boating that this area offers, there are other attractions: the Old Schoolhouse National Trust Museum in Ceduna has a wide range of pioneer artefacts on display as well as items from the Maralinga atomic bomb test sites. Watching whales from the cliffs as they come to these waters to calve is a fascinating experience. On the October long weekend, Ceduna holds Oysterfest, with beach sport events, the opening of the sailing season, a Red Faces competition, and a variety of other entertainment.
Map ref: page 789 G10 A4

NULLARBOR

Nothing more than a roadhouse, motel and caravan park on the edge of the main highway, Nullarbor (population 15) is 300 km (186 miles) west of Ceduna— and 1097 km (681 miles) west of Adelaide—on the edge of the vast, treeless Nullarbor Plain. For most it is nothing more than an overnight stay, or an even shorter refuelling stop, but in winter a major event takes place here. This tiny outpost of civilisation is the closest habitation to the Head of the Bight, where southern right whales come to give birth and to mate.

The roadhouse at the isolated outpost of Nullarbor. The word Nullarbor comes from the Latin words for 'no trees'.

From the cliffs you get a great view of the animals frolicking in the waters. However, you will need a permit to travel across the Yalata Aboriginal land—these are available from the motel. This section of coast is one of the premier whale viewing areas in the world. North of the roadhouse is the Murrawijinie Cave, just one of several large caves found on the Nullarbor but one approved for the public to visit.

Map ref: page 789 C9

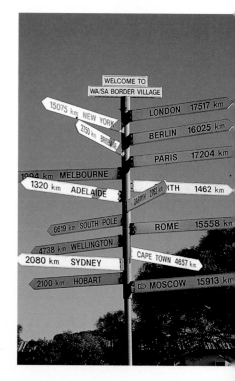

Located 73 km (45 miles) west of Ceduna, the tiny township of Penong is renowned for its many windmills which pump the artesian waters.

PENONG

The small settlement of Penong lies on the western edge of the South Australian grain-growing belt on marginal agricultural land 870 km (540 miles) west of Adelaide. Water is a constant problem. Artesian water pumped by windmill is supplemented by supplies trucked in from the Todd River pipeline 15 km (9.3 miles) to the east. At Lake MacDonnell, to the south, massive deposits of salt and gypsum are mined for export from the port of Thevenard. The Woolshed, on Penong's western outskirts, houses a museum of local history and is an outlet for locally made quandong jam and chutney—quandong is a native fruit. The town also has a surfboard factory.

Map ref: page 789 F10

POINT SINCLAIR

Facing the power of the Southern Ocean, edged by dramatic cliffs and backed by huge sand dunes, Point Sinclair is visited by a steady stream of surfing enthusiasts, as well as sightseers attracted by its stark beauty. Its 500 ha (1236 acres) was the first land in South Australia to come under a 1980 Heritage Agreement where, in exchange for not paying rates, the landholder instead undertakes to maintain the native vegetation and allow access to the public. Like nearby Cactus Beach, Point Sinclair is almost as famous for its white pointer shark population as it is for its waves; with a 1975 fatality and several

maulings. This is also a popular fishing spot, with impressive catches of salmon and mulloway. The point was named by Matthew Flinders during his 1802 exploration of the coast after his midshipman Kennet Sinclair.

Map ref: page 789 F10

UNNAMED CONSERVATION PARK

This large park—2,132,600 ha (5,269,655 acres)—covers desert scrub country of the Great Victoria Desert. It is situated north of the Trans Australian Railway, with the Western Australia–South Australia border as its western boundary. About 1350 km (838 miles) north-west of Adelaide, the park is surrounded by Aboriginal land.

Only two sandy 4WD tracks cut through the park—the Anne Beadell Highway, which runs east–west and is the main access to the area, and the north–south track which runs north from the railway siding at Cook to Vokes Hill Junction, in the east of the park. Permits are required to travel both these routes and only well-equipped and experienced 4WD travellers should attempt them.

The park is one of South Australia's most pristine and remote wilderness areas, and is home to the Alexandra's parrot and a number of rare mammals. The park is mainly mallee scrub land and spinifex sand plains; stands of marble gums, desert poplars and

desert kurrajong provide a delightful change. After a rainfall the desert blooms with a host of brightly coloured ephemerals such as daisies, parakeelya, hakeas and thryptomenes.

Near the border is the long chain of vivid white saltpans known as the Serpentine Lakes. The Anne Beadell Highway gives good access to these remote and interesting landforms. The best time to visit is winter or spring.

Map ref: page 789 A4

A signpost at the Western Australian border in Unnamed Conservation Park.

CENTRAL-EAST SOUTH AUSTRALIA

During his circumnavigation of Australia, Matthew Flinders charted and named Spencer Gulf and Gulf St Vincent, both of which are shallow and provide excellent fishing opportunities. The Eyre and Yorke Peninsulas, the most prominent features on any map of this area, are both rather flat and dry but their coastlines, which are washed by the Southern Ocean, attract thousands of visitors annually.

Many enjoy the camping, fishing and diving opportunities provided by the Lincoln and Coffin Bay National Parks. Dangerous Reef, near Port Lincoln, is a well-known location for the sighting of great white sharks and sea lions

The Adelaide Hills, only half an hour's drive from Adelaide, appear lush compared to much of the state due to a reasonable rainfall. The distinctive European character of the area, which produced Australia's earliest wines, is due in part to its settlement by Germans fleeing religious persecution in their homeland in the nineteenth century and in part to wealthy British settlers who built summer retreats there. Another renowned wine-producing region is the Barossa Valley, also developed by German settlers. A delightful way to view the picturesque landscape, with its German-style cottages and churches, is by hot-air balloon. This pastime is celebrated annually during the valley's Balloon Regatta.

The so-called Copper Triangle is a group of three towns—Kadina, Wallaroo and Moonta—which are located on the Yorke Peninsula. The many splendid old public buildings and private homes located in these towns have survived from the 'copper boom'

of the nineteenth and early twentieth centuries because of the lack of commercial development since the 1920s.

An Australian invention, the stump-jump plough, which made early wheat farming possible, is commemorated in the coastal town of Ardrossan, which is still dominated by wheat silos. At the head of Spencer Gulf is Port Augusta which played a pivotal role in opening up the inland and is still an important crossroads. Further inland the landscape rarely rises beyond 300 m (984 feet) above sea level. The Mount Lofty and Flinders Ranges provide some relief as a spine of hills running 800 km (497 miles) north–south from the coast into the interior .

OPPOSITE: The dead trunks of red river gums (Eucalyptus camaldulensis) in Lake Bonney, near Barmena.

The winery at Bethany in the Barossa Valley produces full-bodied reds typical of this region.

REGIONAL FEATURE

The Flinders Ranges

As the sun rises, the landscape takes on varying hues of blue, then pink, gold and yellow, before the rocks and scrub don their daytime garb of ochre and olive green. At sunset, the scene changes again, as the ranges absorb the colours of a darkening sky, moving through cobalt and navy blue to rich oranges and reds, then finally to purple just as the light fades.

The changing moods of the Flinders Ranges, which stretch 300 km (186 miles) from Gladstone near the Spencer Gulf northward to the edge of the Strzelecki Desert, have enchanted visitors for decades, and it's no wonder that generations of artists ranging from the great painter Sir Hans Heysen, who first came here in the 1930s, to modern-day chroniclers using cameras and film have tried so hard to capture the magic of these mountains.

Situated 446 km (277 miles) north of Adelaide, the Flinders Ranges are, for the majority of South Australians, the most accessible part of the outback. A sealed road leads all the way from the state capital to Wilpena Pound, at the heart of the ranges, and there is also a slightly shorter route through Orroroo and Jamestown, which is all bitumen apart from a 50-km (31-mile) section of smooth gravel south of Hawker. Within the ranges, too, good dirt roads suitable for the family car lead to most points of interest; only after severe rains or floods do they close, and then usually just for a short time.

History

OPPOSITE: The Pichi Richi Railway, based at Quorn in the southern Flinders, offers weekly trips to Stirling North on trains pulled by two historic steam locomotives.

Thrust upward 500 million years ago, the Flinders Ranges originally stood 6000 m (20,000 feet) high. Erosion then gradually reduced the ranges to their present elevation.

Aboriginal peoples have inhabited the Flinders for at least 15,000 years and by the time of European settlement at least six groups dwelled in the area. They lived well off the ranges' rich natural resources, including permanent waterholes, varied vegetation and bountiful game, and left behind records of their lifestyle and culture in the form of abundant artworks, many of which still adorn caves and cliffs throughout the region.

Matthew Flinders, after whom the ranges were named, was the first European to sight these mountains, during his circumnavigation of Australia on the *Investigator* in 1802. But it was Edward John Eyre who opened up the area with his 1839 and 1840 expeditions, inspiring pioneer pastoralists to follow.

Gold, copper and silver drew hordes of prospectors in the 1850s, but the deposits were quickly exhausted. In the 1870s, a period of unusually temperate weather encouraged wheat farmers to flock to the plains around the southern end of the Flinders. When the climate readjusted to its semi-arid norm, crops failed on a huge scale and many of the small settlements that had been built had to be abandoned. Their ruins still dot the landscape.

Tourists began to visit the Flinders in the mid twentieth century and a motel was built at Wilpena Creek in the 1950s. In 1970, the government bought Oraparinna Station and created a national park northeast of Wilpena Pound. This park was extended to include the pound itself in 1972 and further enlarged four years later. Wilpena Station, which covered much of the eastern flank of the Wilpena Pound Range, was incorporated in the park in 1988.

Flinders Ranges National Park

Today, Flinders Ranges National Park encompasses 94,908 ha (234,518 acres) of the central ranges. Its centrepiece, Wilpena Pound, is an enormous natural amphitheatre measuring 11 km (7 miles) by 5 km (3.1 miles) and rimmed by battlement-like ridges, which on their outer edge plummet as much as 300 m (1000 feet) to the surrounding plains. The highest point in the pound, 1188-m (3898-foot) St Mary Peak, is also the tallest mountain in South Australia. The Aboriginal name Wilpena is said to mean 'cupped hand'—a highly appropriate description—while the epithet 'pound' derives from the landform's use as a natural stock enclosure by pioneer graziers.

BUSHWALKING

Several bushwalking tracks departing from Wilpena Resort allow visitors to investigate this dramatic landscape more closely. Shorter tracks lead to the old homestead and up to Wangara Lookout, a return trip of one or two hours depending on your level of fitness and on how long you spend admiring the superb views over the surrounding country. At the entrance to the pound there is also an hour-long nature trail as well as a more strenuous two-hour hike to a lookout on top of Mount Ohlssen Bagge.

Longer walks of a day or more can take you south to Bridle Gap or north to Edeowie Gorge. A circuit route leads via the heart of the pound and Cooinda Camp north to Tanderra Saddle, where there is a detour to the top of St Mary Peak, before returning south along the battlements to Wilpena Creek.

You can also hike part of the Heysen Trail, a long-distance walking track that runs all the way from

Climbing the Great Wall at Wilpena Pound. Rock climbing in the Flinders Ranges can be a great experience.

Cape Jervis, south of Adelaide, to the northern end of the Flinders—an epic journey of around 1500 km (930 miles). It enters the park at Bridle Gap, then leads north along the ABC Range to Aroona Valley.

At Aroona, where the ruins of the homestead face magnificent views, you can follow another trail along the nearby creek or climb to Red Hill Lookout, a 7.5-km (4.7-mile), two-hour trip. You can also hike east to Trezona Bore and the headwaters of Brachina Creek; from there, you can either return along the same route to complete a 14-km (8.5-mile) round trip, or continue south to the road near Trezona camp site and Brachina Creek, and then follow the roads

west and north back to Aroona. All up, this is a 25-km (15.5-mile) hike, requiring at least a day.

EXPLORING THE GORGES

Brachina Creek runs all the way to the western edge of the park, where its waters flow through the Heysen Range at delightful Brachina Gorge. Here, bluffs and gum trees line the creek, creating a shady refuge favoured by local wildlife, including corellas, kangaroos and wallabies. Nearby, a geological trail leads for 20 km (12.5 miles) along the gorge past signs explaining the formation and development of the rocks, some of which date back more than 600 million years.

Wilpena Pound Resort turn-off. A short walk from the car park along a tree-lined creek brings you to the canyon, where engravings, or petroglyphs, of animal tracks, circles and other symbols decorate the walls.

One of the best ways to see some of the park's wildlife is to drive the Yanyanna Hut–Bunyeroo Valley road early in the morning. Red kangaroos are common here and as you get closer to the main range you're likely to spot euros and western grey kangaroos, too. This is also a good area for wildflowers, which bloom profusely after rain, and the views are fantastic, with the pine-clad hills rolling away to the sheer bluffs of the Heysen Range. If you want to make a day of it, continue to the Prairie Hotel in Parachilna for lunch and then take the Moralana Scenic Drive back to Wilpena. This 36-km (22-mile) route provides fabulous views of the western walls of Wilpena.

ACCOMMODATION

Wilpena Pound Resort has a motel, caravan park and store, as well as a fuel outlet, ranger base and information centre. It can get crowded during school holidays, so it is best to book accommodation well in advance.

At Aroona Valley, the main camp site east of the homestead ruins has toilets and water. Further east, along the headwaters of Brachina Creek, at Slippery Dip, Trezona and Youngoona, bush camping areas have been set up; although all have toilets, you need to take your own water. Camping areas are also located at Dingly Dell on the Blinman road, 30 km (18.5 miles) north of Wilpena Pound Resort; along the main road through Bunyeroo Gorge, 27 km (16.5 miles) by road from Wilpena; and at Wilkawillina Gorge.

Another excellent area for camping can be found at Brachina Gorge, where a scenic dirt road leads from Aroona Valley through the Heysen Range to the arid plains surrounding the park. There are no facilities at the gorge, however, so campers must be self-sufficient.

The Flinders Ranges Trek

This trek starts in Quorn, 350 km (217 miles) north of Adelaide, at the southern end of the Flinders Ranges. Originally established as a farming community, Quorn became the hub of the rural rail system but declined in the 1950s following the rerouting of train services through Port Augusta. Tourism has, however, helped it recover and the town now meets all the usual needs of the traveller. In addition, the local Pichi Richi Railway operates short trips on historic steam locomotives into the scenic Pichi Richi Pass, allowing passengers to experience rail travel as it used to be.

From Quorn railway station, take the road heading west toward Port Augusta, but instead of following the main road once you have crossed the railway line, drive straight ahead, keeping the mountains on your left. Continuing north, rolling hills and farmland stretch away to your right; on the left, the ranges rear up dramatically to their ragged battlements. The most prominent peak is Dutchmans Stern, which is protected by a small conservation park reached via a

The western grey kangaroo (Macropus fuliginosus) is often seen grazing in grassy valleys. Joeys remain with their mothers for around eight months.

Another spectacular gorge is located in the far north-east of the park. Wilkawillina Gorge, 25 km (15.5 miles) off the Oraparinna road, was formed as Mount Billy Creek gradually cut its way through the Bunker Range. There is a camping ground at the end of the road, from where a walk of about 1 km (0.6 miles) will take you into the gorge itself. This part of the Flinders is much drier than the Wilpena side, but Wilkawillina usually holds some water.

Aboriginal art sites can be found throughout the Flinders and one of the best is Sacred Canyon, a small chasm reached via a 14-km (8.5-mile) dirt track that branches off the main Blinman road just north of the turn-off 7 km (4.4 miles) out of Quorn. The park encompasses some of the most rugged country in the Flinders, and if you follow the trail to the ridge you will have spectacular views of the ranges to the east and Spencer Gulf to the west.

Continuing along the main dirt road, a track junction 21 km (13 miles) from Quorn marks the turn-off to Warren Gorge. This small, sheer-sided, shady canyon holds water in all but the driest spells. Beyond the far end of the picturesque gorge is an area of rolling hills dotted with native pines, a popular picnic spot.

About 8 km (5 miles) further on along the main dirt road, it's worth making another short detour, to Buckaringa Gorge. The cliff on the right as you enter this small canyon is popular with climbers, and there are camp sites at either end of the gorge. Beyond the gorge, the track continues for 2 km (1.2 miles) to a car park, where there is another camp site and a trail leading to Middle Gorge. If you follow the creek down to the southern extremity of this gorge, you will come to a viewing platform which overlooks a rocky bluff—the home of a small group of rare yellow-footed rock-wallabies.

Back on the main road, the route skirts the eastern side of the ranges and 6 km (3.7 miles) later arrives at Proby's grave. Hugh Proby, proprietor of nearby Kanyaka Station, drowned in Willochra Creek while mustering sheep one stormy night in 1852. You cross the wadi-like creek just past the grave and then come to another junction, 6 km (3.7 miles) beyond the grave, where you should turn right. On your left, you will see the ruins of Simmonston, which was founded in 1872 to service a proposed railway but

Grasstrees are fire- and drought-tolerant.

then abandoned when the railway was rerouted. Continue south for another 6 km (3.7 miles) before turning left again, then drive 9 km (5.6 miles) to the main Quorn–Hawker road, which is sealed. When you reach this road, you will have driven 56 km (35 miles) from Quorn, although it is only 34 km (21 miles) away via the main highway.

Turning left at the junction takes you onto Willochra Plain. Nearby are the ruins of Gordon, a hamlet established, like many others in the late 1800s, in the mistaken belief that conditions here were ideal for growing wheat. The ruins of Kanyaka Homestead and its outbuildings lie just off the main road, 7 km (4.4 miles) nearer Hawker. At its peak in the early 1870s, this was one of the richest properties in the area, accommodating over 70 families and 40,000 sheep. You pass another ruined farm, Wilson, on the way to Yourambulla Peak, 16 km (10 miles) further north, where you can admire Aboriginal rock art and fine views.

The small township of Hawker is 9 km (5.6 miles) north of Yourambulla. To reach the centre of town, turn off the main road at the 'Wilpena Pound' signpost. Hawker has a number of general stores, fuel outlets and a good range of accommodation.

HAWKER TO WILPENA POUND

As you head north-east from Hawker across gently undulating country, the Flinders Ranges loom ever larger on the horizon; to your left you will see the Elder Range and to your right, one after another, the Lower, Druid and Chace Ranges.

Arkaba Station Woolshed, 19 km (12 miles) north of Hawker, sits on a low rise with a panoramic view of the Elder Range. The woolshed is open most days and offers coffee, tea and scones, as well as souvenirs and local art. You can also join guided tours of the property, which is one of the most impressive in the region, and even rent a cabin if you feel like staying longer.

Approximately 5 km (3.1 miles) beyond Arkaba, on the left, the Moralana Scenic Drive branches off the main road. It skirts the southern rim of Wilpena Pound before joining the Hawker–Leigh Creek highway. Staying on the main road, you soon reach Rawnsley Park Station, which is situated below Rawnsley Bluff on the edge of Wilpena Pound. The station has a camping ground and accommodation, and can provide food and fuel.

As you near the pound, the ranges close in from the west and dense stands of native pines grow right up to the edge of the road. Just before you enter Flinders Ranges National Park, 44 km (27 miles) from Hawker, you pass the turn-off to Arkaroo Rock, where a short walk leads to a natural cliff gallery featuring striking Aboriginal rock art.

Beneath 698-m (2290-foot) Yourambulla Peak, an easy 3-km (1.9-mile) loop trail leads to a group of caves whose walls bear historic Aboriginal artworks.

The turn-off to Wilpena Pound is 8 km (5 miles) further along the main road, 52 km (32 miles) from Hawker. Turning left leads to Wilpena Pound Resort, 4 km (2.5 miles) away. It's worth spending a few days here to explore the pound properly.

Continuing north from the Wilpena Pound Resort turn-off, the bitumen soon stops, and after just 1 km (0.6 miles) you pass the track to Sacred Canyon. At the major road junction 5 km (3.1 miles) north of the resort turn-off, head left toward Yanyanna Hut and Bunyeroo Valley. This dirt road initially winds through low hills and valleys of red gums, then climbs through native pine and finally crests a ridge after 14 km (8.5 miles); from here, you enjoy expansive views down the Bunyeroo Valley and across the domes of the ABC Range to the ramparts of the Heysen Range.

From the Bunyeroo Valley Lookout, the road follows the ridgeline for a short distance before winding its way down to Bunyeroo Creek. The next 2 km (1.2 miles) or so lead along the creekbed into the gorge. This is generally no problem for a 4WD, but

the rocks and boulders may damage a low-slung car. Once the road leaves the creek, it swings north between the ABC and Heysen Ranges. Reaching the T-junction 10 km (6 miles) north of the creek and 28 km (17 miles) from Wilpena Pound Resort turn-off, veer left and follow the road along the creek and into Brachina Gorge. There may be water here but a 4WD will cope easily. Brachina is an exquisite place and its camp sites are among the best in the park.

The road crosses the creek for the last time 7 km (4.4 miles) from the T-junction, then climbs a low hill, from where you have fine views back across the creek and down the Heysen Range to the northern walls of Wilpena Pound. It then heads due west for 12 km (7.5 miles) until it strikes the main Hawker–Leigh Creek road 43 km (26.5 miles) north of Hawker, 109 km (68 miles) from Quorn via the main road, and 166 km (103 miles) along the route you have travelled. Here, you can either turn left and return to Hawker along the blacktop, or veer right toward Parachilna, Marree and the deserts of central Australia.

According to local Aboriginal Dreaming stories, the parallel ranges of the central Flinders are the petrified bodies of two giant ancestral serpents, or akurras.

Places in
CENTRAL-EAST
SOUTH AUSTRALIA

ADELAIDE HILLS
WINE REGION

The Adelaide Hills region lies less than half an hour's drive from Adelaide's flat suburban sprawl, up in the steep, wooded ranges that border the city's eastern edge. The region stretches from Mount Pleasant in the neighbouring northerly wine region of Eden Valley, down to Mount Compass and the hills behind McLaren Vale in the south. At about 400 m (1312 feet) above sea level, it is cool, and not just in meteor-ological terms—its restrained whites and elegant reds are fashion-able and attracting increasing in-ternational acclaim. Some of Australia's most respected wine-makers—people like Brian Croser, Stephen and Prue Henschke, Tim Knappstein and Geoff Weaver—have major interests in the area.

But the Adelaide Hills is not simply a trendy new wine region. From 1840–1900, there were as many as 195 grape-growers and winemakers in the area. Legend has it that the Adelaide Hills was even

the source of Australia's first ex-ported wine, a hock from Echunga that was sent to Queen Victoria in 1845. The fact that wine pro-duction in the region had all but died out by 1910 is probably due to the preference of the day for rich, ripe, high-alcohol, warm-climate reds, such as those that come from the Barossa Valley.

The mixed pastoral landscape of steep little valleys, winding roads, orchards and switchback vine rows provides Australia with one of its most picturesque wine regions. English oaks, green pasture and a fair bit of mist and rain give a European feel to the area, and there are numerous microclimates and subregions. This makes any generalisation about conditions and suitable varieties hazardous, but the region's cool, moist climate provides excellent results from the most widely planted white grape, chardonnay, including two of Australia's most prestigious and expensive versions—Petaluma Tiers and Penfolds Yattarna. Ries-ling is also successful here, showing lime-blossom characters when

'Collingrove' at Angaston is furnished with the Angas family's original antiques.

young and ageing well. Nowhere else in Australia can match this region for sauvignon blanc. Not surprisingly, it also produces fruit and base wines for some of Aus-tralia's better sparkling wines.

As for what the most widely planted red is, indeed, what the most widely planted grape is, this would perhaps make a good trivia question. Although the Adelaide Hills is fast gaining a reputation for quality pinot noir, it is really the cabernet franc grape that dom-inates in terms of quantity. This region is still a long way from realising its full potential and, with cellar-door facilities at bou-tique wineries on the increase,

visitors have plenty of choice. Some wineries, such as Petaluma's popular Bridgewater Mill, at Bridgewater, also run fine res-taurants on their premises.
Map ref: page 791 K10

ANGASTON

Situated in the east of the famous and largest wine-growing area in Australia, the Barossa Valley, Anga-ston—77 km (48 miles) north-east of Adelaide—can be reached via Gawler and Nuriootpa, or via a pleasant run through the Eden Valley passing through Birdwood and Hahndorf. Just south of the town is Yalumba Wines, the oldest

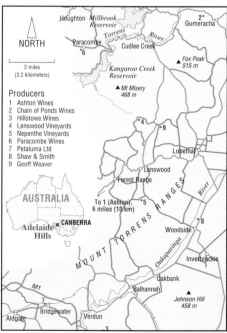

The vineyards of Hillstowe Wines, Hahndorf, in the Adelaide Hills Wine Region.

family-owned winery in the country. The Henschke Estate, established in 1847, just a couple of years before the Yalumba winery, has an exceptional reputation for fine wines and is located a few kilometres east; the Saltram Wine Estate, with its heritage going back to 1859, is a couple of kilometres north. All offer wine-tasting and sales.

The town of Angaston is not large—its population is 2000. It is a rich blend of English and German cultures, contains many fine public buildings, numerous art and craft shops, galleries and tea-rooms. The Lutheran church was built in the 1850s of pink marble; the town hall was constructed from local white marble, which, today, is still cut from a nearby quarry. The Angas Park Fruit Co. provides visitors with a sample of some of the other fare that this region produces—dried fruit, nuts, chocolate, and honey. The Angaston Blacksmith Shop has been fully restored and is open to the public for viewing.

Just to the south of the town is Collingrove Homestead. Built for John Angas in 1853, it is now owned by the National Trust. Nearby is the racehorse stud of Lindsay Park, built in 1848 by George Fife Angas, who took up much of the area. About 10 km (6.2 miles) south-west of the town is the Kaiser Stuhl Conservation Park, which protects a rugged area of natural bushland and is ideal for day walks. Annual events include the show in February and the Yalumba Christmas Carols, at Yalumba Wines, in December.
Map ref: page 791 K9

ARDROSSAN

Named after the town in Ayrshire, Scotland, Ardrossan (population 980) is one of the largest ports on the Yorke Peninsula and the third-largest grain handling outlet in the State. The area is dominated by the wheat silos down near the wharf. The port also handles the shipping

The town of Barmera is on the shores of peaceful-looking Lake Bonney, a popular spot for hiring windsurfers, canoes and catamarans.

of dolomite, which is mined near-by for BHP. Situated on the north-east coast of the Peninsula, 144 km (89 miles) north-west of Adelaide, the Ardrossan area boasts great fishing and crabbing. The town's long jetty is ideal for garfish, tom-my ruff, and whiting. Blue crabs can be caught in the shallows at low tide or from the jetty. Diving in this area is centred on the wreck of the *Zanoni*, 10 nautical miles off the coast—it is considered one of the most interesting wrecks in South Australian waters.

On the cliff-top near the town is a monument to the stump-jump plough, which was developed here. This invention allowed the culti-vation of fields that had been pre-viously deemed useless because of the many mallee roots buried in the ground. The Smith Plough Museum has a series of exhibits; the National Trust Museum is nearby.
Map ref: page 791 H9

BARMERA

This pretty town (with a popu-lation of 4470), located in the heart of the Murray Riverland, on the shores of Lake Bonney— 215 km (134 miles) east of Adelaide—is known today as the capital of the South Australian country music scene. Each June long weekend, the town hosts the

state's Country Music Awards. Rocky's Country Music Hall of Fame is always worth a visit. Being in the centre of the Riverland and the irrigation area, the area around the town produces a vast quantity of fruit, particularly grapes. The Bonneyview Winery, established in 1967, is located just west of town along the Sturt Highway.

Europeans first came across Lake Bonney in the 1830s, and by 1850 Nappers Old Accommodation House was in operation. Its ruins, at the mouth of Chambers Creek, are now classified by the National Trust, while the Cobdogla Irri-gation and Steam Museum houses

the only working Humphrey Pump in the world. This National Trust museum has many other interest-ing displays and photographs.

The lake has many sandy beaches and is popular for swim-ming and waterskiing. In 1964 the flat water of Lake Bonney was the site of Donald Campbell's attempt at the world water-speed record. Barmera's other annual events (apart from the Country Music Awards) include the Easter Sailing Regatta, the Riverland Autumn Floral Spectacular in April and the National Sheepdog Trials in September.
Map ref: page 791 N8

Garfish are commonly caught in the waters off the jetty at Ardrossan.

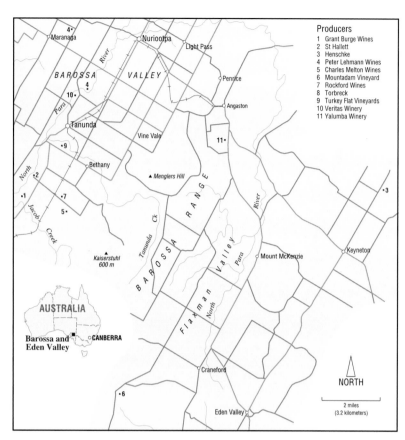

The Charles Melton vineyards in Tanunda, in the Barossa Valley.

BAROSSA VALLEY WINE REGION

Less than 75 km (47 miles) north-east of Adelaide, the Barossa Valley can justifiably claim to be Australia's best-known wine region, and is arguably its most important. Here, among a patchwork spread of neat vineyards and rolling hills are more than 50 wineries, including the home bases and headquarters of most of Australia's leading wine companies. Southcorp (in the form of Penfolds, Tollana and Seppelt), Orlando and Wolf Blass are based here, as are Yalumba, Peter Lehmann and Grant Burge. Around Nuriootpa and Tanunda is the greatest concentration of bottling plants and industry service providers of any Australian wine region.

Many of the country's finest and best-known wines come from the Barossa—Penfolds Grange is born, bred and made in the Barossa (and contains mostly local fruit), as are a raft of highly regarded wines from lesser-known niche producers. The Barossa has also produced some of Australia's best-known brands—from Barossa Pearl, which was popular in the 1950s, to Jacobs Creek today. But it is not simply big business or well-known labels that make the area stand out in

wine terms—its distinct and complex heritage and culture make this wine region quite unlike any other.

At first glance, the Barossa seems dichotomous. There are two regions within it, each producing distinctive styles of wine. The Eden Valley is high-altitude hill country, while the Barossa Valley is on the valley floor, with classic, full-bodied old-vine shiraz and grenache the order of the day. Each area was settled in the late 1830s by two very different groups of migrants, with their own particular cultures, lifestyles and religions. Up in the hills it was English farmers and the gentry, while down in the valley it

Aggie's fruit shop in Berri, with its window display of the fresh local produce.

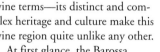

was mainly German-speaking peasant farmers from Silesia (now part of Poland and eastern Germany) who established European-style villages and settlements.

But cultural differences did not stand in the way here. Mixed hamlets, villages and townships sprang up, farms were established and the settlers developed a strong sense of community. Equally important, they quickly realised that grapevines were one of the most suitable and flourishing crops, whether in the hills or the valley. For the English, bottles and casks from Bordeaux and Burgundy suffered badly on their passage through the tropics. And for the Silesians, viticulture and wine-making were as much a part of their tradition as making sausages or pickling vegetables. So, via this unexpectedly successful intertwining and establishment of lifestyle and cultures, the first Barossa wines

were made in the 1840s, and many of the same vineyards planted then are still being worked today. Some of the oldest vines in the world can be found here, and many of the 500-plus growers producing grapes in the Barossa Valley today are fifth- and sixth-generation descendants of the original settlers. The hugely popular biennial Barossa Vintage Festival and similar events were started to rekindle a sense of unity between English descendants and those with German heritage after World War II.

Max Schubert, the first to make Penfolds Grange, was a Barossa winemaker, as was Colin Gramp, who revolutionised winemaking in the region in the 1950s by introducing cold-pressure fermentation for white wines and secondary fermentation for sparkling wine at Orlando. Today, wine producers such as Rockford, Charles Melton, Grant Burge, St Hallett, Elderton and Bethany exemplify the Barossa style with big blockbuster reds packed full of spice, tannin, rich fruit and depth—wines with tar and leather and chocolate. These opulent full-bodied beauties have made the Barossa into a thriving premium winemaking region of global importance.

Map ref: page 791 K9

BERRI

Fruit, fruit juice and wine are what make the town of Berri (with a population of 7100) tick. Located 230 km (143 miles) east of Adelaide on a bend on the Murray River, from where it gains its name—'berri berri' is a word from a local Aboriginal language that means 'big bend'—the surrounding

area is a mosaic of fruit orchards and vineyards. Berrivale Orchards is one of the largest manufacturers of fruit and fruit juice in Australia. Berri Estates, which was founded in 1922 and is located 13 km (8 miles) west of the town, is one of the largest wineries in Australia.

Set on the cliffs overlooking the Murray is the old Reiners homestead, now part of the Wilabalangaloo Reserve. It has a fine collection of riverboat photos and a outdoor display including a small paddleboat. There are numerous walking tracks in this reserve. Just a few kilometres south of town is the Katarapko section of the Murray River National Park; upstream is the park's Lyrup Flats section. These areas of bushland protect the river flats and offer excellent camping, canoeing and fishing. The fish most commonly caught are yellowbelly, redfin and the

occasional Murray cod. Annual events include the Berri Easter Festival and the Berri/Loxton Bowling Carnival in September.
Map ref: page 791 N8

BIRDWOOD

Located in the picturesque Adelaide Hills, 42 km (26 miles) east of Adelaide, Birdwood (with a population of 500) is home to the National Motor Museum, Australia's largest, and most important, collection of motor vehicles. It rates as one of the world's finest collections of vintage, veteran and classic cars and motorcycles, dating from 1899 to the present day. The museum is also the focus of the annual Bay to Birdwood Run by vintage vehicles. The town also hosts the annual Rock & Roll Rendezvous and the very different Medieval Festival. Back 6 km (3.7 miles) along the main road to Adelaide is the small town of Gumeracha with its Toy Factory; at Cudlee Creek, another 7 km (4.3 miles) west, the Gorge Wildlife Park has one of the largest private native animal collections in Australia.
Map ref: page 791 K10

BLINMAN

Blinman is in the heart of the Flinders Ranges, 525 km (326 miles) north of Adelaide—the last 32 km (20 miles), or 55 km (34 miles), of road, depending if you come from Parachilna or from Wilpena, is

reasonable dirt road, passable for a normal car. The drive from Parachilna is exceptional as it winds its way through Parachilna Gorge; the southern route from Wilpena passes what is known as 'The Great Wall of China'. Other natural attractions include Glass Gorge and the secluded, spring-fed Blinman Pools, most easily accessible by following Blinman Creek up from the Angorichina Tourist Village. Further afield is Chambers Gorge with rugged country, ancient Aboriginal stone engravings and wildflowers.

This small town (population 55) was once a booming copper mining town. The remains are well signposted—the self-guided walk is excellent. In October, there is fun and excitement at the Blinman Picnic Race Meeting and Gymkhana.
Map ref: page 791 J2

BURRA

This historic town, 176 km (109 miles) north of Adelaide, once had a population of over 5000 when Adelaide had just 18,000! Its importance in the 1850s was due to the discovery of copper—'The Monster Mine' became the richest mine of its time in Australia. The Burra Burra, as the area was first called, had several distinct villages, Redruth (Cornish), Aberdeen (Scottish), Llwchwr (Welsh), Hampton (English), and the mining company town of Kooringa. The villages eventually became Burra. The mine was abandoned in 1877 but was

reworked during the 1980s. Today, however, the town is small, with a population of 1200, and relies more on tourism and servicing its surrounding rich merino sheep country than anything else.

Burra was declared a State Heritage Town in 1994. There is a self-guided walk or drive leading past 43 heritage sites. The Unicorn Brewery Cellars give an indication of how hard men used to work and drink in that period, while the 'Dugouts' in the Burra Creek are mute testimony to the life many of these workers lived away from the danger of the mines. The Paxton Square Cottages, built around

Vintage truck outside the Hillstowe Wines vineyard cellar door.

1850 to provide the miners with decent housing, are now refurbished and open for visitors to stay in. Annual events include the South Australian Stud Merino Field Days in March and the Antique Fair and Cultural Weekend in May.
Map ref: page 791 K7

The former mining town of Burra now offers tours of its buildings and its mining history, including the miners' 'Dugouts', where over 1500 people lived during the boom time.

Sevenhill Cellars near Clare; Jesuits have produced sacramental wine here since 1851.

CLARE

Just one and a half hours' drive north from Adelaide—132 km (82 miles) north of the city—is the charming Clare Valley. Vineyards and gum trees colour the scene and in the space of a few kilometres you will pass through the small villages of Auburn, Watervale and Sevenhill and will finally arrive in delightful Clare. Home to over 28 wineries, the valley is arguably the finest riesling producing area in Australia, but others would say its shiraz isn't bad. The Riesling Trail—a walking, bike or horse-riding path from Watervale to Sevenhill—emphasises the importance of riesling in the valley.

Edward John Eyre passed this way in 1839—his reports soon had pastoralists taking up land. The Hawker brothers set up Bungaree Station, today one of the most

respected merino studs in Australia, and John Hope established nearby Wolta Wolta, another famous stud and historic homestead. The region also has a rich European heritage. In 1851 the Jesuit Fathers set up a church and school at Sevenhill, and planted a vineyard. The Sevenhill Cellars, the oldest and one of the most famous wineries in the area, is still operated by the Jesuit Society. St Aloysius Church, with its crypt, is also well worth a look. Other wineries in the area include Taylors Wine, Tim Knappstein, Pikes, Leasingham and Jim Barry Wines.

Clare—population 3000—has a large number of heritage-listed buildings, including the former courthouse and police station, which are now the National Trust Museum, and Hill River Station, with its coach-house and stables. Easter sees big racing meets, on the

Anzac weekend there is a Spanish Festival, and in mid-May the Clare Valley Gourmet Weekend is held. There is also a Summer Festival in early December. C.J. Dennis, poet, famous for his *Sentimental Bloke* was born in nearby Auburn in 1876 and is commemorated in an annual festival in the village.
Map ref: page 791 J8

CLARE VALLEY WINE REGION

Fed by four main river systems, the Clare Valley is now one of the most highly regarded wine-producing districts in Australia. This pretty, winding, wooded region just one and a half hours' drive north of Adelaide has a history of wine-making that dates back to the time of first European settlement, when English settler John Horrocks first planted vines at Hope Farm in 1840. His pioneering efforts were followed by plantings at Sevenhill in 1851 and Spring Vale (subsequently Quelltaler) in 1853. Expansion was steady rather than swift until the changes that occurred with the turn of the century.

At the same time as these early viticultural experiments, the Clare area was being populated by a diverse range of settlers, many of whom were heading north to stake a claim on land or search for minerals. They included English miners from Cornwall coming to exploit local sources of tin and copper, German-speaking Silesians venturing a little farther north than most of their contemporaries who had settled in the Barossa, and English and Irish entrepreneurs spreading north from Adelaide.

The beginning of the twentieth century saw the rapid expansion of Clare's fledgling wine industry. In 1890, there were about 100 ha (247 acres) of vineyards; ten years later there were 600 ha (1483 acres). Two producers, Stanley Wine Co. and Quelltaler in Watervale, were the main forces at the

time, making wines mainly for export to England. Development slowed after that period to the point where the area of land under vine actually decreased, but the industry had established itself and continued to advance steadily.

It is a curious region climatically and stylistically. Set in the middle of the hot, dry mid-north wheat belt of South Australia, with hot summers and little ground water, Clare somehow manages to produce wines that seem to come from a considerably cooler, wetter climate. This is perfectly illustrated by Clare's best-performing and best-known wine, riesling, the finest examples of which are found in the Mosel, Germany, and in Alsace, France. Those northern European classics are born in a very different climate to Clare, and yet this South Australian pocket produces similar wines. This apparently odd characteristic is generally attributed to cool afternoon breezes that blow through the Clare Valley in the warmer months, slowing and prolonging the ripening of the grapes.

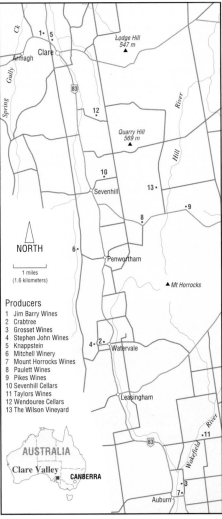

The tasting room at Leasingham Wines, on the outskirts of the town of Clare.

Clare's main competitor in the riesling stakes is much closer though, lying just an hour away in the Eden Valley. Examples from both regions are regarded as Australian classics, but they differ in style: Eden Valley's are all restrained lime juice and steely in character, whereas Clare's add floral, perfumed and spicy characters to the citrus aspects. However, riesling is not the only star in Clare. The region also produces big, firm peppery shiraz and elegant minty cabernets, both with plenty of backbone.

The quality of the wines being made in the region has inevitably attracted the attention of the region's major companies, and there has been much corporate investment since the 1980s. The Clare Valley is now a mix of the large and small, as well as the old and new, but the most renowned producers—such as Grosset in Auburn, Wendouree in Clare and Mitchell in Sevenhill—have maintained their independence and remain small.
Map ref: page 791 J8

CLEVE

This small town (population 820) on Eyre Peninsula lies 25 km (16 miles) inland from Arno Bay and 541 km (336 miles) north-west of Adelaide, and services the surrounding rich cereal and grazing land. It is only a 20 minute drive to the coast. The Cowell Hills have great views of the surrounding plain and Spencer Gulf, and the Carappee Hill Conservation Park offers flora and fauna as well as camping and bushwalking.

The town has an agricultural and folk museum which is opened on request. The Eyre Peninsula Field Days, held in August every two years (in even-numbered years) are huge, attracting exhibits from all over Australia. The Cleve Show, held in October, is one of the biggest on the peninsula.
Map ref: page 790 F7

COFFIN BAY

The small resident population (350) of this idyllic holiday resort is often outnumbered by its many visitors. The town is located on the protected waters of Coffin Bay, 700 km (435 miles) west of Adelaide, and is nearly surrounded by the national park of the same name. Reached by a bitumen road off the Flinders Highway, 35 km (22 miles) northwest of Port Lincoln, Coffin Bay is a great spot for fishing (for whiting), sailing or boating on the protected waters, or just for swimming. The oysters here are considered among the best in Australia. A graded walking track—the Oyster Walk—winds for 2.5 km (1.6 miles) around the foreshore of the bay.

Just a short drive away through the national park, along a graded dirt road, is a wild untamed coast, vastly different from Coffin Bay itself. The national park has many good bush camping sites and is good for fishing from rock or beach. Yachties will not want to miss the 'Queen of the Gulf' Yacht Race, held annually in March.
Map ref: page 790 D9

COFFIN BAY NATIONAL PARK

The Coffin Bay Peninsula is a large wilderness area, almost surrounded by water, reaching out into the Great Australian Bight. Rich in flora, the peninsula is covered in dense coastal heathland and mallee. The park also has a good variety of birds, and the beaches are breeding grounds for many seabirds. Western grey kangaroos are often seen. The area is popular with bushwalkers, divers, campers and birdwatchers; it also has excellent fishing. A 4WD is needed to get around the majority of the park. The park is 720 km (447 miles) west of Adelaide and 50 km (31 miles) west of Port Lincoln.
Map ref: page 790 C9

COPLEY

There is still a little confusion surrounding the naming of Copley, which dates back to when it was just a railway siding, then known as Leigh Creek. When the town of Copley was proclaimed in 1891 the siding was absorbed into the new town, but the locals retained the name of Leigh Creek for the pub, the railway station and the post office. While today there is a much larger township of Leigh Creek (population 1950) just down the road, the Leigh Creek Hotel remains in little Copley (population 95)!

Copley lies at the junction of the main bitumen road north to Marree and the dirt road east to Arkaroola and the Gammon Ranges, 573 km (356 miles) north of Adelaide. It makes a good base from which to explore the surrounding area.
Map ref: page 791 J1

Coffin Bay was named by explorer Matthew Flinders, after his friend Sir Isaac Coffin.

Wheat farm at the foot of the bluff that gives Dutchmans Stern Conservation Park its name.

COWELL

Located on the protected waters of Franklin Harbour on the east coast of Eyre Peninsula, 498 km (309 miles) west of Adelaide, Cowell is a major port servicing the inland grazing and cereal growing area, with a population of 710. Fishing is also an important industry here, while jade, mined in the nearby Minbrie Ranges, has put Cowellon the world gem market. The nephrite jade, from one of the biggest deposits in the world, has a variety of colour and patterns not found elsewhere, and the jade boulders, sometimes weighing tonnes, are brought into the town-based factory for cutting before export or further processing. It is Australia's only commercial jade-mining operation.

The first pioneers arrived in the area in the 1850s, although the bay had been seen, and described as a lagoon, by Matthew Flinders 50 years earlier. The local museum, once the post office, was built in 1885. The real attraction for visitors is the large bay. It offers great fishing for whiting, snapper, garfish and snook, and crabbing at night; the shallow waters of the bay south of the town are a birdwatcher's delight. Nearby Entrance Island has small, lovely beaches. The Cowell Show is held in September.

Map ref: page 790 F7

CRYSTAL BROOK

The 'Gateway to the Flinders Ranges', Crystal Brook lies 198 km (123 miles) north of Adelaide, just off the main highway north, amongst the gentle folds of hills where the Mount Lofty Ranges begin to give way to the more rugged slopes of the Flinders. Edward Eyre was the first European to visit this rich farming area, in 1840, and named the creek Crystal Brook. The land was soon taken up by graziers, while the town came into existence in the 1870s. The town has a population of 2100 today, and services the surrounding sheep, beef and cereal farming community.

The local National Trust museum in the old bakehouse in Brandis Street is worth a visit, as are the two hotels in the town, which date back to the 1870s. The Bowman Fauna Park, located 5 km (3.1 miles) east of town, includes the ruins of the original Bowman family homestead, Crystal Brook Run, which was the heart of one of South Australia's largest sheep stations. Today, it offers backpacker-type accommodation and restricted camping, and a chance to experience quiet bushland. An agricultural show is held annually in August, and in October there is an antiques and collectables fair.

Map ref: page 791 J7

DUTCHMANS STERN CONSERVATION PARK

Dutchmans Stern Conservation Park, 7 km (4.3 miles) north of Quorn, is renowned not only for its dramatic scenery, but also for its bird life and orchids. The car park and picnic area is 3 km (1.9 miles) from the main road, and from this point access to the park is on foot, or by joining one of the 4WD tours into the area. To appreciate the wild grandeur of this park you need to venture into its interior. The view from the top of the range over the flat plains to the distant gulf and back towards the bluffs and escarpments is astonishing, especially in the soft evening light. The rare Quorn wattle is found in this park, and the animal life is varied, with euros and some yellow-footed rock wallabies.

Map ref: page 791 H4

EDEN VALLEY WINE REGION

About 60 km (37 miles) north-east of Adelaide, Eden Valley is the high-altitude hill country within the Barossa region, mostly between 400–600 m (1300–2000 feet) above sea level. The soils are rockier and more acidic than those on the valley floor and winter rainfall is much more significant. Riesling grapes do well here, producing elegant, structured wines, along with chardonnay and cabernet.

The Adelaide Hills area was settled in the late 1830s by English farmers and the gentry, but there is a strong sense of community with descendants of the German-speaking peasant farmers from Silesia, who established European-style villages and settlements lower down on the floor of the Barossa Valley.

While the Barossa Valley is acclaimed for its big reds, Eden Valley producers such as Leo Buring, John Vickery, Pewsey Vale and Steingarten are enjoying similar success with their classically crisp rieslings. Henschke Hill of Grace white wines (and reds), from fifth-generation winemakers Stephen and Prue Henschke at Keyneton, are among the best produced anywhere, and Mountadam Vineyard, on the High Eden Ridge, produces an exceptional chardonnay. White wines are now enjoying a revival in popularity and finding wider distribution and acceptance, with the Australian charge being led by Eden Valley and its northern neighbour the Clare Valley.

Map ref: page 791 K9

EDITHBURGH

Situated on the 'heel' of Yorke Peninsula, 226 km (140 miles) west of Adelaide, Edithburgh is a quiet seaside town (population 450), an easy three hours' drive from the city. The large jetty is a reminder of the days when the port was used to ship large quantities of salt, which was mined on the numerous salt lakes nearby. The town was surveyed in 1869, and retains much of its old-style charm today, including the local hotel, which was built in 1872. Recollections of the old days are relived when the tall ships *One and All* and *Falie* visit the port as they cruise the waters of Gulf St Vincent.

For divers, the nearby coast boasts a number of shipwrecks, the best known being the *Clan Ranald* off Troubridge Point. So many ships were lost here that the Troubridge Light was built on an island

The cellar of Mountadam winery, Eden Valley.

Mural representing the history of the town and district, Elliston Community Agricultural Hall.

lying just offshore Edithburgh in 1856. Today the island, with this old light, is part of a conservation park, and is home to penguins and crested terns. A pleasant scenic drive takes you out to Troubridge Point and Troubridge Hill, where the modern light is. For the angler, the surrounding waters offer excellent fishing for whiting, snapper, tommy ruff and snook; the jetty is probably the best fishing jetty in the region. Edithburgh's Gala Day is held in October.
Map ref: page 791 H10

ELLISTON

The tiny hamlet of Elliston (with a population of just 250), lies 664 km (412 miles) west of Adelaide, on the shores of the cliff-lined Waterloo Bay, and is protected by a near continuous reef across its mouth. This is one of the larger towns on the coast of Eyre Peninsula. Elliston is an important service town for the surrounding farms and a port for the fishing, crayfish and abalone industries.

The nearby coastline is spectacular, with a number of sheltered bays and offshore islands to attract anglers and divers. The surfing too is great, with the famous 'Blackfellows' waves running to the north in Anxious Bay. Locks Well and Sheringa Beach are both superb surf-fishing areas. Walkers Rocks, around 11 km (6.8 miles) to the north, is a popular beach nearby. The Talia Caves region further north is an area of considerable natural beauty, with caves, white sand dunes and a beautiful beach. Lake Newland Conservation Park is excellent for bird life.
Map ref: page 790 C7

GAWLER

Just 35 minutes—about 40 km (25 miles)—north of Adelaide, Gawler is a pleasant rural town nestling between the two arms of the Para River and backed by the rolling hills of the Mount Lofty Ranges. Ordered streets and three town squares are due to Colonel William Light, the far-sighted planner of Adelaide. Fine Victorian architecture complements a town that former British poet laureate, Sir John Betjeman, said, 'was one of the most delightful towns [he] had seen anywhere'.

One of the first major settlements north of Adelaide, the town, begun in 1839, was at first a wayside stop for the miners and load carriers heading for the Burra mine or the copper mines on Yorke Peninsula. The railway arrived in 1857; the present station, built in 1879, is also a telecommunications museum. The town has a population of 11,500 today, and is the centre of a rich agricultural district that produces fat lambs, wool, wheat, poultry and dairy products, as well as being the western gateway to the Barossa Valley. It is also home to the Roseworthy Agricultural College, the oldest agricultural college in Australia, and one of the most prestigious. The regular Gawler races are an important social event, and the annual Gawler Three Day Horse Show, held in June, is a major event.
Map ref: page 791 K9

GLADSTONE

Located on the banks of the Rocky River, 210 km (130 miles) north of Adelaide, Gladstone was once two separate towns: the government town of Booyoolie, and the private town of Gladstone, separated by the railway. While the two towns amalgamated some time ago, it was not until 1940 that the town became officially known as Gladstone.

The town became a major railway junction with all three gauges used in Australia—broad, narrow and standard—running side by side. Today the town is of less importance as far as the railway is concerned, and its population is only 790, but it still acts as a major service centre for the surrounding grazing region. The local jail, built in 1879, was finally closed in 1975 and opened to the public a few years later. It is the town's most famous landmark.
Map ref: page 791 J6

HAHNDORF

Claimed to be South Australia's most popular tourist attraction, Hahndorf is a historic German village (population 1750) situated in the delightful Adelaide Hills, just off the South Eastern Freeway, 25 km (16 miles) south-east of Adelaide. It was originally settled by 52 German migrants in 1839, and is now the oldest German village still surviving in Australia. More than 10 buildings are listed on the National Estate, including the Hahndorf Old Mill, now a motel and restaurant.

Hans Heysen, the painter who celebrated the grandeur of the Flinders Ranges in his paintings, lived here until his death in 1968. The Cedars (his home) and his studio have been preserved as he left them. The Hahndorf Academy originally opened as a school in 1857, but is now an art gallery specialising in the work of Heysen and of other local artists. The town has several festivals that relate to its German heritage: in January the famous Schützenfest German Festival takes place; in March the town holds the Hahndorf Founders Celebration; and the 'St Nicholas Comes to Hahndorf' weekend is in December.
Map ref: page 791 K10

During World War I the German Arms Hotel, Hahndorf, changed its name to the Ambleside Hotel. The name was changed back in 1976.

Anglican Church, Jamestown, founded 1880.

HAWKER

Promoted as 'the Hub of the Flinders', Hawker sits in a broad valley in the central Flinders Ranges, 409 km (254 miles) north of Adelaide. Reached by bitumen via Wilmington and Quorn, the shortest route to Adelaide is actually via Oororoo, but that still has around 100 km (62 miles) of good dirt road. This small town (population 350) has relied nearly completely on tourism since the railway left in 1970. Founded in the 1880s on the promise of wheat, the area was just a little too far north to ensure consistent, good rainfall. However, when the Great Northern Railway passed through in the same decade it took on a more important role. Hawker is the last major town before the Flinders' major attraction, Wilpena Pound, or the Gammon Ranges and Arkaroola.

The town makes a good base from which to explore the surrounding area: just south of the town is Yourambulla Peak, where there are caves and a number of Aboriginal paintings.

A walking trail and scenic lookout have been established on Jarvis Hill, and to the north is the magnificent Arkaba homestead, with its cottage and camping facilities. The Moralana Scenic Drive, running from Parachilna to Wilpena, provides wonderful views of the western wall of Wilpena Pound.
Map ref: page 791 J3

IRON KNOB

Just off the Eyre Highway, 70 km (43 miles) west of Port Augusta and 385 km (239 miles) north-west of Adelaide, is Iron Knob. The small town—its population is only 325—is primarily visited by those interested in mining history. It was here that iron ore was first discovered in Australia, in the 1870s, making it the birthplace of the Australian steel industry. BHP first started mining the iron ore deposit in 1897. Ore is still supplied to the BHP steelworks in Whyalla from these mines and others in the area. Tours of the Iron Knob mine are available, and the tourist centre is a mining museum. To the north are the remote Gawler Ranges, known for their wildflower displays in spring.
Map ref: page 790 G5

JAMESTOWN

A pleasant rural township in the southern Flinders Ranges, 206 km (128 miles) north of Adelaide, Jamestown derives most of its income from the surrounding wheat and sheep farms. Founded in 1871, it was the arrival of the railway soon afterwards that lent permanence to the town. Its population today is 1360. South of the town is the Bundaleer Forest, which was the first government forest reserve in Australia. Tasmanian blue gums and pines were first planted in 1876 and today the forest produces more than 6000 tonnes (6612 tons) of timber annually. There is a pleasant scenic drive in the forest as well as a number of walks. The National Trust Museum, located in the old railway station, has displays of regional interest. The Jamestown Show, held every October Labour Day weekend, is one of the biggest shows in the mid-north of South Australia.
Map ref: page 791 J6

KADINA

One of the three towns of the 'Copper Triangle', the other two being Wallaroo and Moonta, Kadina is the biggest town on the Yorke Peninsula, and the service centre for the rich surrounding agricultural district. It is 144 km (89 miles) north-west of Adelaide, and has a population of 3600. The town was founded after the discovery of copper and the opening of the Wallaroo Mine, a large mine, with workings down to 800 m (2625 feet) or so. The mine is located just south of town and the remains of the pumping station and the tall, square Cornish-built chimney dominate the old mine site.

The town has many reminders of its past, and a number of historic buildings are listed by the National Trust. Kadina has two museums, one of which includes a former mine manager's residence. In celebration of the area's Cornish, Welsh and Scottish heritage, 'Kernewek Lowender' is held every two years in May, with highland games, caber tossing, haggis-eating competitions and much more. The events take place around the three towns of the Triangle.
Map ref: page 791 H8

KAPUNDA

The rich heritage of Kapunda—81 km (50 miles) north-east of Adelaide, on the edge of the Barossa Valley—is easily visible in its fine old buildings, museums and churches, more than 50 of which are listed by the National Trust. Of interest are the fine examples of patterned iron work, 'Kapunda Lace', that graces many of the buildings and fences. The town was established in the 1840s, and was the site of Australia's first significant copper mine. For the next 30 years it was one of the biggest towns in the State—the population was around 5000 and

Iron ore was first mined at Iron Knob by Mount Minden Mining, but due to production problems, BHP took over the mine in 1897.

In pioneering days, bags of wheat from Kimba were carried by bullock drays. Today the town is dominated by huge trucks and silos.

there were 16 hotels in town, and a million pounds' worth of copper was mined— but then the copper finally ran out, and the town was soon nearly deserted. Today it has a population of only 1625, and services the surrounding grazing and farming lands. The Kapunda Copper Mine Walking Trail meanders through the old mine workings, and past one of the earliest miner's cottages in the state. The Kapunda Celtic Festival is held in March, and the Country Music Festival is held in August.
Map ref: page 791 K9

KIMBA

Located in the central north of the Eyre Peninsula, and 484 km (301 miles) north-west of Adelaide, Kimba is one of the largest towns in the region, despite its population being a mere 680, and is the service centre for one of South Australia's major wheat-growing areas. The region was settled in the 1870s, but it was not until 1915 that the town was proclaimed. An excellent local museum opposite the wheat silos traces the development of the area. To the north are the granite domes of the Gawler Ranges, to the north-east is the Lake Gilles Conservation Park, to the north-west is the Pinkawillinie Conservation Park and to the south-west are the Hambridge Conservation Park and Carappee Hill Conservation Park. The annual show is held in September, and the rodeo takes place in October.
Map ref: page 790 E6

LEIGH CREEK

Located on the edge of the Flinders Ranges, 569 km (353 miles) north of Adelaide, this is the state's source of coal which is shipped south to the power stations at Port Augusta. The town was moved to its present location in 1981, when the original site proved to be in the way of the mining operation. Coal was originally discovered here in 1888, but it was not until the 1940s that it was mined in earnest, and now the fields produce over 2 million tonnes (2.2 million tons) annually. The area was first settled in 1841, and the town was named after Harry Leigh, the head stockman on the surrounding sheep station. Today the town is quite small, with a population of 1950, and houses the miners and their families. It is a pleasant spot for passing travellers, but accommodation is very limited. The nearby Aroona Dam is worth a visit, and tours of the coalfields can be arranged.
Map ref: page 791 J1

LINCOLN NATIONAL PARK

The park is on the Eyre Peninsula, 13 km (8 miles) south of Port Lincoln. It is the wild coastline and the fishing and diving that attract most people to this park. A rough walking trail leads down the cliffs on the western side of Wanna Cove, giving access to a short section of rocks that in calm weather is a good spot to cast a line for sweep, salmon and groper. There are also some popular surf fishing spots. There are many pleasant walks in the park, along the beach and on the cliff-tops, where you might find an access track to a small secluded cove.
Map ref: page 790 D10

LOXTON

Situated on a sweep of the Murray River, 243 km (151 miles) east of Adelaide, Loxton is a pleasant town with a number of parks and gardens. Established in the 1850s, the town was proclaimed in 1907, taking its name from a boundary rider who lived in a log hut near the site of the township. After World War II the town became the centre of a large soldier settlement scheme based around the newly declared irrigation area, and with that, the town boomed—today it has a population of 3380. The area is rich with vineyards and orchards. A number of co-operatives were formed in the 1950s, including a winery and distillery which crush more than 20,000 tonnes (22,040 tons) of grapes a year. Much of the early history of the region is re-created in the Loxton Historical Village, which has more than 30 fully furnished buildings.

The Katarapko Island section of the Murray River National Park encompasses a vast area of river flats across the river from the town, nearly all the way to the township of Berri. There is good fishing and excellent walking and canoeing in this region of the park and it is easily accessible, with many fine camping spots dotted along the river. The river is also popular with water sports enthusiasts. The Pyap Reserve, also known as the Daisy Bates Reserve, commemorates the life of a remarkable woman who spent much of her life working with and for Aboriginal people. Annual events include the Apex Fisherama in January and the Show Day in October.
See also Riverland Wine Region
Map ref: page 791 N9

LYNDOCH

Situated in the south of the Barossa Valley, 56 km (35 miles) north-east of Adelaide, Lyndoch is the first town you enter in the Barossa when you come from Adelaide via Gawler. One of the most famous wineries in the valley is located close by: Chateau Yaldara is not only a fine winery, but also has an outstanding collection of artwork, antiques and European porcelain.

Given the name of Lyndoch by Colonel Light in 1837, the town was once known as Hoffnungsthal, the 'Valley of Hope'. A flood in 1854 forced the townspeople, who were mainly Lutheran, to move their settlement to higher ground. The town's population today is 950.

The town is home to the South Australian Museum of Mechanical Music, which has a fine collection of music boxes, player organs and other instruments run by clockwork. Nearby is Lyndoch Lavender Farm. A short distance west of town is the Sandy Creek Conservation Park, a birdwatcher's delight—over 100 species of birds are found in an area of native bush, which is dominated by native pine and pink gum.
Map ref: page 791 K9

Landing a carp with a paternoster rig, in the Murray River at Loxton.

MCLAREN VALE

Home to the famous Hardy and Seaview wineries, McLaren Vale (population 1200) is located in the heart of the Fleurieu Peninsula's 'wine coast', 38 km (24 miles) south of Adelaide, in the rolling plains at the foot of the Mount Lofty Ranges. Dotted amongst the vineyards are orchards of olives, almonds, avocadoes, stone fruits and berries, all of which grow well in this temperate region—the Almond Train in the main street sells the largest range of almond products in Australia. But it is the area's 50-plus wineries for which the district is most famous. Wines have been made here since the region was first settled in the 1850s, but the industry took off with Thomas Hardy's arrival in 1873. The nearby beaches and reefs offer excellent swimming, diving and surfing. Throughout October visitors can participate in the annual Wine Bushing Festival.

See also Adelaide Hills Wine Region

Map ref: page 791 J10

MCLAREN VALE WINE REGION

Only 40 km (25 miles) south of Adelaide, McLaren Vale was settled by a group of Englishmen. Two in particular laid the foundations for the region and really left their

Peaches thrive in the McLaren Vale area.

mark—John Reynell, who first planted vines in the area in 1838, and Thomas Hardy, whose influence has been integral to the region. Wheat dominated in the early days, but the pioneers recognised that this region was perfect for vines. By the early twentieth century, there were 19 wineries in the district, mostly producing dark, high-alcohol, tannic dry reds and fortifieds, predominantly for the English market.

There were serious interruptions to supply and development during the two world wars. Then in the 1970s, taste and fashion switched from big robust red wines to dry light white wines. This caused serious problems for a number of years in McLaren Vale, where plantings of red varieties outnumbered white by about three to one. Many vines were grubbed out and replanted, or regrafted. But this

now seems to have been fortunate, since the introduction of new varieties like chardonnay, sauvignon blanc, merlot and cabernet franc allowed wine producers to expand their repertoires with considerable success.

Bordered to the east by the southern ranges of the Adelaide Hills and to the west the Gulf St Vincent, the diverse landscape of McLaren Vale varies from steep ranges and gorges to wide open plains, with beaches and cliffs, rivers, hills, olive groves, orchards and ocean views in between. The terrain is undulating and soil types vary widely, but red-brown or grey-brown loamy sands are dominant. There is also significant climatic variation, due to differing degrees of exposure to or protection from the nearby sea and its cooling influences. Summer rainfall is low, so vineyard irrigation is generally necessary, but the presence of the Onkaparinga River and its tributaries ensure that water is available.

Because of the geographical and climatic diversity, nearly all grape varieties flourish here, and especially those suited to premium styles. The resulting wines tend to be intense, full-flavoured reds and

powerful, fruit-driven whites. Shiraz is a mainstay, producing deep-coloured, richly flavoured wines with distinctive velvety characters (as opposed to the spicy/peppery characters found, say, in Barossa shiraz). Cabernet sauvignon tends to smoothness, with a ripe richness and hints of chocolate, and merlot also does well.

Among the whites, chardonnay excels here, producing classic examples at many levels, from big rich, buttery, toasty wines to elegant, peach-flavoured fruit-driven examples. Sauvignon blanc thrives here, too, giving herby, asparagus-flavoured wines with a prickly intensity. The region also produces some good fortifieds and is home to a wide range of sparkling wines.

McLaren Vale's 50 wineries are a mixed bunch in size, style and stature, with everything from one-person cellar-door operations to corporate behemoths. But the biggest of them all is no newcomer—BRL Hardy, the current incarnation of the company started by Thomas Hardy in the mid-1800s. He bought Chateau Reynella, now Hardy headquarters, from his contemporary, John Reynell. Hardys have kept expanding, acquiring new businesses at home and abroad, but the heart has always stayed in McLaren Vale. In addition, Southcorp has a significant stake in the region with its Seaview winery

Winetasting at the Coriole winery, McLaren Vale, which specialises in dry red and white table wines.

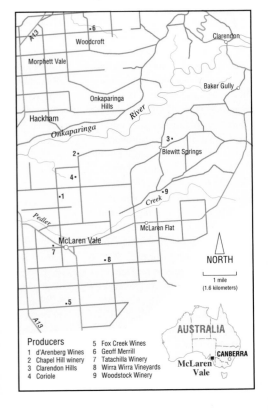

NORTH

1 mile
(1.6 kilometers)

AUSTRALIA

CANBERRA

McLaren Vale

Producers

1 d'Arenberg Wines
2 Chapel Hill winery
3 Clarendon Hills
4 Coriole
5 Fox Creek Wines
6 Geoff Merrill
7 Tatachilla Winery
8 Wirra Wirra Vineyards
9 Woodstock Winery

90, located 15 km (9.3 miles) south-east of Clare and 122 km (76 miles) north of Adelaide, is a declared heritage site, the first complete town in South Australia to be so recognised. Many of the old cottages and buildings date from when the town was first settled, in 1849. The magnificent Martindale Hall is just 2 km (1.2 miles) south of the centre of the town and is a fine example of an oldstyle Georgian mansion. Many cottages offer self-contained accommodation. The town makes a good base from which to explore the Clare Valley and the many local wineries.

The town is also known for its enormous slate deposit, which has been worked for over 150 years. It has been used a great deal in local construction, and also in fine buildings and billiard tables around the world.

The annual Paddy's Market and Street Fair is held in March.
Map ref: page 791 K8

MOONTA

Located just a short distance inland from Moonta Bay and the shores of Yorke Peninsula, and 161 km (100 miles) north-west of Adelaide, Moonta is rich in heritage and fine old buildings.

Moonta owes its existence to the discovery of copper in 1861 and the establishment of the Moonta Mining Co. Most of the mining was undertaken by Cornish immigrant miners, and by 1875 the population had reached 12,000—today it is 2750. Many of the buildings associated with this era are still standing.

The Moonta Mines State Heritage Area, which covers most of the old Moonta Mines lease area, includes Cornish cottages, the local church, a couple of shafts and ore processing plants. The Moonta Mines School is a very good museum.

Nearby Moonta Bay is a popular holiday centre with good beaches for water sports and fishing. The 'Kernewek Lowender Festival', which is held every second May, celebrates the Cornish heritage of the Copper Triangle towns of Moonta, Kadina and Wallaroo. The Moonta Show takes place in October.
Map ref: page 791 H8

Charles Sturt named Mannum on a journey to solve the mystery as to why rivers flowed westwards from the Great Dividing Range.

(given an upmarket re-branding as Edwards & Chaffey in 1999), as have Mildara Blass and Rosemount. But most of the wineries are considerably smaller, resulting in a range and variety of wines that reflects the diversity of the region and its producers.
Map ref: page 791 J10

MANNUM

Founded in 1852, Mannum—one of the oldest towns on the Murray River—became a major port when paddle-boats plied the Murray River, from its mouth upstream as far as Albury in New South Wales. The town is 78 km (48 miles) east of Adelaide, and today has a population of 2030. It is still an important river town, and services the surrounding community. Wool, beef and cereals are produced in the region. A number of vessels are based at Mannum, including the paddle-steamers PS *Marion, Proud Mary* and *Murray Princess*, the last

of which is the largest paddleboat in the Southern Hemisphere. The National Trust museum, housed in an old paddle-steamer, pays homage to the river trade and to Charles Sturt, the first European explorer to come this way. There is good fishing along the river, and the Cowirra Historic Reserve north-east of the township is important to the Aboriginals who once lived here. In July the town hosts the annual River Festival.
Map ref: page 791 L10

MELROSE

This delightful, quiet town in the Flinders Ranges, 271 km (168 miles) north of Adelaide, Melrose nestles at the foot of Mount Remarkable, one of the highest peaks in the range. Melrose was established in 1853—it is one of the oldest towns in the region—and the North Star Hotel was licensed one year later, in 1854. The town is small (population 210), but

is an excellent base from which to explore the surrounding area and the nearby Mount Remarkable National Park. A walking trail from just outside town leads to the top of the mountain, giving splendid views of the countryside, including the Willochra Plain. The walk takes about 5 hours (return). Another walking trail goes past the old copper mines to Bald Hill Lookout. A heritage walk in the town is popular with history buffs. The old police station and courthouse (founded 1862) is worth visiting, as it is now the site of a National Trust museum featuring antique furniture and farm implements. The Melrose Show, held annually in October of each year, is one of the largest in the region.
Map ref: page 791 J5

MINTARO

This small town, nestled among rolling hills and rich agricultural country, with a population of only

MORGAN

Located on the great bend of the Murray River where the river turns south towards the sea, 166 km (103 miles) east of Adelaide, Morgan is a small (population 445), quiet, pleasant town that relies mainly on tourism and servicing the local farm country for its existence. This has not always been the case—Morgan was once one of the most important ports in the State, servicing the paddle-steamers along the Murray. When the railway arrived from Adelaide it was one of only a couple of towns connected to the coast by rail. The area around the port and the railway siding is preserved today, as is a section of the long high wharf.

Ruins of an old farmhouse in Mount Remarkable National Park.

There is an excellent heritage walk around the wharf and nearby town area, and a museum is located down at the railway siding. There are a number of art and craft and antique shops in the town, and trail rides through the nearby bushland on carts, horses or camels can be arranged. Houseboats are also available for hire.
Map ref: page 791 L8

MOUNT REMARKABLE NATIONAL PARK

Mount Remarkable National Park, in the southern Flinders Ranges, is divided into two sections: the Alligator Gorge section in the west and the Mount Remarkable section in the east. A circle of ridges, which encompass a basin of valleys and creeks, form the Alligator Gorge section of the park. The gorge and the creek it feeds are the main attractions of the park. With a varied habitat and a reasonably reliable rainfall for this part of the state,

the park is rich in wildflowers and birds and is home to many animals, including euros and yellow-footed rock wallabies. From Melrose, in the eastern section of the park, there are a number of walking trails that take people to the top of Mount Remarkable. Alligator Creek, in the west, has cut a deep path through the red quartzite along the creek bed, creating a number of impressive gorges. The park is 270 km (168 miles) north of Adelaide and 50 km (31 miles) north of Port Pirie.
Map ref: page 791 H5

MURRAY BRIDGE

Murray Bridge (population 12,570) is an important rural riverside town as well as being a popular tourist retreat. It is sited on the Princes Highway, 80 km (50 miles) east of Adelaide, and is connected to the capital via the South East Freeway. Charles Sturt first passed this way in 1829–30, but it was another 25 years before settlement began. In the 1860s cattle on the overland route from the eastern states swam the Murray at this point, then known as Edward's Crossing and later as Mobilong. The first bridge was built in 1879, and in 1886 the railway passed through. In 1906 the swamps were drained and the land irrigated, allowing for farming of pigs, dairy cattle, fruit and vegetables. The new bridge, just to the south of town, was built in 1979.

The area is well endowed with water sports activities with everything from swimming and fishing to cruising in a houseboat. Another favourite attraction is Dundee's

Cruising on a houseboat is one way to enjoy the Murray River National Park.

Crocodile Farm. Just south of the town is the pioneer village of Old Tailem Town. West of Murray Bridge is the Monarto Zoological Park, which features Asian and African animals, and some pleasant walking trails.
Map ref: page 791 L10

MURRAY RIVER NATIONAL PARK

This park, located about 240 km (149 miles) east of Adelaide, is made up of three distinct sections of floodplain spread along the

Murray River from above Renmark to just north of Loxton. The park protects not only the natural wonders and rich wildlife, but the signs of past inhabitants—middens, canoe trees, ceremonial rings of stone, burial sites, stone chips and tools. The Katarapko section is primarily river flats and is the largest; the Bulyong Island and Lyrup Flats sections are smaller. Fishing, cruising on a houseboat, canoeing, camping and birdwatching are all popular pastimes in the park.
Map ref: page 791 N9

NURIOOTPA

The largest town in the Barossa Valley, and 72 km (45 miles) north-east of Adelaide, this delightful place is an excellent base for those wishing to experience the many wineries in the immediate area. Nuriootpa has a population of 3350, and is the commercial centre of the valley and home to some of Australia's largest wineries. On the edge of town is Penfolds, who for over 150 years have been producing wines; a few kilometres to the west is the Seppelt's winery, and to the north is Wolf Blass. Smaller, lesser-known wineries dot the intervening areas. All have wine-tasting and cellar door sales.

Murray Bridge got its name when a bridge was first built across the Murray in 1879.

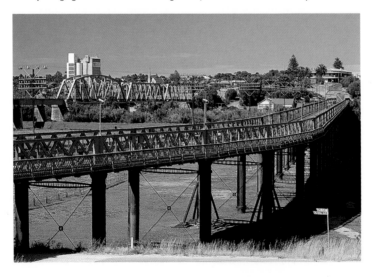

Europeans first arrived here in the 1840s, and William Coulthard built an inn. A town soon sprang up around this watering hole, and while the original building has long gone, there is still a hotel on the site. Coulthard's House, an impressive bluestone building, is now the National Trust Museum. In May of each year there is a hot-air balloon regatta, and in September there is the Barossa in Bloom weekend. *See also* Barossa Valley Wine Region
Map ref: page 791 K9

PARA WIRRA RECREATION PARK

Covering rolling hills and steep-sided valleys, this small park—only 1409 ha (3482 acres)—is located just 40 km (25 miles) north-east of Adelaide, making it popular with day visitors wanting to get away from the city. The main entrance, off Humbug Scrub Road, leads into the heart of the park, passing a range of sporting facilities, such as tennis courts and ovals, along the way. Gas barbecues are also dotted around the main roads through the park, and walking trails lead to a number of scenic spots or lookouts. The walking trails cover a good variety of terrain and distance—most are between 2 and 10 km (1.2 and 6.2 miles). Western grey kangaroos are common in the park, as are emus. Other birds, especially parrots, abound, while smaller birds, such as thornbills, tree-creepers, wrens and honey-eaters can be seen.
Map ref: page 791 K9

PETERBOROUGH

The town of Peterborough, 248 km (154 miles) north of Adelaide, was, and still is, a railway town. A year after it was founded in 1880, the railway arrived from Adelaide, and seven years later the line from Broken Hill to Port Pirie passed through. A short time later the railway to Port Augusta arrived, and Peterborough became one of the few places in the world where three railway gauges—broad, standard and narrow—met. Now most of the lines have been standardised, but the active local Steamtown Railway Preservation Society still uses some of the narrow gauge lines in and around the town to run steam train excursions.

The town is not large—its population is 2140. It now services the surrounding wheat and sheep properties. The State's only gold battery is located here. This battery has been crushing ore for 100 years and has yielded more than 400 kg (14,112 ounces) of gold. The town has many old buildings and a number of museums, mainly centred around the railway and its importance for Peterborough and Australia. Steamtown is open daily and offers narrow-gauge steam-train trips during winter. Being located on the eastern edge of the Flinders Ranges, the town is also a gateway to this area. A night rodeo is held every February.
Map ref: page 791 K6

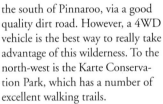

Emu (Dromaius novaehollandiae)

PINNAROO

Pinnaroo is a small town in far eastern South Australia, 244 km (152 miles) east of Adelaide. It is situated on the Ouyen Highway, almost on the South Australia–Victoria border. The township has a population of only 650, and gains its living from the wheat, barley and oat farms that surround it. Established in the 1860s, it was not until the railway arrived in 1906 that the town took on any real importance.

The town has a big aviary and a large collection of grain varieties. The local museum specialises in farm machinery. Part of the mallee lands that once dominated the whole region, Pinnaroo is close to a number of large parks that preserve vast tracks of mallee scrub and heath-covered plains. The Scorpion Springs, Mount Shaugh, Mount Rescue and Ngarkat Conservation Parks all lie to the south of Pinnaroo, via a good quality dirt road. However, a 4WD vehicle is the best way to really take advantage of this wilderness. To the north-west is the Karte Conservation Park, which has a number of excellent walking trails.
Map ref: page 791 N10

The Peterborough area was originally 'a wild place' with 'kangaroos swarming', according to early settler Johann Koch, 1875.

PORT AUGUSTA

Situated at the head of Spencer Gulf, 318 km (197 miles) north of Adelaide, Port Augusta is one of South Australia's major towns, with a population of 14,600, and is known as 'The Crossroads of the North'. For many travellers it is the gateway to outback South Australia, Central Australia and the Northern Territory, and to Eyre Peninsula and places further west. It is also a major rail terminal, and literally the powerhouse of the state—the state's major electricity generating stations are just south of the town on the shores of Spencer Gulf.

Matthew Flinders, on the *Investigator*, was the first European to see this semi-desert country. In 1839 Edward John Eyre pushed north along the coastal plain and followed the western edge of the Flinders Ranges north on his failed quest to find a way inland. The town was founded in 1854 as a major port for the pastoral lands and mining endeavours taking place further north at that time. In the 1870s it became an important base for the construction of the Overland Telegraph line, which linked Adelaide and the rest of Australia with Darwin and the world. In 1878 it also became the major railway town for the Ghan line, which goes to Alice Springs, and in 1917 it was joined to Perth via the Transcontinental line. In 1944 the Morgan–Whyalla pipeline was completed, assuring Port Augusta a steady supply of good water, and 10 years later the first of the state's major power stations was opened. The ships stopped calling at the port in 1973, but by

The wharf at Port Augusta was once a busy with shipping. Nowadays water sports and boating are the main activity around it.

then the large Australian National Railways workshops were located here. The town is also the operational base for the Royal Flying Doctor Service and the School of the Air. Tours of both bases are available by arrangement.

The Arid Lands Botanical Garden is a large area dedicated to Australia's unique arid land plants; the Wadlata Outback Centre is an award-winning display that will take you from the present day back 15 million years. There are a number of historic buildings in the town, including the Institute of Mechanics building, built in 1875. A heritage walk gives a good insight into the history and importance of this town in opening up the outback of Australia. The town also has several other museums, including the Homestead Park Pioneer Museum, which includes a fully furnished 130-year-old homestead as well as hundreds of other historic items and displays.

Being close to the Flinders Ranges, the town is a good base from which to explore the immediate area, through Pichi Richi Pass to Quorn , or south-east via Horrocks Pass to Wilmington and Melrose, or south to Mount Remarkable National Park inland from historic Port Germein. As the town is located on the shores of Spencer Gulf, fishing is also an attraction, with the mighty 'reds' (big snapper) being the fish to chase. Of course other fish, including whiting, mullet and flathead, are around, too. The town has many annual events: the Australia Day Breakfast and Swimming Carnival in January, the Apex Summer Festival and Surf Boat Carnival in March, the Blues & Country Music Festival in April, the Racing Carnival in June, Golf Week and the Camel Cup in August and the BMX Carnival in October.
Map ref: page 791 H5

PORT BROUGHTON

Located on a very well-protected arm of Mundoora Bay, 285 km (177 miles) north of Adelaide, is the small town of Port Broughton (population 680). With its safe family beach, it has become a very popular seaside holiday resort. The town has a protected anchorage where the fishing fleet, renowned for its catches of prawns, is moored. The town was named and established in 1871 after the surrounding area had been divided into wheat farms and a port was needed from which to ship the grain. The first jetty was completed in 1874 and today's long T-shaped jetty makes a good fishing platform. The town's

local museum is housed in the old council chambers. Just to the north of the town is the small village of Fisherman's Bay, and to the south are the copper towns of Moonta, Kadina and Wallaroo.
Map ref: page 791 H7

PORT LINCOLN

Port Lincoln, one of the largest towns on the Eyre Peninsula—with a population of 11,350—as well as one of its busiest ports, is situated 653 km (406 miles) west of Adelaide, on Boston Bay, which covers over three times the area of Sydney Harbour. The bay was named by Matthew Flinders in 1802 and was used by whalers and sealers before a permanent settlement was established. In 1839 it was mooted as the site for the capital of the new colony of South Australia, but Colonel William Light was concerned about the lack of fresh water and therefore chose the site of Adelaide instead.

The Lincoln Hotel, built in 1840, still stands on the waterfront. The first jetty was built in 1875 to handle the ever-increasing load of wheat and wool being shipped from the port. As the 1900s progressed, a web of railway lines brought even more primary products to the harbour, and in 1980 Port Lincoln became the second port in Australia to handle bulk grain export. A cannery was opened in the 1950s, mainly processing tuna, and today the calm waters around Boston Island are dotted with the circular enclosures of great fish traps that house and fatten the tuna. The harbour is also a base for the crayfishing and abalone industries, both

Harvester on wheat farm, near the historic port town of Port Broughton.

of which abound in these waters.

For travellers the city makes a fine base from which to explore the surrounding area and to take in the many delights the region has to offer. The town itself has a number of attractions, including the Mill Cottage Museum, which is operated by the National Trust, the Settler's Cottage Museum, and the nearby Rose-Wal Memorial Shell Museum. The Apex Wheelhouse commemorates the commercial fishing industry, and the Alex Stenross Maritime Museum features an extensive collection of sailing ship memorabilia. Just out of town is the fully restored Mikkira Station, the oldest sheep station on the Peninsula. The station has picnic and camping areas but visits must be booked in advance. Several local art galleries display work of the Constantia Designer Craftsmen, who have been internationally recognised for their fine work; the Mayne Gallery and the Arteyrea Gallery display a wide selection of local arts and crafts.

To the south is a magnificent coastline of white sandy beaches and rugged headlands, much of it protected in the Lincoln National Park. This park offers excellent bush camping, fishing, diving and surfing. To the west of the town and readily accessible are the town and waters of Coffin Bay. Whaler's Way, to the south of the town, is a privately owned scenic drive that takes in some of the most spectacular coastal scenery in Australia. You have to pay to obtain the key to open the gates to the drive. The key, and details on camping on Whaler's Way, are obtainable from the tourist offices in the city.

Offshore there are a host of islands to attract the traveller, including Boston Island and the Spilsby Island group to the north. Dangerous Reef, one of the best known great white shark locations in the world, is offshore and charter boats and cruises include this area on their tours. The reef is also home to one of the largest sea lion colonies in Australia—an underwater viewing platform lets visitors see these magnificent animals in their own environment.

With this protected waterway and all the islands nearby, it is no surprise that Port Lincoln is also a great yachting destination; there are a number of charter boats for hire from here. The fishing is varied and excellent. Offshore there are shark, whiting, snapper and kingfish, while from the jetty and beach there are tommy ruff, whiting and garfish. There are a number of walking trails in the nearby national park, and in town the Parnkalla Walking Trail winds around the delightful harbour. Annual events include the Adelaide to Port Lincoln Yacht Race and the Tunarama Festival, both in January.
Map ref: page 790 D9

Red snapper caught from the jetty at Port Pirie.

PORT PIRIE

Port Pirie is located 228 km (142 miles) north of Adelaide, just off Highway One on the eastern side of Spencer Gulf, a short distance from the ragged bluffs of the southern Flinders Ranges. It is one of South Australia's major cities and ports, and has a population of 15,120. It is also the site of the world's largest lead-smelting and refining plant, as well as a site for a huge bulk silo complex which is used for storing grain before export. The town got its start in 1845, when local pastoralists requested a ship be sent to transport sheep; the schooner *John Pirie* arrived and navigated the mangrove-lined creek that was soon to see a jetty and harbour established. The town was surveyed in 1871 and in 1877 the railway line to Broken Hill was opened, bringing with it the ore that was to see the town grow into the State's first provincial city.

At one stage three railway gauges converged at Port Pirie and ran down the main street, and while these have now been standardised, the town remains an important railway town which services the Indian–Pacific and Ghan railways.

There are a number of historic buildings within the town, including the railway station, Sampson's Cottage, which dates from the 1890s, and the majestic mansion of Carn Brae, built in 1901. Being close to the Flinders Ranges, the town is a good base from which to explore the Mount Remarkable National Park, the Telowie Gorge Conservation Park and the Nelshaby Reserve. All these parks have a number of walking trails, the most spectacular being the one into Alligator Gorge, which is in the national park and accessible from the small township of Wilmington. The walking trail in the Nelshaby Reserve has wheelchair access. Just up the coast is the small hamlet of Port Germein, once an important wheat shipping port but now a beachside holiday destination with a long wooden jetty, ideal for fishing. There is good crabbing along this coast, and the fishing from jetty or shore is likely to land whiting, salmon and garfish. Offshore there is snapper.

Annual events in town include the Easter Speedway and Motocross in March/April; the Blessing of the Fleet in late August/early September; the Country Music Festival and a round of the National Offroad Championships in October. The Athletic and Cycling Carnival is a big event in November.
Map ref: page 791 H6

Matthew Flinders arrived at Port Lincoln bay in 1802 and named it after his native province, Lincolnshire.

PORT VICTORIA

This tranquil seaside town (population 315) is 181 km (112 miles) west of Adelaide, and nestles on the eastern coastline of Spencer Gulf, on Yorke Peninsula, overlooking a protected bay sheltered by the bulk of Wardang Island, a few kilometres offshore. A busy commercial port for grain in the early 1900s, it is known as 'the last of the windjammer ports'. It was from here that the final, great grain race to Great Britain began in June 1939. History buffs can learn more about the area's past by visiting the Maritime Museum. There are a number of wrecks around Wardang Island which are part of the Maritime Heritage Underwater Trail, and these are popular with divers. The area abounds with water-based activities and anglers are likely to get catches of snapper, flathead, snook and whiting.
Map ref: page 790 G9

PORT WAKEFIELD

This historic township, with a population of 515, at the northern end of Gulf St Vincent, 93 km (58 miles) north-west of Adelaide, is at the crossroads of the main route to Yorke Peninsula and the road further north to Port Augusta, so its main thoroughfare is cluttered with fuel outlets and roadhouses. Port Wakefield was the first government town north of Adelaide and traces its beginnings back to 1838 when it was known as Port Henry; it was established to ship copper ore from Burra. The link between Burra and Port Wakefield was of such importance that a horse-drawn tramway was constructed between the two

Wheat silos in the distance, at Port Victoria harbour.

towns and used until the coming of the railway in 1857. Later the port was used to export wheat and wool from the surrounding districts.

Today the town is tranquil, with many of its original buildings still standing and well preserved—a walk around town and along the jetty is most interesting. The jetty is also irresistible to keen anglers, and the surrounding shallow waters and mangrove habitats also make for excellent fishing, with catches of whiting, snapper, mullet and Australian salmon.
Map ref: page 791 J8

QUORN

Nestled in the south-central Flinders Ranges, 344 km (214 miles) north of Adelaide, Quorn, proclaimed in 1878, was founded on farming. It became an important railway centre when the Great Northern Railway pushed north

Ruins of an old pioneer's stone cottage, on farmland near Quorn.

from Port Augusta to Quorn in 1879, eventually reaching Alice Springs some 50 years later. The railway was built by Chinese and British workers, but the line was closed in 1956. With the closure of the railway, Quorn struggled to survive, but today tourism has put some vitality back into this wonderful little country town. Its population today is 1390.

A ride on the historic narrow-gauge Pichi Richi Railway, one of the oldest intact railway systems in the world, should not be missed. A stroll around town will take you past many fine old buildings, and there are also numerous art and craft galleries. Nature lovers will enjoy a tour into the nearby spectacular Dutchmans Stern Conservation Park. The Quorn Show and a country music event under the stars are held annually in September.
Map ref: page 791 H4

RENMARK

Renmark, initially named Bookmark, is located on the Sturt Highway, alongside the Murray River. It is 251 km (156 miles) east of Adelaide, and around 145 km (90 miles) west of Mildura. It is the oldest and largest town in the Riverland, with a population of 4260, and is the centre for South Australia's largest irrigation scheme along the Murray River, covering an area of nearly 7000 ha (17,297 acres). In fact, it was here that two Canadian brothers, George and William Chaffey, established Australia's first irrigation settlement. Their original home in the district, Olivewood Historical Homestead, is open to the public and gives a fine introduction to the region and the development of the scheme.

The lifegiving flow of water allows the growing of grapes, citrus, stone fruit, vegetables and flowers; wheat and wool are also produced in the region. Like many towns along the river, Renmark's businesses were built with a strong sense of community involvement.

Australia's first co-operative winery was opened here in 1916, six years after the first winery and distillery in the Riverland.

Renmark's rich history is portrayed to visitors in many forms, from its magnificent and well-preserved old buildings and monuments to the romantic old paddle-steamers. These haven't quite disappeared from the river, with the PS *Industry* now a floating museum. The *Murray Princess*, the largest stern paddle-steamer in the Southern Hemisphere, still plies the waterways, taking passengers on cruises. For others, a houseboat is an idyllic way to cruise up and down the Murray—there are many to choose from in Renmark. Other water sports, including swimming, sailing and waterskiing, are also popular along the river. Fishing for golden perch and Murray cod is also on the agenda and it is a great way to spend time. Across the river from town is Paringa, which has excellent picnic and recreational facilities centred around the river and water activities.

Visitors will find plenty to keep them occupied in and around Renmark. One of Australia's largest reptile parks, with more than 450 reptiles, birds, and animals, is located here, and Ruston's Rose Garden is the largest in the Southern Hemisphere. There are many conservation and games parks nearby as well. Just to the north of the city is the Bulyong section of the

Murray River National Park, with its natural flood plains, and the Ral Ral Creek canoe trail. In fact, canoeing is a pleasant way to enjoy much of the river and you can hire a canoe at a number of places in town. A short distance south of the town is the Lyrup Flats section of the same national park, which has pleasant camping spots and walking trails. Birdwatchers will find plenty of bird life to keep them occupied along the river and amongst its wetlands and tributaries. When the Calperum Wetlands have water, they become one of the major centres for breeding waterbirds in southern Australia. Orange Week, the local festival, is held in August/ September of each year.
See also Riverland Wine Region
Map ref: page 791 N8

RIVERLAND WINE REGION

With so much attention and emphasis placed on the fashionable premium-wine producing regions, it would be easy to forget that the driving force in Australia's wine industry is the far less glamorous, vast open space of the Riverland that stretches across the border into Victoria. These endless hectares of vines, watered by the mighty Murray River, pump out more than half of South Australia's grapes and a third of the country's total crush. They provide the fruit for the

Australian wine that most people, at home and abroad, drink most of—the big-name brands, the bags-in-boxes, the everyday quaffers. They are honest, enjoyable, good-value wines that are full of flavour.

Without the Riverland, nowhere near the number of people who currently enjoy a glass or two of Oxford Landing, Jacob's Creek, Lindemans Bin 65, or brands with other household names would ever have tasted Australian wine, or perhaps even have known that it existed. Nor would the Australian wine industry be enjoying the enormous global success that it does. Much of the credit for the apparently inexorable rise in wine exports should go to the growers and winemakers of the Riverland (even though it rarely does). Without them, Australia simply couldn't meet the demand for wines or invest in the future of its wine industry.

If you drop in at the cellar-door of some of the larger producers, such as Angoves or Renmano in Renmark, or Berri Estates in Berri, it seems a bit like battery farming

The wineries in the Riverland Wine Region are well known for their golden chardonnays.

for grapes. You'll see endless rows of vines, posts and wires, with computer-controlled irrigation systems stretching to the horizon, or seas of stainless-steel tanks and sheds that resemble chemical refineries more than wineries. The wines produced are simple, straightforward, fruit-driven styles that are made in huge quantities for instant drinking rather than for careful cellaring. But, as in the rest of the industry, fruit quality, technical know-how and the wines themselves are improving all the time, and some enthusiastic producers are now taking the Riverland to a much higher plane.

The showpiece of the Riverland Wine Region is Banrock Station, a good example of what can be achieved in this environmentally sensitive and stretched region. This groundbreaking vineyard property has a wetland reserve and visitor centre near Kingston-on-Murray. Everything has been done with the environment and conservation in mind, from the solar-powered, recycled-water-using visitor centre with stunning views over the wetland lagoons and river, to the computer-controlled vineyard irrigation. Even the packaging used at Banrock Station wines is recycled and recyclable, and a contribution from the sale of every bottle goes to Landcare Australia.

Bonneyview Wines, on the shores of Lake Bonney at Barmera, is a boutique winery that makes an interesting contrast to the more industrial-scale enterprises of its nearest neighbours. Its cellar-door facilities and restaurant are a popular destination.

It's hot and dry in the Riverland region, but the brown sandy loam soils—which are just an hour from the Barossa Valley—are reasonably fertile. Rainfall here is low and the rate of evaporation is high, so there is little risk of disease The main concern for the future of the Riverland region is the health of Murray River, where water levels are dropping and salinity levels are rising fast. It is hoped that new, more sensitive irrigation systems will help to alleviate the pressures on this invaluable water resource.
Map ref: page 791 N8

The Murray River at Renmark. It is thought that Renmark means 'red mud' in a local Aboriginal language.

ROXBY DOWNS

This modern mining town (population 3030) is 570 km (354 miles) north-west of Adelaide, and is reached by bitumen road on the way to Andamooka. It is 85 km (53 miles) from Pimba, off the Stuart Highway. It can also be accessed via the Oodnadatta Track, which is to the north. The community was established in 1987 to service the employees (and their families) of the Olympic Dam mining operations. With the availability of water, thanks to the Great Artesian Basin, the town is developing into a verdant, treed oasis in an otherwise parched landscape. Surface tours of the mine site, 15 km (9.3 miles) north of the town, give visitors an idea how copper, uranium oxide, gold and silver are extracted and refined.
Map ref: page 790 F1

STRATHALBYN

Established beside the peaceful Angas River on the Fleurieu Peninsula in 1839 by Scottish immigrants, Strathalbyn—61 km (38 miles) south-east of Adelaide—is one of the most attractive towns in South Australia. Copper, one of its first enterprises, was mined and smelted in and around the district from 1848–1914. Other operations included flour milling, brewing, a foundry and a gasworks. Today the town has a population of 2630, and the area's primary industries revolve around the production of butter, cheese and cereal crops.

Some of the area's earliest history is depicted within the Anthony's Hill Historic Reserve; there is a small sandstone rock shelter here where the local Aboriginals painted unusual human figures in red ochre on the walls and ceiling.

Strathalbyn has been declared a heritage town, and now has more than 30 vintage heritage-listed buildings. There is even a roving resident town crier. There are also plenty of delicious dining spots, and handicraft enthusiasts will find a wide range of antique, craft and gift shops to browse through.

A pleasant day can be spent visiting the nearby wine-growing districts of Langhorne Creek, or taking a drive to Milang to see the largest freshwater lake in Australia, Lake Alexandrina. For nature lovers, a visit to the Cox Scrub Conservation Park and Kuipto Forest, west of the town, is worthwhile. Here you can enjoy a drive or go for a walk through the natural bushland. Annual events include the Collectors Hobbies and Antiques Fair in August and the Rotary Duck Race in November.
Map ref: page 791 K10

STREAKY BAY

The coastal township of Streaky Bay (population 960) is located in the southern corner of the bay of the same name, on the Flinders Highway, 722 km (448 miles) west of Adelaide and 112 km (70 miles) south of Ceduna. Matthew Flinders sailed into the bay in 1802, naming it after the streaks of colour in the water created by the seaweed. The town itself was not proclaimed until 1865— there is a wealth of information about its early history in the National Trust Museum. The harvesting of wheat played an important role in Streaky Bay's early development, and continues to do so today, along with the production of barley, wool and fat lambs. Fishing has also been a major

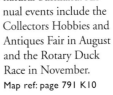

part of the town's economy, along with tourism, and granite mining, the latest commercial venture.

The beautiful coastline around Streaky Bay is dotted with bays and coves, many protected from the relentless motion of the Southern Ocean, and the fishing is excellent. You can also fish close to town, where you stand a chance of catching snook, snapper, garfish, squid and tommy ruff. Of special interest and well worth the drive are a couple of unique attractions within 60 km (37 miles) of Streaky Bay: Point Labat has the only sea lion colony on the Australian mainland, and the impressive rocky outcrops of pink granite boulders known as 'Murphy's Haystacks', 1500-million-year-old granite iselbergs, are a phenomenal sight. Regular events and shows include the Agricultural Show in September, the Snapper Contest in November/ December and Camel Cup Races in November.
Map ref: page 790 B5

SWAN REACH

Swan Reach is a delightful town, first settled by Europeans during the late 1830s, and has long been a popular holiday destination, as the holiday shacks that line the river front attest. Located 26 km (16 miles) south of Blanchetown and 138 km (86 miles) north-east of Adelaide on the Sturt Highway, this small township (population 240) is perched high on the cliff-top on the eastern bank of the Murray River. Spectacular cliff faces tower above the waterline, and a line of vivid green, hugging the cliff base along

Streaky Bay is a small town best known for its coastal scenery and striking rock formations.

The waters at the Murray's end flow extremely slowly through Swan Reach.

the water's edge, provides a beautiful setting for the houseboats that pull up along here. The vehicle ferry that crosses the river here provides the only access from one side of the river to the other. Well known for its excellent water sports, the town also has launching facilities on the river; anglers can pursue golden perch and cod, but are more likely to catch carp. The surrounding area teems with bird life, and the flora and fauna, including many wombats, and kangaroos, are well safeguarded within the Swan Reach and Ridley Conservation Parks. Murray River Educational Tours are available by appointment. The Punyelroo Caravan Park offers fishing, boating and waterskiing.
Map ref: page 791 L9

TANUNDA

The settlement of Tanunda (population 3100), 91 km (57 miles) north-east of Adelaide, was established along the banks of the North Para River in 1843. It was originally called Langmeil, and later renamed Tanunda. The area was first settled by German Lutherans, who established farms and villages in the valley; English settlers took up the surrounding grazing land. Although Tanunda is a focal point in Barossa Central, and is surrounded by wineries, the region also produces wool and wheat.

Tanunda is one of the oldest towns in the Barossa—the first vines here were planted by Samuel Hoffman in the mid-1800s. The town

was then basically a German enclave, with all the stores, school and church German. The Tabor Lutheran Church, built in 1849, is one of four in the town today, its towering spire seeming to overlook the town like a guardian angel. To sample the rich heritage and culture of this delightful town, a stroll around the streets is a must. The feeling that you are wandering round a German village is probably most noticeable while in the vicinity of the old market square, Goat Square—which is classified by the National Trust—as the square is surrounded by century-old cottages. The historical museum is housed in the old Post Office, built in 1866.

To discover all that Tanunda and its surrounds has to offer, visit the Barossa Wine and Visitor Centre in Murray Street. Apart from information on the many attractions and services available, the wine centre will also teach you about the art of making good wine and the history of this wine-growing region. There are wine-tasting tours of the many vineyards in the area, including Langmeil Winery, which is set in the old Tanunda Langmeil settlement. Other attractions include the Keg Factory, makers of traditional handcrafted pot kegs, and Norm's Coolies Performing Sheep Dogs, a working team of sheep dogs. There is a hectic calendar of events for the Barossa region; of special interest in Tanunda are the Jazz and German Night in February, and the Melodienacht in May.
See also Barossa Valley Wine Region
Map ref: page 791 K9

railway line in the 1980s, the town's significance and its economy diminished. However, Terowie has now been declared a historic township, and a walk along the main street is like stepping back in time. The shopfronts have retained their original character and architecture, and the small museum, hardware store and blacksmith shop exhibit artefacts from a bygone era. Other attractions include Terowie Antique Linen and Lace and Collectables.
Map ref: page 791 K6

TUMBY BAY

The small coastal town of Tumby Bay (population 1150) lies on the western shore of Spencer Gulf on Eyre Peninsula, 49 km (30 miles)

Surf fishing for snapper, whiting and bream, is popular at Tumby Bay.

north of Port Lincoln and 608 km (378 miles) west of Adelaide. The blue water of its sheltered bay and its white sandy beaches are backdropped by a grassy foreshore lined with Norfolk Island pines. Named by Matthew Flinders in 1802, the town was settled in the 1840s. It became an important port for vessels visiting the communities which farmed sheep and grew wheat on the offshore islands of the Sir Joseph Banks Group. Two jetties were built in the 1870s for the handling of supplies and produce. Fishing is a favourite activity in the bay and around the jetties.
Map ref: page 790 E9

TEROWIE

The small settlement of Terowie (population 230) is on the Barrier Highway, 63 km (39 miles) north of Burra and 239 km (148 miles) north of Adelaide, in the rural area of the midnorth. It began life in the 1800s as an important railway town, and it was not long before the outlying stations to the north-east became reliant on it for supplies. With the redirection of the

By 1839 large tracts of land were being sold off around Tanunda. German settlers arrived in 1842.

WAIKERIE

The biggest citrus-growing centre in Australia, Waikerie—170 km (106 miles) north-east of Adelaide—is the largest town in the Riverland, with a population of 1750. Founded as a communal settlement in 1894, aimed at relieving unemployment in Adelaide at the time, the new settlers set to with their government-supplied tools and began carving out an oasis in the dry mallee scrub. With irrigation the area boomed, and today the town is home to one of the largest citrus-packing sheds in the Southern Hemisphere, as well as to the popular 'Crusta' fruit juice company.

A large riverside park caters for many sporting activities and from the nearby Rotary cliff-top lookout there is a fine view of the surrounding area and some of Waikerie's one million or so orange trees. On the main highway is The Orange Tree, where you can buy a wide selection of local produce and where you'll find the Heritage Room, which depicts life during the early years of this settlement.

The town is considered by many gliding experts to be one of the best gliding areas in Australia, and each year sees many making the pilgrimage here to take to the clear blue skies. As with most riverside towns, there is also a great selection of bird life along the river and in the nearby lagoons and backwaters,

and, of course, there is also good fishing. The Waikerie International Food Fair takes place in March.
Map ref: page 791 M8

WALLAROO

The third town of the Copper Triangle—the other two being Kadina and Moonta— Wallaroo, 153 km (95 miles) north-west of Adelaide, is now one of the major ports in the State, exporting barley and wheat and shipping in phosphate rock. Surveyed in 1860, the town was established a year later, when rich discoveries of copper were found at Kadina and Moonta. The first jetty was constructed that year to ship the ore from the Wallaroo Mine, located near Kadina. A smelter was built and the port soon became one of the busiest in the State.

The town today has a population of 2470, and is a reminder of those past days—many of the buildings listed by the National Trust. The 'Big Stack' of the smelter still stands as testimony to the craftsmanship of the Welsh builders who built it, while many other buildings in town owe their heritage to the Cornish

At the Soaring Centre in Waikerie, tourists can go for joy rides or take courses in gliding.

immigrants who made up the bulk of the early population. The whitewashed limestone buildings of the Heritage and Nautical Museum, dating back to 1865 and once the post office, now house a fine display of the region's early history.

While the offshore fishing is good, for those without a boat, the grain jetty provides a perfect platform from which to fish for snapper, yellowtail kingfish, mulloway, snook, garfish, and others. Two low-lying islands just offshore Wallaroo, the Bird Islands, are pro-

tected in a conservation park as a breeding area for a good variety of seabirds. The major annual festivity in Wallaroo and surrounding areas is the 'Kernewek Lowender', an 11-day event in May (every second year) celebrating the Cornish history of the Copper Triangle.
Map ref: page 791 H8

WHYALLA

Located nearly 80 km (50 miles) south of Port Augusta and 391 km (243 miles) north-west of Adelaide on the Lincoln Highway, in the north of the Spencer Gulf and on the east side of Eyre Peninsula, Whyalla is the largest provincial town in South Australia. It owes its existence to the nearby great iron ore deposits of Iron Knob, Iron Monarch and Iron Baron—Iron Knob was the first iron ore deposit to be exploited in Australia, at the end of the nineteenth century.

Whyalla, originally called Hummock Hill when Flinders first sailed the Gulf in 1802, became a port for the ore when a tramway was built from the mine. In 1941 the town got a blast furnace and soon became a shipbuilding town. In 1965 it received a big shot in the arm when BHP opened a steelworks there. The shipyard has closed and the steel mill is running down, but the town is still large— population 25,260—and still an industrial giant, with oil and gas

Whyalla—the name means 'deep-water place'—has safe beaches and excellent fishing and boating facilities.

production and a shipping terminal nearby at Port Bonython; tourism and aquaculture have played a more important part in recent times.

The town has a number of attractions, including the Maritime Museum, home of the biggest land-locked ship in Australia, the former warship *Whyalla*; the largest model railway in Australia; the Whyalla Wildlife and Reptile Sanctuary, with its large collection of native reptiles, birds and animals; and the Ada Ryan Gardens, one of the first parks established in the city and still one of the most popular. The National Trust museum is housed in the Mount Laura Homestead, a former sheep station, and consists of a number of buildings relocated and refurbished here as well as displays of stationary engines and many old photographs. For something different, try the Steelworks Tour, the only one of its kind in Australia. The Tanderra Craft Village, located next to the Tourist Centre has a variety of craft markets and specialty shops, a pottery workshop and gallery. There are other attractions further afield, including the historic Point Lowly Lighthouse, Port Bonython and a scenic coastal drive along the Gulf.

Whyalla is considered the best fishing spot for snapper in Australia, with the Australian Amateur Snapper Fishing Championship held here in January. While the fishing is great offshore for salmon and yellowtail kingfish, closer in there are whiting, snook and garfish; along the foreshore you might just catch blue swimmer crabs. Whyalla is also a very active town when it comes to festivals and events, with some of the major highlights being the Sportsfishing Convention held in March or April, the local show in August and the Proclamation Day Concert in December, and harness racing, throughout the year.
Map ref: page 790 G6

WILMINGTON

Located 23 km (14 miles) north of Melrose, 51 km (32 miles) west of Orroroo and 295 km (183 miles) north of Adelaide, in the mid-north of the State, Wilmington lies tucked in beside the Flinders Ranges,

Wilpena Pound is a natural amphitheatre surrounded by high ridges. The word Wilpena is said to mean 'cupped hands'.

with the vast flat Willochra Plain stretching away to the east and north. Formerly known as Beautiful Valley, the name was changed when the town was officially founded in 1876. The town's location, near Horrocks Pass, and with access to the coast and Port Augusta, became an important service centre for the surrounding farms. The railway arrived in 1915. Today the town is tiny, with a population of only 250, but it still services the surrounding district and the tourists who travel through here experiencing the Flinders.

Located at the northern end of Mount Remarkable National Park, Wilmington gives easy access to Alligator Gorge, which is possibly the most spectacular gorge in the Flinders and certainly the most accessible. Walking trails start from near the gorge car park. In town there is a small museum and a number of historic buildings. Further afield there are the Spring Creek Copper Mine ruins, which are worth a look, and the historic settlements of Hammond and Bruce. Hancock's Lookout, which can be accessed from the road

through Horrocks Pass, gives spectacular views of Spencer Gulf and Port Augusta. The major events for the town are the show in September and the Night Rodeo in January.
Map ref: page 791 H5

WILPENA

Arguably South Australia's most famous tourist attraction, Wilpena Pound is located within the confines of the Flinders Ranges National Park. At the only access to the pound is the small hamlet of Wilpena (population nominal). Wilpena is 456 km (283 miles) north of Adelaide, and is little more than a caravan park, motel complex and the national park headquarters. It is a delightful place—a day or two at Wilpena is more than worthwhile. Recently upgraded, the motel and camping area have lost none of their charm, and there are a number of places to camp. You can enjoy a host of walks and some of the best scenic drives in the State while based at Wilpena. For the more active there are some long, hard walks in and around the pound, or further, through the ranges, along the Heysen Trail. Rock climbers can test their mettle on the walls of the pound near Arkaroo Rock.
Map ref: page 791 J3

The butcher on Wilmington's main road, where there is no footpath between shops and busy street.

NORTH-EAST SOUTH AUSTRALIA

Wide horizons, deserts and salt lakes all contribute to the spectacular arid landscape of north-east South Australia. The ruggedness of this area conceals rich mineral resources: oil, natural gas, copper, uranium and opals. Conservation parks and national parks preserve vast areas for today's adventurers, usually experienced and well prepared 4-wheel drivers.

The Stuart Highway, one of the major routes north from Port Augusta to the Northern Territory, passes through much of this region, including the opal-mining town of Coober Pedy. The harshness of the environment and the difficulties of surviving in it are perfectly exemplified by the underground dugouts in which many of the town's population live to escape the extreme heat. The white clay mounds resulting from the extensive opal-mining contribute to the desolate feel of this place which was used as a location for the film 'Mad Max'. Alternatively, it is possible to head north via the Oodnadatta Track, one of the overland tracks originally used to drive cattle south to Adelaide. It follows the route of the old Overland Telegraph Line and the original Ghan Railway, so there are many historic ruins of railway sidings and telegraph stations along the way. It joins the famed Birdsville Track at Marree.

Lake Eyre, the largest salt lake in Australia, drains nearly one-sixth of Australia's land surface but is rarely full due to its location in the dry heart of Australia. Further north lies the impenetrable Simpson Desert which was not crossed on foot until 1973. It had been aerially charted in 1929 by Cecil Madigan—a fellow expeditioner and explorer in Antarctica with Douglas Mawson. To the north-east lies the Sturt Stony Desert, so named because it is covered in gibber, a layer of round stones ranging from pebbles to boulders.

Intrepid naturalists find the Witjira National Park, on the western fringes of the Simpson Desert, a unique environment. A number of springs—outlets for the Great Artesian Basin—have formed mineral deposits and mounds. This permanent water supply supports large flocks of birds as well as rare fish and amphibians.

OPPOSITE: With an area of more than 150,000 sq. km (57,900 sq. miles), the Simpson Desert is one of the world's most significant sand-ridge deserts.

Cooper Creek, near Innamincka. The Innamincka Regional Reserve covers a unique part of Australia.

REGIONAL FEATURE

The Birdsville Track

Originally established in the nineteenth century as a droving highway through some of the harshest terrain in South Australia, the Birdsville Track became one of the country's most notorious highways, accounting for numerous strandings and fatalities. In recent years, it has been tamed—the surface has been improved and comfortable accommodation is available en route—and the track can now be driven in a day or so, even in a conventional vehicle.

That said, it is still a long way between water and supply points on the Birdsville, and the route should therefore be treated with the respect it deserves. Do the wrong thing out here and you could still end up in strife. So make sure you travel in a well-maintained—preferably 4WD—vehicle and carry spares, extra fuel and plentiful supplies of water. Avoid travelling the route in the summer Wet season, when temperatures soar and flood waters rise, and check the road conditions locally before you set off.

History

Aboriginal people lived in the deserts of north-east South Australia for many thousands of years before Europeans arrived, and their trade routes crisscrossed the entire region. Among the most widely bartered goods were Flinders Ranges ochre and Lake Eyre pituri.

The first European to enter this region was Edward John Eyre in 1840; he travelled as far as the southern shore of Lake Eyre, although he thought it was Lake Torrens. Backtracking and then heading north-east, he got as far as Mount Hopeless, at the northern end of the Flinders Ranges, before turning back. Eyre's report of a vast ring of salt beyond the Flinders encouraged Charles Sturt in his search for a large inland sea. In 1844, Sturt set out for the heart of the continent, following the Darling River north, then striking north-west to Innamincka. He subsequently pushed on across the gibber-strewn plain now known as Sturt Stony Desert. Sturt saw the country in the grip of a drought and his disillusioned testimony did little to inspire further exploration. Eventually, however, reports from the search parties sent to look for Burke and Wills in 1861 encouraged others to venture into the area.

In 1874 the surveyor John Lewis explored the Diamantina River system, and in 1880 E.A. Burt blazed the trail that we know as the Birdsville Track. It allowed the cattlemen of south-western Queensland to drive their herds down the track to Adelaide and, subsequently, following the construction of a railway, to the railhead at Marree. In good years, mobs of as many as 2000 head travelled the route, taking about five to six weeks to cover the 500 km (310 miles) or so between Birdsville and Marree.

Numerous sidetracks lead off the Birdsville Track to homesteads or points of interest. Generally, these should be tackled only by experienced off-road drivers.

The railway made Marree the major supply point for north-eastern South Australia and for places further north, including Birdsville. Afghan traders, after whom the Ghan railway was subsequently named, led their camel trains out of the town on the long, dusty haul along the track, carrying all manner of goods. Later the camels were replaced by vehicles, then road trains. During the 1930s, mailman Tom Kruse began working the track and in 1952 the classic documentary 'Back of Beyond' was broadcast, making Kruse a household name. It was during this period that the 'The Track', as it became known, gained its fearful reputation, with stories abounding of travellers losing their lives among the dunes or on the featureless gibber plains.

The Trek

With the closure of the Old Ghan railway in 1980—the new one was built 200 km (124 miles) further west—Marree entered a decline from which it seems unlikely to emerge; yet the town preserves a sense of its historical significance and is still an interesting place to visit. The pub, the Great Northern Hotel, is the tallest building and offers accommodation, meals and cold beer. There are also two caravan parks with camp sites and two general stores providing a wide range of supplies as well as fuel and mechanical repairs.

Head south out of Marree and turn right onto the Birdsville Track; the road sign here is much photographed. Lake Harry, 31 km (19 miles) north, was the site of a large date palm plantation between the 1860s and 1915, but today there is little to remind one of those endeavours. The stone ruins are those of the Lake Harry Homestead, which was built in the 1870s as an outstation of Mundowdna, south of Marree. The low hills nearby provide good views of the surrounding countryside.

You pass through the dog fence 14 km (8.5 miles) north of Lake Harry. The longest fence in the world, it stretches from near the Western Australia border,

Once the principal form of transport in the desert, camels were superseded by motor vehicles in the 1930s. Today, about 100,000 roam free in Central Australia, while only a small number are used for treks and safaris.

A quiet tributary of Cooper Creek. The Cooper floods regularly— its floodpalin is almost 5 km (3.1 miles) wide in places.

across South Australia and along the western and northern boundaries of New South Wales, before veering into central Queensland. North of the wire is dingo and cattle country; south of the barrier is sheep country.

You cross Clayton Creek and pass Clayton Homestead, on your right, 55 km (34 miles) out of Marree. The gibber plain rolls onward, and 30 km (18.5 miles) north of Clayton Homestead you come to Dulkaninna Homestead. Cannuwaukaninna Bore is on the left, 28 km (17 miles) further on, and although it is now controlled and the water piped to many tanks on the property, a mini-wetland around the borehead usually attracts abundant birdlife.

The next notable landmark, Etadunna Homestead, is located on the right of the highway, 127 km (79 miles) from Marree. A cross stands by the side of the road here in memory of the Moravian missionaries who came to this part of the world in the 1860s, attempting to convert the local Aboriginal people to Christianity. Despite incredible hardship and long droughts, they persevered until they were finally defeated by the harsh conditions in 1917.

If Cooper Creek is in flood across the main track, take the detour to the ferry just north of Etadunna Homestead. This sidetrack wanders across gibber plain and sand-ridge country for 33 km (20.5 miles) before arriving at the ferry crossing. Should you have to make this detour, take your time and savour the area's distinctive scenery and birdlife.

Back on the main road, the flood plain of the Cooper can be viewed from a relatively high point 12 km (7.5 miles) north of Etadunna. On the left of the track, stands the MV Tom Brennan, a barge once used to transport stock and goods across the flooded river. A walk through the trees nearby usually provides glimpses of desert wildlife, be it a raucous group of corellas, a gliding, keen-eyed kite, or a dingo hunting for an evening meal.

Continue down the hill and onto the flood plain of the Cooper; it is nearly 5 km (3.1 miles) wide here, but during the Dry the crossing is no problem. The track from the ferry rejoins the main road about 3 km (1.9 miles) north of the crossing.

Beyond the Cooper, the landscape is dominated by yellowish sandhills. In the early twentieth century, this was the horror section for the mail trucks that regularly made the trip to Birdsville, and the next 15 km (9 miles) or so would take postman Tom Kruse and other mailmen of the period at least a day in their heavily loaded vehicles.

About 44 km (27 miles) north of Etadunna Homestead and 171 km (106 miles) from Marree, you come to the ruins of Mulka Homestead and general store, which were abandoned in the 1950s. Continuing north, you enter gibber country again on the edge of Sturt Stony Desert. In fact, three deserts meet here: the sandy Strzelecki Desert to the east, the driest in Australia; the Tirari Desert to the west; and the Sturt Stony Desert to the north.

Another 39 km (24 miles) takes you to Mungeranie Homestead and Roadhouse. This is an ideal place to stop, as the roadhouse offers air-conditioned accommodation, cold drinks, snacks and fuel. If you want

The Simpson Desert has about 1000 sand dunes. They extend mainly north to south and range in height from 3 m (9.8 feet) to the massive 30-m (98-foot) Big Red dune, east of Birdsville.

Marree, at the southern end of the Birdsville Track, is a good base for visits to Lake Eyre. This vast salt lake floods only once every eight years and has filled just three times in the last 150 years.

to camp, there is a small, pleasant site by the adjacent red sandhill. A small wetland here created by artesian bores provides a haven for a large number of birds, making this an interesting spot for ornithologists. For those who like an early morning wake-up call, the corellas usually provide one free of charge!

MUNGERANIE TO BIRDSVILLE

North of the roadhouse, the gibber plains stretch to the horizon and there is generally little to attract the eye until you come to Mirra Mitta Bore, 35 km (21.5 miles) north of Mungeranie. There is quite a bit of greenery here and once again some birdlife, but even so it is hard to believe that this forbidding place had a small store and vegetable garden and catered for travellers until the 1930s.

Mount Gason Bore, 2 km (1.2 miles) west of the road, is 46 km (28.5 miles) north of Mirra Mitta Bore and it too has formed a small wetland that adds a splash of greenery to the parched surroundings. The ruins of Mount Gason Homestead are situated just to the west, and the low mesa to the south is Mount Gason itself. The peak was named after Samuel Gason, the first policeman to patrol the track. A short distance up the road, a small area has been fenced off to protect a stand of Mount Gason wattle, a rare plant found in only one other part of Australia, near Old Andado Station in the Northern Territory.

About 27 km (16.5 miles) north of the Mount Gason Bore turn-off, the Rig Road, which crosses the Simpson Desert, branches off the track on the left. Another 11 km (7 miles) takes you to the turn-off to the main homestead of Clifton Hills, the largest station on the Birdsville Track, which covers 12,500 sq km (4,825 square miles). It's then another 14 km (8.5 miles) to the junction with the Inside Track.

TO BIRDSVILLE VIA THE INSIDE TRACK

The Inside Track, which crosses the flood plain of the Diamantina River just west of Goyder Lagoon, was the original route used by drovers. When the rivers were high, it remained impassable for months on end, and the new route, or Outside Track, was built in the

1960s to bypass the flood plain. Even during the Dry, the Inside Track is rougher, slower and little used compared to the main track, but because it crosses a better-watered area, where trees grow and birds thrive, it is the more scenic route. It is also more enjoyable, as long as you are in a 4WD, and at 155 km (96 miles), as against the Outside Track's 181 km (112 miles), shorter.

From the junction, the Inside Track heads north, then crosses the channels of the Diamantina. On the left-hand side of the road, 46 km (28.5 miles) further north, another track heads off into the Simpson Desert where it meets up with the Rig Road. The Inside Track continues along the edge of the flood plain, passing the turn-off to Alton Downs Station 38 km (23.5 miles) further north. From this junction, it's a straightforward 71 km (44 miles) to Birdsville.

TO BIRDSVILLE VIA THE OUTSIDE TRACK

The Outside Track arcs eastward from the junction, curving round the vast expanse of the Goyder Lagoon. After 57 km (35 miles), you come to a turn-off to the south. This track, which leads through Innamincka Regional Reserve, via Walkers Crossing and Clifton Hills, to the Strzelecki Track, is a private road, so you need to obtain permission to use it. It is, however, the fastest route between Birdsville and Innamincka.

Continuing along the Outside Track for another 5 km (3.1 miles) takes you to the edge of the famous Koonchera Sandhill, the largest sand dune on the Diamantina flood plain. The southbound Walkers Crossing track runs beside it for some distance and conveys a better sense of its size.

You pass the turn-off to Pandie Pandie Homestead 93 km (58 miles) north of the Walkers Crossing track junction, and then cross the South Australia–Queensland border. About 27 km (16.5 miles) north of the Pandie Pandie turn-off you come to a T-junction where you should turn left. The famous Birdsville racetrack is on your right. You then cross the Diamantina River and, 31 km (19 miles) from Pandie Pandie, arrive in the centre of Birdsville, 314 km (195 miles) from Mungeranie Roadhouse and 524 km (325 miles) from Marree.

Especially in the middle of the day, sightings of animals may be few and far between. But abundant tracks, such as these emu prints, indicate that, despite appearances, wildlife flourishes.

Places in
NORTH-EAST
SOUTH AUSTRALIA

The 42-km (26-mile) Ridgetop Tour in Arkaroola, is not for the faint-hearted.

ARKAROOLA

This wildlife sanctuary-cum-resort, with a population of 45, in the very north of the Flinders Ranges, 702 km (436 miles) north of Adelaide, was once a run-down sheep station, and is reached via good dirt roads from either Copley (the closest bitumen) or via Yunta. Today Arkaroola is one of the best outback resorts in South Australia, offering visitors a rich experience of natural attractions in a rugged, wild, inland setting. Located on the edge of the Gammon Ranges National Park and close to a number of historic sites, such as the Bolla Bollana smelter ruins, as well as the geological wonders of the Paralana Hot Springs and Mount Painter, the resort is an ideal base from which to explore the surrounding area. There are a number of pleasant 4WD routes and a host of walking tracks. One of the best ways to experience this place is on the Ridgetop Tour, a 4WD trip, taking in sweeping panoramas, which ends at the spectacular Sillers Lookout. Another unique attraction is the large astronomical telescope located on a peak close to the heart of the resort.
Map ref: page 793 L10

COOBER PEDY

The famed opal mining town of Coober Pedy lies on the Stuart Highway, 857 km (532 miles) north of Adelaide, near the centre of the State, on the main route to the Northern Territory. It is not a pretty place, and the extremely harsh climate—summer temperatures are often in the high 40°Cs (around 117°F)—makes many of the locals live underground. Some shops and motels are buried in the earth to escape the heat. Added to that are the white mounds of clay, littering the red-brown landscape, testimony to how many holes have been dug in search of the elusive opal. While you don't need a permit to 'noodle' for opal, only selected areas are open to noodlers.

The oldest and biggest opal-mining town in South Australia, Coober Pedy is the centre for over 70 different small opal fields scattered around the town. Founded in 1915, the town was only proclaimed in 1969. Over 45 nationalities live in Coober Pedy, which today has a population of 3500, but it is the Greek population that are the most noticeable—each July they hold their Greek Glendi carnival. There are three underground

churches here which should not be missed. The Umoona Mine Museum features the Aboriginal heritage of the area, and there are also underground mine tours. The Breakaways Reserve, located 32 km (20 miles) north along the Stuart Highway, protects an area of stark sandstone mesas and buttes.
Map ref: page 792 C7

GAMMON RANGES
NATIONAL PARK

This wild and formidable landscape forms the far north-east of the Flinders Ranges. The park takes in not only the rough and craggy heart of the ranges, but also a section of the surrounding plain leading to the salt expanse of Lake Frome. Geologically, the ranges consist mainly of heavily dissected granites and allied rocks, and after millions of years of battling nature's elements they are now worn down to awesome chasms, gorges, sheer bluffs and overhangs, with creeks that sometimes plunge downwards as waterfalls. The magnificent Sturt's desert pea and the delicate Sturt's desert rose are found here. Animal life is plentiful, if a little elusive, and includes euros, red kangaroos and the rare yellow-footed rock wallaby. Bird-watching is especially rewarding around the park's water points. The view from Grindells Hut, overlooking the Illinawortinna Pound and the Gammons, is breathtaking. The park is 750 km (466 miles) north of Adelaide and 110 km (68 miles) east of Leigh Creek. Take plenty of drinking water with you.
Map ref: page 793 K10

INNAMINCKA

In the far north-east of South Australia, about 1081 km (671 miles) north of Adelaide and surrounded by deserts in all directions, is an oasis fed by the slow-moving waters of Cooper Creek. Located on the southern bank of the Cooper, not far from the Queensland border, is a motley collection of buildings known as Innamincka. The pub and the general store are the heart of this tiny township; the national park headquarters, with its fine photographic display, is housed in the recently refurbished Australian Inland Mission (AIM) Nursing

Underground living at Coober Pedy is a must due to the heat and lack of building timber.

Home. You can't get to Inna-mincka without travelling a long way on dirt roads, the closest bitumen being to the east, in Queensland, 160 km (99 miles) away. South is the infamous Strze-lecki Track, now tamed because of the Moomba gas fields. While you could take a conventional vehicle to the Cooper via the Strzelecki, the area really is the home of the 4WD—in anything less, take care!

Charles Sturt came this way in 1844 and the Burke and Wills tragedy was played out along the Cooper 16 years later. A number of monuments to these journeys are located near the AIM home as well as by the stream. Before Federation in 1901, the town was an important stopping point for the drovers taking cattle down the Strzelecki Track. A pub was soon followed by a customs office, police station and the AIM home. How-ever, by the 1950s, the town was deserted, and it was not until gas was found around Moomba that a new pub was built at Innamincka in the early 1970s. The town is now the biggest it has ever been, with a population of 105!

While the Cooper is the major attraction, the town is also a step-ping-off point for the magical Coongie Lakes, 112 km (70 miles)

to the north-west. If you are in the area in August, the picnic race meeting is not to be missed.
Map ref: page 793 N4

INNAMINCKA REGIONAL RESERVE

This reserve covers a unique and historic part of Australia, with a contrasting but impressive landscape of sand dunes, claypans and gibber desert and the oasis of the mighty Cooper Creek. The reserve is rich in flora and fauna; one of the most significant habitats in the reserve is the Coongie Lakes system, in the north-west. This large wetland area, made up of myriad lakes, is an important retreat for birds. Unfortunately, visitors are only allowed access to Coongie Lake itself, which is the southernmost lake of the system. Cooper Creek and its waterholes are well stocked with fish, and there is a good chance of catching a feed of yellowbelly.
Map ref: page 793 M3

LAKE EYRE NATIONAL PARK

Lake Eyre National Park protects a major part of the heat-hazed, shimmering salt flats of Lake Eyre, the largest salt lake in Australia.

The almost still waters of Cooper Creek in Innamincka Regional Reserve.

This park encircles all of Lake Eyre North and the adjoining Tirari Desert. A drier, more inhospitable landscape you could hardly ima-gine. Lake Eyre is both a dry salt lake and a playa lake (one that occasionally floods), and is split in two, with the north and south lakes joined by the 13-km (8-mile) Goyder Channel. When the great rivers of the channel country far to the north flood, they set course for Lake Eyre, and occasionally the life-giving waters arrive at the

lower reaches of Lake Eyre and may even span out to fill both lakes, creating an inland sea nearly one-sixth the size of Australia. This then was the inland sea that Charles Sturt and his party set out to discover back in 1844—a sea of salt. At times of flooding, the lakes' waters, fresh for a short time, teem with fish from the rivers, and the lake is a utopia for a variety of water birds, such as pelicans, gulls and ducks. The park is 720 km (447 miles) from Adelaide.
Map ref: page 792 G6

MARLA

Proclaimed in 1981, the modern township of Marla, with a popu-lation of 100, is the government administration centre in northern South Australia. Situated at the junction of the bituminised Stuart Highway and the all-gravel Oodna-datta Track, 1092 km (678 miles) north-west of Adelaide, Marla is located at the site of a reliable water supply, the Marla Bore— an important consideration in this semi-desert country. Just 35 km (22 miles) to the west are the Mintabie opal fields. In recent years, these have outstripped Coo-ber Pedy as the largest suppliers of opals. The Dalhousie Mound Springs in the Witjira National Park are 350 km (217 miles) to the north-east—a virtual stone's throw in this vast desert country—but you will need a 4WD vehicle to get there. The Marla Race Meeting is held annually in April.
Map ref: page 792 A4

Motorists should check road conditions before embarking on a journey along the hazardous Strzelecki Track, near Innamincka.

MARREE

Located at the junction of the Birdsville Track, the Oodnadatta Track and the main road south to Port Augusta, 689 km (428 miles) north of Adelaide, Marree has always been an important service town for this outback area of South Australia. The town is close to Hergott Springs, a natural spring discovered by John McDouall Stuart in 1860, and by which name the town was first known. The area was put on the map by the construction of the Overland Telegraph line in 1871. By the time the railway line arrived in 1882, the town had become an important staging post for the camel trains carrying supplies further north. Only when the railway was shifted west in the 1970s did Marree lose its strategic importance. Today it has a population of only 385, but it continues to service the travellers passing through and the surrounding cattle and sheep stations. A few decaying reminders of the glory days stand close to the old railway siding. The town is bustling annually in June, when the Picnic Race Meeting and Gymkhana are held.
Map ref: page 793 H8

OODNADATTA

A small historic backwater in the desert region of South Australia's far north, 1093 km (679 miles) north of Adelaide, Oodnadatta (population 235) owes its existence to the trains that once ran through here. John McDouall Stuart blazed a route through here on his crossing of the continent in 1861. The Overland Telegraph line arrived in 1870. A few years later a town

A 4WD on the WAA Line track, Simpson Desert Regional Reserve.

was laid out, and from 1891 to 1929 Oodnadatta was the railhead servicing the outposts further north. Tough Afghan camel drivers took their strings of camels loaded with supplies far and wide through the desert country, and when the train line was finally pushed further north to Alice Springs it was named after them—The Ghan. The old Ghan operated through Oodnadatta until 1980, and while the new train line is much further west, it still carries the name of these pioneer camel men. A small section of track and the old railway station, now a museum, are reminders of those days of steam, and

hustle and bustle. The famous, or infamous, Oodnadatta Track links the town with Marree, 410 km (255 miles) to the south, and Marla 220 km (137 miles) to the west. To the north, over rough sandy tracks, is the Witjira National Park, and 200 km (124 miles) to the south-west is the mining town of Coober Pedy. Probably the most famous establishment in town is the Pink Roadhouse, run by Adam and Lynnie Plate and home to the famous Oodnaburger. In May Oodnadatta holds its Picnic Race Meeting.
Map ref: page 792 D4

SIMPSON DESERT REGIONAL RESERVE

Abutting the eastern boundary of the Witjira National Park, the Simpson Desert Regional Reserve is joined by the Conservation Park and (in Queensland) the Simpson Desert National Park, creating a forbidding yet extraordinarily beautiful wilderness area. Endless sand dunes of varying earthy red colours crest in enormous waves and run unimpaired the full length of the park, from south-east to north-west. The landscape is scattered with dry playa lakes and claypans. Hardy plants such as

spinifex and sandhill cane grass cover the sandy slopes and valleys, along with good growths of acacia. In more sheltered areas shrubs such as wattles, grevilleas and emu bush endure. On the rare occasions when it rains, the Simpson's salt lakes fill with water, the clay flats become wet and boggy and a major hazard to cross by vehicle, and the desert blooms. Though you may not see them, the desert is home to a large number of animals, including the hopping mouse, the dunnart and the rabbit-eared bandicoot. The area also supports abundant and varied bird life, even more so after rain. The park is 1200 km (745 miles) from Adelaide.
Map ref: page 792 G3

WITJIRA NATIONAL PARK

The Witjira National Park, forming the western edge of the Simpson Desert, protects a vast desert landscape of sand, stony tablelands, gibber plains, mound springs and transitory river systems, including the Finke River floodplains. The jewel in the crown of this park is Dalhousie Springs, the most active

Showy parrot-pea (Dilwynia sericea) in Witjira National Park.

artesian spring in Australia. The mounds and springs are an important habitat for invertebrates, fish and birds. However, the animal life is not easy to see, most being nocturnal. The Dalhousie ruins lie some 9 km (5.6 miles) south of Dalhousie Springs, near another spring complex that is dominated by date palms. Travel within the park is 4WD only. The Witjira National Park is 120 km (75 miles) north of Oodnadatta and 1200 km (745 miles) from Adelaide.
Map ref: page 792 D1

The Pink Roadhouse is a Mecca for travellers to the town of Oodnadatta.

Adelaide City Centre

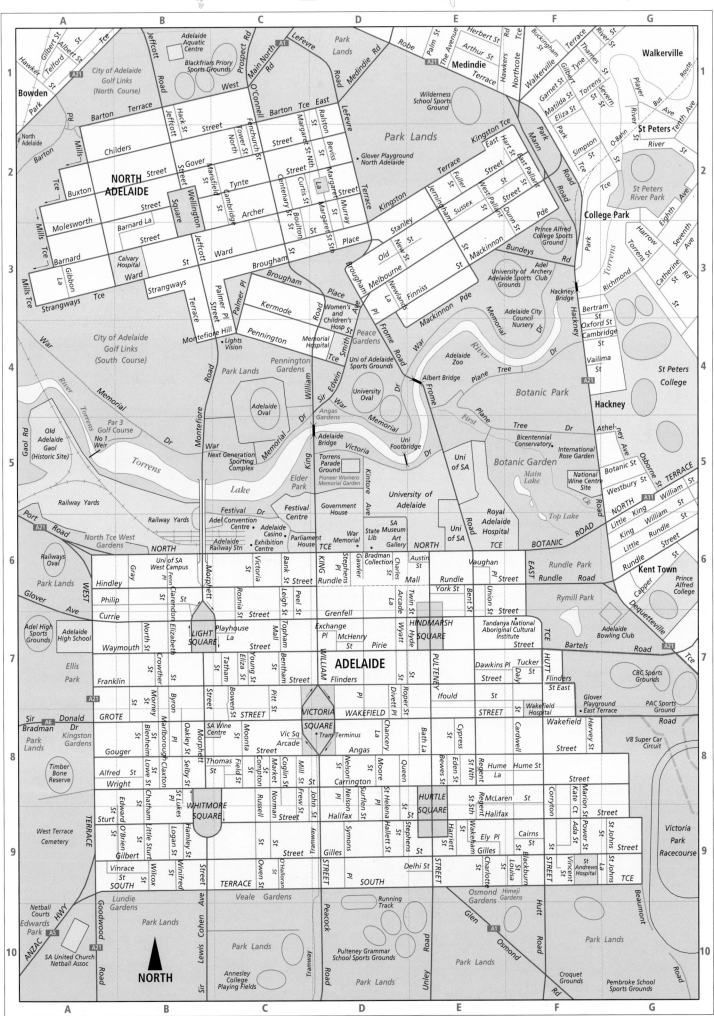

Adelaide Throughroads

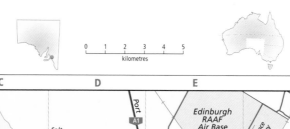

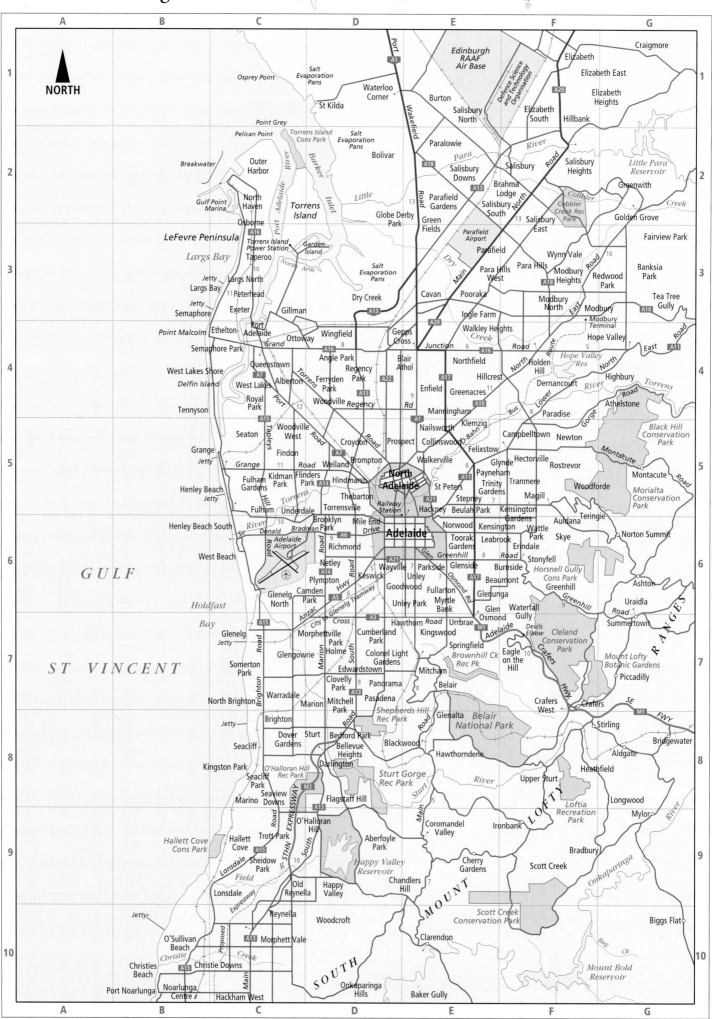

NORTH

Craigmore

Elizabeth

Elizabeth East

Edinburgh RAAF Air Base

Defence Science and Technology Organisation

Elizabeth Heights

Waterloo Corner

Burton

Salisbury North

Elizabeth South

Hillbank

Osprey Point

Salt Evaporation Pans

St Kilda

Para

River

Salisbury Heights

Point Grey

Pelican Point

Torrens Island Cons Park

Salt Evaporation Pans

Bolivar

Paralowie

Salisbury Downs

Salisbury

Brahma Lodge

Salisbury South

Greenwith

Little Para Reservoir

Cobbler Creek

Cobbler Creek Rec Park

Golden Grove

Breakwater

Outer Harbor

Salisbury East

Parafield Gardens

Green Fields

Parafield Airport

Fairview Park

Gulf Point Marina

North Haven

Torrens Island

Little

Dry

Parafield

Wynn Vale

Banksia Park

Osborne

LeFevre Peninsula

Torrens Island Power Station

Taperoo

Garden Island

Salt Evaporation Pans

Para Hills West

Para Hills

Modbury Heights

Redwood Park

Largs Bay

North Arm

Dry Creek

Cavan

Pooraka

Modbury North

Modbury

Tea Tree Gully

Jetty Largs Bay

Largs North

Peterhead

Ingle Farm

Modbury Terminal

Jetty Semaphore

Exeter

Gillman

Walkley Heights

Hope Valley

Point Malcolm

Ethelton

Port Adelaide

Ottoway

Wingfield

Gepps Cross

Junction

Greenacres Creek

Holden Hill

Hope Valley Res

Highbury

Athelstone

Semaphore Park

Queenstown

Angle Park

Blair Athol

Northfield

North

Dernancourt

Black Hill Conservation Park

West Lakes Shore

Ferryden Park

Regency Park

Enfield

Hillcrest

Paradise

Delfin Island

Albert Park

West Lakes

Woodville

Regency Rd

Manningham

Greenacres

Bus

Lower

Gorge

River

Montacute

Tennyson

Royal Park

Nailsworth

Klemzig

Campbelltown

Newton

Seaton

Woodville West

Findon

Croydon

Prospect

Collinswood

Felixstow

Hectorville

Rostrevor

Montacute

Grange

Brompton

North Adelaide

Walkerville

Glynde

Payneham

Trinity Gardens

Tranmere

Magill

Woodforde

Morialta Conservation Park

Henley Beach

Fulham Gardens

Kidman Park

Flinders Park

Hindmarsh

St Peters

Stepney

Paynham

Kensington Gardens

Wattle Park

Skye

Auldana

Teringie

Norton Summit

Henley Beach South

Fulham

Underdale

Thebarton

Torrensville

Railway Station

Hackney

Beulah Park

Norwood

Kensington

Leabrook

Erindale

Stonyfell

Ashton

West Beach

Brooklyn Park

Mile End

Adelaide

Toorak Gardens

Kensington

Beaumont

Horsnell Gully Cons Park

Uraidla

Netley

Richmond

Wayville

Parkside

Glenside

Burnside

Greenhill

Adelaide Airport

Plympton

Keswick

Unley

Goodwood

Fullarton

Glenunga

Glen Osmond

Waterfall Gully

Mount Lofty Botanic Gardens

Summertown

Glenelg North

Camden Park

Unley Park

Myrtle Bank

Urrbrae

Kingswood

Devils Elbow

Cleland Conservation Park

Piccadilly

Holdfast Bay

Glenelg

Morphettville

Park Holme

Cumberland Park

Hawthorn

Springfield

Eagle on the Hill

Crafers West

Crafers

Somerton Park

Glengowrie

Colonel Light Gardens

Mitcham

Brownhill Ck Rec Pk

Stirling

North Brighton

Warradale

Marion

Edwardstown

Clovelly Park

Pasadena

Belair

Shepherds Hill Rec Park

Belair National Park

Bridgewater

Brighton

Mitchell Park

Panorama

Glenalta

Aldgate

Jetty

Dover Gardens

Sturt

Bedford Park

Blackwood

Hawthorndene

Heathfield

Seacliff

Bellevue Heights

Upper Sturt

Kingston Park

Seacliff Park

Darlington

Sturt Gorge Rec Park

Longwood

Marino

Seaview Downs

Flagstaff Hill

Loftia Recreation Park

Hallett Cove Cons Park

O'Halloran Hill Rec Park

O'Halloran Hill

Aberfoyle Park

Coromandel Valley

Ironbank

Mylor

Hallett Cove

Trott Park

Sheidow Park

Happy Valley Reservoir

Cherry Gardens

Bradbury

Scott Creek

Old Reynella

Happy Valley

Chandlers Hill

Reynella

Woodcroft

Clarendon

Scott Creek Conservation Park

Biggs Flat

Jetty

O'Sullivan Beach

Morphett Vale

Christies Beach

Christie Downs

Onkaparinga Hills

Baker Gully

Mount Bold Reservoir

Port Noarlunga

Noarlunga Centre

Hackham West

SOUTH

MOUNT

LOFTY

RANGES

GULF

ST VINCENT

Adelaide and Surrounding Areas

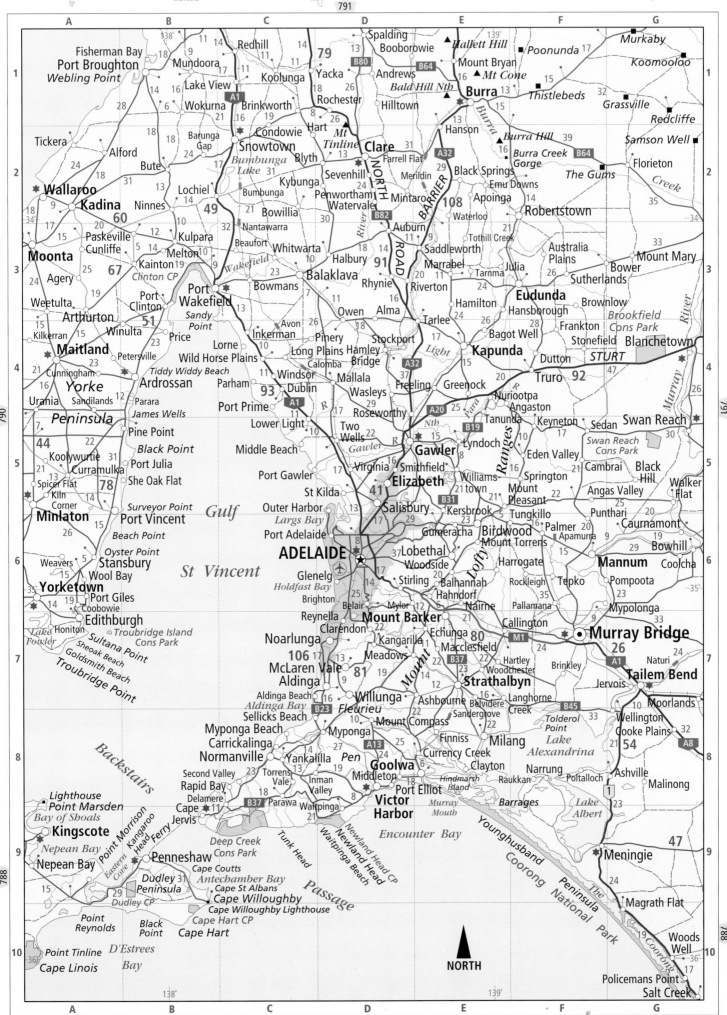

South-East South Australia

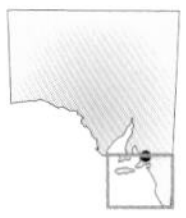

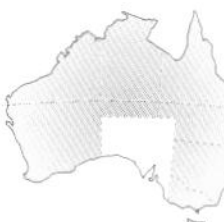

0   20   40   60   80   100

SOUTH AUSTRALIA

VICTORIA

SOUTHERN OCEAN

Big Desert Wilderness Park

Ngarkat Conservation Park

Little Desert NP

Coorong National Park

Canunda National Park

Kangaroo Island

Investigator Strait

Backstairs Passage

Encounter Bay

Lacepede Bay

Flinders Chase National Park

Murray Bridge
Tailem Bend
Mount Barker
Goolwa
Victor Harbor
Strathalbyn
Kingscote
Edithburgh
Bordertown
Keith
Naracoorte
Millicent
Mount Gambier
Port MacDonnell
Robe
Kingston SE
Pinnaroo

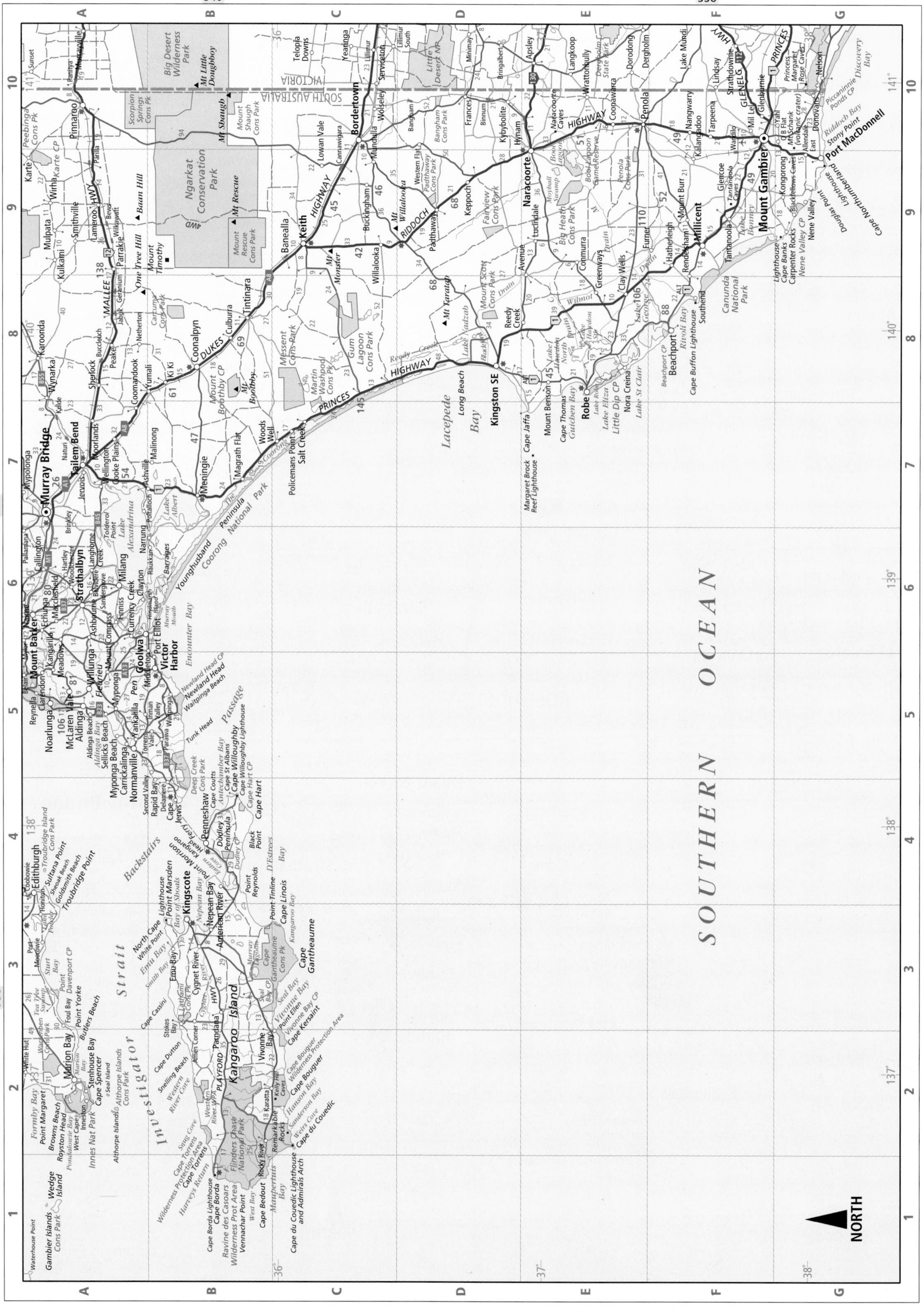

NORTH

SOUTH AUSTRALIA

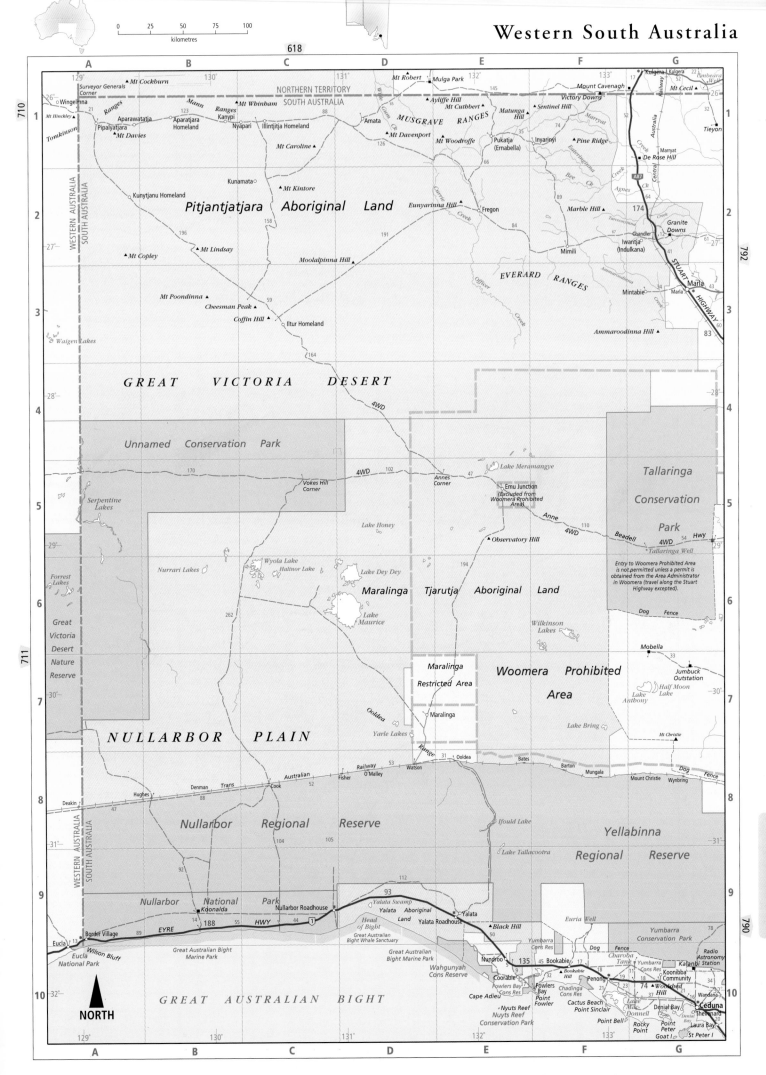

Western South Australia

Central-East South Australia

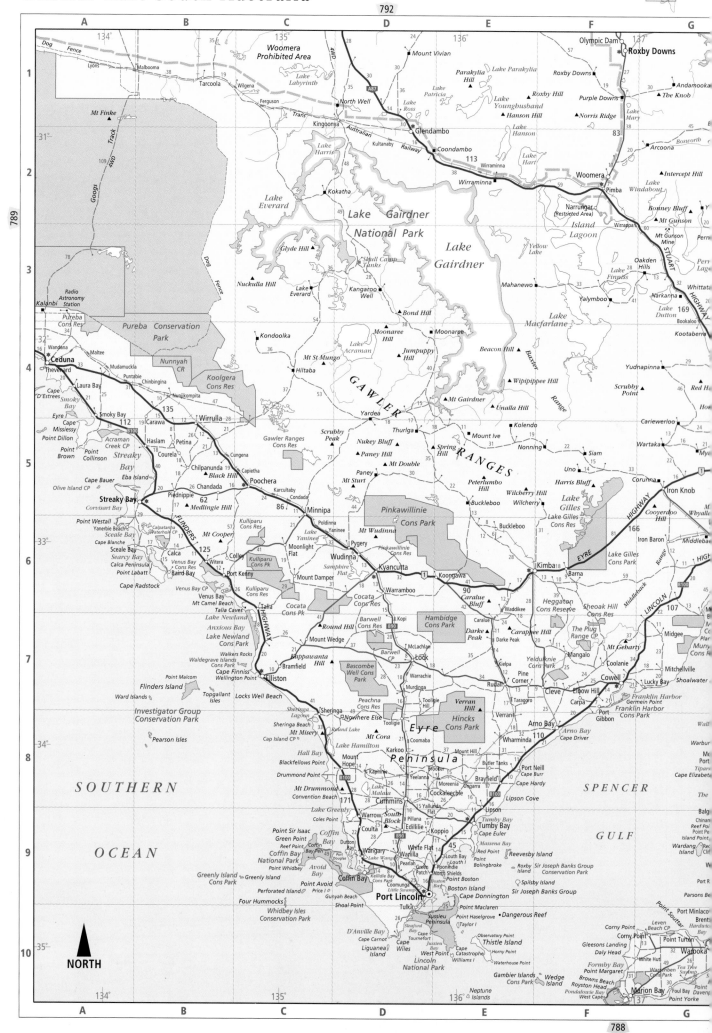

SOUTH AUSTRALIA

NORTH

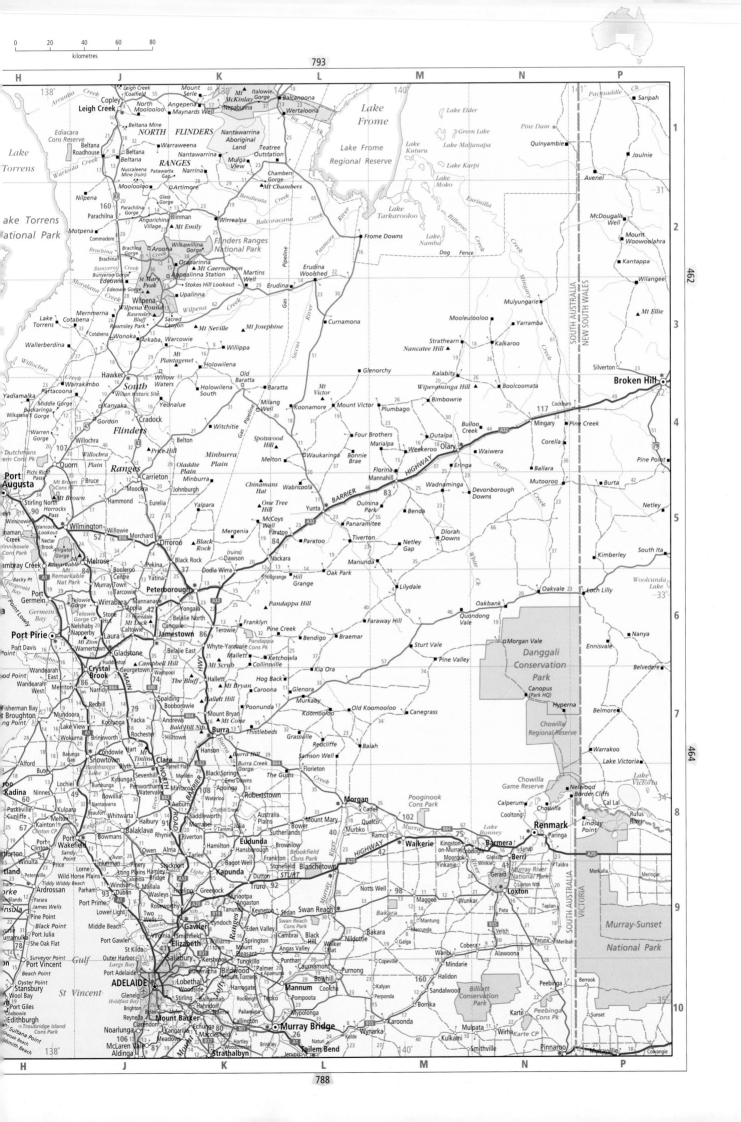

North-East South Australia

NORTH

Finke Aboriginal Land

NORTHERN TERRITORY
SOUTH AUSTRALIA

Witjira
National Park
(Desert Parks Pass required prior to entry)

Umbeara Well
▲ *Mt Cecil*
Duffield
Charlotte Bore
Finke
McDills Well

Tieyon

▲ *Mt Anderson*
Abminga
Mount Dare
Horse Hill ▲
▲ *Mt Apperda*
Bloods Creek
Alka Seltzer Bore
French Line
Macumba Well
Poolo

Eringa
Eyntahyera
Old Ghan Rail Route (Dismantled)
Dalhousie Springs
Purni Bore
Freeth Junction
Rig
Road

▲ *Mt Britton*
Hamilton
Pedirka
Dalhousie

SIMPSON   DESERT

PEDIRKA   DESERT

Mount Sarah
Mt Sarah ▲
Flood detour
Fogartys Claypan

Todmorden
210
Macumba River
Macumba
Simp
Region

Marla
STUART HWY
A87
83
Welbourn Hill ▲
North Branch of Neales
South Branch of Neales
Oodnadatta
Allandale
Freu. Creek
Lake Noolyeana

Wintinna ▲
Mt Willoughby ▲
Arkaringa Creek
River Mt Dutton ▲ Mount Dutton
Neales River
Kooraarina Creek
The Warburton Groove
Lewis Bay

Cadney Park Homestead
Cadney Park
Mt Arckaringa ▲
Arckaringa
Algebuckina Bridge
Algebuckina Waterhole
Browns Creek

Mount Willoughby
Copper Hill
Evelyn Ck
North Peake
Mt Kingston
203 ▲ Mt Denison
Neales River

▲ England Hill
Evelyn Downs
Lora Creek
Mount Barry
Warrina
Peake

Pootnoura
152
Algebullcullia Creek
Mt Barry ▲
Eurelyana Ck
Nilpinna Ck
Edwards Creek
Nilpinna
Umbum Creek

Dog Fence
58
Mount Clarence
STUART
95
Derangunabula Hill ▲
Duff Creek
▲ Mt Margaret
George Creek
Davenport Creek
Sunny Creek
Hambidge Point

Mabel Creek
4WD
Mangun
A87
Coober Pedy
Box Creek
Oodnadatta
Armistice Bore
Elliot Price Cons Park
Bonython Headland

RANGE
Lake Cadibarrawirracanna
Anna Creek
Anna Creek
William Creek
Lake William
Belt Bay

Engenina Creek
Balta Creek
166
Mooloogoorana Swamp
Irrapatana
Lake Callara
Lake Eyre National Park

Pioneers Swamp
Lake Woorong
Lake Phillipson
Warriner Creek
Beresford
Kewson Hill
Lake Eyre South

Wirrida
Lake Wirrida
Brumby Creek
Woomera
Prohibited Area
North Creek
Anna Creek
Margaret River
Coward Springs
Hamilton Hill
Curdimurka
201

Ingomar
McDouall Peak
Millers Creek
Emu Creek
Pound Ck
Lake Phibbs
Stuart Creek

Jumbuck Outstation
Commonwealth Hill
Central Australia Railway
Gina
The Twins
Billa Kalina
Millers Creek
Chamber (or Stuart) Ck
Stuart Creek

257
STUART
Haggard Hill ▲
Mount Eba
Curdlawidny Lagoon
Borefield Road
Mattaweara Lagoon
Stuart Opal D

Mulgathing ▲
Carne Outstation
Carne
Bulgunnia
A87
Mt Sabine ▲
Mount Eba
Dog Fence
Lake Torrens National Park

Partridge Lakes
Mentor Outstation
Bon Bon
Vivian Wells
Parakylia
Red Lake
Olympic Dam Mine
Andamooka
Olympic Dam
Roxby Downs

Dog Fence
134
135
Mount Vivian
136
137

SOUTH AUSTRALIA

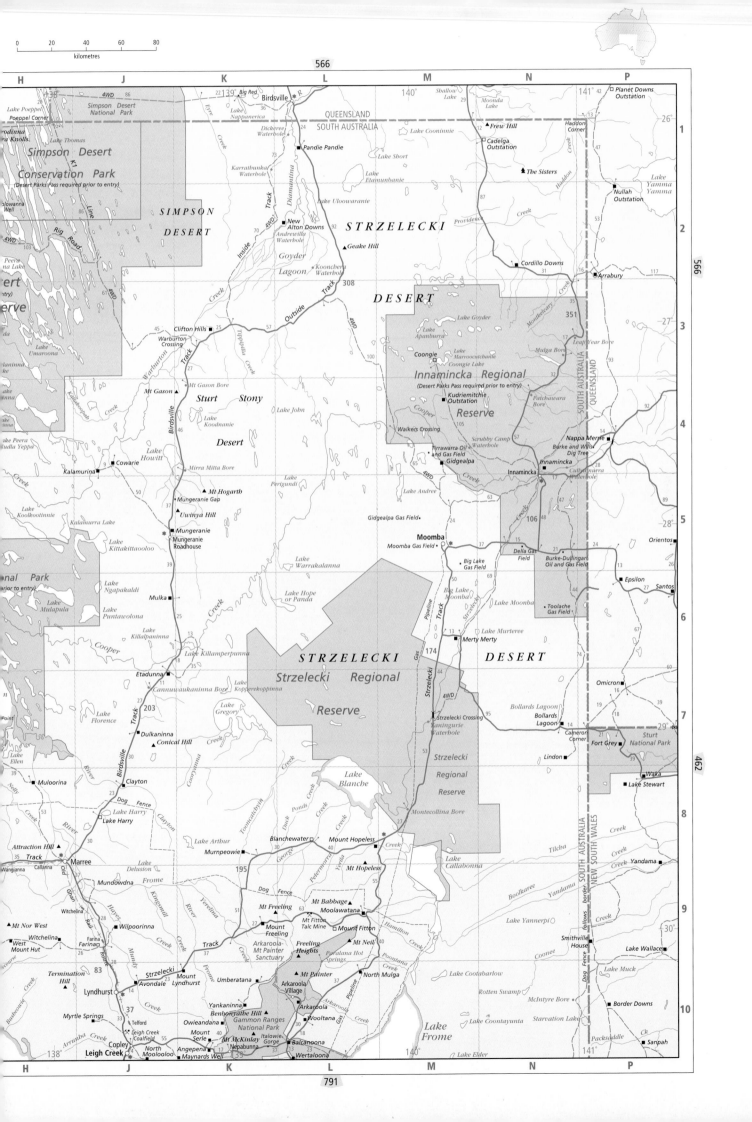

0 20 40 60 80
kilometres

H J K L M N P

566
462

TASMANIA

Rodondo I

Hogan I

Kent Group

Curtis I

Deal I

Outer Sister I

Cape Wickham

Stanley Point

Egg Lagoon

Lavinia Point

Palana

KING
ISLAND

Cowper Point

Cape Frankland

FLINDERS
ISLAND

Babel I

Loorana

Marshall Bay

Fraser Bluff

Prime Seal I

Blue Rocks

Surprise Bay

Grassy

Parrys Bay

Lady Barron

Stokes Point

Badger I

Vansitta

Franklin Sound

Cape Barren Island

BASS STRAIT

Clarke Island

Cape Keraudren

Three Hummock
Island

Banks

Strait

Hunter Island

Walker Island

Cape Portland

Swan Island

Cape Grim

Robbins
Island

North Point

Ringarooma
Bay

West Sandy Point

Cape Naturalis

Perkins
Bay

Stanley

Anderson
Bay

Eddystor

Smithton

Ann Bay

Bridport

Gladstone

Marrawah

Wynyard

Greens Beach

George Town

Arthur

River

Somerset

Burnie

Pipers River

Herrick

Penguin

Devonport

Beaconsfield

Scottsdale

Ulverstone

Lilydale

St Helen

Latrobe

Railton

Rocherlea

St Helens

Lake
Barrington

Sheffield

Launceston

Sandy Cape

Waratah

Liena

Hadspen

Mathinna

Savage River

Mole Creek

Deloraine

Perth

Evandale

River Forth

Liffey

St Marys

Lake
Mackintosh

Lake
Rowallan

Great
Lake

Fingal

Tullah

Rosebery

Lake
Pieman

Mt Ossa
1617 m (5305 ft)

Arthurs
Lake

Campbell Town

Moulting
Lagoon

Zeehan

TASMANIA

Ross

Queenstown

Lake
St Clair

Lake
Sorell

Strahan

Lake
Burbury

Derwent Bridge

Lake King
William

Woods
Lake

Lake
Echo

Swansea

Great
Oyster
Bay

Coles Bay

Cape Sorell

Macquarie
Harbour

Franklin
River

Freycinet
Peninsula

Schouten Isla

Tarraleah

River

Oatlands

Point Hibbs

Gordon
River

Bothwell

Lake
Tiberias

Triabunna

Melton
Mowbray

Derwent
River

Hamilton

Maria Island

Lake
Gordon

Westerway

Buckland

Strathgordon

Richmond

Cape Peron

Maydena

Bridgewater

Sorell

River

New Norfolk

Glenorchy

Midway Point

Low Rocky Point

Lake
Pedder

Huonville

HOBART

Rokeby

Forestier Peninsula

Elliott
Bay

Mt Picton
1327 m (4354 ft)

Kingston

Geeveston

Cygnet

Nubeena

Eaglehawk Neck

Tasman Peninsula

Storm
Bay

Port Arthur

Dover

Cape Queen
Elizabeth

Cape Raoul

Cape Pillar

Port Davey

Bathurst
Harbour

Alonnah

South Bruny
Island

Southport

South West Cape

Prion
Bay

South East Cape

Maatsuyker
Group

De Witt I

Maatsuyker I

NORTH

0   50   100 kilometres

0   50 miles

TASMANIA

Tasmania may be small, but it is a most diverse and interesting state. Separated from the mainland by Bass Strait, the historical and wilderness delights of this magnificent island bring visitors flocking to its shores. Many come by air, but the vehicle and passenger ferries are becoming increasingly popular—with a good road system and many reasonably priced hotels or bed and breakfast establishments, motoring is probably the best way to experience this small island.

Tasmania covers an area of 68,331 sq. km (26,376 sq. miles)—roughly the same size as Ireland. Each region offers quite different natural landscapes and features. The state's northern part is gentle farmlands and rolling pastures between large outcrops such as the Great Western Tiers. This huge mountain range extends across the centre of Tasmania, separating the wilderness of Cradle Mountain–Lake St Clair National Park from the agricultural regions around Launceston to the north. The Tamar Valley, the state's premier wine-growing region, is near Launceston. Along the north and east coasts are many magnificent beaches, some stretching for many kilometres; there are fishing villages with excellent surfing to the north-west. The west coast features wild rivers, which cut through an area of rugged beauty that is rich in mineral wealth and timber; the east is rich in agricultural land.

In the southern part of the state are the magnificent Huon and Derwent valleys and Tasmania's capital city, Hobart. Many of the southern towns, such as Richmond, feature magnificent historic buildings. The Tasman Peninsula in the far south-east is home to Australia's most notorious convict settlement, Port Arthur; Bruny Island is another popular summer holiday destination here.

The climate in Tasmania is pleasant. Spring and autumn are mild to warm, but the nights can become very chilly and it can rain. Summer sees long warm to hot days, with pleasant nights. During winter, much of the mountain country is covered in snow, ideal for skiing. Heading down from the mountain tops, the climate is still chilly and the nights are cold. The west coast boasts 360 days of rain each year, so pack a raincoat if you are heading there. During winter check with authorities on road conditions for the higher peaks.

Originally inhabited by Aboriginals, the island was first sighted by Europeans in 1624. Dutch navigator Abel Tasman arrived off the west coast and named it Van Diemen's Land after the Dutch Governor of Jakarta.

Trout fishing at Cradle Mountain Resort, a calm retreat in the heart of Cradle Mountain–Lake St Clair National Park.

Mount Wellington makes a splendid backdrop to Bellerive Marina on the Derwent River, Hobart.

Capital
Hobart
Area
68,400 sq. km
(26,411 sq. miles)
Proportion of Australia
0.89%
Population of State
471,900
Population Density
6.9 per sq. km
(18 per sq. mile)
Population of Capital
195,000
Time Zone
10 hours ahead of GMT
Climate
Warm-temperate with
no dry season
Highest Point
Mount Ossa 1617 m
(5303 feet)

In 1777 Captain James Cook anchored off Bruny Island, and 27 years later Colonel David Collins established the settlement of Hobart. The white settlement of Tasmania soon led to the near extinction of the Aborigines— the authorities at that time took it upon themselves to rid the state of the Aboriginal people. When Truganini died in Hobart in 1876, for quite a long time it was thought that she was the last of the Tasmanian Aborigines, but there are still descendants of the Tasmanian tribes living today.

Tasmania's beginnings were as a convict colony, and there are remnants of penal settlements found all over the island, with the most notable being Port Arthur. This settlement was set up in 1830, and over the next 47 years an estimated 12,500 convicts passed through its gates. The settlement is extensive, and many of the buildings, including the solitary confinement cells, have been carefully restored. Tours, including the eerie night tours, are highly recommended.

Sarah Island, on Tasmania's wild west coast, is a similar site— the most hardened prisoners were kept in conditions not unlike those of Port Arthur.

Tasmania's vast mineral wealth has led to the establishment and growth of many towns, particularly on the State's west coast. Around Queenstown, gold was mined originally, but after most of the gold had been extracted copper was mined, with the subsequent deforestation causing considerable damage to the surrounding hills. Silver, lead and tin have all been mined at Zeehan, with tin mining continuing today.

With turbulent rivers gorging through the rugged mountain ranges, hydro-electricity is the best source of power for Tasmania— the island produces more energy than it needs. Many power stations are open to the public for inspection.

Much of Tasmania was forested when Europeans first arrived and timber was used for buildings both within Tasmania as well as on the mainland. Among other uses, Tasmanian blue

gum was used to build the wharf areas on the Thames in London, and also to underpin the streets of Melbourne. There are several paper mills in Tasmania: the Australian Newsprint Mill in Boyer, which produces more than 250,000 tonnes (275,500 tons) of paper annually; the Australian Paper Mill in Burnie; and the Tasmanian Pulp and Forest Holdings in Triabunna, which produces woodchip.

Much of the island is World Heritage listed or national park land and it is quite likely that some areas may never have been explored by Europeans. A journey into the parks will reveal stunning lakes (St Clair or Dove Lakes), towering sheer precipices (Ben Lomond National Park), limestone caves (near Mole Creek), and vivid coloured rocks (Freycinet National Park). The most popular area is the Franklin–Gordon Rivers region, which was steeped in controversy during the 1980s when it was proposed that the Franklin River be dammed. Today the wild— and still undammed—waters are World Heritage listed, testimony to a case won by the persistent actions of many environmentalists and campaigning by environmental groups.

A yearling jersey calf from Camlin Jerseys Longford Stud wins pride of place at the Royal Hobart Show, held each October to showcase the State's produce.

ABOVE: Tasmania was the first State to officially recognise its flag (top) and authorise its general use.

LEFT: The farming regions of northern Tasmania form a green blanket of pastures and rolling hills.

The cemetery at Cleveland. Early days as a convict outpost means that Tasmania is steeped in history. This town was a common coach stop in the early days.

There are many outdoor activities on offer in Tasmania, including bushwalking and horse riding. There are easy strolls in gentle, rolling countryside or along coastal heathlands, and more rigorous and lengthy treks through remote areas of the national parks; horse riders can trek along the beaches or across mountain ranges. Other possibilities are rock climbing, downhill and cross-country skiing, canoeing, whitewater rafting, abseiling, hang gliding, mountain biking, jet boat river riding and 4WD touring. You will even find camel riding! Marine reserves provide excellent diving and snorkelling.

Tasmania also has much to offer the gourmet, with excellent wines in the Tamar Valley—Piper's Brook Vineyard produces fine chardonnay, pinot noir and riesling—and at the nearby Heemskerk, Dalmere and Dalrymple. Dairy produce is superb, with many cheeses and creams, including camembert and brie, available, and seafood is abundant.

Tasmania really is an isle of contrasts, with rugged mountain ranges, magnificent scenery, pristine sandy beaches, historic towns and fine food and wine—no wonder it is called the Holiday Isle.

HOBART

A brew operator at Hobart's Cascade Brewery, established in 1824. Cascade's bottle collection tells the history of brewing beer in Tasmania. Hops were first brought to Tasmania in 1822.

Nestled on the Derwent River on the south-east coast of Tasmania is the state's capital, Hobart. The region was first settled by Colonel David Collins in 1804, and the township was soon established. Hobart was named after Robert Hobart, Earl of Buckinghamshire and Secretary for the Colonies. Occupying both banks of the Derwent River, this picturesque city has a relaxed atmosphere, which is why it is so popular with mainland Australians.

The township is focused on its busy docks, where you can watch the local fishing catch coming in and the large icebreaker ships being loaded before they head south to Antarctica. Constitution Dock is an especially popular marina around New Year's Eve, when the yachts arrive from the annual Sydney to Hobart Race, which leaves Sydney Harbour on Boxing Day. This race, Australia's premier yacht race, has been contested since 1949, and is regarded as one of the toughest races in the world.

The docks area and city centre feature many delightful cafés and restaurants, along with boutique stores. There is a shopping precinct at Elizabeth Street Mall, plus many retail stores along Collins, Murray, Liverpool and Argyle Streets.

Hobart has resisted the pressure to modernise—the old buildings add to the city's charm. Tasmania's

Parliament House was built by convicts in the late 1830s, originally as a customs house, and is now fully restored. The Penitentiary, Chapel and Criminal Courts, a National Trust Property and one of Tasmania's oldest convict buildings, sits on Brisbane Street—a tour of this site will reveal eerie underground tunnels which once led to execution yards.

There are historic homes throughout the State; in Hobart there are fine examples of the Colonial, Georgian and Victorian periods, many of which are owned by the National Trust. Runnymede House, a colonial building, was built by a lawyer, Robert Picton, in 1840 in New Town, to the north. Theatre Royal, in Campbell Street, is Australia's oldest theatre, originally opened in 1837—it still boasts a full program of theatre and music. To appreciate the history of Hobart, take the heritage walk—tours depart the Wrest Point Casino at 2 p.m. on Saturdays.

Hobart has many other attractions for visitors. The Anglesea Barracks and Museum on Davey Street is the oldest military barracks in Australia—it is still occupied by the Australian Army. Apart from memorabilia dating back to convict days you can view some of the tombstones from the original burial ground of Hobart Town. Some of Hobart's convict past can be seen in the Cascade Female Factory Site,

Constitution Dock, the end point of the Sydney to Hobart yacht race, is near some of the city's best attractions and offers many tantalising restaurants and cafés.

where women were sent for rehabilitation. The first inmates of this prison arrived in 1828—the complex operated until 1877. It is said that corruption and crime were rife throughout the prison, with frequent prisoner riots. Most of the site on Degraves Street was demolished, but what was left has been restored.

Tasmania is renowned worldwide for its beer, and Cascade Brewery in South Hobart opens the brewery, museum and gardens to the public on weekdays. The brewery was founded by Peter Degraves in 1824, and is the oldest in Australia; it still uses traditional manufacturing methods. Even more popular is chocolate. The Cadbury Chocolate Factory, Australia's largest confectionery factory, is in Claremont; it too opens its nearly 15 ha (37 acres) plant for tours, which show the chocolate manufacturing process and, even better, offer samples. It is essential to book for this tour.

Near the Cadbury Factory is the Alpenrail (this is found on Abbotsfield Road), a piece of Switzerland in Tasmania. This indoor village and model railway display places you in the Alps of Switzerland; you listen to Swiss music while gazing upon rivers, lakes and the magnificent scenery that can only be found in Switzerland. Ten kilometres (6 miles) south of Hobart, at Taroona, is the Tudor Court Model Village, another intricate village model.

The Tasmanian Transport Museum at Glenorchy is a must for tram and train buffs. It boasts a wide collection of steam trains, rail cars, trams and trolley buses. There is even a railway station and signal box. The Hobart-based Classic Rail Tours Tasmania has restored two 1939 rail carriages—these are available for tours and charter bookings. The cars run from the museum in Glenorchy to the town of Ross every third Sunday during the warmer months.

Sandy Bay, a suburb only 2.5 km (1.6 miles) south of Hobart, is home to Wrest Point Casino, Australia's first casino, which was opened in 1973. At that time, Australians used to flock to it to legally play blackjack, roulette and keno although since then,

casinos have now been built in other States. However, Wrest Point is still popular and the complex includes many fine restaurants as well as a large convention centre. Sandy Bay is also home to the John Elliot Classics Museum, situated in the grounds of the University of Tasmania, which contains artefacts from Ancient Mesopotamia, Egypt, Greece and Rome, and the Masterpiece Fine Art and Antique Gallery, which features Australian paintings from the Impressionist, Colonial and Modern periods, plus many Aboriginal paintings.

North of Hobart, on the shores of the Derwent River, is Plasminco Metals–EZ, a zinc mining plant —tours are conducted on weekdays (suitable clothing is required). Further north is Risdon Cove Historical Site, where the first European settlement was begun, during 1803. The site has a visitors' centre, theatre, monument and housing displays.

If your preference is to spend some time outdoors, go to nearby Mount Wellington, which offers superb views of Hobart and the Derwent River. There are numerous walking trails, plus bicycle and even Harley Davidson excursions are possible here.

Dining in Hobart is exquisite, with fresh local seafood, delicious dairy products, crisp vegetables and fruits, and fine wines all being specialties. The Tasmanian Wine Centre can even arrange gourmet tours of the State and has information on wineries; tastings are also held here by arrangement. The Trout Fishing Guides of Tasmania offer tours and advice on trout fishing in the inland waters. The Royal Harbour Regatta is held each February, the Hobart Film Festival is held in September, and the Royal Hobart Show is on in October.

The Wrest Point Casino, which is the dominant feature on the Derwent River foreshore south of Hobart, was Australia's first legal casino. It opened in 1973.

Inside view of Tasmania's House of Representatives. Parliament House was built in Hobart in 1836, mostly by convicts, and the first official meeting was in 1841.

ADVENTURE ACTIVITIES

Tasmania

One of the world's great white-water-rafting trips, the Franklin incorporates numerous grade-four rapids, including the Coruscades, the longest continuous stretch of whitewater on the river.

Despite its often bleak and forbidding weather, Tasmania is a mecca for adventurers. Its mountainous terrain gives rise to an abundance of wild rivers to raft, sheer cliffs to climb, caves to explore and extensive pathways to walk, while its many islands and sheltered bays, especially on the east coast, make for great sea kayaking.

Among the state's most renowned outings are the world-famous whitewater-rafting trips along the Franklin River and the extended hike along the Overland Track in Cradle Mountain–Lake St Clair National Park. Throughout the island, clearly marked and well-formed trails make some of Tasmania's most magnificent wilderness accessible to people with minimal bushwalking skills, and a wide range of guiding and tourist services means that even novice adventurers can travel to remote areas. At the same time, there is plenty of terrain here that will test even the most experienced adventure travellers.

Bushwalking

The Overland Track runs north to south through Cradle Mountain–Lake St Clair National Park, covering a distance of 60 km (37 miles). Much of this classic five-day hike follows boardwalks that have been built to minimise damage to the delicate alpine environment or allow it to recover where damage has already occurred. Boardwalks also line much of another famous Tasmanian walk, the four-day hike to Frenchmans Cap in Franklin–Gordon Wild Rivers National Park, where they have eliminated what used to be a slow and tiring trudge across the deep mud of the Lodden Plains. A dramatic white quartzite peak, Frenchmans Cap rises steeply from the plains and offers one of the best wilderness panoramas in the country from its summit.

Tasmania's wildest region is encompassed by Southwest National Park, most of which is accessible

only on foot—with the word 'accessible' taking on a new meaning when applied to Tasmanian horizontal scrub. An airstrip at Melaleuca allows visitors to fly into the heart of this wilderness. From there, the South Coast Track runs south-east parallel to the coast for 85 km (53 miles), sometimes cutting inland to cross ranges as high as 800 m (2625 feet) above sea level, while the 70-km (43.5-mile) Port Davey Track heads north then east toward Lake Pedder, skirting the rugged Arthur Range.

Other popular walks include the hike to the Walls of Jerusalem in the national park of the same name, and the varied tracks in Mount Field National Park. In contrast to these alpine trails, the two- to three-day circuit in Freycinet National Park, on the east coast, takes in stunning coastal scenery; this area is more likely to be blessed with pleasant weather than the interior.

Rock Climbing

Although most of Tasmania's scalable terrain lies in the middle of remote wilderness, enough of it is accessible to make rock climbing a popular sport on the island. Among the most climber-friendly rocks are the granite slabs and cliffs of Freycinet National Park, which draw mountaineers from the mainland and beyond. Greater challenges are to be found on the basalt cliffs of Mount Wellington, which towers over Hobart. Basalt formations are the commonest kind in Tasmania and generally provide enjoyable but difficult climbing; among the best known are the cliffs surrounding the Ben Lomond plateau near Launceston. Long, serious climbs have also been undertaken on the faces of some of Tasmania's highest mountains, such as Geryon, Frenchmans Cap, the Acropolis and Perpendicular Bluff.

Caving

There are two main caving areas in Tasmania, Mole Creek in the north and Mount Anne in the centre. The two places are very different, with the caves at Mole Creek set among gently rolling hills on the edge of bushland while those at Mount Anne occupy a jagged and exposed ridgetop near the northern perimeter of Southwest National Park.

Mountain Biking

Tasmania is a popular area for cycle touring on sealed roads, and there are great opportunities for off-road riding as well. The forest trails on the slopes of Mount Wellington offer challenging biking, while less steep terrain can be found in the forests to the east of Hobart. The east coast has much to offer, with the best area being from Coles Bay north to Mount Elephant. Varied technical riding can be found on

Bushwalkers wend their way through buttongrass on the Arthur Plains near the end of the gruelling Port Davey Track in Southwest National Park.

the west coast as well: for example, on the old road from Granville Harbour south toward Trial Harbour. Because much of Tasmania is hilly, almost any dirt road provides interesting mountain biking—the more minor and eroded the road, the better.

Canoeing, Kayaking and Rafting

Tasmania is the best state in Australia for adventurous river sports, largely because the mountainous terrain combines with heavy rainfall to guarantee rugged whitewater rivers almost year-round. The journey along the Franklin River is the most famous such trip, not only because of the dramatic conservation battle which prevented the river being dammed for hydro-electricity, but also because, whether it's done in a kayak or on a raft, it offers an unrivalled experience of the Tasmanian wilderness. Although there have been fatalities, professional rafting companies make the expedition a relatively safe undertaking for anyone who is fit and adventurous.

Other worthwhile rivers include the Picton, which is presents few difficulties, the Mersey, and the North and South Esk, with the latter running through Launceston's dramatic Cataract Gorge.

Sea Kayaking

Tasmania has an abundance of great locations for sea kayaking, ranging from Port Arthur and Norfolk Bay to the Freycinet Peninsula and Macquarie Habour. Bruny Island and the D'Entrecasteaux Channel are two other excellent destinations, both located on Hobart's doorstep. Less accessible but worthwhile are Port Davey and Bathurst Harbour on the south-west coast, both reached from Melaleuca Inlet.

Winter Sports

Although it snows in Tasmania every winter, the areas suitable for skiing are relatively few. Ben Lomond is the island's principal downhill ski resort, with eight lifts, while Lake Dobson in Mount Field National Park has more limited alpine skiing facilities. These two locations are the best places on the island for ski touring. Ben Lomond is also a venue for ice-climbing, an exciting form of mountaineering on frozen waterfalls that is as yet in its infancy in Tasmania. Hiking to these vertical ice formations through snow-covered scrub can often be almost as challenging as the climbing itself.

In winter, the majority of visitors to Walls of Jerusalem National Park are cross-country skiiers. Because the park has no facilities, such travellers must be well-equipped and prepared for extreme weather.

NORTHERN TASMANIA

Off the north-east coast of Tasmania lies a group of islands known as the Furneaux Group. The largest, Flinders Island, is well known for the furious seas that often lash its coast. The second largest, Cape Barren, is home to one of the rarest species of geese in the world.

There are more shipwrecks in the vicinity of King Island, off the north-west corner of the state, than anywhere else in Australia. Legend has it that seeds from straw-filled mattresses washed ashore from some of the hapless vessels have created the unique pastures of the island. These grasses give the beef and cheese a flavour that is much sought after by discerning gourmands.

Launceston, the second largest city in Tasmania, is situated at the confluence of the North and South Esk Rivers, at Cataract Gorge, before becoming the Tamar. As is to be expected, the city is lush and green most of the time, showcased in numerous public gardens and parks. Many of Tasmania's towns invite comparision to those of the British Isles and indeed in some cases the earliest European settlers worked hard to create hedgerows, village greens and elegant Georgian homes within the context of the Australian bush. Westbury, about 40 minutes drive west of Launceston, has some charming buildings and a recently planted maze.

Much of the north's wilderness has been preserved by the creation of vast national parks. The most well known of these is Cradle Mountain–Lake St Clair because of the Overland Track, a multiday walk approximately 76 km long. Located right in the heart of the Central Highlands and listed as a World Heritage Area, the landscape includes rugged peaks, deep gorges, rainforests and glacial lakes. The weather is as spectacular as the beauty of the area, so walkers are warned to expect extremes in a single day, from fierce sun to sudden snowstorms.

A much smaller park, Ben Lomond, is Tasmania's main ski resort during winter, offering both cross-country and downhill skiing. Freycinet National Park, a peninsula on the east coast, boasts red granite peaks, forests and glorious white sandy beaches such as Wineglass Bay.

OPPOSITE: It is a gruelling eight-hour climb to the jagged peaks of Cradle Mountain. A pleasant bushwalk around Dove Lake passes through the Ballroom Forest, lush with moss and lichens.

Arcoona Heritage Lodge in Deloraine is one of Tasmania's many grand National Trust buildings.

*Hunted almost to extinction in the early twentieth century, the Cape Barren goose (*Cereopsis novaehollandiae*) now thrives in eastern Tasmania and on the south coast of the mainland.*

The North-East

Tasmania's north-east is largely overlooked by travellers, but it has much to offer those who like to get off the well-worn tourist track. Although it lacks the awesome grandeur and pristine rainforests of the west and south, it has superb and varied scenery, some of the best beaches and fishing in the state, and a wealth of flora and fauna. In addition, it includes two important and contrasting national parks: Ben Lomond, with its prominent and often snow-capped plateau, and Mount William, which encompasses forests, heath and dramatic coastline.

History

The first European to sight the north-east corner of Tasmania was James Cook. He named the Furneaux Islands and Furneaux Strait after mariner Tobias Furneaux, who later visited the islands himself in 1773. In 1798, Matthew Flinders explored the archipelago more fully; in honour of this, his name was later given to the largest island in the group. In the early nineteenth century, the Furneaux Islands were regularly visited by American and British sealers.

Following the founding of Hobart in 1803 and George Town in 1804, European surveyors and explorers spread out across the island. Reports of the north-east's warm climate, plentiful timber and fertile land drew free settlers to the region. As was the case throughout the state, this led to conflict with indigenous peoples, who had inhabited Tasmania for thousands of years. Between 1830 and 1835, the government implemented the brutal and callous policy of resettling Aboriginal peoples on Flinders Island, where, tragically, most succumbed to despair and disease.

Settlement of the north-east was boosted by the discovery of minerals, particularly tin and wolfram, in the 1870s. By the end of the century, there were more than 100 mining settlements in the region, whose populations included significant numbers of Chinese prospectors. Tin and wolfram are still important resources, but the area's economy is now based mainly on farming, timber harvesting, and fishing.

Ben Lomond National Park

Located just 60 km (37 miles) from Launceston, this 16,527-ha (40,838-acre) park is dominated by the massive bulk of the Ben Lomond Plateau. It was named by Lieutenant-Colonel William Paterson, founder of George Town, after the mountain of the same name in western Scotland.

Blanketed with snow for much of the winter, the park incorporates the state's major ski resort, which offers a range of facilities and draws downhill and cross-country skiers from all over Tasmania.

In spring, visitors come to enjoy fine bushwalking and the plateau's impressive scenery, which includes alpine moors, scree slopes and precipitous dolerite cliffs (also popular with climbers). From the ski resort, walkers can either follow an easy 1-km (0.6-mile) walk to Hamilton Crags or undertake the steep climb to Legges Tor. At 1572 m (5157 feet), this is the state's second-highest peak and its summit provides panoramic 360-degree views. Allow two hours each way. As you hike, you will come across a wide range of birds including black currawongs, green rosellas, dusky robins, yellow-throated honeyeaters, Tasmanian thornbills and wedge-tailed eagles.

Reaching the park is an adventure in itself. The road climbs steeply and the final ascent is winding

and narrow. The section known as Jacobs Ladder has six hairpin bends, vertical drops and no safety barriers, and is often closed in winter.

Apart from private ski lodges, the only accommodation is Creek Inn, which opens only in winter and has log-cabin-style units and a licensed restaurant. There are no camp sites, but bush camping is permitted throughout the park.

Mount William National Park

Originally created in 1973 to protect the then-rare forester kangaroo, this 13,812 ha (34,130-acre) park is situated on the north-east tip of Tasmania, 140 km north-east of Launceston. It takes in coastal heathland, dry sclerophyll forest and some of the most beautiful beaches you'll see anywhere.

The forest consists mainly of black peppermint, black and white gums, banksias and casuarinas. Grass trees, or kangaroo tails, are common, and behind the coastal dunes are a number of paperbark salt marshes. In spring, the heathlands blaze with the colours of pink and white heath, white tea-tree, yellow wattles, banksias and guinea flowers.

Forester kangaroos are now abundant, particularly along the 15-km (9-mile) Forester Kangaroo Drive in the park's north. Large numbers of Bennett's wallabies, pademelons, wombats and echidnas also roam the park. Less obvious, since they are nocturnal, but still common, are possums, quolls and Tasmanian devils.

The varied birdlife of over 100 recorded species includes honeyeaters, finches, robins, wrens and pardalotes, Cape Barren geese, and seabirds such as gulls, albatrosses, oystercatchers and white-breasted sea-eagles.

Spectacular Denison Crag looms over Tranquil Tarn in Ben Lomond National Park. Features such as these were sculpted during the last ice age, 15–20,000 years ago.

The north-east coastline is characterised by granite rock formations and boulders coated with striking orange and red lichen.

Some of the most spectacular coastal scenery can be found in the south around Eddystone Point. The Eddystone Light (open Tuesdays and Thursdays), a circular tower built in 1889 from locally quarried granite, is 35 m (115 feet) high and sits 45 m (148 feet) above the ocean on Tasmania's easternmost tip. From the lighthouse, you can enjoy superb panoramas of the Bay of Fires stretching away to the south. Like so much of this coast, the point is fringed with giant granite boulders coated in orange lichen—a colourful contrast to the deep blue-green water. A rough track of about 4 km (2.5 miles) follows the coast northward around Picnic Rocks to Deep Creek, and there is a good boat-launching site in a little natural harbour among the rocks, just north of the lighthouse. At the north end of the park lies the equally scenic Cape Naturaliste, with its magnificent beaches of white sand stretching south through Stumpys Bay to Boulder Point and Cobbler Rocks.

Much of the park is inaccessible to vehicles, with tracks existing only at the northern and southern edges, but the long beaches and an extensive network of fire trails provide varied bushwalking. One of the most popular routes is the easy 30-minute walk from the car park to the top of 216-m (709-foot) Mount William. The summit provides sweeping views,

spanning the wide, sandy beaches and rocky headlands, the forested interior and the mountains of Flinders and Cape Barren Islands in Bass Strait.

In the south, camp sites are dotted among the dunes near Picnic Rocks and on a grassy area beside Deep Creek. In the north, there are several sites near Stumpys Bay and north of Cape Naturaliste. Facilities are limited, however, so campers must be self-sufficient.

The North-East Trek

The north-east is great escape territory for 4WD fanatics, with many options for a round trip from either Launceston or Hobart. Depending on the time available and your particular interests—fishing, surfing, bushwalking or just driving—this trek could vary from 600 to 1000 km (370 to 600 miles).

LAUNCESTON TO EDDYSTONE POINT

From Launceston, head north-east on the Tasman Highway (A3) through undulating farmlands to Scottsdale, and on to Derby, a total distance of 103 km (64 miles). Derby once had a large tin mine, the Briseis, and a population of 3000, but the boom ended when a nearby dam collapsed, destroying the mine and much of the town. There are several other former tin-mining towns in the area, including Ringarooma, Branxholm and Moorina.

A further 15 km (9 miles) or so past Derby, turn left on Gladstone Road (B82) and drive for 26 km (16 miles) to Gladstone. Another tin-mining town, it has food and fuel supplies. From here, take the Brown's Bridge–Eddystone Road (843) for 8 km (5 miles), cross Browns Bridge, then turn left onto Musselroe Road (845) to Poole and Great Musselroe Bay, about 20 km (12.5 miles) away. Along the way you will pass one of the entrances to Mount William National Park.

Poole is a small fishing and holiday hamlet situated on a broad inlet that forms part of Musselroe Bay Coastal Reserve. It offers excellent fishing (especially for bream), lovely coastal views and pleasant campgrounds. Just south of Poole is another entrance to Mount William National Park. You can either enter the park here or, if you need maps, information and camping permits, return to the entrance you passed, which has a ranger station.

In this northern section of the park, you can explore the fabulous coastal scenery at Cape Naturaliste and undertake the short hike to the top of Mount William. When you're ready to move on, retrace your drive along the Musselroe Road (845) for about 12 km (7.5 miles) to the junction with the Gladstone–St Helens Road (843). Turn left here and drive for approximately 17 km (10.5 miles) to the turn-off to Eddystone Point. A rugged 12-km (7.5-mile) drive through open forest takes you to the point itself, with its lighthouse and splendid outlook.

EDDYSTONE POINT TO ST HELENS

Returning to the Gladstone–St Helens Road, turn left (south) for a short distance, then take the next left (843) to Ansons Bay. This little hamlet has holiday shacks spread around the sheltered bay plus a store with food supplies, petrol, gas and diesel (the only fuel on this route between Gladstone and St Helens).

Return to 843, heading south, cross Ansons River and turn left at the next junction. From here, a 5-km (3.1-mile) track runs along the southern shore of Ansons Bay to a delightful spot called Policemans Point. This headland provides the only northern access to the spectacularly beautiful Bay of Fires, a 40-km (25-mile) stretch of coast where white sand beaches stretch between headlands of granite boulders coloured bright orange by lichen. Bush camping is permitted among the dunes at Policemans Point, and you can launch a boat from here onto Ansons Bay, but be aware that the track to the point is extremely rough with some deep, soft sand.

Backtracking once more to route 843, continue south for some 45 km (28 miles) of dusty, but easy, driving through open forest country until you come to the turn-off to Binalong Bay (route 849). Don't worry if it's not signposted; it's the only left-hand turn-off; if you do miss it, you'll end up in St Helens a few minutes later, anyway.

At Binalong Bay there is a popular holiday village and a track (848) that meanders some 13 km (8 miles)

north along the coast to the Gardens, a name coined by an early visitor who first saw the area in spring when it was a mass of wildflowers and flowering shrubs.

The whole Bay of Fires coastline is a wonderful place for a beach-camping holiday, with great swimming and fishing, and over 300 days of sunshine per year. As well as beautiful beaches, there are heathlands dotted with wattle, banksia, tea-tree, casuarina, melaleuca, native pine and a great variety of orchids. Animals are plentiful, too, with large numbers of waterfowl inhabiting the lagoons, which also offer excellent canoeing and swimming. Basic camp sites are dotted along the coast at places such as Cosy Corner, Sloop Lagoon and Grants Lagoon.

A short distance to the east of Binalong Bay is Humbug Point State Recreation Reserve, a jumble of tiny coves and rocky headlands that is popular with the fishing fraternity (and can be crowded at weekends). It has boat ramps, and picnic and camping facilities with toilets and fresh water.

Follow route 850 south for 15 km (9 miles) around the broad expanse of Georges Bay, with its many oyster farms, to St Helens. This is a popular and pretty holiday resort with much to interest the visitor—check out the local Tasmanian Visitor Information Centre for details of its attractions. The sheltered waters of Georges Bay are home to a large fishing fleet and, consequently, seafood, most notably crayfish, features prominently on local restaurant menus.

Head south out of St Helens for about 2 km (1.2 miles), turn left onto St Helens Point Road (851) and follow the shore for approximately 10 km (6 miles) to the headland, which is part of St Helens Point State Recreation Reserve. Here, a great white arc of surf-washed sand borders enormous dunes. Known as the Peron Dunes, these are particularly popular with off-road enthusiasts; however, their steepness and extremely soft sand make them much better suited to dune buggies than 4WDs, unless you're very experienced.

From St Helens, you can return to Launceston either the way you came or by taking highways A3 and A4 and then heading north on the Midland Highway.

Winter on Tasmania's higher peaks always includes heavy snowfalls. Ben Lomond Plateau, west of St Helens, is Tasmania's major ski resort.

Places in
NORTHERN
TASMANIA

The Dalrymple Vineyards, near Bridport, produce a rich yet elegant chardonnay.

ARTHUR–PIEMAN RIVER STATE RESERVE

In the south of this reserve, 206 km (128 miles) south-west of Devonport, lies the serene beauty of the Pieman River; a reserve 800 m (2,625 feet) wide protects the cool, temperate rainforest on the riverbank. Ferns and shrubs grow under the protective canopy of towering beech forests, with lichens and mosses coating tree-trunks, rocks and fallen logs. There are also stands of Huon pine, along with the rare and elegant Cunningham tree fern. With no vehicle access within the reserve, you can discover its many charms by boat, exploring by canoe or joining a wilderness cruise. Other activities to be enjoyed include swimming, fishing, boating and bushwalking.
Map ref: page 840 B6

BICHENO

Bicheno, one of Tasmania's most popular holiday resorts, is 187 km (116 miles) north-east of Hobart, and has a population of 705. It has much to offers the visitor—pristine white beaches, sailing on sparkling ocean waters, and the bustling atmosphere of a seaside town.

The safe waters of the Maclean Bay, today an important port and fishing area, were first used in the early 1800s by European sealers and whalers as a harbour. Today Bicheno is quite a favourite with anglers—they fish off the rocks, in the surf or go deep-sea fishing.

Two lookouts, which can be accessed via walking tracks, offer magnificent views of the harbour. Whaler's Lookout in particular allows visitors to take in much of the coastline vista.

The passageway between nearby Governor's Island and Bicheno is known as the Gulch and this area is generally a mass of colour, with sailboats and fishing vessels all using this waterway for recreation or as a safe refuge. Scuba diving is also a popular sport; a glass-bottomed boat is a dry alternative for those interested in marine life. Under-water life can also be viewed at the Bicheno Sea Centre.

Continuing further north, on the edge of town, is Diamond Island. This is joined to the mainland by Penguin Sandbar, which is accessible only during low tide. Fairy or little penguins that live here can be viewed at night.

Also nearby is the Douglas–Apsley National Park, which is home to a large dry sclerophyll forest. Over half of Tasmania's eucalypt species can be found here, including some of the rarest.
See also Northern Tasmania Wine Regions
Map ref: page 841 P9

BOAT HARBOUR

A popular beach resort on the north coast of the State, 355 km (220 miles) north-west of Hobart, Boat Harbour (population 390) has protected beaches and crystal clear waters, which then lead out into the wild seas of Bass Strait.

These waters are just perfect for fishing, swimming, waterskiing or scuba diving. At low tide, the rock pools provide some insight into the local marine life.

Further west along the coast is the Rocky Cape National Park, Tasmania's smallest national park. It has good walking trails, picnic areas and many Aboriginal sites. A small nearby township, Sisters Beach offers magnificent views of the coastline and accommodation in delightful cottages.
Map ref: page 840 D4

Bicheno's fishing wharf is a popular departure point for anglers as the area offers good deep-sea fishing opportunities.

BRIDPORT

Bridport (population 1165) lies 289 km (179 miles) north-east of Hobart on Tasmania's northern coast, at the mouth of the Forester River, which flows into Anderson Bay. Once a haunt of those wishing to escape from the law, it is now an excellent destination for escaping city life. Lush green forests extend to sandy white swimming beaches.

Among early settlers were the Andersons, the first landowners, after whom the picturesque bay is named. Bowood, a nearby home-stead built in 1839, includes the remains of a cemetery, a school-house and a wildlife park. At certain times of the year, the impressive gardens are open for public viewing.

The Foreshore Walking Trail extends from the Old Pier Beach in the town's north, along the shoreline, continues past Goftons Beach and the mouth of the Great Forester River to the bridge. Another walking track begins near the golf course and heads north to Adams Beach. There are also tours to the Double Sandy Point Coastal Reserve, or to the sand dunes of Waterhouse. The nearby region is a renowned grape-growing area, and wineries such as Pipers Brook give tastings and have cellar door sales. A seaside market is held in town on the first and third Sundays of each month. The Bridport triathlon is staged every January and the Art Exhibition is held in November. *See also* Northern Tasmania Wine Regions

Map ref: page 841 L4

BURNIE

Burnie, 328 km (204 miles) north-west of Hobart on the coast, is the fourth largest city in Tasmania, and has a population of 20,505. It was named after William Burnie, a director of the Van Diemen's Land Company. The original town was established on Emu Bay, where the port is today. It remained a fairly peaceful town up until tin was

discovered in the hills during the 1870s. Then the town began to grow. First a tramway was built, to move tin from Mount Bischoff to the port. Then, in 1900, the Emu Bay Railway was extended to service the mining towns of Zeehan and Rosebery. Today the large deep-water port handles a major portion of the produce exported from Tasmania.

In 1938, the Associated Pulp and Paper Mills opened a factory in South Burnie and it has since become Australia's largest fine-paper manufacturer. There are tours of the mill and of the Lactos Cheese Company, with tastings available at the Cheese Tasting Centre on Old Surrey Road.

The Burnie Regional Art Gallery at the Civic Centre displays Australian contemporary art. Burnie Inn, the oldest building in town, was relocated to Burnie Park, and The Pioneer Village contains replicas of stores such as a black-smith shop, general store and even a boot shop, all from the early 1900s. Outside Burnie is the delightful Emu Valley Rhododendron Garden, a 12 ha (30 acre) property, which flashes the bright colours of thousands of

Inside the General Store at the Pioneer Village at Burnie.

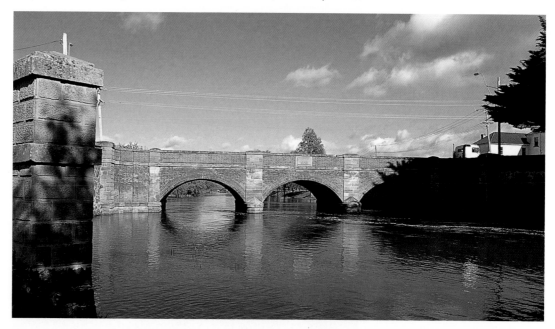

Burnie features a colourful rhododendrom garden.

rhododendrons. Annsleigh Gardens and Tea Rooms is another lovely garden that is open to the public.

The Burnie Athletics Carnival, including the Burnie Gift, is run every year on New Year's Day. The Burnie Festival comes alive each September and the Agricultural Show, the Orchid Show and the Rhododendron Show are all held during October.

Map ref: page 840 E4

CAMPBELL TOWN

The centre of Tasmania's fine wool industry, historic Campbell Town is situated on the Midland Highway between Hobart and Launceston. It is 130 km (81 miles) north of

Hobart. The town was established in the early 1800s as one of the five garrison towns along the main route between Hobart and Launceston, as there was much bushranger activity here—raids by the infamous Matthew Brady and the unfortunate John Quigley, who, in his attempt to hold up a coach on its way to the races, was shot in the leg and captured. The area is now a major primary producing region, one renowned not only for its wool, but also for beef cattle and timber.

Today the town is small, with a population of 820, and far more sedate. It has some buildings of historic interest including the Catholic church, the oldest such building in Australia, and the Campbell Town Inn. The Red Bridge, which takes the main street over the Elizabeth River in the middle of town, was built by convicts in the 1830s.

The Campbell Town markets are held on the fourth Sunday of each month, and the Agricultural Show is on the first Tuesday and Wednesday in June.

Map ref: page 841 L9

Campbell Town's Red Bridge, which crosses the Elizabeth River, was built by convicts.

Olive Lagoon, Central Plateau, is one of many trout-fishing lakes in this World Heritage Area.

CENTRAL PLATEAU CONSERVATION AND PROTECTED AREA

This high, windswept plateau—the Conservation and Protected Area is 89,200 ha (220,412 acres)—is part of the World Heritage Area, and it features a great many lakes, which make the area a world-renowned trout fishing venue. It also abuts the Walls of Jerusalem National Park. Surrounded by mountain peaks, frequently snow-clad, the plateau is often snowbound, and is one of the coldest parts of the State; the little hamlet of Liawenee regularly records Tasmania's lowest temperatures. The area is covered in sparse, alpine scrub, with the occasional stand of eucalypts or pencil pines.

There are few walks and limited facilities in this park. This is strictly trout fishing country, with many shacks scattered along lake shores and a great many anglers are seen waist deep in the freezing waters! Brown trout caught here average 1.5 to 3 kg (3.3 to 6.6 lb), with some catches reaching up to 5 or 6 kg (11 or 13.2 lb). The season runs from August to April and a licence is necessary. If fishing is not your thing an interesting 225 km (140 miles) round trip from Launceston will give a small taste of the Central Plateau, much of which is inaccessible to vehicles. Drive southwards through Longford to Poatina on Route B51, then there is a steep climb—with great views—up the 1000 m (3281 feet) Western Tiers, where you can catch sight of Great

Lake and Arthurs Lake. Then take a right turn onto Lake Highway (this is largely unsealed and is quite often icy or boggy) and go around the bottom of Great Lake passing Shannon Lagoon and Miena. Lake Highway passes through Liawenee, then follows the western shore of Great Lake—views are frequently obscured by thick scrub. Drive on through Breona, follow the descent of the Western Tiers—with some spectacular north coast views—go onto bitumen to Deloraine, then head back to Launceston on the Bass Highway. This drive is

Looking out over Coles Bay towards the adjacent Freycinet National Park.

accessible to regular cars, except when the road is under snow! The round trip from Launceston takes around 3–4 hours.

The Central Plateau is approximately 100 km (62 miles) from Launceston; summer and autumn are the best times to go. Fuel and food are available at Miena; Great Lake Hotel has camping as well as accommodation. Check both road and weather conditions before setting out and take suitable clothing.
Map ref: page 841 J8

COLES BAY

The tiny township of Coles Bay (population 120) is on the east coast of Tasmania, 203 km (126 miles) north-east of Hobart. It is nestled beside the world-famous Freycinet National Park, where spectacular red granite boulders plunge deep into the ocean. Coles Bay is the last stop for supplies before the park.

The park itself was originally proclaimed in 1916 as a flora and fauna reserve. Now it covers over 11,000 ha (27,181 acres) and it

boasts a variety of vegetation, such as wattles, oyster bay pines, banksias and grass trees, with the most predominant feature being its coastal heathlands. The three peaks of the Hazards dominate the skyline from all directions. Bushwalking is the main activity here—there are a number of excellent walks—and the road only ventures about 6 km (3.7 miles) into the park. There are secluded swimming areas, such as Wineglass Bay, with its spectacular sandy beaches, on the east coast of the park. A sea cruise or fishing charter is available from Coles Bay.
Map ref: page 841 P10

CRADLE MOUNTAIN–LAKE ST CLAIR NATIONAL PARK

This park is part of the Tasmanian Wilderness World Heritage Area. It lies in the central west of the State, its landscape features craggy mountain pinnacles, deep forested valleys with gorges and waterfalls, and alpine moorlands. The wildlife most commonly seen in the park are Bennett's wallabies, rufous wallabies and potoroos. Bird life consists of parrots, birds of prey, and numerous smaller bush birds. There is vehicle access only as far as Cradle Valley in the north of the park, and Lake St Clair in the south. Lake St Clair is the deepest lake in Australia. It is ideal for windsurfing and canoeing, and swimming is popular during the warmer months. Fishing for trout in the lakes and rivers is allowed in season, provided you have a licence. The park is a bushwalker's paradise. Cradle Valley, 95 km (59 miles) south of Devonport, is the northernmost point of entry into the World Heritage Area.
Map ref: page 840 F9

DELORAINE

Sitting directly at the base of the towering Cluan and Great Western Tiers, Deloraine (population 2100) and the surrounding district boast fertile soils and a temperate climate, making the area rich in vegetable farming, dairying, lamb, and cattle. Established in 1840, the township is found 231 km (143 miles) north-west of Hobart, and has historical classification. Many impressive old buildings have been restored and some are open to the public. Built in 1853, Deloraine's Bowerbank

Antarctic beech trees displaying autumn colours in the Cradle Mountain area.

Mill Gallery has a selection of paintings, crafts and handmade Tasmanian wood furniture for sale.

Deloraine is surrounded by rather beautiful scenery—Liffey Falls to the south are spectacular. The town is also popular with artists, and its proximity to the Lakes area and Mount St Clair means bushwalkers use it as a base. Showground markets are held on the first Saturday of each month; the Deloraine Agricultural Show takes place in November and the Grand National Steeple Chase is held on Easter Monday.
Map ref: page 841 H7

DEVONPORT

For many Australians, Devonport (population 25,400), 280 km (174 miles) north-west of Hobart, is the first town they visit in Tasmania as it has been the port for ferry crossings from Melbourne since 1959. Today, the *Spirit of Tasmania* car ferry departs from its Melbourne dock three times a week. The port also handles exports of much of the fresh produce from the surrounding agricultural areas. International cruise ships also visit Devonport, and each summer the town comes alive with yachts that have sailed

south from Victoria across the treacherous waters of Bass Strait. Because so many visitors land in Devonport, it is the perfect starting point for a self-drive Tasmanian holiday and many visitors use the town as a base to see the northern part of the island. Popular features in the region, such as Launceston, Boat Harbour, Stanley, Deloraine, Burnie and the Cradle Mountain area can all be quite easily undertaken as day trips.

Perched alongside the Mersey River is the Maritime Museum, which has a library and research centre that contains hundreds of

very detailed models of sailboats, steamboats and ferries.

There are exhibits of Tasmania's earliest inhabitants at Tiagarra, a Tasmanian Aboriginal Cultural Museum established in 1972, where Aboriginal crafts, artefacts and rock engravings, many of which are thousands of years old, are on show. The carvings were initially discovered at Mersey Bluff in 1929 and the site has since been protected. The bluff offers some rather commanding views of the Mersey and Don Rivers, both of which flank the town, as well as of the majestic coastline. Devonport also puts on regular exhibitions of local artwork at the Gallery and Art Centre.

Also especially popular with visitors is the Don River Railway: the old train takes passengers on scenic rides from Don, on the western side of Devonport. On weekdays the train is drawn by a diesel engine; on weekends the passengers take a step back in time as the carriages are hauled along the tracks by a steam engine. The Melbourne–Devonport Yacht Race is held in late December, as is the Cycling and Athletics Carnival. The Devonport Cup takes place in early January while the Food and Wine Fun Fiesta is held in late February. Devonport's Agricultural Show is held in November.
Map ref: page 840 G5

Nichols Cap peeks above the Douglas River in Douglas–Apsley National Park.

DOUGLAS–APSLEY NATIONAL PARK

This park is situated on the east coast, about 150 km (93 miles) south-east of Launceston. It covers a range of landforms and habitats, preserving an area rich in fauna and flora, especially rare eucalypts. Landforms include river gorges, waterfalls, deep pools and rainforest patches; hillsides are covered in dry sclerophyll forest. There is a variety of walks in the park.
Map ref: page 841 N8

EVANDALE

Evandale (population 775) is classified as a historic town and is 182 km (113 miles) north of Hobart. Set in Tasmania's picturesque countryside, with Ben Lomond National Park just to the north-west, it primarily attracts history buffs, who come to see the many original and now restored buildings. Of special interest is Clarendon, a grand Georgian mansion on the South Esk River, 8 km (5 miles) from town at Nile. Originally built in 1836, it has been restored by

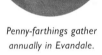

Penny-farthings gather annually in Evandale.

the National Trust. Formal gardens and parklands surround the three-storey mansion. There are also a few art galleries and antique shops, and in nearby Breadalbane there is a traditional glassblower who uses the sand mined from the Savage River on Tasmania's west coast to produce some of the world's finest glassware. Evandale can also claim some significant former residents: John Batman, the founder of the city of Melbourne, lived in the Evandale region for 15 years.

Each year in February, the town hosts the World Penny-farthing Championships. Riders from all around the world gather to exhibit their prowess on this peculiar cycle. Other events in Evandale include the Sunday markets, the Village Fair (held in February), and the Agricultural Show, which takes place in mid-March.
Map ref: page 841 K7

The Farsund, a shipwreck lying just off Flinders Island.

FLINDERS ISLAND

Measuring about 60 km (37 miles) long and 20 km (12 miles) wide, Flinders is the largest of the Furneaux Group of islands off the north-east coast of Tasmania. It is 198 km (123 miles) north of Hobart, and has a population of 1130. First visited by Tobias Furneaux in 1773, this island was later named after the explorer Matthew Flinders. In the early days, sealers established a base on the island. Today fishing and tourism are the main industries. Visitors flock to this isolated island to enjoy its water sports; diving around the many shipwrecks that dot the coastline is very popular. Walking is also a favourite activity, and Mount Strzelecki, which rises 756 m (2480 feet) above sea level, attracts rock climbers. Other interests for visitors include fossicking for Killecranke diamonds (actually white topaz). Flinders island also supports much wildlife, including Cape Barren geese and mutton-birds, which fly many thousands of kilometres each year, then return to their original burrow.

In the early 1800s, as the Aboriginal population decreased at an alarming rate on mainland Tasmania, Aboriginals were relocated onto the island. Today, at the Wybalenna Historic Site, near Emita, and at the Emita Museum, visitors can appreciate the cultural richness of the island's previous inhabitants—Aboriginals, sealers, sailors and fishermen.
Map ref: page 841 J2

FREYCINET NATIONAL PARK

Jutting from the sea along the east coast, remarkable red granite cliffs plunge straight down into the ocean's depths on both sides of the peninsula, broken only where stark white beaches, such as Wineglass Bay, soften the rugged coastline. A variety of vegetation, including grass trees, banksia, wattles, oyster bay pine and bull oak, add to the park's scenic attractions, as do the marshy heathlands all around the shoreline at Wineglass Bay. Vehicle access to the park extends for only 6 km (3.7 miles); after that, the way to explore this park is on foot, and it is well worth the effort. While bushwalking is the main recreational activity, there is some excellent offshore fishing around the peninsula, and water sports such as swimming, waterskiing, sailing, canoeing and scuba diving are popular. The park is 200 km (124 miles) north of Hobart.
Map ref: page 841 P10

GEORGE TOWN

George Town is situated 254 km (158 miles) north of Hobart, near the mouth of the Tamar River. It was first settled in 1811. One of the first major towns in the north of Tasmania, it was not until the early 1950s, when the Comalco Mining Company set up a smelter at the nearby port of Bell Bay, that the town grew. The population of the town today is 5030.

George Town has many historic homes, and these can be viewed by taking the George Town Discovery Trail, a four-part self-guided tour that includes the Grove, one of the finest Georgian mansions in Tasmania. The trail also stops by the Paterson Monument, which marks the exact spot on the banks of the Tamar River where Lieutenant-Colonel Paterson claimed the north of Tasmania for England in 1804 and named the town in honour of King George III.

Outside town are orchards, selling delicious local produce such as apples, and the popular Pipers Brook regional wineries, including Delamere, Rochcombe and Clover Hill, all of which offer wine tastings and cellar door sales.

There is a ferry service that runs from George Town across the river to Beauty Point. Other cruises are available on the river or out to sea, visiting local bird and seal colonies. The SS Furneaux Explorer cruises around the Furneaux Group of islands. There is a fairy penguin colony at Low Head which can be viewed every evening. Low Head is only 5 minutes north of George Town, and also offers magnificent beaches for swimming and surfing.

Clover Hill, a Pipers Brook winery near George Town.

During March, the Bass Strait Challenge, Australia's oldest yacht race, heads from Queenscliff in Victoria to its finish at George Town. Other events in the town include the Tamar Valley Folk Festival in January, and an arts and craft market, which is held on the second Saturday of each month. See also Northern Tasmania Wine Regions
Map ref: page 841 J5

LATROBE

Latrobe, 273 km (170 miles) north-west of Hobart, was a bustling port and major commercial centre in the 1800s, but these days visitors come to this quiet town of 2550 to sample the fine restaurants and view the historic buildings. Bells Parade Park, on the banks of the Mersey River, includes Sherwood Hall, the 1848 home of Thomas and Dolly Johnson, early pioneers of the region, plus a reconstructed wharf and sculptures, reminders of Latrobe's earlier years. The Court House Museum is also worth a visit. There are numerous walking

Wineglass Bay in Freycinet National Park features some of Australia's best bushwalking and coastal scenery.

A swing bridge crosses the churning waters of Cataract Gorge in Launceston.

tracks offering excellent views of the town; the Teddy Shean Walk heads off from the car park on Gilbert Street.

At Christmas the town comes alive as it hosts the Latrobe Wheel Race. Established in 1890, this is one of Australia's biggest cycling carnivals, where both sprinters and cyclists compete for the Latrobe Wheel and the Latrobe Gift. The famous Tasmanian Axemen are also in action here. A market is held in town each Sunday, and the Latrobe Summer Festival takes place sometime around Australia Day.
Map ref: page 840 G5

LAUNCESTON

Tasmania's second-biggest city, with a population of 68,779, Launceston is an important northern regional centre for the surrounding agricultural industry. Situated 201 km (125 miles) north of Hobart, on the edge of the magnificent Tamar Valley, it makes the ideal base for visitors. Launceston is a city of parks and gardens—City Park, which was established in the 1820s is a sanctuary featuring manicured lawns, colourful flowerbeds and towering English deciduous trees, such as oaks and elms. Punchbowl Reserve is 5 km (3 miles) south of the town. This is a 24 ha (59 acre) reserve with extensive lawns, which features the multicoloured blooms of rhododendrons and native trees.

Nestled right down on the edge of the South Esk River, only 2 km (1.2 miles) from Launceston city, are Trevallyn Dam and the State Recreation Reserve. The dam is the storage area for the Trevallyn power station and is open for inspection. The reserve is ideal for horseriding, swimming and bushwalking.

Settled in 1804, Launceston is rich in history. It has a number of museums, including the Community History Museum, situated in a historic warehouse built in 1842, and the Queen Victoria Museum and Art Gallery, which exhibits fine pieces of colonial artwork alongside contemporary Australian artwork. The National Automotive Museum of Tasmania, opposite City Park, contains over 40 classic vintage cars, and a collection of motorcycles that date back as far as 1914. The National Trust of Tasmania has restored many fine historic properties throughout Tasmania; an excellent example is Franklin House, 8 km (5 miles) south of Launceston. This Georgian home built in 1838 has been fully restored and then decorated with furniture from the 1800s. Another fine old building is Macquarie House at Civic Square, a colonial warehouse which was built in 1830 and now houses displays relating to Tasmania's convict past. Penny Royal World sits in an old quarry in the centre of town. Features include a nineteenth-century gunpowder mill, lakes, windmill, waterfalls and a traditional confectionery factory, plus an underground museum that shows how gunpowder was made. Penny Royal World is adjacent to Cataract Gorge and the Paterson Bridge, from where *Lady Stelfox,* a paddle-steamer, offers daily cruises of this picturesque gorge.

The sheep and wool industry has been an economic mainstay for Tasmania. Tours of the Waverley Woollen Mills, which was first established in 1874 and is the oldest in Australia, demonstrate the milling process, from the fleece to the finished product. Tasmanian Woollie Crafts illustrate the process where the hides are tanned. The Tamar Knitting Mill, Tasmania's largest, also offers visitor tours of its working mill.

The Launceston Planetarium is one of only four displays in all of Australia where visitors can view the night-time skies of the Southern Hemisphere. A solar telescope also allows safe viewing of the sun.

Cake at Café Cucina in Launceston.

Launceston's annual Festivale, which features food, wine, arts and entertainment, takes place every year in February; during the same month the Country Club Casino Skyrace is held. Three Peaks Race is on at Easter, followed much later in the year by the Launceston Show in September, and then the Royal Launceston Show is on in October. *See also* Northern Tasmania Wine Regions
Map ref: page 841 K6

Launceston's Penny Royal World is an old gunpowder mill and cannon foundry, just a short walk from Cataract Gorge and the city.

The wild beaches on King Island are not all safe for swimming.

LAVINIA NATURE RESERVE AND WILDLIFE SANCTUARY, KING ISLAND

This stretch of King Island's east coast—the sanctuary is 6800 ha (16,803 acres)—is an important autumn stopover for the very rare orange-bellied parrots as they travel from south-west Tasmania north to Victoria. It is a combination of heathlands, swamps, scrub, beaches and lakes, and home to large numbers of parrots, honey-eaters, sea birds, waterfowl, sea eagles and many other birds, including hundreds of thousands of muttonbirds. The other wildlife on the island includes both Bennett's and rufous wallabies, emus and echidnas.

The sandy soils produce masses of wildflowers. Sea Elephant River, the longest river on King island, is reached via Sea Elephant Road from Naracoopa. It travels through approximately 20 km (12 miles) of heathlands, saltmarshes and impenetrable melaleuca scrub. The tannin-stained river is dotted with swans, but there is not much out here for the visitor. There is no way across the river and the area to the north, along Nine Mile Beach, is wild and virtually inaccessible. The rest of the park is reached from the far northeast.

Lavinia Beach has long, white sands with rolling surf between Lavinia Point and Boulder Point. Named after the *Lavinia*, a ship which was wrecked here, this is a dangerous beach for swimmers or surfers. Inland is Penny's Lagoon, a very pretty, 'suspended' lake, popular with campers, canoeists and swimmers. It is surrounded by most attractive woodlands, which are crisscrossed by innumerable,

Winter vines at Providence Vineyard, a historic winery not far from Lilydale.

very sandy 4WD or 'wallaby' tracks on which it would be easy to get lost. It has a picnic area and toilets. Martha Lavinia Lagoon is also popular with campers and anglers—if they can find it; the poor signposting on King Island leaves a lot to be desired. Access to the Lavinia area is from the top end of North Road, via Haines Road; the beach is approximately 50 km (37 miles) from Currie.
Map ref: page 840 F2

LILYDALE

In the 1800s the small township of Lilydale, 230 km (143 miles) north of Hobart, was renowned for its wine production, but since it was surrounded by forest, the logging industry became the major source of income. Today this pretty town (population 335) is popular with artists, and there are many arts and craft shops which feature paintings, wood-turning, drawings, sculptures and leather work. To the south-east of the town is Mount Arthur—the tracks that originally serviced the nearby Lisle goldfields now allow walkers and climbers to gain some excellent views from the peak. Mount Arthur is particularly popular with bushwalkers, who may use Lilydale as a base.

Lilydale Falls is 3 km (1.9 miles) north of the town, in a nice picnic reserve. There is a very easy walking track to the falls. The W.A.G. Walker Rhododendron Reserve in nearby Lalla has plants that are 60 or more years old and some tower more than 6 m (20 feet) tall. The Bridestowe Estate Lavender Farm at Nabowla, north of Lilydale, is the largest oil-producing lavender farm in the Southern Hemisphere. Open only during January, it is a delight when the heavily scented plants are in full bloom.
See also Southern Tasmania Wine Regions
Map ref: page 841 K5

LONGFORD

Longford is a historic town with a population of 2,605. It is situated where the Macquarie and South Esk Rivers meet, 189 km (117 miles) north of Hobart. The town is noted for its rich agricultural land, which supports the local beef and dairy industry.

Longford's origins were very much influenced by early British settlers who first moved here from Norfolk Island in 1813. Stately homes and rural properties are scattered around the rolling green countryside. Two quite notable properties well worth visiting are Brickendon and Woolmers Estate. Brickendon is one of Tasmania's oldest rural properties, being established in 1824 by a William Archer, and now farmed by his descendants. Located about 5 km (3 miles) out of Longford, the Woolmers Estate offers cottage accommodation and guided house tours. Christ Church, built in 1839, features the graves of many of the early pioneers of this region.

In the town centre there are antique shops, art and craft stores and the Ye Olde Dolls House Shop and Museum, which specialises in dolls and miniatures. Longford Wildlife Park, 12 km (7 miles) to the town's north, is the the first to import deer into Tasmania (in 1834)—these splendid creatures still roam in this pleasant park. The Blessing of the Harvest takes place each March, the Longford Show is held in October, and the Longford Village Green Garden Fair takes place in November.
Map ref: page 841 K7

A Mole Creek apiarist checks the hives.

MOLE CREEK

Mole Creek is 256 km (159 miles) north-west of Hobart, and has a population of 250. It is the centre of Tasmania's apiary industry: the honey that is produced at Mole Creek is considered to be 'liquid gold'—the finest honey found in Australia. The leatherwood forests of the west coast of Tasmania are responsible for giving this honey its very distinctive flavour. Stephens Honey Factory offers visitors honey tastings and sales.

Accommodation in Mole Creek.

Mole Creek is a perfect starting point for a journey through the Great Western Tiers. To the southwest is Mole Creek Karst National Park, and nearby is the Trowunna Wildlife Park, which allows visitors to see Tasmanian animals in their native habitat.

Map ref: page 840 G7

MOLE CREEK KARST NATIONAL PARK

Two of the finest cave systems in Tasmania—Marakoopa and King Solomons—are now combined into one national park, together with over 200 caves and sinkholes, including Scotts, Baldock and Marakoopa Caves.

King Solomons Caves, which are right on the edge of the Emu Plains, are small, dry caves that feature a profusion of light-reflecting calcite crystals that glisten like diamonds. They have some interesting formations, such the vast 'Bridal Chamber' and 'The Temple'. A path leads to the much larger Marakoopa Caves, which have two underground streams and stretch for 6 km (3.7 miles).

Marakoopa is the only cave system in Tasmania with glowworm colonies that is open to the public. Nearby are shelter huts with log fires, which are welcome in winter. The park is situated 85 km (53 miles) west of Launceston.

Map ref: page 840 G7

Cliff House is one of many Tamar Valley wineries offering cellar door sales.

NORTHERN TASMANIAN WINE REGIONS

Tasmania has a sublime landscape, pure air and the long growing season of a cool, temperate climate: the perfect home for the finest culinary produce, with some elegant wine styles to match.

In the colony's early days, hard liquor held sway. Wine production began with optimistic but ill-fated plantings in the mid-nineteenth century; however, this was followed by a century of neglect. The story of a vigneron pinning bunches of grapes to unyielding vines to impress investors is one of several quaint follies.

Although relatively small, Tasmania can be unofficially divided into six subregions with regard to wine production. The four in the northern part are the north-west, the Tamar Valley, Pipers Brook/River and the east coast. The north-west's fertile red soils and 1000 mm (400 inches) of rain make it the most marginal of the subregions. Hawley Vineyard, Hawley Beach and Lake Barrington Estate all produce wines typical of this area.

Some of Tasmania's most spectacularly sited wineries are found in the Tamar Valley; among these are Marion's at Deviot and Strathlynn at Rosevears. With vineyards all over the Pipers Brook and Tamar areas, the Pipers Brook Vineyard accounts for about 40 per cent of Tasmania's wine output. The publicly listed company's Ninth Island label, with a distinct market presence, now has its own cellar door, in addition to those at Pipers Brook Vineyard and Strathlynn Wine Centre. This company's major focus on export has won it a national export award and also a market presence in Europe and North America.

Experience and a willingness to experiment have pared down the grape selections grown in the varied regions of Tasmania. Some more savvy cabernet producers now limit their plantings to the warmer slopes of the Tamar Valley and the east coast. Pinot noir growers have discovered that a combination of microclimate and careful clonal selection for their area, in tandem with immaculate winemaking, is producing good wines with layered bouquets and subtle, yet lingering flavours. Riesling is emerging as a star variety, and is proving its vinous versatility with some

excellent examples from the cool, muggy Pipers Brook area.

A benchmark style of chardonnay is yet to emerge. Tasmanian winemakers, like many of their mainland counterparts, are making very peachy-fruity, buttery styles. At present, chardonnay is finding its perfect expression alongside pinot noir in Tasmania's sparkling wine industry. Freycinet Vineyard, Bicheno, on the east coast, is consistently making one of the best pinot noirs in the country. The vineyard's sun-embracing amphitheatre gives the team ample opportunity to work with ripe fruit—something of a luxury in Tasmania's mostly marginal climate.

PENGUIN

Nestled between Bass Strait and the mountain ranges of northern Tasmania, 309 km (192 miles) north-west of Hobart, this town (population 2880) has magnificent parklands and a beautiful bay lined with pristine sandy beaches.

Originally supplying timber from its lush hinterland, this seaside resort is now more famous for the fairy penguins that inhabit the eastern edge of Penguin Beach.

Along the water's edge, Main Road is perfect for a walk or picnic. For shoppers, the Old School Markets are held in King Edward Street off Main Road every second Sunday featuring regional arts and crafts. Hiscutt Park is home to the town's Bicentennial Project, a large windmill, which was built by the Dutch community of Penguin.

In the area, the road in between Penguin and Ulverstone boasts excellent views of the coastline while the Three Sisters Seabird Sanctuary—on offshore islands—offers refuge to thousands of sea birds. Mount Montgomery has many walking tracks, and for anyone keen on caving, it is a good day trip to the caving district south of Gunns Plains.

Map ref: page 840 F5

PERTH

The township of Perth (population 1575) is 182 km (113 miles) north of Hobart. It was established in 1821 by Governor Lachlan Macquarie when travelling through the South Esk River region towards Hobart. A ferry service was established on the river for transport before the road to Launceston was built. The bridge across the South Esk River that replaced the ferry has an unfortunate history: the first bridge, built in 1836, was destroyed by floods in 1929. The structure was replaced within two years, but was once again washed away in floods 50 years later. The current bridge has, fortunately, remained intact since 1981.

Many old buildings from the nineteenth century remain, these include the Uniting Church, the Old Post Office, Jolly Farmer, Leather Bottell and the Old Crown Inn. The Tasmanian Honey Company, producer of fine Tasmanian honey, is open to the public.
Map ref: page 841 K7

While in Perth, have a taste of Tasmanian honey.

POATINA

Located on the edge of the Great Western Tiers, 203 km (126 miles) north of Hobart, the small township of Poatina (population 120) was built in the 1950s to house workers for the hydro-electric power station 5 km (3 miles) south-west of the town. In 1977 the Great Lake Power Development Scheme was completed, with water diverted north towards Poatina, inaugurating Tasmania's first underground power station. Tours are available of the power station. South-west of the historic towns of Longford and Perth, Poatina is perfect for a day drive and a chance to view part of this State's power system.
Map ref: page 841 J8

PORT SORELL

Port Sorrel is a very popular seaside resort (population 1495) 293 km (182 miles) north-west of Hobart, nestled among its surrounding hills. The town, once known as Burgess, was established in the early 1800s, as a base for sealers, whalers and fishermen. The protected waters of the Port Sorell estuary are particularly good for water sports, and Freers Beach is a favourite with swimmers.

To the east of Port Sorell, across the bay, is Asbestos Range National Park, which has sandy beaches and a wide variety of walks. Being very close to Devonport, the park is quite popular with day trippers and campers, who can take the marked walking trails to explore the heathlands as well as the open plains of the park.
Map ref: page 841 H5

Rocky Cape National Park is near Wynyard on Tasmania's north-eastern coast.

QUEENSTOWN

The bare surrounding hills that crest the mountain range seen on coming into Queenstown (population 3370) testify to this town's mining history. It lies 262 km (163 miles) north-west of Hobart. Gold was discovered in 1881 and the Mount Lyell Gold Mining Company was formed to extract the precious metal. The mining of gold ended in 1891 but then the copper, which had been previously been discarded as rubbish, was mined—this continues today. The mining process has stripped the vegetation and left scarred hillsides.

The remains of the West Lyell Open Cut Mine, once Australia's largest mine, and the Mount Lyell Mine can both be toured. There is An underground tour that shows the working areas of the copper mine, 6 km (3.7 miles) down the main shaft and 340 m (1116 feet) below sea level, is only the second working mine in the world to allow visitors access to the rock face.

Beyond the hills of Queenstown lie Tasmania's magnificent rainforests. 4WD tours here offer spectacular views of the west coast as well as an opportunity to walk some of the Kelly Basin Track, which was once part of the North Lyell Railway Line.

Queenstown is an excellent place from which to gain access to both the Franklin–Gordon Wild Rivers and the Cradle Mountain–Lake St Clair national parks. Whitewater rafting trips on the Franklin River are also on offer. A scenic drive to the King River Power Development south of Queenstown travels through forest with Huon pine, King Billy pine and celery-top pine trees.
Map ref: page 840 D10

ROCKY CAPE NATIONAL PARK

Tasmania's smallest national park contains rocky north coast headlands, small, sheltered beaches, hills covered in heath and woodlands, plus some of this State's richest Aboriginal sites.

Vehicular access is limited to Sisters Beach in the east and Rocky Cape Road in the west. Beautiful Sisters Beach is wide, clean and shaded by she-oaks. At the western end of Sisters Beach, signs lead to cave shelters—Wet Cave and Lee Archer Cave—with interpretive signs detailing some of the history of the Aborigines who lived here up to 10,000 years ago. At the western end of the park the Rocky Cape lighthouse towers above the orange-coated rocks, and sea caves dot the cliffs. Rocky Cape National Park is about 90 km (56 miles) west of Devonport, and is accessed via the Bass Highway.
Map ref: page 840 D4

Untouched forests can be found outside Queenstown in the adjacent World Heritage areas.

ROSEBERY

The mining town of Rosebery lies on the mineral-rich west coast of Tasmania. It has a population of 1640 people and is situated 308 km (191 miles) north-west of Hobart. It was here that gold was first discovered, in 1893. Only one year later, other minerals, including lead, zinc and copper were also found; however, by 1912, the mines had ceased to operate.

Only 2 km (1.2 miles) from Rosebery is the magnificent Montezuma Falls, one of the highest in Tasmania, with a drop of 104 m (341 feet). Lake Pieman and the Pieman River lie on the edge of town, and legend has it that the river took its name from the criminal Alexander 'Pieman' Pearce, who was jailed for selling food that was unfit for humans. He managed to escape from prison and it has been alleged that he ate his fellow escapees in the process.

Rosebery's sporting carnival is held each year in mid-December.
Map ref: page 840 D8

ROSS

The small township of Ross has a population 285 and is 119 km (74 miles) north of Hobart. This town was named by Governor Lachlan Macquarie in 1821 after a town in Scotland, but the town had already been established some

The track to Montezuma Falls, near Rosebery.

St Helens is a quiet fishing town situated on the still waters of Georges Bay.

ten years earlier as a military outpost. While there are a number of historic buildings, the town's most splendid feature is the bridge across the Macquarie River. This rather intricately designed bridge, built by convicts, was completed in 1836. It is one of the oldest such bridges found in Australia.

Ross was the site of one of only two female convict settlements in Tasmania—the 'Female Factory'. It was opened in 1847 and housed female convicts and their offspring until the transportation of convicts to Tasmania had finally ceased, in 1853. It has since been partially restored by the National Parks and Wildlife people.

This region of midland Tasmania is famous for producing fine Merino wool; Ross is home to the Tasmanian Wool Centre, which features woollen garments, arts and

crafts along with a retail store. There are other fine examples of local crafts in the Ross Nursery, Crafts and Antiques Store, and in the Village Toymaker.
Map ref: page 841 L9

ST HELENS

Protected by the tranquil harbour of Georges Bay, St Helens, with a population of 1145, is Tasmania's easternmost town and it is situated 267 km (166 miles) north-east of Hobart. Fishing is one of the main industries in this town, and there are three fish processing plants in the area—with many fishing and charter boats that operate out of St Helens. The town is also a popular place with holiday-makers who come in particular for the beaches, which offer families safe swimming as well as a host of other popular water sports, such as waterskiing, canoeing or sailing.

With quite a number of reserves and parks close by, the area is also ideal for walking, and St Helens Point State Recreation Area is a great place to start. This park features coastal views, impressive sand dunes and also has camp sites. Other walks in the area include

those found in Humbug Point Reserve, and some in the Bay of Fires Coastal Reserve and Goblin Forest Walk. There is also a cycling and walking track that follows the magnificent foreshore right around the bay, starting from the bridge at St Helens.

Only a 20 minute drive north-west of St Helens is Pyengana. This is a small village that has a history of tin mining. From here you can get to the spectacular St Columba Falls, which drop a dramatic 100 m (328 feet) into South George River.

Along the St Columba Falls Road is Healeys Pyengana Cheese Factory, where traditional old-style cheddar cheese is produced and definitely worth sampling.

The Game Fishing Championship is held each year over a long weekend in March and the Surf Angling Champion is determined in late April. During winter, a huge jazz festival takes place over the June long weekend.
Map ref: page 841 P6

ST MARYS

St Marys is situated on the headwaters of the South Esk River, 232 km (144 miles) north-east of Hobart. The town is surrounded by spectacular mountain peaks and it is only a ten-minutes drive from the east coast, making it a good base to explore both the mountains and the sea.

The small township (population 630) once supported a local dairy industry, but most of the farms have gone; the main industries now are cattle, coalmining and timber.

St Patricks Head State Reserve is 7 km (4 miles) east of town. From the top of St Patricks Head, about an hour's climb, there are spectacular views. A trek along the Grey Mare Trail leads to a picnic area and small waterfall; Elephant Pass, south of the town, also offers some splendid coastal views. The drive from Bicheno through St Marys to the seaside town of St Helens has excellent views. Fingal, 20 km (12 miles) west on the Esk Highway, was originally a goldmining town, but now supports farming and a coalmining industry. The Tasmanian Hotel was built in 1860 and is built of stone removed from the local prison barracks.
Map ref: page 841 N7

Eastern black bream from Scamander.

SCAMANDER

Situated right at the mouth of the Scamander River, 247 km (153 miles) north-east of Hobart, Scamander's small resident population of 410 rises to nearer 1000 during the holiday season, when holiday-makers head to this east coast resort for sun, water sports and its magnificent sandy beaches.

Fishing is another popular recreation, both in the river and out at sea, with bream the main catch in the estuary. Wrinklers Beach and Steels Beach, either side of the river mouth, both offer safe swimming in protected waters. Beaumaris, 5 km (3 miles) to the north, has beaches and lagoon areas for water sports. Scamander Forest Reserve is perfect for a picnic, fishing for trout or bushwalking. At Trout Creek Reserve, only ten minutes away, anglers will find a platform built for trout and bream fishing.
Map ref: page 841 P6

SCOTTSDALE

Situated in the regional heart of the north-east of Tasmania, 267 km (166 miles) from Hobart, Scottsdale (population 2020) is the centre of a rich agriculture, dairy and forest industry. The tall pine trees that cover the local hillsides are milled at Tonganah, 7 km (4 miles) south-east of town. Potatoes are harvested here, mainly for the frozen food company Birdseye. The area was first viewed by Europeans in 1855, when the then government surveyor, James Scott, came across this fertile land. It took less than 10 years for the first sawmill to begin production, but over 40 years for the railway to stretch from Launceston, 65 km (40 miles) to the south.

The visitor information centre is in the old Lyric Theatre, which closed in 1972. On show here are old photographs and artefacts from the town's past. Another reminder of the past is the Derby Tin Mine Centre, a reconstructed mining town, which features a tin mine museum with displays, old photographs and artefacts. A bicycle museum is housed at the historic Beulah bed and breakfast.

Sliding Range Lookout, on the highway west of town, offers some superb views of the countryside; North-East Park, on the Tasman Highway to the east, is a pleasant picnic location with interesting walking trails. Cuckoo Falls and the Tonganah hop fields are just outside town, and the Bridestowe Lavender Farm to the west is quite delightful, especially in January when the lavender is in full bloom. The Scottsdale Markets are held each Saturday, and the Scottsdale Show is in early November.
Map ref: page 841 L5

SEAL ROCKS STATE RESERVE, KING ISLAND

King Island's most famous features are its storm-lashed cliffs, which managed to claim over 70 ships in the nineteenth century. Few places are wilder and more forbidding than Seal Rocks in the south-west, where gigantic cliffs overlook the jagged, rocky outcrops that were once home to a great many seals. The seals were almost wiped out in the early 1900s, but numbers have now increased; however, you will see more penguins and mutton-birds here than seals. Adventurous

The Bridestowe Lavender Farm is near Scottsdale.

visitors can explore caves in these steep, dangerous cliffs. On a nearby cliff-top is the Petrified Forest, a lunar-like landscape of 30 million-year-old fossilised tree stumps and branches. Now fenced off for its protection, there is a walkway and a windblown lookout. Seal Rocks is about 32 km (20 miles) south of Currie via South Road.
Map ref: page 840 F3

SHEFFIELD

Sheffield (population 995) is 269 km (167 miles) north-west of Hobart, near the beautiful Lake Barrington on the edge of the Great Western Tiers. The town boasts a most unusual outdoor art gallery, with more than 30 historic murals painted on walls and shop fronts. The project began in 1986 to help boost tourism and Sheffield is now known as the 'Town of Murals'. In the main street you will find art and craft stores, a blacksmith gallery, a pottery, the Kentish School Community Museum as well as the Diversity Theatre, which screens films about the town's murals. In December and January, and for the first weekend each month, the Redwater Creek Steam Railway Society offers the chance to have a steam train ride. A short drive from Sheffield is the Mount Roland Emu Ranch, which is open to the public. Mount Roland is also home to the Paradise Park Deer Farm; you can tour the farm, or fish for trout. There are markets held every third Saturday in March, June, September and December, and the Model Railways and

Fresh salmon: fishing is the mainstay of Smithton.

Collectables Show is held on Australia Day. Daffodil Week is in full bloom in mid-September, and the Triple Top Running Race is held annually in October.
See also Northern Tasmania Wine Regions
Map ref: page 840 G6

SMITHTON

Smithton (population 3495) sits at the mouth of the Duck River in the far north-west of Tasmania, 415 km (258 miles) from Hobart. Not very far from Stanley and the Arthur–Pieman Protected Areas, it is the administrative centre of this region of Tasmania. Forestry and farming provide the basis of employment; there is a strong fishing industry and dolomite is mined nearby. The mouth of the Duck River is popular for fishing and boating. Much of the area, however, is reclaimed swampland, but fossilised bones, including those of a giant wombat and kangaroo, were found by locals in these swamps. These bones are now on display at the Hobart and Launceston museums. The Smithton–Circular Head Heritage Centre features local history of the area, including the history of the Aborigines who lived in the region; Gunn's Timber Mill, the largest mill of its type in the Southern Hemisphere, is open for guided tours.

To the west is the small coastal town of Marrawah, which offers excellent surfing; the surrounding west coast region forms part of the Arthur–Pieman Protected Area, a popular area with bushwalkers and campers. One of the more exciting ways to experience this region's remote wilderness is on a 4-wheeler quad bike, as these are specifically designed to tackle the beaches and rugged timbered terrain.

Smithton holds a food festival in February every even-numbered year, in conjunction with the Tasmanian circumnavigational yacht race. The Tasmania Day Regatta, held in November, is another very popular local event.
Map ref: page 840 C3

Boats at Strahan, a quiet town near the edge of the remote Franklin–Gordon Wild Rivers World Heritage area.

Macquarie Harbour is a magnificent bay, best appreciated from the air. Apart from seaplane flights, this remote region is accessible only to walkers or rafters. Within the harbour lies Sarah Island, an old convict settlement whose history makes Port Arthur seem like a resort. Established in 1822, it was renowned for the harsh treatment inflicted on prisoners and the appalling conditions in which they lived. The island is accessible by boat only—tours are available.

Most visitors to Strahan take the opportunity to cruise the still waters of the Gordon River into the remote wilderness of the Franklin–Gordon Wild Rivers National Park, passing through lush verdant forests and magnificent Huon pines. This region is part of the Tasmanian Wilderness World Heritage Area, with rainforests that are thousands of years old. There are also 4WD tour that take in Ocean Beach, Tasmania's longest, along with the Henty sand dunes, which are close to Strahan. Horse rides through the heavily timbered forests or along the sandy beaches at sunset are also a great way to explore the region.

In town you can wander along the wharf, investigate the local arts and craft stores, gaze at the gem and mineral displays or just enjoy the fine dining at Strahan's many restaurants. The Strahan–Lyell Picnic Day is held in January on Australia Day, and the Tin Miner's Marathon is in February.

Map ref: page 840 C10

STANLEY

Stanley is a historic town and fishing port in the far north-west of Tasmania, 408 km (253 miles) from Hobart or an easy 130 km (81 miles) west of Devonport via the Bass Highway.

This town has one particularly prominent feature, for which it is very well known: Circular Head. It was named by Bass and Flinders, who sailed this region in 1798. This entire landmass forms The Nut State Reserve. 'The Nut', as it is affectionately known among locals, is a gigantic 152 m (499 feet) mound of solidified lava that set hard, with sheer cliffs on three sides dropping into the water. Looming above the town of Stanley, this windy plateau is believed to be many millions of years old.

The town and the plateau are connected to the mainland by a 7 km (4 mile) isthmus and are thus almost surrounded by water. Large muttonbird colonies inhabit this reserve and there is a short nature walk that circumnavigates the summit. A walking track to the top starts opposite the post office, or you can take the chair-lift, which operates from behind The Nut Shop Tea Rooms. From the top there are some really spectacular views up and down the north coast, inland across the township of Stanley and right out over the seas of Bass Strait.

Originally a port for sailors and whalers who fished the treacherous wild seas of Bass Strait, today the town of Stanley has a population 580 and is an important base for many cray and shark fishermen.

Stanley's waterfront features numerous old bluestone buildings, including the quaint old grain store and the customs bond store. There are several other historic buildings in town including Lyons Cottage, which was at one time the home of one of Australia's Prime Ministers, Joseph Lyons.

Stanley holds a number of festivals every year. These include the Circular Head Spring Flower Festival, which offers a colourful display of local blooms. It is on each year in early October. During the following month, the port comes alive on Melbourne Cup Weekend in November, when the Melbourne to Stanley Yacht Race takes place.

Map: page 840 C3

STRAHAN

Situated beside the protected waters of Macquarie Harbour, Strahan (population 600) is in the south-west, 302 km (188 miles) from Hobart. Visitors can experience some of the best natural wilderness on offer in Tasmania.

Surrounded by lush forests, this town was once home to a booming timber industry, plus mining and fishing industries. These declined, and then, during the 1980s, came the controversy over the proposed damming of the Franklin River.

Franklin Manor, a restored heritage building in Strahan, offers elegant lodgings on Macquarie Harbour.

STRZELECKI NATIONAL PARK, FLINDERS ISLAND

Strzelecki National Park, on the south-western tip of Flinders Island, is made up of very rugged country: towering granite peaks rise almost sheer from the sea. The highest peak, Mount Strzelecki, is only 756 m (2480 feet), but the range dominates the south of the island. A rough 4WD track runs along the south coast to Big River. Along this narrow coastal plain are pretty little coves, tannin-stained rivers and salmon-coloured rocks. Bennett's wallabies, wombats, pademelons, echidnas and brush-tailed possums are very common throughout the island, and care should be taken on all roads. Some 150 bird species have been recorded here. In the park's west is the stunningly beautiful Trousers Point, with headlands of jumbled granite boulders thickly encrusted with orange lichen.

There is just one steep walking track to the peaks, but this offers sweeping views from the summit of Mount Strzelecki. Flinders Island is an hour's flight from Melbourne.
Map ref: page 841 J3

Rugged mountain peaks in Strzelecki National Park seen from Mount Strzelecki.

ULVERSTONE

The seaside resorts of Ulverstone and nearby Turners Beach are only a little over an hour's drive from the city of Devonport. Ulverstone, which has a population of 9925, is at the mouth of the Leven River. The town is about 300 km (186 miles) north-west of Hobart.

As with much of Tasmania, the timber industry was the first to thrive in Ulverstone, when paling splitters worked the region's forests for timber to build houses in Tasmania as well as on the mainland. It was actually here that Australia's first axeman competition was held in the 1870s.

Those with a taste for the historical will enjoy Ulverston as in the township there are a number of antique stores that have a large selection of fine furniture and heirlooms. The Local History Museum features many artefacts and photographs that will help preserve the history of the region for future generations.

With its excellent beaches and spectacular parks lining the river and foreshore, Ulverstone is an ideal place for water sports, fishing, or just relaxing. In between Ulverstone and Devonport is Turners Beach, with 2 km (1.2 miles) of pristine sandy beaches which attract beach lovers and anglers. The Twilight Rodeo is a highlight in February and the Agricultural Show is on in October.
Map ref: page 840 F5

WALLS OF JERUSALEM NATIONAL PARK

A subalpine wilderness, the Walls of Jerusalem National Park is a stunningly beautiful but rather fragile place. It is sited 110 km (68 miles) west of Launceston, wedged between Cradle Mountain–Lake St Clair National Park and the windswept Central Plateau. It is part of the World Heritage Area.

This park is strictly for the very fit. Bushwalking, plus some rock climbing and cross-country skiing in winter, are the main activities here; there is no vehicular access. From the car park at Fish River Road a rough walking track heads off into the park. From here, also, it is a strenuous three-hour walk that entails a very steep climb to Trappers Hut and on to Solomons Jewels, a chain of little lakes.
Map ref: page 840 G8

The rugged wilderness in the Walls of Jerusalem National Park demands high-level bush skills.

WESTBURY

Westbury, 216 km (134 miles) north-west of Hobart, was originally a farming village, established in 1828. Today it is a historic town with a population of 1295, full of Georgian and Victorian homes, brilliant green pastures and hedges. There are many historic buildings including the White House, a National Trust property situated on the village green. Originally built in the 1840s, it has been completely restored and furnished with eighteenth-century oak furniture. Culzean is another historic home—it was built in 1841 and is surrounded by a truly magnificent English-style garden.

Mazes often go hand in hand with historic colonial towns and Westbury's young maze, which was planted only in 1984, is sure to provide plenty of family fun.

Gem collectors will be excited by the Westbury Minerals and Gemstones store, which features more than 30,000 specimens of a variety of minerals and gemstones. Visitors can also purchase many Tasmanian stones either polished or roughly cut.

The St Patrick's Day Festival in March is great fun, while over Easter and during November, Pearn's Steam World activates its extensive exhibit of steam engines. The Westbury Markets are held at St Andrew's Church on the third Saturday of each month.
Map ref: page 841 J7

WYBALENNA HISTORIC SITE, FLINDERS ISLAND

Flinders Island is situated in Bass Strait right above the north-eastern corner of Tasmania. The tranquil setting at Wybalenna Point on Flinders Island, with Cape Barren geese feeding on lush green lawns, belies its rather sorry history.

In the years from 1831 to 1847, George Augustus Robinson rounded up the remnants of the Tasmanian Aborigines, some 160 people, and transported them to Flinders Island. He set up a 'sanctuary' at Wybalenna but it was a disastrous experiment. Over 100 people died and those left remaining were finally taken to Oyster Bay near Hobart.

Once Wybalenna was a small village but most of the buildings have now disappeared. However, this place is regarded as one of the most important historical sites in Australia because of its association with the last of the Tasmanian Aboriginal tribes.

The little chapel—used as a shearing shed for many years—was purchased in 1973 and restored by the National Trust Furneaux Group. The little cemetery has only a few headstones left, with memorials to both Aboriginal and white people. The chapel, located between Pea Jacket Hill and Wireless Hill, overlooks this historic site. Being the only building associated with the original Tasmanians, it is rated the third most important historic building in the State of Tasmania.

Superb coastal views from the settlement extend to the beach and the remains of the old Port Davies wharf. Beautiful little bays of opaline water and pure white sand are bounded by headlands of granite boulders. In the nearby hamlet of Emita is a museum full of old archives of sealers, whalers and Straitsmen (descendants of white men and Aboriginal women). Wybalenna Historic Site is situated 20 km (12 miles) north of Whitemark.
Map ref: page 841 J2

A tulip festival with a carnival-like atmostphere is held in Wynyard each March.

The Henty Sand Dunes near Zeehan measure 30 m (98 feet) high and stretch along the coast for 24 km (15 miles).

WYNYARD

Not far from Burnie, on the State's north coast, 345 km (214 miles) from Hobart, is Wynyard, nestled between the Inglis River and the Table Cape. This is a rich agricultural area, with forest reserves, rhododendron gardens and colourful crops of poppies or tulips.

Wynyard (population 4680) is an excellent base for a visit to King Island. Once on the island you can sample the beef and cheeses for which it is particularly famous.

To Wynyard's west is the Rocky Cape National Park and its magnificent Sisters Beach. You can choose between leisurely 15-minute strolls or more energetic walks on the park's well-signposted tracks. One of the smallest parks in Tasmania, Rocky Cape features coastal heathlands, beaches and also has Aboriginal sites.

Perhaps one of Wynyard's biggest events is the annual Tulip Festival, held in early October. The festival is very much a community event—apart from the magnificent tulip displays, there are sailing races, music, fireworks and a running event along with the crowning of the Festival Queen. A must during this festival time is a visit to the Van Diemen's Quality Bulb Farm, where rows of brightly coloured tulips, irises and daffodils cover more than 3 ha (7 acres). The Wynyard Agricultural Show takes place in March.
Map ref: page 840 E4

ZEEHAN

Zeehan, 295 km (183 miles) from Hobart in the State's north-west, is rich in its history and in minerals, and the discovery of both silver and lead in 1882 saw it become the third-largest settlement in the early 1900s. In this peak period there were 26 hotels in town, but after the boom in around 1914, most of the residents left and there are now only two hotels. Today Zeehan has a population 1135 and is a tourist town, although the opening of the Renison Bell tin mine outside town has boosted the town's economy.

Many historic buildings line the main street, including the Gaiety Theatre, Grand Hotel, the local bank, St Luke's Church and the post office. Much of the history of the region and one of the best mining displays can be found at the West Coast Pioneers Memorial Museum. Spray Tunnel Road leads to an old mine site. Also worth a visit are the pioneers' cemetery, and Zeehan smelters, built in 1898.

Granville Harbour, to the north, originally began as a soldier settlement at the end of World War I. It is an excellent spot for fishing. Today there are few permanent residents but many holiday shacks line the coast from Granville to Trial Harbour.

From Zeehan you can visit the Henty Sand Dunes to the south, which are ideal for 4WD, or follow the old railway line, now a road from Zeehan to Strahan. Cruises leave from the old goldmining town of Corinna to the north and take in the spectacular wilderness of the Pieman River State Forest. The Reece Dam and Lake Pieman are also in the region. In February each year Zeehan plays host to the Tin Miners' Marathon.
Map ref: page 840 C9

Southern Tasmania

The south-east corner of Tasmania is a peaceful haven protected by Bruny Island, which was once used as a base for whalers and sealers. One of the first Europeans to chart this area was Frenchman Bruni D'Entrecasteaux, who gave the intervening channel his name.

D'Entrecasteaux also named the Huon River, which originally wound its way through country heavily timbered with the now rare Huon pine. Tasmania was regarded as the 'apple isle' because of the superiority of its fruit but fish farming or aquaculture has since emerged as one of its major industries. The Atlantic salmon bred at Port Esperance on open-water farms are now earning the state a reputation as the 'salmon isle'.

Mount Wellington forms an impressive backdrop to Tasmania's capital city, Hobart, located on the estuary of the Derwent River. Victoria Dock, with its beautifully restored Georgian warehouses is part of Hobart's waterfront that comes to life in late December–early January with the finish of the annual Sydney to Hobart Yacht Race. Kingston, almost a suburb of Hobart, was a popular holiday destination in the early twentieth century because its beach was particularly safe for swimming, although very cold. Today it is the headquarters of Australia's Antarctic Division Research Facility.

Lake Pedder and Lake Gordon are two vast lakes used to create hydro-electricity within some of the most spectacularly wild national parks in Australia. The Franklin–Gordon Wild Rivers National Park contains high, dissected ranges; large, fast-flowing rivers that carved their way through gorges and ravines; and rainforests and dense, closed scrub. Much of it is impenetrable on foot and only experienced rafters should attempt the Franklin. Southwest National Park has many challenging, multiday walks through difficult terrain such as the Western Arthur Range or the isolated South Coast Track.

Port Arthur was opened as a penal settlement in 1830 and as a place for secondary offenders (convicts who had committed further crimes in the colony). It soon became infamous for the harshness of treatment received by the inmates, until its closure in 1877. Some of the buildings have been restored and the site is one of Tasmania's best-known tourist destinations.

OPPOSITE: Lower Marion Falls is in Mount Field National Park where stunning giant tree fern forests may be found.

Ruins of convict buildings at Port Arthur, where the most incorrigible or dangerous convicts were sent.

REGIONAL FEATURE

The Wild South-West

One of the most pristine parts of Australia, south-west Tasmania is a rugged, windswept, rain-lashed land of incomparable beauty, penetrated by few roads and still sparsely populated. In its interior, fast-flowing rivers slice through some of the continent's largest and oldest stands of temperate rainforest, and glacier-scoured peaks rise above sparkling lakes; along the coast, exquisite, tranquil harbours cut deep inland, providing shelter from the winds that regularly buffet exposed cliffs and capes.

Much of the region is encompassed by two immense national parks: Franklin–Gordon Wild Rivers National Park and Southwest National Park. Together with Cradle Mountain–Lake St Clair National Park and Mole Creek Karst National Park to the north, and Hartz Mountains National Park to the south-east, these parks form a continuous corridor of green, which in 1982 was proclaimed the Tasmanian Wilderness World Heritage Area by UNESCO.

The south-west's parks offer limited visitor facilities and there are relatively few access points or marked trails. Exploring these areas in depth therefore requires that you raft or hike over significant distances and are completely self-sufficient for long periods. Less adventurous travellers can, however, make short forays into the fringes of this wilderness, thereby gaining a sense of its splendour and majesty.

History

Some of the earliest evidence of Aboriginal occupation discovered in Tasmania was found in this area. It indicates that places such as Kutikina Cave, on the edge of the Franklin River, not far upstream from its confluence with the Gordon, were inhabited continuously during the last ice age, between 15,000 and 20,000 years ago. As weather patterns changed and the ice retreated, dense temperate rainforest re-

invaded the valleys and people moved closer to the sea. The large numbers of shell middens dotted along the beaches and cliffs testify to sizeable communities around 6000 years ago, and evidence suggests that four different Aboriginal groups have inhabited the south-west coast for the past 3000 years.

The first European to record a visit to the region was Abel Tasman in 1642, but it wasn't until the early nineteenth century, when the British decided to establish penal colonies on what was then known as Van Diemen's Land, that extensive exploration occurred. By 1821, one of the most notorious penal colonies in history had been established on Sarah Island at the head of Macquarie Harbour. By the time the prison closed in 1834, hardy pioneers were also using the rivers to source and transport timber to small settlements at river mouths and on the coast. Toward the end of the century, hordes of prospectors arrived on the west coast to mine deposits of gold, silver and copper.

So wild are the region's rivers that it was not until the 1950s that the longest, the Franklin River, was navigated from end to end. In that same decade, a young immigrant, Olegas Truchanas, paddled a canoe from Lake Pedder to Strahan via the Gordon River.

In 1955, Lake Pedder National Park was proclaimed; it was later expanded and renamed Southwest National Park. In the late 1960s, the government proposed the construction of a dam above Lake Pedder on the upper reaches of the Gordon. The fledgling conservation movement, led by Truchanas, lost the battle to halt this project, but by the time the Tasmanian Hydro-Electric Commission released plans to flood the lower Gordon and Franklin rivers, it was better prepared. The environmentalists generated a huge amount of publicity, attracting widespread support and engendering a keen interest in the region's ecological treasures among the wider population. During this period the first commercial rafting trips took place on the Franklin and pleasure cruises began in the waters of the lower Gordon. The plan for a dam was finally defeated in the High Court in 1981. Soon afterward, several small national parks were amalgamated to form Franklin–Gordon Wild Rivers National Park.

Franklin–Gordon Wild Rivers National Park

West of Derwent Bridge, the Lyell Highway follows a route used by early explorers and pioneers, climbing the broad flanks of mountains, descending into narrow gorges and skirting verdant rainforest, eucalypt forest, buttongrass plains, and sparkling lakes and streams. North of the road lies Cradle Mountain–Lake St Clair National Park; to the south is Franklin–Gordon Wild Rivers National Park. It's here on the southern side of the highway that one of Australia's greatest wilderness adventures begins: the journey

OPPOSITE: *Lake Pedder and neighbouring Lake Gordon form the largest reservoir system in Australia, holding 27 times as much water as Sydney Harbour.*

Some of the buildings in and around Strathgordon were built in the early 1970s to house workers involved in the Gordon River Power Development. They are now used as visitor accommodation.

The expansion of Lake Pedder drowned a unique environment incorporating spectacular pink quartzite beaches. An international campaign is now underway to restore the lake to its original state.

down the Franklin River to its junction with the wider, more tranquil waters of the Gordon.

Most rafting tours of the Franklin begin on one of its tributaries, usually the Collingwood. Soon after you join the Franklin itself, the river carves a great arc around the sheer, gigantic bluff of Frenchmans Cap. The dramatic quartzite peak remains hidden from view by verdant veils of vegetation and high walls of rock, though you can hike to its summit from the small camp site at Irenabyss, one of many delightful glens on the upper Franklin.

Beyond Frenchmans Cap, the river enters a series of gorges. Inception Reach, Serenity Sound and Transcendence Reach are cut by rapids of varying intensity, with descriptive names such as the Churn, Coruscades, Thunder Rush and the Cauldron. You then come to Deliverance Reach, a stretch of placid water in an area called the Great Ravine. Having barely had time to catch your breath, you enter a number of smaller but still impressive gorges, containing further rapids, some quite long, others merely patches of white water. Below Big Fall, the Franklin slows and spreads out as it nears the Gordon, requiring a fair amount of paddling to reach the landing spots at the confluence of the two waterways. By that time, passengers are usually very glad to see their pick-up boat, float plane or chopper!

VARIED PERSPECTIVES

Until the great dams were built, creating Lakes Gordon and Pedder, the Gordon River was also navigable. Now, because of irregular releases of water from the dams, its upper stretches are considered too dangerous to raft or paddle, and only the placid lower reaches can be explored on boat trips from the town

of Strahan on Macquarie Harbour. These tours usually travel upriver as far as Horseshoe Bend, then pause at nearby Heritage Landing, where a boardwalk circuit allows visitors to take a closer look at the ancient rainforest that cloaks the banks. Huon pine, blackwood, myrtle, sassafras, beech and celery-top pine are among the species that form a dense canopy above giant tree-ferns, moss-coated laurels and leatherwoods. One of the highlights of the walk is a 2000-year-old Huon pine.

Walking tracks can also be found along the Lyell Highway. The Donaghys Hill Wilderness Walk is a short, easy 2-km (1.2-mile) return hike that provides superb views of the Franklin River and Frenchmans Cap. Allow about 40 minutes return. A more demanding trail heads south from Victoria Pass to Irenabyss, where you can pick up the well-worn track to the top of Frenchmans Cap. This round trip measures 54 km (33.5 miles), takes at least three days, and requires a good level of fitness and thorough preparation.

Less energetic visitors can always opt to view the interior on a flightseeing tour. Several companies run float-plane trips out of Strahan, with the standard route taking you up the Gordon to a small landing strip. From here, you can walk to Sir John Falls, which lies much further upstream than most of the boat tours are allowed to go.

VEHICLE ACCESS AND CAMPING

There is very limited vehicle access to the Franklin and Gordon areas; in fact, there is only one vehicle track that takes you anywhere near the Franklin River and it is accessible only with a 4WD and a key that has to be obtained from the Queenstown office of the Parks and Wildlife Service. This is the Mount McCall

Although settled earlier by loggers, Strahan was officially founded and named in 1877 as a port for the tin mines at Mount Heemskirk. Today, its main industries are crayfishing, forestry and tourism.

Track, which was constructed by the Hydro-Electric Commission and runs for 22 km (13.5 miles) to the foot of Mount McCall. Even from there, it's a tough descent to the river past the ruins of a steep rail track.

There are only a few established bush camp sites in the national park, including Irenabyss Camp on the Franklin, Warners Landing on the Gordon, and another site at the bridge over the Collingwood. You can, however, generally pitch a tent anywhere—if you can find a space amid the tangle of vegetation.

Southwest National Park

From the southern edge of Franklin–Gordon Wild Rivers National Park, Southwest National Park extends all the way to Tasmania's west and south coasts. Covering more than 600,000 ha (1,482,600 acres), this is the largest national park in Tasmania and undoubtedly one of the wildest in Australia.

SCENIC DRIVES

The most accessible part of the park is the area around Lakes Gordon and Pedder. Here the Gordon River Road runs for 82 km (51 km) from the Maydena Gate entrance to the Gordon Dam and Power Station. This spectacular route threads through narrow valleys and high peaks, traverses wide moors and lush forests, and frequently reveals magnificent views of surrounding mountains such as the Saw Back, Anne and Frankland ranges. Along the way, you may see colourful flowers such as silver wattle, leatherwood and waratah, and native birds including robins, wrens, thornbills, rosellas, honeyeaters and currawongs. At the Maydena Gate entrance station, you can buy or hire an audio cassette that provides an informative commentary on the area.

Lakes Pedder and Gordon, which can be viewed from various points along the way, are huge bodies of water, covering 500 sq. km (193 square miles). Mountain peaks such as Scotts Peak and Mount Solitary now form islands within these artificial lakes.

Visitors with robust vehicles can also take the Scotts Peak Road, which departs from the Gordon River Road at Frodshams Pass, 28 km (17 miles) from Maydena Gate. This corrugated and deeply potholed track runs south for 36 km (22 miles), providing stunning views in all directions. Notable sights include Mount Anne, the highest peak in the southwest, and unusual formations such as the Needles and the Thumbs. A number of lookouts offer breathtaking views of Lake Pedder, the Arthur Plains, the Arthur, Maydena and Jubilee ranges, and the Weld River Valley, while the most dramatic panorama—a full 360 degrees—can be obtained at Red Knoll Lookout, 2 km (1.2 miles) beyond Scotts Peak Dam.

OTHER ACTIVITIES

Several interesting day walks depart from the Gordon River and Scotts Peak roads. From the former, the Timbs Track offers a four-hour return hike through rainforest to the Florentine River, whereas the Mount Wedge Track, a four- or five-hour round trip, leads to the summit of Mount Wedge and its majestic vistas. Just 2 km (1.2 miles) along the Scotts Peak Road is the Creepy Crawly Nature Trail, a 1-km (0.6-mile) trail along a boardwalk which provides a terrific introduction to the temperate rainforest environment. The walk is relatively easy, though not recommended for anyone unable to climb numerous steps and duck under low branches.

The tawny frogmouth (Podargus strigoides) relies on its camouflage to conceal it from predators. When threatened, it narrows its eyes and raises its head, assuming the form of a broken branch.

Further south, two much more arduous trails should be attempted only by experienced, energetic hikers. The gruelling walk to Lake Judd requires eight hours, while the challenging climb to the top of Eliza Plateau takes five or six. On all of these tracks, except for the Creepy Crawly Nature Trail, hikers should register their departure in the park log books provided and sign out when they return.

Southwest National Park also offers two of the country's most challenging long-distance walking tracks. The 70-km (43.5-mile) Port Davey Track, which was originally created as an escape route for survivors of shipwrecks on the wild south-west coast, leads from Lake Pedder to Melaleuca on Bathurst Harbour and requires at least four or five days. As there are no roads to Melaleuca, hikers must then retrace their steps or fly or sail out. Alternatively, they can continue southward along the South Coast Track to Cockle Creek, a gruelling 85-km (53-mile) journey that takes between five and nine days. Both trips should be undertaken only by very experienced and well-prepared bushwalkers.

A much easier way to view the wild heart of the park is to take a sightseeing flight from Hobart to Bathurst Harbour. Some trips include a short stay at Melaleuca and a cruise around the harbour. Boating is also available on Lakes Pedder and Gordon, where between August and April you can enjoy some of the finest fishing in Australia.

ACCESS AND CAMPING

The northern section of the park is situated 75 km (46.5 miles) from Hobart along the Lyell Highway and Gordon River Road. The southern section can be accessed from Cockle Creek, which is about two hours from Hobart along the Huon Highway. All roads are subject to snow and ice and visitors should be prepared for sudden weather changes all year round.

There are camp sites at Edgar Dam and Cockle Creek and at the Huon Campground near Scotts Peak Dam. There is also a motel at Strathgordon.

Places in
SOUTHERN
TASMANIA

Isthmus bays on Bruny Island. The Neck joins North and South Bruny.

BOTHWELL

Set around the magnificent Queens Park, 77 km (48 miles) north-west of Hobart, this small historic town (population 400) is built along the banks of the Clyde River. Bothwell boasts more than 18 National Trust buildings. Among those is a building that was opened in 1837 and became Tasmania's very first public library. Other interesting buildings include the Castle Hotel—which has held its licence since 1829—and Wentworth House—built in 1833 for Major D'Arcy Wentworth. Visitors, many of whom come because of their interest in the history of the area, often stay in one of the many historic hotels. One of these, Bothwell Grange, a heritage building circa 1836, puts on 'Murder Mystery Weekends'.
Map ref: page 843 J2

BRUNY ISLAND

Bruny Island (population 520) is situated just off the coast of southern Tasmania, 33 km (20 miles) south of Hobart. Joined by a thin stretch of sandy shoreline, known as the Neck, are North and South Bruny, two rather distinctly different areas. The north comprises mainly cleared pastoral land, with only a scattering of light brushland

areas. The south, however, is quite different: it is a rugged, mountainous region, and is heavily timbered.

Many explorers navigated their way around this small tract of land, including Tobias Furneaux, James Cook (who came ashore in 1777), Matthew Flinders and William Bligh. The Bligh Museum, which is in Adventure Bay, has excellent displays highlighting the travels of these explorers and the whalers

The pond at Panorama Winery, one of two wineries in the Cygnet region.

who used Bruny as a base from which to hunt. Bruny also has important significance for the Aborigines as the birthplace of Truganini. She was the daughter of an island chief and the last of the full-blooded Tasmanian Aborigines. She died in 1876.

A car and passenger ferry operates from Kettering to North Bruny. The island, although only 55 km (34 miles) in length, has much to offer the visitor, and while many people come on day trips from Hobart, the island is much better appreciated over two or three days. The island's main town is Alonnah. Nearby South Bruny National Park has some truly spectacular scenery and views. The Barnes Bay Regatta is held in early March each year, and there is a rodeo held over Easter.
Map ref: page 843 K8

CYGNET

The centre of a large fruit-growing region, Cygnet (population 925) sits on the banks of Port Cygnet, 58 km (36 miles) south of Hobart, where the Huon River flows out into the D'Entrecasteaux Channel.

Agriculture has always been the mainstay of this town—the con-

victs who were housed for a short period in probation settlements here were used to clear much of the surrounding land for farming. Unlike much of Tasmania, where old buildings were traditionally built from stone, Cygnet's buildings were mainly constructed using timbers cleared from the surrounding land. This tradition continues today, with the wood-turner at the Deepings, on the way to Nicholls Rivulet south-east of town, still manufacturing ornaments and bowls from the magnificent Tasmanian timbers. Nearby, Talune Wildlife Park and Koala Gardens has much in the way of local native wildlife, which includes the infamous Tasmanian devil.

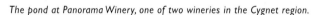

Window at Hartzview Vineyard, near Cygnet.

Also in the Cygnet region are two wineries, the Hartzview Vineyard and the Panorama Winery and both offer cellar door sales. The Huon Folk Festival is held in late January or early February.
See also Southern Tasmanian Wine Regions
Map ref: page 389 J6

DOVER

Dover is situated 87 km (54 miles) south of Hobart. Originally it was a convict station but today the town is a very popular fishing spot, with a sheltered harbour that faces the D'Entrecasteaux Channel and the west side of Bruny Island. The Huon pine was once heavily processed and exported from Dover, but since this magnificent timber has become scarce, fishing and fruit growing are the major sources of income. Tourism is a growth industry and there are numerous cottages that offer bed and breakfast.

Dover (population 570) is an excellent base for exploring the nearby Hartz Mountains National Park, which is part of the World Heritage Area. The park offers some rather spectacular scenery, and has many walking trails that take keen bushwalkers on a varied route through mountain lakes, alpine heathlands, rainforests and rugged ranges. There is also another, much shorter, walk that takes you to the Waratah Lookout.

The wharf at Dunalley, a small town on the Forestier Peninsula.

Here you can view the grandeur of Mount Wellington and take in the surrounding greenery of the lush Huon Valley.
Map ref: page 843 J7

DUNALLEY

The small township of Dunalley (population 310) is 61 km (38 miles) east of Hobart, and stands on the narrow isthmus that connects the Forestier Peninsula to mainland Tasmania—it was the site of the first European landing, in December 1642. The Tasman Memorial 2 km (1.2 miles) northeast of the town bears testament to the landing by Dutch sailors from the ships Heemskirk and Zeehan under the command of Abel Tasman more than 350 years ago. Tasman named the island Van Diemen's Land after Anthony Van Diemen, who was at that time the governor-in-chief of the Dutch East India Company. The name was not changed to Tasmania until as late as 1855.

Dunalley has cafés and local arts and crafts, which are sold in small shops and galleries. There are some guided tours of bushland around Dunalley that take in large tracts of grasslands and native bush, and are ideal for bushwalking. The local lagoons and coastal areas are also of interest to the visitor. The Dennison Bridge connects the peninsula to the mainland, and occasionally vehicles wanting to use the bridge will have to wait a few minutes for boats to pass under the swing-style bridge.
Map ref: page 843 M5

FRANKLIN

Not to be confused with the well-known Franklin River in Tasmania's south-west, this timber milling and orchard town (population 465) is one of the oldest to be found along the Huon River in the State's south-west. Sited only 62 km (39 miles) south-west of Hobart, Franklin was named after Governor Sir John Franklin who lived on the banks of the Huon with his wife Lady Jane Franklin. The settlement expanded rapidly near their home. There are a number of historic buildings in Franklin today, including three churches that were constructed sometime in the mid-1800s.

Although the main industry has always been timber milling, there is a museum in the town highlighting the orchard industry of the region surrounding Franklin.
Map ref: page 843 J6

GEEVESTON

Geeveston (population 830), 65 km (40 miles) south of Hobart, was first settled in 1842 by a William Geeves, who came to the richly treed region and began clearing timber, a process that has continued for more than 150 years. There are many walking trails, such as those off Arve road, and some of these feature trees that are labelled for easy identification. Further west along the Arve Road is the Tahune Reserve, where there is a natural stand of the rare Huon pine. The Forest and Heritage Centre allows you to smell and feel the magnificent local timber. There are some photographs and also displays of wooden artefacts handcrafted by the local wood-turners.

Geeveston is also the perfect starting point for a journey to the Hartz Mountains National Park, a rugged mountain range that is popular with both bushwalkers as well as day trippers in the milder months and cross-country skiers flock there in the winter months to enjoy the snow country.
Map ref: page 843 H6

HARTZ MOUNTAINS NATIONAL PARK

The wild and rugged primeval landscape of this park is made up of many glacially carved mountain lakes, alpine heathlands, snow-gum woodlands and rugged dolerite ranges that run from north to south between the catchments of the Arve and Picton Rivers.

In winter the highlands are popular with cross-country skiers as there are decent snowfalls in the winter months. During spring and summer, the giant, crimson–red blooms of Tasmanian waratahs, as well as many other wildflowers, soften the landscape. This is the ideal time for intrepid, prepared bushwalkers, who venture into what can still be an exposed, cold and windswept region. The park is situated 85 km (53 miles) south-west of Hobart.
Map ref: page 843 H7

The Arve River in the Hartz Mountains National Park, an alpine park not far from Geeveston.

A local Tasmanian salmon farmer.

HUONVILLE

Bruni D'Entrecasteaux, the French admiral who explored much of the region south of Hobart in the early 1790s, was the first European to sight the Huon River. He named it after Captain Huon de Kermedec, his second-in-command. The small township of Huonville has a population of 1525. It sits 42 km (26 miles) south-west of Hobart, beside the Huon River. With the later arrival of settlers, the Huon Valley eventually developed into an excellent fruit-growing district, and fresh produce is still easily obtained from laden roadside stalls. Just outside town is the Huon Apple and Heritage Museum. This place commemorates the early orchard industry with exhibits of restored machinery. There are also the many locally grown varieties of apple on hand for sampling.

In nearby Ranelagh, just to the north of Huonville, is the Tasmanian Antique Motor Museum. It has more than 40 beautifully restored vehicles on display.

For thrill seekers, jet boat rides have become extremely popular on the fast-flowing Huon River. On the calmer Denison River at nearby

Fresh Atlantic salmon can be sampled at the Huonville trout fishery.

Judbury is the Snowy Range Trout Fishery. Its ponds are well-stocked with Tasmanian rainbow trout that weigh in at up to 4 kg (9 lb). Atlantic salmon are available too. Huonville's Sunday markets are held down by the river bank, and the Festival on the Bank is held in April.
Map ref: page 843 J6

KETTERING

Kettering, 33 km (20 miles) south of Hobart, is a small town (population 295) and is the gateway to Bruny Island, being the car and passenger ferry terminal. North of Kettering is Oyster Cove, home of a thriving berry industry, while the larger fruit-growing district of Cygnet is only a short drive to the south-west. On the outskirts of Kettering is the Herons Rise Vineyard, which produces a range of wines, including pinot noir, Rhine riesling and Müller Thurgau. Wine tastings and cellar door sales are available by appointment—accommodation is also offered on this scenic property.

Only 8 km (5 miles) north of town on the Channel Highway is the delightful township of Snug. It is here that you will find Mother's Favourites, Tasmania's finest bakery for pies and quiches. To the south-west of Snug are Snug Falls, these pretty waterfalls are accessible via a walking track.
See also Southern Tasmanian Wine Regions
Map ref: page 843 K6

The eroded sandstone landscape of the Painted Cliffs, on Maria Island.

KINGSTON

The largest town south of Hobart, with a population of 12,910, and known as the gateway to southern Tasmania, Kingston could almost be described as a southern suburb of Hobart—it is a mere 13 km (8 miles) south of the city. Both the town site and river were named Browns River after the botanist Robert Brown who explored this region in 1804. The town's name was later changed to Kingston, after Lieutenant Philip Gidley King, the officer in charge of the first settlement in Tasmania. Browns River flows through the Kingston Beach Golf Course, considered one of the finest in Tasmania, before reaching the sea at Kingston Beach, which is a magnificent safe swimming area.

Kingston is also the home of Australia's Antarctic Division Research Facility, which provides necessary backup services to the research stations in Antarctica—a section of the facility is open to the public on weekdays.

The region around Kingston is perfect for scenic drives. The road south of the town follows the coastline for much of the way to Cygnet, taking in towns such as Middleton, Woodbridge and Snug. Along the way there are many vantage points

from which to view Bruny Island. Continue north along the Channel Highway to Huonville where you can pick up the Huon Highway and make the round trip back to Kingston. The Kingborough Festival is held each year in March, and the Dutch Oliebollen Festival is on in October.
Map ref: page 843 K5

MARIA ISLAND NATIONAL PARK

This tranquil and beautiful island, just 15 km (9 miles) off Tasmania's east coast, was named after Maria, Anthony Van Diemen's wife, and a penal settlement was established there in 1825—many of the settlement's buildings are still standing. There have since been many different ventures on the island, but it is now a national park and wildlife sanctuary. The island boasts quite magnificent coastal scenery and a mountain range high enough to support a rainforest habitat. There are walking tracks that vary from half an hour to several days, taking in the wilder southern areas. Near Darlington lie the Painted Cliffs. The Fossil Cliffs, full of millions of fossilised shellfish, are east of Darlington. Wildlife is abundant, and includes large numbers of tame

New Norfolk overlooks the pleasant tranquil waters of the Derwent River.

Bennett's wallabies. There are many birds on the island including the introduced Cape Barren goose and the endangered forty-spotted pardalote. Seals and whales frequently visit, and some of the waters have been declared a marine reserve.

Much of the western side of the island is perfect for swimming, snorkelling and diving. Access to the island is via ferry; charter boats operate in the bay and are available for fishing or for cruises. There are also scenic flights over the island from Triabunna. Orford, the nearest mainland town, is 77 km (48 miles) from Hobart.

Map ref: page 843 N3

MOUNT FIELD NATIONAL PARK

During the last ice age, glacial movements shaped the landforms of the plateau and the myriad lakes and tarns of this, Tasmania's oldest national park. The striking landscape of the park is bountiful in flora, from rainforest to towering

forests of swamp gum, stringybarks and conifers; gnarled snow gums and alpine moorlands are found on the high country. The bird and animal life, too, is abundant. Lady Barron, Russell and Horseshoe Falls are major attractions. Bushwalking is popular here and for the winter sports enthusiast the high country has been a favourite for over 70 years, although the snowfall in this area is unreliable. Trout fishing in Lakes Webster and Dobson is also popular. The park is 75 km (47 miles) west of Hobart.

Map ref: page 842 G3

NEW NORFOLK

Located on the banks of the Derwent River, New Norfolk is 39 km (24 miles) north-west of Hobart. A major town with a population of 5820, it offers a blend of history, good restaurants and museums. The town took its name from the original settlers who arrived here from Norfolk Island after the penal colony there was abandoned in

1808. These men built quite a magnificent colonial village, which is now registered in its entirety with the National Trust. A town walk is the best way to appreciate it. Of particular interest are the Old Colony Inn, with its art and craft shop and superb gardens, and the Bush Inn, built in 1816, which overlooks the pleasant, tranquil waters of the Derwent River.

During the mid-1800s hops were introduced to the region for brewing Tasmanian beer. Bushy Park produced the first commercial hops in the district and was once the largest hop farm in the Southern Hemisphere. Each March Bushy Park hosts the Derwent Valley Hop Festival.

For thrillseekers there are jet boat rides over the rapids of the Derwent River. Train enthusiasts will enjoy the Derwent Valley Railway, which offers steam train rides through the valley. Tulips in bloom make a delightfully colourful display from the first week in October. Nearby Plenty is home to the Salmon Ponds, where the first brown and rainbow trout were bred in captivity in Australia, in 1864.

Map ref: page 843 J4

OATLANDS

Before the delightful township of Oatlands (population 525) was established, this area was home (in 1827) to a military garrison, one of four strung from the south to the north to control the State. It was to be five more years before the township on the shores of Lake Dulverston—85 km (53 miles) north of Hobart—was surveyed and the community of sandstone buildings erected: High Street has 87 colonial sandstone buildings.

It is claimed that Oatlands has the best collection of pre-1837 houses in Australia, and they include the Carrington Mill, which was extensively renovated by the National Trust in the 1980s, the courthouse, the gaoler's home and three magnificent churches.

Among many interesting shops is the Scottish, Irish and Welsh Shop, which stocks and has on display over 500 different kinds of tartans. The Craft Bear, which is housed in a historic building circa 1845, has a large range of teddy bears, chocolates and biscuits, and Wood and Wife has a wide choice of collectables and antiques.

To the north-west of Oatlands are Lakes Sorell and Crescent, which sit at the base of Mount Franklin. The Lake Sorell Wildlife Sanctuary is well worth visiting while in the area. The lakeland also offers many activities—a walking track that runs through Lake Dulverton Aquatic Reserve, a scenic golf course on the shores of Lake Dulverton and trout fishing in the lake. In February there is a rodeo held in Oatlands.

Map ref: page 843 K2

The spiky foliage of the giant heath (Richea pandanifolia) in Mount Field National Park.

ORFORD

Orford (population 505) is a very popular holiday resort and fishing village located on the east coast of Tasmania, 79 km (49 miles) north-east of Hobart. This is where the Prosser River opens out into Prosser Bay where popular activities include fishing and swimming off sandy beaches such as the popular Shelly Beach or Raspins Beach.

Maria Island, which lies directly off the coast, is a national park and wildlife sanctuary that is worth a visit; the access is via ferry. There are also charter boats to explore the

The Prosser River, upstream from Orford.

bay that are available for fishing or for cruises, and scenic flights over Maria Island from Triabunna. The Wielangta Road Forest Drive, to the south of Orford, is a rather interesting alternative route down to the Tasman Peninsula. The road passes through the Sandspit Forest Reserve, where there are walks that highlight the trees and plants on information boards. Another walk goes through the old Wielangta sawmilling town, most of which is now in ruins.
Map ref: page 843 M3

PONTVILLE

This mid-nineteenth century garrison town was built just 31 km (19 miles) north of Hobart, near a quarry that supplied most of the freestone used in Tasmania in the nineteenth century. Pontville (population 1,125) has a historic town classification. It has numerous interesting buildings dating from the 1800s, including St Matthew's Catholic Church and St Mark's Church of England. The Barracks, formerly the local store, and the Sheiling, built in 1825, are both restored as accommodation houses. A historic bridge, built by convicts, which spans the Jordan River. Less

than 20 km (12 miles) north is the Chauncy Vale Wildlife Sanctuary; south of the town is the Bonorong Park Wildlife Centre.
Map ref: page 843 K4

PORT ARTHUR HISTORIC SITE

No visit to Tasmania is complete without a tour of the Port Arthur Penal Settlement, which is 102 km (63 miles) south-east of Hobart. Started as a timber station in 1828, it became a penal settlement. In 1830 Lieutenant-Governor Arthur chose this site to incarcerate the worst of Tasmania's convicts—there was only one route for escape on land. Tales of man-eating sharks in the surrounding waters deterred any escape by sea.

The penal settlement operated until 1877, and around 12,500 convicts served time here. A bushfire ravaged the settlement in 1897, and a second has swept through the area since, but more than 30 buildings have survived, although badly damaged, as poignant reminders of the harsh conditions the convicts endured. Some of the buildings that can be inspected include the church, the penitentiary, the commandant's residence and the model prison, where prisoners were put into

solitary confinement. The township of Port Arthur then boasted a sawmill, shipbuilding yards, coalmining and brick manufacturing as well as the timber industry. The Bush Mill Steam Railway, a narrow gauge system, gives an insight into the timber industry as it takes passengers on a breathtaking 4 km (2.5 mile) journey around the hillside. The Isle of the Dead, near Point Puer, contains the graves of nearly 2000 convicts as well as many local residents.

Stewarts Bay State Reserve, to the north of the town, has a track that leads from the penitentiary and follows the foreshore around Lakes Bay before joining back up with another track leading into the Reserve and down to Garden Point. The Tasmanian Devil Park, which is also north of the town, is a wildlife rescue centre, with up to 25 species of injured and orphaned animals on display at any time, including Tasmanian devils, quolls, eagles, owls and kangaroos. Further north again is Eaglehawk Neck, the small tract of land that connects the Tasman Peninsula (the total Tasman Peninsula population is 1595) with the mainland. Here the notorious Dog Line, yet another means of preventing any of the prisoners from escaping, was installed. This

Countryside of the Coal River region, near Richmond.

area has many other natural attractions, preserved in State reserves, including the Tessellated Pavement, Tasman Blowhole, Tasman Arch and Devils Kitchen. The township of Port Arthur holds a triathlon, regatta and woodchopping festival on Boxing Day.
Map ref: page 843 M6

RICHMOND

Only 20 minutes' from Hobart—28 km (17 miles) north-east of the city—the town of Richmond (population 755) is one of the finest examples of a Georgian village in Australia. Some buildings date as far back as the 1820s. Richmond Gaol, which is the oldest and best preserved colonial jail in Australia, was built between 1825 and 1840. Australia's oldest complete freestone bridge crosses the Coal River in Richmond. Built by convicts

Port Arthur's notorious convict prison, where regular tours are held by daylight and spooky lantern-lit ghost tours occur by night.

between 1823 and 1825, it gave access from Hobart to the east coast and the Tasman Peninsula. Other structures that are of interest in the town include the post office building (1828) and the Prospect House mansion.

The Peppercorn Gallery is in an old 1850s convict-built cottage that features local artwork. Then there is the Old Hobart Town Historical Model Village. It depicts Hobart in a scale model as it was in the 1920s. The Richmond Maze is always fun, for both children and adults. With toys dating back to 1900, the Richmond Toy Museum contains many reminders of the past—Matchbox and Hornby toys, teddy bears and dolls. The Richmond Village Fair is held in October, and the harvest festival is in May.
Map ref: page 843 K4

SORELL

Not to be mistaken for Port Sorell, the town Sorell, with a population of 3200, is 27 km (17 miles) north-east of Hobart; it is connected to Midway Point by a large causeway that took eight years to build. This route is a link between Hobart and Port Arthur, significantly reducing the distance between the city and the Tasman Peninsula. In the early days this town was an important supplier of grain, but now sheep farming is the main industry in the region.

Bushranger Matthew Brady came upon the small settlement of Sorell not long after it had been established, and captured the guards of the garrison, along with most of the locals. This rather audacious act, however, was short lived: Brady was caught two years later and, in 1826, he was hanged for his crimes.

The town has quite a number of historical attractions, and these include the Blue Bell Inn, which was built in 1863, and two churches, St George's and Scots Church. A short drive from Sorell is the Orani Vineyard, which offers wine tastings and cellar door sales. A food festival is held in the town in November.
Map ref: page 843 L4

Barrels at Lubiana Wines, in one of the Southern Tasmanian Wine Regions.

The war memorial at Sorrel, not far from Hobart.

SOUTH BRUNY NATIONAL PARK

Tasmania's newest national park, South Bruny has wild, rugged scenery and spectacular views. Some areas are inaccessible; others can be reached by walking or by 4WD. Covering the south coast of Bruny Island, the park stretches from Labillardiere Peninsula across Cape Bruny, Cloudy Bay and Tasman Head, then up the east coast to Adventure Bay. The convict-built Cape Bruny Lighthouse is Australia's oldest manned lighthouse. It has breathtaking views of Lighthouse Bay, West Cloudy Head and East Cloudy Head, Tasman Head and the Friars Rocks. Cloudy Bay, a popular surfing spot, can become wild in winter. There is excellent fishing in most areas, plus swimming at Great Taylor and Adventure Bays, and a range of other bushwalks and 4WD tracks. Ferries run frequently from Kettering. Adventure Bay is the 'holiday resort' of Bruny. It has a long sweep of white sands lapped by clear waters, and is safe for swimming and boating.
Map ref: page 843 J8–K8

SOUTHERN TASMANIAN WINE REGIONS

In the southern part of Tasmania there are two unofficial subregions: one is of Hobart and the Derwent and Coal River Valleys, while the other consists of the Huon Valley and D'Entrecasteaux Channel. With its rocky soils and blonde plains, the dry south-east has a good capacity to ripen cabernet sauvignon in good vintages.

Claudio Alcorso, who founded Moorilla Estate, Berriedale, in the Derwent Valley in 1958, and Andrew Pirie (of Pipers Brook Vineyard in the northern part of the State) stand tall in the rebirth of Tasmania's wine industry. Both 'new islanders' with a vision, they followed in the footsteps of another immigrant, Jean Miguet, who established the first modern vineyard at Lalla in 1956. Miguet's influence on the pinot noir aspirations of the young Pirie was significant; Pirie was searching for a Southern-hemisphere equivalent of the great wine-growing regions of France. Moorilla Estate is totally committed to wine tourism: their tasting facilities at Claremont are immaculate, and Claudio Alcorso's fabulous 1960s home on the Derwent River has been converted to an antiquities museum and a quite sophisticated function area. Delightful concerts are held here on the lawns during the summer months.

Other prominent names in the industry include Stefano Lubiana, who took his family to Tasmania to make cool-climate wines, and the State is indebted to his considerable talents. Not only does he make an increasingly interesting range of wines under the Lubiana label, but Stefano has been vital to the development of the State's sparkling wine industry. He provides contract winemaking and consultancy services to small and large makers such as Elsewhere Vineyard at Glaziers Bay, Lake Barrington Estate and the mighty Pipers Brook Vineyard.

Stoney Vineyard, Campania, produces the premium Domaine A cabernet sauvignon and pinot noir that are mostly sold interstate but also overseas and these wines command an influential list of devotees. The more immediate-drinking Stoney Vineyard label includes Aurora, a white wine made from classic red varieties. Riesling is proving its versatility with excellent examples from the warm and dry Coal River Valley.

Meticulous attention to trellising systems allows vignerons in the Huon Valley and D'Entrecasteaux Channel to produce some intensely flavoured wines. Indeed, the high quality of the *méthode champenoise* pinot that is produced by the Elsewhere Vineyard does suggest that sparkling wines could even become a regional specialty.

Vineyard in one of the Southern Tasmanian Wine Regions.

The Morris General Store is on Swansea's history walk.

SWANSEA

Swansea (population 550) lies on the brilliant blue waters of Great Oyster Bay, 137 km (85 miles) north-east of Hobart. It is a very popular fishing destination and seaside resort. The views from the town are spectacular, with the famous Freycinet National Park on the other side of the bay. Anglers fish in the bay or head out to the Tasman Sea to cast their lines. First settled in 1821, six years later, a military garrison was established on Waterloo Point. This point now has a park and picnic area that leads down to the Schouten House Beach on its southern edge.

Whalers set up a base in Swansea but the bark factory, established in 1885, is what made Swansea renowned. The Swansea Bark Mill and East Coast Museum on the Tasman Highway is the only restored black wattle bark mill in Australia. (Bark from the black wattle was often used for tanning leather.) The town has a very good historic walk that takes in the council chambers, the

Winery sign in Swansea.

old Morris General Store, Swan Inn and also the Community Centre, purported to house Australia's last remaining full-sized billiard table. Mayfield and Boltons Beach coastal reserves to the south are easily accessible from the highway; some other seaside attractions include the Rocky Hills Convict Station and the unusual, convict-built stone bridge at Spiky Beach. Two vineyards, Craigie Knowe and Spring Vale, feature in the area. The cellar at Spring Vale was originally a stable built by convicts, and the stone walls and pine rafters are still intact. The Swansea Show is held in September and the Craft Fair is in December.
Map ref: page 843 N1

TESSELLATED PAVEMENT AND TASMAN ARCH STATE RESERVES

These reserves are possibly the most extensively visited State reserves in Tasmania. Being at the entrance to the Tasman Peninsula and Port Arthur, they are easy to access, as a stop off point. The Tessellated Pavement is at Pirates Bay, which is one of the best fishing and surfing spots in the area. A five-minute walk from the car park leads right to the water's edge, with these intriguing geological features that appear remarkably like paving stones. At low tide a beach walk to Clydes Island reveals fascinating sea life in many rockpools. The Tasman Arch Reserve includes the spectacular Blowhole and the Devils Kitchen, a crevice in which the sea boils and churns. These reserves are 70 km (43 miles) from Hobart on the Arthur Highway.
Map ref: page 843 M6

TRIABUNNA

Triabunna is 88 km (55 miles) north-east of Hobart. The town's early claim to fame was as a whaling station—this industry kept it

Tessellated Pavement near Port Arthur.

The Devils Kitchen near Eagle Hawk Neck, in the Tasman Arch State Reserve.

alive during its very early years as a garrison town—but today the small township, with a population of only 925, boasts a large woodchip mill; the paper produced from the woodchip is mainly exported to Japan. Fishing is also a big industry in this historic seaside town.

The grand old buildings in the town can be appreciated on a historic walk, which takes in the police watch-house and the magistrate's office, both built in the 1840s, as well as the Girraween Gardens and Tearooms. These gardens are a truly magnificent sight in both spring and summer when they are in full bloom and alive with colour.

Maria Island, to the south, was a penal settlement in the early 1800s but today it is a national park. A ferry goes from the Eastcoaster Resort, just south of Triabunna, to Darlington on Maria Island. You can visit the ruins of the settlement, or

go bushwalking, swimming or do some fishing, so it is worth spending an entire day there.

A very important attraction in Triabunna is the Spring Bay Crayfish Derby. Held on 4 January each year, it is a gourmet's delight.
Map ref: page 843 M3

Old homes in the historic township of Triabunna.

Hobart City Centre

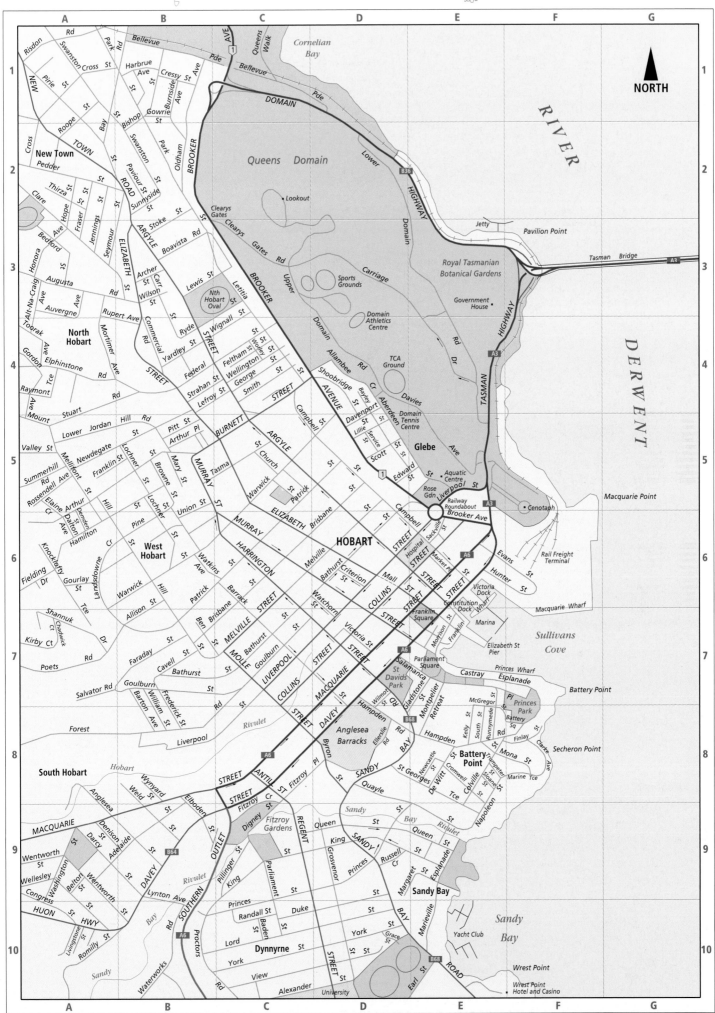

Hobart Throughroads

TASMANIA

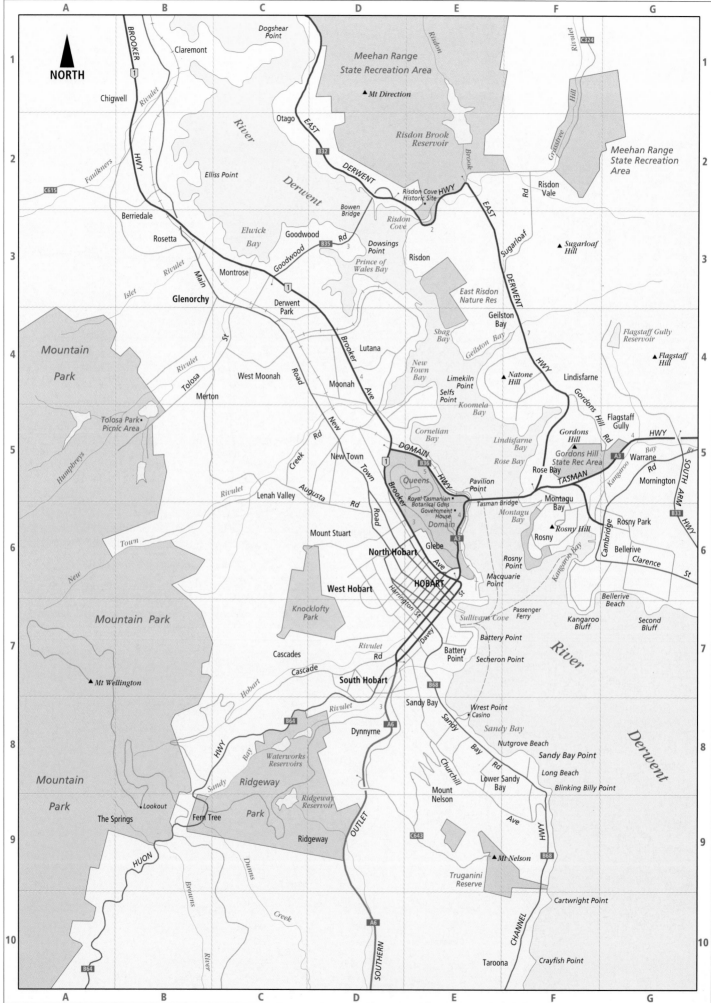

NORTH

0   1   2
kilometres

	A	B	C	D	E	F	G

Claremont
Chigwell
BROOKER
Dogshear Point
Meehan Range State Recreation Area
▲ Mt Direction
Otago
Risdon Brook Reservoir
Grasstree Hill
C324

Ellis Point
River
DERWENT
EAST
B832
Risdon Cove Historic Site
HWY
Meehan Range State Recreation Area
Risdon Vale

Berriedale
Rosetta
Elwick Bay
Goodwood
Bowen Bridge
Dowsings Point
Risdon Cove
Risdon
East Risdon Nature Res
Sugarloaf
▲ Sugarloaf Hill
EAST

Montrose
Glenorchy
Derwent Park
Goodwood Rd
B35
Prince of Wales Bay
Geilston Bay
DERWENT
Flagstaff Gully Reservoir

Mountain Park
Islet
Rivulet
Main
Tolosa
Merton
West Moonah
Brooker Road
Lutana
Moonah
New Town Bay
Shag Bay
Geilston Bay
HWY
Flagstaff Hill ▲
Flagstaff Gully

Tolosa Park Picnic Area
Humphreys
Creek Rd
New Town Rd
Moonah
Ave
Limekiln Point
Selfs Point
Natone Hill ▲
Koomela Bay
Lindisfarne
Gordons Hill Rd
A3
Warrane
Bay
SOUTH ARM HWY

Lenah Valley
Augusta Rd
New Town
Town Rd
DOMAIN HWY
B36
Queens Domain
Cornelian Bay
Lindisfarne Bay
Rose Bay
Gordons Hill State Rec Area
Rosny Hill ▲
Mornington
B33

Mount Stuart
Brooker
Royal Tasmanian Botanical Gdns
Government House
Domain
Pavilion Point
Tasman Bridge
Montagu Bay
TASMAN
Rosny
Montagu Bay
Cambridge
Rosny Park

North Hobart
West Hobart
Glebe
HOBART
Harrington St
Macquarie Point
Rosny Point
Kangaroo Bay
Bellerive
Clarence

Mountain Park
Knocklofty Park
Davey
Sullivans Cove
Passenger Ferry
Kangaroo Bluff
Bellerive Beach
Second Bluff

Cascades
Cascade Rd
South Hobart
Battery Point
Secheron Point
Battery Point
River
Derwent

Mt Wellington ▲
Hobart Rivulet
B64
A6
Sandy Bay
Wrest Point Casino
Sandy Bay
Nutgrove Beach
Sandy Bay Point

HUON HWY
Sandy Bay
Waterworks Reservoirs
Ridgeway
Dynnyrne
Churchill Ave
Lower Sandy Bay
Long Beach
Blinking Billy Point

Mountain Park
Lookout
Fern Tree
Ridgeway Park
Ridgeway Reservoir
OUTLET
Mount Nelson
Ave

The Springs
Ridgeway
C643
B68

HUON
Browns
Dunns
SOUTHERN
A6
▲ Mt Nelson
Truganini Reserve
CHANNEL
B68
Cartwright Point

B64
Creek
Taroona
Crayfish Point

	A	B	C	D	E	F	G

Hobart and Surrounding Areas

kilometres
0 5 10 15 20

843

147° | A | B | C | D | 147°30′ | E | F | 148° | G

Row 1
Nicholas Sugarloaf · 147 · Northumbria Hill · Parattah · 147°30′ · Pt Bailly · 58
Thorpe Water Mill · Green Hill · Jericho · Pike Hill · 17 · Mount Seymour · Little Swanport Hill · Boltons Beach Cons Area
Bothwell · Spring Hill · Whiteford · Buckland Military Training Area · Grindstone Point
A5 · 21 · 18 · Stonor · Baden · 14 · Woodsdale · Bluestone Tier · Mt Murray

Row 2
Mt Reid · Melton Mowbray · Lake Tiberias · Tunnack · Triabunna · Cape Bougainville
42°30′ · B110 · B31 · Rhyndaston · 42°30′
9° · Kempton · Colebrook · Eldon · Levendale · 22 · Louisville · Okehampton Bay
Hollow Tree · 12 · Quoin Mtn · Craigbourne Dam · Prosser · Orford · Lighthouse

Row 3
Mt Spode · Dysart · 36 · 18 · Mt Hobbs · Spring Beach · Darlington
Pelham · Elderslie · Bagdad · 23 · Brown Mtn · 52 · Thumbs Picnic Area · 11 · Rheban · Maria Island
A10 · 48 · 19 · Mangalore · TASMAN · 17 · Buckland · Prossers Sugarloaf · Return Pt
Gretna · Broadmarsh · Pontville · 19 · Lowdina · Runnymede · Mt Morrison · Sandspit River Forest Res · Pt Lesueur
Glenora · Rosegarland · C321 · Campania · A3 · 18 · Nugent · 20 · Booming Bay · Sboal Bay

Row 4
Bushy Park · Macquarie Plains · Mt Dromedary · Brighton · Tea Tree · Richmond · Pawleena · Cape Bernier · Cape Peron
Plenty · Black Hills · Dromedary · Bridgewater · Orielton · Sorell · Wattle Hill · Kellevie · Marion Bay
Salmon Ponds · Hayes · Magra · B10 · Granton · Old Beach · Grasstree Hill · Forcett · ARTHUR · Bream Creek
Moogara · Boyer · Molesworth · Claremont · B31 · Midway Point · 24 · Copping · Cape Paul Lamanon
Feilton · New Norfolk · Malbina · Otago · B32 · Risdon Vale · Cambridge · Lewisham · A9 · North Bay

Row 5
Glenfern · Glenlusk · Glenorchy · 9 · Pitt Water · Dodges Ferry · 10 · Dunalley · Cape Frederick Hendrick
Mount Lloyd · Lachlan · Collinsvale · 21 · HOBART · Seven Mile Beach Protected Area · Primrose Sands · High Yellow Bluff
Collins Cap · Lookout · Rokeby · Seven Mile Beach · Carlton · Dunalley Bay · Mt Forestier · Forestier
Trestle Mtn · Mt Wellington · Ridgeway · Taroona · Lauderdale · Frederick Henry · Green Head · Lime Bay Nat Res · Murdunna · Peninsula
Blue Hill · Fern Tree · B64 · A6 · Shot Tower · Sandford · Sloping I · Smooth I · Cape Surville

Row 6
Mt Misery · Mountain River · Neika · Leslie Vale · Kingston · Cremorne · Coal Mines Historic Site · 75
Crabtree · HWY · Longley · Blackmans Bay · Opossum Bay · Clifton Beach · Norfolk Bay · Eaglehawk Neck · Tessellated Pavement
Judbury · Lucaston · Grove · Lower Longley · 42 · Sandfly · B33 · Cape Deslacs · Saltwater River · Pirates Bay
Glen Huon · Ranelagh · Kaoota · Howden · South Arm · Premaydena · Tasman Blowhole · Tasman Arch
HUON · Huonville · Pelverata · Margate · Tinderbox · Iron Pot · Betsey Island · Koonya · Taranna · Devils Kitchen

Row 7
Franklin · Woodstock · Snug Falls · Snug · Dennes Point · Outer North Head · B37 · A9 · Waterfall Bay
South Franklin · Cradoc · Pelverata Falls · Coningham · Killora · One Tree Point · Tasman · O'Hara Bluff
Castle Forbes Bay · Glaziers Bay · Oyster Cove · Kettering · Barnes Bay · Nubeena · Peninsula · Tasman Trail
Port Huon · Wattle Grove · Nicholls Rivulet · Ferry · The Yellow Bluff · Wedge Bay · White Beach · Fortescue Bay
Geeveston · Petcheys Bay · Gardners Bay · Woodbridge · Birchs Bay · Trumpeter Bay · Two Island Bay · Highcroft · Palmers Lookout · Cape Huay

Row 8
Cairns Bay · Lymington · B68 · Great Bay · STORM · Port Arthur Convict Ruins · Munro Bight
Waterloo · Middleton · B66 · North Bruny Island · Curio Bay · Remarkable Cave · Tasman National Park
Surges Bay · Garden Island Creek · Simpsons Pt · BAY · Tasman National Park · Cape Pillar
Glendevie · Verona Sands · Isthmus Bay · Cape Queen Elizabeth · Maingon Bay · Tasman I Lighthouse
Police Point · Hideaway Bay · 64 · Gordon · Simpsons Bay · Raoul Bay · Cape Raoul

Row 9
Dover · Raminea · Strathblane · Maggot Pt · Esperance Pt · Ventenat Point · Alonnah · Adventure Bay · Fluted Cape
A6 · Partridge Island · South · Lunawanna · Capt Cook's Landing Place · Bligh Museum
Lune River · Hopwood Point · Great Taylors Bay · Bruny Island · Bay of Islands · Mangana Bluff · TASMAN SEA
Southport · South Bruny Nat Park · South Bruny National Park · 43°30′
Ida Bay · Historic Lighthouse · Mt Bruny · Boreel Head

Row 10
Southport Lagoon · Cape Bruny · West Cloudy Head · East Cloudy Head · Tasman Head · The Friars
Eliza Point · Recherche Bay · Cloudy Bay
Catamaran · Whale Sculpture
Cockle Creek
Whale Head · 147° · 147°30′ · 43°30′

NORTH

Northern Tasmania

Flinders Island
Scale same as main map

0 10 20 30
kilometres

148°
147°30'

FURNEAUX GROUP

FLINDERS ISLAND

Inner Sister Island
Stanley Point
Blyth Point
Palana
Mt Killiecrankie
Killiecrankie Bay
Killiecrankie
Cape Frankland
Mt Tanner
Leeka
Roydon Island
Tanners Bay
Marshall Bay
Babel Island
Lighthouse
Cat Island
Sellars Point
Prime Seal Island
Emita
Memana
The Patriachs
Furneaux Lookout
Walkers Lookout
Sellars Lagoon
Arthur Bay
Blue Rocks
Mt Levenstborpe
Cameron Inlet
Chalky Island
Long Point
Parrys Bay
Whitemark
Logan Lagoon
East Kangaroo Island
Big Green Island
Ranga
Strzelecki Peaks
Lady Barron
Fotheringate Bay
Trousers Point
Little Green Island
Pot Boil Point
Mt Chappell Island
Strzelecki Nat Park
Great Dog Island
Franklin
Pigs Head Point
Little Dog I
Vansittart Island
Goose Island
Puncheon Pt
Sound

BANKS STRAIT

Mt Chappell Island
Strzelecki NP
Franklin
Pigs Head Point
Little Dog I
Great Dog Island
Goose Island
Lighthouse
Anderson Island
Tin Kettle Island
Apple Orchard Point
Vansittart Island
Puncheon Pt
Badger Island
Sound
Deep Bay
Long Island
Cape Barren Island
Mt Munro
Double Peak
Cape Barren Island
Mt Kerford
Cape Sir John
Kent Bay
Thunder and Lightning Bay
Preservation Island
Wombat Pt
Sloping Pt
Forsyth Island
Passage Island
Clarke Island
Armstrong Channel
Black Point
Moriarty Bay
Lookout Head
Moriarty Point

Cape Portland
Swan Island
Ringarooma Bay
Waterhouse Island
Musselroe Bay Conservation Area
Great Musselroe Bay
Waterhouse Point
Boobyalla Beach
Poole
Cape Naturaliste
Croppies Point
Sth Croppies Pt
Waterhouse Cons Area
Big Waterhouse Lake
Tomahawk
Boobyalla
Stumpys Bay
Mt William
Mount William National Park
Cod Bay
Purdon Bay
Eddystone Point Lighthouse
Eddystone Point

West Sandy Point
St Albans Bay
East Sandy Point
Anderson Bay
Shortys Point
Double Sandy Pt Cons Area
Granite Point Cons Area
Bridport
Mt Cameron
Gladstone
South Mount Cameron
Ansons Bay
Noland Bay
Sharon Point
Bay of Fires Cons Area
Bay Of Fires

Stony Head
Beechford
Five Mile Bluff
Low Head
Lulworth
Stony Head Military Area
Weymouth
Bellingham
Pipers Brook
Mt Horror
North Scottsdale
Winnaleah
Herrick
Pioneer
The Banca
The Gardens
Big Lagoon

West Head
Greens Beach
Kelso
George Town
Lefroy
Pipers River
Jetsonville
Scottsdale
Derby
Branxholm
Weldborough
Mt Pearson
Binalong Bay
Sloop Lagoon
Clarence Point
Beauty Point
Bell Bay
Nippogoree Hills
Golconda
Blumont
Tonganah
Tulendeena
Mt Paris Dam
Goulds Country
Humbug Point Cons Area
Beaconsfield
Sidmouth
Rowella
Retreat
Lebrina
Wyena
Nabowla
West Scottsdale
Springfield
Cuckoo
Ledgerwood
Ringarooma
St Helens Point Cons Area
The Dazzler Rg
Kayena
Tunnel
Lower Turners Marsh
Lisle
South Springfield
Cuckoo Hill
Pyengana
St Columba Falls State Reserve
St Helens
Stieglitz
Holwell
Deviot
Paper Beach
Gravelly Beach
Hillwood
Mount Direction
Karoola
Lilydale
Lalla
Mt Arthur
Talawa
Mt Victoria
Goulds Country
Parkside
Pamella
St Helens Island
Winkleigh
Exeter
Blackwall
Windermere
Lanena
Turners Marsh
Underwood
Myrtle Bank
Hollybank Forest Reserve
Patricks
Mt Young
Loila Tier
Dianas Basin
Frankford
Rosevears
Dilston
Targa
Patersonia
Mt Saddleback
Mathinna Falls Forest Reserve
Upper Scamander
Beaumaris
Scamander Forest Res
West Frankford
Glengarry
Legana
Rocherlea
Nunamara
Mt Barrow
Ben Nevis
Evercreech Forest Res
Scamander
Birralee
Bridgenorth
Mowbray
Rosevale
Launceston
Norwood
Mt Young
Henderson Lagoon
Falmouth
Reedy Marsh
Weetah
Selbourne
Prospect
Youngtown
White Hills
Musselboro
Burns Creek
Upper Blessington
Mathinna
Mt Nicholas
Cornwall
Four Mile Creek
Ironhouse Point
Hagley
Hadspen
Relbia
Westwood
Blessington
St Marys
Westbury
Carrick
Perth
Western Junction
Ski Village
Legges Tor
Elephant Pass
Chain of Lagoons
Deloraine
Osmaston
Glenore
Whitemore
Oaks
Toiberry
Bishopsbourne
Longford
Evandale
Clarendon
Nile
Deddington
Ben Lomond National Park
Mangana
Fingal
Picaninny Point
Templestowe Lagoon
Golden Valley
Bracknell
Cressy
Drys Bluff
Blackwood Creek
Hummocky Hills
Epping Forest
Cleveland
Stacks Bluff
Storys Creek
Rossarden
Avoca
St Pauls Dome
Douglas Apsley National Park
Seymour
Long Point
Projection Bluff
Liffey
Liffey Forest Res
Mother Lords Plains
Mt Blackwood
Poatina
Conara
Mt St John
Royal George
Mt Henry
Birdlife and Animal Park
Maclean Bay
Breona
Reynolds I
Reynolds Neck
Cramps
Central Plateau Conservation Area
Liawenee
Miena
Bernacchi
Great Lake
Little Lake
Millers Bluff
Campbell Town
Snow Hill
Meetus Falls Forest Res
Bicheno
Cape Lodi
Courland Bay
Shannon Lagoon
Flintstone
Mt Penny West
Mt Augusta
Hobgoblin
Lake Leake
Cranbrook
Friendly Beaches
Freycinet National Park
Barren Tier
Wilburville
Mt Franklin
Ross
Lost Falls Forest Res
Mt Peter
Mt Paul
Penstock Lagoon
Steppes
Woods Lake
Lake Sorell
Old Mans Head
Tunbridge
Nine Mile Beach
Hepburn Point
Coles Bay
Lighthouse Cape Tourville
Waddamana
Lake Echo
Lagoon of Islands
Alma Pass
Interlaken
Woodbury
Antill Ponds
Faddens Tier
Swansea
Fleurieu Pt
Sleepy Bay
Mayfield Bay Cons Area
Great Oyster Bay
Wineglass Bay
Cape Forestier
Table Mtn
Vincent Hill
York Plains
Tooms Lake
Spiky Bridge
Mayfield Bay
Weatherhead Point
Promise Bay
Mt Graham
Mt Freycinet
Freycinet Pen
Buxton Pt
Bryans Beach
Baldy Bluff

TASMANIA

Southern Tasmania

SOUTHERN

OCEAN

NORTH

kilometres

0 10 20 30

H J K L M N P

Steppes Lake Sorell 147°30' C305 O'Connor Rd 148° River Nine Mile Beach Hepburn Point Coles Bay Lighthouse
LAKE Alma Pass Interlaken Tunbridge Swansea Cape Tourville Coles Bay Sleepy Bay
Old Mans Head Woodbury A3 Great Mt Dove Wineglass Bay
81 Table Mtn Antill Ponds Meredith Oyster Fleurieu Pt Cape Forestier 1
Lake Crescent 86 Vincent Hill Faddens Tier Buxton River Spiky Bridge Promise Bay Mt Grabam Mt Freycinet
Woods Quoin York Plains Tooms Lake Mayfield Bay Cons Area Freycinet Pen
15 Oatlands Callington Mill Pawtella Mayfield Bay Weatherhead Point Baldy Bluff
Historic Site Lemont Buxton Pt Bryans Beach Cape Degerando
Nicholas Sugarloaf Northumbria Hill Andover Little Schouten Passage Cape Faure Schouten Island
Thorpe Water Mill Jericho Parattah Swanport Seaford Point Rooster Point 2
Bothwell A5 Green Hill Pike Hill Mount Seymour Little Swanport Pt Bailly Cape Sonnerat
Spring Hill Stonor Swanport Hill Boltons Freycinet National Park
Mt Reid Black Tier Melton Mowbray Whiteford Buckland Military Beach Cons Area
B110 B31 Baden Training Area Grindstone Point
Hollow Tree Kempton Lake Tiberias Rhyndaston Tunnack Woodsdale Bluestone Tier Triabunna Mt Murray
Colebrook Eldon Levendale Mt Hobbs Cape Bougainville 3
Mt Spode Quoin Mtn Craigbourne Dam Prosser Louisville Okebampton Bay
A10 48 Pelham Dysart Brown Mtn 52 Orford Lighthouse Cape Boullanger Maria Island National Park
Elderslie Bagdad Buckland Spring Beach Darlington
Gretna Broadmarsh Mangalore TASMAN Runnymede Rheban Maria Island Mt Maria
Rosegarland Mangalore Tier A3 Mt Morrison Thumbs Picnic Area Mistaken Cape
Macquarie Plains Pontville Campania Prossers Sugarloaf Booming Bay 4
Mt Dromedary Tea Tree Lowdina Sandspit River Forest Res Shoal Bay Riedle Bay
Plenty Black Hills Dromedary Brighton Nugent Oyster Bay
Salmon Ponds Hayes Magra Bridgewater Richmond Orielton Cape Maurouard
Moogara B10 Granton Old Beach Pawleena Cape Peron
Feilton New Norfolk Grasstree Hill Sorell Wattle Hill Kellevie Cape Bernier
Malbina Claremont Midway Point Forcett ARTHUR Bream Creek Marion 5
Glenfern Molesworth Otago Risdon Vale Pitt Water Lewisham Copping Bay
Mount Lloyd Lachlan Cambridge Seven Mile Beach Protected Area Cape Paul Lamanon
Glenlusk Glenorchy Mt Rumney Dodges Ferry A9 North Bay
Trestle Mtn Collinsvale 21 Lookout Carlton Dunalley Cape Frederick Hendrick
Blue Hill Collins Cap HOBART Seven Mile Beach Primrose Sands Dunalley Bay Mt Forestier
Mt Wellington Rokeby Sandford Green Head Forestier
Mt Misery Fern Tree Lauderdale Frederick Henry Lime Bay Nat Res Smooth I Murdunna High Yellow Bluff
Crabtree Ridgeway B64 Sloping I Bay Peninsula Cape Surville
Judbury Lucaston Mountain River A6 Taroona Cremorne Chronicle Pt 75 Eaglehawk Tessellated Pavement
Ranelagh Grove Neika Shot Tower Cape Deslacs Coal Mines Historic Site Neck Pirates Bay
Lower Longley Leslie Vale Kingston Clifton Beach Norfolk Tasman Arch
Glen Huon 42 Sandfly Blackmans Bay B31 Saltwater River Bay Tasmanian Devil Park Devils Kitchen
Huonville Longley Howden South Arm Premaydena Taranna Waterfall Bay
HUON Pelverata Kaoota Opossum Bay Betsey Island Koonya O'Hara Bluff
Electrona Margate Tinderbox Iron Pot Tasman Tasman Trail
Franklin Pelverata Falls Woodstock Snug Lighthouse Nubeena B37 A9 Peninsula Fortescue Bay
South Franklin Cradoc Snug Falls Dennes Point Outer North Head Tasman Port Arthur
Castle Forbes Bay Glaziers Bay Coningham Nth West Bay Wedge Bay White Beach Convict Ruins Cape Huay
Port Huon Wattle Grove Kettering Killora One Tree Point Highcroft Palmers Munro Bight
Geeveston Petcheys Bay Oyster Cove Barnes Bay The Yellow Bluff Lookout Tasman National Park
Cairns Bay Sygnet Ferry Trumpeter Bay Two I Bay Remarkable Cape Pillar
Waterloo Gardners Bay Nicholls Rivulet Woodbridge STORM Curio Bay Cave
Surges Bay Lymington Birchs Bay Variety Bay Tasman Maingon Bay
Glendevie Middleton Great Bay North Bruny National Park Tasman Island
Police Point B68 Island BAY Lighthouse
Hartz Mts NP Garden Island Creek B66 Simpsons Pt Cape Queen Elizabeth
Hideaway Bay Gordon Simpsons Bay
Surveyors Bay Verona Sands Adventure
Dover Huon I Bay
Strathblane Maggot Pt Alonnah Fluted Cape
A6 Esperance Pt South Adventure Bay Capt Cook's Landing Place
Ventenat Point Lunawanna Bligh Museum
Partridge Island Bruny Island Cape Connella Bay of Islands
Hopwood Point Mangana Bluff
Southport South Bruny Nat Park South Bruny National Park
Lune River Historic Lighthouse Mt Bruny
Ida Bay Boreel Head
Southport Lagoon Tasman Head
Eliza Point West Cloudy Head East Cloudy Head The Friars
Recherche Bay Catamaran Whale Sculpture
Cockle Creek Bare Hill
Whale Head

TASMAN SEA

−42°30'
−43°
−43°30'

147° 147°30' 148°

Launceston and Surrounding Areas

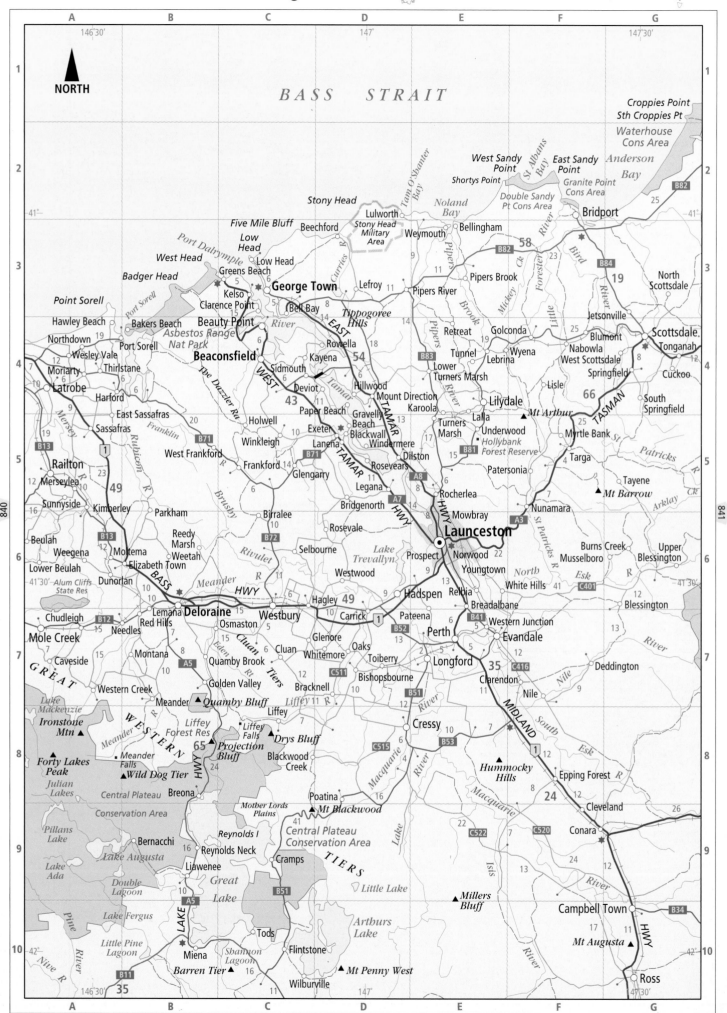

Road Maps Key and Distance Bars

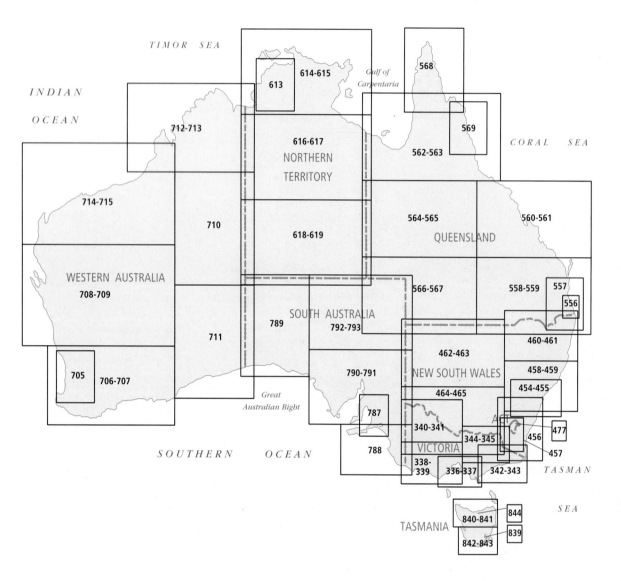

TIMOR SEA

INDIAN

OCEAN

613

614-615

Gulf of Carpentaria

568

712-713

CORAL SEA

569

562-563

616-617

NORTHERN TERRITORY

714-715

564-565

560-561

710

618-619

QUEENSLAND

WESTERN AUSTRALIA

708-709

566-567

558-559

557

556

711

789

SOUTH AUSTRALIA

792-793

460-461

462-463

705

706-707

790-791

NEW SOUTH WALES

458-459

Great Australian Bight

464-465

454-455

787

ACT

477

340-341

344-345

456

457

788

SOUTHERN OCEAN

VICTORIA

338-339

342-343

TASMAN

336-337

840-841

844

SEA

TASMANIA

842-843

839

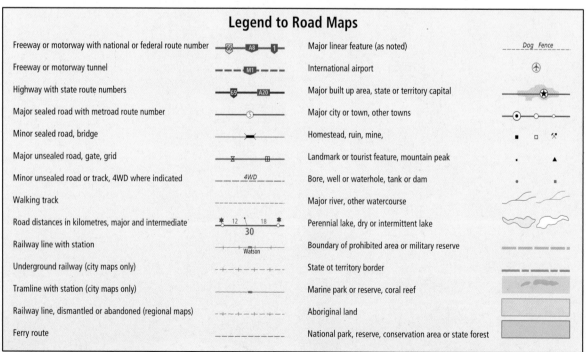

Legend to Road Maps

Freeway or motorway with national or federal route number	Major linear feature (as noted) — *Dog Fence*
Freeway or motorway tunnel	International airport
Highway with state route numbers	Major built up area, state or territory capital
Major sealed road with metroad route number	Major city or town, other towns
Minor sealed road, bridge	Homestead, ruin, mine,
Major unsealed road, gate, grid	Landmark or tourist feature, mountain peak
Minor unsealed road or track, 4WD where indicated	Bore, well or waterhole, tank or dam
Walking track	Major river, other watercourse
Road distances in kilometres, major and intermediate	Perennial lake, dry or intermittent lake
Railway line with station — Watson	Boundary of prohibited area or military reserve
Underground railway (city maps only)	State or territory border
Tramline with station (city maps only)	Marine park or reserve, coral reef
Railway line, dismantled or abandoned (regional maps)	Aboriginal land
Ferry route	National park, reserve, conservation area or state forest

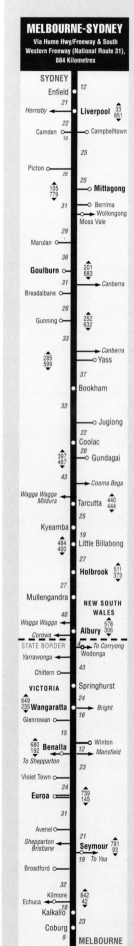

MELBOURNE–SYDNEY
Via Hume Hwy/Freeway & South Western Freeway (National Route 31), 884 Kilometres

SYDNEY
Enfield 12
21
Hornsby — Liverpool 33 / 851
22
Camden — Campbelltown
10
25
Picton 20
25
105 / 779 — Mittagong
31 — Berrima
— Wollongong
Moss Vale
29
Marulan
36
Goulburn 201 / 683
31 — Canberra
Breadalbane
20
Gunning 252 / 632
33
— Canberra
285 / 599 — Yass
37
Bookham
33
— Jugiong
22
Coolac
397 / 487 — Gundagai
20
43
— Cooma Bega
Wagga Wagga / Mildura — Tarcutta 440 / 444
25
Kyeamba
19
484 / 400 — Little Billabong
27
Holbrook 511 / 373
27
Mullengandra — NEW SOUTH WALES
40
Wagga Wagga — Albury 578 / 306
Corowa
STATE BORDER — To Corryong
Yarrawonga — Wodonga
Chiltern
43
VICTORIA — Springhurst
24
649 / 235 — Wangaratta — Bright
Glenrowan
16
15
— Winton
680 / 192 — Benalla 12 — Mansfield
To Shepparton
23
Violet Town
24
Euroa 739 / 145
31
Avenel
21
Shepparton / Brisbane — Seymour 791 / 93
19 — To Yea
Broadford
32
Kilmore 842 / 42
Echuca 10
Kalkallo
23
Coburg
9
MELBOURNE

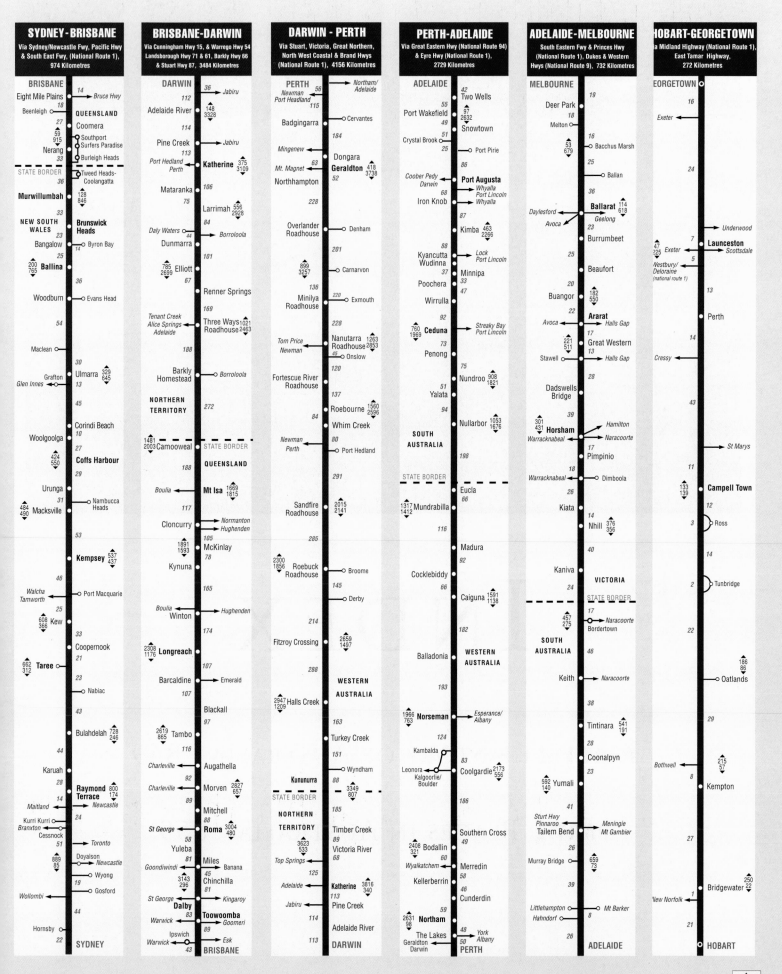

NOTE: On the intercity route maps the distance between centres is indicated in red. The cumulative distance is indicated between triangles, e.g.

▲
33
851
▼

INDEX

PART 1 THE STORY OF AUSTRALIA   849

PART 2 PLACES IN AUSTRALIA   859

INDEX TO PART 1: THE STORY OF AUSTRALIA

This is an index to the subjects in this book (places are in a separate index starting on page 859). Page numbers for pictures are in *italics*, and page numbers for major discussions of a subject are **bold**.

This index was created by Glenda Browne.

A

ABC 186, 210–211, 218
Abdulla, Ian 186
Aboriginal and Torres Strait Islander Commission (ATSIC) 155, 188
Aboriginal art 88, 93, **174–175**, *see also* rock art
  ancestral beings in 176, 179–181
  art styles 90–91, 183–184
  commercial *182*, 182–184, *183, 184*
  urban 185–186
Aboriginal culture 88, 92, *129*, 187–190, *see also* indigenous culture
  CAAMA Radio *218*
  renaissance 90–91
Aboriginal flag *97, 157*, 174
Aboriginal Land Fund Commission 101
Aboriginal Legal Service *102*
Aboriginal people *92, 195, 202, see also* indigenous Australians; remote Aboriginal communities
  1967 referendum 98
  alcohol abuse *101*
  arrival and spread 32, 87, *87*, 88, 104
  history, before colonisation 86–92
  history, colonial 93–96
  history, modern 97–103
  intellectual property 189
  involvement in World Wars *97*, 97–98
  John Batman and *110*, 111
  knowledge construction by 175
  missions and settlements 95–96
  population 88–89, 174, 202
  resistance to Europeans *93*, 93–94, 95, *95*
  science and technology 130
  socioeconomic indicators 185
  sport 234–236, *236*, 239, *240, 241*, 245
  stockmen *99, 113*
  stolen generations 103, 187
  tourism *171*
  use of fire 32, 58, 88, 177

Aboriginal Places 178
Aboriginal Welfare Board 96, 97, 103
Aboriginals Progressive Association 97
Acacia (wattle) 60, 68, *68*
ACT (Australian Capital Territory) 150, 151
Adelaide
  architecture 228–229, *229*
  Light, Colonel William 222
  settlement 111
Adelie penguin 80, *80, 81*
administration, *see* public administration
Admiralty House *153*
Advance Australia Fair 127, 156
AFL (Australian Football League) 239
agriculture (farming)
  early years of settlement 106
  farmers' associations 154
  indigenous Australians 91, 177
  inventions and equipment 135–137, *136, 168*
  land for 106, 109–110, *111*, 131
  land management 38, *38, 39*, 159
  native fauna and 58
  protectionism 158
  raw materials for Britain 110
  research and development *161*
  significance 158, 170
  soil nutrient status 39
  wine shows 162, *163*
aircraft flights and inventions 116, 135, *135*
Akubra hat factory *158*
Albanese, Anthony *154*
albatrosses 82, *82*
algae in Antarctica 79
ALP, *see* Australian Labor Party
alpine areas (snow country) 64, *64*
America's Cup 128, 233–234
amphibians 46
Amundsen, Roald 74
Ananda Marga sect 127
ANARE 77
angiosperms 60
Anglophilia 194
Angus & Robertson 207
ant-eaters, *see* echidnas; numbats
Antarctic Treaty 77
Antarctica 74–75, **74–83**, *see also* Heard Island; Macquarie Island
  bases and territorial claims *74*, 77
  climate 79
  discovery *74*, 74–75

fauna 80–83
flora *78*, 79
  physical geography *78*, 78–79
  resource exploitation 76–77
  scientific research 77
  tourism 77
anti-war moratorium 126
ants 42, 56–57
Anu, Christine 188
Anzac Day 119, 193, 202
ANZAC forces 119–120, *193*
  ingenious tinkering 138
  national identity 192–193
apology for stolen generations 103
aquatic plants 72
Araucariaceae 60–61
Arbitration and Conciliation Commission 149
arboreal marsupials 49–50
Archibald, J.F. 192, *206*, 207
architects 226–228
architecture **222–231**, *see also* housing
  Adelaide 228–229, *229*
  Brisbane 230–231, *231*
  Canberra 231, *231*
  Darwin 229–230, *230*
  Hamilton (Vic.) 224–225
  Hobart *111*, 227
  Melbourne *223*, 228
  Perth 229, *229*
  phases of settlement 222–223
  Sydney *223, 226*, 226–227
  Tasmania *227*
arid or semi-arid regions 68–69
  acacias in 68
  adaptation to 31, 46
  agriculture 38
  ants 56–57
  bandicoots and bilbies 45
  bushfires 58
  diversity *35*
  drying of Australia 30–31
  European impact *32*
  expansion 89
  fauna 46
  population growth 88
  skin bags for carrying water 92
  spinifex grasslands hunters and prey 56–57
  woodland communities 68–69
aristocracy, *see also* Queen Elizabeth II
  absence in Australia 194
armed services *123, see also* ANZAC forces; defence
  women in World War II 122
art galleries 212

arts, *see also* Aboriginal art; indigenous art; painting
  media and the arts **204–221**
Ashes (cricket trophy) 236, *237*
Asian immigrants 199, *199*, 200, *see also* Chinese immigrants
  fears of 117, 124
  federation and 145
Asian nations, trade with 156, 170
assimilation (absorption), *see also* stolen generations
  indigenous Australians 96
  migrants 125
assisted packages for British migrants 200
astronomy 133–134, *134*
Atherton Tablelands 72
athletics *243*, 244
Atriplex spp. 69
ATSIC 155, 188
AUSSAT 1 and 2: *141*
Australasian Antarctic Expedition 75
Australia
  age of culture 190
  area 28
  colonial beginnings 105
  expansion 110–111
  exploration and discovery 93
  Flinders uses the name 108
  flora *60*
  food 196–197
  frontier expands 108–112
  isolation 92
  issues for the future 157
  a new society 113–118
  Australia Act of 1986: 156
  Australia Day 144, 202
  First Fleet arrives 105
  Bicentenary celebrations 128
  Day of Mourning 1938: 97
  Australia II (boat) 128
Australian Aboriginals League 97
Australian Aboriginals Progressive Association 97
Australian Broadcasting Commission (ABC) 186, 218, 219
Australian Capital Territory (ACT) 150, 151
Australian character *190*, 190–191, 193, 194–195, *see also* national identity
Australian Country Party 153
Australian Democrats 129, 154
Australian dollar 171
Australian Film Development Corporation 217
Australian Football League 239
Australian Housing Survey 169
Australian Institute of Sport *242, 243, 244, 245*
Australian Labor Party 118, 125, *127*, 152–153, *see also* labor governments; Labor Party

Australian National Gallery *231*
Australian Rules 238–239,
    238–239, 240
Australian Technology Park *141*
authors 206
autobiographies 207–208
aviation 116, 135, *135*
avifauna, *see* birds
Ayers House (Adelaide) 228

B

Babe (movie) 217, *217*
bag-making, indigenous 183
Baker, Snowy 193
ball and chain *106*
Ballarat 112
banana republic 128
Bancroft, Joseph and Thomas 139
bandicoots *48*, 48–49
    extinctions 58, 59
    first appearance of 45
bands 215
Bangarra Dance Theatre 187, *187*,
    188
banks, foreign 164
Banks, Sir Joseph 60, 130, 134
banksias *62, 65*
Barcaldine (Qld) strike 118
bark paintings 181
Barrens 66
Barunga region (NT) 179, 182–183
basketball 245, *245*
    wheelchair *244*
Bass, George 108
Batman, John *110*, 110–111
bats 43, 44, 50–51
battles, *see* wars
beach volleyball *233*
beaches 35, *35*
    'Bronzed Aussie' culture 193
Bean, C.E.W. and the Anzac legend
    119
Belgian Antarctic Expedition 74
Bell Shakespeare Company 211
Benaud, Richie 237
Bendigo *112*
Bennett, Gordon 186
Beresford, Bruce 217
betting 120, 234–235
bettongs 58, 59
Bicentenary celebrations 128, *128*
Big Guitar, Tamworth *214*
Big Scrub rainforest
bilbies 49
billabongs (permanent waterholes)
    71, 72, *113*
billiards 235
biodiversity 38, 59
biographies 207–208
biological control 59, 139
biological research 139
bird fossils 44

birds 43, 44, 52–54
    Antarctic region 80–81, 82, 83
    diversification 53–54
    evolution 45
    extinctions 58
    Gondwana 54
    inland Australia 46
    introduced species 59
    primitive 52–53
    publications about 206
Black Caesar (Madagascan convict)
    199
black deaths in custody 102
'blackbirding', *see* kanakas
Blainey, Geoffrey
    Asian migration 124–125
    Tyranny of Distance 191
Blaxland, Wentworth and Lawson
    108
Blue Hills (radio serial) *219*
Blue Mountains 62, 108, *108, 109*
blue-tongued lizards *46*
bluebushes *68, 69*
Blundstone boot factory *167*
boab trees 70, *70*
body painting *86, 88*, 175
Bodyline cricket series 236–237
bogs 64
Bond, Alan 128
Bond University 128
Bondi beach *233*
boomerangs, early fragments
    preserved 88
boot-heels
    'Australian to my…' 126
    'British to the…' 125
Borchgrevink, Carsten 74
botany, *see* flora
Botany Bay
    Banks and settlement at 130–131
    First Fleet 105
    named for the variety of plants 60
bowerbirds *44*
bowls (game) *234*
box kites *135*
boxing 235
Boyd, Arthur *213*, 213
Boyd, Robin *229*
Bradman, Don 236–237, *237*
brain drain 138, 141, 160
breeding plants and animals 137
bridges *222–223*
Brisbane
    architecture 197–198, 230–231,
    231
    settlement 107
British Antarctic Expedition 74
British exploration 93–94, 105
British heritage
    Anglophilia 194
    architecture 228
    assumptions in constitution 146
    common law 149

evolution to nationhood 156
    food 196–197
    government 144, *146, 147*
    public administration 155
    shift away in trade 125
British immigrants 116, 124, 200
'British to the boot-heels' 125
broadcasting 210–211, *218*,
    218–219
broadsides (single sheet newspapers)
    220
Bronzed Aussies *192*, 193
Broome (WA) bombed 123
brown falcon *58*
Brown, Robert 131
brush-turkey 53
brushtail possums 49, *49*
Buddhist temples *124*
budgerigar 53
buffalo *59*
Builders Labourers' Federation green
    bans 127
buildings, *see* architecture
bull riding *99*
Bulletin 207
    illustration 213
    influence of 192
Burke and Wills's expedition 109
Burley Griffin, Walter 228, 231
Burma and Thailand railway 122
burning, *see* fire
burrowing animals 46, 49
bush foods *176*, 177, *see also*
    hunting and gathering
    boab trees *70*
    restaurants 197
Bush, The, and national identity
    113–114, 192
bushfires, *see* fire
bushrangers *113*, 113–114
'business' (closed ceremonies) 188

C

cabbage tree palms *61*, 62
cabinet *147*, *see also* ministries
Cainozoic era 27, 30
calicivirus 139
Calwell, Arthur 124
camels *110*
Campbell, Robert Jnr 186
Canberra
    architecture 231, *231*
    as national capital 151
cane toads 139
cannons *131*
canoes 87, 90, 92
Capitol House (Melbourne) 228
car racing *219*
Carey, Peter 206, 209
carnivorous marsupials 48
carp, European 59, *139*
carvings, *see* rock art

Cascade Brewery *227*
cassowaries 52, *52*
casual work 166–167
casuarinas less dominant after fires
    32
Catholicism 199
Cawley (born Goolagong), Evonne
    245, *245*
celebrations 202
    tall ships *128*
central government, *see* federal
    government
Central Land Council office *101*
Centre for Alternative Technology
    103
ceremonies 91, *91*, 181, 188
    body painting *86, 88*
Chamberlain, Azaria 128
Chambers Pillar *25*
Channel 7: 218, 219
Channel 9: 218, 219
Channel 10: 219
Chappell, Ian 237
character, *see* Australian character
Chauvel, Charles *216*
cheese making *161*
Chenopodiaceae 69
Chifley, Ben 218, *218*
children
    benefits and taxes 168
    childcare industry *169*
    indigenous *98*
    literature 208
    surf life-savers *234*
Chinese immigrants *195*, 200
    1980s 124
    goldrushes 112, *112*, 116, 117,
    117, 200
Christian missionaries, *see* missions
    and settlements
churches *106, 116, see also* religion
    architecture 222, *224–225, 226*
cities 114–115, *see also* urbanisation
citizenship 98, 156
city councils 155
city planning 222, 226–231
    Adelaide 228
    Brisbane 230–231
    Canberra 231
    Darwin 229–230
    Hamilton (Vic) *224–225*
    Hobart 227
    Melbourne 227
    Perth 229
    Sydney 226
city versus the bush 192
Clark, Belinda 237
Clarke, Marcus 207, 208
Clarke, Reverend W.B. 133
clay for Wedgwood medallion 131,
    131
climate 33–34
    Antarctica and 77, 79

change and indigenous Australians 89
oceans and 35
Tertiary period 28
trends over past 50 million years *30*
clothing factories *158*
coal deposits and mining 26, 28
coal mining *158, 160*
Coalition governments 154
coastal areas 35, *191*
Customs Service *201*
mangroves 73
sand dunes *30*, 31, *65, 65*
sea and other water rights 178
sea level changes 31, 32, 87
south-west Australia 66
coats of arms *151*
Cobb and Co. 115
cockatoos 53
cod (fish) 55
coins *128, 145*
Collingwood Town Hall *155*
Collins, David 106–107
Colombo Plan 200
colonisation 93–96, 105, 110, *see also* settlement
customs and trade barriers 145
Moreton Bay *94*
new colonies 106–107, 110
states 144
Commonwealth Constitution, *see* Constitution
Commonwealth Games 244
Commonwealth government, *see* federal government
Commonwealth Scientific and Industrial Research Organisation (CSIRO) 140
communications 115–116, *see also* Internet
telegraph line 110, 115, *137*, 221
Communist Party 122, 125
compulsory voting 154
computers *168*, 169
Coniston massacre 95
conscription
Vietnam War 126, 127
World War I 119
conservation 38-41
attitudes to 59
conservation movement 127
Constitution 145, 146, 147, 149, *see also* referenda
dismissal of Whitlam government and 127
Constitutional Convention 157
consumption tax, *see* GST
continental drift 26, 27
convergent evolution 43
convicts 105, 106
Anglo-Saxon origins 199
end of transportation 111

labour in WA 107
literature about 206–207
prison architecture 222
theatre 210
Cook, Captain James 105
Antarctic discovery and 74
contact with Aboriginals *93*, 93–94
scientific research 130
Coolgardie safes 136
Coonawarra wineries *163*
Cooperative Research Centres 140–141
copper-flotation plants *41*
Copper Mines of Tasmania *166*
copyright law, indigenous art 189
coral reefs 36–37, *36–37*
sea level changes 31
cormorants 82
corporate high-flyers 128
corporatisation of government activities 164
corroborees 188
cotton industry 116–117
councils 155, *155*
Countdown 215
counter-culture 126, *127*
country areas, *see* rural areas
'country', importance of 178–181, *see also* Bush, The; land
court sports 245
courts 149, *149*
High Court 149, 156
Cowra, NSW *111*
Japanese prison camp *122*
Cox, Paul *217*
crabeater seals 81
Crescent Head, NSW *178*
crescent nailtail wallabies *59*
Cretaceous era 27
cricket *236*, 236–237, *237*
behaviour of athletes 233
history 232
women's team 237
Crimean War defences 115
crocodiles 44, 55, *55, 71*
crow family 54
Crown Land, native title and 102
CSIRO 140
cultural cringe 194
culture **190–203**, *see also* arts
Aboriginal diversity 92
multicultural society 125
nature of Australian 204
Cunningham, Allan 109
Currency Press 206
currency 126, 128
trading 171
currents, ocean *34*, 35
Curtin, John 122, 123
Customs Service *201*
cyclones 34, 229–230

D
'Dad and Dave' stories 192, 207, *208, 217*
Daintree World Heritage Area 72
Dampier, William 93, *93*, 105
description of journey 206, 212
dance, indigenous 175, *175*, 181, *186*, 187, *187, 188*
Darling Downs 109
Darwin
architecture 229–230, *230*
bombed in World War II 123
cyclones 229–230
settlement 110
Dasyurids 48
Dawes Point *131*
Day of Mourning (Australia Day 1938) 97
de Groot, Captain 121
de Quiros, Pedro Fernandez de 104
de Torres, Luis Vaez de 104
deaths in custody 102
decimal currency 126
defence, *see also* armed services
after Crimean War 115
federation and 145
Demidenko, Helen 208
democracy, struggle for 144
Democratic Labor Party 125, 153
Democrats, Australian 129, 154
demonstrations, *see* marches and demonstrations
Depression 121, *121*
deregulation 128, 164
desert, *see* arid or semi-arid regions
devils, Tasmanian 45, 48, 51
Devils Marbles, NT *176*
Dhuwa moiety *179*, 179–180, 183
didgeridoos *174*, 182, *182, 185*
guide to playing 189
diggers, Australian troops known as 119
Dimboola 211
dingoes 51
arrival in Australia 32, 90
blamed for baby's disappearance 128
dinosaurs *42, 43*
diprotodontid marsupials 32, 44, 45, 89
directors, film *217*
disabled athletes 244, *244*
discovery, *see* exploration and discovery
diseases spread by settlers 95
dismissals
Lang government 121
Whitlam government 127, *127*, 148
DLP (Democratic Labor Party) 125, 153
Dobell, William *213*
Dodson, Pat 103

dollar, Australian 171
floating of 128
dolphins 44
domestic work 160
Donahoe, Bold Jack 113
doves *54*
Dreaming *176*, 176–177
male artists and 183
rock art 179, 180
sacred sites 178–179
drinking restrictions 120
dromornithids 44
droughts *33*, 34, *see also* rainfall
drying of Australia 30–31
dry regions, *see* arid or semi-arid regions
dry sclerophyll forest 62, 65
dry tropics 70–71
dryland salinity 39
dugongs 51
dung beetles 139
Dunlop, Edward 'Weary' 123
Durham, Judith 214
Dutch exploration 93, 104
publications 212
Duyfken 93, 104

E
early settlers, *see* settlement
earnings, *see* income
earthquakes 34
east coast, subtropical 65
Eastern Highlands 25, 26
eating patterns, *see* food
echidnas *47*, 48
economic policies 128, 164–165
ALP 129, 152
Liberal–National Party 153
economy **158–171**
early years 158
geology important to 28
goldrushes 112
Great Depression 121, *121*
World War II 122
egalitarian society 190, 194
egg-laying mammals (monotremes) 47–48
elapids 44, *44*
electoral system 154–155
elephant seals 82, *82*
Elizabeth II *149*, *see also* governors-general
relieved of her powers 156
visit to Australia *194*
embassies *151*
emperor penguins 80, *80*
employment 167, *167*, *see also* unemployment
emus 52, *52, 68*
Endeavour 105
engineering 138, *see also* science and technology

English exploration 93–94, 105
engravings, see rock art
environment, see also land
    management
    attitudes to 59
    changes in Quaternary period
        31–32
    conservation 38–41, 59, 127
    fauna adaptations to 46
    Gordon River below Franklin 128
    human adaptation to 33
    hunting impact on 88
    movements 127
environment and architecture 223
    Adelaide 228–229
    Brisbane 230
    Darwin 230
    Hobart 227
    Perth 229
    Sydney 227
estuaries and rivers
    life in 55
    mangroves 73
etchings 213
ethnic society, see multicultural society
ethnic waves, see immigrants
eucalypts 32, 60
    alpine areas 64, 64
    arid or semi-arid regions 68, 69
    dry sclerophyll forest 62
    dry tropics 70–71
    jarrah forests 66
    koalas in forests 49
    lemon-flowered gum 61
    paintings on bark from 181
    response to fire 61
    south-east Australia 62–63
    south-west Australia 66, 66, 67
    subtropical east coast 65
    Tertiary period 28
    wet tropics 72
eucalyptus oil 133
Eureka Stockade 112
European carp 59
European exploration, see exploration
    and discovery
European immigrants 116, 124,
    124, 200–201, see also British
        immigrants; Irish immigrants
    Greek and Italian 194, 200–201,
        201
    Jewish 199–200, 200
    origin of Australian culture 204
Evatt, Dr H.V. 'Doc' 153, 157
evolution
    birds 53–54
    convergence 43
    interglacials 45
Executive government 147–148
exotic animals, see introduced (feral)
    animals
expansion 110–111
expenditure, see spending patterns

exploration and discovery 93,
    108–110
    Aboriginal contacts 90
    Antarctica 74–75
    Captain Cook 130
    landward 108–110
    maritime 104–105
    publications 206, 212
    surveying and 131
exports 170, 170
    Asian-Pacific nations 156
    wine 162
extinctions 58–59, 58–59
    end of Cretaceous 27
    ice ages 31
    plants 61

F

factory workers 167
Fairfax-Associated Newspapers,
    television station licences 218
Fairfax family 221
farming, see agriculture (farming)
Farr-Jones, Nick 239–240
Farrer, William 136
fauna 42–59
    adaptations to environment 46
    Antarctic region 80–83
    Asian immigrants 44
    coral reefs 37
    extinct and endangered 49,
        58–59, 89
    Gondwana 27, 42–43
    publications 212
Fawkner, John Pascoe 111
FCAATSI (Federal Council for the
    Advancement of Aboriginals and
    Torres Strait Islanders) 98–99
federal government 147–148, see also
    Constitution
    Aboriginal Affairs 98–99
    Gordon River development 128
    Howard Coalition 102, 103, 129,
        153
    labor governments 118, 121, 152
    power 151
federal law 149
Federal–State relations 151
federation 118, 144–146, 145
    sport as a unifying factor 232
Federation bungalows 223
feldmark (alpine area) 64
females, see women
Female Eunuch 127
feral animals, see introduced (feral)
    animals
fibre arts 182–183, 183
fighting, see wars
figs (Ficus) 65
film industry 211, 216–217
financial deregulation 128, 164
financial markets 171

financial services 159–160
fine arts 212–213
fire
    droughts and 34
    firefighting 167
    indigenous Australians 32, 58, 88,
        177
    plants' response to 32, 61, 130
    Sydney bushfires 34
First Fleet 105, 130, 131
First World War, see World War I
Fisher, Andrew 118, 119
fishes 55
    introduced species 59
fishing 35, 40
    indigenous Australians 91, 91, 177
    Macassans 93
flags 156, 156
    indigenous 97, 157, 174
Flinders, Matthew 108, 131
floating of the dollar 128
floodplains in Kakadu National Park
    71
floods 34
flora 60, 60–73
    ancient 27–28, 60–61
    Antarctic region 78, 79
    arid or semi-arid regions 35
    publications about 206
    response to fire 32, 61, 130
    scientific exploration 131
    soils and 34–35
Florey, Sir Howard 134, 134, 138
flour mills 222
flying, see aviation
Flying Doctor Service 116
flying foxes (fruit bats) 50, 50
Flynn, John 116
food 196–197, 196–197
    indigenous Australians 70, 176,
        176–177, 196, 197
food-collecting techniques 91
football codes 238–241
foreign banks 164
foreign debt 171
foreign exchange market 171
foreign investment 170–171, 171
forests 33, 40, 40, see also rainforests
    logging 58, 65
Fort Denison 115
Fortunes of Richard Mahony 208
fossils
    ants 42
    bats 50
    birds 43, 44, 54
    monotremes 47
    relatives of hedgehogs 43
    Riversleigh fossil deposits 28, 31, 50
France, see French exploration
Franklin, Sir John and Lady 132
Fraser Island 30
Fraser, Malcolm 128, 153
    government elected 127

free settlers 106, 110, 116-118, see
    also immigrants
    Adelaide a model town for 111
    goldrushes 112, 116
free trade vs protectionism 158
Freedom Ride 99
Freeman, Cathy 234
French exploration 105, 133
    perceived as threat 106
frilled lizard 56
frogs 43, 43, 46
fruit bats (flying foxes) 50, 50
fur seals 51, 51, 82–83
'fuzzy-wuzzy angels' 123, 123

G

galahs 46
galaxiids 55
Gallipoli 119
    ingenious tinkering 138
    national identity 192–193
gambling 120, 234–235
gaols, see prisons
gathering, see hunting and gathering
gatherings (Aboriginal people), see
    ceremonies
Gay and Lesbian Mardi Gras 127, 202
gay liberation 127
Gaze, Lindsay and Andrew 245
GDP per capita 168
gender differences, see also women
    indigenous art 182–183, 188
    national identity masculine
        192–193
    work 166, 167, 167, 168
genetic improvement 136
gentoo penguins 83, 83
geologic exploration 132
geologic history 25–28
    ice ages 30–32
geological research 133
German immigrants 116
ghost bat 51
Giles Corridor 56
Gill, ST 213
glaciers 78, 78
gliding possums 49
global warming, Antarctic research 77
globalisation
    economic issues 164, 170–171
    fashion 193
    Internet and indigenous issues
        188–189
goannas 56, 56
gold mining, opencut 170
goldrushes 112, 112, 117
    immigrants 116, 200
    money for the arts from 212
    paintings 210, 213
    science and 132
    theatre 210

golf 234
Gondwana *26*, 27, 78
   birds 52, 54
   fauna 42–43
   flora 60
   geologic history 26
   monotremes 47
goods and services tax (GST) 129,
   151, 165
Goolagong (now Cawley), Evonne
   245, *245*
Gordon River below Franklin 128
gorges 70, *71*
Gorton, John Gray 126
government **144–157**, *see also*
   ministries
   Aboriginal policies 96
   British influences *146, 147*
   contribution to economy 160
   local *155*, 155
   responses to globalisation 171
   trend to small 164
   Westminster system 152
Government Houses *144, 229, see
   also* Parliament Houses
governors and governors-general
   147–148, 150
grain silos *38*
Grampians Mountains 62
grass trees *62*
grasses in Antarctic regions 79
grasslands *66–67*, 68, *69*, 70
grazing animals
   effect on environment 38
   kangaroo family 50
Great Barrier Reef 36–37, *36–37*
   management problems 37
   sea level changes and 31
Great Depression 121, *121*
Greek immigrants 200–201, *201*
green bans 127
Greens (political party) 154
Greenway, Francis 226–227
Greer, Germaine 127, 208, *209*
grevillea *67*
Groot, Captain de 121
GST (goods and services tax) 129,
   151, 165
guerilla warfare, *see* wars
Gulf of Carpentaria 109
gymnastics *242*
gymnosperms 60–61
Gyngell, Bruce 218

H

Hall, Ben 113
Hamersley Ranges 53, *69*
Hamilton, Jacinta *245*
Hamilton (Vic.)
   architecture 224–225, *224–225*
   state school *164*
hand stencils 179, 180

Hanson, Pauline 125, 129, 154
harbours, architecture and 226
Hargrave, Lawrence 135, *135*
Hargraves, Edmund 112
Hartog, Dirck 104
Hawke, Bob 128, 129
   on America's Cup 233–234
Hawkesbury sandstone flora 62
headdresses 175
heads of state
   governors-general as 147–148
   models for in a republic 157
   Queen Elizabeth II *149*, 156, *194*
healing techniques, *see* medicine
health care, private 165
Heard Island 78, 79, *79*, 82
heath 64, 65
Heidelberg School 212
helicopter servicing *166*
Henty family 110
Herald and Weekly Times 221
herbivorous marsupials 48–49
Hewson, Dr John 129
High Court 149, 156
high-tech industries 160, 170
highwaymen, *see* bushrangers
Hills hoist rotary clothes lines 125,
   135
Hilton Hotel bombing 127
history
   indigenous **86–103**
   since European contact **104–129**
   1930s 121
   World War II and the 1940s
      122–123
   after World War II 124–125
   1950s and the Menzies years 125
   the old order changes 126–127
   1980s boom and bust 128
   towards a new millennium 128
   1990s and the future 129
Hobart
   architecture 227
   colonial architecture *111*
   fishing boats *114*
   settlement 107
   St George's church *106*
Hockney, David *205*
Holden cars 125, *125*
Holmes a Court, Robert 128
Holocene 30, 32
Holt, Harold 126
home ownership *168*, 169
Homebush Bay Olympic site *129*
honey possums 49
honeyeaters 45, 52, *52*
Horne, Donald 191
horse-drawn coaches 115
horseracing *235*
hotels *96*, 120, *120*
House of Representatives 147–148
Household Expenditure Survey 169
household spending 169

household work, unpaid 160
Houses of Parliament, *see*
   government
housing *125*, 169, 197–198,
   197–198, 222–223, *223, 225,
   227, 229, 230, 231*
   Aboriginal people *87, 98*
Hovell, William 109
Howard, John
   Aboriginal issues and 102, 103
   government 129, 153
   republic 129, 157
Hughes, William 'Billy' 119, *119*,
   152
human arrival, *see* Aboriginal people,
   arrival and spread
Hume, Hamilton 109
humpback whales 51, *51*
hunter animals 44
hunting and gathering *90*, 130, 177
   Aboriginal renaissance 91
   adaptation after arrival 87
   environmental impact 88
Huon pine 63
husbandry, *see* agriculture

I

ice ages (glacials) 30–32
   changes in fauna 45
ice in Antarctica 78
ice-making machinery 136
identity, *see also* national identity
   urban indigenous art 185–186
Ifield, Frank 214
immigrants *124, 195, see also* Asian
   immigrants; European immigrants;
      multicultural society
   early settlement 106, 110, 111,
      116–118
   goldrushes 112, 116
   influences on food 197
   literature 208
   Pacific Islanders 116–117, 200
   post-war 124, 200–201
   proposals to reduce 124–125
Immigration Act, *see* White Australia
   Policy
imports 112, 170
income 168
   decentralised wage fixing 164,
      168
   support 168
   taxes 165, 168
Indian migration 199, *199*
Indian mynahs 59
indigenous art 181–182, 188–189,
   see also Aboriginal art; Torres Strait
      Islanders, art and culture
   commercial *182*, 182–184, *183*,
      184

indigenous Australians 174, *see also*
      Aboriginal people; land rights;
      Torres Strait Islanders
   Australia Day 202
   Bicentenary marches 128
   flags *97, 157*, 174
   food *70*, 176–177, 196, 197
   history **86–103**
   medicine 176–177
   reconciliation *86*, 86, 103, 129,
      175
   sport 234–236, *236*, 239, *240*,
      241, 245
indigenous culture 88, **174–189**, *see
   also* Aboriginal culture
   music *174, 185*, 187–189
indigenous land rights, *see* land rights
Indochinese, *see* Vietnam War
Indonesians, relations with
   Aboriginals 93, 104, *188*
information technology 160, *168,
   169*
inland Australia, *see also* arid or semi-
   arid regions; remote Aboriginal
      communities
   exploration 108–110
   mallee 63
inland seas 26–27, 108, 110
interglacials 30, 45
International Geophysical Year 77
international trade, *see* trade
International Whaling Commission
   76
Internet 169
   indigenous use 188–189, *189*
introduced (feral) animals 59, *139,
   139*
   Acclimatisation Societies 59
   extinctions and 58
   fishes 59
   mammals 51
   Subantarctic islands 82
inventions 135–137, 140
invertebrates 43
investment in Australia 170–171,
   171
Irish immigrants 116
   convicts 199
   egalitarian society and 194
irrigation *39*, 41
Islanders, *see* Pacific Islanders
Italian immigrants 200–201

J

jails, *see* prisons
Japan in World War II 122, *122*, 123
jarrah forests 66
Jewish immigrants 199–200, *200*
job seekers, *see* unemployment
Johnson, Lyndon 126
journalism, *see* newspapers
judicature and legal system 149

K

Kakadu National Park 70–71
kanakas *116*, 116–117, 200
Kangaroo (Lawrence, D.H.) 190
kangaroo paws (*Anigozanthos*) 66, *66*
kangaroos 45, 46, 50, *50*
   prehistoric 44, *45*
   'farming' 41
   joeys *50*
   tooth replacement 50
karri forests 66, *66*
Keating, Paul 129
   banana republic 128
   government 129
   republic 157
Kelly, Ned 113–114, 194, *194*
   arts and 205, 206
   movies and 216
Kerr, Sir John 127, 148, *148*
Kimberley 70–71
king penguins 83
King, Philip Parker 133
King's Park (Perth) 61
Kingsford-Smith, Charles 140
Kirribilli House *153*
Knutsford, Lord 117
koalas 44, 49, *49*
Kokoda Trail 123, *123*
kookaburras *53*
Kooris *202*
Korean War 125
Kosciuzsko National Park 64
krill *76*, 77
Kronosaurus 43

L

La Pérouse, Compte Jean-François de 105
labor governments 152
   early years 118
   Great Depression 121
Labor Party (not the ALP) 118, *see also* Australian Labor Party
labour force, *see* work participation
lace monitors 56
Lacey, G. *210*
Lake Mungo 30
Lambing Flat riots *112*, 116
lamingtons *196*
land, indigenous relationships to 96, 176–181
land management *34, 58*
   agriculture *38, 39*
   conservation and 38–41
   extinctions and 58
   natural resources 41
land rights *99*, 100–102, 178, *see also* native title
   dispossession 96
   legislation 178
   restricted lands *178*

   traditional rules of 92
   Wave Hill cattle station 99–100
Land Rights Commission 101
land transport 115, *see also* railways
landforms in Antarctica 78
landscape *33, see also* soils
   Aboriginal people and 176, 178–179, 183–184
   Heidelberg School 212–213
Lang, Jack 121
languages 93, 198
law 149
Lawler, Ray 210
lawn bowls *234*
lawnmowers 137
Lawrence, D.H. 190
Lawson, Blaxland, and Wentworth 108
Lawson, Henry 192, *206*
leaf-eaters, *see* herbivores
legal system 149
Legislative Assemblies 144
Legislative Councils 144
legless lizards 56
Leichhardt, Ludwig 109, *133*
leisure activities 120
leopard seals 80, 81, *81*
Liberal Party 153
licence fees to mine gold 112
lichens in Antarctica 79
Light, Colonel William 111, 222, 228
lighthouses *222*
Lindrum, Walter 235
Lindsay, Lionel *212*
Lindsay, Norman *207*, 208
linguistics, *see* language
liquor laws 120
literature 190, 206–209
livestock for export *170*
living standards 168–169
lizards *46*, 56–57
local government, voting for 155, *155*
loggerhead turtles *37*
logging *58*, 65
lorikeets 53
lotus flower *71*
Lower House 147–148
Lucky Country 191
Luhrmann, Baz 217
lungfish 55
Lyons, Joe 121

M

Mabo Case 96, 101–102, 149, 178
macaroni penguin 83
MacArthur, General Douglas 123
Macarthur, John and Elizabeth 137
Macassans (of Sulawesi) 93, 104, *188*
MacDonnell Ranges 54

Macfarlane Burnet, Sir Frank 139
Mackellar, Dorothea *208*
Macquarie, Governor Lachlan *108*
   architecture 226, 227
Macquarie Island 78, 79, 82
macropods, *see* kangaroos; wallabies
Magic Pudding 207, 208
magistrates 149
Malangi, David 189
males, *see* men
mallee 63
malleefowl 52–53, *53*
mammals 47–51
   desert 46
   extinctions 58
   introduced species 51
   Quaternary period 31–32
mandatory sentencing 102
mangroves 73, *73*
manufacturing industries 158, 159–160
   gender differences 167
   trade 170
mapping the continent, *see* exploration; surveying
maps, world's first atlas *104*
marches and demonstrations
   anti-war moratorium 126
   land rights *99*
   Sydney Harbour Bridge 86, *86*, 103
   Mardi Gras, Gay and Lesbian 127, 202
marine mammals 51
marine waters, *see* ocean currents
maritime exploration 104–105
   Aboriginal people 87
   Bass and Flinders 108
maritime strike of 1890: 118
marketing boards 158
marsupial lion 32
marsupial moles 43
marsupials 44, 47, 48–50
   diets 48
   fossils 43
   Gondwana 43
   megafauna 32
   reproduction 46, 49
masculinity in the national identity 192–193
masks 175
massacres of Aboriginals 95, *95*
Masters games *233*
mateship 190, 193
Mawson, Douglas 75, 77
   hut *75*
   wind recordings 79
mayors 155
McBride, Dr William 139
McKay, Heather 235
McMahon, William 100, *153*
McNamara, Dame Jean 139
meat-ants 57

Mechanics Institutes 222, *224*
media and the arts **204–221**
media ownership 221
medicine
   Flying Doctor Service 116
   indigenous Australians 176–177
   Nobel Prize winners 134
   research 139
megafauna (large animals) 32, 45, *45*
   decline and extinction of 45, 89
   impact of early Aborigines 32
megapods 52–53
Melaleuca viridiflora 70
Melba, Nellie *204*
Melbourne *114, see also* Port Phillip Bay
   architecture 222, *223*, 227–228, *228*
   founded 110–111
   growth 114
   Olympic Games 125, 242–243, *243*
   rivalry with Sydney 114
   science and 132
Melbourne Cup 120, 234–235
men, *see also* gender differences
   indigenous art 182–183
   workforce *166*, 166–167
Meninga, Mal *241*
men's business 188
Menzies, Sir Robert Gordon 125, 153, *153*
   currency options 126
   World War II 122
merino sheep-breeding 137
meteorological research *79*
mice 51
microbats 50–51
Middle East immigrants 124
migrants, *see* immigrants
Miller, George 217
mimi (spirits) 180
mineral resources 28, *28*
   copper-flotation plant *41*
   Western Australia 25
'Ming' dynasty *153*
mining 158, *158, 170, see also* goldrushes
   Antarctica 76–77
ministries *146*, 147, 155
   Billy Hughes *152*
Minogue, Kylie 214, 215, *215*
missions and settlements 95, 95–96, *96*
   stolen generations 103
Mitchell, Sir Thomas 136
moiety *179*, 179–180, 183
monarchy 144
monotremes 47–48, *see also* echidnas; platypuses
Moore, Maggie *211*
Moreton Bay settlement *94*, 107
mosses 64

motor vehicles (utes) 137
mound-building birds 52–53
Mount Kosciuszko 133
movie industry 211, 216–217
Mt Spurgeon black pine 73
Mt Stromlo Observatory 134
Mt York road construction 109
mulga 68
multicultural society 191, 199–201,
    200, see also immigrants
    celebrations 202
    initially British–Irish 116
    literature 208
    migrant policy 125
    SBS television 219
Mundey, Jack 127
municipal councils 155, 155
Murdoch family 221
museums 131, 131, 140
music 175
    indigenous 174, 185, 187–189
    popular 214–215
Muttaburrasaurus 42
Myilly Point Historic Precinct 230,
    230
myrtle beech 63
myxomatosis virus 139

N

Namatjira, Albert 98, 183, 183–184
national anthem 127
national capital 151
National Competition Policy 164
national flag 156
national identity 191, see also
    Australian character
    Anzac legend 119
    biographies and novels 208
    geologic history and 25
    national celebrations 202
    the bush 113–114
    Whitlam government and 127
National Museum 140, 231
national parks and reserves 61, 65
National Party 153–154
National Soccer League (NSL) 241
national song 156
nationhood, evolution to 156–157
native dog, see dingo
native title 178, 178
    extinguishment 102
    Mabo Case 101–102, 149, 178
    terra nullius 101, 105, 178
    Wik Case 102
Native Title Act 102, 178
natural hazards, see droughts; floods
natural history 206, 207, 212
natural resources 41, see also mineral
    resources
navigators, see exploration and
    discovery
netball 245

New Australians, see immigrants
new economy 160
New Guinea
    communication with 89
    World War II 123, 123
new society 113–118
New South Wales, see also Sydney
    claimed for Britain 105
    representative government 144–145
New Zealand, not in federation 145
Newcastle (NSW) 160
News Corporation 171, 221
newspapers 220–221
Nicholls, Doug 239
night parrots 59
Nobel Prize winners 134, 209
nocturnal animals 46
Nolan, Sidney 114, 205
non-English speaking immigrants
    124
non-profit sector 160, 165
Norfolk Island 104
Northern Territory, see also Darwin
    Central Land Council office 101
    dry tropics 70–71
    Land Rights Commission 101
    mandatory sentencing 102
    self-government 150, 150
    settlement 110
Norton family 120, 221
novels, see literature
NSL (National Soccer League) 241
numbats 48

O

observatories, see astronomy
occupations 166, 167, 168
ocean currents 34, 35
oil extraction from Antarctica 77
O'Keefe, Johnny 214, 214
Olympic Games 129, 242–243
    Cathy Freeman 234
    celebratory graffiti 234
    flame 242
    icons in ceremony 114, 137,
        204–205
    Melbourne 125, 242–243, 243
    Paralympic Games 232, 244,
        244
    spectators 193
    spirit of competition 232
    tent embassy during 100
On Our Selection (Rudd) 192
One Nation 125, 129, 154
    multicultural society and 201
Opera House (Sydney) 227
optical fibre production 141
outback, see inland Australia
outdoor events 193, 204
over-employment 167
Overland Telegraph Line 110, 115,
    137, 221

Oxley, Surveyor-General John
    108–109
ozone hole discovered in Antarctica
    77

P

P & O Steam Navigation Company
    115
Pacific Islanders
    kanakas 116, 116–117
    migrants 200
    trade with 156
Pacific Ocean in World War II 122
painting 204, 212–213
    early settlement 212
    Heidelberg School 212
    Hockney, David 205
    indigenous 88, 91, 92, 98, 175,
        175, 179, 179–181, 184
    modern 213
Palm Valley 61
palms 62
Palorchestes 45
Pangaea 42
paperbarks 70, 71
Papua New Guinea, see New Guinea
Papunya Tula school 182, 184, 189
Paralympic Games 232, 244, 244
parasites in Antarctica 80
Parkes radio telescope 134, 134
Parliament Houses 151, see also
    Government Houses
    Canberra 147, 152, 154, 156,
        231
    Darwin 150
    Hobart 151
Parramatta, settlement 106
parrots 53, 53, 54
part-time work 166–167
pastoral leases and native title 102
Paterson, 'Banjo' 192, 207
pavlova 197
Pay TV 219
penguins 77, 80–83, 80–81, 83
perch (fish) 55, 59
perentie lizard 56
performing arts, see visual and
    performing arts
Peron, Francois 107
Perth, architecture 229, 229
petaurids 49
petrels 80–83 83
Phar Lap 232
Phillip, Captain Arthur 144, 144
    arrival in Australia 105
    landed unopposed 94
    on value of settlement 106
Photonics CRC 141
physical geography 25–41, 28
    Antarctica 78–79
pickups (utes) 137

pig-nosed turtles 55
'pindan' (woodlands) 70
pine plantations 40
pineapple grass 64
place, see land
placental mammals 43, 47, 50
planigale 48
plant foods eaten, see bush foods
plants, see flora
platypuses 47, 47, 132, 132
plays 210–211, see also theatre
    Currency Press 206
Pleistocene fauna 45
political activity by indigenous
    people 97
    art and 175, 186
political history 144–146
political parties 152–154
    Great Depression 121
    minor 154
political system 152–155
popular arts 204–205
popular music 214–215
population
    to 1900: 116
    increase during goldrushes 112
    indigenous Australians 88–89,
        174, 202
    Melbourne 114
'populate or perish' 124–125
Port Arthur 106, 107
    memorial pond 129
Port Kembla steelworks 165
Port Macquarie 106, 109
Port Phillip Bay settlement 106–107,
    110, see also Melbourne
possums 43, 44, 49, 49
post-war migrants 200–201
potoroos 49–50
pouched mammals, see marsupials
precipitation, see rainfall
predators 44
preferential voting system 154–155
President, see head of state; republic
press barons, era of 221
press conferences 154
price and income accords 128
prickly pear 139
primary industries 158–159
prime ministers 147, 148, see also
    names of specific prime ministers,
    eg Keating, Paul
print media 220, 220–221, 221
printing presses 220, 220
prisoners, Aboriginal 102
prisoners of war 123
prisons
    architecture 222
    privatisation of 164–165
    Stuart Town Jail 102
private sector 160, 164–165
proportional representation 155

Proteaceae *28*, 60
    adaptation to poor soils 62
    fossils 60
    Gondwana 27
    response to fire 61
protection boards, *see* Welfare Boards
protectionism 158
protest movements *126*, 126–127
Protestants 120, 199
public administration 155, 164
public sector contributions 160,
    164–165
publishing 206
pubs, *see* hotels
Pukumani poles *91*

Q

Qantas *115*, 116
quail-thrush 53
Quaternary period 27, 30, 31–32
Queen Elizabeth II *149*, *see also*
    governors-general
    relieved of her powers 156
    visit to Australia *194*
Queen Victoria Building 227
Queensland, *see also* Brisbane
    housing 197–198
    National Party 154
    settlement 107
    wet tropics 72–73
Queenslander houses 198, 230, *231*
Quiros, Pedro Fernandez de 104
quokkas *43*

R

rabbits 59, 139
racecourse totalisators *139*, 140
racism and immigration 116, 117,
    124
radio 210–211, 218, *218*
railways 115, *115*, 138, *138*
    architecture *229*
Rainbow Valley Conservation
    Reserve *25*
rainfall 33–34, *see also* drought
    arid or semi-arid regions 68
    ocean currents and *34*
    trends in *30*
rainforests *28–29*, *42*
    fruits *72*
    loss of 44–45, 58
    marsupials 49–50
    subtropical 65
    temperate 62–63, *63*
    Tertiary period 27–28
rat-kangaroos 49–50
rats 51
Rats of Tobruk 122
recessions 166

reconciliation
    friction with government 103
    marches and demonstrations 86,
        86, 129
    notions of time and 175
Reconciliation Council 103
record companies 215
red cedar (*Toona*) 40, 65
red kangaroo 46
reefs, *see* coral reefs
referenda 149, *see also* Constitution
    Aboriginal recognition 98
    Communist Party 125
    conscription 119
    republic 129, 157, 194
refrigeration inventions 136–137
refugees from the Vietnam War *199*
regional variations 198
religion, *see also* churches
    British-Irish 116
    Catholicism 199
    dissenters in Adelaide 111
    Protestantism 120, 199
remote Aboriginal communities *177*
    performing arts 181, 188, *188*
    influence on urban art 185–186
    websites 188
representative government 144–145
reptiles 44, 46, 56–57
republican movement 157, 194
    Keating government 129
    political history 144
    referendum 129, 157, 194
research and development 160
Reserve Bank of Australia
    Australian dollar 171
    painting on $1 note 189
resource exploitation in Antarctica
    76–77
restaurants *196*, 196–197
revenue raising, federal power 151
Rhododendron spp. 72
Richardson, Henry Handel 208
ringtail possums 49, *49*
rivers
    continental plates and 26
    management problems 41
Riversleigh fossil deposits (Qld) 28,
    31, 50
RMIT, architecture 228, *228*
road construction *109*, 164
rock art 88, *89*, *90*, *92*, 179–181,
    180, *181*
    ancestral beings in 179, 180
    technological changes shown in
        90–91
rockhopper penguins 83
rodents 43, 51
rodeos *190*
Roman Catholicism 199
rosellas 53
Ross seals 81

Royal Commission into Black
    Deaths in Custody 102
Royal National Park 61
royal penguin 83
Rudd, Steele 192, *192*, 207, *208*,
    217
rufous hare-wallaby 58
rugby league 240–241, *241*
rugby union 239–240
rural areas, *see also* remote Aboriginal
    communities
    Great Depression 121
    industries decline 159
    National Party 153–154

S

Sabbath day maintenance 120
sacred sites 178
sailing 235, *235*
    communications on ships 115
Salamanca Place (Hobart) 227
salinity 38–40, *39*, 58
salt lakes 27, *27*
saltbush plains 69
Salvation Army feature film 216,
    216
sand dunes, coastal *30*, 31, 65, *65*
sandplains 66–67, *66–67*
sandstone bluffs, Sydney *26*
satellites *141*
Sauvage, Louise 244
SBS television 219
science and technology **130–141**
    Antarctica 77
    indigenous 90–92, *103*
    institutions 138, 140–141
    wine industry 162
Scott, Robert Falcon 74
scribbly gums 62
scrubfowl 53
Scullin, James 121
sculpture *205*
sea and other water rights 178
sea discovery, *see* maritime
    exploration
sea level changes 31, 32, 87
sea lions 51
seals 51, *51*, 76, *77*, 80, 81, *81*,
    82–83
Second Fleet 106
Seekers 214
self-government 144–145, 156
semi-arid regions, *see* arid or semi-
    arid regions
Senate 147, *148*
services sector 159–160, *169*
    economic contribution *159*
    gender differences 167
settlement 105–107, 110 *see also*
    colonisation
    Aboriginal people and *87*, 94–95,
        95, 186

architecture 222–223
    Australian fauna and 58–59
    food 196
    housing 197–198
    land exploitation 38
    Moreton Bay *94*
    Parramatta *106*
    science and technology 131
settlements, Aboriginal, *see* missions
    and settlements
Shackleton, Ernest 74, 75
share ownership *164*, 165
shearers *118*
sheep breeding 137
shelters, Aboriginal *87*
ships, communications 115
shire councils 155, *155*
shorelines, *see* coastal areas
shrublands, *see* woodlands and
    shrublands
silos *38*, *137*
Skase, Christopher 128
sketches 213
skills-based economy 170
skin bags for carrying water 92
skinks, limb reduction in 57
skuas *83*
Skyhooks 215
Smith, Robert Bowyer 135–136
smoke bush *66–67*
snakes 44, *44*, *57*
snow country, *see* alpine areas
snow gums 64, *64*
Snowy Mountains hydroelectric
    scheme 138
Snowy River 41, 138
Snugglepot and Cuddlepie 208
soccer 241
social democratic parties, ALP as
    152
social security 168
society, *see also* culture
    indigenous art and 174–175
socioeconomic indicators 185
soils *34*, 34–35, 39
Solander, Daniel 60, 130
sole parents' income 168
songs 175, 187–188
    ceremonial 181
'sorry' (stolen generations apology)
    103
South Australia 111, *see also*
    Adelaide
south-east Australian flora 62–63
South Georgia 74–76, *76*
South Pole 74, 77
south-west Australian flora 66–67
Southcorp Wines 163
southern right whale 51
Spanish exploration 104
sparrows 59
spending patterns 169, *169*
sphagnum moss 64

spinifex grasslands *56, 56–57, 66–67,* 68, *69*
spinifex hopping mouse 46
Spofforth, Demon 236, *237*
sport *232,* **232–245**
   attitudes to *242*
   breadth of participation 233–235
   culture of 232–235
   spectators *193, 232*
   television 219
squash (game) 235
standard of living, *see* living standards
State of Origin rugby league 241
states, *see also* federation
   colonisation of 144
   Federal–State relations 151
   governments 150–151
   law 149
   powers in constitution 146
   revenue raising 151
   role of Senate 147
   statutory authorities 155
Stead, Christina *208*
steelworks *165*
Stirling, Captain James 107
Stirling Ranges 66
stock exchange *164*
stockmen *99, 113*
stolen generations (Aboriginal children removed) 103, 187
stone tools *86, 88, 88,* 90, 91
street theatre *211*
Strickland, Shirley *243*
strikes *118*
   1850-1915: 118
   Wave Hill cattle station 99–100, *100*
string bags 183
stripper harvesters 136
Strzelecki, Count Paul Edmond de 133
Stuart, John McDouall 110
Stuart Town Jail, Alice Springs *102*
students, Asian 200
stump-jump plough 135–136
Sturt, Captain Charles 109
Subantarctic islands, *see* Antarctic region; Heard Island; Macquarie Island
subtropical rainforest 65
sugar industry 116–117
Sulawesi, *see* Macassans (of Sulawesi)
Summer of the Seventeenth Doll 210
Sunday as the Sabbath 120
sundews 64
Super Pit goldmine, Kalgoorlie *170*
Supreme Courts *149*
surf life-savers *192, 203*
   Nippers *234*
surf rescue reels 140
Sutton, Henry 135
swagmen 121
swamp buffalo *59*

Swan River *107,* 107
swimming 243
Sydney
   Aboriginal people 86, 93–94
   architecture *223, 226,* 226–227
   British arrival at 105, 131
   sandstone bluffs *26*
   science and 132
Sydney 2000 Olympic Games, *see* Olympic Games
Sydney Harbour
   bicentennial celebrations *128*
   First Fleet entering *130*
   Japanese midget submarines 123
Sydney Harbour Bridge *121,* 138, *138*
   marches *86, 86,* 103
   opening 121
Sydney Mail *221*
Sydney–Melbourne rivalry 114
Sydney Morning Herald 220, 221
Sydney Opera House 227
Sydney University students on Freedom Ride 99
Sydney–Hobart yacht race 235, *235*

T

tall poppy syndrome 194
Tamworth country music festival *214*
tariffs 158, 164
Tasman, Abel 104
Tasman peninsula *105*
Tasmania, *see also* Hobart; Van Diemen's Land
   Aboriginal people in *32, 89,* 92, *94*
   architecture *227*
   cut off from mainland 89
   fauna retreated to 45
   wet sclerophyll forests 63
Tasmanian Aborigines *32, 89,* 92, *94*
Tasmanian devils 45, 48, 51
Tasmanian tigers, *see* thylacines
tawny frogmouths *54*
taxes 165, *165, see also* GST
   changes and redistribution 168
   federal right to levy 151
   living standards and 168
tea plantations *38*
Tebbutt, John 134
technology, *see* science and technology
telegraph line 110, 115, *137,* 221
Telegraph Station, Alice Springs *137*
telephone services 115–116
telescopes 134, *134*
television 218–219
temperance movement 120
temperate rainforests *28–29,* 62–63, *63*

tennis 245, *245*
tent embassies *100,* 100–101
termites 48, 57, *57*
terra nullius, see native title
territories, *see also* Australian Capital Territory (ACT); Northern Territory
   governments 150–151
terrorism 127
Tertiary period 27
The Bulletin 192, 207, 213
The Bush and national identity 113–114
The Lucky Country 191
The Seekers 214
theatre 210–211, *211*
   Currency Press 206
thorny devil 56
threatened plants 61
Thunderbolt (bushranger) *113*
thylacines (Tasmanian tigers) 38, 44, 45, 48, *48,* 51, *59*
time, notions of 175
Tjapukai dance theatre *186,* 187, *187*
Todd River *27*
Tooloom Falls 178
tools *86, 88, 88,* 90, 91
Torres, Luis Vaez de 104
Torres Strait Islanders *177, see also* indigenous Australians; Mabo case; native title
   agriculture 177
   art and culture *88,* **174–175**
   flag 174
   interchange with mainland 92
   land ownership 101–102
   population 174
   trading 90
tortoises, *see* turtles
totalisators, racecourse *139,* 140
tourism 159, *171*
   Antarctic region *76,* 77, *77*
   Great Barrier Reef 37
   wine 162
Town Hall, Collingwood *155*
town planning, *see* city planning
trade 170, *170*
   Aboriginal people *90,* 90–91
   Asian-Pacific nations 156
trade unions
   1850-1915: 118
   associated with ALP 152
   changes in membership 159
   green bans 127
   protectionism and 158
training for indigenous people *103*
trains, *see* railways
Trans-Australia railway 138, *138*
transits of Venus 134
transport 115–116, *see also* aviation; railways
transportation of convicts, *see* convicts

Treaty (Yothu Yindi) 188
tree-dwelling marsupials 49–50
tree ferns 62, *65, 72*
tree kangaroos 46
tree plantations *40*
tribunals 149
tropical cyclones 34
tropical rainforests 72, *72*
Troppo Architects 230
Truganini *94*
Truth newspaper 221
Tudor precinct, Perth 229
turtles *37,* 55, *55*
tussock grasslands, *see* spinifex grasslands
TV channels 218–219
'two-up' (game) 120, *120*
tyranny of distance in transport 115

U

ultrasound scans *139*
under-employment 167
unemployment 128, 166, 168
   Great Depression 121
unions, *see* trade unions
United Australia Party 121
United Nations 156
United States
   defense ties with 123, 156
University of Sydney *132–133*
unpaid work 167
Upper House 147, *148*
urbanisation 114–115, *191, see also* cities
   Australia 190
   indigenous art and 185–186
utes (pickups) 137

V

Van Diemen's Land, *see also* Hobart; Tasmania
   discovery and naming of 104
   farmers moved to Victoria 110
   independence from NSW 107
   settlement 106–107
Vanuatu, kanakas from *116,* 116–117
varanids in spinifex 56
vegetation, *see* flora
velvet worms 43
VFL 238
vice-regal representation, *see* governors-general
Victa mowers 137
Victoria, *see also* Melbourne
   goldrushes 112
   growth 114
   settlement 110–111
Victorian Football League 238
Vietnam War 126, *126*
   refugees *199*
   Whitlam and 127

vine forests 71
vineyards 163
visual and performing arts 175, *see also* arts; dance; music
    commercial vs ceremonial 181, 182
    indigenous 91, *175, 179, 185,* 185–186
volcanoes 26
voluntary workers 167, *167*
voting 154–155, *155*
    women 118

W

wages, *see* income
Wakefield, Edmund Gibbon 111
wallabies *43*, 59
Wallabies (rugby union) 239–240
Walls of Jerusalem (Tasmania) *31*
wallum (coastal heath) 65
Waltzing Matilda *113*
war memorials *119*
waratah *63*
warrungs (wallabies) *59*
wars, *see also* World War I; World War II
    Aboriginals and settlers 95, *95*
Warung, Price 192
water bags 92, 136
water conservation 46, *see also* arid and semi-arid areas
water-holding frogs 46
water management 41
water rats 51
water tables 39, *58*
waterholes, *see* billabongs (permanent waterholes)
Watson, Judy 186
wattles (*Acacia*) 60, *68*, 68
Wave Hill cattle station strike 99–100, *100*
weapons *90*
weather systems
    Antarctica 79, *79*
    oceans and 35
websites, indigenous 188–189, *189*
Weddell seals 80
Wedgwood medallion from Australian clay 131, *131*
weeds 65
Welfare Boards 96, 97, 103
Wentworth, Blaxland, and Lawson 108
Western Australia, *see also* Perth
    convicts 111
    geology 25
    settlement 107
Western Desert art style 184, *184*
wet and dry seasons 65, 70
wet sclerophyll forests 62, 65
wet tropics 72–73
wetlands *30*, 71, 72

whales 51, 76, *77*
wharf labourers *118*
wheat 38, 67, 136, *136, 137*
wheelchair sports 244, *244*
White Australia Policy 117–118, 200
    abandoned 124, 152
White, Patrick 208, 209, *209*
    rural themes 205
Whiteley, Brett *212*, 213
Whitlam, Gough *148, 153*
    land handover 101
    government 126–127, 148
Wik Case 102
wildfires, *see* fire
Wilkes, Charles 74
Williamson, David *210*, 211
Williamson, JC *211*
wine industry *162,* 162–163, *163*
    university wineries 161
wine tourism 162, *162*
Wollemi pine *60*, 60–61
wombats 49
women, *see also* gender differences
    basketball 245, *245*
    cricket 237
    indigenous art 182–183
    right to vote 118
    temperance movement 120
workforce 167
World War II 122
women's business 188
women's liberation movement 127
woodlands and shrublands
    arid or semi-arid regions 68–69
    dry tropics 70
    flora 66
    wet tropics 72
Woods, Reverend Julian Tenison 133
woodworking 90, *90*
wool industry *159*
Woolley, Leigh 227, *227*
work participation
    gender differences 166, 167, *167*
    migration and 124, 199
    pay and conditions 118
work patterns *166,* 166–167
working class utopia, Australia as a 190–191
world economic activity, *see* globalisation
World Series Cricket 237
World War I 119–120, *193*
    Aboriginal involvement in 98
    conscription proposed 119
    ingenious tinkering 138
    losses 120
    national identity 192–193
World War II 122–123
    Aboriginal involvement in *97,* 97–98
    Australian deaths 123

    defences *122*
    Japanese prison camp at Cowra *122*
    Middle East and Greece 122
    Papua New Guinea *123*
wowser, origin of the word 120
wrens *54*
writing, *see* literature
Wynn's Coonawarra winery *163*

X

Xanthorrhoea 62

Y

yacht races 235, *235*
Yellow Peril 117, 124
Yirritja moiety *179,* 179–180, 183
Yothu Yindi 188
Yuendumu, art movements 184, *184*

INDEX TO PART 2: PLACES IN AUSTRALIA

Abbreviations used in the index

CA   Conservation Area
CP   Conservation Park
CR   Conservation Reserve
FP   Forest Park
FR   Forest Reserve
GR   Game Reserve
NP   National Park
NR   Nature Reserve
PA   Protected Area
RP   Recreation Park
RR   Regional Reserve
SF   State Forest
SP   State Park
SR   State Reserve
SRA   State Recreation Area
WP   Wildlife Park
WPA   Wilderness Protection Area

Numbers in **bold** indicate an entry in the text

A

A1 Mine Settlement Vic 337 N1, 344 E9
Abbeyard Vic 342 B2, 344 G7
Abbieglassie Qld 558 C6
Abbotsford NSW 453 D6
Abbotsford NSW 462 G10, 464 G1
Abbotsham Tas 840 F5
Aberbaldie NSW 459 J1, 461 J9
Abercorn Qld 559 J2
Abercrombie NSW 454 C7, 456 D1, 458 C9
Abercrombie River NP NSW 454 D7, 456 D2, 458 D9
Abercrombie River NSW 458 D9
Aberdeen NSW 458 G4
Aberfeldy Vic 337 N2, 344 F10
Aberfoyle NSW 461 K7
Aberfoyle Qld 565 N5
Aberfoyle Park SA 786 D9
Abergowrie Qld 563 L8
Abermain NSW 455 L2, 459 H5
Abingdon Downs Qld 563 H6
Abington NSW 461 H7
Abminga SA 792 C1
Acacia Gardens NSW 453 A3
Acacia Ridge Qld 555 C8, 557 C3
Acacia Store NT 613 D3, 614 D5
Acheron Vic 344 D8
Acland Qld 556 A5, 559 K6
Acraman Creek CP SA 790 A5
Acton ACT 477 D3
Acton Downs Qld 565 K3
Adaminaby NSW **364**, 456 B6, 457 D5

Adavale Qld 567 M4
Adcock Gorge WA 713 J6
Addington Vic 336 B1, 339 K4
Adelaide SA **722–723**, 786 D6, 787 D6, 791 J10
Adelaide Hills Wine Region SA **754**
Adelaide Lead Vic 339 K3
Adelaide River NT **588**, 613 D5, 614 D5
Adelaide River NT 613 D2
Adelong NSW 456 A5, 457 A2, 465 P6
Adels Grove Qld 562 B8
Adjungbilly NSW 456 B4, 457 C1
Admiralty Gulf WA 713 J2
Advance Qld 567 K3
Advancetown Qld 557 E7
Adventure Bay Tas 839 C8, 843 K8
Afton Downs Qld 565 L4
Agery SA 787 A3, 791 H8
Agnes Vic 341 P8
Agnes Water Qld **514**, 561 M10
Agnew Qld 568 C5
Agnew WA 709 K7
Aileron NT 618 G4
Ailsa Vic 340 F10
Ainslie ACT 477 D2
Aireys Inlet Vic **266**, 336 D6, 339 L8
Airlie Beach Qld **514**, 560 F2
Airly Vic 342 C7
Airport West Vic 335 B2
Ajana WA 708 C7
Akuna Bay NSW 453 F2
Alawa NT 612 E3
Alawoona SA 791 N9
Alba Qld 565 L4
Albacutya Vic 340 D8
Albany WA **638**, 706 F10
Albany Creek Qld 555 B2, 557 C1
Albany Downs Qld 558 D6
Albemarle NSW 462 E9
Alberrie Creek SA 792 G8
Albert NSW 463 N9
Albert Park Vic 335 C4
Alberton SA 786 C4
Alberton Vic 342 B9
Alberton West Vic 337 P7, 342 A9
Albion Qld 555 D4
Albion Vic 335 B3
Albion Downs WA 709 K6
Albion Park NSW 455 J9, 456 G3
Albro Qld 560 C7
Albury NSW **444**, 465 M8
Alcala Qld 562 D10, 564 E1
Alcomie Tas 840 C4
Alcoota NT 619 J4
Alderley Qld 555 C4

Alderley Qld 564 D6
Aldersyde WA 705 F6, 706 E5
Aldgate SA 786 G8
Aldinga SA 787 D7, 788 A5, 791 J10
Aldinga Bay SA 787 C7
Aldinga Beach SA 787 C7, 788 A5
Aldingham Qld 565 K6
Alectown NSW 458 A6, 463 P10, 465 P1
Alehvale Qld 562 G8
Alexander Heights WA 704 D2
Alexander Morrison NP WA 706 B1, 708 D10
Alexandra Vic **324**, 344 D8
Alexandria NT 617 M7
Alford SA 787 A2, 791 H7
Alfords Point NSW 453 B8
Alfred Cove WA 704 C7
Alfred NP Vic 343 M5
Alfred Town NSW 465 N6
Algester Qld 555 D9
Ali-Curung NT 617 J10, 619 J1
Alice NSW 461 L3
Alice Downs Qld 560 A10, 565 N10, 567 N1
Alice Downs WA 713 M8
Alice Springs NT **606–607**, 619 H6
Alkira Qld 559 H6
Allambee Vic 337 M6
Allambee South Vic 337 M6
Allambi NT 619 J7
Allambie NSW 453 F4
Allambie NSW 462 E8
Allambie Heights NSW 453 F4
Allan Qld 556 B7, 559 L8
Allandale SA 792 D4
Allandy NSW 462 D4
Allans Flat Vic 345 H4
Allansford Vic 338 F8
Allawah Qld 559 J8
Alleena NSW 465 M4
Allendale Vic 336 C1, 339 K4
Allendale East SA 788 G9
Allies Creek Qld 559 J4
Alligator Creek Qld 563 N9
Allora Qld 556 B7, 559 L8
Allworth NSW 455 N1, 459 K5
Allynbrook NSW 459 J4
Alma NSW 465 H3
Alma SA 787 D3, 791 J8
Alma Vic 339 K3
Alma Park NSW 465 M7
Almaden Qld 563 K6, 569 B9
Almonds Vic 344 E4
Almoola Qld 560 E3
Almora Qld 562 C8
Alonnah Tas 839 C8, 843 K7
Alpha Qld 558 A6, 567 P6
Alpha Qld 560 C10
Alpha Qld 560 C9
Alpine NP Vic **320–323**, 342 B4, 344 G9, 843 M7
Alroy Qld 565 K8

Alroy Qld 567 M7
Alroy Downs NT 617 L7
Alsace Qld 560 G8
Alsace Qld 562 C10, 564 D1
Alstonville NSW **412**, 461 P3
Althorpe Islands CP SA 788 A2
Altona Vic 335 B5, 336 G3, 339 N6
Altona Bay Vic 335 B5
Altona East Vic 335 B4
Altona Meadows Vic 335 B5
Altona North Vic 335 B4
Alum Cliffs SR Tas 844 A6, 840 G7
Alva Qld 560 D1, 563 P9
Alva Qld 567 N2
Alvie Vic 336 A5, 339 J7
Alyangula NT 615 M6
Amamoor Qld 556 D2, 559 M5
Amanbidji NT 616 B2
Amaroo Qld 567 N2
Amata SA 789 D1
Ambalindum NT 619 J5
Ambathala Qld 567 N4
Amberley Qld 557 A4
Amboola Qld 558 D5
Ambrose Qld 561 K9
Amburla NT 618 G5
Amby Qld 558 D5
Amby Downs Qld 558 E5
Amelup WA 706 F8
Amen Corner SA 788 B3
American River SA **732**, 787 A9, 788 B4
Amery WA 705 F3, 706 E3
Amherst Vic 339 K3
Amity Point Qld 556 F5, 557 F2, 559 N7
Ammaroo NT 619 K3
Amoonguna NT 619 H6
Amor Downs Qld 565 L9
Amosfield NSW 461 K2
Amphitheatre Vic 339 J3
Amungee Mungee NT 617 H2
Anakie Qld **514**, 560 E8
Anakie Vic 336 D4, 339 L6
Anavale Qld 560 B1, 563 M10
Andado NT 619 K9
Andamooka SA 790 G1
Andamooka SA 792 F10
Anderson Vic 337 J7
Ando NSW 456 C8, 457 F9
Andoom Qld 568 B5
Andover Tas 843 K2
Andrews SA 787 D1, 791 J7
Angahook–Lorne SP Vic **264**, 336 C6, 339 L8
Angas Downs NT 618 F8
Angas Valley SA 787 F5, 791 L9
Angaston SA **754–755**, 787 E4, 791 K9
Angellala Qld 558 B5
Angellala Qld 558 C4
Angepena SA 791 K1, 793 K10
Angip Vic 340 E9

Angle Park SA 786 D4
Angle Point WA 714 E6
Angledool NSW 463 P2
Anglers Paradise Qld 557 E6
Anglers Reach NSW 456 B6, 457 D5
Anglers Rest Vic 342 E2, 345 K7
Anglesea Vic **266**, 336 D6, 339 L8
Angourie NSW 461 N5
Angurugu NT 615 M7
Anketell WA 709 H7
Anna Bay NSW 455 P2, 459 K5
Anna Creek SA 792 E7
Anna Plains WA 715 M3
Annaburroo NT 613 E4, 614 E5
Annandale NSW 453 E6
Annangrove NSW 453 A2
Annean WA 708 G5
Annerley Qld 555 D6
Anningie NT 618 G3
Annitowa NT 617 M10, 619 M2
Annuello Vic 340 G4
Anson Bay NT 613 A5
Ansons Bay Tas 841 P4
Answer Downs Qld 564 F5
Anthony Lagoon NT 617 K5
Antill Plains Qld 563 N9
Antill Ponds Tas 843 K1, 841 L10
Antwerp Vic 340 E9
Anula NT 612 F4
Apamurra SA 787 F6, 791 K10
Aparatjara Homeland SA 789 B1
Aparawatatja SA 789 A1
Apoinga SA 791 K8, 787 E2
Apollo Bay Vic **266–267**, 336 B8, 339 K9
Appealinna Station SA 791 J2
Appila SA 791 J6
Appin NSW 455 J8, 456 G2, 458 G10
Appin South Vic 341 K8
Apple Tree Flat NSW 459 L2
Applecross WA 704 C6
Apsley NSW 454 B1, 458 C5
Apsley Vic 338 B3
Apsley River NSW 461 K9
Aqua Downs Qld 558 B6
Arabella Qld 558 B5
Arakoola NR NSW 460 G4
Arakoon NSW 461 N9
Araluen NSW **364**, 456 E6
Araluen North NSW 456 E6
Aramac Qld 565 N7
Arana Hills Qld 555 B3
Aranda ACT 477 D3
Arapunya NT 619 L4
Ararat Vic **267**, 338 G4
Arawata Vic 337 L6
Arawee Qld 567 L4
Arcadia NSW 453 C1
Arcadia Vic 344 B5
Archdale Vic 339 J2
Archdale Junction Vic 339 J2

Archer River Roadhouse Qld 568 D7
Archerfield Qld 555 C8
Archervale Qld 564 G6
Archies Creek Vic 337 K7
Archipelago of the Recherche WA 707 N8
Arckaringa SA 792 C5
Arcoona SA 790 G2
Arcturus Downs Qld 560 F9
Ardath WA 706 F4
Ardeer Vic 335 A4
Ardglen NSW 458 G2
Ardlethan NSW 465 M4
Ardmona Vic 344 B4
Ardmore Qld 564 C5
Ardno Qld 558 E5
Ardno Vic 338 A6
Ardoch Qld 567 L7
Ardross WA 704 C7
Ardrossan Qld 558 A7, 567 P7
Ardrossan SA **755**, 787 B4, 791 H9
Area Vic 340 B7
Areegra Vic 340 F9
Areyonga NT 618 F6
Argadargada NT 619 M2
Argyle Qld 558 D8
Argyle Vic 339 N3
Ariah Park NSW 465 M4
Arizona Qld 562 E10, 564 F1
Arkaba SA 791 J3
Arkaroola SA **782**, 793 L10
Arkaroola–Mount Painter Sanctuary SA 793 K9
Arkaroola Village SA 793 L10
Arklay Creek Tas 841 L6
Arkona Vic 338 E1, 340 E10
Arlparra NT 619 J3
Arltunga Historical Reserve NT **607**, 619 J5
Armadale Vic 335 D4
Armadale WA 704 G10, 705 C6, 706 C5
Armatree NSW 458 A2, 460 A10
Armdobilla Qld 567 N6
Armidale NSW **412**, 461 J8
Armraynald Qld 562 C7
Armstrong Vic 338 G4
Armstrong Beach Qld 560 G4
Armuna Qld 560 E2
Arncliffe NSW 453 D7
Arnhem Land NT 615 J5
Arno Qld 567 K1
Arno Bay SA 790 F8
Arnold Vic 339 K2
Aroona SA 791 J2
Arrabury Qld 566 F5
Arranfield Qld 567 N5
Arrawarra NSW 461 N6
Arrilalah Qld 565 L9
Arrino WA 708 D9
Artarmon NSW 453 E5
Arthur Pieman CA Tas 840 A7
Arthur Range Tas 842 F6

Arthur River Tas 840 A4
Arthur River WA 705 F9, 706 D7
Arthurs Creek Vic 337 H2, 339 P5, 344 B10
Arthurs Lake Tas 844 D10, 841 J9
Arthurs Seat SP Vic 336 G6
Arthurton SA 787 A3, 791 H8
Arthurville NSW 454 A1, 458 B5
Artimore SA 791 K2
Arubiddy WA 711 C7
Arumpo NSW 464 D3
Asbestos Range NP Tas 844 B4, 841 H5
Ascot Qld 555 D4
Ascot WA 704 E4
Ascot Vale NSW 462 B8
Ascot Vale Vic 335 C3
Ashbourne SA 787 E7, 788 A6
Ashburton Vic 335 E4
Ashburton Downs WA 714 F9
Ashburton River WA 714 D8
Ashbury NSW 453 D7
Ashcroft NSW 453 A7
Ashens Vic 338 F2
Ashfield NSW 453 D6
Ashfield WA 704 E4
Ashford NSW 461 H4
Ashgrove Qld 555 C4
Ashley NSW 460 E4
Ashmont NSW 462 D9
Ashover Qld 564 D4
Ashton Qld 565 M4
Ashton SA 786 G6
Ashville SA 787 G8, 788 B7
Aspendale Vic 335 E6
Aspley Qld 555 C2
Asquith NSW 453 C2
Astrebla Downs NP Qld 564 E10
Atartinga NT 619 J4
Athelstone SA 786 G4
Atherfield Qld 565 N4
Atherton Qld **526**, 563 L6, 569 D8
Athlone Vic 337 L5
Athley WA 709 J7
Atnarpa NT 619 J6
Attadale WA 704 C7
Attunga NSW 460 G9
Attwood Vic 335 B2
Atula NT 619 M5
Aubrey Vic 340 E9
Auburn NSW 453 B6
Auburn Qld 559 H4
Auburn SA 787 D3, 791 J8
Auburn Vic 335 D4
Auburn River NP Qld 559 J3
Auchenflower Qld 555 C5
Audley NSW 453 C10
Augathella Qld 558 B4
Augusta WA **638–639**, 706 B8
Augustus Downs Qld 562 C8
Auldana SA 786 F6
Aurukun Aboriginal Community Qld 568 B7

Auski Roadhouse WA 715 H8
Austin Downs WA 708 G6
Austral Downs NT 617 P9
Australia Plains SA 787 F3, 791 K8
Australian Capital Territory **468–469**
Australind WA 705 B9, 706 B7
Auteuil Qld 565 N8
Authoringa Qld 558 B5
Auvergne NT 614 B10, 616 B1
Avalon NSW 453 G1
Avalon Vic 336 E4, 339 M7
Avenel NSW 462 A5
Avenel Vic 344 B7
Avenue SA 788 E9
Avisford NR NSW 458 D5
Avoca Qld 560 D9
Avoca Tas 841 M8
Avoca Vic **267**, 339 J3
Avoca Downs WA 707 M3
Avoca River Vic 341 H10
Avon NSW 462 D9
Avon SA 787 C4, 791 J8
Avon Downs NT 617 N8
Avon Downs Qld 560 D5
Avon Downs Police Station NT 617 N8
Avon River WA 705 C4
Avon Valley NP WA 705 D4, 706 C4
Avon Wilderness Park Vic 342 B5, 345 H10
Avondale NSW 463 H4
Avondale SA 793 J10
Avondale Heights Vic 335 B3
Avonmore Qld 560 C9
Avonmore Vic 339 M1, 341 M10
Avonsleigh Vic 337 J4
Axe Creek Vic 339 M2
Axedale Vic 339 M2
Aylmerton NSW 455 H9, 456 F3, 458 F10
Ayr Qld 560 D1, 563 P10
Ayrford Vic 338 G8
Ayton Qld 563 L4, 569 C4

B

Baan Baa NSW 460 E8
Babakin WA 706 F5
Babbiloora Qld 558 C2
Babinda NSW 463 L8
Babinda Qld 563 M6, 569 E9
Bacchus Marsh Vic 336 E2, 339 M5
Back Creek Vic 345 H4
Back River NR NSW 459 H2
Back Springs NSW 463 H2
Back Yamma NSW 465 P2
Backstairs Passage SA 787 B9, 788 B4
Backwater NSW 461 K6
Backwell NSW 462 B9
Badalia Qld 564 C7
Baddaginnie Vic 344 D5
Baden Tas 839 D1, 843 K2
Baden Park NSW 462 G8
Badgebup WA 706 F7

Badgingarra WA 706 B2, 708 D10
Badgingarra NP WA 706 B2
Badja WA 708 F8
Badjaling WA 705 G5, 706 E4
Badwin NR NSW 461 L8
Bael Bael Vic 341 K7
Baerami NSW 458 F4
Baerami Creek NSW 455 H1, 458 F5
Bagdad Tas 839 C3, 843 J3
Bagnoo NSW 459 L2
Bago Blutt NP NSW 459 M2
Bagot Park Velodrome NT 612 D4
Bagot Well SA 787 E4, 791 K8
Bagshot Vic 339 M2
Bagshot North Vic 339 M1
Bahgallah Vic 338 C5
Baikal NT 619 L4
Baird Bay SA 790 B6
Bairnsdale Vic 302, 342 E6
Bajool Qld 561 J9
Bakara SA 791 L9
Bakara CP SA 791 M9
Baker Gully SA 786 E10
Bakers Beach Tas 844 B4, 841 H5
Bakers Creek Qld 560 G4
Bakers Swamp NSW 454 B2, 458 B5
Baladjie Lake NR WA 706 G2
Balah SA 791 L7
Balaklava SA 787 C3, 791 J8
Balbirini NT 617 L3
Balcanoona SA 791 L1, 793 L10
Balcatta WA 704 C3
Bald Hills Qld 555 C1, 557 C1
Bald Hills Vic 336 B1, 339 K4
Bald Nob NSW 461 K5
Bald Rock Vic 341 L8
Bald Rock NP NSW 412–413,
    461 K3
Baldersleigh NSW 461 H7
Baldivis WA 705 B6, 706 C5
Baldry NSW 458 A6
Balfes Creek Qld 560 A2, 565 P2
Balfour Tas 840 B5
Balfour Downs WA 715 L8
Balga WA 704 C2
Balgo WA 710 F2
Balgowan SA 790 G9
Balgowlah NSW 453 F5
Balgownie NSW 455 J9, 456 G2,
    458 G10
Balhannah SA 787 E6, 791 K10
Balingup WA 705 C10, 706 C7
Balladonia WA 676, 707 P5, 711 A8
Balladoran NSW 458 B3
Ballajura WA 704 E2
Ballalaba NSW 456 D5
Ballan Vic 336 D2, 339 L5
Ballandean Qld 556 B9, 559 L9
Ballangeich Vic 338 F7
Ballara SA 791 N4
Ballarat Vic 268, 336 B2, 339 K5
Ballatherie NSW 465 J2
Ballatta NSW 463 M9

Ballbank NSW 464 F7
Balldale NSW 465 L8
Ballendella Vic 341 N9
Balliang Vic 336 E3, 339 M6
Balliang East Vic 336 E3, 339 M6
Ballidu WA 705 E1, 706 D2
Ballimore NSW 458 B4
Ballina NSW 413, 461 P3
Ballyrogan Vic 339 H4
Balmain NSW 453 E6
Balmoral NSW 453 F5
Balmoral Qld 555 D5, 557 C2
Balmoral Qld 561 J7
Balmoral Vic 338 D4
Balmoral Village NSW 455 H8,
    456 F2, 458 F10
Balnarring Vic 302, 337 H6, 339 P8
Balonne River Qld 558 E 9
Balook Qld 560 G5
Balook Vic 337 P6, 342 A8
Balranald NSW 444, 464 F5
Balwyn Vic 335 D3
Bamaga Qld 550, 568 C2
Bamawm Vic 341 M9
Bamawm Extension Vic 341 N9
Bambaroo Qld 563 M8
Bambill Vic 340 C3
Bamboo Springs NT 616 A3
Bamboo Springs WA 715 J7
Bambra Vic 336 C6, 339 L8
Bamganie Vic 336 C4, 339 L6
Ban Ban Qld 565 K10
Ban Ban Springs NT 613 E5, 614 E6
Ban Ban Springs Qld 559 L3
Banana Qld 559 H1, 561 J10
Bandiana Vic 345 H3
Bandon Grove NSW 459 J4
Bandon Grove Qld 565 K9
Bandya WA 709 M6
Banealla SA 788 C9
Bang Bang Qld 562 D8
Bangalow NSW 413, 461 P2
Bangham SA 788 D10
Bangham CP SA 788 D10
Bangholme Vic 335 F6
Bangor NSW 453 C9
Banjawarn WA 709 M6
Banjup WA 704 D10
Banka Banka NT 617 H6
Banks ACT 477 D5
Banks Strait Tas 841 N3
Banksia NSW 453 D7
Banksia Qld 561 H7
Banksia Park SA 786 G3
Banksmeadow NSW 453 E8
Bankstown NSW 453 B7, 455 K7,
    456 G1, 459 H9
Bannerton Vic 340 G4
Bannister WA 705 D7, 706 D6
Bannockburn Qld 565 N5
Bannockburn Vic 336 D4, 339 L7
Banoon NSW 464 D4
Banora Point NSW 461 P1

Banyabba NR NSW 461 M4
Banyena Vic 338 G1, 340 G10
Banyena South Vic 338 G1
Banyenong Vic 341 H9
Banyo Qld 555 D3, 557 C2
Baradine NSW 460 C9
Barakee NR NSW 459 K2
Barakula Qld 559 H5
Baralaba Qld 561 H10
Barataria Qld 565 K7
Baratta SA 791 K4
Barbigal NSW 458 B4
Barcaldine Qld 534, 560 A8, 565 N9
Bardon Qld 555 B5
Bardwell Park NSW 453 D7
Barellan NSW 465 L4
Barenya Qld 565 L5
Barfield Qld 559 H1
Barfold Vic 339 M3
Bargara Qld 559 M2
Bargo NSW 455 H8, 456 F2,
    458 F10
Barham NSW 464 G7
Baring Vic 340 E6
Baringhup Vic 339 L3
Barjarg Vic 344 E7
Barkers Creek Vic 339 L3
Barkly Vic 339 H3
Barkly Downs Qld 564 B3
Barkly Homestead Roadhouse NT
    598, 617 L8
Barkly Tableland NT 617 M8
Barlee Range NR WA 714 E9
Barmah Vic 341 P8, 344 A3
Barmah SF Vic 324
Barmah SP Vic 324, 341 P8, 344 A2
Barmedman NSW 465 N4
Barmera SA 755, 791 N8
Barmundu Qld 561 K10
Barna SA 790 F6
Barnadown Vic 339 M2
Barnato NSW 463 H7
Barnawartha Vic 344 G3
Barnawartha South Vic 344 G4
Barnes Bay Tas 839 C6, 843 K6
Barngo Qld 558 C2
Barnhill WA 712 C9, 715 M2
Barnie Bolac Vic 339 H6
Barnong WA 708 E8
Barongarook Vic 336 A6, 339 J8
Barooga NSW 444, 465 K8
Barool NP NSW 461 K5
Baroona NSW 460 B5
Baroona Qld 567 P8
Baroona Downs Qld 564 G3
Baroondah Qld 558 F3
Barossa Valley Wine Region SA 756
Barpinba Vic 336 B5, 339 K7
Barra Brui NSW 453 E4
Barraba NSW 413, 460 G7
Barradale NSW 462 E7
Barradeen Qld 558 B4
Barrakee NSW 463 H4

Barrakee Vic 341 J9
Barram Qld 559 J2
Barrambie WA 709 J6
Barramornie Qld 559 H6
Barramunga Vic 336 B7, 339 K9
Barranyi NP NT 615 M9, 617 N1
Barraport Vic 341 K8
Barraroo NSW 462 D8
Barretts Creek NSW 461 M4
Barrington Tas 840 G6
Barrington Tops NP NSW 384,
    459 H4
Barringun NSW 463 K1
Barrow Creek NT 619 H2
Barrow Island NR WA 714 D5
Barry NSW 454 C5, 456 C1, 458 C8
Barry NSW 459 H2
Barry Beach Vic 337 P8, 342 A10
Barrys Reef Vic 336 D1, 339 M4
Bartle Frere Qld 563 M6, 569 E9
Bartlett Bluff WA 711 B4
Barton ACT 477 D3
Barton SA 789 F8
Barton Vic 338 G4
Barton NR NSW 454 B4, 458 B7
Barton Plains WA 713 K2
Barton Springs Qld 558 F4
Barunduda Vic 345 H4
Barunga NT 614 G8
Barunga Gap SA 787 B2, 791 H7
Barwell CP SA 790 D7
Barwell CR SA 790 D7
Barwidgee WA 709 L5
Barwidgee Creek Vic 345 H5
Barwidgi Qld 563 K7, 569 A10
Barwo Vic 341 P8, 344 B3
Barwon Downs Vic 336 B6, 339 K8
Barwon Heads Vic 278, 336 E6,
    339 M8
Barwon Park Qld 560 F8
Barwon River NSW 460 A5, 463 L3
Baryulgil NSW 461 M4
Basalt Creek Qld 558 F1
Bascombe Well CP SA 790 D7
Baskerville WA 704 G1
Basket Swamp NP NSW 461 K3
Bass Vic 337 K7
Bass Hill NSW 453 B7
Bassendean WA 704 F4
Bat Cave Point WA 707 J8
Batavia Downs Qld 568 D6
Batavia Outstation Qld 568 B5
Batchelor NT 588, 613 C4, 614 D5
Batchica Vic 340 F9
Bate Bay NSW 453 E10
Batehaven NSW 456 E6
Bateman WA 704 C7
Batemans Bay NSW 364, 456 E6
Batemans Bay NSW 456 F6
Bates SA 789 E8
Batesford Vic 336 D5, 339 L7
Batheaston Qld 560 F6
Bathurst NSW 384, 454 D4, 458 D7

Bathurst Head Qld 563 J1, 568 F9
Bathurst Island NT 614 C3
Batlow NSW **364–365**, 456 A5, 457 B3, 465 P7
Battery Qld 560 A1, 563 L9, 565 P1
Battery Point Tas 838 E7
Battle Camp Qld 563 K3, 568 G10, 569 B3
Bauhinia Downs NT 615 K10, 617 K2
Bauhinia Downs Qld 558 F1, 560 G10
Baulkham Hills NSW 453 B4
Bauple Qld 559 M4
Baw Baw Alpine Village Vic 337 N3
Baw Baw NP Vic **302**, 337 N4
Bawley Point NSW 456 F5
Baxter Vic 335 F8, 337 H5, 339 P7
Baxter Cliffs WA 711 C8
Bay of Fires CA Tas 841 P5
Bay of Islands Coastal Reserve Vic 338 F8
Bayindeen Vic 339 H4
Baykool Qld 567 N3
Bayles Vic 337 K5
Bayrick Qld 558 A3, 567 P3
Bayswater Vic 335 F4
Bayswater WA 704 E4
Bayswater North Vic 335 G3
Bayview NSW 453 F2
Beachmere Qld 556 E4, 559 N6
Beachport SA 788 F8
Beachport CP SA 788 F8
Beacon WA 706 F2
Beacon Hill NSW 453 F4
Beaconsfield NSW 453 E7
Beaconsfield Qld 565 M8
Beaconsfield Tas 844 C4, 841 J5
Beaconsfield Vic 337 J4
Beaconsfield WA 704 B8
Beagle Bay WA 712 D7
Beagle Gulf NT 612 A4, 613 B2, 614 C4
Bealbah NSW 463 P6
Bealiba Vic 339 J2
Beames Brook Qld 562 C7
Bearbung NSW 458 B2
Beardmore Vic 337 P3, 342 A6
Bearii Vic 344 B2
Bears Lagoon Vic 341 L10
Beatrice Downs Qld 565 J10
Beauchamp Vic 341 J7
Beaudesert Qld **496**, 556 E7, 557 C6, 559 M8
Beaudesert Qld 564 F5
Beaufort Qld 560 C9
Beaufort Qld 560 C9
Beaufort SA 787 C3, 791 J8
Beaufort Vic 339 J4
Beaumaris Tas 841 P6
Beaumaris Vic 335 D6
Beaumont SA 786 E6
Beaumont NR WA 707 N7

Beauty Point NSW 453 F5
Beauty Point Tas 844 C4, 841 J5
Beazleys Bridge Vic 339 H2
Beckenham WA 704 F6
Bedford WA 704 D4
Bedford Downs WA 713 L7
Bedford Park SA 786 D8
Bedgerebong NSW 465 N2
Bedooba NSW 463 K9
Bedourie Qld 558 F2
Bedourie Qld 564 C10, 566 C1
Bee Creek SA 789 F2
Beeac Vic 336 B5, 339 K7
Beebo Qld 559 J9
Beech Forest Vic 336 A7, 339 J9
Beechboro WA 704 E2
Beechford Tas 844 D3, 841 J4
Beechmont Qld 557 D7
Beechwood NSW 459 M2, 461 M10
Beechworth Vic **324**, 344 G4
Beechworth Historic Park Vic 344 G4
Beecroft NSW 453 C4
Beedelup NP WA 706 C9
Beekeepers NR WA 708 D9
Beelbangera NSW 465 K4
Beeliar WA 704 C9
Beenleigh Qld 556 E6, 557 D4, 559 N7
Beerburrum Qld 556 D4, 559 M6
Beerwah Qld 556 D3, 559 M6
Beetaloo NT 617 H3
Beetoomba Vic 345 L4
Bega NSW **365**, 456 E8
Beggan Beggan NSW 456 A3, 465 P5
Beilpajah NSW 462 F10, 464 F1
Belah NSW 463 J5
Belair SA 786 E7, 787 D6, 788 A5, 791 J10
Belair NP SA 786 E8
Belalie East SA 791 J6
Belalie North SA 791 J6
Belarabon NSW 463 H8
Belaringar NSW 463 N7
Belconnen ACT 477 C2, 456 C5, 457 E2
Beldene Qld 558 E6
Belele WA 708 G4
Belfast Qld 565 H5
Belfield NSW 453 D7
Belford NSW 455 K1, 459 H5
Belgamba NSW 458 G1, 460 G10
Belgrave Vic 337 J4
Belhus WA 704 G1
Belinar NSW 464 D3
Belka WA 706 F4
Bell Qld 556 A4, 559 K6
Bell Bay Tas 844 C3, 841 J5
Bellalie Qld 567 J6
Bellangry NSW 459 M1, 461 M10
Bellarine Vic 335 A9, 336 F5, 339 N7
Bellarwi NSW 465 M4
Bellata NSW 460 E6

Bellbird NSW 455 L2, 459 H6
Bellbird Creek Vic 343 K5
Bellbrae Vic 336 D6, 339 L8
Bellbridge Vic 345 J3
Bellbrook NSW 461 L9
Belle Creek Qld 558 D7
Bellellen Vic 338 G3
Bellenden Ker Qld 563 M6, 569 E8
Bellerive Tas 838 G6
Bellevue NSW 464 G2
Bellevue Qld 563 J5
Bellevue WA 704 G4
Bellevue Heights SA 786 D8
Bellevue Hill NSW 453 F6
Bellfield Qld 563 H9
Bellingen NSW **413**, 461 M8
Bellinger River NP NSW 461 M8
Bellingham Tas 844 E3, 841 K4
Bellman Qld 562 D10, 564 E1
Bellmount Forest NSW 456 C4, 457 F1
Bellrose Qld 558 B4
Belltrees NSW 459 H3
Belmont NSW **384**, 455 M3, 459 J6
Belmont Qld 555 F6, 557 D3
Belmont Vic 336 E5, 339 M7
Belmont WA 704 E5
Belmore NSW 453 C7
Belmore NSW 464 A3
Beloka NSW 456 B8, 457 D8
Belrose NSW 453 E3
Beltana SA 791 J1
Beltana Roadhouse SA 791 J1
Belton SA 791 K4
Belvedere NSW 463 K3
Belvedere SA 791 P7
Belvidere SA 787 E7, 788 A6
Belyuen NT 613 C3, 614 C4
Bemboka NSW 456 D8, 457 G8
Bemboka NP NSW 456 D8, 457 G8
Bemm River NSW 456 C8, 457 E9
Bemm River Vic 343 K4
Ben Boyd NP NSW **365**, 456 E9
Ben Bullen NSW 454 F3, 458 E7
Ben Halls Gap NP NSW 459 H2
Ben Lomond NSW 461 J6
Ben Lomond NSW 463 K5
Ben Lomond NP Tas **806–807**, 841 M7
Bena NSW 465 M2
Bena Vic 337 L6
Benalla Vic **324–325**, 344 E5
Benambra Vic 342 E2, 345 L7
Benanee NSW 464 D5
Benaraby Qld 561 L9
Benayeo Vic 338 B2
Bencubbin WA 706 F2
Benda SA 791 M5
Bendalong NSW 456 F5
Bendemeer NSW 461 H9
Bendemeer Qld 565 H5
Bendemere Qld 558 F5
Bendering WA 706 F5

Bendick Murrell NSW 456 B2, 458 A9
Bendidee NP Qld 559 H8
Bendigo SA 791 L6
Bendigo Vic **268–269**, 339 M2
Bendigo Park Qld 562 E10, 564 F2
Bendoc Vic 343 K3
Bendoc North Vic 343 K3
Bendolba NSW 459 J4
Benetook Vic 340 E2
Bengerang NSW 460 D4
Bengworden Vic 342 E6
Beni NSW 458 B4
Benjaberring WA 705 F3, 706 E3
Benjeroop Vic 341 K7
Benlidi Qld 565 M10, 567 M1
Benmara NT 617 M5
Bennison Vic 337 N8
Benobble Qld 557 D6
Bentinck Island Qld 562 C6
Bentleigh Vic 335 D5
Bentleigh East Vic 335 E5
Bentley NSW 461 N3
Bentley WA 704 E6
Bents Basin SRA NSW 455 H7, 456 G1, 458 G9
Benwerrin Vic 336 C7, 339 K8
Berala NSW 453 B6
Berangabah NSW 463 H9
Beremboke Vic 336 D3, 339 L6
Beresfield NSW 455 M2, 459 J6
Beresford Qld 560 C6
Beresford SA 792 F8
Beringarra WA 708 F4
Berkshire Valley WA 705 C1, 706 C2
Bermagui NSW **365**, 456 E8
Bermagui South NSW 456 E8
Bernacchi Tas 844 B9, 841 H8
Bernfels Qld 565 J5
Bernier and Dorre Islands NR WA 708 A2
Berowra NSW 453 D1
Berowra Creek NSW 453 D1
Berowra Heights Regional Park NSW 453 D1
Berowra Valley Regional Park NSW 453 D2
Berowra Waters NSW 455 K5, 459 H8
Berri SA **756–757**, 791 N8
Berridale NSW 456 C7, 457 E7
Berriedale Tas 838 B3
Berrigan NSW **444**, 465 K7
Berrilee NSW 453 C1
Berrima NSW **365**, 454 G9, 456 F3, 458 F10
Berrimal Vic 339 J1, 341 J10
Berrinba Qld 555 E10
Berringama Vic 345 L4
Berriwillock Vic 341 H7
Berrook Vic 340 A5
Berry NSW **366**, 455 H10, 456 G3
Berry Springs NT 613 D3, 614 D4

Berrybank Vic 336 A4, 339 J6
Bertiehaugh Qld 568 C5
Berwick Vic 335 G6, 337 J4
Bessiebelle Vic 338 D7
Beswick NT 614 G8
Bet Bet Vic 339 K3
Beta Qld 560 B9
Bete Bolong Vic 343 H5, 345 N10
Bethana Qld 555 G10
Bethanga Vic 345 J3
Bethungra NSW 465 P5
Betley Vic 339 K3
Betoota Qld 566 E3
Beulah NSW 463 L2
Beulah Tas 844 A6, 840 G6
Beulah Vic 340 F8
Beulah East Vic 340 F8
Beulah Park SA 786 E5
Beulah West Vic 340 E8
Bevendale NSW 454 C9, 456 C3
Beverford Vic 341 J6
Beveridge Vic 336 G1, 339 P5, 344 A9
Beverley WA **639**, 705 E5, 706 D5
Beverley Group NP Qld 561 J4
Beverley Park NSW 453 D8
Beverley Springs WA 713 H6
Beverly Hills NSW 453 C7
Bews SA 788 A9
Bexhill NSW 461 N3
Bexley NSW 453 D8
Bexley North NSW 453 D7
Beyondie WA 709 K2
Biala NSW 454 C10, 456 C3
Biamanga NP NSW 456 E8
Bibbenluke NSW 456 D9, 457 F9
Biboohra Qld 563 L5, 569 D7
Bibra Lake WA 704 C8
Bicentennial Park NT 612 C10
Bicheno Tas **810**, 841 P8
Bicton Qld 558 B6
Bicton WA 704 B6
Biddon NSW 458 B2
Bidgeemia NSW 465 L7
Bidgemia WA 708 D3
Bidura NSW 464 E4
Bierbank Qld 567 N5
Big Brush NR NSW 465 N4
Big Creek Qld 567 M7
Big Desert Wilderness Park Vic 340 B7
Big Heath CP SA 788 E9
Big Hill Vic 339 L2
Big River Vic 337 M1
Big River Country NSW **406–411**
Big Rivers Wine Region NSW **444–445**
Bigga NSW 454 C7, 456 C2, 458 C9
Biggara Vic 345 M4
Biggenden Qld 559 L3
Biggs Flat SA 786 G10
Bilambil NSW 461 N1
Bilbah Downs Qld 565 L10, 567 L1

Bilbarin WA 706 F5
Bilbul NSW 465 K4
Billa Kalina SA 792 E9
Billabalong WA 708 E6
Billabong Roadhouse WA 708 C5
Billenbah Qld 558 F7
Billengarrah NT 617 L2
Billeroy NSW 460 A8
Billiatt CP SA 791 M10
Billilla NSW 462 E8
Billiluna WA 710 E1
Billimari NSW 454 A6, 456 B1, 458 B8
Billinnooka WA 715 L9
Billybingbone NSW 463 M4
Billyrimba NSW 461 L4
Billys Creek NSW 461 L7
Biloela Qld **496**, 559 H1, 561 J10
Bilpa Morea Claypan Qld 566 D2
Bilpin NSW 455 H5, 458 F8
Bimbi NSW 456 A2, 465 P4
Bimbijy WA 708 G9
Bimbowrie SA 791 M4
Bimerah Qld 565 K10, 567 K1
Binalong NSW 454 A10, 456 B3
Binalong Bay Tas 841 P5
Binbee Qld 560 E2
Binda NSW 454 C8, 456 D2, 458 C10
Binda NSW 464 F3
Bindara NSW 462 C10, 464 C1
Bindarri NP NSW 461 M7
Bindawalla Qld 561 K10
Bindebango Qld 558 C7
Bindi NSW 463 J8
Bindi Vic 342 F3, 345 L8
Bindi Bindi WA 705 D1, 706 C2
Bindle Qld 558 E7
Bindogundra NSW 458 A6
Bindoon WA 705 C3, 706 C3
Binerah Downs NSW 462 B1
Bing Bong NT 615 M10, 617 M1
Bingara NSW 460 F6
Bingil Bay Qld 563 M7, 569 E10
Binginwarri Vic 337 P7, 342 A9
Bingo Munjie North Vic 342 E2, 345 L7
Biniguy NSW 460 F5
Binjour Qld 559 K3
Binnaway NSW 458 D2
Binnaway NR NSW 458 D2
Binningup Beach WA 705 B8, 706 B6
Binnu WA 708 C7
Binnum SA 788 D10
Binya NSW 465 L4
Binyeah Qld 564 B5
Birchip Vic 340 G8
Birchs Bay Tas 839 C7, 843 K7
Birdsville Qld **542**, 566 C4
Birdsville Track SA **778–781**
Birdwood SA **757**, 787 E6, 791 K10
Birdwoodton Vic 340 E2
Birkdale Qld 555 G6

Birkhead Qld 558 A1, 560 B10
Birralee Qld 560 E3
Birralee Tas 844 C6, 841 J6
Birrego NSW 465 L6
Birregurra Vic 336 B6, 339 K8
Birricannia Qld 565 M5
Birrimba NT 616 E2
Birrindudu NT 616 B6
Birriwa NSW 458 D4
Birrong NSW 453 B7
Bishopsbourne Tas 844 D7, 841 J7
Bittern Vic 335 F10, 337 H6, 339 P8
Black Flag WA 707 L2
Black Gate NSW 462 D8
Black Hill SA 787 G5, 791 L9
Black Hill WA 709 J7
Black Hill CP SA 786 G5
Black Hills Tas 839 A3, 843 J4
Black Mountain NSW 461 J7
Black Mountain Qld 560 G5
Black Mountain NP Qld 563 L3, 569 C4
Black Range WA 709 J7
Black Range SP Vic 338 E3
Black Rock SA 791 K5
Black Rock Vic 335 D6
Black Springs NSW 454 E6, 456 E1, 458 D9
Black Springs SA 787 E2, 791 K8
Blackall Qld **534**, 560 A10, 565 N10, 567 N1
Blackboy Lake NSW 462 B10, 464 B1
Blackbraes Qld 563 J9, 565 L1
Blackbraes NP Qld 563 J9
Blackbull Qld 562 F7
Blackburn Vic 335 E4
Blackburn North Vic 335 E3
Blackburn South Vic 335 E4
Blackbutt Qld 556 B4, 559 L6
Blackdown Qld 563 J6
Blackdown Tableland NP Qld 560 G9
Blackfellows Caves SA 788 G9
Blackheath NSW 454 G5, 456 F1, 458 F8
Blackheath Vic 338 E1, 340 E10
Blackmans Bay Tas 839 C5, 843 K5
Blackmans Point NSW 459 M1, 461 M10
Blackstone Qld 557 B4
Blacktown NSW 453 A4, 455 J6, 456 G1, 458 G8
Blackville NSW 458 F2
Blackwall Tas 844 D5, 841 J6
Blackwarry Vic 342 A8
Blackwater Qld **514–515**, 560 F9
Blackwood SA 786 D8
Blackwood Vic 336 D1, 339 M5
Blackwood Creek Tas 844 C8, 841 J8
Blackwood NP Qld 560 C4
Blackwood River WA 706 B8
Bladensburg NP Qld 565 J7
Blair Athol Qld 560 D7

Blair Athol Qld 564 D7
Blair Athol SA 786 D4
Blairgowrie Qld 565 M10, 567 M1
Blairgowrie Vic 336 F6, 339 N8
Blairmore Qld 558 B8
Blakehurst NSW 453 D8
Blakeville Vic 336 D1, 339 L5
Blakney Creek NSW 454 B10, 456 C3
Blamey WA 707 M3
Blampied Vic 336 C1, 339 L4
Blanchetown SA 787 G4, 791 L9
Blanchewater SA 793 K8
Bland NSW 465 N3
Blandford NSW 458 G3
Blanket Flat NSW 454 C8, 456 C2, 458 C9
Blantyre Qld 565 M3
Blaxland NSW 455 H6, 456 F1, 458 G8
Blayney NSW **384**, 454 C5, 458 C8
Blenheim Qld 558 G7
Blessington Tas 844 G6, 841 L7
Blighty NSW 465 J7
Blina WA 712 G8
Blinman SA **757**, 791 J2
Bloods Creek SA 792 C1
Bloomfield NSW 454 C4, 458 C7
Bloomfield NSW 463 J8
Bloomfield Qld 567 N1
Bloomsbury Qld 560 F3
Blow Clear NSW 463 P10, 465 P1
Blow Clear NSW 465 M3
Blowering Reservoir NSW 456 A5, 457 B3
Blue Creek Qld 566 G2
Blue Hills Qld 558 G1, 561 H10
Blue Knob NSW 461 N2
Blue Lake NP Qld 557 F3
Blue Mountain Qld 560 G5
Blue Mountains NP NSW **384–385**, 454 G7, 455 H6, 456 F2, 458 F9
Blue Range Qld 563 L9
Blue Rocks Tas 841 J2
Blue Water Springs Roadhouse Qld 563 L9
Bluewater Qld 563 M9
Blueys Beach NSW 459 L4
Bluff Qld 560 G9
Bluff Downs Qld 560 A1, 563 L10, 565 P1
Bluff Rock NSW 461 K4
Blumont Tas 844 F4, 841 L5
Blyth SA 787 D2, 791 J8
Blythdale Qld 558 F5
Boambee NSW 461 N7
Boat Harbour NSW 455 P2, 459 K5
Boat Harbour Tas **810**, 840 D4
Boat Harbour Beach Tas 840 D4
Boatman Qld 558 B6
Bobadah NSW 463 L9
Bobawaba Qld 560 D1, 563 P10
Bobbin Head NSW 453 D2

Bobby Towns Hut Qld 562 G6
Bobin NSW 459 L2
Bobinawarrah Vic 344 G5
Bobundara NSW 456 C8, 457 E8
Bodalla NSW **366**, 456 E7
Bodallin WA 706 G3
Boddington WA 705 D7, 706 D6
Bogan Gate NSW 463 N10, 465 N2
Bogangar NSW 461 P1
Bogantungan Qld 560 D9
Bogarella Qld 558 C3
Bogee NSW 454 F2, 458 E6
Bogewong Qld 565 K9
Boggabilla NSW 460 F2
Boggabri NSW **414**, 460 E8
Boginderra Hills NR NSW 465 N4
Bogolo NSW 463 L10, 465 L1
Bogong Qld 558 D8
Bogong Vic 342 D1, 345 J6
Bogong High Plains Vic 345 J7
Bohemia Downs WA 710 D1,
    713 J10
Bohnock NSW 459 L3
Boho South Vic 344 D6
Boigbeat Vic 340 G7
Boinka Vic 340 C5
Boisdale Vic 342 C6
Bokhara Plains NSW 463 M3
Bolgart WA 705 D3, 706 D3
Bolinda Vic 336 F1, 339 N4
Bolingbroke Qld 560 G5
Bolivar SA 786 D2
Bolivia NSW 461 K4
Bollards Lagoon SA 793 N7
Bollon Qld 558 C8
Bolton Vic 340 G5
Boltons Beach CA Tas 839 G1,
    843 N2
Bolwarra Qld 563 J6
Bolwarra Vic 338 C7
Bomaderry NSW 456 F4
Bomali NSW 463 N2
Bombah NSW 463 M9
Bombah Point NSW 459 L5
Bombala NSW 456 C9, 457 F9
Bomera NSW 458 E2
Bon Bon SA 792 D10
Bonalbo NSW 461 M3
Bonang Vic 343 J3
Bonaparte Archipelago WA 712 G2
Bonathorne Qld 558 E9
Bonbeach Vic 335 E7
Bond Springs NT 619 H6
Bondi NSW 453 F6
Bondi Bay NSW 453 G7
Bondi Beach NSW 453 F6
Bondi Gulf NP NSW 456 C9
Bondi Junction NSW 453 F6,
    455 L7, 459 H9
Bondo NSW 456 B5, 457 C2
Bonegilla Vic 345 H3
Boneo Vic 336 G6, 339 N8
Boney Point NT 615 M3

Bongaree Qld 556 E4, 559 N6
Bonna Vonna Qld 558 B8
Bonnet Bay NSW 453 C9
Bonnie Brae SA 791 L4
Bonnie Doon Qld 560 F9
Bonnie Doon Qld 567 N2
Bonnie Doon Vic 344 D7
Bonnie Downs WA 715 K8
Bonnie Rock WA 706 F2
Bonnie Vale WA 707 L2
Bonny Hills NSW 459 M2
Bonrook NT 613 F6, 614 E6
Bonshaw NSW 461 H3
Bonton NSW 462 F9, 464 F1
Bonus Downs Qld 558 D5
Bonville NSW 461 N7
Bonython ACT 477 D4
Boobera Qld 567 N7
Booberoi NSW 558 G9
Booborowie SA 787 D1, 791 K7
Boobyalla Tas 841 M4
Boogardie WA 708 G7
Book Book Qld 558 D9
Bookabie SA 789 F10
Bookaloo SA 790 G3
Bookar Vic 339 H7
Bookham NSW 456 B4
Bool Lagoon SA 788 E9
Bool Lagoon GR SA 788 E9
Boola Boolka NSW 462 E9
Boolambayte NSW 459 L4
Boolardy WA 708 E5
Boolaroo NSW 455 M2, 459 J6
Boolarra Vic 337 N6
Boolarra South Vic 337 N6
Boolba Qld 558 D8
Boolbanna Qld 567 L5
Boolburra Qld 561 H9
Boolcoomata SA 791 N4
Booleroo Centre SA 791 J6
Booligal NSW 465 H3
Boolite Vic 340 F10
Boologooro WA 708 B2
Boomahnoomoonah Vic 344 E3
Boomi NSW 460 D2
Boomley NSW 458 C3
Boonah Qld 556 D7, 557 A6,
    559 M8
Boonanghi NR NSW 461 L9
Boonarga Qld 559 J6
Boonarring NR WA 705 C3, 706 C3
Boondall Qld 555 D2, 557 C1
Boondall Wetlands Park Qld 555 E2
Boondandilla Qld 559 H8
Boondarra NSW 465 H2
Boonderoo Qld 565 L2
Boongoondoo Qld 560 B7, 565 P7
Boonoo Boonoo NSW 461 K3
Boonoo Boonoo NP NSW 461 K3
Boorabbin WA 707 J3
Boorabbin NP WA 707 J3
Booragoon WA 704 C7
Booral NSW 459 K5

Boorara Qld 560 A9, 565 P9
Boorara Qld 567 L9
Boorcan Vic 339 H7
Boorhaman Vic 344 F4
Boorolite Vic 344 E8
Boorongie Vic 340 F5
Booroolong NR NSW 461 J7
Boorooma NSW 463 N4
Booroomba ACT 477 C5
Booroondarra Downs NSW 463 J6
Booroopki Vic 338 B2
Booroorban NSW 465 H6
Boorowa NSW 454 A9, 456 B3,
    458 B10
Boort Vic 341 K9
Boort East Vic 341 K9
Boothulla Qld 567 N5
Booti Booti NP NSW **385**, 459 L4
Bootra NSW 462 D4
Booyal Qld 559 L2
Booylgoo Spring WA 709 K7
Boppy Mount NSW 463 L7
Borallon Qld 557 A3
Borambil NSW 458 E3
Borambola NSW 465 N6
Borden WA 706 F8
Border Cliffs SA 791 P8
Border Downs NSW 462 A4
Border Ranges NP NSW **414**,
    461 N2
Border Village SA 789 A9
Bordertown SA **732**, 788 C10
Boree NSW 454 A4, 458 B7
Boree Qld 565 L3
Boree Creek NSW 465 L6
Boree Plains NSW 464 E3
Boreen Qld 556 E2, 559 M5
Borenore NSW 454 B4, 458 B7
Boro NSW 456 D4
Boronia Vic 335 G4
Bororen Qld 559 K1, 561 L10
Borrika SA 791 M10
Borroloola NT **598**, 615 M10,
    617 M1
Borung Vic 341 K9
Boscabel WA 705 F10, 706 E7
Bostobrick NSW 461 M7
Bostock Creek Vic 339 H7
Bosworth SA 790 G1
Botany NSW 455 K7, 459 H9
Botany Bay NSW 453 E8, 455 K7,
    459 H9
Botany Bay NP NSW 453 F8
Bothwell Tas **830**, 839 A1, 843 J2
Bouddi NP NSW 455 L5, 459 J8
Bouillia NSW 462 B4
Boulder WA 707 L2
Bouldercombe Qld 561 J9
Boulia Qld **534**, 564 D7
Boundary Bend Vic 341 H4
Bourke NSW **434**, 463 K4
Bournda NP NSW 456 E9
Bow NSW 458 F4

Bow Bridge WA 706 D10
Bow River WA 713 M6
Bowalli Qld 567 L6
Bowan Park NSW 454 A4, 458 B7
Bowelling WA 705 D9, 706 D7
Bowen Qld **515**, 560 E2
Bowen Hills Qld 555 D4
Bowenville Qld 556 A5, 559 K6
Bower SA 787 G3, 791 L8
Bowgada WA 708 E9
Bowhill SA 791 L10
Bowie Qld 560 B5, 565 P5
Bowillia SA 787 C2, 791 J8
Bowling Alley Point NSW 459 H1,
    461 H10
Bowling Green Bay NP Qld 563 N9
Bowmans SA 787 C3, 791 J8
Bowmans Creek NSW 459 H4
Bowna NSW 465 M8
Bowning NSW 454 A10, 456 B3
Bowral NSW **366–367**, 454 G9,
    456 F3, 458 F10
Bowraville NSW 461 M8
Bowser Vic 344 F4
Bowthorn Qld 562 A7
Box Creek SA 792 D7
Box Hill NSW 455 J5, 456 G1,
    458 G8
Box Hill Vic 335 E4, 337 H3, 339 P6
Box Hill North Vic 335 E3
Boxvale Qld 558 E3
Boxwood Hill WA 706 G9
Boyanup WA 705 B9, 706 B7
Boyben NSW 458 C3
Boyeo Vic 340 C9
Boyer Tas 839 B4, 843 J4
Boyland Qld 557 D6
Boyne Island Qld 561 L9
Boys Town Qld 557 C6
Boyup Brook WA 705 D10, 706 C8
Brachina SA 791 J2
Bracken Ridge Qld 555 D1
Brackendale NSW 459 J1, 461 J10
Brackenley Qld 560 G10
Bracknell Tas 844 D7, 841 J7
Bradbury SA 786 F9
Braddon ACT 477 D3, 456 C5,
    457 F2
Bradvale Vic 339 J6
Braefield NSW 458 G2
Braemar NSW 460 E3
Braemar Qld 565 L4
Braemar SA 791 L6
Braeside Qld 560 F5
Braeside Qld 564 G5
Braeside Vic 335 E6
Brahma Lodge SA 786 E2
Braidwood NSW **367**, 456 E5
Braidwood Qld 567 J2
Bramfield SA 790 C7
Bramston Beach Qld 563 M6, 569 E9
Bramwell Qld 568 C5
Brandon Qld 560 D1, 563 N10

Brandy Creek Vic 337 M5
Bransby Qld 567 H8
Branxholm Tas 841 M5
Branxholme Vic 338 D6
Branxton NSW 455 L1, 459 H5
Brassall Qld 557 A3
Braunstone NSW 461 M6
Brawlin NSW 456 A3, 465 P5
Braybrook Vic 335 B3
Brayfield SA 790 E8
Breadalbane NSW 456 D4
Breadalbane Qld 564 C9
Breadalbane Tas 844 E6, 841 K7
Break O'Day Vic 337 J1, 344 B9
Breakaway Ridge NR WA 706 G6
Breakfast Creek NSW 454 A7, 456 B2, 458 B9
Breakfast Creek NSW 454 F1, 458 E5
Bream Creek Tas 839 F4, 843 M4
Breamlea Vic 336 E6, 339 M8
Bredbo NSW 456 C6, 457 F5
Breelong NSW 458 B3
Breeza NSW 458 F1, 460 F10
Breeza Plains Outstation Qld 563 J2, 568 F10
Bremer Bay WA 639, 707 H9
Brenda NSW 463 N1
Brenda Gate Qld 558 C10
Brendale Qld 555 B1
Brentwood SA 790 G10
Brentwood Vic 340 E8
Brentwood WA 704 C7
Breona Tas 844 B8, 841 H8
Bretti NSW 459 K3
Bretti NR NSW 459 K2
Brewarrina NSW 434, 463 M3
Brewongle NSW 454 E5, 458 D8
Brewster Vic 336 A1, 339 J5
Briaba Qld 560 E2
Briagolong Vic 342 C6
Bribbaree NSW 465 P4
Bribie Island Qld 496, 556 E3
Bribie Island NP Qld 556 E4, 559 N6
Bridge Creek Vic 344 E7
Bridgeman Downs Qld 555 C2
Bridgenorth Tas 844 D5, 841 J6
Bridgetown WA 640, 706 C8
Bridgewater SA 786 G8
Bridgewater Tas 839 C4, 843 K4
Bridgewater Vic 339 K1
Bridport Tas 811, 844 F2, 841 L4
Brierfield NSW 461 M8
Brigalow NSW 458 B1, 460 B10
Brigalow Qld 559 J6
Bright Vic 325, 342 C1, 345 H6
Brightlands Qld 564 E4
Brighton Qld 555 D1, 557 C1
Brighton SA 786 C8, 787 D6, 791 J10
Brighton Tas 839 C3, 843 J4
Brighton Vic 335 D5, 336 G4, 339 P6
Brighton Downs Qld 564 G8

Brighton-le-Sands NSW 453 E8
Brim Vic 340 F9
Brim East Vic 340 F9
Brimboal Vic 338 C4
Brimpaen Vic 338 E3
Brinawa Qld 562 B7
Brindabella NSW 456 B5, 457 D3
Brindabella NP NSW 477 A2, 456 C5, 457 D2
Brindabella Range ACT 477 A4
Brindingabba NSW 463 H2
Brindiwilpa NSW 462 D3
Bringagee NSW 465 K5
Bringalbert Vic 338 B2
Bringelly NSW 455 H7, 456 G1, 458 G9
Bringle NSW 458 B1, 460 B10
Brinkin NT 612 E2
Brinkley SA 787 F7, 788 A7, 791 K10
Brinkworth SA 787 C1, 791 J7
Brisbane Qld 484–485, 555 C5, 556 E5, 557 C2, 559 N7
Brisbane Forest Park Qld 555 A4, 557 A1
Brisbane Ranges NP Vic 269, 336 D3, 339 M6
Brisbane River Qld 555 E4, 556 D5
Brisbane Water NP NSW 385, 455 L5, 459 H8
Brit Brit Vic 338 D5
Brittons Swamp Tas 840 B4
Brixton Qld 565 N8
Broad Arrow WA 707 L2, 709 L10
Broadbeach Qld 557 F7
Broadford Qld 565 L5
Broadford Vic 269, 339 P4, 344 A8
Broadleigh Downs Qld 560 B3
Broadmarsh Tas 839 B3, 843 J4
Broadmeadow NSW 455 M2, 459 J6
Broadmeadows Vic 335 B2, 336 G2, 339 N5, 344 A10
Broadmere NT 617 K2
Broadmere Qld 558 G3
Broadmount Qld 561 K8
Broadwater NSW 461 P3
Broadwater Vic 338 E7
Broadwater NP NSW 461 P4
Brocklehurst NSW 458 B4
Brocklesby NSW 465 L7
Brodribb River Vic 343 J5, 345 P10
Brogo NSW 456 E8
Broke NSW 455 K2, 459 H5
Broke Inlet WA 706 C10
Broken Bay NSW 455 L5, 459 H8
Broken Hill NSW 434–435, 462 B8
Brolgan NSW 463 P10, 465 P2
Bromelton Qld 556 D7, 557 B6, 559 M8
Brompton SA 786 D5
Bronte NSW 453 F7
Bronte Qld 567 N3
Bronte Park Tas 842 F1, 840 G10
Bronzewing Vic 340 F5

Brookdale Qld 562 C7
Brooker SA 790 E8
Brookfield NSW 459 J5
Brookfield Qld 555 A5
Brookfield CP SA 787 G4, 791 L9
Brooking Gorge CP WA 713 H8
Brooking Springs WA 713 H9
Brooklana NSW 461 M7
Brooklands Qld 563 J7
Brooklyn NSW 455 K5, 459 H8
Brooklyn Qld 565 J5
Brooklyn Vic 335 B4
Brooklyn Park SA 786 D6
Brookstead Qld 556 A6, 559 K7
Brookton WA 705 F6, 706 D5
Brookvale NSW 453 F4
Brookville Vic 342 E4, 345 L9
Brooloo Qld 556 D2, 559 M5
Broome WA 696, 712 C8, 715 N1
Broomehill WA 705 G10, 706 E8
Brooms Head NSW 461 N5
Broughton Qld 560 B2, 563 M10
Broughton Vic 340 B9
Broulee NSW 456 E6
Brownhill Creek RP SA 786 E7
Brownleigh NSW 460 E3
Brownlow SA 787 F3, 791 L8
Browns Plains Qld 555 D10, 556 E6, 557 C4, 559 N7
Browns Plains Vic 344 G3
Bruce ACT 477 D2
Bruce SA 791 J5
Bruce Rock WA 706 F4
Brucedale Qld 558 F6
Bruinbun NSW 454 D3, 458 D6
Brunchilly NT 617 J6
Brunette Downs NT 617 L6
Brungle NSW 456 A4, 457 B2, 465 P6
Brunkerville NSW 455 L2, 459 J6
Brunswick Vic 335 C3, 336 G3, 339 P6
Brunswick Bay WA 712 G4
Brunswick Heads NSW 414, 461 P2
Brunswick Junction WA 705 C9, 706 C7
Bruny Island Tas 830, 839 C8, 843 K7
Bruthen Vic 342 F5, 345 L10
Bryah WA 709 H3
Bryans Gap NSW 461 K3
Buangor Vic 339 H4
Bubialo Qld 560 F2
Bucasia Qld 560 G4
Buccaneer Archipelago WA 712 E5
Buccarumbi NSW 461 L6
Buccleuch SA 788 A8
Buchan Vic 302, 342 G4, 345 N9
Buchan South Vic 342 G5, 345 N10
Bucheen Creek Vic 345 K5
Buckalow NSW 462 A9, 464 A1
Buckenderra NSW 456 B7, 457 D6
Bucket Claypan Qld 564 B9

Bucketty NSW 455 K3, 459 H6
Buckeys Creek Qld 558 A3
Buckhorst Vic 340 A8
Buckingham SA 788 C9
Buckland Tas 839 E3, 843 L3
Buckland Vic 342 B1, 345 H6
Buckleboo SA 790 E5
Buckleboo SA 790 E6
Buckley Swamp Vic 338 E6
Buckrabanyule Vic 341 J9
Buckwaroon NSW 463 J6
Budawang NP NSW 367, 456 E5
Buddabaddah NSW 463 M8
Budderoo NP NSW 455 J10, 456 G3
Buddigower NSW 465 M4
Buddigower NR NSW 465 M3
Buderim Qld 556 E3, 559 N5
Budgee Budgee NSW 458 D5
Budgeree Vic 337 N6
Budgerum Vic 341 J7
Budgerygar Qld 567 K3
Budgewoi NSW 455 M4, 459 J7
Buffalo Vic 337 M7
Buffalo Creek Vic 344 G5
Buffalo River Vic 342 B1, 344 G6
Bug Creek SA 786 G10
Bugaldie NSW 458 C1, 460 C10
Bugilbone NSW 460 B6
Bugtown NSW 456 B6, 457 D5
Bukalong NSW 456 C9, 457 F9
Bukkula NSW 461 H5
Bukulla NSW 460 A4
Bulahdelah NSW 385, 459 L4
Bulart Vic 338 D5
Buldah Vic 343 L3
Bulga NSW 455 K1, 459 H5
Bulga NSW 459 L2
Bulga Downs WA 709 J8
Bulgamurra NSW 462 E10, 464 E2
Bulgandramine NSW 463 P9
Bulgandry NSW 465 L7
Bulgary NSW 465 M6
Bulgroo Outstation Qld 567 K4
Bulgunnia SA 792 C10
Bulimba Qld 555 D4
Bulimba Qld 563 H5
Bulingary NSW 461 M8
Bull Creek WA 704 D7
Bulla NSW 463 H7
Bulla Vic 335 A2, 336 G2, 339 N5
Bullabulling WA 707 K3
Bullamon Plains Qld 558 F9
Bullara WA 714 B8
Bullardoo WA 708 D7
Bullargreen NSW 463 P7
Bullaring WA 705 G7, 706 F5
Bullarto Vic 336 D1, 339 L4
Bullawarrie Qld 558 E9
Bullecourt Qld 564 A3
Bulleen Vic 335 D3
Bullen Bullen Qld 558 D2
Bullen Range NP ACT 477 C4
Bullenbong NSW 465 M6

Bullengarook Vic 336 E1, 339 M5
Bulleringa NP Qld 563 J6
Bullfinch WA 707 H3
Bullhead Creek Vic 345 K4
Bullioh Vic 345 K4
Bullita NT 614 C10, 616 C2
Bulliwallah Qld 560 C5
Bullo River NT 614 B9
Bullock Creek Qld 563 K7, 569 A10
Bulloo Creek SA 791 N4
Bulloo Downs Qld 567 J9
Bulloo Downs WA 709 J1, 715 J10
Bulloo River Qld 567 L7
Bulls Gully Qld 567 M4
Bullsbrook WA 705 C4, 706 C4
Bullumwaal Vic 342 E5, 345 K10
Bulman NT 615 J6
Buln Buln Vic 337 M5
Bulyee WA 705 G6, 706 E5
Bulyeroi NSW 460 C6
Bumberry NSW 458 A7
Bumbunga SA 787 C2, 791 J8
Bunbartha Vic 344 B4
Bunbury WA **640–641**, 705 B9,
    706 B7
Bunda NT 616 A5
Bunda Bunda Qld 562 F10, 565 H2
Bundaberg Qld **496–497**, 559 L2
Bundaburrah NSW 465 N2
Bundalaguah Vic 342 B7
Bundaleer Qld 558 B9
Bundalong Vic 344 E3
Bundalong South Vic 344 E3
Bundamba Qld 557 B3
Bundanoon NSW **367**, 454 G10,
    456 F3
Bundarra NSW 461 H7
Bundarra NSW 462 E3
Bundeena NSW 453 D10, 455 K7,
    459 H9
Bundeena Qld 567 J7
Bundella NSW 458 E2
Bundemar NSW 458 A3, 463 P8
Bundjalung NP NSW **406**, 461 N4
Bundoo Qld 558 B4
Bundooma NT 619 J8
Bundoona Qld 567 M8
Bundoora Vic 335 D2
Bundure NSW 465 K6
Bung Bong Vic 339 J3
Bunga NSW 456 E8
Bungador Vic 339 J8
Bungal Vic 336 D2, 339 L5
Bungalien Qld 564 D4
Bungalla WA 705 G4, 706 E4
Bungarby NSW 456 C8, 457 E8
Bungaree Vic 336 C2, 339 L5
Bungaringa Qld 558 D4
Bungawalbin NP NSW 461 M3
Bungeet Vic 344 E4
Bungendore NSW **477** G2, 456 D5,
    457 G2
Bungil Vic 345 K3

Bungobine Qld 560 D4
Bungonia NSW 456 E4
Bungowannah NSW 465 M8
Bunguluke Vic 341 J9
Bungunya Qld 558 G9
Bungwahl NSW 459 L4
Buninyong Vic 336 C2, 339 K5
Bunjil WA 708 E9
Bunketch WA 705 F1, 706 E2
Bunna Bunna NSW 460 C6
Bunnaloo NSW 465 H7
Bunnan NSW 458 G3
Bunnawarra WA 708 F8
Bunnerungee NSW 464 B3
Buntine WA 706 D1, 708 F10
Bunya Qld 555 B2
Bunya Mountains NP Qld **497**,
    556 A3, 559 K5
Bunyah NSW 459 L4
Bunyan NSW 456 C7, 457 F6
Bunyaville SF Qld 555 B2
Bunyip Vic 337 L5
Bunyip SP Vic 337 K4
Buranda Qld 555 D6
Burbank Qld 555 F7
Burbong ACT 457 F3
Burcher NSW 465 M2
Burdekin Downs Qld 560 B1,
    563 M10
Burdett South NR WA 707 M7
Burekup WA 705 B9
Burgooney NSW 465 L2
Burgoyne Qld 560 B9, 565 P9
Burkan Qld 560 G8
Burke and Wills Roadhouse Qld
    562 D9
Burkes Flat Vic 339 J2
Burketown Qld **526**, 562 C7
Burleigh Qld 565 J2
Burleigh Heads Qld 556 F7, 557 F7,
    559 N8
Burlington Qld 563 J7, 569 A10
Burma Road NR WA 708 D8
Burnabinmah WA 708 G8
Burnbank Vic 339 J4
Burngrove Qld 560 F9
Burnie Tas **811**, 840 E4
Burns Creek Tas 844 G6, 841 L6
Burnside Qld 565 L5
Burnside SA 786 E6
Burnt Down Scrub NR NSW 461 L4
Burnt Yards NSW 454 B5, 458 B8
Buronga NSW 464 C4
Burra Qld 565 N3
Burra SA **757**, 787 E1, 791 K7
Burra Bee Dee NSW 458 D1,
    460 D10
Burra Creek SA 787 E1
Burra NR WA 707 L3
Burraboi NSW 464 G7
Burracoppin WA 706 G3
Burraga NSW 454 D7, 456 D1,
    458 D9

Burragate NSW 456 D9, 457 G10
Burramine Vic 344 D3
Burrandana NSW 465 N7
Burraneer NSW 453 D10
Burrangong NSW 456 A2, 458 A10,
    465 P4
Burrapine NSW 461 M8
Burraway NSW 458 A3, 463 P8
Burrell Creek NSW 459 L3
Burren Junction NSW 460 B7
Burrenbilla Qld 567 P8
Burrereo Vic 338 G1, 340 G10
Burrill Lake NSW 456 F5
Burringbar NSW 461 P2
Burringurrah (Mount Augustus) NP
    WA **664**
Burrinjuck NSW 456 B4, 457 D1
Burrinjuck Waters SP NSW 456 B4,
    457 C1
Burrowa–Pine Mountain NP Vic
    345 L3
Burrowye Vic 345 K3
Burrum Heads Qld 559 M2
Burrumbeet Vic 336 B1, 339 K5
Burrumbuttock NSW 465 M8
Burslem Qld 565 L6
Burswood WA 704 D5
Burta NSW 462 A9
Burthong NSW 463 L9
Burtle Qld 560 C8
Burton SA 786 E1
Burton Downs Qld 560 E5
Burtundy NSW 464 C3
Burua Qld 561 K9
Burunga NSW 558 G4
Burwood NSW 453 D6
Burwood Vic 335 E4
·Burwood East Vic 335 E4
Busbys Flat NSW 461 M3
Bushy Park NT 619 H4
Bushy Park Qld 564 D4
Bushy Park Tas 839 A3, 843 H4
Bushy Park Vic 342 C6
Busselton WA **641**, 705 A10, 706 B7
Butcher Lake WA 710 E4
Butchers Creek Qld 563 L6, 569 D9
Butchers Ridge Vic 342 G3, 345 N8
Bute SA 787 B2, 791 H8
Butler Tanks SA 790 E8
Butru Qld 564 D4
Butterleaf NP NSW 461 K5
Buxton NSW 455 H8, 456 F2,
    458 F10
Buxton Vic 337 L1, 344 D9
Byabarra NSW 459 L2
Byaduk Vic 338 D6
Byaduk North Vic 338 D6
Byalong Qld 558 B8
Byerawering NSW 463 M2
Byerwen Qld 560 E4
Byfield Qld 561 J7
Byfield NP Qld 561 K7
Byford WA 705 C6, 706 C5

Bylands Vic 336 G1, 339 P4, 344 A9
Bylong NSW 458 E4
Bylong Qld 565 J2
Byrnes Scrub NR NSW 461 M6
Byrneside Vic 339 P1, 341 P10, 3
    44 B5
Byrneville Vic 338 E1, 340 E10
Byro WA 708 E4
Byrock NSW 463 L5
Byron Bay NSW **414**, 461 P2
Bywong NSW 456 D4, 457 F2

C

C Lake NSW 462 E10, 464 E2
Cabana Qld 563 J7
Cabanandra Vic 343 J3
Cabanda Qld 564 G2
Cabbage Lake NSW 464 G3
Cabbage Tree Creek Vic 343 J5
Cabbage Tree Point Qld 557 E4
Caboolture Qld 556 D4, 559 M6
Cabramatta NSW 453 A7
Cabramatta West NSW 453 A6
Cabramurra NSW 456 B6, 457 C5
Cactus Beach SA **744**
Caddens Flat Vic 338 D4
Cadelga Outstation SA 793 N1
Cadell SA 791 L8
Cadney Homestead (Roadhouse) SA
    792 A5
Cadney Park SA 792 A5
Cadoux WA 705 F1, 706 E2
Caiguna WA 711 C8
Cairn Curran Reservoir Vic 339 L3
Cairns Qld **550**, 563 L5, 569 D7
Cairns Bay Tas 839 A7, 843 H7
Cairo Qld 560 D6
Caiwarra Qld 564 F3
Caiwarro Qld 567 M9
Cal Lal NSW 464 A4
Calala NSW 458 G1, 460 G10
Calamvale Qld 555 D9
Calca SA 790 B6
Calcifer Qld 563 K6, 569 A8
Calcium Qld 560 C1, 563 N10
Calder Tas 840 D5
Caldermeade Vic 337 K5
Caldervale Qld 558 B2
Caldwell NSW 464 G7
Calen Qld 560 F3
Calga NSW 455 K4, 459 H7
Calindary NSW 462 D4
Calingiri WA 705 D2, 706 D3
Calivil Vic 341 L9
Callagiddy WA 708 B3
Callala Bay NSW 456 G4
Callawa WA 715 K5
Callawadda Vic 338 G2
Calleen NSW 465 M3
Callide Qld 559 H1, 561 J10
Callington SA 787 E7, 788 A6,
    791 K10
Calliope Qld 561 K9

Callytharra Springs WA 708 D4
Calomba SA 787 C4, 791 J9
Caloola NSW 454 D5, 456 D1, 458 D8
Caloona NSW 460 C3
Caloundra Qld 556 E3, 559 N6
Calpatanna Waterhole CP SA 790 B6
Calperum SA 791 N8
Calton Hills Qld 562 C10, 564 C2
Caltowie SA 791 J6
Calvert Vic 338 G5
Calvert Hills NT 617 N3
Calwell ACT 477 D5
Calwynyardah WA 712 G8
Camballin WA 712 F8
Cambarville Vic 337 L2, 344 D10
Camberwell NSW 459 H5
Camberwell Vic 335 D4, 337 H3, 339 P6
Camboon Qld 559 H2
Cambooya Qld 556 B6, 559 L7
Cambrai SA 787 F5, 791 L9
Cambridge Tas 839 D4, 843 K5
Camburinga Village NT 615 M5
Camden NSW 455 H7, 456 G2, 458 G9
Camden Park SA 786 C6
Camel Creek Qld 563 L8
Camel Lake NR WA 706 F8
Camena Tas 840 F5
Camfield NT 616 D3
Camira Qld 555 A9, 557 B4
Camira Creek NSW 461 M4
Cammeray NSW 453 E5
Camooweal Qld 534–535, 562 A10, 564 A1
Camooweal Caves NP Qld 562 A10, 564 A2
Camp Hill Qld 555 E5
Campania Tas 839 D3, 843 K4
Campbell ACT 477 E3
Campbell Range WA 713 M3
Campbell Town Tas 811, 844 G10, 841 L9
Campbellfield Vic 335 C2, 336 G2, 339 P5, 344 A10
Campbells Bridge Vic 338 G2
Campbells Creek Vic 339 L3
Campbells Forest Vic 339 L1
Campbelltown NSW 368, 455 J7, 456 G2, 458 G9
Campbelltown SA 786 F5
Campbelltown Vic 339 L4
Camperdown NSW 453 E6
Camperdown Vic 339 H7
Campsie NSW 453 D7
Camurra NSW 460 E4
Canada Bay NSW 453 D6
Canaga Qld 559 J5
Canary Qld 564 E8
Canary Island Vic 341 K8
Canaway Downs Qld 567 L4
Canbelego NSW 463 L7

Canberra ACT 470–473, 477 D3, 456 C5, 457 F2
Canberra District Wine Region 368
Canberra Nature Park ACT 477 E2
Candelo NSW 456 D8
Cane River WA 714 D7
Canegrass SA 791 M7
Cangai NSW 461 L5
Cania Gorge NP Qld 497, 559 J1
Canley Heights NSW 453 A6
Canley Vale NSW 453 A6
Cann River Vic 343 L5
Canna WA 708 E8
Cannawigara SA 788 C9
Canning River WA 704 E7
Canning Vale WA 704 E8
Cannington Qld 564 F5
Cannington WA 704 E6
Cannon Hill Qld 555 E5
Cannonvale Qld 560 F2
Canobie Qld 562 E9, 564 F1
Canonba NSW 463 N6
Canoona Qld 561 J8
Canopus SA 791 N7
Canowie SA 791 K6
Canowindra NSW 386, 454 A5, 458 B8
Canteen Creek NT 617 L9, 619 L1
Canterbury NSW 453 D7
Canterbury Qld 566 G3
Canterbury Vic 335 E4
Canunda NP SA 732, 788 F8
Canungra Qld 557 D6
Canyonleigh NSW 454 F10, 456 E3
Cap Island CP SA 790 C8
Capalaba Qld 555 G7, 556 E5, 557 D3, 559 N7
Capalaba West Qld 555 G6
Capamauro NR WA 706 C1, 708 E10
Cape Arid NP WA 641, 707 P7, 711 A9
Cape Barren Island Tas 841 P1
Cape Bougainville WA 713 J1
Cape Bouguer WPA SA 788 C2
Cape Bridgewater Vic 338 C8
Cape Burney WA 708 C8
Cape Clear Vic 336 A3, 339 J6
Cape Crawford NT 617 L3
Cape Gantheaume CP SA 788 B3
Cape Hart CP SA 787 B10, 788 B4
Cape Jaffa SA 788 E7
Cape Jervis SA 787 B9, 788 B4
Cape Le Grand NP WA 641, 707 M8
Cape Leeuwin WA 706 B9
Cape Londonderry WA 713 K1
Cape Melville NP Qld 563 K2, 568 G9, 569 B1
Cape Nelson SP Vic 338 C8
Cape Onslow WA 713 M2
Cape Palmerston NP Qld 561 H5
Cape Paterson Vic 337 K8
Cape Range NP WA 693–694,

714 B7
Cape Riche WA 706 G9
Cape River Qld 560 A3, 565 N3
Cape Schanck Vic 336 G6, 339 N8
Cape Torrens WPA SA 788 B2
Cape Tribulation NP Qld 563 L4, 569 D5
Cape Upstart NP Qld 560 E1, 563 P10
Cape York Peninsula Qld 568 C5
Capel WA 705 B10, 706 B7
Capella Qld 560 E8
Capels Crossing Vic 341 L7
Capertee NSW 454 F3, 458 E7
Capietha SA 790 C5
Capricorn Coast Qld 561 K8
Capricorn Group Qld 561 M8
Capricorn Roadhouse WA 715 K9
Captain Billy Landing Qld 568 D4
Captains Creek NR NSW 461 L2
Captains Flat NSW 456 D5, 457 G4
Carabost NSW 465 N7
Caradoc NSW 462 E5
Carag Carag Vic 339 N1, 341 N10, 344 A5
Caragabel NSW 465 N3
Caralue SA 790 E7
Caramut Vic 338 F6
Carandotta Qld 564 B5
Caranna Qld 567 N3
Carapooee Vic 339 J2
Carapook Vic 338 C5
Caravan Head NSW 453 C9
Carawa SA 790 B5
Carbeen NSW 460 C7
Carbeen Park NT 613 F9, 614 E8
Carbine WA 707 K2
Carbla WA 708 C4
Carboor Vic 344 G5
Carboor Upper Vic 342 A1, 344 G6
Carcoar NSW 454 C5, 456 C1, 458 C8
Carcoory Qld 566 D3
Carcuma CP SA 788 B8
Cardabia WA 714 B9
Cardigan Qld 560 C2
Cardigan Vic 336 B1, 339 K5
Cardigan Village Vic 336 B1, 339 K5
Cardington Qld 560 C1, 563 N10
Cardinia Vic 337 J5
Cardinia Reservoir Vic 337 J4
Cardowan Qld 560 G6
Cardross Vic 340 E2
Cardstone Qld 563 L7, 569 D10
Cardwell Qld 526, 563 M7
Careel Bay NSW 453 G1
Carey Downs WA 708 D3
Carfax Qld 560 F6
Cargo NSW 454 A4, 458 B7
Cargoon Qld 563 K10, 565 M2
Cariewerloo SA 790 G5
Carina Qld 555 E5
Carina Vic 340 B6
Carina Heights Qld 555 E6

Carinda NSW 463 N5
Carindale Qld 555 E6
Carine WA 704 B2
Caringbah NSW 453 D9, 455 K7, 459 H9
Carinya NSW 464 F2
Carinya Qld 558 E4
Carisbrook Vic 339 K3
Carlindi WA 715 J5
Carlingford NSW 453 C4
Carlisle WA 704 E5
Carlisle River Vic 339 J9
Carlisle SP Vic 336 A7, 339 J9
Carlsruhe Vic 339 M4
Carlton NSW 453 D8
Carlton Tas 839 E5, 843 L5
Carlton Vic 335 C3
Carlton Hill WA 713 N4
Carlyarn NR WA 706 E1, 708 G10
Carmichael Qld 560 B5, 565 P5
Carmila Qld 560 G5
Carmor Plain NT 613 F2, 614 E4
Carnamah WA 708 E9
Carnarvon Qld 558 D2
Carnarvon WA 664, 708 B2
Carnarvon NP Qld 497, 558 D1
Carnarvon Range WA 709 L3
Carne Outstation SA 792 B10
Carnegie Vic 335 D5
Carnegie WA 664, 709 N4
Carney NSW 463 H5
Carngham Vic 336 A2, 339 J5
Caroda NSW 460 F6
Carole Park Qld 555 A9
Caroling WA 705 G5
Caroona NSW 458 F1, 460 F10
Caroona SA 791 K7
Carpa SA 790 F7
Carpendeit Vic 339 H8
Carpentaria Downs Qld 563 J8
Carpenter Rocks SA 788 G9
Carpet Springs Qld 567 M8
Carpolac Vic 338 B2
Carrai NP NSW 461 L9
Carrajung Vic 342 B8
Carrajung South Vic 342 B8
Carramar NSW 453 A6
Carranballac Vic 339 H5
Carranya Qld 567 H3
Carranya WA 710 E1
Carrarang WA 708 B5
Carrathool NSW 465 J4
Carrick Tas 844 D7, 841 J7
Carrickalinga SA 787 C8, 788 A5
Carrieton SA 791 J5
Carroll NSW 460 F9
Carroll Gap NSW 460 F9
Carron Vic 340 G9
Carrow Brook NSW 459 H4
Carrum Qld 564 G3
Carrum Vic 335 E7
Carrum Downs Vic 335 F7, 337 H5, 339 P7

Carseldine Qld 555 C2
Carson River WA 713 K2
Carss Park NSW 453 D8
Carwarp Vic 340 E3
Carwell Qld 558 B2
Cascade NSW 461 M7
Cascade WA 707 K7
Cascade NP NSW 461 L7
Cascades Tas 838 C7
Cashew Nut Farm NT 613 F3,
   614 E4
Cashmere Qld 555 A1
Cashmere Qld 558 E8
Cashmere Downs WA 709 J8
Cashmore Vic 338 C8
Casino NSW 414–415, 461 N3
Cassidy Gap Vic 338 F5
Cassilis NSW 458 E3
Cassilis Vic 342 E3, 345 L8
Casterton Vic 269, 338 C5
Castle Doyle NSW 461 J8
Castle Forbes Bay Tas 839 A7, 843 H6
Castle Hill NSW 453 B3
Castle Rock NSW 458 G4
Castle Tower NP Qld 561 L10
Castleburn Vic 342 D5, 345 J10
Castlemaine Vic 269, 339 L3
Castlevale Qld 558 B1, 560 C10
Casuarina NT 612 F2
Casuarina Coastal Reserve NT
   612 D2
Casula NSW 453 A7
Cataby WA 705 B1, 706 B2
Catamaran Tas 839 A10, 843 H9
Cathcart NSW 456 D9, 457 G9
Cathcart Vic 338 G4
Cathedral Hill Qld 565 H6
Cathedral Range SP Vic 337 L1,
   344 D9
Cathedral Rock NP NSW 461 L7
Catherine Hill Bay NSW 455 M3,
   459 J7
Cathkin Vic 344 C8
Cathundral NSW 463 P8
Cattai NSW 455 J5, 458 G8
Cattle Creek NT 616 E4
Catumnal Vic 341 K9
Caulfield Vic 335 D4
Caulfield North Vic 335 D4
Caurnamont SA 791 L10
Cavan NSW 456 C4, 457 E1
Cavan SA 786 E3
Cave Creek NSW 460 G7
Cave Hill NR WA 707 L4
Caveat Vic 344 C8
Cavendish Vic 338 E5
Caversham WA 704 F3
Caveside Tas 844 A7, 840 G7
Cavillon Qld 558 D9
Cawarral Qld 561 J8
Cawnalmurtee NSW 462 E5
Cawongla NSW 461 N2
Cecil Plains Qld 559 J7

Cedar Bay NP Qld 563 L4, 569 C4
Cedar Brush Creek NSW 455 L3,
   459 H6
Cedar Grove Qld 557 C5
Cedar Party NSW 459 L2
Cedar Point NSW 461 N2
Ceduna SA 744, 789 G10, 790 A4
Centennial Park NSW 453 F6
Central Castra Tas 840 F6
Central Lansdowne NSW 459 L2
Central Mangrove NSW 455 K4,
   459 H7
Central Mt Stuart Historical Reserve
   NT 619 H3
Central Plateau CA Tas 812, 844 A8,
   841 H8
Central Plateau PA Tas 812, 844 C9,
   841 J9
Central Tilba NSW 368, 456 E7
Central Victoria Wine Region Vic 270
Ceres Vic 336 D5, 339 L7
Cerito Qld 560 E4
Cervantes WA 641, 705 A1, 706 B2
Cessnock NSW 386, 455 L2, 459 H6
Chadinga CR SA 789 F10
Chadshunt Qld 562 G7
Chadstone Vic 335 E4
Chaelundi NP NSW 461 L6
Chain of Lagoons Tas 841 P7
Chakola NSW 456 C7, 457 F6
Chalky Well NSW 462 C10, 464 C2
Challa WA 709 H7
Challambra Vic 340 F9
Chamberlain River WA 713 L6
Chambers Bay NT 613 E2
Chambers Flat Qld 557 D4
Chambers Pillar Historical Reserve
   NT 607, 619 H8
Chandada SA 790 B5
Chandler Qld 555 F6
Chandler SA 789 G2
Chandlers Creek Vic 343 L4
Chandlers Hill SA 786 D9
Channing Qld 558 G5
Chapel Hill Qld 555 B6
Chapman ACT 477 C4
Chapple Vale Vic 339 J9
Charam Vic 338 C3
Charbon NSW 454 F2, 458 E6
Charlestown NSW 455 M2, 459 J6
Charleville Qld 498, 558 A5
Charleyong NSW 456 E5
Charleys Creek Vic 336 A7, 339 J9
Charlotte Plains Qld 558 A8, 567 P8
Charlotte Plains Qld 565 L2
Charlotte Vale Qld 558 A7, 567 P7
Charlottes Pass NSW 456 A8,
   457 B7, 465 P9
Charlton NSW 463 M4
Charlton Vic 341 J9
Charnwood ACT 477 C2
Charters Towers Qld 515, 560 B2,
   563 M10

Chartwell Vic 336 F3, 339 N6
Chatham Village NSW 453 A8
Chatsbury NSW 454 E9, 456 E3
Chatswood NSW 453 D5, 455 K6,
   459 H8
Chatswood West NSW 453 E4
Chatsworth NSW 461 N4
Chatsworth Qld 564 E6
Chatsworth Vic 338 G6
Cheadanup NR WA 707 K7
Cheepie Qld 567 M5
Chelmer Qld 555 B6
Chelmer Qld 558 F8
Chelsea Vic 335 E7, 337 H4, 339 P7
Chelsea Heights Vic 335 E6
Cheltenham Vic 335 E5
Cheriton Qld 558 F8
Chermside Qld 555 C3, 557 C2
Chermside West Qld 555 C3
Cherrabun WA 710 C1, 713 H10
Cherry Gardens SA 786 E9
Cherry Tree Hill NSW 461 H5
Cherrybrook NSW 453 C3
Cherrypool Vic 338 E3
Chesalon Qld 560 C9
Cheshire Qld 558 B1, 560 B10
Cheshunt Vic 342 A1, 344 F6
Cheshunt South Vic 344 F7
Chesney Vic 344 E5
Chester Hill NSW 453 B6
Chesterfield Qld 560 D5
Chesterton Range NP Qld 558 C4
Chetwynd Vic 338 C4
Chewton Vic 339 M3
Cheyne Bay WA 706 G9
Cheyne Beach WA 706 F9
Chichester NSW 459 J4
Chichester Range WA 714 G7
Chiddarcooping NR WA 706 G2
Chidlow WA 705 D5, 706 C4
Chidna Qld 562 C9, 564 C1
Chifley NSW 453 F8
Chifley WA 707 N3
Chigwell Tas 838 A1
Childers Qld 498, 559 L2
Childers Vic 337 M6
Chilla Well NT 618 D2
Chillagoe Qld 526, 563 K6, 569 A8
Chillagoe–Mungana Caves NP Qld
   563 K6, 569 A8
Chillingham NSW 461 N1
Chillingollah Vic 341 H6
Chilpanunda SA 790 B5
Chiltern Vic 344 G3
Chiltern Box – Ironbark NP Vic
   344 G3
Chiltern Hills Qld 564 G7
Chinaman Creek SA 791 H5
Chinaman Wells SA 790 G9
Chinbi Qld 565 K4
Chinbingina SA 790 A4
Chinchilla Qld 498, 559 J5
Chinderah NSW 461 P1

Chinghee Creek Qld 557 C8
Chinkapook Vic 340 G5
Chinocup NR WA 706 F7
Chipping Norton NSW 453 A7
Chipping Norton Lake NSW 453 A7
Chirnside Park Vic 335 G2
Chirrup Vic 341 H9
Chiswick NSW 453 D6
Chorregon Qld 565 K7
Chowilla SA 791 N8
Chowilla GR SA 791 N8
Chowilla RR SA 791 N7
Christie Downs SA 786 B10
Christies Beach SA 786 B10
Christmas Creek Qld 563 L9
Christmas Creek Vic 342 E1, 345 K6
Christmas Creek WA 710 C1,
   713 J10
Christmas Hills Tas 840 B4
Christmas Hills Vic 335 F1
Christmas Point Qld 562 F1, 568 B9
Chudleigh Tas 844 A7, 840 G7
Chudleigh Park Qld 563 J10, 565 L1
Chullora NSW 453 C6
Church Plain Camp NSW 460 F4
Church Point NSW 453 F2
Churchill Qld 557 B4
Churchill Vic 337 P6, 342 A8
Churchill NP Vic 335 G5
Churchlands WA 704 B4
Churinga NSW 462 D7
Chute Vic 339 J4
Circle Valley WA 707 L6
City Beach WA 704 B4
Clackline WA 705 D4, 706 D4
Clairview Qld 561 H6
Clandulla NSW 454 F2, 458 E6
Clarafield Qld 565 H4
Claravale NT 613 E8, 614 E7
Claravale Qld 558 D4
Claraville NT 619 J5
Claraville Qld 562 F8
Clare NSW 464 F2
Clare Qld 560 A7, 565 P7
Clare Qld 560 D1, 563 N10
Clare SA 758, 791 J7, 787 D2
Clare Calpa NSW 464 G3
Clare Valley Wine Region SA
   758–759
Claremont Tas 838 B1, 839 C4,
   843 K4
Claremont WA 704 B5
Clarence Point Tas 844 C3, 841 J5
Clarence River NSW 461 L2
Clarence Strait NT 613 C1
Clarence Town NSW 459 K5,
   455 N1
Clarendon SA 786 E10, 787 D7,
   788 A5, 791 J10
Clarendon Tas 844 F7, 841 K7
Clarendon Vic 336 C3, 339 L5
Clarinda Vic 335 E5
Clarke Hills Qld 563 K10, 565 M1

Clarke River Qld 563 L9
Clarkefield Vic 336 F1, 339 N5
Clarkes Hill Vic 336 C1, 339 L5
Claude Road Tas 840 G6
Claverton Qld 558 A7, 567 P7
Clay Wells SA 788 E8
Clayfield Qld 555 D4
Clayton SA 787 E8, 788 A6
Clayton SA 793 J8
Clayton Vic 335 E5
Clayton South Vic 335 E5
Clear Creek ACT 477 B8
Clear Lake Vic 338 D3
Clear Ridge NSW 465 N3
Cleland CP SA 786 F7
Clemton Park NSW 453 D7
Clermont Qld 515, 560 D7
Cleve SA 759, 790 F7
Cleveland Qld 556 E5, 557 E3, 559 N7
Cleveland Tas 844 F9, 841 L8
Cliffdale Qld 567 P6
Clifford Qld 558 F4
Cliffordville WA 705 G7, 706 E6
Clifton Qld 556 B6, 559 L8
Clifton Qld 567 J3
Clifton Beach Qld 563 L5, 569 D7
Clifton Beach Tas 839 D5, 843 L5
Clifton Creek Vic 342 E5, 345 L10
Clifton Downs NSW 462 D3
Clifton Gardens NSW 453 F5
Clifton Hill Vic 335 D3
Clifton Hills SA 793 J3
Clifton Springs Vic 336 E5, 339 M7
Clinton Centre SA 787 B3, 791 H8
Clinton CP SA 787 B3, 791 H8
Clio Qld 565 J5
Clive Qld 560 G7
Clonagh Qld 562 D10, 564 E2
Cloncose Qld 559 J3
Cloncurry Qld 535, 564 E3
Clontarf NSW 453 F5
Clontarf Qld 559 K8
Closeburn Qld 557 B1
Clouds Creek NSW 461 M6
Clough Creek NT 619 N3
Clovelly NSW 453 F7
Clovelly Qld 565 M9
Clovelly Park SA 786 D7
Cloverdale WA 704 E5
Cloverlea Vic 337 M5
Cloyna Qld 556 B1, 559 L4
Cluan Tas 844 C7, 841 J7
Club Terrace Vic 343 K5
Clunes Vic 339 K4
Cluny Qld 564 C10, 566 C1
Clybucca NSW 461 M9
Clyde NSW 453 B6
Clyde Vic 337 J5
Clydebank Vic 342 D7
Coal Mines Historic Site Tas 839 E5, 843 L5

Coalcliff NSW 455 J8, 456 G2, 458 G10
Coaldale NSW 461 M4
Coalstoun Lakes Qld 559 L3
Coalville Vic 337 N5
Coan Downs NSW 463 K9, 465 K1
Cobains Vic 342 C7
Cobar NSW 435, 463 K7
Cobargo NSW 456 E7
Cobbadah NSW 460 F7
Cobbannah Vic 342 D5, 345 J10
Cobbler Creek RP SA 786 F2
Cobbora NSW 458 C3
Cobbrum Qld 558 A7
Cobourg Marine Park NT 589, 614 F1
Cobourg Peninsula NT 614 F2
Cobra WA 708 E1
Cobram Vic 325, 344 C2
Cobrico Vic 339 H8
Cobungra Vic 342 D3, 345 K8
Coburg Vic 335 C3, 336 G3, 339 P6, 344 A10
Coburg North Vic 335 C2
Coburn WA 708 C5
Cocamba Vic 340 G5
Cocata CP SA 790 C6
Cocata CR SA 790 D6
Cochranes Creek Vic 339 J2
Cockaleechie SA 790 D8
Cockatoo Qld 559 H3
Cockatoo Vic 337 K4
Cockburn SA 791 P4
Cockburn Sound WA 705 B6, 706 B5
Cockenzie Qld 560 F5
Cocklarina Qld 567 N7
Cockle Creek Tas 839 A10, 843 H9
Cocklebiddy WA 676, 711 D7
Coconut Grove NT 612 C4
Cocoparra NP NSW 465 L4
Codrington Vic 338 D7
Coen Qld 563 H1, 568 D8
Coffin Bay SA 759, 790 D9
Coffin Bay NP SA 759, 790 C9
Coffs Harbour NSW 415, 461 N7
Coghills Creek Vic 336 B1, 339 K4
Cogla Downs WA 709 H6
Cohuna Vic 290, 341 L8
Coimadai Vic 336 E2, 339 M5
Cokum Vic 341 H7
Colac Vic 270, 336 A6, 339 J8
Colac Colac Vic 345 L4
Colane NSW 462 E3
Colbinabbin Vic 339 N1, 341 N10
Colbinabbin West Vic 339 N1
Coldstream Vic 337 J3, 344 B10
Coleambally Irrigation Area NSW 465 K5
Colebrook Tas 839 C2, 843 K3

Coleman Bend Vic 345 M4
Coleraine Qld 565 J4
Coleraine Vic 338 D5
Coles Bay Tas 812, 843 P1, 841 P10
Colignan Vic 340 F3
Colinroobie NSW 465 L5
Colinton NSW 456 C6, 457 F5
Collapy Qld 560 C1, 563 N10
Collarenebri NSW 460 B5
Collaroy NSW 453 G3
Collaroy Qld 558 A5
Collaroy Qld 560 G6
Collaroy Plateau NSW 453 F3
Collector NSW 456 D4, 457 G1
Collerina NSW 463 L3
Colley SA 790 B6
Collie NSW 458 A2, 463 P7
Collie WA 642, 705 C9, 706 C7
Collier Bay WA 712 F5
Collier Range NP WA 709 J2
Collingullie NSW 465 M6
Collingwood Qld 559 H4
Collingwood Qld 565 H6
Collingwood Vic 335 D3
Collinsvale Tas 839 B4, 843 J5
Collinsville Qld 560 E3
Collinsville SA 791 K6
Collinswood SA 786 E5
Collymongle NSW 460 B5
Colmslie Qld 555 E4
Colo Heights NSW 455 J4, 458 G7
Colo River NSW 458 F7
Colonel Light Gardens SA 786 D7
Colossal NSW 463 M5
Colosseum Qld 559 K1, 561 L10
Colston Qld 565 J7
Colston Park Qld 560 G5
Columboola Qld 559 H5
Colwell Qld 564 F4
Comara NSW 461 L8
Combaning NSW 465 N5
Combara NSW 458 A1, 460 A10
Combienbar Vic 343 K4
Comboyne NSW 459 L2
Come by Chance NSW 460 A7
Comeroo NSW 463 H2
Comet Qld 560 F9
Commodore SA 791 J2
Commonwealth Hill SA 792 A9
Como NSW 453 C9, 455 K7, 459 H9
Como Qld 567 L5
Como WA 704 D6
Comobella NSW 458 C4
Comongin Qld 567 L5
Compton Downs NSW 463 L4
Conara Tas 844 F9, 841 L8
Conargo NSW 465 J6
Concongella Vic 338 G3
Concord NSW 453 D6
Concord West NSW 453 C6
Condada SA 790 C5
Condah Vic 338 D6

Condamine Qld 559 H6
Condell Park NSW 453 B7
Conder ACT 477 D5
Condingup WA 707 N7
Condobolin NSW 445, 463 M10, 465 M1
Condong NSW 461 P1
Condoulpe NSW 464 F5
Condowie SA /8/ C1, 791 J7
Congie Qld 567 K6
Congo NSW 456 E6
Congupna Vic 344 C4
Conimbla NP NSW 456 A1, 458 A8
Coningham Tas 839 C6, 843 K6
Coniston NT 618 F3
Coniston Qld 558 B7
Coniston Qld 567 J3
Conjola NSW 456 F5
Conjuboy Qld 563 K8
Conmurra SA 788 E9
Connells Lagoon CR NT 617 M6
Connells Point NSW 453 C8
Connemara Qld 558 B3
Connemara Qld 565 H10, 567 H1
Connemarra NSW 458 D2
Connemarra Qld 560 E9
Connewarre Vic 336 E5, 339 M7
Connewirrecoo Vic 338 C4
Connolly Qld 560 C2
Conoble NSW 463 H10, 465 H1
Conondale Qld 556 D3, 559 M5
Conondale NP Qld 556 C3, 559 M5
Conway Qld 560 F2
Conway Beach Qld 560 F3
Conway NP Qld 560 G3
Cooba NSW 457 A1, 465 P6
Coober Pedy SA 782, 792 C7
Cooberrie Qld 561 K8
Coobowie SA 788 A4, 791 H10
Coodardy WA 708 G6
Coogee NSW 453 F7
Coogee WA 704 B9
Coogee Bay NSW 453 F7
Cooinda NT 613 G4, 614 F5
Coojar Vic 338 C4
Cook ACT 477 D3
Cook SA 789 C8
Cookamidgera NSW 458 A7, 465 P2
Cookardinia NSW 465 M7
Cooke Plains SA 787 G8, 788 A7
Cooks Well Outstation Qld 566 G5
Cooktown Qld 551, 563 L3, 569 C3
Cool Creek Vic 337 M3, 344 E10
Coolabah NSW 463 L6
Coolabah Qld 567 N6
Coolabara Qld 567 M2
Coolabri Qld 558 B3
Coolabunia Qld 556 B3, 559 L5
Coolac NSW 456 A4, 457 B1, 465 P6
Cooladdi Qld 567 N5
Coolah NSW 458 D3
Coolah Tops NP NSW 458 E2

Coolamon NSW **445**, 465 M5
Coolangatta Qld 556 F7, 557 F8, 559 N8
Coolangubra NP NSW 456 D9, 457 G10
Coolanie SA 790 F7
Coolaroo Vic 335 C2
Coolatai NSW 460 G4
Coolbaggie NSW 458 A3
Coolbaggie NR NSW 458 B3
Coolbellup WA 704 C8
Coolbinia WA 704 D4
Coolcalalaya WA 708 D6
Coolcha SA 787 G6, 791 L10
Coolgardie WA **642**, 707 L3
Coolibah NT 614 D9
Coolimba WA 706 A1, 708 D10
Coolongolook NSW 459 L4
Cooltong SA 791 N8
Coolullah Qld 562 D10, 564 D1
Coolum Beach Qld 556 E2, 559 N5
Coolup WA 705 C7, 706 C6
Cooma NSW **368–369**, 456 C7, 457 F6
Cooma Qld 558 F7
Cooma Qld 567 J5
Cooma Vic 339 P1, 341 P10, 344 A5
Coomaba SA 790 D8
Coomallo NR WA 706 B1, 708 D10
Coomandook SA 788 A7
Coomba NSW 459 L4
Coombah Roadhouse NSW 462 B10, 464 B1
Coombell NSW 461 M3
Coombie NSW 463 J10, 465 J1
Coombogolong NSW 463 P5
Coomera Qld 557 E5
Coomeratta NSW 462 G7
Coominglah Qld 559 J1
Coominya Qld 556 C5, 559 M7
Coomooboolaroo Qld 561 H9
Coomoora Vic 336 D1, 339 L4
Coomrith Qld 558 G7
Coomunga SA 790 D9
Coonabarabran NSW **415**, 458 C1, 460 C10
Coonalpyn SA 788 B8
Coonamble NSW **416**, 460 A9
Coonana WA 707 N3
Coonawarra NT 612 G7
Coonawarra SA 788 E10
Coonawarra and the Limestone Coast SA **728–731**
Coondambo SA 790 D2
Coondarra Qld 559 H4
Cooneel Qld 561 J9
Coonerang NSW 456 C8, 457 F7
Coongan WA 715 J5
Coongie Qld 566 D6
Coongie SA 793 M3
Coongie Lake SA 793 M3
Coongoola Qld 558 A7, 567 P7
Coongulla Vic 342 B6

Coonooer Bridge Vic 339 J1, 341 J10
Cooper Creek Qld 566 G5
Cooper Creek SA 793 J6
Coopernook NSW 459 M3
Coopers Plains Qld 555 D7
Coopracambra NP Vic 343 L3
Coorabah Qld 560 A7
Coorabah Qld 565 N7
Coorabelle Qld 565 K5
Coorabie SA 789 E10
Coorabulka Qld 564 E9
Coorada Qld 558 G2
Cooralya WA 708 C2
Cooran Qld 556 D2, 559 M5
Cooranbong NSW 455 L3, 459 J6
Cooranga North Qld 559 K5
Coordewandy WA 708 E3
Cooriemungle Vic 339 H8
Coorong NP SA **732–733**, 787 F9, 788 B6
Cooroorah Qld 560 F8
Coorow WA 706 C1, 708 E10
Cooroy Qld 556 D2, 559 M5
Coorparoo Qld 555 D6
Cootamundra NSW **445**, 456 A3, 465 P5
Cootawundi NSW 462 D6
Cooyal NSW 458 D4
Cooyar Qld 556 B4, 559 L6
Coparella Qld 567 M6
Cope Cope Vic 339 H1, 341 H10
Copeland NSW 459 K3
Copeton Dam NSW 461 H6
Copeton Waters SP NSW 460 G6
Copeville SA 791 M10
Copley SA **759**, 791 J1, 793 J10
Copmanhurst NSW 461 M5
Coppabella Qld 560 F5
Copper Hill SA 792 B5
Copperhania NR NSW 454 C6, 456 C1, 458 C8
Copping Tas 839 F4, 843 M5
Cora Lynn Vic 337 K5
Corack East Vic 341 H9
Corackerup NR WA 706 G8
Coragulac Vic 336 A5, 339 J7
Coraki NSW 461 N3
Coral Bank Vic 345 J5
Coral Bay WA **697**, 714 B9
Coral Coast WA **692–695**
Coral Sea Qld 563 N5
Coralie Qld 562 F7
Coralville NSW 459 M3
Coramba NSW 461 N7
Cordelia Qld 563 M8
Cordering WA 705 E9, 706 D7
Cordillo Downs SA 793 N2
Corea Plains Qld 560 B3, 565 P3
Coreen NSW 465 L7
Corella NSW 463 L3
Corella SA 791 N4
Corella Lakes NSW 463 M3
Corfield Qld 565 K5

Corin Dam ACT 477 A6
Corinda Qld 555 C7
Corindhap Vic 336 B3, 339 K6
Corindi Beach NSW 461 N6
Corinella NSW 465 N2
Corinella Vic 337 J6
Corinna Tas 840 B7
Corinthia WA 707 H3
Corio Vic 336 E4, 339 M7
Corio Bay Vic 336 E5
Cork Qld 565 H7
Cornella Vic 339 N2
Cornella East Vic 339 N2
Corner Camp NSW 460 G7
Corner Country NSW **428–433**
Corner Inlet Vic 337 N8
Cornwall Qld 558 E4
Cornwall Tas 841 N7
Corny Point SA 790 G10
Corobimilla NSW 465 L5
Coromandel Valley SA 786 E9
Coromby Vic 338 F1, 340 F10
Corona NSW 462 B6
Corona Qld 567 M4
Coronet Bay Vic 337 J6
Coronga Peak NSW 463 L5
Corop Vic 339 N1, 341 N10
Cororooke Vic 336 A6, 339 J8
Corowa NSW **446**, 465 L8
Corridgery NSW 465 N2
Corrie Downs Qld 564 D6
Corrigin WA 706 F5
Corrimal NSW 455 J9, 456 G2, 458 G10
Corroboree Park Tavern NT 613 E3, 614 E5
Corrong NSW 464 G4
Corrowong NSW 456 B9, 457 D9
Corryong Vic **325**, 345 M4
Corunna SA 790 G5
Corunna Downs WA 715 K6
Cosgrove Vic 344 C4
Cosmo Newbery WA 709 N7
Cosmos Qld 560 F7
Cossack WA **697**, 714 F5
Costerfield Vic 339 N2
Cotabena SA 791 J3
Cotswold Qld 564 E2
Cottage Point NSW 453 E1
Cottesloe WA 704 A6
Cottles Bridge Vic 335 F1
Coturaundee NR NSW 462 D6
Couangalt Vic 336 F2, 339 N5
Cougal NSW 461 M1
Coulson Qld 556 D7, 557 A6, 559 M8
Coulta SA 790 D9
Countegany NSW 456 D7, 457 G6
Country Downs WA 712 D7
Courela SA 790 B5
Couta Rocks Tas 840 A5
Coutts Crossing NSW 461 M6
Cowabbie West NSW 465 M5

Cowan NSW 453 D1
Cowan Creek NSW 453 E1
Cowan Downs Qld 562 D9
Cowangie Vic 340 C6
Cowaramup WA 705 A10, 706 B8
Coward Springs SA 792 F8
Cowarie SA 793 J4
Cowarna Downs WA 707 M3
Cowary NSW 462 F8
Cowcowing Lakes WA 705 F2, 706 E3
Cowell SA **760**, 790 F7
Cowes Vic **302–303**, 337 J6
Cowl Cowl NSW 465 J3
Cowley Qld 563 M7, 569 E10
Cowley Qld 567 M6
Cowra NSW **386–387**, 454 A6, 456 B1, 458 B9
Cowra Wine Region NSW **387**
Cowwarr Vic 342 B7
Cowwarr Weir Vic 342 B6
Cox River NT 615 J10, 617 J1
Coyrecup WA 706 F7
Craboon NSW 458 D3
Crabtree Tas 839 B5, 843 J5
Cracow Qld 559 H3
Cradle Mountain Tas 840 F8
Cradle Mountain Lake St Clair NP Tas **812**, 840 E8
Cradle Valley Tas 840 E7
Cradoc Tas 839 A6, 843 J6
Cradock SA 791 J4
Crafers SA 786 F7
Crafers West SA 786 F7
Craigie NSW 456 C9, 457 E10
Craigie WA 704 B1
Craigieburn Vic 336 G2, 339 P5, 344 A10
Craiglie Qld 563 L5, 569 D6
Craigmore Qld 560 E9
Craigmore SA 786 G1
Cramenton Vic 340 F4
Cramps Tas 844 C9, 841 J9
Cramsie Qld 565 L8
Cranbourne Vic 335 G7, 337 J5
Cranbourne North Vic 335 G6
Cranbourne South Vic 335 G8
Cranbrook Tas 841 N9
Cranbrook WA **642**, 706 E8
Cranebrook NSW 455 J6, 456 G1, 458 G8
Craven NSW 459 K4
Craven Qld 560 D8
Craven NR NSW 459 K4
Crawley WA 704 C5
Crayfish Creek Tas 840 D4
Crediton Qld 560 F4
Credo WA 707 K2
Creighton Creek Vic 344 C7
Cremorne NSW 453 F5
Cremorne Qld 560 C8
Cremorne Tas 839 D5, 843 L5
Cremorne Point NSW 453 F6

Crendon Qld 565 H4
Crescent Head NSW 459 M1, 461 M10
Cresswell Downs NT 617 L5
Cressy Tas 844 E8, 841 K8
Cressy Vic 336 B4, 339 K7
Crestwood NSW 477 E3
Creswick Vic 336 C1, 339 K4
Creswick North Vic 336 C1, 339 K4
Crew Qld 560 F8
Crib Point Vic 337 H6, 339 P8
Cringadale NSW 464 E5
Croajingolong NP Vic 303, 343 N5
Crocodile Qld 563 K3, 569 B4
Cromer NSW 453 F3
Cronulla NSW 453 E10, 455 K7, 459 H9
Crooble NSW 460 F4
Crooked Corner NSW 454 C8, 456 D2, 458 C10
Crooked River Vic 342 C4, 345 J9
Crookwell NSW 454 D9, 456 D3, 458 D10
Croppa Creek NSW 460 F4
Crossley Vic 338 E8
Crossman WA 705 E7, 706 D6
Crossmoor Qld 565 M7
Crowdy Bay NP NSW 459 M2
Crowdy Head NSW 387, 459 M3
Crowlands Vic 339 H3
Crows Nest Qld 556 B4, 559 L6
Crowther NSW 456 B2, 458 A9
Croydon NSW 453 D6
Croydon Qld 560 G6
Croydon Qld 562 G7
Croydon SA 786 D5
Croydon Vic 335 F3, 337 J3
Croydon Hills Vic 335 F3
Croydon North Vic 335 F2
Croydon South Vic 335 G3
Crusher NSW 460 B9
Cryon NSW 460 B6
Crystal Brook SA 760, 791 J7
Crystalbrook Qld 558 D3
Cuba Plains Qld 563 K10, 565 N1
Cuballing WA 705 F7, 706 E6
Cubbaroo NSW 460 C7
Cubbaroo Qld 562 D10, 564 E2
Cuckadoo Qld 564 E5
Cuckoo Tas 844 G4, 841 L5
Cudal NSW 454 A4, 458 B7
Cuddapan Qld 566 G3
Cudgee Vic 338 G8
Cudgewa Vic 345 L4
Cudgewa North Vic 345 L3
Cudmirrah NSW 456 F4
Cudmore NP Qld 560 B7
Cue WA 664–665, 708 G6
Culbin WA 705 E8, 706 D6
Culburra NSW 456 G4
Culburra SA 788 B8
Culcairn NSW 465 M7
Culfearne Vic 341 L7

Culgoa Vic 341 H7
Culgoa Floodplain NP Qld 558 C9
Culgoa NP NSW 463 M2
Culgoora NSW 460 D7
Culgowie Qld 558 G4
Culla Vic 338 C4
Cullacabardee WA 704 D1
Culladar Qld 565 K6
Cullculli WA 709 H6
Cullen Bay NT 612 A8
Cullen Bullen NSW 454 F4, 458 E7
Culloden Vic 342 C6
Cullulleraine Vic 340 C2
Culpataro NSW 464 G3
Culpaulin NSW 462 E7
Cultowa NSW 462 G7
Cumberland Downs Qld 560 E6
Cumberland Park SA 786 D7
Cumbijowa NSW 465 P2
Cumboogle NSW 458 B4
Cumborah NSW 463 N3
Cummins SA 790 D8
Cumnock NSW 454 A2, 458 B6
Cundeelee Community WA 707 P2, 711 A6
Cunderdin WA 705 F4, 706 E4
Cundumbul NSW 454 B2, 458 B6
Cungelella Qld 558 C1
Cungena SA 790 B5
Cunliffe SA 787 A3, 791 H8
Cunnamulla Qld 542, 567 P8
Cunningar NSW 456 B3
Cunningham SA 787 A4, 791 H9
Cunno Creek Qld 558 B2
Cunyu WA 709 K4
Cuprona Tas 840 F5
Curban NSW 458 B2
Curbur WA 708 E5
Curdie Vale Vic 338 G8
Curdimurka SA 792 G8
Curl Curl NSW 453 G4
Curlewis NSW 458 F1, 460 F10
Curlwaa NSW 464 C4
Curnamona SA 791 L3
Curra Creek NSW 454 B1, 458 B5
Currabubula NSW 458 G1, 460 G10
Curragh NSW 464 F3
Curragh Qld 560 F8
Currajong Qld 558 G7
Currajong Qld 559 H8
Curramulka SA 787 A5, 791 H9
Currareva Qld 567 J3
Currarong NSW 456 G4
Currawarna NSW 465 M6
Currawilla Qld 566 F2
Currawinya Qld 567 M9
Currawinya NP Qld 542–543, 567 L9
Currawong Qld 558 E10
Currency Creek SA 787 E8, 788 A6
Currie Tas 840 F2
Currumbin Qld 557 F7
Curtin ACT 477 D3

Curtin WA 707 M2
Curtin Springs NT 618 E9
Curtis Channel Qld 561 L8
Curtis Island Qld 561 K9
Curtis Island NP Qld 561 K8
Curyo Vic 340 G8
Cuthero NSW 462 C10, 464 C1
Cutta Cutta Caves Nature Park NT 588
Cuttabri NSW 460 C7
Cygnet Tas 830, 839 B7, 843 J6
Cygnet River SA 788 B3
Cytherea Qld 558 D6

D

Daandine Qld 559 J6
Daceyville NSW 453 F7
Dadswells Bridge Vic 338 F3
Daglish WA 704 B5
D'Aguilar NP Qld 499, 556 D5, 557 B1, 559 M7
Dagaragu NT 616 C4
Dagworth Qld 563 H7
Dagworth Qld 565 H5
Dahwilly NSW 465 H7
Daintree Qld 551, 563 L4, 569 C5
Daintree Qld 565 K6
Daintree NP Qld 546–549, 563 K4, 569 C5
Dairy Creek WA 708 E3
Daisy Hill Qld 555 G9
Daisy Hill Vic 339 K3
Daisy Hill SF Qld 555 F9
Daisy Plains NSW 461 L9
Dajarra Qld 564 C5
Dalbeg Qld 560 D2
Dalby Qld 559 K6
Dalgaranga WA 708 F7
Dalgety NSW 456 B8, 457 D8
Dalgety Downs WA 708 E3
Dalgonally Qld 562 E10, 564 F2
Dalhousie SA 792 D2
Dalkeith WA 704 B6
Dallarnil Qld 559 L3
Dalma Qld 561 J8
Dalman NSW 461 L1
Dalmeny NSW 456 E7
Dalmore Qld 565 L8
Dalmorino NSW 462 E10, 464 E1
Dalmorton NSW 461 L6
Dalmuir NSW 462 C4
Dalrymple NP Qld 560 B1, 563 M10
Dalton NSW 454 C10, 456 C3
Dalveen Qld 556 B8, 559 L9
Dalwallinu WA 706 D1, 708 F10
Dalwood NSW 463 L2
Daly River NT 588–589, 613 C6, 614 C6
Daly River NT 613 B5, 614 C6
Daly Waters NT 598, 616 G2
Dalyup WA 707 L7
Damboring WA 705 E1, 706 D2

Dampier WA 697, 714 F5
Dampier Archipelago WA 714 E5
Dampier Downs WA 712 E9, 715 P2
Dancers Valley Qld 564 G5
Dandabilla NR NSW 456 B2, 458 A10
Dandaloo NSW 463 N8
Dandaraga Qld 565 M9
Dandaraga WA 709 J7
Dandaragan WA 705 B1, 706 B2
Dandelong NR NSW 456 D8, 457 F7
Dandenong Vic 335 F6, 337 H4, 339 P6
Dandenong Creek Vic 335 F4
Dandenong North Vic 335 F5
Dandenong Park Qld 560 C3
Dandenong Ranges NP Vic 303, 335 G4, 337 H3
Dandenong South Vic 335 F6
Dandongadale Vic 342 B1, 344 G6
Dangarfield NSW 458 G4
Danggali CP SA 791 N6
Dangin WA 705 F5, 706 E4
Danyo Vic 340 B6
Dapper NR NSW 458 C4
Dapto NSW 455 J9, 456 G3, 458 G10
Daradgee Qld 563 M6, 569 E9
Darbys Falls NSW 454 B7, 456 C1, 458 B9
Darbyshire Vic 345 K3
Dardanup WA 705 B9, 706 C7
Dareton NSW 464 C4
Dargo Vic 342 D4, 345 J9
Dargo River Vic 345 K8
Darkan WA 705 E9, 706 D7
Darke Peak SA 790 E7
Darkwood NSW 461 M8
Darling Point NSW 453 F6
Darling River NSW 462 D8, 463 H5, 464 C3
Darlington NSW 453 E6
Darlington SA 786 C8
Darlington Tas 839 G2, 843 N3
Darlington Vic 339 H7
Darlington Point NSW 465 K5
Darnick NSW 462 F10, 464 F1
Darnum Vic 337 M5
Daroobalgie NSW 465 P2
Darr Qld 565 L8
Darra Qld 555 B7, 557 C3
Darraweit Vic 336 G1
Darraweit Guim Vic 339 N4, 344 A9
Darriman Vic 342 C9
Dartmoor Vic 338 B6
Dartmouth Vic 345 K5
Darwin NT 576–577, 612 C9, 613 C2, 614 D4
Darwin River Dam NT 613 C4
Darwin Water Gardens NT 612 E3
Daubeny NSW 462 D6
Daunia Qld 560 F6

Davenport Downs Qld 564 F10
Davenport Range NT **596–597**, 617 J9
Davenport Range NP NT **596–597**, 617 J10, 619 J1
Davidson NSW 453 E3
Davis Creek NSW 459 H4
Davyhurst WA 707 K1, 709 L10
Dawes Qld 559 J1
Dawesville WA 705 B7, 706 B5
Dawson SA 791 K5
Dawson City Vic 342 E4, 345 L9
Dawson Vale Qld 559 H3
Dawson Vale Qld 560 B4
Dayboro Qld 556 D4, 559 M6
Daylesford Vic **270**, 336 D1, 339 L4
Daymar Qld 558 F9
Daysdale NSW 465 L7
Daytrap Vic 340 G5
De Grey WA 715 J5
De La Poer Range NR WA 709 N6
De Rose Hill SA 789 G1
de Salis NSW 477 E4
Deagon Qld 555 D1
Deakin ACT 477 D3
Deakin WA 711 G6
Dean Vic 336 C1, 339 L5
Deans Marsh Vic 336 C6, 339 K8
Debella Qld 562 F10, 564 G1
Deception Bay Qld 556 E4, 559 N6
Deddick Vic 343 H2, 345 P7
Deddington Tas 844 F7, 841 L7
Dederang Vic 345 H5
Dee Tas 842 G2
Dee Why NSW 453 F4
Deep Creek WA 714 D9
Deep Creek CP SA 787 C9, 788 B4
Deep Lead Vic 338 G3
Deep Well NT 619 H7
Deepwater NSW 461 K5
Deepwater NP Qld 559 L1, 561 M10
Deer Park Vic 335 A4, 336 F3, 339 N6
Deeral Qld 563 M6, 569 E8
Degarra Qld 563 L4, 569 C5
Delahey Vic 335 A3
Delalah House NSW 462 E2
Delamere NT 614 E9, 616 E1
Delamere SA 787 C8, 788 B4
Delegate NSW 456 C9, 457 E10
Delegate River Vic 343 K2
Dellicknora Vic 343 J3
Dellyannie WA 705 F9, 706 E7
Delmore Downs NT 619 J4
Delny NT 619 J4
Deloraine Tas **812–813**, 844 B6, 841 H7
Delray Beach Vic 342 D8
Delta Qld 560 E2
Delta Downs Qld 562 E5
Delta South Qld 560 A9, 565 N9
Delungra NSW 460 G5
Delvine Vic 342 D6

Demon NR NSW 461 L4
Denham WA **665**, 708 B4
Denham Sound WA 708 A4
Denial Bay SA 789 G10
Denian NSW 462 E9
Denicull Creek Vic 338 G4
Deniliquin NSW **446**, 465 H7
Denison Vic 342 B7
Denistone NSW 453 C5
Denistone East NSW 453 D4
Denman NSW **388**, 458 G4
Denman SA 789 B8
Denmark WA **642–643**, 706 E10
Dennes Point Tas 839 C6, 843 K6
Dennington Vic 338 F8
D'Entrecasteaux NP **643**, WA 706 C9
Depot Creek SA 791 H4
Depot Springs WA 709 K7
Deptford Vic 342 E5, 345 L10
Derby Tas 841 M5
Derby Vic 339 L2
Derby WA **686**, 712 E7
Dereel Vic 336 B3, 339 K6
Dergholm Vic 338 B4
Dergholm SP Vic 338 B4
Dering Vic 340 E6
Deringulla NSW 458 C1, 460 C10
Dernancourt SA 786 F4
Derrinallum Vic 339 H6
Derriwong NSW 463 N10, 465 N2
Derry Downs NT 619 K3
Derwent NT 618 F5
Derwent Bridge Tas 842 E1, 100 F10
Derwent Park Tas 838 C3
Detpa Vic 340 D9
Deua NP NSW **369**, 456 E6
Devenish Vic 344 D4
Deverill Qld 560 F6
Devils Marbles CR NT **598**, 617 J9
Deviot Tas 844 D4, 841 J5
Devlins Bridge Vic 337 K1, 344 C9
Devon NSW 462 D7
Devon Vic 342 A9
Devon Meadows Vic 335 G8
Devonborough Downs SA 791 M5
Devoncourt Qld 564 E4
Devonport Tas **813**, 840 G5
Devonshire Qld 565 M9
Dharawal SRA NSW 455 J8, 456 G2, 458 G9
Dharug NP NSW 455 K4, 459 H7
Dhuragoon NSW 464 G6
Dhurringile Vic 344 B5
Diamantina Lakes Qld 564 F9
Diamantina NP Qld 564 F9
Diamantina River Qld 565 H7, 566 E2
Diamond Beach NSW 459 L3
Diamond Creek Vic 335 E1, 337 H2, 339 P5, 344 B10
Diamond Downs Qld 560 D5
Diamond Well WA 709 J4
Dianella WA 704 D3

Diapur Vic 340 C10
Dickson ACT 477 D2
Diemals WA 709 J9
Digby Vic 338 C6
Diggers Rest Vic 336 F2, 339 N5
Diggora Vic 341 M10
Diggora West Vic 339 M1, 341 M10
Dillalah Qld 558 A6, 567 P6
Dillcar Qld 565 K6
Dilpurra NSW 464 F6
Dilston Tas 844 D5, 841 K6
Dilulla Qld 565 M8
Dimboola Vic 338 E1, 340 E10
Dimbulah Qld 563 K6, 569 C8
Dimora Qld 565 H4
Dingee Vic 339 L1, 341 L10
Dingley Vic 335 E6
Dingo Qld 560 G9
Dingo Beach Qld 560 F2
Dingo Tops NP NSW 459 K2
Dingwall Vic 341 K8
Dinmore Qld 557 B3
Dinner Plain Vic **328–329**, 342 D2, 345 J7
Dinoga NSW 460 G6
Dinyarrak Vic 340 B10
Dipperu NP Qld 560 F5
Dirnasser NSW 465 N5
Dirranbandi Qld 558 E9
Dirrung NSW 465 J3
Disaster Bay NSW 456 E10
Discovery Bay Vic 338 B7
Discovery Bay Coastal Park Vic 338 B7
Disney Qld 560 C5
Dittmer Qld 560 F3
Dixie Vic 338 G8
Dixie Outstation Qld 563 H2, 568 E10
Dixons Creek Vic 337 J2, 344 B10
Djukbinj NP NT 613 D1, 613 D2, 614 D3, 614 D4
Dlorah Downs SA 791 M5
Dneiper NT 619 K4
Dobbyn Qld 562 C10, 564 D1
Dobie Vic 339 H4
Dobroyd Point NSW 453 D6
Docker Vic 344 F5
Doctors Flat Vic 342 F3, 345 L8
Dodges Ferry Tas 839 E4, 843 L5
Dodsworth NSW 477 F3
Dogs Grave Vic 342 D3, 345 K8
Dogtown Vic 342 E4, 345 L9
Dolans Bay NSW 453 D10
Dollar Vic 337 N7
Dolls Point NSW 453 E8
Dolphin Island NR WA 714 F5
Don Qld 562 A10, 564 A2
Don Tas 840 G5
Don Valley Vic 337 K3, 344 C10
Donald Vic 338 G1, 341 H10
Doncaster Qld 565 K2

Doncaster Vic 335 E3, 337 H3, 339 P6
Doncaster East Vic 335 E3
Donga Qld 558 F7
Dongara WA **665**, 708 C9
Donnelly WA 706 C8
Donnybrook Vic **644**, 336 G2, 339 P5, 344 A9
Donnybrook WA 705 B10, 706 C7
Donnyville Qld 563 H8
Donors Hill Qld 562 D8
Donovans SA 788 G10
Donvale Vic 335 E3
Doobibla Qld 567 N6
Dooboobetic Vic 339 H1, 341 H10
Doodlakine WA 706 F4
Dooen Vic 338 E2
Dookie Vic 344 C4
Dookie College Vic 344 D4
Doolandella Qld 555 C9
Dooley Downs WA 708 F1, 714 F10
Doolgunna WA 709 J4
Doomadgee Qld 562 B7
Doomben Qld 555 E4
Doon Doon WA 713 M5
Doongan WA 713 K4
Doongmabulla Qld 560 B6
Dooralong NSW 455 L3, 459 H7
Doorawarrah WA 708 C2
Doorstop Bay Tas 842 E8
Dooruna Qld 560 D5
Dora Creek NSW 455 L3, 459 J6
Dora Vale Qld 562 E9, 564 F1
Doreen NSW 460 C6
Dorisvale NT 613 D8, 614 D8
Dornock WA 706 G6
Dorodong Vic 338 B4
Dorrigo NSW **416**, 461 M7
Dorrigo NP NSW **416**, 461 M7
Dorunda Qld 562 F5
Dotswood Qld 560 B1, 563 M10
Double Bridges Vic 342 F5, 345 M10
Double Gates NSW 463 J7
Double Lagoon Qld 562 E6
Double Sandy Point CA Tas 844 F2, 841 K4
Doubleview WA 704 B4
Doubtful Bay WA 712 G5
Doubtful Creek NSW 461 M3
Douglas Vic 338 D3
Douglas Apsley NP Tas **813**, 841 N8
Douglas Downs Qld 564 B5
Dover Qld 564 F7
Dover Tas **830–831**, 839 A8, 843 J7
Dover Gardens SA 786 C8
Dover Heights NSW 453 G6
Doveton Vic 335 F6
Dowerin WA 705 F3, 706 D3
Downer ACT 477 E2
Downside NSW 465 N6
Doyalson NSW 455 L3, 459 J7
Doyles Creek NSW 455 J1, 458 G5
Doyles River NP NSW 459 K2

Dragon Rocks NR WA 706 G5

Dragon Tree Soak NR WA 710 A2, 715 P4

Drain C SA 788 E8

Drake NSW 461 L3

Dreeite Vic 336 A5, 339 J7

Drewvale Qld 555 D10

Driftway NSW 456 A1, 465 P3

Drik Drik Vic 338 B6

Dripstone NSW 454 B1, 458 C5

Dripstone Park NT 612 E1

Dromana Vic 336 G6, 339 P8

Dromedary Tas 839 B4, 843 J4

Dronfield Qld 564 D4

Dropmore Vic 344 B7

Drouin Vic 337 L5

Drovers Cave NP WA **644**, 706 B1, 708 D10

Drumanure Vic 344 C3

Drumborg Vic 338 C7

Drumduff Qld 563 H4

Drummond Qld 560 D9

Drummond Vic 339 M4

Drummond Cove WA 708 C8

Drummoyne NSW 453 D6

Drung Drung Vic 338 F2

Drung Drung South Vic 338 E2

Dry Creek SA 786 D4

Dry Creek Vic 344 D7

Dry Creek WA 711 D6

Dry River NT 614 F9

Dryander NP Qld 560 F2

Drysdale Vic 336 F5, 339 M7

Drysdale River WA 713 K4

Drysdale River NP WA **686**, 713 L3

Duaringa Qld 561 H9

Dubbo NSW **388**, 458 B4

Dublin SA 787 C4, 791 J9

Duchess Qld 564 D4

Duck Creek WA 714 F8

Dudinin WA 706 F6

Dudley CP SA 787 B9, 788 B4

Dudley South Vic 337 K7

Duff Creek SA 792 D6

Duffield NT 619 J10

Duffy ACT 477 C3

Duffys Forest NSW 453 E2

Dulacca Qld 558 G5

Dulbydilla Qld 558 C5

Dulcie Ranges NP NT 619 K4

Dulkaninna SA 793 J7

Dululu Qld 561 J9

Dulwich Hill NSW 453 D7

Dumbalk Vic 337 M7

Dumbalk North Vic 337 N7

Dumbleyung WA 705 G9, 706 E7

Dumbleyung Lake WA 705 G9, 706 E7

Dumosa Vic 341 H8

Dunach Vic 339 K4

Dunalley Tas **831**, 839 F5, 843 M5

Dunbar Qld 562 G4

Duncraig WA 704 B2

Dundas Qld 557 A1

Dundas NR WA 707 N5

Dundas Strait NT 614 E2

Dundas Valley NSW 453 C4

Dundee NSW 461 K5

Dundee Qld 565 J4

Dundee Rail NSW 461 K5

Dundoo Qld 567 M7

Dundula Qld 560 G4

Dundurrabin NSW 461 L7

Dunedoo NSW 458 D3

Dungarubba NSW 461 N3

Dungarvon NSW 463 H2

Dunggir NP NSW 461 M8

Dungog NSW **388**, 459 J4

Dungowan NSW 459 H1, 461 H10

Dungowan NT 616 F3

Dunk Island Qld 563 M7, 569 E10

Dunkeld Qld 558 D6

Dunkeld Vic 338 F5

Dunkerry Qld 559 H6

Dunmarra NT 616 G3

Dunmore NSW 463 P9, 465 P1

Dunmore Vic 338 E7

Dunn Rock NR WA 707 H7

Dunneworthy Vic 339 H4

Dunnstown Vic 336 C2, 339 L5

Dunoak NSW 462 G6

Dunolly Vic **270–271**, 339 K2

Dunoon NSW 461 N2

Dunorlan Tas 844 A6, 841 H7

Dunrobin Qld 560 B7, 565 P7

Dunrobin Vic 338 C5

Dunrobin Bridge Tas 842 G3

Dunsborough WA 705 A10, 706 B7

Duntroon NSW 462 E6

Duntulla Qld 564 C5

Dunwich Qld 556 F5, 557 F3

Durack Qld 555 C8

Durack River WA 713 L5

Durah Qld 559 J4

Dural NSW 453 B2

Duramana NSW 454 D4, 458 D7

Duranillin WA 705 E10, 706 D7

Durdidwarrah Vic 336 D3, 339 L6

Durella Qld 558 C5

Durham Qld 563 H7

Durham Downs Qld 558 F4

Durham Downs Qld 566 G6

Durham Ox Vic 341 K9

Duri NSW 458 G1, 460 G10

Durong South Qld 559 J5

Durras NSW 456 F6

Durras North NSW 456 F6

Durrie Qld 566 E3

Dutchmans Stern CP SA **760**, 791 H4

Dutson Vic 342 D7

Dutton SA 787 F4, 791 K9

Dutton Bay SA 790 D9

Dutton Park Qld 555 C6

Dwellingup WA **644–645**, 705 C7, 706 C6

Dwyers NSW 463 L5

Dyers Crossing NSW 459 L3

Dynevor Downs Qld 567 L8

Dynnyrne Tas 838 D8

Dyraaba Central NSW 461 M2

Dysart Qld 560 F7

Dysart Tas 839 C2, 843 J3

E

Eagle Bay WA 712 G5

Eagle Farm Qld 555 E4

Eagle Heights Qld 557 D6

Eagle Junction Qld 555 D3

Eagle on the Hill SA 786 F7

Eagle Point Vic 342 E6

Eagle Vale NSW 455 J7, 456 G2, 458 G9

Eaglebar Qld 558 G8

Eaglefield Qld 560 E4

Eaglehawk NSW 462 B9

Eaglehawk Vic 339 L2

Eaglehawk Neck Tas 839 F6, 843 M6

Earaheedy WA 709 M3

Earlando Qld 560 F2

Earlwood NSW 453 D7

East Botany NSW 453 E8

East Boyd NSW 456 E9

East Brisbane Qld 555 D5

East Cannington WA 704 F6

East Creek Qld 560 E7

East End Qld 561 K9

East Fremantle WA 704 B7

East Hills NSW 453 B8

East Jindabyne NSW 456 B7, 457 D7

East Lindfield NSW 453 E4

East Loddon Vic 339 L1, 341 L10

East Lynne NSW 456 F5

East Lynne Qld 558 A1, 560 A10, 565 P10, 567 P1

East Malvern Vic 335 E4

East Perth WA 704 D5

East Point NT 612 B5

East Point Recreation Reserve NT 612 B5

East Risdon NR Tas 838 E3

East Ryde NSW 453 D5

East Sassafras Tas 844 A5, 841 H6

East Victoria Park WA 704 E6

East View ACT 477 E1

East Yuna NR WA 708 D7

Eastbourne NSW 456 B7, 457 D6

Eastbrook Qld 560 G9

Eastbrook WA 706 C9

Eastern View Vic 336 C6, 339 L8

Eastlakes NSW 453 E7

Eastmere Qld 560 B6, 565 P6

Eastville Vic 339 L2

Eastwood NSW 453 C4

Eastwood Qld 567 N2

Eatons Hill Qld 555 A2

Ebden Vic 345 H3

Ebor NSW 461 L7

Echo Hills Qld 560 D10

Echuca Vic **290**, 341 N9

Echuca Village Vic 341 N9

Echunga SA 787 E7, 788 A6, 791 K10

Ecklin South Vic 338 G8

Ecobeach WA 712 C9, 715 M2

Edaggee WA 708 C3

Eddington Qld 564 G3

Eddington Vic 339 K2

Eden NSW **369**, 456 E9

Eden Creek NSW 461 M2

Eden Hill WA 704 E3

Eden Vale Qld 563 H7

Eden Valley SA 787 F5, 791 K9

Eden Valley Wine Region SA **760**

Edenhope Vic **271**, 338 B3

Edeowie SA 791 J3

Edgecliff NSW 453 F6

Edgecombe Vic 339 M4

Edgeroi NSW 460 E7

Edi Vic 342 A1, 344 F6

Ediacara CR SA 791 H1

Edillilie SA 790 D9

Edith NSW 454 F6, 456 E1, 458 E8

Edith Creek Tas 840 C4

Edith Downs Qld 565 H3

Edithburgh SA **760**, 787 A7, 788 A4, 791 H10

Edithvale Vic 335 E6

Edjudina WA 709 N10

Edmonton Qld 563 L5, 569 D8

Edmund WA 708 E1, 714 E10

Edmund Kennedy NP Qld 563 M7

Edwards Creek SA 792 D6

Edwards Point Reserve Vic 335 B9

Edwardstown SA 786 D7

Edwinstowe Qld 560 B8, 565 P8

Eenaweenah NSW 463 N7

Eganstown Vic 336 C1, 339 L4

Egelabra NSW 463 N7

Egera Qld 560 B4, 565 P4

Egg Lagoon Tas 840 F1

Eginbah WA 715 K6

Eglinton NSW 454 D4, 458 D7

Ehlma Qld 559 J6

Eidsvold Qld 559 J3

Eight Mile Plains Qld 555 E8

Eighty Mile Beach WA 715 L4

Eildon Vic **326**, 344 D8

Eildon Park Qld 565 H8

Eildon SP Vic 344 E8

Eimeo Qld 560 G4

Einasleigh Qld 563 J8

Ejanding WA 705 F2, 706 E3

Ekibin Qld 555 D6

El Alamein SA 791 H5

El Arish Qld 563 M7, 569 E10

El Questro WA 713 M5

El Trune NSW 463 L6

Elaine Vic 336 C3, 339 L6

Elands NSW 459 L2

Elanora Heights NSW 453 F3

Elbow Hill SA 790 F7
Elderslie Qld 563 K3, 568 G10, 569 C2
Elderslie Tas 839 B3, 843 J3
Eldon Tas 839 D2, 843 K3
Eldorado Qld 565 L4
Eldorado Vic 344 G4
Electrona Tas 839 C6, 843 K6
Elgin Down Qld 560 C5
Elgin Vale Qld 556 C2, 559 L5
Elizabeth SA 786 F1, 787 D5, 791 J9
Elizabeth Beach NSW 459 L4
Elizabeth Downs NT 613 B6, 614 C6
Elizabeth East SA 786 F1
Elizabeth Heights SA 786 F1
Elizabeth South SA 786 F1
Elizabeth Town Tas 844 B6, 841 H7
Elkedra NT 617 K10, 619 K2
Ella Vale NSW 463 J2
Ellalong NSW 455 L2, 459 H6
Ellam Vic 340 E9
Ellangowan NSW 461 N3
Ellavalla WA 708 C3
Ellen Grove Qld 555 B9
Ellenborough NSW 459 L2, 461 L10
Ellenbrae WA 713 L5
Ellenbrook WA 704 F1
Ellendale Tas 842 G3
Ellendale WA 712 G8
Ellerside Vic 337 L7
Ellerslie Vic 338 G7
Ellerston NSW 459 H3
Elliminyt Vic 336 A6, 339 J8
Ellinbank Vic 337 L5
Elliot Price CP SA 792 G7
Elliott NT 598–599, 617 H4
Elliott Tas 840 E5
Elliott Heads Qld 559 M2
Ellis Crossing Vic 338 D1, 340 D10
Elliston SA 761, 790 C7
Elmhurst Vic 339 H4
Elmina Qld 558 B7
Elmore Qld 562 G10, 565 J2
Elmore Vic 339 N1, 341 N10
Elong Elong NSW 458 C3
Elphin WA 705 E2, 706 D2
Elphinstone Qld 560 E5
Elphinstone Vic 339 M3
Elrose Qld 564 D7
Elrose Qld 564 F4
Elsey NT 614 G8
Elsey NP NT 589, 614 G8
Elsie Hills Qld 560 B10, 565 P10
Elsmore NSW 461 H6
Elsternwick Vic 335 D4
Eltham Vic 335 E2, 337 H3, 339 P5, 344 B10
Elton Downs Qld 565 K4
Elverston Qld 558 B6
Elvina Bay NSW 453 F1
Elvira Qld 565 K4
Elvo Qld 565 H8

Elwood Vic 335 C5
Emaroo NSW 462 G4
Embleton WA 704 E3
Emerald Qld 515, 560 E8
Emerald Vic 303, 337 J4
Emerald Beach NSW 461 N7
Emerald Hill NSW 460 E9
Emerald Springs Roadhouse NT 613 E6, 614 E6
Emily and Jessie Gap NP NT 619 H6
Emita Tas 841 J2
Emmaville NSW 461 J5
Emmdale Roadhouse NSW 462 G7
Emmet Qld 567 M1
Emmet Downs Qld 567 M2
Empire Vale NSW 461 P3
Emu Vic 339 J2
Emu Bay SA 788 B3
Emu Creek Vic 339 M2
Emu Downs SA 787 E2, 791 K8
Emu Flat Vic 339 N3
Emu Junction SA 789 E5
Emu Lake WA 715 N10
Emu Mountain Qld 564 E4
Emu Park Qld 561 K8
Emu Plains Qld 560 E3
Emudilla Qld 567 L4
Encounter Bay SA 787 D9, 788 B5
Endeavour Qld 563 K3, 569 C3
Endeavour Hills Vic 335 F5
Endeavour River NP Qld 563 L3, 569 C3
Eneabba WA 706 B1, 708 D10
Enfield NSW 453 D7
Enfield SA 786 E4
Enfield Vic 336 B3, 339 K5
Enfield South NSW 453 C7
Enfield SP Vic 336 B3
Engadine NSW 453 B10
Englefield Vic 338 D4
Engoordina NT 619 J8
Enmore NSW 453 E7
Enmore NSW 461 J8
Enngonia NSW 463 K2
Ennisvale NSW 464 A2
Enoch Point Vic 337 M1
Enoggera Qld 555 C4
Enryb Downs Qld 565 K5
Ensay Qld 565 L4
Ensay Vic 342 F4, 345 M9
Ensay North Vic 342 F4, 345 M9
Epala Qld 561 K9
Epenarra NT 617 K9
Eppalock Vic 339 M2
Epping NSW 453 C4
Epping Vic 335 D1, 337 H2, 339 P5, 344 A10
Epping Forest Qld 560 C6
Epping Forest Tas 844 F8, 841 L8
Epping Forest NP Qld 560 C6
Epsilon Qld 566 F8
Epsom Qld 560 F5
Epsom Vic 339 M2

Erambie Qld 558 G6
Eremaran NSW 463 L9
Eribung NSW 463 N9, 465 N1
Erica Vic 337 P4, 342 A6
Erigolia NSW 465 L3
Erikin WA 706 F4
Erindale SA 786 F6
Eringa SA 791 M4, 792 B1
Erldunda NT 618 G9
Erlistoun WA 709 M7
Ermington NSW 453 C5
Erne Qld 558 A1, 560 B10, 565 P10, 567 P1
Eromanga Qld 567 K5
Erong Springs WA 708 F3
Errabiddy WA 708 F3
Erriba Tas 840 F6
Erringibba NP Qld 558 G7
Errinundra Vic 343 K4
Errinundra NP Vic 304, 343 K4
Erskine Park NSW 455 J6, 456 G1, 458 G8
Erskineville NSW 453 E7
Erudgere NSW 454 D1, 458 D5
Erudina SA 791 L3
Erudina Woolshed SA 791 L3
Escombe Qld 565 K5
Escott Qld 562 C7
Esk Qld 499, 556 C4, 559 L6
Eskdale Qld 565 L6
Eskdale Vic 345 J5
Esmeralda Qld 562 G8
Esperance WA 645, 707 M8
Essendon Vic 335 C3
Essex Downs Qld 565 J4
Etadunna SA 793 J7
Ethel Creek WA 715 K9
Etheldale Qld 562 G10, 565 J1
Etona Qld 558 B4
Etta Plains Qld 562 E10, 564 F1
Ettrick NSW 461 M2
Etty Bay Qld 563 M6, 569 E9
Euabalong NSW 463 L10, 465 L2
Euabalong West NSW 463 L10, 465 L1
Euchareena NSW 454 B2, 458 C6
Eucla WA 676, 711 G7
Eucla NP WA 711 G7
Eucumbene NSW 456 B7, 457 D6
Eudamullah WA 708 D2
Eudunda SA 787 F3, 791 K8
Eugenana Tas 840 G5
Eugowra NSW 458 A7
Eulo NSW 464 D2
Eulo Qld 543, 567 N8
Eulolo Qld 564 G4
Eulomogo NSW 458 B4
Euminbah NSW 463 P3
Eumundi Qld 556 D2, 559 M5
Eumungerie NSW 458 B3
Eungai NSW 461 M9
Eungella Qld 560 F4
Eungella NP Qld 516, 560 F3

Eurack Vic 336 B5, 339 K7
Euramo Qld 563 M7
Eurardy WA 708 C6
Eureka Plains NSW 463 K1
Eurelia SA 791 J5
Eurimbula NSW 454 B2, 458 B6
Eurimbula NP Qld 561 L10
Euroa Vic 344 C6
Eurobin Vic 342 B1, 345 H6
Eurobodalla NSW 456 E7
Euroka Qld 559 J3
Euroka Springs Qld 562 F10, 564 G1
Eurong Qld 559 N3
Eurongilly NSW 465 N6
Euston NSW 464 D5
Euston Qld 565 K8
Eva Downs NT 617 J5
Eva Valley NT 614 G7
Evandale Tas 813, 844 E7, 841 K7
Evangy Qld 565 J10, 567 J1
Evans Head NSW 416–417, 461 P4
Evansford Vic 339 K4
Eveleigh Qld 563 J7
Evelyn Downs SA 792 B5
Evercreech FR Tas 841 N6
Everton Vic 344 G4
Everton Hills Qld 555 B3
Everton Park Qld 555 C3
Evesham Qld 565 K8
Evora Qld 560 A10, 565 N10
Ewan Qld 563 L9
Ewaninga NT 619 H6
Ewaninga CR NT 607
Ewaninga Rock Carvings CR NT 619 H6
Exeter NSW 454 G10, 456 F3
Exeter SA 786 C3
Exeter Tas 844 D5, 841 J6
Exevale Qld 560 F4
Exford Vic 336 F3, 339 M6
Exmoor Qld 560 E3
Exmoor Qld 565 J4
Exmouth WA 698, 714 C7
Exmouth Gulf WA 714 B8
Exmouth Gulf WA 714 C7
Exmouth Homestead WA 714 C8
Expedition NP Qld 558 F2

F

Fadden ACT 477 D4
Failford NSW 459 L3
Fairfield NSW 453 A6
Fairfield Qld 555 C6
Fairfield Qld 558 F1
Fairfield Qld 565 M8
Fairfield Vic 335 D3
Fairfield WA 713 H8
Fairfield East NSW 453 B6
Fairfield Heights NSW 453 A6
Fairfield West NSW 453 A6
Fairhaven Vic 336 C6, 339 L8
Fairhaven Vic 343 N4
Fairhill Qld 560 F8

Fairholme NSW 465 N2
Fairlight NSW 463 M5
Fairlight Qld 563 J3
Fairneyview Qld 557 A2
Fairview Qld 563 J3, 569 A3
Fairview CP SA 788 D9
Fairview Park SA 786 G3
Fairy Hill NSW 461 M3
Fairyland Qld 559 H3
Fairyland Qld 559 J5
Falls Creek NSW 456 F4
Falls Creek Vic 342 D2, 345 J7
Falmouth Tas 841 P7
Fannie Bay NT 612 A6
Fannie Bay NT 612 B7
Fanning River Qld 560 B1, 563 M10
Faraway Hill SA 791 L6
Farina SA 793 J9
Farleigh Qld 560 G4
Farrell Flat SA 787 E2, 791 K8
Farrendale NSW 463 P9
Farrer ACT 477 D4
Faulkland NSW 459 K3
Fawcett Vic 344 D8
Fawkner Vic 335 C2
Feilton Tas 839 A4, 843 H4
Felixstow SA 786 E5
Felton East Qld 556 A6, 559 K8
Fentonbury Tas 843 H4
Fentons Creek Vic 339 J1, 341 J10
Ferguson SA 790 C1
Ferguson Vic 336 A7, 339 J9
Fermoy Qld 565 J8
Fern Bay NSW 455 N2, 459 K6
Fern Hill Vic 336 E1, 339 M4
Fern Tree Tas 838 B9, 839 C5, 843 K5
Fernbank Vic 342 D6
Fernbrook NSW 461 L7
Ferndale Qld 558 B7
Ferndale WA 704 E7
Fernihurst Vic 341 K9
Fernlee Qld 558 C8
Fernlees Qld 560 E9
Fernshaw Vic 337 K2, 344 C10
Ferntree Gully Vic 335 G4
Fernvale Qld 556 D5, 557 A2, 559 M7
Fernvale Vic 345 J4
Ferny Creek Vic 335 G4
Ferny Grove Qld 555 A3, 557 C2
Ferny Hills Qld 555 A3
Ferryden Park SA 786 D4
Fiddlers Green Vic 337 P2, 342 A5, 344 F10
Fiddletown NSW 453 C1
Fifield NSW 463 N10, 465 N1
Fig Tree Pocket Qld 555 B6
Finch Hatton Qld 560 F4
Findon SA 786 C5
Fingal Tas 841 N7
Fingal Head NSW 461 P1
Finke NT 619 J9

Finke Bay NT 613 F2
Finke Gorge NP NT **607**, 618 F7
Finke River NT 618 G7
Finley NSW 465 J7
Finniss SA 787 E8, 788 A6
Finniss Springs SA 792 G9
Fischerton Qld 563 J6, 569 A9
Fish Creek Vic 337 M8
Fish Point Vic 341 K6
Fisher SA 789 D8
Fisherman Bay SA 787 B1, 791 H7
Fishermens Bend Vic 335 C4
Fiskville Vic 336 D2, 339 L5
Fitzgerald Tas 842 G4
Fitzgerald River NP WA **645**, 707 H8
Fitzgibbon Qld 555 C2
Fitzmaurice River NT 613 B9
Fitzroy NT 614 D9, 616 D1
Fitzroy Vic 335 C3
Fitzroy Crossing WA **686**, 713 H9
Fitzroy Island NP Qld 563 M5, 569 E7
Fitzroy River Vic 338 C7
Fitzroy River WA 712 F8
Five Day Creek NSW 461 L8
Five Dock NSW 453 D6
Five Ways NSW 463 M8
Flaggy Rock Qld 560 G5
Flagstaff Gully Tas 838 G5
Flagstaff Hill SA 786 D8
Flamingo NSW 463 M10, 465 M1
Flamingo Beach Vic 342 D8
Flemington Vic 335 C3
Fletcher Vale Qld 560 A1, 563 L10, 565 P1
Fleurieu Peninsula SA 787 D8, 788 A5
Flinders Qld 557 A5
Flinders Vic 337 H7, 339 P8
Flinders Bay WA 706 B9
Flinders Chase NP SA **733**, 788 B2
Flinders Group NP Qld 563 J1, 568 F8
Flinders Island Tas **814**, 841 J2
Flinders Park SA 786 C5
Flinders Ranges SA **748–753**
Flinders Ranges NP SA **748**, 791 K2
Flinders River Qld 562 E8, 565 K3
Flintstone Tas 844 C10, 841 J9
Floods Creek NSW 462 B6
Flora Valley WA 713 N9
Floraville Qld 562 C7
Floreat WA 704 B4
Florence Vale Qld 560 D8
Florey ACT 477 C2
Florida NSW 463 L7
Florieton SA 787 G2, 791 L8
Florina NT 613 E8, 614 E7
Florina SA 791 M4
Flowerdale Tas 840 E4
Flowerdale Vic 337 J1, 344 B9
Fluorspar Qld 563 K6, 569 A8
Flyers Creek NSW 454 B5, 458 C8

Flying Fish Point Qld 563 M6, 569 E9
Flying Fox Qld 557 D7
Flynn ACT 477 C2
Flynn Vic 342 B7
Flynns Creek Vic 342 A8
Fog Bay NT 613 B4
Fog Creek Qld 563 H9
Fogg Dam CR NT 613 D3, 614 D4
Foleyvale Qld 561 H8
Footscray Vic 335 C4, 336 G3, 339 N6
Forbes NSW **446–447**, 465 P2
Forbes River NSW 459 L1, 461 L10
Forbesdale NSW 459 K3
Forcett Tas 839 E4, 843 L4
Fords Bridge NSW 463 J3
Fordsdale Qld 556 B6, 559 L7
Forest Tas 840 C3
Forest Hill NSW 465 N6
Forest Hill Vic 335 E4
Forest Hills Qld 558 G2
Forest Home Qld 560 B2, 563 M10
Forest Home Qld 563 H7
Forest Lake Qld 555 B9, 557 C3
Forest Reefs NSW 454 B5, 458 C7
Forest Vale Qld 558 D4
Forestdale Qld 555 C10
Forestville NSW 453 E4
Forge Creek Vic 342 E6
Forktown Vic 342 E4, 345 L9
Forrest Vic 336 B7, 339 K8
Forrest WA 711 F6
Forrest Beach Qld 563 M8
Forrestdale WA 704 E10
Forrestdale Lake WA 704 F10
Forrester Qld 560 C7
Forrestfield WA 704 G5
Forsayth Qld 563 H8
Forster NSW **388**, 459 L4
Forster Keys NSW 459 L4
Fort Constantine Qld 564 E3
Fort Grey NSW 462 A2
Fort William Outstation Qld 564 D6
Fortescue Roadhouse WA 714 E6
Forth Tas 840 G5
Fortis Creek NP NSW 461 M5
Fortitude Valley Qld 555 D5
Fortland Qld 558 B6
Fortuna Qld 560 A7, 565 N7
Fortville House NSW 462 A1
Forty Mile Scrub NP Qld 563 K7
Fossil Downs WA 713 J9
Foster Vic **304**, 337 N7
Fosterton NSW 459 J4
Fosterville Vic 339 M2
Foul Bay SA 788 A3, 790 G10
Four Brothers SA 791 L4
Four Corners NSW 465 J5
Four Mile Clump NSW 460 D3
Four Mile Creek NSW 454 B4, 458 B7
Four Mile Creek Tas 841 P7

Four Pegs Qld 559 H7
Four Ways NSW 458 A7
Fowlers Bay SA 789 F10
Fowlers Bay CR SA 789 E10
Fowlers Gap NSW 462 B6
Fox Creek Qld 562 G2, 568 D9
Fox Valley NSW 453 D3
Foxdale Qld 560 F2
Foxhow Vic 336 A4, 339 J7
Framlingham Vic 338 G7
Frances SA 788 D10
Frances Bay NT 612 D9
Francois Peron NP WA **612**, 708 B4
Frank Hann NP WA 707 J6
Frankfield Qld 560 C6
Frankford Tas 844 C5, 841 H6
Frankland WA 706 E9
Franklin Qld 564 G7
Franklin Tas **831**, 839 A6, 843 J6
Franklin Harbor CP SA 790 F7
Franklin River Tas 842 D3, 840 E10
Franklin–Gordon Wild Rivers NP Tas **826–829**, 842 D2
Franklyn SA 791 K6
Frankston Vic 335 F8, 337 H5, 339 P7
Frankston North Vic 335 F7
Frankton SA 791 K8, 787 F4
Fraser ACT 477 D2
Fraser Island Qld **490–495**, 559 N2
Fraser Range WA 707 N4
Frazier Downs WA 712 C10, 715 M3
Frederick Henry Bay Tas 839 D5
Frederickton NSW 461 M9
Freeburgh Vic 342 C1, 345 H6
Freeling SA 787 E4, 791 K9
Freemantle NR NSW 454 C3, 458 C6
Fregon SA 789 E2
Fremantle WA 704 B7, 705 B5, 706 C4
French Island NP Vic 337 J6
French Park NSW 465 M6
Frenchman Bay WA 706 F10
Frenchs Forest NSW 453 F3
Freshford ACT 477 C5
Freshwater Creek Vic 336 D5, 339 M7
Frewhurst Qld 563 J7
Freycinet NP Tas **814**, 843 P1, 841 P10
Freycinet Peninsula Tas 843 P1
Frogmore NSW 454 B8, 456 C2, 458 B10
Frome Downs SA 791 L2
Fry Qld 561 K10
Fryerstown Vic 339 L3
Fulham SA 786 C5
Fulham Vic 342 C7
Fulham Gardens SA 786 C5
Fullarton SA 786 E6
Fumina Vic 337 M4
Fumina South Vic 337 M4

Furneaux Group Tas 841 K2
Furnell Vic 343 L5
Furner SA 788 F9
Fyansford Vic 336 D5, 339 M7
Fyshwick ACT 477 E3, 456 C5, 457 F2

G

Gabbin WA 705 G2, 706 E2
Gabyon WA 708 E7
Gaffneys Creek Vic 337 N1, 344 E9
Gailes Qld 555 A9, 557 C3
Gairdner WA 706 G8
Galah Vic 340 E5
Galah Creek NT 615 K6
Galaquil Vic 340 F8
Galaquil East Vic 340 F8
Galbraith Qld 562 F5
Gale NSW 477 F4
Galena WA 708 C7
Galga SA 791 M9
Galiwinku NT 615 L3
Gallipoli NT 617 P7
Galong NSW 456 B3
Galore NSW 465 M6
Galston NSW 453 C2
Galway Downs Qld 567 J2
Gama Vic 340 F7
Gambier Islands CP SA 788 A1
Gamboola Qld 563 H5
Gammon Ranges NP SA 782, 793 K10
Ganmain NSW 465 M5
Gannawarra Vic 341 L7
Gapuwiyak NT 615 L4
Garah NSW 460 D4
Garbutt Qld 563 N9
Garden Island Creek Tas 839 B7, 843 J7
Garden Vale NSW 462 F4
Gardens of Stone NP NSW 458 E7
Gardners Bay Tas 839 B7, 843 J7
Garema NSW 465 P3
Garfield Qld 560 B8, 565 P8
Garfield Vic 337 K5
Gargett Qld 560 F4
Garigal NP NSW 453 F3
Garlands NSW 463 K3
Garlandtown NSW 456 E6
Garnpung Lake NSW 464 E2
Garran ACT 477 D3
Garrawilla NSW 458 D1, 460 D10
Garthowen NSW 460 G9
Gartmore Qld 558 A2
Garvoc Vic 338 G8
Gascoyne Junction WA 666, 708 D3
Gascoyne River WA 708 B2
Gatton Qld 556 C5, 559 L7
Gatum Vic 338 D4
Gavial Qld 561 J8
Gawler SA 761, 787 E5, 791 K9
Gawler Tas 840 F5
Gawler Ranges SA 790 D4

Gawler Ranges CR SA 790 C5
Gayndah Qld 559 K3
Gaythorne Qld 555 C4, 557 C2
Gaza Qld 565 L10
Geebung Qld 555 D3, 557 C2
Geehi NSW 456 A7, 465 P9, 457 B7
Geelong Vic 271, 336 E5, 339 M7
Geera Qld 560 A9, 565 N9
Geeveston Tas 831, 839 A7, 843 H6
Geikie Gorge NP WA 689, 713 J9
Geilston Bay Tas 838 E4
Gelantipy Vic 343 H3, 345 N8
Gellibrand Vic 336 A7, 339 J8
Gellibrand Hill Park Vic 335 B1
Gelorup WA 705 B9
Gem Creek Qld 560 A4, 565 P4
Gembrook Vic 337 K4
Gemfields Reserve Qld 516, 560 E9
Gemoka Qld 565 J3
Gemtree Roadhouse NT 608, 619 J5
Genoa Vic 343 M4
Genoa NP NSW 456 D9, 457 G10
Genoa River Vic 343 M3
Geographe Bay WA 705 A9, 706 B7
Geographe Wine Region WA 646
George Town Tas 814, 844 C3, 841 J5
Georges Creek NSW 461 K8
Georges Hall NSW 453 B7
Georges Plains NSW 454 D5, 458 D8
Georges River NSW 453 B8
Georges River NP NSW 453 B9
Georgetown Qld 526, 563 H7
Georgetown SA 791 J7
Georgina Downs NT 617 P10, 619 P1
Gepps Cross SA 786 D4
Geraldton WA 666, 708 C8
Gerang Gerung Vic 338 D1, 340 D10
Geranium SA 788 A8
Gerara NSW 463 L2
Gerard SA 791 N9
Gerata Qld 562 C10, 564 D2
Germantown Vic 342 C1, 345 H6
Gerogery NSW 465 M8
Gerringong NSW 370, 456 G3, 455 J10
Gerroa NSW 455 J10, 456 G3
Geurie NSW 458 B4
Ghin Ghin Vic 344 B8
Gibb River WA 713 K5
Gibb River Road WA 680–685
Gibihi Qld 559 H1
Gibraltar Range NP NSW 411, 461 L5
Gibson WA 707 M7
Gibson Desert WA 710 C7
Gibson Desert NR WA 677, 710 C8
Gidgealpa SA 793 M4
Gidgee NSW 463 J6
Gidgee WA 709 J6
Gidgegannup WA 705 C4, 706 C4
Gidginbung NSW 465 N4
Giffard Vic 342 C8

Giffard West Vic 342 C8
Gifford Creek WA 708 E1, 714 E10
Gilbert River Qld 562 G7
Giles Meteorological Station WA 710 F8
Gilgai NSW 461 H6
Gilgandra NSW 389, 458 B2
Gilgooma NSW 460 A8
Gilgunnia NSW 463 K9
Giligulgul Qld 559 H5
Gilliat Qld 564 G3
Gillieston Vic 344 B4
Gillingall Vic 342 G4, 345 N9
Gillingarra WA 705 C2, 706 C2
Gillman SA 786 C3
Gilmore ACT 477 D4
Gilmore NSW 457 B3, 456 A5, 465 P6
Gilroyd WA 708 D4
Gilston Qld 557 E7
Gin Gin NSW 463 P8
Gin Gin Qld 499, 559 L2
Gina SA 792 B9
Ginburra Qld 564 E3
Gindie Qld 560 E9
Gingerella Qld 563 K7, 569 B10
Gingin WA 705 C3, 706 C3
Ginninderra ACT 456 C4, 457 E2, 477 D2
Gippsland Lakes Coastal Park Vic 304, 342 E7
Gippsland Wine Region Vic 304
Gipsy Point Vic 343 N4
Giralang ACT 477 D2
Giralia WA 714 C8
Girgarre Vic 339 P1, 341 P10, 344 A5
Girgarre East Vic 339 P1, 341 P10, 344 A5
Girilambone NSW 463 M6
Girragulang NSW 458 D3
Girral NSW 465 M3
Girralong NR NSW 454 C3, 458 C6
Girraween NSW 453 A5
Girraween NP Qld 499, 556 B9, 559 L9
Girrawheen NSW 462 F10, 464 F1
Girrawheen WA 704 C2
Giru Qld 560 D1, 563 N9
Girvan NSW 459 K5
Gisborne Vic 336 F1, 339 N5
Gladesville NSW 453 D5
Gladfield Vic 341 L8
Gladstone NSW 461 M9
Gladstone Qld 516, 561 K9
Gladstone SA 761, 791 J6
Gladstone Tas 841 N4
Gladstone WA 708 C4
Gladstone Park Vic 335 B2
Glamorganvale Qld 557 A3
Glandore Qld 559 H2
Glanworth Qld 567 P3
Glastonbury Qld 556 C2, 559 M4

Glaziers Bay Tas 839 A7, 843 J6
Glebe NSW 453 E6
Glebe Tas 838 E6
Gleeson Qld 562 D10, 564 D1
Glen WA 708 G6
Glen Afton Qld 565 L10, 567 L1
Glen Albyn NSW 462 F9
Glen Alice NSW 454 G3, 458 F6
Glen Alvie Vic 337 K7
Glen Aplin Qld 556 B9, 559 L9
Glen Avon Qld 560 C10
Glen Ayle WA 709 M3
Glen Creek Vic 345 H5
Glen Davis NSW 454 G3, 458 F6
Glen Elgin NSW 461 K5
Glen Eva Qld 560 D4
Glen Florrie WA 714 E9
Glen Forbes Vic 337 K6
Glen Gallic NSW 455 J1, 458 G5
Glen Garland Qld 563 H2, 568 E10
Glen Gowrie NSW 462 E6
Glen Harding Qld 563 L7
Glen Helen NT 618 F5
Glen Helen Tourist Camp NT 618 F6
Glen Hill WA 713 N6
Glen Hope NSW 462 E5
Glen Hope NSW 463 L6
Glen Huon Tas 839 A6, 843 H6
Glen Innes NSW 417, 461 J6
Glen Iris Vic 335 E4
Glen Isla Qld 564 E2
Glen Morrison NSW 459 J1, 461 J10
Glen Ora NSW 462 F9
Glen Osmond SA 786 E6
Glen Ruth Qld 563 L7
Glen Valley Vic 342 E2, 345 K7
Glen Waverley Vic 335 F4, 337 H3, 339 P6
Glen Wills Vic 342 E1, 345 K6
Glenaire Vic 336 A8, 339 J9
Glenaladale Vic 342 D5, 345 K10
Glenalbyn Vic 339 K1, 341 K10
Glenalta SA 786 E8
Glenapp Qld 557 B8
Glenarbon Qld 559 J9
Glenariff NSW 463 L5
Glenariff Qld 567 J1
Glenaroua Vic 339 P3, 344 A8
Glenavon Qld 560 D5
Glenbervie Qld 564 G4
Glenbrae Vic 336 A1, 339 J4
Glenburgh WA 708 E3
Glenburn Vic 337 J1, 344 C9
Glenburnie SA 788 F10
Glencairn Vic 337 P2, 342 A4, 344 G9
Glencoe NSW 461 J6
Glencoe Qld 559 J2
Glencoe SA 788 F9
Glendalough WA 704 C4
Glendambo SA 790 D2
Glenden Qld 560 E4
Glendevie Tas 839 A7, 843 H7

Glendilla Qld 567 N7
Glendinning Vic 338 D4
Glendon Brook NSW 459 H5
Gleneagle Qld 557 C6
Glenelg SA 786 C7, 787 D6, 791 J10
Glenelg North SA 786 C6
Glenelg River Vic 338 B7
Glenfern Tas 839 A4, 843 H5
Glenferrie Vic 335 D3
Glengalla Qld 562 G10, 565 H2
Glengarry Qld 558 E4
Glengarry Qld 558 G7
Glengarry Tas 844 C5, 841 J6
Glengarry Vic 337 P5, 342 A7
Glengeera NSW 458 B4
Glengower Vic 339 K4
Glengowrie SA 786 C7
Glengyle Qld 566 D2
Glenhaughton Qld 558 F3
Glenhaven NSW 453 B3
Glenhope NSW 462 G2
Glenhope NSW 464 G5
Glenhope Vic 339 N3
Glenhuntly Vic 335 D5
Glenidal Qld 558 F2
Glenisla Vic 338 E4
Glenlee Vic 340 D9
Glenlofty Vic 339 H3
Glenloth Vic 341 J9
Glenlusk Tas 839 B4, 843 J5
Glenlyon Qld 556 A9, 559 K9
Glenlyon Qld 565 J4
Glenlyon Vic 339 L4
Glenmaggie Vic **305**, 342 A6
Glenmaggie Reservoir Vic 342 B6
Glenmore Qld 558 F7
Glenmore Downs Qld 560 D7
Glenmorgan Qld 558 G6
Glenora NSW 462 C7
Glenora NSW 463 H4
Glenora SA 791 L7
Glenora Tas 839 A3, 843 H4
Glenorchy SA 791 L3
Glenorchy Tas 838 B3, 839 C4, 843 K5
Glenorchy Vic 338 G3
Glenore Qld 562 E7
Glenore Tas 844 C7, 841 J7
Glenorie NSW 453 B1
Glenormiston Qld 564 B7
Glenormiston Vic 338 G7
Glenorn WA 709 M9
Glenpatrick Vic 339 J3
Glenprairie Qld 561 H7
Glenreagh NSW 461 M6
Glenrock Qld 563 K2, 568 G10, 569 C2
Glenrowan Qld 559 H5
Glenrowan Vic **326**, 344 F5
Glenroy Qld 565 K10, 567 K1
Glenroy Vic 335 C2
Glenroy WA 713 J7
Glenside SA 786 E6

Glenstuart Qld 565 N10, 567 N1
Glenthompson Vic 338 F5
Glenunga SA 786 E6
Glenusk Qld 560 A10, 565 N10, 567 N1
Glenvalley Qld 567 J2
Glenwood NSW 463 K8
Glenwood Qld 556 D1, 559 M4
Glenwood Park NSW 453 A3
Glomar Beach Vic 342 D8
Glossop SA 791 N8
Gloucester NSW **389**, 459 K3
Gloucester Island NP Qld 560 F2
Glynde SA 786 E5
Gnalta Qld 564 F6
Gnangara WA 704 C1
Gnangara Lake WA 704 D1
Gnaraloo WA 708 B1, 714 B10
Gnarwarre Vic 336 D5, 339 L7
Gnotuk Vic 339 H7
Gnowangerup WA 706 F8
Gobarralong NSW 456 A4, 457 B1, 465 P6
Gobur Vic 344 C7
Gocup NSW 456 A4, 457 B2, 465 P6
Godfreys Creek NSW 454 A8, 456 B2, 458 B9
Gogango Qld 561 H9
Gogeldrie NSW 465 L5
Gogo WA 713 H9
Gol Gol NSW 464 C4
Gol Gol NSW 464 E2
Golconda Tas 844 F4, 841 K5
Gold Coast Qld **500**, 556 F7, 557 F7, 559 N8
Golden Beach Vic 342 D8
Golden Grove SA 786 G2
Golden Grove WA 708 F8
Golden Valley Tas 844 B7, 841 H7
Goldsborough Vic 339 K2
Gollan NSW 458 C4
Golspie NSW 454 E8, 456 D2, 458 D10
Goneaway NP Qld 565 H9
Gongolgon NSW 463 M4
Goobang NSW 458 A6, 463 P10, 465 P1
Goobang NP NSW 458 A5
Goobarragandra NSW 456 B5, 457 C3
Goode River Qld 556 A2, 559 K4
Goodedulla NP Qld 561 H8
Goodna Qld 555 A9, 557 B4
Goodnight Scrub NP Qld 559 K3
Goodooga NSW 463 N2
Goodparla NT 613 F5, 614 F5
Goodwill Point Tas 840 A2
Goodwood NSW 462 E5
Goodwood Qld 564 D7
Goodwood SA 786 D6
Goodwood Tas 838 C3
Googong Reservoir NSW 477 F5
Goold Island NP Qld 563 M7

Goolgowi NSW 465 K3
Goolma NSW 458 C4
Goolmangar NSW 461 N3
Gooloogong NSW 456 B1, 458 A8
Goolwa SA **733**, 787 E8, 788 A6
Goomalibee Vic 344 D5
Goomalling WA 705 E3, 706 D3
Goomally Qld 558 F1, 560 G10
Goombie Qld 567 L4
Goomboorian Qld 556 D1, 559 M4
Goombungee Qld 556 B5, 559 L6
Goomburra Qld 556 B7, 559 L8
Goomeri Qld 556 B1, 559 L4
Goon Goon Qld 565 K10, 567 K1
Goon Nure Vic 342 E6
Goonalah Qld 559 H5
Goonalga NSW 462 F7
Goonawarra NR NSW 465 H4
Goondah NSW 454 A10, 456 B3
Goondi Qld 563 M6, 569 E9
Goondiwindi Qld **500–501**, 559 H9
Goondoola Qld 558 F8
Goondooloo NT 614 G8
Goonengerry NSW 461 P2
Goonery NSW 463 H4
Goongarrie WA 707 K1, 709 L10
Goongarrie NP WA 707 L1, 709 M10
Goongee Vic 340 B5
Goongerah Vic 343 J4
Goonoo Goonoo NSW 458 G1, 460 G10
Goora Qld 567 N7
Gooram Vic 344 C7
Gooramadda Vic 344 G3
Goorambat Vic 344 D5
Gooray Qld 559 H9
Goorianawa NSW 460 B9
Goorimpa NSW 462 G4
Goornong Vic 339 M1
Gooroc Vic 339 H1, 341 H10
Goorooyaroo NR ACT 477 F2
Goovigen Qld 561 J10
Gooyer Qld 567 L3
Gorae Vic 338 C7
Gorae West Vic 338 C7
Goranba Qld 559 H6
Gordon ACT 477 D5
Gordon NSW 453 D4
Gordon SA 791 J4
Gordon Tas 839 C8, 843 K7
Gordon Vic 336 D2, 339 L5
Gordon Brook NSW 461 M5
Gordon Downs WA 713 N10
Gordon Park Qld 555 C4
Gordon River Tas 842 C3
Gordons Hill SRA Tas 838 F5
Gordonvale Qld 563 L6, 569 E8
Gorge Rock WA 706 F5
Gormandale Vic 342 B8
Gormanston Tas 840 D10
Goroke Vic 338 C2
Gorrie NT 614 F9, 616 F1
Goschen Vic 341 J7

Gosford NSW **389**, 455 L4, 459 H7
Gosnells WA 704 G8, 705 C5, 706 C4
Gostwyck NSW 461 J8
Goughs Bay Vic 344 E8
Goulburn NSW **370–371**, 454 E10, 456 D3
Goulburn River Vic 344 B8
Goulburn River NP NSW 458 E4
Goulburn Weir Vic 339 P2, 344 A6
Goulds Country Tas 841 N5
Govana Qld 559 H6
Gove Peninsula NT 615 M4
Gowan NSW 454 C3, 458 C7
Gowan Hills Qld 565 M10, 567 M1
Gowanford Vic 341 H6
Gowangardie Vic 344 D5
Gowar East Vic 339 J1, 341 J10
Gowrie Park Tas 840 G7
Goyura Vic 340 F8
Grabben Gullen NSW 454 D9, 456 D3
Grabine SP NSW 454 B7, 456 C1, 458 C9
Gracemere Qld 561 J8
Gracetown WA 706 A8
Graceville Qld 555 B6, 557 C3
Gradgery NSW 463 P6
Gradule Qld 558 F9
Grafton NSW **417**, 461 M5
Graman NSW 460 G5
Grampians and Pyrenees Wine Region Vic **272**
Grampians NP Vic **272**, 338 F4
Granada Qld 562 D10, 564 E2
Grange Qld 555 C4
Grange SA 786 C5
Granite Belt Wine Region Qld **506–507**
Granite Downs SA 789 G2
Granite Peak WA 709 L3
Granite Point CA Tas 844 F2, 841 L4
Granite Tor CA Tas 840 E8
Grant Qld 560 A8, 565 P8
Grantham Qld 556 C6, 559 L7
Grantham Downs Qld 558 F6
Grantleigh Qld 561 H9
Granton Tas 839 B4, 843 J4
Grantville Vic 337 K6
Granville NSW 453 B5
Granville Harbour Tas 840 B8
Granya Vic 345 K3
Grasmere NSW 462 D7
Grass Patch WA 707 L7
Grass Valley WA 705 E4, 706 D4
Grassdale Vic 338 C6
Grassmere Qld 558 C7
Grasstree Qld 560 G4
Grasstree Hill Tas 839 C4, 843 K4
Grassville SA 787 G1, 791 L7
Grassy Tas 840 F3
Grassy Head NSW 461 N9
Gravelly Beach Tas 844 D5, 841 J6

Gravesend NSW 460 F5
Grays Point NSW 453 C10
Graytown Vic 339 P2, 344 A6
Gre Gre Vic 339 H2
Gre Gre North Vic 339 H1
Great Australian Bight SA 789 B10
Great Australian Bight MP SA 789 B10
Great Australian Bight Whale Sanctuary SA 789 D9
Great Barrier Reef Qld 561 K3
Great Barrier Reef Marine Park (Cairns Section) Qld 563 M3, 569 E4
Great Barrier Reef Marine Park (Central Section) Qld 560 F1, 563 N7
Great Barrier Reef Marine Park (Far North Section) Qld 568 G5
Great Barrier Reef Marine Park (Mackay–Capricorn Section) Qld 559 M1, 561 M6
Great Basalt Wall NP Qld 560 A2, 563 L10, 565 N2
Great Dividing Range NSW 456 D6, 458 E5, 461 L3
Great Dividing Range Qld 560 A2
Great Lake Tas 844 C9, 841 H9
Great Oyster Bay Tas 843 N1
Great Sandy Desert WA 710 B2
Great Sandy Island NR WA 714 D6
Great Sandy NP Qld **490–491**, 556 E1, 559 N2, 559 N4
Great Southern Wine Region WA **646**
Great Victoria Desert SA 789 B4
Great Victoria Desert WA 711 C4
Great Victoria Desert NR WA 711 F4
Great Western Vic 338 G3
Great Western Tiers Tas 841 H8
Gredgwin Vic 341 K8
Green Fields SA 786 E2
Green Head WA 706 A1, 708 D10
Green Hill Creek Vic 339 J3
Green Hills WA 705 E5, 706 D4
Green Island NP Qld 563 M5, 569 E7
Green Lake SA 791 M1
Green Patch SA 790 D9
Green Point SA 790 C9
Greenacre NSW 453 C7
Greenacres SA 786 E4
Greenbank NT 615 N10, 617 N2
Greenbushes WA 705 C10, 706 C8
Greendale Vic 336 D2, 339 M5
Greenethorpe NSW 456 B1, 458 A9
Greenhill SA 786 F6
Greenland NSW 459 H4
Greenly Island CP SA 790 C9
Greenmount Qld 556 B6, 559 L7
Greenmount Vic 342 B9
Greenock SA 787 E4, 791 K9
Greenough WA 708 C8

Greenridge NSW 461 N3
Greens Beach Tas 844 C3, 841 H5
Greens Creek Vic 338 G3
Greensborough Vic 335 E2
Greenslopes Qld 555 D6, 557 C3
Greenvale NSW 464 C2
Greenvale NSW 465 L6
Greenvale Qld 563 K9
Greenvale Qld 563 K9
Greenvale Vic 335 B1, 336 G2, 339 N5
Greenvale Reservoir Vic 335 B1
Greenwald Vic 338 C6
Greenway ACT 477 D4
Greenways SA 788 E8
Greenwich NSW 453 E5
Greenwith SA 786 G2
Greenwood Qld 564 F3
Greenwood WA 704 B2
Greenwoods Qld 565 L10
Gregadoo NSW 465 N6
Gregory WA 708 C7
Gregory Downs Qld 562 C8
Gregory NP NT **589**, 614 C10, 614 D10, 616 C2, 616 D1
Gregory Range Qld 562 G8
Gregory Range WA 715 L6
Grenfell NSW **447**, 456 A1, 465 P3
Grenfield Qld 567 M4
Grenville Vic 336 C3, 339 K6
Gresford NSW 459 J4
Greta NSW 455 L1, 459 H5
Greta Vic 344 F5
Greta South Vic 344 F6
Greta West Vic 344 F5
Gretna Tas 839 A3, 843 H4
Grevillia NSW 461 M2
Grey WA 705 A1, 706 B2
Grey Peaks NP Qld 563 L6, 569 E8
Grey Range Qld 566 G10
Greycroft Qld 565 N10
Greystanes NSW 453 A5
Greythorn Vic 335 D3
Griffith ACT 477 D3
Griffith NSW **447**, 465 K4
Griffiths NR WA 707 L7
Gringegalgona Vic 338 D4
Gritjurk Vic 338 D5
Grogan NSW 465 P4
Groganville Qld 563 J5, 569 A6
Grong Grong NSW 465 M5
Groote Eylandt NT 615 M7
Grosvenor Downs Qld 560 E6
Grove Tas 839 B5, 843 J5
Grove Creek Qld 568 D5
Grovedale Vic 336 E5, 339 M7
Grovely Qld 555 B3
Gruyere Vic 337 J3, 344 C10
Gubbata NSW 465 L3
Guilderton WA 705 B3, 706 B3
Guildford NSW 453 B6
Guildford Tas 840 E6
Guildford Vic 339 L3

Guildford WA 704 F3, 705 C5, 706 C4
Guim Vic 336 G1
Gular NSW 458 A1, 460 A10
Gulargambone NSW 458 A1, 460 A10
Gulera Qld 559 J6
Gulf Country Qld **520–525**
Gulf Creek NSW 460 G7
Gulf of Carpentaria NT 615 M8
Gulf of Carpentaria Qld 562 C3
Gulf St Vincent SA 787 B6, 791 H10
Gulgoa NP NSW 463 M2
Gulgong NSW **390**, 458 D4
Gulley Point Tas 842 A3
Gulnare SA 791 J7
Guluguba Qld 559 H4
Gum Creek NSW 465 J5
Gum Creek Qld 562 F7
Gum Flat NSW 461 H6
Gum Lagoon CP SA 788 C8
Gum Lake NSW 462 E9, 464 E1
Gum Vale NSW 462 B2
Gumahah Qld 567 N9
Gumbalie NSW 463 J3
Gumbardo Qld 567 M4
Gumble NSW 454 A3, 458 B6
Gumdale Qld 555 F6, 557 D3
Gumeracha SA 787 E6, 791 K10
Gumlu Qld 560 E1, 563 P10
Gunalda Qld 556 C1, 559 M4
Gunbar NSW 465 J3
Gunbar NSW 465 J4
Gunbarrel Highway WA **672–675**
Gunbarwood Qld 559 H6
Gunbower Vic 341 M8
Gundagai NSW **371**, 456 A4, 457 B1, 465 P6
Gundaring WA 705 G9, 706 E7
Gundaroo NSW 456 C4, 457 F1
Gundary Qld 567 M4
Gundowring Vic 345 J5
Gundy NSW 459 H3
Gunebang NSW 463 L10, 465 L1
Gungahlin ACT 477 D2
Gungal NSW 458 F4
Gunnawarra Qld 558 B6
Gunnawarra Qld 563 L7, 569 C10
Gunnedah NSW **417**, 460 F9
Gunnewin Qld 558 E4
Gunning NSW **371**, 454 C10, 456 C3
Gunningbland NSW 463 P10, 465 P2
Gunns Plains Tas 840 F6
Gunpowder Qld 562 C10, 564 C1
Guntawang NSW 458 D4
Gununa Qld 562 B5
Gurig NP NT **589**, 614 E2
Gurley NSW 460 E5
Gurner NT 618 D4
Gutha WA 708 E8
Guthalungra Qld 560 E1, 563 P10

Guthega NSW 456 A7, 457 C7
Guy Fawkes River NP NSW 461 L6
Guyra NSW 461 J7
Guys Forest Vic 345 L3
Gwabegar NSW 460 B8
Gwambagwine Qld 558 G3
Gwandalan NSW 459 J6, 455 M3
Gwelup WA 704 B3
Gwydir River NSW 460 C5
Gymbowen Vic 338 C2
Gymea NSW 453 C9
Gymea Bay NSW 453 C10
Gympie Qld **501**, 556 D1, 559 M4
Gypsum Vic 340 F6

H

Habana Qld 560 G4
Hackham West SA 786 C10
Hackney SA 786 E5
Haddon Vic 336 B2, 339 K5
Haddon Rig NSW 463 P7
Haden Qld 556 B4, 559 L6
Hadfield Vic 335 C2
Hadleigh NSW 460 F5
Hadspen Tas 844 D6, 841 K7
Hagley Tas 844 C6, 841 J7
Hahndorf SA **761**, 787 E6, 791 K10
Haig WA 711 D6
Haigslea Qld 557 A3
Haines Junction Vic 336 B7, 339 K9
Halbury SA 787 D3, 791 J8
Halfway Creek NSW 461 N6
Halidon SA 791 M10
Halifax Qld 563 M8
Hall ACT 477 D2, 456 C4, 457 E2
Hallam Vic 335 G6, 337 H4
Hallett SA 791 K7
Hallett Cove SA 786 C9
Hallett Cove CP SA 786 C9
Hallidays Point NSW 459 L3
Halls Creek WA **686**, 713 L9
Halls Gap Vic **272–273**, 338 F3
Hallsville NSW 460 G9
Halton NSW 459 J4
Hambidge CP SA 790 D7
Hamel WA 705 C8, 706 C6
Hamelin WA 708 C5
Hamelin Bay WA 706 A8
Hamelin Pool Marine NR WA 708 B4
Hamersley WA 704 C2
Hamersley WA 714 G8
Hamersley Range WA 714 F7
Hamilton NSW 462 F7
Hamilton Qld 555 D4
Hamilton SA 787 E3, 791 K8
Hamilton SA 792 C2
Hamilton Tas 843 H3
Hamilton Vic **273**, 338 D6
Hamilton Downs NT 618 G6
Hamilton Downs Youth Camp NT 618 G6
Hamilton Hill WA 704 B8

Hamilton Hotel Qld 564 E7
Hamilton Island Qld 560 G2
Hamilton Park NSW 463 J4
Hamley Bridge SA 787 D4, 791 J9
Hammond SA 791 J5
Hammond Downs Qld 567 J3
Hammondville NSW 453 A8
Hampden Downs Qld 564 G5
Hampshire Tas 840 E5
Hampton NSW 454 F5, 456 E1,
   458 E8
Hampton Vic 335 D5
Hampton Park Vic 335 G6, 337 J4
Hampton Tableland WA 711 F7
Hanging Rock NSW 459 H2
Hann River Roadhouse Qld 563 J3,
   568 E10
Hann Tableland NP Qld 563 L5,
   569 C7
Hannaford Qld 559 H7
Hannahs Bridge NSW 458 D3
Hannan NSW 465 L3
Hannaville Qld 560 F4
Hansborough SA 787 E3, 791 K8
Hanson SA 787 E2, 791 K7
Hanwood NSW 465 K4
Happy Valley Qld 559 N3
Happy Valley SA 786 D9
Happy Valley Vic 340 G4
Happy Valley Vic 345 H5
Happy Valley Reservoir SA 786 D9
Haran Qld 559 H7
Harcourt Vic 339 L3
Harden NSW 456 A3
Harding Falls FR Tas 841 N8
Hardings Ranges Qld 564 G10
Hardington Qld 565 M6
Hardwicke Bay SA 790 G10
Harefield NSW 465 N6
Harford Tas 844 B4, 841 H5
Hargrave Park NSW 453 A7
Hargraves NSW 454 D2, 458 D5
Harkaway Vic 335 G6
Harrami Qld 559 J2
Harriedale NSW 462 B10, 464 B1
Harrietville Vic **326**, 342 C2, 345
   J7
Harrington NSW 459 M3
Harris NR WA 706 G6
Harris Park NSW 453 B5
Harrismith WA 706 F6
Harrisville Qld 556 D6, 557 A5,
   559 M7
Harrogate SA 787 E6, 791 K10
Harrow Vic 338 C3
Harrys Creek Vic 344 D6
Harston Vic 339 P1, 341 P10, 344 B5
Hart SA 787 C2, 791 J7
Hartley NSW **390**, 454 F5, 458 E8
Hartley SA 787 E7, 788 A6, 791 K10
Harts Range Police Station NT
   619 K5
Hartwell Vic 335 E4

Hartz Mountains NP Tas **831**,
   843 H7
Harvest Home Qld 560 C3
Harvey WA 705 C8, 706 C6
Harvey Estuary WA 705 B7
Harwood NSW 461 N5
Haslam SA 790 B5
Hassell NP WA 706 F9
Hastings NSW 463 L4
Hastings Vic 335 F10, 337 H6,
   339 P8
Hat Head NSW 461 N9
Hat Head NP NSW 459 N1, 461 N9
Hatches Creek NT 617 K10, 619 K1
Hatfield NSW 464 F3
Hatherleigh SA 788 F9
Hattah Vic 340 E4
Hattah–Kulkyne NP Vic **290**, 340 E3
Hatton Vale Qld 556 C5, 559 M7
Havelock Vic 339 K3
Haven Vic 338 E2
Havilah Qld 560 E3
Hawker ACT 477 C2
Hawker SA **762**, 791 J3
Hawkesdale Vic 338 E7
Hawkesdale West Vic 338 E7
Hawks Nest NSW 455 P1, 459 K5
Hawkwood Qld 559 J4
Hawley Beach Tas 844 A4, 841 H5
Hawthorn SA 786 D7
Hawthorn Vic 335 D4
Hawthorn East Vic 335 D4
Hawthorndene SA 786 E8
Hawthorne Qld 555 D5
Hay NSW **448**, 465 H5
Hay Point Qld 560 G4
Haydens Bog Vic 343 K3
Haydon Qld 562 F7
Hayes Tas 839 A4, 843 J4
Hayes Creek NT 613 E6, 614 D6
Hayman Island Qld 560 F2
Haysdale Vic 341 H4
Hazel Park Vic 337 P7
Hazelbush Qld 560 B8
Hazelmere Qld 560 A6, 565 P6
Hazelmere Qld 563 K3, 569 C3
Hazelmere WA 704 G4
Hazelwood Qld 565 J3
Hazelwood Qld 565 L9
Headingly Qld 564 A4
Healesville Vic **305**, 337 K2, 344 C10
Healesville West Vic 337 K2,
   344 C10
Heathcote NSW 453 B10, 455 K7,
   456 G2, 459 H9
Heathcote Vic **273**, 339 N3
Heathcote Junction Vic 337 H1, 339
   P4, 842 A9
Heathcote NP NSW 453 B10
Heather Qld 558 C8
Heather Downs Qld 558 D5
Heatherton Vic 335 E5
Heathfield NSW 463 P3

Heathfield SA 786 F8
Heathfield West Qld 560 C2,
   563 M10
Heathlands Qld 568 C4
Heathmere Vic 338 C7
Heathmont Vic 335 F3
Heathvale Vic 338 E3
Heathwood Qld 555 C9, 557 C4
Hebel Qld 558 D10
Hectorville SA 786 F5
Hedley Vic 337 P7, 342 A9
Heggaton CR SA 790 F7
Heidelberg Qld 560 D3
Heidelberg Vic 335 D3, 337 H3,
   339 P6, 842 A10
Heidelberg West Vic 335 D2
Heka Tas 840 F6
Helen Springs NT 617 H5
Helen Vale Qld 560 B9, 565 P9
Helena Valley WA 704 G4
Helensburgh NSW 455 J8, 456 G2,
   458 G10
Helensvale Qld 557 E6
Helenvale Qld 563 L3, 569 C4
Helidon Qld 556 B5, 559 L7
Hell Hole Gorge NP Qld 567 L3
Hells Gate Roadhouse Qld 562 A6
Hellyer Tas 840 D4
Hellyer Gorge SR Tas 840 D5
Hemmant Qld 555 F4
Henbury NT 618 G7
Henbury Meteorite CR NT 618 G7
Henderson WA 704 B10
Hendra Qld 555 D4, 557 C2
Henley Beach SA 786 C5
Henley Beach South SA 786 C6
Henley Brook WA 704 F1
Henlow Vic 345 K4
Henrietta Tas 840 E5
Henty NSW **448**, 465 M7
Henty Vic 338 C5
Hepburn Springs Vic 339 L4
Herbert Downs Qld 564 C8
Herbert Vale Qld 562 A9
Herberton Qld 563 L6, 569 C9
Herdsman WA 704 B4
Herdsman Lake WA 704 B4
Hereward Qld 565 L7
Heritage Park Qld 555 E10
Hermannsburg NT 618 F6
Hermidale NSW 463 L7
Hernani NSW 461 L7
Herne Hill WA 704 G2
Herons Creek NSW 459 M2
Herrick Tas 841 M5
Herston Qld 555 C4
Hervey Bay Qld **501**, 559 M3
Hervey Bay Qld 559 M2
Hervey Bay Marine Park Qld 559 M1
Hesket Vic 336 F1, 339 N4
Hesso SA 790 G4
Hewart Downs NSW 462 A2
Hexham Qld 565 J6

Hexham Vic 338 G6
Heybridge Tas 840 F5
Heyfield Vic 342 B6
Heywood Vic 338 C7
Heywood Islands WA 712 G4
Hi-Way Inn NT 616 G2
Hiamdale Vic 342 B8
Hiawatha Vic 337 P7, 342 A9
Hibiscus Coast Qld 561 G4
Hidden Valley NT 616 G2
Hidden Valley Qld 560 D3
Hidden Valley Qld 563 M9
Hideaway Bay Tas 839 B8, 843 J7
Higginsville WA 707 L4
High Camp Vic 339 N4, 344 A8
High Range NSW 454 G9, 456 F2,
   458 F10
High Wycombe WA 704 G5
Highbury Qld 563 H5
Highbury SA 786 G4
Highbury WA 705 F8, 706 E6
Highclere Tas 840 E5
Highcroft Tas 839 F7, 843 M6
Highgate WA 704 D4
Highgate Hill Qld 555 C5
Highlands Qld 558 A1
Highlands Qld 567 M2
Highlands Vic 344 B8
Highton Vic 336 D5, 339 M7
Highvale Qld 557 B2
Hill End NSW **390**, 454 D3, 458 D6
Hill End Qld 555 C5
Hill End Vic 337 N4
Hill Grange SA 791 L6
Hill Springs WA 708 C2
Hill Top NSW 455 H9, 456 F2,
   458 F10
Hill View NSW 463 K7
Hillarys WA 704 A1
Hillbank SA 786 F1
Hillcrest Qld 555 D10
Hillcrest SA 786 E4
Hillcroft NSW 458 C4
Hillgrange SA 791 K6
Hillgrove NSW 461 K8
Hillgrove Qld 560 A1, 563 L10,
   565 P1
Hillsdale NSW 453 F8
Hillside NSW 453 A1
Hillside NSW 462 F2
Hillside Qld 558 C3
Hillside WA 715 J7
Hillston NSW 465 J2
Hilltops Wine Region NSW **371**
Hilltown SA 787 D1, 791 J7
Hillview Qld 557 C8
Hillview Qld 558 D1, 560 E10
Hillview Qld 565 L4
Hillview WA 709 H5
Hillwood Tas 844 D4, 841 J5
Hiltaba SA 790 C4
Hilton WA 704 B8
Hilton Qld 564 C3

Hinchinbrook Island NP Qld **527**, 563 M8
Hincks CP SA 790 E8
Hindmarsh SA 786 D5
Hinemoa Qld 558 G1, 561 H10
Hines Hill WA 706 F4
Hinnomunjie Vic 342 E2, 345 L7
Hivesville Qld 556 A1, 559 K4
Hobart Tas **800–801**, 838 E6, 839 C5, 843 K5
Hobartville Qld 560 B8
Hobbys Yards NSW 454 C6, 456 D1, 458 C8
Hobsons Bay Vic 335 C4
Hoddle Vic 337 M8
Hoddles Creek Vic 337 K3
Hodgson Qld 558 E5
Hodgson Downs NT 615 H9
Hodgson River NT 615 H9, 617 H1
Hog Back SA 791 K7
Hoganthulla Qld 558 C3
Hogarth Range NP NSW 461 M3
Holbrook NSW 454 G1, 458 F5
Holbrook NSW 465 N7
Holdfast Bay SA 786 C6, 787 D6
Holey Creek NT 613 B7, 614 C7
Holey Plains SP Vic 342 B7
Holland Landing Vic 342 D7
Holland Park Qld 555 D6, 557 C3
Holland Park West Qld 555 D6
Hollow Tree Tas 839 A2, 843 H3
Holly Downs Qld 558 B4
Hollybank FR Tas 844 E5, 841 K6
Hollywell Qld 557 E6
Holmwood NSW 454 A6, 456 B1, 458 B8
Holowilena SA 791 K3
Holowilena South SA 791 K4
Holroyd NSW 453 A5
Holstons Vic 342 F4, 345 M9
Holsworthy NSW 453 A8
Holt ACT 477 C2
Holt Rock WA 707 H6
Holwell Tas 844 C5, 841 J6
Home Hill Qld 560 D1, 563 P10
Home Rule NSW 458 D4
Home Valley WA 713 M4
Homeboin Qld 558 C7
Homebush NSW 453 C6
Homebush Qld 560 G4
Homebush Vic 339 J3
Homebush Bay NSW 453 C5
Homecroft Vic 340 F9
Homestead Qld 560 A2, 565 P2
Homevale Qld 560 F4
Homevale NP Qld 560 F4
Homewood Vic 344 B8
Honan Downs Qld 565 M9
Honiton SA 787 A7, 788 A3, 791 H10
Hooley WA 715 H7
Hoomooloo Park Qld 567 M4

Hope Vale Aboriginal Community Qld 563 L3, 569 C3
Hope Valley SA 786 F4
Hopefield NSW 465 L8
Hopetoun Vic 340 F7
Hopetoun WA **646–647**, 707 J8
Hopetoun West Vic 340 E7
Hopevale Vic 340 E8
Hopkins River Vic 338 G7
Hoppers Crossing Vic 335 A5, 336 F3, 339 N6
Hornet Bank Qld 558 G4
Hornsby NSW 453 C3, 455 K6, 456 G1, 459 H8
Hornsby Heights NSW 453 C2
Hornsdale SA 791 J6
Horrocks WA 708 C7
Horseshoe Bend NT 619 J9
Horseshoe Creek NSW 461 N2
Horsham Vic **273**, 338 E2
Horsnell Gully CP SA 786 F6
Horton Vale Qld 567 P8
Hoskinstown NSW 456 D5, 457 G3
Hotham Heights Vic 342 C2, 345 J7
Hotspur Vic 338 C6
Hovells Creek NSW 454 B7, 456 C2, 458 B9
Howard Qld 559 M3
Howard Springs NT 613 D2, 614 D4
Howden Tas 839 C6, 843 K6
Howes Valley NSW 455 J2, 458 G6
Howick Group NP Qld 563 K2, 568 G9
Howittville Vic 342 C4, 345 H9
Howqua Vic 344 E8
Howth Tas 840 F5
Hoyleton SA 787 D3, 791 J8
Huckitta NT 619 K4
Huddleston SA 791 J6
Hugh River NT 619 H7
Hugh River NT 619 H7
Hughenden Qld **535**, 565 L3
Hughes ACT 477 D3
Hughes SA 789 B8
Hull Heads Qld 563 M7
Humbert River Ranger Station NT 616 C2
Humboldt Qld 560 F10
Humbug Point CA Tas 841 P5
Hume Weir NSW 465 M8
Humeburn Qld 567 N7
Humevale Vic 337 H1, 339 P5, 344 B9
Humpty Doo NT 613 D3, 614 D4
Humula NSW 465 N7
Hungerford Qld 567 M10
Hunter Vic 339 M1, 341 M10
Hunter River NSW 458 G5
Hunter Valley NSW **380–383**
Hunters Hill NSW 453 E5
Hunterston Vic 342 B9
Huntingdale WA 704 F8
Huntingfield NSW 464 A3

Huntly Vic 339 M2
Huon Vic 345 J4
Huon River Tas 843 J7
Huonville Tas **832**, 839 B6, 843 J6
Hurricane Qld 563 K5, 569 B6
Hurstbridge Vic 335 E1, 337 H2, 339 P5, 842 B10
Hurstville NSW 453 D8, 455 K7, 459 H9
Hurstville Grove NSW 453 D8
Huskisson NSW **371**, 456 G4
Hy Brazil WA 708 G7
Hyden WA **647**, 706 G5
Hynam SA 788 D10
Hyperna SA 791 N7

I

Ibis Creek Qld 560 D4
Icy Creek Vic 337 M3
Ida Bay Tas 839 A9, 843 H8
Ida Valley WA 709 K8
Idalia Qld 562 G8
Idalia NP Qld 567 M2
Idracowra NT 619 H8
Iffley Qld 560 F6
Iffley Qld 562 E8
Iguana Creek Vic 342 D5, 345 K10
Ilbilbie Qld 560 G5
Ilford NSW 454 E2, 458 E6
Ilfracombe Qld 565 M8
Illabarook Vic 336 B3, 339 K6
Illabo NSW 465 N5
Illawarra Vic 338 G3
Illawong NSW 453 C9
Illawong WA 708 D9
Illilliwa NSW 465 H4
Illintjitja Homeland SA 789 C1
Illistrin Qld 562 D10, 564 E1
Illowa Vic 338 F8
Iltur Homeland SA 789 C3
Iluka NSW 461 N4
Imanpa NT 618 F8
Imbil Qld 556 D2, 559 M5
Impadna NT 619 H8
Inala Qld 555 B8, 557 C3
Indee WA 715 H6
Indented Head Vic 335 A8, 336 F5, 339 N7
Indiana NT 619 K5
Indooroopilly Qld 555 C6, 557 C3
Ingalba NR NSW 465 N5
Ingeberry Qld 567 L6
Ingebyra NSW 456 B8, 457 C8
Ingham Qld **527**, 563 M8
Ingle Farm SA 786 E3
Ingleby Vic 336 C6, 339 K8
Ingleside NSW 453 F2
Inglewood Qld 559 J9
Inglewood Vic 339 K1, 341 K10
Inglewood WA 704 D4
Ingomar SA 792 B8
Injinoo Aboriginal Community Qld 568 C3

Injune Qld **501**, 558 E4
Inkerman Qld 560 D1, 563 P10
Inkerman Qld 562 E4
Inkerman SA 787 C4, 791 J9
Inman Valley SA 787 C8, 788 A5
Innaloo WA 704 B3
Innamincka SA **782–783**, 793 N4
Innamincka RR SA **783**, 793 M3
Innes NP SA **733**, 788 A2
Innesowen NSW 463 H6
Inneston SA 788 A2
Innesvale NT 614 D9
Innis Downs Qld 558 A2, 567 P2
Innisfail Qld **527**, 563 M6, 569 E9
Innot Hot Springs Qld 563 L7, 569 C10
Innouendy WA 708 E3
Inorunie Qld 562 G7
Interlaken Tas 843 J1, 841 K10
Inveralochy NSW 456 D4
Inverell NSW **418**, 461 H6
Invergordon Vic 344 C3
Inverleigh Qld 562 D7
Inverleigh Vic 336 C5, 339 L7
Inverloch Vic **305**, 337 L7
Inverway NT 616 B5
Investigator Group CP SA 790 B8
Investigator Strait SA 788 A2
Inyarinyi SA 789 F1
Iona NSW 464 E3
Iowna WA 708 G7
Ipolera NT 618 F6
Ipswich Qld **502**, 556 D6, 557 B4, 559 M7
Irishtown Tas 840 C4
Iron Baron SA 790 G6
Iron Knob SA **762**, 790 G5
Iron Range Qld 568 E6
Iron Range NP Qld 568 E6
Ironbank SA 786 E9
Ironbark NR NSW 460 G7
Ironbark Dam Camp NSW 460 G4
Ironhurst Qld 563 H7
Ironpot Qld 556 A3, 559 K5
Ironside Qld 555 C6
Irrapatana SA 792 F7
Irrewarra Vic 336 A6, 339 K8
Irrewillipe Vic 339 J8
Irvinebank Qld 563 L6, 569 C9
Irymple Vic 340 E2
Isaacs ACT 477 D4
Isis Downs Qld 565 M10
Isisford Qld 565 M10, 567 M1
Isla Gorge NP Qld 558 G2
Isla Plains Qld 559 H2
Island Bend NSW 456 B7, 457 C7
Island Lagoon SA 790 F3
Israelite Bay WA 711 A9
Italian Gully Vic 336 B3, 339 K5
Ithaca Qld 555 C4
Ivanhoe NSW 462 G10, 464 G1
Ivanhoe Qld 558 A2
Ivanhoe Vic 335 D3

Ivanhoe WA 713 N4
Iwantja (Indulkana) SA 789 G2
Iwupataka NT 619 H6

J

J Trotter Memorial Park Qld 555 G7
Jaaningga NR NSW 461 M8
Jabiru NT **590**, 614 G4
Jabuk SA 788 A8
Jackadgery NSW 461 L5
Jackson Qld 558 G5
Jackson Vic 338 F2
Jacobs Well Qld 556 F6, 557 E5, 559 N7
Jallukar Vic 338 G4
Jallumba Vic 338 D3
Jamberoo NSW 455 J10, 456 G3
Jamberoo Qld 558 G2
Jambin Qld 561 J10
Jamboree Heights Qld 555 A7
Jamestown SA **762**, 791 J6
Jamieson Vic **326–327**, 344 E8
Jan Juc Vic 336 D6, 339 M8
Jancourt East Vic 339 H8
Jandakot WA 704 D8
Jandowae Qld 559 J5
Jane River Tas 840 D7
Janina NSW 463 H4
Jannali NSW 453 C9
Japoon Qld 563 M7, 569 E10
Jardine River NP Qld 568 C3
Jarklin Vic 341 L9
Jarrahdale WA 705 C6, 706 C5
Jarrahmond Vic 343 H5, 345 P10
Jarvis Field Qld 565 H7
Jarvisfield Qld 560 D1, 563 P10
Jaspers Brush NSW 455 H10, 456 G3
Jay Park Qld 555 B6
JC Hotel Qld 566 G3
Jecundars Park WA 706 D2
Jeedamya WA 709 L9
Jeffcott Vic 341 H9
Jefferson Lakes WA 709 K9
Jellat Jellat NSW 456 E8
Jellinbah Qld 560 F8
Jennacubbine WA 705 E3, 706 D3
Jenolan Caves NSW 454 F6, 456 E1, 458 E8
Jeogla NSW 461 K8
Jeparit Vic 340 D9
Jerangle NSW 456 D6, 457 G5
Jericho Qld 560 B9, 565 P9
Jericho Tas 839 C1, 843 K2
Jerilderie NSW **448**, 465 K6
Jerona Qld 560 D1, 563 N9
Jerrabomberra NSW 477 E4
Jerramungup WA 706 G8
Jerrys Plains NSW 458 G5
Jerseyville NSW 461 N9
Jervis Bay NSW **372**, 456 G4
Jervis Bay NP NSW 456 G4
Jervois NT **608**, 619 L5

Jervois SA 787 G7, 788 A7
Jetsonville Tas 841 L5, 844 G3
Jigalong WA 715 L9
Jil Jil Vic 341 H8
Jilbadji NR WA 707 J4
Jilliby NSW 455 L4, 459 H7
Jimb Creek Qld 557 B5
Jimba Jimba WA 708 D3
Jimboola Qld 564 B6
Jimboomba Qld 557 C5
Jimboomba Qld 557 C5
Jimbour Qld 559 K6
Jimna Qld 556 C3, 559 L5
Jindabyne NSW **372**, 456 B8, 457 D7
Jindalee NSW 456 A3, 465 P5
Jindalee Qld 555 A7
Jindare NT 613 E7, 614 E7
Jindera NSW 465 M8
Jindivick Vic 337 L4
Jingellic NSW 465 N8
Jingemarra WA 708 F7
Jingera NSW 477 F8, 456 D6, 457 G4
Jingili NT 612 E4
Jinka NT 619 L5
Jitarning WA 706 F6
Jobs Gate NSW 463 M1
Joel Vic 339 H3
Joel South Vic 339 H3
Johanna Vic 339 J9
John Forrest NP WA **647**
Johnburgh SA 791 K5
Johns River NSW 459 M2
Johnsonville Vic 342 F6
Jolimont WA 704 C5
Jomara NSW 460 A3
Jondaryan Qld 556 A5, 559 K7
Joondanna WA 704 C4
Jooro Qld 561 J10
Jordan Avon Qld 560 B8
Joseph Bonaparte Gulf NT 614 A8
Joseph Bonaparte Gulf WA 713 N2
Josephville Qld 557 C7
Joulnie NSW 462 A5
Joycedale Qld 560 B9, 565 P9
Joyces Creek Vic 339 L3
Joylands Qld 558 B5
Jubilee Qld 555 B5
Jubilee Downs WA 713 H9
Jubilee Lake WA 711 D4
Judbury Tas 839 A5, 843 H5
Jugiong NSW 456 A4, 465 P5
Jugiong Qld 565 K8
Julatten Qld 563 L5, 569 C7
Julia SA 787 E3, 791 K8
Julia Creek Qld **536**, 564 G3
Julius River FR Tas 840 B5
Jumbuck Outstation SA 789 E7, 792 A9
Juna Downs WA 715 H9
Junction Village Vic 337 J5
Jundah Qld 567 J2

Jundee WA 709 L4
Junee NSW **449**, 465 N5
Junee Qld 560 G7
Junee Reefs NSW 465 N5
Jung Vic 338 F1
Junortoun Vic 339 M2
Jurema Qld 560 E8
Jurien WA **647**, 706 A1, 708 D10

K

Kaarimba Vic 344 B3
Kaban Qld 563 L6, 569 D9
Kabelbara Qld 560 E8
Kabra Qld 561 J8
Kadina SA **762**, 787 A2, 791 H8
Kadji Kadji WA 708 E9
Kadnook Vic 338 C3
Kadungle NSW 463 N10, 465 N1
Kagaru Qld 557 C5
Kaimkillenbun Qld 556 A4, 559 K6
Kainton SA 787 B3, 791 H8
Kaiuroo Qld 560 G8
Kajabbi Qld 562 D10, 564 D2
Kajuligah NSW 463 H9
Kajuligah NR NSW 463 H9, 465 H1
Kakadu NP NT **582–587**, 613 G4, 614 F5
Kalabity SA 791 M4
Kalala NT 614 G10, 616 G2
Kalamurina SA 793 J4
Kalanbi SA 789 G10, 790 A3
Kalang Qld 560 D6
Kalangadoo SA 788 F9
Kalannie WA 706 E2, 708 F10
Kalarka Qld 561 H6
Kalaru NSW 456 E8
Kalbar Qld 556 D6, 557 A6, 559 M8
Kalbarri WA **666–667**, 708 C7
Kalbarri NP WA **667**, 708 C6
Kaleen ACT 477 D2
Kaleno NSW 463 H8
Kalgoorlie WA **648**, 707 L2
Kalimna Vic 342 F6
Kalimna West Vic 342 F6
Kalinga Qld 555 D3
Kalinga Qld 563 J3, 568 E10
Kalkadoon Qld 565 H6
Kalkallo Vic 336 G2, 339 P5, 344 A9
Kalkarindji NT **599**, 616 D4
Kalkaroo NSW 462 F6
Kalkaroo SA 791 N3
Kalkee Vic 338 E1, 340 E10
Kallangur Qld 557 C1
Kallara NSW 462 G5
Kallaroo WA 704 A1
Kalli WA 708 F5
Kalmeta Qld 562 E10, 564 F1
Kalpienung Vic 341 H8
Kalpowar Qld 563 J2, 568 F10
Kalpower Qld 559 K1
Kaltukatjara Community (Docker River) NT 618 A8
Kalumburu WA **686–687**, 713 K2

Kaluwiri WA 709 K6
Kalyan SA 791 M10
Kalyeeda WA 712 G10
Kamarah NSW 465 M4
Kamaran Downs Qld 564 C10, 566 C1
Kamarooka Vic 339 M1, 341 M10
Kamarooka East Vic 339 M1, 341 M10
Kamarooka SP Vic 339 M1, 341 M10
Kambah ACT 477 D4
Kambalda WA **648**, 707 L3
Kambalda NR WA 707 L3
Kambalda West WA 707 L3
Kamballup WA 706 F9
Kameruka NSW 456 D8
Kamileroi Qld 562 D9
Kanagulk Vic 338 D3
Kanandah WA 711 B6
Kanangra–Boyd NP NSW **390–391**, 454 F6, 456 E1, 458 E9
Kanawalla Vic 338 E5
Kancoona Vic 345 H5
Kandanga Qld 556 D2, 559 M5
Kandos NSW 454 F2, 458 E6
Kangaloon NSW 455 H9, 456 F3
Kangan WA 715 H6
Kangarilla SA 787 D7, 788 A5, 791 J10
Kangaroo Bay SA 788 C3
Kangaroo Camp NSW 461 H6
Kangaroo Flat NSW 459 K1, 461 K10
Kangaroo Flat Vic 339 L2
Kangaroo Ground Vic 335 E2
Kangaroo Hills Qld 563 L9
Kangaroo Island SA 788 B2
Kangaroo Point NSW 453 C9
Kangaroo Point Qld 555 D5
Kangaroo Valley NSW 455 H10, 456 F3
Kangaroo Well SA 790 D3
Kangawall Vic 338 C2
Kangiara NSW 454 A10, 456 B3
Kaniva Vic 338 B1, 340 B10
Kanoloo Qld 560 D9
Kanowna Qld 558 C9, 560 E8
Kanowna WA 707 L2
Kantappa NSW 462 A7
Kanumbra Vic 344 C7
Kanunnah Bridge Tas 840 B5
Kanya Vic 339 H2
Kanyaka SA 791 J4
Kanyapella Vic 341 N9, 344 A3
Kanyapella South Vic 341 N9
Kanypi SA 789 B1
Kaoota Tas 839 B6, 843 J6
Kapinnie SA 790 D8
Kapunda SA **762–763**, 787 E4, 791 K9
Kara NSW 462 C5
Kara Kara SP Vic 339 J2
Karabeal Vic 338 E5

Karadoc Vic 340 E2
Karalee WA 707 J3
Karalundi WA 709 H4
Karanja Tas 843 H4
Karara Qld 556 A7, 559 K8
Karara WA 708 F9
Karatta SA 788 B2
Karawara WA 704 D6
Karawatha Qld 555 E9
Karawinna Vic 340 D3
Karbar WA 708 G6
Karcultaby SA 790 C5
Kardella Vic 337 L6
Kardinya WA 704 C8
Kareela NSW 453 C9
Kariah Vic 339 H7
Karidi Creek NT 618 E2
Karijini NP WA 698, 715 H9
Kariong NSW 455 L5, 459 H7
Karkoo SA 790 D8
Karlamilyi (Rudall River) NP WA 698
Karlgarin WA 706 G5
Karmona Qld 566 G7
Karn Vic 344 E6
Karnak Vic 338 C2
Karnup WA 705 B6, 706 C5
Karonie WA 707 N3
Karoola NSW 462 C10, 464 C1
Karoola Tas 844 E4, 841 K6
Karoonda SA 788 A8, 791 M10
Karpa Kora NSW 462 E10, 464 E1
Karrabin Qld 557 A3
Karragullen WA 705 C5, 706 C5
Karrakatta WA 704 B5
Karratha WA 699, 714 F5
Karratha WA 714 F6
Karratha Roadhouse WA 714 F5
Karridale WA 706 B8
Karrinyup WA 704 B3
Karroun Hill NR WA 706 F1, 709 H10
Kars NSW 462 C8
Kars Springs NSW 458 F3
Karte SA 788 A9, 791 N10
Karte CP SA 788 A9, 791 N10
Karuah NSW 455 N1, 459 K5
Karumba Qld 527, 562 E6
Karwarn NSW 463 J9
Karween Vic 340 B2
Karyrie Vic 340 G8
Katamatite Vic 344 D3
Katamatite East Vic 344 D3
Katandra Qld 565 L5
Katandra Vic 344 C4
Katandra West Vic 344 C4
Katanning WA 648, 705 G10, 706 E7
Katarvon Qld 558 D6
Katherine NT 590–591, 613 G8, 614 F7
Katherine River NT 613 F9
Kathida NSW 461 J4

Katoomba NSW 391, 454 G6, 456 F1, 458 F8
Katunga Vic 344 C3
Katyil Vic 340 E10
Kau Rock NR WA 707 M7
Kawarren Vic 336 A7, 339 J8
Kayena Tas 844 C4, 841 J5
Kayrunnera NSW 462 D5
Kealba Vic 335 B3
Kearsley NSW 455 L2, 459 J6
Kedron Qld 555 D3
Keelambra NSW 462 G5
Keep River WA 713 P4
Keep River NP NT 591, 614 A10, 616 A1
Keeroongooloo Qld 567 J4
Keewong NSW 463 H8
Keilor Vic 335 B3, 336 G3, 339 N5
Keilor Downs Vic 335 A2
Keilor East Vic 335 B3
Keith SA 733, 788 C9
Kellalac Vic 338 F1, 340 F10
Kellerberrin WA 705 G4, 706 E4
Kellevie Tas 839 F4, 843 M4
Kellidie Bay CP SA 790 D9
Kellyville NSW 453 A3
Kelmscott WA 704 G9, 705 C5, 706 C5
Kelsey Creek Qld 560 F2
Kelso NSW 454 D4, 458 D7
Kelso Tas 844 C3, 841 H5
Kelvin NSW 460 F9
Kelvin Grove Qld 555 C4
Kemps Creek NSW 455 J6, 456 G1, 458 G9
Kempsey NSW 418, 461 M9
Kempton NSW 454 D8, 456 D2, 458 D10
Kempton Tas 839 B2, 843 J3
Kendall NSW 459 M2
Kendenup WA 706 E9
Kenebri NSW 460 C8
Kenilworth Qld 556 D3, 559 M5
Kenley Vic 341 J4
Kenmare Vic 340 E8
Kenmore NSW 454 E10, 456 E3
Kenmore Qld 555 A6, 557 B3
Kenmore Qld 558 A6
Kenmore Hills Qld 555 A6
Kennedy Qld 563 M7
Kennedy Range WA 708 D2
Kennedy Range NP WA 667, 708 D2
Kennedys Creek Vic 339 H9
Kennett River Vic 336 B8, 339 K9
Kensington NSW 453 E7
Kensington SA 786 E6
Kensington Vic 335 C3
Kensington WA 704 D5
Kensington Gardens SA 786 F5
Kentbruck Vic 338 B7
Kenthurst NSW 453 B2
Kentucky NSW 461 J8
Kentucky Qld 559 H5

Kenwick WA 704 F7
Keperra Qld 555 B4
Keppel Sands Qld 561 K8
Keppoch SA 788 D9
Kerang Vic 290–291, 341 K7
Kerang East Vic 341 L8
Kerein Hills NSW 463 M9
Kergunyah Vic 345 H4
Kergunyah South Vic 345 J4
Keri NT 613 B5, 614 C5
Kernot Vic 337 K6
Kerrabee NSW 458 F4
Kerrisdale Vic 344 B8
Kerriwah NSW 463 N9
Kerry Qld 557 C7
Kersbrook SA 787 E5, 791 K9
Keswick SA 786 D6
Ketchowla SA 791 K6
Kettering Tas 832, 839 C6, 843 K6
Kevington Vic 337 N1, 344 E9
Kew NSW 459 M2
Kew Vic 335 D3, 337 H3, 339 P6
Kew East Vic 335 D3
Kewdale WA 704 F5
Kewell Vic 338 F1, 340 F10
Keyneton SA 787 F5, 791 K9
Keysborough Vic 335 F6
Keysbrook WA 705 C6, 706 C5
Khancoban NSW 456 A7, 457 B6, 465 P8
Khappinghat NR NSW 459 L3
Ki Ki SA 788 B8
Kia Ora NSW 463 N3
Kia Ora Qld 558 C1, 560 D10
Kia Ora SA 791 L7
Kiacatoo NSW 463 M10, 465 M1
Kiah NSW 456 E9
Kialla Vic 344 C5
Kialla West Vic 344 B5
Kiama NSW 372, 455 J10, 456 G3
Kiama NSW 463 H8
Kiamal Vic 340 E5
Kiana NT 617 L4
Kiandool NSW 460 D7
Kiandra NSW 456 B6, 457 C5
Kiandra Qld 567 L7
Kianga NSW 456 E7
Kianga Qld 559 H2
Kiara WA 704 E3
Kiata Vic 338 D1, 340 D10
Kiata East Vic 340 D9
Kickabil NSW 458 A3
Kiddell Plains Qld 558 G1
Kidman Park SA 786 C5
Kidston Qld 563 J8
Kielpa SA 790 E7
Kiewa Vic 345 H4
Kiewa River Vic 345 J5
Kihee Qld 567 J7
Kikoira NSW 465 L3
Kilcowera Qld 567 L9
Kilcoy Qld 556 C4, 559 M6
Kilcummin Qld 560 D6

Kilcunda Vic 337 K7
Kilfeera Vic 344 E5
Kilfera NSW 462 G10, 464 G1
Kilkerran SA 791 H9
Kilkivan Qld 556 C1, 559 L4
Killara NSW 453 E4
Killara WA 709 J4
Killarney NT 616 E2
Killarney Qld 556 C8, 559 L8
Killarney Qld 563 H3
Killarney Qld 563 L10, 565 N2
Killarney Vic 338 E8
Killarney Heights NSW 453 F4
Killarney Park Qld 558 B1
Killawarra NSW 459 L3
Killawarra Qld 559 H5
Killawarra Vic 344 F4
Killcare NSW 455 L5, 459 H8
Killeen Qld 565 K3
Killiecrankie Tas 841 H2
Killora Tas 839 C6, 843 K6
Kilmany Vic 342 B7
Kilmany South Vic 342 C7
Kilmore Vic 274, 339 P4, 344 A8
Kilmorey Qld 558 D4
Kiln Corner SA 787 A5, 791 H9
Kilsyth Vic 335 G3
Kilsyth South Vic 335 G3
Kilterry Qld 565 H2
Kilto WA 712 D8, 715 N1
Kimba Qld 563 H3
Kimba SA 763, 790 F6
Kimberley NSW 462 A10, 464 A1
Kimberley Tas 844 A5, 840 G6
Kimberley Downs WA 712 G7
Kimbriki NSW 459 L3
Kimovale NSW 456 A4, 457 B1, 465 P6
Kin Kin Qld 556 D2, 559 M4
Kinalung NSW 462 C8
Kinchega NP NSW 435, 462 C9
Kinchela NSW 461 M9
Kincora Qld 558 D5
Kindee NSW 459 L1, 461 L10
Kindon Qld 559 J8
Kindred Tas 840 G5
King Ash Bay NT 615 M10, 617 M1
King George Sound WA 706 F10
King Island Tas 840 F2
King Junction Qld 563 H4
King Leopold Ranges WA 713 H7
King River WA 706 F9
King Sound WA 712 E7
King Valley Vic 342 A1, 344 F6
Kingaroy Qld 502, 556 B2, 559 L5
Kinglake Vic 337 J2, 344 B9
Kinglake NP Vic 306, 337 J1, 344 B10
Kinglake West Vic 337 J1, 344 B9
Kingoonya SA 790 D1
Kingower Vic 339 K1
Kings Canyon Resort NT 618 E7
Kings Creek NT 618 E7

Kings Cross NSW 453 F6
Kings Langley NSW 453 A4
Kings Park Vic 335 A3
Kings Park WA 704 C5
Kings Plains NSW 461 J5
Kings Plains NP NSW 461 H5
Kingsborough Qld 563 K5, 569 C7
Kingsborough Qld 565 N7
Kingsbury Vic 335 D2
Kingscliff NSW 461 P1
Kingscote SA 734, 787 A9, 788 B3
Kingsdale NSW 454 E10, 456 D3
Kingsford NSW 453 F7
Kingsgrove NSW 453 D7
Kingsley WA 704 B1
Kingston ACT 477 D3
Kingston Qld 555 E10, 557 D4
Kingston Qld 560 C8
Kingston Tas 832, 839 C5, 843 K5
Kingston Vic 336 C1, 339 L4
Kingston-on-Murray SA 791 M8
Kingston Park SA 786 C8
Kingston SE SA 734, 788 D8
Kingstown NSW 461 H8
Kingsvale NSW 456 A3, 458 A10,
    465 P4
Kingswood SA 786 E7
Kinimakatka Vic 338 C1, 340 C10
Kinkuna NP Qld 559 M2
Kinnabulla Vic 340 G8
Kinnoul Qld 558 G3
Kio Ora Vic 338 G5
Kioloa NSW 456 F5
Kiora Qld 560 A2, 565 N2
Kirkalocka WA 708 G8
Kirkimbie NT 616 A4
Kirkstall Vic 338 E7
Kirrama Qld 563 L7
Kirrawee NSW 453 C9
Kirribilli NSW 453 F6
Kirup WA 705 C10, 706 C7
Kitchener NSW 455 L2, 459 H6
Kitchener WA 711 B6
Kiwirrkurra WA 710 E6
Klemzig SA 786 E5
Klori NSW 460 G9
Knebsworth Vic 338 D7
Knocklofty Park Tas 838 D7
Knockwood Vic 337 N1, 344 F9
Knowsley Vic 339 N2
Knoxfield Vic 335 F4
Koah Qld 563 L5, 569 D7
Koberinga Qld 560 D1, 563 P10
Kobyboyn Vic 344 B7
Koetong Vic 345 K3
Kogan Qld 559 J6
Kogarah NSW 453 D8
Kogarah Bay NSW 453 D8
Koimbo Vic 340 G4
Kojonup WA 705 F10, 706 E8
Kokardine WA 705 F1, 706 E2
Kokatha SA 790 C2
Kokotungo Qld 561 H10

Kolendo SA 790 E5
Koloona NSW 460 G5
Komungla NSW 456 D4
Kondinin WA 706 F5
Kondoolka SA 790 C4
Kondut WA 705 E1, 706 D2
Kongorong SA 788 G9
Kongwak Vic 337 K7
Konnongorring WA 705 E2, 706 D3
Konong Wootong Vic 338 C5
Koo-Wee-Rup Vic 306, 337 K5
Kooemba Qld 561 H10
Koojan WA 705 C2, 706 C2
Kookaburra NSW 461 L9
Kookynie WA 709 M9
Koolamarra Qld 564 E2
Koolan WA 712 F5
Koolanooka WA 708 E9
Koolatah Qld 562 G4
Koolburra Outstation Qld 563 J3
Koolgera CP SA 790 B4
Kooline WA 714 E9
Koolkhan NSW 461 M5
Kooloonong Vic 341 H4
Koolpinyah NT 613 D2, 614 D4
Kooltandra Qld 561 H7
Koolunga SA 787 C1, 791 J7
Koolyanobbing WA 707 H2
Koolywurtie SA 787 A5, 791 H9
Koombana Bay WA 705 B9
Koombooloomba Qld 563 L7,
    569 D10
Koomooloo SA 787 G1, 791 L7
Koonadgin WA 706 G4
Koonalda SA 789 B9
Koonamore SA 791 L4
Koonawarra NSW 462 C6
Koonda Vic 344 D5
Koondoo Qld 567 N2
Koondoola WA 704 D2
Koondrook Vic 341 L7
Koongawa SA 790 E6
Koongie Park WA 713 L9
Koonibba Community SA 789 G10
Koonkool Qld 559 H1, 561 J10
Koonmarra WA 708 G4
Koonoomoo Vic 344 C2
Koonunga SA 787 E4, 791 K9
Koonwarra Vic 337 M7
Koonya Tas 839 F6, 843 M6
Koorawatha NSW 456 B2, 458 A9
Koorboora Qld 563 K6, 569 B9
Koorda WA 705 G2, 706 E2
Koordarrie WA 714 D8
Kooreh Vic 339 J1
Kooringal Qld 557 F1
Koorkab Vic 341 H4
Koornalla Vic 337 P6, 342 A8
Koorongara Qld 559 K8
Kooroora Qld 564 G4
Kootaberra SA 790 G4
Kootchee Qld 567 P2
Koothney NSW 460 A6

Kootingal NSW 461 H9
Kooyong Vic 335 D4
Kooyoora SP Vic 339 K1, 341 J10
Kopi SA 790 D7
Koppio SA 790 D9
Kopyje NSW 463 L7
Korbel WA 706 F4
Korcha Qld 558 E3
Koreelah NP NSW 461 L1
Korenan Qld 559 K1, 561 L10
Koriella Vic 344 C8
Korobeit Vic 336 E2, 339 M5
Koroit Vic 274, 338 F8
Korong Vale Vic 341 K10
Koroop Vic 341 L7
Korora NSW 461 N7
Korrelocking WA 705 G3, 706 E3
Korumburra Vic 337 L6
Kosciuszko NP NSW 360–363, 477
    A7, 456 B5, 457 C3, 465 P9
Kotta Vic 341 M9
Koukandowie NR NSW 461 M6
Koumala Qld 560 G5
Koumala South Qld 560 G5
Kowanyama Aboriginal Community
    Qld 562 F3
Kowguran Qld 559 H5
Koyuga Vic 341 N9, 344 A4
Krambach NSW 459 L3
Kroombit Tops NP Qld 559 J1,
    561 K10
Krowera Vic 337 K6
Ku-ring-gai Chase NP NSW 391,
    453 E1, 455 L5, 459 H8
Kubill Qld 558 A7, 567 P7
Kudardup WA 706 B8
Kudriemitchie Outstation SA 793 M4
Kuender WA 706 G6
Kukerin WA 706 F6
Kulde SA 788 A7, 791 L10
Kulgera NT 608, 618 G10
Kulgera Rail Head NT 618 G10
Kulin WA 706 F6
Kulja WA 705 F1, 706 E2
Kulkami SA 788 A9, 791 M10
Kulki Qld 567 K8
Kulkyne Vic 340 F3
Kulkyne Park Vic 340 F4
Kulliparu CP SA 790 C6
Kulliparu CR SA 790 C6
Kulnine Vic 340 C2
Kulnura NSW 455 K4, 459 H7
Kulpara SA 787 B3, 791 H8
Kulpi Qld 556 A4, 559 K6
Kultanaby SA 790 D2
Kulwin Vic 340 F5
Kulwyne Vic 340 G5
Kumari WA 707 L6
Kumarina Roadhouse WA 709 J2
Kumbarilla Qld 559 J7
Kumbatine NP NSW 459 L1,
    461 L10
Kumbia Qld 556 A3, 559 K5

Kunamata SA 789 C2
Kunat Vic 341 J7
Kundabung NSW 459 M1, 461 M10
Kundip NR WA 707 J7
Kungala NSW 461 N6
Kunghur NSW 461 N2
Kunjin WA 706 F5
Kunmunya Mission WA 712 G4
Kununoppin WA 706 F3
Kununurra WA 687, 713 N5
Kunwarara Qld 561 J7
Kunytjanu Homeland SA 789 A2
Kuraby Qld 555 E9, 557 D3
Kuranda Qld 563 L5, 569 D7
Kurbayia Qld 564 D4
Kuri Bay WA 712 G4
Kuridala Qld 564 E4
Kurnell NSW 453 E9
Kurnwill Vic 340 C3
Kurraca West Vic 339 J1, 341 J10
Kurrajong NSW 455 H5, 458 G8
Kurrajong Qld 559 H1
Kurray Qld 558 E8
Kurri Kurri NSW 455 L2, 459 J6
Kurrimine Beach Qld 563 M7,
    569 E10
Kurting Vic 339 K1, 341 K10
Kurundi NT 617 J9
Kurunjie (Pentecost Downs) WA
    713 L5
Kuttabul Qld 560 G4
Kwinana WA 705 B6, 706 C5
Kwobrup WA 706 F7
Kwolyin WA 706 F4
Kyabra Qld 567 J4
Kyabram Vic 327, 341 P9, 344 A4
Kyalite NSW 464 E6
Kyancutta SA 790 D6
Kybeyan NSW 456 D7, 457 G7
Kybunga SA 787 D2, 791 J8
Kybybolite SA 788 D10
Kyeamba NSW 465 N7
Kyeemagh NSW 453 D8
Kyle Bay NSW 453 D8
Kyndalyn Vic 340 G4
Kyneton Vic 274, 339 M4
Kynnersley Qld 558 A6, 567 P6
Kynuna Qld 536, 564 G5
Kyogle NSW 418, 461 N2
Kyong Qld 560 A5, 565 P5
Kyvalley Vic 341 P9, 344 A4
Kywong NSW 465 M6
Kywong Qld 565 K6

L

La Grange Aboriginal Community
    WA 712 C10, 715 M2
La Perouse NSW 453 F8
Laanecoorie Vic 339 K2
Laanecoorie Reservoir Vic 339 K2
Laang Vic 338 G8
Labelle Downs Outstation NT 613
    B4, 614 C5

Laceby Vic 344 F5

Lacepede Bay SA 788 D7

Lachlan Tas 839 B4, 843 J5

Lachlan River NSW 454 B8, 456 C2, 458 C10, 464 G4

Lacmalac NSW 456 A5, 457 C2

Lady Barron Tas 841 K3

Ladys Pass Vic 339 N2

Laen Vic 338 G1, 340 G10

Laen East Vic 338 G1, 340 G10

Laen North Vic 338 G1, 340 G10

Lagaven Qld 564 G4

Laggan NSW 454 D9, 456 D2, 458 D10

Laglan Qld 560 C6

Laguna NSW 455 K3, 459 H6

Laguna Qld 558 A3

Laguna Quays Qld 560 F3

Lah Vic 340 F9

Lah-Arum Vic 338 E3

Laheys Creek NSW 458 C4

Laidley Qld 556 C6, 559 L7

Lajamanu NT 616 C5

Lake Ace NR WA 707 J6

Lake Albacutya Vic 340 D7

Lake Albert SA 787 F9

Lake Alexandrina SA 787 F8, 788 A6

Lake Amadeus NT 618 C7

Lake Argyle WA 713 N5

Lake Argyle Tourist Village WA 713 N5

Lake Auld WA 710 A5

Lake Austin WA 708 G6

Lake Ballard WA 709 L9

Lake Banksiadale WA 705 C7

Lake Barlee WA 709 J9

Lake Barlee WA 709 J9

Lake Bathurst NSW 456 D4

Lake Benetook Vic 340 E2

Lake Biddy WA 706 G6

Lake Bindegolly NP Qld 567 L8

Lake Blanche SA 793 L8

Lake Boga Vic 341 K6

Lake Bolac Vic 338 G5

Lake Bolac Vic 338 G5

Lake Brewster NSW 465 K2

Lake Buloke Vic 340 G9

Lake Burbury Tas 840 E9

Lake Burley Griffin ACT 477 E3, 457 E2

Lake Burragorang NSW 454 G7, 456 F1, 458 F9

Lake Burrendong NSW 454 C1, 458 C5

Lake Burrendong SP NSW 454 B1, 458 B5

Lake Burrinjuck NSW 456 B4, 457 D1

Lake Burrumbeet Vic 336 A2, 339 K5

Lake Cadibarrawirracanna SA 792 D7

Lake Callabonna SA 793 M9

Lake Campion NR WA 706 G3

Lake Carey WA 709 N9

Lake Cargelligo NSW 465 L2

Lake Carnegie WA 709 N4

Lake Cathie NSW 459 M2

Lake Charm Vic 341 K7

Lake Chisholm FR Tas 840 B5

Lake Clifton WA 705 B7

Lake Colac Vic 336 A6

Lake Condah Vic 338 D7

Lake Conjola NSW 456 F5

Lake Connewarte Vic 336 E5

Lake Corangamite Vic 336 A5, 339 J7

Lake Cowal NSW 465 N3

Lake Cowan WA 707 M4

Lake Dalrymple Qld 560 C3

Lake Dartmouth Vic 345 L5

Lake De Burgh NT 617 L7

Lake Deborah East WA 707 H2

Lake Deborah West WA 706 G2

Lake Delusion SA 793 J9

Lake Disappointment WA 715 N10

Lake Dora WA 715 P8

Lake Dundas WA 707 M5

Lake Eildon NP Vic 327, 344 D8

Lake Eppalock Vic 339 M2

Lake Eppalock Vic 339 M2

Lake Eucumbene NSW 456 B7, 457 D6

Lake Eulo NSW 462 E8

Lake Everard SA 790 C2

Lake Everard SA 790 C3

Lake Eyre North SA 792 G6

Lake Eyre NP SA 783, 792 G6

Lake Eyre South SA 792 G8

Lake Frome SA 791 L1, 793 M10

Lake Frome RR SA 791 L1

Lake Gairdner SA 790 E3

Lake Gairdner NP SA 790 D2

Lake Galilee Qld 565 P6

Lake George NSW 477 G1, 456 D4, 457 G2

Lake Gilles SA 790 F5

Lake Gilles CP SA 790 F6

Lake Goldsmith Vic 339 J5

Lake Goran NSW 460 E10

Lake Gordon Tas 842 E4

Lake Grace WA 706 G6

Lake Gregory SA 793 K7

Lake Harry SA 793 J8

Lake Hattah Vic 340 F4

Lake Hindmarsh Vic 340 D8

Lake Honey SA 789 D5

Lake Hope WA 707 J5

Lake Hopkins WA 710 F7

Lake Hume NSW 465 M8

Lake Hume Vic 345 J4

Lake Hurlstone NR WA 707 H5

Lake Illawarra NSW 455 J9, 456 G3

Lake Innes NR NSW 459 M2

Lake Jindabyne NSW 456 B7, 457 D7

Lake John SA 793 K4

Lake Johnston WA 707 K5

Lake Jones WA 710 B7

Lake Keepit NSW 460 F9

Lake King Vic 342 F6

Lake King WA 649, 707 H6

Lake King NR WA 707 H6

Lake King William Tas 840 G10

Lake Leake Tas 841 M9

Lake Learmonth Vic 336 B1

Lake Lefroy WA 707 L3

Lake Lewis NT 618 F5

Lake Logue NR WA 706 B1, 708 D10

Lake Lonsdale Vic 338 F3

Lake Lucy Qld 563 L8

Lake Macfarlane SA 790 F4

Lake Mackay NT 618 A4

Lake Mackay WA 710 F5

Lake MacLeod WA 708 B1, 714 B10

Lake Macquarie NSW 455 M3, 459 J6

Lake Magenta NR WA 706 G7

Lake Marmal Vic 341 J9

Lake Martin Vic 336 A5

Lake Mason WA 709 J6

Lake Meran Vic 341 K8

Lake Mere NSW 463 H4

Lake Mindona NSW 464 C2

Lake Minigwal WA 709 P9

Lake Mokoan Vic 344 E5

Lake Moore WA 706 E1, 708 G9

Lake Muir WA 706 D9

Lake Muir NR WA 706 D9

Lake Mulwala NSW 465 K8

Lake Mulwala Vic 344 E3

Lake Mundi Vic 338 B5

Lake Munmorah NSW 455 M3, 459 J7

Lake Murdeduke Vic 336 C5

Lake Nash NT 617 P10, 619 P1

Lake Neale NT 618 B7

Lake Newland CP SA 790 C7

Lake Noondie WA 709 J8

Lake Parrara NT 618 D8

Lake Pedder Tas 842 F5

Lake Pieman Tas 840 C8

Lake Raeside WA 709 M9

Lake Rason WA 711 B3

Lake Rebecca WA 707 M1, 709 N10

Lake Reeve Vic 342 D8

Lake Robin WA 707 J4

Lake Rowan Vic 344 E4

Lake St Clair Tas 840 F9

Lake Samsonvale Qld 557 B1

Lake Sharpe WA 707 K6

Lake Somerset Qld 556 D4

Lake Sorell Tas 841 K10

Lake Stewart NSW 462 A2

Lake Sylvester NT 617 L6

Lake Tay WA 707 K6

Lake Theo WA 708 F7

Lake Thistle WA 711 E2

Lake Thompson Vic 337 N3

Lake Tiberias Tas 839 C1

Lake Timboram Vic 341 H6

Lake Torrens SA 791 H1, 792 G10

Lake Torrens SA 791 H3

Lake Torrens NP SA 791 H2

Lake Tyers Vic 342 G6

Lake Tyers SP Vic 342 G5

Lake Tyrrell Vic 340 G6

Lake Valerie NT 619 M7

Lake Varley NR WA 707 H6

Lake Victoria NSW 464 A3

Lake Victoria Vic 342 E7

Lake View NSW 462 C7

Lake View SA 787 C1, 791 J7

Lake Violet WA 709 L5

Lake Wahpool Vic 340 G6

Lake Wallace NSW 462 B4

Lake Wallambin WA 705 G2, 706 E3

Lake Wasby NSW 462 D2

Lake Waukarlycarly WA 715 M6

Lake Way WA 709 K5

Lake Way WA 709 K5

Lake Wellington Vic 342 D7

Lake Wells WA 709 P5

Lake Wivenhoe Qld 556 C5, 557 A2

Lake Woods NT 616 G5

Lake Wyangala NSW 454 B7, 456 C1, 458 C9

Lake Yamma Yamma Qld 566 G5

Lake Yarrunga NSW 454 G10

Lake Yindarlgooda WA 707 M2

Lakefield Qld 563 J2, 568 F10, 569 A2

Lakefield NP Qld 563 J2, 568 F10, 569 A2

Lakeland Qld 563 K4, 569 B4

Lakemba NSW 453 C7

Lakes and Streams of the Capital ACT 474–475

Lakes Entrance Vic 306, 342 G6

Lakeside WA 708 G6

Lal Lal Vic 336 C2, 339 L5

Lal Lal Reservoir Vic 336 C2

Lalbert Vic 341 J7

Lalbert Road Vic 341 J7

Lalla Tas 844 E4, 841 K6

Lalla Rookh WA 715 J6

Lalor Vic 335 D2

Lalor Park NSW 453 A4

Lambina SA 792 A3

Lamboo WA 713 L9

Lameroo SA 788 A9

Lamington Qld 557 C8

Lamington NP Qld 502, 556 E7, 557 D8, 559 N8

Lamorbey Qld 560 C8

Lamplough Vic 339 J3

Lana Downs Qld 565 J5

Lancaster Vic 341 P10, 344 B4

Lancefield Qld 561 J9

Lancefield Vic 339 N4

Lancelin WA 649, 705 A2, 706 B3

Lancevale Qld 560 B9, 565 P9

Lancewood Qld 560 E4
Landor WA 708 F3
Landreath Qld 558 E5
Landsborough Qld 556 D3, 559 M6
Landsborough Vic 339 H3
Landsborough West Vic 339 H3
Landsdale WA 704 D1
Landsdowne Qld 558 A2
Lane Cove NSW 453 E5
Lane Cove NP NSW 453 C4
Lane Cove River NSW 453 D4
Lane Poole Reserve WA 705 D8, 706 C6
Lanena Tas 844 D5, 841 J6
Lang Creek Vic 341 L9
Lang Lang Vic 337 K5
Langdale Qld 565 H3
Langford WA 704 F7
Langhorne Creek SA 787 E7, 788 A6
Langi Ghiran SP Vic 339 H4
Langi Logan Vic 338 G4
Langidoon NSW 462 C7
Langkoop Vic 338 A3
Langley Qld 560 G7
Langley Vic 339 M3
Langleydale NSW 464 F3
Langlo Crossing Qld 567 P4
Langlo Downs Qld 567 P3
Langtree NSW 465 J3
Langville Vic 341 K8
Langwarrin Vic 335 F8, 337 H5, 339 P7
Langwell NSW 462 B9
Lankeys Creek NSW 465 N7
Lansdale NSW 463 M8
Lansdowne NSW 453 B7
Lansdowne NSW 459 L2
Lansdowne WA 713 K8
Lansvale NSW 453 A7
Lapoinya Tas 840 D4
Lara Vic 336 E4, 339 M7
Larapinta Qld 555 C9
Laravale Qld 556 D7, 557 C7, 559 M8
Lardner Vic 337 L5
Largs Bay SA 786 B3
Larmer NSW 477 E3
Laroona Qld 563 M9
Larpent Vic 336 A6, 339 J8
Larrakeyah NT 612 A9
Larras Lee NSW 454 B3, 458 B6
Larrawa WA 710 D1, 713 K10
Larrimah NT 614 G9, 616 G1
Lascelles Qld 560 B3, 565 P3
Lascelles Vic 340 F7
Latham ACT 477 C2
Latham WA 708 E9
Lathami CP SA 788 B3
Lathlain WA 704 E5
LaTrobe River Vic 337 M4
Latrobe Tas 814–815, 844 A4, 840 G5
Lauderdale Tas 839 D5, 843 L5

Launceston Tas 815, 844 E6, 841 K6
Laura Qld 563 K3, 569 A3
Laura SA 791 J6
Laura Bay SA 789 G10, 790 A4
Lauradale NSW 463 J3
Laurel Hill NSW 457 B4
Laurieton NSW 459 M2
Lauriston Vic 339 M4
Lavers Hill Vic 339 J9
Laverton Vic 335 A5, 336 F3, 339 N6
Laverton WA 668, 709 N8
Laverton Downs WA 709 N8
Laverton North Vic 335 A4
Laverton South Vic 335 A5
Lavington NSW 465 M8
Lavinia NR Tas 816, 840 F1
Lawloit Vic 338 C1, 340 C10
Lawn Hill Qld 562 B8
Lawn Hill NP Qld 528, 562 A8
Lawnton Qld 557 C1
Lawrence NSW 461 N5
Lawrenny Tas 843 H3
Lawson NSW 454 G6, 456 F1, 458 F8
Lea Creek Qld 562 D8
Leabrook SA 786 E6
Leadville NSW 458 D3
Leaghur Vic 341 K8
Leaghur SP Vic 341 K8
Leander NSW 463 M2
Leanyer NT 612 G2
Learmonth Vic 336 B1, 339 K4
Learmonth WA 714 B8
Lebrina Tas 844 E4, 841 K5
Ledcourt Vic 338 F3
Ledge Point WA 705 A2, 706 B3
Ledgerwood Tas 841 M5
Lee Point NT 612 G1
Leechs Gully NSW 461 K3
Leederville WA 704 C4
Leeka Tas 841 H2
Leeman WA 706 A1, 708 D10
Leeming WA 704 D8
Leeor Vic 338 B1, 340 B10
Leeson Qld 565 J6
Leeton NSW 449, 465 L5
Leeuwin–Naturaliste Coast WA 632–637
Leeuwin–Naturaliste NP WA 632–635, 706 A8
Leeville NSW 461 M3
Lefroy Tas 844 D3, 841 J5
Lefroy WA 707 L3
Legana Tas 844 D5, 841 J6
Legume NSW 461 L2
Legune NT 614 B9
Leichardt Vic 339 L2
Leichhardt NSW 453 D6
Leichhardt Range Qld 560 D2
Leigh Creek SA 763, 791 J1, 793 J10
Leigh Creek Vic 336 C2, 339 K5
Leightonfield NSW 453 B6

Leinster WA 709 L7
Leinster Downs WA 709 L7
Leitchville Vic 341 M8
Leith Tas 840 G5
Leitpar Vic 340 G5
Lemana Tas 844 B6, 841 H7
Lemnos Vic 344 C4
Lemont Tas 843 L2
Lenah Valley Tas 838 C5
Leneva Vic 345 H4
Lennox Qld 560 B7, 565 P7
Lennox Head NSW 461 P3
Leonards Hill Vic 336 D1, 339 L4
Leongatha Vic 306–307, 337 M7
Leongatha South Vic 337 L7
Leonora WA 668, 709 L8
Leonora Downs NSW 462 C9
Leopold Vic 336 E5, 339 M7
Leopold Downs WA 713 H8
Lerderderg SP Vic 274–275, 336 E2, 339 M5
Lerida NSW 463 K7
Leslie Harrison Reservoir Qld 555 G7
Leslie Manor Vic 339 J7
Leslie Vale Tas 839 C5, 843 K5
Lesmurdie Falls NP WA 704 G6
Lesueur NP WA 649, 706 B1, 708 D10
Lethbridge Vic 336 D4, 339 L6
Lethebrook Qld 560 F3
Leura NSW 391, 454 G6, 456 F1, 458 F8
Leura Qld 561 H8
Leven Beach CP SA 790 G10
Levendale Tas 839 D2, 843 L3
Lewis Ponds NSW 454 C4, 458 C7
Lewisham NSW 453 E7
Lewisham Tas 839 E4, 843 L5
Lexton Vic 339 J4,
Leyburn Qld 556 A7, 559 K8
Liawenee Tas 844 B9, 841 H9
Licola Vic 342 A5, 344 G10
Lidcombe NSW 453 C6
Liena Tas 840 G7
Liffey Tas 844 C8, 841 H8
Liffey FR Tas 844 B8, 841 J8
Lightning Creek Vic 342 D1, 345 K6
Lightning Ridge NSW 436, 463 P2
Lila NT 618 E7
Lilarea Qld 565 M6
Lileah Tas 840 C4
Lilla Creek NT 619 H9
Lilli Pilli NSW 453 D10
Lillimur Vic 340 B10
Lillimur South Vic 338 B1, 340 B10
Lilliput Vic 344 F3
Lily Vale Qld 563 H1, 568 E9
Lilydale SA 791 M6
Lilydale Tas 816, 844 E4, 841 K5
Lilydale Vic 335 G2, 337 J3, 344 B10
Lilyfield NSW 453 E6
Lilyvale NSW 463 H7
Lilyvale Downs Qld 558 G3

Lima Vic 344 D6
Lima South Vic 344 E6
Limbla NT 619 K6
Limbri NSW 461 H9
Limbunya NT 616 B3
Lime Bay NR Tas 839 E5, 843 L5
Limeburners Creek NSW 455 N1, 459 K5
Limeburners Creek NR NSW 459 M1, 461 M10
Limestone Vic 344 C8
Limevale Qld 559 J9
Limmen Bight NT 615 K8
Limpinwood NR NSW 461 M1
Lincoln NSW 458 C4
Lincoln Gap SA 790 G5
Lincoln NP SA 763, 790 D10
Lind NP Vic 343 K5
Linda Downs Qld 564 B6
Lindeman Group Qld 560 G2
Linden NSW 455 H6, 456 F1, 458 F8
Lindenow Vic 342 E6
Lindenow South Vic 342 D6
Lindesay View NSW 461 M2
Lindfield NSW 453 D4
Lindfield Qld 564 G2
Lindisfarne Tas 838 F4
Lindon SA 793 N7
Lindsay Vic 338 A5
Lindsay Point Vic 340 A1
Lindum Qld 555 F4
Linga Vic 340 C5
Linley Point NSW 453 D5
Linton Vic 336 A2, 339 J5
Linville Qld 556 C3, 559 L6
Lipson SA 790 E8
Liptrap Vic 337 M8
Lirambenda NSW 456 A2, 465 P4
Lisle Tas 844 F4, 841 K5
Lismore Qld 559 J4
Lismore NSW 419, 461 N3
Lismore Vic 339 J6
Lissadell WA 713 N6
Liston NSW 461 K2
Listowel Downs Qld 567 N2
Listowel Valley Qld 567 N3
Litchfield NT 613 B5, 614 C6
Litchfield Vic 340 G9
Litchfield NP NT 591, 613 C5, 614 D5
Lithgow NSW 392, 454 F5, 458 E7
Littabella NP Qld 559 L1
Little Bay NSW 453 F8
Little Billabong NSW 465 N7
Little Desert NP Vic 275, 338 C1, 340 C10
Little Dip CP SA 734, 788 E8
Little Hampton Vic 336 D1, 339 M4
Little Hartley NSW 454 G5, 458 F8
Little Myall River NP NSW 459 K4
Little Para Reservoir SA 786 G2
Little Para River SA 786 D2

Little Plain NSW 460 G5
Little River Vic 336 E4, 339 M6
Little Sandy Desert WA 709 M1
Little Snowy Creek Vic 345 J5
Little Swanport Tas 843 M2
Little Topar Roadhouse NSW 462 C7
Littlemore Qld 559 K1, 561 L10
Liveringa WA 712 F9
Liverpool NSW 453 A7, 455 J7, 456 G1, 458 G9
Liverpool Range NSW 458 F3
Lizard Island NP Qld 563 L2, 569 D1
Llanelly Vic 339 K2
Llangothlin NSW 461 J7
Llidem Vale Qld 558 G8
Llorac Qld 565 M6
Lobethal SA 787 E6, 791 K10
Loch Vic 337 L6
Loch Lilly NSW 462 A10, 464 A1
Loch Sport Vic 342 E7
Loch Valley Vic 337 M3
Lochanger Qld 558 F7
Lochern Qld 565 K10
Lochern NP Qld 565 K10
Lochiel NSW 456 E9
Lochiel SA 787 B2, 791 J8
Lochnagar Qld 560 A9, 565 P9
Lochnagar Qld 562 F3
Lock SA 790 D7
Lockhart NSW 465 L6
Lockhart River Aboriginal Community Qld 568 E6
Lockington Vic 341 M9
Lockridge WA 704 F3
Locksley Vic 344 B6
Lockwood NSW 454 A5, 458 B7
Lockwood Vic 339 L2
Loddon Qld 567 P5
Loddon River Vic 341 K8
Loddon Vale Vic 341 L8
Loftia RP SA 786 F8
Loftus NSW 453 C10
Logan Vic 339 J1
Logan Central Qld 555 E9
Logan Downs Qld 560 E6
Logan Reserve Qld 557 D4
Loganholme Qld 555 G10, 556 E6, 559 N7
Loganlea Qld 555 F10, 557 D4
Logie Brae NSW 465 J7
Lolworth Qld 565 N2
Lombadina Mission WA 712 D6
Londonderry NSW 455 H5, 456 G1, 458 G8
Lonesome Creek Qld 559 H2
Long Beach NSW 456 F6
Long Creek Qld 557 B9
Long Plains SA 787 C4, 791 J9
Long Plains Vic 340 G6
Long Pocket Qld 555 C6
Long Pocket Qld 563 M8
Longerenong Vic 338 F2

Longford NSW 461 H8
Longford Qld 564 F3
Longford Qld 567 J2
Longford Tas 816, 844 E7, 841 K7
Longford Vic 342 C7
Longlea Vic 339 M2
Longley Tas 839 B5, 843 J5
Longreach Qld 536, 565 L8
Longs Corner NSW 454 A4, 458 B7
Longton Qld 560 B3, 565 P3
Longueville NSW 453 E5
Longwarry Vic 337 L5
Longwood SA 786 G8
Longwood Vic 344 B6
Lonnavale Tas 843 H5
Lonsdale SA 786 C9
Loomberah NSW 459 H1, 461 H10
Loongana Tas 840 F6
Loongana WA 711 E6
Loorana Tas 840 F2
Lord Howe Island NSW 392
Lorinna Tas 840 F7
Lorna Downs Qld 564 D8
Lorna Glen WA 709 M4
Lorne NSW 459 M2
Lorne Qld 558 C3
Lorne Qld 567 N2
Lorne SA 787 C4, 791 J9
Lorne Vic 275, 336 C7, 339 L8
Lornesleigh Qld 560 C3
Lornvale Qld 563 H8
Lorquon Vic 340 D9
Lorraine Qld 562 C9
Lorraine Station Qld 565 K7
Lorrett Downs Qld 564 E6
Lost Falls FR Tas 841 M9
Lota Qld 555 G5, 557 D2
Lotus Vale Qld 562 E6
Lou Lou Park Qld 560 B6
Louis Point NSW 461 L6
Louisa Downs WA 713 K10
Louisiana Qld 563 K3, 569 C3
Louisville Tas 839 F2, 843 M3
Louth NSW 463 J5
Louth Bay SA 790 E9
Lovely Banks Vic 336 D4, 339 M7
Lovett Bay NSW 453 F1
Low Head Tas 844 C3, 841 J5
Lowan Vale SA 788 C9
Lowanna NSW 461 M7
Lowden WA 705 C10
Lowdina Tas 839 D3, 843 K3
Lower Barrington Tas 840 G6
Lower Beechmont Qld 557 D7
Lower Beulah Tas 844 A6, 840 G7
Lower Boro NSW 456 E4
Lower Glenelg NP Vic 276, 338 C7
Lower Light SA 787 C5, 791 J9
Lower Longley Tas 839 B5, 843 J5
Lower Mookerawa NSW 454 C2, 458 C5
Lower Mount Hicks Tas 840 E4
Lower Norton Vic 338 E2

Lower Plenty Vic 335 E2
Lower Quipolly NSW 458 G1, 460 G10
Lower Sandy Bay Tas 838 E8
Lower Turners Marsh Tas 844 E4, 841 K5
Lower Wilmot Tas 840 F6
Lowesdale NSW 465 L7
Lowlands NSW 463 J10, 465 J2
Lowmead Qld 559 K1, 561 L10
Lowood Qld 558 B5
Lowther NSW 454 F5, 456 E1, 458 E8
Loxton SA 763, 791 N9
Loxton North SA 791 N9
Lubeck Vic 338 F2
Lucas Heights NSW 453 B9
Lucaston Tas 839 B5, 843 J5
Lucinda Qld 563 M8
Lucindale Qld 565 J3
Lucindale SA 788 E9
Lucknow NSW 454 C4, 458 C7
Lucknow Qld 564 F7
Lucknow Vic 342 E6
Lucky Bay SA 790 G7
Lucy Creek NT 619 M4
Lucyvale Vic 345 L4
Ludmilla NT 612 C6
Lue NSW 454 E1, 458 E5
Lugarno NSW 453 C8
Luina Tas 840 D7
Luluigui WA 712 F9
Lulworth Tas 844 D2, 841 J4
Lumholtz NP Qld 563 M8
Lunawanna Tas 839 C8, 843 J8
Lundavra Qld 558 G8
Lune River Tas 839 A9, 843 H8
Lurnea Qld 558 B5
Lurnea NSW 453 A8
Lutana Tas 838 D4
Lutwyche Qld 555 C4
Lyal Vic 339 M3
Lymington Tas 839 B7, 843 J7
Lymwood Tas 840 F2
Lynchford Tas 842 C1, 840 D10
Lyndavale NT 618 G9
Lyndbrook Qld 563 K7, 569 A10
Lyndhurst NSW 454 B6, 456 C1, 458 C8
Lyndhurst Qld 563 J9
Lyndhurst SA 793 J10
Lyndhurst Vic 335 F6
Lyndoch SA 763, 787 E5, 791 K9
Lyndon WA 708 D1, 714 D10
Lyneham ACT 477 D2
Lynwood Qld 567 K3
Lynwood WA 704 E7
Lyons ACT 477 D3
Lyons SA 790 A1
Lyons Vic 338 C7
Lyons River WA 708 D2
Lyonville Vic 336 D1, 339 L4
Lyrian Qld 562 E9, 564 F1
Lyrup SA 791 N8

Lysterfield Vic 335 G5, 337 J4
Lysterfield Lake Park Vic 335 G5, 337 J4
Lytton Qld 555 F4, 557 D2

M

Mabel Creek SA 792 A7
Mabel Downs WA 713 M7
Mac Clark (Acacia Peuce) CR NT 619 L8
Macalister Qld 559 J6
Macalister Qld 562 D7
Macalister River Vic 342 A4
Macaroni Qld 562 F5
Macarthur ACT 477 D4
Macarthur Vic 338 E7
McArthur River NT 617 L2
McCallum Park NSW 462 D5
Macclesfield SA 787 E7, 788 A6, 791 K10
McClintock Range WA 713 L10
McColl Vic 341 M10
McCoys Well SA 791 K5
McCrae Vic 336 G6, 339 N8
MacDonald Downs NT 619 K4
Macdonald River NSW 458 G6
MacDonnell Ranges NT 619 K6
McDouall Peak SA 792 B9
McDougalls Well NSW 462 A6
McDowall Qld 555 C2
Macedon Vic 276, 336 F1, 339 M4
Macgregor Qld 555 E7, 557 C3
McGullys Gap NSW 458 G4
Machans Beach Qld 563 L5, 569 D7
Macintyre River NSW 460 C3
Mackay Qld 516–517, 560 G4
Mackenzie Qld 555 F7
McKenzie Creek Vic 338 E2
Mackenzie River Vic 338 E2
McKinlay Qld 564 F4
McKinnon Vic 335 D5
Macknade Qld 563 M8
Macks Creek Vic 342 A9
Macksville NSW 419, 461 M8
Mackunda Downs Qld 564 F6
McLachlan SA 790 D7
McLaren Creek NT 617 H9
McLaren Vale SA 764, 787 D7, 788 A5, 791 J10
McLaren Vale Wine Region SA 764–765
Maclean NSW 419, 461 N5
Macleay River NSW 461 L9
Macleod Vic 335 D2
McLoughlins Beach Vic 342 B9
McMahons Creek Vic 337 L3, 344 D10
McMahons Reef NSW 456 B3
Macorna Vic 341 L8
Macquarie Harbour Tas 842 B2
Macquarie Marshes NR NSW 463 N5
Macquarie Plains Tas 839 A3, 843 H4

Macquarie River NSW 454 C3, 458 B4, 463 N7
Macquarie River Tas 844 E8
Macrossan Qld 560 B2, 563 M10
Macs Cove Vic 344 E8
Macumba SA 792 D3
Macumba River SA 792 C3, 792 F4
Maddington WA 704 G7
Madoonga WA 708 G5
Madura WA 711 E7
Madura Hotel WA 711 E7
Mafeking Qld 560 A9, 565 P9
Mafeking Vic 338 F4
Maffra Vic **307**, 342 B6
Maffra West Upper Vic 342 B6
Magenta NSW 464 F3
Maggea SA 791 M9
Maggieville Qld 562 E6
Maggot Point Tas 839 B8, 843 J7
Maggy Creek Qld 564 E5
Magill SA 786 F5
Magnetic Island Qld **528**
Magnetic Island NP Qld 563 N9
Magowra Qld 562 E7
Magra Tas 839 B4, 843 J4
Magrath Flat SA 787 G10, 788 B7
Mahanewo SA 790 E3
Mahrigong Qld 565 K6
Maianbar NSW 453 D10
Maida Vale WA 704 G5
Maiden Gully Vic 339 L2
Maiden Springs Qld 563 J10, 565 L1
Maidenhead Qld 559 K10
Maidstone Vic 335 B4
Mailors Flat Vic 338 F8
Main Creek NSW 459 K4
Main Range NP Qld **502**, 556 C7, 559 L8
Main Ridge Vic 336 G6, 339 P8
Maindample Vic 344 E7
Mainoru NT 615 H7
Maison Dieu NSW 459 H5
Maitland NSW **392–393**, 455 M2, 459 J5
Maitland SA 787 A4, 791 H9
Maitland Downs Qld 563 K4, 569 B5
Majorca Vic 339 K3
Majors Creek NSW 456 E5
Malabar NSW 453 F8
Malacura Qld 563 H8
Malaga WA 704 D2
Malak NT 612 G4
Malak Park NT 612 G4
Malanda Qld 563 L6, 569 D9
Malbina Tas 839 B4, 843 J4
Malbon Qld 564 E4
Malbooma SA 790 B1
Malcolm WA 709 M8
Maldon Vic **276**, 339 L3
Malebo NSW 465 N6
Maleny Qld 556 D3, 559 M5
Malinong SA 787 G8, 788 B7

Mallacoota Vic **307**, 343 N5
Mallacoota Inlet Vic 343 N5
Mallala SA 787 D4, 791 J9
Mallanganee NSW 461 M3
Mallanganee NP NSW 461 M3
Mallapunyah NT 617 L3
Mallee WA 708 D7
Mallee Cliffs NP NSW 464 D4
Mallett SA 791 K6
Mallina WA 714 G6
Mallowa NSW 460 C5
Malmsbury Vic 339 M3
Maloneys Qld 558 G1
Maltee SA 790 A4
Malua Bay NSW 456 F6
Malvern Vic 335 D4
Mambray Creek SA 791 H5
Manangatang Vic 340 G5
Manangoora NT 615 M10, 617 M1
Manara NSW 462 E10, 464 E1
Manara NSW 462 G7
Manberry WA 708 C1, 714 C10
Manbulloo NT 613 F8, 614 F8
Manchester NSW 460 A5
Mandagery NSW 458 A7
Mandalay NSW 462 E5
Mandemar NSW 454 G9, 456 F3, 458 F10
Mandora WA 715 L4
Mandorah NT 613 C2, 614 C4
Mandurah WA 705 B7, 706 B5
Mandurama NSW 454 B5, 456 C1, 458 C8
Maneroo Qld 565 L8
Manfred NSW 464 F2
Manfred WA 708 E5
Manfred Downs Qld 564 G2
Mangalo SA 790 F7
Mangalore NSW 463 L7
Mangalore Tas 839 C3, 843 K4
Mangalore Vic 339 P3, 344 B7
Mangana Tas 841 M7
Mangaroon WA 708 D1, 714 D10
Mangkili Claypan NR WA 710 B9
Mangooya Vic 340 G4
Mangoplah NSW 465 M7
Manguel Creek WA 712 E8, 715 P1
Manguri SA 792 B7
Manildra NSW 454 A3, 458 B7
Manilla NSW 460 G8
Manilla NSW 464 C2
Maningrida NT 615 J3
Manjimup WA 706 C8
Manly NSW 453 G4, 455 L6, 459 H8
Manly Qld 555 G5, 557 D2
Manly Vale NSW 453 F4
Manly West Qld 555 G5
Manmanning WA 705 F2, 706 E2
Mann River NR NSW 461 K5
Mannahill SA 791 M5
Mannanarie SA 791 J6

Mannerim Vic 335 A10, 336 F5, 339 M7
Manners Creek NT 619 P3
Manning WA 704 D6
Manning Point NSW 459 M3
Manningham SA 786 E4
Manns Beach Vic 342 B9
Mannum SA **765**, 787 F6, 791 L10
Mannus NSW 456 A6, 457 A4, 465 P7
Manobalai NSW 458 G4
Manobalai NR NSW 458 F3
Manoora SA 787 E2, 791 K8
Mansfield Qld 555 E7
Mansfield Vic **327**, 344 E7
Manton Dam Park NT 613 D3, 614 D5
Mantuan Downs Qld 558 C1, 560 D10
Mantung SA 791 M9
Manuka ACT 477 D3
Manumbar Qld 556 C2, 559 L5
Manunda SA 791 M5
Many Peaks Qld 559 K1, 561 L10
Manya Vic 340 B5
Manypeaks WA 706 F9
Mapala Qld 558 F2
Mapleton Qld 556 D3, 559 M5
Mapoon Aboriginal Community Qld 568 B4
Mapperley Park Qld 564 F3
Maralinga SA 789 D7
Marambir NSW 460 E5
Maranalgo WA 708 G9
Maranboy NT 614 F8
Marandoo WA 714 G8
Marangaroo WA 704 C2
Marathon Qld 565 K3
Marayong NSW 453 A4
Marble Bar WA **699**, 715 J6
Marburg Qld 556 D5, 557 A3, 559 M7
March NSW 454 C4, 458 C7
Marchagee WA 706 C1, 708 E10
Mardan Vic 337 M6
Mardathuna WA 708 C2
Mardie WA 714 E6
Mareeba Qld **552**, 563 L5, 569 D8
Marengo Vic 336 B8, 339 K9
Marengo Plain NSW 461 L7
Marfield NSW 462 G9
Margaret River NT 613 D4
Margaret River WA **650**, 706 A8
Margaret River WA 706 B8
Margaret River WA 713 K10
Margaret River Wine Region WA **635–637**
Margate Qld 557 D1
Margate Tas 839 C6, 843 K6
Maria Downs Qld 558 E6
Maria Island Tas 843 N3

Maria Island NP Tas **832–833**, 843 N3
Maria River NP NSW 459 M1, 461 M10
Mariala NP Qld 567 N4
Marialpa SA 791 M4
Marian Qld 560 G4
Maribyrnong Vic 335 C3
Maribyrnong River Vic 335 B2
Marillana WA 715 J8
Marimo Qld 564 E3
Marina Plains Qld 563 J2, 568 E9
Marino SA 786 C8
Marion SA 786 C7
Marion Bay SA 788 A2, 790 F10
Marion Bay Tas 839 F4
Marion Downs Qld 564 D8
Marita Downs Qld 565 K6
Markwell NSW 459 K4
Markwood Vic 344 G5
Marla SA **783**, 789 G3, 792 A4
Marlborough Qld 561 H7
Marlo Vic **308**, 343 J6
Marmion WA 704 A2
Marmion Marine Park WA 705 B4, 706 B4
Marnoo Vic 338 G2
Marnoo East Vic 338 G2
Maronan Qld 564 F4
Marong Vic 339 L2
Maronga Qld 558 E7
Maroochydore Qld 556 E3, 559 N5
Maroon Qld 556 D7, 557 A8, 559 M8
Maroona Vic 338 G4
Maroonah WA 714 D9
Maroota NSW 455 K5, 459 H7
Maroubra NSW 453 F8
Maroubra Junction NSW 453 F7
Marqua NT 619 N4
Marra NSW 462 G6
Marrabel SA 787 E3, 791 K8
Marradong WA 705 D8, 706 D6
Marramarra NP NSW 455 K5, 459 H8
Marrapina NSW 462 C6
Marrar NSW 465 N5
Marrara NT 612 E4
Marrara Sporting Complex NT 612 F4
Marrawah Tas 840 A4
Marree SA **784**, 793 H8
Marrickville NSW 453 E7
Marrilla WA 714 C9
Marron WA 708 C3
Marryat SA 789 G1
Marsden NSW 465 N3
Marsden Qld 555 E10
Marsfield NSW 453 C4
Marshall Vic 336 E5, 339 M7
Martin WA 704 G7
Martin Washpool CP SA 788 C8

Martins Creek NSW 455 M1, 459 J5
Martins Well SA 791 K3
Marton Qld 563 L3, 569 C3
Marulan NSW 454 F10, 456 E3
Marungi Vic 344 C4
Marvel Loch WA 707 H3
Mary Kathleen Qld 564 D3
Mary River NT 613 E3
Mary River NT 613 F5, 614 E6
Mary River NP NT 613 E2, 614 E4
Mary River Roadhouse NT 613 G6, 614 F6
Mary Springs WA 708 C6
Maryborough Qld 502–503, 559 M3
Maryborough Vic 276–277, 339 K3
Maryfarms Qld 563 L5, 569 C6
Maryfield NT 614 G10, 616 G1
Maryknoll Vic 337 K4
Maryland NP NSW 461 K2
Marysville Vic 328, 337 L2, 344 D9
Maryvale NSW 458 B5
Maryvale NT 619 H8
Maryvale Qld 556 C7, 559 L8
Maryvale Qld 558 B5
Maryvale Qld 563 L10, 565 N1
Mascot NSW 453 E7
Massey Vic 340 G9
Massey Downs Qld 558 E5
Matakana NSW 463 K10, 465 K1
Mataranka NT 591, 614 G8
Matheson NSW 461 J5
Mathiesons Vic 339 P1, 344 A5
Mathinna Tas 841 M7
Mathinna Falls FR Tas 841 M6
Mathoura NSW 465 H7
Matilda Highway Qld 532–533
Matlock Vic 337 N2, 344 F10
Matong NSW 465 M5
Matraville NSW 453 F8
Maude NSW 464 G5
Maude Vic 336 D4, 339 L6
Maudsland Qld 557 E6
Maudville NSW 459 J3
Maules Creek NSW 460 E8
Mawbanna Tas 840 D4
Mawson ACT 477 D4
Mawson WA 705 F5, 706 E4
Maxwelton Qld 565 J3
Maxwelton Qld 565 J3
May Downs Qld 560 G7
May Vale Qld 562 F7
Maya WA 706 D1, 708 E10
Mayberry Tas 840 G7
Maybole NSW 461 J6
Maydena Tas 842 G4
Mayfield Qld 558 A5, 567 P5
Mayfield Bay CA Tas 843 N1, 841 N10
Maylands WA 704 D4
Maynards Well SA 791 K1, 793 K10
Mayne Qld 555 D4
Mayneside Qld 565 H8
Mayrung NSW 465 J7

Mays Hill NSW 453 B5
Maytown (ruins) Qld 563 J4, 569 A5
Mayvale Qld 558 A8, 567 P8
Mazeppa NP Qld 560 D6
Mead Vic 341 L8
Meadow Flat NSW 454 F5, 458 E7
Meadow Glen NSW 463 J7
Meadowbank Qld 563 K7
Meadowbrook Qld 555 F10
Meadows SA 787 D7, 788 A6, 791 K10
Meadowvale Qld 560 C1, 563 M10
Meandarra Qld 558 G6
Meander Tas 844 B7, 841 H7
Meatian Vic 341 J7
Meckering WA 705 F4, 706 D4
Meda WA 712 F7
Medlow Bath NSW 454 G5, 456 F1, 458 F8
Medowie NSW 459 K5
Meeberrie WA 708 E5
Meedo WA 708 C4
Meehan Range SRA Tas 838 D1
Meekatharra WA 668–669, 709 H5
Meeline WA 709 H8
Meeniyan Vic 337 M7
Meeragoolia WA 708 C2
Meerlieu Vic 342 D6
Meetus Falls FR Tas 841 M9
Megan NSW 461 M7
Megine Qld 558 E6
Meka WA 708 F6
Mekaree Qld 567 M1
Melangata WA 708 F7
Melba Gully SP Vic 339 J9
Melbourne Vic 254–257, 335 C4, 336 G3, 339 P6
Melinda Downs Qld 562 D10, 564 E1
Melita WA 709 M8
Mella Tas 840 B3
Mellenbye WA 708 E8
Melmoth Qld 560 G8
Melrose NSW 463 M9, 465 M1
Melrose SA 765, 791 J5
Melrose Tas 840 G5
Melrose WA 709 L7
Melton SA 787 B3, 791 H8
Melton SA 791 L4
Melton Vic 336 F2, 339 M5
Melton Grove NSW 464 F2
Melton Mowbray Tas 839 B2, 843 J3
Melton South Vic 336 F3, 339 M5
Melville WA 704 B7
Melville Forest Vic 338 D5
Melville Island NT 614 D2
Memana Tas 841 J2
Memerambi Qld 556 B2, 559 L5
Mena Murtee NSW 462 E7
Mena Park Qld 560 A10, 565 N10
Mena Park Vic 336 A2, 339 J5
Menai NSW 453 B9
Menangina WA 707 M1, 709 M10

Mendip Hills Qld 560 B9, 565 P9
Mendleyarri WA 709 M9
Mendooran NSW 458 C3
Mengha Tas 840 C4
Menin Downs Qld 564 G6
Menindee NSW 436, 462 D9
Menindee Lake NSW 462 C9
Meningie SA 787 F9, 788 B7
Menora WA 704 D4
Mentone Vic 335 E6, 337 H4, 339 P6
Mentor Outstation SA 792 C10
Menzies WA 669, 709 L9
Merah North NSW 460 C7
Meran West Vic 341 K8
Merapah Qld 568 C8
Merbein Vic 340 E2
Merbein South Vic 340 D2
Mercadool NSW 460 A6
Mercunda SA 791 M9
Meredith Vic 336 C3, 339 L6
Mergenia SA 791 K5
Meribah SA 791 N9
Merildin SA 787 E2, 791 K8
Merimbula NSW 372, 456 E9
Merinda Park Vic 335 G7
Meringandan Qld 556 B5, 559 L7
Meringur Vic 340 B2
Meringur North Vic 340 B2
Merino Vic 338 C5
Merivale Qld 558 E3
Merluna Qld 568 C6
Mermaid Beach Qld 557 F7
Mernda Vic 337 H2, 339 P5, 344 A10
Mernmerna SA 791 J3
Mernot NR NSW 459 J2
Merolia WA 709 N8
Merredin WA 650, 706 F3
Merriang Vic 337 H1, 339 P5, 344 A9
Merriang Vic 344 G5
Merricks Vic 337 H6, 339 P8
Merrigang Qld 558 B5
Merrigum Vic 339 P1, 341 P10, 344 B4
Merrijig Vic 344 F8
Merrinee Vic 340 D2
Merrinee North Vic 340 D2
Merriot Qld 558 F9
Merriton SA 791 J7
Merriula Qld 565 J3
Merriwa NSW 393, 458 F4
Merriwagga NSW 465 J3
Merrygoen NSW 458 C3
Merrylands NSW 453 B5
Merrywinebone NSW 460 B5
Merseylea Tas 844 A5, 840 G6
Merthyr Qld 555 D5
Merton Vic 344 D7
Merton Vale NSW 465 L8
Mertondale WA 709 M8
Merty Merty SA 793 M6

Merungle NSW 465 H3
Messent CP SA 788 C8
Metcalfe Vic 339 M3
Metford NSW 455 M2, 459 J5
Methul NSW 465 M5
Metung Vic 342 F6
Meunna Tas 840 D5
Mexico Qld 560 B9
Mia Mia Vic 339 M3
Mia Mia WA 714 C9
Miakite Vic 338 D6
Miallo Qld 563 L5, 569 C6
Miandetta NSW 463 M7
Miawood Qld 558 F5
Michaelmas Reef Qld 563 M5, 569 E6
Michelago NSW 477 E8, 456 C6, 457 F4
Mickibri NSW 458 A6, 463 P10, 465 P1
Mickleham Vic 336 G2, 339 N5
Middalya WA 708 C1, 714 C10
Middle Beach SA 787 C5, 791 J9
Middle Camp NSW 462 B9, 464 B1
Middle Cove NSW 453 E4
Middle Dural NSW 453 B2
Middle Harbour NSW 453 F5
Middle Park Qld 555 A7
Middle Park Qld 563 H10, 565 K1
Middle Park Vic 335 C4
Middle Point NT 613 D3, 614 D4
Middle Swan WA 704 G2
Middle Tarwin Vic 337 L8
Middleback SA 790 G6
Middlemount Qld 560 F7
Middleton Qld 564 G6
Middleton SA 787 D8, 788 A5
Middleton Tas 839 C7, 843 K7
Middleton Park Qld 564 G6
Midge Point Qld 560 F3
Midgee Qld 561 J8
Midgee SA 790 G7
Midkin NR NSW 460 D4
Midland WA 704 G3, 705 C5, 706 C4
Midvale WA 704 G3
Midway Point Tas 839 D4, 843 L4
Miena Tas 844 B10, 841 H9
Miepoll Vic 344 C5
Miga Lake Vic 338 C3
Mil Lel SA 788 F10
Mila NSW 456 C9, 457 F10
Milabena Tas 840 D4
Milang SA 787 E8, 788 A6
Milang Well SA 791 K4
Milawa Vic 344 F5
Milbong Qld 556 D6, 557 A5, 559 M8
Milbrulong NSW 465 M6
Mildura Vic 291, 340 E2
Mile End SA 786 D6
Miles Qld 559 H5
Mileura WA 708 G5

Milgarra Qld 562 E7
Milgery Qld 564 G4
Milgun WA 709 H3
Milguy NSW 460 F4
Milikapiti NT 614 C2
Miling WA 705 D1, 706 C2
Milingimbi NT 615 K3
Milkengay NSW 464 C2
Milkshakes Hills FR Tas 840 C5
Mill Park Vic 335 D2
Millaa Millaa Qld 563 L6, 569 D9
Millajiddee WA 712 G10
Millaroo Qld 560 D2, 563 N10
Millbillillie WA 709 K5
Millbrook Vic 336 C2, 339 L5
Millers Creek SA 792 E9
Millgrove Vic 337 K3, 344 C10
Millicent SA 734–735, 788 F9
Millie NSW 460 D6
Millie Windie WA 713 J7
Millmerran Qld 503, 559 K8
Milloo Vic 341 M10
Millrose WA 709 L5
Millstream WA 714 F7
Millstream–Chichester NP WA 700, 714 G6
Millthorpe NSW 454 C5, 458 C7
Milltown Vic 338 D7
Millungera Qld 562 F10, 564 G1
Millwood NSW 465 M6
Milly Milly WA 708 F4
Milman Qld 561 J8
Milo Qld 567 M3
Milparinka NSW 462 C3
Milperra NSW 453 B7
Milray Qld 560 A3, 565 P3
Milsons Point NSW 453 E5
Milton NSW 456 F5
Milton Qld 555 C5
Milton Park NT 618 G5
Milton Park Qld 567 N1
Milvale NSW 465 P4
Milyakburra NT 615 L6
Mimili SA 789 F2
Mimong Qld 564 G4
Mimosa NSW 465 N5
Mimosa Park Qld 561 H10
Mimosa Rocks NP NSW 373, 456 E8
Minamere Qld 565 H3
Minara WA 709 M8
Minburra SA 791 K5
Mincha Vic 341 L8
Minda NSW 464 D2
Mindarie SA 791 M10
Minderoo WA 714 D7
Mindie Qld 564 E3
Mindil Beach Reserve NT 612 B8
Miners Rest Vic 336 B1, 339 K5
Minerva Hills NP Qld 560 E10
Minetta NSW 463 H3
Mingah Springs WA 709 H2
Mingary SA 791 N4

Mingay Vic 339 J6
Mingela Qld 560 C1, 563 N10
Mingenew WA 708 D9
Mingoola NSW 461 J3
Minhamite Vic 338 E6
Minilya WA 708 B1, 714 B10
Minilya Roadhouse WA 708 B1, 714 B10
Minimay Vic 338 B2
Mininera Vic 338 G5
Minjah Vic 338 F7
Minjilang NT 614 F2
Minlaton SA 791 H9
Minmindie Vic 341 K8
Minnamoolka Qld 563 K7
Minnamurra NSW 455 J10, 456 G3
Minnel Qld 558 G8
Minnie Creek WA 708 D1, 714 D10
Minnie Water NSW 461 N6
Minnies Outstation Qld 562 G6
Minnipa SA 790 C5
Minnippi Parklands Qld 555 E5
Minnivale WA 705 F3, 706 E3
Minore NSW 458 A4
Mintabie SA 789 G3
Mintaro SA 765, 787 D2, 791 K8
Minyip Vic 338 F1, 340 F10
Miram Vic 340 B10
Miram South Vic 338 C1, 340 C10
Miranda NSW 453 D9
Miranda Downs Qld 562 F6
Mirani Qld 560 F4
Mirboo Vic 337 N7
Mirboo East Vic 337 N7
Mirboo North Vic 337 N6
Miriam Vale Qld 559 K1, 561 L10
Mirima (Hidden Valley) NP WA 688, 713 N4
Mirimbah Vic 342 A3, 344 F8
Miriwinni Qld 563 M6, 569 E9
Mirrabooka WA 704 D2
Mirranatwa Vic 338 F4
Mirrool NSW 465 M4
Mirtna Qld 560 B4
Missabotti NSW 461 M8
Mission Beach Qld 528–529, 563 M7, 569 E10
Mistake Creek Community NT 616 A3, 713 P7
Mitakoodi Qld 564 E3
Mitcham SA 786 E7
Mitcham Vic 335 F3
Mitchell ACT 477 D2
Mitchell Qld 503, 558 D5
Mitchell and Alice Rivers NP Qld 562 F3
Mitchell Park SA 786 D7
Mitchell River Qld 562 F3
Mitchell River Vic 342 D5
Mitchell River WA 713 J3
Mitchell River NP Vic 342 D5, 345 K10
Mitchells Flat NSW 461 J8

Mitchellstown Vic 339 P2, 344 A6
Mitchellville SA 790 G7
Mitchelton Qld 555 B4
Mitiamo Vic 341 L9
Mitre Vic 338 D2
Mitta Junction Vic 345 H3
Mitta Mitta Vic 345 K5
Mitta Mitta River Vic 345 J4
Mittagong NSW 373, 455 H9, 456 F3, 458 F10
Mittagong Qld 562 G8
Mittebah NT 617 N6
Mittyack Vic 340 G5
Moalie Park NSW 462 D3
Moama NSW 449, 465 H8
Mobbs Hill NSW 453 C4
Mobella SA 789 G7
Moble Qld 567 L6
Moble Springs Qld 567 M5
Mockinya Vic 338 E3
Moculta NSW 463 K4
Modanville NSW 461 N2
Modbury SA 786 F3
Modbury Heights SA 786 F3
Modbury North SA 786 F3
Model Farms NSW 453 B4
Modella Vic 337 L5
Moe Vic 308, 337 N5
Mogal Plain NSW 463 M9
Moggill Qld 557 B3
Moglonemby Vic 344 C6
Mogo NSW 456 E6
Mogong NSW 454 A5, 458 B7
Mogriguy NSW 458 B3
Mogumber WA 705 C2, 706 C3
Moil NT 612 E3
Moil Park NT 612 F4
Moina Tas 840 F7
Mokepilly Vic 338 F3
Mole Creek Tas 816–817, 844 A7, 840 G7
Mole Creek Karst NP Tas 817, 840 G7
Mole River NSW 461 J3
Molendinar Qld 557 E6
Molesworth Qld 565 J3
Molesworth Tas 839 B4, 843 J4
Molesworth Vic 344 C8
Moliagul Vic 339 K2
Molka Vic 344 C6
Mollerin WA 705 G1
Mollerin NR WA 705 G1, 706 E2
Mollongghip Vic 336 C1, 339 L5
Mollymook NSW 456 F5
Mologa Vic 341 L9
Molong NSW 393, 454 B3, 458 B6
Moltema Tas 844 A6, 841 H6
Momba NSW 462 F6
Momba Qld 562 F9
Mona Qld 558 D8
Mona Vale NSW 453 G2, 455 L6, 459 H8
Mona Vale Qld 567 M4

Monadnocks CP WA 705 D6, 706 C5
Monak NSW 464 C4
Monash ACT 477 D4
Monbulk Vic 308, 337 J3
Mondure Qld 556 A1, 559 K4
Monegeeta Vic 336 F1, 339 N4
Mongarlowe NSW 456 E5
Monia Gap NSW 465 K3
Monivea NSW 462 G10, 464 G1
Monkey Mia WA 708 B4
Monkira Qld 566 E2
Monogorilby Qld 559 J4
Monolon NSW 462 E4
Mons Qld 565 M10, 567 M1
Monstraven Qld 562 E10, 564 F1
Mont Albert Vic 335 D3
Montacute SA 786 G5
Montagu Tas 840 B3
Montagu Bay Tas 838 F5
Montana Tas 844 B7, 841 H7
Montarna NSW 464 D3
Monteagle NSW 456 A2, 458 A10
Montebello Islands CP WA 714 D5
Montefiores NSW 458 B5
Montejinni NT 616 E2
Monterey NSW 453 E8
Montmorency Vic 335 E2
Monto Qld 559 J2
Montrose Tas 838 C3
Montrose Vic 335 G3
Montumana Tas 840 D4
Montville Qld 556 D3, 559 M5
Montys Hut Vic 337 M2, 344 E10
Moockra SA 791 J5
Moodiarrup WA 705 E10, 706 D7
Moogara Tas 839 A4, 843 H4
Moojebing WA 705 G10, 706 E7
Mooka WA 708 C2
Mookerawa SRA NSW 454 B2, 458 B5
Moolah NSW 463 H9
Moolawatana SA 793 L9
Moolbong NSW 465 H2
Mooleulooloo SA 791 N3
Mooleyarrah NSW 462 G2
Mooloo Downs WA 708 E3
Mooloogool WA 709 J4
Mooloolaba Qld 556 E3, 559 N5
Mooloolerie NSW 462 D10, 464 D1
Moolooloo SA 791 J2
Moolooloo Outstation NT 616 E2
Moolort Vic 339 K3
Moolpa NSW 464 F6
Moomba SA 793 M5
Moombidary Qld 567 L10
Moombooldool NSW 465 L4
Moona Plains NSW 461 K9
Moonagee NSW 463 M6
Moonah Tas 838 D4
Moonan Flat NSW 459 H3
Moonaran NSW 460 G9
Moonaree SA 790 D4

Moonbah NSW 456 B8, 457 C8
Moonbi NSW 461 H9
Moondarra Vic 337 N4
Moondarra SP Vic 337 N4
Moondene NSW 462 G10, 464 G1
Moonee Beach NSW 461 N7
Moonee Beach NP NSW 461 N7
Moonee Ponds Vic 335 C3
Moonford Qld 559 J2
Moongobulla Qld 563 M9
Moonie Qld 559 H7
Moonlight Flat SA 790 C6
Moonta SA 765, 787 A3, 791 H8
Moonta Bay SA 790 G8
Moonyoonooka WA 708 C8
Moora WA 705 C1, 706 C2
Moorabbin Vic 335 D5, 337 H4, 339 P6
Mooraberree Qld 566 F2
Moorabie NSW 462 A4
Moorak Qld 558 C4
Mooral Creek NSW 459 L2
Mooralla Vic 338 E4
Mooramanna Qld 558 E8
Moorarie WA 708 G4
Moore NSW 460 G9
Moore Qld 556 C3, 559 L6
Moore Park NSW 453 F6
Moore Park Qld 559 L1
Moore River WA 705 B2
Moore River NP WA 705 B2, 706 B3
Moorebank NSW 453 A7
Mooreland Downs NSW 462 G2
Mooren Creek NSW 458 D2
Mooreville Tas 840 E5
Moorine Rock WA 707 H3
Moorinya NP Qld 565 M4
Moorland NSW 459 M3
Moorland Qld 559 L2
Moorlands SA 788 A7
Moorleah Tas 840 D4
Moorooduc Vic 335 F9, 337 H5, 339 P7
Moorook SA 791 M8
Moorooka Qld 555 C7
Mooroolbark Vic 335 G2
Mooroopna Vic 344 B5
Mooroopna North Vic 344 B4
Moorumbine WA 705 F7, 706 E5
Moothandella Qld 567 J3
Mootwingee NSW 462 C6
Moppin NSW 460 D4
Moquilambo NSW 463 K6
Moraby Qld 558 G6
Morago NSW 465 H6
Moranbah Qld 560 E6
Morang South Vic 335 D1, 337 H2, 339 P5, 344 A10
Morangarell NSW 465 N4
Morapoi WA 709 M9
Morawa WA 669, 708 E9
Moray Downs Qld 560 C5
Morbining WA 705 F5, 706 E5

Morchard SA 791 J5
Morden NSW 462 C5
Mordialloc Vic 335 E6, 337 H4, 339 P6
Morecambe Qld 563 K7, 569 C10
Moree NSW 419, 460 E5
Moree Vic 338 C4
Moreenia SA 790 E8
Morella Qld 565 L7
Morestone Qld 564 B1
Moreton Bay Qld 555 F2, 556 E4
Moreton Island Qld 556 F4, 557 F1, 559 N6
Moreton Island NP Qld 556 F4, 557 F1, 559 N6
Morgan SA 766, 791 L8
Morgan Vic 342 C5
Morgan Vale SA 791 N6
Moriac Vic 336 D5, 339 L7
Morialta CP SA 786 G5
Moriarty Tas 844 A4, 840 G5
Morisset NSW 455 L3, 459 J6
Morkalla Vic 340 B2
Morley WA 704 E3
Morney Qld 566 G3
Morning Side NSW 462 G10, 464 G1
Morningside Qld 555 E5
Mornington Tas 838 G5
Mornington Vic 308–309, 335 E9, 337 H5, 339 P7
Mornington WA 713 J8
Mornington Island Qld 562 C5
Mornington Peninsula Vic 300–301
Mornington Peninsula NP Vic 309, 336 F6, 339 N8
Moroak NT 615 H8
Morongla Creek NSW 454 A7, 456 B1, 458 B9
Mororo NSW 461 N4
Morpeth NSW 393, 455 M1, 459 J5
Morpeth Qld 560 F6
Morphett Vale SA 786 C10
Morphettville SA 786 C7
Morri Morri Vic 338 G2
Morstone Qld 562 A9
Mortchup Vic 336 A2, 339 J5
Mortdale NSW 453 C8
Mortlake NSW 453 D5
Mortlake Vic 338 G7
Morton NP NSW 373, 456 E4
Morton Plains NSW 463 L1
Morton Plains Vic 340 G9
Morundah NSW 465 L6
Moruya NSW 373, 456 E6
Moruya Heads NSW 456 E6
Morven Qld 558 C5
Morwell Vic 309, 337 P5, 342 A8
Morwell NP Vic 337 P6
Moselle Qld 565 K3
Mosman NSW 453 F5
Mosman Park WA 704 B6

Moss Vale NSW 374, 454 G9, 456 F3
Mossgiel NSW 464 G2
Mossiface Vic 342 F5, 345 L10
Mossman Qld 563 L5, 569 C6
Mossy Point NSW 456 E6
Motpena SA 791 J2
Moulamein NSW 464 G6
Moulyinning WA 706 F7
Mount Aberdeen Qld 560 E2
Mount Aberdeen NP Qld 560 E2
Mount Adrah NSW 457 A2, 465 P6
Mount Alfred Qld 567 N6
Mount Alfred Vic 345 L3
Mount Amhurst WA 713 L9
Mount Anderson WA 712 F9
Mount Arapiles–Tooan SP Vic 338 C2
Mount Archer NP Qld 561 J8
Mount Arrowsmith NSW 462 B4
Mount Augustus WA 708 F2
Mount Augustus NP WA 664, 708 F2
Mount Barker SA 787 E6, 788 A6, 791 K10
Mount Barker WA 650, 706 E9
Mount Barkly NT 618 F2
Mount Barnett WA 688, 713 J6
Mount Barney NP Qld 556 D7, 557 A8, 559 M8
Mount Barry SA 792 C6
Mount Beauty Vic 328, 342 D1, 345 J6
Mount Beckworth Vic 336 B1, 339 K4
Mount Benson SA 788 E8
Mount Best Vic 337 N7
Mount Bold Reservoir SA 786 F10
Mount Boothby CP SA 788 B7
Mount Brockman WA 714 F8
Mount Brown CP SA 791 H5
Mount Bryan SA 787 E1, 791 K7
Mount Buangor SP Vic 339 H4
Mount Buckley Qld 560 E2
Mount Buffalo NP Vic 328, 342 B1, 345 H6
Mount Buller Alpine Village Vic 342 A3, 344 F8
Mount Bundy NT 613 D5, 614 D5
Mount Burges WA 707 K2
Mount Burr SA 788 F9
Mount Bute Vic 336 A3, 339 J6
Mount Campbell Qld 565 H5
Mount Carbine Qld 563 K5, 569 C6
Mount Cavenagh NT 618 G10
Mount Celia WA 709 N9
Mount Charlton Qld 560 F4
Mount Chinghee NP Qld 557 C8
Mount Christie SA 789 G8
Mount Claremont WA 704 B5
Mount Clarence SA 792 B7
Mount Clear Vic 336 C2, 339 K5
Mount Clere WA 708 G3

Mount Colah NSW 453 D2
Mount Colreavy WA 706 G2
Mount Compass SA 787 D8, 788 A5
Mount Cook NP Qld 563 L3, 569 C3
Mount Coolon Qld 560 D4
Mount Coot-tha Qld 555 B5
Mount Coot-tha Qld 555 B5
Mount Coot-tha Park Qld 555 A5
Mount Cornish Qld 565 M7
Mount Cotton Qld 555 G9, 557 D4
Mount Crosby Qld 557 B3
Mount Damper SA 790 C6
Mount Dandenong Vic 337 J3
Mount Dangar Qld 560 E2
Mount Dare SA 792 C1
Mount Darrah NSW 456 D9, 457 G9
Mount David NSW 454 D6, 456 D1, 458 D8
Mount Denison NT 618 E3
Mount Direction Tas 844 D4, 841 J5
Mount Doran Vic 336 C3, 339 L5
Mount Douglas Qld 560 C5
Mount Driven Qld 558 F8
Mount Dutton SA 792 D5
Mount Eba SA 793 D10
Mount Ebenezer NT 618 F8
Mount Eccles Vic 337 M6
Mount Eccles NP Vic 338 D7
Mount Edgar WA 715 K6
Mount Egerton Vic 336 D2, 339 L5
Mount Eliza Vic 335 E8, 337 H5, 339 P7
Mount Elizabeth WA 713 J5
Mount Elsie Qld 560 C4
Mount Emu Vic 336 A2, 339 J5
Mount Emu Plains Qld 563 K10, 565 M2
Mount Etna Qld 565 H5
Mount Evelyn Vic 337 J3
Mount Farmer WA 708 G7
Mount Field NP Tas 833, 842 G3
Mount Fitton SA 793 L9
Mount Florance WA 714 G7
Mount Frankland NP WA 706 D9
Mount Freeling SA 793 K9
Mount Gambier SA 735, 788 F10
Mount Gap NSW 463 H6
Mount Garnet Qld 563 K7, 569 C10
Mount George NSW 459 K3
Mount Gibson WA 708 G9
Mount Gipps NSW 462 B7
Mount Gipps NSW 462 B8
Mount Glorious Qld 557 B1
Mount Gould WA 708 G4
Mount Granya SP Vic 345 K3
Mount Gravatt Qld 555 D7, 557 C3
Mount Gravatt East Qld 555 E6
Mount Grenfell NSW 463 J6
Mount Gunderbooka NP NSW 463 K5
Mount Hale WA 708 G4

Mount Harden Qld 567 M2
Mount Hart WA 712 G6
Mount Hawthorn WA 704 C4
Mount Helen Vic 336 C2, 339 K5
Mount Hill SA 790 E8
Mount Hope NSW 463 K10, 465 K1
Mount Hope Qld 560 C4
Mount Hope SA 790 D8
Mount Hopeless SA 793 L8
Mount Horeb NSW 456 A4, 457 A2, 465 P6
Mount Hotham Vic 328–329
Mount House WA 713 J7
Mount Howe Qld 558 D2
Mount Howitt Qld 567 H5
Mount Hyland NR NSW 461 L7
Mount Imlay NP NSW 456 D9
Mount Irvine NSW 455 H5, 458 F7
Mount Isa Qld 536–537, 564 C3
Mount Ive SA 790 E5
Mount Jack NSW 462 F5
Mount Jackson WA 707 H1, 709 J10
Mount James WA 708 F2
Mount Jerusalem NP NSW 461 N2
Mount Jowlaenga WA 712 E8, 715 P1
Mount Julian Qld 560 F2
Mount Kaputar NP NSW 420, 460 E7
Mount Keith WA 709 K6
Mount Kosciuszko NSW 456 A8, 457 B7
Mount Kuring-gai NSW 453 D1
Mount Larcom Qld 561 K9
Mount Lawley WA 704 D4
Mount Lawson SP Vic 345 K3
Mount Leonard Qld 566 E3
Mount Lewis NSW 453 C7
Mount Lewis NSW 463 L7
Mount Liebig NT 618 D5
Mount Lion NSW 461 M2
Mount Lloyd Tas 839 A4, 843 H5
Mount Lofty Botanic Gardens SA 786 G7
Mount Lofty Ranges SA 787 E7, 791 K10
Mount Lonarch Vic 339 J4
Mount Lonsdale Qld 558 D5
Mount Lyndhurst SA 793 J10
Mount Macedon Vic 336 F1, 339 N4
Mount Madden WA 707 J7
Mount Magnet WA 669, 708 G7
Mount Manara NSW 462 F9
Mount Manning NR WA 707 J1, 709 K10
Mount Manning Range WA 709 J10
Mount Margaret Qld 567 K6
Mount Margaret WA 709 N8
Mount Maria Qld 558 C5
Mount Marlow Qld 567 K2
Mount Martha Vic 335 E10, 337 H5, 339 P7
Mount Mary SA 787 G3, 791 L8

Mount McConnel Qld 560 C3
Mount McLaren Qld 560 E6
Mount Mee Qld 556 D4, 559 M6
Mount Mercer Vic 336 C3, 339 K6
Mount Minnie WA 714 D7
Mount Mistake NP Qld 556 C6, 559 L8
Mount Mitchell NSW 461 K6
Mount Molloy Qld 563 L5, 569 C7
Mount Monger WA 707 M3
Mount Morgan Qld 517, 561 J9
Mount Moriac Vic 336 D5, 339 L7
Mount Morris Qld 567 N4
Mount Mulgrave Qld 563 J4
Mount Mulligan Qld 563 K5, 569 B7
Mount Mulyah NSW 462 G4
Mount Murchison NSW 462 F7
Mount Napier SP Vic 338 E6
Mount Narryer WA 708 E5
Mount Nebo Qld 556 D5, 557 B2, 559 M7
Mount Nelson Tas 838 E8
Mount Neville NR NSW 461 M4
Mount Norman Qld 563 H10, 565 K1
Mount Numinbah NR NSW 461 N1
Mount O'Connell NP Qld 561 H7
Mount Ommaney Qld 555 A7
Mount Ossa Qld 560 F3
Mount Padbury WA 708 G4
Mount Pelion Qld 560 F3
Mount Perry Qld 559 K2
Mount Phillip WA 708 E2
Mount Pierre WA 713 J10
Mount Pikapene NP NSW 461 M4
Mount Playfair Qld 558 B2
Mount Pleasant NSW 462 F6
Mount Pleasant Qld 558 E1
Mount Pleasant Qld 560 D9
Mount Pleasant SA 787 E5, 791 K9
Mount Pleasant WA 704 C6
Mount Poole NSW 462 B3
Mount Pritchard NSW 453 A7
Mount Prospect Vic 336 C1, 339 L4
Mount Remarkable WA 709 M9
Mount Remarkable NP SA 766, 791 H5
Mount Rescue CP SA 788 B9
Mount Richmond Vic 338 C7
Mount Richmond NP Vic 338 C7
Mount Riddock NT 619 J5
Mount Ringwood NT 613 D4, 614 D5
Mount Royal NP NSW 459 H4
Mount Russell NSW 460 G5
Mount Samaria SP Vic 344 E7
Mount Samson Qld 557 B1
Mount Sandiman WA 708 D2
Mount Sanford NT 616 C3
Mount Sarah SA 792 C3
Mount Scott CP SA 788 D8
Mount Seaview NSW 459 K1, 461 K10

Mount Serle SA 791 K1, 793 K10
Mount Seymour Tas 839 D1, 843 K2
Mount Shannon NSW 462 B3
Mount Shaugh CP SA 788 B10
Mount Skinner NT 619 H3
Mount Stuart NSW 462 C2
Mount Stuart Qld 560 F7
Mount Stuart Tas 838 D6
Mount Stuart WA 714 E8
Mount Sturgeon Qld 563 J10, 565 L2
Mount Sturt NSW 462 B3
Mount Surprise Qld 563 J7
Mount Tamborine Qld 557 D6
Mount Taylor Vic 342 E5, 345 L10
Mount Tenandra NSW 458 B1, 460 B10
Mount Timothy SA 788 B9
Mount Torrens SA 787 E6, 791 K10
Mount Tyson Qld 556 A5, 559 K7
Mount Vernon WA 709 H1
Mount Vetters WA 707 L1, 709 L10
Mount Victor SA 791 L4
Mount Victoria NSW 454 G5, 458 F8
Mount Vivian SA 790 D1, 792 D10
Mount Walker WA 706 G5
Mount Wallace Vic 336 D3, 339 L6
Mount Walsh NP Qld 559 L3
Mount Warning NP NSW 461 N2
Mount Waverley Vic 335 E4
Mount Wedge NT 618 E4
Mount Wedge SA 790 C7
Mount Wedge FR Tas 842 F5
Mount Weld WA 709 N8
Mount Wellington Tas 838 A7, 839 C5, 843 J5
Mount Westwood NSW 462 B6
Mount William NP Tas 807–808, 841 P4
Mount Willoughby SA 792 A5
Mount Wilson NSW 393, 454 G5, 458 F8
Mount Windsor Qld 564 G9
Mount Wittenoom WA 708 F6
Mount Wood NSW 462 C2
Mount Woowoolahra NSW 462 A6
Mount Worth SP Vic 337 M6
Mountain Park Tas 838 A7
Mountain River Tas 839 B5, 843 J5
Mountain Valley NT 615 H7
Mountain View Qld 560 D1, 563 N10
Mountain View Qld 560 D7
Moura Qld 558 G1
Mourilyan Qld 558 D8
Mourilyan Qld 563 M6, 569 E9
Mourilyan Harbour Qld 563 M6, 569 E9
Mouroubra WA 706 E1, 708 G10
Moutajup Vic 338 E5
Mowanjum Community WA 712 F7, 715 P1

Mowbray Tas 844 E6, 841 K6
Mowla Bluff WA 712 E10, 715 P2
Moyhu Vic 344 F5
Moyston Vic 338 G4
Muccan WA 715 K5
Muchea WA 705 C4, 706 C4
Muckadilla Qld 558 E5
Muckatah Vic 344 C3
Muckaty NT 617 H6
Mudamuckla SA 790 A4
Mudgeacca Qld 564 D8
Mudgee NSW 393, 454 D1, 458 D5
Mudgee Wine Region NSW 394
Mudgeegonga Vic 345 H5
Mudgeeraba Qld 556 E7, 557 E7, 559 N8
Mudginberri NT 614 F4
Muggleton Qld 558 F5
Muggon WA 708 D5
Mukinbudin WA 706 F2
Mulga Downs WA 715 H7
Mulga Park NT 618 E10
Mulga Valley NSW 462 E4
Mulga View SA 791 K1
Mulgaria SA 792 G9
Mulgathing SA 792 A10
Mulgowie Qld 556 C6, 559 L7
Mulgrave Vic 335 F5
Mulgul WA 709 H2
Mulka SA 793 J6
Mullaley NSW 458 E1, 460 E9
Mullaloo WA 705 B4, 706 B4
Mullamuddy NSW 454 E1, 458 D5
Mullengandra NSW 465 M8
Mullengudgery NSW 463 N7
Mullewa WA 669, 708 D8
Mullion Creek NSW 454 C3, 458 C6
Mulloway Point NSW 461 N4
Mullumbimby NSW 420, 461 P2
Muloorina SA 793 H8
Mulpata SA 788 A9, 791 N10
Multi Qld 559 H2
Muludja Community WA 713 J9
Mulwala NSW 465 K8
Mulya NSW 463 J5
Mulyandry NSW 465 P2
Mulyungarie SA 791 N3
Mumbannar Vic 338 B6
Mumbil NSW 454 B1, 458 C5
Mummel Gulf NP NSW 459 J1, 461 J10
Mummulgum NSW 461 M3
Mumu Qld 565 L3
Munarra WA 709 H4
Munburra Qld 563 K2, 568 G10, 569 C1
Mundabullangana WA 714 G5
Mundadoo NSW 463 M5
Mundaring WA 650, 705 C5, 706 C4
Mundarlo NSW 457 A1, 465 P6
Munderoo NSW 457 A5, 465 P8

Mundijong WA 705 C6, 706 C5
Mundiwindi WA 709 K1, 715 K10
Mundoo Bluff Qld 560 A5, 565 N5
Mundoona Vic 344 B3
Mundoora SA 787 B1, 791 H7
Mundowdna SA 793 J9
Mundrabilla WA **677**, 711 E7
Mundrabilla WA 711 E6
Mundrabilla Motel WA 711 F7
Mundubbera Qld **503**, 559 K3
Mundulla SA 788 C9
Munduran Qld 564 G7
Mungabroom NT 617 J5
Mungala SA 789 F8
Mungallala Qld 558 C5
Mungana Qld 563 J6, 569 A8
Mungeranie SA 793 K5
Mungeranie Roadhouse SA 793 J5
Mungeribar NSW 463 P8
Mungerup WA 706 F8
Mungery NSW 463 P9
Munghorn Gap NR NSW 458 E4
Mungindi NSW 460 C3
Mungkan Kandju NP Qld 568 C7
Mungle NSW 460 F3
Munglinup WA 707 K7
Mungo NSW 464 E3
Mungo Brush NSW 455 P1, 459 L5
Mungo NP NSW **442–443**, 464 E3
Mungunburra Qld 560 A2, 565 P2
Munni NSW 459 J4
Munro Vic 342 C6
Munster WA 704 C10
Muntadgin WA 706 G4
Muntz NR WA 707 N7
Munyaroo CP SA 790 G7
Munyaroo CR SA 790 G7
Muradup WA 705 E10, 706 D8
Muralgarra WA 708 F8
Murarrie Qld 555 E5
Murbko SA 791 L8
Murchison Vic 339 P1, 344 B5
Murchison Downs WA 709 J5
Murchison East Vic 344 B5
Murchison House WA 708 C6
Murchison River WA 708 E5
Murchison Roadhouse WA 708 E5
Murdinga SA 790 D7
Murdoch WA 704 C8
Murdong WA 705 G10, 706 E7
Murdunna Tas 839 F5, 843 M5
Murgenella NT 614 G2
Murgheboluc Vic 336 D5, 339 L7
Murgon Qld 556 B2, 559 L4
Murgoo WA 708 E6
Murkaby SA 787 G1, 791 L7
Murmungee Vic 344 G5
Murninnie Beach SA 790 G7
Murnpeowie SA 793 K8
Muronbong NSW 458 B4
Murphys Creek Qld 556 B5, 559 L7
Murra Murra Qld 558 B8
Murra Warra Vic 338 E1, 340 E10

Murrabit Vic 341 L7
Murradoc Vic 335 A9
Murramarang NP NSW **374**, 456 F5
Murrami NSW 465 L4
Murranji NT 616 G3
Murrawal NSW 458 C2
Murray Bridge SA **766**, 787 F7, 788 A7, 791 L10
Murray Downs NSW 464 F6
Murray Downs NT 617 J10, 619 J1
Murray Mouth SA 787 E8
Murray River NSW 456 A7, 457 A6, 465 J8
Murray River SA 787 G4, 791 L9
Murray River Vic 340 F3, 341 K6, 344 B2
Murray River NP SA **766**, 791 N9
Murray Town SA 791 J6
Murray–Kulkyne NP Vic 340 F4
Murray–Sunset NP Vic **287**, 340 B4
Murrayville Vic 340 B6
Murrin Bridge NSW 465 L2
Murrindal Vic 345 N9
Murrindindi Vic 337 K1, 344 C9
Murringo NSW 456 B2, 458 A10
Murroon Vic 336 B6, 339 K8
Murrum WA 708 G7
Murrumbateman NSW 456 C4, 457 E1
Murrumbeena Vic 335 D5
Murrumbidgee River ACT 477 D4
Murrumbidgee River NSW 464 F5
Murrumburrah NSW 456 A3
Murrungowar Vic 343 J5
Murrurundi NSW **394**, 458 G2
Murtoa Vic 338 F1
Murwillumbah NSW **420**, 461 P1
Musgrave Qld 563 H2, 568 E10
Musk Vic 336 D1, 339 L4
Muskerry East Vic 339 N2
Musselboro Tas 844 F6, 841 L7
Musselroe Bay CA Tas 841 N3
Muswellbrook NSW **394**, 458 G4
Mutawintji NP NSW **431**, 462 D6
Mutchilba Qld 563 L6, 569 C8
Mutdapilly Qld 557 A5
Mutooroo SA 791 N5
Muttaburra Qld **537**, 565 M7
Muttama NSW 456 A4, 465 P5
Mutton Hole Qld 562 E6
Myall NSW 462 F1
Myall Vic 341 L7
Myall Creek NSW 460 G6
Myall Creek Qld 567 P2
Myall Creek SA 790 G5
Myall Lakes NP NSW **394**, 459 M5
Myalla Tas 840 D4
Myalup Beach WA 705 B8, 706 B6
Myamyn Vic 338 D6
Myaree WA 704 C7
Myaring Vic 338 B6
Myers Flat Vic 339 L2
Mylestom NSW 461 N8

Mylor SA 786 G9, 787 D6, 791 K10
Myola Qld 562 E9
Myola Vic 339 N1
Myora Qld 557 F2
Mypolonga SA 787 G6, 788 A7, 791 L10
Myponga SA 787 D8, 788 A5
Myponga Beach SA 787 C8, 788 A5
Myra Vale Qld 562 E6
Myrniong Vic 336 E2, 339 M5
Myrnong NSW 462 F3
Myro NSW 462 E4
Myroodah WA 712 F9
Myrrhee Vic 337 N3
Myrrlumbing Qld 560 A2, 563 L10, 565 P2
Myrtle Bank SA 786 E6
Myrtle Bank Tas 844 F5, 841 L6
Myrtle Scrub NSW 459 K1, 461 K10
Myrtle Springs SA 793 J10
Myrtle Vale NSW 463 J4
Myrtlebank Vic 342 C7
Myrtleford Vic **329**, 344 G5
Myrtletown Qld 555 F3
Myrtleville NSW 454 E9, 456 E3, 458 E10
Myrtleville Qld 558 E3
Mysia Vic 341 K9
Mystic Park Vic 341 K7
Myubee Qld 564 D4
Myuna Qld 565 J4
Mywee Vic 344 C2
Mywyn Qld 563 J8

N

Naas ACT 477 D6
Nabageena Tas 840 C4
Nabarlek NT 614 G4
Nabawa WA 708 C8
Nabiac NSW 459 L3
Nabowla Tas 844 F4, 841 L5
Nackara SA 791 K5
Nadgee NR NSW 456 E10
Nadgee NR NSW 456 E10
Nagambie Vic **277**, 339 P2, 344 A6
Nagoorin Qld 559 K1, 561 K10
Nailsworth SA 786 E5
Nairana Qld 560 C5
Nairne SA 787 E6, 791 K10
Nakara NT 612 E2
Nakara Park NT 612 E2
Nalangil Vic 336 A6, 339 J8
Nalbarra WA 708 G8
Nalcoombie Qld 558 D1, 560 E10
Naldera Qld 558 E6
Nalinga Vic 344 D5
Nalkain WA 705 G2, 706 E3
Nallan WA 708 G6
Namadgi NP ACT 477 B7, 456 C6, 457 E4
Nambi WA 709 M7
Nambour Qld **503**, 556 D3, 559 M5
Nambrok Vic 342 B7
Nambrok West Vic 342 B7

Nambucca Heads NSW **420–421**, 461 N8
Nambung NP WA **651**, 705 A1, 706 B2
Namming NR WA 705 B2, 706 B3
Namoi River NSW 460 E8
Nana Glen NSW 461 N7
Nanami NSW 458 A8
Nanango Qld **503**, 556 B3, 559 L5
Nanardine NSW 463 P10, 465 P1
Nandaly Vic 340 G6
Nanga Bay WA 708 B4
Nangar NP NSW 458 A7
Nangara NSW 462 G6
Nangeela Vic 338 B5
Nangerybone NSW 463 L9
Nangiloc Vic 340 F3
Nangus NSW 457 A1, 465 P6
Nangwarry SA 788 F10
Nanneella Vic 341 N9
Nannup WA **651**, 706 C8
Nanson WA 708 C8
Nantawarra SA 787 C3, 791 J8
Nantawarrina SA 791 K1
Nantilla NSW 462 F4
Nanutarra WA 714 D8
Nanutarra Roadhouse WA 714 D8
Nanya NSW 464 A2
Nanya Qld 560 E7
Napier Broome Bay WA 713 K2
Napier Downs WA 712 G7
Napoleons Vic 336 B2, 339 K5
Nappa Merrie Qld 566 F7
Napperby NT 618 F4
Napperby SA 791 H6
Napranum Qld 568 B6
Napunyah NSW 462 G5
Naracoopa Tas 840 G2
Naracoorte SA **735**, 788 E9
Naracoorte Caves CP SA 788 E10
Naradhan NSW 465 L3
Naraling WA 708 C8
Narbethong Vic 337 K2, 344 C10
Narcowla NSW 462 C2
Nardoo NSW 462 G2
Nardoo Qld 558 A7, 567 P7
Nardoo Qld 562 C8
Nareen Vic 338 C4
Narellan NSW 455 J7, 456 G2, 458 G9
Narembeen WA 706 F5
Naretha Qld 567 L5
Naretha WA 711 B6
Nariel Vic 345 L5
Nariel Creek Vic 345 L4
Narine Qld 558 E10
Naringal Vic 338 G8
Narkal WA 705 G2, 706 E2
Narkanna SA 790 G3
Narline Qld 558 D9
Narloo WA 708 E7
Narndee WA 709 H8
Narooma NSW **374**, 456 E7

Narounyah Qld 560 C9
Narrabarba NSW 456 E10
Narrabeen NSW 453 G3, 455 L6, 459 H8
Narrabeen Lakes NSW 453 F3
Narrabri NSW 421, 460 E7
Narrabri West NSW 460 D7
Narrabundah ACT 477 E3
Narraburra NSW 465 N4
Narracan Vic 337 N5
Narran Lake NSW 463 N3
Narran Lake NR NSW 463 N3
Narran Park NSW 463 N3
Narrandera NSW 449, 465 L5
Narraport Vic 341 H8
Narrawa NSW 454 C9, 456 C3, 458 C10
Narrawa Qld 563 J8
Narraway NSW 463 P6
Narraweena NSW 453 F3
Narrawong Vic 338 D7
Narre Warren Vic 335 G6, 337 J4
Narre Warren North Vic 335 G5
Narrewillock Vic 341 J9
Narridy SA 791 J7
Narrien Qld 560 C7
Narrien Range NP Qld 560 C7
Narrierra NSW 462 D2
Narrikup WA 706 E9
Narrina SA 791 K1
Narrogin WA 651, 705 F8, 706 E6
Narromine NSW 436–437, 458 A4, 463 P8
Narrung SA 787 F8, 788 B6
Narrung Vic 341 H4
Narrungar SA 790 F2
Narwee NSW 453 C8
Narwietooma NT 618 F5
Naryilco Qld 566 G9
Nashua NSW 461 P3
Natal Downs Qld 565 P4
Nathalia Vic 341 P9
Nathan Qld 555 D7
Nathan River NT 615 K9, 617 K1
Natimuk Vic 338 D2
National Park Tas 842 G4
Natone Tas 840 E5
Nattai NP NSW 454 G8, 456 F2, 458 F10
Natte Yallock Vic 339 J3
Natural Bridge Qld 557 D8
Naturi SA 787 G7, 788 A7, 791 L10
Natya Vic 341 H5
Nauiyu NT 613 C6, 614 C6
Navarre Vic 339 H2
Nayook Vic 337 M4
N'Dhala Gorge NP NT 608, 619 J6
Nea NSW 458 F1, 460 F10
Neale Junction NR WA 711 C3
Nebo Qld 560 F5
Nectar Brook SA 791 H5
Nedlands WA 704 C6
Neds Corner Vic 340 C2

Neds Creek WA 709 J3
Needle Creek Qld 567 K1
Needles Tas 844 B7, 841 H7
Neerabup NP WA 705 B4, 706 B4
Neerim Vic 337 M4
Neerim South Vic 337 M4
Neeworra NSW 460 C3
Neika Tas 839 C5, 843 J5
Neilrex NSW 458 C2
Nelia Qld 565 H3
Nelia Ponds Qld 565 H3
Nelligen NSW 456 E6
Nellys Hut Qld 562 G6
Nelshaby SA 791 H6
Nelson NSW 453 A2
Nelson Vic 277, 338 A7
Nelson Bay NSW 394–395, 455 P2, 459 K5
Nelson Springs NT 616 A4
Nelwood SA 791 N8
Nemeena NSW 463 M5
Nemingha NSW 461 H10
Nene Valley SA 788 G9
Nene Valley CP SA 788 G9
Nepabunna SA 791 K1, 793 K10
Nepean Bay SA 788 B3
Nepean River NSW 455 H7, 458 F9
Nerang Qld 556 E7, 557 E6, 559 N8
Neranwood Qld 557 E7
Nereena Qld 565 L9
Nerong NSW 459 L5
Nerren Nerren WA 708 C6
Nerriga NSW 456 E4
Nerrigundah NSW 456 E7
Nerrigundah Qld 567 L6
Nerrima WA 712 G9
Nerrin Nerrin Vic 339 H6
Nerring Vic 336 A1, 339 J5
Netherby Vic 340 C9
Netherton SA 788 A8
Netley NSW 462 B9
Netley SA 786 D6
Netley Gap SA 791 M5
Neuarpur Vic 338 B2
Neumayer Valley Qld 562 D8
Neutral Bay NSW 453 F5
Neutral Junction NT 619 H2
Nevertire NSW 463 N8
Neville NSW 454 C6, 456 C1, 458 C8
New Alton Downs SA 793 L2
New Armraynald Qld 562 C7
New Bamboo Qld 563 H2, 568 E9
New Chum NSW 463 H5
New Crown NT 619 J9
New Deer Qld 567 L1
New Dixie Qld 563 H2, 568 E10
New Dunmore Qld 559 J7
New England NP NSW 421, 461 L8
New Farm Qld 555 D5
New Forest WA 708 D6
New Gisborne Vic 336 F1, 339 N4
New Mollyan NSW 458 C2

New Moon Qld 563 L9
New Norcia WA 652, 705 D2, 706 C3
New Norfolk Tas 833, 839 B4, 843 J4
New South Wales 349–351
New Strathgordon Qld 562 G2, 568 C10
New Town Tas 838 D5
New Victoria Downs Qld 560 B3
Newborough Vic 337 N5
Newbridge NSW 454 C5, 458 C8
Newbridge Vic 339 K2
Newburn WA 704 F5
Newbury Vic 336 D1, 339 M4
Newcastle NSW 395, 455 M2, 459 J6
Newcastle Bight NSW 455 N2
Newcastle Waters NT 616 G4
Newdegate WA 706 G6
Newell Qld 563 L5, 569 D6
Newham Vic 339 N4
Newhaven NT 618 D4
Newhaven Vic 337 J7
Newland Head CP SA 787 D9, 788 B5
Newlyn Vic 336 C1, 339 L4
Newman WA 700, 715 J9
Newmarket Qld 555 C4
Newmerella Vic 343 H5, 345 P10
Newminster WA 705 G7, 706 E5
Newnes NSW 454 G3, 458 F7
Newport NSW 453 G2
Newport Qld 561 H6
Newport Vic 335 B4
Newry NT 614 A10, 616 A1
Newry Vic 342 B6
Newstead Qld 555 D4
Newstead Qld 558 F6
Newstead Vic 339 L3
Newton SA 786 F5
Newton Boyd NSW 461 L6
Newtown NSW 453 E7
Newtown Vic 336 B2, 339 K5
Ngambaa NR NSW 461 M9
Ngangganawili WA 709 K5
Ngarkat CP SA 736, 788 B9
Nguiu NT 614 C3
Ngukurr NT 615 J8
Ngunnawal ACT 477 D1
Nhill Vic 291, 340 C10
Nhulunbuy NT 592, 615 M4
Niagara Qld 560 D6
Niall Qld 563 L9
Niangala NSW 459 J1, 461 J10
Nicholls ACT 477 D2
Nicholls Rivulet Tas 839 B7, 843 J6
Nicholson Vic 342 F6
Nicholson WA 713 N9
Nicholson River Vic 342 E4, 345 K9
Niddrie Vic 335 B3
Nidgery Downs NSW 463 M5
Nietta Tas 840 F6

Nightcap NP NSW 421, 461 N2
Nightcliff NT 612 C3
Nildottie SA 791 L9
Nile Tas 844 F7, 841 K7
Nilgen NR WA 705 A2, 706 B3
Nilma Vic 337 M5
Nilpena SA 791 J2
Nilpinna SA 792 E6
Nimaru Qld 558 A5, 567 P5
Nimbin NSW 421, 461 N2
Nimboy Qld 567 N5
Nimby Creek NSW 456 B2
Niminja WA 709 N4
Nimmitabel NSW 456 D8, 457 F8
Ninda Vic 340 G6
Nindigully Qld 558 F9
Ningaloo WA 714 B8
Ningaloo Marine Park WA 692–693, 714 B8
Ninghan WA 708 F9
Ninnes SA 787 B2, 791 H8
Ninyeunook Vic 341 J8
Nipan Qld 559 H2
Nippering WA 705 G9, 706 E7
Nirranda Vic 338 G8
Nita Downs WA 712 C10, 715 M3
Nithsdale Qld 564 F5
Nitmiluk (Katherine Gorge) NP NT 592, 613 G7, 614 F7
Nive Downs Qld 558 B3
Noarlunga SA 787 D7, 788 A5, 791 J10
Noarlunga Centre SA 786 B10
Nobby Beach Qld 557 F7
Noble Park Vic 335 F5, 337 H4
Noccundra Qld 567 J7
Nockatunga Qld 567 J7
Nocoleche NSW 462 G3
Nocoleche NR NSW 462 G3
Noella Qld 558 A3, 567 P3
Nollamara WA 704 C3
Nombinnie NR NSW 463 K10, 465 K1
Nome Qld 563 N9
Nonda Qld 565 H3
Nonnamah NSW 462 F4
Nonning SA 790 F5
Noojee Vic 337 M4
Nook Tas 840 G6
Nookawarra WA 708 F4
Noona NSW 463 H7
Noonamah NT 613 D3, 614 D4
Noonbah Qld 565 J10
Noonbinna NSW 454 A6, 456 B1, 458 B9
Noondie WA 708 F6
Noondoo Qld 558 E9
Noondoonia WA 707 P5, 711 A8
Noonga Qld 558 G5
Noongal WA 708 F7
Noonkanbah WA 712 G9
Noorama Qld 558 A9, 567 P9
Noorat Vic 338 G7

Noorinbee Vic 343 L4
Noorinbee North Vic 343 L4
Noosa Heads Qld **504**, 556 E2, 559 N5
Noosa NP Qld 556 E2, 559 N5
Nooyeah Downs Qld 567 K8
Nora Creina SA 788 E8
Noradjuha Vic 338 D2
Noranda WA 704 E3
Noreena Downs WA 715 K8
Norfolk Qld 562 A9
Norie WA 709 H5
Norlane Vic 336 E5, 339 M7
Norley Qld 567 L7
Norman Park Qld 555 D5
Normanhurst NSW 453 C3
Normanton Qld **529**, 562 E7
Normanville Vic 341 K8
Normanville SA 787 C8, 788 A5
Nornalup WA 706 D10
Norong Vic 344 F3
Norong Central Vic 344 F3
Norseman WA **652**, 707 M5
North Adelaide SA 786 D5
North Bannister WA 705 D7, 706 D5
North Beach WA 704 B3
North Bondi NSW 453 F6
North Bourke NSW 463 K4
North Brighton SA 786 C7
North Brighton Vic 335 D5
North Cronulla NSW 453 E10
North Dandalup WA 705 C7, 706 C5
North Dorrigo NSW 461 M7
North East Island NP Qld 561 J5
North-East Tasmania **806–809**
North-East Wine Region Vic **329**
North Engadine NSW 453 B10
North Epping NSW 453 C4
North Fremantle WA 704 A7
North Haven NSW 459 M2
North Haven SA 786 C2
North Head Qld 563 H8
North Hobart Tas 838 D6
North Huntly Vic 339 M1
North Karlgarin NR WA 706 G5
North Keppel Island NP Qld 561 K8
North Maclean Qld 557 C5
North Manly NSW 453 F4
North Melbourne Vic 335 C3
North Molle Island Qld 560 F2
North Moolooloo SA 791 J1
North Motton Tas 840 F5
North Mulga SA 793 L10
North Narrabeen NSW 453 G3
North Peake SA 792 D5
North Perth WA 704 D4
North Rocks NSW 453 B4
North Ryde NSW 453 D4
North Scottsdale Tas 844 G3, 841 L5
North Seaforth NSW 453 F4
North Shields SA 790 D9

North St Ives NSW 453 E3
North Star NSW 460 F3
North Stradbroke Island Qld 556 F5, 557 F3
North Strathfield NSW 453 D6
North Sydney NSW 453 E5, 455 K6, 459 H8
North Tamborine Qld 557 D6
North Well SA 790 D1
North-West Victoria Wine Region Vic **291**
Northam WA **652**, 705 E4, 706 D4
Northampton WA 708 C7
Northbridge NSW 453 E5
Northbridge WA 704 D5
Northcliffe WA 706 C9
Northcote Vic 335 D3
Northdown Tas 844 A4, 840 G5
Northern Rivers Wine Region NSW **396**
Northern Tasmanian Wine Regions Tas **817**
Northern Territory **573–575**
Northfield SA 786 E4
Northgate Qld 555 D3
Northlakes Golf Course NT 612 G4
Northmead NSW 453 B4
Norton Summit SA 786 G6
Norval Vic 338 G4
Norway NSW 454 E6, 456 E1, 458 E8
Norwell Qld 557 E5
Norwich Park Qld 560 F7
Norwood SA 786 E6
Norwood Tas 844 E6, 841 K6
Notting Hill Vic 335 E5
Nottingham Downs Qld 565 K4
Notts Well SA 791 L9
Nowa Nowa Vic 342 G5, 345 M10
Nowendoc NSW 459 J2
Nowendoc NP NSW 459 J1, 461 J10
Nowhere Else SA 790 D8
Nowie North Vic 341 J6
Nowingi Vic 340 E3
Nowley NSW 460 C6
Nowra NSW **374**, 456 F4
Nubeena Tas 839 E6, 843 M6
Nudgee Qld 555 E2, 557 C1
Nudgee Beach Qld 555 E2
Nuga Nuga NP Qld 558 E2
Nugent Tas 839 E3, 843 M4
Nuggetty Vic 339 L3
Nukarni WA 706 F3
Nulla Qld 567 P8
Nulla Nulla Qld 563 L10, 565 N1
Nullagine WA 715 K7
Nullah Outstation Qld 566 F5
Nullamanna NSW 461 H5
Nullarbor NP SA **740–742**, 789 B9
Nullarbor Plain SA **740–743**, 789 B7
Nullarbor Plain WA 711 F6
Nullarbor Roadhouse SA **744–745**, 789 C9

Nullarbor RR SA 789 B8
Nullawa NSW 463 P2
Nullawarre Vic 338 G8
Nullawil Vic 341 H8
Nulty NSW 463 J4
Number One NSW 459 K2
Numbla Vale NSW 456 B8, 457 D8
Numbugga NSW 456 D8
Numbulwar NT 615 L7
Numeralla NSW 456 D7, 457 F6
Numery NT 619 K6
Numil Downs Qld 562 E10, 564 G1
Numinbah NSW 461 N1
Numinbah Valley Qld 556 E7, 557 D7, 559 N8
Numurkah Vic 344 C3
Nunamara Tas 844 F5, 841 K6
Nunawading Vic 335 F3
Nundah Qld 555 D3, 557 C2
Nundle NSW **396**, 459 H2
Nundora NSW 462 C5
Nundroo SA 789 E10
Nunga Vic 340 F5
Nungarin WA 706 F3
Nungatta NSW 456 D10
Nungunyah NSW 462 G2
Nunjikompita SA 790 B4
Nunnyah CR SA 790 B4
Nuntherungie NSW 462 D5
Nurcoung Vic 338 D2
Nurina WA 711 D6
Nuriootpa SA **766–767**, 787 E4, 791 K9
Nurrabiel Vic 338 E3
Nutwood Downs NT 615 H10, 617 H1
Nuyts Reef SA 789 E10
Nuytsland NR WA 711 B8
Nyabing WA 706 F7
Nyah Vic 341 J5
Nyah West Vic 341 J5
Nyang WA 714 D9
Nyapari SA 789 C1
Nyarrin Vic 340 G6
Nychum Qld 563 K5, 569 A7
Nymagee NSW 463 L8
Nymboi Binderay NP NSW 461 M7
Nymboida NSW **422**, 461 M6
Nymboida NP NSW **411**, 461 L5
Nymboida River NSW 461 L6
Nyngan NSW **437**, 463 M7
Nyngynderry NSW 462 E8
Nyora Vic 337 K6
Nypo Vic 340 E7

O

O B Flat SA 788 G10
Oak Park Qld 563 J9
Oak Park SA 791 L6
Oak Park Vic 335 B2
Oak Vale NSW 462 D5
Oak Vale Qld 565 N2
Oak Valley Qld 563 J10, 565 L1

Oakbank SA 791 N6
Oakdale NSW 455 H7, 456 F2, 458 F9
Oakden Hills SA 790 G3
Oakenden Qld 560 G4
Oakey Qld 556 A5, 559 K7
Oakey Creek ACT 477 C4
Oakey Creek NSW 458 D2
Oakey Park Qld 558 D9
Oakham Qld 567 K3
Oaklands NSW 465 K7
Oaklands Junction Vic 335 A1, 336 G2, 339 N5
Oakleigh Qld 558 A4, 567 P4
Oakleigh Qld 560 C9
Oakleigh Vic 335 E5, 337 H4, 339 P6
Oakley Qld 565 N4
Oakpark Qld 558 A4, 567 P4
Oaks Tas 844 D7, 841 J7
Oakvale SA 791 N6
Oakvale Vic 341 J8
Oakwood NSW 461 H5
Oakwood Qld 558 A3, 567 P3
Oasis Roadhouse Qld 563 K8
Oatlands Tas **833**, 843 K2
Oatley NSW 453 C8
Oban Qld 564 C4
Oberon NSW 454 E6, 456 E1, 458 E8
Obley NSW 458 A5
OBX Creek NSW 461 M6
Ocean Grove Vic **278**, 336 E5, 339 M7
Ocean Shores NSW 461 P2
O'Connell NSW 454 E5, 458 D8
O'Connor WA 704 C7
Oenpelli NT 614 G4
Offham Qld 558 A7, 567 P7
Officer Vic 337 J4
Ogmore Qld 561 H7
Ogunbil NSW 459 H1, 461 H10
O'Halloran Hill SA 786 C9
O'Halloran Hill RP SA 786 C8
O'Haras Creek NSW 453 B1
Olary SA 791 M4
Old Adaminaby NSW 456 B7, 457 D6
Old Andado NT 619 K9
Old Banchory Qld 560 D7
Old Bar NSW 459 L3
Old Beach Tas 839 C4, 843 K4
Old Bonalbo NSW 461 L2
Old Bowenfels NSW 454 F5, 458 E8
Old Burren NSW 460 B6
Old Cherrabun WA 713 H9
Old Cork Qld 564 G7
Old Creek Vic 339 L2
Old Delamere NT 614 E10, 616 E1
Old Grevillia NSW 461 M2
Old Guildford NSW 453 B6
Old Junee NSW 465 N5
Old Koomooloo SA 791 L7

Old Koreelah NSW 461 L2
Old Laura Qld 563 K3, 569 A3
Old May Downs Qld 564 C2
Old Roseberth Qld 566 C3
Old Rowena NSW 462 C6
Old Silver Plains Qld 563 H1,
  568 E8
Old Strathgordon Qld 562 F2,
  568 C9
Old Warrah NSW 458 G2
Oldina Tas 840 E5
Olinda NSW 454 F2, 458 E6
Olio Qld 565 K5
Olive Downs NSW 462 B1
Olive Island CP SA 790 A5
Olive Vale Qld 563 K3, 569 A3
Olympic Dam SA 790 F1, 792 F10
Oma Qld 565 L10, 567 L1
O'Malley ACT 477 D4
O'Malley SA 789 D8
Omeo Vic 330, 342 E3, 345 L8
Omicron Qld 566 F9
One Arm Point WA 712 E6
One Tree NSW 462 C4
One Tree NSW 465 H4
Onepah NSW 462 C1
Ongerup WA 706 G8
Onkaparinga Hills SA 786 D10
Onkaparinga River SA 786 G9
Onoto Qld 565 H10
Onslow WA 700–701, 714 D7
Oobagooma WA 712 F6
Oodla Wirra SA 791 K6
Oodnadatta SA 784, 792 D4
Ooldea SA 789 E8
Oolloo NT 613 D7, 614 D7
Oolloo Crossing NT 613 D7, 614 D7
Oombabeer Qld 558 G1, 561 H10
Oombulgurri WA 713 M4
Oondooroo Qld 565 J6
Oonoomurra Qld 564 E3
Ooratippra NT 619 L3
Oorindi Qld 564 F3
Ootann Qld 563 K6, 569 B9
Ootha NSW 463 N10, 465 N2
Opalton Qld 565 J8
Ophir NSW 454 C3, 458 C7
Opium Creek NT 613 E3, 614 E4
Opossum Bay Tas 839 D5, 843 K5
Ora Banda WA 707 K2, 709 L10
Orana NSW 462 G10, 464 G1
Orange NSW 396–397, 454 B4,
  458 C7
Orange Creek NT 618 G7
Orange Grove NSW 464 F3
Orange Grove WA 704 G6
Orange Wine Region NSW 397
Oraparinna SA 791 K2
Orbost Vic 310, 343 H5, 345 P10
Orchid Beach Qld 559 N2
Ord River WA 713 N4
Ord River WA 713 N7
Ord River NR WA 713 N3

Orford Tas 834, 839 F2, 843 M3
Orford Vic 338 E7
Organ Pipes NP Vic 335 A2
Orielton Tas 839 D4, 843 L4
Orientos Qld 566 G8
Orion Downs Qld 560 F10
Ormeau Qld 557 E5
Ormiston Qld 557 E3
Ormond Vic 335 D5
Oroners Outstation Qld 562 G3
Orpheus Island NP Qld 563 M8
Orroroo SA 791 J5
Osborne NSW 465 M6
Osborne SA 786 C3
Osborne Vic 335 E10
Osborne Park WA 704 B3
Osborne Well NSW 465 K7
Osbornes Flat Vic 345 H4
Osmaston Tas 844 C7, 841 H7
Osmond Valley WA 713 M7
Osprey Point SA 786 C1
Osterley Tas 843 H2
O'Sullivan Beach SA 786 B10
OT Downs NT 617 K2
Otago Tas 838 C2, 839 D4
Ottoway SA 786 C4
Otway NP Vic 263, 336 A8, 339 J9
Otway Range Vic 262–265, 336 A8,
  339 K9
Ouchy Qld 562 E10, 564 F1
Oulnina Park SA 791 M5
Ourimbah NSW 455 L4, 459 H7
Ourimbah NSW 462 F2
Ournie NSW 457 A5, 465 P8
Ouse Tas 842 G3
Outalpa SA 791 M4
Outer Harbor SA 786 C2, 787 D5,
  791 J9
Outtrim Vic 337 L7
Ouyen Vic 292, 340 E5
Ovens Vic 345 H5
Overlander Roadhouse WA 708 C5
Overnewton NSW 462 F10, 464 F1
Owen SA 787 D3, 791 J8
Owen Anchorage WA 704 A9
Owen Downs NSW 462 E2
Owens Gap NSW 458 G3
Owieandana SA 793 K10
Oxenford Qld 556 E6, 557 E6,
  559 N8
Oxenhope Outstation Qld 560 A4,
  565 P4
Oxford Downs Qld 558 A3
Oxford Park Qld 555 B3
Oxley ACT 477 D4
Oxley NSW 464 G4
Oxley Qld 555 B7, 557 C3
Oxley Vic 344 F5
Oxley Vale NSW 460 G9
Oxley Wild Rivers NP NSW 422,
  459 K1, 461 K9
Oyster Cove Tas 839 B6, 843 J6
Ozenkadnook Vic 338 B2

P

Paaratte Vic 338 G8
Pacific Palms NSW 459 L4
Packsaddle NSW 462 C5
Padbury WA 704 B1
Paddington NSW 453 F6
Paddington NSW 463 H8
Paddington Qld 555 C5
Paddys Flat NSW 461 L3
Paddys Plain NSW 461 L7
Paddys Ranges SP Vic 339 K3
Paddys River ACT 477 C5
Padstow NSW 453 B8
Padthaway SA 788 D9
Padthaway CP SA 788 D9
Page ACT 477 D2
Pagewood NSW 453 F7
Pago WA 713 K2
Paignie Vic 340 E5
Painters Bore Camp NSW 460 F4
Pajingo Qld 560 B3, 565 P3
Pakenham Vic 337 K5
Pakenham South Vic 337 K5
Pakenham Upper Vic 337 K4
Palana Tas 841 J1
Palen Creek Qld 557 B8
Paling Yards NSW 454 E3, 458 D7
Pallamana SA 787 F6, 788 A6,
  791 K10
Pallara Qld 555 C9
Pallarang Vic 340 B5
Pallarenda Qld 563 N9
Pallarup NR WA 707 H6
Palm Beach NSW 453 G1, 455 L5,
  459 H8
Palm Beach Qld 557 F7
Palmer SA 787 F6, 791 K10
Palmer River Roadhouse Qld 563 K4,
  569 B5
Palmer Valley NT 618 G8
Palmerston ACT 477 D2
Palmerston NT 613 C2, 614 D4
Palmerville Qld 563 J4
Palmgrove NP Qld 558 G2
Palmwoods Qld 556 D3, 559 M5
Palmyra WA 704 B7
Paloona Tas 840 G6
Palparara Qld 566 G2
Paluma Qld 563 M9
Paluma Range NP Qld 563 M9
Palumpa NT 613 A8, 614 B7
Pambula NSW 456 E9
Pambula Beach NSW 456 E9
Panania NSW 453 B8
Panaramitee SA 791 L5
Pandanus Creek Qld 563 K9
Pandappa CP SA 791 K6
Pandie Pandie SA 793 L1
Pandora Park Qld 565 K10, 567 K1
Paney SA 790 D5
Panitya Vic 340 A6
Panmure Vic 338 G8
Pannawonica WA 714 E7

Panorama SA 786 D7
Pantapin WA 705 G5, 706 E4
Pantijan WA 713 H5
Panton Hill Vic 335 F1, 337 H2,
  339 P5, 842 B10
Paper Beach Tas 844 D4, 841 J5
Pappinbarra NSW 459 L1, 461 L10
Papulankutja WA 710 F10
Papunya Aboriginal Community NT
  618 E5
Para Hills SA 786 F3
Para Wirra RP SA 767
Paraburdoo WA 714 G9
Parachilna SA 791 J2
Paradise SA 786 F4
Paradise Tas 840 G6
Paradise Vic 336 A8, 339 J9
Paradise Vic 339 H2
Paradise WA 712 G9
Paradise Beach Vic 342 D7
Paradise Point Qld 556 F6, 559 N8
Parafield SA 786 E3
Parafield Gardens SA 786 E2
Parakylia SA 792 E10
Paralowie SA 786 E2
Parap NT 612 C7
Parara SA 787 B4, 791 H9
Paratoo SA 791 L5
Parattah Tas 839 D1, 843 K2
Parawa SA 787 C8, 788 B5
Parawee Tas 840 D6
Pardoo WA 715 J5
Pardoo Roadhouse WA 715 K4
Parenna Tas 840 F2
Parham SA 787 C4, 791 J9
Parilla SA 788 A9
Paringa NSW 462 B7
Paringa SA 791 N8
Park Holme SA 786 D7
Park Orchards Vic 335 F3
Park Ridge Qld 556 E6, 557 C4,
  559 N7
Parkdale Vic 335 E6
Parkes NSW 437, 458 A6, 463 P10,
  465 P2
Parkham Tas 844 B5, 841 H6
Parkhurst Qld 561 J8
Parkinson Qld 555 D9
Parklea NSW 455 J6, 456 G1,
  458 G8
Parkside SA 786 E6
Parkside Tas 841 P6
Parkville NSW 458 G3
Parkville Vic 335 C3
Parkwood WA 704 E7
Parnabal Qld 560 G9
Parndana SA 788 B3
Parnella Tas 841 P6
Paroo WA 709 J4
Parrakie SA 788 A9
Parramatta NSW 453 B5, 455 J6,
  456 G1, 459 H8
Parramatta River NSW 453 C5

Parry Lagoons NR WA 713 N4
Partacoona SA 791 H4
Partridge Lakes SA 792 B10
Paru NT 614 C3
Paruna SA 791 N9
Parwan Vic 336 E3, 339 M5
Pasadena SA 786 D7
Paschendale Vic 338 C5
Pascoe Vale Vic 335 C2
Pasha Qld 560 D5
Paskeville SA 787 B3, 791 H8
Pata SA 791 N9
Patchewollock Vic 340 E6
Pateena Tas 844 E7, 841 K7
Paterson NSW 397, 455 M1, 459 J5
Paterson Bay Vic 336 C7, 339 L8
Patersonia Tas 844 F5, 841 K6
Patho Vic 341 M8
Patterson Lakes Vic 335 F7
Patyah Vic 338 B2
Paupong NSW 456 B8, 457 D8
Pawleena Tas 839 E4, 843 L4
Pawtella Tas 843 L2
Paxton NSW 455 K2, 459 H6
Payneham SA 786 E5
Paynes Find WA 708 G9
Paynesville Vic 310, 342 E6
Peachna CR SA 790 D7
Peak Charles NP WA 707 L6
Peak Creek NSW 454 B5, 458 B8
Peak Crossing Qld 557 A5
Peak Downs Qld 560 E7
Peak Hill NSW 458 A5, 463 P9,
    465 P1
Peak Hill WA 709 H3
Peak Range NP Qld 560 E7
Peak Vale Qld 560 D8
Peak View NSW 456 D7, 457 G6
Peaka NSW 464 D2
Peake SA 788 A8
Peakhurst NSW 453 C8
Peakhurst Heights NSW 453 C8
Pearce ACT 477 D4
Pearcedale Vic 335 G8, 337 H5
Pearlah SA 790 D9
Peats Ridge NSW 455 K4, 459 H7
Peawaddy Qld 558 E1
Pedirka SA 792 C2
Pedirka Desert SA 792 B3
Peebinga SA 791 N10
Peebinga CP SA 791 N10
Peechelba Vic 344 E4
Peechelba East Vic 344 F3
Peedamulla WA 714 D7
Peekadoo Qld 558 G4
Peel NSW 454 D4, 458 D7
Peel Inlet WA 705 B7
Peelwood NSW 454 D8, 456 D2,
    458 D9
Pegarah Tas 840 F2
Pekina SA 791 J5
Pelaw Main NSW 455 L2, 459 J6
Pelham Qld 562 G9, 565 J1

Pelham Tas 839 A2, 843 J3
Pella Vic 340 D8
Pelverata Tas 839 B6, 843 J6
Pemberton WA 652, 706 C9
Pemberton Wine Region WA
    652–653
Pembrooke NSW 459 M1, 461 M10
Penarie NSW 464 F4
Pencil Pine Tas 840 F7
Pendle Hill NSW 453 A5
Penguin Tas 817, 840 F5
Penneshaw SA 787 B9, 788 B4
Penola SA 736, 788 E10
Penola CP SA 788 E9
Penong SA 745, 789 F10
Penrice Qld 565 M3
Penrith NSW 397, 455 H6, 456 G1,
    458 G8
Penshurst NSW 453 C8
Penshurst Vic 278, 338 E6
Pentland Qld 560 A3, 565 N3
Penwortham SA 787 D2, 791 J8
Peppermint Grove WA 704 B6
Peppers Plains Vic 340 E9
Peppimenarti NT 613 A7, 614 C7
Peranga Qld 556 A4, 559 K6
Perch Creek Qld 561 H10
Percival Lakes WA 710 B4
Perekerten NSW 464 F6
Perenjori WA 708 E9
Perenna Vic 340 D9
Pericoe NSW 456 D9, 457 G10
Perisher Valley NSW 456 B8, 457 C7
Pernatty SA 790 G3
Peron WA 708 B4
Peronne Vic 338 C2
Perponda SA 791 M10
Perrinvale Outcamp WA 709 K8
Perry Bridge Vic 342 D7
Perth Tas 818, 844 E7, 841 K7
Perth WA 626–627, 704 D5,
    705 B5, 706 C4
Perth Airport WA 704 G4
Perth Hills Wine Region WA 653
Perth Water WA 704 D5
Perthville NSW 454 D5, 458 D8
Petcheys Bay Tas 839 A7, 843 J7
Peterborough SA 767, 791 J6
Peterborough Vic 278, 338 G9
Petersham NSW 453 E6
Petersville SA 787 A4, 791 H9
Petford Qld 563 K6, 569 B9
Petina SA 790 B5
Petita NSW 462 E4
Petrie Qld 556 E5, 557 C1, 559 M6
Petro NSW 464 D3
Pettit NSW 456 A4, 457 B1, 465 P6
Pheasant Creek Vic 337 J1, 344 B9
Phillip Bay NSW 453 F8
Phillip Creek NT 617 H7
Phillip Island Vic 310–311
Piallamore NSW 459 H1, 461 H10
Piallaway NSW 458 F1, 460 F10

Piambie Vic 341 H4
Piambra NSW 458 D2
Piangil Vic 341 J5
Piangil North Vic 341 H5
Piavella Vic 341 M9
Piawaning WA 705 D2, 706 C2
Picaninny Outstation NT 616 B8
Picardy Qld 560 F7
Piccadilly SA 786 G7
Piccaninnie Ponds CP SA 788 G10
Pickabox Qld 558 B5
Pickering Brook WA 705 C5, 706 C4
Pickertaramoor NT 614 D3
Picnic Bay Qld 563 N9
Picnic Point NSW 453 B8
Picola Vic 341 P8, 344 A3
Picton NSW 455 H8, 456 G2, 458
    G10
Picton WA 705 B9, 706 B7
Piedmont Vic 337 M4
Piednippie SA 790 B5
Pieman River SR Tas 840 B8
Pier Millan Vic 340 G6
Piesseville WA 705 F9, 706 E6
Pigeon Hole NT 616 D3
Pigeon Ponds Vic 338 C4
Pikedale Qld 556 A9, 559 K9
Pilbara WA 714 E8
Pilga WA 715 J7
Pillana SA 790 D9
Pillar Valley NSW 461 N6
Pilliga NSW 460 B7
Pilliga NR NSW 460 D9
Pimba SA 790 F2
Pimbee WA 708 C3
Pimpama Qld 556 E6, 557 E5,
    559 N7
Pimpara Lake NSW 462 B4
Pimpinio Vic 338 E1
Pincally NSW 462 B4
Pindabunna WA 708 G9
Pindar WA 708 E8
Pindera Downs NSW 462 D2
Pindi Pindi Qld 560 F3
Pine Clump NSW 463 P7
Pine Corner SA 790 E7
Pine Creek NT 592, 613 F6, 614 E6
Pine Creek SA 791 L6
Pine Creek SA 791 N4
Pine Gap NT 619 H6
Pine Grove NSW 460 B9
Pine Lodge Vic 344 C4
Pine Lodge South Vic 344 C5
Pine Plains Vic 340 D6
Pine Point SA 787 A5, 791 H9
Pine Ridge NSW 458 F2
Pine Valley SA 791 M6
Pine View NSW 462 A5
Pine View NSW 463 J3
Pinedale Qld 559 H4
Pinegrove WA 708 D7
Pinery SA 787 C4, 791 J9
Piney Range NSW 456 A1, 465 P3

Pingandy WA 708 G1, 714 G10
Pingaring WA 706 G6
Pingelly WA 705 F7, 706 E5
Pingine Qld 567 M5
Pingrup WA 706 G7
Pinjarra WA 653, 705 C7, 706 C5
Pinjarra Hills Qld 555 A7
Pinjarrega NR WA 706 C1, 708 E10
Pinjin WA 707 N1, 709 N10
Pinkawillinie CP SA 790 D5
Pinkawillinie CR SA 790 D6
Pinkenba Qld 555 F4
Pinkett NSW 461 K6
Pinkilla Qld 567 K5
Pinnacle Qld 560 F4
Pinnacle Reefs NSW 465 P3
Pinnacles Qld 563 H3
Pinnacles WA 709 K7
Pinnaroo SA 767, 788 A10, 791 N10
Pintharuka WA 708 E9
Pioneer Qld 560 D1, 563 N9
Pioneer Qld 560 D7
Pioneer Tas 841 N5
Pipalyatjara SA 789 A1
Pipers Brook Tas 844 E3, 841 K5
Pipers River Tas 844 E3, 841 K5
Pira Vic 341 J6
Piries Vic 344 E8
Pirlta Vic 340 D2
Pirron Yallock Vic 336 A6, 339 J8
Pitfield Vic 336 A3, 339 J6
Pithara WA 706 D2, 708 F10
Pittong Vic 336 A2, 339 J5
Pittsworth Qld 556 A6, 559 K7
Pittwater NSW 453 G1
Plain Creek Qld 560 C5
Planet Downs Qld 562 C8
Planet Downs Outstation Qld 566 F4
Pleasant Hills NSW 465 M7
Pleasure Point NSW 453 B8
Plenty Tas 839 A4, 843 H4
Plenty Vic 335 D1
Plenty River Vic 335 D1
Plevna Downs Qld 567 J5
Plumbago SA 791 M4
Plumridge Lakes NR WA 711 B4
Plympton SA 786 D6
Pmara Jutunta NT 618 G3
Poatina Tas 818, 844 D8, 841 J8
Poinsetta Qld 560 E8
Point Cook Vic 335 A5, 336 F4,
    339 N6
Point Coulomb NR WA 712 C7,
    715 N1
Point Davenport CP SA 788 A3,
    790 G10
Point Gordo WA 706 G9
Point Lonsdale Vic 278, 336 F6,
    339 N8
Point Lookout Qld 556 F5, 557 F2,
    559 N7
Point Pass SA 787 E3, 791 K8
Point Pearce SA 790 G9

Point Percy Vic 338 E8
Point Piper NSW 453 F6
Point Samson WA 714 F5
Point Sinclair SA 745
Point Stuart Coastal Reserve NT 613 F2, 614 E4
Point Turton SA 790 G10
Poison Gate NSW 460 C5
Poitrel Qld 560 E6
Polblue CR NSW 459 H3
Poldinna SA 790 C6
Polelle WA 709 H5
Police Point Tas 839 A7, 843 J7
Policemans Point SA 787 G10, 788 C7
Polkemmet Vic 338 D2
Pollappa Qld 563 H1, 568 D9
Polocara NSW 462 G5
Poltalloch SA 787 F8, 788 A7
Pomborneit Vic 339 J8
Pomona Qld 556 D2, 559 M5
Pomonal Vic 338 F4
Pompoota SA 787 G6, 791 L10
Ponto NSW 458 B4
Pontville Tas 834, 839 C3, 843 K4
Pony Hills Qld 558 F4
Poochera SA 790 C5
Pooginook CP SA 791 M8
Poolaijelo Vic 338 B4
Poolamacca NSW 462 B7
Poole Tas 841 N3
Poona NP Qld 559 M3
Pooncarie NSW 464 D2
Poonindie SA 790 E9
Poonunda SA 787 F1, 791 K7
Pooraka SA 786 E3
Pootilla Vic 336 C2, 339 L5
Pootnoura SA 792 A6
Poowong Vic 337 L6
Poowong East Vic 337 L6
Popanyinning WA 705 F7, 706 E6
Popiltah NSW 464 B2
Popiltah Lake NSW 464 B2
Popio NSW 462 B10, 464 B1
Popran NP NSW 455 K4, 459 H7
Porcupine Flat Vic 339 L3
Porcupine Gorge NP Qld 565 L2
Porepunkah Vic 330, 342 C1, 345 H6
Pormpuraaw Aboriginal Community Qld 562 F2, 568 B10
Porongurup WA 706 F9
Porongurup NP WA 706 F9
Port Adelaide SA 786 C4, 787 D6, 791 J10
Port Adelaide River SA 786 C2
Port Albert Vic 342 B9
Port Alma Qld 561 K9
Port Arthur Tas 839 F7, 843 M6
Port Arthur Historic Site Tas 834, 839 F7, 843 M6
Port Augusta SA 768, 791 H5
Port Botany NSW 453 E8

Port Broughton SA 768, 787 B1, 791 H7
Port Campbell Vic 279, 339 H9
Port Campbell NP Vic 339 H9
Port Clinton SA 787 B3, 791 H8
Port Davis SA 791 H6
Port Denison WA 708 C9
Port Douglas Qld 552, 563 L5, 569 D6
Port Elliot SA 787 D8, 788 B5
Port Fairy Vic 279, 338 E8
Port Franklin Vic 337 N8
Port Gawler SA 787 C5, 791 J9
Port Germein SA 791 H6
Port Gibbon SA 790 F7
Port Giles SA 787 A6, 791 H10
Port Hacking NSW 453 D10
Port Hacking NSW 453 E10, 455 K7, 459 H9
Port Hedland WA 701, 715 H5
Port Hughes SA 790 G8
Port Huon Tas 839 A7, 843 H6
Port Jackson NSW 453 F6, 455 L6, 459 H9
Port Julia SA 787 B5, 791 H9
Port Kembla NSW 455 J9, 456 G3, 458 G10
Port Kenny SA 790 B6
Port Latta Tas 840 C3
Port Lincoln SA 768–769, 790 D9
Port MacDonnell SA 736, 788 G9
Port Macquarie NSW 398, 459 M2, 461 M10
Port Melbourne Vic 335 C4
Port Minlacowie SA 790 G10
Port Moorowie SA 788 A3, 790 G10
Port Neill SA 790 E8
Port Noarlunga SA 786 B10
Port of Brisbane Qld 557 D2
Port Phillip Vic 335 B7, 336 F4, 339 N7
Port Phillip Bay Wine Region Vic 280
Port Pirie SA 769, 791 H6
Port Prime SA 787 C4, 791 J9
Port Rickaby SA 790 G9
Port Roper NT 615 K8
Port Smith WA 712 C9, 715 M2
Port Sorell Tas 818, 844 A4, 841 H5
Port Stephens NSW 455 N1, 459 K5
Port Victoria SA 770, 790 G9
Port Vincent SA 787 A5, 791 H10
Port Wakefield SA 770, 787 B3, 791 J8
Port Warrender WA 713 J2
Port Welshpool Vic 337 P8, 342 A10
Portarlington Vic 278–279, 335 A8, 336 F5, 339 N7
Porters Retreat NSW 454 E7, 456 E1, 458 D9
Portland NSW 454 F4, 458 E7
Portland Vic 280, 338 C8
Portland Bay Vic 338 D8

Portland Downs Qld 565 M10
Portland North Vic 338 C8
Portland Roads Qld 568 E6
Portsea Vic 311, 336 F6, 339 N8
Poseidon Qld 558 B3
Possession Island NP Qld 568 C2
Potato Point NSW 456 E7
Potts Point NSW 453 F6
Pottsville Beach NSW 461 P2
Powell Creek NT 617 H5
Powelltown Vic 311, 337 L3
Powers Creek Vic 338 B3
Powlathanga Qld 560 B2, 565 P2
Powlett Plains Vic 339 K1, 341 K10
Powlett River Vic 337 K7
Prahran Vic 335 D4
Prairie Qld 565 M3
Prairie Qld 567 L7
Prairie Vic 341 L9
Prairie Downs WA 715 J10
Prairiewood NSW 453 A6
Pranjip Vic 344 B6
Pratten Qld 556 A7, 559 K8
Precipice NP Qld 559 H3
Premaydena Tas 839 F6, 843 M6
Premer NSW 458 E2, 460 E10
Premier Downs WA 711 C6
Prenti Downs WA 709 N5
Preolenna Tas 840 D5
Preston Qld 558 C6
Preston Tas 840 F6
Preston Vic 335 C3, 336 G3, 339 P6, 344 A10
Preston Beach WA 705 B8, 706 B6
Pretty Bend Qld 560 E2
Pretty Plains Qld 563 K10, 565 L2
Prevelly WA 706 A8
Price SA 787 B4, 791 H8
Priestdale Qld 555 G8
Primrose Sands Tas 839 E5, 843 L5
Prince Frederick Harbour WA 713 H3
Prince Regent NR WA 713 H4
Princetown Vic 339 H9
Princhester Qld 561 H7
Priors Pocket Qld 555 A8
Prooinga Vic 341 H5
Proserpine Qld 517, 560 F2
Prospect NSW 453 A5
Prospect Qld 558 A2, 567 P2
Prospect Qld 562 G9
Prospect SA 786 D5
Prospect Tas 844 E6, 841 K6
Prospect Reservoir NSW 453 A5
Proston Qld 556 A1, 559 K4
Prubi Qld 565 J6
Prungle NSW 464 E4
Pucawan NSW 465 N4
Puckapunyal Vic 339 P3, 344 A7
Pudman Creek NSW 454 B10, 456 C3
Pukatja (Ernabella) SA 789 E1
Pularumpi NT 614 C2

Pulgamurtie NSW 462 C4
Pullabooka NSW 465 N3
Pullagaroo WA 708 G9
Pulletop NSW 465 N7
Pullut Vic 340 E8
Punchbowl NSW 453 C7
Pungalina NT 617 N3
Punjaub Qld 562 B7
Puntabie SA 790 B4
Punthari SA 787 F6, 791 L10
Pura Pura Vic 339 H6
Puralka Vic 338 B6
Pureba CP SA 790 B4
Purga Qld 556 D6, 557 A4, 559 M7
Purlewaugh NSW 458 D1, 460 D10
Purnanga NSW 462 E4
Purnim Vic 338 F8
Purnong SA 791 L10
Purnululu CR WA 713 M8
Purnululu NP WA 688, 713 N7
Purple Downs SA 790 F1
Putney NSW 453 D5
Putty NSW 455 H2, 458 G6
Pyalong Vic 339 N3
Pyengana Tas 841 N6
Pygery SA 790 D6
Pymble NSW 453 D4, 455 K6, 459 H8
Pyramid Qld 560 D3
Pyramid WA 714 G6
Pyramid Hill Vic 341 L9
Pyramul NSW 454 D2, 458 D6
Pyrmont NSW 453 E6

Q

Quaama NSW 456 E8
Quairading WA 705 G5, 706 E4
Qualco SA 791 M8
Quambatook Vic 341 J8
Quambetook Qld 565 H4
Quambone NSW 463 P6
Quamby Qld 564 E2
Quamby Brook Tas 844 B7, 841 H7
Quanbun WA 713 H9
Quanda NR NSW 463 M7
Quandialla NSW 465 P4
Quandong NSW 462 C8
Quangallin WA 705 F9, 706 E7
Quantong Vic 338 E2
Quarrum NR WA 706 D9
Quarry View NSW 462 D4
Quartz Hill NT 619 K5
Queanbeyan NSW 477 E4, 456 C5, 457 F3
Queanbeyan River NSW 477 F4
Queen Victoria Spring NR WA 707 P1, 709 P10, 711 A5
Queens Beach Qld 560 E2
Queens Domain Tas 838 D5
Queens Park NSW 453 F7
Queens Park WA 704 F6
Queenscliff NSW 453 G4

Queenscliff Vic **280**, 335 A10, 336 F5, 339 N7
Queensland **482–483**
Queensport Qld 555 E4
Queenstown SA 786 C4
Queenstown Tas **818**, 840 D10
Questa Park NSW 462 E4
Quibet Qld 558 E7
Quida Downs Qld 558 C4
Quilpie Qld **543**, 567 L5
Quinalow Qld 556 A4, 559 K6
Quindanning WA 705 D8, 706 D6
Quindinup NR WA 706 D9
Quinninup WA 706 C9
Quinns Rocks WA 705 B4, 706 B4
Quinyambie SA 791 N1
Quirindi NSW **398**, 458 G2
Quobba WA 708 B2
Quondong Vale SA 791 M6
Quorn SA **770**, 791 H4

R

RAAF East Sale Vic 342 C7
RAAF Golf and Bowls Club NT 612 D5
Rabbit Flat Roadhouse NT **599**, 616 B9
Raglan NSW 454 E5, 458 D7
Raglan Qld 561 K9
Raglan Vic 339 J4
Railton Tas 844 A5, 840 G6
Rainbar NSW 463 H3
Rainbow Vic 340 E8
Rainbow Beach Qld 556 E1, 559 N4
Rainbow Flat NSW 459 L3
Rainbow Valley CR NT 619 H7
Rainsby Qld 565 N5
Rainworth Qld 555 B5
Raleigh NSW 461 N8
Raluana Vic 338 G2
Ralvona NSW 465 M7
Ramco SA 791 M8
Raminea Tas 839 A8, 843 H7
Ramingining NT 615 K4
Ramornie NP NSW 461 M6
Ramsgate NSW 453 D8
Ranceby Vic 337 L6
Rand NSW 465 L7
Randwick NSW 453 F7
Ranelagh Tas 839 A6, 843 J6
Ranga Tas 841 J3
Ranges Valley Qld 564 G5
Rangeview Qld 560 D2
Ranken NT 617 M8
Rankins Springs NSW 465 L3
Rannes Qld 561 J10
Ransome Qld 555 G5
Rapid Bay SA 787 C8, 788 B4
Rapid Creek NT 612 D3
Rapid Creek NT 612 E4
Rappville NSW 461 M4
Rathdowney Qld 556 D7, 557 B8, 559 M8

Rathscar Vic 339 J3
Raukkan SA 787 F8, 788 B6
Ravendale NSW 462 C6
Ravenshoe Qld 563 L6, 569 D9
Ravensthorpe WA 707 J7
Ravenswood Qld 560 A7, 565 N7
Ravenswood Qld 560 C2, 563 N10
Ravenswood Vic 339 L2
Ravenswood WA 705 B7, 706 C5
Ravenswood South Vic 339 L3
Ravensworth NSW 459 H4
Ravine des Casoars WPA SA 788 B1
Rawbelle Qld 559 J2
Rawdon Vale NSW 459 J3
Rawlinna WA 711 C6
Rawson Vic 337 P4, 342 A6
Ray Qld 567 K4
Raymond Terrace NSW **398**, 455 M2, 459 J5
Raymore Qld 567 J4
Raywood Vic 339 L1, 341 L10
Razorback NR NSW 454 C7, 456 C2, 458 C9
Recherche Archipelago NR WA 707 N8
Red Bank Qld 560 G9
Red Bluff WA 708 C7
Red Cap Creek Vic 338 B5
Red Cliffs SA 790 G9
Red Cliffs Vic **292**, 340 E2
Red Creek WA 709 D2
Red Hill ACT 477 D3
Red Hill Qld 555 C5
Red Hill Vic 337 H6, 339 P8
Red Hill WA 714 E7
Red Hills Tas 844 B7, 841 H7
Red Lake WA 707 L6
Red Range NSW 461 K6
Red Rock NSW 461 N6
Redbank Qld 557 B3
Redbank Qld 559 H3
Redbank Vic 339 J3
Redbank Plains Qld 557 B4
Redbournberry NSW 455 K1, 459 H5
Redcastle Vic 339 N2
Redcliffe Qld 556 E5, 557 D1, 559 N6
Redcliffe Qld 558 G1, 561 H10
Redcliffe SA 787 G1, 791 L7
Redcliffe WA 704 E4
Redesdale Vic 339 M3
Redfern NSW 453 E7
Redford Qld 558 C4
Redhead NSW 455 M3, 459 J6
Redhill SA 787 C1, 791 J7
Redland Bay Qld 557 E4
Redmond WA 706 E9
Redpa Tas 840 A4
Redrock Qld 560 D7
Redwood Park SA 786 F3
Reedy Corner NSW 463 N7
Reedy Creek SA 788 D8

Reedy Creek Vic 339 P4, 344 A8
Reedy Dam Vic 340 G8
Reedy Marsh Tas 844 B6, 841 H6
Reedy Spring Qld 563 K10, 565 M2
Reedys WA 709 H6
Reefton NSW 465 N4
Reekara Tas 840 F1
Regatta Point Tas 842 B1, 840 C10
Regency Park SA 786 D4
Regents Park NSW 453 C6
Regents Park Qld 555 D10
Reichardt Creek NT 612 F8
Reid ACT 477 D3
Reid WA 711 F6
Reid River Qld 560 C1, 563 N10
Reids Creek Vic 344 G4
Reids Flat NSW 454 B8, 456 C2, 458 C9
Reindeer Lake NT 616 C8
Relbia Tas 844 E6, 841 K7
Remington NSW 463 N3
Remlap WA 706 E1, 708 G10
Rendelsham SA 788 F9
Renison Bell Tas 840 D8
Renmark SA **770–771**, 791 N8
Renner Springs NT 617 H5
Rennick Vic 338 A6
Rennie NSW 465 K7
Reola NSW 462 E3
Repton NSW 461 N8
Retreat Qld 567 K2
Retreat Tas 844 E4, 841 K5
Retro Qld 560 E7
Retro Qld 560 E7
Revesby NSW 453 B8
Revesby Heights NSW 453 C8
Revilo Qld 558 D5
Reynella SA 786 C10, 787 D7, 788 A5, 791 J10
Reynolds Neck Tas 844 B9, 841 H8
Rheban Tas 839 F3, 843 M3
Rheola Vic 339 K2
Rhodes NSW 453 C5
Rhyll Vic 337 J6
Rhyndaston Tas 839 C2, 843 K3
Rhynie SA 787 D3, 791 J8
Riachella Vic 338 G2
Riamukka NSW 459 J1, 461 J10
Riana Tas 840 F5
Rich Avon Vic 338 G1, 340 G10
Richardson ACT 477 D4
Richlands NSW 454 E8, 456 E2, 458 E10
Richlands Qld 555 B8, 557 C3
Richmond NSW **398**, 455 J5, 458 G8
Richmond Qld 565 J3
Richmond SA 786 D6
Richmond Tas **834–835**, 839 D4, 843 K4
Richmond Vic 335 D4
Richmond Downs Qld 558 F5
Richmond Hills Qld 560 A8, 565 P8

Richmond Plains Vic 339 J1, 341 J10
Richmond Range NP NSW 461 L3
Riddells Creek Vic 336 F1, 339 N5
Ridgeland Qld 558 E3
Ridgelands Qld 561 J8
Ridgeway Tas 839 C5, 843 K5
Ridgeway Park Tas 838 C8
Ridgley Tas 840 E5
Rifle Creek Qld 564 C3
Rimbanda Qld 565 K7
Ringarooma Tas 841 M5
Ringwood NT 619 K6
Ringwood Vic 335 F3, 337 J3
Ringwood East Vic 335 F3
Ringwood North Vic 335 F3
Ripplebrook Vic 337 L5
Ripponhurst Vic 338 E7
Risdon Tas 838 E3
Risdon Vale Tas 838 F2, 839 C4, 843 K4
Rita Island Qld 560 D1, 563 P10
River Derwent Tas 838 F7, 839 C5, 842 G3, 843 H3
River Heads Qld 559 M3
River Light SA 787 E4
River Tamar Tas 844 D4, 841 J5
River Torrens SA 786 C5
River View Qld 560 A3, 565 N3
River View Vic 342 B1
Riverdale Qld 565 K3
Riveren NT 616 C5
Riverhills Qld 555 A8
Riverina WA 709 K9
Riverland Wine Region SA **771**
Riverside NSW 462 E7
Riverside Qld 558 C1, 560 D10
Riverslea Vic 342 C7
Riversleigh Qld 558 B5
Riversleigh Qld 562 B9
Riverton SA 787 D3, 791 K8
Riverton WA 704 E7
Rivervale WA 704 E5
Riverview NSW 453 D5
Riverview Qld 563 H8
Riverwood NSW 453 C8
Rivett ACT 477 C4
Rivington Qld 560 C9
Roadvale Qld 557 A6
Robbins Island Tas 840 B3
Robe SA **736–737**, 788 E8
Robertson NSW **374–375**, 455 H10, 456 F3
Robertson Qld 555 D7
Robertson Range WA 715 L9
Robertstown SA 787 F2, 791 K8
Robin Hood Vic 337 L4
Robinhood Qld 563 J8
Robins Qld 565 H6
Robinson River NT 617 N3
Robinvale Vic 340 G3
Rochedale Qld 555 F7, 557 D3
Rochedale South Qld 555 F8
Rocherlea Tas 844 E5, 841 K6

Rochester SA 787 D1, 791 J7
Rochester Vic 339 N1, 341 N10
Rochford Vic 336 F1, 339 N4
Rock Flat NSW 456 C7, 457 F7
Rock Valley NSW 461 N2
Rockbank Vic 336 F3, 339 N6
Rockbrae Qld 556 C7, 559 L8
Rockdale NSW 453 D8
Rockdale Qld 558 F6
Rockhampton Qld **517**, 561 J8
Rockhampton Downs NT 617 K6
Rockingham WA **653**, 705 B6,
   706 B5
Rocklands Qld 562 A10, 564 A1
Rocklands Reservoir Vic 338 D4
Rocklea Qld 555 C7
Rocklea WA 714 G9
Rockleigh SA 787 F6, 791 K10
Rockley NSW 454 D6, 456 D1,
   458 D8
Rocksville Qld 558 A4, 567 P4
Rockvale Qld 565 H3
Rocky Qld 558 B5
Rocky Cape Tas 840 D4
Rocky Cape NP Tas **818**, 840 D4
Rocky Creek NSW 460 F6
Rocky Creek NT 616 A3
Rocky Dam NSW 460 G4
Rocky Glen NSW 460 D9
Rocky Gully WA 706 D9
Rocky Islets NP Qld 563 L2, 569 D2
Rocky Plains NSW 456 B7, 457 D6
Rocky Ponds Qld 560 D1, 563 P10
Rocky River NSW 461 J8
Rocky River SA 788 B2
Rodd Point NSW 453 D6
Rodinga NT 619 H7
Rodney Downs Qld 565 M8
Roebourne WA **702**, 714 F6
Roebuck Bay WA 712 C9
Roebuck Plains WA 712 D8, 715 N1
Roebuck Roadhouse WA 712 D8,
   715 N1
Roeburne Qld 558 G2
Roger Corner SA 790 G10
Roger River Tas 840 B4
Rokeby Qld 565 L3
Rokeby Qld 568 C8
Rokeby Tas 839 D5, 843 K5
Rokeby Vic 337 M4
Rokewood Vic 336 B4, 339 K6
Rokewood Junction Vic 336 B3,
   339 K6
Roland Tas 840 G6
Rollands Plains NSW 459 M1,
   461 M10
Rolleston Qld 558 E1, 560 F10
Rollingstone Qld 563 M9
Roma Qld **504**, 558 F5
Romani NSW 463 J3
Romsey Vic 336 F1, 339 N4
Rooken Glen Qld 560 D9
Rookhurst NSW 459 K3

Rookwood Qld 563 J6, 569 A8
Rooster Point Tas 843 P2
Roper Bar NT 615 J8
Rosa Brook WA 706 B8
Rosalie Qld 555 C5
Rosanna Vic 335 D2
Rose Bay NSW 453 F6
Rose Bay Tas 838 F5
Rose Bay North NSW 453 G6
Rose Hill ACT 477 E5
Rosebank NSW 461 N2
Rosebank Qld 567 P4
Roseberry NSW 461 M2
Roseberth Qld 566 C4
Rosebery NSW 453 E7
Rosebery Tas **819**, 840 D8
Rosebery Vic 340 F8
Rosebery Downs Qld 565 M7
Rosebery East Vic 340 F8
Rosebrook Vic 338 E8
Rosebud Vic **312**, 336 G6, 339 N8
Rosedale NSW 456 C6, 457 E5
Rosedale Qld 559 L1
Rosedale Qld 560 B8, 565 P8
Rosedale Qld 560 G5
Rosedale Vic 342 B7
Rosegarland Tas 839 A3, 843 H4
Rosehill NSW 453 C5
Roselands NSW 453 C7
Rosella Plains Qld 563 K8
Roseneath Vic 338 B4
Rosetta Tas 838 B3
Rosevale Qld 556 C6, 559 M8
Rosevale Qld 558 A6, 567 P6
Rosevale Qld 559 K1, 561 L10
Rosevale Tas 844 D6, 841 J6
Rosevears Tas 844 D5, 841 J6
Roseville NSW 453 E4
Rosewood NSW 462 F8
Rosewood NSW 465 P7, 457 A4
Rosewood NT 616 A2
Rosewood Qld 556 D6, 559 M7
Roseworthy SA 787 D4, 791 K9
Roslyn NSW 454 D9, 456 D3,
   458 D10
Roslynmead Vic 341 M9
Rosny Tas 838 F6
Rosny Park Tas 838 G6
Ross Tas **819**, 844 G10, 841 L9
Ross Creek Vic 336 B2, 339 K5
Ross River NT **608**, 619 J6
Rossarden Tas 841 M8
Rossbridge Vic 338 G5
Rossi NSW 456 D5, 457 G3
Rosslyn Qld 559 K2
Rossmoya Qld 561 J7
Rossmoyne WA 704 D7
Rossville Qld 563 L3, 569 C4
Rostella NSW 463 J1
Rostock Qld 558 G6
Rostrevor SA 786 F5
Rostron Vic 339 H2
Rothbury NSW 455 L1, 459 H5

Roto NSW 463 J10, 465 J1
Rottnest Island WA 705 B5, 706 B4
Round Corner NSW 453 B3
Round Hill NR NSW 463 K10,
   465 K1
Round Lake Vic 338 C2
Rouse Hill NSW 453 A2
Rowella Tas 844 D4, 841 J5
Rowena NSW 460 B6
Rowles Lagoon NR WA 707 K2,
   709 L10
Rowley Shoals Marine Park WA
   715 J1
Rowsley Vic 336 E3, 339 M5
Rowville Vic 335 F5
Roxburgh Downs Qld 564 B6
Roxburgh Park Vic 335 B1
Roxby Downs SA **772**, 790 F1
Roxby Downs SA 790 F1, 792 F10
Roy Hill WA 715 K8
Royal George Tas 841 M8
Royal NP NSW **399**, 453 C10,
   455 K8, 459 H9
Royal Oak NSW 462 D5
Royal Park SA 786 C4
Royal Park Vic 335 C3
Royalla NSW 477 E5, 456 C5,
   457 F3
Royston Qld 558 E6
Rubicon Vic 337 L1, 344 D9
Ruby Vic 337 L6
Ruby Gap Nature Park NT 619 K5
Ruby Plains WA 713 L9
Rubyvale Qld 560 E8
Rudall SA 790 E7
Rudall River NP WA **698–699**,
   715 N8
Ruffy Vic 344 C7
Rufus River NSW 464 A4
Rugby NSW 454 B9, 456 C2,
   458 C10
Rules Beach Qld 559 L1, 561 M10
Rules Point NSW 456 B6, 457 C4
Rum Jungle NT 613 C4, 614 D5
Rumbalara NT 619 J9
Rumula Qld 563 L5, 569 C6
Runcorn Qld 555 E8
Rundle Range NP Qld 561 K9
Running Creek Vic 345 J5
Running Stream NSW 454 E3,
   458 E6
Runnymede Qld 558 C8
Runnymede Qld 565 J2
Runnymede Tas 839 D3, 843 L4
Runnymede Vic 339 N1, 341 N10
Rupanyup Vic 338 F1
Rupanyup North Vic 338 F1,
   340 F10
Rushcutters Bay NSW 453 F6
Rushworth Vic **280–281**, 339 P1,
   341 P10, 344 A5
Russell Lea NSW 453 D6
Russell Park Qld 560 E6

Rutchillo Qld 564 G3
Rutherford NSW 455 L1, 459 J5
Rutherglen Vic **330–331**, 344 F3
Rutland Qld 560 D9
Rutland Park Qld 565 M10, 567 M1
Rutland Plains Qld 562 F3
Rydal NSW 454 F5, 458 E7
Rydalmere NSW 453 C5
Ryde NSW 453 D5
Rye Vic **312**, 336 G6, 339 N8
Rye Park NSW 454 B9, 456 C3,
   458 B10
Ryeford Qld 556 B7, 559 K8
Rylstone NSW **399**, 454 F2, 458 E5
Ryton Vic 337 P7
Rywung Qld 559 H5

S

Saddleworth SA 787 E3, 791 K8
Sadgroves Creek NT 612 D8
Safety Beach Vic 335 E10, 336 G6,
   339 P8
St Albans NSW 455 J4, 458 G7
St Albans Qld 560 F5
St Albans Vic 335 A3
St Albans East Vic 335 B3
St Andrews Vic 337 J2, 344 B10
St Andrews Beach Vic 336 G6,
   339 N8
St Anns Qld 560 C4
St Arnaud Vic 339 H1
St Clair NSW 459 H4
St Clair Vic 337 N2, 344 E10
St Columba Falls SR Tas 841 N6
St Fillans Vic 337 K2, 344 C10
St George Qld **504–505**, 558 E8
St Germains Vic 341 P9, 344 B4
St Helena Is NP Qld 557 E2
St Helens Tas **819**, 841 P6
St Helens Vic 338 E7
St Helens Beach Qld 560 F3
St Helens Plains Vic 338 F2
St Helens Point CA Tas 841 P6
Saint Hilliers Qld 559 H7
St Ives NSW 453 E3
St Ives Chase NSW 453 D3
St James Vic 344 D4
St James WA 704 E6
St Johns Wood Qld 555 B4
St Kilda SA 786 D1, 787 D5, 791 J9
St Kilda Vic 335 C4, 336 G3, 339 P6
St Lawrence Qld 561 H6
St Leonards NSW 453 E5
St Leonards Vic **281**, 335 A9, 336 F5,
   339 N7
St Lucia Qld 555 C6
St Marys NSW 455 J6, 456 G1,
   458 G8
St Marys Tas **819**, 841 P7
St Peters NSW 453 E7
St Peters SA 786 E5
St Vidgeon NT 615 K8
Sale Vic **312**, 342 C7

Salisbury NSW 459 J4
Salisbury Qld 555 D7
Salisbury SA 786 F2, 787 D5, 791 J9
Salisbury Vic 340 D10
Salisbury Downs NSW 462 D3
Salisbury Downs SA 786 E2
Salisbury East SA 786 F2
Salisbury Heights SA 786 F2
Salisbury North SA 786 E1
Salisbury South SA 786 E2
Sallys Flat NSW 454 D2, 458 D6
Salmon Gums WA 707 L6
Salt Creek Qld 568 B9
Salt Creek SA 788 C7
Salt Lake NSW 462 G4
Salt Water Point NT 614 F3
Saltbush Park Qld 560 F6
Salter Point WA 704 D6
Saltwater River Tas 839 E6, 843 L6
Samford Qld 556 D5, 557 B2,
    559 M7
Samford SF Qld 555 A3
Samson WA 704 C8
Samson Well SA 787 G2, 791 L7
Samsonvale Qld 557 B1
San Remo Vic 337 J7
Sanctuary Cove Qld 557 E5
Sandalwood SA 791 M10
Sandergrove SA 787 E8, 788 A6
Sandfire Roadhouse WA 702, 715 L4
Sandfly Tas 839 B5, 843 J5
Sandford Tas 839 D5, 843 L5
Sandford Vic 338 C5
Sandgate NSW 455 M2, 459 J6
Sandgate Qld 555 D1, 556 E5,
    557 C1, 559 N6
Sandhill Lake Vic 341 K7
Sandigo NSW 465 L6
Sandilands SA 787 A4, 791 H9
Sandmount Vic 344 C3
Sandon NSW 461 N5
Sandringham NSW 453 D9
Sandringham Qld 564 C9
Sandringham Vic 335 D6, 337 H4,
    339 P6
Sandsmere Vic 340 B9
Sandspit River FR Tas 839 F3,
    843 M4
Sandstone WA 709 J7
Sandy Bay Tas 838 E8
Sandy Beach NSW 461 N7
Sandy Camp NSW 463 N5
Sandy Creek Vic 345 J4
Sandy Flat NSW 461 K4
Sandy Hill NSW 461 L3
Sandy Hollow NSW 458 F4
Sandy Lake WA 712 E9, 715 P2
Sandy Point NSW 453 B8
Sandy Point NSW 456 E4
Sandy Point Vic 337 M8
Sangar NSW 465 K7
Sanpah NSW 462 A5
Sans Souci NSW 453 D9

Santa Teresa NT 619 J7
Santos Qld 566 G8
Sapphire NSW 461 H5
Sapphire Qld 560 E8
Sardine Creek Vic 343 J4, 345 P9
Sarina Qld 560 G4
Sarina Beach Qld 560 G4
Sarsfield Vic 342 E5, 345 L10
Sassafras NSW 456 F4
Sassafras Tas 844 A5, 840 G6
Saunders Beach Qld 563 N9
Savage River Tas 840 C7
Savage River NP Tas 840 D6
Savernake NSW 465 K7
Sawmill Settlement Vic 344 F8
Sawpit Creek NSW 456 B7, 457 C7
Sawtell NSW 422, 461 N7
Saxa NSW 458 C4
Sayers Lake NSW 462 E9, 464 E1
Scabby Range NP NSW 477 B9,
    457 D4
Scaddan WA 707 L7
Scamander Tas 820, 841 P6
Scamander FR Tas 841 P6
Scarborough WA 704 B3, 705 B5,
    706 C4
Scarsdale Vic 336 B2, 339 K5
Scartwater Qld 560 C4
Sceale Bay SA 790 B6
Scone NSW 399, 458 G3
Scoresby Vic 335 F4
Scoria Qld 559 H1, 561 J10
Scorpion Springs CP SA 788 A10
Scotsburn Vic 336 C2, 339 K5
Scott Creek NT 613 F9, 614 E8
Scott Creek SA 786 F9
Scott Creek CP SA 786 E9
Scott NP WA 706 B8
Scotts Creek Vic 339 H8
Scotts Head NSW 461 N8
Scottsdale Tas 820, 844 G4, 841 L5
Scullin ACT 477 C2
Sea Lake Vic 292, 340 G7
Seabird WA 705 B3, 706 B3
Seabrook Tas 840 E4
Seacliff SA 786 C8
Seacliff Park SA 786 C8
Seacombe Vic 342 D7
Seaford Vic 335 F7, 337 H5, 339 P7
Seaforth NSW 453 F4
Seaforth Qld 560 G3
Seaham NSW 459 J5, 455 M1
Seal Bay CP SA 737, 788 B3
Seal Rocks NSW 459 L4
Seal Rocks SR Tas 820, 840 F3
Seaspray Vic 342 D8
Seaton SA 786 C5
Seaton Vic 342 A6
Seaview Downs SA 786 C8
Sebastapol NSW 465 N5
Sebastian Vic 339 L1
Sebastopol Vic 336 B2, 339 K5
Second Valley SA 787 C8, 788 B5

Sedan SA 787 F5, 791 L9
Sedan Dip Qld 562 E10, 564 F2
Sedgwick Vic 339 M2
Sefton NSW 453 B6
Selbourne Tas 844 C6, 841 J6
Seldom Seen Vic 342 E4, 345 K9
Sellicks Beach SA 787 C8, 788 A5
Selwyn Qld 564 E5
Semaphore SA 786 B3
Semaphore Park SA 786 B4
Separation Creek Vic 336 C7, 339 K9
Serpentine Vic 339 L1, 341 L10
Serpentine WA 705 C6, 706 C5
Serpentine NP WA 705 C6, 706 C5
Serviceton Vic 338 A1, 340 A10
Sesbania Qld 565 J4
Seven Emu NT 617 N2
Seven Hills NSW 453 A4
Seven Hills Qld 555 E5, 557 C2
Seven Mile Beach Tas 839 D5,
    843 L5
Seven Mile Beach PA Tas 839 D4,
    843 L5
Sevenhill SA 787 D2, 791 J8
Seventeen Mile Rocks Qld 555 B7
Seventeen Seventy Qld 561 L10
Severn River NP NSW 461 H4
Seville Vic 337 K3
Seymour Tas 841 P8
Seymour Vic 331, 339 P3, 344 B7
Shackleton WA 706 F4
Shadeville Qld 560 E10
Shadforth NSW 454 C4, 458 C7
Shady Lagoon Qld 562 E7
Shailer Park Qld 555 G9
Shandon Vale Qld 560 A8, 565 N8
Shannon NP WA 654, 706 D9
Shannons Flat NSW 477 C10,
    456 C6, 457 E5
Shark Bay WA 660–663, 708 B3
Shark Bay Marine Park WA 661,
    708 B3
Sharon Point Tas 841 P5
Shaw Vic 337 M2, 344 E10
She Oak Flat SA 787 B5, 791 H9
Sheans Creek Vic 344 C6
Shearwater Tas 844 A4
Sheep Hills Vic 340 F10
Sheffield Tas 820, 840 G6
Sheidow Park SA 786 C9
Sheila Outstation Qld 564 B4
Shelbourne Vic 339 L2
Sheldon Qld 555 G8, 557 D3
Shelford Vic 336 C4, 339 L7
Shelley Vic 345 K4
Shelley WA 704 D7
Shellharbour NSW 375, 455 J9,
    456 G3
Shenandoah NT 616 G3
Shenton Park WA 704 B5
Sheoak Hill CR SA 790 F7
Sheoaks Vic 336 D4, 339 L6
Shepherds Hill RP SA 786 D8

Shepparton Vic 331, 344 C4
Sheringa SA 790 C8
Sherlock SA 788 A8
Sherlock WA 714 G6
Sherwood NSW 461 M9
Sherwood Qld 555 C6
Sherwood WA 709 H5
Sherwood NR NSW 461 N6
Shinfield Qld 560 G4
Shirley Qld 558 E9
Shirley Vic 339 H4
Shoal Bay NSW 455 P1, 459 K5
Shoalhaven Heads NSW 456 G4
Shoalhaven River NSW 456 E4
Shoalwater Islands Marine Park WA
    705 B6, 706 B5
Shooters Hill NSW 454 E7, 456 E1,
    458 E9
Shoreham Vic 337 H6, 339 P8
Shorncliffe Qld 555 E1
Shortys Point Tas 844 E2, 841 K4
Shovel Lake WA 715 M3
Shutehaven Qld 560 F2
Shuttleworth Qld 560 B6, 565 P6
Shy Creek NSW 463 L7
Siam SA 790 F5
Sidmouth Tas 844 C4, 841 J5
Silent Grove WA 713 H7
Silkwood Qld 563 M7, 569 E10
Silky Oak Creek Qld 563 M7
Silvan Vic 337 J3
Silver Hills Qld 565 J3
Silver Plains Qld 563 H1, 568 E8
Silver Spur Qld 559 K10
Silverton NSW 438, 462 A8
Silverwater NSW 453 C5
Simmie Vic 341 N9
Simpson Vic 339 H8
Simpson Desert NT 619 M9
Simpson Desert SA 792 F2
Simpson Desert CP SA 793 H1
Simpson Desert NP Qld 566 A3
Simpson Desert RR SA 784, 792 G3
Simpsons Bay Tas 839 C8, 843 K7
Simson Vic 339 K3
Sinclair Vic 338 C7
Single NP NSW 461 J6
Singleton NSW 400, 455 K1, 459 H5
Singleton NT 617 J9, 619 J1
Sinnamon Park Qld 555 B7
Sir Joseph Banks Group CP SA
    790 F9
Sisters Beach Tas 840 D4
Sisters Creek Tas 840 D4
Skenes Creek Vic 336 B8, 339 K9
Skipton Vic 339 J5
Skye SA 786 F6
Skye Vic 335 F7, 337 H5, 339 P7
Slacks Creek Qld 555 F9, 557 D4
Slade Point Qld 560 G4
Slamannon NSW 462 F8
Slashers Creek Qld 564 E7
Slaty Creek Vic 339 J1, 341 J10

Smeaton Vic 336 C1, 339 K4
Smiggin Holes NSW 456 B7, 457 C7
Smith Islands NP Qld 560 G3
Smithfield NSW 453 A6
Smithfield Qld 559 J9
Smithfield SA 787 D5, 791 K9
Smithton Tas **820**, 840 C3
Smithtown NSW 461 M9
Smithville House NSW 462 A4
Smokers Bank Tas 840 C4
Smoky Bay SA 790 A4
Smoky Creek NSW 465 N5
Smythesdale Vic 336 B2, 339 K5
Snake Creek NT 617 J2
Snake Creek WA 705 E2, 706 D2
Snake Range NP Qld 560 D10
Snake Valley Vic 336 A2, 339 J5
Snowball NSW 456 D6, 457 G5
Snowtown SA 787 C2, 791 J7
Snowy Mountains NSW 457 B7
Snowy River NSW 456 B8, 457 D7
Snowy River Vic 343 H3, 345 N9
Snowy River NP Vic **312**, 343 H3, 345 P8
Snug Tas 839 C6, 843 K6
Sofala NSW **400**, 454 E3, 458 D6
Soil Creek Qld 563 H6
Soldiers Point NSW 455 P1, 459 K5
Somers Vic 337 H6, 339 P8
Somers Park Vic 337 L2, 344 D10
Somerset Qld 560 B1, 563 M10, 565 P1
Somerset Qld 565 L9
Somerset Qld 568 C2
Somerset Tas 840 E4
Somerset Dam Qld 556 C4, 559 M6
Somerton NSW 460 G9
Somerton Vic 335 C1, 336 G2, 339 P5, 842 A10
Somerton Park SA 786 C7
Somerville Qld 562 G10, 565 J2
Somerville Vic 337 H5, 339 P7
Sophie Downs WA 713 M9
Sorell Tas **835**, 839 D4, 843 L4
Sorrel Hills Qld 561 H9
Sorrento Vic **312–313**, 336 F6, 339 N8
Sorrento WA 704 A2
Soudan NT 617 N8
South Alligator NT 613 G3, 614 F4
South Alligator River NT 613 G2, 614 F4
South Arm Tas 839 D6, 843 K6
South Australia **720–721**
South Bank Qld 555 C5
South Blackwater Qld 560 F9
South Brisbane Qld 555 C5
South Bruny Island Tas 843 K8
South Bruny NP Tas **835**, 839 C9, 843 J8
South Burnett Wine Region Qld **505**
South Canberra ACT 456 C5, 457 F2

South Coast Wine Region NSW **375**
South Comongin Qld 567 L6
South Coogee NSW 453 F7
South Cumberland Islands NP Qld 561 H3
South East Forest NP NSW 456 D9
South-East Queensland Wine Region Qld **505**
South End Qld 561 L9
South Eneabba NR WA 706 B1, 708 D10
South Flinders Ranges SA 791 J4
South Forest Tas 840 C4
South Franklin Tas 839 A6, 843 H6
South Fremantle WA 704 B8
South Galway Qld 567 H3
South Gap SA 791 H3
South Glen Qld 559 H7
South Grafton NSW 461 M5
South Guildford WA 704 F4
South Head Qld 563 H9
South Hobart Tas 838 C8
South Island NP Qld 561 J5
South Ita NSW 462 B10, 464 B1
South Johnstone Qld 563 M6, 569 E9
South Kempsey NSW 459 M1, 461 M9
South Kilkerran SA 787 A4, 791 H9
South Kumminin WA 706 F5
South Lake WA 704 C9
South Melbourne Vic 335 C4
South Mission Beach Qld 563 M7, 569 E10
South Mount Cameron Tas 841 N4
South Nietta Tas 840 F6
South Perth WA 704 D5
South Riana Tas 840 F5
South Springfield Tas 844 G4, 841 L5
South Stradbroke Island Qld 556 F6
South Trayning WA 706 F3
South Turramurra NSW 453 D4
South West Rocks NSW **422–423**, 461 N9
Southend SA 788 F8
Southern Beekeepers NR WA 706 B2, 708 D10
Southern Cross Qld 560 B2, 563 M10, 565 P2
Southern Cross WA **654**, 707 H3
Southern Hills WA 707 N5
Southern River WA 704 F9
Southern Tasmanian Wine Regions Tas **835**
Southport Qld 556 F7, 557 F6, 559 N8
Southport Tas 839 A9, 843 H8
Southwest CA Tas 842 B4
Southwest NP Tas **829**, 842 F7
Southwood NP Qld 559 H7
Spalding SA 791 J7
Spalford Tas 840 F5
Spargo Creek Vic 336 D1, 339 L5

Spearwood WA 704 B9
Speddingup WA 707 M7
Speed Vic 340 F6
Speewa Vic 341 J5
Spence ACT 477 D2
Spencer Gulf SA 790 F8
Spencers Brook WA 705 E4, 706 D4
Spicer Flat SA 787 A5, 791 H9
Spicers Creek NSW 458 C4
Spirabo NP NSW 461 K4
Split Rock Qld 562 B10, 564 B1
Spotswood Vic 335 B4
Sprent Tas 840 F6
Spreyton Qld 564 G4
Spreyton Tas 840 G5
Spring ACT 477 D5
Spring Beach Tas 839 F2, 843 M3
Spring Creek NT 617 M2
Spring Creek Qld 556 B7, 559 L8
Spring Creek Qld 563 K8
Spring Creek WA 713 N6
Spring Grove Qld 558 F6
Spring Hill NSW 454 C4, 458 C7
Spring Hill Qld 555 C5
Spring Hill Qld 558 E1, 560 E10
Spring Hill Vic 339 M4
Spring Mount Qld 558 G8
Spring Plain NSW 460 C6
Spring Plains Qld 565 K9
Spring Ridge NSW 458 C4
Spring Ridge NSW 458 F1, 460 F10
Spring Vale Qld 560 B9, 565 P9
Spring Valley Qld 565 L3
Springbank Vic 336 C2, 339 L5
Springbrook Qld 557 E8
Springbrook NP Qld 556 E7, 557 E8, 559 N8
Springdale NSW 465 N5
Springfield Qld 558 D6
Springfield Qld 563 K7
Springfield Qld 567 J4
Springfield SA 786 E7
Springfield Tas 838 B4
Springfield Tas 844 G4, 841 L5
Springhurst Vic 344 F4
Springside Qld 556 A6, 559 K7
Springsure Qld 560 E10
Springton SA 787 F5, 791 K9
Springvale Qld 560 C7
Springvale Qld 563 K4, 569 B4
Springvale Qld 564 E9
Springvale Vic 335 E5, 337 H4, 339 P6
Springvale WA 713 L8
Springvale South Vic 335 E5
Springwood NSW 455 H6, 456 F1, 458 F8
Springwood NSW **400**, 464 B2
Springwood Qld 555 F9, 557 D4
Staaten River NP Qld 562 G5
Staceys Bridge Vic 337 P7, 342 A9
Stafford Qld 555 C3, 557 C2
Stafford Heights Qld 555 C3

Staghorn Flat Vic 345 H4
Stagmount Qld 565 N7
Stamford Qld 565 L4
Stanage Qld 561 H6
Stanborough NSW 461 H6
Standley Chasm NT 618 G6
Stanhope Vic 339 P1, 341 P10, 344 A5
Stanhope Park NSW 453 A3
Stanley Tas **821**, 840 C3
Stanley Vic 344 G5
Stanley Park NSW 455 J5, 458 G7
Stannifer NSW 461 H6
Stannum NSW 461 J4
Stansbury SA 787 A6, 791 H10
Stanthorpe Qld **505**, 556 B9, 559 L9
Stanwell Qld 561 J8
Stanwell Park NSW 455 K8, 456 G2, 458 G10
Stapylton Qld 557 D4
Star Qld 563 M9
Starcke Qld 563 K2, 568 G10, 569 C2
Starcke NP Qld 563 K2, 568 G10, 569 C2
Stavely Vic 338 F5
Staverton Tas 840 F6
Stawell Vic **281**, 338 G3
Steiglitz Vic 336 D3, 339 L6
Stenhouse Bay SA 788 A2
Stephens Creek NSW 462 B8
Stepney SA 786 E5
Steppes Tas 843 H1, 841 J10
Stieglitz Tas 841 P6
Stirling NT 619 H2
Stirling Qld 558 E4
Stirling Qld 562 F6
Stirling SA 786 F8, 787 D6, 791 K10
Stirling Vic 342 F4, 345 L9
Stirling WA 704 C3
Stirling North SA 791 H5
Stirling Range NP WA **654**, 706 F9
Stirrat Qld 561 K9
Stockdale Vic 342 C6
Stockinbingal NSW 465 P5
Stockleigh Qld 557 C5
Stockmans Reward Vic 337 M2, 344 E9
Stockport Qld 564 D7
Stockport SA 787 D4, 791 J9
Stockton NSW 455 M2, 459 J6
Stockyard Gully NP WA **655**
Stockyard Hill Vic 339 J5
Stokes Bay SA 788 B3
Stokes NP WA **655**, 707 K8
Stone Hut SA 791 J6
Stonecraft Qld 558 G2
Stonefield SA 787 F4, 791 L9
Stonehaven Vic 336 D5, 339 L7
Stonehenge NSW 461 J6
Stonehenge Qld 565 K10, 567 K1
Stones Corner Qld 555 D6
Stoneville WA 707 L2

Stoneyford Vic 339 J8
Stonor Tas 839 D1, 843 K2
Stony Creek NSW 458 D5
Stony Creek SA 792 A3
Stony Creek Vic 337 M7
Stony Point Vic 337 H6, 339 P8
Stony Rivulet Tas 839 E2, 843 L3
Store Creek NSW 454 B2, 458 C6
Storm Bay Tas 839 D7, 843 L7
Storys Creek Tas 841 M7
Stowport Tas 840 F5
Stradbroke Vic 342 C8
Stradbroke West Vic 342 C8
Strahan Tas **821**, 842 B1, 840 C10
Stratford NSW 459 K4
Stratford Qld 563 L5, 569 D7
Stratford Vic 342 C6
Strath Creek Vic 339 P4, 344 B8
Strathalbyn Qld 560 D2
Strathalbyn SA **772**, 787 E7, 788 A6, 791 K10
Strathallan Vic 341 N9
Stratham WA 705 B9, 706 B7
Strathaven Qld 563 H2, 568 D10
Strathblane Tas 839 A8, 843 H7
Strathbogie NSW 461 J5
Strathbogie Qld 560 D2
Strathbogie Vic 344 D6
Strathbogie Ranges Vic 344 C7
Strathbowen Qld 560 D3
Strathburn Qld 562 G1, 568 D9
Strathdownie Vic 338 B5
Strathearn SA 791 M3
Strathelbiss Qld 564 D7
Strathern NSW 463 J2
Strathewen Vic 337 J2, 344 B10
Strathfield NSW 453 C6
Strathfield Qld 560 F5
Strathfield Qld 564 F4
Strathfield South NSW 453 C6
Strathfield West NSW 453 C6
Strathfieldsaye Vic 339 M2
Strathfillan Qld 565 J6
Strathgordon Tas 842 E4
Strathkellar Vic 338 E5
Strathlea Vic 339 L3
Strathleven Qld 563 H4
Strathmay Qld 562 G2, 568 D10
Strathmerton Vic 344 C2
Strathmore Qld 560 D3
Strathmore Qld 562 G7
Strathmore Qld 565 L8
Strathmore Vic 335 C3
Strathpark Qld 563 H10, 565 J1
Strathpine Qld 555 B1, 556 D5, 557 C1, 559 M6
Stratton Vic 340 F6
Streaky Bay SA **772**, 790 B5
Streatham Vic 339 H5
Strelley WA 715 J5
Stretton Qld 555 E9
Strickland Tas 842 G2
Striped Lake WA 709 N2

Stromlo Pine Forest ACT 477 C3
Stroud NSW **400**, 459 K4
Stroud Road NSW 459 K4
Strzelecki Vic 337 L6
Strzelecki Desert SA 793 L6
Strzelecki NP Tas **822**, 841 J3, 841 N1
Strzelecki RR SA 793 L7
Stuart Qld 563 N9
Stuart Creek SA 792 G9
Stuart Mill Vic 339 H2
Stuart Park NT 612 C8
Stuart Town NSW 454 B2, 458 C6
Stuarts Point NSW 461 M9
Stuarts Well NT 618 G7
Studfield Vic 335 F4
Sturt SA 786 C8
Sturt Gorge RP SA 786 D8
Sturt Meadows WA 709 L8
Sturt NP NSW **430**, 462 B2
Sturt River SA 786 E8
Sturt Stony Desert SA 793 K4
Sturt Vale SA 791 M6
Sturts Meadows NSW 462 B6
Styx Qld 561 H7
Subiaco WA 704 C5
Success WA 704 D10
Sudley Qld 568 C6
Sue City Camp NSW 456 A6, 457 C5
Suffolk Park NSW 461 P2
Sugar River NSW 459 J2
Suggan Buggan Vic 343 H2, 345 N7
Sullivan WA 708 E8
Sullivans Vic 337 P3, 342 A6
Sulphur Creek Tas 840 F5
Summer Hill NSW 453 D7
Summerfield Vic 339 L1, 341 L10
Summertown SA 786 G7
Summervale Qld 567 N2
Sumner Qld 555 A8
Sunbury Vic 336 F2, 339 N5
Sunday Creek NT 614 G10, 616 G2
Sundown Qld 563 K7, 569 B10
Sundown NP Qld **505**, 556 A9, 559 K9
Sunny Corner NSW 454 E4, 458 E7
Sunnybank Qld 555 E8, 557 C3
Sunnybank Hills Qld 555 D8
Sunnyside NSW 461 K3
Sunnyside Tas 844 A5, 840 G6
Sunrise Qld 558 D3
Sunset Vic 340 A5
Sunset Country Vic 340 B3
Sunset Strip NSW 462 C8
Sunshine Vic 335 B4, 336 G3, 339 N6
Sunshine Coast Qld **506**, 556 E3, 559 N5
Suplejack NT 616 B7
Surat Qld 558 F6
Surbiton Qld 560 C8
Surface Hill NSW 461 L4

Surfers Paradise Qld 556 F7, 557 F6, 559 N8
Surges Bay Tas 839 A7, 843 J7
Surrey Hills Vic 335 E3
Surry Hills NSW 453 E6
Surveyors Bay Tas 839 B8, 843 J7
Surveyors Lake NSW 462 F9
Sussex NSW 463 L7
Sussex Inlet NSW 456 F4
Sutherland NSW 453 C9, 455 K7, 456 G2, 459 H9
Sutherland Vic 339 H1, 341 H10
Sutherlands SA 787 F3, 791 K8
Sutton NSW 477 F1, 456 C4, 457 F2
Sutton Vic 341 H7
Sutton Grange Vic 339 M3
Swan Bay NSW 455 N1, 459 K5
Swan Bay Vic 336 F5
Swan Hill Vic **293**, 341 J6
Swan Marsh Vic 339 J8
Swan Reach SA **772–773**, 787 G5, 791 L9
Swan Reach Vic 342 F6
Swan Reach CP SA 787 G5, 791 L9
Swan River WA 704 C6, 705 C5
Swan Vale NSW 461 J6
Swan Vale Qld 567 K1
Swan Valley Wine Region WA **655**
Swanbourne WA 704 B5
Swanlean Qld 565 P6
Swanpool Vic 344 E6
Swansea NSW 455 M3, 459 J6
Swansea Tas **836**, 843 N1, 841 N10
Swanwater Vic 339 H1, 341 H10
Swanwater West Vic 339 H1, 341 H10
Swifts Creek Vic 342 F3, 345 L8
Swim Creek Plains NT 613 F2, 614 E4
Sydenham NSW 453 E7
Sydenham Vic 335 A2, 336 F2, 339 N5
Sydenham Inlet Vic 343 K6
Sydenham West Vic 336 F2, 339 N5
Sydney NSW **352–355**, 453 E6, 455 K6, 459 H9
Sydney Harbour NP NSW **400–401**, 453 G5
Sylvania NSW 453 D9
Sylvania WA 715 K10
Sylvania Heights NSW 453 D9
Sylvania Waters NSW 453 D9
Syndal Vic 335 E4
Synnot Range WA 713 H6

T
Tabba Tabba WA 715 H6
Tabberabbera Vic 342 D5, 345 K10
Tabbimoble NSW 461 N4
Tabbimoble Swamp NP NSW 461 N4
Tabbita NSW 465 K4

Table Top NSW 465 M8
Tableland WA 713 K7
Tabletop Qld 562 G7
Tabletop Qld 563 M9
Tabor Vic 338 E6
Tabourie Lake NSW 456 F5
Tabratong NSW 463 N8
Tabulam NSW 461 L3
Taggerty Vic 337 L1, 344 D9
Tahara Vic 338 D6
Tahara West Vic 338 C5
Tahmoor NSW 455 H8, 456 F2, 458 F10
Tahune FR Tas 843 H6
Taigum Qld 555 D2
Tailem Bend SA **737**, 788 A7, 791 L10
Takone Tas 840 D5
Talarm NSW 461 M8
Talaroo Qld 563 J7
Talavera Qld 560 A1, 563 L10, 565 N1
Talawa Tas 841 M6
Talawanta NSW 463 M2
Talawanta Qld 562 D8
Talbingo NSW 456 A5, 457 B4, 465 P7
Talbingo Reservoir NSW 457 C4
Talbot Vic 339 K3
Talbot Well NT 616 B7
Talbragar River NSW 458 B4
Taldora Qld 562 E9
Taldra SA 791 N9
Taleeban NSW 465 L3
Talgarno Vic 345 J3
Talia SA 790 C6
Talisker WA 708 D4
Tallageira Vic 338 A2
Tallalara NSW 462 F5
Tallandoon Vic 345 J5
Tallangatta Vic 345 J4
Tallangatta East Vic 345 J4
Tallangatta Valley Vic 345 K4
Tallaringa CP SA 789 G5, 792 A7
Tallarook Vic 339 P3, 344 A8
Tallebudgera Qld 557 F7
Tallebudgera Beach Qld 557 F7
Tallebung NSW 463 L9, 465 L1
Tallering WA 708 E7
Tallimba NSW 465 M3
Tallong NSW 454 F10, 456 E3
Tallygaroopna Vic 344 C4
Talmalmo NSW 465 N8
Talwood Qld 558 G9
Talyawalka NSW 462 E9
Tamala WA 708 B5
Tamarama NSW 453 F7
Tamarang NSW 458 E2
Tambar Springs NSW 458 E1, 460 E10
Tambellup WA 706 E8
Tambo Qld **506**, 558 A2
Tambo Crossing Vic 342 F4, 345 L9

Tambo Upper Vic 342 F6
Tamboon Vic 343 L5
Tamborine Qld 556 E6, 557 D5, 559 N8
Tamborine NP Qld 556 D6, 557 D5, 559 M8
Tambua NSW 463 J7
Taminick Vic 344 E5
Tamleugh Vic 344 C5
Tamleugh North Vic 344 C5
Tamleugh West Vic 344 C5
Tammin WA 705 G4, 706 E4
Tamrookum Qld 557 B7
Tamrookum Qld 557 C7
Tamworth NSW 423, 458 G1, 460 G9
Tanah Merah Qld 555 G10
Tanami Desert NT 616 D9
Tanami Downs NT 616 B9
Tanby Qld 561 K8
Tandarook Vic 339 H8
Tandarra Vic 339 L1, 341 L10
Tanderra Qld 558 D1
Tandou NSW 462 C10, 464 C1
Tangadee WA 709 H2
Tangalooma Qld 556 F4, 559 N6
Tangambalanga Vic 345 H4
Tangorin Qld 565 L5
Tanja NSW 456 E8
Tanjil Bren Vic 337 N3
Tanjil South Vic 337 N5
Tankerton Vic 337 J6
Tanners Spring NSW 458 A5
Tannum Sands Qld 561 L9
Tansey Qld 556 B1, 559 L4
Tantangara Reservoir NSW 456 B6, 457 D4
Tantanoola SA 788 F9
Tantawangalo NP NSW 456 D8, 457 G9
Tanumbirini NT 617 J2
Tanunda SA 773, 787 E4, 791 K9
Tanwood Vic 339 J3
Taperoo SA 786 C3
Taplan SA 791 N9
Tara NSW 463 H5
Tara Qld 559 H6
Taradale Vic 339 M3
Tarago NSW 456 D4
Tarago Vic 337 L4
Tarago Reservoir Vic 337 L4
Taragoro SA 790 E7
Taralba NSW 463 M2
Taralga NSW 454 E9, 456 E2, 458 E10
Tarana NSW 454 F5, 458 E8
Taranna Tas 839 F6, 843 M6
Taravale Qld 563 M9
Tarawi NR NSW 464 A3
Tarban NSW 461 K3
Tarcombe Vic 344 B7
Tarcoola SA 790 B1
Tarcoon NSW 463 L4

Tarcowie SA 791 J6
Tarcutta NSW 465 N6
Tardie WA 708 E7
Tardun WA 708 E8
Taree NSW 401, 459 L3
Taree Qld 560 A8, 565 N8
Tareleton Tas 840 G5
Tarella NSW 462 E6
Taren Point NSW 453 D9
Targa Tas 844 F5, 841 L6
Tarin Rock WA 706 F6
Tarin Rock NR WA 706 F6
Taringa Qld 555 B5, 557 C3
Taringo Downs NSW 463 J8
Tarlee SA 787 E4, 791 K8
Tarlo NSW 454 E10, 456 E3
Tarlo River NP NSW 454 F9, 456 E3, 458 E10
Tarlton Downs NT 619 M4
Tarmoola Qld 558 E7
Tarmoola WA 709 L8
Tarnagulla Vic 339 K2
Tarnma SA 787 E3, 791 K8
Tarnook Vic 344 D5
Taroborah Qld 560 E8
Tarome Qld 556 C7, 559 M8
Tarong NP Qld 556 B3, 559 L5
Taroom Qld 506, 558 G3
Taroona Tas 839 C5, 843 K5
Tarpeena SA 788 F10
Tarra Valley Vic 337 P7, 342 A9
Tarra–Bulga NP Vic 342 A8
Tarragal Vic 338 C8
Tarragindi Qld 555 D6
Tarragona Qld 565 L6
Tarraleah Tas 842 F2
Tarranginnie Vic 340 C10
Tarrango Vic 340 D3
Tarranyurk Vic 340 E9
Tarraville Vic 342 B9
Tarrawingee Vic 344 F5
Tarrayoukyan Vic 338 C4
Tarrenlea Vic 338 D5
Tarrina Qld 558 A2, 567 P2
Tarrington Vic 338 E6
Tarrion NSW 463 M4
Tartrus Qld 560 G7
Tarvano Qld 565 K5
Tarwin East Vic 337 N7
Tarwin Lower Vic 337 L8
Tarwong NSW 464 G3
Tarzali Qld 563 L6, 569 D9
Tasman NSW 463 H9
Tasman Arch SR Tas 836
Tasman NP Tas 839 E7/G7, 843 M7
Tasmania 797–799
Tatham NSW 461 N3
Tathra NSW 375, 456 E8
Tathra NP WA 706 B1, 708 D10
Tatong Vic 344 E6
Tatura Vic 332, 339 P1, 341 P10, 344 B5
Tatyoon Vic 338 G5

Tatyoon North Vic 339 H5
Taunton Qld 559 L1, 561 L10
Tawallah NT 617 L2
Tawonga Vic 342 C1, 345 J6
Tayene Tas 844 G5, 841 L6
Taylors Flat NSW 454 B8, 456 C2, 458 C10
Taylors Lakes Vic 335 A2
Tchelery NSW 464 G5
Tea Gardens NSW 455 P1, 459 K5
Tea Tree Tas 839 C3, 843 K4
Tea Tree Gully SA 786 G3
Teal Point Vic 341 L7
Teatree Outstation SA 791 L1
Tebin Qld 567 L5
Tecoma Vic 335 G4
Teddywaddy Vic 341 J9
Teddywaddy West Vic 341 H9
Teds Beach Tas 842 E4
Teesdale Vic 336 C4, 339 L7
Tego Qld 558 B9
Teilta NSW 462 A6
Telangatuk East Vic 338 D3
Telegraph Point NSW 459 M1, 461 M10
Telfer Mine WA 715 N7
Telford SA 793 J10
Telford Vic 344 D3
Telleraga NSW 460 D5
Telopea NSW 453 C5
Telopea Downs Vic 340 B9
Telowie Gorge CP SA 791 J6
Temma Tas 840 A5
Temora NSW 450, 465 N4
Tempe NSW 453 E7
Tempe Downs NT 618 F7
Templestowe Vic 337 H3, 339 P6, 344 A10
Templestowe Lower Vic 335 E3
Templeton Qld 562 G8
Templin Qld 557 A6
Tempy Vic 340 F6
Ten Mile Vic 337 N1, 344 E9
Tenham Qld 567 J3
Tennant Creek NT 599, 617 H8
Tennappera Qld 566 G8
Tennyson NSW 453 D5
Tennyson Qld 555 C6
Tennyson SA 786 B4
Tennyson Vic 341 M9
Tent Creek NSW 461 K4
Tent Hill NSW 461 J5
Tent Hill SA 791 H4
Tent Island NR WA 714 C7
Tenterden NSW 461 J7
Tenterden WA 706 E9
Tenterfield NSW 423, 461 K3
Tepko SA 787 F6, 791 K10
Terang Vic 338 G7
Teridgerie NSW 460 B9
Teringie SA 786 F6
Termeil NSW 456 F5
Tero Creek NSW 462 D4

Terowie NSW 463 P9
Terowie SA 773, 791 K6
Terragong NSW 458 F3
Terrey Hills NSW 453 E2, 455 K6, 459 H8
Terrick Terrick Qld 567 N2
Terrick Terrick Vic 341 L9
Terrick Terrick NP Vic 341 L9
Terrigal NSW 401, 455 L5, 459 J7
Terry Hie Hie NSW 460 E6
Teryawynia NSW 462 E8
Tessellated Pavement SR Tas 836, 839 G6, 843 M6
Tetoora Road Vic 337 L6
Teurika NSW 462 D2
Teutonic WA 709 L7
Teviot Qld 565 J6
Teviotville Qld 557 A6
Tewantin Qld 556 E2, 559 M5
Tewkesbury Tas 840 E5
Texas Qld 506, 559 J10
Texas Qld 560 A8, 565 P8
Texas Downs WA 713 N7
Thagoona Qld 557 A4
Thalia Vic 341 H9
Thallon Qld 558 F9
Thane Qld 556 A7, 559 K8
Thangoo WA 712 D9, 715 N2
Thangool Qld 559 H1, 561 J10
Thargomindah Qld 543, 567 K8
Tharwa ACT 477 D5, 456 C5, 457 E3
The Banca Tas 841 M4
The Bark Hut Inn NT 613 E4, 614 E5
The Basin NSW 453 F1
The Basin Vic 335 G3
The Basin NR NSW 461 H7
The Bluff NSW 463 K7
The Brothers Vic 342 F2, 345 L7
The Cap Vic 336 C5, 339 K7
The Cascade Vic 345 K4
The Caves Qld 561 J8
The Channon NSW 461 N2
The Chase Qld 560 G4
The Coorong SA 787 G10
The Cove Vic 338 G8
The Cross Roads NSW 453 A8
The Cups Vic 336 G6, 339 N8
The Entrance NSW 401, 455 L4, 459 J7
The Fingerboards Vic 342 D6
The Gap Qld 555 B4, 557 C2
The Garden NT 619 J5
The Gardens NT 612 B8
The Gardens Tas 841 P5
The Granites NT 616 C9, 618 C1
The Gums Qld 559 H7
The Gums SA 787 F2, 791 L8
The Gurdies Vic 337 K6
The Heart Vic 342 C7
The Honeysuckles Vic 342 D8
The Lagoon NSW 454 D5, 458 D8

The Lagoon NSW 463 L3
The Lake Qld 560 A7, 565 P7
The Lakes WA 705 D5, 706 C4
The Lakes NP Vic 342 E6
The Lynd Qld 563 K9
The Monument Qld 564 D5
The Narrows NT 612 D6
The Nut SR Tas 840 C3
The Oaks Qld 561 J7
The Oaks Qld 563 J8
The Oaks Vic 337 N2, 344 E10
The Peaks Qld 558 D5
The Plug Range CR SA 790 F7
The Quiet Corner NSW 463 P6
The Ranch Qld 565 K8
The Range NSW 462 F4
The Range WA 714 D8
The Rock NSW **450**, 465 M6
The Rock NR NSW 465 M6
The Rocks NSW 453 E6
The Rookery NSW 463 K7
The Sisters Vic 338 G7
The Spit NSW 453 F5
The Springs Tas 838 B9
The Summit Qld 556 B8, 559 L9
The Twins SA 792 D9
The Vale NSW 464 F3
The Veldt NSW 462 B5
The Whitsundays Qld 560 G2
Thebarton SA 786 D5
Theda WA 713 K3
Theodore ACT 477 D5
Theodore Qld 559 H2
Theresa Creek NSW 461 M3
Thevenard SA 789 G10, 790 A4
Thirlestone Qld 560 A5, 565 N5
Thirlstane Tas 844 A4, 841 H5
Thirroul NSW 455 J8, 456 G2, 458 G10
Thistlebank Qld 565 N6
Thistlebank NP Qld 565 N6
Thistlebeds SA 787 F1, 791 K7
Thomastown Vic 335 C2, 337 H2, 339 P5, 344 A10
Thomby Qld 558 F8
Thomby Qld 558 G2
Thompson River Vic 342 A6
Thomson River Qld 565 L8
Thomsons Lake WA 704 C10
Thoona Vic 344 E4
Thoopara Qld 560 F3
Thora NSW 461 M7
Thordon Park Qld 558 G4
Thornborough Qld 563 K5, 569 C8
Thornbury Vic 335 D3
Thorneside Qld 555 G5, 557 D3
Thornhill Qld 558 E5
Thornlands Qld 557 E3
Thornleigh NSW 453 C3
Thornleigh Qld 565 M10, 567 M1
Thornlie WA 704 F7
Thornton Qld 565 M6
Thornton Vic 344 D8

Thornton Beach Qld 563 L4, 569 D5
Thorntonia Qld 562 B9, 564 B1
Thorpdale Vic 337 N6
Thoura NSW 463 H2
Thowgla Vic 345 M4
Thowgla Upper Vic 345 M4
Thredbo Village NSW 456 A8, 457 C8
Three Bridges Vic 337 K3
Three Rivers WA 709 J3
Three Springs WA 708 E9
Three Ways Roadhouse NT 617 J7
Thrushton NP Qld 558 D7
Thuddungra NSW 456 A2, 465 P4
Thule NSW 464 G7
Thulloo NSW 465 M3
Thunda Qld 567 J3
Thundelarra WA 708 F8
Thurgoona NSW 465 M8
Thuringowa Qld 563 N9
Thurla Vic 340 E2
Thurlga SA 790 D5
Thurloo Downs NSW 462 E2
Thurrulgoonia Qld 567 P9
Thursday Island Qld **553**, 568 C2
Thylungra Qld 567 K4
Ti-Tree NT 618 G3
Ti-Tree Farm NT 618 G3
Tiaro Qld 559 M3
Tiarri NSW 463 H10, 465 H1
Tibarri Qld 564 F3
Tibbuc NSW 459 K3
Tibooburra NSW **438**, 462 C2
Tichborne NSW 465 P2
Tickalara Qld 567 H9
Tickera SA 787 A2, 791 H7
Tidal River Vic 337 N9
Tidbinbilla NR ACT 477 B5
Tieri Qld 560 F8
Tieyon SA 789 G1, 792 A1
Tilba Tilba NSW 456 E7
Tilboroo Qld 567 N7
Tilmouth Well NT **608**, 618 F4
Tilpa NSW 462 G6
Tilpilly NSW 462 G6
Tiltagoona NSW 463 H6
Timbarra Vic 342 G4, 345 M9
Timber Creek NT **593**, 614 C9, 616 C1
Timberfield WA 707 J2
Timberoo South Vic 340 E6
Timbillica NSW 456 D10
Timboon Vic 339 H8
Timmering Vic 341 N10
Timor NSW 459 H2
Timor Qld 558 E3
Timor Vic 339 K3
Timora Qld 562 F7
Tims Channel Vic 341 H6
Tin Can Bay Qld 556 E1, 559 M4
Tinamba Vic 342 B6
Tinderry NR ACT 477 F7
Tinderbox Tas 839 C6, 843 K6

Tinderry Qld 567 L7
Tindo Qld 565 L3
Tingalpa Qld 555 F5
Tingha NSW **423**, 461 H6
Tingoora Qld 556 A2
Tingoora Qld 559 K5
Tinnenburra Qld 567 N9
Tinonee NSW 459 L3
Tinowon Qld 558 F6
Tintaldra Vic 345 M3
Tintinara SA 788 B8
Tipperary NT 613 D6, 614 D6
Tiranna Qld 567 N5
Tiree Qld 565 N5
Tireen Qld 559 J3
Tirlta NSW 462 C6
Tirranna Roadhouse Qld 562 C7
Tittybong Vic 341 J7
Tiverton SA 791 L5
Tivoli Qld 557 B3
Tiwi NT 612 E1
Tiwi Park NT 612 E2
Tjukayirla Roadhouse WA 711 B1
Tjuwaliyn (Douglas Hot Springs) NP NT 613 D6, 614 D6
Tnorala CR NT **608–609**, 618 F6
Tobermorey NT 619 P3
Tobermory Qld 567 K6
Tocumwal NSW **450**, 465 J7
Todd River NT 619 J6
Todmorden SA 792 B3
Tods Tas 844 C10, 841 J9
Togari Tas 840 B4
Togganoggera NSW 456 D6, 457 G4
Toiberry Tas 844 D7, 841 J7
Tolga Qld 563 L6, 569 D8
Tollingo NR NSW 463 M9
Tolmie Vic 344 F7
Tolosa Park Picnic Area Tas 838 B5
Tom Groggin NSW 456 A8, 457 B8, 465 P9
Tom Price WA **702**, 714 G8
Tomahawk Qld 560 B6, 565 P6
Tomahawk Tas 841 M4
Tomakin NSW 456 E6
Tomaree NP NSW 455 P2, 459 K5
Tomerong NSW 456 F4
Tomingley NSW 458 A5, 463 P9
Tomoo Qld 558 C6
Toms Cap Creek Vic 342 B8
Toms Lake NSW 465 H3
Tonderburine NSW 458 B1, 460 B10
Tongala Vic 341 P9, 344 A4
Tonganah Tas 844 G4, 841 L5
Tonghi Creek Vic 343 K4
Tongio Vic 342 E3, 345 L8
Tongio West Vic 342 E3, 345 L8
Tongo NSW 462 F5
Tonkoro Qld 565 H9
Tooan Vic 338 D2
Toobanna Qld 563 M8
Toobeah Qld 558 G9
Tooborac Vic 339 N3

Toodyay WA **656**, 705 D4, 706 D4
Toogong NSW 454 A4, 458 B7
Toogoolawah Qld 556 C4, 559 L6
Toohey FP Qld 555 D7
Toolakea Qld 563 M9
Toolamba Vic 344 B5
Toolamba West Vic 344 B5
Toolangi Vic 337 K2, 344 C9
Toolebuc Qld 564 F6
Toolern Vale Vic 336 F2, 339 M5
Tooleybuc NSW 464 E6
Toolibin WA 705 G8, 706 E6
Tooligie SA 790 D8
Tooligie Hill SA 790 D7
Toolleen Vic 339 N2
Toolondo Vic 338 D3
Toolondo Reservoir Vic 338 D3
Toolong Vic 338 E8
Toolonga NR WA 708 D5
Tooloom NSW 461 L2
Tooloom NP NSW 461 L2
Tooloombah Qld 561 H7
Tooloombilla Qld 558 D4
Tooloon NSW 460 A9, 463 P6
Tooma NSW 456 A6, 457 A5, 465 P8
Toomba Qld 560 A2, 563 L10, 565 N2
Toombul Qld 555 D3
Toombullup Vic 344 F7
Toompine Qld 567 L6
Toongabbie NSW 453 A5
Toongabbie Vic 342 A7
Toongi NSW 458 B4
Toonumbar NP NSW 461 M2
Toora Vic 337 N7
Tooradin Vic 337 J5
Toorak Vic 335 D4
Toorak Gardens SA 786 E6
Toorale NSW 463 J4
Toorale East NSW 463 J4
Tooraweenah NSW **401**, 458 B2
Toorongo Vic 337 M3
Toorooka NSW 461 M9
Tootool NSW 465 M6
Tootoolah Qld 560 F5
Toowong Qld 555 B5, 557 C2
Toowoomba Qld **507**, 556 B5, 559 L7
Top Hut NSW 464 D3
Top Springs NT 616 E2
Topiram Vic 337 L6
Torbanlea Qld 559 M3
Torbreck Station Vic 337 M1, 344 E9
Torndirrup NP WA **656**, 706 F10
Toronto NSW 455 M3, 459 J6
Torquay Vic **282**, 336 D6, 339 M8
Torrens ACT 477 D4
Torrens Creek Qld 565 N3
Torrens Island CP SA 786 C2
Torrens Vale SA 787 C8, 788 B5
Torrensville SA 786 D5
Torres Strait Qld 568 B1

Torrington NSW 461 J4
Torrington SRA NSW 461 J4
Torrita Vic 340 D5
Torrumbarry Vic 341 M9
Torryburn NSW 461 H8
Tortilla Flats NT 613 D4, 614 D5
Torver Valley Qld 565 L3
Torwood Qld 555 C5
Torwood Qld 563 J6
Tostaree Vic 342 G5, 345 N10
Tothill Creek SA 787 E3, 791 K8
Tottenham NSW 463 N8
Tottenham Vic 335 B4
Tottington Vic 339 H2
Toukley NSW **402**, 455 M4, 459 J7
Toulby Gate NSW 463 M1
Towallum NSW 461 M6
Towamba NSW 456 D9
Towan Vic 341 H5
Towaninny Vic 341 J8
Towaninny South Vic 341 J8
Towarry NP NSW 458 G3
Tower Hill Vic 338 F8
Towlers Bay NSW 453 F1
Townson Qld 556 C6, 559 L8
Townsville Qld **529**, 563 N9
Towong Vic 345 M3
Towong Upper Vic 345 M4
Towra Point NR NSW 453 E9
Towrana WA 708 D3
Towrang NSW 454 E10, 456 E3
Trafalgar Qld 567 K2
Trafalgar Vic 337 N5
Tragowell Vic 341 L8
Trangie NSW **438–439**, 463 P8
Tranmere SA 786 F5
Traralgon Vic **313**, 337 P5, 342 A7
Traralgon South Vic 337 P6, 342 A8
Travellers Lake NSW 464 C2
Trawalla Vic 336 A1, 339 J4
Trawool Vic 339 P3, 344 B8
Trayning WA 706 F3
Traynors Lagoon Vic 339 H1,
   341 H10
Treasure Vic 342 D3, 345 J8
Treasures Vic 342 D3, 345 J8
Trebonne Qld 563 M8
Tregoning Qld 558 C5
Trelega NSW 464 C2
Trent Qld 560 A9, 565 N9
Trentham Vic 336 E1, 339 M4
Trentham East Vic 336 E1, 339 M4
Trephina Gorge Nature Park NT
   609, 619 J6
Tresco Vic 341 K7
Trewalla Qld 567 J1
Trewalla Vic 338 C8
Trewilga NSW 458 A5, 463 P10,
   465 P1
Triabunna Tas 839 F2, 843 M3
Trial Harbour Tas 840 C9
Triamble NSW 454 C2, 458 C6

Triangle Flat NSW 454 D6, 456 D1,
   458 D8
Trida NSW 463 H10, 465 H1
Trigg WA 704 A3
Trinidad Qld 567 L3
Trinita Vic 340 E4
Trinity Beach Qld 563 L5, 569 D7
Trinity Gardens SA 786 E5
Trott Park SA 786 C9
Troubridge Island CP SA 787 A7,
   788 A4, 791 H10
Trowutta Tas 840 B4
Truganina Vic 336 F3, 339 N6
Truganini Reserve Tas 838 E9
Trundle NSW 463 N10, 465 N1
Trungley Hall NSW 465 N4
Trunkey NSW 454 C6, 456 D1,
   458 C8
Truro SA 787 F4, 791 K9
Truslove WA 707 L7
Truslove Townsite NR WA 707 M7
Tuan Qld 559 M3
Tuart Forest NP WA 705 B10,
   706 B7
Tuart Hill WA 704 C3
Tubbul NSW 456 A2, 465 P4
Tubbut Vic 343 J2, 345 P7
Tucabia NSW 461 N5
Tuckanarra WA 708 G6
Tucklan NSW 458 D4
Tuckurimba NSW 461 N3
Tudor Vic 341 H5
Tuen Qld 567 P9
Tuena NSW 454 C7, 456 D2,
   458 C9
Tugan Qld 557 F7
Tuggerah NSW 455 L4, 459 J7
Tuggeranong ACT 477 D4, 456 C5,
   457 E3
Tulendeena Tas 841 M5
Tulka SA 790 D10
Tulkara Vic 339 H3
Tullah Tas 840 D8
Tullakool NSW 464 G7
Tullamarine Vic 335 B2, 336 G2,
   339 N5
Tullamore NSW 463 N9
Tullaroop Reservoir Vic 339 K3
Tullibigeal NSW 465 M2
Tulloh Vic 336 A6, 339 J8
Tully Qld 563 M7, 569 E10
Tully Heads Qld 563 M7
Tulmur Qld 565 H7
Tumbar Qld 560 B9
Tumbarumba NSW **375**, 456 A6,
   457 A5, 465 P7
Tumbarumba Wine Region NSW
   376
Tumblong NSW 456 A4, 457 A2,
   465 P6
Tumbulgum NSW 461 P1
Tumby Bay SA **773**, 790 E9
Tummaville Qld 556 A6, 559 K8

Tumorrama NSW 456 B4, 457 C2
Tumut NSW **376**, 456 A5, 457 B2,
   465 P6
Tumut Pond Reservoir NSW 457 C5
Tumut River NSW 456 A5
Tunart Vic 340 B3
Tunbridge Tas 843 K1, 841 L10
Tuncurry NSW 459 L4
Tungamah Vic 344 D3
Tungkillo SA 787 E6, 791 K10
Tunnack Tas 839 D1, 843 K2
Tunnel Tas 844 E4, 841 K5
Tunnel Creek NP WA **689**, 713 H8
Tunney WA 706 E8
Tuppal NSW 465 J7
Turee NSW 458 E3
Turee Creek WA 715 H10
Turill NSW 458 E3
Turkey Beach Qld 561 L10
Turkey Creek Qld 560 F9
Turlee NSW 464 E3
Turlinjah NSW 456 E7
Turner ACT 477 D3
Turner WA 713 M8
Turners Beach Tas 840 G5
Turners Flat NSW 461 M9
Turners Marsh Tas 844 E5, 841 K6
Tuross Head NSW 456 E7
Turramurra NSW 453 D3
Turrawalla Qld 560 E4
Turrawan NSW 460 E8
Turrella NSW 453 D7
Turriff Vic 340 F6
Turriff West Vic 340 F6
Turtons Creek Vic 337 N7
Tutanning NR WA 705 F7, 706 E5
Tutye Vic 340 C5
Tweed Heads NSW **424**, 461 P1
Twelve Mile NSW 458 C5
Twin Hills Qld 560 C5
Twin Peaks WA 708 E6
Twin Wells NSW 462 B10, 464 B2
Two Mile Flat NSW 458 D4
Two Peoples Bay NR WA 706 F10
Two Rocks WA 705 B4, 706 B4
Two Wells SA 787 D5, 791 J9
Twyford Qld 563 L4, 569 C6
Tyaak Vic 339 P4, 344 A8
Tyabb Vic 335 F9, 337 H5
Tyagong NSW 456 A2, 458 A9,
   465 P4
Tyalgum NSW 461 N1
Tycannah NSW 460 E5
Tyenna Tas 842 G4
Tyers Vic 337 P5, 342 A7
Tyers Junction Vic 337 N4
Tyers Park Vic 337 P5, 342 A7
Tylden Vic 336 E1, 339 M4
Tylerville Qld 557 B9
Tyndale NSW 461 N5
Tynong Vic 337 K4
Tyntynder Central Vic 341 J6
Typo Vic 342 A2, 344 G7

Tyraman NSW 459 J4
Tyrendarra Vic 338 D7
Tyrendarra East Vic 338 D7
Tyringham NSW 461 L7
Tyrrell Downs Vic 340 G6

U

Uanda Qld 565 M5
Uarbry NSW 458 D3
Uardry NSW 465 J4
Uaroo WA 714 D8
Ubobo Qld 559 K1, 561 L10
Ucharonidge NT 617 J4
Udialla WA 712 F8, 715 P1
Uki NSW 461 N2
Ulalie NSW 462 F6
Ulamambri NSW 458 D1, 460 D10
Ulan NSW 458 D4
Ulandra NR NSW 465 P5
Uley NSW 465 M4
Ulidarra NP NSW 461 N7
Ulimaroa Qld 558 G5
Ulinda NSW 458 D2
Ulladulla NSW **376**, 456 F5
Ullawarra WA 714 E9
Ullina Vic 339 K4
Ullswater Vic 338 C3
Ulmarra NSW 461 N5
Ulong NSW 461 M7
Ultima Vic 341 H6
Ultimo NSW 453 E6
Uluru–Katatjuta NP NT **602–605**,
   618 D9
Ulva Qld 565 N4
Ulverstone Tas **822**, 840 F5
Umbakumba NT 615 M6
Umbango NSW 465 N7
Umbeara NT 619 H9
Umberatana SA 793 K10
Umbrawarra Gorge NP NT 613 E7,
   614 E7
Umina NSW 455 L5, 459 H8
Unanderra NSW 455 J9, 456 G3,
   458 G10
Undara Volcanic NP Qld 563 K8
Undera Vic 341 P9, 344 B4
Underbank NSW 459 J4
Underbool Vic 340 D5
Undercliff Qld 560 G5
Undercliffe NSW 453 D7
Underdale SA 786 C5
Underwood Qld 555 E8
Underwood Tas 844 E5, 841 K6
Undilla Qld 562 B10, 564 B1
Undina Qld 564 F3
Undoolya NT 619 H6
Undulla Qld 558 G6
Ungarie NSW 465 M3
Ungarra SA 790 E8
Ungo Qld 567 L2
Unicup NR WA 706 D8
Unley SA 786 E6
Unley Park SA 786 E6

Unnamed CP SA **745**, 789 A4
Uno SA 790 F5
Upalinna SA 791 K3
Uplands Vic 342 E2, 345 L7
Upper Beaconsfield Vic 337 J4
Upper Bingara NSW 460 G6
Upper Blessington Tas 844 G6, 841 L7
Upper Bowman NSW 459 J3
Upper Castra Tas 840 F6
Upper Coomera Qld 557 E6
Upper Ferntree Gully Vic 335 G4
Upper Horton NSW 460 F7
Upper Kedron Qld 555 A4
Upper Manilla NSW 460 G8
Upper Mount Gravatt Qld 555 E7
Upper Mount Hicks Tas 840 E5
Upper Natone Tas 840 E5
Upper Rollands Plains NSW 459 L1, 461 L10
Upper Scamander Tas 841 N6
Upper Stone Qld 563 M8
Upper Stowport Tas 840 E5
Upper Sturt SA 786 F8
Upper Swan WA 705 C4, 706 C4
Upper Yarra Reservoir Vic 344 D10
Upson Downs NSW 464 E4
Upwey Vic 335 G4
Uraidla SA 786 G6
Urala WA 714 C7
Uralla NSW **424**, 461 J8
Urambie Qld 565 N9
Urana NSW 465 L6
Urana West Qld 558 B6
Urandangi Qld 564 A5
Urangeline NSW 465 L7
Urangeline East NSW 465 L7
Urania SA 787 A4, 791 H9
Urannah Qld 560 F3
Uranquinty NSW 465 N6
Urapunga NT 615 J8
Urawa NR WA 708 D7
Urbenville NSW 461 L2
Urella Downs NSW 462 E3
Urisino NSW 462 F3
Urquhart Qld 564 E2
Urrbrae SA 786 E7
Urunga NSW **424**, 461 N8
Useless Loop WA 708 B4
Uteara NSW 463 J4
Utopia NT 619 J3
Uxbridge Tas 843 H4

V

Vacy NSW 455 M1, 459 J5
Valencia Creek Vic 342 C6
Valery NSW 461 M7
Valla Beach NSW 461 N8
Valley of Lagoons Qld 563 K8
Valroona NSW 465 K2
Van Diemen Gulf NT 613 F1, 614 E3
Van Lee Qld 563 J7

Vandyke Qld 560 E10
Vanrook Qld 562 F5
Varley WA 707 H6
Vasey Vic 338 D4
Vauchan Vic 339 L3
Vaughan Springs NT 618 D3
Veitch SA 791 N9
Velox Hut Qld 562 G6
Vena Park Qld 562 E8
Venman Bushland NP Qld 555 G9
Ventnor Vic 337 H7, 339 P8
Venus Bay SA 790 B6
Venus Bay Vic 337 L8
Venus Bay CP SA 790 B6
Venus Bay CR SA 790 B6
Verdun Valley Qld 564 G8
Verdure Qld 563 K6, 569 C8
Vergemont Qld 565 J9
Vermont Qld 560 F6
Vermont Vic 335 F4
Vermont Hill NSW 463 M9
Vermont South Vic 335 F4
Verona Sands Tas 839 B8, 843 J7
Verran SA 790 E8
Vervale Vic 337 K5
Vesper Vic 337 M3
Victor Harbor SA **737**, 787 D8, 788 B5
Victoria **251–253**
Victoria Downs Qld 560 B3
Victoria Park WA 704 D5
Victoria Point Qld 556 E6, 557 E3, 559 N7
Victoria River NT 614 B9, 616 D4
Victoria River Crossing NT **593**
Victoria River Downs NT 616 D2
Victoria River Wayside Inn NT 614 D9, 616 D1
Victoria Rock NR WA 707 K3
Victoria Vale Qld 562 G9
Victoria Valley Vic 338 E5
Victorian Alps Vic **318–323**
Victoria's Outback Vic **286–289**
Victory Downs NT 618 G10
View Bank Vic 335 D2
View Point Outstation NSW 462 G4
Viewmont NSW 462 D8
Villa Dale Qld 565 K3
Villafranca Qld 560 E6
Villawood NSW 453 B6
Vimy Qld 561 J9
Vinabel Qld 560 C8
Vincentia NSW 456 G4
Vindex Qld 565 K7
Vinifera Vic 341 J5
Violet Town Vic 344 D6
Violet Vale Qld 562 E10, 564 F1
Virginia Qld 555 D2
Virginia SA 787 D5, 791 J9
Vite Vite Vic 339 H6
Vite Vite North Vic 339 H6

Viveash WA 704 G3
Vivian Wells SA 792 D10
Vivonne Bay SA 788 B2
Vivonne Bay CP SA 788 C2
Voyager Point NSW 453 B8

W

Waaia Vic 344 B3
Waar Waar Qld 559 J7
Wabba Wilderness Park Vic 345 L4
Wabricola SA 791 L5
Wacol Qld 555 A8
Wadbilliga NP NSW **376**, 456 D7, 457 G7
Waddamana Tas 843 H1, 841 H10
Waddi NSW 465 K5
Waddikee SA 790 E6
Waddington WA 705 D2, 706 C2
Wade Hill Qld 567 M4
Wadeye NT 614 B7
Wadnaminga SA 791 M5
Wagaman NT 612 F3
Wagaman Park NT 612 F3
Wagant Vic 340 F5
Wagga Wagga NSW **450–451**, 465 N6
Wagga Wagga WA 708 F7
Waggarandall Vic 344 D4
Wagin WA 705 F9, 706 E7
Wagoora Qld 560 F3
Wahgunyah Vic 344 F3
Wahgunyah CR SA 789 E10
Wahring Vic 339 P2, 344 B6
Wahroonga NSW 453 D3
Wahroonga WA 708 C3
Waikerie SA **774**, 791 M8
Wail Vic 338 E1, 340 E10
Wairewa Vic 342 G5, 345 N10
Wairuna Qld 563 L8
Waitara NSW 453 D3
Waitara Qld 560 F5
Waitchie Vic 341 H6
Waite River NT 619 J4
Waitpinga SA 787 D9, 788 B5
Waiwera SA 791 N4
Waka NSW 462 A2
Wakefield River SA 787 C3
Wakeley NSW 453 A6
Wakerley Qld 555 F5
Wakes Lagoon Qld 567 M3
Wakooka Outstation Qld 563 K2, 568 F9
Wakool NSW 464 G7
Wal Wal Vic 338 F2
Walba Qld 558 G1, 561 H10
Walbundrie NSW 465 L7
Walcha NSW **424**, 461 J9
Walcha Road NSW 461 J9
Waldburg WA 708 G2
Walebing WA 705 C1, 706 C2
Walenda NSW 462 G9, 464 G1
Walgett NSW **439**, 463 P4

Walgunya WA 715 L9
Walhalla Vic **313**, 337 P4, 342 A6
Walhallow NT 617 L4
Walkamin Qld 563 L6, 569 D8
Walkaway WA 708 C8
Walker Flat SA 791 L9
Walkers Hill NSW 463 M9
Walkerston Qld 560 G4
Walkerville SA 786 E5
Walkerville Vic 337 M9
Walla Walla NSW 465 M7
Wallabadah NSW 458 G2
Wallabadah Qld 562 G7
Wallabadah NR NSW 458 G2
Wallabella Qld 558 F6
Wallabi Point NSW 459 L3
Wallace Vic 336 C2, 339 L5
Wallace Rock Station NT 618 G7
Wallacedale Vic 338 D6
Wallaga Lake NP NSW 456 E7
Wallal Qld 558 A5, 567 P5
Wallalong NSW 455 M1, 459 J5
Wallaloo Vic 338 G2
Wallaloo East Vic 338 G2
Wallamunga NT 616 A5
Wallan Vic 336 G1, 339 P4, 344 A9
Wallan East Vic 337 H1, 339 P4, 344 A9
Wallangarra Qld 559 L10
Wallangra NSW 460 G4
Wallareenya WA 715 H5
Wallarobba NSW 459 J5
Wallaroo Qld 561 H9
Wallaroo SA **774**, 787 A2, 791 H8
Wallaroo NR NSW 455 M1, 459 J5
Wallen Qld 567 P7
Wallendbeen NSW 456 A3, 465 P5
Wallerawang NSW 454 F4, 458 E7
Wallerberdina SA 791 H3
Walleroobie NSW 465 M5
Walli NSW 454 B5, 456 C1, 458 B8
Wallinduc Vic 336 A3, 339 J6
Walling Rock WA 709 K9
Wallingat NR NSW 459 L4
Wallington Vic 336 E5, 339 M7
Walloon Qld 557 A3
Walls of Jerusalem NP Tas **822**, 840 G8
Wallsend NSW 455 M2, 459 J6
Wallumbilla Qld 558 F5
Wallumburrawang NSW 458 B2
Wallundry NSW 465 N4
Wallup Vic 340 E10
Walmer NSW 454 A1, 458 B5
Walpa Vic 342 D6
Walpeup Vic 340 E5
Walpole WA **656**, 706 D10
Walpole–Nornalup NP WA **656**, 706 D10
Walungurru NT 618 A5
Walwa Vic 345 L3
Walyahmoning NR WA 706 G2
Wamberra NSW 464 C3

Wamboin NSW 463 M5
Wamboyne NSW 465 N3
Wammadoo Qld 565 K8
Wammutta Qld 564 D4
Wamoon NSW 465 L5
Wampo NSW 464 E3
Wampra NSW 463 H3
Wamuran Qld 556 D4, 559 M6
Wanaaring NSW 462 G3
Wanagarren NR WA 705 A1, 706 B2
Wanbi SA 791 M9
Wanda NSW 462 D9
Wandagee WA 708 C1, 714 C10
Wandana SA 789 G10, 790 A4
Wandana NR WA 708 D7
Wandandian NSW 456 F4
Wandarrie WA 708 G7
Wandearah East SA 791 H7
Wandearah West SA 791 H7
Wandering WA 705 E7, 706 D6
Wandiligong Vic 342 C1, 345 H6
Wandilo SA 788 F10
Wandin Vic 337 J3
Wandina WA 708 D7
Wando Bridge Vic 338 C5
Wando Vale Vic 338 C5
Wandoan Qld 558 G4
Wandong Vic 337 H1, 339 P4,
    344 A9
Wandoona NSW 460 C4
Wandsworth NSW 461 J6
Wandsworth Qld 567 K2
Wanganella NSW 465 H6
Wangara WA 704 C1
Wangarabell Vic 343 M4
Wangaratta Vic **332**, 344 F4
Wangareena NSW 462 G3
Wangary SA 790 D9
Wangianna SA 793 H9
Wangoom Vic 338 F8
Wanguri NT 612 F2
Wanguri Park NT 612 F2
Wanilla SA 790 D9
Wanjarri NR WA 709 L6
Wanna WA 708 F1, 714 F10
Wannamal WA 705 C3, 706 C3
Wannarra WA 708 F9
Wanneroo WA 705 B4, 706 C4
Wanniassa ACT 477 D4
Wannon Vic 338 D5
Wannon Vic 338 F4
Wannon River Vic 338 D5
Wanora Qld 557 A3
Wanora Downs Qld 565 H5
Wantabadgery NSW 465 N6
Wantagong Qld 565 J9
Wantirna Vic 335 F4
Wantirna South Vic 335 F4
Wanwin Vic 338 B6
Wapengo NSW 456 E8
Wapet Camp WA 714 D6
Wappinguy NSW 458 F4
Waramanga ACT 477 D4

Warambie WA 714 F6
Waranga Basin Vic 344 A5
Waratah NSW 463 L2
Waratah NSW 463 M4
Waratah Tas 840 D6
Waratah Bay Vic 337 M8
Waratah Bay Vic 337 M9
Waratah North Vic 337 M8
Warbreccan Qld 565 J10, 567 J1
Warburn NSW 465 K4
Warburton Vic **314**, 337 L3,
    344 D10
Warburton WA **677**, 710 D10
Warburton Creek SA 792 G5
Warburton East Vic 337 L3, 344 D10
Warby Range SP Vic 344 F4
Warcowie SA 791 J3
Wardell NSW 461 P3
Wards Mistake NSW 461 K7
Wards River NSW 459 K4
Wareek Vic 339 K3
Warenda Qld 564 E7
Wareo Qld 567 M6
Wargambegal NSW 465 L2
Warge Rock NSW 463 N9
Warialda NSW **424**, 460 F5
Warialda Rail NSW 460 F5
Warianna Qld 565 L4
Warida Qld 558 C5
Warkton NSW 458 C1, 460 C10
Warkworth NSW 455 K1, 459 H5
Warmun (Turkey Creek) WA 713 M7
Warnambool Downs Qld 565 J7
Warncoort Vic 336 B6, 339 K8
Warne Vic 341 H8
Warnecliffe NSW 454 B3, 458 C6
Warneet Vic 337 J5
Warner Qld 555 B1
Warners Bay NSW 455 M3, 459 J6
Warnertown SA 791 J6
Warooka SA 790 G10
Waroon Qld 558 F7
Waroona WA 705 C8, 706 C6
Waroula Qld 561 J8
Warra Qld 559 J6
Warra Qld 564 E8
Warra NP NSW 461 K6
Warrabah NP NSW 460 G8
Warrabin Qld 567 K5
Warrabkook Vic 338 E6
Warrachie SA 790 D7
Warracknabeal Vic **293**, 340 F9
Warradale SA 786 C7
Warraderry NSW 456 A1, 458 A8,
    465 P3
Warragamba NSW 455 H7, 456 F1,
    458 G9
Warragoon NSW 465 K8
Warragul Vic **314**, 337 M5
Warrak Vic 339 H4
Warrakimbo SA 791 H4
Warrakoo SA 791 P7
Warral NSW 458 G1, 460 G10

Warrambine Vic 336 B4, 339 K6
Warramboo SA 790 D6
Warrananga NSW 464 B3
Warrandyte Vic 335 F2
Warrandyte South Vic 335 F2
Warrandyte SP Vic 335 F2
Warrane Tas 838 G5
Warranwood Vic 335 F3
Warrawagine WA 715 L6
Warraweena SA 791 J1
Warrayure Vic 338 E5
Warreah Qld 565 M3
Warregal NSW 465 P2
Warregal Qld 560 D5
Warrego Park Qld 558 A6, 567 P6
Warrego River NSW 463 J3
Warrego River Qld 558 A5
Warrell Creek NSW 461 M8
Warren NSW **439**, 463 P7
Warren NP WA 706 C9
Warren Vale Qld 562 E8
Warrenbayne Vic 344 D6
Warrenben CP SA 788 A2, 790 G10
Warrenmang Vic 339 J3
Warrentinna Tas 841 M5
Warriedar WA 708 F9
Warriewood NSW 453 F2
Warrigal NSW 463 N7
Warrigal Qld 560 A3, 565 N3
Warrill View Qld 556 D6, 557 A5,
    559 M8
Warrimbah WA 713 H9
Warrina SA 792 D5
Warringa Tas 840 F6
Warrinilla NSW 460 A5, 463 P2
Warrion Vic 336 A5, 339 J7
Warrnambool Vic **282–283**, 338 F8
Warrong Qld 558 D2
Warrong Vic 338 E7
Warroo NSW 465 N2
Warrow SA 790 D9
Warrumbungle NSW 458 B1,
    460 B10
Warrumbungle NP NSW **424–425**,
    458 C1, 460 C10
Warrumbungle Range NSW 458 C1
Warruwi NT 614 G3
Wartaka SA 790 G5
Wartook Vic 338 F3
Wartook Reservoir Vic 338 F3
Warumbul NSW 453 D10
Warwick Qld **507**, 556 B7, 559 L8
Warwick Qld 560 F7
Warwick WA 704 B2
Washpool SA 791 J7
Washpool NP NSW **410–411**,
    461 L4
Wasleys SA 787 D4, 791 J9
Watagans NP NSW 455 K3, 459 H6
Watarrka (Kings Canyon) NP NT
    610, 618 D7
Watchem Vic 340 G9
Watchupga Vic 340 G7

Waterbag NSW 462 C7
Waterfall NSW 455 J8, 456 G2,
    459 H9
Waterfall Gully SA 786 F6
Waterford Qld 557 D4
Waterford Vic 342 D4, 345 J9
Waterford WA 704 D6
Waterhouse CA Tas 844 G2, 841 L4
Waterloo NSW 453 E7
Waterloo NT 616 A2
Waterloo Qld 558 E7
Waterloo SA 787 E2, 791 K8
Waterloo Tas 839 A7, 843 H7
Waterloo Vic 336 A1, 339 J4
Waterloo Corner SA 786 D1
Waterman WA 704 B2
Watermark NSW 458 F1, 460 F10
Watervale SA 787 D2, 791 J8
Watheroo WA 706 C1, 708 E10
Watheroo NP WA 706 C1, 708 E10
Watson ACT 477 E2
Watson SA 789 D8
Watsonia Vic 335 D2
Watsons Bay NSW 453 F5
Watsons Creek NSW 461 H8
Watsons Creek Vic 337 J2, 344 B10
Watsons Creek NR NSW 461 H8
Wattamondara NSW 456 B1, 458 B9
Wattle Vic 339 H9
Wattle Creek Vic 339 H3
Wattle Flat NSW 458 D6, 454 E3
Wattle Glen Vic 335 E1
Wattle Grove NSW 453 A8
Wattle Grove Tas 839 A7, 843 J6
Wattle Grove WA 704 G6
Wattle Hill Tas 839 E4, 843 L4
Wattle Park SA 786 F6
Wattle Vale NSW 462 E4
Wattleup WA 704 C10
Waubra Vic 336 A1, 339 K4
Wauchope NSW **402**, 459 M2
Wauchope NT 617 J9, 619 J1
Waukaringa SA 791 L4
Wauraltee SA 790 G9
Waurn Ponds Vic 339 M7
Wave Hill NSW 462 F8
Wave Hill NSW 463 L4
Wave Hill NT 616 D4
Wavell Heights Qld 555 D3
Waverley NSW 453 F7
Waverley Downs NSW 462 F2
Wayatinah Tas 842 G2
Waygara Vic 343 H5, 345 N10
Wayville SA 786 D6
Weabonga NSW 459 H1, 461 H10
Wealwandangie Qld 558 D1,
    560 E10
Weaner Creek Qld 567 P5
Weavers SA 787 A6, 791 H10
Wedderburn Vic **283**, 339 J1,
    341 J10
Wedderburn Junction Vic 339 K1,
    341 K10

Weddin Mountains NP NSW 456 A1, 465 P3
Wedge Island WA 705 A2, 706 B2
Wee Jasper NSW 456 B4, 457 D2
Wee Jasper NR NSW 456 B4, 457 C2
Wee Waa NSW **425**, 460 D7
Wee Wee Rup Vic 341 M8
Weeaproinah Vic 336 A7, 339 J9
Weebo WA 709 L7
Weegena Tas 844 A6, 840 G7
Weekeroo SA 791 M4
Weelamurra Qld 558 A8
Weelarrana WA 709 K1, 715 K10
Weemelah NSW 460 C3
Weeragua Vic 343 L4
Weeraman NSW 458 D3
Weerangourt Vic 338 D6
Weerite Vic 339 H7
Weetah Tas 844 B6, 841 H6
Weetalaba Qld 560 E4
Weetaliba NSW 458 D2
Weetalibah NR NSW 458 D2
Weetangera ACT 477 D2
Weethalle NSW 465 L3
Weetulta SA 791 H8
Wehla Vic 339 J1
Weilmoringle NSW 463 M2
Weimby NSW 464 E5
Weipa Qld **553**, 568 B6
Weja NSW 465 M3
Welaregang NSW 456 A7, 457 A5, 465 P8
Welbourn Hill SA 792 A4
Welbungin WA 706 F2
Weldborough Tas 841 M5
Welford NP Qld 567 J2
Welland SA 786 D5
Wellers Hill Qld 555 D6
Wellesley Islands Qld 562 C5
Wellingrove NSW 461 J5
Wellington NSW **402**, 454 B1, 458 B5
Wellington SA 788 A7, 787 G8
Wellington Dam WA 705 C9, 706 C7
Wellington Point Qld 557 E2
Wellshot Qld 565 M9
Wellstead WA 706 G9
Welltree NT 613 B5, 614 C5
Welshmans Reef Vic 339 L3
Welshpool Vic 337 P8, 342 A9
Welshpool WA 704 F6
Wembley WA 704 C4
Wembley Downs WA 704 B4
Wemen Vic 340 G4
Wendouree Vic 336 B2, 339 K5
Wengenville Qld 556 A3, 559 K6
Wenlock (ruins) Qld 568 D7
Wentworth NSW **451**, 464 C4
Wentworth Falls NSW 454 G6, 456 F1, 458 F8
Wentworthville NSW 453 B5
Weranga Qld 559 J6

Weribone Qld 558 F7
Werna Qld 565 J5
Wernadinga Qld 562 C7
Werneth Vic 336 A4, 339 K6
Werombi NSW 455 H7, 456 F1, 458 G9
Werrap Vic 340 D8
Werri Beach NSW 455 J10, 456 G3
Werribee Vic 335 A5, 336 F3, 339 N6
Werribee Gorge SP Vic 336 D2, 339 M5
Werribee South Vic 335 A6, 336 F4, 339 N6
Werrikimbe NP NSW **425**, 459 L1, 461 L10
Werrimull Vic 340 C3
Werrina Qld 564 G2
Werrington Qld 563 J9
Werris Creek NSW 458 G1, 460 G10
Wertaloona SA 791 L1, 793 L10
Wesburn Vic 337 K3
Wesley Vale Tas 844 A4, 840 G5
West Beach SA 786 C6
West Burleigh Qld 557 F7
West Cape Howe NP WA 706 E10
West End Qld 555 C5
West Footscray Vic 335 B4
West Frankford Tas 844 C5, 841 H6
West Hill Qld 560 G5
West Hill NP Qld 561 H5
West Hobart Tas 838 D6
West Kalgoorlie WA 707 L2
West Kentish Tas 840 G6
West Lakes SA 786 C4
West Lakes Shore SA 786 B4
West Lynne NSW 456 B8, 457 D8
West MacDonnell NP NT **610**, 618 G5
West Moonah Tas 838 C4
West Mount Hut SA 793 H9
West Pennant Hills NSW 453 C4
West Perth WA 704 C5
West Pine Tas 840 F5
West Point Qld 561 H6
West Pymble NSW 453 D4
West Ridgley Tas 840 E5
West Ryde NSW 453 C5
West Scottsdale Tas 844 G4, 841 L5
West Swan WA 704 F2
West Tamworth NSW 460 G9
West Wyalong NSW **451**, 465 M3
Westall Vic 335 E5
Westbourne Qld 565 N9
Westbrook NSW 457 A3, 465 P7
Westbury Tas **822**, 844 C7, 841 J7
Westby NSW 465 N7
Westby Vic 341 L7
Westcourt Qld 558 C6
Western Australia **623–625**
Western Creek NT 614 F10, 616 F1
Western Creek Tas 844 A7, 841 H7
Western Flat SA 788 D10

Western Gardens Vic 335 A5
Western Junction Tas 844 E7, 841 K7
Western Port Vic 335 G9, 337 J5
Western River WPA SA 788 B2
Westerton Qld 565 J9
Westerway Tas 843 H4
Westfield WA 704 G9
Westgrove Qld 558 E3
Westlake Qld 555 A7
Westland Qld 565 L9
Westlea Qld 567 P9
Westleigh NSW 453 C3
Westmar Qld 558 G8
Westmead NSW 453 B5
Westmeadows Vic 335 B2
Westmere Vic 338 G5
Westmoreland Qld 562 A6
Weston ACT 477 D3
Weston Creek ACT 477 C4, 456 C5, 457 E3
Westonia WA 706 G3
Westward Ho Qld 564 E8
Westwood Qld 561 J9
Westwood Tas 844 D6, 841 J7
Westwood Downs NSW 462 B5
Wet Creek NT 614 E9
Wetherill Park NSW 453 A6
Wetlands Qld 558 C3
Weymouth Tas 844 E3, 841 K4
Whale Beach NSW 453 G1
Wharminda SA 790 E8
Wharparilla Vic 341 N9
Wharparilla North Vic 341 N9
Whealbah NSW 465 J3
Wheelers Hill Vic 335 F4
Whetstone Qld 559 J9
Whidbey Islands CP SA 790 C10
Whim Creek WA 714 G6
Whinstanes Qld 555 E4
Whiporie NSW 461 M4
Whipstick SP Vic 339 M1
Whirily Vic 341 H8
White Beach Tas 839 E7, 843 M6
White Cliffs NSW **439**, 462 E5
White Cliffs WA 709 N8
White Creek SA 791 N5
White Flat SA 790 D9
White Gate Vic 344 E6
White Gum Valley WA 704 B7
White Hills Tas 844 E6, 841 K7
White Hut SA 788 A2, 790 G10
White Leeds NSW 462 B8
White Mountains Qld 565 M2
White Mountains NP Qld 565 M2
White Rock Qld 563 L5, 569 D8
Whitefoord Tas 839 D1, 843 L2
Whiteheads Creek Vic 344 B7
Whiteman WA 704 E2
Whiteman Park WA 704 E2
Whitemark Tas 841 J3
Whitemore Tas 844 D7, 841 J7
Whites Corner Vic 337 M4
Whitewells WA 708 F9

Whitewood Qld 565 K5
Whitfield Vic 342 A1, 344 F6
Whitlands Vic 344 F6
Whitsunday Group Qld **510–513**, 560 G2
Whitsunday Islands NP Qld 560 G3
Whittata SA 790 G3
Whittlesea Vic 337 H2, 339 P5, 344 A9
Whitton NSW 465 K5
Whitwarta SA 787 C3, 791 J8
Whorouly Vic 344 G5
Whorouly East Vic 344 G5
Whroo Vic 339 P2, 344 A6
Whyalla NSW 460 A4
Whyalla SA **774–775**, 790 G6
Whyalla CP SA 790 G6
Whyjonta NSW 462 D3
Whyralla Qld 565 H7
Whyte Yarcowie SA 791 K6
Wialki WA 706 F2
Wiangaree NSW 461 M2
Wickepin WA 705 G7, 706 E6
Wickham WA 714 F5
Wickliffe Vic 338 G5
Widbury Qld 559 J3
Widden NSW 454 G1, 458 F5
Widgelli NSW 465 K4
Widgeman Qld 560 B7, 565 P7
Widgiemooltha WA 707 L3
Widgiewa NSW 465 L6
Wiesners Swamp NR NSW 465 M7
Wietalaba Qld 559 K1, 561 K10
Wilangee NSW 462 A7
Wilban WA 711 C6
Wilburville Tas 844 C10, 841 J9
Wilby Vic 344 E3
Wilcannia NSW **439**, 462 E7
Wilcherry SA 790 E5
Wild Duck Island NP Qld 561 H6
Wild Horse Plains SA 787 C4, 791 J9
Wild South-West Tasmania **826–829**
Wildman Reserve NT **593**
Wiley Park NSW 453 C7
Wilfred Downs Qld 565 L4
Wilga NSW 462 F7
Wilga Downs NSW 463 K5
Wilga Downs Qld 559 H6
Wilgalong NSW 463 L7
Wilgaroon NSW 463 K5
Wilgena SA 790 C1
Wilkatana SA 791 H4
Wilkawatt SA 788 A9
Wilkur Vic 340 G8
Wilkur South Vic 340 F9
Wilkurra NSW 462 E10, 464 E2
Willa Vic 340 E6
Willaba NSW 462 C10, 464 C1
Willagee WA 704 C7
Willalooka SA 788 C9
Willandra NP NSW **451**, 465 H2
Willandspey Qld 560 C5
Willara Qld 558 B3

Willare Bridge Roadhouse WA 712 F8, 715 P1
Willarie Qld 558 F9
Willaroy NSW 462 E4
Willatook Vic 338 E7
Willaura Vic 338 G5
Willawa Qld 558 H2
Willawarrin NSW 461 M9
Willawong Qld 555 C8
Willbriggie NSW 465 K5
Willenabrina Vic 340 E9
Willeroo NT 614 E9
Willesley Qld 560 D6
Willetton WA 704 D7
Willi Willi NP NSW 459 L1, 461 L10
William Bay NP WA 656, 706 E10
William Creek SA 792 E7
Williambury WA 708 D1, 714 D10
Williams WA 705 E8, 706 D6
Williamsdale ACT 477 D6, 456 C5, 457 F4
Williamsford Tas 840 D8
Williamstown SA 787 E5, 791 K9
Williamstown Vic 335 C4, 336 G3, 339 N6
Williamstown North Vic 335 C4
Williamtown NSW 455 N2, 459 K6
Willippa SA 791 K3
Willis Vic 343 H2, 345 P7
Willochra SA 791 J4
Willoughby NSW 453 E5
Willow Grove Vic 337 N4
Willow Tree NSW 458 G2
Willow Waters SA 791 J4
Willowie SA 791 J5
Willowmavin Vic 339 N4, 344 A8
Willowra NT 616 F10, 618 F2
Willows Qld 560 D9
Willowvale Vic 336 A3, 339 J6
Willung Vic 342 B8
Willung South Vic 342 B8
Willunga SA 787 D7, 788 A5
Wilmington Qld 560 E2, 563 P10
Wilmington SA 775, 791 H5
Wilmot Tas 840 F6
Wilora NT 619 H2
Wilpena SA 775, 791 J3
Wilpoorinna SA 793 J9
Wilroy WA 708 D8
Wilson SA 791 J4
Wilson WA 704 E6
Wilsons Hut Qld 562 F6
Wilsons Promontory Vic 337 N9
Wilsons Promontory NP Vic 314–315, 337 N9
Wilston Qld 555 C4
Wilton NSW 455 H8, 456 G2, 458 G10
Wilton Qld 565 M7
Wiltshire Tas 840 C3
Wiluna WA 669, 709 K5

Winbar NSW 463 H5
Winburdale NR NSW 454 E4, 458 E7
Winchelsea Vic 283, 336 C5, 339 L7
Winchester WA 706 C1, 708 E10
Windah Qld 561 J9
Windamere Dam NSW 454 E1, 458 E5
Windara NSW 463 H7
Windarra WA 709 N8
Windellama NSW 456 E4
Windera NSW 463 K6
Windera Qld 556 B1, 559 L4
Winderie WA 708 D3
Windermere Tas 844 D5, 841 J6
Windermere Vic 336 B1, 339 K5
Windeyer NSW 454 D2, 458 D5
Windidda WA 709 N5
Windimurra WA 709 H7
Windjana Gorge NP WA 689, 712 G8
Windorah Qld 567 J3
Windsor NSW 402–403, 455 J5, 456 G1, 458 G8
Windsor Qld 555 D4
Windsor SA 787 C4, 791 J9
Windsor Vic 335 D4
Windsor WA 709 H7
Windsor Park Qld 564 D6
Windurong NSW 458 B2
Windy Harbour WA 706 C9
Wineries of the South-East Vic 296–301
Wingadee NSW 460 A8
Wingala NSW 453 G4
Wingan Bay Vic 343 N5
Wingan Swamp Vic 343 M4
Wingeel Vic 336 B4, 339 K7
Wingelinna WA 710 G10
Wingello NSW 454 F10, 456 E3
Wingen NSW 458 G3
Wingfield Qld 559 J2
Wingfield SA 786 D4
Wingham NSW 403, 459 L3
Winiam Vic 338 C1, 340 C10
Winiam East Vic 338 D1, 340 D10
Winjallok Vic 339 H2
Winkie SA 791 N9
Winkle Creek NT 617 M7
Winkleigh Tas 844 C5, 841 J6
Winlaton Vic 341 K7
Winnaleah Tas 841 M5
Winnambool Vic 340 G5
Winnap Vic 338 B6
Winnathee NSW 462 A3
Winneba Qld 558 C4
Winnellie NT 612 E7
Winnellie Park NT 612 G7
Winnindoo Vic 342 B7
Winning WA 714 C9
Winninowie SA 791 H5
Winninowie CP SA 791 H5
Winnungra NSW 465 M3

Winslow Vic 338 F7
Winston Hills NSW 453 B4
Winthrop WA 704 C7
Wintinna SA 792 A4
Winton Qld 537, 565 J6
Winton Vic 344 E5
Winulta SA 787 B4, 791 H8
Wirega NSW 456 A1, 458 A9, 465 P3
Wirha SA 788 A9, 791 N10
Wirra Wirra Qld 563 J8
Wirrabara SA 791 J6
Wirraminna SA 790 E2
Wirrappa SA 790 F3
Wirrawa NSW 463 N2
Wirrawarra NSW 463 J2
Wirrealpa SA 791 K2
Wirrida SA 792 B8
Wirrimah NSW 456 A2, 458 A9
Wirrinya NSW 465 P3
Wirrulla SA 790 B5
Wiseleigh Vic 342 F5, 345 L10
Wisemans Creek NSW 454 E5, 456 D1, 458 D8
Wisemans Ferry NSW 403, 455 K4, 459 H7
Wishart Qld 555 E7
Witchcliffe WA 706 B8
Witchelina SA 793 H9
Witchitie SA 791 K4
Witera SA 790 B6
Witheren Qld 557 D7
Withersfield Qld 560 D9
Withywine Qld 565 K9
Witjira NP SA 784, 792 D1
Wittenbra NSW 460 C9
Wittenoom WA 702, 715 H8
Woden ACT 477 D4
Woden Valley ACT 456 C5, 457 E3
Wodonga Vic 332–333, 345 H3
Wogarl WA 706 G4
Wogarno WA 708 G7
Woggoon NR NSW 463 M10, 465 M1
Woko NP NSW 459 J2
Wokurna SA 787 B1, 791 H7
Wolfe Creek Crater NP WA 710 E1, 713 M10
Wolffdene Qld 556 E6, 557 D5, 559 N7
Wolfram Qld 563 K6, 569 B8
Wollar NSW 458 E4
Wollemi NP NSW 403, 455 H1, 458 F5, 454 G3
Wollert Vic 337 H2, 339 P5, 344 A10
Wollogorang NT 617 P3
Wollogorang Qld 562 A6
Wollombi NSW 403, 455 K2, 459 H6
Wollombi Qld 560 E4
Wollomombi NSW 461 K8
Wollongbar NSW 461 P3

Wollongong NSW 377, 455 J9, 456 G3, 458 G10
Wollstonecraft NSW 453 E5
Wollun NSW 461 J9
Wololla Qld 560 B9, 565 P9
Wolonga Camp NSW 460 F3
Wolseley SA 788 C10
Wolseley Park NSW 457 A4, 465 P7
Wolumla NSW 456 E9
Wolverton Qld 568 D7
Wolvi Qld 556 D1, 559 M4
Womal Park Qld 558 D5
Womalilla Qld 558 D5
Wombat NSW 456 A3, 458 A10, 465 P4
Wombelano Vic 338 C3
Womblebank Qld 558 D3
Womboota NSW 465 H8
Wombramurra NSW 459 H2
Wombungi NT 613 C9, 614 D8
Wompah House NSW 462 C1
Wonaminta NSW 462 C5
Wonboyn Lake NSW 456 E10
Wondai Qld 556 B2, 559 L5
Wondinong WA 709 H7
Wondoola Qld 562 E8
Wonga NSW 462 A9
Wonga NSW 462 E3
Wonga Qld 563 L4, 569 D6
Wonga Creek Vic 345 J5
Wonga Lilli NSW 462 F4
Wonga Park Vic 335 F2, 337 J3, 344 B10
Wongabinda NSW 460 E4
Wongalara NSW 462 G7
Wongalea NSW 465 J4
Wongalee Qld 565 M3
Wongamere Qld 558 B7
Wongan Hills WA 705 E2, 706 D2
Wonganoo WA 709 M6
Wongarbon NSW 458 B4
Wongarra Vic 336 B8, 339 K9
Wongawol WA 709 M4
Wonglepong Qld 557 D6
Wongoni NSW 458 C3
Wongungarra Vic 342 C4, 345 J9
Wongwibinda NSW 461 K7
Wonoka SA 791 J3
Wonolga Qld 558 E8
Wonthaggi Vic 315, 337 K7
Wonthaggi North Vic 337 K7
Wonwondah North Vic 338 E2
Wonwron Vic 342 B9
Wonyip Vic 337 P7, 342 A9
Woobera Qld 564 D4
Wood Wood Vic 341 J5
Woodanilling WA 705 G10, 706 E7
Woodbourne Vic 336 C3, 339 L6
Woodbridge Tas 839 C7, 843 K6
Woodburn NSW 461 N4
Woodbury Tas 843 K1, 841 L10
Woodchester SA 787 E7, 788 A6, 791 K10

Woodcroft SA 786 D10
Woodenbong NSW 461 M2
Woodend Vic 336 E1, 339 M4
Woodend North Vic 336 F1, 339 M4
Woodford NSW 455 H6, 456 F1, 458 F8
Woodford Qld 556 D4, 559 M6
Woodford Vic 338 F8
Woodford Dale NSW 461 N5
Woodforde SA 786 F5
Woodgate Qld 559 M2
Woodgate NP Qld 559 M2
Woodglen Vic 342 D6
Woodhill Qld 557 C6
Woodhouse Qld 560 D1, 563 N10
Woodhouselee NSW 454 D9, 456 D3
Woodlands Qld 558 A7
Woodlands Qld 558 D6
Woodlands WA 704 B4
Woodlands WA 708 G2
Woodlawn Qld 558 F8
Woodleigh Vic 337 K6
Woodleigh WA 708 C4
Woodpark NSW 453 A5
Woodridge Qld 555 E9, 557 D4
Woods Point Vic 337 N2, 344 F10
Woods Well SA 788 C7
Woodsdale Tas 839 E1, 843 L3
Woodside Qld 558 B5
Woodside SA 787 E6, 791 K10
Woodside Vic 342 B9
Woodside Beach Vic 342 C9
Woodstock NSW 454 B6, 456 C1, 458 B8
Woodstock NSW 463 K4
Woodstock Qld 560 C1, 563 N10
Woodstock Qld 564 G6
Woodstock Tas 839 B6, 843 J6
Woodstock Vic 339 L2
Woodstock WA 715 H7
Woodvale Qld 558 B7
Woodvale Vic 339 L2
Woodvale WA 704 B1
Woodview NSW 461 M3
Woodville NSW 455 M1, 459 J5
Woodville SA 786 D4
Woodville West SA 786 C5
Woody Point Qld 557 D1
Woohlpooer Vic 338 E4
Wool Bay SA 787 A6, 791 H10
Wool Wool Vic 336 A5, 339 J7
Woolabra Qld 558 B4
Woolamai Vic 337 K7
Woolamai Waters Vic 337 J7
Woolbrook NSW 461 H9
Woolcunda NSW 462 B10, 464 B1
Wooleen WA 708 E6
Woolerbilla Qld 558 D9
Woolerina Qld 558 C9
Woolfield Qld 559 H6
Woolfield Qld 565 K5
Woolgangi SA 791 L7

Woolgoolga NSW 425, 461 N7
Woolgorong WA 708 E7
Wooli NSW 425, 461 N6
Woolianna NT 613 C6, 614 C6
Woolibar WA 707 L3
Woolla Downs NT 619 H3
Woollahra NSW 453 F6
Woolloongabba Qld 555 D5
Woolner NT 613 E2, 614 D4
Woolnorth Tas 840 A3
Woolomin NSW 459 H1, 461 H10
Woolooga Qld 556 C1, 559 L4
Woolooma NSW 459 H3
Woolooware NSW 453 D9
Wooloowin Qld 555 D4
Wooloweyah Estuary NSW 461 N5
Woolshed Corner Vic 339 L1, 341 L10
Woolshed Flat SA 791 H5
Woolsthorpe Vic 338 F7
Wooltana SA 793 L10
Woomargama NSW 465 N8
Woomelang Vic 340 G7
Woomera SA 790 F2
Woomera Prohibited Area SA 789 F7, 790 C1, 792 D8
Woongoolba Qld 556 E6, 557 E4, 559 N7
Woonigan Qld 564 D4
Woorabinda Qld 560 G10
Woorak Vic 340 D9
Woorak West Vic 340 D9
Wooramel WA 708 C4
Wooramel Roadhouse WA 708 C4
Woorarra Vic 337 P7, 342 A9
Wooreen Vic 337 M6
Woori Yallock Vic 337 K3
Woorinen Vic 341 J6
Woorndoo Vic 338 G6
Woorndoo Upper Vic 338 G6
Wooroloo WA 705 D4, 706 C4
Wooroonook Vic 341 H9
Wooroonooran NP Qld 569 E8
Woorragee Vic 344 G4
Woosang Vic 341 J10
Wootton NSW 459 L4
Wooyung NSW 461 P2
Woronora NSW 453 C9
Woronora Heights NSW 453 C9
Wotonga Qld 560 E5
Wotto NR WA 708 D9
Wowan Qld 561 J9
Woy Woy NSW 403, 455 L5, 459 H8
Wrangrawally NSW 463 P4
Wrightley Vic 344 E6
Wrotham Park Qld 563 J5
Wroxham Vic 343 M4
Wubbera NSW 460 E5
Wubin WA 706 D1, 708 F10
Wudinna SA 790 D6
Wujal Wujal Qld 563 L4, 569 C5
Wulagi NT 612 G3

Wulagi Park NT 612 G3
Wulgulmerang Vic 342 G2, 345 N7
Wumalgi Qld 561 H6
Wumbulgal NSW 465 L4
Wundowie WA 705 D4, 706 C4
Wunghnu Vic 344 C3
Wungong WA 704 G10
Wunkar SA 791 M9
Wunurra NT 617 M8
Wurarga WA 708 E8
Wurruk Vic 342 C7
Wurung Qld 562 D9
Wutul Qld 556 B4, 559 K6
Wy Yung Vic 342 E6
Wyalkatchem WA 705 G3, 706 E3
Wyalong NSW 465 M3
Wyan NSW 461 M4
Wyandotte Qld 563 K8
Wyandra Qld 558 A6, 567 P6
Wyangala NSW 454 B7, 456 C1, 458 B9
Wyangala Waters SP NSW 454 B6, 456 C1, 458 B9
Wybalenna Historic Site, Flinders Island Tas 823
Wycarbah Qld 561 J9
Wycheproof Vic 341 H9
Wychitella Vic 341 J9
Wycliffe Well Roadhouse NT 617 J10, 619 J1
Wye River Vic 336 C7, 339 K9
Wyee NSW 455 L3, 459 J7
Wyeebo Vic 345 K4
Wyelangta Vic 336 A7, 339 J9
Wyena Qld 560 D5
Wyena Tas 844 F4, 841 K5
Wylie Creek NSW 461 K2
Wylie Scarp WA 711 A9
Wyloo WA 714 E8
Wymah NSW 465 N8
Wynarka SA 788 A8, 791 L10
Wynbring SA 789 G8
Wyndham NSW 456 D9
Wyndham WA 689, 713 M4
Wyndonga NSW 462 B5
Wynn Vale SA 786 F3
Wynnum Qld 555 G4, 557 D2
Wynnum West Qld 555 G5
Wynyangoo WA 709 H7
Wynyard Tas 823, 840 E4
Wyong NSW 403, 455 L4, 459 J7
Wyperfeld NP Vic 293, 340 C7
Wyreema Downs Qld 565 H5
Wyseby Qld 558 E2
Wyuna Vic 341 P9, 344 A4
Wyuna Downs NSW 463 L5

Y

Yaamba Qld 561 J8
Yaapeet Vic 340 E7
Yabba North Vic 344 D4
Yabbro NP NSW 461 L2
Yabulu Qld 563 M9

Yacka SA 787 C1, 791 J7
Yackabindie WA 709 K6
Yackandandah Vic 333, 345 H4
Yadboro Flat NSW 456 F5
Yadlamalka SA 791 H4
Yagoona NSW 453 C7
Yahl SA 788 G10
Yakara Qld 567 L9
Yalamurra Qld 567 N5
Yalardy WA 708 D4
Yalata SA 789 E9
Yalata Roadhouse SA 789 E9
Yalbalgo WA 708 C3
Yalbarrin WA 706 F4
Yalboroo Qld 560 F3
Yalbra WA 708 E3
Yalca North Vic 344 B2
Yalca South Vic 344 B3
Yalgogrin NSW 465 M3
Yalgoo WA 708 F7
Yalgorup NP WA 705 B8, 706 B6
Yalla Y Poora Vic 339 H5
Yallalong WA 708 D6
Yallambie Vic 335 D2
Yallaroi NSW 460 F4
Yalleen WA 714 E7
Yalleroi Qld 560 A10, 565 P10
Yallingup WA 657, 706 A7
Yallock NSW 463 H9
Yallourn North Vic 337 P5
Yallunda Flat SA 790 E9
Yalpara SA 791 K5
Yalwal NSW 456 F4
Yalymboo SA 790 F3
Yamala Qld 560 F9
Yamanto Qld 557 A4
Yamarna WA 709 P7, 711 A3
Yamba NSW 461 N5
Yamba NSW 425, 462 E3
Yambacoona NSW 463 L3
Yambacoona Tas 840 F1
Yambah NT 619 H5
Yambuk Vic 338 E8
Yambungan Qld 562 D10, 564 E1
Yan Yan Qld 560 F8
Yan Yean Vic 337 H2, 339 P5, 344 A10
Yanac Vic 340 C9
Yanakie Vic 337 N8
Yancannia NSW 462 D4
Yanchep WA 657, 705 B4, 706 B4
Yanchep NP WA 657, 705 B4, 706 B4
Yanco NSW 451, 465 L5
Yanco Glen NSW 462 B7
Yandal WA 709 L6
Yandama NSW 462 B3
Yandaminta NSW 462 B3
Yandaminta South NSW 462 B3
Yandaran Qld 559 L1
Yandarlo Qld 558 B2
Yandaroo NSW 463 J4
Yandeyarra WA 715 H6

Yanderra NSW 455 H8, 456 F2, 458 F10

Yandi WA 708 C7

Yandil WA 709 K5

Yandilla Qld 565 K8

Yandina Qld 556 D2, 559 M5

Yando Vic 341 K9

Yandoit Vic 339 L4

Yanerbie Beach SA 790 A6

Yanka NR NSW 464 F5

Yangebup WA 704 C9

Yaninee SA 790 C6

Yanipy Vic 338 B1, 340 B10

Yankalilla SA 787 C8, 788 A5

Yankaninna SA 793 K10

Yannathan Vic 337 K5

Yannergee NSW 458 E2

Yanrey WA 714 C8

Yantabangee NSW 462 F5

Yantabulla NSW 463 H2

Yantara NSW 462 C3

Yanyula Park NT 612 F4

Yaouk NSW 477 A9, 456 B6, 457 D5

Yaraka Qld 567 L2

Yaramulla Qld 563 K7

Yarck Vic 344 C8

Yard Creek WA 713 L7

Yardanogo NR WA 708 D9

Yardea SA 790 D4

Yaringa WA 708 C4

Yarlarweelor WA 708 G3

Yarloop WA 705 C8, 706 C6

Yarmouth Qld 558 A7

Yarra NSW 454 D10, 456 D3

Yarra Glen Vic 315, 335 G1, 337 J2, 344 B10

Yarra Junction Vic 315, 337 K3

Yarra Ranges NP Vic 337 K2, 344 C10

Yarra River Vic 335 D3

Yarra Valley Vic 296–300

Yarra Yarra Lakes WA 708 E9

Yarrabah Qld 563 L5, 569 E7

Yarrabandai NSW 463 N10, 465 N2

Yarraberb Vic 339 L1

Yarrabin NSW 454 C1, 458 C5

Yarrabubba WA 709 H6

Yarraden Qld 563 H1, 568 E9

Yarragadee WA 708 D8

Yarragon Vic 337 M5

Yarragrin NSW 458 C2

Yarrah Creek Tas 840 F2

Yarralin NT 616 D2

Yarraloola WA 714 E7

Yarram Vic 342 B9

Yarrama NSW 463 L8

Yarramalong NSW 455 L4, 459 H7

Yarraman NSW 458 F2

Yarraman Qld 556 B3, 559 L6

Yarramba SA 791 N3

Yarrambat Vic 335 E1

Yarrangobilly NSW 377, 456 B6, 457 C4

Yarranlea Qld 556 A6, 559 K7

Yarranvale NSW 463 K8

Yarrara Vic 340 C3

Yarras NSW 459 L1, 461 L10

Yarraville Vic 335 C4

Yarrawalla Vic 341 L9

Yarrawalla South Vic 341 L9

Yarrawarrah NSW 453 B10

Yarrawin NSW 463 M4

Yarrawonga Vic 333, 344 E3

Yarriambiack Creek Vic 340 F10

Yarrock Vic 340 B9

Yarronvale Qld 567 N6

Yarroweyah Vic 344 C2

Yarrowford NSW 461 K5

Yarrowitch NSW 459 K1, 461 K10

Yarrowmere Qld 560 A4, 565 P4

Yarrowyck NSW 461 H8

Yarrum Qld 562 C7

Yarto Vic 340 E7

Yarwun Qld 561 K9

Yass NSW 377, 456 C4

Yatala Qld 557 D4

Yatchaw Vic 338 E6

Yathong NSW 463 J9

Yathong NR NSW 463 J9

Yatina SA 791 J6

Yatpool Vic 340 E2

Yatteyattah NSW 456 F5

Yea Vic 344 B8

Yeal NR WA 705 B3, 706 C3

Yealering WA 705 G7, 706 E5

Yearinan NSW 458 C1, 460 C10

Yearinga Vic 340 B9

Yednalue SA 791 J4

Yednia Qld 556 C3, 559 M5

Yeeda WA 712 E8, 715 P1

Yeelanna SA 790 D8

Yeelirrie WA 709 K6

Yeerip Vic 344 E4

Yeerongpilly Qld 555 C6

Yelarbon Qld 559 J9

Yelbeni WA 705 G3, 706 E3

Yeldulknie CP SA 790 F7

Yelka NSW 462 B5

Yellabinna RR SA 789 F8

Yellangip Vic 340 E9

Yellingbo Vic 337 K3

Yellow Lake SA 790 E3

Yellowdine WA 707 H3

Yellowdine NR WA 707 H3

Yelma WA 709 M5

Yeltacowie SA 790 G2

Yelty NSW 462 G10, 464 G1

Yelvertoft Qld 564 B2

Yenda NSW 465 L4

Yendon Vic 336 C2, 339 L5

Yengo NP NSW 455 J3, 458 G6

Yenlora Qld 567 L9

Yennora NSW 453 B6

Yenyening Lakes NR WA 705 F6, 706 E5

Yeo Lake WA 711 B2

Yeo Lake NR WA 711 B2

Yeo Yeo NSW 456 A3, 465 P5

Yeodene Vic 336 B6, 339 K8

Yeoval NSW 454 A1, 458 B5

Yeppoon Qld 561 K8

Yerda SA 790 C2

Yerecoin WA 705 D2, 706 C2

Yerilla Qld 559 J3

Yering Vic 337 J2, 344 B10

Yerong Creek NSW 465 M7

Yeronga Qld 555 C6, 557 C3

Yerrinbool NSW 455 H9, 456 F2, 458 F10

Yethera NSW 463 N9

Yetholme NSW 454 E5, 458 E7

Yetman NSW 460 G3

Yeungroon Vic 339 J1, 341 J10

Yeungroon East Vic 341 J10

Yiddah NSW 465 N4

Yilliminning WA 705 F8, 706 E6

Yindi WA 707 N2, 709 N10

Yinkanie SA 791 M9

Yinnar Vic 337 N6

Yinnetharra WA 708 E2

Yirrkala NT 615 M4

Yo Yo Creek Qld 558 B3

Yo Yo Park Qld 558 B4

Yokine WA 704 D3

Yolla Tas 840 E5

Yongala SA 791 K6

Yoogali NSW 465 K4

Yoorooga Qld 558 F7

Yoothapina WA 709 H5

York WA 657, 705 E5, 706 D4

York Plains Tas 843 K2, 841 L10

Yorketown SA 787 A6, 791 H10

Yorkeys Knob Qld 563 L5, 569 D7

Yorklea NSW 461 N3

Yorkrakine WA 705 G3, 706 E3

Yorkshire Downs Qld 564 G3

Yornaning WA 705 F7, 706 E6

You Yangs RP Vic 336 E4, 339 M6

Youangarra WA 709 H8

Youanmi WA 709 H8

Youanmite Vic 344 D3

Youndegin WA 705 F4, 706 E4

Young NSW 377, 456 A2, 458 A10, 465 P4

Youngs WA 706 E10

Youngtown Tas 844 E6, 841 K7

Youno Downs WA 709 J6

Yowah Qld 567 M8

Yowaka NP NSW 456 E9

Yoweragabbie WA 708 G7

Yowie Bay NSW 453 D9

Yowrie NSW 456 E7

Yudnapinna SA 790 G4

Yuelamu NT 618 F3

Yuendumu NT 618 E3

Yugar Qld 557 B1

Yugilbar NSW 460 B8

Yuin WA 708 E7

Yuinmery WA 709 J8

Yulabilla Qld 558 G6

Yulama NSW 465 L6

Yulara NT 618 D8

Yuleba Qld 558 F5

Yulecart Vic 338 D6

Yullundry NSW 454 A2, 458 B6

Yumali SA 788 B8

Yumbarra CP SA 789 F9

Yuna WA 708 D7

Yundamindra WA 709 M9

Yunderup WA 705 B7, 706 C5

Yundool Vic 344 D4

Yungaburra Qld 563 L6, 569 D8

Yunta SA 791 L5

Yurammie NSW 456 D9

Yuraraba Qld 559 K9

Yuraygir NP NSW 406–408, 461 N5

Yuroke Vic 336 G2, 339 N5

Yuulong Vic 339 J9

Z

Zanthus WA 707 P3, 711 A6

Zeehan Tas 823, 840 C9

Zenonie Qld 567 K9

Zetland NSW 453 E7

Zillmere Qld 555 D2

Zumsteins Vic 338 F3

Zuytdorp Cliffs WA 708 B6

Zuytdorp NR WA 708 C6

ACKNOWLEDGEMENTS

The Publisher believes that permission for use of the historical images in this publication, listed below, has been correctly obtained, however if any errors or omissions have occurred, Global Book Publishing would be pleased to hear from copyright owners.

National Library of Australia

77; 86; 89; 92; 93; 94 bottom; 94 top; 96; 99; 100; 104; 106; 107 bottom; 107 top; 108; 109; 110; 112 bottom; 112 top; 113; 114; 116; 117; 118 top; 119; 121 bottom; 126; 130; 131; 132; 132; 134; 138 bottom; 138 top; 146; 152; 190; 204 bottom; 206 bottom; 206 top; 207 top; 208; 210 bottom; 210 top; 211; 213 bottom left; 213 top; 216 bottom; 216 middle; 236; 237; 239

State Library of New South Wales
90 top left; 91 bottom

Australian War Memorial
97; 123 top; 123 bottom; 191

Universal City Studios, Inc.
217 top

Robert Clancy map collection
104

PHOTOGRAPHERS

Fred Adler, Chris Bell, Rob Blakers, Lorraine Blyth, John Borthwick, Martin Bowerman, Ken Brass, Peter Brennan, Adam Bruzzone, John Callanan, Claver Carroll, Alexander Craig, Frank Dalgity, Kevin Deacon, Grant Dixon, Heather Donovan, Richard Eastwood, Joy Eckermann, Mike Edmondson, Stuart Owen Fox, Greg French, Graham Gittins, Philip Gostelow, Ivy Hansen, Dennis Harding, Paul Huntley, Richard I'Anson, Alex Julius, Ionas Kaltenbach, Judith Kempen, Colin Kerr, Albert Kuhnigk, Mike Langford, Gary Lewis, Malcolm Ludgate, Valerie Martin, John McCann, David McGonigal, Richard McKenna, Shane Mensforth, Ron Moon, Siobhan O'Connor, Peter O'Reilly, Nolen Oayada, Lee Pearce, Craig Potton, Geof Prigge, Nick Rains, Brendan Read, Rob Reichenfeld, Christo Reid, Jamie Robertson, Tony Rodd, Don Skirrow, Raoul Slater, Heidi Smith, Peter Solness, Phil Stanley, Steve Starling, Ken Stepnell, Warren Steptoe, Oliver Strewe, Glenn Tempest, J. Peter Thoeming, Sharyn Vanderhorst, Colleen Vigar, Carmen Vila, Neil Wehlack, Kim Westerskov, Murray White, Vic Widman, Geoff Woods, Paul Worsteling, James Young

CAPTIONS FOR DOUBLE PAGE PICTURES

16–17: left to right, see pages 28, 35, 43, 72, 75, 93, 124, 136, 156, 182, 189, 191, 228, 232.

20–21: Carnarvon Gorge in rain, Carnarvon National Park, Queensland.

84–85: Tall ships on Sydney Harbour; a celebration of the bicentenary of European settlement, 26 January, 1988.

142–43: Sheep shearing at Silvester Station near Blackall in Queensland.

172–73: Rock art in Kakadu National Park, Northern Territory. The park's World Heritage status was granted as much for sites like this as for its spectacular wildlife and landscapes.

246–47: left to right, see pages 251, 332, 366, 370, 443, 231, 516, 500, 593, 606, 698, 726, 733, 816.

248-49: Lake Eildon, north-east Victoria, pictured at dawn.

346–47: Morning mist rises above the New South Wales township of Tumut, northern gateway to Kosciuszko National Park.

466–67: Old Parliament House built in 1927, and released from its parliamentary duties in 1988, Canberra, ACT.

478–79: Spectators watch a campdraft event at the Warwick rodeo, Queensland. In a campdraft, a rider selects a steer from a group in a corral, corners it and takes it round a set course in a certain time.

570–71: Aboriginal children playing in the waters of the Finke River, at Hermannsburg Aboriginal Settlement, Northern Territory.

620–21: The Pinnacles, in Nambung National Park are formed by the interaction of water, quartz, sand and limestone, Western Australia.

716–17: The Knappstein Wines vineyard, in the Clare Valley Wine Region, South Australia.

794–95: Twisted Lakes, Cradle Mountain–Lake St Clair National Park, Tasmania.

845: Rock wall, Macdonnell Ranges, Northern Territory.

848: Mullumbimby, north-east New South Wales.